GREEK-ENGLISH CONCORDANCE

To the New Testament

A TABULAR AND STATISTICAL
GREEK-ENGLISH CONCORDANCE
BASED ON THE KING JAMES VERSION
WITH AN ENGLISH-TO-GREEK INDEX

BY J. B. SMITH
INTRODUCTION BY BRUCE M. METZGER
Princeton Theological Seminary

HERALD PRESS · SCOTTDALE, PENNSYLVANIA · 1955

LIBRARY OF CONGRESS CATALOG NUMBER: 55-12260

PHOTOLITHOPRINTED BY CUSHING - MALLOY, INC.
ANN ARBOR, MICHIGAN, UNITED STATES OF AMERICA
1955

Introduction

JOSEPH J. SCALIGER, that illustrious philologist of the Renaissance, once remarked that "a part of the daily prayer of every educated man should be thanksgiving to God that He had been pleased to make lexicographers and grammarians." It need scarcely be remarked that in the category of lexicographers there fall also the makers of concordances or indexes of all the words in a body of literature.

It was the late J. B. Smith's ambition to provide a tool for the study of the New Testament which would enable the ordinary reader of the English New Testament to gather at a glance basic information regarding the original Greek text. Like the earlier work entitled, *The Englishman's Greek Concordance* (1839), Smith's volume indicates the varying translations in the King James Version which represent the same Greek word. But, unlike the earlier volume, this CONCORDANCE is arranged statistically so as to disclose at once the relative frequency of occurrence of a given Greek word in each book of the New Testament. Furthermore, by consulting the Index at the close of the CONCORDANCE, the user can ascertain all the Greek words (as well as their frequency) which are translated by the same English word.

The compiler chose as the basis of his work the King James Version of the Bible. Involved in this choice were certain advantages as well as disadvantages. Among the former is the fact that this translation has been justly regarded as the classic English version of the Scriptures. As regards the number of copies in circulation, the translation of 1611 has held an undisputed place of pre-eminence. On the other hand, however, is the fact that scholars today have access to Greek manuscripts of the New Testament which are far older and more accurate copies than those which were available to the King James translators. Inevitably, therefore, there will be differences, smaller or greater, between the Greek evidence presented in this or any other concordance of the King James Version and a concordance which reflects an edition of the Greek New Testament that embodies the evidence of the earlier and better manuscripts.

Despite these differences, however, the ordinary reader who knows no Greek and whose favorite translation of the Scriptures is the King James Version can consult Smith's work with profit. In fact, there is no other concordance of the 1611 New Testament which will provide him with as much information so conveniently displayed. At the same time the technical scholar of the New Testament will also find certain information conveniently set forth in Smith's tabular and statistical arrangement of words which will assist him in making a comparative study of English versions and their underlying Greek texts. Both types of users of the CONCORDANCE, therefore, will find that Smith's painstaking research will not only lighten their labors, but will enlighten them as well.

As in other walks of life so also in the making of concordances it is true that "other men laboured, and ye are entered into their labours." A man of energetic temperament, amid the press of other duties, J. B. Smith found time during the last twenty years of his life to tabulate the statistics embodied in this CONCORDANCE. He did not "despise the day of small things," but by adding "line upon line, here a little, and there a little," he produced a labor of love for which the user will rise up and call him blessed. Although Samuel Johnson lamented in the Preface of his famous *English Dictionary* that the writer of dictionaries is "doomed only to remove rubbish and clear obstructions from the path through which learning and genius press forward to conquest and glory, without bestowing a smile on the humble drudge that facilitates their progress," the late compiler of this statistical CONCORDANCE sought no other praise than the dominical words of commendation, "Well done, thou good and faithful servant!"

BRUCE M. METZGER
Professor of New Testament
Language and Literature
Princeton Theological Seminary
Princeton, New Jersey

Preface

THIS VOLUME consists of two main parts—the Concordance and the Index. The author has developed the Concordance from the *Textus Receptus* of the Greek New Testament, substantially the third edition of Robert Stephanus published in 1550. The Concordance gives in alphabetical order the Greek words of the New Testament with English translations and verse references for the translations.

While the Concordance provides a Greek-to-English treatment of the New Testament, the Index offers in English-to-Greek a comprehensive list of words of the King James Version. Through the use of serial numbers the Index refers the reader to the tables in the Concordance.

The complete title of this work, "Greek-English Concordance to the New Testament, A Tabular and Statistical Greek-English Concordance Based on the King James Version with an English-to-Greek Index" indicates the important functions of the Concordance. The tabular arrangement and statistical treatment of the translations of the Greek words are unique to this Concordance. By means of tables the Concordance provides easily and quickly a "picture" of the translations and related meanings of a given Greek word. The statistical treatment of the Greek word shows the number of occurrences according to books of the New Testament and according to translations. In addition, each table gives the number of occurrences of the Greek word by verse references and according to books of the New Testament.

In the construction of the Concordance, *The Englishman's Greek Concordance of the New Testament*, 9th edition, 1903, was used as a guide for words presenting no difficulty. For words of frequent occurrence or such as are beset with irregularities the *Concordance of the Greek New Testament* (1880 edition), by Karl Hermann Bruder, based on the work of Erasmus Schmid, served as a constant guide to the author. The author verified by his own count in the Greek text words of most frequent occurrence.

The Author

The publisher deeply regrets that the author was suddenly taken by death in 1951 before the work was published and that of necessity this volume must be published posthumously. The work stands as a unique monument to the sincere devotion and intense interest of J. B. Smith in the origination and development of this Concordance. Since the preparation of the manuscript for publication was of considerable magnitude, more time was required for its publication than had been anticipated.

The manuscript for both the Concordance and the Index was completed and in the hands of the publisher before the passing of the author. Until the time of the author's death, the publisher's editor, Dorothy C. Kemrer, Associate Professor of Latin and New Testament Greek at Eastern Mennonite College, Harrisonburg, Va., consulted with him regularly on all points in question with regard to translations, the formation and arrangement of tables, statistical data, and other editorial questions.

The author had written in rough draft various parts of the introductory material and these have been available to the publisher for incorporation in the Preface. Some of these notes have to do with the beginnings of Smith's interest in the preparation of the Concordance as well as suggestions on the use of the Concordance and the Index. From these notes we wish to share with the reader his personal testimony of how he began this task:

"From a child I delighted in figures, and were it not that I recognized to be 'mighty in the Scriptures' is more important than to be mighty in mathematics, I would have decided to become a mathematician. After my conversion at twenty-one, I was impelled by an upward urge to prepare for Christian service in spite of the fact that my father offered to start me out in life on a fertile farm of 175 acres. During my scholastic career I came across the dictum:

'Study thyself and above all note well
Wherein kind Nature invites thee to excel.'

"As a consequence I decided to specialize in the languages: Latin, Greek, and Hebrew, even though I took delight in the sciences and mathematics and history.

"At the age of twenty-eight a call came for my ordination to the ministry. I early came in contact with well-known religious leaders: Torrey, Jowett, Moorehead, Griffith Thomas, John R. Mott, Robert Dick Wilson, and others. It was Dr. Wilson who aroused my innate love for mathematics by associating this science with the words of Scripture. My first meeting with him was at Lake Winona where he gave a series of lectures on the Book of Daniel, but later I was attracted by his exhibiting and enumerating of the occurrences of 'God' in the Old Testament. I immediately took my Hebrew concordance in order to ascertain whether his enumeration was correct. To my surprise I found that there were numerous errors in the summations. Following this I became suspicious of all statistics cited by authors."

Smith held that the usage of a word determined its meaning. He wrote: "In matters of interpretation no greater authority spoke truer words than did Cremer in his *Biblico-Theological Lexicon:* 'In order to attain a sure result we must consult linguistic usage.' " With this principle as a base Smith used the statistical and tabular method in the construction of the Concordance.

Smith was also intensely interested in making available the treasures of the Greek New Testament to Christian laymen and ministers not familiar with the Greek. In order to provide this opportunity he prepared a complete English-to-Greek Index of New Testament English words which, besides serving as an Index to all Greek words and their meanings, is also of considerable value in itself.

Explanation of the Tabular Form

The sample table below explains the meaning and use of the tables in the Concordance. In this sample, nine numbers and notes above the table refer to the explanations that follow.

1. *N.T. Book.* In the book column appear abbreviations to titles of the New Testament books in which the Greek word is found. In many instances a Greek word appears only once in the New Testament; in other cases common Greek words appear in most of the New Testament books.

2. *Times Occurring.* This column gives the number of occurrences of a particular English translation in each book in which the Greek word appears. The total at the foot of the column indicates the total number of occurrences of a particular translation of the Greek word in the New Testament. Each translation of a Greek word has with it an occurrence column.

3. *Translation.* The main body of the tabulation is made up of verse references in which the translations of the Greek word appear. In the translations of nouns the nominative singular is used, and in verbs, the present active, first person singular. In the listing of certain pronouns the tabulation is broken down by gender, case, and number. The same translation may be found in a number of tables, since several Greek words may oftentimes have an identical English translation.

4. *Word Serial Number.* Each Greek word has a serial number. The total number of Greek words in the Concordance is 5,524. Where a Greek word has been tabulated by case, number, voice, gender, or in some other way, these tables appear under the same serial number with the designation of "a," "b," "c," and so on. For an example, see Table 846. The total number of tables in the Concordance therefore exceeds considerably the number 5,524. The enumeration of the Greek words corresponds with the enumeration of the "Greek Dictionary of the New Testament" in Strong's *Exhaustive Concordance of the Bible.* The variation in the final total by Strong of 5,624 as compared with Smith's total of 5,524 is due to Strong's omission of certain numbers. On p. 79 of the "Dictionary," Strong notes as follows: "Owing to changes in the enumeration while in progress, there were no words left for Nos. 2717 and 3203-3302, which were therefore silently dropped out of the vocabulary and references as redundant." The addition by Smith of the Greek word καταφάγω with serial number 2702, compensates for the omission by Strong of number 2717, thus making the variation in the total number of words equal 100.

5. *Greek Word.* The Greek words in the Concordance appear in alphabetical order as table headings in Greek characters with breathing marks and accents. Nouns appear in the nominative singular form; verbs, in the present active, first person singular; and adjectives, in the nominative singular masculine.

6. *English Transliteration.* Immediately following each Greek word is the transliterated form in English letters. The transliterated word carries an accent and diacritical marks which will assist the reader in the correct pronunciation of the Greek word. The following explanations, taken from *New Testament Greek for Beginners* by J. Gresham Machen, will show the mode of pronunciation of the English spelling of the Greek words where English pronunciation varies:

a as in *father*
g as in *got*
e as in *get*

1. N. T. Book — **2. Times Occurring** — **3. Translation** — **4. Word Serial Number** — **5. Greek Word** — **6. English Transliteration** — **7. Not Translated** — **8. Miscellaneous** — **9. Total Occurrences**

4283. πρόσωπον, pros'ōpon

Book	Oc.	face	Oc.	person	Oc.	presence	Oc.	countenance	Oc.	Not Tr.	Oc.	Misc.	Total
Mt.	9	6:16, 17; 11:10; 16:3; 17:2, 6; 18:10; 26:39, 67	1	22:16									10
Mk.	2	1:2; 14:65	1	12:14									3
Lk.	13	1:76; 2:31; 5:12; 7:27; 9:51, 52, 53; 10:1; 12:56; 17:16; 21:35; 22:64; 24:5	1	20:21			1	9:29					15
Ac.	6	6:15, 15; 7:45; 17:26; 20:25, 38			3	3:13, 19; 5:41	1	2:28	1	13:24	1	25:16	12
1 Co.	3	13:12, 12; 14:25											3
2 Co.	5	3:7a, 13, 18; 4:6; 11:20	2	1:11; 2:10	1	10:1	1	3:7b			3	5:12; 8:24; 10:7	12
Gal.	2	1:22; 2:11	1	2:6									3
Col.	1	2:1											1
1 Th.	2	2:17b; 3:10			1	2:17a							3
2 Th.					1	1:9							1
Heb.					1	9:24							1
Jas.	1	1:23									1	1:11	2
1 Pt.	1	3:12											1
Jd.			1	1:16									1
Rev.	10	4:7; 6:16; 7:11; 9:7, 7; 10:1; 11:16; 12:14; 20:11; 22:4											10
Total	55		7		7		3		1		5		78

Miscellaneous: Ac. 25:16 (with 2596), face to face; 2 Co. 5:12, appearance; 2 Co. 8:24 (with 1519), before; 2 Co. 10:7, outward appearance; Jas. 1:11, fashion.

z like dz
ẹ as "a" in *late*
i as in *pit*
o as in *obey*
u as German ü
ph like f
ch like German ch in *Ach*
ō as in *note*
ai like ai in *aisle*
ei as a in *fate*
oi as oi in *oil*
au as ow in *cow*
eu as eu in *feud*
ou as oo in *food*
ui as uee in *queen*

The mark (ʽ) placed over the initial vowel of the Greek word is called a rough breathing mark and is represented in the transliterated word by the English letter "h." The equivalent of the letter "r" in the Greek also occasionally carries a rough breathing mark. In such instances the letter "h" appears with this consonant.

7. *Not Translated.* The King James translators did not provide an equivalent English word for every Greek word in the New Testament. In such cases the column "Not Translated" gives the references in which no English translation appears.

8. *Miscellaneous.* The miscellaneous column contains references to translations with only one or two occurrences. The translations, with the references, appear in a note immediately under the table. This column permits a more feasible arrangement of the table, in that translations of one or two occurrences are usually provided for in this column.

9. *Total Occurrences.* Two kinds of totals are found in each table. The vertical total column at the right of the table gives the total occurrences of the Greek word according to each book in the New Testament. The horizontal total line at the foot of the table gives the total number of occurrences according to translations.

Explanation of the Index

The Index will serve as the key to the Concordance for the non-Greek student. It lists alphabetically all English words of the New Testament as found in the column headings in the tables except such words as prepositions, articles, and pronouns which are not direct translations of a Greek word. Verbs which appear in a tense other than the present tense, or in the passive voice, or in the second or third person, will always be listed in the present active in the Index. For example, "found" is listed under "find;" "saw" under "see." In nouns, the singular form will be listed instead of the plural; e.g., "women" is found under "woman." The reader should be aware of this fact when searching for a New Testament word in the Index.

A sample entry for "abide" taken from the Index appears here to explain its use.

abide,	390 anastreph'ō, 1	2650 katamen'ō, 1
	835 aulid'zomai, 1	3206 men'ō, 61
	1304 diatri'bō, 5	3787 paramen'ō, 1
	1961 epimen'ō, 2	4060 poie'ō, 1
	2476 his'temi, 1	5178 hupomen'ō, 1

With each English entry appear one or more serial numbers referring to the tables in the Concordance where that word can be found. For example, the word, "abide," is a translation of ten Greek words in the New Testament. Serial numbers are arranged in numerical order. Following the serial number is the Greek word in transliterated form. The last number indicates the number of occurrences of that translation of the Greek word. For example in Table 3206 the word μένω is translated "abide" 61 times. By turning to this table one will find that μένω is translated "remain" 17 times; "dwell," 15 times; "continue," 11 times; "tarry," 9 times; and so on.

The Index is keyed to table numbers rather than page numbers. At the top of each page of the Concordance will be found the serial numbers of the tables which appear on that page.

The Index should put at the disposal of the user many insights into the meaning and use of the words of the New Testament. It will prevent students from attaching undue importance to English translations. The Index along with the Concordance will offer the opportunity to analyze through philological and exegetical study the meanings of the translations of the Greek words.

Special Tables and Word Combinations

Occasionally more than one table for a Greek word appears in the Concordance. Additional tables are classified and tabulated according to usage, form, or some other method. For example, see Tables 165 and 846.

In numerous instances one English word represents the translation of two or more Greek words. In such cases the English translation is accompanied by a parenthesis showing the numbers of other Greek words in the combination. For example in Table 444 under Miscellaneous appears the reference Lk. 19:12 (with 2104) and this combination of two Greek words is translated "nobleman." The number 2104 refers to the table for the other Greek word.

The Values of the Concordance

In describing the use of the Concordance, Smith wrote as follows: "Notice carefully in the tables the various translations of a word. The thought expressed by each is inherent in the Greek word. In other words the Greek word has a larger meaning or content than what is expressed in each single translation. Some concordances use English words as their basis, and those who use them build up their sermonic material by using English words that have no affiliation in fact. Much confusion and factionalism might be avoided if Christian people would learn to think from the sense of the original Greek word as expressed in the various English words of which they are translations."

Smith wrote further that one should observe the word or words having the most frequent occurrences. Note the frequency of the use of a word by the different New Testament writers. Which writers use it most frequently and which rarely use it at all? The reader "will see in what books of the New Testament the word occurs, how often it occurs in each book, and not only so, but he will be able to see at a glance in parallel columns all other English words which are translations of the same Greek word." In this manner the Concordance presents a new and simplified approach to New Testament word study.

The Index makes it possible for the English student to use the Concordance. He may take an English word occurring in the New Testament and in a few minutes' time he will be able to turn to the pages where all the occurrences of that word will appear before his eyes.

The tabular presentation provides a quick and easy way to study related word meanings and translations classified according to writers and books of the New Testament. Through the Concordance one may work from Greek to English, and through the Index from English to Greek. It puts at the disposal of the reader of the English Bible many of the insights which come through a knowledge of the Greek language.

English students of the Bible, as well as Greek students, should find the Concordance and the Index of much value in uncovering the deeper meanings and insights of the New Testament. Scholars, teachers, writers, translators, editors, ministers, and laymen will find the Concordance an invaluable guide and help in Bible study.

Abbreviations in the Concordance

Mt., Matthew	Phi., Philemon
Mk., Mark	Heb., Hebrews
Lk., Luke	Jas., James
Jn., John	1 Pt., I Peter
Ac., Acts	2 Pt., II Peter
Ro., Romans	1 Jn., I John
1 Co., I Corinthians	2 Jn., II John
2 Co., II Corinthians	3 Jn., III John
Gal., Galatians	Jd., Jude
Eph., Ephesians	Rev., Revelation
Phl., Philippians	*
Col., Colossians	Acc., Accusative
1 Th., I Thessalonians	Dat., Dative
2 Th., II Thessalonians	Gen., Genitive
1 Ti., I Timothy	Misc., Miscellaneous
2 Ti., II Timothy	Not Tr., Not Translated
Tit., Titus	Oc., Occurrences

Acknowledgments

The publisher acknowledges with deep appreciation the assistance given by many persons who have shared in offering counsel and help in the production of this work; to members of the J. B. Smith family for their assistance and counsel and making available papers from the files of the author; to numerous persons who assisted the author in the detailed work of compilation, checking, and typing of the manuscript; to Dorothy C. Kemrer, Associate Professor of Latin and New Testament Greek at Eastern Mennonite College, for her editorial assistance in the preparation of the manuscript for printing; to the consultants, H. S. Bender, Dean of Goshen College Biblical Seminary; Chester K. Lehman, Professor of Doctrinal and Apologetical Theology at Eastern Mennonite College; and John C. Wenger, Professor of Theology and Philosophy at Goshen College, for their valuable counsel and suggestions in the publishing of the Concordance; to Paul Erb and Millard C. Lind, members of the editorial staff of the Mennonite Publishing House; and to the staff of Cushing and Malloy, Inc., who provided counsel and special skills in the lithographic production of the volume. Last, the publisher acknowledges sincerely the providence of God in permitting the author to live until the manuscript was finished. He hereby commits the work to all earnest Bible students with the intent that it may serve them well and bring glory to God and His Holy Word.

Errata

Following are listed the errata that were discovered in the process of indexing, which was done after the body of the book was printed.

In Table 29 the translation for Mt. 5:41 should read "compel to go." In Table 224 the Greek word ἄλευρον should read ἀλίσγημα. In Table 665 the Greek word ἀποστρέπω should read ἀποτρέπω. In Table 1223a under Miscellaneous the translation in Ro. 4:11 should read "though" instead of "through." In Table 1352 the reference "1 Co. 4:16" should be "2 Co. 4:16." In Table 1389 the translation should read "handle . . . deceitfully." In Table 1410 under translation "cannot (with 3656)," "Jn. 1:3,5" should read "Jn. 3:3,5." In Table 1437 on page 95 "whosoever (with 3639)" should read "whosoever (with 3639 and 3261)." In Table 1508 under Miscellaneous "(with 1623)" should read in each of the three occurrences "(with 1622)." In Table 2007 the reference "Mk. 10:30" in the Not Translated column should read "Lk. 10:30." In Table 2256 the translation "half" should read "half an hour." In Table 2369 the Greek word Θυμιαστήριον should read θυμιατήριον. In Table 2736b the Greek word κατωτέρο should read κατωτέρω. In Table 3173 under Miscellaneous the translation "sign" for Acts 8:13 (with 1411) should read "miracle." In Table 3665b "Mk. 22:16" should read "Lk. 22:16." In Table 3836a the Greek word παρίστημι should read παριστάνω. In Table 3864 the translation "murder of a father" should read "murderer of a father." In Table 4235 the translation "pray earnestly" should read "pray earnestly (with 3246)." In Table 4573 the translation is "bier" and has one occurrence, Lk. 7:14. In Table 4924 the words "as Adverb" should be omitted from the explanatory note. In Table 5024 in Miscellaneous the reference "1 Cor. 12:15,16 (with 1519)" should read "1 Co. 12:15,16 (with 3744)." In Table 5077 under Miscellaneous the reference "Ac. 19:11 (with 3656)" should read "Ac. 19:11 (with 3656 and 3488)." In Table 5116 under Miscellaneous the reference "2 Co. 8:7" should read "2 Co. 8:7(with 1537)." In Table 5326 under Miscellaneous the reference "Phl. 2:5 (with 3678)" should read "Phl. 2:5 (with 5024)." In Table 5384 the translation "forsake" should read "for . . . sake."

October 1, 1955 THE PUBLISHER.

THE CONCORDANCE

1. Α, al'pha

Book	Alpha	Total
Rev.	1:8, 11; 21:6; 22:13	4

2. Ἀαρών, Aarōn'

Book	Aaron	Total
Lk.	1:5	1
Ac.	7:40	1
Heb.	5:4; 7:11; 9:4	3
Total		5

3. Ἀβαδδών, Abaddōn'

Book	Abaddon	Total
Rev.	9:11	1

4. ἀβαρής, abarēs'

Book	burdensome	Total
2 Co.	11:9	1

5. Ἀββᾶ, Abba'

Book	Abba	Total
Mk.	14:36	1
Ro.	8:15	1
Gal.	4:6	1
Total		3

6. Ἄβελ, Ab'el

Book	Abel	Total
Mt.	23:35	1
Lk.	11:51	1
Heb.	11:4; 12:24	2
Total		4

7. Ἀβιά, Abia'

Book	Abia	Total
Mt.	1:7, 7	2
Lk.	1:5	1
Total		3

8. Ἀβιάθαρ, Abiath'ar

Book	Abiathar	Total
Mk.	2:26	1

9. Ἀβιληνή, Abilēnē'

Book	Abilene	Total
Lk.	3:1	1

10. Ἀβιούδ, Abioud'

Book	Abioud	Total
Mt.	1:13, 13	2

11. Ἀβραάμ, Abraam'

Book	Abraham	Total
Mt.	1:1, 2, 17; 3:9, 9; 8:11; 22:32	7
Mk.	12:26	1
Lk.	1:55, 73; 3:8, 8, 34; 13:16, 28; 16:22, 23, 24, 25, 29, 30; 19:9; 20:37	15
Jn.	8:33, 37, 39, 39, 39, 40, 52, 53, 56, 57, 58	11
Ac.	3:13, 25; 7:2, 16, 17, 32; 13:26	7
Ro.	4:1, 2, 3, 9, 12, 13, 16; 9:7; 11:1	9
2 Co.	11:22	1
Gal.	3:6, 7, 8, 9, 14, 16, 18, 29; 4:22	9
Heb.	2:16; 6:13; 7:1, 2, 4, 5, 6, 9; 11:8, 17	10
Jas.	2:21, 23	2
1 Pt.	3:6	1
Total		73

12. ἄβυσσος, ab'ussos

Book	Oc.	bottomless pit	Oc.	deep	Oc.	bottomless	Total
Lk.			1	8:31			1
Ro.			1	10:7			1
Rev.	5	9:11; 11:7; 17:8; 20:1, 3			2	9:1, 2	7
Total	5		2		2		9

13. Ἄγαβος, Ag'abos

Book	Agabus	Total
Ac.	11:28; 21:10	2

14. ἀγαθοεργέω, agathoerge'ō

Book	do good	Total
1 Ti.	6:18	1

15. ἀγαθοποιέω, agathopoie'ō

Book	Oc.	do good	Oc.	well doing	Oc.	do well	Total
Mk.	1	3:4					1
Lk.	4	6:9, 33, 33, 35					4
Ac.	1	14:17					1
1 Pt.			2	2:15; 3:17	2	2:20; 3:6	4
3 Jn.	1	1:11					1
Total	7		2		2		11

16. ἀγαθοποιΐα, agathopoii'a

Book	well doing	Total
1 Pt.	4:19	1

17. ἀγαθοποιός, agathopoios'

Book	do well	Total
1 Pt.	2:14	1

18. ἀγαθός, agathos'

Book	Oc.	good	Oc.	good thing	Oc.	that which is good (with 3488)	Oc.	the thing which is good (with 3488)	Oc.	well	Oc.	benefit	Total
Mt.	13	5:45; 7:11a, 17, 18; 12:35a, 35b; 19:16a, 17, 17; 20:15; 22:10; 25:21, 23	4	7:11b; 12:34, 35c: 19:16b									17
Mk.	3	10:17, 18, 18											3
Lk.	13	6:45a, 45b; 8:8, 15; 10:42; 11:13; 12:18, 19; 18:18, 19, 19; 19:17; 23:50	2	1:53; 16:25	1	6:45c							16
Jn.	2	5:29; 7:12	1	1:46									3
Ac.	3	9:36; 11:24; 23:1											3
Ro.	13	2:10; 3:8; 5:7; 7:12, 19; 8:28; 9:11; 12:2, 21; 13:3a, 4; 14:16; 15:2	2	7:18; 10:15	5	7:13, 13; 12:9; 13:3b; 16:19			1	2:7			21
2 Co.	2	5:10; 9:8											2
Gal.	1	6:10	1	6:6									2
Eph.	2	2:10; 4:29	1	6:8			1	4:28					4
Phl.	1	1:6											1
Col.	1	1:10											1
1 Th.	1	3:6			1	5:15							2
2 Th.	2	2:16, 17											2
1 Ti.	4	1:5, 19; 2:10; 5:10											4
2 Ti.	2	2:21; 3:17											2
Tit.	4	1:16; 2:5, 10; 3:1											4
Phe.			1	1:6							1	1:14	2
Heb.	1	13:21	2	9:11; 10:1									3
Jas.	2	1:17; 3:17											2
1 Pt.	6	2:18; 3:10, 11, 16, 16, 21			1	3:13							7
3 Jn.	1	1:11											1
Total	77		14		8		1		1		1		102

19. ἀγαθωσύνη, agathōsu'nē

Book	goodness	Total
Ro.	15:14	1
Gal.	5:22	1
Eph.	5:9	1
2 Th.	1:11	1
Total		4

20. ἀγαλλίασις, agalli'asis

Book	Oc.	gladness	Oc.	joy	Oc.	exceeding joy	Total
Lk.	1	1:14	1	1:44			2
Ac.	1	2:46					1
Heb.	1	1:9					1
Jd.					1	1:24	1
Total	3		1		1		5

22. ἄγαμος, ag'amos

Book	unmarried	Total
1 Co.	7:8, 11, 32, 34	4

21. ἀγαλλιάω, agallia'ō

Book	Oc.	rejoice	Oc.	be exceeding glad	Oc.	be glad	Oc.	greatly rejoice	Oc.	with exceeding joy	Total
Mt.			1	5:12							1
Lk.	2	1:47; 10:21									2
Jn.	2	5:35; 8:56									2
Ac.	1	16:34			1	2:26					2
1 Pt.	1	1:8					1	1:6	1	4:13	3
Rev.	1	19:7									1
Total	7		1		1		1		1		11

23. ἀγανακτέω, aganakte′ō

Book	Oc.	have indignation	Oc.	be much displeased	Oc.	be moved with indignation	Oc.	with indignation	Oc.	be sore displeased	Total
Mt.	1	26:8			1	20:24			1	21:15	3
Mk.	1	14:4	2	10:14, 41							3
Lk.							1	13:14			1
Total	2		2		1		1		1		7

24. ἀγανάκτησις, aganak′tesis

Book	indignation	Total
2 Co.	7:11	1

25. ἀγαπάω, agapa′ō

Book	Oc.	love	Oc.	beloved	Total
Mt.	8	5:43, 44, 46, 46; 6:24; 19:19; 22:37, 39			8
Mk.	5	10:21; 12:30, 31, 33, 33			5
Lk.	13	6:27, 32, 32, 32, 32. 35; 7:5, 42, 47, 47; 10:27; 11:43; 16:13			13
Jn.	37	3:16, 19, 35; 8:42; 10:17; 11:5; 12:43; 13:1, 1, 23; 13:34, 34, 34; 14:15, 21, 21, 21, 21, 23, 23, 24, 28, 31; 15:9, 9, 12, 12, 17; 17:23, 23, 24, 26; 19:26; 21:7, 15, 16, 20			37
Ro.	6	8:28, 37; 9:13; 13:8, 8, 9	2	9:25, 25	8
1 Co.	2	2:9; 8:3			2
2 Co.	4	9:7; 11:11; 12:15, 15			4
Gal.	2	2:20; 5:14			2
Eph.	9	2:4; 5:2, 25, 25. 28, 28, 28, 33; 6:24	1	1:6	10
Col.	1	3:19	1	3:12	2
1 Th.	1	4:9	1	1:4	2
2 Th.	1	2:16	1	2:13	2
2 Ti.	2	4:8, 10			2
Heb.	2	1:9; 12:6			2
Jas.	3	1:12; 2:5, 8			3
1 Pt.	4	1:8, 22; 2:17; 3:10			4
2 Pt.	1	2:15			1
1 Jn.	28	2:10, 15, 15; 3:10, 11, 14, 14, 18, 23; 4:7, 7, 8, 10, 10, 11, 11, 12, 19, 19, 20, 20, 20, 21, 21; 5:1, 1, 2, 2			28
2 Jn.	2	1:1, 5			2
3 Jn.	1	1:1			1
Rev.	3	1:5; 3:9; 12:11	1	20:9	4
Total	135		7		142

26. ἀγάπη, aga′pe

Book	Oc.	love	Oc.	charity	Oc.	dear	Oc.	charitably (with 2596)	Oc.	feast of charity	Total
Mt.	1	24:12									1
Lk.	1	11:42									1
Jn.	7	5:42; 13:35; 15:9, 10, 10, 13; 17:26									7
Ro.	8	5:5, 8; 8:35, 39; 12:9; 13:10, 10; 15:30					1	14:15			9
1 Co.	2	4:21; 16:24	12	8:1; 13:1, 2, 3, 4, 4, 4, 8, 13, 13; 14:1; 16:14							14
2 Co.	9	2:4, 8; 5:14; 6:6; 8:7, 8, 24; 13:11, 14									9
Gal.	3	5:6, 13, 22									3
Eph.	10	1:4, 15; 2:4; 3:17, 19; 4:2, 15, 16; 5:2; 6:23									10
Phl.	4	1:9, 17; 2:1, 2									4
Col.	3	1:4, 8; 2:2	1	3:14	1	1:13					5
1 Th.	4	1:3; 3:12; 5:8, 13	1	3:6							5
2 Th.	2	2:10; 3:5	1	1:3							3
1 Ti.	2	1:14; 6:11	3	1:5; 2:15; 4:12							5
2 Ti.	2	1:7, 13	2	2:22; 3:10							4
Tit.			1	2:2							1
Phe.	3	1:5, 7, 9									3
Heb.	2	6:10; 10:24									2
1 Pt.			3	4:8, 8; 5:14							3
2 Pt.			1	1:7							1
1 Jn.	18	2:5, 15; 3:1, 16, 17; 4:7, 8, 9, 10, 12, 16, 16, 16, 17, 18, 18, 18; 5:3									18
2 Jn.	2	1:3, 6									2
3 Jn.			1	1:6							1
Jd.	2	1:2, 21							1	1:12	3
Rev.	1	2:4	1	2:19							2
Total	86		27		1		1		1		116

27. ἀγαπητός, agapetos′

Book	Oc.	beloved	Oc.	dearly beloved	Oc.	well beloved	Oc.	dear	Total
Mt.	3	3:17; 12:18; 17:5							3
Mk.	2	1:11; 9:7			1	12:6			3
Lk.	3	3:22; 9:35; 20:13							3
Ac.	1	15:25							1
Ro.	5	1:7; 11:28; 16:8, 9. 12	1	12:19	1	16:5			7
1 Co.	3	4:14, 17; 15:58	1	10:14					4
2 Co.			2	7:1; 12:19					2
Eph.	1	6:21					1	5:1	2
Phl.	1	2:12	2	4:1, 1					3
Col.	3	4:7, 9, 14					1	1:7	4
1 Th.							1	2:8	1
1 Ti.	1	6:2							1
2 Ti.			1	1:2					1
Phe.	2	1:2, 16	1	1:1					3
Heb.	1	6:9							1
Jas.	3	1:16, 19: 2:5							3
1 Pt.	1	4:12	1	2:11					2
2 Pt.	6	1:17; 3:1, 8, 14, 15, 17							6
1 Jn.	5	3:2, 21; 4:1, 7, 11							5
3 Jn.	3	1:2, 5, 11			1	1:1			4
Jd.	3	1:3, 17, 20							3
Total	47		9		3		3		62

28. ῎Αγαρ, Ag′ar

Book	Agar	Total
Gal.	4:24, 25	2

29. ἀγγαρεύω, anggareu′ō

Book	compel	Total
Mt.	5:41; 27:32	2
Mk.	15:21	1
Total		3

30. ἀγγεῖον, anggei′on

Book	vessel	Total
Mt.	13:48; 25:4	2

31. ἀγγελία, anggeli′a

Book	message	Total
1 Jn.	3:11	1

32. ἄγγελος, ang'gelos

Book	Oc.	angel	Oc.	messenger	Total
Mt.	19	1:20, 24; 2:13, 19; 4:6, 11; 13:39, 41, 49; 16:27; 18:10; 22:30; 24:31, 36; 25:31, 41; 26:53; 28:2, 5	1	11:10	20
Mk.	5	1:13; 8:38; 12:25; 13:27, 32	1	1:2	6
Lk.	23	1:11, 13, 18, 19, 26, 28, 30, 34, 35, 38; 2:9, 10, 13, 15, 21; 4:10; 9:26; 12:8, 9; 15:10; 16:22; 22:43; 24:23	3	7:24, 27; 9:52	26
Jn.	4	1:51; 5:4; 12:29; 20:12			4
Ac.	21	5:19; 6:15; 7:30, 35, 38, 53; 8:26; 10:3, 7, 22; 11:13; 12:7, 8, 9, 10, 11, 15, 23; 23:8, 9; 27:23			21
Ro.	1	8:38			1
1 Co.	4	4:9; 6:3; 11:10; 13:1			4
2 Co.	1	11:14	1	12:7	2
Gal.	3	1:8; 3:19; 4:14			3
Col.	1	2:18			1
2 Th.	1	1:7			1
1 Ti.	2	3:16; 5:21			2
Heb.	13	1:4, 5, 6, 7, 7, 13; 2:2, 5, 7, 9, 16; 12:22; 13:2			13
Jas.			1	2:25	1
1 Pt.	2	1:12; 3:22			2
2 Pt.	2	2:4, 11			2
Jd.	1	1:6			1
Rev.	76	1:1, 20; 2:1, 8, 12, 18; 3:1, 5, 7, 14; 5:2, 11; 7:1, 2, 2, 11; 8:2, 3, 4, 5, 6, 7, 8 10, 12, 13, 13; 9:1, 11, 13, 14, 14, 15; 10:1, 5, 7, 8, 9, 10; 11:1, 15; 12:7, 7, 9; 14:6, 8, 9, 10, 15, 17, 18, 19; 15:1, 6, 7, 8; 16:1, 3, 4, 5, 8, 10, 12, 17; 17:1, 7; 18:1, 21; 19:17; 20:1; 21:9, 12, 17; 22:6, 8, 16			76
Total	179		7		186

33. ἄγε, ag'e

Book	go to	Total
Jas.	4:13; 5:1	2

34. ἀγέλη, agel'ē

Book	herd	Total
Mt.	8:30, 31, 32, 32	4
Mk.	5:11, 13	2
Lk.	8:32, 33	2
Total		8

35. ἀγενεαλόγητος, agenealog'ētos

Book	without descent	Total
Heb.	7:3	1

36. ἀγενής, agenēs'

Book	base things	Total
1 Co.	1:28	1

37. ἁγιάζω, hagiad'zō

Book	Oc.	sanctify	Oc.	hallow	Oc.	be holy	Total
Mt.	2	23:17, 19	1	6:9			3
Lk.			1	11:2			1
Jn.	4	10:36; 17:17, 19, 19					4
Ac.	2	20:32; 26:18					2
Ro.	1	15:16					1
1 Co	4	1:2; 6:11; 7:14, 14					4
Eph.	1	5:26					1
1 Th.	1	5:23					1
1 Ti.	1	4:5					1
2 Ti.	1	2:21					1
Heb.	7	2:11, 11; 9:13; 10:10, 14, 29; 13:12					7
1 Pt.	1	3:15					1
Jd.	1	1:1					1
Rev.					1	22:11	1
Total	26		2		1		29

38. ἁγιασμός, hagiasmos'

Book	Oc.	holiness	Oc.	sanctification	Total
Ro.	2	6:19, 22			2
1 Co.			1	1:30	1
1 Th.	1	4:7	2	4:3, 4	3
2 Th.			1	2:13	1
1 Ti.	1	2:15			1
Heb.	1	12:14			1
1 Pt.			1	1:2	1
Total	5		5		10

39. ἅγιον, hag'ion

Book	Oc.	sanctuary	Oc.	holy place	Oc.	holiest of all	Oc.	holiest	Total
Heb.	4	8:2; 9:1, 2; 13:11	3	9:12, 24, 25	3	9:3, 3, 8	1	10:19	11

40. ἅγιος, hag'ios

Book	Oc.	holy	Oc.	saints	Oc.	Holy One	Oc.	Misc.	Total
Mt.	10	1:18, 20; 3:11; 4:5; 7:6; 12:32; 24:15; 25:31; 27:53; 28:19	1	27:52					11
Mk.	6	1:8; 3:29; 6:20; 8:38; 12:36; 13:11			1	1:24			7
Lk.	17	1:15, 35a, 41, 49, 67, 70, 72; 2:23, 25, 26; 3:16, 22; 4:1; 9:26; 11:13; 12:10, 12			1	4:34	1	1:35b	19
Jn.	5	1:33; 7:39; 14:26; 17:11; 20:22							5
Ac.	49	1:2, 5, 8, 16; 2:4, 33, 38; 3:21; 4:8, 27, 30, 31; 5:3, 32; 6:3, 5, 13; 7:33, 51, 55; 8:15, 17, 18, 19; 9:17, 31; 10:22, 38, 44, 45, 47; 11:15, 16, 24; 13:2, 4, 9, 52; 15:8, 28; 16:6; 19:2, 2, 6; 20:23, 28; 21:11, 28; 28:25	4	9:13, 32, 41; 26:10	1	3:14			54
Ro.	12	1:2; 5:5; 7:12, 12; 9:1; 11:16, 16; 12:1; 14:17; 15:13, 16; 16:16	8	1:7; 8:27; 12:13; 15 25, 26, 31; 16:2, 15					20
1 Co.	7	2:13; 3:17; 6:19; 7:14, 34; 12:3; 16:20	6	1:2; 6:1, 2; 14:33; 16:1, 15					13
2 Co.	3	6:6; 13:12, 14	5	1:1; 8:4; 9:1, 12; 13:13					8
Eph.	6	1:4, 13; 2:21; 3:5; 4:30; 5:27	9	1:1, 15, 18; 2:19; 3:8, 18; 4:12; 5:3; 6:18					15
Phl.			2	1:1; 4:22			1	4:21	3
Col.	2	1:22; 3:12	4	1:2, 4, 12, 26					6
1 Th.	5	1:5, 6; 4:8; 5:26, 27	1	3:13					6
2 Th.			1	1:10					1
1 Ti.			1	5:10					1
2 Ti.	2	1:9, 14							2
Tit.	1	3:5							1
Phe.			2	1:5, 7					2
Heb.	6	2:4; 3:1, 7; 6:4; 9:8; 10:15	2	6:10; 13:24					8
1 Pt.	8	1:12, 15, 15, 16, 16; 2:5, 9; 3:5							8
2 Pt.	6	1:18, 21, 21; 2:21; 3:2, 11							6
1 Jn.	1	5:7			1	2:20			2
Jd.	1	1:20b	2	1:3, 14			1	1:20a	4
Rev.	14	3:7; 4:8, 8, 8; 6:10; 11:2; 14:10; 18:20; 20:6; 21:2, 10; 22:6, 11, 19	13	5:8; 8:3, 4; 11:18; 13: 7, 10; 14:12; 15:3; 16: 6; 17:6; 18:24; 19:8; 20:9					27
Total	161		61		4		3		229

Miscellaneous: Lk. 1:35b, holy thing; Phl. 4:21, saint; Jd. 1:20a, most holy.

41. ἁγιότης, hagiot'ēs

Book	holiness	Total
Heb.	12:10	1

42. ἁγιωσύνη, hagiōsu'nē

Book	holiness	Total
Ro.	1:4	1
2 Co.	7:1	1
1 Th.	3:13	1
Total		3

43. ἀγκάλη, angkal'ē

Book	arm	Total
Lk.	2:28	1

44. ἄγκιστρον, ang'kistron

Book	hook	Total
Mt.	17:27	1

45. ἄγκυρα, ang'kura

Book	anchor	Total
Ac.	27:29, 30, 40	3
Heb.	6:19	1
Total		4

46. ἄγναφος, ag'naphos

Book	new	Total
Mt.	9:16	1
Mk.	2:21	1
Total		2

47. ἁγνεία, hagnei'a

Book	purity	Total
1 Ti.	4:12; 5:2	2

48. ἁγνίζω, hagnid'zō

Book	Oc.	purify	Oc.	purify (one's) self	Total
Jn.	1	11:55			1
Ac.	1	24:18	2	21:24, 26	3
Jas.	1	4:8			1
1 Pt.	1	1:22			1
1 Jn.	1	3:3			1
Total	5		2		7

49. ἁγνισμός, hagnismos'

Book	purification	Total
Ac.	21:26	1

51. ἀγνόημα, agno'ēma

Book	error	Total
Heb.	9:7	1

50. ἀγνοέω, agnoe'ō

Book	Oc.	be ignorant	Oc.	ignorant	Oc.	know not	Oc.	understand not	Oc.	ignorantly	Oc.	unknown	Total
Mk.							1	9:32					1
Lk.							1	9:45					1
Ac.					1	13:27			1	17:23			2
Ro.	2	10:3; 11:25	1	1:13	3	2:4; 6:3; 7:1							6
1 Co.	3	10:1; 14:38, 38	1	12:1									4
2 Co.	1	2:11	1	1:8							1	6:9	3
Gal.											1	1:22	1
1 Th.	1	4:13											1
1 Ti.									1	1:13			1
Heb.			1	5:2									1
2 Pt.							1	2:12					1
Total	7		4		4		3		2		2		22

53. ἁγνός, hagnos'

Book	Oc.	pure	Oc.	chaste	Oc.	clear	Total
2 Co.			1	11:2	1	7:11	2
Phl.	1	4:8					1
1 Ti.	1	5:22					1
Tit.			1	2:5			1
Jas.	1	3:17					1
1 Pt.			1	3:2			1
1 Jn.	1	3:3					1
Total	4		3		1		8

52. ἄγνοια, ag'noia

Book	ignorance	Total
Ac.	3:17; 17:30	2
Eph.	4:18	1
1 Pt.	1:14	1
Total		4

55. ἁγνῶς, hagnōs'

Book	sincerely	Total
Phl.	1:16	1

54. ἁγνότης, hagnot'ēs

Book	pureness	Total
2 Co.	6:6	1

57. ἄγνωστος, ag'nōstos

Book	unknown	Total
Ac.	17:23	1

56. ἀγνωσία, agnōsi'a

Book	Oc.	not the knowledge	Oc.	ignorance	Total
1 Co.	1	15:34			1
1 Pt.			1	2:15	1
Total	1		1		2

58. ἀγορά, agora'

Book	Oc.	market	Oc.	marketplace	Oc.	street	Total
Mt.	2	11:16; 23:7	1	20:3			3
Mk.	1	7:4	1	12:38	1	6:56	3
Lk.	2	11:43; 20:46	1	7:32			3
Ac.	1	17:17	1	16:19			2
Total	6		4		1		11

59. ἀγοράζω, agorad'zō

Book	Oc.	buy	Oc.	redeem	Total
Mt.	7	13:44, 46; 14:15; 21:12; 25:9, 10; 27:7			7
Mk.	5	6:36, 37; 11:15; 15:46; 16:1			5
Lk.	6	9:13; 14:18, 19; 17:28; 19:45; 22:36			6
Jn.	3	4:8; 6:5; 13:29			3
1 Co.	3	6:20; 7:23, 30			3
2 Pt.	1	2:1			1
Rev.	3	3:18; 13:17; 18:11	3	5:9; 14:3, 4	6
Total	28		3		31

60. ἀγοραῖος, agorai'os

Book	Oc.	baser sort	Oc.	law	Total
Ac.	1	17:5	1	19:38	2

61. ἄγρα, ag'ra

Book	draught	Total
Lk.	5:4, 9	2

63. ἀγραυλέω, agraule'ō

Book	abide in the field	Total
Lk.	2:8	1

62. ἀγράμματος, agram'matos

Book	unlearned	Total
Ac.	4:13	1

64. ἀγρεύω, agreu'ō

Book	catch	Total
Mk.	12:13	1

65. ἀγριέλαιος, agriel'aios

Book	Oc.	wild olive tree	Oc.	olive tree which is wild	Total
Ro.	1	11:17	1	11:24	2

66. ἄγριος, ag'rios

Book	Oc.	wild	Oc.	raging	Total
Mt.	1	3:4			1
Mk.	1	1:6			1
Jd.			1	1:13	1
Total	2		1		3

67. Ἀγρίππας, Agrip'pas

Book	Agrippa	Total
Ac.	25:13, 22, 23, 24, 26; 26:1, 2, 7, 19, 27, 28, 32	12

68. ἀγρός, agros'

Book	Oc.	field	Oc.	country	Oc.	land	Oc.	farm	Oc.	piece of ground	Total
Mt.	15	6:28, 30; 13:24, 27, 31, 36, 38, 44, 44; 24:18, 40; 27:7, 8, 8, 10			1	19:29	1	22:5			17
Mk.	1	13:16	5	5:14; 6:36, 56; 15:21; 16:12	2	10:29, 30					8
Lk.	6	12:28; 15:15, 25; 17:7, 31, 36	3	8:34; 9:12; 23:26					1	14:18	10
Ac.					1	4:37					1
Total	22		8		4		1		1		36

69. ἀγρυπνέω, agrupne'ō

Book	watch	Total
Mk.	13:33	1
Lk.	21:36	1
Eph.	6:18	1
Heb.	13:17	1
Total		4

70. ἀγρυπνία, agrupni'a

Book	watching	Total
2 Co.	6:5; 11:27	2

72. ἀγωγή, agōgē'

Book	manner of life	Total
2 Ti.	3:10	1

71. ἄγω, ag'ō

Book	Oc.	bring	Oc.	lead	Oc.	go	Oc.	bring forth	Oc.	Misc.	Total
Mt.	3	10:18; 21:2, 7			1	26:46			1	14:6	5
Mk.	2	11:2, 7	1	13:11	2	1:38; 14:42					5
Lk.	8	4:9, 40; 10:34; 18:40; 19:27, 30, 35; 21:12	5	4:1, 29; 22:54; 23:1, 32					1	24:21	14
Jn.	7	1:42; 7:45; 8:3; 9:13; 10:16; 19:4, 13	1	18:28	4	11:7, 15, 16; 14:31					12
Ac.	22	5:21, 26, 27; 6:12; 9:2, 21, 27; 11:26; 17:5, 15, 19; 18:12; 19:37; 20:12; 21:16; 22:5, 24; 23:10, 18, 18, 31; 25:6	1	8:32			2	25:17, 23	2	19:38 21:34	27
Ro.			2	2:4; 8:14							2
1 Co.			1	12:2							1
Gal.			1	5:18							1
1 Th.	1	4:14									1
2 Ti.	1	4:11							1	3:6	2
Heb.	1	2:10									1
Total	45		12		7		2		5		71

Miscellaneous: Mt. 14:6, keep; Lk. 24:21, be; Ac. 19:38, be open; Ac. 21:34, carry; 2 Ti. 3:6, lead away.

73. ἀγών, agōn′

Book	Oc.	conflict	Oc.	fight	Oc.	contention	Oc.	race	Total
Phl.	1	1:30							1
Col.	1	2:1							1
1 Th.					1	2:2			1
1 Ti.			1	6:12					1
2 Ti.			1	4:7					1
Heb.							1	12:1	1
Total	2		2		1		1		6

74. ἀγωνία, agōni′a

Book	agony	Total
Lk.	22:44	1

76. Ἀδάμ, Adam′

Book	Adam	Total
Lk.	3:38	1
Ro.	5:14, 14	2
1 Co.	15:22, 45, 45	3
1 Ti.	2:13, 14	2
Jd.	1:14	1
Total		9

75. ἀγωνίζομαι, agōnid′zomai

Book	Oc.	strive	Oc.	fight	Oc.	labour fervently	Total
Lk.	1	13:24					1
Jn.			1	18:36			1
1 Co	1	9:25					1
Co	1	1:29			1	4:12	2
1 Ti.			1	6:12			1
2 Ti.			1	4:7			1
Total	3		3		1		7

77. ἀδάπανος, adap′anos

Book	without charge	Total
1 Co.	9:18	1

78. Ἀδδί, Addi′

Book	Addi	Total
Lk.	3:28	1

79. ἀδελφή, adelphẹ′

Book	sister	Total
Mt.	12:50; 13:56; 19:29	3
Mk.	3:35; 6:3; 10:29, 30	4
Lk.	10:39, 40; 14:26	3
Jn.	11:1, 3, 5, 28, 39; 19:25	6
Ac.	23:16	1
Ro.	16:1, 15	2
1 Co.	7:15; 9:5	2
1 Ti.	5:2	1
Jas.	2:15	1
2 Jn.	1:13	1
Total		24

80. ἀδελφός, adelphos′

Book	brother	Total
Mt.	1:2, 11; 4:18, 18, 21, 21; 5:22, 22, 23, 24, 47; 7:3, 4, 5; 10:2, 2, 21, 21; 12:46, 47, 48, 49, 50; 13:55; 14:3; 17:1; 18:15, 15, 21, 35; 19:29; 20:24; 22:24, 24, 25, 25; 23:8; 25:40; 28:10	39
Mk.	1:16, 19; 3:17, 31, 32, 33, 34, 35; 5:37; 6:3, 17, 18; 10:29, 30; 12:19, 19, 19, 20; 13:12, 12	20
Lk.	3:1, 19; 6:14, 41, 42, 42, 42; 8:19, 20, 21; 12:13; 14:12, 26; 15:27, 32; 16:28; 17:3; 18:29; 20:28, 28, 28, 29; 21:16; 22:32	24
Jn.	1:40, 41; 2:12; 6:8; 7:3, 5, 10; 11:2, 19, 21, 23, 32; 20:17; 21:23	14
Ac.	1:14, 16; 2:29, 37; 3:17, 22; 6:3; 7:2, 13, 23, 25, 26, 37; 9:17, 30; 10:23; 11:1, 12, 29; 12:2, 17; 13:15, 26, 38; 14:2; 15:1, 3, 7, 13, 22, 23, 23, 32, 33, 36, 40; 16:2, 40; 17:6, 10, 14; 18:18, 27; 20:32; 21:7, 17, 20; 22:1, 5, 13; 23:1, 5, 6; 28:14, 15, 17, 21	57
Ro.	1:13; 7:1, 4; 8:12, 29; 9:3; 10:1; 11:25; 12:1; 14:10, 10, 13, 15, 21; 15:14, 15, 30; 16:14, 17, 23	20
1 Co.	1:1, 10, 11, 26; 2:1; 3:1; 4:6; 5:11; 6:5, 6, 6, 8; 7:12, 15, 24, 29; 8:11, 12, 13, 13; 9:5; 10:1; 11:2, 33; 12:1; 14:6, 20, 26, 39; 15:1, 6, 50, 58; 16:11, 12, 12, 15, 20	38
2 Co.	1:1, 8; 2:13; 8:1, 18, 22, 23; 9:3, 5; 11:9; 12:18; 13:11	12
Gal.	1:2, 11, 19; 3:15; 4:12, 28, 31; 5:11, 13; 6:1, 18	11
Eph.	6:10, 21, 23	3
Phl.	1:12, 14; 2:25; 3:1, 13, 17; 4:1, 8, 21	9
Col.	1:1, 2; 4:7, 9, 15	5
1 Th.	1:4; 2:1, 9, 14, 17; 3:2, 7; 4:1, 6, 10, 10, 13; 5:1, 4, 12, 14, 25, 26, 27	19
2 Th	1:3; 2:1, 13, 15; 3:1, 6, 6, 13, 15	9
1 Ti.	4:6; 5:1; 6:2	3
2 Ti.	4:21	1
Phe.	1:1, 7, 16, 20	4
Heb.	2:11, 12, 17; 3:1, 12; 7:5; 8:11; 10:19; 13:22, 23	10
Jas.	1:2, 9, 16, 19; 2:1, 5, 14, 15; 3:1, 10, 12; 4:11, 11, 11; 5:7, 9, 10, 12, 19	19
1 Pt.	5:12	1
2 Pt.	1:10; 3:15	2
1 Jn.	2:7, 9, 10, 11; 3:10, 12, 12, 13, 14, 14, 15, 16, 17; 4:20, 20, 21; 5:16	17
3 Jn.	1:3, 5, 10	3
Jd.	1:1	1
Rev.	1:9; 6:11; 12:10; 19:10; 22:9	5
Total		346

83. ἀδηλότης, adẹlot′ẹs

Book	uncertain	Total
1 Ti.	6:17	1

84. ἀδήλως, adẹ′lōs

Book	uncertainly	Total
1 Co.	9:26	1

87. ἀδιάκριτος, adiak′ritos

Book	without partiality	Total
Jas.	3:17	1

89. ἀδιαλείπτως, adialeip′tōs

Book	without ceasing	Total
Ro.	1:9	1
1 Th.	1:3; 2:13; 5:17	3
Total		4

90. ἀδιαφθορία, adiaphthori′a

Book	uncorruptness	Total
Tit.	2:7	1

81. ἀδελφότης, adelphot′ẹs

Book	Oc.	brothernood	Oc.	brethren	Total
1 Pt.	1	2:17	1	5:9	2

82. ἄδηλος, ad′ẹlos

Book	Oc.	appear not	Oc.	uncertain	Total
Lk.	1	11:44			1
1 Co.			1	14:8	1
Total	1		1		2

85. ἀδημονέω, adẹmone′ō

Book	Oc.	be very heavy	Oc.	be full of heaviness	Total
Mt.	1	26:37			1
Mk.	1	14:33			1
Phl.			1	2:26	1
Total	2		1		3

86. ᾅδης, ha′dẹs

Book	Oc.	hell	Oc.	grave	Total
Mt.	2	11:23; 16:18			2
Lk.	2	10:15; 16:23			2
Ac.	2	2:27, 31			2
1 Co.			1	15:55	1
Rev.	4	1:18; 6:8; 20:13, 14			4
Total	10		1		11

88. ἀδιάλειπτος, adial′eiptos

Book	Oc.	continual	Oc.	without ceasing	Total
Ro.	1	9:2			1
2 Ti.			1	1:3	1
Total	1		1		2

91. ἀδικέω, adike′ō

Book	Oc.	hurt	Oc.	do wrong	Oc.	wrong	Oc.	suffer wrong	Oc.	be unjust	Oc.	take wrong	Oc.	injure	Oc.	be an offender	Total
Mt.			1	20:13													1
Lk.	1	10:19															1
Ac.			3	7:26, 27; 25:10			1	7:24							1	25:11	5
1 Co.			1	6:8							1	6:7					2
2 Co.			1	7:12a	1	7:2	1	7:12b									3
Gal.													1	4:12			1
Col.			2	3:25, 25													2
Phe.					1	1:18											1
Rev.	9	2:11; 6:6; 7:2, 3; 9:4, 10, 19; 11:5, 5							2	22:11, 11							11
Total	10		8		2		2		2		1		1		1		27

92. ἀδίκημα, adik'ẹma

Book	Oc.	matter of wrong	Oc.	evil doing	Oc.	iniquity	Total
Ac.	1	18:14	1	24:20			2
Rev.					1	18:5	1
Total	1		1		1		3

95. ἀδίκως, adi'kōs

Book	wrongfully	Total
1 Pt.	2:19	1

93. ἀδικία, adiki'a

Book	Oc.	unrighteousness	Oc.	iniquity	Oc.	unjust	Oc.	wrong	Total
Lk.	1	16:9	1	13:27	2	16:8; 18:6			4
Jn.	1	7:18							1
Ac.			2	1:18; 8:23					2
Ro.	7	1:18, 18, 29; 2:8; 3:5; 6:13; 9:14							7
1 Co.			1	13:6					1
2 Co.							1	12:13	1
2 Th.	2	2:10, 12							2
2 Ti.			1	2:19					1
Heb.	1	8:12							1
Jas.			1	3:6					1
2 Pt.	2	2:13, 15							2
1 Jn.	2	1:9; 5:17							2
Total	16		6		2		1		25

94. ἄδικος, ad'ikos

Book	Oc.	unjust	Oc.	unrighteous	Total
Mt.	1	5:45			1
Lk.	3	16:10, 10; 18:11	1	16:11	4
Ac.	1	24:15			1
Ro.			1	3:5	1
1 Co.	1	6:1	1	6:9	2
Heb.			1	6:10	1
1 Pt.	1	3:18			1
2 Pt.	1	2:9			1
Total	8		4		12

96. ἀδόκιμος, adok'imos

Book	Oc.	reprobate	Oc.	castaway	Oc.	rejected	Total
Ro.	1	1:28					1
1 Co.			1	9:27			1
2 Co.	3	13:5, 6, 7					3
2 Ti.	1	3:8					1
Tit.	1	1:16					1
Heb.					1	6:8	1
Total	6		1		1		8

97. ἄδολος, ad'olos

Book	sincere	Total
1 Pt.	2:2	1

98. Ἀδραμυττηνός Adramuttẹnos'

Book	Adramyttium	Total
Ac.	27:2	1

99. Ἀδρίας, Adri'as

Book	Adria	Total
Ac.	27:27	1

100. ἁδρότης, hadrot'ẹs

Book	abundance	Total
2 Co.	8:20	1

101. ἀδυνατέω, adunate'ō

Book	be impossible	Total
Mt.	17:20	1
Lk.	1:37	1
Total		2

102. ἀδύνατος, adu'natos

Book	Oc.	impossible	Oc.	impotent	Oc.	could not do	Oc.	weak	Oc.	not possible	Total
Mt.	1	19:26									1
Mk.	1	10:27									1
Lk.	1	18:27									1
Ac.			1	14:8							1
Ro.					1	8:3	1	15:1			2
Heb.	3	6:4, 18; 11:6							1	10:4	4
Total	6		1		1		1		1		10

104. ἀεί, aei'

Book	Oc.	alway	Oc.	always	Oc.	ever	Total
Mk.					1	15:8	1
Ac.			1	7:51			1
2 Co.	2	4:11; 6:10					2
Tit.	1	1:12					1
Heb.	1	3:10					1
1 Pt.			1	3:15			1
2 Pt.			1	1:12			1
Total	4		3		1		8

103. ᾄδω, ad'ō

Book	sing	Total
Eph.	5:19	1
Col.	3:16	1
Rev.	5:9; 14:3; 15:3	3
Total		5

105. ἀετός, aetos'

Book	eagle	Total
Mt.	24:28	1
Lk.	17:37	1
Rev.	4:7; 12:14	2
Total		4

106. ἄζυμος, ad'zumos

Book	Oc.	unleavened bread	Oc.	unleavened	Total
Mt.	1	26:17			1
Mk.	2	14:1, 12			2
Lk.	2	22:1, 7			2
Ac.	2	12:3; 20:6			2
1 Co.	1	5:8	1	5:7	2
Total	8		1		9

107. Ἀζώρ, Adzōr'

Book	Azor	Total
Mt.	1:13, 14	2

108. Ἄζωτος, Ad'zōtos

Book	Azotus	Total
Ac.	8:40	1

109. ἀήρ, aẹr'

Book	air	Total
Ac.	22:23	1
1 Co.	9:26; 14:9	2
Eph.	2:2	1
1 Th.	4:17	1
Rev.	9:2; 16:17	2
Total		7

110. ἀθανασία, athanasi'a

Book	immortality	Total
1 Co.	15:53, 54	2
1 Ti.	6:16	1
Total		3

111. ἀθέμιτος, athem'itos

Book	Oc.	unlawful thing	Oc.	abominable	Total
Ac.	1	10:28			1
1 Pt.			1	4:3	1
Total	1		1		2

112. ἄθεος, ath'eos

Book	without God	Total
Eph.	2:12	1

113. ἄθεσμος, ath'esmos

Book	wicked	Total
2 Pt.	2:7; 3:17	2

114. ἀθετέω, athete'ō

Book	Oc.	despise	Oc.	reject	Oc.	bring to nothing	Oc.	frustrate	Oc.	disannul	Oc.	cast off	Total
Mk.			2	6:26; 7:9									2
Lk.	4	10:16, 16, 16, 16	1	7:30									5
Jn.			1	12:48									1
1 Co.					1	1:19							1
Gal.							1	2:21	1	3:15			2
1 Th.	2	4:8, 8											2
1 Ti.											1	5:12	1
Heb.	1	10:28											1
Jd.	1	1:8											1
Total	8		4		1		1		1		1		16

115. ἀθέτησις, athet'ĕsis

Book	Oc.	disannulling	Oc.	to put away (with 1519)	Total
Heb.	1	7:18	1	9:26	2

116. 'Αθῆναι, Athē'nai

Book	Athens	Total
Ac.	17:15, 16; 18:1	3
1 Th.	3:1	1
Total		4

119. ἄθλησις, ath'lĕsis

Book	fight	Total
Heb.	10:32	1

120. ἀθυμέω, athume'ō

Book	be discouraged	Total
Col.	3:21	1

117. 'Αθηναῖος, Athēnai'os

Book	Oc.	Athenians	Oc.	of Athens	Total
Ac.	1	17:21	1	17:22	2

118. ἀθλέω, athle'ō

Book	strive	Total
2 Ti.	2:5, 5	2

124. Αἰγύπτιος, Aigup'tios

Book	Oc.	Egyptian	Oc.	Egyptians	Total
Ac.	3	7:24, 28; 21:38	1	7:22	4
Heb.			1	11:29	1
Total	3		2		5

121. ἄθῳος, ath'ōos

Book	innocent	Total
Mt.	27:4, 24	2

125. Αἴγυπτος, Ai'guptos

Book	Egypt	Total
Mt.	2:13, 14, 15, 19	4
Ac.	2:10; 7:9, 10, 10, 11, 12, 15, 17, 34, 34, 36, 39, 40; 13:17	14
Heb.	3:16; 8:9; 11:26, 27	4
Jd.	1:5	1
Rev.	11:8	1
Total		24

122. αἴγειος, ai'geios

Book	goatskin (with 1192)	Total
Heb.	11:37	1

126. ἀΐδιος, ai'dios

Book	Oc.	eternal	Oc.	everlasting	Total
Ro.	1	1:20			1
Jd.			1	1:6	1
Total	1		1		2

123. αἰγιαλός, aigialos'

Book	shore	Total
Mt.	13:2, 48	2
Jn.	21:4	1
Ac.	21:5; 27:39, 40	3
Total		6

127. αἰδώς, aidōs'

Book	Oc.	shamefacedness	Oc.	reverence	Total
1 Ti.	1	2:9			1
Heb.			1	12:28	1
Total	1		1		2

128. Αἰθίοψ, Aithi'ops

Book	Ethiopian	Total
Ac.	8:27, 27	2

129. αἷμα, hai'ma

Book	blood	Total
Mt.	16:17; 23:30, 35, 35, 35; 26:28; 27:4, 6, 8, 24, 25	11
Mk.	5:25, 29; 14:24	3
Lk.	8:43, 44; 11:50, 51, 51; 13:1; 22:20, 44	8
Jn.	1:13; 6:53, 54, 55, 56; 19:34	6
Ac.	1:19; 2:19, 20; 5:28; 15:20, 29; 17:26; 18:6; 20:26, 28; 21:25; 22:20	12
Ro.	3:15, 25; 5:9	3
1 Co.	10:16; 11:25, 27; 15:50	4
Gal.	1:16	1
Eph.	1:7; 2:13; 6:12	3
Col.	1:14, 20	2
Heb	2:14; 9:7, 12, 12, 13, 14; 9:18, 19, 20, 21, 22, 25; 10:4, 19, 29; 11:28; 12:4, 24; 13:11, 12, 20	21
1 Pt.	1:2, 19	2
1 Jn.	1:7; 5:6, 6, 8	4
Rev.	1:5; 5:9; 6:10, 12; 7:14; 8:7, 8; 11:6; 12:11; 14:20; 16:3, 4, 6, 6; 17:6, 6; 18:24; 19:2, 13	19
Total		99

130. αἱματεκχυσία haimatekchusi'a

Book	shedding of blood	Total
Heb.	9:22	1

131. αἱμορρέω, haimorhre'ō

Book	diseased with an issue of blood	Total
Mt.	9:20	1

132. Αἰνέας, Aine'as

Book	Aeneas	Total
Ac.	9:33, 34	2

133. αἴνεσις, ai'nesis

Book	praise	Total
Heb.	13:15	1

136. αἶνος, ai'nos

Book	praise	Total
Mt.	21:16	1
Lk.	18:43	1
Total		2

139. αἵρεσις, hai'resis

Book	Oc.	sect	Oc.	heresy	Total
Ac.	5	5:17; 15:5; 24:5; 26:5; 28:22	1	24:14	6
1 Co.			1	11:19	1
Gal.			1	5:20	1
2 Pt.			1	2:1	1
Total	5		4		9

134. αἰνέω, aine'ō

Book	praise	Total
Lk.	2:13, 20; 19:37; 24:53	4
Ac.	2:47; 3:8, 9	3
Ro.	15:11	1
Rev.	19:5	1
Total		9

137. Αἰνών, Ainōn'

Book	Aenon	Total
Jn.	3:23	1

140. αἱρετίζω, hairetid'zō

Book	choose	Total
Mt.	12:18	1

143. αἰσθάνομαι, aisthan'omai

Book	perceive	Total
Lk.	9:45	1

135. αἴνιγμα, ai'nigma

Book	darkly (with 1722)	Total
1 Co.	13:12	1

138. αἱρέομαι, haire'omai

Book	choose	Total
Phl.	1:22	1
2 Th.	2:13	1
Heb.	11:25	1
Total		3

141. αἱρετικός, hairetikos'

Book	that is an heretic	Total
Tit.	3:10	1

144. αἴσθησις, ai'sthēsis

Book	judgment	Total
Phl.	1:9	1

142. αἴρω, ai'rō

Book	Oc.	take up	Oc.	take away	Oc.	take	Oc.	away with	Oc.	lift up	Oc.	bear	Oc.	Misc.	Total
Mt.	6	9:6; 14:12, 20; 15:37; 16:24; 17:27	4	13:12; 22:13; 24:39; 25:29	7	9:16; 11:29; 20:14; 21:43; 24:17, 18; 25:28					1	27:32	2	4:6; 21:21	20
Mk.	12	2:9, 11, 12; 6:29, 43; 8:8, 19, 20, 34; 10:21; 13:16; 16:18	2	2:21; 4:15	4	4:25; 6:8; 13:15; 15:24					2	2:3; 15:21	1	11:23	21
Lk.	6	5:24, 25; 9:17, 23; 19:21, 22	6	6:29, 30; 8:12; 11:52; 17:31; 19:26	5	8:18; 9:3; 11:22; 19:24; 22:36	1	23:18	1	17:13			1	4:11	20
Jn.	5	5:8, 9, 11, 12; 8:59	11	1:29; 11:39, 41a, 48; 15:2; 19:31, 38a; 20:1, 2, 13, 15	5	2:16; 10:18; 16:22; 17:15; 19:38b	2	19:15, 15	1	11:41b			2	5:10; 10:24	26
Ac.	2	20:9; 27:17	1	8:33a	2	8:33b; 21:11	2	21:36; 22:22	1	4:24			1	27:13	9
1 Co.					1	6:15									1
Eph.													1	4:31	1
Col.					1	2:14									1
1 Jn.			1	3:5											1
Rev.	1	18:21							1	10:5					2
Total	32		25		25		5		4		3		8		102

Miscellaneous: Mt. 4:6, bear up; Mt. 21:21; Mk. 11:23, remove; Lk. 4:11, bear up; Jn. 5:10, carry; Jn. 10:24 (with 5490), make (one) to doubt; Ac. 27:13, loose; Eph. 4:31, put away.

145. αἰσθητήριον, aisthete'rion

Book	senses	Total
Heb.	5:14	1

147. αἰσχροκερδῶς, aischrokerdōs'

Book	for filthy lucre	Total
1 Pt.	5:2	1

150. αἰσχρός, aischros'

Book	filthy	Total
Tit.	1:11	1

151. αἰσχρότης, aischrot'es

Book	filthiness	Total
Eph.	5:4	1

146. αἰσχροκερδής, aischrokerdes'

Book	Oc.	greedy of filthy lucre	Oc.	given to filthy lucre	Total
1 Ti.	2	3:3, 8			2
Tit.			1	1:7	1
Total	2		1		3

152. αἰσχύνη, aischu'ne

Book	Oc.	shame	Oc.	dishonesty	Total
Lk.	1	14:9			1
2 Co.			1	4:2	1
Phl.	1	3:19			1
Heb.	1	12:2			1
Jd.	1	1:13			1
Rev.	1	3:18			1
Total	5		1		6

148. αἰσχρολογία, aischrologi'a

Book	filthy communication	Total
Col.	3:8	1

153. αἰσχύνομαι, aischu'nomai

Book	be ashamed	Total
Lk.	16:3	1
2 Co.	10:8	1
Phl.	1:20	1
1 Pt.	4:16	1
1 Jn.	2:28	1
Total		5

149. αἰσχρόν, aischron'

Book	shame	Total
1 Co.	11:6; 14:35	2
Eph.	5:12	1
Total		3

155. αἴτημα, ai'tema

Book	Oc.	require	Oc.	request	Oc.	petition	Total
Lk.	1	23:24					1
Phl.			1	4:6			1
1 Jn.					1	5:15	1
Total	1		1		1		3

154. αἰτέω, aite'ō

Book	Oc.	ask	Oc.	desire	Oc.	beg	Oc.	require	Oc.	crave	Oc.	call for	Total
Mt.	12	5:42; 6:8; 7:7, 8, 9, 10, 11; 14:7; 18:19; 20:22; 21:22; 27:20	1	20:20	1	27:58							14
Mk.	5	6:22, 23, 24, 25; 10:38	4	10:35; 11:24; 15:6, 8					1	15:43			10
Lk.	8	1:63; 6:30; 11:9, 10, 11, 12, 13; 12:48	1	23:25	1	23:52	1	23:23					11
Jn.	11	4:9, 10; 11:22; 14:13, 14; 15:7, 16; 16:23, 24, 24, 26											11
Ac.	1	3:2	8	3:14; 7:46; 9:2; 12:20; 13:21, 28; 25:3, 15							1	16:29	10
1 Co.							1	1:22					1
Eph.	1	3:20	1	3:13									2
Col.			1	1:9									1
Jas.	5	1:5, 6; 4:2, 3, 3											5
1 Pt.	1	3:15											1
1 Jn.	4	3:22; 5:14, 15a, 16	1	5:15b									5
Total	48		17		2		2		1		1		71

156. αἰτία, aiti'a

Book	Oc.	cause	Oc.	wherefore (with 1223 and 3639)	Oc.	accusation	Oc.	fault	Oc.	case	Oc.	crime	Total
Mt.	1	19:3			1	27:37			1	19:10			3
Mk.					1	15:26							1
Lk.	1	8:47											1
Jn.							3	18:38; 19:4, 6					3
Ac.	5	10:21; 13:28; 23:28; 28:18, 20	1	22:24	1	25:18					1	25:27	8
2 Ti.	1	1:12	1	1:6									2
Tit.			1	1:13									1
Heb.	1	2:11											1
Total	9		3		3		3		1		1		20

157. αἰτίαμα, aiti'ama

Book	complaint	Total
Ac.	25:7	1

158. αἴτιον, ai'tion

Book	Oc.	fault	Oc.	cause	Total
Lk.	2	23:4, 14	1	23:22	3
Ac.			1	19:40	1
Total	2		2		4

159. αἴτιος, ai'tios

Book	author	Total
Heb	5:9	1

160. αἰφνίδιος, aiphnid'ios

Book	Oc.	unawares	Oc.	sudden	Total
Lk.	1	21:34			1
1 Th.			1	5:3	1
Total	1		1		2

161. αἰχμαλωσία, aichmalōsi'a

Book	captivity	Total
Eph.	4:8	1
Rev.	13:10, 10	2
Total		3

162. αἰχμαλωτεύω, aichmalōteu'ō

Book	lead captive	Total
Eph.	4:8	1
2 Ti.	3:6	1
Total		2

163. αἰχμαλωτίζω, aichmalōtid'zō

Book	Oc.	bring into captivity	Oc.	lead away captive	Total
Lk.			1	21:24	1
Ro.	1	7:23			1
2 Co.	1	10:5			1
Total	2		1		3

164. αἰχμαλωτός, aichmalōtos'

Book	captive	Total
Lk.	4:18	1

165a. αἰών, aiōn′

Book	Oc.	ever	Oc.	world	Oc.	never (with 3264, 1519, and 3488)	Oc.	ever-more	Oc.	age	Oc.	eternal	Oc.	Misc.	Total
Mt.	2	6:13; 21:19	7	12:32; 13:22, 39, 40, 49; 24:3; 28:20											9
Mk.	1	11:14	2	4:19; 10:30									1	3:29	4
Lk.	2	1:33, 55	5	1:70; 16:8; 18:30; 20:34, 35											7
Jn.	6	6:51, 58; 8:35, 35; 12:34; 14:16	1	9:32	6	4:14; 8:51, 52; 10:28; 11:26; 13:8									13
Ac.			2	3:21; 15:18											2
Ro.	4	1:25; 9:5; 11:36; 16:27	1	12:2											5
1 Co.			8	1:20; 2:6, 6, 7, 8; 3:18; 8:13; 10:11											8
2 Co.	1	9:9	1	4:4			1	11:31							3
Gal.	2	1:5, 5	1	1:4											3
Eph.			3	1:21; 3:9; 6:12					1	2:7	1	3:11	3	2:2; 3:21, 21	8
Phl.	2	4:20, 20													2
Col.									1	1:26					1
1 Ti.	2	1:17b, 17c	1	6:17							1	1:17a			4
2 Ti.	2	4:18, 18	1	4:10											3
Tit.			1	2:12											1
Heb.	10	1:8, 8; 5:6; 6:20; 7:17, 21, 24; 13:8, 21, 21	4	1:2; 6:5; 9:26; 11:3			1	7:28							15
1 Pt.	6	1:23, 25; 4:11, 11; 5:11, 11													6
2 Pt.	2	2:17; 3:18													2
1 Jn.	1	2:17													1
2 Jn.	1	1:2													1
Jd.	1	1:13											1	1:25	2
Rev.	26	1:6, 6; 4:9, 9, 10, 10; 5:13, 13, 14, 14; 7:12, 12; 10:6, 6; 11:15, 15; 14:11, 11; 15:7, 7; 19:3, 3; 20:10, 10; 22:5, 5					2	1:18, 18							28
Total	71		38		6		4		2		2		5		128

Miscellaneous: Mk. 3:29 (with 3656, 1519, and 3488), never; Eph. 2:2, course; Eph. 3:21, 21 (with 3488), world without end; Jd. 1:25 (with 1519, 3856, and 3488), ever.

165b. αἰών, aiōn′

An exhibit on the usage of the word "age" according to Greek phraseology

Book	Oc.	εἰς τοὺς αἰῶνας τῶν αἰώνων unto the ages of the ages	Oc.	εἰς τὸν αἰῶνα unto the age	Oc.	ὁ αἰὼν οὗτος this age	Oc.	εἰς τοὺς αἰῶνας unto the ages	Oc.	συντέλεια τοῦ αἰῶνος end of the age	Oc.	ἀπ' αἰῶνος or ἐκ αἰῶνος from the age	Oc.	Misc.	Total
Mt.			1	21:19	2	12:32; 13:22	1	6:13	5	13:39, 40, 49; 24:3; 28:20					9
Mk.			2	3:29; 11:14	1	4:19							1	10:30	4
Lk.			1	1:55	2	16:8; 20:34	1	1:33			1	1:70	2	18:30; 20:35	7
Jn.			12	4:14; 6:51, 58; 8:35, 35, 51, 52; 10:28; 11:26; 12:34; 13:8; 14:16							1	9:32			13
Ac.											2	3:21; 15:18			2
Ro.					1	12:2	4	1:25; 9:5; 11:36; 16:27							5
1 Co.			1	8:13	5	1:20; 2:6, 6, 8; 3:18							2	2:7; 10:11	8
2 Co.			1	9:9			1	11:31					1	4:4	3
Gal.	2	1:5, 5											1	1:4	3
Eph.					3	1:21; 2:2; 6:12							5	2:7; 3:9, 11, 21, 21	8
Phl.	2	4:20, 20													2
Col.											1	1:26			1
1 Ti.	2	1:17b, 17c			1	6:17							1	1:17a	4
2 Ti.	2	4:18, 18											1	4:10	3
Tit.													1	2:12	1
Heb.	2	13:21, 21	6	5:6; 6:20; 7:17, 21, 24, 28			1	13:8	1	9:26			5	1:2, 8, 8; 6:5; 11:3	15
1 Pt.	4	4:11, 11; 5:11, 11	2	1:23, 25											6
2 Pt.													2	2:17; 3:18	2
1 Jn.			1	2:17											1
2 Jn.			1	1:2											1
Jd.			1	1:13									1	1:25	2
Rev.	28	1:6, 6, 18, 18; 4:9, 9, 10, 10; 5:13, 13, 14, 14; 7:12, 12; 10:6, 6; 11:15, 15; 14:11, 11; 15:7, 7; 19:3, 3; 20:10, 10; 22:5, 5													28
Total	42		29		15		8		6		5		23		128

Miscellaneous: Mk. 10:30; Lk. 18:30, the age to come; Lk. 20:35, that age; 1 Co. 2:7, before the ages; 1 Co. 10:11, the ends of the ages; 2 Co. 4:4, the god of this age; Gal. 1:4, this present evil age; Eph. 2:7, the ages to come; Eph. 3:9, from the ages; Eph. 3:11, purpose of the ages; Eph. 3:21, 21, the age of the ages; 1 Ti. 1:17a, King of the ages; 2 Ti. 4:10, Tit. 2:12, the present age; Heb. 1:2, the ages; Heb. 1:8, 8, unto the age of the age; Heb. 6:5, the age to come; Heb. 11:3, the ages; 2 Pt. 2:17, unto an age; 2 Pt. 3:18, unto a day of an age; Jd. 1:25, unto all the ages. Note: The word "age" is to be understood in Mt. 12:32 and Eph. 1:21, viz., "in the coming (age)," thus making these passages parallel with Mk. 10:30, Lk. 18:30 and Heb. 6:5.

166. αἰώνιος, aiō'nios

Book	Oc.	eternal	Oc.	everlasting	Oc.	the world began (with 5450)	Oc.	since the world began (with 5450)	Oc.	for ever	Total
Mt.	2	19:16; 25:46b	4	18:8; 19:29; 25:41, 46a							6
Mk.	3	3:29; 10:17, 30									3
Lk.	2	10:25; 18:18	2	16:9; 18:30							4
Jn.	9	3:15; 4:36; 5:39; 6:54, 68; 10:28; 12:25; 17:2, 3	8	3:16, 36; 4:14; 5:24; 6:27, 40, 47; 12:50							17
Ac.	1	13:48	1	13:46							2
Ro.	3	2:7; 5:21; 6:23	2	6:22; 16:26			1	16:25			6
2 Co.	3	4:17, 18; 5:1									3
Gal.			1	6:8							1
2 Th.			2	1:9; 2:16							2
1 Ti.	2	6:12, 19	2	1:16; 6:16							4
2 Ti.	1	2:10			1	1:9					2
Tit.	2	1:2a; 3:7			1	1:2b					3
Phe.									1	1:15	1
Heb.	5	5:9; 6:2; 9:12, 14, 15	1	13:20							6
1 Pt.	1	5:10									1
2 Pt.			1	1:11							1
1 Jn.	6	1:2; 2:25; 3:15; 5:11, 13, 20									6
Jd.	2	1:7, 21									2
Rev.			1	14:6							1
Total	42		25		2		1		1		71

167. ἀκαθαρσία, akatharsi'a

Book	uncleanness	Total
Mt.	23:27	1
Ro.	1:24; 6:19	2
2 Co.	12:21	1
Gal.	5:19	1
Eph.	4:19; 5:3	2
Col.	3:5	1
1 Th.	2:3; 4:7	2
Total		10

168. ἀκαθάρτης, akathar'tēs

Book	filthiness	Total
Rev.	17:4	1

170. ἀκαιρέομαι, akaire'omai

Book	lack of opportunity	Total
Phl.	4:10	1

171. ἀκαίρως, akai'rōs

Book	out of season	Total
2 Ti.	4:2	1

173. ἄκανθα, ak'antha

Book	thorns	Total
Mt.	7:16; 13:7, 7, 22; 27:29	5
Mk.	4:7, 7, 18	3
Lk.	6:44; 8:7, 7, 14	4
Jn.	19:2	1
Heb.	6:8	1
Total		14

174. ἀκάνθινος, akan'thinos

Book	of thorns	Total
Mk.	15:17	1
Jn.	19:5	1
Total		2

176. ἀκατάγνωστος akatag'nōstos

Book	cannot be condemned	Total
Tit.	2:8	1

169. ἀκάθαρτος, akath'artos

Book	Oc.	unclean	Oc.	foul	Total
Mt.	2	10:1; 12:43			2
Mk.	10	1:23, 26, 27; 3:11, 30; 5:2, 8, 13; 6:7; 7:25	1	9:25	11
Lk.	6	4:33, 36; 6:18; 8:29; 9:42; 11:24			6
Ac.	5	5:16; 8:7; 10:14, 28; 11:8			5
1 Co.	1	7:14			1
2 Co.	1	6:17			1
Eph.	1	5:5			1
Rev.	2	16:13; 18:2b	1	18:2a	3
Total	28		2		30

172. ἄκακος, ak'akos

Book	Oc.	simple	Oc.	harmless	Total
Ro.	1	16:18			1
Heb.			1	7:26	1
Total	1		1		2

175. ἄκαρπος, ak'arpos

Book	Oc.	unfruitful	Oc.	without fruit	Total
Mt.	1	13:22			1
Mk.	1	4:19			1
1 Co.	1	14:14			1
Eph.	1	5:11			1
Tit.	1	3:14			1
2 Pt.	1	1:8			1
Jd.			1	1:12	1
Total	6		1		7

181. ἀκαταστασία, akatastasi'a

Book	Oc.	confusion	Oc.	tumult	Oc.	commotion	Total
Lk.					1	21:9	1
1 Co.	1	14:33					1
2 Co.			2	6:5; 12:20			2
Jas.	1	3:16					1
Total	2		2		1		5

185. ἀκέραιος, aker'aios

Book	Oc.	harmless	Oc.	simple	Total
Mt.	1	10:16			1
Ro.			1	16:19	1
Phl.	1	2:15			1
Total	2		1		3

177. ἀκατακάλυπτος akatakal'uptos

Book	uncovered	Total
1 Co.	11:5, 13	2

178. ἀκατάκριτος, akatak'ritos

Book	uncondemned	Total
Ac.	16:37; 22:25	2

179. ἀκατάλυτος, akatal'utos

Book	endless	Total
Heb.	7:16	1

180. ἀκατάπαυστος akatap'austos

Book	cannot cease	Total
2 Pt.	2:14	1

182. ἀκατάστατος, akatas'tatos

Book	unstable	Total
Jas.	1:8	1

183. ἀκατάσχετος, akatas'chetos

Book	unruly	Total
Jas.	3:8	1

184. Ἀκελδαμά, Akeldama'

Book	Aceldama	Total
Ac.	1:19	1

186. ἀκλινής, aklinēs'

Book	without wavering	Total
Heb.	10:23	1

187. ἀκμάζω, akmad'zō

Book	be fully ripe	Total
Rev.	14:18	1

188. ἀκμήν, akmēn'

Book	yet	Total
Mt.	15:16	1

189. ἀκοή, akoē'

Book	Oc.	hearing	Oc.	ears	Oc.	fame	Oc.	rumour	Oc.	report	Oc.	audience	Oc.	Misc.	Total
Mt.	1	13:14			2	4:24; 14:1	1	24:6							4
Mk.			1	7:35	1	1:28	1	13:7							3
Lk.											1	7:1			1
Jn.									1	12:38					1
Ac.	1	28:26	1	17:20											2
Ro.	2	10:17, 17							1	10:16					3
1 Co.	2	12:17, 17													2
Gal.	2	3:2, 5													2
1 Th.													1	2:13	1
2 Ti.			2	4:3, 4											2
Heb.	1	5:11											1	4:2	2
2 Pt.	1	2:8													1
Total	10		4		3		2		2		1		2		24

Miscellaneous: 1 Th. 2:13, which ye heard; Heb. 4:2, preached.

190. ἀκολουθέω, akolouthe'ō

Book	Oc.	follow	Oc.	reach	Total
Mt.	25	4:20, 22, 25; 8:1, 10, 19, 22, 23; 9:9, 9, 19, 27; 10:38; 12:15; 14:13; 16:24; 19:2, 21, 27, 28; 20:29, 34; 21:9; 26:58; 27:55			25
Mk.	19	1:18; 2:14, 14, 15; 3:7; 5:24; 6:1; 8:34; 9:38, 38; 10:21, 28, 32, 52; 11:9; 14:13, 51, 54; 15:41			19
Lk.	17	5:11, 27, 28; 7:9; 9:11, 23, 49, 57, 59, 61; 18:22, 28, 43; 22:10, 39, 54; 23:27			17
Jn.	19	1:37, 38, 40, 43; 6:2; 8:12; 10:4, 5, 27; 11:31; 12:26; 13:36, 36, 37; 18:15; 20:6; 21:19, 20, 22			19
Ac.	4	12:8, 9; 13:43; 21:36			4
1 Co.	1	10:4			1
Rev.	6	6:8; 14:4, 8, 9, 13; 19:14	1	18:5	7
Total	91		1		92

191. ἀκούω, akou'ō

Book	Oc.	hear	Oc.	hearken	Oc.	give audience	Oc.	hearer	Oc.	Misc.	Total
Mt.	65	2:3, 9, 18, 22; 4:12; 5:21, 27, 33, 38, 43; 7:24, 26; 8:10; 9:12; 10:14, 27; 11:2, 4, 5, 15, 15; 12:19, 24, 42; 13:9, 9, 13, 13, 14, 15, 16, 17, 17, 17, 18, 19, 20, 22, 23, 43, 43; 14:1, 13, 13; 15:10, 12; 17:5, 6; 18:15, 16; 19:22, 25; 20:24, 30; 21:16, 33, 45; 22:7 22, 33, 34; 24:6; 26:65; 27:13. 47							2	13:15; 28:14	67
Mk.	45	2:17; 3:8, 21; 4:9, 9, 12, 12, 15, 16, 18, 20, 23, 23, 24, 24, 33; 5:27, 36; 6:2, 11, 14, 16; 6:20, 20, 29, 55; 7:16, 16, 25, 37; 8:18; 9:7; 10:41, 47; 11:14, 18; 12:28, 29, 37; 13:7; 14:11, 58, 64; 15:35; 16:11	2	4:3; 7:14					1	2:1	48
Lk.	64	1:41, 58, 66; 2:18, 20, 46, 47; 4:23, 28; 5:1, 15; 6:17, 27, 47, 49; 7:3, 9, 22, 22, 29; 8:8, 8, 10, 12, 13, 14, 15, 18, 21, 50; 9:7, 9, 35; 10:16, 16, 24, 24, 24, 39; 11:28, 31; 12:3; 14:15, 35, 35; 15:1, 25; 16:2, 14, 29, 31; 18:6, 22, 23, 26, 36; 19:11, 48; 20:16; 21:9, 38; 22:71; 23:6, 8							1	20:45	65
Jn.	58	1:37, 40; 3:8, 29, 32; 4:1, 42, 47; 5:24, 25, 25, 28, 30, 37; 6:45, 60, 60; 7:32, 40, 51; 8:9, 26, 40, 43, 47, 47; 9:27, 27, 31, 31, 32, 35, 40; 10:3, 8, 16, 20, 27; 11:4, 6, 20, 29, 41, 42; 12:12, 18, 29, 34, 47; 14: 24, 28; 15:15; 16:13; 18:21, 37; 19:8, 13; 21:7									58
Ac.	83	1:4; 2:6, 8, 11, 22, 33, 37; 3:22, 23; 4:4, 20, 24; 5:5, 5, 11, 21, 24, 33; 6:11, 14; 7:12, 34, 37, 54; 8:6, 14, 30; 9:4, 7, 13, 21, 38; 10:22, 33, 44, 46; 11:1, 7, 18; 13:7, 44, 48; 14:9, 14; 15:7, 24; 16:14, 38; 17:8, 21, 32, 32; 18:8, 26; 19:2, 5, 10, 26, 28; 21:12, 20, 22; 22:1, 2, 7, 9, 14, 15, 26; 23:16; 24:4, 22, 24; 25:22, 22; 26:3, 14, 29; 28:15, 22, 26, 27, 28	3	4:19; 7:2; 15:13	3	13:16; 15:12; 22:22			2	11:22; 28:27	91
Ro.	5	10:14, 14, 18; 11:8; 15:21									5
1 Co.	2	2:9; 11:18							2	5:1; 14:2	4
2 Co.	2	12:4, 6									2
Gal.	3	1:13, 23; 4:21									3
Eph.	4	1:13, 15; 3:2; 4:21					1	4:29			5
Phl.	4	1:27, 30; 2:26; 4:9									4
Col.	4	1:4, 6, 9, 23									4
2 Th.	1	3:11									1
1 Ti.	1	4:16									1
2 Ti.	3	1:13; 2:2; 4:17					1	2:14			4
Phe.	1	1:5									1
Heb.	8	2:1, 3; 3:7, 15, 16; 4:2, 7; 12:19									8
Jas.	2	1:19; 5:11	1	2:5							3
2 Pt.	1	1:18									1
1 Jn.	14	1:1, 3, 5; 2:7, 18, 24, 24; 3:11; 4:3, 5, 6, 6; 5:14, 15									14
2 Jn.	1	1:6									1
3 Jn.	1	1:4									1
Rev.	46	1:3, 10; 2:7, 11, 17, 29; 3:3, 6, 13, 20, 22; 4:1; 5:11, 13; 6:1, 3, 5, 6, 7; 7:4; 8:13; 9:13, 16, 20; 10:4, 8; 11:12; 12:10; 13:9; 14:2, 2, 13; 16:1, 5, 7; 18:4, 22, 22, 23; 19:1, 6; 21:3; 22:8, 8, 17, 18									46
Total	418		6		3		2		8		437

Miscellaneous: Mt. 13:15, of hearing; Mt. 28:14, to come to (one's) ears; Mk. 2:1, be noised; Lk. 20:45, in the audience of; Ac. 11:22 (with 3056), tidings come; Ac. 28:27, of hearing; 1 Co. 5:1, be reported; 1 Co. 14:2, understand.

192. ἀκρασία, akrasi'a

Book	Oc.	excess	Oc.	incontinency	Total
Mt.	1	23:25			1
1 Co.			1	7:5	1
Total	1		1		2

193. ἀκράτης, akrat'ēs

Book	incontinent	Total
2 Ti.	3:3	1

194. ἄκρατος, ak'ratos

Book	without mixture	Total
Rev.	14:10	1

195. ἀκρίβεια, akri'beia

Book	perfect manner	Total
Ac.	22:3	1

196. ἀκριβέστατος, akribes'tatos

Book	most straitest	Total
Ac.	26:5	1

197. ἀκριβέστερον, akribes'teron

Book	Oc.	more perfectly	Oc.	more perfect	Total
Ac.	3	18:26; 23:15, 20	1	24:22	4

198. ἀκριβόω, akribo'ō

Book	enquire diligently	Total
Mt.	2:7, 16	2

199. ἀκριβῶς, akribōs'

Book	Oc.	diligently	Oc.	perfect	Oc.	perfectly	Oc.	circumspectly	Total
Mt.	1	2:8							1
Lk.			1	1:3					1
Ac.	1	18:25							1
Eph.							1	5:15	1
1 Th.					1	5:2			1
Total	2		1		1		1		5

200. ἀκρίς, akris'

Book	locust	Total
Mt.	3:4	1
Mk.	1:6	1
Rev.	9:3, 7	2
Total		4

201. ἀκροατήριον, akroatē'rion

Book	place of hearing	Total
Ac.	25:23	1

202. ἀκροατής, akroatēs'

Book	hearer	Total
Ro.	2:13	1
Jas.	1:22, 23, 25	3
Total		4

203. ἀκροβυστία, akrobusti'a

Book	Oc.	uncircumcision	Oc.	being uncircumcised (with 1722)	Oc.	uncircumcised (with 2192)	Oc.	though not circumcised (with 1223)	Total
Ac.					1	11:3			1
Ro.	8	2:25, 26, 26, 27; 3:30; 4:9, 10, 10	2	4:11a, 12			1	4:11b	11
1 Co.	2	7:18, 19							2
Gal.	3	2:7; 5:6; 6:15							3
Eph.	1	2:11							1
Col.	2	2:13; 3:11							2
Total	16		2		1		1		20

204. ἀκρογωνιαῖος akrogōniai'os

Book	chief corner	Total
Eph.	2:20	1
1 Pt.	2:6	1
Total		2

205. ἀκροθίνιον, akrothin'ion

Book	spoils	Total
Heb.	7:4	1

206. ἄκρον, ak'ron

Book	Oc.	uttermost part	Oc.	one end	Oc.	other (with 846)	Oc.	tip	Oc.	top	Total
Mt.			1	24:31a	1	24:31b					2
Mk.	2	13:27, 27									2
Lk.							1	16:24			1
Heb.									1	11:21	1
Total	2		1		1		1		1		6

207. Ἀκύλας, Aku'las

Book	Aquila	Total
Ac.	18:2, 18, 26	3
Ro.	16:3	1
1 Co	16:19	1
2 Ti.	4:19	1
Total		6

208. ἀκυρόω, akuro'ō

Book	Oc.	make of none effect	Oc.	disannul	Total
Mt.	1	15:6			1
Mk.	1	7:13			1
Gal.			1	3:17	1
Total	2		1		3

209. ἀκωλύτως akōlu'tōs

Book	no man forbidding him	Total
Ac.	28:31	1

210. ἄκων, ak'ōn

Book	against (one's) will	Total
1 Co.	9:17	1

211. ἀλάβαστρον, alab'astron

Book	Oc.	alabaster box	Oc.	box	Total
Mt.	1	26:7			1
Mk.	1	14:3a	1	14:3b	2
Lk.	1	7:37			1
Total	3		1		4

212. ἀλαζονεία, aladzonei'a

Book	Oc.	boasting	Oc.	pride	Total
Jas.	1	4:16			1
1 Jn.			1	2:16	1
Total	1		1		2

213. ἀλαζών, aladzōn'

Book	boaster	Total
Ro.	1:30	1
2 Ti.	3:2	1
Total		2

214. ἀλαλάζω, alalad'zō

Book	Oc.	wail	Oc.	tinkle	Total
Mk.	1	5:38			1
1 Co.			1	13:1	1
Total	1		1		2

215. ἀλάλητος, alal'ētos

Book	which cannot be uttered	Total
Ro.	8:26	1

216. ἄλαλος, al'alos

Book	dumb	Total
Mk.	7:37; 9:17, 25	3

217. ἅλας, hal'as

Book	salt	Total
Mt.	5:13, 13	2
Mk.	9:50, 50, 50	3
Lk.	14:34, 34	2
Col.	4:6	1
Total		8

218. ἀλείφω, alei'phō

Book	anoint	Total
Mt.	6:17	1
Mk.	6:13; 16:1	2
Lk.	7:38, 46, 46	3
Jn.	11:2; 12:3	2
Jas.	5:14	1
Total		9

219. ἀλεκτοροφωνία alektorophōni'a

Book	cockcrowing	Total
Mk.	13:35	1

220. ἀλέκτωρ, alek'tōr

Book	cock	Total
Mt.	26:34, 74, 75	3
Mk.	14:30, 68, 72, 72	4
Lk.	22:34, 60, 61	3
Jn.	13:38; 18:27	2
Total		12

221. Ἀλεξανδρεύς, Alexandreus'

Book	Oc.	Alexandrian	Oc.	born at Alexandria (with 1085)	Total
Ac.	1	6:9	1	18:24	2

222. Ἀλεξανδρῖνος Alexandri'nos

Book	of Alexandria	Total
Ac.	27:6; 28:11	2

223. Ἀλέξανδρος, Alex'andros

Book	Oc.	Alexander (of Ephesus)	Oc.	Alexander (the coppersmith)	Oc.	Alexander (son of Simon)	Oc.	Alexander (of Jerusalem)	Total
Mk.					1	15:21			1
Ac.	2	19:33, 33					1	4:6	3
1 Ti.			1	1:20					1
2 Ti.			1	4:14					1
Total	2		2		1		1		6

224. ἀλίσγεμα, alis'gema

Book	meal	Total
Mt.	13:33	1
Lk.	13:21	1
Total		2

225. ἀλήθεια, alē'theia

Book	Oc.	truth	Oc.	truly (with 1909)	Oc.	true	Oc.	verity	Total
Mt.	1	22:16							1
Mk.	3	5:33; 12:14, 32							3
Lk.	2	4:25; 22:59	1	20:21					3
Jn.	25	1:14, 17; 3:21; 4:23, 24; 5:33; 8:32, 32, 40, 44, 44, 45, 46; 14:6, 17; 15:26; 16:7, 13, 13; 17:17, 17, 19; 18:37, 37, 38							25
Ac.	3	4:27; 10:34; 26:25							3
Ro.	8	1:18, 25; 2:2, 8, 20; 3:7; 9:1; 15:8							8
1 Co.	2	5:8; 13:6							2
2 Co.	8	4:2; 6:7; 7:14, 14; 11:10; 12:6; 13:8, 8							8
Gal.	4	2:5, 14; 3:1; 5:7							4
Eph.	5	1:13; 4:21, 25; 5:9; 6:14			1	4:24			6
Phl.	1	1:18							1
Col.	2	1:5, 6							2
2 Th.	3	2:10, 12, 13							3
1 Ti.	5	2:4, 7a; 3:15; 4:3; 6:5					1	2:7b	6
2 Ti.	6	2:15, 18, 25; 3:7, 8; 4:4							6
Tit.	2	1:1, 14							2
Heb.	1	10:26							1
Jas.	3	1:18; 3:14; 5:19							3
1 Pt.	1	1:22							1
2 Pt.	2	1:12; 2:2							2
1 Jn.	9	1:6, 8; 2:4, 21, 21; 3:18, 19; 4:6; 5:6							9
2 Jn.	5	1:1, 1, 2, 3, 4							5
3 Jn.	6	1:1, 3, 3, 4, 8, 12							6
Total	107		1		1		1		110

226. ἀληθεύω, ale̱theu'ō

Book	Oc.	tell the truth	Oc.	speak the truth	Total
Gal.	1	4:16			1
Eph.			1	4:15	1
Total	1		1		2

227. ἀληθής, ale̱the̱s'

Book	Oc.	true	Oc.	truly	Oc.	truth	Total
Mt.	1	22:16					1
Mk.	1	12:14					1
Jn.	12	3:33; 5:31, 32; 7:18; 8:13, 14, 16, 17, 26; 10:41; 19:35; 21:24	1	4:18			13
Ac.	1	12:9					1
Ro.	1	3:4					1
2 Co.	1	6:8					1
Phl.	1	4:8					1
Tit.	1	1:13					1
1 Pt.	1	5:12					1
2 Pt.	1	2:22					1
1 Jn.	1	2:8			1	2:27	2
3 Jn.	1	1:12					1
Total	23		1		1		25

228. ἀληθινός, ale̱thinos'

Book	true	Total
Lk.	16:11	1
Jn.	1:9; 4:23,37; 6:32; 7:28; 15:1; 17:3; 19:35	8
1 Th.	1:9	1
Heb.	8:2; 9:24; 10:22	3
1 Jn.	2:8; 5:20, 20, 20	4
Rev.	3:7, 14; 6:10; 15:3; 16:7; 19:2, 9, 11; 21:5; 22:6	10
Total		27

229. ἀλήθω, ale̱'thō

Book	grinding	Total
Mt.	24:41	1
Lk.	17:35	1
Total		2

231. ἁλιεύς, halieus'

Book	Oc.	fishers	Oc.	fishermen	Total
Mt.	2	4:18, 19			2
Mk.	2	1:16, 17			2
Lk.			1	5:2	1
Total	4		1		5

232. ἁλιεύω, halieu'ō

Book	a fishing	Total
Jn.	21:3	1

230. ἀληθῶς, ale̱thōs'

Book	Oc.	of a truth	Oc.	indeed	Oc.	surely	Oc.	truly	Oc.	very	Oc.	Misc.	Total
Mt.	1	14:33			1	26:73	1	27:54					3
Mk.					1	14:70	1	15:39					2
Lk.	3	9:27; 12:44; 21:3											3
Jn.	2	6:14; 7:40	6	1:47; 4:42; 6:55, 55; 7:26a; 8:31	1	17:8			1	7:26b			10
Ac.											1	12:11	1
1 Th.											1	2:13	1
1 Jn.											1	2:5	1
Total	6		6		3		2		1		3		21

Miscellaneous: Ac. 12:11, of a surety; 1 Th. 2:13, in truth; 1 Jn. 2:5, verily.

233. ἁλίζω, halid'zō

Book	to salt	Total
Mt.	5:13	1
Mk.	9:49, 49	2
Total		3

See page 14 for Word 235.

236. ἀλλάσσω, allas'sō

Book	change	Total
Ac.	6:14	1
Ro.	1:23	1
1 Co.	15:51, 52	2
Gal.	4:20	1
Heb.	1:12	1
Total		6

238. ἀλληγορέω, alle̱gore'ō

Book	be an allegory	Total
Gal.	4:24	1

234. ἀλίσγεμα, alis'gema

Book	pollution	Total
Ac.	15:20	1

237. ἀλλαχόθεν, allachoth'en

Book	some other way	Total
Jn.	10:1	1

239. ἀλληλουϊα, alle̱lou'ia

Book	alleluia	Total
Rev.	19:1, 3, 4, 6	4

240. ἀλλήλων, alle̱'lōn

Book	Oc.	one another	Oc.	themselves	Oc.	yourselves	Oc.	Misc.	Total
Mt.	3	24:10, 10; 25:32							3
Mk.	2	4:41; 9:50	3	8:16; 9:34; 15:31					5
Lk.	7	2:15; 6:11; 7:32; 8:25; 12:1; 24:17, 32	1	4:36			2	23:12; 24:14	10
Jn.	9	4:33; 5:44; 13:14, 22, 34, 34, 35; 15:12, 17	4	6:52; 11:56; 16:17; 19:24	2	6:43; 16:19			15
Ac.	4	2:7; 7:26; 19:38; 21:6	4	4:15; 26:31; 28:4, 25			1	15:39	9
Ro.	13	1:27; 2:15; 12:5, 10, 10, 16; 13:8; 14:13, 19; 15:5, 7, 14; 16:16					1	1:12	14
1 Co.	3	11:33; 12:25; 16:20					1	7:5	4
2 Co.	1	13:12							1
Gal.	6	5:13, 15, 15, 26, 26; 6:2					1	5:17	7
Eph.	4	4:2, 25, 32; 5:21							4
Phl.							1	2:3	1
Col.	2	3:9, 13							2
1 Th.	3	3:12; 4:9, 18			1	5:15	1	5:11	5
2 Th.							1	1:3	1
Tit.	1	3:3							1
Heb.	1	10:24							1
Jas.	4	4:11; 5:9, 16, 16							4
1 Pt.	4	1:22; 4:9; 5:5, 14							4
1 Jn.	6	1:7; 3:11, 23; 4:7, 11, 12							6
2 Jn.	1	1:5							1
Rev.	2	6:4; 11:10							2
Total	76		12		3		9		100

Miscellaneous: Lk. 23:12 (with 3226), together; Lk. 24:14 (with 4214), together; Ac. 15:39, one the other; Ro. 1:12 (with 1722), mutual; 1 Co. 7:5, one the other; Gal. 5:17, the one the other; Phl. 2:3, each other; 1 Th. 5:11, yourselves together; 2 Th. 1:3, each other.

242. ἅλλομαι, hal'lomai

Book	Oc.	leap	Oc.	spring up	Total
Jn.			1	4:14	1
Ac.	2	3:8; 14:10			2
Total	2		1		3

241. ἀλλογενής, allogene̱s'

Book	stranger	Total
Lk.	17:18	1

243. ἄλλος, al′los

Book	Oc.	other(s)	Oc.	another	Oc.	some	Oc.	one	Oc.	Misc.	Total
Mt.	17	4:21; 5:39; 12:13; 13:8; 20:3, 6; 21:8, 36, 41; 22:4; 25:16, 17, 20a, 22; 27:42, 61; 28:1	9	2:12; 8:9; 10:23; 13:24, 31, 33; 19:9; 21:33; 26:71	3	13:5, 7; 16:14			1	25:20b	30
Mk.	15	3:5; 4:8, 36; 6:15, 15; 7:4, 8; 8:28b; 11:8; 12:5b, 9, 31, 32; 15:31, 41	6	10:11, 12; 12:4, 5a; 14:19, 58	3	4:5, 7; 8:28a					24
Lk.	7	5:29; 6:10, 29; 9:8, 19b; 20:16; 23:35	4	7:8, 19, 20; 22:59	1	9:19a					12
Jn.	24	4:38; 6:22, 23; 7:12, 41a; 9:9b, 16; 10:16, 21; 12:29; 15:24; 18:16, 34; 19:18, 32; 20:2, 3, 4, 8, 25, 30; 21: 2, 8, 25	7	4:37b; 5:7, 32, 43; 14:16; 18:15; 21:18	2	7:41b; 9:9a	1	4:37a			34
Ac.	2	4:12; 15:2	3	2:12b; 19:32b; 21:34b	2	19:32a; 21: 34a	1	2:12a			8
1 Co.	7	1:16; 3:11; 9:2, 12, 27; 14:19, 29	14	3:10; 10:29; 12:8, 9, 10, 10, 10, 10; 14:30; 15:39b, 39c, 39d, 41b, 41c			2	15:39a; 15:41a			23
2 Co.	3	1:13; 8:13; 11:8	1	11:4							4
Gal.			1	1:7					1	5:10	2
Phl.	1	3:4									1
1 Th.	1	2:6									1
Heb.	1	11:35	1	4:8							2
Jas.	1	5:12									1
Rev.	2	2:24; 17:10	16	6:4; 7:2; 8:3; 10:1; 12: 3; 13:11; 14:6, 8, 15, 17, 18; 15:1; 16:7; 18:1, 4; 20:12							18
Total	81		62		11		4		2		160

Miscellaneous: Mt. 25:20b, more; Gal. 5:10, otherwise.

244. ἀλλοτριεπίσκοπος allotriepis′kopos

Book	a busybody in other men's matters	Total
1 Pt.	4:15	1

245. ἀλλότριος, allot′rios

Book	Oc.	stranger	Oc.	another man's	Oc.	strange	Oc.	other men's	Oc.	other	Oc.	alien	Total
Mt.	2	17:25, 26											2
Lk.			1	16:12									1
Jn.	2	10:5, 5											2
Ac.					1	7:6							1
Ro.			2	14:4; 15:20									2
2 Co.			1	10:16			1	10:15					2
1 Ti.							1	5:22					1
Heb.					1	11:9			1	9:25	1	11:34	3
Total	4		4		2		2		1		1		14

246. ἀλλόφυλος, alloph′ulos

Book	one of another nation	Total
Ac.	10:28	1

247. ἄλλως, al′lōs

Book	otherwise	Total
1 Ti.	5:25	1

248. ἀλοάω, aloa′ō

Book	Oc.	tread out the corn	Oc.	thresh	Total
1 Co.	1	9:9	1	9:10	2
1 Ti.	1	5:18			1
Total	2		1		3

249. ἄλογος, al′ogos

Book	Oc.	unreasonable	Oc.	brute	Total
Ac.	1	25:27			1
2 Pt.			1	2:12	1
Jd.			1	1:10	1
Total	1		2		3

235. ἀλλά, alla′

Book	Oc.	but	Oc.	yea	Oc.	yet
Mt.	36	4:4; 5:15, 17, 39; 6:13, 18; 7:21; 8:4, 8; 9:12, 13, 17, 18, 24; 10:20, 34; 11:8, 9; 13:21; 15:11; 16:12, 17, 23; 17:12; 18:22, 30; 19:6; 20:23, 26, 28; 21:21; 22:30, 32; 24:6; 26:39; 27:24				
Mk.	39	1:44, 45; 2:17, 17, 22; 3:26, 29; 4:17, 22; 5:19, 26, 39; 6:9; 7:5, 15, 19; 8:33; 9:13, 22, 37; 10:8, 27, 40, 43, 45; 11: 23, 32; 12:14, 25, 27; 13:7, 11, 11, 20, 24; 14:28 36b, 49; 16:7			1	14:29
Lk.	33	1:60; 4:4; 5:14, 31, 32, 38; 6:27; 7:7, 25, 26; 8:16, 27, 52; 9:56; 11:4, 33, 42; 12:7, 51; 13:3, 5; 14:10, 13; 16:30; 18: 13; 20:21, 38; 21:9; 22:26, 36, 42, 53; 24:6	1	24:22		
Jn.	99	1:8, 13, 31, 33; 3:8, 15, 16, 17, 28, 36; 4:2, 14, 23; 5:18, 22, 24, 30, 34, 42; 6:9, 22, 26, 27, 32, 36, 38, 39, 64; 7:10, 12, 16, 22, 24, 28, 44, 49; 8:12, 16, 26,28, 37, 42, 49, 55; 9:3, 31; 10:1, 5, 8, 18, 26, 33; 11:4, 11, 22, 30, 42, 51, 52, 54; 12: 6, 9, 16, 27, 30, 42, 44, 47, 49; 13:9, 10,10, 18; 14:24, 31; 15:16, 19, 21, 25; 16:4, 6, 12, 13, 20, 25, 25, 33; 17:9, 15, 20; 18:28, 40; 19:21, 24, 34; 20:7, 27; 21:8, 23.	1	16:2		
Ac.	26	1:4, 8; 2:16; 4:17, 32; 5:4, 13; 7:39; 10:35, 41; 13:25; 15:11, 20; 16:37; 18:9, 21; 19:26, 27; 20:24; 21:13, 24; 26:16, 20, 25, 29; 27:10				
Ro.	64	1:21, 32; 2:13, 29, 29; 3:27; 4:2, 4, 10, 12, 13, 16, 20, 24; 5:3, 11, 15; 6:13, 14, 15; 7:13, 15, 17, 19, 20; 8:1, 4, 9, 15, 20, 23, 26, 32; 9:7, 8, 10, 11, 16, 24, 32; 10:2, 8, 16, 18, 19; 11:4, 11, 18, 20; 12:2, 3, 16, 19, 21; 13:3, 5, 14; 14:13, 17, 20; 15:3, 21; 16:4, 18	1	3:31		
1 Co.	61	1:17, 27; 2:4, 5, 7, 9, 12, 13; 3:1, 5, 6, 7; 4:14, 19, 20; 5:8; 6:6, 11, 11, 11, 12, 12, 13; 7:4, 4, 7, 10, 19, 21, 35; 8:6; 9: 12b, 21, 27; 10:5, 13, 20, 23, 23, 24, 29, 33; 11:8, 9, 17; 12:14, 24, 25; 14:2, 17, 22, 22, 33, 34; 15:10, 10, 35, 37, 39, 40, 46b	1	4:3	4	4:4, 15; 9:2; 14:19
2 Co.	52	1:9, 9, 12, 19, 24; 2:4, 5, 13, 17, 17; 3:3, 3, 5, 6, 14, 15; 4:2, 2, 5, 8b,9, 9, 16b, 18; 5:4, 12, 15; 6:4; 7:5, 7, 9, 12, 14; 8:5, 8, 10, 14, 19, 21; 9:12; 10:4, 12, 13, 18; 11:6b, 17; 12:14, 14; 13:3, 4b, 7, 8	6	7:11, 11, 11, 11, 11, 11	5	4:8a, 16a; 5:16; 11: 6a; 13:4a
Gal.	20	1:1, 8, 12, 17; 2:3, 7, 14; 3:12, 16, 22; 4:2, 7, 14, 23, 29, 31; 5:6, 13; 6:13, 15	1	4:17		
Eph.	12	1:21; 2:19; 4:29; 5:4, 15, 17, 18, 27, 29; 6:4, 6, 12				
Phl.	12	1:20, 29; 2:3, 4, 7, 12, 27, 27; 3:7, 9, 4:6, 17	3	1:18; 2:17; 3:8		
Col.	2	3:11, 22			1	2:5
1 Th.	13	1:5, 8; 2:2, 4, 4, 7, 8, 13; 4:7, 8; 5:6, 9, 15				
2 Th.	5	2:12; 3:8, 9, 11, 15				
1 Ti.	11	1:13; 2:10, 12; 3:3; 4:12; 5:1, 13, 23; 6:2, 4, 17				
2 Ti.	11	1:7, 8, 9, 17; 2:9, 20, 24; 3:9; 4:3, 8, 16				
Tit.	4	1:8, 15; 2:10; 3:5				
Phe.	2	1:14, 16				
Heb.	15	2:16; 3:13; 4:2; 5:4, 5; 7:16; 9:24; 10:3, 25, 39; 11:13; 12:11, 22, 26; 13:14				
Jas.	4	1:25, 26; 3:15; 4:11	1	2:18		
1 Pt.	15	1:15, 19, 23; 2:16, 18, 20, 25; 3:4, 14, 21; 4:2, 13; 5:2, 2, 3				
2 Pt.	6	2:4, 5; 3:9, 9				
1 Jn.	13	2:2, 7, 16, 19, 19, 21, 27; 3:18; 4:1, 10, 18; 5:6, 18				
2 Jn.	4	1:1, 5, 8, 12				
3 Jn.	3	1:9, 11, 13				
Jd.	2	1:6, 9				
Rev.	9	2:6, 9, 14; 3:9; 9:5; 10:7, 9; 17:12; 20:6				
Total	573		15		11	

250. ἀλοή, aloe̤′

Book	aloes	Total
Jn.	19:39	1

251. ἅλς, hals

Book	salt	Total
Mk.	9:49	1

252. ἁλυκός, halukos′

Book	salt	Total
Jas.	3:12	1

253. ἀλυπότερος, alupot′eros

Book	less sorrowful	Total
Phl.	2:28	1

254. ἅλυσις, hal′usis

Book	Oc.	chain	Oc.	bonds	Total
Mk.	3	5:3, 4, 4			3
Lk.	1	8:29			1
Ac.	4	12:6, 7; 21:33; 28:20			4
Eph.			1	6:20	1
2 Ti.	1	1:16			1
Rev.	1	20:1			1
Total	10		1		11

256. Ἀλφαῖος, Alphai′os

Book	Oc.	Alphaeus (father of James)	Oc.	Alphaeus (father of Levi)	Total
Mt.	1	10:3			1
Mk.	1	3:18	1	2:14	2
Lk.	1	6:15			1
Ac.	1	1:13			1
Total	4		1		5

255. ἀλυσιτελής, alusitele̤s′

Book	unprofitable	Total
Heb.	13:17	1

257. ἅλων, hal′ōn

Book	floor	Total
Mt.	3:12	1
Lk.	3:17	1
Total		2

258. ἀλώπηξ, alō′pe̤x

Book	fox	Total
Mt.	8:20	1
Lk.	9:58; 13:32	2
Total		3

259. ἅλωσις, hal′ōsis

Book	to be taken (with 1519)	Total
2 Pt.	2:12	1

261. ἀμαθής, amathe̤s′

Book	unlearned	Total
2 Pt.	3:16	1

260. ἅμα, ham′a

Book	Oc.	together	Oc.	withal	Oc.	with	Oc.	and	Oc.	Not Tr.	Total
Mt.					1	13:29			1	20:1	2
Ac.							1	27:40	1	24:26	2
Ro.	1	3:12									1
Col.			1	4:3							1
1 Th.	2	4:17; 5:10									2
1 Ti.			1	5:13							1
Phe.			1	1:22							1
Total	3		3		1		1		2		10

262. ἀμαράντινος, amaran′tinos

Book	that fadeth not away	Total
1 Pt.	5.4	1

263. ἀμάραντος, amar′antos

Book	that fadeth not away	Total
1 Pt.	1:4	1

235. ἀλλά, alla′ (continued)

Book	Oc.	nevertheless	Oc.	howbeit	Oc.	nay	Oc.	therefore	Oc.	save	Oc.	Not Tr.	Oc.	Misc.	Total
Mt.									1	19:11					37
Mk.	1	14:36a							1	9:8					42
Lk.													4	16:21; 17:8; 23:15; 24:21	38
Jn.	2	11:15; 16:7	1	7:27											103
Ac.			1	7:48			1	10:20					1	19:2	29
Ro.	1	5:14			2	7:7; 8:37					1	6:5			69
1 Co.	1	9:12a	3	8:7; 14:20; 15:46a	2	6:8; 12:22							1	3:2	73
2 Co.	2	7:6; 12:16					1	8:7			1	1:13	1	11:1	68
Gal.	1	4:30	1	4:8											23
Eph.							1	5:24							13
Phl.															15
Col.															3
1 Th.															13
2 Th.															5
1 Ti.			1	1:16											12
2 Ti.	1	1:12													12
Tit.															4
Phe.															2
Heb.			1	3:16											16
Jas.															5
1 Pt.															15
2 Pt.															6
1 Jn.															13
2 Jn.															4
3 Jn.															3
Jd.															2
Rev.	1	2:4											1	2:20	11
Total	10		8		4		3		2		2		8		636

Miscellaneous: Lk. 16:21 (with 2532), moreover; Lk. 17:8, and rather; Lk. 23:15, no; Lk. 24:21 (with 1065), and; Ac. 19:2 (with 3661), not so much as; 1 Co. 3:2 (with 3677), neither: 2 Co. 11:1, indeed; Rev. 2:20, notwithstanding.

264. ἁμαρτάνω, hamartan'ō

Book	Oc.	sin	Oc.	trespass	Oc.	offend	Oc.	for your faults	Total
Mt.	2	18:21; 27:4	1	18:15					3
Lk.	2	15:18, 21	2	17:3, 4					4
Jn.	4	5:14; 8:11; 9:2, 3							4
Ac.					1	25:8			1
Ro.	7	2:12, 12; 3:23; 5:12, 14, 16; 6:15							7
1 Co.	7	6:18; 7:28, 28, 36; 8:12, 12; 15:34							7
Eph.	1	4:26							1
1 Ti.	1	5:20							1
Tit.	1	3:11							1
Heb.	2	3:17; 10:26							2
1 Pt.							1	2:20	1
2 Pt.	1	2:4							1
1 Jn.	10	1:10; 2:1, 1; 3:6, 6, 8, 9; 5:16, 16, 18							10
Total	38		3		1		1		43

266. ἁμαρτία, hamarti'a

Book	Oc.	sin	Oc.	sinful	Oc.	offence	Total
Mt.	7	1:21; 3:6; 9:2, 5, 6; 12:31; 26:28					7
Mk.	6	1:4, 5; 2:5, 7, 9, 10					6
Lk.	11	1:77; 3:3; 5:20, 21, 23, 24; 7:47, 48, 49; 11:4; 24:47					11
Jn.	17	1:29; 8:21, 24, 24, 34, 34, 46; 9:34, 41, 41; 15:22, 22, 24; 16:8, 9; 19:11; 20:23					17
Ac.	8	2:38; 3:19; 5:31; 7:60; 10:43; 13:38; 22:16; 26:18					8
Ro.	47	3:9, 20; 4:7, 8; 5:12, 12, 13, 13, 20, 21; 6:1, 2, 6, 6, 7, 10, 11, 12, 13, 14, 16, 17, 18, 20, 22, 23; 7:5, 7, 7, 8, 8, 9, 11, 13, 13, 13, 14, 17, 20, 23, 25; 8:2, 3b, 3c, 10; 11:27; 14:23	1	8:3a			48
1 Co.	4	15:3, 17, 56, 56					4
2 Co.	2	5:21, 21			1	11:7	3
Gal.	3	1:4; 2:17; 3:22					3
Eph.	1	2:1					1
Col.	2	1:14; 2:11					2
1 Th.	1	2:16					1
2 Th.	1	2:3					1
1 Ti.	2	5:22, 24					2
2 Ti.	1	3:6					1
Heb.	25	1:3; 2:17; 3:13; 4:15; 5:1, 3; 7:27; 8:12; 9:26, 28, 28; 10:2, 3, 4, 6, 8, 11, 12, 17, 18, 26; 11:25; 12:1, 4; 13:11					25
Jas.	6	1:15, 15; 2:9; 4:17; 5:15, 20					6
1 Pt.	6	2:22, 24, 24; 3:18; 4:1, 8					6
2 Pt.	2	1:9; 2:14					2
1 Jn.	17	1:7, 8, 9, 9; 2:2, 12; 3:4, 4, 5, 5, 8, 9; 4:10; 5:16, 16, 17, 17					17
Rev.	3	1:5; 18:4, 5					3
Total	172		1		1		174

265. ἁμάρτημα, hamar'tẹma

Book	sin	Total
Mk.	3:28; 4:12	2
Ro.	3:25	1
1 Co.	6:18	1
Total		4

268. ἁμαρτωλός, hamartōlos'

Book	Oc.	sinner	Oc.	sinful	Total
Mt.	5	9:10, 11, 13; 11:19; 26:45			5
Mk.	5	2:15, 16, 16, 17; 14:41	1	8:38	6
Lk.	16	5:30, 32; 6:32, 33, 34, 34; 7:34, 37, 39; 13:2; 15:1, 2, 7, 10; 18:13; 19:7	2	5:8; 24:7	18
Jn.	4	9:16, 24, 25, 31			4
Ro.	3	3:7; 5:8, 19	1	7:13	4
Gal.	2	2:15, 17			2
1 Ti.	2	1:9, 15			2
Heb.	2	7:26; 12:3			2
Jas.	2	4:8; 5:20			2
1 Pt.	1	4:18			1
Jd.	1	1:15			1
Total	43		4		47

267. ἀμάρτυρος, amar'turos

Book	without witness	Total
Ac.	14:17	1

269. ἄμαχος, am'achos

Book	Oc.	not a brawler	Oc.	no brawler	Total
1 Ti.	1	3:3			1
Tit.			1	3:2	1
Total	1		1		2

270. ἀμάω, ama'ō

Book	reap down	Total
Jas.	5:4	1

271. ἀμέθυστος, ameth'ustos

Book	amethyst	Total
Rev.	21:20	1

272. ἀμελέω, amele'ō

Book	Oc.	neglect	Oc.	make light of	Oc.	regard not	Oc.	be negligent	Total
Mt.			1	22:5					1
1 Ti.	1	4:14							1
Heb.	1	2:3			1	8:9			2
2 Pt.							1	1:12	1
Total	2		1		1		1		5

273. ἄμεμπτος, am'emptos

Book	Oc.	blameless	Oc.	unblameable	Oc.	faultless	Total
Lk.	1	1:6					1
Phl.	2	2:15; 3:6					2
1 Th.			1	3:13			1
Heb.					1	8:7	1
Total	3		1		1		5

274. ἀμέμπτως, amemp'tōs

Book	Oc.	unblameably	Oc.	blameless	Total
1 Th.	1	2:10	1	5:23	2

275. ἀμέριμνος, amer'imnos

Book	Oc.	secure (with 4060)	Oc.	without carefulness	Total
Mt.	1	28:14			1
1 Co.			1	7:32	1
Total	1		1		2

276. ἀμετάθετος, ametath'etos

Book	Oc.	immutability	Oc.	immutable	Total
Heb.	1	6:17	1	6:18	2

277. ἀμετακίνητος, ametakin'ẹtos

Book	unmoveable	Total
1 Co.	15:58	1

279. ἀμετανόητος, ametano'ẹtos

Book	impenitent	Total
Ro.	2:5	1

278. ἀμεταμέλητος, ametamel'ẹtos

Book	Oc.	without repentance	Oc.	not to be repented of	Total
Ro.	1	11:29			1
2 Co.			1	7:10	1
Total	1		1		2

280. ἄμετρος, am'etros

Book	things without measure	Total
2 Co.	10:13, 15	2

281. ἀμήν, amen′

Book	Oc.	verily	Oc.	amen	Total
Mt.	30	5:18, 26; 6:2, 5, 16; 8:10; 10:15. 23, 42; 11:11; 13:17; 16:28; 17:20; 18:3, 13, 18; 19:23, 28; 21:21, 31; 23:36; 24:2, 34, 47; 25:12, 40, 45; 26:13, 21, 34	2	6:13; 28:20	32
Mk.	14	3:28; 6:11; 8:12; 9:1, 41; 10:15, 29; 11:23; 12:43; 13:30; 14:9, 18, 25, 30	1	16:20	15
Lk.	7	4:24; 12:37; 13:35; 18:17, 29; 21:32; 23:43	1	24:53	8
Jn.	50	1:51, 51; 3:3, 3, 5, 5, 11, 11; 5:19, 19, 24, 24, 25, 25; 6:26, 26, 32, 32, 47, 47, 53, 53; 8:34, 34, 51, 51, 58, 58; 10:1, 1, 7, 7; 12:24, 24; 13:16, 16, 20, 20, 21, 21, 38, 38; 14:12, 12; 16:20, 20, 23, 23; 21:18, 18	1	21:25	51
Ro.			7	1:25; 9:5; 11:36; 15:33; 16:20, 24, 27	7
1 Co.			2	14:16; 16:24	2
2 Co.			2	1:20; 13:14	2
Gal.			2	1:5; 6:18	2
Eph.			2	3:21; 6:24	2
Phl.			2	4:20, 23	2
Col.			1	4:18	1
1 Th.			1	5:28	1
2 Th.			1	3:18	1
1 Ti.			3	1:17; 6:16, 21	3
2 Ti.			2	4:18, 22	2
Tit.			1	3:15	1
Phe.			1	1:25	1
Heb.			2	13:21, 25	2
1 Pt.			3	4:11; 5:11, 14	3
2 Pt.			1	3:18	1
1 Jn.			1	5:21	1
2 Jn.			1	1:13	1
Jd.			1	1:25	1
Rev.			10	1:6, 7, 18; 3:14; 5:14; 7:12, 12; 19:4; 22:20, 21	10
Total	101		51		152

282. ἀμήτωρ, amē′tōr

Book	without mother	Total
Heb.	7:3	1

283. ἀμίαντος, ami′antos

Book	undefiled	Total
Heb.	7:26; 13:4	2
Jas.	1:27	1
1 Pt.	1:4	1
Total		4

284. Ἀμιναδάβ, Aminadab′

Book	Aminadab	Total
Mt.	1:4, 4	2
Lk.	3:33	1
Total		3

285. ἄμμος, am′mos

Book	sand	Total
Mt.	7:26	1
Ro.	9:27	1
Heb.	11:12	1
Rev.	13:1; 20:8	2
Total		5

286. ἀμνός, amnos′

Book	lamb	Total
Jn.	1:29, 36	2
Ac.	8:32	1
1 Pt.	1:19	1
Total		4

287. ἀμοιβή, amoibē′

Book	requite (with 591)	Total
1 Ti.	5:4	1

288. ἄμπελος, am′pelos

Book	vine	Total
Mt.	26:29	1
Mk.	14:25	1
Lk.	22:18	1
Jn.	15:1, 4, 5	3
Jas.	3:12	1
Rev.	14:19	1
Total		8

289. ἀμπελουργός, ampelourgos′

Book	dresser of vineyard	Total
Lk.	13:7	1

290. ἀμπελών, ampelōn′

Book	vineyard	Total
Mt.	20:1, 2, 4, 7, 8; 21:28, 33, 39, 40, 41	10
Mk.	12:1, 2, 8, 9, 9	5
Lk.	13:6; 20:9, 10, 13, 15, 15, 16	7
1 Co.	9:7	1
Total		23

291. Ἀμπλίας, Ampli′as

Book	Amplias	Total
Ro.	16:8	1

292. ἀμύνομαι, amu′nomai

Book	defend	Total
Ac.	7:24	1

293. ἀμφίβληστρον, amphib′lēstron

Book	net	Total
Mt.	4:18	1
Mk.	1:16	1
Total		2

294. ἀμφιέννυμι, amphien′numi

Book	clothe	Total
Mt.	6:30; 11:8	2
Lk.	7:25; 12:28	2
Total		4

295. Ἀμφίπολις, Amphip′olis

Book	Amphipolis	Total
Ac.	17:1	1

296. ἄμφοδον, am′phodon

Book	place where two ways meet	Total
Mk.	11:4	1

297. ἀμφότερος, amphot′eros

Book	both	Total
Mt.	9:17; 13:30; 15:14	3
Lk.	1:6, 7; 5:7, 38; 6:39; 7:42	6
Ac.	8:38; 23:8	2
Eph.	2:14, 16, 18	3
Total		14

299. ἄμωμος, am′ōmos

Book	Oc.	without blemish	Oc.	without blame	Oc.	unblameable	Oc.	without spot	Oc.	faultless	Oc.	without fault	Total
Eph.	1	5:27	1	1:4									2
Col.					1	1:22							1
Heb.							1	9:14					1
1 Pt.	1	1:19											1
Jd.									1	1:24			1
Rev.											1	14:5	1
Total	2		1		1		1		1		1		7

298. ἀμώμητος, amō′mētos

Book	Oc.	without rebuke	Oc.	blameless	Total
Phl.	1	2:15			1
2 Pt.			1	3:14	1
Total	1		1		2

300. Ἀμών, Amōn′

Book	Amon	Total
Mt.	1:10, 10	2

301. Ἀμώς, Amōs′

Book	Amos	Total
Lk.	3:25	1

302a. ἄν, an

Translations with the relative 3639, ending in "-soever" and indicating indefiniteness.

Book	Oc.	whosoever	Oc.	whatsoever	Oc.	whomsoever	Oc.	whereinsoever	Oc.	what things soever	Total
Mt.	15	5:19, 21, 22, 22, 31, 32; 12:32, 32; 15:5; 16:25, 25; 19:9; 23:16, 16, 18	1	10:11a	2	21:44; 26:48					18
Mk.	8	3:35; 8:35, 35, 38; 9:41, 42; 10:44; 11:23			1	14:44					9
Lk.	6	8:18, 18; 9:24, 24, 26; 12:8	4	9:4; 10:5, 8, 10	1	20:18					11
Jn.	1	4:14							1	5:19	2
Ac.	1	2:21			1	8:19					2
Ro.	1	10:13	1	16:2							2
1 Co.	1	11:27									1
2 Co.							1	11:21			1
Jas.	1	4:4									1
1 Jn.	1	4:15	1	5:15							2
Total	35		7		5		1		1		49

302b. ἄν, an

(with 3645)

Book	Oc.	whatsoever	Oc.	as many as	Oc.	whosoever	Oc.	what things soever	Oc.	wherewith soever	Total
Mt.	3	7:12; 21:22; 23:3	1	22:9							4
Mk.			1	6:56b	1	6:11	1	11:24	1	3:28	4
Lk.					1	9:5					1
Jn.	3	11:22; 16:13, 23									3
Ac.	1	3:22	1	2:39							2
Rev.			1	13:15							1
Total	7		4		2		1		1		15

302c. ἄν, an

(with 3599)

Book	Oc.	whithersoever	Oc.	wheresoever	Total
Mk.	1	6:56a	2	9:18; 14:9	3
Lk.	1	9:57			1
Jas.	1	3:4			1
Rev.	1	14:4			1
Total	4		2		6

302d. ἄν, an

(with 3648)

Book	Oc.	whatsoever	Oc.	whosoever	Total
Mt.			2	10:33; 12:50	2
Lk.	1	10:35			1
Jn.	3	2:5; 14:13; 15:16			3
Gal.			1	5:10	1
Col.	1	3:17			1
Total	5		3		8

302e. ἄν, an

(with 5000)

Book	whose soever	Total
Jn.	20:23, 23	2

302f. ἄν, an

Book	Not Tr.	Total
Mt.	2:13; 5:18, 18, 26; 6:5; 10:11b, 23; 11:21, 23; 12:7, 20; 16:28; 18:6; 22:44; 23:30, 39; 24:22, 34, 43, 43; 25:27	21
Mk.	3:29; 4:25; 6:10; 9:1; 12:36; 13:20	6
Lk.	1:62; 2:35; 6:11; 7:39; 9:27, 46; 10:13; 12:39, 39; 13:25, 35; 17:6, 6; 19:23; 20:43; 21:32	16
Jn.	1:33; 4:10, 10; 5:46; 8:19, 39, 42; 9:41; 11:21, 32; 13:24; 14:2, 7, 28; 15:19; 18:30, 36	17
Ac.	2:12, 35, 45; 3:19, 23; 4:35; 5:24; 7:3; 8:31; 10:17; 15:17; 17:18, 20; 18:14; 21:33; 26:29	16
Ro.	3:4; 9:15, 15, 29, 29	5
1 Co.	2:8; 4:5; 7:5; 11:25, 26, 26, 31, 34; 12:2; 15:25; 16:2	11
2 Co.	3:16; 10:9	2
Gal.	1:10; 3:21; 4:15; 5:17	4
Phl.	2:23	1
1 Th.	2:7	1
Heb.	1:13; 4:8; 8:4, 7; 10:2; 11:15	6
Jas.	5:7	1
1 Jn.	2:5, 19; 3:17	3
Rev.	2:25	1
Total		111

Word 302 has 191 occurrences.

305. ἀναβαίνω, anabai´nō

Book	Oc.	go up	Oc.	come up	Oc.	ascend	Oc.	ascend up	Oc.	climb up
Mt.	6	3:16; 5:1; 14:23; 15:29; 20:17, 18	1	17:27						
Mk.	4	3:13; 6:51; 10:32, 33	1	1:10						
Lk.	5	2:4, 42; 9:28; 18:10, 31					1	19:28	1	19:4
Jn.	9	2:13; 5:1; 7:8, 8; 7:10, 10, 14; 11:55; 21:11	1	12:20	3	1:51; 20:17, 17	2	3:13; 6:62	1	10:1
Ac.	10	1:13; 3:1; 10:9; 15:2; 18:22; 21:4, 12, 15; 24:11; 25:9	4	8:31, 39; 10:4; 11:2	2	2:34; 25:1				
Ro.					1	10:6				
1 Co.										
Gal.	2	2:1, 2								
Eph.					1	4:9	2	4:8, 10		
Rev.	1	20:9	3	4:1; 11:12a; 13:11	3	7:2; 11:7; 17:8	3	8:4; 11:12b; 14:11		
Total	37		10		10		8		2	

303a. ἀνά, ana′ (adverb)

Book	Oc.	by	Oc.	apiece	Oc.	every man	Oc.	each	Oc.	several	Oc.	two and two (with 1417)	Total
Mt.					2	20:9, 10							2
Mk.	2	6:40, 40											2
Lk.	1	9:14	1	9:3							1	10:1	3
Jn.			1	2:6									1
Rev.							1	4:8	1	21:21			2
Total	3		2		2		1		1		1		10

303b. ἀνά, ana′ (preposition)

Book	Oc.	among	Oc.	through	Oc.	between	Oc.	by	Oc.	in	Total
Mt.	1	13:25									1
Mk.			1	7:31	1	6:5					2
1 Co.							1	14:27			1
Rev.									1	7:17	1
Total	1		1		1		1		1		5

Word 303 has 15 occurrences.

304. ἀναβαθμός, anabathmos′

Book	stairs	Total
Ac.	21:35, 40	2

See page 18 for Word 305.

306. ἀναβάλλομαι, anabal′lomai

Book	defer	Total
Ac.	24:22	1

307. ἀναβιβάζω, anabibad′zō

Book	draw	Total
Mt.	13·48	1

309. ἀνάβλεψις, anab′lepsis

Book	recovering of sight	Total
Lk.	4:18	1

311. ἀναβολή, anabolē′

Book	delay (with 4060)	Total
Ac.	25:17	1

308. ἀναβλέπω, anablep′ō

Book	Oc.	receive sight	Oc.	look up	Oc.	look	Oc.	see	Total
Mt.	2	11:5; 20:34	1	14:19					3
Mk.	2	10:51, 52	4	6:41; 7:34; 8:24, 25	1	16:4			7
Lk.	3	18:41, 42, 43	3	9:16; 19:5; 21:1			1	7:22	7
Jn.	4	9:11, 15, 18, 18							4
Ac.	4	9:12, 17, 18; 22:13a	1	22:13b					5
Total	15		9		1		1		26

310. ἀναβοάω, anaboa′ō

Book	Oc.	cry	Oc.	cry aloud	Oc.	cry out	Total
Mt.	1	27:46					1
Mk.			1	15:8			1
Lk.					1	9:38	1
Total	1		1		1		3

312. ἀναγγέλλω, ananggel′lō

Book	Oc.	tell	Oc.	shew	Oc.	declare	Oc.	rehearse	Oc.	speak	Oc.	report	Total
Mk.	2	5:14, 19											2
Jn.	2	4:25; 5:15	4	16:13, 14, 15, 25									6
Ac.	1	16:38	2	19:18; 20:20	2	15:4; 20:27	1	14:27					6
Ro.									1	15:21			1
2 Co.	1	7:7											1
1 Pt.											1	1:12	1
1 Jn.					1	1:5							1
Total	6		6		3		1		1		1		18

313. ἀναγεννάω, anagenna′ō

Book	Oc.	beget again	Oc.	be born again	Total
1 Pt.	1	1:3	1	1:23	2

315. ἀναγκάζω, anangkad′zō

Book	Oc.	compel	Oc.	constrain	Total
Mt.			1	14:22	1
Mk.			1	6:45	1
Lk.	1	14:23			1
Ac.	1	26:11	1	28:19	2
2 Co.	1	12:11			1
Gal.	2	2:3, 14	1	6:12	3
Total	5		4		9

314. ἀναγινώσκω, anaginōs′kō

Book	read	Total
Mt.	12:3, 5; 19:4; 21:16, 42; 22:31; 24:15	7
Mk.	2:25; 12:10, 26; 13:14	4
Lk.	4:16; 6:3; 10:26	3
Jn.	19:20	1
Ac.	8:28, 30, 30, 32; 13:27; 15:21, 31; 23:34	8
2 Co.	1:13; 3:2, 15	3
Eph.	3:4	1
Col.	4:16, 16, 16	3
1 Th.	5:27	1
Rev.	1:3; 5:4	2
Total		33

305. ἀναβαίνω, anabai′nō (continued)

Book	Oc.	spring up	Oc.	grow up	Oc.	come	Oc.	enter	Oc.	arise	Oc.	rise up	Oc.	Misc.	Total
Mt.	1	13:7													8
Mk.	1	4:8	2	4:7, 32											8
Lk.									1	24:38			1	5:19	9
Jn.							1	21:3							17
Ac.					2	7:23; 21:31							1	20:11	19
Ro.															1
1 Co.							1	2:9							1
Gal.															2
Eph.															3
Rev.									1	9:2	2	13:1; 19:3			13
Total	2		2		2		2		2		2		2		81

Miscellaneous: Lk. 5:19, go; Ac. 20:11, come up again.

316. ἀναγκαῖος, anangkai′os

Book	Oc.	necessary	Oc.	near	Oc.	more needful	Oc.	of necessity	Total
Ac.	1	13:46	1	10:24					2
1 Co.	1	12:22							1
2 Co.	1	9:5							1
Phl.	1	2:25			1	1:24			2
Tit.	1	3:14							1
Heb.							1	8:3	1
Total	5		1		1		1		8

317. ἀναγκαστῶς, anangkastōs′

Book	by constraint	Total
1 Pt.	5:2	1

319. ἀναγνωρίζομαι, anagnōrid′zomai

Book	be made known	Total
Ac.	7:13	1

318. ἀναγκή, anangke̱′

Book	Oc.	necessity	Oc.	must needs	Oc.	distress	Oc	must of necessity	Oc.	need (with 2192)	Oc.	necessary	Oc.	needful	Total
Mt.			1	18:7											1
Lk.			1	14:18	1	21:23	1	23:17							3
Ro.			1	13:5											1
1 Co.	2	7:37; 9:16			1	7:26									3
2 Co.	3	6:4; 9:7; 12:10													3
1 Th.					1	3:7									1
Phe.	1	1:14													1
Heb.	1	7:12					1	9:16	1	7:27	1	9:23			4
Jd.													1	1:3	1
Total	7		3		3		2		1		1		1		18

321. ἀνάγω, anag′ō

Book	Oc.	bring	Oc.	loose	Oc.	sail	Oc.	launch	Oc.	depart	Oc.	Misc.	Total
Mt.											1	4:1	1
Lk.	1	2:22									3	4:5; 8:22; 22:66	4
Ac.	2	9:39; 16:34	3	13:13; 16:11; 27:21	3	18:21; 20:3, 13	3	21:1; 27:2, 4	3	27:12; 28:10, 11	3	7:41; 12:4; 21:2	17
Ro.											1	10:7	1
Heb.											1	13:20	1
Total	3		3		3		3		3		9		24

Miscellaneous: Mt. 4:1, lead up; Lk. 4:5, take up; Lk. 8:22, launch forth; Lk. 22:66, lead; Ac. 7:41, offer; Ac. 12:4, bring forth; Ac. 21:2, set forth; Ro. 10:7, bring up again; Heb. 13:20, bring again.

320. ἀνάγνωσις, anag′nōsis

Book	reading	Total
Ac.	13:15	1
2 Co.	3:14	1
1 Ti.	4:13	1
Total		3

322. ἀναδείκνυμι, anadeik′numi

Book	Oc.	appoint	Oc.	shew	Total
Lk.	1	10:1			1
Ac.			1	1:24	1
Total	1		1		2

323. ἀνάδειξις, anad′eixis

Book	shewing	Total
Lk.	1:80	1

324. ἀναδέχομαι, anadech′omai

Book	receive	Total
Ac.	28:7	1
Heb.	11:17	1
Total		2

325. ἀναδίδωμι, anadid′ōmi

Book	deliver	Total
Ac.	23:33	1

326. ἀναζάω, anadza′ō

Book	Oc.	be alive again	Oc.	revive	Oc.	live again	Total
Lk.	2	15:24, 32					2
Ro.			2	7:9; 14:9			2
Rev.					1	20:5	1
Total	2		2		1		5

327. ἀναζητέω, anadze̱te′ō

Book	seek	Total
Lk.	2:44	1
Ac.	11:25	1
Total		2

328. ἀναζώννυμι, anadzōn′numi

Book	gird up	Total
1 Pt.	1:13	1

329. ἀναζωπυρέω, anadzōpure′ō

Book	stir up	Total
2 Ti.	1:6	1

330. ἀναθάλλω, anathal′lō

Book	flourish	Total
Phl.	4:10	1

331. ἀνάθεμα, anath′ema

Book	Oc.	accursed	Oc.	anathema	Oc.	bind under a great curse (with 332)	Total
Ac.					1	23:14	1
Ro.	1	9:3					1
1 Co.	1	12:3	1	16:22			2
Gal.	2	1:8, 9					2
Total	4		1		1		6

334. ἀνάθημα, anath′e̱ma

Book	gift	Total
Lk.	21:5	1

335. ἀναίδεια, anai′deia

Book	importunity	Total
Lk.	11:8	1

332. ἀναθεματίζω, anathematid′zō

Book	Oc.	curse	Oc.	bind under a curse	Oc.	bind with an oath	Oc.	bind under a great curse (with 331)	Total
Mk.	1	14:71							1
Ac.			1	23:12	1	23:21	1	23:14	3
Total	1		1		1		1		4

336. ἀναίρεσις, anai′resis

Book	death	Total
Ac.	8:1; 22:20	2

333. ἀναθεωρέω, anatheōre′ō

Book	Oc.	behold	Oc.	consider	Total
Ac.	1	17:23			1
Heb.			1	13:7	1
Total	1		1		2

338. ἀναίτιος, anai′tios

Book	Oc.	blameless	Oc.	guiltless	Total
Mt.	1	12:5	1	12:7	2

337. ἀναιρέω, anaire′ō

Book	Oc.	kill	Oc.	slay	Oc.	put to death	Oc.	take up	Oc.	do	Oc.	take away	Total
Mt.			1	2:16									1
Lk.	1	22:2			1	23:32							2
Ac.	9	7:28a; 9:23, 24; 12:2; 16:27; 23:15, 21, 27; 25:3	7	2:23; 5:33, 36; 9:29; 10:39; 13:28; 22:20	1	26:10	1	7:21	1	7:28b			19
Heb.											1	10:9	1
Total	10		8		2		1		1		1		23

339. ἀνακαθίζω, anakathid'zō

Book	sit up	Total
Lk.	7:15	1
Ac.	9:40	1
Total		2

340. ἀνακαινίζω, anakainid'zō

Book	renew	Total
Heb.	6:6	1

341. ἀνακαινόω, anakaino'ō

Book	renew	Total
2 Co.	4:16	1
Col.	3:10	1
Total		2

342. ἀνακαίνωσις, anakai'nōsis

Book	renewing	Total
Ro.	12:2	1
Tit.	3:5	1
Total		2

343. ἀνακαλύπτω, anakalup'tō

Book	Oc.	untaken away (with 3261)	Oc.	open	Total
2 Co.	1	3:14	1	3:18	2

344. ἀνακάμπτω, anakamp'tō

Book	Oc.	return	Oc.	turn again	Total
Mt.	1	2:12			1
Lk.			1	10:6	1
Ac.	1	18:21			1
Heb.	1	11:15			1
Total	3		1		4

345. ἀνάκειμαι, anak'eimai

Book	Oc.	sit at meat	Oc.	guests	Oc.	sit	Oc.	sit down	Oc.	be set down	Oc.	lie	Oc.	lean	Oc.	at the table	Total
Mt.	1	9:10	2	22:10, 11	1	26:7	1	26:20									5
Mk.	1	16:14			1	14:18					1	5:40					3
Lk.	3	7:37; 22:27, 27															3
Jn.									1	6:11			1	13:23	1	13:28	3
Total	5		2		2		1		1		1		1		1		14

346. ἀνακεφαλαιόω, anakephalaio'ō

Book	Oc.	briefly comprehend	Oc.	gather together in one	Total
Ro.	1	13:9			1
Eph.			1	1:10	1
Total	1		1		2

347. ἀνακλίνω, anakli'nō

Book	Oc.	sit down	Oc.	make sit down	Oc.	sit down to meat	Oc.	make sit down to meat	Oc.	lay	Total
Mt.	2	8:11; 14:19									2
Mk.			1	6:39							1
Lk.	1	13:29	1	9:15	1	7:36	1	12:37	1	2:7	5
Total	3		2		1		1		1		8

348. ἀνακόπτω, anakop'tō

Book	hinder	Total
Gal.	5:7	1

350. ἀνακρίνω, anakri'nō

Book	Oc.	examine	Oc.	judge	Oc.	ask question	Oc.	search	Oc.	discern	Total
Lk.	1	23:14									1
Ac.	4	4:9; 12:19; 24:8; 28:18					1	17:11			5
1 Co.	1	9:3	6	2:15, 15; 4:3, 3, 4; 14:24	2	10:25, 27			1	2:14	10
Total	6		6		2		1		1		16

349. ἀνακράζω, anakrad'zō

Book	cry out	Total
Mk.	1:23; 6:49	2
Lk.	4:33; 8:28; 23:18	3
Total		5

351. ἀνάκρισις, anak'risis

Book	examination	Total
Ac.	25:26	1

352. ἀνακύπτω, anakup'tō

Book	Oc.	lift up (one's) self	Oc.	look up	Total
Lk.	1	13:11	1	21:28	2
Jn.	2	8:7, 10			2
Total	3		1		4

353. ἀναλαμβάνω, analamban'ō

Book	Oc.	take up	Oc.	receive up	Oc.	take	Oc.	take in	Oc.	take unto	Total
Mk.			1	16:19							1
Ac.	4	1:2, 11, 22; 7:43	1	10:16	1	23:31	2	20:13, 14			8
Eph.					1	6:16			1	6:13	2
1 Ti.			1	3:16							1
2 Ti.					1	4:11					1
Total	4		3		3		2		1		13

354. ἀνάληψις, anal'ẹpsis

Book	receive up	Total
Lk.	9:51	1

355. ἀναλίσκω, analis'kō

Book	consume	Total
Lk.	9:54	1
Gal.	5:15	1
2 Ti.	2:8	1
Total		3

356. ἀναλογία, analogi'a

Book	proportion	Total
Ro.	12:6	1

357. ἀναλογίζομαι analogid'zomai

Book	consider	Total
Heb.	12:3	1

358. ἄναλος, an'alos

Book	lose saltness (with 1096)	Total
Mk.	9:50	1

359. ἀνάλυσις, anal'usis

Book	departure	Total
2 Ti.	4:6	1

360. ἀναλύω, analu'ō

Book	Oc.	return	Oc.	depart	Total
Lk.	1	12:36			1
Phl.			1	1:23	1
Total	1		1		2

361. ἀναμάρτητος, anamar'tẹtos

Book	without sin	Total
Jn.	8:7	1

362. ἀναμένω, anamen'ō

Book	wait for	Total
1 Th.	1:10	1

363. ἀναμιμνήσκω, anamimnẹs'kō

Book	Oc.	call to remembrance	Oc.	call to mind	Oc.	bring into remembrance	Oc.	remember	Oc.	put in remembrance	Total
Mk.	1	11:21	1	14:72							2
1 Co.					1	4:17					1
2 Co.							1	7:15			1
2 Ti.									1	1:6	1
Heb.	1	10:32									1
Total	2		1		1		1		1		6

364. ἀνάμνησις, anam'nẹsis

Book	Oc.	remembrance	Oc.	remembrance again	Total
Lk.	1	22:19			1
1 Co.	2	11:24, 25			2
Heb.			1	10:3	1
Total	3		1		4

365. ἀνανεόω, ananeo'ō

Book	renew	Total
Eph.	4:23	1

366. ἀνανήφω, ananẹphō

Book	recover (one's) self	Total
2 Ti.	2:26	1

367. Ἀνανίας, Anani'as

Book	Oc.	Ananias (of Damascus)	Oc.	Ananias (of Jerusalem)	Oc.	Ananias (high priest)	Total
Ac.	6	9:10, 10, 12, 13, 17; 22:12	3	5:1, 3, 5	2	23:2; 24:1	11

368. ἀναντίῤῥητος, anantir'hrētos

Book	cannot be spoken against (with 5507)	Total
Ac.	19:36	1

369. ἀναντιῤῥήτως, anantirhrē'tōs

Book	without gainsaying	Total
Ac.	10:29	1

370. ἀνάξιος, anax'ios

Book	unworthy	Total
1 Co.	6:2	1

371. ἀναξίως, anaxi'ōs

Book	unworthily	Total
1 Co.	11:27, 29	2

372. ἀνάπαυσις, anap'ausis

Book	Oc.	rest	Oc.	rest (with 2192)	Total
Mt.	2	11:29; 12:43			2
Lk.	1	11:24			1
Rev.	1	14:11	1	4:8	2
Total	4		1		5

375. ἀναπέμπω, anapem'pō

Book	Oc.	send	Oc.	send again	Total
Lk.	2	23:7, 15	1	23:11	3
Phe.			1	1:12	1
Total	2		2		4

373. ἀναπαύω, anapau'ō

Book	Oc.	rest	Oc.	refresh	Oc.	take rest	Oc.	give rest	Oc.	take ease	Total
Mt.					1	26:45	1	11:28			2
Mk.	1	6:31			1	14:41					2
Lk.									1	12:19	1
1 Co.			1	16:18							1
2 Co.			1	7:13							1
Phe.			2	1:7, 20							2
1 Pt.	1	4:14									1
Rev.	2	6:11; 14:13									2
Total	4		4		2		1		1		12

374. ἀναπείθω, anapei'thō

Book	persuade	Total
Ac.	18:13	1

376. ἀνάπηρος, anap'ēros

Book	maimed	Total
Lk.	14:13, 21	2

377. ἀναπίπτω, anapip'tō

Book	Oc.	sit down	Oc.	sit down to meat	Oc.	be set down	Oc.	lean	Total
Mt.	1	15:35							1
Mk.	2	6:40; 8:6							2
Lk.	2	14:10; 22:14	2	11:37; 17:7					4
Jn.	2	6:10, 10			1	13:12	1	21:20	4
Total	7		2		1		1		11

380. ἀναπτύσσω, anaptus'sō

Book	open	Total
Lk.	4:17	1

381. ἀνάπτω, anap'tō

Book	kindle	Total
Lk.	12:49	1
Ac.	28:2	1
Jas.	3:5	1
Total		3

378. ἀναπληρόω, anaplēro'ō

Book	Oc.	fulfill	Oc.	supply	Oc.	occupy	Oc.	fill up	Total
Mt.	1	13:14							1
1 Co.			1	16:17	1	14:16			2
Gal.	1	6:2							1
Phl.			1	2:30					1
1 Th.							1	2:16	1
Total	2		2		1		1		6

382. ἀναρίθμητος, anarith'mētos

Book	innumerable	Total
Heb.	11:12	1

379. ἀναπολόγητος, anapolog'ētos

Book	Oc.	without excuse	Oc.	inexcusable	Total
Ro.	1	1:20	1	2:1	2

383. ἀνασείω, anasei'ō

Book	Oc.	move	Oc.	stir up	Total
Mk.	1	15:11			1
Lk.			1	23:5	1
Total	1		1		2

384. ἀνασκευάζω, anaskeuad'zō

Book	subvert	Total
Ac.	15:24	1

385. ἀνασπάω, anaspa'ō

Book	Oc.	pull out	Oc.	draw up	Total
Lk.	1	14:5			1
Ac.			1	11:10	1
Total	1		1		2

386. ἀνάστασις, anas'tasis

Book	Oc.	resurrection	Oc.	rising again	Oc.	that should rise	Oc.	raised to life again (with 1537)	Total
Mt.	4	22:23, 28, 30, 31							4
Mk.	2	12:18, 23							2
Lk.	5	14:14; 20:27, 33, 35, 36	1	2:34					6
Jn.	4	5:29, 29; 11:24, 25							4
Ac.	10	1:22; 2:31; 4:2, 33; 17:18, 32; 23:6, 8; 24:15, 21			1	26:23			11
Ro.	2	1:4; 6:5							2
1 Co.	4	15:12, 13, 21, 42							4
Phl.	1	3:10							1
2 Ti.	1	2:18							1
Heb.	2	6:2; 11:35b					1	11:35a	3
1 Pt.	2	1:3; 3:21							2
Rev.	2	20:5, 6							2
Total	39		1		1		1		42

387. ἀναστατόω, anastato'ō

Book	Oc.	turn upside down	Oc.	make an uproar	Oc.	trouble	Total
Ac.	1	17:6	1	21:38			2
Gal.					1	5:12	1
Total	1		1		1		3

388. ἀνασταυρόω, anastauro'ō

Book	crucify afresh	Total
Heb.	6:6	1

389. ἀναστενάζω, anastenad'zō

Book	sigh deeply	Total
Mk.	8:12	1

390. ἀναστρέφω, anastreph'ō

Book	Oc.	return	Oc.	have conversation	Oc.	live	Oc.	abide	Oc.	over-throw	Oc.	behave (one's) self	Oc.	be used	Oc.	pass	Total
Mt.							1	17:22									1
Jn.									1	2:15							1
Ac.	2	5:22; 15:16															2
2 Co.			1	1:12													1
Eph.			1	2:3													1
1 Ti.											1	3:15					1
Heb.					1	13:18							1	10:33			2
1 Pt.															1	1:17	1
2 Pt.					1	2:18											1
Total	2		2		2		1		1		1		1		1		11

391. ἀναστροφή, anastrophẹ'

Book	conversation	Total
Gal.	1:13	1
Eph.	4:22	1
1 Ti.	4:12	1
Heb.	13:7	1
Jas.	3:13	1
1 Pt.	1:15, 18; 2:12; 3:1, 2, 16	6
2 Pt.	2:7; 3:11	2
Total		13

392. ἀνατάσσομαι, anatas'somai

Book	set forth in order	Total
Lk.	1:1	1

394. ἀνατίθημι, anatith'ẹmi

Book	Oc.	declare	Oc.	communicate	Total
Ac.	1	25:14			1
Gal.			1	2:2	1
Total	1		1		2

395. ἀνατολή, anatolẹ'

Book	Oc.	east	Oc.	dayspring	Total
Mt.	5	2:1, 2, 9; 8:11; 24:27			5
Lk.	1	13:29	1	1:78	2
Rev.	3	7:2; 16:12; 21:13			3
Total	9		1		10

393. ἀνατέλλω, anatel'lō

Book	Oc.	be up	Oc.	rise	Oc.	spring up	Oc.	make rise	Oc.	at the rising of	Oc.	spring	Oc.	arise	Total
Mt.	1	13:6			1	4:16	1	5:45							3
Mk.	1	4:6							1	16:2					2
Lk.			1	12:54											1
Heb.											1	7:14			1
Jas.			1	1:11											1
2 Pt.													1	1:19	1
Total	2		2		1		1		1		1		1		9

396. ἀνατρέπω, anatrep'ō

Book	Oc.	overthrow	Oc.	subvert	Total
2 Ti.	1	2:18			1
Tit.			1	1:11	1
Total	1		1		2

398. ἀναφαίνω, anaphai'nō

Book	Oc.	appear	Oc.	discover	Total
Lk.	1	19:11			1
Ac.			1	21:3	1
Total	1		1		2

397. ἀνατρέφω, anatreph'ō

Book	Oc.	nourish	Oc.	nourish up	Oc.	bring up	Total
Ac.	1	7:21	1	7:20	1	22:3	3

400. ἀναφωνέω, anaphōne'ō

Book	speak out	Total
Lk.	1:42	1

401. ἀνάχυσις, anach'usis

Book	excess	Total
1 Pt.	4:4	1

399. ἀναφέρω, anapher'ō

Book	Oc.	offer up	Oc.	bear	Oc.	offer	Oc.	bring up	Oc.	lead up	Oc.	carry up	Total
Mt.							1	17:1					1
Mk.									1	9:2			1
Lk.											1	24:51	1
Heb.	2	7:27, 27	1	9:28	1	13:15							4
Jas.					1	2:21							1
1 Pt.	1	2:5	1	2:24									2
Total	3		2		2		1		1		1		10

402. ἀναχωρέω, anachōre'ō

Book	Oc.	depart	Oc.	withdraw (one's) self	Oc.	go aside	Oc.	turn aside	Oc.	give place	Total
Mt.	7	2:12, 13, 14; 4:12; 14:13; 15:21; 27:5	1	12:15			1	2:22	1	9:24	10
Mk.			1	3:7							1
Jn.	1	6:15									1
Ac.					2	23:19; 26:31					2
Total	8		2		2		1		1		14

403. ἀνάψυξις, anaps'uxis

Book	refreshing	Total
Ac.	3:19	1

404. ἀναψύχω, anapsu'chō

Book	refresh	Total
2 Ti.	1:16	1

405. ἀνδραποδιστής andrapodistẹs'

Book	manstealer	Total
1 Ti.	1:10	1

406. 'Ανδρέας, Andre'as

Book	Andrew	Total
Mt.	4:18; 10:2	2
Mk.	1:16, 29; 3:18; 13:3	4
Lk.	6:14	1
Jn.	1:40, 44; 6:8; 12:22, 22	5
Ac.	1:13	1
Total		13

407. ἀνδρίζομαι, andrid'zomai

Book	quit you like men	Total
1 Co.	16:13	1

408. 'Ανδρόνικος, Andron'ikos

Book	Andronicus	Total
Ro.	16:7	1

409. ἀνδροφόνος, androphon'os

Book	manslayer	Total
1 Ti.	1:9	1

410. ἀνέγκλητος, aneng'klẹtos

Book	Oc.	blameless	Oc.	unreprovable	Total
1 Co.	1	1:8			1
Col.			1	1:22	1
1 Ti.	1	3:10			1
Tit.	2	1:6, 7			2
Total	4		1		5

411. ἀνεκδιήγητος anekdie̱'ge̱tos

Book	unspeakable	Total
2 Co.	9:15	1

412. ἀνεκλάλητος, aneklal'e̱tos

Book	unspeakable	Total
1 Pt.	1:8	1

413. ἀνέκλειπτος, anek'leiptos

Book	not to fail	Total
Lk.	12:33	1

414. ἀνεκτότερος, anektot'eros

Book	more tolerable	Total
Mt.	10:15; 11:22, 24	3
Mk.	6:11	1
Lk.	10:12, 14	2
Total		6

415. ἀνελεήμων, anelee̱'mōn

Book	unmerciful	Total
Ro.	1:31	1

416. ἀνεμίζω, anemid'zō

Book	driven with the wind	Total
Jas.	1:6	1

417. ἄνεμος, an'emos

Book	wind	Total
Mt.	7:25, 27; 8:26, 27; 11:7; 14:24, 30, 32; 24:31	9
Mk.	4:37, 39, 39, 41; 6:48, 51; 13:27	7
Lk.	7:24; 8:23, 24, 25	4
Jn.	6:18	1
Ac.	27:4, 7, 14, 15	4
Eph.	4:14	1
Jas.	3:4	1
Jd.	1:12	1
Rev.	6:13; 7:1, 1	3
Total		31

418. ἀνένδεκτος, anen'dektos

Book	impossible	Total
Lk.	17:1	1

419. ἀνεξερεύνητος anexereu'ne̱tos

Book	unsearchable	Total
Ro.	11:33	1

420. ἀνεξίκακος, anexik'akos

Book	patient	Total
2 Ti.	2:24	1

421. ἀνεξιχνίαστος, anexichni'astos

Book	Oc.	past finding out	Oc.	unsearchable	Total
Ro.	1	11:33			1
Eph.			1	3:8	1
Total	1		1		2

422. ἀνεπαίσχυντος anepai'schuntos

Book	that needeth not to be ashamed	Total
2 Ti.	2:15	1

423. ἀνεπίληπτος, anepil'e̱ptos

Book	Oc.	blameless	Oc.	unrebukeable	Total
1 Ti.	2	3:2; 5:7	1	6:14	3

424. ἀνέρχομαι, anerch'omai

Book	go up	Total
Jn.	6:3	1
Gal.	1:17, 18	2
Total		3

425. ἄνεσις, an'esis

Book	Oc.	rest	Oc.	liberty	Oc.	be eased	Total
Ac.			1	24:23			1
2 Co.	2	2:13; 7:5			1	8:13	3
2 Th.	1	1:7					1
Total	3		1		1		5

426. ἀνετάζω, anetad'zō

Book	examine	Total
Ac.	22:24, 29	2

427. ἄνευ, an'eu

Book	without	Total
Mt.	10:29	1
1 Pt.	3:1; 4:9	2
Total		3

428. ἀνεύθετος, aneu'thetos

Book	not commodious	Total
Ac.	27:12	1

429. ἀνευρίσκω, aneuris'kō

Book	find	Total
Lk.	2:16	1
Ac.	21:4	1
Total		2

430. ἀνέχομαι, anech'omai

Book	Oc.	suffer	Oc.	bear with	Oc.	forbear	Oc.	endure	Total
Mt.	1	17:17							1
Mk.	1	9:19							1
Lk.	1	9:41							1
Ac.			1	18:14					1
1 Co.	1	4:12							1
2 Co.	2	11:19, 20	3	11:1, 1, 4					5
Eph.					1	4:2			1
Col.					1	3:13			1
2 Th.							1	1:4	1
2 Ti.							1	4:3	1
Heb.	1	13:22							1
Total	7		4		2		2		15

431. ἀνέψιος, aneps'ios

Book	sister's son	Total
Col.	4:10	1

432. ἄνηθον, an'e̱thon

Book	anise	Total
Mt.	23:23	1

434. ἀνήμερος, ane̱'meros

Book	fierce	Total
2 Ti.	3:3	1

433. ἀνήκω, ane̱'kō

Book	Oc.	be convenient	Oc.	be fit	Total
Eph.	1	5:4			1
Col.			1	3:18	1
Phe.	1	1:8			1
Total	2		1		3

435. ἀνήρ, ane̱r'

Book	Oc.	man	Oc.	husband	Oc.	sir	Oc.	fellow	Oc.	Not Tr.	Total
Mt.	6	7:24, 26; 12:41; 14:21, 35; 15:38	2	1:16, 19							8
Mk.	3	6:20, 44; 10:2	1	10:12							4
Lk.	23	1:27, 34; 5:8, 12, 18; 7:20; 8:27, 38, 41; 9:14, 30, 32, 38; 11:31, 32; 14:24; 17:12; 19:2, 7; 22:63; 23:50, 50; 24:4	2	2:36; 16:18					1	24:19	26
Jn.	3	1:13, 30; 6:10	5	4:16, 17, 17, 18, 18							8
Ac.	90	1:10, 11, 16, 21; 2:5, 14, 22, 22, 29, 37; 3:2, 12; 4:4; 5:1, 14, 25, 35, 36; 6:3, 5, 11; 7:2; 8:2, 3, 9, 12, 27; 9:2, 7, 12, 13, 38; 10:1, 5, 17, 19, 21, 22, 28, 30; 11:3, 11, 12, 13, 20, 24; 13:7, 15, 16, 21, 22, 26, 38; 14:8; 15:7, 13, 22, 22, 25; 16:9; 17:12, 22, 31, 34; 18:24; 19:7, 35, 37; 20:30; 21:11, 23, 26, 28, 38; 22:1, 3, 4, 12; 23:1, 6, 21. 27, 30; 24:5; 25:5, 14, 17, 23, 24; 28:17	2	5:9, 10	6	7:26; 14:15; 19:25; 27:10, 21, 25	1	17:5	1	3:14	100
Ro.	4	4:8; 7:3b, 3d; 11:4	5	7:2, 2, 2, 3a,3c							9
1 Co.	16	7:16b; 11:3, 3, 4, 7, 7, 8, 8, 9, 9, 11, 11, 12, 12, 14; 13:11	16	7:2, 3, 3, 4, 4, 10, 11, 11, 13, 14, 14, 16a, 34, 39, 39; 14:35							32
2 Co.			1	11:2							1
Gal.			1	4:27							1
Eph.	2	4:13; 5:28	5	5:22, 23, 24, 25, 33							7
Col.			2	3:18, 19							2
1 Ti.	3	2:8, 12; 5:9	2	3:2, 12							5
Tit.			2	1:6; 2:5							2
Jas.	6	1:8, 12, 20, 23; 2:2; 3:2									6
1 Pt.			3	3:1, 5, 7							3
Rev.			1	21:2							1
Total	156		50		6		1		2		215

436. ἀνθίστημι, anthis'tēmi

Book	Oc.	resist	Oc.	withstand	Total
Mt.	1	5:39			1
Lk.	1	21:15			1
Ac.	1	6:10	1	13:8	2
Ro.	3	9:19; 13:2, 2			3
Gal.			1	2:11	1
Eph.			1	6:13	1
2 Ti.	1	3:8b	2	3:8a; 4:15	3
Jas.	1	4:7			1
1 Pt.	1	5:9			1
Total	9		5		14

440. ἄνθραξ, anth'rax

Book	coals of fire	Total
Ro.	12:20	1

441. ἀνθρωπάρεσκος anthrōpar'eskos

Book	menpleaser	Total
Eph.	6:6	1
Col.	3:22	1
Total		2

437. ἀνθομολογέομαι anthomologe'omai

Book	give thanks	Total
Lk.	2:38	1

438. ἄνθος, anth'os

Book	flower	Total
Jas.	1:10, 11	2
1 Pt.	1:24, 24	2
Total		4

439. ἀνθρακιά, anthrakia'

Book	fire of coals	Total
Jn.	18:18; 21:9	2

443. ἀνθρωποκτόνος anthrōpokton'os

Book	murderer	Total
Jn.	8:44	1
1 Jn.	3:15, 15	2
Total		3

442. ἀνθρώπινος, anthrō'pinos

Book	Oc.	man's	Oc.	after the manner of man	Oc.	of man	Oc.	common to man	Oc.	mankind (with 5349)	Total
Ro.			1	6:19							1
1 Co.	3	2:4, 13; 4:3					1	10:13			4
Jas.									1	3:7	1
1 Pt.					1	2:13					1
Total	3		1		1		1		1		7

444. ἄνθρωπος, anth'rōpos

Book	Oc.	man	Oc.	Not Tr.	Oc.	Misc.	Total
Mt.	114	4:4, 19; 5:13, 16, 19; 6:1, 2, 5, 14, 15, 16, 18; 7:9, 12; 8:9, 20, 27; 9:6, 8, 9, 32; 10:17, 23, 32, 33, 35, 36; 11:8, 19, 19; 12:8, 10, 11, 12, 13, 31, 31, 32, 35, 35, 36, 40, 43, 45; 13:24, 25, 31, 37, 41, 44, 45, 52; 15:9, 11, 11, 18, 20, 20; 16:13, 13, 23, 26, 26, 27, 28; 17:9, 12, 14, 22, 22; 18:7, 11, 12; 19:3, 5, 6, 10, 12, 26, 28; 20:1, 18, 28; 21:25, 26, 28; 22:11, 16; 23:4, 5, 7, 13, 28; 24:27, 30, 30, 37, 39, 44; 25:13, 14, 24, 31; 26:2, 24, 24, 24, 24, 45, 64, 72, 74; 27:32, 57	2	13:28; 21:33	2	18:23; 22:2	118
Mk.	55	1:17, 23; 2:10,27, 27, 28; 3:1, 3, 5, 28; 4:26; 5:2, 8; 7:7, 8, 11, 15, 15, 18, 20, 20, 21, 23; 8:24, 27, 31, 33, 36, 37, 38; 9:9, 12, 31, 31; 10:7, 9, 27, 33, 45; 11:2, 30, 32; 12:1, 14; 13:26, 34; 14:13, 21, 21, 21, 21, 41, 62, 71; 15:39					55
Lk.	99	1:25; 2:14, 25, 25, 52; 4:4, 33; 5:10, 18, 20, 24; 6:5, 6, 8, 10, 22, 22, 26, 31, 45, 45, 48, 49; 7:8, 25, 31, 34, 34; 8:29, 33, 35; 9:22, 25, 26, 44, 44, 56, 56, 58; 10:30; 11:24, 26, 30, 44, 46; 12:8, 8, 9, 10, 14, 16,36, 40; 13:4, 19; 14:2, 16, 30; 15:4, 11; 16:1, 15, 15, 19; 17:22, 24, 26, 30; 18:2, 4, 8, 10, 11, 27, 31; 19:10, 21, 22, 30; 20:4, 6, 9; 21:26, 27, 36; 22:10, 22, 22, 48, 58, 60, 69; 23:4, 6, 14, 14, 47; 24:7, 7	1	2:15	1	19:12	101
Jn.	59	1:4, 6, 9, 51; 2:10, 25, 25; 3:1, 4, 13, 14, 19, 27; 4:28, 29, 50; 5:5, 7, 9, 12, 15, 27, 34, 41; 6:10. 14, 27, 53, 62; 7:22, 23, 23, 46, 46, 51; 8:17, 28, 40; 9:1, 11, 16, 16, 24, 24, 30; 10:33; 11:47, 50; 12:23, 34, 34, 43; 13:31; 16:21; 17:6; 18:14, 17, 29; 19:5					59
Ac.	45	4:9, 12, 13, 14, 16, 17, 22; 5:4, 28, 29, 35, 38, 38; 6:13; 7:56; 9:33; 10:26, 28; 12:22; 14:11, 15; 15:17, 26; 16: 17, 20, 35; 17:25, 26, 29, 30; 18:13; 19:16, 35; 21:28, 39; 22:15, 25, 26; 23:9; 24:16; 25:16, 22; 26:31, 32; 28:4	1	16:37			46
Ro.	27	1:18, 23; 2:1, 3, 9, 16, 29; 3:4, 5, 28; 4:6; 5:12, 12, 15, 18, 18, 19; 6:6; 7:1, 22, 24; 9:20; 10:5; 12:17, 18; 14: 18, 20					27
1 Co.	30	1:25, 25; 2:5, 9, 11, 11, 11, 14; 3:3, 21; 4:1, 9; 6:18; 7:1, 7, 23, 26; 9:8; 11:28; 13:1; 14:2, 3; 15:19, 21, 21, 32, 39, 45, 47, 47					30
2 Co.	8	3:2; 4:2, 16; 5:11; 8:21; 12:2, 3, 4					8
Gal.	15	1:1, 1, 10, 10, 10, 11, 12; 2:6, 16; 3:12, 15, 15; 5:3; 6:1, 7					15
Eph.	9	2:15; 3:5, 16; 4:8, 14, 22, 24; 5:31; 6:7					9
Phl.	3	2:7, 8; 4:5					3
Col.	7	1:28, 28, 28; 2:8, 22; 3:9, 23					7
1 Th.	5	2:4, 6, 13, 15; 4:8					5
2 Th.	2	2:3; 3:2					2
1 Ti.	10	2:1, 4, 5, 5; 4:10; 5:24; 6:5, 9, 11, 16					10
2 Ti.	5	2:2; 3:2, 8, 13, 17					5
Tit.	5	1:14; 2:11; 3:2, 8, 10					5
Heb.	10	2:6, 6; 5:1, 1; 6:16; 7:8, 28; 8:2; 9:27; 13:6					10
Jas.	7	1:7, 19; 2:20, 24; 3:8, 9; 5:17					7
1 Pt.	6	1:24; 2:4, 15; 3:4; 4:2, 6					6
2 Pt.	4	1:21, 21; 2:16; 3:7					4
1 Jn.	1	5:9					1
Jd.	1	1:4					1
Rev.	25	1:13; 4:7; 8:11; 9:4, 5, 6, 7, 10, 15, 18, 20; 11:13; 13:13, 18; 14:4, 14; 16:2, 8, 9, 18, 21, 21; 18:13; 21:3, 17					25
Total	552		4		3		559

Miscellaneous: Mt. 18:23; 22:2, certain; Lk. 19:12 (with 2104), nobleman.

445. ἀνθυπατεύω, anthupateu'ō

Book	be deputy	Total
Ac.	18:12	1

446. ἀνθύπατος, anthu'patos

Book	deputy	Total
Ac.	13:7, 8, 12; 19:38	4

447. ἀνίημι, ani'ēmi

Book	Oc.	loose	Oc.	forbear	Oc.	leave	Total
Ac.	2	16:26; 27:40					2
Eph.			1	6:9			1
Heb.					1	13:5	1
Total	2		1		1		4

448. ἀνίλεως, ani'leōs

Book	without mercy	Total
Jas.	2:13	1

449. ἄνιπτος, an'iptos

Book	unwashen	Total
Mt.	15:20	1
Mk.	7:2, 5	2
Total		3

450. ἀνίστημι, anis′te̱mi

Book	Oc.	arise	Oc.	rise	Oc.	rise up	Oc.	rise again	Oc.	raise up	Oc.	stand up	Oc.	raise up again	Oc.	Misc.	Total
Mt.	2	9:9; 26:62	1	12:41			2	17:9; 20:19	1	22:24							6
Mk.	6	2:14; 5:42; 7:24; 9:27; 10:1; 14:57	6	9:9, 31; 10: 50; 12:23, 25; 16:9	2	1:35; 3:26	2	8:31; 10:34			1	14:60			1	9:10	18
Lk.	10	1:39; 4:38, 39; 6:8; 8: 55; 15:18, 20; 17:19; 23:1; 24:12	5	11:7, 8; 16:31; 22: 46; 24: 46	6	4:29; 5: 25, 28; 11:32; 22:45; 24:33	4	9:8, 19; 18:33; 24:7			2	4:16; 10:25					27
Jn.					1	11:31	3	11:23, 24; 20:9	3	6:40, 44, 54			1	6:39			8
Ac.	18	5:6; 6:9; 7: 18; 8:26, 27; 9:6, 11, 18, 34, 34, 39, 40; 10:20; 11:7; 20:30; 22:10, 16; 23:9	3	10:13, 41; 26:16	6	5:17, 36, 37; 14:20; 15:7; 26:30	1	17:3	7	2:24, 30, 32; 3:22, 26; 7:37; 13:34	5	1:15; 5:34; 10:26; 11:28; 13:16	1	13:33	4	9:41; 12:7; 14:10; 17:31	45
Ro.			2	14:9; 15:12													2
1 Co.					1	10:7											1
Eph.	1	5:14															1
1 Th.			1	4:16			1	4:14									2
Heb.	1	7:15	1	7:11													2
Total	38		19		16		13		11		8		2		5		112

Miscellaneous: Mk. 9:10, rising; Ac. 9:41, lift up; Ac. 12:7, arise up; Ac. 14:10. stand upright; Ac. 17:31, raise.

451. Ἄννα, An′na

Book	Anna	Total
Lk.	2:36	1

452. Ἄννας, An′nas

Book	Annas	Total
Lk	3:2	1
Jn.	18:13, 24	2
Ac.	4:6	1
Total		4

453. ἀνόητος, ano′e̱tos

Book	Oc.	foolish	Oc.	fool	Oc.	unwise	Total
Lk.			1	24:25			1
Ro.					1	1:14	1
Gal.	2	3:1, 3					2
1 Ti.	1	6:9					1
Tit.	1	3:3					1
Total	4		1		1		6

454. ἄνοια, an′oia

Book	Oc.	madness	Oc.	folly	Total
Lk.	1	6:11			1
2 Ti.			1	3:9	1
Total	1		1		2

455. ἀνοίγω, anoi′gō

Book	open	Total
Mt.	2:11; 3:16; 5:2; 7:7, 8; 9:30; 13:35; 17:27; 20:33; 25:11; 27:52	11
Lk.	1:64; 3:21; 11:9, 10; 12:36; 13:25	6
Jn.	1:51; 9:10, 14, 17, 21, 26, 30, 32; 10:3, 21; 11:37	11
Ac.	5:19, 23; 7:56; 8:32, 35; 9:8, 40; 10:11, 34; 12:10, 14, 16; 14:27; 16:26, 27; 18:14; 26:18	17
Ro.	3:13	1
1 Co.	16:9	1
2 Co.	2:12; 6:11	2
Col.	4:3	1
Rev.	3:7, 7, 8, 20; 4:1; 5:2, 3, 4, 5, 9; 6:1, 3, 5, 7, 9, 12; 8:1; 9:2; 10:2, 8; 11:19; 12:16; 13:6; 15:5; 19:11; 20:12, 12	27
Total		77

456. ἀνοικοδομέω, anoikodome′ō

Book	build again	Total
Ac.	15:16, 16	2

457. ἄνοιξις, an′oixis

Book	that (one) may open (with 1722)	Total
Eph.	6:19	1

458. ἀνομία, anomi′a

Book	Oc.	iniquity	Oc.	unrighteousness	Oc.	transgress the law (with 4060)	Oc.	transgression of the law	Total
Mt.	4	7:23; 13:41; 23:28; 24:12							4
Ro.	3	4:7; 6:19, 19							3
2 Co.			1	6:14					1
2 Th.	1	2:7							1
Tit.	1	2:14							1
Heb.	3	1:9; 8:12; 10:17							3
1 Jn.					1	3:4a	1	3:4b	2
Total	12		1		1		1		15

459. ἄνομος, an′omos

Book	Oc.	without law	Oc.	transgressor	Oc.	wicked	Oc.	lawless	Oc.	unlawful	Total
Mk.			1	15:28							1
Lk.			1	22:37							1
Ac.					1	2:23					1
1 Co.	4	9:21, 21, 21, 21									4
2 Th.					1	2:8					1
1 Ti.							1	1:9			1
2 Pt.									1	2:8	1
Total	4		2		2		1		1		10

460. ἀνόμως, anom′ōs

Book	without law	Total
Ro.	2:12, 12	2

461. ἀνορθόω, anortho′ō

Book	Oc.	make straight	Oc.	set up	Oc.	lift up	Total
Lk.	1	13:13					1
Ac.			1	15:16			1
Heb.					1	12:12	1
Total	1		1		1		3

462. ἀνόσιος, anos′ios

Book	unholy	Total
1 Ti.	1:9	1
2 Ti.	3:2	1
Total		2

463. ἀνοχή, anoche̱′

Book	forbearance	Total
Ro.	2:4; 3:25	2

464. ἀνταγωνίζομαι antagōnid′zomai

Book	strive against	Total
Heb.	12:4	1

465. ἀντάλλαγμα, antall′agma

Book	in exchange	Total
Mt.	16:26	1
Mk.	8:37	1
Total		2

466. ἀνταναπληρόω antanaple̱ro′ō

Book	fill up	Total
Col.	1:24	1

467. ἀνταποδίδωμι, antapodi'dōmi

Book	Oc.	recompense	Oc.	recompense again	Oc.	repay	Oc.	render	Total
Lk.	2	14:14, 14							2
Ro.			1	11:35	1	12:19			2
1 Th.							1	3:9	1
2 Th.	1	1:6							1
Heb.	1	10:30							1
Total	4		1		1		1		7

468. ἀνταπόδομα, antapod'oma

Book	recompence	Total
Lk.	14:12	1
Ro.	11:9	1
Total		2

469. ἀνταπόδοσις, antapod'osis

Book	reward	Total
Col.	3:24	1

470. ἀνταποκρίνομαι, antapokri'nomai

Book	Oc.	answer again	Oc.	reply against	Total
Lk.	1	14:6			1
Ro.			1	9:20	1
Total	1		1		2

471. ἀντέπω, antep'ō

Book	Oc.	gainsay	Oc.	say against	Total
Lk.	1	21:15			1
Ac.			1	4:14	1
Total	1		1		2

472. ἀντέχομαι, antech'omai

Book	Oc.	hold to	Oc.	support	Oc.	hold fast	Total
Mt.	1	6:24					1
Lk.	1	16:13					1
1 Th.			1	5:14			1
Tit.					1	1:9	1
Total	2		1		1		4

473. ἀντί, anti'

Book	Oc.	for	Oc.	because (with 3639)	Oc.	for...cause	Oc.	therefore (with 3639)	Oc.	in the room of	Total
Mt.	4	5:38, 38; 17:27; 20:28							1	2:22	5
Mk.	1	10:45									1
Lk.	1	11:11	2	1:20; 19:44			1	12:3			4
Jn.	1	1:16									1
Ac.			1	12:23							1
Ro.	1	12:17									1
1 Co.	1	11:15									1
Eph.					1	5:31					1
1 Th.	1	5:15									1
2 Th.			1	2:10							1
Heb.	2	12:2, 16									2
Jas.	1	4:15									1
1 Pt.	2	3:9, 9									2
Total	15		4		1		1		1		22

474. ἀντιβάλλω, antibal'lō

Book	have	Total
Lk.	24:17	1

475. ἀντιδιατίθεμαι antidiatith'emai

Book	oppose (one's) self	Total
2 Ti.	2:25	1

476. ἀντίδικος, antid'ikos

Book	adversary	Total
Mt.	5:25, 25	2
Lk.	12:58; 18:3	2
1 Pt.	5:8	1
Total		5

477. ἀντίθεσις, antith'esis

Book	opposition	Total
1 Ti.	6:20	1

478. ἀντικαθίστημι antikathis'tēmi

Book	resist	Total
Heb.	12:4	1

479. ἀντικαλέω, antikale'ō

Book	bid again	Total
Lk.	14:12	1

480. ἀντίκειμαι, antik'eimai

Book	Oc.	adversary	Oc.	be contrary	Oc.	oppose	Total
Lk.	2	13:17; 21:15					2
1 Co.	1	16:9					1
Gal.			1	5:17			1
Phl.	1	1:28					1
2 Th.					1	2:4	1
1 Ti.	1	5:14	1	1:10			2
Total	5		2		1		8

481. ἀντικρύ, antikru'

Book	over against	Total
Ac.	20:15	1

482. ἀντιλαμβάνομαι, antilamban'omai

Book	Oc.	help	Oc.	support	Oc.	partaker	Total
Lk.	1	1:54					1
Ac.			1	20:35			1
1 Ti.					1	6:2	1
Total	1		1		1		3

484. ἀντίληψις, antil'ēpsis

Book	help	Total
1 Co.	12:28	1

483. ἀντιλέγω, antileg'ō

Book	Oc.	speak against	Oc.	deny	Oc.	contradict	Oc.	gainsay	Oc.	gainsayer	Oc.	answer again	Total
Lk.	1	2:34	1	20:27									2
Jn.	1	19:12											1
Ac.	3	13:45a; 28:19, 22			1	13:45b							4
Ro.							1	10:21					1
Tit.									1	1:9	1	2:9	2
Total	5		1		1		1		1		1		10

485. ἀντιλογία, antilogi'a

Book	Oc.	contradiction	Oc.	strife	Oc.	gainsaying	Total
Heb.	2	7:7; 12:3	1	6:16			3
Jd.					1	1:11	1
Total	2		1		1		4

486. ἀντιλοιδορέω, antiloidore'ō

Book	revile again	Total
1 Pt.	2:23	1

487. ἀντίλυτρον, antil'utron

Book	ransom	Total
1 Ti.	2:6	1

488. ἀντιμετρέω, antimetre´ō

Book	measure again	Total
Mt.	7:2	1
Lk.	6:38	1
Total		2

489. ἀντιμισθία, antimisthi´a

Book	recompence	Total
Ro.	1:27	1
2 Co.	6:13	1
Total		2

490. Ἀντιόχεια, Antioch´eia

Book	Oc.	Antioch (of Syria)	Oc.	Antioch (of Pisidia)	Total
Ac.	13	11:19, 20, 22, 26, 26, 27; 13:1; 14:26; 15:22, 23, 30, 35; 18:22	3	13:14; 14:19, 21	16
Gal.	1	2:11			1
2 Ti.			1	3:11	1
Total	14		4		18

491. Ἀντιοχεύς, Antiocheus´

Book	of Antioch	Total
Ac.	6:5	1

492. ἀντιπαρέρχομαι, antiparer´chomai

Book	pass by on the other side	Total
Lk.	10:31, 32	2

493. Ἀντίπας, Anti´pas

Book	Antipas	Total
Rev.	2:13	1

494. Ἀντιπατρίς, Antipatris´

Book	Antipatris	Total
Ac.	23:31	1

495. ἀντιπέραν, antiper´an

Book	over against	Total
Lk.	8:26	1

496. ἀντιπίπτω, antipip´tō

Book	resist	Total
Ac.	7:51	1

497. ἀντιστρατεύομαι, antistrateu´omai

Book	war against	Total
Ro.	7:23	1

500. ἀντίχριστος, anti´christos

Book	antichrist	Total
1 Jn.	2:18, 18, 22; 4:3	4
2 Jn.	1:7	1
Total		5

498. ἀντιτάσσομαι, antitas´somai

Book	Oc.	resist	Oc.	oppose (one's) self	Total
Ac.			1	18:6	1
Ro.	1	13:2			1
Jas.	2	4:6; 5:6			2
1 Pt.	1	5:5			1
Total	4		1		5

499. ἀντίτυπον, antit´upon

Book	Oc.	figure	Oc.	like figure whereunto	Total
Heb.	1	9:24			1
1 Pt.			1	3:21	1
Total	1		1		2

502. ἄντλημα, ant´lẹma

Book	nothing to draw with (with 3677)	Total
Jn.	4:11	1

503. ἀντοφθαλμέω, antophthalme´ō

Book	bear up into	Total
Ac.	27:15	1

501. ἀντλέω, antle´ō

Book	Oc.	draw	Oc.	draw out	Total
Jn.	3	2:9; 4:7, 15	1	2:8	4

505. ἀνυπόκριτος, anupok´ritos

Book	Oc.	unfeigned	Oc.	without dissimulation	Oc.	without hypocrisy	Total
Ro.			1	12:9			1
2 Co.	1	6:6					1
1 Ti.	1	1:5					1
2 Ti.	1	1:5					1
1 Pt.	1	1:22					1
Jas.					1	3:17	1
Total	4		1		1		6

504. ἄνυδρος, an´udros

Book	Oc.	dry	Oc.	without water	Total
Mt.	1	12:43			1
Lk.	1	11:24			1
2 Pt.			1	2:17	1
Jd.			1	1:12	1
Total	2		2		4

507. ἄνω, an´ō

Book	Oc.	above	Oc.	up	Oc.	high	Oc.	brim	Total
Jn.	1	8:23	1	11:41			1	2:7	3
Ac.	1	2:19							1
Gal.	1	4:26							1
Phl.					1	3:14			1
Col.	2	3:1, 2							2
Heb.			1	12:15					1
Total	5		2		1		1		9

506. ἀνυπότακτος, anupot´aktos

Book	Oc.	unruly	Oc.	disobedient	Oc.	that is not put under	Total
1 Ti.			1	1:9			1
Tit.	2	1:6, 10					2
Heb.					1	2:8	1
Total	2		1		1		4

508. ἀνώγεον, anōg´eon

Book	upper room	Total
Mk.	14:15	1
Lk.	22:12	1
Total		2

509. ἄνωθεν, an´ōthen

Book	Oc.	from above	Oc.	top	Oc.	again	Oc.	from the very first	Oc.	from the beginning	Oc.	Not Tr.	Total
Mt.			1	27:51									1
Mk.			1	15:38									1
Lk.							1	1:3					1
Jn.	2	3:31; 19:11	1	19:23	2	3:3, 7							5
Ac.									1	26:5			1
Gal.											1	4:9	1
Jas.	3	1:17; 3:15, 17											3
Total	5		3		2		1		1		1		13

510. ἀνωτερικός, anōterikos´

Book	upper	Total
Ac.	19:1	1

511. ἀνώτερος, anō´teros

Book	Oc.	higher	Oc.	above	Total
Lk.	1	14:10			1
Heb.			1	10:8	1
Total	1		1		2

512. ἀνωφέλες, anōphel´es

Book	Oc.	unprofitable	Oc.	unprofitableness	Total
Tit.	1	3:9			1
Heb.			1	7:18	1
Total	1		1		2

513. ἀξίνη, axi´nẹ

Book	axe	Total
Mt.	3:10	1
Lk.	3:9	1
Total		2

514. ἄξιος, ax´ios

Book	Oc.	worthy	Oc.	meet	Oc.	due reward	Oc.	unworthy (with 3656)	Total
Mt.	8	10:10, 11, 13, 13, 37, 37, 38; 22:8	1	3:8					9
Lk.	7	3:8; 7:4; 10:7; 12:48; 15:19, 21; 23:15			1	23:41			8
Jn.	1	1:27							1
Ac.	5	13:25; 23:29; 25:11, 25; 26:31	1	26:20			1	13:46	7
Ro.	2	1:32; 8:18							2
1 Co.			1	16:4					1
2 Th.			1	1:3					1
1 Ti.	4	1:15; 4:9; 5:18; 6:1							4
Heb.	1	11:38							1
Rev.	7	3:4; 4:11; 5:2, 4, 9, 12; 16:6							7
Total	35		4		1		1		41

515. ἀξιόω, axio′ō

Book	Oc.	count worthy	Oc.	think worthy	Oc.	think good	Oc.	desire	Total
Lk.			1	7:7					1
Ac.					1	15:38	1	28:22	2
2 Th.	1	1:11							1
1 Ti.	1	5:17							1
Heb.	1	3:3	1	10:29					2
Total	3		2		1		1		7

516. ἀξίως, axi′ōs

Book	Oc.	worthy	Oc.	as becometh	Oc.	after a godly sort (with 2316)	Total
Ro.			1	16:2			1
Eph.	1	4:1					1
Phl.			1	1:27			1
Col.	1	1:10					1
1 Th.	1	2:12					1
3 Jn.					1	1:6	1
Total	3		2		1		6

517. ἀόρατος, aor′atos

Book	Oc.	invisible	Oc.	invisible things	Total
Ro.			1	1:20	1
Col.	2	1:15, 16			2
1 Ti.	1	1:17			1
Heb.	1	11:27			1
Total	4		1		5

518. ἀπαγγέλλω, apanggel′lō

Book	Oc.	tell	Oc.	shew	Oc.	declare	Oc.	report	Oc.	bring word	Oc.	bring word again	Oc.	shew again	Total
Mt.	4	8:33; 14:12; 28:9, 10	2	12:18; 28:11					1	28:8	1	2:8	1	11:4	9
Mk.	3	6:30; 16:10, 13													3
Lk.	8	7:22; 8:20, 34, 36; 9:36; 13:1; 18:37; 24:9	2	7:18; 14:21	1	8:47									11
Jn.	2	4:51; 20:18													2
Ac.	9	5:22, 25; 12:14; 15:27; 16:36; 22:26; 23:16, 17, 19	4	11:13; 12: 17; 26:20; 28:21			1	4:23							14
1 Co.							1	14:25							1
1 Th.			1	1:9											1
Heb.					1	2:12									1
1 Jn.			1	1:2	1	1:3									2
Total	26		10		3		2		1		1		1		44

519. ἀπάγχομαι, apang′chomai

Book	hang (one's) self	Total
Mt.	27:5	1

520. ἀπάγω, apag′ō

Book	Oc.	lead away	Oc.	lead	Oc.	put to death	Oc.	bring	Oc.	take away	Oc.	carry away	Total
Mt.	3	26:57; 27:2, 31	2	7:13, 14									5
Mk.	3	14:44, 53; 15:16											3
Lk.	2	13:15; 23:26											2
Jn.	2	18:13; 19:16											2
Ac.					1	12:19	1	23:17	1	24:7			3
1 Co.											1	12:2	1
Total	10		2		1		1		1		1		16

521. ἀπαίδευτος, apai′deutos

Book	unlearned	Total
2 Ti.	2:23	1

522. ἀπαίρω, apai′rō

Book	Oc.	take away	Oc.	take	Total
Mt.			1	9:15	1
Mk.	1	2:20			1
Lk.	1	5:35			1
Total	2		1		3

523. ἀπαιτέω, apaite′ō

Book	Oc.	ask again	Oc.	require	Total
Lk.	1	6:30	1	12:20	2

524. ἀπαλγέω, apalge′ō

Book	be past feeling	Total
Eph.	4:19	1

525. ἀπαλλάσσω, apallas′sō

Book	Oc.	deliver	Oc.	depart	Total
Lk.	1	12:58			1
Ac.			1	19:12	1
Heb.	1	2:15			1
Total	2		1		3

526. ἀπαλλοτριόω, apallotrio′ō

Book	Oc.	be alienated (with 5507)	Oc.	be alien	Total
Eph.	1	4:18	1	2:12	2
Col.	1	1:21			1
Total	2		1		3

527. ἁπαλός, apalos′

Book	tender	Total
Mt.	24:32	1
Mk.	13:28	1
Total		2

528. ἀπαντάω, apanta′ō

Book	meet	Total
Mt.	28:9	1
Mk.	5:2; 14:13	2
Lk.	14:31; 17:12	2
Jn.	4:51	1
Ac.	16:16	1
Total		7

529. ἀπάντησις, apan′tēsis

Book	to meet (with 1519)	Total
Mt.	25:1, 6	2
Ac.	28:15	1
1 Th.	4:17	1
Total		4

530. ἅπαξ, hap′ax

Book	once	Total
2 Co.	11:25	1
Phl.	4:16	1
1 Th.	2:18	1
Heb.	6:4; 9:7, 26, 27, 28; 10:2; 12:26, 27	8
1 Pt.	3:18, 20	2
Jd.	1:3, 5	2
Total		15

531. ἀπαράβατος, aparab′atos

Book	unchangeable	Total
Heb.	7:24	1

532. ἀπαρασκεύαστος
aparaskeu′astos

Book	unprepared	Total
2 Co.	9:4	1

533. ἀπαρνέομαι, aparne′omai

Book	deny	Total
Mt.	16:24; 26:34, 35, 75	4
Mk.	8:34; 14:30, 31, 72	4
Lk.	9:23; 12:9; 22:34, 61	4
Jn.	13:38	1
Total		13

534. ἀπάρτι, apar′ti

Book	from henceforth	Total
Rev.	14:13	1

535. ἀπαρτισμός, apartismos′

Book	finish	Total
Lk.	14:28	1

536. ἀπαρχή, aparchē′

Book	firstfruits	Total
Ro.	8:23; 11:16; 16:5	3
1 Co.	15:20, 23; 16:15	3
Jas.	1:18	1
Rev.	14:4	1
Total		8

537. ἅπας, hap'as

Book	Oc.	all	Oc.	all things	Oc.	whole	Oc.	every one	Oc.	every	Total
Mt.	2	6:32; 24:39	1	28:11							3
Mk.	3	5:40; 11:32; 16:15							1	8:25	4
Lk.	16	3:16, 21; 4:6; 5:11, 26, 28; 7:16; 9:15; 15:13; 17:27, 29; 19:7, 48; 21:4, 4, 12	1	2:39	3	8:37; 19:37; 23:1					20
Ac.	11	2:1, 4, 14; 4:31; 5:12; 6:15; 11:10; 13:29; 16:3, 28; 27:33	3	2:44; 4:32; 10:8			1	5:16			15
Eph.	1	6:13									1
Jas.	1	3:2									1
Total	34		5		3		1		1		44

538. ἀπατάω, apata'ō

Book	deceive	Total
Eph.	5:6	1
1 Ti.	2:14, 14	2
Jas.	1:26	1
Total		4

539. ἀπάτη, apat'ẹ

Book	Oc.	deceitfulness	Oc.	deceitful	Oc.	deceit	Oc.	deceiv-ableness	Oc.	deceivings	Total
Mt.	1	13:22									1
Mk.	1	4:19									1
Eph.			1	4:22							1
Col.					1	2:8					1
2 Th.							1	2:10			1
Heb.	1	3:13									1
2 Pt.									1	2:13	1
Total	3		1		1		1		1		7

540. ἀπάτωρ, apat'ōr

Book	without father	Total
Heb.	7:3	1

541. ἀπαύγασμα, apau'gasma

Book	brightness	Total
Heb.	1:3	1

542. ἀπείδω, apei'dō

Book	see	Total
Phl.	2:23	1

543. ἀπείθεια, apei'theia

Book	Oc.	unbelief	Oc.	disobedience	Total
Ro.	2	11:30, 32			2
Eph.			2	2:2; 5:6	2
Col.			1	3:6	1
Heb.	2	4:6, 11			2
Total	4		3		7

544. ἀπειθέω, apeithe'ō

Book	Oc.	believe not	Oc.	disobedient	Oc.	obey not	Oc.	unbelieving	Total
Jn.	1	3:36							1
Ac.	2	17:5; 19:9					1	14:2	3
Ro.	3	11:30, 31; 15:31	1	10:21	1	2:8			5
Heb.	2	3:18; 11:31							2
1 Pt.			3	2:7, 8; 3:20	2	3:1; 4:17			5
Total	8		4		3		1		16

545. ἀπειθής, apeithẹs'

Book	disobedient	Total
Lk.	1:17	1
Ac.	26:19	1
Ro.	1:30	1
2 Ti.	3:2	1
Tit.	1:16; 3:3	2
Total		6

546. ἀπειλέω, apeile'ō

Book	threaten	Total
Ac.	4:17	1
1 Pt.	2:23	1
Total		2

547. ἀπειλή, apeilẹ'

Book	Oc.	threatening	Oc.	straitly	Total
Ac.	2	4:29; 9:1	1	4:17	3
Eph.	1	6:9			1
Total	3		1		4

548. ἄπειμι, ap'eimi

Book	Oc.	be absent	Oc.	absent	Total
1 Co.			1	5:3	1
2 Co.	4	10:1, 11; 13:2, 10			4
Phl.	1	1:27			1
Col.	1	2:5			1
Total	6		1		7

549. ἄπειμι, ap'eimi

Book	go	Total
Ac.	17:10	1

550. ἀπεῖπον, apei'pon

Book	renounce	Total
2 Co.	4:2	1

551. ἀπείραστος, apei'rastos

Book	cannot be tempted (with 2076)	Total
Jas.	1:13	1

552. ἄπειρος, ap'eiros

Book	unskilful	Total
Heb.	5:13	1

553. ἀπεκδέχομαι, apekdech'omai

Book	Oc.	wait for	Oc.	look for	Total
Ro.	3	8:19, 23, 25			3
1 Co.	1	1:7			1
Gal.	1	5:5			1
Phl.			1	3:20	1
Heb.			1	9:28	1
Total	5		2		7

554. ἀπεκδύομαι, apekdu'omai

Book	Oc.	spoil	Oc.	put off	Total
Col.	1	2:15	1	3:9	2

555. ἀπέκδυσις, apek'dusis

Book	putting off	Total
Col.	2:11	1

556. ἀπελαύνω, apelau'nō

Book	drive	Total
Ac.	18:16	1

557. ἀπελεγμός, apelegmos'

Book	nought	Total
Ac.	19:27	1

558. ἀπελεύθερος, apeleu'theros

Book	freeman	Total
1 Co.	7:22	1

559. Ἀπελλῆς, Apellẹs'

Book	Apelles	Total
Ro.	16:10	1

560. ἀπελπίζω, apelpid'zō

Book	hope for again	Total
Lk.	6:35	1

561. ἀπέναντι, apen'anti

Book	Oc.	over against	Oc.	before	Oc.	in the presence of	Oc.	contrary	Total
Mt.	2	21:2; 27:61	1	27:24					3
Ac.					1	3:16	1	17:7	2
Ro.			1	3:18					1
Total	2		2		1		1		6

562. ἀπέραντος, aper'antos

Book	endless	Total
1 Ti.	1:4	1

563. ἀπερισπάστως, aperispas'tōs

Book	without distraction	Total
Co.	7:35	1

564. ἀπερίτμητος, aperit'mẹtos

Book	uncircumcised	Total
Ac.	7:51	1

566. ἀπέχει, apech'ei

Book	be enough	Total
Mk.	14:41	1

567. ἀπέχομαι, apech'omai

Book	abstain	Total
Ac.	15:20, 29	2
1 Th.	4:3; 5:22	2
1 Ti.	4:3	1
1 Pt.	2:11	1
Total		6

565. ἀπέρχομαι, aper'chomai

Book	Oc.	go	Oc.	depart	Oc.	go (one's) way	Oc.	go away	Oc.	come	Oc.	Misc.	Total
Mt.	20	2:22; 4:24; 8:19, 21; 8:32; 10:5; 13: 28, 46; 14:15, 25; 16:21; 18:30; 21: 29, 30; 25:10, 18, 25; 26:36; 27:5; 28:10	5	8:18; 9:7; 14:16; 16:4; 27:60	5	8:33; 13:25; 20:4; 22:5, 22	5	8:31; 19: 22; 25:46; 26:42, 44					35
Mk.	10	1:20; 5:24; 6:27, 36, 37; 7:24; 9:43; 14:10, 12; 16:13	7	1:35, 42; 5:17, 20; 6:32, 46; 8:13	2	11:4; 12:12	2	10:22; 14: 39	2	3:13; 7:30			23
Lk.	9	5:14; 8:34; 9:12, 57, 59, 60; 17:23; 22:13; 24:24	8	1:23, 38; 5:13, 25; 7:24; 8:37; 10:30; 24:12	3	8:39; 19:32; 22:4	1	2:15	1	23:33	1	8:31	23
Jn.	8	4:43, 47; 6:1, 68; 9:11; 11:54; 12: 19; 18:6	3	4:3; 5:15; 12:36	4	4:28; 9:7; 11:28, 46	6	4:8; 6:22; 10:40; 16: 7, 7; 20:10			1	6:66	22
Ac.	1	5:26	2	10:7; 28:29	1	9:17					1	4:15	5
Ro.									1	15:28			1
Gal.	1	1:17											1
Jas.					1	1:24							1
Jd.	1	1:7											1
Rev.	3	10:9; 12:17; 16:2	2	18:14, 14							3	9:12; 11: 14; 21:4	8
Total	53		27		16		14		4		6		120

Miscellaneous: Lk. 8:31, go out; Jn. 6:66, go back; Ac. 4:15, go aside; Rev. 9:12; 11:14, be past; Rev. 21:4, pass away.

568. ἀπέχω, apech'ō

Book	Oc.	be	Oc.	have	Oc.	receive	Total
Mt.	1	15:8	3	6:2, 5, 16			4
Mk.	1	7:6					1
Lk.	3	7:6; 15:20; 24:13			1	6:24	4
Phl.			1	4:18			1
Phe.					1	1:15	1
Total	5		4		2		11

569. ἀπιστέω, apiste'ō

Book	believe not	Total
Mk.	16:11, 16	2
Lk.	24:11, 41	2
Ac.	28:24	1
Ro.	3:3	1
2 Ti.	2:13	1
Total		7

570. ἀπιστία, apisti'a

Book	unbelief	Total
Mt.	13:58; 17:20	2
Mk.	6:6; 9:24; 16:14	3
Ro.	3:3; 4:20; 11:20, 23	4
1 Ti.	1:13	1
Heb.	3:12, 19	2
Total		12

571. ἄπιστος, ap'istos

Book	Oc.	that believe not	Oc.	unbelieving	Oc.	faithless	Oc.	unbeliever	Oc.	infidel	Oc.	thing incredible	Oc.	which believe not	Total
Mt.					1	17:17									1
Mk.					1	9:19									1
Lk.					1	9:41	1	12:46							2
Jn.					1	20:27									1
Ac.											1	26:8			1
1 Co.	6	7:12, 13; 10:27; 14: 22, 22, 24	3	7:14, 14, 15			2	6:6; 14:23							11
2 Co.							1	6:14	1	6:15			1	4:4	3
1 Ti.									1	5:8					1
Tit.			1	1:15											1
Rev.			1	21:8											1
Total	6		5		4		4		2		1		1		23

572. ἁπλότης, haplot'ẹs

Book	Oc.	simplicity	Oc.	singleness	Oc.	liberality	Oc.	bountifulness	Oc.	liberal	Total
Ro.	1	12:8									1
2 Co.	2	1:12; 11:3			1	8:2	1	9:11	1	9:13	5
Eph.			1	6:5							1
Col.			1	3:22							1
Total	3		2		1		1		1		8

573. ἁπλοῦς, haplous'

Book	single	Total
Mt.	6:22	1
Lk.	11:34	1
Total		2

574. ἁπλῶς, haplōs'

Book	liberal	Total
Jas.	1:5	1

575. ἀπό, apo′

Book	Oc.	from	Oc.	of	Oc.	out of	Oc.	for	Oc.	off	Oc.	by
Mt.	67	1:17, 17, 17, 21, 24; 2:1, 16; 3:7, 13; 4:17, 25; 5: 18, 29; 5:30; 6:13; 7:23; 8:1, 11, 30; 9:15, 16, 22; 11:12, 25; 12:38; 13:12, 35; 14:2; 15:8, 27b, 28; 17:9, 18b; 18:8, 9, 35; 19:1, 8; 20:8, 29; 21:8, 43; 22:46; 23:34, 35; 24:1, 29, 31; 25:28, 29, 32, 32, 34, 41; 26:16,39, 42, 47; 27:40, 42, 45, 51, 55b, 64; 28:2, 7, 8	25	3:4; 5:42; 7:15, 16b, 16c; 10:17; 11:19, 29; 15:1, 27a; 16:6, 11, 12, 12; 16: 21b; 17:25, 25, 25, 26; 21:11; 24:32; 27:9, 21, 24, 57	10	3:16; 7:4; 8: 34; 12:43; 13: 1; 14:13; 14: 29; 15:22; 17: 18a; 24:27	3	13:44; 14: 26; 28:4	2	26:58; 27: 55a	2	7:16a, 20
Mk.	29	1:9, 42; 2:20; 3:7, 7, 8, 8, 22; 4:25; 5:35; 7:1, 4, 6,17, 33; 8:11; 9:9; 10: 6; 11:12; 12:34; 13:19, 27; 14:35, 36, 52; 15:30, 32, 38; 16:8	11	5:29, 34; 6:43; 7:28; 8: 15, 31; 12:2, 38; 13:28; 15:43, 45	7	1:10; 5:17; 6: 33; 7:15; 10: 46; 15:21; 16: 9			3	5:6; 14:54; 15:40		
Lk.	61	1:2, 38, 48, 52; 2:4, 15, 36, 37; 3:7; 4:1, 13, 42; 5:3, 8, 10, 13, 35; 7:6; 8:18, 37; 9:5b, 33, 37, 39, 45, 54; 10:21, 30, 42; 11:4, 50a, 51a; 12:52, 58; 13:15, 16, 27, 29, 29; 16:3, 18, 21b, 30; 17:29b; 18: 34; 19:24, 26, 26, 39, 42; 21:11; 22:41, 42, 43, 45a; 23:5, 49; 24:2, 9, 13, 51	26	5:15; 6:13, 17b, 30; 7:21, 35; 8:2a, 3; 9:22, 38; 11:50b, 51b; 12:1, 4, 15, 20, 57; 17:25; 18:3; 20: 10, 46; 21:30; 22:18; 22: 71; 23:51; 24:42	18	4:35, 41; 5:2, 36; 6:17a; 8: 2b, 12, 29, 33, 35, 38, 46; 9: 5a; 11:24; 12: 54; 17:29a; 23:26; 24:31	4	19:3; 21:26; 22:45b; 24:41	1	16:23		
Jn.	14	3:2; 8:44; 10:5, 18a; 11: 53; 12:36; 13:3; 14:7; 15:27; 16:22, 30; 18:28; 19:27; 21:8a	20	1:44, 45; 5:19, 30; 7:17, 18, 28; 8:28, 42; 10:18b; 11:1, 51; 12:21; 14:10; 15:4; 16:13; 18:34; 19: 38; 21:2, 10	1	7:42	1	21:6	1	11:18		
Ac.	68	1:4, 11, 12, 22, 22; 2:40; 3:19, 24, 26; 5:38, 41; 8: 10, 26, 33; 9:3, 8, 18; 10: 17, 21, 23, 37; 11:11, 27; 12:10, 19; 13:8, 13, 13, 14, 29, 31, 39; 14:15, 19; 15:1, 20, 33, 38, 38, 39; 16:11; 17:27; 18:2, 5, 6, 16, 21; 19:9, 12a, 12b; 20:6, 9b, 17, 18a, 26; 21: 1, 7, 10; 22:22, 29, 30; 23:21; 24:18; 25:1, 7; 26:18; 27:21; 28:23b	17	2:17, 18, 22; 5:2, 3; 6:9; 8:22; 10:38; 12:1; 13: 23; 15:5; 17:13; 19:13; 21:16; 21:27; 23:34; 27: 44	8	1:9; 2:5; 13:50; 16:18; 17:2; 19: 12c; 28:21, 23a	2	22:11; 12: 14			2	9:13; 12:20
Ro.	19	1:7, 18, 20; 5:9, 14; 6:7, 18, 22; 7:2, 3, 6; 8:2, 21, 35, 39; 9:3; 11:26; 15: 19, 31	1	13:1								
1 Co.	5	1:3; 7:10, 27; 10:14; 14: 36	4	1:30; 4:5; 6:19; 11:23								
2 Co.	7	1:2; 3:18a; 5:6; 7:1; 11: 3, 9; 12:8	3	2:3; 3:5; 10:7	1	1:16					2	3:18b; 7:13
Gal.	4	1:3, 6; 2:12; 4:24	3	1:1; 2:6; 3:2								
Eph.	3	1:2; 4:31; 6:23										
Phl.	3	1:2, 5; 4:15	1	1:28								
Col.	5	1:2, 23, 26, 26; 2:20	2	1:7; 3:24								
1 Th.	9	1:1, 8, 9, 10; 2:17; 3:6; 4:3, 16; 5:22	2	2:6, 6								
2 Th	8	1:2, 7, 9, 9; 2:13; 3:2, 3, 6										
1 Ti.	3	1:2; 6:5, 10	1	3:7								
2 Ti.	7	1:2, 3; 2:19, 21; 3:15; 4:4, 18										
Tit.	2	1:4; 2:14										
Phe.	1	1:3										
Heb.	14	3:12; 4:3, 4, 10, 10; 6:1, 7; 7:1, 26; 8:11; 9:14; 10:22; 11:15; 12:25	5	7:2, 13; 11:12; 12:15; 13:24	1	11:34					1	5:8
Jas.	4	1:17, 27; 4:7; 5:19	2	1:13; 5:4								
1 Pt.	2	1:12; 3:10										
2 Pt.	1	3:4b										
1 Jn.	15	1:1, 7, 9; 2:7, 7, 13, 14, 20, 24, 24; 3:8, 11, 17; 4:21; 5:21	2	1:5, 27								
2 Jn.	2	1:5, 6										
3 Jn.			1	1:7								
Jd.	1	1:14									1	1:23
Rev.	25	1:4, 4, 5, 5; 3:12; 6:4, 16, 16; 7:2, 17; 9:6; 12:14; 13:8; 14:3, 4; 16:17b; 17: 8; 18:14, 14; 20:9, 11; 21:2, 4, 10; 22:19a	3	2:17; 12:6; 16:12	2	16:17a; 22:19b			3	18:10; 18: 15b, 17	1	18:15a
Total	379		129		48		10		10		9	

575. ἀπό, apo′ (continued)

Book	Oc.	at	Oc.	in	Oc.	since (with 3639)	Oc.	on	Oc.	Not Tr.	Oc.	Misc.	Total
Mt.	1	19:4			1	24:21			2	10:28; 23:33	5	16:21a; 18:7; 23:39; 26:29, 64	118
Mk.													50
Lk.	2	24:27, 47			1	16:16			2	6:29; 8:43	9	1:70; 7:45; 13:25; 14:18; 15:16; 16:21a; 19:39; 22:69; 24:21	124
Jn.	1	8:9							2	13:19; 21:8b	1	1:51	41
Ac.	3	8:35; 23:23; 26:4							3	16:33; 20:18b; 21:21	9	3:21; 7:45; 10:30; 11:19; 15:7, 18, 19; 20:9a; 24:11	112
Ro.			2	11:25; 15:15					3	15:23, 24; 16:17			25
1 Co.													9
2 Co.			2	1:14; 2:5							3	5:16; 8:10; 9:2	18
Gal.									1	5:4			8
Eph.											1	3:9	4
Phl.													4
Col.					2	1:6, 9							9
1 Th.													11
2 Th.			1	2:2									9
1 Ti.													4
2 Ti.													7
Tit.													2
Phe.													1
Heb.			1	5:7	1	9:26							23
Jas.													6
1 Pt.	2	4:17, 17							1	3:11			5
2 Pt.											1	3:4a	2
1 Jn.											1	2:28	18
2 Jn.													2
3 Jn.													1
Jd.													2
Rev.							5	6:10; 21:13, 13, 13, 13	1	16:18	1	14:20	41
Total	9		6		5		5		15		31		656

Miscellaneous: Mt. 16:21a, from ... forth; Mt. 18:7, because of; Mt. 23:39; 26:29 (with 737), henceforth; Mt. 26:64 (with 737), hereafter; Lk. 1:70, since ... began; Lk. 7:45, since; Lk. 13:25 (with 3639 and 302), when once; Lk. 14:18; 15:16; 16:21a, with; Lk. 19:39, from among; Lk. 22:69, hereafter; Lk. 24:21, since; Jn. 1:51 (with 737), hereafter; Ac. 3:21, since ... began; Ac. 7:45, before; Ac. 10:30, ago; Ac. 11:19, upon; Ac. 15:7, ago; Ac. 15:18, from the beginning; Ac. 15:19, from among; Ac. 20:9a, with; Ac. 24:11, since; 2 Co. 5:16, henceforth; 2 Co. 8:10; 9:2, ago; Eph. 3:9, from the beginning; 2 Pt. 3:4a, since; 1 Jn. 2:28, before; Rev. 14:20, by the space of.

576. ἀποβαίνω, apobai'nō

Book	Oc.	turn	Oc.	go out	Oc.	come	Total
Lk.	1	21:13	1	5:2			2
Jn.					1	21:9	1
Phl.	1	1:19					1
Total	2		1		1		4

577. ἀποβάλλω, apobal'lō

Book	cast away	Total
Mk.	10:50	1
Heb.	10:35	1
Total		2

578. ἀποβλέπω, apoblep'ō

Book	have respect	Total
Heb.	11:26	1

579. ἀπόβλητος, apob'le̱tos

Book	be refused	Total
1 Ti.	4:4	1

580. ἀποβολή, apobole̱'

Book	Oc.	loss	Oc.	casting away	Total
Ac.	1	27:22			1
Ro.			1	11:15	1
Total	1		1		2

581. ἀπογενόμενος, apogenom'enos

Book	being dead	Total
1 Pt.	2:24	1

582. ἀπογραφή, apographe̱'

Book	taxing	Total
Lk.	2:2	1
Ac.	5:37	1
Total		2

583. ἀπογράφω, apograph'ō

Book	Oc.	tax	Oc.	write	Total
Lk.	3	2:1, 3, 5			3
Heb.			1	12:23	1
Total	3		1		4

584. ἀποδείκνυμι, apodeik'numi

Book	Oc.	approve	Oc.	prove	Oc.	set forth	Oc.	shew	Total
Ac.	1	2:22	1	25:7					2
1 Co.					1	4:9			1
2 Th.							1	2:4	1
Total	1		1		1		1		4

585. ἀπόδειξις, apod'eixis

Book	demonstration	Total
1 Co.	2:4	1

586. ἀποδεκατόω, apodekato'ō

Book	Oc.	pay tithe	Oc.	tithe	Oc.	give tithe	Oc.	take tithe	Total
Mt.	1	23:23							1
Lk.			1	11:42	1	18:12			2
Heb.							1	7:5	1
Total	1		1		1		1		4

587. ἀπόδεκτος, apod'ektos

Book	acceptable	Total
1 Ti.	2:3; 5:4	2

588. ἀποδέχομαι, apodech'omai

Book	Oc.	receive	Oc.	receive gladly	Oc.	accept	Total
Lk.			1	8:40			1
Ac.	3	15:4; 18:27; 28:30	1	2:41	1	24:3	5
Total	3		2		1		6

590. ἀπόδημος, apod'e̱mos

Book	taking a far journey	Total
Mk.	13:34	1

589. ἀποδημέω, apode̱me'ō

Book	Oc.	go into a far country	Oc.	take (one's) journey	Oc.	travel into a far country	Total
Mt.	1	21:33	1	25:15	1	25:14	3
Mk.	1	12:1					1
Lk.	1	20:9	1	15:13			2
Total	3		2		1		6

591. ἀποδίδωμι, apodid'ōmi

Book	Oc.	pay	Oc.	give	Oc.	render	Oc.	reward	Oc.	sell	Oc.	yield	Oc.	Misc.	Total
Mt.	7	5:26; 18:25a, 26, 28, 29, 30, 34	2	12:36; 20:8	2	21:41; 22:21	4	6:4, 6, 18; 16:27					3	5:33; 18:25b; 27:58	18
Mk.					1	12:17									1
Lk.	2	7:42; 12:59	1	16:2	1	20:25							4	4:20; 9:42; 10:35; 19:8	8
Ac.			2	4:33; 19:40					2	5:8; 7:9					4
Ro.					2	2:6; 13:7							1	12:17	3
1 Co.					1	7:3									1
1 Th.					1	5:15									1
1 Ti.													1	5:4	1
2 Ti.			1	4:8			1	4:14							2
Heb.			1	13:17					1	12:16	1	12:11			3
1 Pt.			1	4:5	1	3:9									2
Rev.			1	22:12			2	18:6, 6			1	22:2			4
Total	9		9		9		7		3		2		9		48

Miscellaneous: Mt. 5:33, perform; Mt. 18:25b, payment to be made; Mt. 27:58, deliver; Lk. 4:20, give again; Lk. 9:42, deliver again; Lk. 10:35, repay; Lk. 19:8, restore; Ro. 12:17, recompense; 1 Ti. 5:4 (with 287), requite.

592. ἀποδιορίζω, apodiorid'zō

Book	separate (one's) self	Total
Jd.	1:19	1

593. ἀποδοκιμάζω, apodokimad'zō

Book	Oc.	reject	Oc.	disallow	Total
Mt.	1	21:42			1
Mk.	2	8:31; 12:10			2
Lk.	3	9:22; 17:25; 20:17			3
Heb.	1	12:17			1
1 Pt.			2	2:4, 7	2
Total	7		2		9

594. ἀποδοχή, apodoche̱'

Book	acceptation	Total
1 Ti.	1:15; 4:9	2

597. ἀποθησαυρίζω, apothe̱saurid'zō

Book	lay up in store	Total
1 Ti.	6:19	1

598. ἀποθλίβω, apothli'bō

Book	press	Total
Lk.	8:45	1

595. ἀπόθεσις, apoth'esis

Book	Oc.	putting away	Oc.	must put off (with 2076)	Total
1 Pt.	1	3:21			1
2 Pt.			1	1:14	1
Total	1		1		2

596. ἀποθήκη, apothe̱'ke̱

Book	Oc.	barn	Oc.	garner	Total
Mt.	2	6:26; 13:30	1	3:12	3
Lk.	2	12:18, 24	1	3:17	3
Total	4		2		6

599. ἀποθνήσκω, apothnęs'kō

Book	Oc.	die	Oc.	be dead	Oc.	be at the point of death (with 3195)	Oc.	perish	Oc.	lie a dying	Oc.	be slain (with 5308)	Total
Mt.	3	22:24, 27; 26:35	1	9:24			1	8:32					5
Mk.	4	12:19, 20, 21, 22	4	5:35, 39; 9:26; 15:44									3
Lk.	9	16:22, 22; 20:28, 28, 29,30, 31, 32, 36	2	8:52, 53					1	8:42			12
Jn.	18	4:49; 6:50; 8:21, 24, 24: 11: 16, 26, 32, 37, 50, 51; 12:24, 24, 33; 18:32; 19:7; 21:23, 23	7	6:49, 58; 8:52, 53, 53; 11:14, 25	1	4:47							26
Ac.	3	9:37; 21:13; 25:11	1	7:4									4
Ro.	16	5:6, 7, 7, 8; 6:9, 10, 10; 7:9; 8:13, 34; 14:7, 8, 8, 8, 9, 15	7	5:15; 6:2, 7, 8; 7:2, 3, 6									23
1 Co.	7	8:11; 9:15; 15:3, 22, 31, 32, 36											7
2 Co.	4	5:14a, 15, 15; 6:9	1	5:14b									5
Gal.			2	2:19, 21									2
Phl.	1	1:21											1
Col.			2	2:20; 3:3									2
1 Th.	2	4:14; 5:10											2
Heb.	5	7:8; 9:27; 10:28; 11:13, 21	1	11:4							1	11:37	7
Jd.			1	1:12									1
Rev.	6	3:2; 8:9, 11; 9:6; 14:13; 16:3											6
Total	78		29		1		1		1		1		111

600. ἀποκαθίστημι, apokathis'tęmi

Book	Oc.	restore	Oc.	restore again	Total
Mt.	2	12:13; 17:11			2
Mk.	3	3:5; 8:25; 9:12			3
Lk.	1	6:10			1
Ac.			1	1:6	1
Heb.	1	13:19			1
Total	7		1		8

601. ἀποκαλύπτω, apokalup'tō

Book	reveal	Total
Mt.	10:26; 11:25, 27; 16:17	4
Lk.	2:35; 10:21, 22; 12:2; 17:30	5
Jn.	12:38	1
Ro.	1:17, 18; 8:18	3
1 Co.	2:10; 3:13; 14:30	3
Gal.	1:16; 3:23	2
Eph.	3:5	1
Phl.	3:15	1
2 Th.	2:3, 6, 8	3
1 Pt.	1:5, 12; 5:1	3
Total		26

603. ἀποκαραδοκία apokaradoki'a

Book	earnest expectation	Total
Ro.	8:19	1
Phl.	1:20	1
Total		2

604. ἀποκαταλλάσσω apokatallas'sō

Book	reconcile	Total
Eph.	2:16	1
Col.	1:20, 21	2
Total		3

602. ἀποκάλυψις, apokal'upsis

Book	Oc.	revelation	Oc.	be revealed	Oc.	to lighten (with 1519)	Oc.	manifestation	Oc.	coming	Oc.	appearing	Total
Lk.					1	2:32							1
Ro.	2	2:5; 16:25					1	8:19					3
1 Co.	2	14:6, 26							1	1:7			3
2 Co.	2	12:1, 7											2
Gal.	2	1:12; 2:2											2
Eph.	2	1:17; 3:3											2
2 Th.			1	1:7									1
1 Pt.	1	1:13	1	4:13							1	1:7	3
Rev.	1	1:1											1
Total	12		2		1		1		1		1		18

605. ἀποκατάστασις apokatas'tasis

Book	restitution	Total
Ac.	3:21	1

607. ἀποκεφαλίζω apokephalid'zō

Book	behead	Total
Mt.	14:10	1
Mk.	6:16, 27	2
Lk.	9:9	1
Total		4

606. ἀπόκειμαι, apok'eimai

Book	Oc.	lay up	Oc.	appoint	Total
Lk.	1	19:20			1
Col.	1	1:5			1
2 Ti.	1	4:8			1
Heb.			1	9:27	1
Total	3		1		4

608. ἀποκλείω, apoklei'ō

Book	shut to	Total
Lk.	13:25	1

610. ἀπόκριμα, apok'rima

Book	sentence	Total
2 Co.	1:9	1

609. ἀποκόπτω, apokop'tō

Book	cut off	Total
Mk.	9:43, 45	2
Jn.	18:10, 26	2
Ac.	27:32	1
Gal.	5:12	1
Total		6

611. ἀποκρίνομαι, apokri'nomai

Book	answer	Total
Mt.	3:15; 4:4; 8:8; 11:4, 25; 12:38, 39, 48; 13:11, 37; 14:28; 15:3, 13, 15, 23, 24, 26, 28; 16:2, 16, 17; 17:4, 11, 17; 19:4, 27; 20:13, 22; 21:21, 24, 27, 29, 30; 22:1, 29, 46; 24:4; 25:9, 12, 26, 37, 40, 44, 45; 26:23, 25, 33, 62, 63, 66; 27:12, 14, 21, 25; 28:5	55
Mk.	3:33; 5:9; 6:37; 7:6, 28; 8:4, 28, 29; 9:5, 12, 17, 19, 38; 10:3, 5, 20, 24, 29, 51; 11:14, 22, 29, 29, 30, 33, 33; 12:17, 24, 28, 29, 34, 35; 13:2, 5; 14:20, 40, 48, 60, 61; 15:2, 4, 5, 9, 12	44
Lk.	1:19, 35, 60; 3:11, 16; 4:4, 8, 12; 5:5, 22, 31; 6:3; 7:22, 40, 43; 8:21, 50; 9:19, 20, 41, 49; 10:27, 28, 41; 11:7, 45; 13:2, 8, 14, 15, 25; 14:3, 5; 15:29; 17:17, 20, 37; 19:40; 20:3, 7, 24, 34, 39; 22:51, 68; 23:3, 9, 40; 24:18	49
Jn.	1:21, 26, 48, 49, 50; 2:18, 19; 3:3, 5, 9, 10, 27; 4:10, 13, 17; 5:7, 11, 17, 19; 6:7, 26, 29, 43, 68, 70; 7:16, 20, 21, 46, 47, 52; 8:14, 19, 33, 34, 39, 48, 49, 54; 9:3, 11, 20, 25, 27, 30, 34, 36; 10:25, 32, 33, 34; 11:9; 12:23, 30, 34; 13:7, 8, 26, 36, 38; 14:23; 16:31; 18:5, 8, 20, 22, 23, 30, 34, 35, 36, 37; 19:7, 11, 15, 22; 20:28; 21:5	78
Ac.	3:12; 4:19; 5:8, 29; 8:24, 34, 37; 9:13; 10:46; 11:9; 15:13; 19:15; 21:13; 22:8, 28; 24:10, 25; 25:4, 9, 12, 16	21
Col.	4:6	1
Rev.	7:13	1
Total		249

612. ἀπόκρισις, apok'risis

Book	answer	Total
Lk.	2:47; 20:26	2
Jn.	1:22; 19:9	2
Total		4

613. ἀποκρύπτω, apokrup'tō

Book	hide	Total
Mt.	11:25; 25:18	2
Lk.	10:21	1
1 Co.	2:7	1
Eph.	3:9	1
Col.	1:26	1
Total		6

614. ἀπόκρυφος, apok'ruphos

Book	Oc.	hid	Oc.	kept secret	Total
Mk.			1	4:22	1
Lk.	1	8:17			1
Col.	1	2:3			1
Total	2		1		3

615. ἀποκτείνω, apoktei΄nō

Book	Oc.	kill	Oc.	slay	Oc.	put to death	Total
Mt.	10	10:28, 28; 16:21; 17:23; 21:35, 38; 23:34, 37; 24:9; 26:4	2	21:39; 22:6	1	14:5	13
Mk.	10	3:4; 6:19; 8:31; 9:31, 31; 10:34; 12:5, 5, 7, 8			1	14:1	11
Lk.	8	11:47, 48; 12:4, 5; 13:31, 34; 20:14, 15	3	9:22; 11:49; 13:4	1	18:33	12
Jn.	9	5:18; 7:1, 19, 20, 25; 8:22, 37, 40; 16:2	1	5:16	3	11:53; 12:10; 18:31	13
Ac.	4	3:15; 21:31; 23:12; 27:42	2	7:52; 23:14			6
Ro.	1	11:3	1	7:11			2
2 Co.	1	3:6					1
Eph.			1	2:16			1
1 Th.	1	2:15					1
Rev.	11	2:23; 6:8, 11; 9:5, 18, 20; 11:5, 7; 13:10, 10, 15	4	2:13; 9:15; 11:13; 19:21			15
Total	55		14		6		75

616. ἀποκυέω, apokue΄ō

Book	Oc.	bring forth	Oc.	beget	Total
Jas.	1	1:15	1	1:18	2

617. ἀποκυλίω, apokuli΄ō

Book	Oc.	roll away	Oc.	roll back	Total
Mt.			1	28:2	1
Mk.	2	16:3, 4			2
Lk.	1	24:2			1
Total	3		1		4

618. ἀπολαμβάνω, apolamban΄ō

Book	Oc.	receive	Oc.	take aside	Oc.	receive . . . again	Total
Mk.			1	7:33			1
Lk.	5	6:34a, 15:27; 16: 25; 18:30; 23:41			1	6:34b	6
Ro.	1	1:27					1
Gal.	1	4:5					1
Col.	1	3:24					1
2 Jn.	1	1:8					1
3 Jn.	1	1:8					1
Total	10		1		1		12

620. ἀπολείπω, apoleip΄ō

Book	Oc.	leave	Oc.	remain	Total
2 Ti.	2	4:13, 20			2
Heb.			3	4:6, 9; 10:26	3
Jd.	1	1:6			1
Total	3		3		6

619. ἀπόλαυσις, apol΄ausis

Book	Oc.	to enjoy (with 1519)	Oc.	enjoy the pleasures (with 2192)	Total
1 Ti.	1	6:17			1
Heb.			1	11:25	1
Total	1		1		2

621. ἀπολείχω, apolei΄chō

Book	lick	Total
Lk.	16:21	1

623. Ἀπολλύων, Apollu΄ōn

Book	Apollyon	Total
Rev.	9:11	1

624. Ἀπολλωνία, Apollōni΄a

Book	Apollonia	Total
Ac.	17:1	1

625. Ἀπολλῶς, Apollōs΄

Book	Apollos	Total
Ac.	18:24; 19:1	2
1 Co.	1:12; 3:4, 5, 6, 22; 4: 6; 16:12	7
Tit.	3:13	1
Total		10

622. ἀπόλλυμι, apol΄lumi

Book	Oc.	perish	Oc.	destroy	Oc.	lose	Oc.	be lost	Oc.	lost	Oc.	Misc.	Total
Mt.	6	5:29, 30; 8:25; 9:17; 18: 14; 26:52	6	2:13; 10:28; 12:14; 21:41; 22:7; 27:20	5	10:39, 39, 42; 16:25, 25	1	18:11	2	10:6; 15:24			20
Mk.	1	4:38	5	1:24; 3:6; 9:22; 11:18; 12:9	3	8:35, 35; 9:41					1	2:22	10
Lk.	8	5:37; 8:24; 11:51; 13:3, 5, 33; 15:17; 21:18	7	4:34; 6:9; 9:56; 17:27, 29; 19:47; 20:16	8	9:24, 24, 25; 15:4, 8, 9; 17: 33, 33	3	15:4b, 6; 19:10	2	15:24, 32			28
Jn.	5	3:15,16; 6:27; 10:28; 11: 50	1	10:10	5	6:12, 39; 12: 25; 17:12; 18:9					1	18:14	12
Ac.	1	5:37											1
Ro.	1	2:12	1	14:15									2
1 Co.	3	1:18; 8:11; 15:18	3	1:19; 10:9, 10									6
2 Co.	1	2:15	1	4:9			1	4:3					3
2 Th.	1	2:10											1
Heb.	1	1:11											1
Jas.	1	1:11	1	4:12									2
1 Pt.	1	1:7											1
2 Pt.	2	3:6, 9											2
2 Jn.					1	1:8							1
Jd.	1	1:11	1	1:5									2
Total	33		26		22		5		4		2		92

Miscellaneous: Mk. 2:22, be marred; Jn. 18:14, die.

626. ἀπολογέομαι, apologe΄omai

Book	Oc.	answer	Oc.	answer for (one's) self	Oc.	make defence	Oc.	excuse	Oc.	excuse (one's) self	Oc.	speak for (one's) self	Total
Lk.	2	12:11; 21:14											2
Ac.	1	24:10	3	25:8; 26:1, 2	1	19:33					1	26:24	6
Ro.							1	2:15					1
2 Co.									1	12:19			1
Total	3		3		1		1		1		1		10

627. ἀπολογία, apologi΄a

Book	Oc.	defence	Oc.	answer	Oc.	answer for (one's) self	Oc.	clearing of (one's) self	Total
Ac.	1	22:1			1	25:16			2
1 Co.			1	9:3					1
2 Co.							1	7:11	1
Phl.	2	1:7, 17							2
2 Ti.			1	4:16					1
1 Pt.			1	3:15					1
Total	3		3		1		1		8

628. ἀπολούω, apolou΄ō

Book	Oc.	wash away	Oc.	wash	Total
Ac.	1	22:16			1
1 Co.			1	6:11	1
Total	1		1		2

629. ἀπολύτρωσις, apolu΄trōsis

Book	Oc.	redemption	Oc.	deliverance	Total
Lk.	1	21:28			1
Ro.	2	3:24; 8:23			2
1 Co.	1	1:30			1
Eph.	3	1:7, 14; 4:30			3
Col.	1	1:14			1
Heb.	1	9:15	1	11:35	2
Total	9		1		10

630. ἀπολύω, apolu'ō

Book	Oc.	release	Oc.	put away	Oc.	send away	Oc.	let go	Oc.	set at liberty	Oc.	let depart	Oc.	dismiss	Oc.	Misc.	Total
Mt.	4	27:15, 17, 21, 26	8	1:19; 5:31, 32a; 19:3, 7, 8, 9, 9	6	14:15, 22, 23; 15:23, 32, 39									2	5:32b; 18:27	20
Mk.	4	15:6, 9, 11, 15	4	10:2, 4, 11, 12	4	6:36, 45; 8: 3, 9											12
Lk.	5	23:16, 17, 18, 20; 23: 25	2	16:18, 18	2	8:38; 9:12	3	14:4; 22:68; 23:22			1	2:29			3	6:37, 37; 13: 12	16
Jn.	4	18:39, 39; 19:10, 12a					1	19:12b									5
Ac.					1	13:3	9	3:13; 4: 21; 4:23; 5:40; 15: 33; 16: 35, 36; 17:9; 28: 18	1	26:32	1	23:22	2	15:30; 19:41	1	28:25	15
Heb.									1	13:23							1
Total	17		14		13		13		2		2		2		6		69

Miscellaneous: Mt. 5:32b, divorce; Mt. 18:27, loose; Lk. 6:37, 37, forgive; Lk. 13:12, loose; Ac. 28:25, depart.

631. ἀπομάσσομαι apomas'somai

Book	wipe off	Total
Lk.	10:11	1

632. ἀπονέμω, aponem'ō

Book	give	Total
1 Pt.	3:7	1

633. ἀπονίπτω, aponip'tō

Book	wash	Total
Mt.	27:24	1

634. ἀποπίπτω, apopip'tō

Book	fall	Total
Ac.	9:18	1

635. ἀποπλανάω, apoplana'ō

Book	Oc.	seduce	Oc.	err	Total
Mk.	1	13:22			1
1 Ti.			1	6:10	1
Total	1		1		2

636. ἀποπλέω, apople'ō

Book	sail	Total
Ac.	13:4; 14:26; 20:15; 27:1	4

637. ἀποπλύνω, apoplu'nō

Book	wash	Total
Lk.	5:2	1

638. ἀποπνίγω, apopni'gō

Book	choke	Total
Mt.	13:7	1
Lk.	8:7, 33	2
Total		3

639. ἀπορέω, apore'ō

Book	Oc.	doubt	Oc.	be perplexed	Oc.	stand in doubt	Total
Jn.	1	13:22					1
Ac.	1	25:20					1
2 Co.			1	4:8			1
Gal.					1	4:20	1
Total	2		1		1		4

640. ἀπορία, apori'a

Book	perplexity	Total
Lk.	21:25	1

641. ἀποῤῥίπτω, aporhrip'tō

Book	cast (one's) self	Total
Ac.	27:43	1

642. ἀπορφανίζω, aporphanid'zō

Book	take	Total
1 Th.	2:17	1

643. ἀποσκευάζω, aposkeuad'zō

Book	take up (one's) carriages	Total
Ac.	21:15	1

644. ἀποσκίασμα, aposki'asma

Book	shadow	Total
Jas.	1:17	1

645. ἀποσπάω, apospa'ō

Book	Oc.	draw	Oc.	withdraw	Oc.	draw away	Oc.	be gotten	Total
Mt.	1	26:51							1
Lk.			1	22:41					1
Ac.					1	20:30	1	21:1	2
Total	1		1		1		1		4

648. ἀποστεγάζω, apostegad'zō

Book	uncover	Total
Mk.	2:4	1

646. ἀποστασία, apostasi'a

Book	Oc.	to forsake (with 575)	Oc.	falling away	Total
Ac.	1	21:21			1
2 Th.			1	2:3	1
Total	1		1		2

647. ἀποστάσιον, apostas'ion

Book	Oc.	divorcement	Oc.	writing of divorcement	Total
Mt.	1	19:7	1	5:31	2
Mk.	1	10:4			1
Total	2		1		3

649. ἀποστέλλω, apostel'lō

Book	Oc.	send	Oc.	send forth	Oc.	send away	Oc.	send out	Oc.	Misc.	Total
Mt.	13	10:40; 11:10; 15:24; 20:2; 21:1, 3, 34, 36, 37; 23:34, 37; 24:31; 27:19	6	2:16; 10:5, 16; 13: 41; 22:3, 4			2	14:35; 22:16			21
Mk.	11	1:2; 3:31; 6:27; 9:37; 11:3; 12:2, 4a, 5, 6, 13; 13:27	5	3:14; 6:7, 17; 11:1; 14:13	4	5:10; 8:26; 12:3, 4b			1	4:29	21
Lk.	23	1:19, 26; 4:18a, 43; 7:3, 20, 27; 9:2, 48, 52; 10: 1, 16; 11:49; 13:34; 14:17, 32; 19:14, 29, 32; 20: 10; 22:8, 35; 24:49	2	10:3; 20:20					1	4:18b	26
Jn.	28	1:6, 19, 24; 3:17, 28, 34; 4:38; 5:33, 36, 38; 6: 29, 57; 7:29, 32; 8:42; 9:7; 10:36; 11:3, 42; 17:3, 8, 18, 18, 21, 23, 25; 18:24; 20:21									28
Ac.	25	3:20, 26; 5:21; 7:14, 34, 35; 8:14; 9:17, 38; 10: 8, 17, 20, 21, 36; 11:11, 13, 30; 13:15, 26; 15:27; 16:35, 36; 19:22; 26:17; 28:28									25
Ro.	1	10:15									1
1 Co.	1	1:17									1
2 Co.	1	12:17									1
2 Ti.	1	4:12									1
Heb.			1	1:14							1
1 Pt.	1	1:12									1
1 Jn.	3	4:9, 10, 14									3
Rev.	2	1:1; 22:6	1	5:6							3
Total	110		15		4		2		2		133

Miscellaneous: Mk. 4:29, put in; Lk. 4:18b, set.

650. ἀποστερέω, apostere´ō

Book	Oc.	defraud	Oc.	destitute	Oc.	keep back by fraud	Total
Mk.	1	10:19					1
1 Co.	3	6:7, 8; 7:5					3
1 Ti.			1	6:5			1
Jas.					1	5:4	1
Total	4		1		1		6

651. ἀποστολή, apostolẹ´

Book	apostleship	Total
Ac.	1:25	1
Ro.	1:5	1
1 Co.	9:2	1
Gal.	2:8	1
Total		4

652. ἀπόστολος, apos´tolos

Book	Oc.	apostle	Oc.	messenger	Oc.	he that is sent	Total
Mt.	1	10:2					1
Mk.	1	6:30					1
Lk.	6	6:13; 9:10; 11:49; 17:5; 22:14; 24:10					6
Jn.					1	13:16	1
Ac.	30	1:2, 26; 2:37, 42, 43; 4:33, 35, 36, 37; 5:2, 12, 18, 29, 34, 40; 6:6; 8:1, 14, 18; 9:27; 11:1; 14:4, 14; 15:2, 4, 6, 22, 23, 33; 16:4					30
Ro.	3	1:1; 11:13; 16:7					3
1 Co.	10	1:1; 4:9; 9:1, 2, 5; 12:28, 29; 15:7, 9, 9					10
2 Co.	5	1:1; 11:5, 13; 12:11, 12	1	8:23			6
Gal.	3	1:1, 17, 19					3
Eph.	4	1:1; 2:20; 3:5; 4:11					4
Phl.			1	2:25			1
Col.	1	1:1					1
1 Th.	1	2:6					1
1 Ti.	2	1:1; 2:7					2
2 Ti.	2	1:1, 11					2
Tit.	1	1:1					1
Heb.	1	3:1					1
1 Pt.	1	1:1					1
2 Pt.	2	1:1; 3:2					2
Jd.	1	1:17					1
Rev.	3	2:2; 18:20; 21:14					3
Total	78		2		1		81

653. ἀποστοματίζω apostomatid´zō

Book	provoke to speak	Total
Lk.	11:53	1

655. ἀποστυγέω, apostuge´ō

Book	abhor	Total
Ro.	12:9	1

656. ἀποσυνάγωγος, aposunag´ōgos

Book	Oc.	be put out of the synagogue (with 1096)	Oc.	put out of the synagogue (with 4060)	Total
Jn.	2	9:22; 12:42	1	16:2	3

654. ἀποστρέφω, apostreph´ō

Book	Oc.	turn away	Oc.	turn away from	Oc.	put up again	Oc.	turn from	Oc.	bring again	Oc.	pervert	Total
Mt.	1	5:42			1	26:52			1	27:3			3
Lk.											1	23:14	1
Ac.	1	3:26											1
Ro.	1	11:26											1
2 Ti.	1	4:4	1	1:15									2
Tit.							1	1:14					1
Heb.			1	12:25									1
Total	4		2		1		1		1		1		10

657. ἀποτάσσομαι, apotas´somai

Book	Oc.	bid farewell	Oc.	take leave	Oc.	send away	Oc.	forsake	Total
Mk.					1	6:46			1
Lk.	1	9:61					1	14:33	2
Ac.	1	18:21	1	18:18					2
2 Co.			1	2:13					1
Total	2		2		1		1		6

658. ἀποτελέω, apotele´ō

Book	finish	Total
Jas.	1:15	1

659. ἀποτίθημι, apotith´ẹmi

Book	Oc.	put off	Oc.	lay aside	Oc.	lay down	Oc.	cast off	Oc.	put away	Oc.	lay apart	Total
Ac.					1	7:58							1
Ro.							1	13:12					1
Eph.	1	4:22							1	4:25			2
Col.	1	3:8											1
Heb.			1	12:1									1
Jas.											1	1:21	1
1 Pt.			1	2:1									1
Total	2		2		1		1		1		1		8

660. ἀποτινάσσω, apotinas´sō

Book	shake off	Total
Lk.	9:5	1
Ac.	28:5	1
Total		2

661. ἀποτίνω, apoti´nō

Book	repay	Total
Phe.	1:19	1

662. ἀποτολμάω, apotolma´ō

Book	be very bold	Total
Ro.	10:20	1

663. ἀποτομία, apotomi´a

Book	severity	Total
Ro.	11:22, 22	2

664. ἀποτόμως, apotom´ōs

Book	Oc.	sharpness	Oc.	sharply	Total
2 Co.	1	13:10			1
Tit.			1	1:13	1
Total	1		1		2

665. ἀποστρέπω, apostrep´ō

Book	turn away	Total
2 Ti.	3:5	1

666. ἀπουσία, apousi´a

Book	absence	Total
Phl.	2:12	1

667. ἀποφέρω, apopher´ō

Book	Oc.	carry away	Oc.	carry	Oc.	bring	Total
Mk.	1	15:1					1
Lk.			1	16:22			1
1 Co.					1	16:3	1
Rev.	2	17:3; 21:10					2
Total	3		1		1		5

668. ἀποφεύγω, apopheu´gō

Book	Oc.	escape	Oc.	escape from	Total
2 Pt.	2	1:4; 2:20	1	2:18	3

669. ἀποφθέγγομαι, apophtheng´gomai

Book	Oc.	utterance	Oc.	speak forth	Oc.	say	Total
Ac.	1	2:4	1	26:25	1	2:14	3

670. ἀποφορτίζομαι apophortid'zomai

Book	unlade	Total
Ac.	21:3	1

671. ἀπόχρησις, apoch'rēsis

Book	using	Total
Col.	2:22	1

674. ἀποψύχω, apopsu'chō

Book	heart failing	Total
Lk.	21:26	1

675. Ἄππιος, Ap'pios

Book	Appii	Total
Ac.	28:15	1

672. ἀποχωρέω, apochōre'ō

Book	depart	Total
Mt.	7:23	1
Lk.	9:39	1
Ac.	13:13	1
Total		3

673. ἀποχωρίζω, apochōrid'zō

Book	Oc.	depart asunder	Oc.	depart	Total
Ac.	1	15:39			1
Rev.			1	6:14	1
Total	1		1		2

677. ἀπρόσκοπος, apros'kopos

Book	Oc.	void of offence	Oc.	none offence	Oc.	without offence	Total
Ac.	1	24:16					1
1 Co.			1	20:32			1
Phl.					1	1:10	1
Total	1		1		1		3

676. ἀπρόσιτος, apros'itos

Book	which no man can approach unto	Total
1 Ti.	6:16	1

678. ἀπροσωπολήπτως aprosōpolēp'tōs

Book	without respect of persons	Total
1 Pt.	1:17	1

679. ἄπταιστος, ap'taistos

Book	keep from falling (with 5342)	Total
Jd.	1:24	1

680. ἅπτομαι, hap'tomai

Book	touch	Total
Mt.	8:3, 15; 9:20, 21, 29; 14:36, 36; 17:7; 20:34	9
Mk.	1:41; 3:10; 5:27, 28, 30, 31; 6:56, 56; 7:33; 8:22; 10:13	11
Lk.	5:13; 6:19; 7:14, 39; 8:44, 45, 45, 46, 47; 18:15; 22:51	11
Jn.	20:17	1
1 Co.	7:1	1
2 Co.	6:17	1
Col.	2:21	1
1 Jn.	5:18	1
Total		36

681. ἅπτω, hap'tō

Book	Oc.	light	Oc.	kindle	Total
Lk.	3	8:16; 11:33; 15:8	1	22:55	4

682. Ἀπφία, Apphi'a

Book	Apphia	Total
Phe.	1:2	1

685. ἀρά, ara' (noun)

Book	cursing	Total
Ro.	3:14	1

683. ἀπωθέομαι, apōthe'omai

Book	Oc.	cast away	Oc.	thrust away	Oc.	put from	Oc.	thrust from	Oc.	put away	Total
Ac.			1	7:27	1	13:46	1	7:39			3
Ro.	2	11:1, 2									2
1 Ti.									1	1:19	1
Total	2		1		1		1		1		6

684. ἀπώλεια, apō'leia

Book	Oc.	perdition	Oc.	destruction	Oc.	waste	Oc.	damnable	Oc.	damnation	Oc.	to die (with 1519)	Oc.	perish (with 1498 and 1519)	Oc.	pernicious way	Total
Mt.			1	7:13	1	26:8											2
Mk.					1	14:4											1
Jn.	1	17:12															1
Ac.											1	25:16	1	8:20			2
Ro.			1	9:22													1
Phl.	1	1:28	1	3:19													2
2 Th.	1	2:3															1
1 Ti.	1	6:9															1
Heb.	1	10:39															1
2 Pt.	1	3:7	2	2:1b; 3:16			1	2:1a	1	2:3					1	2:2	6
Rev.	2	17:8, 11															2
Total	8		5		2		1		1		1		1		1		20

686. ἄρα, ar'a

Book	Oc.	therefore (with 3667)	Oc.	so then (with 3667)	Oc.	now therefore (with 3667)	Oc.	then (with 1065)	Oc.	wherefore (with 1065)	Oc.	haply (with 1065)	Oc.	then	Oc.	Not Tr. (Interrogative)	Oc.	Misc.	Total
Mt.							1	17:26	1	7:20			3	12:28; 19:25; 24:45	1	18:1	1	19:27	7
Mk.																	2	4:41; 11:13	2
Lk.													1	12:42	1	22:23	4	1:66; 8: 25; 11: 20, 48	6
Ac.							1	11:18			1	17:27			3	7:1; 12: 18; 21:38	1	8:22	6
Ro.	4	5:18; 8: 12; 9:18; 14:19	4	7:3, 25; 9:16; 14: 12									1	7:21			2	8:1; 10:17	11
1 Co.													3	5:10; 15:14, 18	1	7:14	1	15:15	5
2 Co.													1	5:14	1	1:17	1	7:12	3
Gal.	1	6:10											3	2:21; 3:29; 5:11			2	3:7; 4:31	6
Eph.					1	2:19													1
1 Th.	1	5:6																	1
2 Th.	1	2:15																	1
Heb.													1	12:8			1	4:9	2
Total	7		4		1		2		1		1		13		7		7		51

Miscellaneous: Mt. 19:27, therefore; Mk. 4:41, manner of man; Mk. 11:13, haply; Lk. 1:66, manner of; Lk. 8:25, manner of man; Lk. 11:20, no doubt; Lk. 11:48, truly; Ac. 8:22, perhaps; Ro. 8:1, therefore; Ro. 10:17, so then; 1 Co. 15:15, so be; 2 Co. 7:12, wherefore; Gal. 3:7, therefore; Gal. 4:31, so then; Heb. 4:9, therefore.

687. ἄρα, ar'a (adverb)

Book	Oc.	therefore	Oc.	Not Tr.	Total
Lk.			1	18:8	1
Ac.			1	8:30	1
Gal.	1	2:17			1
Total	1		2		3

688. Ἀραβία, Arabi'a

Book	Arabia	Total
Gal.	1:17; 4:25	2

689. Ἀράμ, Aram'

Book	Aram	Total
Mt.	1:3, 4	2
Lk.	3:33	1
Total		3

690. Ἄραψ, Ar'aps

Book	Arabians	Total
Ac.	2:11	1

691. ἀργέω, arge'ō

Book	linger	Total
2 Pt.	2:3	1

692. ἀργός, argos'

Book	Oc.	idle	Oc.	slow	Oc.	barren	Total
Mt.	4	12:36; 20:3, 6, 6					4
1 Ti.	2	5:13, 13					2
Tit.			1	1:12			1
2 Pt.					1	1:8	1
Total	6		1		1		8

693. ἀργύρεος, argu'reos

Book	Oc.	silver	Oc.	of silver	Total
Ac.	1	19:24			1
2 Ti.			1	2:20	1
Rev.	1	9:20			1
Total	2		1		3

694. ἀργύριον, argu'rion

Book	Oc.	money	Oc.	piece of silver	Oc.	silver	Oc.	silver piece	Total
Mt.	4	25:18, 27; 28:12, 15	4	26:15; 27:3, 5, 9			1	27:6	9
Mk.	1	14:11							1
Lk.	4	9:3; 19:15, 23; 22:5							4
Ac.	2	7:16; 8:20	1	19:19	2	3:6; 20:33			5
1 Pt.					1	1:18			1
Total	11		5		3		1		20

695. ἀργυροκόπος, argurokop'os

Book	silversmith	Total
Ac.	19:24	1

696. ἄργυρος, ar'guros

Book	silver	Total
Mt.	10:9	1
Ac.	17:29	1
1 Co.	3:12	1
Jas.	5:3	1
Rev.	18:12	1
Total		5

697. Ἄρειος Πάγος, Ar'eios Pag'os

Book	Oc.	Areopagus	Oc.	Mars' Hill	Total
Ac.	1	17:19	1	17:22	2

698. Ἀρεοπαγίτης, Areopagit'ẹs

Book	Areopagite	Total
Ac.	17:34	1

699. ἀρέσκεια, ares'keia

Book	pleasing	Total
Col.	1:10	1

700. ἀρέσκω, ares'kō

Book	please	Total
Mt.	14:6	1
Mk.	6:22	1
Ac.	6:5	1
Ro.	8:8; 15:1, 2, 3	4
1 Co.	7:32, 33, 34; 10:33	4
Gal.	1:10, 10	2
1 Th.	2:4, 15; 4:1	3
2 Ti.	2:4	1
Total		17

701. ἀρεστός, arestos'

Book	Oc.	those things that please	Oc.	reason	Oc.	please (with 2076)	Oc.	those things that are pleasing	Total
Jn.	1	8:29							1
Ac.			1	6:2	1	12:3			2
1 Jn.							1	3:22	1
Total	1		1		1		1		4

702. Ἀρέτας, Aret'as

Book	Aretas	Total
2 Co.	11:32	1

703. ἀρέτη, aret'ẹ

Book	Oc.	virtue	Oc.	praise	Total
Phl.	1	4:8			1
1 Pt.			1	2:9	1
2 Pt.	3	1:3, 5, 5			3
Total	4		1		5

704. ἀρήν, arẹn'

Book	lamb	Total
Lk.	10:3	1

705. ἀριθμέω, arithme'ō

Book	number	Total
Mt.	10:30	1
Lk.	12:7	1
Rev.	7:9	1
Total		3

706. ἀριθμός, arithmos'

Book	number	Total
Lk.	22:3	1
Jn.	6:10	1
Ac.	4:4; 5:36; 6:7; 11:21; 16:5	5
Ro.	9:27	1
Rev.	5:11; 7:4; 9:16, 16; 13:17, 18, 18, 18; 15:2; 20:8	10
Total		18

707. Ἀριμαθαία, Arimathai'a

Book	Arimathaea	Total
Mt.	27:57	1
Mk.	15:43	1
Lk.	23:51	1
Jn.	19:38	1
Total		4

708. Ἀρίσταρχος, Aris'tarchos

Book	Aristarchus	Total
Ac.	19:29; 20:4; 27:2	3
Col.	4:10	1
Phe.	1:24	1
Total		5

709. ἀριστάω, arista'ō

Book	dine	Total
Lk.	11:37	1
Jn.	21:12, 15	2
Total		3

710. ἀριστερός, aristeros'

Book	Oc.	left hand	Oc.	left	Oc.	on the left	Total
Mt.	1	6:3					1
Lk.			1	23:33			1
2 Co.					1	6:7	1
Total	1		1		1		3

711. Ἀριστόβουλος Aristob'oulos

Book	Aristobulus	Total
Ro.	16:10	1

712. ἄριστον, ar'iston

Book	dinner	Total
Mt.	22:4	1
Lk.	11:38; 14:12	2
Total		3

713. ἀρκετός, arketos'

Book	Oc.	sufficient	Oc.	enough	Oc.	suffice	Total
Mt.	1	6:34	1	10:25			2
1 Pt.					1	4:3	1
Total	1		1		1		3

714. ἀρκέω, arke'ō

Book	Oc.	be content	Oc.	be sufficient	Oc.	be enough	Oc.	suffice	Oc.	content	Total
Mt.					1	25:9					1
Lk.	1	3:14									1
Jn.			1	6:7			1	14:8			2
2 Co.			1	12:9							1
1 Ti.	1	6:8									1
Heb.	1	13:5									1
3 Jn.									1	1:10	1
Total	3		2		1		1		1		8

715. ἄρκτος, ark'tos

Book	bear	Total
Rev.	13:2	1

716. ἅρμα, har′ma

Book	chariot	Total
Ac.	8:28, 29, 38	3
Rev.	9:9	1
Total		4

717. Ἀρμαγεδδών, Armageddōn′

Book	Armageddon	Total
Rev.	16:16	1

718. ἁρμόζω, harmod′zō

Book	espouse	Total
2 Co.	11:2	1

719. ἁρμός, harmos′

Book	joint	Total
Heb.	4:12	1

720. ἀρνέομαι, arne′omai

Book	Oc.	deny	Oc.	refuse	Total
Mt.	4	10:33, 33; 26:70, 72			4
Mk.	2	14:68, 70			2
Lk.	3	8:45; 12:9; 22:57			3
Jn.	3	1:20; 18:25, 27			3
Ac.	3	3:13, 14; 4:16	1	7:35	4
1 Ti.	1	5:8			1
2 Ti.	4	2:12, 12, 13; 3:5			4
Tit.	2	1:16; 2:12			2
Heb.			1	11:24	1
2 Pt.	1	2:1			1
1 Jn.	3	2:22, 22, 23			3
Jd.	1	1:4			1
Rev.	2	2:13; 3:8			2
Total	29		2		31

721. ἀρνίον, arni′on

Book	Oc.	Lamb (Christ)	Oc.	lamb (young believer)	Oc.	lamb (false prophet)	Total
Jn.			1	21:15			1
Rev.	28	5:6, 8, 12, 13; 6:1, 16; 7:9, 10, 14, 17; 12:11; 13:8; 14:1, 4, 4, 10; 15:3; 17:14, 14; 19:7, 9; 21:9, 14, 22, 23, 27; 22:1, 3			1	13:11	29
Total	28		1		1		30

722. ἀροτριόω, arotrio′ō

Book	plow	Total
Lk.	17:7	1
1 Co.	9:10, 10	2
Total		3

723. ἄροτρον, ar′otron

Book	plough	Total
Lk.	9:62	1

724. ἁρπαγή, harpagē′

Book	Oc.	extortion	Oc.	ravening	Oc.	spoiling	Total
Mt.	1	23:25					1
Lk.			1	11:39			1
Heb.					1	10:34	1
Total	1		1		1		3

725. ἁρπαγμός, harpagmos′

Book	robbery	Total
Phl.	2:6	1

726. ἁρπάζω, harpad′zō

Book	Oc.	catch up	Oc.	take by force	Oc.	catch away	Oc.	pluck	Oc.	catch	Oc.	pull	Total
Mt.			1	11:12	1	13:19							2
Jn.			1	6:15			2	10:28, 29	1	10:12			4
Ac.			1	23:10	1	8:39							2
2 Co.	2	12:2, 4											2
1 Th.	1	4:17											1
Jd.											1	1:23	1
Rev.	1	12:5											1
Total	4		3		2		2		1		1		13

727. ἅρπαξ, har′pax

Book	Oc.	extortioner	Oc.	ravening	Total
Mt.			1	7:15	1
Lk.	1	18:11			1
1 Co.	3	5:10, 11; 6:10			3
Total	4		1		5

728. ἀῤῥαβών, arhrabōn′

Book	earnest	Total
2 Co.	1:22; 5:5	2
Eph.	1:14	1
Total		3

729. ἄῤῥαφος, ar′hraphos

Book	without seam	Total
Jn.	19:23	1

730a. ἄῤῥην, ar′hren

Book	Oc.	man	Oc.	man child	Oc.	man child (with 5107)	Total
Ro.	1	1:27a					1
Rev.			1	12:13	1	12:5	2
Total	1		1		1		3

730b. ἄρσην, ar′sen

Book	Oc.	male	Oc.	man	Total
Mt.	1	19:4			1
Mk.	1	10:6			1
Lk.	1	2:23			1
Ro.			2	1:27b, 27c	2
Gal.	1	3:28			1
Total	4		2		6

Word 730 has 9 occurrences.

731. ἄῤῥητος, ar′hretos

Book	unspeakable	Total
2 Co.	12:4	1

732. ἄῤῥωστος, ar′hrōstos

Book	Oc.	sick	Oc.	sick folk	Oc.	be sick	Oc.	sickly	Total
Mt.	1	14:14							1
Mk.	1	16:18	1	6:5	1	6:13			3
1 Co.							1	11:30	1
Total	2		1		1		1		5

734. Ἀρτεμᾶς, Artemas′

Book	Artemas	Total
Tit.	3:12	1

735. Ἄρτεμις, Ar′temis

Book	Diana	Total
Ac.	19:24, 27, 28, 34, 35	5

733. ἀρσενοκοίτης, arsenokoi′tes

Book	Oc.	abuser of (one's) self with mankind	Oc.	defile (one's) self with mankind	Total
1 Co.	1	6:9			1
1 Ti.			1	1:10	1
Total	1		1		2

736. ἀρτέμων, artem′ōn

Book	mainsail	Total
Ac.	27:40	1

737. ἄρτι, ar′ti

Book	Oc.	now	Oc.	henceforth (with 575)	Oc.	hereafter (with 575)	Oc.	this present	Oc.	hitherto (with 2193)	Oc.	Misc.	Total
Mt.	3	3:15; 11:12; 26:53	2	23:39; 26:29	1	26:64					1	9:18	7
Jn.	9	2:10; 9:19, 25; 13:7, 19, 33, 37; 16:12, 31			1	1:51			2	5:17; 16:24	1	14:7	13
1 Co.	3	13:12, 12; 16:7					2	4:11; 15:6			2	8:7; 4:13	7
Gal.	3	1:9, 10; 4:20											3
1 Th.	1	3:6											1
2 Th.	1	2:7											1
1 Pt.	2	1:6, 8											2
1 Jn.	1	2:9											1
Rev.	1	12:10											1
Total	24		2		2		2		2		4		36

Miscellaneous: Mt. 9:18, even now; Jn. 14:7, henceforth; 1 Co. 8:7, this hour; 1 Co. 4:13, this day.

738. ἀρτιγέννητος, artigen'ne̱tos

Book	newborn	Total
1 Pt.	2:2	1

739. ἄρτιος, ar'tios

Book	perfect	Total
2 Ti.	3:17	1

741. ἀρτύω, artu'ō

Book	season	Total
Mk.	9:50	1
Lk.	14:34	1
Col.	4:6	1
Total		3

742. Ἀρφαξάδ, Arphaxad'

Book	Arphaxad	Total
Lk.	3:36	1

743. ἀρχάγγελος, archang'gelos

Book	archangel	Total
1 Th.	4:16	1
Jd.	1:9	1
Total		2

740. ἄρτος, ar'tos

Book	Oc.	bread	Oc.	loaf	Oc.	shewbread (with 4186 and 3488)	Total
Mt.	13	4:3, 4; 6:11; 7:9; 15:2, 26, 33; 16:5, 7, 8, 11, 12; 26:26	7	14:17, 19, 19; 15:34, 36; 16:9, 10	1	12:4	21
Mk.	13	3:20; 6:8, 36, 37, 52; 7:2, 5, 27; 8:4, 14a, 16, 17; 14:22	9	6:38, 41, 41, 44, 52; 8:5, 6, 14b, 19	1	2:26	23
Lk.	12	4:3, 4; 7:33; 9:3; 11:3, 11; 14:1, 15; 15:17; 22:19; 24:30, 35	3	9:13, 16; 11:5	1	6:4	16
Jn.	20	6:5, 7, 23, 31, 32, 32, 33, 34, 35, 41, 48, 50, 51, 51, 51, 58, 58; 13:18; 21:9, 13	4	6:9, 11, 13, 26			24
Ac.	5	2:42, 46; 20:7, 11; 27:35					5
1 Co.	7	10:16, 17, 17; 11:23, 26, 27, 28					7
2 Co.	1	9:10					1
2 Th.	2	3:8, 12					2
Heb.					1	9:2	1
Total	73		23		4		100

744. ἀρχαῖος, archai'os

Book	Oc.	old	Oc.	of old time	Oc.	a good while ago (with 575 and 2250)	Total
Mt.			3	5:21, 27, 33			3
Lk.	2	9:8, 19					2
Ac.	2	15:21; 21:16			1	15:7	3
2 Co.	1	5:17					1
2 Pt.	1	2:5					1
Rev.	2	12:9; 20:2					2
Total	8		3		1		12

747. ἀρχηγός, arche̱gos'

Book	Oc.	prince	Oc.	captain	Oc.	author	Total
Ac.	2	3:15; 5:31					2
Heb.			1	2:10	1	12:2	2
Total	2		1		1		4

745. Ἀρχέλαος, Archel'aos

Book	Archelaus	Total
Mt.	2:22	1

748. ἀρχιερατικός, archieratikos'

Book	of the high priest	Total
Ac.	4:6	1

746. ἀρχή, arche̱'

Book	Oc.	beginning	Oc.	principality	Oc.	corner	Oc.	first	Oc.	Misc.	Total
Mt.	4	19:4, 8; 24:8, 21									4
Mk.	4	1:1; 10:6; 13:8, 19									4
Lk.	1	1:2							2	12:11; 20:20	3
Jn.	8	1:1, 2; 2:11; 6:64; 8:25, 44; 15:27; 16:4									8
Ac.	1	11:15			2	10:11; 11:5	1	26:4			4
Ro.			1	8:38							1
1 Co.									1	15:24	1
Eph.			3	1:21; 3:10; 6:12							3
Phl.	1	4:15									1
Col.	1	1:18	3	1:16; 2:10, 15							4
2 Th.	1	2:13									1
Tit.			1	3:1							1
Heb.	3	1:10; 3:14; 7:3					1	5:12	2	2:3; 6:1	6
2 Pt.	1	3:4									1
1 Jn.	9	1:1; 2:7, 7, 13, 14, 24, 24; 3:8, 11									9
2 Jn.	2	1:5, 6									2
Jd.									1	1:6	1
Rev.	4	1:8; 3:14; 21:6; 22:13									4
Total	40		8		2		2		6		58

Miscellaneous: Lk. 12:11, magistrate; Lk. 20:20, power; 1 Co. 15:24, rule; Heb. 2:3, at the first; Heb. 6:1, principles; Jd. 1:6, first estate.

749. ἀρχιερεύς, archiereus'

Book	Oc.	chief priest	Oc.	high priest	Oc.	high priest (Christ)	Oc.	chief of the priests	Total
Mt.	18	2:4; 16:21; 20:18; 21:15, 23, 45; 26:3a, 14, 47, 59; 27:1, 3, 6, 12, 20, 41, 62; 28:11	7	26:3b, 51, 57, 58, 62, 63, 65					25
Mk.	14	8:31; 10:33; 11:18, 27; 14:1, 10, 43, 53b, 55; 15:1, 3, 10, 11, 31	8	2:26; 14:47, 53a, 54, 60, 61, 63, 66					22
Lk.	13	9:22; 19:47; 20:1, 19; 22:2, 4, 52; 66; 23:4, 10, 13, 23; 24:20	3	3:2; 22:50, 54					16
Jn.	10	7:32, 45; 11:47, 57; 12:10; 18:3, 35; 19:6, 15, 21	11	11:49, 51; 18:10, 13, 15, 15, 16, 19, 22, 24, 26					21
Ac.	9	4:23; 5:24; 9:14, 21; 22:30; 23:14; 25:15; 26:10, 12	12	4:6; 5:17, 21, 27; 7:1; 9:1; 22:5; 23:2, 4, 5; 24:1; 25:2			1	19:14	22
Heb.			9	4:15; 5:1, 5; 7:27, 28; 8:3; 9:7, 25; 13:11	8	2:17; 3:1; 4:14; 5:10; 6:20; 7:26; 8:1; 9:11			17
Total	64		50		8		1		123

750. ἀρχιποίμην, archipoi'me̱n

Book	chief shepherd	Total
1 Pt.	5:4	1

751. Ἄρχιππος, Ar'chippos

Book	Archippus	Total
Col.	4:17	1
Phe.	1:2	1
Total		2

752. ἀρχισυνάγωγος, archisunag'ōgos

Book	Oc.	ruler of the synagogue	Oc.	chief ruler of the synagogue	Total
Mk.	4	5:22, 35, 36, 38			4
Lk.	2	8:49; 13:14			2
Ac.	1	13:15	2	18:8, 17	3
Total	7		2		9

753. ἀρχιτέκτων, architek'tōn

Book	masterbuilder	Total
1 Co.	3:10	1

754. ἀρχιτελώνης, architelō'nēs

Book	chief among the publicans	Total
Lk.	19:2	1

755. ἀρχιτρίκλινος, architri'klinos

Book	Oc.	governor of the feast	Oc.	ruler of the feast	Total
Jn.	2	2:8, 9b	1	2:9a	3

756. ἄρχομαι, ar'chomai

Book	Oc.	begin	Oc.	rehearse from the beginning	Total
Mt.	13	4:17; 11:7, 20; 12:1; 14:30; 16:21, 22; 18:24; 20:8; 24:49; 26:22, 37, 74			13
Mk.	26	1:45; 2:23; 4:1; 5:17, 20; 6:2, 7, 34, 55; 8:11, 31, 32; 10:28, 32, 41, 47; 11:15; 12:1; 13:5; 14:19, 33, 65, 69, 71; 15:8, 18			26
Lk.	31	3:8, 23; 4:21; 5:21; 7:15, 24, 38, 49; 9:12; 11:29, 53; 12:1, 45; 13:25, 26; 14:9, 18, 29, 30; 15:14, 24; 19:37, 45; 20:9; 21:28; 22:23; 23:2, 5, 30; 24:27, 47			31
Jn.	2	8:9; 13:5			2
Ac.	9	1:1, 22; 2:4; 8:35; 10:37; 11:15; 18:26; 24:2; 27:35	1	11:4	10
2 Co.	1	3:1			1
1 Pt.	1	4:17			1
Total	83		1		84

757. ἄρχω, ar'chō

Book	Oc.	rule over	Oc.	reign over	Total
Mk.	1	10:42			1
Ro.			1	15:12	1
Total	1		1		2

759. ἄρωμα, ar'ōma

Book	Oc.	spices	Oc.	sweet spices	Total
Mk.			1	16:1	1
Lk.	2	23:56; 24:1			2
Jn.	1	19:40			1
Total	3		1		4

760. Ἀσά, Asa'

Book	Asa	Total
Mt.	1:7, 8	2

758. ἄρχων, ar'chōn

Book	Oc.	ruler	Oc.	prince	Oc.	chief	Oc.	magistrate	Oc.	chief ruler	Total
Mt.	2	9:18, 23	3	9:34; 12:24; 20:25							5
Mk.			1	3:22							1
Lk.	5	8:41; 18:18; 23:13, 35; 24:20			2	11:15; 14:1	1	12:58			8
Jn.	3	3:1; 7:26, 48	3	12:31; 14:30; 16:11					1	12:42	7
Ac.	11	3:17; 4:5, 8, 26; 7:27, 35, 35; 13:27; 14:5; 16:19; 23:5									11
Ro.	1	13:3									1
1 Co.			2	2:6, 8							2
Eph.			1	2:2							1
Rev.			1	1:5							1
Total	22		11		2		1		1		37

761. ἀσάλευτος, asal'eutos

Book	Oc.	unmoveable	Oc.	which cannot be moved	Total
Ac.	1	27:41			1
Heb.			1	12:28	1
Total	1		1		2

762. ἄσβεστος, as'bestos

Book	Oc.	unquenchable	Oc.	never shall be quenched	Total
Mt.	1	3:12			1
Mk.			2	9:43, 45	2
Lk.	1	3:17			1
Total	2		2		4

763. ἀσέβεια, aseb'eia

Book	Oc.	ungodliness	Oc.	ungodly	Total
Ro.	2	1:18; 11:26			2
2 Ti.	1	2:16			1
Tit.	1	2:12			1
Jd.			2	1:15, 18	2
Total	4		2		6

764. ἀσεβέω, asebe'ō

Book	Oc.	live ungodly	Oc.	commit ungodly	Total
2 Pt.	1	2:6			1
Jd.			1	1:15	1
Total	1		1		2

765. ἀσεβής, asebēs'

Book	Oc.	ungodly	Oc.	ungodly men	Total
Ro.	2	4:5; 5:6			2
1 Ti.	1	1:9			1
1 Pt.	1	4:18			1
2 Pt.	2	2:5; 3:7			2
Jd.	2	1:15, 15	1	1:4	3
Total	8		1		9

766. ἀσέλγεια, aselg'eia

Book	Oc.	lascivious-ness	Oc.	wantonness	Oc.	filthy (with 1722)	Total
Mk.	1	7:22					1
Ro.			1	13:13			1
2 Co.	1	12:21					1
Gal.	1	5:19					1
Eph.	1	4:19					1
1 Pt.	1	4:3					1
2 Pt.			1	2:18	1	2:7	2
Jd.	1	1:4					1
Total	6		2		1		9

767. ἄσημος, as'ēmos

Book	mean	Total
Ac.	21:39	1

768. Ἀσήρ, Asēr'

Book	Aser	Total
Lk.	2:36	1
Rev.	7:6	1
Total		2

769. ἀσθένεια, asthen'eia

Book	Oc.	infirmity	Oc.	weakness	Oc.	disease	Oc.	sickness	Total
Mt.	1	8:17							1
Lk.	4	5:15; 8:2; 13:11, 12							4
Jn.	1	5:5					1	11:4	2
Ac.					1	28:9			1
Ro.	2	6:19; 8:26							2
1 Co.			2	2:3; 15:43					2
2 Co.	4	11:30; 12:5, 9b, 10	2	12:9a; 13:4					6
Gal.	1	4:13							1
1 Ti.	1	5:23							1
Heb.	3	4:15; 5:2; 7:28	1	11:34					4
Total	17		5		1		1		24

770. ἀσθενέω, asthene′ō

Book	Oc.	be weak	Oc.	be sick	Oc.	sick	Oc.	weak	Oc.	impotent folk	Oc.	impotent man	Oc.	be diseased	Oc.	be made weak	Total
Mt.			1	25:36	1	10:8											2
Mk.					1	6:56											1
Lk.			1	7:10	2	4:40; 9:2											3
Jn.			4	4:46; 11: 2, 3, 6	1	11:1			1	5:3	1	5:7	1	6:2			8
Ac.			1	9:37	1	19:12	1	20:35									3
Ro.	4	4:19; 8:3; 14:1, 2													1	14:21	5
1 Co.	1	8:9					2	8:11, 12									3
2 Co.	7	11:21, 29, 29; 12:10; 13:3, 4, 9															7
Phl.			2	2:26, 27													2
2 Ti.					1	4:20											1
Jas.			1	5:14													1
Total	12		10		7		3		1		1		1		1		36

772. ἀσθενής, asthenẹs′

Book	Oc.	weak	Oc.	sick	Oc.	weakness	Oc.	weaker	Oc.	weak things	Oc.	impotent	Oc.	more feeble	Oc.	without strength	Total
Mt.	1	26:41	3	25:39, 43, 44													4
Mk.	1	14:38															1
Lk.			1	10:9													1
Ac.			2	5:15, 16							1	4:9					3
Ro.															1	5:6	1
1 Co.	7	4:10; 8:7, 10; 9:22, 22, 22; 11: 30			1	1:25			1	1:27			1	12:22			10
2 Co.	1	10:10															1
Gal.	1	4:9															1
1 Th.	1	5:14															1
Heb.					1	7:18											1
1 Pt.							1	3:7									1
Total	12		6		2		1		1		1		1		1		25

771. ἀσθένημα, asthen′ẹma

Book	infirmity	Total
Ro.	15:1	1

773. Ἀσία, Asi′a

Book	Asia	Total
Ac.	2:9; 6:9; 16:6; 19:10, 22, 26, 27; 20:4, 16, 18; 21:27; 24:18; 27:2	13
1 Co.	16:19	1
2 Co.	1:8	1
2 Ti.	1:15	1
1 Pt.	1:1	1
Rev.	1:4, 11	2
Total		19

774. Ἀσιανός, Asianos′

Book	of Asia	Total
Ac.	20:4	1

775. Ἀσιάρχης, Asiar′chẹs

Book	chief of Asia	Total
Ac.	19:31	1

776. ἀσιτία, asiti′a

Book	abstinence	Total
Ac.	27:21	1

777. ἄσιτος, as′itos

Book	fasting	Total
Ac.	27:33	1

778. ἀσκέω, aske′ō

Book	exercise	Total
Ac.	24:16	1

779. ἀσκός, askos′

Book	bottle	Total
Mt.	9:17, 17, 17, 17	4
Mk.	2:22, 22, 22, 22	4
Lk.	5:37, 37, 37, 38	4
Total		12

780. ἀσμένως, asmen′ōs

Book	gladly	Total
Ac.	2:41; 21:17	2

781. ἄσοφος, as′ophos

Book	fool	Total
Eph.	5:15	1

782. ἀσπάζομαι, aspad′zomai

Book	Oc.	salute	Oc.	greet	Oc.	embrace	Oc.	take leave	Total
Mt.	2	5:47; 10:12							2
Mk.	2	9:15; 15:18							2
Lk.	2	1:40; 10:4							2
Ac.	4	18:22; 21:7, 19; 25:13			1	20:1	1	21:6	6
Ro.	17	16:5, 7, 9, 10, 10, 11a, 12, 12, 13, 14, 15, 16, 16, 21, 22, 23, 23	4	16:3, 6, 8, 11b					21
1 Co.	2	16:19, 19	2	16:20, 20					4
2 Co.	1	13:13	1	13:12					2
Phl.	2	4:21a, 22	1	4:21b					3
Col.	3	4:10, 12, 15	1	4:14					4
1 Th.			1	5:26					1
2 Ti.	1	4:19	1	4:21					2
Tit.	1	3:15a	1	3:15b					2
Phe.	1	1:23							1
Heb.	2	13:24, 24			1	11:13			3
1 Pt.	1	5:13	1	5:14					2
2 Jn.			1	1:13					1
3 Jn.	1	1:14a	1	1:14b					2
Total	42		15		2		1		60

783. ἀσπασμός, aspasmos′

Book	Oc.	salutation	Oc.	greeting	Total
Mt.			1	23:7	1
Mk.	1	12:38			1
Lk.	3	1:29, 41, 44	2	11:43; 20:46	5
1 Co.	1	16:21			1
Col.	1	4:18			1
2 Th.	1	3:17			1
Total	7		3		10

784. ἄσπιλος, as′pilos

Book	Oc.	without spot	Oc.	unspotted	Total
1 Ti.	1	6:14			1
Jas.			1	1:27	1
1 Pt.	1	1:19			1
2 Pt.	1	3:14			1
Total	3		1		4

785. ἀσπίς, aspis'

Book	asp	Total
Ro.	3:13	1

786. ἄσπονδος, as'pondos

Book	Oc.	implacable	Oc.	trucebreaker	Total
Ro.	1	1:31			1
2 Ti.			1	3:3	1
Total	1		1		2

787. ἀσσάριον, assar'ion

Book	farthing	Total
Mt.	10:29	1
Lk.	12:6	1
Total		2

788. ἆσσον, as'son

Book	close	Total
Ac.	27:13	1

789. Ἄσσος, As'sos

Book	Assos	Total
Ac.	20:13, 14	2

790. ἀστατέω, astate'ō

Book	have no certain dwelling place	Total
1 Co.	4:11	1

791. ἀστεῖος, astei'os

Book	Oc.	fair	Oc.	proper	Total
Ac.	1	7:20			1
Heb.			1	11:23	1
Total	1		1		2

792. ἀστήρ, aster'

Book	star	Total
Mt.	2:2, 7, 9, 10; 24:29	5
Mk.	13:25	1
1 Co.	15:41, 41, 41	3
Jd.	1:13	1
Rev.	1:16, 20, 20; 2:1, 28; 3:1; 6:13; 8:10, 11, 12; 9:1; 12:1, 4; 22:16	14
Total		24

793. ἀστήρικτος aste'riktos

Book	unstable	Total
2 Pt.	2:14; 3:16	2

795. ἀστοχέω, astoche'ō

Book	Oc.	err	Oc.	swerve	Total
1 Ti.	1	6:21	1	1:6	2
2 Ti.	1	2:18			1
Total	2		1		3

794. ἄστοργος, as'torgos

Book	without natural affection	Total
Ro.	1:31	1
2 Ti.	3:3	1
Total		2

796. ἀστραπή, astrape'

Book	Oc.	lightning	Oc.	light shining	Total
Mt.	2	24:27; 28:3			2
Lk.	2	10:18; 17:24	1	11:36	3
Rev.	4	4:5; 8:5; 11:19; 16:18			4
Total	8		1		9

797. ἀστράπτω, astrap'tō

Book	Oc.	lighten	Oc.	shine	Total
Lk.	1	17:24	1	24:4	2

798. ἄστρον, as'tron

Book	star	Total
Lk.	21:25	1
Ac.	7:43; 27:20	2
Heb.	11:12	1
Total		4

799. Ἀσύγκριτος, Asung'kritos

Book	Asyncritus	Total
Ro.	16:14	1

800. ἀσύμφωνος, asum'phōnos

Book	agreed not (with 5507)	Total
Ac.	28:25	1

801. ἀσύνετος, asun'etos

Book	Oc.	without understanding	Oc.	foolish	Total
Mt.	1	15:16			1
Mk.	1	7:18			1
Ro.	1	1:31	2	1:21; 10:19	3
Total	3		2		5

802. ἀσύνθετος, asun'thetos

Book	covenant breaker	Total
Ro.	1:31	1

803. ἀσφάλεια, asphal'eia

Book	Oc.	safety	Oc.	certainty	Total
Lk.			1	1:4	1
Ac.	1	5:23			1
1 Th.	1	5:3			1
Total	2		1		3

804. ἀσφαλής, asphales'

Book	Oc.	certainty	Oc.	certain	Oc.	safe	Oc.	sure	Total
Ac.	2	21:34; 22:30	1	25:26					3
Phl.					1	3:1			1
Heb.							1	6:19	1
Total	2		1		1		1		5

805. ἀσφαλίζω, asphalid'zō

Book	Oc.	make sure	Oc.	make fast	Total
Mt.	3	27:64, 65, 66			3
Ac.			1	16:24	1
Total	3		1		4

806. ἀσφαλῶς, asphalōs'

Book	Oc.	safely	Oc.	assuredly	Total
Mk.	1	14:44			1
Ac.	1	16:23	1	2:36	2
Total	2		1		3

807. ἀσχημονέω, aschemone'ō

Book	Oc.	behave (one's) self uncomely	Oc.	behave (one's) self unseemly	Total
1 Co.	1	7:36	1	13:5	2

808. ἀσχημοσύνη, aschemosu'ne

Book	Oc.	that which is unseemly	Oc.	shame	Total
Ro.	1	1:27			1
Rev.			1	16:15	1
Total	1		1		2

809. ἀσχήμων, asche'mōn

Book	uncomely	Total
1 Co.	12:23	1

810. ἀσωτία, asōti'a

Book	Oc.	riot	Oc.	excess	Total
Eph.			1	5:18	1
Tit.	1	1:6			1
1 Pt.	1	4:4			1
Total	2		1		3

812. ἀτακτέω, atakte'ō

Book	behave (one's) self disorderly	Total
2 Th.	3:7	1

811. ἀσώτως, asō'tōs

Book	riotous	Total
Lk.	15:13	1

813. ἄτακτος, at'aktos

Book	unruly	Total
1 Th.	5:14	1

814. ἀτάκτως, atak'tōs

Book	disorderly	Total
2 Th.	3:6, 11	2

815. ἄτεκνος, at'eknos

Book	Oc.	without children	Oc.	childless	Total
Lk.	2	20:28, 29	1	20:30	3

816. ἀτενίζω, atenid'zō

Book	Oc.	look steadfastly	Oc.	behold steadfastly	Oc.	fasten (one's) eyes	Oc.	look earnestly upon	Oc.	look earnestly on	Oc.	look up steadfastly	Oc.	behold earnestly	Oc.	Misc.	Total
Lk.							1	22:56							1	4:20	2
Ac.	1	6:15	1	14:9	2	3:4; 11:6			1	3:12	1	7:55	1	23:1	3	1:10; 10:4; 13:9	10
2 Co.	1	3:13	1	3:7													2
Total	2		2		2		1		1		1		1		4		14

Miscellaneous: Lk. 4:20, fastened on; Ac. 1:10, looked steadfastly; Ac. 10:4, look on; Ac. 13:9, set (one's) eyes.

817. ἄτερ, at'er

Book	Oc.	in the absence of	Oc.	without	Total
Lk.	1	22:6	1	22:35	2

818. ἀτιμάζω, atimad'zō

Book	Oc.	dishonour	Oc.	entreat shamefully	Oc.	suffer shame	Oc.	despise	Total
Lk.			1	20:11					1
Jn.	1	8:49							1
Ac.					1	5:41			1
Ro.	2	1:24; 2:23							2
Jas.							1	2:6	1
Total	3		1		1		1		6

819. ἀτιμία, atimi'a

Book	Oc.	dishonour	Oc.	vile	Oc.	shame	Oc.	reproach	Total
Ro.	1	9:21	1	1:26					2
1 Co.	1	15:43			1	11:14			2
2 Co.	1	6:8					1	11:21	2
2 Ti.	1	2:20							1
Total	4		1		1		1		7

820. ἄτιμος, at'imos

Book	Oc.	without honour	Oc.	despised	Oc.	less honourable	Total
Mt.	1	13:57					1
Mk.	1	6:4					1
1 Co.			1	4:10	1	12:23	2
Total	2		1		1		4

821. ἀτιμόω, atimo'ō

Book	handle shamefully	Total
Mk.	12:4	1

822. ἀτμίς, atmis'

Book	vapour	Total
Ac.	2:19	1
Jas.	4:14	1
Total		2

823. ἄτομος, at'omos

Book	moment	Total
1 Co.	15:52	1

824. ἄτοπος, at'opos

Book	Oc.	amiss	Oc.	harm	Oc.	unreasonable	Total
Lk.	1	23:41					1
Ac.			1	28:6			1
2 Th.					1	3:2	1
Total	1		1		1		3

825. Ἀττάλεια, Attal'eia

Book	Attalia	Total
Ac.	14:25	1

826. αὐγάζω, augad'zō

Book	shine	Total
2 Co.	4:4	1

827. αὐγή, augē'

Book	break of day	Total
Ac.	20:11	1

828. Αὔγουστος, Au'goustos

Book	Augustus	Total
Lk.	2:1	1

829. αὐθάδης, authad'ēs

Book	self-willed	Total
Tit.	1:7	1
2 Pt.	2:10	1
Total		2

830. αὐθαίρετος, authai'retos

Book	Oc.	willing of (one's) self	Oc.	of (one's) own accord	Total
2 Co.	1	8:3	1	8:17	2

831. αὐθεντέω, authente'ō

Book	usurp authority over	Total
1 Ti.	2:12	1

832. αὐλέω, aule'ō

Book	pipe	Total
Mt.	11:17	1
Lk.	7:32	1
1 Co.	14:7	1
Total		3

833. αὐλή, aulē'

Book	Oc.	palace	Oc.	hall	Oc.	sheepfold (with 4163)	Oc.	fold	Oc.	court	Total
Mt.	3	26:3, 58, 69									3
Mk.	2	14:54, 66	1	15:16							3
Lk.	1	11:21	1	22:55							2
Jn.	1	18:15			1	10:1	1	10:16			3
Rev.									1	11:2	1
Total	7		2		1		1		1		12

834. αὐλητής, aulētēs'

Book	Oc.	minstrel	Oc.	piper	Total
Mt.	1	9:23			1
Rev.			1	18:22	1
Total	1		1		2

835. αὐλίζομαι, aulid'zomai

Book	Oc.	lodge	Oc.	abide	Total
Mt.	1	21:17			1
Lk.			1	21:37	1
Total	1		1		2

837a. αὐξάνω, auxan'ō

Book	Oc.	grow	Oc.	increase	Oc.	give the increase	Oc.	grow up	Total
Mt.	2	6:28; 13:32							2
Mk.			1	4:8					1
Lk.	4	1:80; 2:40; 12:27; 13:19							4
Jn.			1	3:30					1
Ac.	3	7:17; 12:24; 19:20	1	6:7					4
1 Co.					2	3:6, 7			2
2 Co.			2	9:10; 10:15					2
Eph.							1	4:15	1
Col.			1	1:10					1
1 Pt.	1	2:2							1
2 Pt.	1	3:18							1
Total	11		6		2		1		20

836. αὐλός, aulos'

Book	pipe	Total
1 Co.	14:7	1

837b. αὐξάνω, auxan'ō

Book	Oc.	increase	Oc.	grow	Total
Eph.			1	2:21	1
Col.	1	2:19			1
Total	1		1		2

Word 837 has 22 occurrences.

838. αὔξησις, aux'ēsis

Book	increase	Total
Eph.	4:16	1
Col.	2:19	1
Total		2

839. αὔριον, au'rion

Book	Oc.	tomorrow	Oc.	morrow	Oc.	next day	Total
Mt.	1	6:30	2	6:34, 34			3
Lk.	3	12:28; 13:32, 33	1	10:35			4
Ac.	3	23:15, 20; 25:22	1	4:5	1	4:3	5
1 Co.	1	15:32					1
Jas.	1	4:13	1	4:14			2
Total	9		5		1		15

841. αὐτάρκεια, autar'keia

Book	Oc.	sufficiency	Oc.	contentment	Total
2 Co.	1	9:8			1
1 Ti.			1	6:6	1
Total	1		1		2

840. αὐστηρός, austēros'

Book	austere	Total
Lk.	19:21, 22	2

842. αὐτάρκης, autar'kēs

Book	content	Total
Phl.	4:11	1

843. αὐτοκατάκριτος, autokatak'ritos

Book	condemned of (one's) self	Total
Tit.	3:11	1

844. αὐτόματος, autom'atos

Book	Oc.	of (one's) self	Oc.	of (one's) own accord	Total
Mk.	1	4:28			1
Ac.			1	12:10	1
Total	1		1		2

845. αὐτόπτης, autop'tes

Book	eyewitness	Total
Lk.	1:2	1

The following are the seventeen different forms in which Word 846, the personal pronoun, appears in the varying forms of their gender, number, person, and case. In the nominative case it means "self" (e.g., himself, herself, itself, etc.); in the oblique cases it is used as the personal pronoun, meaning "he," "she," "it," etc.

846a. αὐτά, auta'

Book	Oc.	them	Oc.	the same	Oc.	they	Oc.	it	Oc.	very	Oc.	those things	Oc.	the thing	Oc.	themselves	Oc.	Not Tr.	Total
Mt.	14	6:26a; 10:1b; 11:25; 13:4b, 7, 28c, 30, 30, 39; 18:8; 19:14; 23:4; 27:6, 10																	14
Mk.	6	8:7; 10:14b, 16, 16, 16; 15:24c																	6
Lk.	5	4:41a; 10:21b; 14:19; 18:16, 16			1	5:7	1	17:31b											7
Jn.	6	10:3b, 12, 27, 28b; 13:17; 15:6	1	5:36b					1	14:11							1	5:36a	9
Ac.	1	2:45																	1
Ro.			2	1:32; 2:3							1	10:5							3
Gal.	2	3:10, 12a																	2
Eph.	1	6:4																	1
Heb.															1	9:23			1
1 Pt.													1	1:12					1
Rev.	2	11:6b; 18:14																	2
Total	37		3		1		1		1		1		1		1		1		47

846b. αὐταῖς, autais'

Book	Oc.	them	Oc.	their	Oc.	those (women)	Oc.	those (sacrifices)	Total
Mt.	2	28:9b, 10							2
Mk.	1	16:6a							1
Lk.	4	24:1, 4b, 10, 11c	1	8:3b					5
Jn.	1	5:39							1
1 Co.	1	14:34							1
Phl.					1	4:3			1
1 Ti.	2	1:18; 5:16							2
Heb.							1	10:3	1
2 Pt.	1	3:16							1
Rev.	5	9:3, 4, 5a, 19d; 15:1							5
Total	17		1		1		1		20

846c. αὐτάς, autas'

Book	Oc.	them	Oc.	they	Total
Mk.			1	16:8	1
Lk.	2	23:28; 24:5b	1	24:4a	3
Jn.	3	2:7b; 11:19a; 14:21a			3
Col.	1	3:19			1
Heb.	1	11:13			1
Jd.	1	1:7			1
Total	8		2		10

846d. αὐτή, aute'

Book	Oc.	she	Oc.	itself	Oc.	herself	Total
Lk.	1	1:36a					1
Ro.			1	8:21			1
1 Co.	1	7:12a	1	11:14a			2
Heb.					1	11:11	1
Rev.	1	18:6b					1
Total	3		2		1		6

846e. αὐτῇ, aute'

Book	Oc.	her	Oc.	it	Oc.	the same	Oc.	therein (with 1722)	Oc.	thereon (with 1722)	Oc.	there (with 1722)	Oc.	Misc.	Total
Mt.	6	1:20c; 5:31; 14:7; 15:23a, 28a; 20:21a	5	10:11; 12:39b; 16:4a; 21:19c; 22:39					1	21:19b					12
Mk.	10	5:23b, 33a, 34, 41, 43b; 6:23; 7:27, 29; 14:5, 6b	1	11:14a					1	11:13a					12
Lk.	16	1:30, 35, 36b, 45, 46, 58c; 7:12, 13b, 13c, 48; 8:48, 55b; 10:40, 41; 13:12b, 13	2	11:29; 19:41	7	2:8; 10:7a; 12:12; 13:31a; 20:19b; 23:12; 24:33a	1	10:9a	1	13:6	1	24:18	4	2:38a; 7:21; 10:21a; 24:13b	32
Jn.	21	2:4; 4:7, 10a, 13, 16, 17, 21, 26; 8:7c, 10, 11; 11:23, 25, 31c, 33b, 40; 20:13a, 15a, 16a, 17a, 18													21
Ac.	2	5:8; 9:41a	1	7:5b	2	16:18b; 22:13	1	1:20b			2	9:38a; 20:22			8
Ro.	2	9:12; 16:2b	1	6:12a			1	6:2							4
1 Co.	2	11:15, 15													2
Col.					1	4:2	1	2:7b							2
Heb.			1	7:11											1
Jas.													2	3:9, 9	2
2 Pt.							1	3:10							1
2 Jn.			1	1:6											1
Rev.	10	2:21; 16:19; 18:6a, 6c, 6e, 7a, 9b, 11a, 24; 19:8	4	19:15b; 20:13a; 21:23a; 22:3a			5	1:3; 10:6b, 6c; 13:12b; 21:22a							19
Total	69		16		10		10		3		3		6		117

Miscellaneous: Lk. 2:38a, in that; Lk. 7:21, that same; Lk. 10:21a, that; Lk. 24:13b, that same; Jas. 3:9, 9 (with 1722), therewith.

846f. αὐτήν, autēn′

Book	Oc.	it	Oc.	her	Oc.	she	Oc.	therein (with 1519)	Oc.	thereinto (with 1519)	Oc.	Misc.	Total
Mt.	12	5:30; 7:14; 10:12, 13, 39, 39; 11: 12; 12:41, 42; 16:25, 25; 21:19a	12	1:19b, 19c, 25a; 5:28b,32; 8: 15b; 9:18d, 22; 14:4b; 15:23d; 19:7b; 22:28									24
Mk.	8	4:30; 6:28c, 28d; 8:35, 35; 9:43; 11:2b,13b	9	1:31a, 31c; 6:17c, 26; 10:11b; 12:21a, 22, 23b; 14:6a			1	10:15					18
Lk.	13	4:6c; 6:48; 9:24, 24; 11:32; 13: 7, 8b, 8c, 9; 13:18; 16:16; 17: 33a, 33c	9	1:28, 61; 4:39b; 7:13a; 8:52; 13:12a; 18:5; 20:31, 33b	2	1:57; 2:6b	1	18:17	1	21:21	1	17:33b	27
Jn.	8	10:17, 18, 18, 18, 18; 12:25, 25; 18:10a	5	8:3b; 11:31b, 33a; 12:7a; 19:27									13
Ac.	5	7:5d, 44; 15:16b; 21:3; 27:8	7	5:9, 10b; 9:37b, 41b, 41c; 12: 15a; 27:32	1	9:37a							13
Ro.			1	16:2a	1	7:3							2
1 Co.			1	7:12c									1
Gal.	1	1:13											1
Eph.	3	5:26, 27, 29											3
Col.	1	4:17											1
Heb.	1	12:17					1	4:6			1	10:1	3
1 Pt.	1	3:11											1
1 Jn.	1	2:21											1
Rev.	6	3:8; 11:2; 21:23b, 24b, 26, 27	9	2:22a; 12:6; 17:6, 7, 16a, 16c; 18:8b, 9a, 20a									15
Total	60		53		4		3		1		2		123

Miscellaneous: Lk. 17:33b, his life; Heb. 10:1, the very.

846g. αὐτῆς, autēs′

Book	Oc.	her	Oc.	it	Oc.	thereof	Oc.	thereby (with 1223)	Oc.	the same	Oc.	his	Oc.	Not Tr.	Oc.	Misc.	Total
Mt.	7	1:19a; 5:28a; 8: 15a; 9:25; 15:28b; 21:2b, 26:13	2	7:27; 16:18	3	2:16; 6:34; 21:43					2	24:32; 26: 52b			1	7:13	15
Mk.	6	1:30b, 31b; 5:29; 13:28; 14:9; 16:11											1	7:25b	1	6:22	8
Lk.	13	1:5b, 38, 41, 58a, 58b; 4:38b,39a; 7: 47; 8:44b, 54b, 55a, 56a; 10:42	1	21:21	1	21:20			1	10:10					1	2:35	17
Jn.	5	4:27b; 11:1, 5, 31a; 16:21					1	11:4									6
Ac.	6	5:10c; 8:27; 16:15, 18a, 19; 19:27	2	13:17b; 27:14	1	15:16a											9
Ro.			1	7:11					1	13:3							2
1 Co.	3	7:13b, 39, 39			2	10:26, 28											5
Gal.	1	4:30															1
Eph.			1	5:25													1
2 Ti.					1	3:5											1
Heb.			3	6:7; 9: 5; 11:4	1	7:18	1	12:11									5
2 Jn.	1	1:1															1
3 Jn.															1	1:12	1
Rev.	31	2:22b, 23; 12:1, 1, 4c, 5a, 17; 14:18; 17:2, 16b; 18:3, 3, 3, 4, 4, 4, 5, 5, 6d, 8a, 9c, 9d, 10, 15, 15, 18, 19, 20b; 19: 2b, 3; 21:11	6	21:16b, 18, 22b, 24a, 25; 22:2	5	16:21; 21: 15, 15, 17, 23c							1	21:16			43
Total	73		16		14		2		2		2		2		4		115

Miscellaneous: Mt. 7:13 (with 1223), thereat; Mk. 6:22, the said; Lk. 2:35, thy; 3 Jn. 1:12, itself.

846h. αὐτό, auto´

Book	Oc.	it	Oc.	him	Oc.	itself	Oc.	same	Oc.	self-same thing	Oc.	very thing	Oc.	thereon	Oc.	Not Tr.	Oc.	Misc.	Total
Mt.	7	12:11b; 14:12b; 18:13a; 26:29, 42; 27:59, 60	3	2:13c; 17:19; 18:2a															10
Mk.	6	4:4, 7, 37; 6:29c; 9:50; 14:25	5	9:18c, 28d, 36a, 36c, 50															11
Lk.	9	8:5b, 7; 9:45b; 11:14; 14:35; 15:4b; 23:53, 53, 53	5	1:59a; 2:28b, 40; 9:40, 47b													1	19:23	15
Jn.	6	1:5; 6:39b; 15:2b; 18:11; 19:40; 21:6b	3	14:17, 17, 17											1	15:2a	2	12:7b, 14	12
Ac.	1	5:39															2	7:6b; 27:6	3
Ro.	2	7:17, 20			2	8:16, 26											2	9:17; 13:6	6
2 Co.							1	2:3	2	5:5; 7:11									3
Gal.	1	1:12					1	2:10											2
Eph.																	2	6:18, 22	2
Phl.	1	3:21a									1	1:6							2
Col.	3	2:14, 14; 4:4									1	4:8							4
1 Th.	1	4:10																	1
Heb.															1	9:19			1
1 Pt.																	1	4:10	1
2 Pt.																	1	1:5	1
Rev.	4	8:5; 10:9b, 10, 10											2	5:3, 4					6
Total	41		16		2		2		2		2		2		2		11		80

Miscellaneous: Lk. 19:23, mine own; Jn. 12:7b, this; Jn. 12:14 (with 1909), thereon; Ac. 7:6b, them; Ac. 27:6 (with 1519), therein; Ro. 9:17, same purpose; Ro. 13:6, same thing; Eph. 6:18 (with 1519 and 5024), thereunto; Eph. 6:22 (with 1519), itself; 1 Pt. 4:10, the same; 2 Pt. 1:5, beside.

846i. αὐτοί, autoi´

Book	Oc.	they	Oc.	yourselves	Oc.	themselves	Oc.	we ourselves	Oc.	ye	Oc.	ye yourselves	Oc.	they themselves	Oc.	Not Tr.	Oc.	Misc.	Total
Mt.	9	5:4, 5, 6, 7, 8, 9; 12:27; 20:10; 25:44b																	9
Mk.			1	6:31															1
Lk.	14	2:50a; 6:11; 9:36; 11:19, 48a; 14:1b, 12b; 16:28b; 17:13; 18:34a; 22:23a; 24:14, 35, 52a					1	22:71a			2	11:46, 52					1	11:4	18
Jn.	5	4:45b; 6:24b; 17:8b, 19, 21	1	3:28			1	4:42					1	18:28					8
Ac.	4	13:14; 22:19; 27:36; 28:28			3	15:32; 16:37b; 24:15			1	18:15	2	2:22; 20:34					1	24:20	11
Ro.	1	11:31							1	15:14b							2	8:23, 23	4
2 Co.	2	6:16c; 10:12					1	1:4									1	1:9	4
Gal.	1	2:9			1	6:13	1	2:17											3
1 Th.	1	2:14	4	2:1; 3:3; 4:9; 5:2									1	1:9					6
2 Th.			1	3:7															1
2 Ti.	1	2:10																	1
Heb.	5	1:11; 3:10; 8:9d, 10e; 13:17	1	13:3															6
Jas.	1	2:7													1	2:6			2
1 Pt.									2	1:15; 2:5									2
2 Pt.													1	2:19b					1
1 Jn.	1	4:5a																	1
Rev.	[illegible]	6:11d; 12:11; 21:3b																	3
Total	48		8		4		4		4		4		3		1		5		81

Miscellaneous: Lk. 11:4, we; Ac. 24:20, same; Ro. 8:23, 23, ourselves; 2 Co. 1:9, we.

846j. αὐτοῖς, autois′

Book	Oc.	them	Oc.	their	Oc.	Not Tr.	Oc.	Misc.	Total
Mt.	109	3:7; 4:16, 19; 6:1, 8a; 7:12, 23; 8:4b, 15c, 26, 32; 9:12, 15a, 18b, 24a, 28b, 30b; 10:1a, 5, 18; 11:4; 12:3a, 11a, 16a, 39a; 12:25b; 13:3, 10b, 11, 13, 14, 24, 28a, 29, 31, 33, 34, 37, 51a, 52, 57b; 14:16, 16, 27; 15:3, 10, 34; 16:1b, 2, 6, 8, 15; 17:3a, 9b, 11, 13, 20, 22b, 27c; 18:19; 19:4a, 8, 11, 13b, 13c, 15, 26, 28; 20:6, 7b, 8, 17, 23, 31; 21:2a, 6, 13a, 16b, 21, 24, 27a, 31b, 36, 42; 22:1, 20, 21b, 29, 43a; 24:2, 4, 45b; 25:14, 20, 22, 40, 45; 26:10, 19, 27a, 31, 38, 45, 48b; 27:17b, 21, 22a, 26, 65; 28:16					1	25:16	110
Mk.	120	1:17, 31d, 38, 44b; 2:2, 8, 17, 19a, 25b, 27; 3:4, 12a, 17, 23b, 33; 4:2b, 9, 11, 12, 13, 21, 24, 33, 34, 35, 40; 5:13, 16, 19c, 39, 43a; 6:4, 7b, 8, 10, 11, 31a, 34a, 37a, 37b, 37d, 38, 39, 41, 46, 48b, 50c; 7:6a, 9, 14, 18a, 36a, 36c; 8:1, 15, 17, 21, 27b, 29b, 30a, 34; 9:1, 4, 7a, 9b, 12, 14b, 29, 31a, 35, 36d; 10:3, 5, 11a, 14a, 24b, 27, 32b, 36, 38, 39b, 42b; 11:2a, 5, 6a, 17a, 22, 29, 33; 12:1a, 15b, 16a, 17a, 24, 28b, 38, 43; 13:5, 9; 14:10b, 13a, 16b, 20, 22b, 23a, 24, 27, 34, 41, 44b, 48; 15:6, 8, 9, 11, 12, 14a, 15; 16:15, 19	1	12:44			1	16:14a	122
Lk.	94	1:7, 22a, 22c; 2:7c, 9a, 10, 17, 50b, 51b; 3:11; 4:39c; 5:7, 14c; 6:2, 5, 31, 39; 7:6a, 22; 8:25a, 31b, 32b, 32c, 36, 56b; 9:1, 11c, 13b, 17, 20, 21, 46a, 48, 55; 10:9b, 18; 11:2, 17c; 12:37b; 13:2, 32; 15:2, 6, 12b; 16:15, 28a; 17:14a, 20, 37b; 18:1, 7b, 15c, 29; 19:13a, 32, 40, 46a; 20:8, 15b, 17, 25, 34; 21:10, 29; 22:4b, 6b, 10a, 13, 19, 24a, 25a, 35, 36, 38, 40, 46, 67; 23:17, 25a, 34a, 35; 24:15c, 19a, 27, 29b, 30c, 33b, 35b, 36d, 38, 40, 41b, 44, 46	1	21:4					95
Jn.	104	1:12b, 26, 38b, 39; 2:7a, 8, 19a, 22b, 24b; 4:32, 34a, 40c; 5:11, 17, 19; 6:7b, 20, 26, 29, 31, 32, 35, 43, 53a, 61b, 70; 7:6, 9, 16, 21, 33, 45a, 47; 8:12, 14, 21, 23, 25b, 27, 28, 34, 39b, 42, 58; 9:15b, 16, 20a, 27a, 30, 41; 10:6, 6, 7, 25, 28a, 32a, 34; 11:11. 14, 44b, 46b, 49b; 12:23, 35; 13:12b; 15:22, 24; 16:19b, 31; 17:2c, 8a, 10, 14a, 22, 23a, 26, 26, 26; 18:4b, 5b, 6, 21, 31a, 38b; 19:4a, 5, 6b, 15b, 16b; 20:2a, 13b, 17b, 19, 20, 21, 22, 23, 25b; 21:3a, 5a, 6a, 10, 12a, 13							104
Ac.	74	1:3b, 4, 10b; 2:3a, 4, 14; 3:5a, 8; 4:1b, 3, 14, 17, 18b, 24, 34; 5:13a, 25; 6:6; 7:25b, 26a, 43; 8:5, 18; 9:27b, 39a; 10:8a, 20a, 23b; 11:3, 4, 12, 17; 12:10a, 17a, 17b; 13:3, 8a, 19a, 21, 22b, 43a; 14:18, 23a; 15:8, 8, 20, 38b; 16:4, 23a; 17:2b, 18b, 34b; 18:2b, 3, 11, 20b, 21; 19:6a; 20:7, 18b, 36; 21:7, 24a, 24b, 26a; 22:2; 23:21a, 31; 24:21; 25:6, 11; 26:11b, 30b; 27:10; 28:14	1	4:32b			2	7:60; 14:15	77
Ro.	14	1:19, 19; 4:11b; 9:26; 10:2, 5; 11:8, 9b, 17, 27a; 15:27c, 28; 16:14, 15b							14
1 Co.	2	1:24; 7:8					1	11:13	3
2 Co.	5	2:13; 4:4; 5:19a; 6:16a; 8:22							5
Gal.	2	2:2; 3:12b							2
Eph.	2	2:10b; 4:18a							2
Phl.	1	1:28							1
Col.	1	3:7							1
1 Th.	2	4:17; 5:3							2
2 Th.	1	2:11a							1
1 Ti.	1	4:16							1
2 Ti.	1	2:25	1	4:16					2
Tit.	1	3:13							1
Heb.	5	6:16; 8:8, 10d; 11:16c; 12:19					1	12:10a	6
Jas.	2	2:16, 16							2
1 Pt.	1	1:11							1
2 Pt.	6	2:8, 19a, 20, 21, 21, 22							6
Jd.	1	1:11							1
Rev.	13	5:13; 6:8d, 11a; 8:2; 11:10, 12a; 12:12; 14:9a; 16:6; 20:4b, 11b, 13b; 21:14			2	7:2; 13:16a			15
Total	562		4		2		6		574

Miscellaneous: Mt. 25:16, the same; Mk. 16:14a, they; Ac. 7:60, their charge; Ac. 14:15 (with 1722), therein; 1 Co. 11:13 (with 5113), yourselves; Heb. 12:10a, their own.

See page 51 for Word 846k.

846l. αὐτός, autos′

Book	Oc.	he	Oc.	himself	Oc.	he himself	Oc.	myself	Oc.	Not Tr.	Oc.	Misc.	Total
Mt.	8	1:21b; 3:11; 8:24; 12:3b; 14:2a; 16:20; 21:27b; 25:17	3	6:4; 8:17; 27:57							4	3:4a; 11:14; 12:50; 26:48c	15
Mk.	13	1:8; 2:25a, 25c; 3:13a; 4:27; 4:38a; 6:16, 45, 47; 7:36b; 8:29a; 12:21b; 14:15	3	6:17a; 12:36, 37a					1	15:43	1	14:44c	18
Lk.	36	1:17a, 22b; 2:28a; 3:15, 16b; 4:15a, 30a; 5:1b, 14a, 16, 17a; 6:8a, 20, 35; 7:5; 8:1a, 22a, 37c, 41a, 54a; 9:51b; 10:38b; 11:17a, 28a; 15:14b; 16:24; 17:11b, 16c; 18:39b; 19:9b; 22:41a; 23:9b; 24:21, 25a, 28, 31c	6	3:23; 6:3b; 20:42; 23:51b; 24:15b; 36b	1	10:1b	1	24:39	1	5:37	2	6:42; 19:2	47
Jn.	10	1:27a; 2:12a, 24a, 25; 7:10b; 9:21b, 21d; 12:49; 14:10; 18:1a	7	4:2a, 12a, 44, 53b; 5:20, 37a; 16:27	3	6:6b, 15c; 7:4					1	12:24	21
Ac.	6	7:15; 10:42; 14:12; 16:33b; 17:25; 20:35	2	8:13; 20:13	3	2:34; 18:19; 19:22b	1	10:26b	1	8:32	5	21:24c; 22:20a; 24:8b, 16; 25:22a	18
Ro.							3	7:25; 9:3; 15:14a					3
1 Co.	1	7:13a	1	15:28b	2	2:15; 3:15					1	9:27	5
2 Co.	1	10:7	1	11:14			2	10:1; 12:13					4
Eph.	3	2:14; 4:11; 5:23									1	4:10	4
Phl.											1	2:24	1
Col.	3	1:17a, 18, 18											3
1 Th.			2	3:11; 4:16							1	5:23	3
2 Th.			2	2:16; 3:16									2
Heb.	3	1:5b; 4:10b; 13:5			3	2:14a, 18; 5:2					1	10:12	7
Jas.	1	1:13											1
1 Pt.									1	5:10	1	2:24a	2
1 Jn.	8	1:7a; 2:2, 25; 3:24c; 4:10, 13b, 15b, 19b	1	2:6b									9
3 Jn.					1	1:10b							1
Rev.	6	3:20c; 14:17; 17:11; 19:15c, 15e; 21:7b	1	21:3d	1	19:12c					1	14:10a	9
Total	99		29		14		7		4		20		173

Miscellaneous: Mt. 3:4a, the same; Mt. 11:14, this; Mt. 12:50, the same; Mt. 26:48c; Mk. 14:44c, that same; Lk. 6:42, thou thyself; Lk. 19:2, which; Jn. 12:24, it; Ac. 21:24c, thou thyself; Ac. 22:20a, I; Ac. 24:8b, thyself; Ac. 24:16; Ac. 25:22a; 1 Co. 9:27, I myself; Eph. 4:10, the same; Phl. 2:24, I myself; 1 Th. 5:23, very; Heb. 10:12, this man; 1 Pt. 2:24a, his own self; Rev. 14:10a, the same.

846k. αὐτόν, auton′

Book	Oc.	him	Oc.	he	Oc.	it	Oc.	that he	Oc.	Not Tr.	Oc.	Misc.	Total
Mt.	106	3:5, 14, 15, 15, 16b; 4:5, 5, 8a, 11a; 6:8b; 7:11, 24b; 8:5b, 7b, 25b, 31, 34a; 10:4, 33; 12:10a, 14b, 16b, 18, 22b; 13:2a; 14:3, 5, 5, 22, 26, 35a, 36a; 15:23c; 16:1a, 22a; 17:10a, 12a, 16, 16, 17, 23, 25; 18:15a, 25b, 27a, 28b, 29c, 30, 32a, 34b; 19:3b; 20:18, 19; 21:38a, 39, 44, 46, 46; 22:13b, 15, 22, 23b, 35b, 43b, 45a, 46b; 23:15; 24:47, 51a; 26:15a, 16, 25a, 48a, 48d, 49, 50b, 56, 59, 67b, 71b; 27:1, 2, 2, 3, 11a, 18, 19b, 19d, 27, 28a, 30a, 31b, 31c, 31e, 35a, 36, 39, 43, 43, 48b, 49, 64b; 28:7b, 13b, 14, 17a	5	13:2b, 4a; 16:21; 26:71a; 27:12	8	5:15, 29; 13:20, 46; 18:9; 21:13b, 33c; 26:61					2	9:31; 23:21b	121
Mk.	171	1:5a, 10, 12, 26a, 32, 34, 36a, 37a, 40a, 40b, 40c, 43b, 45b; 2:3, 13a, 16a; 3:2a, 2b, 6b, 8, 9b, 11a, 12b, 13b, 19, 21b, 31b, 31c, 32a; 4:1a, 10, 10, 36a, 38b; 5:3, 4c, 9, 10a, 12a, 17a, 18b, 19a, 21, 22a, 23a, 24c; 6:17b, 19b, 20b, 27b, 33b, 33d, 49, 50a, 54b, 56a; 7:1, 5, 12, 15a, 15b, 17a, 18b, 26, 32b, 33a; 8:11c, 22b, 23a, 23d, 25b, 26a, 32a, 38; 9:11, 13b, 15, 15, 18a, 18b, 19b, 20, 20, 20, 20, 22, 22, 25c, 26, 27, 27, 28c, 31b, 32, 38b, 39; 10:1a, 2, 2, 10c, 17b, 17c, 21b, 33, 33, 34b, 34d, 49a; 11:2c, 3b, 4, 18a, 18b, 27b; 12:3, 6a, 7, 8, 12a, 12c, 13, 13, 18, 18, 28c, 33, 34c, 37b; 13:3b; 14:1, 10a, 11b, 44a, 44d, 45b, 46, 46, 50, 51b, 55, 61a, 64, 65c, 65e, 69a; 15:2a, 4, 10, 13, 14b, 16, 17a, 18, 20b, 20c, 20d, 20e, 22, 24a, 25, 29, 32b, 36, 36, 44, 46, 46; 16:1, 6b, 7b, 14c	5	2:23a; 4:1b; 5:4a; 6:20a; 9:28a	5	4:16; 9:45, 47; 11:17b; 12:1b			1	12:34a	2	1:45a; 2:15a	184
Lk.	182	1:12, 13a, 50b, 62b; 2:7a, 7b, 22b, 25, 44, 44, 45, 45, 46a, 48a, 48b; 3:10, 12, 14a, 22; 4:4, 5a, 9a, 9b, 29a, 29b, 29d, 35c, 35e, 38a, 40b, 42a, 42c; 5:3, 18a, 19, 19, 33; 6:7a; 7:3, 3, 4, 6c, 9a, 15a, 20, 36a, 39a, 40, 42c; 8:4, 9a, 19a, 24, 29, 30, 30, 31a, 32a, 37a, 38c, 40, 40, 41b, 42c; 9:9, 39a, 39b, 39d, 42b, 42c, 45c, 49, 50, 53a, 57b, 62; 10:25, 26, 30, 31, 33b, 34b, 34c, 38c; 11:1c, 5b, 13, 22b, 37a, 39, 53c, 54a; 12:44, 46a, 48b; 14:1c, 4, 5b, 9, 12a, 31; 15:15, 20b, 20e, 22a, 27b, 28b; 16:2a, 14, 27; 18:3, 7a, 18, 33, 40a, 40c; 19:4, 5, 5, 6, 9a, 14b, 30, 35, 39, 47; 20:2, 10b, 14, 14, 15a, 18, 19a, 20b, 21, 27, 40, 44a; 21:7, 38a; 22:2, 4a, 6a, 43b, 47c, 49a, 51b, 52, 54, 54, 56a, 57, 57, 58a, 64a, 64c, 65, 66; 23:1b, 3a, 7a, 8a, 9a, 11, 11, 11, 15a, 16, 21, 22c, 26a, 27b, 33, 39; 24:16b, 18a, 20, 20, 24, 29a, 31b, 52b	25	1:8a, 21; 2:4, 21b; 4:41b; 5:9a, 12a; 6:1a, 6a; 8:5a, 42b; 9:18a, 29a; 11:1a, 27a; 14:1a, 18b; 17:11a, 25; 18:35; 19:11b, 15; 23:23a; 24:30a, 51a	6	8:16, 21b; 10:6; 11:28b; 19:46b; 20:9	2	18:24; 24:23b	1	16:22	2	10:33a; 23:7b	218
Jn.	161	1:10b, 11, 12a, 19, 21, 25a, 29, 31, 32, 33, 33, 42a, 47a; 2:3, 11a; 3:4, 15, 16, 18, 26b, 36; 4:10b, 15, 23, 24, 30, 31, 39, 40a, 40b, 45a, 47a, 47b, 48, 49, 52c; 5:12, 14a, 15, 16, 18, 23; 6:6a, 15a, 15b, 21, 25a, 28, 34, 40, 40, 44, 44, 54, 64, 71; 7:1, 3a, 5b, 11, 18a, 29a, 30a, 30b, 31, 32b, 35, 39, 43, 44b, 44c, 45b, 48, 50b; 8:2a, 3a, 6a, 7a, 20a, 30b, 55a, 55b, 55c, 55d, 57, 59a; 9:2a, 8, 13, 15a, 21c, 23b, 28, 34b, 35a, 35b, 36, 37b; 10:24a, 31, 39a, 41, 42; 11:3, 11, 15, 29, 32a, 34a, 36, 44c, 45, 48, 48, 53, 57; 12:4b, 11, 17b, 21, 26, 37c, 42, 47, 48, 48; 13:2, 11, 16, 32b, 32c; 14:7, 7, 21b, 23b, 23c; 16:7, 19a; 18:2, 4a, 5c, 12, 13, 24, 30b, 31b, 31c; 19:2b, 4b, 6a, 6c, 12, 15a, 16a, 18a; 20:2b, 13b, 15c, 15d, 15e; 21:12b	4	2:24c; 4:4; 12:18b; 19:33a	3	2:19b, 20; 19:24a	5	9:22b; 11:17; 20:9; 21:22b, 23b			1	21:25	174
Ac.	138	1:6, 9b, 11; 2:25; 3:4, 7a, 9, 13, 26; 5:6; 6:12, 15a; 7:3, 4b, 5f, 8b, 10a, 10d, 21b, 21c, 27, 31b, 54, 57; 8:20, 38, 39; 9:3, 3, 6, 8, 10, 11, 15, 17, 23, 24b, 25, 26, 27a, 29, 30, 30, 35, 38b; 10:3a, 11, 13, 15, 21, 26a, 35a, 38a, 40, 43b, 48b; 11:2, 26a, 26b; 12:4, 4, 6, 7a, 8a, 16, 17c, 19, 20a, 23; 13:9, 11, 22a, 30, 34; 14:19, 20; 15:21; 16:3a, 9; 17:15, 15, 27, 31; 18:12, 26b, 27b; 19:2b, 4, 30, 31b, 33; 20:14, 18a, 37, 38b; 21:12, 27, 27, 30, 31, 34, 36; 22:13, 18, 20c, 24a, 25, 29b, 29c, 30a; 23:3, 10b, 15a, 15d, 18, 21b, 21d, 27b, 28b, 30, 35; 24:26b, 26c; 25:2b, 3b, 3c, 19, 21, 21, 25c, 26; 26:26; 28:6c, 8b, 16, 21, 23b, 30	16	2:24a; 7:2, 21a; 8:40; 9:3, 16b, 43; 10:10, 41b; 13:28; 21:35; 23:15c; 25:24, 25a; 28:6a, 6d	1	13:46	2	22:22b, 24b	1	3:10a	4	1:3a; 2:36; 3:12; 8:32	162
Ro.	9	8:32a; 10:9, 12b; 11:36c; 12:20a, 20b; 14:3, 4; 15:11	5	3:26; 4:11a, 13b, 18; 8:29							1	4:23a	15
1 Co.	8	2:9, 16; 7:13c; 8:6a; 16:11, 11, 11, 12	1	15:25a									9
2 Co.	2	2:8; 7:15b											2
Gal.	3	1:1, 16, 18											3
Eph.	4	1:20, 22b; 4:15, 21a											4
Phl.	8	1:29a; 2:9a, 27, 27, 28, 28, 29; 3:10a	1	3:21c									9
Col.	4	1:16c; 2:12b; 3:10; 4:10									1	1:20b	5
2 Th.	1	2:1	2	2:4, 6									3
1 Ti.			1	3:7									1
Phe.	3	1:12, 15, 17											3
Heb.	14	2:6b, 7, 7, 7; 3:2a; 5:5, 7; 7:1, 21; 9:28; 11:5a, 6, 19; 13:13a	2	7:24; 9:26							2	3:3; 9:24	18
Jas.	7	1:12; 2:5, 14; 5:14, 14, 15a, 19											7
1 Pt.	3	1:21b; 3:6; 5:7a											3
1 Jn.	11	1:10a; 2:3a, 4a; 3:1, 2b, 6b, 6c, 12a; 4:19a; 5:10, 14a											11
2 Jn.	1	1:10a											1
Rev.	14	1:7, 7, 7, 17a; 3:12, 12, 20a; 12:11; 19:5b, 11; 20:2, 3a, 3b; 22:18	3	11:5e; 17:10; 20:3d	1	9:6a			2	7:9a; 13:10			20
Total	850		70		24		9		5		15		973

Miscellaneous: Mt. 9:31, his fame; Mt. 23:21b, therein; Mk. 1:45a; 2:15a, Jesus; Lk. 10:33a, where he was; Lk. 23:7b, himself; Jn. 21:25, itself; Ac. 1:3a, his; Ac. 2:36, that same; Ac. 3:12, this man; Ac. 8:32, his; Ro. 4:23a (with 1223), for his sake; Col. 1:20b, himself; Heb. 3:3, the house; Heb. 9:24, itself.

846m. αὐτοῦ, autou′

Book	Oc.	his	Oc.	him	Oc.	he	Oc.	it	Oc.	thereof
Mt.	121	1:2, 11, 18a, 21a, 23, 25b; 2:2a, 11a, 13b, 14, 20, 21, 22; 3:3, 4b, 12; 4:18, 24a; 5:1c, 35; 6:33; 7:9a, 28; 8:3b, 13, 14, 21a, 23c, 25a; 9:10b, 11, 19b, 20, 21; 10: 2, 2, 25, 25, 25, 36; 11:20; 12:1, 19, 21, 26, 29, 29, 33, 33, 46b; 13:19, 25, 36b, 41, 55, 55, 56; 14:11, 12a, 15b, 36b; 15:12a, 23b, 33b; 16:5, 27; 17:1a, 2b, 2c, 10b, 27b; 18:6b, 25c, 25d, 29a, 29b, 31, 32b, 34a; 19:10b, 25; 21:35, 38b, 45a; 22:6, 24, 24, 33, 45b; 24:1a, 31a, 45a, 46, 51b; 25:21b, 23b, 26a, 41; 26:7b, 8, 51, 65, 67a; 27:19c, 25, 29a, 29b, 30b, 31d, 32, 35b, 37, 37, 53, 64a; 28:3, 3, 4, 7a, 8, 9a, 13a	31	2:3; 3:6, 13; 4:21a; 5:25, 41; 8: 3a; 9:24; 12:3c, 4b, 10b, 14a; 13: 12b; 14:31a; 17:3b, 5c, 18b; 18: 15b; 20:20b; 22:13a; 25:6, 10b, 28, 29, 31, 32a; 26:24a, 47b; 27: 29c, 54; 28:9c	12	1:20a; 5:1a; 9:18a; 11: 11; 12:46a; 17:5a; 18: 24a, 25a; 21: 10; 24:3a; 26:47a; 27: 19a	7	9:16; 13:32, 44; 21: 34; 23: 18; 26: 27b; 28: 2		
Mk.	64	1:3, 16, 19a, 22a, 28; 2:15b, 15c, 16b, 23b; 3:5c, 21a, 27, 27, 31a; 5:22b, 27, 28, 31b; 6:1b, 2b, 3a, 14a, 27a, 28b, 29a, 29b, 35b, 56a; 7:2, 17b, 19, 25c, 33b, 33c, 35, 35; 8:4b, 23b, 25a, 26b, 27a; 9:3, 21a, 28b, 42b; 10:10a, 24a, 46b; 11:14b, 18c; 12:19, 19, 37c; 13:1c; 14:3c, 12b, 16a, 47, 65b; 15:21, 24b, 26, 27b; 16:7a	41	1:5b, 20b, 25b, 26b, 36b, 41a, 42b; 2:25d; 3:2c, 6a, 10b, 14a; 4:25b, 36b; 5:4b, 18c, 24a, 40, 40; 6: 20c, 20d, 56c; 7:15c, 25a; 8:11b, 22c, 30b; 9:7b, 25b; 11:3a; 12: 37d; 14:21a, 35, 43b, 56, 57, 58; 15:3, 19a, 39; 16:10	11	1:42a; 5:18a, 35; 10:17a, 46a; 11:27a; 12:32b; 13: 1a, 3a; 14: 3b, 43a	3	2:21; 4:32; 14:23b		
Lk.	103	1:5a, 8b, 13b, 14, 23, 24, 29, 31, 32b, 33, 49, 50a, 55, 59b, 60, 62a, 63, 64, 64, 67, 76, 77a, 80; 2:21a, 33a, 34b, 41, 43b, 47b, 48c, 51c; 3:1, 4, 17, 19b; 4:22b, 32, 32; 5:30b; 6:1, 6b, 10b, 14, 17b, 40, 45; 7:11b, 15b, 18, 38, 38, 38; 8:9b, 19b, 22b, 44a; 9:29b, 29c, 31, 32b, 33b, 42d, 53b, 54a; 10:34a, 39; 11:1b, 8b, 8c, 18, 21, 22c, 22d, 54b; 12:43, 46b, 47; 15:20c, 20d, 22b, 25, 26, 28a; 16:1a, 20, 21, 23; 17:2b, 16a, 31a; 19:14a; 20:20a, 44b; 22:39b, 44, 50b, 51a; 23:34b, 49a, 55b; 24:8, 23a, 47	67	1:17b, 66, 75; 2:27b, 33b, 38b, 47a; 3:7, 19a; 4:13, 14, 35b, 35d, 37, 42b; 5:12b, 13, 13, 15a, 15b, 18b; 6:3c, 4, 7b, 17c, 19, 19; 7: 17, 30, 36b, 39b; 8:18b, 38a, 45, 47b, 53; 9:7, 35, 39c; 10:34d, 35b, 37a; 11:16, 54c; 12:48a, 58; 13: 17c; 14:2, 8; 15:1b; 19:14c, 24, 26, 31b, 34, 48; 20:26, 26, 28; 21: 38b; 22:59, 64b; 23:2, 8b, 8c, 10, 14b	19	7:6b, 28; 8: 49a; 9:34a, 42a, 51a; 11:22a, 53a; 12:15c; 13: 17a; 15: 14a, 20a; 17: 12a; 18:40b; 19:36, 37; 20:1; 22:47a, 60	1	13:19	1	19:33b
Jn.	103	1:12c, 14, 16, 35, 37; 2:2, 5, 11b, 12b, 12c, 12d, 17, 22a, 23a, 23b; 3:20, 21, 22a, 32, 33, 35; 4:2b, 8, 12c, 12d, 27a, 34b, 41, 47c, 51b, 53c; 5:28, 35, 37b, 37c, 38; 6:2b, 8b, 16, 22, 22, 24a, 53b, 60a, 61a, 66a; 7:3b, 5a, 10a, 17, 30c, 38; 8:20b, 55e; 9:2b, 2c, 3a, 14, 20b, 21a, 22a, 23a, 27b, 31; 10:3a, 4c; 11:2, 12, 13, 32b, 44a; 12: 3, 4a, 16a, 41a, 50; 13:1a, 23; 15:10, 15; 16:17, 29b; 18:1b, 10b, 19, 19, 25b; 19:2a, 23, 25, 25, 29, 33b, 34, 35; 20:7, 25c, 25d, 26a, 31; 21:2, 20, 24	30	1:3, 3, 7, 10a, 15, 47b; 3:2b, 17, 29; 6:41, 66b; 7:12, 13, 29b, 32a, 51; 8:6b, 26; 9:17, 18, 18, 40a; 10:5, 20b; 11:16; 12:17a, 19, 41b; 18:26; 19:18b	4	4:51a; 8:30a; 12:37a; 18:22	4	6:60b; 7:7a; 8:44b; 19:24b	2	3:8; 7:7b
Ac.	57	1:14, 18, 20a, 20c, 22; 2:29, 30b, 30c, 31, 31, 41; 3: 7b, 16a, 16b; 4:26b; 5:2, 7, 10a, 32a, 41; 6:15b; 7:4a, 5e, 6a, 10b, 23b, 25a; 8:1, 33, 33, 33, 33; 9:18; 10: 43a; 11:13a; 12:7b, 15b; 13:8b, 24, 31b; 16:3b, 32b, 33c; 17:16b; 18:2a; 19:12a; 20:10b, 32, 38a; 21:19b; 22:14, 20b; 24:8a, 23a, 24a; 28:3, 4	26	2:22; 3:16c, 22; 6:11, 14; 7:9, 37; 8:30; 9:2; 10:38b; 12:5, 10b; 13: 29; 17:19; 21:33; 22:22a, 29a; 23:2b, 15b, 20; 24:8c, 24b; 25: 3a, 15, 22b, 27	13	1:10a; 7: 31a; 18: 27a; 21: 14, 40; 23:7; 24:2, 25; 25: 7, 8; 26:24, 30a; 28:29	1	2:24b		
Ro.	25	1:5, 9, 20b; 2:4, 6, 26; 3:7, 24, 25; 4:5, 13a; 5:9a, 10, 10; 6:3, 5; 8:9, 11; 9:19; 11:33, 33, 34; 12:20c; 16: 13, 15a	6	1:20a; 5:9b; 6:9; 11:36a, 36b; 15:10					1	6:12b
1 Co.	6	1:9; 14:25; 15:10, 23, 25b, 27a	6	1:30; 7:12b; 8:3, 6b, 10, 18	1	10:22			2	9:7, 23
2 Co.	9	2:11; 3:7; 7:7, 13, 15a; 9:9, 15; 11:15a, 33								
Gal.	1	3:16								
Eph.	14	1:18, 18, 19, 19, 22a, 23; 2:10a; 3:5, 6, 7; 5:30, 30, 30; 6:10	8	1:4b, 7, 7, 12, 14, 17; 2:18; 3:12						
Phl.	4	3:10b, 10c, 10d, 21b	1	2:22						
Col.	9	1:9, 11, 14, 20c, 24, 26, 29; 3:9; 4:15	4	1:16b, 20a, 20d; 3:17						
1 Th.	3	1:10; 2:19; 3:13								
2 Th.	1	1:9								
2 Ti.	3	1:8; 4:8, 14b	1	2:26						
Heb.	18	1:3a; 2:8a; 3:2b, 5, 7, 15; 4:1, 7, 10a; 6:10; 10:13, 13; 11:4a, 5b; 12:10b; 13:13b, 15b, 21a	5	2:6a; 4:13b; 7:25a; 12:5; 13:15a						
Jas.	2	2:22; 5:20					1	1:11b	1	1:11a
1 Pt.	4	2:21a, 22; 3:12a; 4:13	2	1:21; 2:14					1	1:24
2 Pt.	3	1:3; 3:4, 13								
1 Jn.	22	1:3, 10b; 2:3b, 4b, 5a, 11, 12, 28b; 3:9a, 12b, 12c, 22b, 23, 23, 24a; 4:12; 5:2, 3, 3, 11, 14b, 20	14	1:5a, 6, 7b; 2:27a, 28c, 29; 3:17a, 19, 22a; 4:9, 21; 5:1, 15, 18					1	2:17
2 Jn.	2	1:6a, 11b								
3 Jn.	1	1:7	1	1:10a						
Jd.			1	1:15c						
Rev.	68	1:4, 14, 14, 15, 15, 16, 16, 17b; 2:18; 3:5, 5, 5; 6:17; 7:15b; 10:1, 1; 11:15, 19, 19; 12:4a, 5b, 7, 7, 9a, 10a; 13:1, 1, 2a, 2b, 3, 3, 6, 6, 17, 18; 14:1b, 7b, 9b, 10b, 11b, 11c; 15:2, 2, 2, 8; 16:2, 10, 15; 18:1; 19:2a, 5a, 7b, 10a, 12a, 12b, 13, 15a, 19b, 20b, 21a; 20:4c; 21:3c; 22:3b, 4a, 4b, 12, 14a, 19	12	3:20b, 21b; 6:8a, 8c; 12:9b; 13: 4, 12a; 14:1a; 17:14b; 19:20a; 20:3c, 6			1	20:11a	4	5:2, 5, 9; 16:12
Total	643		256		60		18		13	

846m. αὐτοῦ, autou′ (continued)

Book	Oc.	in his sight (with 1799)	Oc.	thereof (with 1537)	Oc.	thereon (with 1883)	Oc.	his own	Oc.	whose	Oc.	the	Oc.	Not Tr.	Oc.	Misc.	Total
Mt.					2	23:20b, 22									2	9:10a; 12:36	175
Mk.							1	6:1b					2	1:7; 14:3a			122
Lk.			1	22:16			1	22:71b			1	14:29a	1	3:16a	2	12:15b; 14:32	197
Jn.			2	4:12b; 6:50									1	1:27b	2	6:39a; 19:36	148
Ac.											1	23:19			3	18:26a; 25:5, 25b	101
Ro.	1	3:20											1	15:21	1	16:2c	35
1 Co.															1	1:29	16
2 Co.													1	12:17	1	8:19	11
Gal.																	1
Eph.															1	2:20	23
Phl.															1	1:29b	6
Col.																	13
1 Th.																	3
2 Th.																	1
2 Ti.																	4
Heb.	2	4:13a; 13:21b															25
Jas.																	4
1 Pt.									1	2:24b							8
2 Pt.															1	3:7	4
1 Jn.	1	3:22c															38
2 Jn.																	2
3 Jn.																	2
Jd.																	1
Rev.									1	13:12c							86
Total	4		3		2		2		2		2		6		15		1026

Miscellaneous: Mt. 9:10a, Jesus; Mt. 12:36 (with 3912), thereof; Lk. 12:15b, man's; Lk. 14:32, the other; Jn. 6:39a (with 1537 and 3261), nothing; Jn. 19:36, of him; Ac. 18:26a, whom; Ac. 25:5, this man; Ac. 25:25b, he himself; Ro. 16:2c (with 1700), myself; 1 Co. 1:29 (with 1799), in his presence; 2 Co. 8:19, same; Eph. 2:20, himself; Phl. 1:29b (with 5128), for his sake; 2 Pt. 3:7, the same.

846n. αὐτούς, autous′

Book	Oc.	them
Mt.	46	2:8a, 9; 4:21c, 24c; 5:2; 7:6, 16b, 20b, 24a, 26, 29; 10:21, 26; 12:15b; 13:15, 42, 50, 54a; 14:14a, 18, 25; 15:14, 30b, 30c, 32; 16:4b; 17:1b, 5b,27a; 19:2b, 4b; 20:2, 12, 25a, 32; 21:3b, 14b, 17, 37; 22:41b; 25:32b; 26:40, 43a, 44a; 28:19, 20
Mk.	40	1:20a, 22b; 2:13b; 3:5a, 14b, 23a; 4:2a; 5:10b, 12b; 6:7a, 33a, 33c, 34b, 36, 48a, 48c, 48d, 51; 8:3a, 5, 9, 13, 31; 9:2a, 14a, 16, 33; 10:1b, 6, 32a, 42a; 11:6b; 12:4, 6b, 12b; 13:12; 14:7, 37, 40a; 16:18
Lk.	76	1:65; 2:9b, 18, 20, 27a, 34a, 46c, 49; 3:13, 14b; 4:21, 23, 31, 40a, 40d, 43; 5:17b, 22b, 31, 34a, 36; 6:3a, 9, 10a, 32, 47; 8:21a, 22c; 9:2, 3, 5, 10b, 11b, 13a, 14, 16, 18c, 34b, 54b; 10:1a, 2; 11:5a, 31, 47, 48b, 49a, 53b; 12:15a, 16, 24, 37a; 13:4, 23b; 14:5a, 7, 25b; 15:3; 16:30; 18:31; 19:13b, 27, 33c; 20: 3, 19c, 23b, 41; 22:15, 45, 70; 23:14a, 22a; 24:17, 25b, 50, 50, 51b
Jn.	19	1:38a; 6:17; 7:50a; 8:2b, 7b; 9:19; 12:40c; 13:1b; 17:6, 11, 12b, 14b, 15, 15, 17, 18, 23b; 18:7, 29
Ac.	87	1:7; 2:38; 3:11; 4:7, 8, 13, 15, 18a, 19, 21, 21, 23, 33; 5:13b, 18, 19, 21b, 22, 26, 27, 27, 33, 35, 38, 40b; 7:26b, 34b, 36, 42; 8:11b, 14, 17; 9:21; 10:8b,20b, 23a, 24, 28, 48a; 11:15; 12:21; 13:2b, 15, 17a, 43b, 50, 51; 14:5b, 23b; 15:2a, 5, 7; 16:7, 10, 20, 23b, 24a, 30, 33a, 34, 37a, 39, 40; 17:2a, 5, 6, 9, 16a; 18: 6b, 16; 19:2a, 3, 6b, 16a, 17; 20:2, 6; 21:19a, 21, 32; 22:30c; 24:22; 26:11a; 27:43; 28:17b, 23c, 27
Ro.	5	1:24a, 26a, 28; 11:11b, 23
2 Co.	2	8:24; 9:13
Gal.	2	4:17; 6:16
Eph.	1	6:9b
Col.	1	2:15
1 Th.	1	5:13a
2 Th.		
Tit.	2	1:13; 3:1
Heb.	7	1:12; 2:11; 4:8; 8:9c, 10c; 10:16a, 16d
Jas.		
1 Pt.		
2 Pt.	1	2:1
1 Jn.	1	4:4
Jd.		
Rev.	23	2:2, 27; 3:9; 7:15c, 16, 17a, 17b; 9:5b; 11:5a, 5d, 7b, 7c, 11, 11, 12b; 12:4b; 13:7b; 16:14, 16; 17:14a; 19:15d; 20:10; 22:5
Total	314	

846o. αὐτῷ, autō′

Book	Oc.	him
Mt.	172	1:20b, 24; 2:2b, 5, 8b, 11b, 11c; 3:16a; 4:3, 6, 7, 8b, 9, 10, 10, 11b, 20, 22, 24b, 25; 5:1b, 39, 40; 7:9b, 10; 8:1b, 2, 4a, 5a, 7a, 16, 19, 20, 21b, 22, 23b, 27, 28b; 9:2a, 9, 9, 14, 18c, 19a, 27, 28a, 28c, 32b; 10:32; 11:3; 12:2, 4a, 15a, 22a, 32, 32, 46c, 47, 48; 13:10a, 12a, 27, 28b, 36a, 51b, 57a; 14:2b, 4a, 13, 15a, 17, 28, 31b, 33, 35b; 15:12b, 15, 22, 25, 30a, 33a; 16:17, 22b; 17:12b, 14b, 14c, 26, 26; 18:6a, 21, 21, 22, 24b, 26, 27b, 28a, 32c, 34c; 19:2a, 3a, 3c, 7a, 10a, 13a, 16, 17, 18, 20, 21, 27; 20:7a, 20a, 21b, 22, 29b, 33, 34c; 21:14a, 16a, 23b, 25, 31a, 32, 32, 32, 41a, 41c; 22:12, 16, 19, 21a, 23a, 37, 42, 46a; 24:1b, 3b; 25:21a, 23a, 26b, 37, 44a; 26:7a, 15b, 17, 18, 22a, 24b, 25b, 33, 34, 35, 50a, 52a, 58, 62, 63, 64, 69, 75; 27:11b, 13, 14, 22b, 28b, 29d, 31a, 34, 38, 42, 44b, 55; 28:9d, 17b
Mk.	119	1:13, 18, 25a, 27, 30a, 37b, 40d, 41b, 43a, 44a; 2:4, 14, 14, 15d, 18, 24, 26; 3:7, 9a, 10a, 11b,32b; 4:25a, 38c, 41; 5:2b, 6, 8, 19b, 20, 24b, 31a, 33b, 33c, 37; 6:1a, 2a, 3b, 14b, 19a, 30, 35a, 37c; 7:28, 32a, 32c, 34; 8:4a, 11a, 19, 22a, 23c, 29c, 32b; 9:13a, 19a, 21b, 23, 25a, 38a, 42a; 10:13a, 18, 20, 21a, 21c, 28, 32, 34a, 34c, 35, 37, 39a, 48, 49b, 51a, 51b, 52; 11:7,7, 21, 28, 31; 12:14, 16b, 17b, 26, 29, 32a, 34b; 13:1b, 2; 14:11a, 12a, 13b, 19, 29, 30, 40c, 45a, 51a, 53, 54, 61b, 65a, 65d, 67, 72; 15:2b, 17b, 19b, 19c, 20a, 23, 27a, 32a, 41, 41, 41
Lk.	156	1:11, 19, 32a, 74; 2:26; 4:3, 5b, 6a, 8, 8, 9c, 12, 17, 20, 22a,35a; 5:1a, 5, 9b, 11, 14b, 20b, 27, 28, 29a; 7:2, 6d, 9b, 11a, 43; 8:1b, 3a, 18a, 19c, 20, 25b, 27, 27, 28, 38b, 39, 42a, 47a, 47c, 49b, 50; 9:10a, 11a, 12, 18b, 30, 32a, 32c, 37b, 52, 58, 60; 10:28, 35a, 37b; 11:5c, 6, 8a, 8d, 11, 11, 12, 27b, 37b, 45; 12:8,10, 13, 14, 20, 36, 41; 13:1b, 8a, 15a, 17b,23a, 31b; 14:6, 15, 16, 18a, 25a, 29b; 15:1a, 16, 18, 21, 27a, 30, 31; 16:1b, 2b, 6, 7, 29a, 31; 17:2a, 3, 3, 4, 8, 9, 12b, 16b, 19, 37a; 18:15a, 19, 22, 37, 39a, 42, 43; 19:17, 22, 25, 31a; 45; 20:5, 10a, 38; 22:5, 9, 10b, 14, 33, 39a, 43a, 48, 49b, 56b, 56c, 61, 63; 23:3b, 9c, 15b, 22b, 26b, 27a, 32, 36, 36, 38, 40a, 43, 49b, 55a; 24:19b, 42
Jn.	167	1:4, 22, 25b, 38c, 39, 40, 41, 42b, 43, 45, 46, 46, 48, 48, 49, 50, 51; 2:10, 18; 3:2a, 3, 9, 10, 26a, 27; 4:9, 11, 14, 14, 14, 19, 25, 33, 50, 50, 51c, 52b, 53a; 5:6, 7, 8, 14b, 20a, 20c, 27; 6:2a, 7a, 8a, 25b, 30, 56, 65, 68; 7:18b, 26, 52; 8:4, 13, 19, 25a, 29, 31, 33, 39a, 41, 44a, 48, 52; 9:3b, 7, 9, 10, 12, 24, 26, 34a, 35c, 37a,38, 40b; 10:4b, 24b, 33, 38; 11:8, 10, 20, 24, 27, 30, 32c,34b, 39; 12:2, 2, 13, 16b, 16c, 18a, 29, 34; 13:6, 7, 8, 8, 9, 10, 25, 27, 28, 29, 31, 32a, 36, 36, 37, 38; 14:5, 6, 8, 9, 21c, 22, 23a, 23d; 15:5; 16:29a; 17:2a, 2b; 18:5a, 20, 23, 25a, 30a, 31d, 33, 34, 37, 38a, 38c; 19:3, 4c, 6d, 7, 9, 10, 32; 20:6, 15b, 16b, 25a, 28, 29; 21:3b, 5b, 15, 15, 16, 16, 16, 17, 17, 17, 17, 19, 22a, 23a
Ac.	77	2:30a; 3:10b, 16d; 5:17, 21a, 32b, 36, 37, 40a; 7:5a, 5c, 8a, 10c, 30, 33, 35, 38, 40, 47; 8:2, 11a, 31, 35; 9:7, 12, 16a, 27c, 34, 39b; 10:3b, 4, 4, 7, 19, 23c, 25, 27, 35b, 41a; 11:13b; 12:8b, 9; 13:31a; 14:9; 16:32a; 17:16c, 18a, 28, 34a; 18:18, 26c; 19:22a, 38; 20:3, 4, 10a, 10c, 16b; 21:8, 20, 29; 22:24c, 27; 23:2a, 9, 11, 17, 28a, 32, 33; 24:10, 23b, 26a, 26d; 25:2a; 28:8a, 23a
Ro.	12	4:3, 22, 23b; 6:4, 8; 8:32b; 9:33; 10:11; 11:4, 35, 35; 15:12
1 Co.	7	1:5; 2:11, 14; 11:14b; 15:27b, 28a, 28c
2 Co.	8	1:19, 20, 20; 5:9, 21; 7:14; 13:4, 4
Gal.	3	2:11, 13a; 3:6
Eph.	5	1:4a, 10; 3:21; 4:21b; 6:9d
Phl.	2	2:9b; 3:9
Col.	10	1:16a, 17b, 19; 2:6, 9, 10, 12a, 13; 3:4; 4:13
1 Th.	2	4:14; 5:10
2 Th.	2	1:12; 3:14
1 Ti.	1	1:16
2 Ti.	2	1:18; 4:14a
Heb.	10	1:5a, 6; 2:8b, 8c, 8d, 10a, 13; 5:9; 7:10; 10:38
Jas.	5	1:5; 2:3, 23; 4:17; 5:15b
1 Pt.	5	1:21c; 2:2, 6; 3:22; 5:11
2 Pt.	5	1:17, 18; 3:14, 15, 18
1 Jn.	20	1:5b; 2:5b, 6a, 8, 10, 15, 27c, 28a; 3:2a, 3, 5, 6a, 9b, 15, 17b, 24b, 24d; 4:13a, 15, 16; 5:16
2 Jn.	2	1:10b, 11a
Rev.	32	1:1, 6; 2:7, 17, 17, 26, 28; 3:21a; 6:2, 2, 4a, 4c, 5, 8b; 7:14, 15a; 8:3; 9:1; 10:9a; 13:2c, 5, 5, 7a, 7c, 8; 14:7a; 16:8, 9; 19:7a, 10b, 14; 22:3c
Total	824	

846n. αὐτούς, autous' (continued)

Book	Oc.	they	Oc.	their	Oc.	who	Oc.	Not Tr.	Oc.	Misc.	Total
Mt.	2	1:18b; 13:54c							1	21:41b	49
Mk.	1	3:20			1	1:19b					42
Lk.	7	2:6a, 43a; 9:33a; 10:38a; 17:14b; 19:11c; 24:15a									83
Jn.											19
Ac.	7	4:2; 11:26c; 14:1b; 15:13, 39; 21:25a; 26:18b	1	13:18	1	15:27a	2	8:6; 15:17	1	21:25b	99
Ro.	1	1:20c									6
2 Co.											2
Gal.											2
Eph.											1
Col.											1
1 Th.			1	2:16							2
2 Th.	2	2:10, 11b							1	1:4	3
Tit.											2
Heb.	1	1:4					1	11:16a			9
Jas.	1	3:3a									1
1 Pt.			1	4:14							1
2 Pt.	1	3:5									2
1 Jn.											1
Jd.									1	1:24	1
Rev.			3	20:4a, 8, 9							26
Total	23		6		2		3		4		352

Miscellaneous: Mt. 21:41b, those; Ac. 21:25b, themselves; 2 Th. 1:4, ourselves; Jd. 1:24, you.

846o. αὐτῷ, autō' (continued)

Book	Oc.	he	Oc.	it	Oc.	therein (with 1722)	Oc.	his	Oc.	thereby (with 1722)	Oc.	Not Tr.	Oc.	Misc.	Total
Mt.	4	8:1a, 23a, 28a; 21:23a	4	21:33a, 33b; 23:20a, 21a			1	27:44c					2	17:18a; 18:13b	183
Mk.	2	5:2a; 11:23									1	14:21b			122
Lk.							2	2:5; 4:16					1	13:1a	159
Jn.	1	12:6	1	11:38			1	13:3			2	3:1; 10:13	1	1:6	173
Ac.	4	4:32a; 7:5g, 23a; 20:16a	2	19:31a; 22:15	1	17:24					1	4:37			85
Ro.					1	1:17							1	11:36d	14
1 Co.			1	15:38											8
2 Co.															8
Gal.															3
Eph.					1	6:20			1	2:16					7
Phl.															2
Col.					1	2:7a									11
1 Th.															2
2 Th.															2
1 Ti.			1	1:8											2
2 Ti.															2
Heb.															10
Jas.			1	5:7											6
1 Pt.	1	5:7b							1	2:2					7
2 Pt.															5
1 Jn.															20
2 Jn.															2
Rev.	2	13:14, 15			2	10:6a; 11:1	1	21:7a					2	6:4b; 9:11	39
Total	14		10		6		5		2		4		7		872

Miscellaneous: Mt. 17:18a, the devil; Mt. 18:13b, that sheep; Lk. 13:1a, that; Jn. 1:6, whose; Ro. 11:36d, whom; Rev. 6:4b (with 1909), thereon; Rev. 9:11, whose.

846p. αὐτῶν, autōn′

Book	Oc.	them	Oc.	their	Oc.	they	Oc.	their own	Oc.	Not Tr.	Oc.	Misc.	Total
Mt.	35	2:4, 7; 4:8c, 23; 8:30; 9:15b, 15c, 36; 10:29; 17:2a, 7, 12c; 18:2b, 12, 17, 20, 35; 20:13, 25b, 25c; 21:3a, 7a, 45b; 22:35a; 23:26, 30, 34, 34; 25:2, 19; 26:22b, 36, 73; 27:7, 48a	27	1:21c; 4:21b; 6:14, 15; 7:16a, 20a; 8:34b; 9:2b, 4, 29, 30a, 35; 11:1; 12:9, 25a; 13:54b, 58; 14:14b; 15:8; 18:10; 20:34a, 34b; 21:41d; 22:7, 18; 23:3; 26:43b	14	2:13a; 6:26b; 9:32a; 14:32; 17:9a, 14a, 22a, 24; 20:29a; 25:10a; 26:21, 26; 27:17a; 28:11					4	5:3, 10; 21:7b; 24:31b	80
Mk.	20	2:19b, 20; 6:50b, 52, 54a; 7:6b; 8:3b; 9:2b, 36b; 10:13b, 42c, 42d, 42e; 12:15a, 23a, 28a; 14:52, 69b, 70; 16:12	13	1:23, 39; 2:5; 3:5b; 4:15; 5:17b; 6:6; 9:44, 46, 48; 14:40b, 59; 16:14b	4	9:9a; 11:12; 14:18, 22a							37
Lk.	51	2:15, 46b, 51a; 4:6b, 26, 27, 30b, 40c, 42d; 5:2, 25, 29b, 34b, 35; 6:13, 17a; 7:42b; 8:37b; 9:45a, 46b; 11:15, 49b; 12:6; 15:4a, 12a; 16:29b; 17:15; 18:8, 15b, 34b; 20:33a; 21:8; 22:23b, 24b, 25b, 25c, 41b, 47b, 50a, 55b, 58b; 23:1a, 23b, 51a; 24:11a, 13a, 30b, 31d, 36c, 43, 51c	23	1:16, 51, 77b; 4:15b, 29c; 5:6, 20a, 22a, 30a; 6:8b, 23, 26; 8:12; 9:47a; 11:17b, 48c; 13:1c; 20:23a; 23:25b; 24:11b, 16a, 31a, 45	12	2:42; 4:2; 7:42a; 8:23; 9:37a, 57a; 19:11a, 33a; 23:24; 24:5a, 36a, 41a			1	22:55a	2	2:22a; 10:7b	89
Jn.	23	3:22b; 4:52a; 6:7c; 7:44a, 50c; 8:59b; 10:4a, 8, 20a; 11:37, 46a, 49a; 12:36, 37b; 16:4; 17:9, 12a, 12c; 18:5d, 9, 18; 20:24, 26b	10	3:19; 4:38; 10:39b; 11:19b; 12:40a, 40b; 13:12a; 15:25; 17:20; 19:31							2	10:32b; 17:19	35
Ac.	44	2:3b, 6, 11; 3:5b; 4:16; 5:15, 24; 8:15, 16; 9:28, 38c, 39c; 10:46; 11:20, 21, 28; 13:13; 14:27; 15:2b, 4, 9, 9, 12, 23, 38a; 16:22a, 25; 17:4, 12, 33; 19:9, 12b, 12c, 16b, 16c, 19; 21:1, 26b; 23:10a, 10c, 21c, 27a; 26:10; 27:21	23	1:9c, 19, 26; 4:5, 29; 6:1; 7:19, 34a; 9:24a; 12:20b; 13:19b, 27, 32; 14:3, 5a, 13; 16:22b, 24b; 17:26; 22:30b; 23:28c, 29; 26:18a	10	1:9a; 4:1a, 31; 13:2a; 18:6a, 20a; 22:23; 25:17; 28:6b, 17a			1	11:29	3	11:22; 15:22; 20:30	81
Ro.	5	11:12a, 12b, 14, 15; 16:17	20	1:21, 26b; 2:15; 3:3, 13, 13, 15, 16, 18; 10:18, 18; 11:9a, 10, 10, 11a, 12c, 27b; 15:27a, 27b; 16:5			2	1:24b, 24c					27
1 Co.	7	10:5, 7, 8, 9, 10; 12:18; 14:10	3	8:7, 12; 16:19	1	15:10	1	3:19			3	1:2; 5:13; 7:35	15
2 Co.	2	5:15; 6:17	9	3:14a, 15; 5:19b; 6:16b; 8:2, 2, 2; 9:14; 11:15b									11
Gal.			1	2:13b									1
Eph.	2	5:7, 12	1	4:18b					1	6:9c			4
Phl.			1	3:19									1
Col.			1	2:2									1
1 Th.			1	5:13b									1
2 Ti.			2	2:17; 3:9									2
Tit.			2	1:12b, 15							1	1:12a	3
Heb.	4	7:6, 25b; 8:9e; 11:28	13	2:10b; 8:9a, 9b, 10a, 10b, 12, 12, 12; 10:16b, 16c, 17, 17; 11:16b					2	8:11, 11			19
Jas.	1	5:3	2	1:27; 3:3b									3
1 Pt.			2	3:12b, 14									2
2 Pt.	1	2:11	2	2:2, 3									3
1 Jn.	1	4:5b											1
3 Jn.	1	1:9											1
Jd.	1	1:15a	2	1:15b, 16									3
Rev.	12	2:16; 5:11; 8:12; 9:6b, 16, 17a; 11:7a; 12:10b; 14:13b; 19:18; 21:3a, 3e	40	6:11b, 11c; 7:3, 9b, 17c; 9:5c, 7, 7, 8, 9, 10, 10, 17b, 18, 19a, 19b, 19c; 11:5b, 5c, 6a, 8, 9, 9, 12c; 12:8; 13:16b, 16c; 14:5, 11a, 13a; 17:17; 18:11b; 19:19a, 21b; 20:12, 13c; 21:3f, 4, 8; 22:4c	1	22:14b					1	17:9	54
Total	210		198		42		3		5		16		474

Miscellaneous: Mt. 5:3, 10, theirs; Mt. 21:7b (with 1883), thereon; Mt. 24:31b (with 206), the other; Lk. 2:22a, her; Lk. 10:7b (with 3744), as they give; Jn. 10:32b, those; Jn. 17:19, their sakes; Ac. 11:22, these things; Ac. 15:22, their own company; Ac. 20:30, own selves; 1 Co. 1:2, theirs; 1 Co. 5:13 (with 5116), yourselves; 1 Co. 7:35, your own; Tit. 1:12a, themselves; Rev. 17:9, which.

846q. ὁ αὐτός, ho autos′

Book	Oc.	the same	Oc.	together (with 1909)	Oc.	the same thing	Oc.	one place	Oc.	be like minded (with 5326)	Oc.	be of the same mind (with 5326)	Oc.	Not Tr.	Oc.	Misc.	Total
Mt.	3	5:46; 26:44b; 27:44a	1	22:34													4
Mk.	1	14:39													1	10:10b	2
Lk.	4	2:8; 6:33, 38; 23:40b	1	17:35													5
Ac.			4	1:15; 2:44; 3:1; 4:26a	1	15:27b	1	2:1							1	14:1a	7
Ro.	3	9:21; 10:12; 12:4			1	2:1			1	15:5	1	12:16					6
1 Co.	12	1:10b, 10c; 10: 3, 4; 12:4, 5, 6, 8, 9, 9, 25; 15: 39			1	1:10a	2	11:20; 14:23					1	7:5	2	11:5; 12:11	18
2 Co.	8	1:6; 3:14b, 18; 4:13; 6:13; 8: 16; 12:18, 18													1	13:11	9
Eph.					1	6:9											1
Phl.	3	1:30; 2:2b; 3: 16a			1	3:1			1	2:2a	1	4:2			2	2:18; 3:16b	8
Heb.	7	1:12; 2:14b; 4:11; 6:11; 10: 11; 11:9; 13:8													1	10:1	8
Jas.	2	3:10, 11															2
1 Pt.	3	4:1, 4; 5:9															3
1 Jn.	1	2:27b															1
Total	47		6		5		3		2		2		1		8		74

Miscellaneous: Mk. 10:10b, the same matter; Ac. 14:1a (with 2596), together; 1 Co. 11:5, all as if; 1 Co. 12:11, the self same; 2 Co. 13:11 (with 5326), be of one mind; Phl. 2:18, the same cause; Phl. 3:16b (with 5326), mind the same thing; Heb. 10:1, those.

Word 846 has 5117 occurrences.

847. αὐτοῦ, autou′

Book	Oc.	there	Oc.	here	Total
Mt.			1	26:36	1
Ac.	3	15:34; 18:19; 21:4			3
Total	3		1		4

The following word is a reflexive pronoun and is formed by the oblique cases of Word 846. It is only distinguished in all its forms from the cases of Word 846 by the aspirate or rough breathing mark. Note the breathing mark is in reverse order to the breathing mark on Word 846.

848a. αὑτοῦ, hautou′

Book	Oc.	his	Oc.	his own	Oc.	he	Oc.	Misc.	Total
Mt.	97	1:21, 24; 3:4, 4, 7, 12, 12; 4:6; 5:2, 22, 22, 28, 31, 32, 45; 6:27, 29; 7:24, 26; 9:7, 37, 38; 10:1, 10, 24, 35a, 38, 39, 39, 42; 11:1, 2; 12:49, 49; 13:24, 31, 41, 52; 14:2, 3, 22; 15:6, 6, 32, 36; 16:13, 20, 21, 24, 24, 25, 25, 26b, 27, 27, 28; 18:23, 28, 35; 19:3, 5, 9, 23, 28; 20:1, 2, 8,28; 21:34, 37; 22:2, 3, 5, 7, 8, 24, 25, 25; 23:1; 24:17, 18, 31, 43, 45, 47, 48; 25:14, 18, 31, 31, 33, 34; 26:1, 39, 45, 51, 65	5	13:54, 57, 57; 16:26a; 27: 60					102
Mk.	51	1:6; 2:8; 3:7, 9; 4:2, 34; 6:17, 21, 21, 41, 45; 7:12, 12, 33; 8:1, 6, 10, 12, 27, 33, 34, 34, 35, 35, 37, 38; 9:18, 31, 41; 10:7, 7, 11, 23, 45, 50; 11:1, 23; 12:6, 19, 38, 43a; 13:15, 16, 27, 27, 34, 34, 34; 14:13, 32,63	4	6:1, 4, 4; 8:36			1	5:30	56
Lk.	70	1:15, 48, 51, 54, 68, 69, 70, 72; 2:28; 3:17, 17; 4:10; 6:13, 20, 20, 40, 45, 45; 7:1, 3, 12, 16, 19; 8:5, 41; 9:1, 14, 23, 24, 24, 43, 51, 52, 62; 10:1, 2, 7; 11:1; 12:1, 22, 25, 27, 39, 42, 45; 13:6, 15; 14:17, 21, 21, 27; 15:13, 15, 16, 22; 16:1, 18, 23, 24; 17:24, 33; 18:13, 14; 19:29; 20:28, 45; 22:36; 23:11; 24:26, 50	6	1:23; 4:24; 5: 25, 29; 9:26; 18:7	1	12:44	1	1:58	78
Jn.	28	2:11, 21; 3:4, 16, 17; 4:5; 5:9; 6:3, 12, 22; 10:11; 11:54; 12:25, 25; 13:12, 16, 18; 15:13, 13, 20; 17:1; 18:1, 2; 19:17, 26; 20:20, 30; 21:14	1	7:53			1	9:21	30
Ac.	34	2:14; 3:2, 13, 18, 21, 26; 5:1, 31; 7:10, 13, 14, 14, 20, 23, 25; 8:28, 32, 35, 39; 9:8; 10:2, 7, 22, 24; 12:11; 13:36; 14:3, 8; 15:14, 18; 16:34; 18:8; 22:14; 24:24	1	21:11	1	20:36	1	5:37	37
Ro.	9	1:2, 3; 3:25, 26; 8:29; 9:22, 23; 11:1, 2							9
1 Co.	6	2:10; 6:5; 7:36, 37; 9:10; 11:4	1	6:14					7
2 Co.	2	2:14; 11:3							2
Gal.	4	1:15, 16; 4:4, 6							4
Eph.	13	1:5b, 6, 9a, 9b, 17; 2:4, 7, 15; 3:16, 16; 4:25; 5:31, 31	2	1:11, 20					15
Phl.	1	4:19							1
Col.	4	1:13, 22, 22; 2:18							4
1 Th.	2	4:6, 8							2
2 Th.	4	1:7, 10; 2:8, 8							4
1 Ti.	1	5:18							1
2 Ti.	4	2:19; 4:1, 1, 18							4
Tit.	2	1:3; 3:5							2
Heb.	18	1:3, 7, 7; 3:18; 4:4; 5:7; 6:17; 8:11, 11; 10:20, 30; 11:7, 21, 22, 23; 12:16; 13:21, 21	3	2:4; 3:6; 4:10			1	9:26	22
Jas.	9	1:8, 11, 18, 23, 25, 26a; 2:21; 3:13; 4:11	1	1:26b	2	1:9, 10			12
1 Pt.	5	1:3; 2:9; 3:10, 10; 5:10	1	2:24					6
2 Pt.	1	1:9							1
1 Jn.	18	2:9, 10, 11; 3:10, 12, 15a, 16, 17, 17; 4:9, 10, 13, 20, 20, 21; 5:9, 10, 16							18
Jd.	2	1:14, 24							2
Rev.	42	1:1, 1, 1, 6, 16, 16, 17; 2:1, 5, 18; 6:5; 10:2, 2, 5; 12:3, 15, 16b; 13:2, 2, 6; 14:9, 9, 14, 14, 16, 19; 16:2, 3, 4, 8, 10a, 12, 15, 17, 19; 17:17a; 19:2b, 16; 20:1, 7; 22:6, 6	1	1:5					43
Total	427		26		4		5		462

Miscellaneous: Mk. 5:30, him; Lk. 1:58, great; Jn. 9:21, himself; Ac. 5:37, him; Heb. 9:26, himself.

848b. αὐτῶν, hautōn′

Book	Oc.	their	Oc.	their own	Oc.	Not Tr.	Oc.	Misc.	Total
Mt.	31	2:11; 3:6; 4:21, 22; 6:2, 5, 7, 16, 16; 7:6; 10:17; 11:16; 13:15, 43; 15:2, 8, 27; 17:6, 8; 18:31; 21:7; 22:16; 23:4, 5, 5, 5; 25:1, 4, 4, 7; 27:39	2	2:12; 17:25					33
Mk.	8	1:5, 18, 20; 2:6; 11:7, 8; 14:46; 15:29	1	8:3					9
Lk.	10	1:20, 66; 2:8; 3:15; 5:15; 6:17; 16:4; 19:36; 21:1, 12	1	2:39	1	1:7			12
Jn.	1	15:22							1
Ac.	13	5:18; 7:39, 57, 58; 13:50, 51; 14:11, 14; 15:26; 16:19; 19:18; 22:22; 28:27	2	7:41; 14:16			2	7:54; 20:30	17
Ro.	5	1:21, 27, 27; 2:15; 3:13							5
Eph.	1	4:17							1
1 Th.	1	2:16							1
Heb.	2	7:5; 11:35							2
2 Pt.	2	3:3, 16	2	2:12, 13					4
Jd.			1	1:16					1
Rev.	31	2:22; 3:4; 4:4, 10; 6:14; 7:11, 14a; 9:4, 20, 21, 21, 21, 21; 11:7, 11, 16, 16; 12:11, 11; 14:1, 2, 13; 16:10b, 11, 11, 11; 17:17; 18:19; 20:4, 4; 21:24					2	7:14b; 9:11	33
Total	105		9		1		4		119

Miscellaneous: Ac. 7:54, the; Ac. 20:30, them; Rev. 7:14b (with 4649), them; Rev. 9:11, them.

848c. αὐτῆς, hautẹs′

Book	Oc.	her	Oc.	her own	Oc.	it	Oc.	his	Oc.	Not Tr.	Total
Mt.	9	1:25; 2:18; 10:35b, 35c; 11:19; 14:8, 11; 20:20; 24:29									9
Mk.	9	6:24, 28; 7:26, 30; 10:12; 12:43b, 44, 44; 13:24									9
Lk.	12	1:36; 2:7, 19, 36, 51; 7:35, 38, 44; 10:38; 12:53, 53; 21:4	1	1:56					1	1:18	14
Jn.	4	4:28; 11:2, 28; 12:3									4
Ac.	2	9:40; 16:16									2
Gal.	1	4:25									1
Jas.	1	5:18									1
Rev.	12	2:21; 6:13; 12:14, 16a; 14:8; 17:4, 4, 5; 18:7; 19:2a; 21:2; 22:2			1	8:12	1	2:5			14
Total	50		1		1		1		1		54

848d. αὐτούς, hautous′

Book	themselves	Total
Mk.	1:27	1

848e. αὐτήν, hautẹn′

Book	thee	Total
Mt.	23:37	1
Lk.	13:34	1
Total		2

848f. αὐτοῖς, hautois′

Book	Oc.	them-selves	Oc.	they	Oc.	their own	Oc.	them	Total
Jn.	1	17:13							1
Ac.			1	27:27			1	13:42	2
Heb.					1	12:10			1
Total	1		1		1		1		4

848g. αὐτόν, hauton′

Book	Oc.	him	Oc.	himself	Oc.	Not Tr.	Total
Mt.	1	8:18					1
Mk.	1	3:34					1
Lk.	1	18:40					1
Jn.	1	6:5	1	19:12			2
Ac.					1	25:21	1
Eph.			1	1:5			1
Col.			1	1:20			1
Heb.			1	12:3			1
Total	4		4		1		9

848h. αὐτῷ, hautō′

Book	Oc.	him	Oc.	himself	Total
Lk.	1	19:15			1
Ac.	3	9:4; 16:3; 23:2			3
Eph.			1	1:9c	1
Col.	1	2:15			1
Heb.	1	12:2			1
1 Jn.	1	3:15b			1
Total	7		1		8

Word 848 has 659 occurrences.

849. αὐτόχειρ, autoch′eir

Book	with (one's) own hands	Total
Ac.	27:19	1

850. αὐχμηρός, auchmẹros′

Book	dark	Total
2 Pt.	1:19	1

851. ἀφαιρέω, aphaire′ō

Book	Oc.	take away	Oc.	cut off	Oc.	smite off	Total
Mt.					1	26:51	1
Mk.			1	14:47			1
Lk.	3	1:25; 10:42; 16:3	1	22:50			4
Ro.	1	11:27					1
Heb.	1	10:4					1
Rev.	2	22:19, 19					2
Total	7		2		1		10

852. ἀφανής, aphanẹs′

Book	that is not manifest	Total
Heb.	4:13	1

853. ἀφανίζω, aphanid′zō

Book	Oc.	corrupt	Oc.	disfigure	Oc.	perish	Oc.	vanish away	Total
Mt.	2	6:19, 20	1	6:16					3
Ac.					1	13:41			1
Jas.							1	4:14	1
Total	2		1		1		1		5

854. ἀφανισμός, aphanismos′

Book	vanish away	Total
Heb.	8:13	1

855. ἄφαντος, aph′antos

Book	vanish out of sight (with 575)	Total
Lk.	24:31	1

856. ἀφεδρών, aphedrōn′

Book	draught	Total
Mt.	15:17	1
Mk.	7:19	1
Total		2

857. ἀφειδία, apheidi′a

Book	neglecting	Total
Col.	2:23	1

858. ἀφελότης, aphelot′ẹs

Book	singleness	Total
Ac.	2:46	1

859. ἄφεσις, aph′esis

Book	Oc.	remission	Oc.	forgiveness	Oc.	deliverance	Oc.	liberty	Total
Mt.	1	26:28							1
Mk.	1	1:4	1	3:29					2
Lk.	3	1:77; 3:3; 24:47			1	4:18a	1	4:18b	5
Ac.	2	2:38; 10:43	3	5:31; 13:38; 26:18					5
Eph.			1	1:7					1
Col.			1	1:14					1
Heb.	2	9:22; 10:18							2
Total	9		6		1		1		17

860. ἀφή, haphē′

Book	joint	Total
Eph.	4:16	1
Col.	2:19	1
Total		2

861. ἀφθαρσία, aphtharsi′a

Book	Oc.	incorruption	Oc.	immortality	Oc.	sincerity	Total
Ro.			1	2:7			1
1 Co.	4	15:42, 50, 53, 54					4
Eph.					1	6:24	1
2 Ti.			1	1:10			1
Tit.					1	2:7	1
Total	4		2		2		8

862. ἄφθαρτος, aph′thartos

Book	Oc.	incorruptible	Oc.	uncorruptible	Oc.	immortal	Oc.	not corruptible	Total
Ro.			1	1:23					1
1 Co.	2	9:25; 15:52							2
1 Ti.					1	1:17			1
1 Pt.	2	1:4, 23					1	3:4	3
Total	4		1		1		1		7

863. ἀφίημι, aphi′ēmi

Book	Oc.	leave	Oc.	forgive	Oc.	suffer	Oc.	let	Oc.	forsake	Oc.	let alone	Oc.	Misc.	Total
Mt.	14	4:11, 20, 22; 5:24; 8:15; 18:12; 22:22, 25; 23:23b, 38; 24:2, 40, 41; 26:44	17	6:12, 12, 14, 14, 15, 15; 9:2, 5, 6; 12:31, 31, 32, 32; 18:21, 27, 32, 35	4	3:15, 15; 19:14; 23:13	3	7:4; 8:22; 13:30	3	19:27, 29; 26:56	1	15:14	5	5:40; 13:36; 23:23a; 27:49, 50	47
Mk.	12	1:20, 31; 8:13; 10:28, 29; 12:12, 19, 20, 21, 22; 13:2, 34	10	2:5, 7, 9, 10; 3:28; 4:12; 11:25, 25, 26, 26	6	1:34; 5:19, 37; 7:12; 10:14; 11:16	1	7:27	2	1:18; 14:50	2	14:6; 15:36	4	4:36; 7:8; 11:6; 15:37	37
Lk.	11	4:39; 10:30; 11:42; 13:35; 17:34, 35, 36; 18:28, 29; 19:44; 21:6	15	5:20, 21, 23, 24; 7:47, 47, 48, 49; 11:4, 4; 12:10, 10; 17:3, 4; 23:34	3	8:51; 12:39; 18:16	2	6:42; 9:60	1	5:11	1	13:8			33
Jn.	9	4:3, 28, 52; 8:29; 10:12; 14:18, 27; 16:28, 32					2	11:44; 18:8			2	11:48; 12:7	2	20:23, 23	15
Ac.	1	14:17	1	8:22											2
Ro.	1	1:27	1	4:7											2
1 Co.	1	7:13											2	7:11, 12	3
Heb.	2	2:8; 6:1													2
Jas.			1	5:15											1
1 Jn.			2	1:9; 2:12											2
Rev.	1	2:4			1	11:9									2
Total	52		47		14		8		6		6		13		146

Miscellaneous: Mt. 5:40, let have; Mt. 13:36, send away; Mt. 23:23a, omit; Mt. 27:49, let be; Mt. 27:50, yield up; Mk. 4:36, send away; Mk. 7:8, lay aside; Mk. 11:6, let go; Mk. 15:37, cry; Jn. 20:23, 23, remit; 1 Co. 7:11, 12, put away.

864. ἀφικνέομαι, aphikne′omai

Book	come abroad	Total
Ro.	16:19	1

865. ἀφιλάγαθος, aphilag′athos

Book	despiser of those that are good	Total
2 Ti.	3:3	1

866. ἀφιλάργυρος, aphilar′guros

Book	Oc.	not covetous	Oc.	without covetousness	Total
1 Ti.	1	3:3			1
Heb.			1	13:5	1
Total	1		1		2

867. ἄφιξις, aph′ixis

Book	departing	Total
Ac.	20:29	1

868. ἀφίστημι, aphis′tēmi

Book	Oc.	depart	Oc.	draw away	Oc.	fall away	Oc.	refrain	Oc.	withdraw self	Oc.	depart from	Total
Lk.	3	2:37; 4:13; 13:27			1	8:13							4
Ac.	4	12:10; 15:38; 19:9; 22:29	1	5:37			1	5:38					6
2 Co.	1	12:8											1
1 Ti.									1	6:5	1	4:1	2
2 Ti.	1	2:19											1
Heb.	1	3:12											1
Total	10		1		1		1		1		1		15

869. ἄφνω, aph′nō

Book	suddenly	Total
Ac.	2:2; 16:26; 28:6	3

870. ἀφόβως, aphob′ōs

Book	without fear	Total
Lk.	1:74	1
1 Co.	16:10	1
Phl.	1:14	1
Jd.	1:12	1
Total		4

871. ἀφομοιόω, aphomoio′ō

Book	make like	Total
Heb.	7:3	1

872. ἀφοράω, aphora′ō

Book	Oc.	look	Oc.	see	Total
Phl.			1	2:23	1
Heb.	1	12:2			1
Total	1		1		2

873. ἀφορίζω, aphorid′zō

Book	Oc.	separate	Oc.	divide	Oc.	sever	Total
Mt.	1	25:32a	1	25:32b	1	13:49	3
Lk.	1	6:22					1
Ac.	2	13:2; 19:9					2
Ro.	1	1:1					1
2 Co.	1	6:17					1
Gal.	2	1:15; 2:12					2
Total	8		1		1		10

874. ἀφορμή, aphormē′

Book	occasion	Total
Ro.	7:8, 11	2
2 Co.	5:12; 11:12, 12	3
Gal.	5:13	1
1 Ti.	5:14	1
Total		7

875. ἀφρίζω, aphrid'zō

Book	foam	Total
Mk.	9:18, 20	2

876. ἀφρός, aphros'

Book	that (one) foameth again (with 3226)	Total
Lk.	9:39	1

877. ἀφροσύνη, aphrosu'nē

Book	Oc.	foolishly (with 1722)	Oc.	foolishness	Oc.	folly	Total
Mk.			1	7:22			1
2 Co.	2	11:17, 21			1	11:1	3
Total	2		1		1		4

878. ἄφρων, aph'rōn

Book	Oc.	fool	Oc.	foolish	Oc.	unwise	Total
Lk.	2	11:40; 12:20					2
Ro.			1	2:20			1
1 Co.	1	15:36					1
2 Co.	5	11:16, 16, 19; 12:6, 11					5
Eph.					1	5:17	1
1 Pt.			1	2:15			1
Total	8		2		1		11

880. ἄφωνος, aph'ōnos

Book	Oc.	dumb	Oc.	without signification	Total
Ac.	1	8:32			1
1 Co.	1	12:2	1	14:10	2
2 Pt.	1	2:16			1
Total	3		1		4

879. ἀφυπνόω, aphupno'ō

Book	fall asleep	Total
Lk.	8:23	1

881. 'Αχάζ, Achadz'

Book	Achaz	Total
Mt.	1:9, 9	2

882. 'Αχαΐα, Achai'a

Book	Achaia	Total
Ac.	18:12, 27; 19:21	3
Ro.	15:26; 16:5	2
1 Co.	16:15	1
2 Co.	1:1; 9:2; 11:10	3
1 Th.	1:7, 8	2
Total		11

883. 'Αχαϊκός, Achaikos'

Book	Achaicus	Total
1 Co.	16:17	1

884. ἀχάριστος, achar'istos

Book	unthankful	Total
Lk.	6:35	1
2 Ti.	3:2	1
Total		2

885. 'Αχείμ, Acheim'

Book	Achim	Total
Mt.	1:14	1

886. ἀχειροποίητος, acheiropoi'ētos

Book	Oc.	made without hands	Oc.	not made with hands	Total
Mk.	1	14:58			1
2 Co.			1	5:1	1
Col.	1	2:11			1
Total	2		1		3

887. ἀχλύς, achlus'

Book	mist	Total
Ac.	13:11	1

888. ἀχρεῖος, achrei'os

Book	unprofitable	Total
Mt.	25:30	1
Lk.	17:10	1
Total		2

889. ἀχρειόω, achreio'ō

Book	become unprofitable	Total
Ro.	3:12	1

890. ἄχρηστος, ach'rēstos

Book	unprofitable	Total
Phe.	1:11	1

892. ἄχυρον, ach'uron

Book	chaff	Total
Mt.	3:12	1
Lk.	3:17	1
Total		2

891. ἄχρι, ach' ri

Book	Oc.	until	Oc.	unto	Oc.	till	Oc.	till (with 3639 and 302)	Oc.	till (with 3639)	Oc.	until (with 3639)	Oc.	while (with 3639)	Oc.	even to	Oc.	Misc.	Total
Mt.	1	24:38																	1
Lk.	3	1:20; 17:27; 21:24															1	4:13	4
Ac.	3	1:2; 3:21; 23:1	5	2:29; 13:6; 22:4, 22; 26:22	1	20:11			1	7:18			1	27:33	1	11:5	4	13:11; 20:4, 6; 28:15	16
Ro.	2	5:13; 8:22									1	11:25					1	1:13	4
1 Co.			1	4:11			2	11:26; 15:25											3
2 Co.	1	3:14	1	10:13													1	10:14	3
Gal.	1	4:2							1	3:19	1	4:19							3
Phl.	2	1:5, 6																	2
Heb.			1	6:11									1	3:13	1	4:12			3
Rev.	1	17:17	5	2:10, 26; 12:11; 14:20; 18:5	2	15:8; 20:3	1	2:25	1	7:3									10
Total	14		13		3		3		3		2		2		2		7		49

Miscellaneous: Lk. 4:13; Ac. 13:11, for; Ac. 20:4, into; Ac. 20:6, in; Ac. 28:15, as far as; Ro. 1:13 (with 1204 and 3488), hitherto; 2 Co. 10:14, as far as.

893. ἀψευδής, apseudēs'

Book	that cannot lie	Total
Tit.	1:2	1

894a. "Αψινθος, Ap'sinthos

Book	Wormwood	Total
Rev.	8:11a	1

894b. ἄψινθος, ap'sinthos

Book	wormwood	Total
Rev.	8:11b	1

Word 894 has 2 occurrences.

895. ἄψυχος, ap'suchos

Book	without life	Total
1 Co.	14:7	1

896. Βάαλ, Ba'al

Book	Baal	Total
Ro.	11:4	1

897. Βαβυλών, Babulōn'

Book	Babylon	Total
Mt.	1:11, 12, 17, 17	4
Ac.	7:43	1
1 Pt.	5:13	1
Rev.	14:8; 16:19; 17:5; 18:2, 10, 21	6
Total		12

898. βαθμός, bathmos'

Book	degree	Total
1 Ti.	3:13	1

899. βάθος, bath'os

Book	Oc.	depth	Oc.	deep	Oc.	deep (with 2596)	Oc.	deepness	Oc.	deep thing	Total
Mt.							1	13:5			1
Mk.	1	4:5									1
Lk.			1	5:4							1
Ro.	2	8:39; 11:33									2
1 Co.									1	2:10	1
2 Co.					1	8:2					1
Eph.	1	3:18									1
Rev.	1	2:24									1
Total	5		1		1		1		1		9

900. βαθύνω, bathu'nō

Book	dig deep (with 4526)	Total
Lk.	6:48	1

901. βαθύς, bathus'

Book	Oc.	deep	Oc.	very early in the morning (with 3622)	Total
Lk.			1	24:1	1
Jn.	1	4:11			1
Ac.	1	20:9			1
Total	2		1		3

902. βαΐον, bai'on

Book	branch	Total
Jn.	12:13	1

903. Βαλαάμ, Balaam'

Book	Balaam	Total
2 Pt.	2:15	1
Jd.	1:11	1
Rev.	2:14	1
Total		3

904. Βαλάκ, Balak'

Book	Balac	Total
Rev.	2:14	1

905. βαλάντιον, balan'tion

Book	Oc.	purse	Oc.	bag	Total
Lk.	3	10:4; 22:35, 36	1	12:33	4

906. βάλλω, bal'lō

Book	Oc.	cast	Oc.	put	Oc.	thrust	Oc.	cast out	Oc.	lay	Oc.	lie	Oc.	Misc.	Total
Mt.	26	3:10; 4:6, 18; 5:13, 25, 29, 29, 30, 30; 6:30; 7:6, 19; 13:42, 47, 48, 50; 15:26; 17:27; 18:8, 8, 9, 9, 30; 21:21; 27:35, 35	4	9:17, 17; 25: 27; 27:6					1	8:14	2	8:6; 9:2	3	10:34, 34; 26:12	36
Mk.	15	1:16; 4:26; 7:27; 9:22, 42, 45, 47; 11: 23; 12:41, 41, 43, 43, 44, 44; 15:24	2	2:22; 7:33					1	7:30			2	12:42; 14: 65	20
Lk.	13	3:9; 4:9; 12:28, 58; 13:19; 21:1, 2, 3, 4, 4; 23:19, 25, 34	1	5:37			1	14:35	1	16:20			2	12:49; 13: 8	18
Jn.	9	3:24; 8:7, 59; 15:6, 6; 19:24; 21:6, 6, 7	4	5:7; 12:6; 13:2; 20:25	2	20:25, 27							2	13:5; 18:11	17
Ac.	2	16:23, 37			1	16:24							2	22:23; 27: 14	5
Jas.			1	3:3											1
1 Jn.	1	4:18													1
Rev.	20	2:10, 14, 22; 4:10; 6:13; 8:5, 7, 8; 12: 4, 13, 15, 16; 14:19b; 18:19, 21; 19:20; 20:3, 10, 14, 15	1	2:24	2	14:16, 19a	3	12:9, 9, 9					1	18:21	27
Total	86		13		5		4		3		2		12		125

Miscellaneous: Mt. 10:34, 34, send; Mt. 26:12, pour; Mk. 12:42, throw; Mk. 14:65, strike; Lk. 12:49, send; Lk. 13:8 (with 2874), dung; Jn. 13:5, pour; Jn. 18:11, put up; Ac. 22:23, throw; Ac. 27:14, arise; Rev. 18:21, throw down.

907. βαπτίζω, baptid'zō

Book	Oc.	baptize	Oc.	wash	Oc.	baptist	Oc.	baptized (with 2258)	Total
Mt.	11	3:6, 11, 11, 13, 14, 16; 20:22, 22, 23, 23; 28:19							11
Mk.	10	1:4, 5, 8, 8, 9; 10:38, 38, 39, 39; 16:16	1	7:4	1	6:14			12
Lk.	9	3:7, 12, 16, 16, 21, 21; 7:29, 30; 12:50	1	11:38					10
Jn.	12	1:25, 26, 28, 31, 33, 33; 3:22, 23, 23, 26; 4:1, 2					1	10:40	13
Ac.	21	1:5, 5; 2:38, 41; 8:12, 13, 16, 36, 38; 9:18; 10:47, 48; 11:16, 16; 16:15, 33; 18: 8; 19:3, 4, 5; 22:16							21
Ro.	2	6:3, 3							2
1 Co.	10	1:13, 14, 15, 16, 16, 17; 10:2; 12:13; 15:29, 29							10
Gal.	1	3:27							1
Total	76		2		1		1		80

908. βάπτισμα, bap'tisma

Book	baptism	Total
Mt.	3:7; 20:22, 23; 21:25	4
Mk.	1:4; 10:38, 39; 11:30	4
Lk.	3:3; 7:29; 12:50; 20:4	4
Ac.	1:22; 10:37; 13:24; 18: 25; 19:3, 4	6
Ro.	6:4	1
Eph.	4:5	1
Col.	2:12	1
1 Pt.	3:21	1
Total		22

909. βαπτισμός, baptismos'

Book	Oc.	washing	Oc.	baptism	Total
Mk.	2	7:4, 8			2
Heb.	1	9:10	1	6:2	2
Total	3		1		4

910. Βαπτιστής, Baptistes'

Book	Baptist	Total
Mt.	3:1; 11:11, 12; 14:2, 8; 16:14; 17:13	7
Mk.	6:24, 25; 8:28	3
Lk.	7:20, 28, 33; 9:19	4
Total		14

911. βάπτω, bap'tō

Book	dip	Total
Lk.	16:24	1
Jn.	13:26	1
Rev.	19:13	1
Total		3

912. βαραββᾶς, Barabbas'

Book	Barabbas	Total
Mt.	27:16, 17, 20, 21, 26	5
Mk.	15:7, 11, 15	3
Lk.	23:18	1
Jn.	18:40, 40	2
Total		11

913. Βαράκ, Barak'

Book	Barak	Total
Heb.	11:32	1

914. Βαραχίας, Barachi'as

Book	Barachias	Total
Mt.	23:35	1

915. βάρβαρος, bar'baros

Book	Oc.	barbarian	Oc.	barbarous	Total
Ac.	1	28:4	1	28:2	2
Ro.	1	1:14			1
1 Co.	2	14:11, 11			2
Col.	1	3:11			1
Total	5		1		6

916. βαρέω, bare'ō

Book	Oc.	be heavy	Oc.	be pressed	Oc.	be burdened	Oc.	be charged	Total
Mt.	1	26:43							1
Mk.	1	14:40							1
Lk.	1	9:32							1
2 Co.			1	1:8	1	5:4			2
1 Ti.							1	5:16	1
Total	3		1		1		1		6

917. βαρέως, bare'ōs

Book	dull	Total
Mt.	13:15	1
Ac.	28:27	1
Total		2

918. Βαρθολομαῖος Bartholomai'os

Book	Bartholomew	Total
Mt.	10:3	1
Mk.	3:18	1
Lk.	6:14	1
Ac.	1:13	1
Total		4

919. Βαριησοῦς, Bariesous'

Book	Barjesus	Total
Ac.	13:6	1

920. Βαριωνᾶς, Bariōnas'

Book	Barjona	Total
Mt.	16:17	1

921. Βαρνάβας, Barnab'as

Book	Barnabas	Total
Ac.	4:36; 9:27; 11:22, 25, 30; 12:25; 13:1, 2, 7, 43, 46, 50; 14:12, 14, 20; 15:2, 2, 12, 22, 25, 35, 36, 37, 39	24
1 Co.	9:6	1
Gal.	2:1, 9, 13	3
Col.	4:10	1
Total		29

922. βάρος, bar′os

Book	Oc.	burden	Oc.	burdensome (with 1722)	Oc.	weight	Total
Mt.	1	20:12					1
Ac.	1	15:28					1
2 Co.					1	4:17	1
Gal.	1	6:2					1
1 Th.			1	2:6			1
Rev.	1	2:24					1
Total	4		1		1		6

923. Βαρσαβᾶς, Barsabas′

Book	Oc.	Joseph	Oc.	Judas	Total
Ac.	1	1:23	1	15:22	2

924. Βαρτιμαῖος, Bartimai′os

Book	Bartimaeus	Total
Mk.	10:46	1

925. βαρύνω, baru′nō

Book	be overcharged	Total
Lk.	21:34	1

926. βαρύς, barus′

Book	Oc.	grievous	Oc.	heavy	Oc.	weighty	Oc.	weightier	Total
Mt.			1	23:4			1	23:23	2
Ac.	2	20:29; 25:7							2
2 Co.					1	10:10			1
1 Jn.	1	5:3							1
Total	3		1		1		1		6

927. βαρύτιμος, baru′timos

Book	very precious	Total
Mt.	26:7	1

929. βασανισμός, basanismos′

Book	torment	Total
Rev.	9:5, 5; 14:11; 18:7, 10, 15	6

930. βασανιστής, basanistes′

Book	tormentor	Total
Mt.	18:34	1

931. βάσανος, bas′anos

Book	torment	Total
Mt.	4:24	1
Lk.	16:23, 28	2
Total		3

928. βασανίζω, basanid′zō

Book	Oc.	torment	Oc.	pain	Oc.	toss	Oc.	vex	Oc.	toil	Total
Mt.	2	8:6, 29			1	14:24					3
Mk.	1	5:7							1	6:48	2
Lk.	1	8:28									1
2 Pt.							1	2:8			1
Rev.	4	9:5; 11:10; 14:10; 20:10	1	12:2							5
Total	8		1		1		1		1		12

933. βασίλειον, basil′eion

Book	king's court (with 3488)	Total
Lk.	7:25	1

934. βασίλειος, basil′eios

Book	royal	Total
1 Pt.	2:9	1

932. βασιλεία, basilei′a

Book	Oc.	kingdom (of God)	Oc.	kingdom (of heaven)	Oc.	kingdom (general or evil)	Oc.	(Thy or Thine) kingdom	Oc.	(His) kingdom	Oc.	the kingdom	Oc.	(My) kingdom	Oc.	Misc.	Total
Mt.	5	6:33; 12:28; 19:24; 21:31, 43	32	3:2; 4:17; 5:3, 10, 19, 19, 20; 7:21; 8:11; 10:7; 11:11, 12; 13:11, 24, 31, 33, 44, 45, 47, 52; 16:19; 18:1, 3, 4, 23; 19:12, 14, 23; 20:1; 22:2; 23:13; 25:1	5	4:8; 12:25, 26; 24:7, 7	3	6:10, 13; 20:21	2	13:41; 16:28					9	4:23; 8:12; 9:35; 13:19, 38, 43; 24:14; 25:34; 26:29	56
Mk.	15	1:14, 15; 4:11, 26, 30; 9:1, 47; 10:14, 15, 23, 24, 25; 12:34; 14:25; 15:43			5	3:24, 24; 6:23; 13:8, 8									1	11:10	21
Lk.	33	4:43; 6:20; 7:28; 8:1, 10; 9:2, 11, 27, 60, 62; 10:9, 11; 11:20; 12:31; 13:18, 20, 28, 29; 14:15; 16:16; 17:20, 20, 21; 18:16, 17, 24, 25, 29; 19:11; 21:31; 22:16, 18; 23:51			5	4:5; 11:17, 18; 21:10, 10	2	11:2; 23:42	1	1:33	2	12:32; 19:15	1	22:30	2	19:12; 22:29	46
Jn.	2	3:3, 5											3	18:36, 36, 36			5
Ac.	7	1:3; 8:12; 14:22; 19:8; 20:25; 28:23, 31									1	1:6					8
Ro.	1	14:17															1
1 Co.	4	4:20; 6:9, 10; 15:50									1	15:24					5
Gal.	1	5:21															1
Eph.															1	5:5	1
Col.	1	4:11													1	1:13	2
1 Th.									1	2:12							1
2 Th.	1	1:5															1
2 Ti.									2	4:1, 18							2
Heb.					1	11:33	1	1:8							1	12:28	3
Jas.															1	2:5	1
2 Pt.															1	1:11	1
Rev.	1	12:10			4	11:15; 16:10; 17:12, 17					1	1:9			1	17:18	7
Total	71		32		20		6		6		5		4		18		162

Miscellaneous: Mt. 4:23, Gospel of the kingdom; Mt. 8:12, children of the kingdom; Mt. 9:35, Gospel of the kingdom; Mt. 13:19, word of the kingdom; Mt. 13:38, children of the kingdom; Mt. 13:43, kingdom of their Father; Mt. 24:14, Gospel of the kingdom; Mt. 25:34, kingdom prepared; Mt. 26:29, My Father's kingdom; Mk. 11:10, kingdom of our father David; Lk. 19:12; 22:29, a kingdom; Eph. 5:5, the kingdom of Christ and of God; Col. 1:13, the kingdom of His dear Son; Heb. 12:28, a kingdom; Jas. 2:5, heirs of the kingdom; 2 Pt. 1:11, kingdom of our Lord; Rev. 17:18 (with 2192), reign.

935. βασιλεύς, basileus′

Book	Oc.	king	Oc.	King (of Jews)	Oc.	King (God or Christ)	Oc.	King (of Israel)	Total
Mt.	14	1:6, 6; 2:1, 3, 9; 10:18; 11:8; 14:9; 17:25; 18:23; 22:2, 7, 11, 13	4	2:2; 27:11, 29, 27, 37	4	5:35; 21:5; 25:34, 40	1	27:42	23
Mk.	6	6:14, 22, 25, 26, 27; 13:9	5	15:2, 9, 12, 18, 26			1	15:32	12
Lk.	6	1:5; 10:24; 14:31, 31; 21:12; 22:25	3	23:3, 37, 38	2	19:38; 23:2			11
Jn.	5	6:15; 18:37, 37; 19:12, 15b	9	12:15; 18:33, 39; 19:3, 14, 15a; 19:19, 21, 21			2	1:49; 12:13	16
Ac.	20	4:26; 7:10, 18; 9:15; 12:1, 20; 13:21, 22; 17:7; 25:13, 14, 24, 26; 26:2, 7, 13, 19, 26, 27, 30							20
2 Co.	1	11:32							1
1 Ti.	1	2:2			2	1:17; 6:15			3
Heb.	7	7:1, 1, 2, 2, 2; 11:23, 27							7
1 Pt.	2	2:13, 17							2
Rev.	20	1:5, 6; 5:10; 6:15; 9:11; 10:11; 16:12, 14; 17:2, 10, 12, 12; 17:14b, 18; 18:3, 9; 19:16b, 18, 19; 21:24			3	15:3; 17:14a; 19:16a			23
Total	82		21		11		4		118

936. βασιλεύω, basileu′ō

Book	Oc.	reign	Oc.	king	Total
Mt.	1	2:22			1
Lk.	3	1:33; 19:14, 27			3
Ro.	6	5:14, 17, 17, 21, 21; 6:12			6
1 Co.	3	4:8, 8; 15:25			3
1 Ti.			1	6:15	1
Rev.	7	5:10; 11:15, 17; 19:6; 20:4, 6; 22:5			7
Total	20		1		21

937. βασιλικός, basilikos′

Book	Oc.	nobleman	Oc.	royal	Oc.	king's country (with 3488)	Total
Jn.	2	4:46, 49					2
Ac.			1	12:21	1	12:20	2
Jas.			1	2:8			1
Total	2		2		1		5

938. βασίλισσα, basil′issa

Book	queen	Total
Mt.	12:42	1
Lk.	11:31	1
Ac.	8:27	1
Rev.	18:7	1
Total		4

939. βάσις, bas′is

Book	foot	Total
Ac.	3:7	1

940. βασκαίνω, baskai′nō

Book	bewitch	Total
Gal.	3:1	1

941. βαστάζω, bastad′zō

Book	Oc.	bear	Oc.	carry	Oc.	take up	Total
Mt.	3	3:11; 8:17; 20:12					3
Mk.	1	14:13					1
Lk.	4	7:14; 11:27; 14:27; 22:10	1	10:4			5
Jn.	4	12:6; 16:12; 19:17; 20:15			1	10:31	5
Ac.	3	9:15; 15:10; 21:35	1	3:2			4
Ro.	2	11:18; 15:1					2
Gal.	4	5:10; 6:2, 5, 17					4
Rev.	2	2:2, 3	1	17:7			3
Total	23		3		1		27

942. βάτος, bat′os

Book	measure	Total
Lk.	16:6	1

943. βάτος, bat′os

Book	Oc.	bush	Oc.	bramble bush	Total
Mk.	1	12:26			1
Lk.	1	20:37	1	6:44	2
Ac.	2	7:30, 35			2
Total	4		1		5

944. βάτραχος, bat′rachos

Book	frog	Total
Rev.	16:13	1

945. βαττολογέω, battologe′ō

Book	use vain repetitions	Total
Mt.	6:7	1

946. βδέλυγμα, bdel′ugma

Book	abomination	Total
Mt.	24:15	1
Mk.	13:14	1
Lk.	16:15	1
Rev.	17:4, 5; 21:27	3
Total		6

947. βδελυκτός, bdeluktos′

Book	abominable	Total
Tit.	1:16	1

948. βδελύσσω, bdelus′sō

Book	Oc.	abhor	Oc.	abominable	Total
Ro.	1	2:22			1
Rev.			1	21:8	1
Total	1		1		2

949. βέβαιος, beb′aios

Book	Oc.	stedfast	Oc.	sure	Oc.	firm	Oc.	of force	Oc.	more sure	Total
Ro.			1	4:16							1
2 Co.	1	1:7									1
Heb.	3	2:2; 3:14; 6:19			1	3:6	1	9:17			5
2 Pt.			1	1:10					1	1:19	2
Total	4		2		1		1		1		9

950. βεβαιόω, bebaio′ō

Book	Oc.	confirm	Oc.	establish	Oc.	stablish	Total
Mk.	1	16:20					1
Ro.	1	15:8					1
1 Co.	2	1:6, 8					2
2 Co.			1	1:21			1
Col.					1	2:7	1
Heb.	1	2:3	1	13:9			2
Total	5		2		1		8

951. βεβαίωσις, bebai′ōsis

Book	confirmation	Total
Phl.	1:7	1
Heb.	6:16	1
Total		2

952. βέβηλος, beb′ēlos

Book	Oc.	profane	Oc.	profane person	Total
1 Ti.	3	1:9; 4:7; 6:20			3
2 Ti.	1	2:16			1
Heb.			1	12:16	1
Total	4		1		5

953. βεβηλόω, bebēlo′ō

Book	profane	Total
Mt.	12:5	1
Ac.	24:6	1
Total		2

954. Βεελζεβούλ, Beeldzeboul′

Book	Beelzebub	Total
Mt.	10:25; 12:24, 27	3
Mk.	3:22	1
Lk.	11:15, 18, 19	3
Total		7

955. βελίαλ, Beli'al

Book	Belial	Total
2 Co.	6:15	1

956. βέλος, bel'os

Book	dart	Total
Eph.	6:16	1

957. βελτίον, belti'on

Book	very well	Total
2 Ti.	1:18	1

958. Βενιαμίν, Beniamin'

Book	Benjamin	Total
Ac.	13:21	1
Ro.	11:1	1
Phl.	3:5	1
Rev.	7:8	1
Total		4

959. Βερνίκη, Berni'ke

Book	Bernice	Total
Ac.	25:13, 23; 26:30	3

960. Βέροια, Ber'oia

Book	Berea	Total
Ac.	17:10, 13	2

961. Βεροιαῖος, Beroiai'os

Book	of Berea	Total
Ac.	20:4	1

962. Βηθαβαρά, Bethabara'

Book	Bethabara	Total
Jn.	1:28	1

963. Βηθανία, Bethani'a

Book	Bethany	Total
Mt.	21:17; 26:6	2
Mk.	11:1, 11, 12; 14:3	4
Lk.	19:29; 24:50	2
Jn.	11:1, 18; 12:1	3
Total		11

964. Βηθεσδά, Bethesda'

Book	Bethesda	Total
Jn.	5:2	1

965. Βηθλεέμ, Bethleem'

Book	Bethlehem	Total
Mt.	2:1, 5, 6, 8, 16	5
Lk.	2:4, 15	2
Jn.	7:42	1
Total		8

966. Βηθσαϊδά, Bethsaida'

Book	Oc.	Bethsaida (of Galilee)	Oc.	Bethsaida (of Gaulonitis)	Total
Mt.	1	11:21			1
Mk.	2	6:45; 8:22			2
Lk.	1	10:13	1	9:10	2
Jn.	2	1:44; 12:21			2
Total	6		1		7

967. Βηθφαγή, Bethphage'

Book	Bethphage	Total
Mt.	21:1	1
Mk.	11:1	1
Lk.	19:29	1
Total		3

968. βῆμα, be'ma

Book	Oc.	judgment seat	Oc.	throne	Oc.	to set (one's) foot on (with 4128)	Total
Mt.	1	27:19					1
Jn.	1	19:13					1
Ac.	6	18:12, 16, 17; 25:6, 10, 17	1	12:21	1	7:5	8
Ro.	1	14:10					1
2 Co.	1	5:10					1
Total	10		1		1		12

969. Βήρυλλος, Be'rullos

Book	beryl	Total
Rev.	21:20	1

970. βία, bi'a

Book	violence	Total
Ac.	5:26; 21:35; 24:7; 27:41	4

971. βιάζω, biad'zō

Book	Oc.	suffer violence	Oc.	press	Total
Mt.	1	11:12			1
Lk.			1	16:16	1
Total	1		1		2

972. βίαιος, bi'aios

Book	mighty	Total
Ac.	2:2	1

973. βιαστής, biastes'

Book	violent	Total
Mt.	11:12	1

974. βιβλιαρίδιον, bibliarid'ion

Book	little book	Total
Rev.	10:2, 8, 9, 10	4

975. βιβλίον, bibli'on

Book	Oc.	book	Oc.	bill	Oc.	scroll	Oc.	writing	Total
Mt.							1	19:7	1
Mk.			1	10:4					1
Lk.	3	4:17, 17, 20							3
Jn.	2	20:30; 21:25							2
Gal.	1	3:10							1
2 Ti.	1	4:13							1
Heb.	2	9:19; 10:7							2
Rev.	20	1:11; 5:1, 2, 3, 4, 5, 7, 8, 9; 17:8; 20:12, 12, 12; 21:27; 22:7, 9, 10, 18, 18, 19			1	6:14			21
Total	29		1		1		1		32

976. βίβλος, bib'los

Book	book	Total
Mt.	1:1	1
Mk.	12:26	1
Lk.	3:4; 20:42	2
Ac.	1:20; 7:42; 19:19	3
Phl.	4:3	1
Rev.	3:5; 13:8; 20:15; 22:19, 19	5
Total		13

977. βιβρώσκω, bibrō'skō

Book	eat	Total
Jn.	6:13	1

978. Βιθυνία, Bithuni'a

Book	Bithynia	Total
Ac.	16:7	1
1 Pt.	1:1	1
Total		2

979. βίος, bi'os

Book	Oc.	life	Oc.	living	Oc.	good	Total
Mk.			1	12:44			1
Lk.	1	8:14	4	8:43; 15:12, 30; 21:4			5
1 Ti.	1	2:2					1
2 Ti.	1	2:4					1
1 Pt.	1	4:3					1
1 Jn.	1	2:16			1	3:17	2
Total	5		5		1		11

980. βιόω, bio'ō

Book	live	Total
1 Pt.	4:2	1

981. βίωσις, bi'ōsis

Book	manner of life	Total
Ac.	26:4	1

982. βιωτικός, biōtikos'

Book	Oc.	things pertaining to this life	Oc.	things that pertain to this life	Oc.	of this life	Total
Lk.					1	21:34	1
1 Co.	1	6:4	1	6:3			2
Total	1		1		1		3

983. βλαβερός, blaberos'

Book	hurtful	Total
1 Ti.	6:9	1

984. βλάπτω, blap'tō

Book	hurt	Total
Mk.	16:18	1
Lk.	4:35	1
Total		2

985. βλαστάνω, blastan'ō

Book	Oc.	spring up	Oc.	bud	Oc.	bring forth	Total
Mt.	1	13:26					1
Mk.	1	4:27					1
Heb.			1	9:4			1
Jas.					1	5:18	1
Total	2		1		1		4

986. Βλάστος, Blas'tos

Book	Blastus	Total
Ac.	12:20	1

987. βλασφημέω, blasphe̱me'ō

Book	Oc.	blaspheme	Oc.	speak evil of	Oc.	rail on	Oc.	blasphemer	Oc.	speak blasphemy	Oc.	blasphemously	Oc.	Misc.	Total
Mt.	1	9:3							1	26:65			1	27:39	3
Mk.	2	3:28, 29			1	15:29									3
Lk.	1	12:10			1	23:39					1	22:65			3
Jn.	1	10:36													1
Ac.	3	13:45; 18:6; 26:11					1	19:37							4
Ro.	1	2:24	1	14:16									1	3:8	3
1 Co.			1	10:30									1	4:13	2
1 Ti.	2	1:20; 6:1													2
Tit.	1	2:5	1	3:2											2
Jas.	1	2:7													1
1 Pt.			2	4:4, 14											2
2 Pt.			3	2:2, 10, 12											3
Jd.			2	1:8, 10											2
Rev.	4	13:6; 16:9, 11, 21													4
Total	17		10		2		1		1		1		3		35

Miscellaneous: Mt. 27:39, revile; Ro. 3:8, be slanderously reported; 1 Co. 4:13, defame.

988. βλασφημία, blasphe̱mi'a

Book	Oc.	blasphemy	Oc.	railing	Oc.	evil speaking	Total
Mt.	4	12:31, 31; 15:19; 26:65					4
Mk.	4	2:7; 3:28; 7:22; 14:64					4
Lk.	1	5:21					1
Jn.	1	10:33					1
Eph.					1	4:31	1
Col.	1	3:8					1
1 Ti.			1	6:4			1
Jd.			1	1:9			1
Rev.	5	2:9; 13:1, 5, 6; 17:3					5
Total	16		2		1		19

989. βλάσφημος, blas'phe̱mos

Book	Oc.	blasphemous	Oc.	blasphemer	Oc.	railing	Total
Ac.	2	6:11, 13					2
1 Ti.			1	1:13			1
2 Ti.			1	3:2			1
2 Pt.					1	2:11	1
Total	2		2		1		5

990. βλέμμα, blem'ma

Book	seeing	Total
2 Pt.	2:8	1

991. βλέπω, blep'ō

Book	Oc.	see	Oc.	take heed	Oc.	behold	Oc.	beware	Oc.	look on	Oc.	look	Oc.	beware of	Oc.	Misc.	Total
Mt.	15	6:4, 6, 18; 11:4; 12:22; 13:13, 13, 14, 14, 16, 17; 14:30; 15:31, 31; 24:2	1	24:4	2	7:3; 18:10			1	5:28					1	22:16	20
Mk.	7	4:12, 12; 5:31; 8:18, 23, 24; 13:2	4	4:24; 13:5, 23, 33			2	8:15; 12:38							2	12:14; 13:9	15
Lk.	9	7:44; 8:10, 10, 16; 10:23, 23, 24; 11:33; 21:30	2	8:18; 21:8	3	6:41, 42; 24:12					1	9:62			1	7:21	16
Jn.	16	1:29; 5:19; 9:7, 15, 19, 21, 25, 39, 39, 39, 41; 11:9; 20:1, 5; 21:9, 20									1	13:22					17
Ac.	7	2:33; 8:6; 9:8; 12:9; 13:11; 28:26, 26			2	1:9; 4:14	i	13:40			1	3:4			2	9:9; 27:12	13
Ro.	6	7:23; 8:24, 24, 25; 11:8, 10															6
1 Co.	3	1:26; 13:12; 16:10	3	3:10; 8:9; 10:12	1	10:18											7
2 Co.	5	4:18, 18, 18, 18; 12:6							1	10:7					1	7:8	7
Gal.			1	5:15													1
Eph.	1	5:15															1
Phl.													3	3:2, 2, 2			3
Col.					1	2:5	1	2:8							1	4:17	3
Heb.	7	2:9; 3:19; 10:25; 11:1, 3, 7; 12:25	1	3:12													8
Jas.	1	2:22															1
2 Jn.															1	1:8	1
Rev.	13	1:11, 12; 3:18; 6:1, 3, 5, 7; 9:20; 11:9; 16:15; 18:9; 22:8, 8			1	17:8			2	5:3, 4							16
Total	90		12		10		4		4		3		3		9		135

Miscellaneous: Mt. 22:16 (with 1519), Mk. 12:14 (with 1519), regard; Mk. 13:9, take heed to; Lk. 7:21, sight; Ac. 9:9 (with 3261), without sight; Ac. 27:12, lie; 2 Co. 7:8, perceive; Col. 4:17, take heed to; 2 Jn. 1:8, look to.

992. βλητέος, ble̤te'os

Book	must be put	Total
Mk.	2:22	1
Lk.	5:38	1
Total		2

993. Βοανεργές, Boanerges'

Book	Boanerges	Total
Mk.	3:17	1

994. βοάω, boa'ō

Book	cry	Total
Mt.	3:3	1
Mk.	1:3; 15:34	2
Lk.	3:4; 18:7, 38	3
Jn.	1:23	1
Ac.	8:7; 17:6; 21:34	3
Gal.	4:27	1
Total		11

995. βοή, boe̤'

Book	cry	Total
Jas.	5:4	1

996. βοήθεια, boe̤'theia

Book	help	Total
Ac.	27:17	1
Heb.	4:16	1
Total		2

998. βοηθός, boe̤thos'

Book	helper	Total
Heb.	13:6	1

997. βοηθέω, boe̤the'ō

Book	Oc.	help	Oc.	succour	Total
Mt.	1	15:25			1
Mk.	2	9:22, 24			2
Ac.	2	16:9; 21:28			2
2 Co.			1	6:2	1
Heb.			1	2:18	1
Rev.	1	12:16			1
Total	6		2		8

999. βόθυνος, both'unos

Book	Oc.	ditch	Oc.	pit	Total
Mt.	1	15:14	1	12:11	2
Lk.	1	6:39			1
Total	2		1		3

1000. βολή, bole̤'

Book	cast	Total
Lk.	22:41	1

1001. βολίζω, bolid'zō

Book	sound	Total
Ac.	27:28, 28	2

1002. βολίς, bolis'

Book	dart	Total
Heb.	12:20	1

1003. Βοόζ, Booz'

Book	Booz	Total
Mt.	1:5	1
Lk.	3:32	1
Total		2

1004. βόρβορος, bor'boros

Book	mire	Total
2 Pt.	2:22	1

1005. βοῤῥᾶς, borhras'

Book	north	Total
Lk.	13:29	1
Rev.	21:13	1
Total		2

1006. βόσκω, bos'kō

Book	Oc.	feed	Oc.	keep	Total
Mt.	1	8:30	1	8:33	2
Mk.	2	5:11, 14			2
Lk.	3	8:32, 34; 15:15			3
Jn.	2	21:15, 17			2
Total	8		1		9

1007. Βοσόρ, Bosor'

Book	Bosor	Total
2 Pt.	2:15	1

1008. βοτάνη, botan'e̤

Book	herb	Total
Heb.	6:7	1

1009. βότρυς, bot'rus

Book	cluster of the vine	Total
Rev.	14:18	1

1010. βουλευτής, bouleute̤s'

Book	counsellor	Total
Mk.	15:43	1
Lk.	23:50	1
Total		2

1011. βουλεύω, boule̤u'ō

Book	Oc.	consult	Oc.	be minded	Oc.	purpose	Oc.	determine	Oc.	take counsel	Total
Lk.	1	14:31									1
Jn.	1	12:10									1
Ac.			1	27:39			1	15:37	1	5:33	3
2 Co.			1	1:17a	2	1:17b, 17c					3
Total	2		2		2		1		1		8

1012. βουλή, boule̤'

Book	Oc.	counsel	Oc.	will	Oc.	advise (with 4987)	Total
Lk.	2	7:30; 23:51					2
Ac.	5	2:23; 4:28; 5:38; 20:27; 27:42	1	13:36	1	27:12	7
1 Co.	1	4:5					1
Eph.	1	1:11					1
Heb.	1	6:17					1
Total	10		1		1		12

1013. βούλημα, bou'le̤ma

Book	Oc.	purpose	Oc.	will	Total
Ac.	1	27:43			1
Ro.			1	9:19	1
Total	1		1		2

1014. βούλομαι, bou'lomai

Book	Oc.	will	Oc.	would	Oc.	be minded	Oc.	intend	Oc.	be disposed	Oc.	be willing	Oc.	list	Oc.	of his own will	Total
Mt.	1	11:27			1	1:19											2
Mk.	1	15:15															1
Lk.	1	10:22									1	22:42					2
Jn.	1	18:39															1
Ac.	2	18:15; 27:43	7	17:20; 19:30; 22:30; 23:28; 25:20, 22; 28:18			2	5:28; 12:4	1	18:27							12
1 Co.	1	12:11															1
2 Co.					1	1:15											1
Phl.			1	1:12													1
1 Ti.	3	2:8; 5:14; 6:9															3
Tit.	1	3:8															1
Phe.			1	1:13													1
Heb.	1	6:17															1
Jas.	1	4:4											1	3:4	1	1:18	3
2 Pt.	1	3:9															1
2 Jn.			1	1:12													1
3 Jn.			1	1:10													1
Jd.	1	1:5															1
Total	15		11		2		2		1		1		1		1		34

1015. βουνός, bounos′

Book	hill	Total
Lk.	3:5; 23:30	2

1016. βοῦς, bous

Book	ox	Total
Lk.	13:15; 14:5, 19	3
Jn.	2:14, 15	2
1 Co.	9:9, 9	2
1 Ti.	5:18	1
Total		8

1017. βραβεῖον, brabei′on

Book	prize	Total
1 Co.	9:24	1
Phl.	3:14	1
Total		2

1018. βραβεύω, brabeu′ō

Book	rule	Total
Col.	3:15	1

1020. βραδυπλοέω, braduploe′ō

Book	sail slowly	Total
Ac.	27:7	1

1021. βραδύς, bradus′

Book	slow	Total
Lk.	24:25	1
Jas	1:19, 19	2
Total		3

1022. βραδύτης, bradu′tes

Book	slackness	Total
2 Pt.	3:9	1

1023. βραχίων, brachi′ōn

Book	arm	Total
Lk.	1:51	1
Jn.	12:38	1
Ac.	13:17	1
Total		3

1019. βραδύνω, bradu′nō

Book	Oc.	tarry	Oc.	be slack	Total
1 Ti.	1	3:15			1
2 Pt.			1	3:9	1
Total	1		1		2

1024. βραχύς, brachus′

Book	Oc.	a little	Oc.	a little space	Oc.	a little while	Oc.	few words	Total
Lk.					1	22:58			1
Jn.	1	6:7							1
Ac.	1	27:28	1	5:34					2
Heb.	2	2:7, 9					1	13:22	3
Total	4		1		1		1		7

1025. βρέφος, breph′os

Book	Oc.	babe	Oc.	child	Oc.	infant	Oc.	young child	Total
Lk.	4	1:41, 44; 2: 12, 16			1	18:15			5
Ac.							1	7:19	1
2 Ti.			1	3:15					1
1 Pt.	1	2:2							1
Total	5		1		1		1		8

1026. βρέχω, brech′ō

Book	Oc.	rain	Oc.	wash	Oc.	rain (with 5105)	Oc.	send rain	Total
Mt.							1	5:45	1
Lk.	1	17:29	2	7:38, 44					3
Jas.	2	5:17, 17							2
Rev.					1	11:6			1
Total	3		2		1		1		7

1027. βροντή, bronte′

Book	Oc.	thunder	Oc.	thundering	Total
Mk.	1	3:17			1
Jn.	1	12:29			1
Rev.	6	6:1; 10:3, 4, 4; 14:2; 16:18	4	4:5; 8:5; 11:19; 19:6	10
Total	8		4		12

1028. βροχή, broche′

Book	rain	Total
Mt.	7:25, 27	2

1029. βρόχος, broch′os

Book	snare	Total
1 Co.	7:35	1

1030. βρυγμός, brugmos′

Book	gnashing	Total
Mt.	8:12; 13:42, 50; 22:13; 24:51; 25:30	6
Lk.	13:28	1
Total		7

1031. βρύχω, bru′chō

Book	gnash	Total
Ac.	7:54	1

1032. βρύω, bru′ō

Book	send forth	Total
Jas.	3:11	1

1034. βρώσιμος, brō′simos

Book	meat	Total
Lk.	24:41	1

1033. βρῶμα, brō′ma

Book	Oc.	meat	Oc.	victual	Total
Mt.			1	14:15	1
Mk.	1	7:19			1
Lk.	2	3:11; 9:13			2
Jn.	1	4:34			1
Ro.	3	14:15, 15, 20			3
1 Co.	6	3:2; 6:13, 13; 8:8, 13; 10:3			6
1 Ti.	1	4:3			1
Heb.	2	9:10; 13:9			2
Total	16		1		17

1035. βρῶσις, brō′sis

Book	Oc.	meat	Oc.	rust	Oc.	morsel of meat	Oc.	eating	Oc.	food	Total
Mt.			2	6:19, 20							2
Jn.	4	4:32; 6:27, 27, 55									4
Ro.	1	14:17									1
1 Co.							1	8:4			1
2 Co.									1	9:10	1
Col.	1	2:16									1
Heb.					1	12:16					1
Total	6		2		1		1		1		11

1036. βυθίζω, buthid′zō

Book	Oc.	begin to sink	Oc.	drown	Total
Lk.	1	5:7			1
1 Ti.			1	6:9	1
Total	1		1		2

1037. βυθός, buthos′

Book	deep	Total
2 Co.	11:25	1

1038. βυρσεύς, burseus′

Book	tanner	Total
Ac.	9:43; 10:6, 32	3

1039. βύσσινος, bus′sinos

Book	fine linen	Total
Rev.	18:16; 19:8, 8, 14	4

1040. βύσσος, bus′sos

Book	fine linen	Total
Lk.	16:19	1
Rev.	18:12	1
Total		2

1041. βῶμος, bō′mos

Book	altar	Total
Ac.	17:23	1

1042. Γαββαθά, Gabbatha′

Book	Gabbatha	Total
Jn.	19:13	1

1043. Γαβριήλ, Gabriel′

Book	Gabriel	Total
Lk.	1:19, 26	2

1044. γάγγραινα, gang′graina

Book	canker	Total
2 Ti.	2:17	1

1045. Γάδ, Gad

Book	Gad	Total
Rev.	7:5	1

1046. Γαδαρηνός, Gadarenos′

Book	Gadarene	Total
Mk.	5:1	1
Lk.	8:26, 37	2
Total		3

1047. γάζα, gad′za

Book	treasure	Total
Ac.	8:27	1

1048. Γάζα, Gad′za

Book	Gaza	Total
Ac.	8:26	1

1049. γαζοφυλάκιον gadzophulak′ion

Book	treasury	Total
Mk.	12:41, 41, 43	3
Lk.	21:1	1
Jn.	8:20	1
Total		5

1050. Γάϊος, Gai′os

Book	Oc.	Gaius (of Corinth)	Oc.	Gaius (of Macedonia)	Oc.	Gaius (of Derbe)	Oc.	Gaius (a Christian)	Total
Ac.			1	19:29	1	20:4			2
Ro.	1	16:23							1
1 Co.	1	1:14							1
3 Jn.							1	1:1	1
Total	2		1		1		1		5

1051. γάλα, gal′a

Book	milk	Total
1 Co.	3:2; 9:7	2
Heb.	5:12, 13	2
1 Pt.	2:2	1
Total		5

1052. Γαλάτης, Galat′ēs

Book	Galatian	Total
Gal.	3:1	1

1053. Γαλατία, Galati′a

Book	Galatia	Total
1 Co.	16:1	1
Gal.	1:2	1
2 Ti.	4:10	1
1 Pt.	1:1	1
Total		4

1054. Γαλατικός, Galatikos′

Book	of Galatia	Total
Ac.	16:6; 18:23	2

1055. γαλήνη, galē′nē

Book	calm	Total
Mt.	8:26	1
Mk.	4:39	1
Lk.	8:24	1
Total		3

1056. Γαλιλαία, Galilai′a

Book	Galilee	Total
Mt.	2:22; 3:13; 4:12, 15, 18, 23, 25; 15:29; 17:22; 19:1; 21:11; 26:32; 27:55; 28:7, 10, 16	16
Mk.	1:9, 14, 16, 28, 39; 3:7; 6:21; 7:31; 9:30; 14:28; 15:41; 16:7	12
Lk.	1:26; 2:4, 39; 3:1; 4:14, 31, 44; 5:17; 8:26; 17:11; 23:5, 6, 49, 55; 24:6	15
Jn.	1:43; 2:1, 11; 4:3, 43, 45, 46, 47, 54; 6:1; 7:1, 9, 41, 52, 52; 12:21; 21:2	17
Ac.	9:31; 10:37; 13:31	3
Total		63

1057. Γαλιλαῖος, Galilai′os

Book	Oc.	Galilaean	Oc.	of Galilee	Total
Mt.			1	26:69	1
Mk.	1	14:70			1
Lk.	5	13:1, 2, 2; 22:59; 23:6			5
Jn.	1	4:45			1
Ac.	1	2:7	2	1:11; 5:37	3
Total	8		3		11

1058. Γαλλίων, Galli′ōn

Book	Gallio	Total
Ac.	18:12, 14, 17	3

1059. Γαμαλιήλ, Gamaliēl′

Book	Gamaliel	Total
Ac.	5:34; 22:3	2

1061. γαμίσκω, gamis′kō

Book	give in marriage	Total
Mk.	12:25	1

1060. γαμέω, game′ō

Book	Oc.	marry	Oc.	married	Oc.	marry a wife	Total
Mt.	6	5:32; 19:9, 9, 10; 22:30; 24:38			1	22:25	7
Mk.	4	6:17; 10:11, 12; 12:25					4
Lk.	5	14:20; 16:18, 18; 20:34, 35			1	17:27	6
1 Co.	6	7:9, 9, 28, 28, 36, 39	3	7:10, 33, 34			9
1 Ti.	3	4:3; 5:11, 14					3
Total	24		3		2		29

1062. γάμος, gam′os

Book	Oc.	marriage	Oc.	wedding	Total
Mt.	4	22:2, 4, 9; 25:10	5	22:3, 8, 10, 11, 12	9
Lk.			2	12:36; 14:8	2
Jn.	2	2:1, 2			2
Heb.	1	13:4			1
Rev.	2	19:7, 9			2
Total	9		7		16

1063. γάρ, gar

Book	Oc.	for
Mt.	126	1:20, 21; 2:2, 5, 6, 13, 20; 3:2, 3, 9, 15; 4:6, 10, 17, 18; 5:12, 18, 20, 29, 30, 46; 6:7, 8, 14, 16, 21, 24, 32, 32, 34; 7:2, 8, 12, 25, 29; 8:9; 9:5, 13, 16, 21, 24; 10:10, 17, 19, 20, 23, 26, 35; 11:10, 13, 18, 30; 12:8, 33, 34, 37, 40, 50; 13:12, 15, 17; 14:3, 4, 24; 15:2, 4, 19; 16:2, 3, 25, 26, 27; 17:15, 20; 18:7, 10, 11, 20; 19:12, 14, 22; 20:1, 16; 21:26, 32; 22:14, 16, 28, 30; 23:3, 4, 8, 9, 10, 13, 17, 19, 39; 24:5, 6, 7, 21, 24, 27, 28, 38; 25:14, 29, 35, 42; 26:9, 10, 11, 12, 28, 31, 43, 52, 73; 27:1, 8, 19, 43; 28:2, 5, 6
Mt.	71	1:16, 22, 38; 2:15; 3:10, 21, 35; 4:22, 25, 28; 5:8, 28, 42; 6:14, 17, 18, 20, 31, 36, 48, 50, 52, 52; 7:3, 8, 10, 21, 25, 27; 8:3, 35, 36; 9:6, 6, 31, 34, 39, 40, 41, 49; 10:14, 22, 27, 45; 11:13, 18, 23, 32; 12:12, 14, 23, 25, 36, 44; 13:6, 7, 8, 9, 11, 19, 22, 33, 35; 14:5, 7, 40, 56, 70; 15:10; 16:4, 8
Lk.	94	1:15, 18, 30, 44, 48, 76; 2:10; 3:8; 4:8, 10; 5:9, 39; 6:23, 23, 26, 32, 33, 34, 38, 43, 44, 44, 45, 48; 7:5, 6, 8, 28, 33; 8:17, 18, 29, 29, 40, 46; 9:14, 24, 25, 26, 44, 48, 50, 56; 10:7, 24; 11:4, 10, 30; 12:12, 30, 34, 52; 14:14, 24, 28; 16:2, 13, 28; 17:21, 24; 18:16, 23, 25, 32; 19:5, 10, 21, 26, 48; 20:6, 19, 33, 36b, 38; 21:4, 8, 9, 15, 23, 26, 35; 22:2, 16, 18, 27, 37, 37, 59, 71; 23:8, 12, 15, 34, 41
Jn.	59	2:25; 3:2, 16, 17, 20, 24, 34, 34; 4:8, 9, 18, 23, 42, 44, 45, 47; 5:4, 13, 19, 20, 21, 22, 26, 36, 46, 46; 6:6, 27, 33, 55, 64, 71; 7:1, 4, 5, 39; 8:24, 42a; 9:22; 11:39; 12:8, 43, 47; 13:11, 13, 15, 29; 14:30; 16:7, 13, 27; 18:13; 19:6, 31, 36; 20:9, 17; 21:7, 8
Ac.	78	1:20; 2:15a, 25, 34, 39; 3:22; 4:3, 12, 16, 20, 22, 27, 34b; 5:26, 36; 6:14; 7:33, 40; 8:7, 16, 21, 23; 9:11, 16; 10:46; 13:8, 27, 36, 47; 15:21, 28; 16:3, 28; 17:20, 23, 28, 28; 18:3, 15, 18, 28; 19:24, 32, 37, 40; 20:10, 13, 16, 16, 27, 29; 21:3, 13, 22, 29, 36; 22:22, 26; 23:5, 8, 11, 17, 21; 24:5; 25:11, 27; 26:16, 26, 26, 26; 27:22, 23, 25, 34, 34; 28:2, 22, 27
Ro.	140	1:9, 11, 16, 16, 17, 18, 19, 20, 26; 2:1, 1, 11, 12, 13, 14, 24, 25, 28; 3:3, 7, 9, 20, 22, 23; 4:2, 3, 9, 13, 14, 15b; 5:6, 7a, 10, 13, 15, 16, 17, 19; 6:5, 7, 10, 14. 14, 19, 20, 21, 23; 7:1, 2, 5, 7, 8, 11, 14, 15, 15, 18, 18, 19, 22; 8:2, 3, 5, 6, 7a, 13, 14, 15, 18, 19, 20, 22, 24, 24, 26, 38; 9:3, 6, 9, 11, 15, 17, 19, 28, 32; 10: 2, 3, 4, 5, 10, 11, 12, 12, 13, 16; 11:1, 13, 15, 21, 23, 24, 25, 29, 30, 32, 34; 12:3, 4, 19, 20; 13:1, 3, 4, 4, 4, 6, 6, 8, 9, 11; 14:3, 4, 6, 7, 8, 9, 10, 11, 17, 18; 15:3, 4, 18, 24, 26, 27b; 16:2, 18, 19
1 Co.	103	1:11, 17, 18, 19, 21, 26; 2:2, 8, 10, 11, 14, 16; 3:2, 3, 3, 4, 9, 11, 13, 17, 19, 19, 21; 4:4, 7, 9, 15, 15, 20; 5:3, 7, 12; 6:16, 20; 7:7, 9, 14, 16, 22, 31; 8:5, 8,10; 9:2, 9, 15, 16, 16, 17, 19; 10:4, 5, 17, 26, 28, 29; 11:5, 6, 7, 8, 12, 18, 19, 21, 23, 26, 29, 31; 12:8, 12, 13, 14; 13:9, 12; 14:2, 2, 5, 8, 9, 14, 17, 31, 33, 34, 35; 15:3, 9, 16, 21, 22, 25, 27, 32, 34, 41, 52, 53; 16:5, 7, 9, 10, 11, 18
2 Co.	77	1:8, 12, 13, 19, 20, 24; 2:2, 4, 9, 10, 11, 17; 3:6, 9, 10, 11, 14; 4:5, 11, 15, 17, 18; 5:1, 2, 4, 7, 10, 12, 13, 14, 21; 6:2, 14, 16; 7:3, 5, 8, 9, 10, 11; 8:9, 10, 12, 13; 9:1, 2, 7; 10:3, 4, 8, 12, 14, 14, 18; 11:2, 2, 4, 5, 9, 13, 14, 19, 20; 12:6, 6, 9, 10. 11, 11, 13, 14, 14, 20; 13:4, 4, 8, 9
Gal.	36	1:10, 10, 12, 13; 2:6, 8, 12, 18, 19, 21; 3:10, 10, 13, 18, 21, 26, 27, 28; 4:15, 22, 24, 25, 27, 30; 5:5, 6, 13, 14, 17; 6:3, 5, 7, 9, 13, 15, 17
Eph.	11	2:8, 10, 14; 5:5, 6, 8, 9, 12, 13, 29; 6:1
Phl.	12	1:8, 19, 21, 23; 2:13, 20, 21, 27; 3:3, 18, 20; 4:11
Col.	6	2:1, 5; 3:3, 20, 24; 4:13
1 Th.	23	1:8, 9; 2:1, 3, 5, 9, 9, 14, 19, 20; 3:3, 4, 9; 4:2, 3, 7, 9, 14, 15; 5:2, 3, 7, 18
2 Th.	5	2:7; 3:2, 7, 10, 11
1 Ti.	14	2:3, 5, 13; 3:13; 4:5, 8, 10, 16; 5:4, 11, 15, 18; 6:7, 10
2 Ti.	12	1:7, 12; 2:11, 16; 3:2, 6, 9; 4:3, 6, 10, 11, 15
Tit.	6	1:7, 10; 2:11; 3:3, 9, 12
Phe.	3	1:7, 15, 22
Heb.	91	1:5; 2:2, 5, 8, 10, 11, 16, 18; 3:3, 4, 14, 16; 4:2, 3, 4, 8, 10, 12, 15; 5:1, 12, 13, 13; 6:4, 7, 10, 13, 16; 7:1, 10, 11, 12, 13, 14, 17, 18, 19, 21, 26, 27, 28; 8:3, 4, 5, 7, 8; 9:2, 13, 16, 17, 19, 24; 10:1, 4, 14, 15, 23, 26, 30, 34, 36, 37; 11:2, 5, 6, 10, 14, 16, 26, 27, 32; 12:3, 6, 7, 10, 17, 17, 18, 20, 25, 29; 13:2, 5, 9, 11, 14, 16, 17, 17, 18, 22
Jas.	15	1:6, 7, 11, 13, 20, 24; 2:2, 10, 11, 13, 26; 3:2, 7, 16; 4:14a
1 Pt.	9	2:19, 20, 21, 25; 3:5, 10, 17; 4:3, 6
2 Pt.	14	1:8, 10, 11, 16, 17, 21; 2:4, 8, 18, 19, 20, 21; 3:4, 5
1 Jn.	3	2:19; 4:20; 5:3
2 Jn.	1	1:11
3 Jn.	1	1:3
Jd.	1	1:4
Rev.	18	1:3; 3:2; 9:19, 19; 13:18; 14:4, 5; 16:6, 14; 17:17; 19:8, 10; 21:1, 22, 23, 25; 22:9, 18
Total	1029	

1064. γαστήρ, gaster′

Book	Oc.	be with child (with 1722 and 2192)	Oc.	with child (with 1722 and 2192)	Oc.	womb	Oc.	belly	Total
Mt.	2	1:23; 24:19	1	1:18					3
Mk.	1	13:17							1
Lk.	1	21:23			1	1:31			2
1 Th.			1	5:3					1
Tit.							1	1:12	1
Rev.	1	12:2							1
Total	5		2		1		1		9

1065. γέ, ge

Book	Oc.	yet	Oc.	at least	Oc.	beside	Oc.	doubtless	Oc.	Not Tr.	Total
Lk.	2	11:8; 18:5	1	19:42	1	24:21					4
Ac.									3	2:18; 8:30; 11:18	3
Ro.									1	8:32	1
1 Co.							1	9:2	2	4:8; 6:3	3
Total	2		1		1		1		6		11

1066. Γεδεών, Gedeōn′

Book	Gedeon	Total
Heb.	11:32	1

1067. γέεννα, ge′enna

Book	Oc.	hell	Oc.	hell fire (with 3488 and 4342)	Total
Mt.	5	5:29, 30; 10:28; 23:15, 33	2	5:22; 18:9	7
Mk.	2	9:43, 45	1	9:47	3
Lk.	1	12:5			1
Jas.	1	3:6			1
Total	9		3		12

1068. Γεθσημανῆ, Gethsemane′

Book	Gethsemane	Total
Mt.	26:36	1
Mk.	14:32	1
Total		2

1069. γείτων, gei′tōn

Book	neighbour	Total
Lk.	14:12; 15:6, 9	3
Jn.	9:8	1
Total		4

1070. γελάω, gela′ō

Book	laugh	Total
Lk.	6:21, 25	2

1071. γέλως, gel′ōs

Book	laughter	Total
Jas.	4:9	1

1072. γεμίζω, gemid′zō

Book	Oc.	fill	Oc.	be full	Oc.	fill . . . full	Total
Mk.			1	4:37	1	15:36	2
Lk.	2	14:23; 15:16					2
Jn.	3	2:7, 7; 6:13					3
Rev.	2	8:5; 15:8					2
Total	7		1		1		9

1073. γέμω, gem′ō

Book	Oc.	full	Oc.	be full	Total
Mt.			2	23:25, 27	2
Lk.			1	11:39	1
Ro.	1	3:14			1
Rev.	7	4:6, 8; 5:8; 15:7; 17:3, 4; 21:9			7
Total	8		3		11

1063. γάρ, gar (continued)

Book	Oc.	why	Oc.	and	Oc.	because	Oc.	yet	Oc.	but	Oc.	because that	Oc.	verily	Oc.	indeed	Oc.	Not Tr.	Oc.	Misc.	Total
Mt.	1	27:23					1	15:27											1	1:18	129
Mk.	1	15:14					1	7:28											1	8:38	74
Lk.	1	23:22															2	12:58; 20:36a			97
Jn.	1	9:30	1	4:37	2	3:19; 10:26											2	7:41; 8:42b			65
Ac.			1	8:39							1	28:20	1	16:37			3	4:34a; 8:31; 19:35	1	2:15b	85
Ro.					1	4:15a	1	5:7b					1	15:27a	1	8:7b	2	3:2; 15:2			146
1 Co.																	1	11:9	2	9:10; 11:22	106
2 Co.																	1	12:1			78
Gal.																					36
Eph.																					11
Phl.																	1	2:5	1	1:18	14
Col.																					6
1 Th.															1	4:10					24
2 Th.																					5
1 Ti.																					14
2 Ti.			1	2:7																	13
Tit.																					6
Phe.																					3
Heb.																					91
Jas.																			1	4:14b	16
1 Pt.									1	4:15											10
2 Pt.									1	1:9											15
1 Jn.																					3
2 Jn.																					1
3 Jn.											1	1:7									2
Jd.																					1
Rev.																					18
Total	4		3		3		3		2		2		2		2		12		7		1069

Miscellaneous: Mt. 1:18, as; Mk. 8:38, therefore; Ac. 2:15b, seeing; 1 Co. 9:10, no doubt; 1 Co. 11:22, what; Phl. 1:18, then; Jas. 4:14b, even.

1074. γενεά, genea′

Book	Oc.	generation	Oc.	time	Oc.	age	Oc.	nation	Total
Mt.	13	1:17, 17, 17, 17; 11:16; 12:39, 41, 42, 45; 16:4; 17:17; 23:36; 24:34							13
Mk.	5	8:12, 12, 38; 9:19; 13:30							5
Lk.	14	1:48, 50, 50; 7:31; 9:41; 11:29, 30, 31, 32, 50, 51; 16:8; 17:25; 21:32							14
Ac.	3	2:40; 8:33; 13:36	2	14:16; 15:21					5
Eph.					2	3:5, 21			2
Phl.							1	2:15	1
Col.	1	1:26							1
Heb.	1	3:10							1
Total	37		2		2		1		42

1075. γενεαλογέω, genealoge′ō

Book	count (one's) descent	Total
Heb.	7:6	1

1076. γενεαλογία, genealogi′a

Book	genealogy	Total
1 Ti.	1:4	1
Tit.	3:9	1
Total		2

1077. γενέσια, genes′ia

Book	birthday	Total
Mt.	14:6	1
Mk.	6:21	1
Total		2

1079. γενετή, gene̱te′

Book	birth	Total
Jn.	9:1	1

1078. γένεσις, gen′esis

Book	Oc.	generation	Oc.	natural	Oc.	nature	Total
Mt.	1	1:1					1
Jas.			1	1:23	1	3:6	2
Total	1		1		1		3

1081. γέννημα, gen′ne̱ma

Book	Oc.	fruit	Oc.	generation	Total
Mt.	1	26:29	3	3:7; 12:34; 23:33	4
Mk.	1	14:25			1
Lk.	2	12:18; 22:18	1	3:7	3
2 Co.	1	9:10			1
Total	5		4		9

1080. γεννάω, genna′ō

Book	Oc.	beget	Oc.	be born	Oc.	bear	Oc.	gender	Oc.	bring forth	Oc.	be delivered of	Oc.	Misc.	Total
Mt.	39	1:2, 2, 2, 3, 3, 3, 4, 4, 4, 5, 5, 5, 6, 6, 7, 7, 7, 8, 8, 8, 9, 9, 9, 10, 10, 10, 11, 12, 12, 13, 13, 13, 14, 14, 14, 15, 15, 15, 16a	5	1:16b; 2:1, 4; 19:12; 26:24									1	1:20	45
Mk.			1	14:21											1
Lk.			1	1:35	2	1:13; 23:29			1	1:57					4
Jn.			17	1:13; 3:3, 4, 4, 5, 6, 6, 7, 8; 8:41; 9:2, 19, 20, 32, 34; 16: 21b; 18:37							1	16:21a			18
Ac.	3	7:8, 29; 13:33	4	2:8; 7:20; 22:3, 28											7
Ro.			1	9:11											1
1 Co.	1	4:15													1
Gal.			2	4:23, 29			1	4:24							3
2 Ti.							1	2:23							1
Phe.	1	1:10													1
Heb.	2	1:5; 5:5	1	11:23									1	11:12	4
2 Pt.													1	2:12	1
1 Jn.	3	5:1b, 1c, 18b	7	2:29; 3:9, 9; 4:7; 5: 1a, 4; 5:18a											10
Total	49		39		2		2		1		1		3		97

Miscellaneous: Mt. 1:20, conceive; Heb. 11:12, spring; 2 Pt. 2:12, be made.

1082. Γεννησαρέτ, Genne̱saret′

Book	Gennesaret	Total
Mt.	14:34	1
Mk.	6:53	1
Lk.	5:1	1
Total		3

1083. γέννησις, gen′ne̱sis

Book	birth	Total
Mt.	1:18	1
Lk.	1:14	1
Total		2

1084. γεννητός, genne̱tos′

Book	that is born	Total
Mt.	11:11	1
Lk.	7:28	1
Total		2

1086. Γεργεσηνός, Gergese̱nos′

Book	Gergesenes	Total
Mt.	8:28	1

1085. γένος, gen′os

Book	Oc.	kind	Oc.	kindred	Oc.	offspring	Oc.	nation	Oc.	stock	Oc.	born	Oc.	diversity	Oc.	Misc.	Total
Mt.	2	13:47; 17:21															2
Mk.	1	9:29					1	7:26									2
Ac.			3	4:6; 7:13, 19	2	17:28, 29			1	13:26	2	18:2, 24			1	4:36	9
1 Co.	2	12:10; 14:10											1	12:28			3
2 Co.															1	11:26	1
Gal.							1	1:14									1
1 Pt.															1	2:9	1
Phl.									1	3:5							1
Rev.					1	22:16											1
Total	5		3		3		2		2		2		1		3		21

Miscellaneous: Ac. 4:36, country; 2 Co. 11:26, countryman; 1 Pt. 2:9, generation.

1087. γερουσία, gerousi′a

Book	senate	Total
Ac.	5:21	1

1088. γέρων, ger′ōn

Book	old	Total
Jn.	3:4	1

1089. γεύομαι, geu′omai

Book	Oc.	taste	Oc.	eat	Total
Mt.	2	16:28; 27:34			2
Mk.	1	9:1			1
Lk.	2	9:27; 14:24			2
Jn.	2	2:9; 8:52			2
Ac.			3	10:10; 20:11; 23:14	3
Col.	1	2:21			1
Heb.	3	2:9; 6:4, 5			3
1 Pt.	1	2:3			1
Total	12		3		15

1090. γεωργέω, geōrge′ō

Book	dress	Total
Heb.	6:7	1

1091. γεώργιον, geōr′gion

Book	husbandry	Total
1 Co.	3:9	1

1092. γεωργός, geōrgos′

Book	husbandman	Total
Mt.	21:33, 34, 35, 38, 40, 41	6
Mk.	12:1, 2, 2, 7, 9	5
Lk.	20:9, 10, 10, 14, 16	5
Jn.	15:1	1
2 Ti.	2:6	1
Jas.	5:7	1
Total		19

1094. γῆρας, gē′ras

Book	old age	Total
Lk.	1:36	1

1095. γηράσκω, gēras′kō

Book	Oc.	be old	Oc.	wax old	Total
Jn.	1	21:18			1
Heb.			1	8:13	1
Total	1		1		2

1093. γῆ, gē

Book	Oc.	earth	Oc.	land	Oc.	ground	Oc.	country	Oc.	world	Oc.	earthly (with 1537 and 3488)	Total
Mt.	27	5:5, 13, 18, 35; 6:10, 19; 9:6; 10:34; 11: 25; 12:40, 42; 13:5, 5; 16:19, 19; 17:25; 18:18, 18, 19; 23:9, 35; 24:30, 35; 25: 18, 25; 27:51; 28:18	10	2:6, 20, 21; 4:15; 15; 9:26; 10:15; 11:24; 14:34; 27: 45	4	10:29; 13:8, 23; 15:35	1	9:31					42
Mk.	9	2:10; 4:5, 5, 28, 31, 31; 9:3; 13:27, 31	4	4:1; 6:47, 53; 15: 33	6	4:8, 20, 26; 8:6; 9:20; 14:35							19
Lk.	16	2:14; 5:24; 6:49; 10:21; 11:2, 31; 12:49, 51, 56; 16:17; 18:8; 21:25, 33, 35; 23: 44; 24:5	6	4:25; 5:3, 11; 8: 27; 14:35; 21:23	4	8:8, 15; 13: 7; 22:44							26
Jn.	4	3:31a, 31c; 12:32; 17:4	5	3:22; 6:21; 21:8, 9, 11	3	8:6, 8; 12:24					1	3:31b	13
Ac.	18	1:8; 2:19; 3:25; 4:24, 26; 7:49; 8:33; 9: 4, 8; 10:11, 12; 11:6; 13:47; 14:15; 17: 24, 26; 22:22; 26:14	14	7:3b, 4, 4, 6, 11, 29, 36, 40; 13: 17, 19, 19; 27: 39, 43, 44	1	7:33	1	7:3a					34
Ro.	3	9:17, 28; 10:18											3
1 Co.	4	8:5; 10:26, 28; 15:47											4
Eph.	4	1:10; 3:15; 4:9; 6:3											4
Col.	4	1:16, 20; 3:2, 5											4
Heb.	8	1:10; 6:7; 8:4; 11:13, 38; 12:25, 26, 26	2	8:9; 11:9									10
Jas.	5	5:5, 7, 12, 17, 18											5
2 Pt.	4	3:5, 7, 10, 13											4
1 Jn.	1	5:8											1
Jd.			1	1:5									1
Rev.	81	1:5, 7; 3:10; 5:3, 3, 6, 10, 13, 13; 6:4, 8, 8, 10, 13, 15; 7:1, 1, 1, 2, 3; 8:5, 7, 13; 9: 1, 3, 3, 4; 10:2, 5, 6, 8; 11:4, 6, 10, 10, 18; 12:4, 9, 12, 13, 16, 16; 13:8, 11, 12, 13, 14, 14; 14:3, 6, 7, 15, 16, 16, 18, 19, 19; 16:1, 2, 14, 18; 17:2, 2, 5, 8, 18; 18:1, 3, 3, 9, 11, 23, 24; 19:2, 19; 20:8, 9, 11; 21:1, 1, 24							1	13:3			82
Total	188		42		18		2		1		1		252

See pages 72 and 73 for Word 1096.

1097. γινώσκω, ginōs′kō

Book	Oc.	know	Oc.	perceive	Oc.	understand	Oc.	Misc.	Total
Mt.	14	1:25; 6:3; 7:23; 9:30; 10:26; 12:7, 15, 33; 13:11; 24:32, 33, 39, 43; 25:24	3	16:8; 21:45; 22:18	1	26:10	2	16:3; 24:50	20
Mk.	12	4:11, 13; 5:43; 6:38; 7:24; 8:17; 9:30; 12:12; 13:28, 29; 15: 10, 45					1	5:29	13
Lk.	23	1:18, 34; 2:43; 6:44; 7:39; 8:10, 17; 9:11; 10:22; 12:2, 39, 47, 48; 16:15; 18:34; 19:15, 42, 44; 21:20, 30, 31; 24:18, 35	2	8:46; 20:19			3	10:11; 12:46; 16: 14	28
Jn.	50	1:10, 48; 2:24, 25; 3:10; 4:1, 53; 5:6, 42; 7:17, 26, 27, 49, 51; 8:28, 32, 52, 55; 10:14, 14, 15, 15, 27, 38; 11:57; 12:9; 13:7, 12, 28, 35; 14:7, 7, 7, 9, 17, 17, 20, 31; 15:18; 16:3, 19; 17:3, 7, 8, 23, 25, 25, 25; 19:4; 21:17	1	6:15	4	8:27, 43; 10:6; 12:16	1	6:69	56
Ac.	13	1:7; 2:36; 9:24; 17:19, 20; 19:15, 35; 20:34; 21:24, 34; 22:14, 30; 23:28	1	23:6	2	8:30; 24:11	2	17:13; 21:37	18
Ro.	8	1:21; 2:18; 3:17; 6:6; 7:1, 7; 10:19; 11:34					1	7:15	9
1 Co.	14	1:21; 2:8, 8, 14, 16; 3:20; 4:19; 8:2, 2, 3; 13:9, 12; 14:7, 9							14
2 Co.	8	2:4, 9; 3:2; 5:16, 16, 21; 8:9; 13:6							8
Gal.	3	3:7; 4:9, 9	1	2:9					4
Eph.	3	3:19; 5:5; 6:22							3
Phl.	4	2:19, 22; 3:10; 4:5			1	1:12			5
Col.	1	4:8							1
1 Th.	1	3:5							1
2 Ti.	3	1:18; 2:19; 3:1							3
Heb.	4	3:10; 8:11; 10:34; 13:23							4
Jas.	3	1:3; 2:20; 5:20							3
2 Pt.	2	1:20; 3:3							2
1 Jn.	24	2:3, 3, 4, 5, 13, 13, 14, 18, 29; 3:1, 1, 6, 19, 20, 24; 4:2, 6, 6, 7, 8, 13, 16; 5:2, 20	1	3:16					25
2 Jn.	1	1:1							1
Rev.	5	2:17, 23, 24; 3:3, 9							5
Total	196		9		8		10		223

Miscellaneous: Mt. 16:3, can; Mt. 24:50, be aware of; Mk. 5:29, feel; Lk. 10:11, be sure; Lk. 12:46, be aware; Lk. 16:4, be resolved; Jn. 6:69, be sure; Ac. 17:13, have knowledge; Ac. 21:37, can speak; Ro. 7:15, allow.

1098. γλεῦκος, gleu′kos

Book	new wine	Total
Ac.	2:13	1

1099. γλυκύς, glukus′

Book	Oc.	sweet	Oc.	fresh	Total
Jas.	1	3:11	1	3:12	2
Rev.	2	10:9, 10			2
Total	3		1		4

1100. γλῶσσα, glōs'sa

Book	tongue	Total
Mk.	7:33, 35; 16:17	3
Lk.	1:64; 16:24	2
Ac.	2:3, 4, 11, 26; 10:46; 19:6	6
Ro.	3:13; 14:11	2
1 Co.	12:10, 10, 28, 30; 13:1, 8; 14:2, 4, 5, 5, 6, 9, 13, 14, 18, 19, 22, 23, 26, 27, 39	21
Phl.	2:11	1
Jas.	1:26; 3:5, 6, 6, 8	5
1 Pt.	3:10	1
1 Jn.	3:18	1
Rev.	5:9; 7:9; 10:11; 11:9; 13:7; 14:6; 16:10; 17:15	8
Total		50

1101. γλωσσόκομον glōssok'omon

Book	bag	Total
Jn.	12:6; 13:29	2

1102. γναφεύς, gnapheus'

Book	fuller	Total
Mk.	9:3	1

1103. γνήσιος, gnē'sios

Book	Oc.	own	Oc.	sincerity	Oc.	true	Total
2 Co.			1	8:8			1
Phl.					1	4:3	1
1 Ti.	1	1:2					1
Tit.	1	1:4					1
Total	2		1		1		4

1096. γίνομαι, gin'omai

Book	Oc.	be (is, being, been, was, were)	Oc.	come to pass	Oc.	be made	Oc.	be done	Oc.	come
Mt.	26	5:45; 6:16; 8:26; 9:29; 10:16, 25; 12:45; 14:15; 15:28; 16:2; 17:2; 18:13; 19:8; 20:26; 23:26; 24:20, 21, 21, 32, 44; 26:2, 5, 6, 54; 27:45; 28:2	7	7:28; 9:10; 11:1; 13:53; 19:1; 24:6; 26:1	5	4:3; 9:16; 23:15; 25:6; 27:24	17	1:22; 6:10; 8:13; 11:20, 21, 21, 23, 23; 18:19, 31, 31; 21:4, 21; 26:42, 56; 27:54; 28:11	6	8:16; 14:23; 20:8; 26:20; 27:1, 57
Mk.	17	4:10, 39; 6:14, 26, 35; 9:7, 26, 33; 10:43, 44; 13:7, 18, 19, 19, 28; 15:33b; 16:10	6	1:9; 2:15, 23; 4:4; 11:23; 13:29	3	2:21, 27; 14:4	4	4:11; 5:14, 33; 13:30	9	1:11; 4:35; 6:2a, 21, 47; 9:21; 11:19; 15:33a, 42
Lk.	45	1:2, 5, 38; 2:6, 13, 42; 4:25, 36, 42; 6:13, 16, 36, 49; 8:24; 10:32, 36; 11:26, 30; 12:40, 54; 13:2, 4; 15:10; 16:11, 12; 17:26, 28; 18:23, 24; 19:17, 19; 20:14, 33; 22:24, 26, 40, 44, 44, 66; 23:24, 44; 24:5, 19, 22, 37	49	1:8, 23, 41, 59; 2:1, 15, 15, 46; 3:21; 5:1, 12, 17; 6:1, 6, 12; 7:11; 8:1, 22, 40; 9:18, 28, 33, 37, 51, 57; 10:38; 11:1, 14, 27; 12:55; 14:1; 16:22; 17:11, 14; 18:35; 19:15, 29; 20:1; 21:7, 9, 28, 31, 36; 24:4, 12, 15, 18, 30, 51	6	2:2; 4:3; 8:17; 14:12; 23:12, 19	16	4:23; 8:34, 35, 56; 9:7; 10:13, 13; 11:2; 13:17; 14:22; 22:42; 23:8, 31, 47, 48; 24:21	7	1:65; 3:2, 22; 9:34, 35; 19:9; 22:14
Jn.	18	1:6; 2:1; 3:9; 4:14; 6:17, 21; 7:43; 8:58; 9:22, 27; 10:16, 19, 22; 12:36, 42; 14:22; 15:8; 20:27	3	13:19b; 14:29, 29	12	1:3, 3, 3, 10, 14; 2:9; 5:4, 6, 9, 14a; 8:33; 9:39	3	1:28; 15:7; 19:36	8	1:17; 5:14b; 6:16, 25; 10:35; 12:30; 13:19a; 21:4
Ac.	38	1:16, 19, 20; 2:6; 4:4; 5:7a; 7:29, 38, 52; 8:1, 8; 9:19, 42; 10:4, 25; 12:18a, 23; 13:5; 15:7, 39; 16:26, 35; 19:17, 21, 28; 20:16b, 18; 22:9, 17b; 23:12; 25:15; 26:4, 19, 28, 29; 27:36, 39, 42	15	4:5; 9:32, 37, 43; 11:26, 28; 14:1; 16:16; 19:1; 21:1; 22:6, 17a; 27:44; 28:8, 17	7	7:13; 12:5; 13:32; 14:5; 19:26; 21:40; 26:6	15	2:43b; 4:16, 21, 28, 30; 5:7b; 8:13; 10:16; 11:10; 12:9; 13:12; 14:3; 21:14; 24:2; 28:9	15	2:2, 43a; 5:5, 11; 7:31; 10:13; 12:11; 16:29; 21:17, 35; 26:22; 27:7, 16, 27; 28:6
Ro.	12	3:4b; 6:5; 9:29; 11:5, 6, 34; 12:16; 15:8, 16, 31; 16:2, 7			5	1:3; 2:25; 7:13a; 10:20; 11:9				
1 Co.	16	2:3; 3:18b; 4:16; 7:23; 9:23, 27; 10:6, 7; 11:1; 14:20, 20; 15:10, 37, 58; 16:2, 10			9	1:30; 3:13; 4:9, 13; 7:21; 9:22b; 11:19; 14:25; 15:45	4	9:15; 14:26, 40; 16:14		
2 Co.	7	1:18, 19, 19; 3:7; 6:14; 8:14, 14			1	5:21			1	1:8
Gal.	4	3:17, 24; 4:12; 5:26			3	3:13; 4:4, 4			1	3:14
Eph.	5	4:32; 5:1, 7, 17; 6:3			2	2:13; 3:7	1	5:12		
Phl.	4	1:13; 2:15; 3:17, 21			1	2:7				
Col.	2	3:15; 4:11			2	1:23, 25				
1 Th.	6	1:5b, 7; 2:1, 7, 8; 3:5	1	3:4					1	1:5a
2 Th.										
1 Ti.	3	2:14; 4:12; 5:9							1	6:4
2 Ti.	2	1:17; 3:9							1	3:11
Tit.					1	3:7				
Phe.										
Heb.	8	2:2, 17; 5:11; 6:12; 7:18; 9:22; 11:6; 12:8			10	1:4; 3:14; 5:5; 6:4, 20; 7:12, 16, 22, 26; 11:3			1	11:24
Jas.	7	1:12, 22, 25; 2:10; 3:1, 10; 5:2			1	3:9				
1 Pt.	6	1:15, 16; 3:6, 13; 4:12; 5:3			1	2:7				
2 Pt.	5	1:4, 16, 20; 2:1, 20								
1 Jn.	1	2:18								
3 Jn.	1	1:8								
Rev.	22	1:9, 10, 18, 19; 2:8, 10; 3:2; 4:1, 2; 6:12a; 8:1, 5; 11:13, 13, 15a, 19; 12:7; 16:10, 18, 18, 18, 18	1	1:1			3	16:17; 21:6; 22:6	1	12:10
Total	255		82		69		63		52	

Miscellaneous: Mt. 11:26, seem; Mt. 21:19, grow; Mt. 21:42b, be (one's) doing; Mk. 1:4, do; Mk. 1:32, at; Mk. 4:22, be kept; Mk. 5:16, befall; Mk. 6:2b, be wrought; Mk. 9:50 (with 358), lose ... saltness; Mk. 12:11, be (one's) doing; Mk. 14:17 (with 3698), in the evening; Lk. 1:20, be performed; Lk. 1:44, sound; Lk. 9:29 (with 2087), be altered; Lk. 9:36, be past; Lk. 10:21, seem; Lk. 13:19, wax; Jn. 6:19, draw; Jn. 12:29 (with 1027), it thundered; Jn. 13:2, be ended; Jn. 16:20, be turned; Ac. 1:18, fall; Ac. 1:22, be ordained to be; Ac. 4:22, be shewed; Ac. 5:12, be wrought; Ac. 5:24, grow; Ac. 5:36, be

1104. γνησίως, gnesi'ōs

Book	naturally	Total
Phl.	2:20	1

1105. γνόφος, gnoph'os

Book	blackness	Total
Heb.	12:18	1

1106. γνώμη, gnō'me

Book	Oc.	judgment	Oc.	mind	Oc.	purpose (with 1096)	Oc.	advice	Oc.	will	Oc.	agree (with 4060 and 3291)	Total
Ac.					1	20:3							1
1 Co.	3	1:10; 7:25, 40											3
2 Co.							1	8:10					1
Phe.			1	1:14									1
Rev.			1	17:13					1	17:17a	1	17:17b	3
Total	3		2		1		1		1		1		9

1096. γίνομαι, gin'omai (continued)

Book	Oc.	become	Oc.	God forbid (with 3261)	Oc.	arise	Oc.	have	Oc.	be fulfilled	Oc.	be married to	Oc.	be preferred	Oc.	Not Tr.	Oc.	Misc.	Total
Mt.	5	13:22, 32; 18:3; 21:42a; 28:4			2	8:24; 13:21	1	18:12	2	5:18; 24:34							3	11:26; 21:19, 42b	74
Mk.	5	1:17; 4:19, 32; 9:3; 12:10			2	4:17, 37											8	1:4, 32; 4:22; 5:16; 6:2b; 9:50; 12:11; 14:17	54
Lk.	1	20:17	1	20:16	2	6:48; 15:14			1	21:32					1	24:31	6	1:20, 44; 9:29, 36; 10:21; 13:19	135
Jn.	1	1:12			1	3:25							3	1:15, 27, 30			4	6:19; 12:29; 13:2; 16:20	53
Ac.	4	4:11; 7:40; 10:10; 12:18b			6	6:1; 11:19; 19:23; 23:7, 9, 10	1	15:2							12	7:32, 39; 9:3; 10:40; 16:27; 19:34; 20:3, 3, 37; 21:5; 24:25; 27:29	14	1:18, 22; 4:22; 5:12, 24, 36; 10:37; 15:25; 19:10; 20:3, 16a; 21:30; 25:26; 27:33	127
Ro.	3	3:19; 4:18; 7:13c	10	3:4a, 6, 31; 6:2, 15; 7:7, 13b; 9:14; 11:1, 11							3	7:3, 3, 4					2	11:17, 25	35
1 Co.	7	3:18a; 8:9; 9:20, 22a; 13:1, 11; 15:20	1	6:15			2	4:5; 10:20									3	7:36; 10:32; 15:54	42
2 Co.	2	5:17; 12:11															1	7:14	12
Gal.	1	4:16	3	2:17; 3:21; 6:14															12
Eph.																			8
Phl.	1	2:8													1	3:6			7
Col.							1	1:18											5
1 Th.	2	1:6; 2:14															2	2:5, 10	12
2 Th.																	1	2:7	1
1 Ti.																			4
2 Ti.																	1	2:18	4
Tit.																			1
Phe.	1	1:6																	1
Heb.	4	5:9, 12; 10:33; 11:7															5	4:3; 7:21, 23; 9:15; 11:34	28
Jas.	2	2:4, 11																	10
1 Pt.																			7
2 Pt.																			5
1 Jn.																			1
3 Jn.																			1
Rev.	8	6:12b, 12c; 8:8, 11; 11:15b; 16:3, 4; 18:2															3	8:7; 16:2, 19	38
Total	47		15		13		5		3		3		3		14		53		677

brought; Ac. 10:37, be published; Ac. 15:25, be assembled; Ac. 19:10, continue; Ac. 20:3 (with 1917), lay wait for; Ac. 20:16a, would; Ac. 21:30 (with 4790), run together; Ac. 25:26, be had; Ac. 27:33 (with 3195), be coming; Ro. 11:17 (with 4691), partake with; Ro. 11:25, happen; 1 Co. 7:36, require; 1 Co. 10:32, give; 1 Co. 15:54, be brought to pass; 2 Co. 7:14, be found; 1 Th. 2:5 (with 1722), to use; 1 Th. 2:10, behave (one's) self; 2 Th. 2:7, be taken; 2 Ti. 2:18, be past; Heb. 4:3, be finished; Heb. 7:21 (with 1526), be made; Heb. 7:23 (with 1526), were; Heb. 9:15, by means of; Heb. 11:34, wax; Rev. 8:7, follow; Rev. 16:2, fall; Rev. 16:19, be divided.

1107. γνωρίζω, gnōrid′zō

Book	Oc.	make known	Oc.	declare	Oc.	certify	Oc.	give to understand	Oc.	do to wit	Oc.	wot	Total
Lk.	1	2:15											1
Jn.	1	15:15	2	17:26, 26									3
Ac.	1	2:28											1
Ro.	3	9:22, 23; 16:26											3
1 Co.			1	15:1			1	12:3					2
2 Co.									1	8:1			1
Gal.					1	1:11							1
Eph.	6	1:9; 3:3, 5, 10; 6:19, 21											6
Phl.	1	4:6									1	1:22	2
Col.	2	1:27; 4:9	1	4:7									3
2 Pt.	1	1:16											1
Total	16		4		1		1		1		1		24

1108. γνῶσις, gnō′sis

Book	Oc.	knowledge	Oc.	science	Total
Lk.	2	1:77; 11:52			2
Ro.	3	2:20; 11:33; 15:14			3
1 Co.	10	1:5; 8:1, 1, 7, 10, 11; 12:8; 13:2, 8; 14:6			10
2 Co.	6	2:14; 4:6; 6:6; 8:7; 10:5; 11:6			6
Eph.	1	3:19			1
Phl.	1	3:8			1
Col.	1	2:3			1
1 Ti.			1	6:20	1
1 Pt.	1	3:7			1
2 Pt.	3	1:5, 6; 3:18			3
Total	28		1		29

1110. γνωστός, gnōstos′

Book	Oc.	known	Oc.	acquaintance	Oc.	notable	Total
Lk.			2	2:44; 23:49			2
Jn.	2	18:15, 16					2
Ac.	9	1:19; 2:14; 4:10; 9:42; 13:38; 15:18; 19:17; 28:22, 28			1	4:16	10
Ro.	1	1:19					1
Total	12		2		1		15

1109. γνώστης, gnōs′tes

Book	expert	Total
Ac.	26:3	1

1113. γογγυστής, gonggustes′

Book	murmurer	Total
Jd.	1:16	1

1111. γογγύζω, gonggud′zō

Book	murmur	Total
Mt.	20:11	1
Lk.	5:30	1
Jn.	6:41, 43, 61; 7:32	4
1 Co.	10:10, 10	2
Total		8

1112. γογγυσμός, gonggusmos′

Book	Oc.	murmuring	Oc.	grudging	Total
Jn.	1	7:12			1
Ac.	1	6:1			1
Phl.	1	2:14			1
1 Pt.			1	4:9	1
Total	3		1		4

1114. γόης, go′es

Book	seducer	Total
2 Ti.	3:13	1

1115. Γολγοθᾶ, Golgotha′

Book	Golgotha	Total
Mt.	27:33	1
Mk.	15:22	1
Jn.	19:17	1
Total		3

1116. Γόμοῤῥα, Gom′orhra

Book	Gomorrha	Total
Mt.	10:15	1
Mk.	6:11	1
Ro.	9:29	1
2 Pt.	2:6	1
Jd.	1:7	1
Total		5

1117. γόμος, gom′os

Book	Oc.	merchandise	Oc.	burden	Total
Ac.			1	21:3	1
Rev.	2	18:11, 12			2
Total	2		1		3

1118. γονεύς, goneus′

Book	parents	Total
Mt.	10:21	1
Mk.	13:12	1
Lk.	2:27, 41; 8:56; 18:29; 21:16	5
Jn.	9:2, 3, 18, 20, 22, 23	6
Ro.	1:30	1
2 Co.	12:14, 14	2
Eph.	6:1	1
Col.	3:20	1
2 Ti.	3:2	1
Total		19

1121. γράμμα, gram′ma

Book	Oc.	letter	Oc.	bill	Oc.	writing	Oc.	learning	Oc.	scripture	Oc.	written (with 1722)	Total
Lk.	1	23:38	2	16:6, 7									3
Jn.	1	7:15			1	5:47							2
Ac.	1	28:21					1	26:24					2
Ro.	3	2:27, 29; 7:6											3
2 Co.	2	3:6, 6									1	3:7	3
Gal.	1	6:11											1
2 Ti.									1	3:15			1
Total	9		2		1		1		1		1		15

1119. γονύ, gonu′

Book	Oc.	knee	Oc.	kneel (with 4987 and 3488)	Total
Mk.	1	15:19			1
Lk.	1	5:8	1	22:41	2
Ac.			4	7:60; 9:40; 20:36; 21:5	4
Ro.	2	11:4; 14:11			2
Eph.	1	3:14			1
Phl.	1	2:10			1
Heb.	1	12:12			1
Total	7		5		12

1120. γονυπετέω, gonupete′ō

Book	Oc.	kneel down to	Oc.	bow the knee	Oc.	kneel to	Total
Mt.	1	17:14	1	27:29			2
Mk.	1	1:40			1	10:17	2
Total	2		1		1		4

1123. γραπτός, graptos′

Book	written	Total
Ro.	2:15	1

1122. γραμματεύς, grammateus′

Book	Oc.	scribe	Oc.	townclerk	Total
Mt.	24	2:4; 5:20; 7:29; 8:19; 9:3; 12:38; 13:52; 15:1; 16:21; 17:10; 20:18; 21:15; 23:2, 13, 14, 15, 23, 25, 27, 29, 34; 26:3, 57; 27:41			24
Mk.	22	1:22; 2:6, 16; 3:22; 7:1, 5; 8:31; 9:11, 14, 16; 10:33; 11:18, 27; 12:28, 32, 35, 38; 14:1, 43, 53; 15:1, 31			22
Lk.	15	5:21, 30; 6:7; 9:22; 11:44, 53; 15:2; 19:47; 20:1, 19, 39, 46; 22:2, 66; 23:10			15
Jn.	1	8:3			1
Ac.	3	4:5; 6:12; 23:9	1	19:35	4
1 Co.	1	1:20			1
Total	66		1		67

1124. γραφή, graphe′

Book	scripture	Total
Mt.	21:42; 22:29; 26:54, 56	4
Mk.	12:10, 24; 14:49; 15:28	4
Lk.	4:21; 24:27, 32, 45	4
Jn.	2:22; 5:39; 7:38, 42; 10:35; 13:18; 17:12; 19:24, 28, 36, 37; 20:9	12
Ac.	1:16; 8:32, 35; 17:2, 11; 18:24, 28	7
Ro.	1:2; 4:3; 9:17; 10:11; 11:2; 15:4; 16:26	7
1 Co.	15:3, 4	2
Gal.	3:8, 22; 4:30	3
1 Ti.	5:18	1
2 Ti.	3:16	1
Jas.	2:8, 23; 4:5	3
1 Pt.	2:6	1
2 Pt.	1:20; 3:16	2
Total		51

1125. γράφω, graph´ō

Book	Oc.	write	Oc.	writing	Oc.	describe	Total
Mt.	10	2:5; 4:4, 6, 7, 10; 11:10; 21:13; 26:24, 31; 27:37					10
Mk.	10	1:2; 7:6; 9:12, 13; 10:4, 5; 11:17; 12:19; 14:21, 27					10
Lk.	22	1:3, 63; 2:23; 3:4; 4:4, 8, 10, 17; 7:27; 10:20, 26; 16:6, 7; 18:31; 19:46; 20:17, 28; 21:22; 22:37; 23: 38; 24:44, 46					22
Jn.	22	1:45; 2:17; 5:46; 6:31, 45; 8:6, 8, 17; 10:34; 12:14, 16; 15:25; 19:19a, 20, 21, 22, 22; 20:30, 31; 21:24, 25, 25	1	19:19b			23
Ac.	12	1:20; 7:42; 13:29, 33; 15:15, 23; 18:27; 23:5, 25; 24:14; 25:26, 26					12
Ro.	19	1:17; 2:24; 3:4, 10; 4:17, 23; 8:36; 9:13, 33; 10:15; 11:8, 26; 12:19; 14:11; 15:3, 9, 15, 21; 16:22			1	10:5	20
1 Co.	18	1:19, 31; 2:9; 3:19; 4:6, 14; 5:9, 11; 7:1; 9:9, 10, 15; 10:7, 11; 14:21, 37; 15:45, 54					18
2 Co.	11	1:13; 2:3, 4, 9; 4:13; 7:12; 8:15; 9:1, 9; 13:2, 10					11
Gal.	7	1:20; 3:10, 10, 13; 4:22, 27; 6:11					7
Phl.	1	3:1					1
1 Th.	2	4:9; 5:1					2
2 Th.	1	3:17					1
1 Ti.	1	3:14					1
Phe.	2	1:19, 21					2
Heb.	1	10:7					1
1 Pt.	2	1:16; 5:12					2
2 Pt.	2	3:1, 15					2
1 Jn.	13	1:4; 2:1, 7, 8, 12, 13, 13, 13, 14, 14, 21, 26; 5:13					13
2 Jn.	2	1:5, 12					2
3 Jn.	3	1:9, 13, 13					3
Jd.	2	1:3, 3					2
Rev.	29	1:3, 11, 19; 2:1, 8, 12, 17, 18; 3:1, 7, 12, 14; 5:1; 10:4, 4; 13:8; 14:1, 13; 17:5, 8; 19:9, 12, 16; 20:12, 15; 21:5, 27; 22:18, 19					29
Total	192		1		1		194

1126. γραώδης, graō´dēs

Book	old wife	Total
1 Ti.	4:7	1

1127. γρηγορεύω, grēgoreu´ō

Book	Oc.	watch	Oc.	wake	Oc.	be vigilant	Total
Mt.	6	24:42, 43; 25:13; 26:38, 40, 41					6
Mk.	6	13:34, 35, 37; 14:34, 37, 38					6
Lk.	2	12:37, 39					2
Ac.	1	20:31					1
1 Co.	1	16:13					1
Col.	1	4:2					1
1 Th.	1	5:6	1	5:10			2
1 Pt.					1	5:8	1
Rev.	3	3:2, 3; 16:15					3
Total	21		1		1		23

1128. γυμνάζω, gumnad´zō

Book	exercise	Total
1 Ti.	4:7	1
Heb.	5:14; 12:11	2
2 Pt.	2:14	1
Total		4

1129. γυμνασία, gumnasi´a

Book	exercise	Total
1 Ti.	4:8	1

1130. γυμνητεύω, gumnēteu´ō

Book	be naked	Total
1 Co.	4:11	1

1131. γυμνός, gumnos´

Book	Oc.	naked	Oc.	bare	Total
Mt.	4	25:36, 38, 43, 44			4
Mk.	2	14:51, 52			2
Jn.	1	21:7			1
Ac.	1	19:16			1
1 Co.			1	15:37	1
2 Co.	1	5:3			1
Heb.	1	4:13			1
Jas.	1	2:15			1
Rev.	3	3:17; 16:15; 17:16			3
Total	14		1		15

1132. γυμνότης, gumnot´ēs

Book	nakedness	Total
Ro.	8:35	1
2 Co.	11:27	1
Rev.	3:18	1
Total		3

1133. γυναικάριον, gunaikar´ion

Book	silly woman	Total
2 Ti.	3:6	1

1136. Γώγ, Gōg

Book	Gog	Total
Rev.	20:8	1

1134. γυναικεῖος, gunaikei´os

Book	wife	Total
1 Pt.	3:7	1

1135. γυνή, gunē´

Book	Oc.	woman	Oc.	wife	Total
Mt.	14	5:28; 9:20, 22; 11:11; 13:33; 14:21; 15:22, 28, 38; 22:27; 26:7, 10; 27:55; 28:5	16	1:20, 24; 5:31, 32; 14:3; 18:25; 19:3, 5, 8, 9, 10, 29; 22:24, 25, 28; 27:19	30
Mk.	8	5:25, 33; 7:25, 26; 10:12; 12:22; 14:3; 15:40	11	6:17, 18; 10:2, 7, 11, 29; 12:19, 19, 20, 23, 23	19
Lk.	25	1:28, 42; 4:26; 7:28, 37, 39, 44, 44, 50; 8:2, 43, 47; 10:38; 11:27; 13:11, 12, 21; 15:8; 20:32; 22:57; 23:27, 49, 55; 24:22, 24	18	1:5, 13, 18, 24; 2:5; 3:19; 8:3; 14:20, 26; 16:18; 17:32; 18: 29; 20:28, 28, 29, 30, 33, 33	43
Jn.	23	2:4; 4:7, 9, 9, 11, 15, 17, 19, 21, 25, 27, 28, 39, 42; 8:3, 4, 9, 10, 10; 16:21; 19:26; 20:13, 15			23
Ac.	13	1:14; 5:14; 8:3, 12; 9:2; 13:50; 16:1, 13, 14; 17:4, 12, 34; 22:4	6	5:1, 2, 7; 18:2; 21:5; 24:24	19
Ro.	1	7:2			1
1 Co.	20	7:1, 13; 11:3, 5, 6, 6, 7, 8, 8, 9, 9, 10, 11, 11, 12, 12, 13, 15; 14:34, 35	21	5:1; 7:2, 3, 3, 4, 4, 10, 11, 12, 14, 14, 16, 16, 27, 27, 27, 29, 33, 34, 39; 9:5	41
Gal.	1	4:4			1
Eph.			9	5:22, 23, 24, 25, 28, 28, 31, 33, 33	9
Col.			2	3:18, 19	2
1 Ti.	5	2:9, 10, 11, 12, 14	4	3:2, 11, 12; 5:9	9
Tit.			1	1:6	1
Heb.	1	11:35			1
1 Pt.	1	3:5	2	3:1, 1	3
Rev.	17	2:20; 9:8; 12:1, 4, 6, 13, 14, 15, 16, 17; 14:4; 17:3, 4, 6, 7, 9, 18	2	19:7; 21:9	19
Total	129		92		221

1137. γωνία, gōni´a

Book	Oc.	corner	Oc.	quarter	Total
Mt.	2	6:5; 21:42			2
Mk.	1	12:10			1
Lk.	1	20:17			1
Ac.	2	4:11; 26:26			2
1 Pt.	1	2:7			1
Rev.	1	7:1	1	20:8	2
Total	8		1		9

1138. Δαβίδ, Dabid´

Book	David	Total
Mt.	1:1, 6, 6, 17, 17, 20; 9:27; 12:3, 23; 15:22; 20:30, 31; 21:9, 15; 22:42, 43, 45	17
Mk.	2:25; 10:47, 48; 11:10; 12:35, 36, 37	7
Lk.	1:27, 32, 69; 2:4, 4, 11; 3:31; 6:3; 18:38, 39; 20:41, 42, 44	13
Jn.	7:42, 42	2
Ac.	1:16; 2:25, 29, 34; 4:25; 7:45; 13:22, 22, 34, 36; 15:16	11
Ro.	1:3; 4:6; 11:9	3
2 Ti.	2:8	1
Heb.	4:7; 11:32	2
Rev.	3:7; 5:5; 22:16	3
Total		59

1139. δαιμονίζομαι, daimonid′zomai

Book	Oc.	possessed with devils	Oc.	possessed with the devil	Oc.	possessed of the devils	Oc.	possessed with a devil	Oc.	vexed with a devil	Oc.	have a devil	Total
Mt.	3	4:24; 8:16; 8:28			1	8:33	2	9:32; 12:22	1	15:22			7
Mk.	1	1:32	3	5:15, 16, 18									4
Lk.					1	8:36							1
Jn.											1	10:21	1
Total	4		3		2		2		1		1		13

1140. δαιμόνιον, daimon′ion

Book	Oc.	devil	Oc.	god	Total
Mt.	11	7:22; 9:33, 34, 34; 10:8; 11:18; 12:24, 24, 27, 28; 17:18			11
Mk.	13	1:34, 34, 39; 3:15, 22, 22; 6:13; 7:26, 29, 30; 9:38; 16:9, 17			13
Lk.	22	4:33, 35, 41; 7:33; 8:2, 27, 30, 33, 35, 38; 9: 1, 42, 49; 10:17; 11:14, 14, 15, 15, 18, 19, 20; 13:32			22
Jn.	6	7:20; 8:48, 49, 52; 10:20, 21			6
Ac.			1	17:18	1
1 Co.	4	10:20, 20, 21, 21			4
1 Ti.	1	4:1			1
Jas.	1	2:19			1
Rev.	1	9:20			1
Total	59		1		60

1141. δαιμονιώδης, daimoniō′dēs

Book	devilish	Total
Jas.	3:15	1

1142. δαίμων, dai′mōn

Book	Oc.	devils	Oc.	devil	Total
Mt.	1	8:31			1
Mk.	1	5:12			1
Lk.			1	8:29	1
Rev.	2	16:14; 18:2			2
Total	4		1		5

1143. δάκνω, dak′nō

Book	bite	Total
Gal.	5:15	1

1144a. δάκρυ, dak′ru

Book	tear	Total
Mk.	9:24	1
Lk.	7:38, 44	2
Ac.	20:19, 31	2
2 Co.	2:4	1
2 Ti.	1:4	1
Heb.	5:7; 12:17	2
Total		9

1144b. δάκρυον, dak′ruon

Book	tear	Total
Rev.	7:17; 21:4	2

Word 1144 has 11 occurrences.

1145. δακρύω, dakru′ō

Book	weep	Total
Jn.	11:35	1

1146. δακτύλιος, daktu′lios

Book	ring	Total
Lk.	15:22	1

1147. δάκτυλος, dak′tulos

Book	finger	Total
Mt.	23:4	1
Mk.	7:23	1
Lk.	11:20, 46; 16:24	3
Jn.	8:6; 20:25, 27	3
Total		8

1148. Δαλμανουθά Dalmanoutha′

Book	Dalmanutha	Total
Mk.	8:10	1

1149. Δαλματία, Dalmati′a

Book	Dalmatia	Total
2 Ti.	4:10	1

1150. δαμάζω, damad′zō

Book	tame	Total
Mk.	5:4	1
Jas.	3:7, 7, 8	3
Total		4

1151. δάμαλις, dam′alis

Book	heifer	Total
Heb.	9:13	1

1152. Δάμαρις, Dam′aris

Book	Damaris	Total
Ac.	17:34	1

1153. Δαμασκηνός, Damaskēnos′

Book	Damascenes	Total
2 Co.	11:32	1

1154. Δαμασκός, Damaskos′

Book	Damascus	Total
Ac.	9:2, 3, 8, 10, 19, 22, 27; 22:5, 6, 10, 11; 26:12, 20	13
2 Co.	11:32	1
Gal.	1:17	1
Total		15

1155. δανείζω, daneid′zō

Book	Oc.	lend	Oc.	borrow	Total
Mt.			1	5:42	1
Lk.	3	6:34, 34, 35			3
Total	3		1		4

1161. δέ, de

(Occurrences rendered other than "and, " "but" and "not translated")

Book	Oc.	now	Oc.	then	Oc.	also	Oc.	yet
Mt.	20	1:18, 22; 2:1; 4:12; 8:18; 10:2; 11:2; 21:18; 22:25; 24: 32; 26:6, 17, 20, 48, 69; 27:15, 45, 54, 62; 28:11	17	1:19, 24; 12:14; 13:52; 14:33; 15:15, 25, 32; 16:6; 17:4, 17; 18:27; 19:23; 25:16, 24; 26:25; 28:16	3	13:22; 16: 18; 27:41	1	13:21
Mk.	7	1:14, 16; 5:11; 13:12, 28; 15:6; 16:9	3	10:21; 14:63; 15:14	1	4:36		
Lk.	17	1:57; 3:1, 21; 4:40; 5:4; 7:1, 12, 39; 8:11, 38; 9:7; 10: 38; 15:25; 18:22; 20:37; 22:1; 23:47	41	1:34; 3:12; 7:6; 8:19, 24, 33, 35; 9:1, 12, 16, 46; 11:45; 12:20, 28, 41; 13:7, 18, 23; 14:12, 16; 15:1; 16:27; 17:1; 18:28, 31; 19:16; 20: 9, 13, 27, 39, 45; 22:3, 7, 52, 54, 70; 23:4, 9, 34; 24:12, 25	2	12:8; 13:6		
Jn.	22	1:44; 2:23; 4:6, 43; 5:2; 6:10; 7:2; 8:5; 9:31; 11:1, 5, 18, 30, 57; 13:1, 23, 28; 18:14, 40; 19:23, 25, 41	4	1:38; 9:26; 13:25; 21:20	2	8:17; 15: 27	1	8:16
Ac.	21	2:6, 37; 3:1; 4:13; 5:24; 7:11; 8:14; 9:36; 10:17; 12:1, 18; 13:1, 13, 43; 16:6; 17:1, 16; 18:14; 21:3; 24:17; 27:9	59	2:38; 3:6; 5:9, 10, 17, 25, 29, 34; 6:2, 9; 7:1, 14, 29, 32, 33, 42, 57; 8:5, 13, 24, 29, 35; 9:13, 19, 25, 39; 10:21, 34; 11:16, 22, 25, 29; 12:3, 15; 13:9, 16, 46; 14:13; 15:12; 16:1, 29; 17:18, 22; 18:9, 17; 19:4, 13; 21:13; 22:27; 23:17, 19; 24: 10; 25:2, 10, 22; 26:1, 28, 32; 27:36	4	5:32; 15: 35; 19:19; 22:29		
Ro.	15	1:13; 3:19; 4:4, 23; 6:8; 7:20; 8:9; 11:12; 15:5, 8, 13, 30, 33; 16:17, 25	7	6:18; 7:16, 17; 8:8; 12:6; 13:3; 15:1	2	9:27; 11: 23		
1 Co.	23	1:10, 12; 2:1, 12; 3:8, 12; 4:18; 6:13; 7:1, 25a; 8:1; 10:6, 11; 11:2, 17; 12:1, 4, 27; 15:12, 50; 16:1, 5, 10					4	2:6b, 15b; 7: 25b; 15:10b
2 Co.	8	1:21; 2:14; 3:17; 5:5; 6:13; 9:10; 10:1; 13:7					4	6:10, 10; 9: 3; 12:5
Gal.	6	1:20; 3:16, 20; 4:1, 28; 5:19	1	5:16				
Eph.	2	3:20; 4:9						
Phl.	2	4:15, 20					1	2:25
Col.							1	1:21
1 Th.	2	3:11; 5:14						
2 Th.	5	2:1, 16; 3:6, 12, 16						
1 Ti.	4	1:5, 17; 4:1; 5:5			1	3:10		
2 Ti.	1	3:8			2	2:22; 3:1		
Heb.	9	7:4; 8:1, 13; 9:6; 10:18, 38; 11:1; 12:11; 13:20						
Jas.	1	2:11a					2	2:11b; 4:2
1 Pt.							1	1:8
2 Pt.								
1 Jn.								
3 Jn.					1	1:12		
Jd.	1	1:24					1	1:9
Total	166		132		18		16	

1156. δάνειον, dan'eion

Book	debt	Total
Mt.	18:27	1

1157. δανειστής, daneistes'

Book	creditor	Total
Lk.	7:41	1

1158. Δανιήλ, Daniel'

Book	Daniel	Total
Mt.	24:15	1
Mk.	13:14	1
Total		2

1160. δαπάνη, dapan'e

Book	cost	Total
Lk.	14:28	1

1159. δαπανάω, dapana'ō

Book	Oc.	spend	Oc.	be at charges with	Oc.	consume	Total
Mk.	1	5:26					1
Lk.	1	15:14					1
Ac.			1	21:24			1
2 Co.	1	12:15					1
Jas.					1	4:3	1
Total	3		1		1		5

1162. δέησις, de'esis

Book	Oc.	prayer	Oc.	supplication	Oc.	request	Total
Lk.	3	1:13; 2:37; 5:33					3
Ac.			1	1:14			1
Ro.	1	10:1					1
2 Co.	2	1:11; 9:14					2
Eph.			2	6:18, 18			2
Phl.	2	1:4a, 19	1	4:6	1	1:4b	4
1 Ti.			2	2:1; 5:5			2
2 Ti.	1	1:3					1
Heb.	1	5:7					1
Jas.	1	5:16					1
1 Pt.	1	3:12					1
Total	12		6		1		19

1164. δεῖγμα, deig'ma

Book	example	Total
Jd.	1:7	1

1165. δειγματίζω, deigmatid'zō

Book	make a shew	Total
Col.	2:15	1

1163. δεῖ, dei

Book	Oc.	must	Oc.	ought	Oc.	must needs	Oc.	should	Oc.	Misc.	Total
Mt.	4	16:21; 17:10; 24:6; 26:54	2	23:23; 25:27			2	18:33; 26:35			8
Mk.	3	8:31; 9:11; 13:10	1	13:14	1	13:7	1	14:31			6
Lk.	11	2:49; 4:43; 9:22; 13:33; 17:25; 19:5; 21:9; 22:7, 37; 24:7, 44	6	11:42; 12:12; 13:14, 16; 18:1; 24:26					2	15:32; 24:46	19
Jn.	8	3:7, 14, 30; 4:24; 9:4; 10:16; 12:34; 20:9	1	4:20	1	4:4					10
Ac.	12	**1:22; 3:21; 4:12; 9:6, 16; 14:22; 16:30; 18:21; 19:21; 23:11; 27:24, 26**	7	5:29; 10:6; 20:35; 24:19; 25:10; 25:24; 26:9	2	1:16; 17:3	1	27:21	3	15:5; 19:36; 21:22	25
Ro.			2	8:26; 12:3					1	1:27	3
1 Co.	3	11:19; 15:25, 53	1	8:2							4
2 Co.	1	5:10	1	2:3	1	11:30					3
Eph.			1	6:20							1
Col.			2	4:4, 6							2
1 Th.			1	4:1							1
2 Th.			1	3:7							1
1 Ti.	2	3:2, 7	2	3:15; 5:13							4
2 Ti.	2	2:6, 24									2
Tit.	2	1:7, 11a	1	1:11b							3
Heb.	2	9:26; 11:6	1	2:1							3
1 Pt.									1	1:6	1
2 Pt.			1	3:11							1
Rev.	8	1:1; 4:1; 10:11; 11:5; 13:10; 17:10; 20:3; 22:6									8
Total	58		31		5		4		7		105

Miscellaneous: Lk. 15:32, be meet; Lk. 24:46, behove; Ac. 15:5, be needful; Ac. 19:36 (with 2076), ought; Ac. 21:22 (with 3743), must needs; Ro. 1:27, be meet; 1 Pt. 1:6, be need.

1161. δέ, de (continued)

Book	Oc.	yea	Oc.	moreover	Oc.	so	Oc.	nevertheless	Oc.	for	Oc.	even	Oc.	Misc.	Total
Mt.			2	6:16; 18:15	7	8:31; 13:27; 18:31; 20:8, 34; 27:66; 28:15							1	6:29	51
Mk.					1	8:8			1	16:8					13
Lk.	1	2:35					1	5:5	.1	23:17					63
Jn.					2	8:7; 20:4							1	6:23	32
Ac.	3	3:16, 24; 20:34	1	11:12	2	4:21; 7:15	1	27:11					1	25:25b	92
Ro.	2	3:4; 8:34	2	5:20; 8:30			1	15:15	1	11:16	2	3:22; 9:30			32
1 Co.	2	9:16; 15:15	2	10:1; 15:1	1	15:54	3	7:2, 28, 37					3	2:6a; 4:2; 7:8	38
2 Co.	1	5:16	2	1:23; 8:1			1	3:16					1	2:12	17
Gal.							1	2:20							8
Eph.															2
Phl.							1	1:24	1	2:18	1	2:8			6
Col.															1
1 Th.															2
2 Th.															5
1 Ti.			1	3:7											6
2 Ti.	1	3:12													4
Heb.	1	11:36	2	9:21; 11:36			1	12:11							13
Jas.															3
1 Pt.	1	5:5													2
2 Pt.	1	1:13	1	1:15			1	3:13					1	1:5	4
1 Jn.													1	1:3	1
3 Jn.															1
Jd.															2
Total	13		13		13		11		4		3		9		398

Miscellaneous: Mt. 6:29, and yet; Jn. 6:23, howbeit; Ac. 25:25b, that; 1 Co. 2:6a, howbeit; 1 Co. 4:2 (with 3063 and 3639), moreover; 1 Co. 7:8, therefore; 2 Co. 2:12, furthermore; 2 Pt. 1:5, beside; 1 Jn. 1:3, truly.

1166a. δείκνυμι, deik'numi

Book	shew	Total
Mt.	4:8; 8:4	2
Mk.	1:44; 14:15	2
Lk.	4:5; 5:14; 22:12	3
Jn.	5:20, 20; 10:32; 14:8, 9; 20:20	6
Ac.	7:3; 10:28	2
1 Co.	12:31	1
1 Ti.	6:15	1
Heb.	8:5	1
Jas.	2:18, 18; 3:13	3
Rev.	1:1; 4:1; 17:1; 21:9, 10; 22:1, 6	7
Total		28

1166b. δεικνύω, deiknu'ō

Book	shew	Total
Mt.	16:21	1
Jn.	2:18	1
Rev.	22:8	1
Total		3

Word 1166 has 31 occurrences.

1167. δειλία, deili'a

Book	fear	Total
2 Ti.	1:7	1

1168. δειλιάω, deilia'ō

Book	be afraid	Total
Jn.	14:27	1

1169. δειλός, deilos'

Book	fearful	Total
Mt.	8:26	1
Mk.	4:40	1
Rev.	21:8	1
Total		3

1170. δεῖνα, dei'na

Book	such a man	Total
Mt.	26:18	1

1174. δεισιδαιμονέστερος deisidaimones'teros

Book	too superstitious	Total
Ac.	17:22	1

1175. δεισιδαιμονία deisidaimoni'a

Book	superstition	Total
Ac.	25:19	1

1177. δεκαδύο, dekadu'o

Book	twelve	Total
Ac.	19:7; 24:11	2

1178. δεκαπέντε, dekapen'te

Book	fifteen	Total
Jn.	11:18	1
Ac.	27:28	1
Gal.	1:18	1
Total		3

1179. Δεκάπολις, Dekap'olis

Book	Decapolis	Total
Mt.	4:25	1
Mk.	5:20; 7:31	2
Total		3

1180. δεκατέσσαρες dekates'sares

Book	fourteen	Total
Mt.	1:17, 17, 17	3
2 Co.	12:2	1
Gal.	2:1	1
Total		5

1182. δέκατος, dek'atos

Book	tenth	Total
Jn.	1:39	1
Rev.	11:13; 21:20	2
Total		3

1171. δεινῶς, deinōs'

Book	Oc.	grievously	Oc.	vehemently	Total
Mt.	1	8:6			1
Lk.			1	11:53	1
Total	1		1		2

1172. δειπνέω, deipne'ō

Book	Oc.	sup	Oc.	supper	Total
Lk.	1	17:8	1	22:20	2
1 Co.	1	11:25			1
Rev.	1	3:20			1
Total	3		1		4

1173. δεῖπνον, deip'non

Book	Oc.	supper	Oc.	feast	Total
Mt.			1	23:6	1
Mk.	1	6:21	1	12:39	2
Lk.	4	14:12, 16, 17, 24	1	20:46	5
Jn.	4	12:2; 13:2, 4; 21:20			4
1 Co.	2	11:20, 21			2
Rev.	2	19:9, 17			2
Total	13		3		16

1176. δέκα, dek'a

Book	Oc.	ten	Oc.	eighteen (with 2532 and 3538)	Total
Mt.	3	20:24; 25:1, 28			3
Mk.	1	10:41			1
Lk.	10	14:31; 15:8; 17:12, 17; 19:13, 13, 16, 17, 24, 25	3	13:4, 11, 16	13
Ac.	1	25:6			1
Rev.	9	2:10; 12:3; 13:1, 1; 17:3, 7, 12, 12, 16			9
Total	24		3		27

1181. δεκάτη, dekat'ē

Book	Oc.	tithe	Oc.	tenth part	Oc.	tenth	Total
Heb.	2	7:8, 9	1	7:2	1	7:4	4

1183. δεκατόω, dekato'ō

Book	Oc.	receive tithes	Oc.	pay tithes	Total
Heb.	1	7:6	1	7:9	2

1185. δελεάζω, delead'zō

Book	Oc.	entice	Oc.	beguile	Oc.	allure	Total
Jas.	1	1:14					1
2 Pt.			1	2:14	1	2:18	2
Total	1		1		1		3

1184. δεκτός, dektos'

Book	Oc.	accepted	Oc.	acceptable	Total
Lk.	1	4:24	1	4:19	2
Ac.	1	10:35			1
2 Co.	1	6:2			1
Phl.			1	4:18	1
Total	3		2		5

1186. δένδρον, den'dron

Book	tree	Total
Mt.	3:10, 10; 7:17, 17, 18, 18, 19; 12:33, 33, 33; 13:32; 21:8	12
Mk.	8:24; 11:8	2
Lk.	3:9, 9; 6:43, 43, 44; 13:19; 21:29	7
Jd.	1:12	1
Rev.	7:1, 3; 8:7; 9:4	4
Total		26

1187. δεξιολάβος, dexiolab'os

Book	spearman	Total
Ac.	23:23	1

1188a. δεξιός, dexios'

Book	Oc.	right hand	Oc.	right	Oc.	right side	Total
Mt.	9	6:3; 20:21, 23; 22:44; 25:33, 34; 26:64; 27:29, 38	3	5:29, 30, 39			12
Mk.	6	10:37, 40; 12:36; 14:62; 15:27; 16:19			1	16:5	7
Lk.	3	20:42; 22:69; 23:33	2	6:6; 22:50	1	1:11	6
Jn.			2	18:10; 21:6			2
Ac.	6	2:25, 33, 34; 5:31; 7:55, 56	1	3:7			7
Ro.	1	8:34					1
2 Co.	1	6:7					1
Gal.	1	2:9					1
Eph.	1	1:20					1
Col.	1	3:1					1
Heb.	5	1:3, 13; 8:1; 10:12; 12:2					5
1 Pt.	1	3:22					1
Rev.	4	1:20; 2:1; 5:1, 7	4	1:16, 17; 10:2; 13:16			8
Total	39		12		2		53

1188b. δεξιός, dexios'

Word 1188 has 73 occurrences.

The following passages pertain to the session of Jesus at the right hand of God.

Book	Oc.	sit (or set) on the right hand of God	Oc.	sit on my right hand till (or until) (with Psalm 110:1)	Oc.	sit on the right hand of power (of God)	Oc.	set with my Father on his throne	Total
Mt.			1	22:44	1	26:64			2
Mk.	1	16:19	1	12:36	1	14:62			3
Lk.			1	20:42	1	22:69			2
Ac.	2	7:55, 56	1	2:34 (35)					3
Ro.	1	(8:34)							1
Eph.	1	1:20							1
Col.	1	3:1							1
Heb.	3	1:3; 8:1; 12:2	2	1:13; 10:12 (13)					5
1 Pt.	1	(3:22)							1
Rev.							1	3:21	1
Total	10		6		3		1		20

1189. δέομαι, de′omai

Book	Oc.	pray	Oc.	beseech	Oc.	make request	Total
Mt.	1	9:38					1
Lk.	3	10:2; 21:36; 22:32	5	5:12; 8:28, 38; 9:38, 40			8
Ac.	5	4:31; 8:22, 24, 34; 10:2	2	21:39; 26:3			7
Ro.					1	1:10	1
2 Co.	2	5:20; 8:4	1	10:2			3
Gal.			1	4:12			1
1 Th.	1	3:10					1
Total	12		9		1		22

1190. Δερβαῖος, Derbai′os

Book	of Derbe	Total
Ac.	20:4	1

1191. Δέρβη, Der′bē

Book	Derbe	Total
Ac.	14:6, 20; 16:1	3

1192. δέρμα, der′ma

Book	skin (with 122)	Total
Heb.	11:37	1

1193. δερμάτινος, dermat′inos

Book	Oc.	leathern	Oc.	of a skin	Total
Mt.	1	3:4			1
Mk.			1	1:6	1
Total	1		1		2

1195. δεσμεύω, desmeu′ō

Book	bind	Total
Mt.	23:4	1
Ac.	22:4	1
Total		2

1194. δέρω, der′ō

Book	Oc.	beat	Oc.	smite	Total
Mt.	1	21:35			1
Mk.	3	12:3, 5; 13:9			3
Lk.	4	12:47, 48; 20:10, 11	1	22:63	5
Jn.			1	18:23	1
Ac.	3	5:40; 16:37; 22:19			3
1 Co.	1	9:26			1
2 Co.			1	11:20	1
Total	12		3		15

1196. δεσμέω, desme′ō

Book	bind	Total
Lk.	8:29	1

1197. δεσμή, desmē′

Book	bundle	Total
Mt.	13:30	1

1198. δέσμιος, des′mios

Book	Oc.	prisoner	Oc.	be in bonds	Oc.	in bonds	Total
Mt.	2	27:15, 16					2
Mk.	1	15:6					1
Ac.	6	16:25, 27; 23:18; 25:27; 28:16, 17			1	25:14	7
Eph.	2	3:1; 4:1					2
2 Ti.	1	1:8					1
Phe.	2	1:1, 9					2
Heb.			1	13:3			1
Total	14		1		1		16

1200. δεσμοφύλαξ, desmophu′lax

Book	Oc.	keeper of the prison	Oc.	jailor	Total
Ac.	2	16:27, 36	1	16:23	3

1201. δεσμωτήριον, desmōtē′rion

Book	prison	Total
Mt.	11:2	1
Ac.	5:21, 23; 16:26	3
Total		4

1199. δεσμός, desmos′

Book	Oc.	bond	Oc.	band	Oc.	string	Oc.	chain	Total
Mk.					1	7:35			1
Lk.	1	13:16	1	8:29					2
Ac.	4	20:23; 23:29; 26:29, 31	2	16:26; 22:30					6
Phl.	4	1:7, 13, 14, 16							4
Col.	1	4:18							1
2 Ti.	1	2:9							1
Phe.	2	1:10, 13							2
Heb.	2	10:34; 11:36							2
Jd.							1	1:6	1
Total	15		3		1		1		20

1202. δεσμώτης, desmō′tēs

Book	prisoner	Total
Ac.	27:1, 42	2

1203. δεσπότης, despot′ēs

Book	Oc.	Lord	Oc.	master	Oc.	master (Lord)	Total
Lk.	1	2:29					1
Ac.	1	4:24					1
1 Ti.			2	6:1, 2			2
2 Ti.					1	2:21	1
Tit.			1	2:9			1
1 Pt.			1	2:18			1
2 Pt.	1	2:1					1
Jd.	1	1:4					1
Rev.	1	6:10					1
Total	5		4		1		10

1204. δεῦρο, deu′ro

Book	Oc.	come	Oc.	come hither	Oc.	hitherto (with 891 and 3488)	Total
Mt.	1	19:21					1
Mk.	1	10:21					1
Lk.	1	18:22					1
Jn.	1	11:43					1
Ac.	2	7:3, 34					2
Ro.					1	1:13	1
Rev.			2	17:1; 21:9			2
Total	6		2		1		9

1205. δεῦτε, deu′te

Book	Oc.	come	Oc.	follow (with 3594)	Total
Mt.	5	11:28; 21:38; 22:4; 25:34; 28:6	1	4:19	6
Mk.	3	1:17; 6:31; 12:7			3
Lk.	1	20:14			1
Jn.	2	4:29; 21:12			2
Rev.	1	19:17			1
Total	12		1		13

1206. δευτεραῖος, deuterai′os

Book	next day	Total
Ac.	28:13	1

1207. δευτερόπρωτος deuterop′rōtos

Book	second after the first	Total
Lk.	6:1	1

1208. δεύτερος, deu′teros

Book	Oc.	second	Oc.	the second time (with 1537)	Oc.	the second time	Oc.	again (with 1537)	Oc.	again	Oc.	secondarily	Oc.	afterward	Total
Mt.	3	21:20; 22:26, 39	1	26:42											4
Mk.	2	12:21, 31	1	14:72											3
Lk.	3	12:38; 19:18; 20:30													3
Jn.	1	4:54			2	3:4; 21:16	1	9:24							4
Ac.	2	12:10; 13:33	1	10:15	1	7:13	1	11:9							5
1 Co.	1	15:47									1	12:28			2
2 Co.	1	1:15			1	13:2									2
Tit.	1	3:10													1
Heb.	4	8:7; 9:3, 7; 10:9	1	9:28											5
2 Pt.	1	3:1													1
Jd.													1	1:5	1
Rev.	11	2:11; 4:7; 6:3, 3; 8:8; 11:14; 16:3; 20:6, 14; 21:8, 19							1	19:3					12
Total	30		4		4		2		1		1		1		43

1209. δέχομαι dech'omai

Book	Oc.	receive	Oc.	take	Oc.	accept	Oc.	take up	Total
Mt.	10	10:14, 40, 40, 40, 40, 41, 41; 11:14; 18:5, 5							10
Mk.	6	6:11; 9:37, 37, 37, 37; 10:15							6
Lk.	13	8:13; 9:5, 11, 48, 48, 48, 48, 53; 10:8, 10; 16:4, 9; 18:17	3	16:6, 7; 22:17			1	2:28	17
Jn.	1	4:45							1
Ac.	9	3:21; 7:38, 59; 8:14; 11:1; 17:11; 21:17; 22:5; 28:21							9
1 Co.	1	2:14							1
2 Co.	4	6:1; 7:15; 8:4; 11:16			2	8:17; 11:4			6
Gal.	1	4:14							1
Eph.			1	6:17					1
Phl.	1	4:18							1
Col.	1	4:10							1
1 Th.	2	1:6; 2:13							2
2 Th.	1	2:10							1
Heb.	1	11:31							1
Jas.	1	1:21							1
Total	52		4		2		1		59

1210. δέω, de'ō

Book	Oc.	bind	Oc.	tie	Oc.	knit	Oc.	be in bonds	Oc.	wind	Total
Mt.	9	12:29; 13:30; 14:3; 16:19, 19; 18:18, 18; 22:13; 27:2	1	21:2							10
Mk.	6	3:27; 5:3, 4; 6:17; 15:1, 7	2	11:2, 4							8
Lk.	1	13:16	1	19:30							2
Jn.	3	11:44; 18:12, 24							1	19:40	4
Ac.	12	9:2, 14, 21; 12:6; 20:22; 21:11, 11, 13, 33; 22:5, 29; 24:27			1	10:11					13
Ro.	1	7:2									1
1 Co.	2	7:27, 39									2
Col.							1	4:3			1
2 Ti.	1	2:9									1
Rev.	2	9:14; 20:2									2
Total	37		4		1		1		1		44

1211. δή, dē

Book	Oc.	also	Oc.	now	Oc.	and	Oc.	therefore	Oc.	doubtless	Oc.	Not Tr.	Total
Mt.	1	13:23											1
Lk.			1	2:15									1
Ac.					1	15:36					1	13:2	2
1 Co.							1	6:20					1
2 Co.									1	12:1			1
Total	1		1		1		1		1		1		6

1212. δῆλος, dē'los

Book	Oc.	bewray (with 4060)	Oc.	manifest	Oc.	evident	Oc.	certain	Total
Mt.	1	26:73							1
1 Co.			1	15:27					1
Gal.					1	3:11			1
1 Ti.							1	6:7	1
Total	1		1		1		1		4

1213. δηλόω, dēlo'ō

Book	Oc.	declare	Oc.	signify	Oc.	shew	Total
1 Co.	2	1:11; 3:13					2
Col.	1	1:8					1
Heb.			2	9:8; 12:27			2
1 Pt.			1	1:11			1
2 Pt.					1	1:14	1
Total	3		3		1		7

1214. Δημᾶς, Dēmas'

Book	Demas	Total
Col.	4:14	1
2 Ti.	4:10	1
Phe.	1:24	1
Total		3

1215. δημηγορέω, dēmēgore'ō

Book	make an oration	Total
Ac.	12:21	1

1216. Δημήτριος, Dēmē'trios

Book	Oc.	Demetrius (the silversmith)	Oc.	Demetrius (a Christian)	Total
Ac.	2	19:24, 38			2
3 Jn.			1	1:12	1
Total	2		1		3

1217. δημιουργός, dēmiourgos'

Book	maker	Total
Heb.	11:10	1

1218. δῆμος, dē'mos

Book	people	Total
Ac.	12:22; 17:5; 19:30, 33	4

1219. δημόσιος, dēmos'ios

Book	Oc.	common	Oc.	openly	Oc.	publicly	Total
Ac.	1	5:18	1	16:37	2	18:28; 20:20	4

1220. δηνάριον, dēnar'ion

Book	Oc.	penny	Oc.	pence	Oc.	pennyworth	Total
Mt.	5	20:2, 9, 10, 13; 22:19	1	18:28			6
Mk.	1	12:15	1	14:5	1	6:37	3
Lk.	1	20:24	2	7:41; 10:35			3
Jn.			1	12:5	1	6:7	2
Rev.	2	6:6, 6					2
Total	9		5		2		16

1221. δήποτε, dē'pote

Book	whatsoever (with 3639)	Total
Jn.	5:4	1

1222. δήπου, dē'pou

Book	verily	Total
Heb.	2:16	1

1224. διαβαίνω, diabai'nō

Book	Oc.	pass	Oc.	come over	Oc.	pass through	Total
Lk.	1	16:26					1
Ac.			1	16:9			1
Heb.					1	11:29	1
Total	1		1		1		3

See page 82 for Word 1223.

1225. διαβάλλω, diabal'lō

Book	accuse	Total
Lk.	16:1	1

1226. διαβεβαιόομαι, diabebaio'omai

Book	Oc.	affirm	Oc.	affirm constantly	Total
1 Ti.	1	1:7			1
Tit.			1	3:8	1
Total	1		1		2

1227. διαβλέπω, diablep'ō

Book	see clearly	Total
Mt.	7:5	1
Lk.	6:42	1
Total		2

1228. διάβολος, diab′olos

Book	Oc.	devil	Oc.	false accuser	Oc.	slanderer	Total
Mt.	6	4:1, 5, 8, 11; 13:39; 25:41					6
Lk.	6	4:2, 3, 5, 6, 13; 8:12					6
Jn.	3	6:70; 8:44; 13:2					3
Ac.	2	10:38; 13:10					2
Eph.	2	4:27; 6:11					2
1 Ti.	2	3:6, 7			1	3:11	3
2 Ti.	1	2:26	1	3:3			2
Tit.			1	2:3			1
Heb.	1	2:14					1
Jas.	1	4:7					1
1 Pt.	1	5:8					1
1 Jn.	4	3:8, 8, 8, 10					4
Jd.	1	1:9					1
Rev.	5	2:10; 12:9, 12; 20:2, 10					5
Total	35		2		1		38

1229. διαγγέλλω, dianggel′lō

Book	Oc.	preach	Oc.	signify	Oc.	declare	Total
Lk.	1	9:60					1
Ac.			1	21:26			1
Ro.					1	9:17	1
Total	1		1		1		3

1230. διαγίνομαι, diagin′omai

Book	Oc.	be past	Oc.	after	Oc.	be spent	Total
Mk.	1	16:1					1
Ac.			1	25:13	1	27:9	2
Total	1		1		1		3

1231. διαγινώσκω, diaginō′skō

Book	Oc.	enquire	Oc.	know the uttermost	Total
Ac.	1	23:15	1	24:22	2

1232. διαγνωρίζω, diagnōrid′zō

Book	make known abroad	Total
Lk.	2:17	1

1233. διάγνωσις, diag′nōsis

Book	hearing	Total
Ac.	25:21	1

1234. διαγογγύζω diagonggud′zō

Book	murmur	Total
Lk.	15:2; 19:7	2

1235. διαγρηγορέω diagrẹgore′ō

Book	be awake	Total
Lk.	9:32	1

1236. διάγω, diag′ō

Book	Oc.	lead a life (with 979)	Oc.	living	Total
1 Ti.	1	2:2			1
Tit.			1	3:3	1
Total	1		1		2

1237. διαδέχομαι, diadech′omai

Book	come after	Total
Ac.	7:45	1

1238. διάδημα, diad′ẹma

Book	crown	Total
Rev.	12:3; 13:1; 19:12	3

1239. διαδίδωμι, diadid′ōmi

Book	Oc.	distribute	Oc.	make distribution	Oc.	divide	Oc.	give	Total
Lk.	1	18:22			1	11:22			2
Jn.	1	6:11							1
Ac.			1	4:35					1
Rev.							1	17:13	1
Total	2		1		1		1		5

1240. διάδοχος, diad′ochos

Book	come into (one's) room (with 2983)	Total
Ac.	24:27	1

1241. διαζώννυμι, diadzōn′numi

Book	gird	Total
Jn.	13:4, 5; 21:7	3

1242. διαθήκη, diathẹ′kẹ

Book	Oc.	covenant	Oc.	testament	Total
Mt.			1	26:28	1
Mk.			1	14:24	1
Lk.	1	1:72	1	22:20	2
Ac.	2	3:25; 7:8			2
Ro.	2	9:4; 11:27			2
1 Co.			1	11:25	1
2 Co.			2	3:6, 14	2
Gal.	3	3:15, 17; 4:24			3
Eph.	1	2:12			1
Heb.	11	8:6, 8, 9, 9, 10; 9:4, 4; 10: 16, 29; 12:24; 13:20	6	7:22; 9:15, 15, 16, 17, 20	17
Rev.			1	11:19	1
Total	20		13		33

1243. διαίρεσις, diai′resis

Book	Oc.	diversity	Oc.	difference	Total
1 Co.	2	12:4, 6	1	12:5	3

1244. διαιρέω, diaire′ō

Book	divide	Total
Lk.	15:12	1
1 Co.	12:11	1
Total		2

1245. διακαθαρίζω diakatharid′zō

Book	throughly purge	Total
Mt.	3:12	1
Lk.	3:17	1
Total		2

1246. διακατελέγχομαι diakateleng′chomai

Book	convince	Total
Ac.	18:28	1

1247. διακονέω, diakone′ō

Book	Oc.	minister unto	Oc.	serve	Oc.	minister	Oc.	Misc.	Total
Mt.	5	4:11; 8:15; 20:28a; 25:44; 27:55			1	20:28b			6
Mk.	4	1:13, 31; 10:45a; 15:41			1	10:45b			5
Lk.	2	4:39; 8:3	6	10:40; 12:37; 17:8; 22:26, 27, 27					8
Jn.			3	12:2, 26, 26					3
Ac.	1	19:22	1	6:2					2
Ro.	1	15:25							1
2 Co.					1	3:3	2	8:19, 20	3
1 Ti.							2	3:10, 13	2
2 Ti.	1	1:18							1
Phe.	1	1:13							1
Heb.					1	6:10b	1	6:10a	2
1 Pt.					3	1:12; 4:10, 11			3
Total	15		10		7		5		37

Miscellaneous: 2 Co. 8:19, 20, administer; 1 Ti. 3:10, 13, use the office of a deacon; Heb. 6:10a, minister to.

1248. διακονία, diakoni′a

Book	Oc.	ministry	Oc.	ministration	Oc.	ministering	Oc.	Misc.	Total
Lk.							1	10:40	1
Ac.	6	1:17, 25; 6:4; 12:25; 20:24; 21:19	1	6:1			1	11:29	8
Ro.	1	12:7a			1	12:7b	2	11:13; 15:31	4
1 Co.	1	16:15					1	12:5	2
2 Co.	3	4:1; 5:18; 6:3	5	3:7, 8, 9, 9; 9:13	2	8:4; 9:1	2	9:12; 11:8	12
Eph.	1	4:12							1
Col.	1	4:17							1
1 Ti.	1	1:12							1
2 Ti.	2	4:5, 11							2
Heb.							1	1:14	1
Rev.							1	2:19	1
Total	16		6		3		9		34

Miscellaneous: Lk. 10:40, serving; Ac. 11:29, relief; Ro. 11:13, office; Ro. 15:31, service; 1 Co. 12:5, 2 Co. 9:12, administration; 2 Co. 11:8, do service; Heb. 1:14 (with 1519), to minister; Rev. 2:19, service.

1223a. διά, dia′ (WITH THE GENITIVE)

Book	Oc.	by	Oc.	through	Oc.	with
Mt.	14	1:22; 2:5, 15, 23; 4:14; 8:17, 28; 12:17; 13:35; 18:7; 21:4; 24:15; 26:24; 27:9	3	12:1, 43; 19:24		
Mk.	3	6:2; 10:1; 14:21	4	2:23; 9:30; 10:25; 11:16	1	16:20
Lk.	5	1:70; 5:19a; 8:4; 18:31: 22:22	7	4:30; 5:19c; 6:1; 11:24; 17:1, 11; 18:25		
Jn.	8	1:3, 10, 17, 17; 10:1, 2, 9; 14:6	5	1:7; 3:17; 4:4; 8:59; 17:20		
Ac.	33	1:16; 2:16, 22, 23, 43; 3:16, 18, 21; 4:16, 25, 30; 5:12, 19; 7:25; 9:25; 10:36; 11:28, 30; 12:9; 14:3; 15:7, 12, 23, 27; 17:10; 18:9, 28; 19:11; 21:19; 23:31; 24:2, 2; 28:25	9	1:2; 8:18; 10:43; 13:38; 14:22; 15:11; 18:27; 20:3; 21:4	4	8:20; 15:32; 19:26; 20:28
Ro.	41	1:2, 5, 12; 2:12, 16, 27; 3:20, 22, 27, 27; 5:2, 5, 10, 11b, 12b, 12c, 16, 17, 17, 18, 18, 19, 19, 21b; 6:4, 4; 7:4, 5, 7, 8, 11, 11, 13, 13; 10:17; 12:1; 15:18, 28, 32; 16:18, 26	19	1:8; 2:23; 3:24, 25a, 30, 31; 4:13, 13; 5:1, 9, 11a, 21a; 7:25; 8:3, 37; 11:36; 12:3; 15:4; 16:27	2	8:25; 14:20
1 Co.	17	1:9, 10, 21, 21; 2:10; 3:5, 15; 6:14; 8:6, 6; 11:12; 12:8; 14:9; 15:2, 21, 21; 16:3	5	1:1; 4:15; 10:1; 13:12; 15:57	1	14:19
2 Co.	25	1:1, 4, 5, 11, 16, 19, 19, 20; 2:14; 4:14; 5:7, 7, 18, 20; 6:7, 8, 8; 8:5; 9:12, 13; 10:1, 9, 11; 11:33b; 12:17	4	3:4; 4:15b; 9:11; 11:33a	1	2:4
Gal.	13	1:1, 1, 12, 15; 2:16, 21; 3:18, 19, 26; 4:23; 5:6, 13; 6:14	3	2:19; 3:14; 4:7		
Eph.	10	1:1, 5; 2:16; 3:6, 9, 10, 12, 16, 17; 4:16	4	1:7; 2:8, 18; 4:6	1	6:18
Phl.	4	1:11, 20, 20, 26	2	1:19; 3:9		
Col.	6	1:1, 16, 20b, 20c; 2:19; 3:17	5	1:14, 20a, 22; 2:8, 12		
1 Th.	3	3:7b; 4:2; 5:9				
2 Th.	7	2:2a, 2b, 2c, 14, 15a; 3:12, 14				
1 Ti.	2	4:5, 14			1	2:10
2 Ti.	5	1:1, 6b, 10a, 14; 4:17	2	1:10b; 3:15		
Tit.	1	3:5	1	3:6		
Phe.	1	1:7	1	1:22		
Heb.	21	1:2, 3; 2:2, 3, 10b; 3:16; 6:18; 7:11, 19, 21, 25; 9:11, 12, 12, 26; 11:4, 4, 7, 29; 13:11, 15	9	2:10c, 14; 6:12; 9:14; 10:10, 20; 11:33, 39; 13:21	2	12:1; 13:12
Jas.	1	2:12				
1 Pt.	10	1:3, 12, 21, 23; 2:5, 14; 3:1, 20, 21; 5:12a	3	1:5, 22; 4:11	1	1:7
2 Pt.	1	1:4b	1	1:3a		
1 Jn.	1	5:6	1	4:9		
2 Jn.					1	1:12
3 Jn.					1	1:13
Rev.	1	1:1				
Total	233		88		16	

1223b. διά, dia′ (WITH THE ACCUSATIVE)

Book	Oc.	for	Oc.	for . . . sake	Oc.	therefore (with 5024)	Oc.	for this cause (with 5024)	Oc.	wherefore (with 5024)
Mt.	1	27:18	6	10:22; 14:3, 9; 19:12; 24:9, 22	9	6:25; 12:27; 13:13, 52; 14:2; 18:23; 21:43; 23:14; 24:44			2	12:31; 23:34
Mk.	5	2:4, 27, 27; 7:29; 15:10	5	4:17; 6:17, 26; 13:13, 20	3	6:14; 11:24; 12:24				
Lk.	4	8:19, 47; 23:19, 25	1	21:17	4	11:19, 49; 12:22; 14:20				
Jn.	7	4:39; 7:13; 10:19, 32; 16:21; 19:38; 20:19	5	11:15; 12:9, 30b; 14:11; 15:21	13	1:31; 5:16, 18; 6:65; 7:22; 8:47; 9:23; 10:17; 12:39; 13:11; 15:19; 16:15; 19:11	2	12:18a, 27		
Ac.	3	21:34, 35; 28:20			1	2:26				
Ro.	5	3:25b; 13:5a; 4:24, 25, 25	5	4:23; 11:8, 8; 13:5b; 15:30a	1	4:16	3	1:26; 13:6a; 15:9	1	5:12a
1 Co.	5	7:5, 26; 8:11; 11:9, 9	8	4:6, 10; 9:10, 10, 23; 10:25, 27, 28			3	4:17; 11:10a, 30		
2 Co.	2	3:7; 9:14	5	2:10; 4:5, 11, 15a; 8:9	3	4:1; 7:13; 13:10				
Gal.										
Eph.	1	2:4							3	1:15; 5:17; 6:13
Phl.	5	1:24; 2:30; 3:7, 8, 8								
Col.	2	1:5; 4:3	1	3:6			1	1:9		
1 Th.			3	1:5; 3:9; 5:13	1	3:7a	2	2:13; 3:5		
2 Th.							1	2:11		
1 Ti.			1	5:23			1	1:16		
2 Ti.	1	1:12	1	2:10b	1	2:10a				
Tit.										
Phe.			1	1:9	1	1:15				
Heb.	6	1:14; 2:9, 10a, 11; 5:12; 7:18			2	1:9; 2:1	1	9:15		
Jas.										
1 Pt.	2	1:20; 2:19	2	2:13; 3:14						
2 Pt.										
1 Jn.			1	2:12	2	3:1; 4:5				
2 Jn.			1	1:2						
3 Jn.									1	1:10
Rev.	9	1:9, 9; 4:11; 6:9, 9; 18:10, 15; 20:4, 4	1	2:3	3	7:15; 12:12; 18:8				
Total	58		47		44		14		7	

1223a. διά, dia′ (WITH THE GENITIVE) (continued)

Book	Oc.	in	Oc.	after	Oc.	throughout	Oc.	always (with 3856)	Oc.	whereby (with 3639)	Oc.	Not Tr.	Oc.	Misc.	Total
Mt.	1	26:61					1	18:10			1	2:12	3	4:4; 7:13a, 13b	23
Mk.			1	2:1									1	14:58	10
Lk.											2	5:5; 19:4	1	13:24	15
Jn.													2	11:4; 19:23	15
Ac.	1	16:9	1	24:17	2	9:32; 13:49	1	2:25			1	1:3			52
Ro.													4	4:11; 14:14; 15:30, 30	66
1 Co.															23
2 Co.	1	5:10			1	8:18					1	3:11	1	8:8	34
Gal.			1	2:1											17
Eph.															15
Phl.															6
Col.															11
1 Th.	1	4:14													4
2 Th.							1	3:16			1	2:15b	1	2:2d	10
1 Ti.	1	2:15													4
2 Ti.													1	2:2	8
Tit.															2
Phe.															2
Heb.	2	7:9; 13:22							1	12:28	1	2:15	3	12:11, 15; 13:2	39
Jas.															1
1 Pt.													1	5:12b	15
2 Pt.	1	3:5							2	1:4a; 3:6			1	1:3b	6
1 Jn.															2
2 Jn.															1
3 Jn.															1
Rev.															1
Total	8		3		3		3		3		7		19		383

Miscellaneous: Mt. 4:4, of; Mt. 7:13a, at; Mt. 7:13b (with 846), thereat; Mk. 14:58, within; Lk. 13:24, at; Jn. 11:4 (with 846), thereby; Jn. 19:23 (with 3550), throughout; Ro. 4:11, through; Ro. 14:14, of; Ro. 15:30, 30, for; 2 Co. 8:8, by occasion of; 2 Th. 2:2d, from; 2 Ti. 2:2, among; Heb. 12:11 (with 846), thereby; Heb. 12:15 and 13:2 (with 4926c), thereby; 1 Pt. 5:12b (with 3541), briefly; 2 Pt. 1:3b, to.

1223b. διά, dia′ (WITH THE ACCUSATIVE) (continued)

Book	Oc.	because of	Oc.	because (with infinitive)	Oc.	by	Oc.	through	Oc.	by reason of	Oc.	wherefore (with 156 and 3639)	Oc.	Not Tr.	Oc.	Misc.	Total
Mt.	4	13:21, 58; 17:20; 27:19	3	13:5, 6; 24:12	2	15:3, 6											27
Mk.	2	3:9; 6:6	3	4:5, 6; 5:4													18
Lk.	2	5:19b; 11:8b	7	2:4; 8:6; 9:7; 11:8a; 18:5; 19:11; 23:8			1	1:78									19
Jn.	8	3:29; 4:41, 42; 7:43; 11:42; 12:30a, 42; 19:42	1	2:24	2	6:57, 57	1	15:3	1	12:11							40
Ac.	4	4:21; 16:3; 28:2, 2	5	12:20; 18:3; 27:4, 9; 28:18							1	22:24			5	4:2; 8:11; 10:21; 18:2; 23:28;	19
Ro.	4	6:19; 8:10, 10; 15:15			1	8:11	1	2:24	1	8:20					1	4:15	23
1 Co.	1	11:10b													1	7:2	18
2 Co.																	10
Gal.	1	2:4					1	4:13									2
Eph.	2	4:18b; 5:6					1	4:18a									7
Phl.			1	1:7											2	1:15, 15	8
Col.																	4
1 Th.																	6
2 Th.																	1
1 Ti.																	2
2 Ti.											1	1:6a					4
Tit.											1	1:13					1
Phe.																	2
Heb.	2	3:19; 4:6	2	7:24; 10:2	1	6:7			1	5:14			1	2:15	2	5:3; 7:23	18
Jas.			1	4:2													1
1 Pt.																	4
2 Pt.									1	2:2					1	3:12	2
1 Jn.																	3
2 Jn.																	1
3 Jn.																	1
Rev.					3	12:11, 11; 13:14											16
Total	30		23		9		5		4		3		1		12		257

Miscellaneous: Ac. 4:2, that; Ac. 8:11 (with infinitive), because that; Ac. 10:21 (with 3639), wherefore; Ac. 18:2 (with infinitive), because that; Ac. 23:28 (with 3639), wherefore; Ro. 14:15, with; 1 Co. 7:2, to avoid; Phl. 1:15, 15, of; Heb. 5:3 (with 4926b), by reason hereof; Heb. 7:23 (with infinitive), by reason of; 2 Pt. 3:12 (with 3639), wherein.

Word 1223 has 640 occurrences.

1249. διάκονος, diak'onos

Book	Oc.	minister	Oc.	servant	Oc.	deacon	Total
Mt.	1	20:26	2	22:13; 23:11			3
Mk.	1	10:43	1	9:35			2
Jn.			3	2:5, 9; 12:26			3
Ro.	3	13:4, 4; 15:8	1	16:1			4
1 Co.	1	3:5					1
2 Co.	5	3:6; 6:4; 11:15, 15, 23					5
Gal.	1	2:17					1
Eph.	2	3:7; 6:21					2
Phl.					1	1:1	1
Col.	4	1:7, 23, 25; 4:7					4
1 Th.	1	3:2					1
1 Ti.	1	4:6			2	3:8, 12	3
Total	20		7		3		30

1250. διακόσιοι, diakos'ioi

Book	two hundred	Total
Mk.	6:37	1
Jn.	6:7; 21:8	2
Ac.	23:23, 23; 27:37	3
Rev.	11:3; 12:6	2
Total		8

1251. διακούομαι, diakou'omai

Book	hear	Total
Ac.	23:35	1

1252. διακρίνω, diakri'nō

Book	Oc.	doubt	Oc.	judge	Oc.	discern	Oc.	contend	Oc.	waver	Oc.	Misc.	Total
Mt.	1	21:21			1	16:3							2
Mk.	1	11:23											1
Ac.	2	10:20; 11:12					1	11:2			1	15:9	4
Ro.	1	14:23									1	4:20	2
1 Co.			3	6:5; 11:31; 14:29	1	11:29					1	4:7	5
Jas.									2	1:6, 6	1	2:4	3
Jd.							1	1:9			1	1:22	2
Total	5		3		2		2		2		5		19

Miscellaneous: Ac. 15:9, put difference; Ro. 4:20, stagger; 1 Co. 4:7, make to differ; Jas. 2:4, be partial; Jd. 1:22, make a difference.

1253. διάκρισις, diak'risis

Book	Oc.	discerning	Oc.	discern	Oc.	disputation	Total
Ro.					1	14:1	1
1 Co.	1	12:10					1
Heb.			1	5:14			1
Total	1		1		1		3

1254. διακωλύω, diakōlu'ō

Book	forbid	Total
Mt.	3:14	1

1257. διαλείπω, dialei'pō

Book	cease	Total
Lk.	7:45	1

1255. διαλαλέω, dialale'ō

Book	Oc.	noise abroad	Oc.	commune	Total
Lk.	1	1:65	1	6:11	2

1256. διαλέγομαι, dialeg'omai

Book	Oc.	dispute	Oc.	reason with	Oc.	reason	Oc.	preach unto	Oc.	preach	Oc.	speak	Total
Mk.	1	9:34											1
Ac.	4	17:17; 19:8, 9; 24:12	2	17:2; 18:19	2	18:4; 24:25	1	20:7	1	20:9			10
Heb.											1	12:5	1
Jd.	1	1:9											1
Total	6		2		2		1		1		1		13

1258. διάλεκτος, dial'ektos

Book	Oc.	tongue	Oc.	language	Total
Ac.	5	1:19; 2:8; 21:40; 22:2; 26:14	1	2:6	6

1259. διαλλάσσω, diallas'sō

Book	reconcile	Total
Mt.	5:24	1

1262. διαλύω, dialu'ō

Book	scatter	Total
Ac.	5:36	1

1260. διαλογίζομαι, dialogid'zomai

Book	Oc.	reason	Oc.	dispute	Oc.	cast in the mind	Oc.	muse	Oc.	think	Oc.	consider	Total
Mt.	3	16:7, 8; 21:25											3
Mk.	5	2:6, 8, 8; 8:16, 17	1	9:33									6
Lk.	3	5:21, 22; 20:14			1	1:29	1	3:15	1	12:17			6
Jn.											1	11:50	1
Total	11		1		1		1		1		1		16

1261. διαλογισμός, dialogismos'

Book	Oc.	thought	Oc.	reasoning	Oc.	imagination	Oc.	doubtful	Oc.	disputing	Oc.	doubting	Total
Mt.	1	15:19											1
Mk.	1	7:21											1
Lk.	5	2:35; 5:22; 6:8; 9:47; 24:38	1	9:46									6
Ro.					1	1:21	1	14:1					2
1 Co.	1	3:20											1
Phl.									1	2:14			1
1 Ti.											1	2:8	1
Jas.	1	2:4											1
Total	9		1		1		1		1		1		14

1263. διαμαρτύρομαι, diamartu'romai

Book	Oc.	testify	Oc.	charge	Oc.	witness	Total
Lk.	1	16:28					1
Ac.	8	2:40; 8:25; 10:42; 18:5; 20:21, 24; 23:11; 28:23			1	20:23	9
1 Th.	1	4:6					1
1 Ti.			1	5:21			1
2 Ti.			2	2:14; 4:1			2
Heb.	1	2:6					1
Total	11		3		1		15

1265. διαμένω, diamen'ō

Book	Oc.	continue	Oc.	remain	Total
Lk.	1	22:28	1	1:22	2
Gal.	1	2:5			1
Heb.			1	1:11	1
2 Pt.	1	3:4			1
Total	3		2		5

1264. διαμάχομαι, diamach'omai

Book	strive	Total
Ac.	23:9	1

1270. διανόημα, diano'ema

Book	thought	Total
Lk.	11:17	1

1266. διαμερίζω, diamerid'zō

Book	Oc.	part	Oc.	diviae	Oc.	cloven	Total
Mt.	2	27:35, 35					2
Mk.	1	15:24					1
Lk.	1	23:34	5	11:17, 18; 12:52, 53; 22:17			6
Jn.	1	19:24					1
Ac.	1	2:45			1	2:3	2
Total	6		5		1		12

1272. διανοίγω, dianoi'gō

Book	open	Total
Mk.	7:34, 35	2
Lk.	2:23; 24:31, 32, 45	4
Ac.	16:14; 17:3	2
Total		8

1267. διαμερισμός, diamerismos'

Book	division	Total
Lk.	12:51	1

1273. διανυκτερεύω dianuktereu'ō

Book	continued all night (with 2258)	Total
Lk.	6:12	1

1271. διάνοια, dian'oia

Book	Oc.	mind	Oc.	understanding	Oc.	imagination	Total
Mt.	1	22:37					1
Mk.	1	12:30					1
Lk.	1	10:27			1	1:51	2
Eph.	1	2:3	2	1:18; 4:18			3
Col.	1	1:21					1
Heb.	2	8:10; 10:16					2
1 Pt.	1	1:13					1
2 Pt.	1	3:1					1
1 Jn.			1	5:20			1
Total	9		3		1		13

1268. διανέμω, dianem'ō

Book	spread	Total
Ac.	4:17	1

1269. διανεύω, dianeu'ō

Book	beckoned (with 2258)	Total
Lk.	1:22	1

1274. διανύω, dianu'ō

Book	finish	Total
Ac.	21:7	1

1275. διαπαντός, diapantos'

Book	Oc.	always	Oc.	continually	Total
Mk.	1	5:5			1
Lk.			1	24:53	1
Ac.	2	10:2; 24:16			2
Ro.	1	11:10			1
Heb.	1	9:6	1	13:15	2
Total	5		2		7

1276. διαπεράω, diapera'ō

Book	Oc.	pass over	Oc.	go over	Oc.	pass	Oc.	sail over	Total
Mt.	1	9:1	1	14:34					2
Mk.	2	5:21; 6:53							2
Lk.					1	16:26			1
Ac.							1	21:2	1
Total	3		1		1		1		6

1277. διαπλέω, diaple'ō

Book	sail over	Total
Ac.	27:5	1

1278. διαπονέω, diapone'ō

Book	grieve	Total
Ac.	4:2; 16:18	2

1279. διαπορεύομαι, diaporeu'omai

Book	Oc.	go through	Oc.	pass by	Oc.	in (one's) journey	Total
Lk.	2	6:1; 13:22	1	18:36			3
Ac.	1	16:4					1
Ro.					1	15:24	1
Total	3		1		1		5

1280. διαπορέω, diapore'ō

Book	Oc.	doubt	Oc.	be perplexed	Oc.	be much perplexed	Oc.	be in doubt	Total
Lk.			1	9:7	1	24:4			2
Ac.	2	5:24; 10:17					1	2:12	3
Total	2		1		1		1		5

1281. διαπραγματεύομαι diapragmateu'omai

Book	gain by trading	Total
Lk.	19:15	1

1283. διαρπάζω, diarpad'zō

Book	spoil	Total
Mt.	12:29, 29	2
Mk.	3:27, 27	2
Total		4

1282. διαπρίω, diapri'ō

Book	Oc.	be cut to the heart	Oc.	be cut	Total
Ac.	1	5:33	1	7:54	2

1285. διασαφέω, diasaphe'ō

Book	tell unto	Total
Mt.	18:31	1

1284a. διαῤῥήγνυμι, diarhreg'numi

Book	Oc.	rend	Oc.	break	Total
Mt.	1	26:65			1
Mk.	1	14:63			1
Lk.			1	5:6	1
Ac.	1	14:14			1
Total	3		1		4

1284b. διαῤῥήσσω, diarhres'sō

Book	break	Total
Lk.	8:29	1

Word 1284 has 5 occurrences.

1286. διασείω, diasei'ō

Book	do violence to	Total
Lk.	3:14	1

1287. διασκορπίζω, diaskorpid'zō

Book	Oc.	straw	Oc.	scatter abroad	Oc.	scatter	Oc.	waste	Oc.	disperse	Total
Mt.	2	25:24, 26	1	26:31							3
Mk.					1	14:27					1
Lk.					1	1:51	2	15:13; 16:1			3
Jn.			1	11:52							1
Ac.									1	5:37	1
Total	2		2		2		2		1		9

1288. διασπάω, diaspa'ō

Book	Oc.	pluck asunder	Oc.	pull in pieces	Total
Mk.	1	5:4			1
Ac.			1	23:10	1
Total	1		1		2

1290. διασπορά, diaspora'

Book	Oc.	dispersed	Oc.	scattered abroad	Oc.	scattered	Total
Jn.	1	7:35					1
Jas.			1	1:1			1
1 Pt.					1	1:1	1
Total	1		1		1		3

1291. διαστέλλομαι, diastel'lomai

Book	Oc.	charge	Oc.	give commandment	Oc.	be commanded	Total
Mt.	1	16:20					1
Mk.	5	5:43; 7:36, 36; 8:15; 9:9					5
Ac.			1	15:24			1
Heb.					1	12:20	1
Total	6		1		1		8

1289. διασπείρω, diaspei'rō

Book	scatter abroad	Total
Ac.	8:1, 4; 11:19	3

1292. διάστημα, dias'tēma

Book	space	Total
Ac.	5:7	1

1293. διαστολή, diastolē'

Book	Oc.	difference	Oc.	distinction	Total
Ro.	2	3:22; 10:12			2
1 Co.			1	14:7	1
Total	2		1		3

1294. διαστρέφω, diastreph'ō

Book	Oc.	perverse	Oc.	pervert	Oc.	turn away	Total
Mt.	1	17:17					1
Lk.	1	9:41	1	23:2			2
Ac.	1	20:30	1	13:10	1	13:8	3
Phl.	1	2:15					1
Total	4		2		1		7

1295. διασώζω, diasōd'zō

Book	Oc.	escape	Oc.	save	Oc.	make perfectly whole	Oc.	escape safe	Oc.	bring safe	Oc.	heal	Total
Mt.					1	14:36							1
Lk.											1	7:3	1
Ac.	2	28:1, 4	1	27:43			1	27:44	1	23:24			5
1 Pt.			1	3:20									1
Total	2		2		1		1		1		1		8

1296. διαταγή, diatagē'

Book	Oc.	disposition	Oc.	ordinance	Total
Ac.	1	7:53			1
Ro.			1	13:2	1
Total	1		1		2

1297. διάταγμα, diat'agma

Book	commandment	Total
Heb.	11:23	1

1298. διαταράσσω, diataras'sō

Book	trouble	Total
Lk.	1:29	1

1299. διατάσσω, diatas'sō

Book	Oc.	command	Oc.	appoint	Oc.	ordain	Oc.	set in order	Oc.	give order	Total
Mt.	1	11:1									1
Lk.	3	8:55; 17:9, 10	1	3:13							4
Ac.	3	18:2; 23:31; 24:23	2	7:44; 20:13							5
1 Co.					2	7:17; 9:14	1	11:34	1	16:1	4
Gal.					1	3:19					1
Tit.			1	1:5							1
Total	7		4		3		1		1		16

1300. διατελέω, diatele'ō

Book	continue	Total
Ac.	27:33	1

1301. διατηρέω, diatēre'ō

Book	keep	Total
Lk.	2:51	1
Ac.	15:29	1
Total		2

1302. διατί, diati'

Book	Oc.	why	Oc.	wherefore	Total
Mt.	7	9:11, 14; 13:10; 15:2, 3; 17:19; 21:25			7
Mk.	3	2:18; 7:5; 11:31			3
Lk.	5	5:30, 33; 19:31; 20:5; 24:38	1	19:23	6
Jn.	5	7:45; 8:43, 46; 12:5; 13:37			5
Ac.	1	5:3			1
Ro.			1	9:32	1
1 Co.	2	6:7, 7			2
2 Co.			1	11:11	1
Rev.			1	17:7	1
Total	23		4		27

1303. διατίθεμαι, diatith'emai

Book	Oc.	make	Oc.	testator	Oc.	appoint	Total
Lk.					2	22:29, 29	2
Ac.	1	3;25					1
Heb.	2	8:10; 10:16	2	9:16, 17			4
Total	3		2		2		7

1305. διατροφή, diatrophē'

Book	food	Total
1 Ti.	6:8	1

1306. διαυγάζω, diaugad'zō

Book	dawn	Total
2 Pt.	1:19	1

1304. διατρίβω, diatri'bō

Book	Oc.	abide	Oc.	tarry	Oc.	continue	Oc.	be	Total
Jn.			1	3:22	1	11:54			2
Ac.	5	12:19; 14:3, 28; 16:12; 20:6	1	25:6	1	15:35	1	25:14	8
Total	5		2		2		1		10

1307. διαφανής, diaphanēs'

Book	transparent	Total
Rev.	21:21	1

1308. διαφέρω, diapher'ō

Book	Oc.	be better	Oc.	be of more value	Oc.	differ from	Oc.	should carry	Oc.	publish	Oc.	drive up and down	Oc.	Misc.	Total
Mt.	2	6:26; 12:12	1	10:31											3
Mk.							1	11:16							1
Lk.	1	12:24	1	12:7											2
Ac.									1	13:49	1	27:27			2
Ro.													1	2:18	1
1 Co.					1	15:41									1
Gal.					1	4:1							1	2:6	2
Phl.													1	1:10	1
Total	3		2		2		1		1		1		3		13

Miscellaneous: Ro. 2:18, be more excellent; Gal. 2:6, make matter; Phl. 1:10, be excellent.

1309. διαφεύγω, diapheu'gō

Book	escape	Total
Ac.	27:42	1

1310. διαφημίζω, diaphe̱mid'zō

Book	Oc.	spread abroad (one's) fame	Oc.	be commonly reported	Oc.	blaze abroad	Total
Mt.	1	9:31	1	28:15			2
Mk.					1	1:45	1
Total	1		1		1		3

1311. διαφθείρω, diaphthei'rō

Book	Oc.	destroy	Oc.	corrupt	Oc.	perish	Total
Lk.			1	12:33			1
2 Co.					1	4:16	1
1 Ti.			1	6:5			1
Rev.	3	8:9; 11:18, 18					3
Total	3		2		1		6

1313. διάφορος, diaph'oros

Book	Oc.	more excellent	Oc.	differing	Oc.	divers	Total
Ro.			1	12:6			1
Heb.	2	1:4; 8:6			1	9:10	3
Total	2		1		1		4

1312. διαφθορά, diaphthora'

Book	corruption	Total
Ac.	2:27, 31; 13:34, 35, 36, 37	6

1314. διαφυλάσσω, diaphulas'sō

Book	keep	Total
Lk.	4:10	1

1315. διαχειρίζομαι, diacheirid'zomai

Book	Oc.	slay	Oc.	kill	Total
Ac.	1	5:30	1	26:21	2

1316. διαχωρίζομαι diachōrid'zomai

Book	depart	Total
Lk.	9:33	1

1317. διδακτικός, didaktikos'

Book	apt to teach	Total
1 Ti.	3:2	1
2 Ti.	2:24	1
Total		2

1318. διδακτός, didaktos'

Book	Oc.	which (one) teacheth	Oc.	taught	Total
Jn.			1	6:45	1
1 Co.	2	2:13, 13			2
Total	2		1		3

1319. διδασκαλία, didaskali'a

Book	Oc.	doctrine	Oc.	teaching	Oc.	learning	Total
Mt.	1	15:9					1
Mk.	1	7:7					1
Ro.			1	12:7	1	15:4	2
Eph.	1	4:14					1
Col.	1	2:22					1
1 Ti.	8	1:10; 4:1, 6, 13, 16; 5:17; 6:1, 3					8
2 Ti.	3	3:10, 16; 4:3					3
Tit.	4	1:9; 2:1, 7, 10					4
Total	19		1		1		21

1320. διδάσκαλος, didas'kalos

Book	Oc.	Master (Jesus)	Oc.	teacher	Oc.	master	Oc.	doctor	Total
Mt.	9	8:19; 9:11; 12:38; 17:24; 19:16; 22:16, 24, 36; 26:18			2	10:24, 25			11
Mk.	12	4:38; 5:35; 9:17, 38; 10:17, 20, 35; 12:14, 19; 12:32; 13:1; 14:14							12
Lk.	13	7:40; 8:49; 9:38; 10:25; 11:45; 12:13; 18:18; 19:39; 20:21, 28, 39; 21:7; 22:11			3	3:12; 6:40, 40	1	2:46	17
Jn.	6	1:38; 8:4; 11:28; 13:13, 14; 20:16	1	3:2	1	3:10			8
Ac.			1	13:1					1
Ro.			1	2:20					1
1 Co.			2	12:28, 29					2
Eph.			1	4:11					1
1 Ti.			1	2:7					1
2 Ti.			2	1:11; 4:3					2
Heb.			1	5:12					1
Jas.					1	3:1			1
Total	40		10		7		1		58

1321. διδάσκω, didas'kō

Book	Oc.	teach	Oc.	taught (with 2258)	Total
Mt.	13	4:23; 5:2, 19, 19; 9:35; 11:1; 13:54; 15:9; 21:23; 22:16; 26:55; 28:15, 20	1	7:29	14
Mk.	16	1:21; 2:13; 4:1, 2; 6:2, 6, 30, 34; 7:7; 8:31; 9:31; 10:1; 11:17; 12:14, 35; 14:49	1	1:22	17
Lk.	15	4:15; 5:3, 17; 6:6; 11:1, 1; 12:12; 13:10, 22, 26; 20:1, 21, 21; 21:37; 23:5	2	4:31; 19:47	17
Jn.	10	6:59; 7:14, 28, 35; 8:2, 20, 28; 9:34; 14:26; 18:20			10
Ac.	16	1:1; 4:2, 18; 5:21, 25, 28, 42; 11:26; 15:1, 35; 18:11, 25; 20:20; 21:21, 28; 28:31			16
Ro.	3	2:21, 21; 12:7			3
1 Co.	2	4:17; 11:14			2
Gal.	1	1:12			1
Eph.	1	4:21			1
Col.	3	1:28; 2:7; 3:16			3
2 Th.	1	2:15			1
1 Ti.	3	2:12; 4:11; 6:2			3
2 Ti.	1	2:2			1
Tit.	1	1:11			1
Heb.	2	5:12; 8:11			2
1 Jn.	3	2:27, 27, 27			3
Rev.	2	2:14, 20			2
Total	93		4		97

1322. διδαχή, didache̱'

Book	Oc.	doctrine	Oc.	has been taught	Total
Mt.	3	7:28; 16:12; 22:33			3
Mk.	5	1:22, 27; 4:2; 11:18; 12:38			5
Lk.	1	4:32			1
Jn.	3	7:16, 17; 18:19			3
Ac.	4	2:42; 5:28; 13:12; 17:19			4
Ro.	2	6:17; 16:17			2
1 Co.	2	14:6, 26			2
2 Ti.	1	4:2			1
Tit.			1	1:9	1
Heb.	2	6:2; 13:9			2
2 Jn.	3	1:9, 9, 10			3
Rev.	3	2:14, 15, 24			3
Total	29		1		30

1323. δίδραχμον, did'rachmon

Book	Oc.	tribute	Oc.	tribute money	Total
Mt.	1	17:24b	1	17:24a	2

1324. Δίδυμος, Did'umos

Book	Didymus	Total
Jn.	11:16; 20:24; 21:2	3

1325. δίδωμι, did'ōmi

Book	Oc.	give	Oc.	grant	Oc.	put	Oc.	shew	Oc.	deliver	Oc.	make	Oc.	Misc.	Total
Mt.	54	4:9; 5:31, 42; 6:11; 7:6, 7, 11, 11; 9:8; 10:1, 8, 19; 12:39; 13:11, 11, 12; 14:7, 8, 9, 11, 16, 19; 15:36; 16:4, 19, 26; 17:27; 19:7, 11, 21; 20:4, 14, 23, 28; 21:23, 43; 22:17; 24:29, 45; 25:8, 15, 28, 29, 35, 42; 26:9, 15, 26, 27, 48; 27:10, 34; 28:12, 18					1	24:24					1	13:8	56
Mk.	34	2:26; 4:11, 25; 5:43; 6:2, 7, 22, 23, 25, 28, 28, 37, 37, 41; 8:6, 12, 37; 10:21, 40, 45; 11:28; 12:9, 14, 15, 15; 13:11, 24, 34; 14:5, 11, 22, 23, 44; 15:23	1	10:37			1	13:22					2	4:7, 8	38
Lk.	55	1:32, 77; 4:6, 6; 6:4, 30, 38, 38, 38; 7:44, 45; 8:10, 18, 55; 9:1, 13, 16; 10:19, 35; 11:3, 7, 8, 9, 13, 13, 29, 41; 12:32, 33, 42, 48, 51, 58; 14:9; 15:12, 16, 29; 16:12; 17:18; 18:43; 19:8, 15, 23, 24, 26; 20:2, 10, 16, 22; 21:15; 22:5, 19, 19; 23:2	1	1:74	1	15:22			2	7:15; 19:13			1	2:24	60
Jn.	72	1:12, 17, 22; 3:16, 27, 34, 35; 4:5, 7, 10, 10, 12, 14, 14, 15; 5:26, 27, 36; 6:27, 31, 32, 32, 33, 34, 37, 39, 51, 51, 52, 65; 7:19, 22; 9:24; 10:28, 29; 11:22, 57; 12:5, 49; 13:3, 15, 26, 29, 34; 14:16, 27, 27, 27; 15:16; 16:23; 17:2, 2, 2, 4, 6, 6, 7, 8, 8, 9, 11, 12, 14, 22, 22, 24, 24; 18:9, 11; 19:9, 11; 21:13											3	5:22; 18:22; 19:3	75
Ac.	25	2:4; 3:6, 16; 4:12; 5:31, 32; 7:5, 5, 8, 10, 38; 8:18, 19; 9:41; 11:17; 12:23; 13:20, 21, 34; 14:17; 15:8; 17:25; 20:32, 35; 24:26	3	4:29; 11:18; 14:3			2	2:19; 10:40					5	1:26; 2:27; 7:25; 13:35; 19:31	35
Ro.	8	4:20; 5:5; 11:8; 12:3, 6, 19; 14:12; 15:15	1	15:5											9
1 Co.	13	1:4; 3:5, 10; 7:25; 11:15; 12:7, 8, 24; 14:7, 7, 8; 15:38, 57											2	9:12; 14:9	15
2 Co.	11	1:22; 5:5, 12, 18; 6:3; 8:5, 10; 9:9; 10:8; 12:7; 13:10			1	8:16							1	8:1	13
Gal.	6	1:4; 2:9, 9; 3:21, 22; 4:15													6
Eph.	10	1:17, 22; 3:2, 7, 8; 4:7, 8, 11, 27; 6:19	1	3:16									1	4:29	12
Col.	1	1:25													1
1 Th.	2	4:2, 8													2
2 Th.	2	2:16; 3:16									1	3:9	1	1:8	4
1 Ti.	3	2:6; 4:14; 5:14													3
2 Ti.	5	1:7, 9, 16; 2:7, 25	1	1:18											6
Tit.	1	2:14													1
Heb.	2	2:13; 7:4			2	8:10; 10:16									4
Jas.	6	1:5, 5; 2:16; 4:6, 6; 5:18													6
1 Pt.	2	1:21; 5:5													2
2 Pt.	1	3:15													1
1 Jn.	6	3:23, 24; 4:13; 5:11, 16, 20											1	3:1	7
Rev.	46	1:1; 2:7, 10, 17, 17, 21, 23, 26, 28; 4:9; 6:2, 4, 4, 8, 11; 7:2; 8:2, 3a; 9:1, 3, 5; 10:9; 11:1, 2, 3, 13, 18; 12:14; 13:2, 4, 5, 5, 7, 7, 15b; 14:7; 15:7; 16:6, 8, 9, 19; 17:17b; 18:7; 19:7; 20:4; 21:6	2	3:21; 19:8	1	17:17a					1	3:9	7	3:8; 8:3b; 13:14, 15a, 16; 20:13a, 13b	57
Total	365		10		5		4		2		2		25		413

Miscellaneous: Mt. 13:8, bring forth; Mk. 4:7, 8, yield; Lk. 2:24, offer; Jn. 5:22, commit; Jn. 18:22 (with 4375), strike with the palm of (one's) hand; Jn. 19:3, smite; Ac. 1:26, give forth; Ac. 2:27, suffer; Ac. 7:25 (with 4891), deliver; Ac. 13:35, suffer; Ac. 19:31, adventure; 1 Co. 9:12 (with 1464), hinder; 1 Co. 14:9, utter; 2 Co. 8:1, bestow; Eph. 4:29, minister; 2 Th. 1:8, take; 1 Jn. 3:1, bestow; Rev. 3:8, set; Rev. 8:3b, offer; Rev. 13:14, 15a, have power; Rev. 13:16, receive; Rev. 20:13a, give up; Rev. 20:13b, deliver up.

1326. διεγείρω, diegei'rō

Book	Oc.	awake	Oc.	arise	Oc.	stir up	Oc.	raise	Total
Mt.							1	1:24	1
Mk.	1	4:38	1	4:39					2
Lk.	1	8:24							1
Jn.			1	6:18					1
2 Pt.					2	1:13; 3:1			2
Total	2		2		2		1		7

1327. διέξοδος, diex'odos

Book	highway (with 3498 and 3488)	Total
Mt.	22:9	1

1328. διερμηνευτής diermēneutēs'

Book	interpreter	Total
1 Co.	14:28	1

1329. διερμηνεύω, diermēneu'ō

Book	Oc.	interpret	Oc.	by interpretation	Oc.	expound	Total
Lk.					1	24:27	1
Ac.			1	9:36			1
1 Co.	4	12:30; 14:5, 13, 27					4
Total	4		1		1		6

1330. διέρχομαι, dier'chomai

Book	Oc.	pass	Oc.	pass through	Oc.	go	Oc.	go over	Oc.	go through	Oc.	walk	Oc.	Misc.	Total
Mt.					1	19:24					1	12:43			2
Mk.													1	4:35	1
Lk.	3	4:30; 17:11; 19:4	1	19:1	2	2:15; 9:6	1	8:22			1	11:24	2	2:35; 5:15	10
Jn.					2	4:4; 8:59									2
Ac.	2	9:32; 18:27	4	8:40; 15:3; 19:1, 21	2	11:22; 20:25	2	18:23; 20:2	2	13:6; 15:41			9	8:4; 9:38; 10:38; 11:19; 12:10; 13:14; 14:24; 16:6; 17:23	21
Ro.	1	5:12													1
1 Co.	1	10:1	2	16:5, 5											3
2 Co.	1	1:16													1
Heb.													1	4:14	1
Total	8		7		7		3		2		2		13		42

Miscellaneous: Mk. 4:35, pass over; Lk. 2:35, pierce through; Lk. 5:15, go abroad; Ac. 8:4, go everywhere; Ac. 9:38, come; Ac. 10:38, go about; Ac. 11:19, travel; Ac. 12:10, be past; Ac. 13:14, depart; Ac. 14:24, pass throughout; Ac. 16:6, go throughout; Ac. 17:23, pass by; Heb. 4:14, pass into.

1331. διερωτάω, dierōta'ō

Book	make inquiry for	Total
Ac.	10:17	1

1332. διετής, dietes'

Book	two years old	Total
Mt.	2:16	1

1333. διετία, dieti'a

Book	two years	Total
Ac.	24:27; 28:30	2

1334. διηγέομαι, diege'omai

Book	Oc.	tell	Oc.	declare	Oc.	shew	Total
Mk.	2	5:16; 9:9					2
Lk.	1	9:10			1	8:39	2
Ac.			3	8:33; 9:27; 12:17			3
Heb.	1	11:32					1
Total	4		3		1		8

1335. διήγεσις, dieg'esis

Book	declaration	Total
Lk.	1:1	1

1336. διηνεκές, dienekes'

Book	Oc.	continually (with 1519)	Oc.	for ever (with 1519)	Total
Heb.	2	7:3; 10:1	2	10:12, 14	4

1337. διθάλασσος, dithal'assos

Book	where two seas meet	Total
Ac.	27:41	1

1338. διϊκνέομαι, diikne'omai

Book	pierce	Total
Heb.	4:12	1

1339. διΐστημι, diis'temi

Book	Oc.	the space of . . . after	Oc.	go further	Oc.	be parted	Total
Lk.	1	22:59			1	24:51	2
Ac.			1	27:28			1
Total	1		1		1		3

1340. διϊσχυρίζομαι, diischurid'zomai

Book	Oc.	confidently affirm	Oc.	constantly affirm	Total
Lk.	1	22:59			1
Ac.			1	12:15	1
Total	1		1		2

1341. δικαιοκρισία, dikaiokrisi'a

Book	righteous judgment	Total
Ro.	2:5	1

1342. δίκαιος, dik'aios

Book	Oc.	righteous	Oc.	just	Oc.	right	Oc.	meet	Total
Mt.	12	9:13; 10:41, 41, 41; 13:17, 43; 23:28, 29, 35, 35; 25:37, 46	5	1:19; 5:45; 13:49; 27:19, 24	2	20:4, 7			19
Mk.	1	2:17	1	6:20					2
Lk.	4	1:6; 5:32; 18:9; 23:47	6	1:17; 2:25; 14:14; 15:7; 20:20; 23:50	1	12:57			11
Jn.	2	7:24; 17:25	1	5:30					3
Ac.			5	3:14; 7:52; 10:22; 22:14; 24:15	1	4:19			6
Ro.	3	3:10; 5:7, 19	4	1:17; 2:13; 3:26; 7:12					7
Gal.			1	3:11					1
Eph.					1	6:1			1
Phl.			1	4:8			1	1:7	2
Col.			1	4:1					1
2 Th.	2	1:5, 6							2
1 Ti.	1	1:9							1
2 Ti.	1	4:8							1
Tit.			1	1:8					1
Heb.	1	11:4	2	10:38; 12:23					3
Jas.	1	5:16	1	5:6					2
1 Pt.	2	3:12; 4:18	1	3:18					3
2 Pt.	2	2:8, 8	1	2:7			1	1:13	4
1 Jn.	5	2:1, 29; 3:7, 7, 12	1	1:9					6
Rev.	4	16:5, 7; 19:2; 22:11	1	15:3					5
Total	41		33		5		2		81

1343. δικαιοσύνη, dikaiosu'ne

Book	righteousness	Total
Mt.	3:15; 5:6, 10, 20; 6:33; 21:32	6
Lk.	1:75	1
Jn.	16:8, 10	2
Ac.	10:35; 13:10; 17:31; 24:25	4
Ro.	1:17; 3:5, 21, 22, 25, 26; 4:3, 5, 6, 9, 11, 11, 13, 22; 5:17, 21; 6:13, 16, 18, 19, 20; 8:10; 9:28, 30, 30, 30, 31, 31; 10:3, 3, 3, 4, 5, 6, 10; 14:17	36
1 Co.	1:30	1
2 Co.	3:9; 5:21; 6:7, 14; 9:9, 10; 11:15	7
Gal.	2:21; 3:6, 21; 5:5	4
Eph.	4:24; 5:9; 6:14	3
Phl.	1:11; 3:6, 9, 9	4
1 Ti.	6:11	1
2 Ti.	2:22; 3:16; 4:8	3
Tit.	3:5	1
Heb.	1:9; 5:13; 7:2; 11:7, 33; 12:11	6
Jas.	1:20; 2:23; 3:18	3
1 Pt.	2:24; 3:14	2
2 Pt.	1:1; 2:5, 21; 3:13	4
1 Jn.	2:29; 3:7, 10	3
Rev.	19:11	1
Total		92

1344. δικαιόω, dikaio'ō

Book	Oc.	justify	Oc.	be freed	Oc.	be righteous	Oc.	justifier	Total
Mt.	2	11:19; 12:37							2
Lk.	5	7:29, 35; 10:29; 16:15; 18:14							5
Ac.	2	13:39, 39							2
Ro.	13	2:13; 3:4, 20, 24, 28, 30; 4:2, 5; 5:1, 9; 8:30, 30, 33	1	6:7			1	3:26	15
1 Co.	2	4:4; 6:11							2
Gal.	8	2:16, 16, 16, 17; 3:8, 11, 24; 5:4							8
1 Ti.	1	3:16							1
Tit.	1	3:7							1
Jas.	3	2:21, 24, 25							3
Rev.					1	22:11			1
Total	37		1		1		1		40

1345. δικαίωμα, dikai'ōma

Book	Oc.	righteousness	Oc.	ordinance	Oc.	judgment	Oc.	justification	Total
Lk.			1	1:6					1
Ro.	3	2:26; 5:18; 8:4			1	1:32	1	5:16	5
Heb.			2	9:1, 10					2
Rev.	1	19:8			1	15:4			2
Total	4		3		2		1		10

1346. δικαίως, dikai'ōs

Book	Oc.	justly	Oc.	righteously	Oc.	to righteousness	Total
Lk.	1	23:41					1
1 Co.					1	15:34	1
1 Th.	1	2:10					1
Tit.			1	2:12			1
1 Pt.			1	2:23			1
Total	2		2		1		5

1347. δικαίωσις, dikai'ōsis

Book	justification	Total
Ro.	4:25; 5:18	2

1348. δικαστής, dikastes'

Book	judge	Total
Lk.	12:14	1
Ac.	7:27, 35	2
Total		3

1349. δίκη, di'kē

Book	Oc.	vengeance	Oc.	judgment	Oc.	punish (with 4999)	Total
Ac.	1	28:4	1	25:15			2
2 Th.					1	1:9	1
Jd.	1	1:7					1
Total	2		1		1		4

1350. δίκτυον, dik'tuon

Book	net	Total
Mt.	4:20, 21	2
Mk.	1:18, 19	2
Lk.	5:2, 4, 5, 6	4
Jn.	21:6, 8, 11, 11	4
Total		12

1351. δίλογος, dil'ogos

Book	doubletongued	Total
1 Ti.	3:8	1

1352. διό, dio'

Book	Oc.	wherefore	Oc.	therefore	Oc.	for which cause	Total
Mt.	1	27:8					1
Lk.	1	7:7	1	1:35			2
Ac.	8	13:35; 15:19; 20:26; 24:26; 25:26; 26:3; 27:25, 34	2	10:29; 20:31			10
Ro.	3	1:24; 13:5; 15:7	2	2:1; 4:22	1	15:22	6
1 Co.	1	12:3			1	4:16	2
2 Co.	3	2:8; 5:9; 6:17	3	4:13, 13; 12:10			6
Eph.	5	2:11; 3:13; 4:8, 25; 5:14					5
Phl.	1	2:9					1
1 Th.	3	2:18; 3:1; 5:11					3
Phe.	1	1:8					1
Heb.	7	3:7, 10; 10:5; 11:16; 12:12, 28; 13:12	2	6:1; 11:12			9
Jas.	2	1:21; 4:6					2
1 Pt.	2	1:13; 2:6					2
2 Pt.	3	1:10, 12; 3:14					3
Total	41		10		2		53

1353. διοδεύω, diodeu'ō

Book	Oc.	go throughout	Oc.	pass through	Total
Lk.	1	8:1			1
Ac.			1	17:1	1
Total	1		1		2

1354. Διονύσιος, Dionu'sios

Book	Dionysius	Total
Ac.	17:34	1

1355. διόπερ, diop'er

Book	wherefore	Total
1 Co.	8:13; 10:14; 14:13	3

1356. διοπετής, diopetēs'

Book	which fell down from Jupiter	Total
Ac.	19:35	1

1357. διόρθωσις, dior'thōsis

Book	reformation	Total
Heb.	9:10	1

1358. διορύσσω, diorus'sō

Book	Oc.	break through	Oc.	be broken up	Oc.	be broken through	Total
Mt.	2	6:19, 20	1	24:43			3
Lk.					1	12:39	1
Total	2		1		1		4

1360. διότι, diot'i

Book	Oc.	because	Oc.	for	Oc.	because that	Oc.	therefore	Total
Lk.	1	2:7	2	1:13; 21:28					3
Ac.	1	17:31	4	10:20; 18:10, 10; 22:18					5
Ro.	2	1:19; 8:7			1	1:21	1	3:20	4
1 Co.	1	15:9							1
Gal.			1	2:16					1
Phl.					1	2:26			1
1 Th.	1	2:8			1	4:6			2
Heb.	2	11:5, 23							2
Jas.	1	4:3							1
1 Pt.	1	1:16	1	1:24					2
Total	10		8		3		1		22

1359. Διόσκουροι, Dios'kouroi

Book	Castor and Pollux	Total
Ac.	28:11	1

1361. Διοτρεφής, Diotrephēs'

Book	Diotrephes	Total
3 Jn.	1:9	1

1363. διπλόω, diplo'ō

Book	double	Total
Rev.	18:6	1

1362. διπλοῦς, diplous'

Book	Oc.	double	Oc.	twofold more	Total
Mt.			1	23:15	1
1 Ti.	1	5:17			1
Rev.	2	18:6, 6			2
Total	3		1		4

1364. δίς, dis

Book	Oc.	twice	Oc.	again	Total
Mk.	2	14:30, 72			2
Lk.	1	18:12			1
Phl.			1	4:16	1
1 Th.			1	2:18	1
Jd.	1	1:12			1
Total	4		2		6

1365. διστάζω, distad'zō

Book	doubt	Total
Mt.	14:31; 28:17	2

1368. διυλίζω, diulid'zō

Book	strain at	Total
Mt.	23:24	1

1366. δίστομος, dis'tomos

Book	Oc.	twoedged	Oc.	with two edges	Total
Heb.	1	4:12			1
Rev.	1	1:16	1	2:12	2
Total	2		1		3

1367. δισχίλιοι, dischil'ioi

Book	two thousand	Total
Mk.	5:13	1

1369. διχάζω, dichad'zō

Book	to set at variance	Total
Mt.	10:35	1

1370. διχοστασία, dichostasi'a

Book	Oc.	division	Oc.	sedition	Total
Ro.	1	16:17			1
1 Co.	1	3:3			1
Gal.			1	5:20	1
Total	2		1		3

1371. διχοτομέω, dichotome'ō

Book	Oc.	cut asunder	Oc.	cut in sunder	Total
Mt.	1	24:51			1
Lk.			1	12:46	1
Total	1		1		2

1372. διψάω, dipsa'ō

Book	Oc.	thirst	Oc.	be thirsty	Oc.	be athirst	Total
Mt.	1	5:6	3	25:35, 37, 42	1	25:44	5
Jn.	6	4:13, 14, 15; 6:35; 7:37; 19:28					6
Ro.	1	12:20					1
1 Co.	1	4:11					1
Rev.	1	7:16			2	21:6; 22:17	3
Total	10		3		3		16

1373. δίψος, dip'sos

Book	thirst	Total
2 Co.	11:27	1

1374. δίψυχος, dip'suchos

Book	double minded	Total
Jas.	1:8; 4:8	2

1375. διωγμός, diōgmos′

Book	persecution	Total
Mt.	13:21	1
Mk.	4:17; 10:30	2
Ac.	8:1; 13:50	2
Ro.	8:35	1
2 Co.	12:10	1
2 Th.	1:4	1
2 Ti.	3:11, 11	2
Total		10

1376. διώκτης, diōk′tēs

Book	persecutor	Total
1 Ti.	1:13	1

1379. δογματίζω, dogmatid′zō

Book	be subject to ordinances	Total
Col.	2:20	1

1378. δόγμα, dog′ma

Book	Oc.	decree	Oc.	ordinance	Total
Lk.	1	2:1			1
Ac.	2	16:4; 17:7			2
Eph.			1	2:15	1
Col.			1	2:14	1
Total	3		2		5

1377. διώκω, diō′kō

Book	Oc.	persecute	Oc.	follow after	Oc.	follow	Oc.	suffer persecution	Oc.	Misc.	Total
Mt.	6	5:10, 11, 12, 44; 10:23; 23:34									6
Lk.	1	21:12			1	17:23					2
Jn.	3	5:16; 15:20, 20									3
Ac.	9	7:52; 9:4, 5; 22:4, 7, 8; 26:11, 14, 15									9
Ro.	1	12:14	3	9:30, 31; 14:19					1	12:13	5
1 Co.	2	4:12; 15:9	1	14:1							3
2 Co.	1	4:9									1
Gal.	3	1:13, 23; 4:29					2	5:11; 6:12			5
Phl.	1	3:6	1	3:12					1	3:14	3
1 Th.					1	5:15					1
1 Ti.			1	6:11							1
2 Ti.					1	2:22	1	3:12			2
Heb.					1	12:14					1
1 Pt.									1	3:11	1
Rev.	1	12:13									1
Total	28		6		4		3		3		44

Miscellaneous: Ro. 12:13, given to; Phl. 3:14, press toward; 1 Pt. 3:11, ensue.

1380. δοκέω, doke′ō

Book	Oc.	think	Oc.	seem	Oc.	suppose	Oc.	seem good	Oc.	please	Oc.	Misc.	Total
Mt.	10	3:9; 6:7; 17:25; 18:12; 21:28; 22:17, 42; 24:44; 26:53, 66											10
Mk.					1	6:49					1	10:42	2
Lk.	4	10:36; 12:40; 13:4; 19:11	1	8:18	3	12:51; 13:2; 24:37	1	1:3			2	17:9; 22:24	11
Jn.	6	5:39, 45; 11:13, 56; 13:29; 16:2			1	20:15							7
Ac.	2	12:9; 26:9	2	17:18; 25:27	1	27:13	2	15:25, 28	2	15:22, 34			9
1 Co.	6	4:9; 7:40; 8:2; 10:12; 12:23; 14:37	3	3:18; 11:16; 12:22									9
2 Co.	2	11:16; 12:19	1	10:9									3
Gal.	1	6:3	3	2:6, 6, 9							1	2:2	5
Phl.	1	3:4											1
Heb.			2	4:1; 12:11	1	10:29					1	12:10	4
Jas.	1	4:5	1	1:26									2
Total	33		13		7		3		2		5		63

Miscellaneous: Mk. 10:42, be accounted; Lk. 17:9, trow; Lk. 22:24, be accounted; Gal. 2:2, be of reputation; Heb. 12:10, own pleasure.

1381. δοκιμάζω, dokimad′zō

Book	Oc.	prove	Oc.	try	Oc.	approve	Oc.	discern	Oc.	allow	Oc.	like	Oc.	examine	Total
Lk.	1	14:19					2	12:56, 56							3
Ro.	1	12:2			1	2:18			1	14:22	1	1:28			4
1 Co.			1	3:13	1	16:3							1	11:28	3
2 Co.	3	8:8, 22; 13:5													3
Gal.	1	6:4													1
Eph.	1	5:10													1
Phl.					1	1:10									1
1 Th.	1	5:21	1	2:4b					1	2:4a					3
1 Ti.	1	3:10													1
Heb.	1	3:9													1
1 Pt.			1	1:7											1
1 Jn.			1	4:1											1
Total	10		4		3		2		2		1		1		23

1382. δοκιμή, dokimē′

Book	Oc.	proof	Oc.	experience	Oc.	trial	Oc.	experiment	Total
Ro.			2	5:4, 4					2
2 Co.	2	2:9; 13:3			1	8:2	1	9:13	4
Phl.	1	2:22							1
Total	3		2		1		1		7

1383. δοκίμιον, dokim′ion

Book	Oc.	trying	Oc.	trial	Total
Jas.	1	1:3			1
1 Pt.			1	1:7	1
Total	1		1		2

1384. δόκιμος, dok′imos

Book	Oc.	approved	Oc.	tried	Total
Ro.	2	14:18; 16:10			2
1 Co.	1	11:19			1
2 Co.	2	10:18; 13:7			2
2 Ti.	1	2:15			1
Jas.			1	1:12	1
Total	6		1		7

1385. δοκός, dokos′

Book	beam	Total
Mt.	7:3, 4, 5	3
Lk.	6:41, 42, 42,	3
Total		6

1386. δόλιος, dol′ios

Book	deceitful	Total
2 Co.	11:3	1

1387. δολιόω, dolio′ō

Book	use deceit	Total
Ro.	3:13	1

1388. δόλος, dol'os

Book	Oc.	guile	Oc.	subtilty	Oc.	deceit	Oc.	craft	Total
Mt.			1	26:4					1
Mk.					1	7:22	1	14:1	2
Jn.	1	1:47							1
Ac.			1	13:10					1
Ro.					1	1:29			1
2 Co.	1	12:16							1
1 Th.	1	2:3							1
1 Pt.	3	2:1, 22; 3:10							3
Rev.	1	14:5							1
Total	7		2		2		1		12

1389. δολόω, dolo'ō

Book	handling deceit	Total
2 Co.	4:2	1

1390. δόμα, dom'a

Book	gift	Total
Mt.	7:11	1
Lk.	11:13	1
Eph.	4:8	1
Phl.	4:17	1
Total		4

1391. δόξα, dox'a

Book	Oc.	glory	Oc.	glorious	Oc.	honour	Oc.	praise	Oc.	dignity	Oc.	worship	Total
Mt.	8	4:8; 6:13, 29; 16:27; 19:28; 24:30; 25:31, 31											8
Mk.	3	8:38; 10:37; 13:26											3
Lk.	12	2:9, 14, 32; 4:6; 9:26, 31, 32; 12:27; 17:18; 19:38; 21:27; 24:26									1	14:10	13
Jn.	12	1:14, 14; 2:11; 7:18, 18; 8:50; 11:4, 40; 12:41; 17:5, 22, 24			4	5:41, 44, 44; 8:54	3	9:24; 12:43, 43					19
Ac.	4	7:2, 55; 12:23; 22:11											4
Ro.	15	1:23; 2:7, 10; 3:7, 23; 4:20; 5:2; 6:4; 8:18; 9:4, 23, 23; 11:36; 15:7; 16:27	1	8:21									16
1 Co.	12	2:7, 8; 10:31; 11:7, 7, 15; 15:40, 41, 41, 41, 41, 43											12
2 Co.	13	1:20; 3:7b, 9, 9, 10, 18, 18, 18; 4:6, 15, 17; 8:19, 23	5	3:7a, 8, 11, 11; 4:4	1	6:8							19
Gal.	1	1:5											1
Eph.	8	1:6, 12, 14, 17, 18; 3:13, 16, 21											8
Phl.	5	1:11; 2:11; 3:19; 4:19, 20	1	3:21									6
Col.	3	1:27, 27; 3:4	1	1:11									4
1 Th.	3	2:6, 12, 20											3
2 Th.	2	1:9; 2:14											2
1 Ti.	2	1:17; 3:16	1	1:11									3
2 Ti.	2	2:10; 4:18											2
Tit.			1	2:13									1
Heb.	7	1:3; 2:7, 9, 10; 3:3; 9:5; 13:21											7
Jas.	1	2:1											1
1 Pt.	10	1:7, 11, 21, 24; 4:13, 14; 5:1, 4, 10, 11					1	4:11					11
2 Pt.	4	1:3, 17, 17; 3:18							1	2:10			5
Jd.	2	1:24, 25							1	1:8			3
Rev.	16	1:6; 4:9, 11; 5:12, 13; 7:12; 11:13; 14:7; 15:8; 16:9; 18:1; 19:1; 21:11, 23, 24, 26			1	19:7							17
Total	145		10		6		4		2		1		168

1392. δοξάζω, doxad'zō

Book	Oc.	glorify	Oc.	honour	Oc.	have glory	Oc.	magnify	Oc.	make glorious	Oc.	full of glory	Total
Mt.	3	5:16; 9:8; 15:31			1	6:2							4
Mk.	1	2:12											1
Lk.	9	2:20; 4:15; 5:25, 26; 7:16; 13:13; 17:15; 18:43; 23:47											9
Jn.	21	7:39; 11:4; 12:16, 23, 28, 28, 28; 13:31, 31, 32, 32, 32; 14:13; 15:8; 16:14; 17:1, 1, 4, 5, 10; 21:19	2	8:54, 54									23
Ac.	5	3:13; 4:21; 11:18; 13:48; 21:20											5
Ro.	4	1:21; 8:30; 15:6, 9					1	11:13					5
1 Co.	1	6:20	1	12:26									2
2 Co.	1	9:13			1	3:10b			1	3:10a			3
Gal.	1	1:24											1
2 Th.	1	3:1											1
Heb.	1	5:5											1
1 Pt.	4	2:12; 4:11, 14, 16									1	1:8	5
Rev.	2	15:4; 18:7											2
Total	54		3		2		1		1		1		62

1393. Δορκάς, Dorkas'

Book	Dorcas	Total
Ac.	9:36, 39	2

1394. δόσις, dos'is

Book	Oc.	giving	Oc.	gift	Total
Phl.	1	4:1			1
Jas.			1	1:17	1
Total	1		1		2

1395. δότης, dot'ẹs

Book	giver	Total
2 Co.	9:7	1

1396. δουλαγωγέω, doulagōge'ō

Book	bring into subjection	Total
1 Co.	9:27	1

1397. δουλεία, doulei'a

Book	bondage	Total
Ro.	8:15, 21	2
Gal.	4:24; 5:1	2
Heb.	2:15	1
Total		5

1398. δουλεύω, douleu'ō

Book	Oc.	serve	Oc.	be in bondage	Oc.	do service	Total
Mt.	2	6:24, 24					2
Lk.	3	15:29; 16:13, 13					3
Jn.			1	8:33			1
Ac.	1	20:19	1	7:7			2
Ro.	7	6:6; 7:6, 25; 9:12; 12:11; 14:18; 16:18					7
Gal.	1	5:13	2	4:9, 25	1	4:8	4
Eph.					1	6:7	1
Phl.	1	2:22					1
Col.	1	3:24					1
1 Th.	1	1:9					1
1 Ti.					1	6:2	1
Tit.	1	3:3					1
Total	18		4		3		25

1399. δούλη, dou'lẹ

Book	Oc.	handmaiden	Oc.	handmaid	Total
Lk.	1	1:48	1	1:38	2
Ac.	1	2:18			1
Total	2		1		3

1400. δοῦλον, dou'lon

Book	servant	Total
Ro.	6:19, 19	2

1401. δοῦλος, dou'los

Book	Oc.	servant	Oc.	bond	Oc.	bondman	Total
Mt.	30	8:9; 10:24, 25; 13:27, 28; 18:23, 26, 27, 28, 32; 20:27; 21:34, 35, 36; 22:3, 4, 6, 8, 10; 24:45, 46, 48, 50; 25:14, 19, 21, 23, 26, 30; 26:51					30
Mk.	5	10:44; 12:2, 4; 13:34; 14:47					5
Lk.	27	2:29; 7:2, 3, 8, 10; 12:37, 38, 43, 45, 46, 47; 14:17, 21, 21, 22, 23; 15:22; 17:7, 9, 10; 19:13, 15, 17, 22; 20:10, 11; 22:50					27
Jn.	11	4:51; 8:34, 35; 13:16; 15:15, 15, 20; 18:10, 10, 18, 26					11
Ac.	3	2:18; 4:29; 16:17					3
Ro.	5	1:1; 6:16, 16, 17, 20					5
1 Co.	4	7:21, 22, 22, 23	1	12:13			5
2 Co.	1	4:5					1
Gal.	3	1:10; 4:1, 7	1	3:28			4
Eph.	2	6:5, 6	1	6:8			3
Phl.	2	1:1; 2:7					2
Col.	3	3:22; 4:1, 12	1	3:11			4
1 Ti.	1	6:1					1
2 Ti.	1	2:24					1
Tit.	2	1:1; 2:9					2
Phe.	2	1:16, 16					2
Jas.	1	1:1					1
1 Pt.	1	2:16					1
2 Pt.	2	1:1; 2:19					2
Jd.	1	1:1					1
Rev.	11	1:1, 1; 2:20; 7:3; 10:7; 11:18; 15:3; 19:2, 5; 22:3, 6	2	13:16; 19:18	1	6:15	14
Total	118		6		1		125

1402. δουλόω, doulo'ō

Book	Oc.	become servant	Oc.	bring into bondage	Oc.	be under bondage	Oc.	given	Oc.	make servant	Oc.	in bondage	Total
Ac.			1	7:6									1
Ro.	2	6:18, 22											2
1 Co.					1	7:15			1	9:19			2
Gal.											1	4:3	1
Tit.							1	2:3					1
2 Pt.			1	2:19									1
Total	2		2		1		1		1		1		8

1403. δοχή, dochē'

Book	feast	Total
Lk.	5:29; 14:13	2

1404. δράκων, drak'ōn

Book	dragon	Total
Rev.	12:3, 4, 7, 7, 9, 13, 16, 17; 13:2, 4, 11; 16:13; 20:2	13

1405. δράσσομαι, dras'somai

Book	take	Total
1 Co.	3:19	1

1407. δρέπανον, drep'anon

Book	sickle	Total
Mk.	4:29	1
Rev.	14:14, 15, 16, 17, 18, 18, 19	7
Total		8

1406. δραχμή, drachmē'

Book	Oc.	piece	Oc.	piece of silver	Total
Lk.	2	15:8b, 9	1	15:8a	3

1408. δρόμος, drom'os

Book	course	Total
Ac.	13:25; 20:24	2
2 Ti.	4:7	1
Total		3

1409. Δρούσιλλα, Drou'silla

Book	Drusilla	Total
Ac.	24:24	1

1410. δύναμαι, du'namai

Book	Oc.	can (could)	Oc.	cannot (with 3656)	Oc.	be able	Oc.	may (might)	Oc.	able	Oc.	Misc.	Total
Mt.	11	5:36; 6:24a, 27; 8:2; 9:15; 12:29, 34; 16:3; 17:16, 19; 19:25	5	5:14; 6:24b; 7:18; 26:53; 27:42	9	3:9; 9:28; 10:28, 28; 19:12; 20:22, 22; 22:46; 26:61	2	26:9, 42					27
Mk.	22	1:40, 45; 2:4, 7, 19a; 3:20, 23, 27; 5:3; 6:5, 19; 7:15, 24; 8:4; 9:3, 23, 28, 29, 39; 10:26, 38, 39	6	2:19b; 3:24, 25, 26; 7:18; 15:31	1	4:33	3	4:32; 14:5, 7			1	9:22	33
Lk.	14	1:22; 5:12, 21, 34; 6:39, 42; 8:19; 9:40; 12:25; 13:11; 16:13a; 18:26; 19:3; 20:36	6	11:7; 14:20, 26, 27, 33; 16:13b	2	3:8; 21:15	1	16:2	1	1:20	2	12:26; 16:26	26
Jn.	22	1:46; 3:2, 4, 4, 9, 27; 5:19, 30, 44; 6:44, 52, 60, 65; 9:4, 16, 33; 10:21; 11:37; 12:39; 13:36; 14:5; 15:5	14	1:3, 5; 7:7, 34, 36; 8:21, 22, 43; 10:35; 13:33, 37; 14:17; 15:4; 16:12	1	10:29							37
Ac.	7	8:31; 10:47; 13:39; 21:34; 24:13; 27:15, 43	5	4:16, 20; 5:39; 15:1; 27:31	1	20:32	7	17:19; 19:40; 24:8, 11; 25:11; 26:32; 27:12			1	27:39	21
Ro.	1	8:7	1	8:8	1	8:39			1	15:14	1	16:25	5
1 Co.	4	2:14; 3:1, 11; 12:3	4	10:21, 21; 12:21; 15:50	5	3:2, 2; 6:5; 10:13, 13	2	7:21; 14:31					15
2 Co.	1	3:7			1	1:4					1	13:8	3
Gal.	1	3:21											1
Eph.					4	3:20; 6:11, 13, 16	1	3:4					5
Phl.					1	3:21							1
1 Th.	1	3:9					1	2:6					2
1 Ti.	2	6:7, 16	1	5:25									3
2 Ti.			1	2:13	1	3:15			1	3:7			3
Heb.	5	3:19; 5:2; 9:9; 10:1, 11			3	2:18; 5:7; 7:25					1	4:15	9
Jas.	3	2:14; 3:8, 12	1	4:2	2	1:21; 4:12							6
1 Jn.	1	4:20	1	3:9									2
Jd.					1	1:24							1
Rev.	5	2:2; 3:8; 7:9; 9:20; 14:3			4	5:3; 6:17; 13:4; 15:8	1	13:17					10
Total	100		45		37		18		3		7		210

Miscellaneous: Mk. 9:22, can do; Lk. 12:26, be able to do; Lk. 16:26 (with 3261), cannot; Ac. 27:39, be possible; Ro. 16:25, that is of power; 2 Co. 13:8, can do; Heb. 4:15 (with 3261), cannot.

1411. δύναμις, du'namis

Book	Oc.	power	Oc.	mighty work	Oc.	strength	Oc.	miracle	Oc.	might	Oc.	virtue	Oc.	mighty	Oc.	Misc.	Total
Mt.	5	6:13; 22:29; 24: 29, 30; 26:64	6	11:20, 21, 23; 13:54, 58; 14:2											2	7:22; 25: 15	13
Mk.	5	9:1; 12:24; 13: 25, 26; 14:62	3	6:2, 5, 14			1	9:39			1	5:30					10
Lk.	11	1:17, 35; 4:14, 36; 5:17; 9:1; 10:19; 21:26, 27; 22:69; 24:49	2	10:13; 19:37							2	6:19; 8:46					15
Ac.	7	1:8; 3:12; 4:7, 33; 6:8; 8:10; 10:38					2	2:22; 19: 11							1	8:13	10
Ro.	7	1:4, 16, 20; 8: 38; 9:17; 15: 13, 19											1	15:19a			8
1 Co.	10	1:18, 24; 2:4, 5; 4:19, 20; 5:4; 6: 14; 15:24, 43			1	15:56	2	12:10, 28							2	12:29; 14:11	15
2 Co.	7	4:7; 6:7; 8:3, 3; 12:9b; 13:4, 4			2	1:8; 12:9a									1	12:12	10
Gal.							1	3:5									1
Eph.	3	1:19; 3:7, 20							2	1:21; 3:16							5
Phl.	1	3:10															1
Col.									1	1:11					1	1:29	2
1 Th.	1	1:5															1
2 Th.	2	1:11; 2:9											1	1:7			3
2 Ti.	3	1:7, 8; 3:5															3
Heb.	3	1:3; 6:5; 7:16			1	11:11	1	2:4							1	11:34	6
1 Pt.	2	1:5; 3:22															2
2 Pt.	2	1:3, 16							1	2:11							3
Rev.	8	4:11; 5:12; 7: 12; 11:17; 13:2; 15:8; 17:13; 19:1			3	1:16; 3:8; 12:10									1	18:3	12
Total	77		11		7		7		4		3		2		9		120

Miscellaneous: Mt. 7:22, wonderful work; Mt. 25:15, ability; Ac. 8:13 (with 3173), miracles; 1 Co. 12:29, worker of miracles; 1 Co. 14:11, meaning; 2 Co. 12:12, mighty deed; Col. 1:29 (with 1722) mightily; Heb. 11:34, violence; Rev. 18:3, abundance.

1412. δυναμόω, dunamo'ō

Book	strengthen	Total
Col.	1:11	1

1413. δυνάστης, dunas'tes

Book	Oc.	mighty	Oc.	of great authority	Oc.	Potentante	Total
Lk.	1	1:52					1
Ac.			1	8:27			1
1 Ti.					1	6:15	1
Total	1		1		1		3

1414. δυνατέω, dunate'ō

Book	be mighty	Total
2 Co.	13:3	1

1437. ἐάν, ean'

Book	Oc.	if	Oc.	except (with 3261)	Oc.	whosoever (with 3639)	Oc.	if (with 3261)	Oc.	whatsoever (with 3639)
Mt.	33	4:9; 5:13, 23, 46, 47; 6:14, 22, 23; 7:9, 10; 8:2; 9:21; 10:13a; 12:11; 15:14; 16:26; 17:20; 18:12, 15, 15, 17, 17, 19a; 21:3, 21, 24, 25, 26; 22: 24; 24:23, 26, 48; 28:14	4	5:20; 12:29; 18:3; 26:42	8	5:19, 32; 10:14, 42; 11:6; 20:26, 27; 23: 18	4	6:15; 10:13b; 18: 16, 35	6	14:7; 15:5; 16:19, 19; 20:4, 7
Mk.	18	1:40; 3:24, 25; 4:26; 7:11a; 8:3, 36; 9:43, 45, 47, 50; 10:12; 11:3, 31, 32; 12:19; 13:21; 14:31	3	3:27; 7:3, 4	5	9:37, 37; 10:11, 15, 43			6	6:22, 23; 7:11b; 10:35; 11:23; 13: 11
Lk.	21	4:7; 5:12; 6:33, 34; 10:6; 11:12; 12:38, 45; 14:34; 15:8; 16:30; 17: 3, 3, 4; 19:31, 40; 20:5, 6, 28; 22: 67, 68	2	13:3, 5	6	7:23; 9:48, 48; 17: 33, 33; 18:17				
Jn.	41	3:12; 5:31, 43; 6:51, 62; 7:17, 37; 8:16, 31, 36, 51, 52, 54, 55; 9:22, 31; 10:9; 11:9, 10, 40, 48, 57; 12: 24b, 26, 26, 32, 47; 13:17, 35; 14: 3, 14, 15, 23; 15:7a, 10, 14; 16:7b; 19:12; 21:22, 23, 25	12	3:2, 3, 5, 27; 4:48; 6:44, 53, 65; 12:24a; 15:4, 4; 20:25			5	8:24; 12:47; 13:8; 15:6; 16:7a		
Ac.	3	5:38; 9:2; 26:5	3	8:31; 15:1; 27:31						
Ro.	13	2:25, 25, 26; 7:2, 3, 3; 10:9; 11:22; 12:20, 20; 13:4; 14:23; 15:24b	1	10:15			1	11:23		
1 Co.	26	4:19; 5:11; 6:4; 7:8, 11, 28, 28, 36, 39, 40; 8:8a, 10; 10:28; 11:14, 15; 12:15, 16; 14:6a, 8, 14, 23, 24, 30; 16:4, 7, 10	4	14:6b, 7, 9; 15:36			4	8:8b; 9:16b; 14:11, 28		
2 Co.	3	5:1; 9:4; 13:2								
Gal.	2	5:2; 6:1							1	6:7
Eph.									1	6:8
Col.	2	3:13; 4:10								
1 Th.	1	3:8								
2 Th.			1	2:3						
1 Ti.	3	1:8; 2:15; 3:15								
2 Ti.	2	2:5a, 21	1	2:5b						
Heb.	8	3:6, 7, 14, 15; 4:7; 6:3; 10:38; 13: 23								
Jas.	4	2:2, 15; 4:15; 5:19					1	2:17		
1 Pt.	1	3:13								
1 Jn.	16	1:6, 7, 8, 9, 10; 2:1, 3, 15, 24, 29; 3: 20; 4:12, 20; 5:14, 15, 16					1	3:21	1	3:22
3 Jn.	1	1:10							1	1:5
Rev.	3	3:20; 22:18, 19	2	2:5, 22			1	3:3		
Total	201		33		19		17		16	

1415. δυνατός, dunatos′

Book	Oc.	possible	Oc.	able	Oc.	mighty	Oc.	strong	Oc.	could	Oc.	power	Oc.	mighty man	Total
Mt.	3	19:26; 24:24; 26:39													3
Mk.	5	9:23; 10:27; 13:22; 14:35, 36													5
Lk.	1	18:27	1	14:31	2	1:49; 24:19									4
Ac.	2	2:24; 20:16	1	25:5	2	7:22; 18:24			1	11:17					6
Ro.	1	12:18	3	4:21; 11:23; 14:4			1	15:1			1	9:22			6
1 Co.					1	1:26									1
2 Co.			1	9:8	1	10:4	2	12:10; 13:9							4
Gal.	1	4:15													1
2 Ti.			1	1:12											1
Tit.			1	1:9											1
Heb.			1	11:19											1
Jas.			1	3:2											1
Rev.													1	6:15	1
Total	13		10		6		3		1		1		1		35

1417. δύο, du′o

Book	Oc.	two	Oc.	twain	Oc.	both	Oc.	two and two (with 303)	Total
Mt.	35	4:18, 21; 6:24; 8:28; 9:27; 10:10, 29; 11:2; 14:17, 19; 18:8, 8, 9, 16, 16, 19, 20; 20:21, 24, 30; 21:1, 28; 22:40; 24:40, 41; 25:15, 17, 17, 22, 22, 22; 26:2, 37, 60; 27:38	6	5:41; 19:5, 6; 21:31; 27:21, 51					41
Mk.	15	6:7, 7, 9, 38, 41, 41; 9:43, 45, 47; 11:1; 12:42; 14:1, 13; 15:27; 16:12	3	10:8, 8; 15:38					18
Lk.	26	2:24; 3:11; 5:2; 7:19, 41; 9:3, 13, 16, 30, 32; 10:35; 12:6, 52, 52; 15:11; 16:13; 17:34, 35, 36; 18:10; 19:29; 21:2; 22:38; 23:32; 24:4, 13					1	10:1	27
Jn.	12	1:35, 37, 40; 2:6; 4:40, 43; 6:9; 8:17; 11:6; 19:18; 20:12; 21:2			1	20:4			13
Ac.	13	1:10, 23, 24; 7:29; 9:38; 10:7; 12:6, 6; 19:10, 22, 34; 21:33; 23:23							13
1 Co.	3	6:16; 14:27, 29							3
2 Co.	1	13:1							1
Gal.	2	4:22, 24							2
Eph.	1	5:31	1	2:15					2
Phl.	1	1:23							1
1 Ti.	1	5:19							1
Heb.	2	6:18; 10:28							2
Rev.	10	9:12, 16; 11:2, 3, 4, 4, 10; 12:14; 13:5, 11			1	19:20			11
Total	122		10		2		1		135

1416. δύγω or δῦμι

du′nō or du′mi

Book	set	Total
Mk.	1:32	1
Lk.	4:40	1
Total		2

1418. δυσ-, dus-

Used only in composition as a prefix. Means "hard" or "with difficulty."

1419. δυσβάστακτος

dusbas′taktos

Book	grievous to be borne	Total
Mt.	23:4	1
Lk.	11:46	1
Total		2

1437. ἐάν, ean′ (continued)

Book	Oc.	though	Oc.	whosoever (with 3639)	Oc.	whomsoever (with 3639)	Oc.	but (with 3261)	Oc.	wheresoever (with 3599)	Oc.	whether	Oc.	Not Tr.	Oc.	Misc.	Total
Mt.			2	10:14; 11:6	1	11:27			2	24:28; 26:13			2	12:36; 18:19b	5	8:19; 18:5, 13, 18, 18	67
Mk.			1	10:15			1	10:30	1	14:14			1	4:22	1	6:10	37
Lk.	1	16:31	2	7:23; 18:17	1	4:6							1	10:22			34
Jn.							1	5:19					2	7:51; 15:7b	1	13:20	62
Ac.	1	13:41											1	7:7			8
Ro.	1	9:27									3	14:8a, 8b, 8c			2	14:8d; 15:24a	21
1 Co.	7	4:15; 9:16a; 13:1, 2, 2, 3, 3			1	16:3							1	6:18	2	14:16; 16:6	45
2 Co.	2	10:8; 12:6											1	8:12			6
Gal.	1	1:8					1	2:16									5
Eph.																	1
Col.															1	3:23	3
1 Th.																	1
2 Th.																	1
1 Ti.																	3
2 Ti.																	3
Heb.																	8
Jas.	1	2:14															6
1 Pt.																	1
1 Jn.															1	3:2	19
3 Jn.																	2
Rev.													2	3:19; 11:6			8
Total	14		5		3		3		3				11		13		341

Miscellaneous: Mt. 8:19 (with 3599), whithersoever; Mt. 18:5 (with 3639), whoso; Mt. 18:13, if so; Mt. 18:18, 18 (with 3645), whatsoever; Mk. 6:10 (with 3599), in what place soever; Jn. 13:20 (with 5000), whomsoever; Ro. 14:8d, or; Ro. 15:24a (with 5513), whensoever; 1 Co. 14:16, when; 1 Co. 16:6 (with 3657), whithersoever; Col. 3:23 (with 3648) whatsoever; 1 Jn. 3:2, when.

1420. δυσεντερία, dusenteri'a

Book	bloody flux	Total
Ac.	28:8	1

1421. δυσερμήνευτος dusermen'eutos

Book	hard to be uttered	Total
Heb.	5:11	1

1422. δύσκολος, dus'kolos

Book	hard	Total
Mk.	10:24	1

1423. δυσκόλως, duskol'ōs

Book	hardly	Total
Mt.	19:23	1
Mk.	10:23	1
Lk.	18:24	1
Total		3

1424. δυσμή, dusme'

Book	west	Total
Mt.	8:11; 24:27	2
Lk.	12:54; 13:29	2
Rev.	21:13	1
Total		5

1425. δυσνόητος, dusno'etos

Book	hard to be understood	Total
2 Pt.	3:16	1

1426. δυσφημία, dusphemi'a

Book	evil report	Total
2 Co.	6:8	1

1427. δώδεκα, dō'deka

Book	twelve	Total
Mt.	9:20; 10:1, 2, 5; 11:1; 14:20; 19:28, 28; 20:17; 26:14, 20, 47, 53	13
Mk.	3:14; 4:10; 5:25, 42; 6:7, 43; 8:19; 9:35; 10:32; 11:11; 14:10, 17, 20, 43	14
Lk.	2:42; 6:13; 8:1, 42, 43; 9:1, 12, 17; 18:31; 22:3, 14, 30, 47	13
Jn.	6:13, 67, 70, 71; 11:9; 20:24	6
Ac.	6:2; 7:8	2
1 Co.	15:5	1
Jas.	1:1	1
Rev.	7:5, 5, 5, 6, 6, 6, 7, 7, 7, 8, 8, 8; 12:1; 21:12, 12, 12, 14, 14, 16, 21, 21; 22:2	22
Total		72

1428. δωδέκατος, dōdek'atos

Book	twelfth	Total
Rev.	21:20	1

1429. δωδεκάφυλον dōdekaph'ulon

Book	twelve tribes	Total
Ac.	26:7	1

1430. δῶμα, dō'ma

Book	housetop	Total
Mt.	10:27; 24:17	2
Mk.	13:15	1
Lk.	5:19; 12:3; 17:31	3
Ac.	10:9	1
Total		7

1431. δωρεά, dōrea'

Book	gift	Total
Jn.	4:10	1
Ac.	2:38; 8:20; 10:45; 11:17	4
Ro.	5:15, 17	2
2 Co.	9:15	1
Eph.	3:7; 4:7	2
Heb.	6:4	1
Total		11

1432. δωρεάν, dōrean

Book	Oc.	freely	Oc.	without a cause	Oc.	in vain	Oc.	for nought	Total
Mt.	2	10:8, 8							2
Jn.			1	15:25					1
Ro.	1	3:24							1
2 Co.	1	11:7							1
Gal.					1	2:21			1
2 Th.							1	3:8	1
Rev.	2	21:6; 22:17							2
Total	6		1		1		1		9

1433. δωρέομαι, dōre'omai

Book	give	Total
Mk.	15:45	1
2 Pt.	1:3, 4	2
Total		3

1434. δώρημα, dō'rema

Book	gift	Total
Ro.	5:16	1
Jas.	1:17	1
Total		2

1435. δῶρον, dō'ron

Book	Oc.	gift	Oc.	offering	Total
Mt.	9	2:11; 5:23, 24, 24; 8:4; 15:5; 23:18, 19, 19			9
Mk.	1	7:11			1
Lk.	1	21:1	1	21:4	2
Eph.	1	2:8			1
Heb.	5	5:1; 8:3, 4; 9:9; 11:4			5
Rev.	1	11:10			1
Total	18		1		19

1436. ἔα, e'a

Book	alone	Total
Mk.	1:24	1
Lk.	4:34	1
Total		2

See pages 94 and 95 for Word 1437.

1438. ἑαυτοῦ, heautou'

Book	Oc.	himself	Oc.	themselves	Oc.	yourselves	Oc.	ourselves	Oc.	his	Oc.	their	Oc.	itself
Mt.	9	12:26, 45, 45; 13:21; 16:24; 18:4; 23:12, 12; 27:42	6	9:3; 14:15; 16:17; 19:12; 21:25, 38	4	3:9; 16:8; 23:31; 25:9					3	8:22; 21:8; 25:3a	3	6:34; 12:25, 25
Mk.	6	3:26; 5:5, 30; 8:34; 12:33; 15:31	11	2:8; 4:17; 6:36, 51; 9:8, 10; 10:26; 11:31; 12:7; 14:4; 16:3	3	9:33, 50; 13:9							2	3:24, 25
Lk.	20	7:39; 9:23, 25; 10:29; 11:18, 26; 12:17, 21; 14:11, 11; 15:17; 16:3; 18:4, 11; 18:14, 14; 19:12; 23:35; 24:12, 27	8	7:30, 49; 18:9; 20:5, 14, 20; 22:23; 23:12	10	3:8; 12:33, 57; 16:9, 15; 17:3, 14; 21:34; 22:17; 23:28			8	11:21; 12:47; 13:19; 14:26a; 15:5, 20; 16:5; 19:13	6	9:60; 12:36; 16:8; 19:35; 22:66; 23:48	1	11:17
Jn.	16	2:24; 5:18, 19, 26, 26; 6:61; 7:18; 8:22; 11:38; 11:51; 13:4, 32; 16:13; 19:7; 21:1, 7	3	7:35; 11:55; 12:19									1	15:4
Ac.	10	1:3; 5:36; 8:9, 34; 10:17; 12:11; 14:17; 16:27; 19:31; 28:16	3	23:12, 21; 28:29	4	5:35; 13:46; 15:29; 20:38	1	23:14						
Ro.	5	14:7, 7, 12, 22; 15:3	4	1:24, 27; 2:14; 13:2	4	6:11, 13, 16; 12:19	2	8:23; 15:1	1	5:8			1	14:14
1 Co.	5	3:18; 11:28, 29; 14:4, 28	1	16:15			1	11:31	1	7:37				
2 Co.	5	5:18, 19; 10:7, 7, 18	6	5:15; 10:12b, 12c, 12d, 12e, 12f	2	7:11; 13:5a	13	1:9, 9; 3:1, 5, 5; 4:2, 5, 5; 5:12; 6:4; 7:1; 10:12a, 14	1	3:13				
Gal.	5	1:4; 2:12, 20; 6:3, 4b							1	6:8				
Eph.	6	2:15; 5:2, 25b, 27, 28d, 33b	1	4:19	1	5:19			2	5:28c, 33a	1	5:28a	1	4:16
Phl.	3	2:7, 8; 3:21	1	2:3										
Col.														
1 Th.					1	5:13			3	2:11, 12; 4:4				
2 Th.	1	2:4					1	3:9	1	2:6				
1 Ti.	1	2:6	4	2:9; 3:13; 6:10, 19										
2 Ti.	2	2:13, 21	1	4:3										
Tit.	2	2:14, 14												
Heb.	9	1:3; 5:3, 4, 5; 6:13; 7:27; 9:7, 14, 25	1	6:6	1	10:34	1	10:25						
Jas.	2	1:24, 27			1	2:4								
1 Pt.			2	1:12; 3:5	1	4:8					1	4:19		
2 Pt.			1	2:1										
1 Jn.	3	3:3; 5:10, 18			1	5:21	1	1:8						
2 Jn.					1	1:8								
Jd.			2	1:12, 19	2	1:20, 21					1	1:6		
Rev.			2	6:15; 8:6					1	10:7	3	10:3, 4; 17:13		
Total	110		57		36		20		19		15		9	

Miscellaneous: Mt. 23:37, her; Mk. 5:26 (with 3744), that (one) has; Mk. 14:33, him; Lk. 9:47, him; Lk. 13:34, her; Lk. 14:33, he; Lk. 21:30, your own selves; Lk. 23:2, he himself; Jn. 18:34, thyself; Jn. 20:10, their own house; Ac. 7:21, her own; Ac. 25:4, he himself; Ro. 11:25; 12:16, your own conceits; Ro. 13:9, thyself; 1 Co. 6:19, your own; 1 Co. 10:29, thine own; 1 Co. 11:5, her; 1 Co. 13:5, her own; 1 Co. 16:2, him; 2 Co. 8:5, their own selves;

1439. ἐάω, ea'ō

Book	Oc.	suffer	Oc.	let alone	Oc.	leave	Oc.	let	Oc.	commit	Total
Mt.	1	24:43									1
Lk.	2	4:41; 22:51									2
Ac.	4	14:16; 16:7; 19:30; 28:4	1	5:38	1	23:32	1	27:32	1	27:40	8
1 Co.	1	10:13									1
Rev.	1	2:20									1
Total	9		1		1		1		1		13

1440. ἑβδομήκοντα, hebdomē'konta

Book	Oc.	seventy	Oc.	three score and ten	Oc.	three score and fifteen (with 3902)	Oc.	three score and sixteen (with 1803)	Total
Lk.	2	10:1, 17							2
Ac.			1	23:23	1	7:14	1	27:37	3
Total	2		1		1		1		5

1441. ἑβδομηκοντακίς hebdomēkontakis'

Book	seventy times	Total
Mt.	18:22	1

1442. ἕβδομος, heb'domos

Book	seventh	Total
Jn.	4:52	1
Heb.	4:4, 4	2
Jd.	1:14	1
Rev.	8:1; 10:7; 11:15; 16: 17; 21:20	5
Total		9

1443. Ἐβέρ, Eber'

Book	Heber	Total
Lk.	3:35	1

1444. Ἑβραϊκός, Hebraikos'

Book	Hebrew	Total
Lk.	23:38	1

1445. Ἑβραῖος, Hebrai'os

Book	Hebrew	Total
Ac.	6:1	1
2 Co.	11:22	1
Phl.	3:5, 5	2
Total		4

1446. Ἑβραΐς, Hebrais'

Book	Hebrew	Total
Ac.	21:40; 22:2; 26:14	3

1447. Ἑβραϊστί, Hebraisti'

Book	Oc.	in the Hebrew tongue	Oc.	in the Hebrew	Oc.	in Hebrew	Total
Jn.	1	5:2	2	19:13, 17	1	19:20	4
Rev.	2	9:11; 16:16					2
Total	3		2		1		6

1448. ἐγγίζω, enggid'zō

Book	Oc.	draw nigh	Oc.	be at hand	Oc.	come nigh	Oc.	come near	Oc.	draw near	Oc.	Misc.	Total
Mt.	2	15:8; 21:1	5	3:2; 4:17; 10:7; 26: 45, 46					1	21:34			8
Mk.			2	1:15; 14:42	1	11:1							3
Lk.	4	15:25; 21:28; 22:1; 24:28			6	7:12; 10:9, 11; 18:35; 19:29, 37	2	18:40; 19:41	3	21:8; 22:47; 24: 15	3	12:33; 15:1; 21:20	18
Ac.	2	7:17; 10:9			1	22:6	3	9:3; 21:33; 23:15					6
Ro.			1	13:12									1
Phl.											1	2:30	1
Heb.	1	7:19									1	10:25	2
Jas.	3	4:8, 8; 5:8											3
1 Pt.			1	4:7									1
Total	12		9		8		5		4		5		43

Miscellanous: Lk. 12:33, approach; Lk. 15:1 (with 2258), drew near; Lk. 21:20; Phl. 2:30, be nigh; Heb. 10:25, approach.

1438. ἑαυτοῦ, heautou' (continued)

Book	Oc.	them	Oc.	his own	Oc.	their own	Oc.	herself	Oc.	you	Oc.	one another	Oc.	Not Tr.	Oc.	Misc.	Total
Mt.	3	15:30; 25: 3b; 27:35					1	9:21	1	26:11					1	23:37	31
Mk.	2	2:19; 8:14							1	14:7					2	5:26; 14:33	27
Lk.			1	14:26b			1	1:24					1	12:1	5	9:47; 13:34; 14:33; 21:30; 23:2	61
Jn.	1	19:24							3	5:42; 6:53; 12:8			1	11:33	2	18:34; 20:10	27
Ac.	1	21:23													2	7:21; 25:4	21
Ro.			2	4:19; 8:3	2	16:4, 18									3	11:25; 12:16; 13:9	24
1 Co.			2	7:2; 10:24							1	6:7			5	6:19; 10:29; 11:5; 13:5; 16:2	16
2 Co.															3	8:5; 13:5b, 5c	30
Gal.			1	6:4a											1	5:14	8
Eph.			1	5:29	1	5:28b					1	4:32			1	5:25a	16
Phl.			1	2:4	1	2:21									1	2:12	7
Col.											2	3:13, 16					2
1 Th.															2	2:7, 8	6
2 Th.					1	3:12											4
1 Ti.																	5
2 Ti.																	3
Tit.																	2
Heb.											1	3:13					13
Jas.															2	1:22; 2:17	5
1 Pt.															1	4:10	5
2 Pt.																	1
1 Jn.																	5
2 Jn.																	1
Jd.					2	1:13, 18											7
Rev.	1	4:8					3	2:20; 18: 7; 19:7							2	2:9; 3:9	12
Total	8		8		7		5		5		5		2		33		339

2 Co. 13:5b, 5c, your own selves; Gal. 5:14, thyself; Eph. 5:25a, your; Phl. 2:12, your own; 1 Th. 2:7, her; 1 Th. 2:8, our own; Jas. 1:22, your own selves; Jas. 2:17 (with 2596), being alone; 1 Pt. 4:10, one (to) another; Rev. 2:9; 3:9, they.

1449. ἐγγράφω, enggraph'ō

Book	write	Total
2 Co.	3:2, 3	2

1450. ἔγγυος, eng'guos

Book	surety	Total
Heb.	7:22	1

1452. ἐγγύτερον, enggu'teron

Book	nearer	Total
Ro.	13:11	1

1454. ἔγερσις, eg'ersis

Book	resurrection	Total
Mt.	27:53	1

1451. ἐγγύς, enggus'

Book	Oc.	nigh	Oc.	at hand	Oc.	nigh at hand	Oc.	near	Oc.	from	Oc.	nigh unto	Oc.	ready	Total
Mt.	1	24:32	1	26:18			1	24:33							3
Mk.	1	13:29					1	13:28							2
Lk.	1	19:11			2	21:30, 31									3
Jn.	5	6:4, 19, 23; 11:18; 19:20	2	2:13; 7:2	2	11:55; 19:42	2	3:23; 11:54							11
Ac.	2	9:38; 27:8							1	1:12					3
Ro.	1	10:8													1
Eph.	2	2:13, 17													2
Phl.			1	4:5											1
Heb.											1	6:8	1	8:13	2
Rev.			2	1:3; 22:10											2
Total	13		6		4		4		1		1		1		30

1453. ἐγείρω, egei'rō

Book	Oc.	rise	Oc.	raise	Oc.	arise	Oc.	raise up	Oc.	rise up	Oc.	rise again	Oc.	raise again	Oc.	Misc.	Total
Mt.	8	11:11; 14:2; 24:7, 11; 26:46; 27:64; 28:6, 7	1	10:8	15	2:13, 14, 20, 21; 8: 15, 26; 9: 5, 6, 7, 19, 25; 17:7; 24:24; 25: 7; 27:52	2	3:9; 11:5	1	12:42	2	26:32; 27:63	2	16:21; 17:23	2	8:25; 12:11	33
Mk.	10	4:27; 6:14, 16; 10:49; 12:26; 13:8, 22; 14:28; 16:6, 14			4	2:9, 11, 12; 5:41			1	14:42					3	1:31; 3: 3; 9:27	18
Lk.	5	9:7; 11:8; 21:10; 24:6, 34	3	7:22; 9: 22; 20:37	4	5:24; 7:14; 8:24, 54	2	1:69; 3:8	5	5:23; 6:8; 7:16; 11: 31; 13:25							19
Jn.	4	2:22; 5:8; 13:4; 21:14	3	12:1, 9, 17	3	7:52; 11: 29; 14:31	2	2:19; 5:21							1	2:20	13
Ac.			5	3:15; 4:10; 13:23, 30; 26:8	1	9:8	4	5:30; 10:40; 12:7; 13:22	1	3:6			1	13:37	2	3:7; 10: 26	14
Ro.			3	6:9; 7:4; 10:9			4	4:24; 6:4; 8: 11, 11			1	8:34	1	4:25	1	13:11	10
1 Co.	8	15:12, 13, 14, 15c, 16a, 20, 29, 32	7	15:16b, 17, 42, 43, 43, 44, 52			4	6:14; 15: 15a, 15b, 35			1	15:4					20
2 Co.			1	1:9			2	4:14, 14			1	5:15					4
Gal.			1	1:1													1
Eph.			1	1:20											1	5:14	2
Col.			1	2:12													1
1 Th.			1	1:10													1
2 Ti.			1	2:8													1
Heb.							1	11:19									1
Jas.							1	5:15									1
1 Pt.							1	1:21									1
Rev.	1	11:1															1
Total	36		28		27		23		8		5		4		10		141

Miscellaneous: Mt. 8:25, awake; Mt. 12:11, lift out; Mk. 1:31, lift up; Mk. 3:3, stand; Mk. 9:27, lift up; Jn. 2:20, rear up; Ac. 3:7, lift up; Ac. 10:26, take up; Ro. 13:11; Eph. 5:14, awake.

1455. ἐγκάθετος, engkath'etos

Book	spy	Total
Lk.	20:20	1

1456. ἐγκαίνια, engkai'nia

Book	feast of dedication	Total
Jn.	10:22	1

1457. ἐγκαινίζω, engkainid'zō

Book	Oc.	dedicate	Oc.	consecrate	Total
Heb.	1	9:18	1	10:20	2

1458. ἐγκαλέω, engkale'ō

Book	Oc.	accuse	Oc.	implead	Oc.	call in question	Oc.	lay anything to the charge	Total
Ac.	4	23:28, 29; 26:2, 7	1	19:38	1	19:40			6
Ro.							1	8:33	1
Total	4		1		1		1		7

1460. ἐγκατοικέω, engkatoike'ō

Book	dwell among	Total
2 Pt.	2:8	1

1459. ἐγκαταλείπω, engkatalei'pō

Book	Oc.	forsake	Oc.	leave	Total
Mt.	1	27:46			1
Mk.	1	15:34			1
Ac.			1	2:27	1
Ro.			1	9:29	1
2 Co.	1	4:9			1
2 Ti.	2	4:10, 16			2
Heb.	2	10:25; 13:5			2
Total	7		2		9

1461. ἐγκεντρίζω, engkentrid'zō

Book	Oc.	graff in	Oc.	graff	Oc.	graff into	Total
Ro.	4	11:17, 19, 23, 23	1	11:24a	1	11:24b	6

1462. ἔγκλημα, eng'klēma

Book	Oc.	laid to (one's) charge	Oc.	crime laid against (one)	Total
Ac.	1	23:29	1	25:16	2

1463. ἐγκομβόομαι engkombo'omai

Book	be clothed with	Total
1 Pt.	5:5	1

1464. ἐγκοπή, engkopē'

Book	hinder	Total
1 Co.	9:12	1

1465. ἐγκόπτω, engkop'tō

Book	Oc.	hinder	Oc.	be tedious unto	Total
Ac.			1	24:4	1
Ro.	1	15:22			1
Gal.	1	5:7			1
1 Th.	1	2:18			1
1 Pt.	1	3:7			1
Total	4		1		5

1466. ἐγκράτεια, engkrat'eia

Book	temperance	Total
Ac.	24:25	1
Gal.	5:23	1
2 Pt.	1:6, 6	2
Total		4

1467. ἐγκρατεύομαι, engkrateu′omai

Book	Oc.	can contain	Oc.	be temperate	Total
1 Co.	1	7:9	1	9:25	2

1468. ἐγκρατής, engkratẹs′

Book	temperate	Total
Tit.	1:8	1

1469. ἐγκρίνω, engkri′nō

Book	make of the number	Total
2 Co.	10:12	1

1470. ἐγκρύπτω, engkrup′tō

Book	hide in	Total
Mt.	13:33	1
Lk.	13:21	1
Total		2

1471. ἔγκυος, eng′kuos

Book	great with child	Total
Lk.	2:5	1

1472. ἐγχρίω, engchri′ō

Book	anoint	Total
Rev.	3:18	1

1474. ἐδαφίζω, edaphid′zō

Book	lay even with the ground	Total
Lk.	19:44	1

1473. ἐγώ, egō′

Book	Oc.	I	Oc.	my	Oc.	me	Oc.	Not Tr.	Total
Mt.	31	3:11, 14; 5:22, 28, 32, 34, 39, 44; 8:7, 9; 10:16; 11:10; 12:27, 28; 14:27; 18:33; 20:15, 22, 22, 23; 21:27, 30; 22:32; 23:34; 24:5; 25:27; 26:22, 25, 33, 39; 28:20							31
Mk.	18	1:2, 8; 6:16, 50; 9:25; 10:38, 38, 39, 39; 11:33; 12:26; 13:6; 14:19, 19, 29, 36, 58, 62							18
Lk.	23	1:18, 19; 3:16; 7:8, 27; 8:46; 9:9, 9; 10:3, 35; 11:19; 15:17; 19:22, 23; 20:8; 21:8, 15; 22:27, 32, 70; 23:14; 24:39, 49							23
Jn.	142	1:20, 23, 26, 27, 30, 31; 3:28; 4:14, 26, 32, 38; 5:7, 30, 31, 34, 36, 36, 43, 45; 6:20, 35, 40, 41, 44, 48, 51, 51, 51, 54, 63, 70; 7:7, 8, 17, 29, 34, 36; 8:11, 12, 14, 15, 16, 16, 18, 21, 21, 22, 23, 23, 24, 28, 29, 38, 42, 45, 49, 50, 54, 55, 58; 9:9, 39; 10:7, 9, 10, 11, 14, 17, 18, 25, 30, 34; 11:25, 27, 42; 12:26, 46, 47, 49, 50; 13:7, 14, 15, 18, 19, 26, 33; 14:3, 4, 6, 10, 10, 11, 12, 12, 14, 16, 19, 20, 21, 27, 28; 15:1, 5, 10, 14, 16, 19, 20, 26; 16:4, 7, 7, 16, 17, 26, 27, 33; 17:4, 9, 11, 12, 14, 14, 16, 19, 22, 23, 24, 25; 18:5, 6, 8, 20, 20, 21, 26, 35, 37, 37, 38; 19:6							142
Ac.	42	7:7, 32; 9:5, 10, 16; 10:20, 21; 11:5, 17; 13:25, 33, 41; 17:3, 23; 18:6, 10, 15; 20:22, 25, 26, 29; 21:13, 39; 22:3, 8, 8, 19, 21, 28, 28; 23:1, 6, 6; 24:21; 25:18, 20, 25; 26:9, 10, 15, 15; 28:17	1	15:19					43
Ro.	17	7:9, 9, 14, 17, 20, 20, 24, 25; 10:19; 11:1, 13, 19; 12:19; 14:11; 15:14; 16:4, 22					1	9:3	18
1 Co.	25	1:12, 12, 12, 12; 2:3; 3:1, 4, 4, 6; 4:15; 5:3; 6:12; 7:10, 12, 28; 9:6, 15, 26; 10:30, 30; 11:23; 15:9, 10, 11; 16:10							25
2 Co.	11	1:23; 2:2, 10, 10; 10:1; 11:23, 29; 12:11, 13, 15, 16							11
Gal.	8	1:12; 2:19, 20; 4:12; 5:2, 10, 11; 6:17							8
Eph.	3	3:1; 4:1; 5:32							3
Phl.	4	3:4, 4, 13; 4:11							4
Col.	2	1:23, 25							2
1 Th.	1	2:18							1
1 Ti.	2	1:15; 2:7	1	1:11					3
2 Ti.	3	1:11; 4:1, 6							3
Tit.	1	1:5			1	1:3			2
Phe.	3	1:13, 19, 19			1	1:20			4
Heb.	7	1:5, 5; 2:13, 13; 5:5; 10:30; 12:26							7
1 Pt.	1	1:16							1
2 Pt.	1	1:17							1
2 Jn.	2	1:1, 1							2
3 Jn.	1	1:1							1
Rev.	17	1:8, 9, 11, 17; 2:22, 23; 3:9, 19; 5:4; 17:7; 21:2, 6, 6; 22:8, 13, 16, 16							17
Total	365		2		2		1		370

1475. ἔδαφος, ed′aphos

Book	ground	Total
Ac.	22:7	1

1476. ἑδραῖος, hedraï′os

Book	Oc.	stedfast	Oc.	settled	Total
1 Co.	2	7:37; 15:58			2
Col.			1	1:23	1
Total	2		1		3

1477. ἑδραίωμα, hedrai′ōma

Book	ground	Total
1 Ti.	3:15	1

1478. Ἐζεκίας, Edzeki′as

Book	Ezekias	Total
Mt.	1:9, 10	2

1479. ἐθελοθρησκεία, ethelothrẹskei′a

Book	will worship	Total
Col.	2:23	1

1480. ἐθίζω, ethid′zō

Book	custom	Total
Lk.	2:27	1

1481. ἐθνάρχης, ethnar′chẹs

Book	governor	Total
2 Co.	11:32	1

1482. ἐθνικός, ethnikos′

Book	Oc.	heathen	Oc.	heathen man	Total
Mt.	1	6:7	1	18:17	2

1483. ἐθνικῶς, ethnikōs′

Book	after the manner of Gentiles	Total
Gal.	2:14	1

1484. ἔθνος, eth′nos

Book	Oc.	Gentiles	Oc.	nation	Oc.	heathen	Oc.	people	Total
Mt.	8	4:15; 6:32; 10:5, 18; 12:18, 21; 20:19, 25	7	21:43; 24:7, 7, 9, 14; 25:32; 28:19					15
Mk.	2	10:33, 42	4	11:17; 13:8, 8, 10					6
Lk.	5	2:32; 18:32; 21:24b, 24c; 22:25	8	7:5; 12:30; 21:10, 10, 24a, 25; 23:2; 24:47					13
Jn.			5	11:48, 50, 51, 52; 18:35					5
Ac.	30	4:27; 7:45; 9:15; 10:45; 11:1, 18; 13:42, 46, 47, 48; 14:2, 5, 27; 15:3, 7, 12, 14, 17, 19, 23; 18:6; 21:11, 19, 21, 25; 22:21; 26:17, 20, 23; 28:28	12	2·5; 7:7; 10:22, 35; 13:19; 14:16; 17:26; 24:2, 10, 17; 26:4; 28:19	1	4:25	1	8:9	44
Ro.	23	1:13; 2:14, 24; 3:29, 29; 9:24, 30; 11:11, 12, 13, 13, 25; 15:9, 9, 10, 11, 12, 12, 16, 16, 18, 27; 16:4	5	1:5; 4:17, 18; 10:19b; 16:26			1	10:19a	29
1 Co.	3	5:1; 10:20; 12:2							3
2 Co.					1	11:26			1
Gal.	6	2:2, 8, 12, 14, 15; 3:14	1	3:8b	3	1:16; 2:9; 3:8a			10
Eph.	5	2:11; 3:1, 6, 8; 4:17							5
Col.	1	1:27							1
1 Th.	2	2:16; 4:5							2
1 Ti.	2	2:7; 3:16							2
2 Ti.	2	1:11; 4:17							2
1 Pt.	2	2:12; 4:3	1	2:9					3
3 Jn.	1	1:7							1
Rev.	1	11:2	21	2:26; 5:9; 7:9; 10:11; 11:9, 18; 12:5; 13:7; 14:6, 8; 15:4; 16:19; 17:15; 18:3, 23; 19:15; 20:3, 8; 21:24, 26; 22:2					22
Total	93		64		5		2		164

1485. ἔθος, eth′os

Book	Oc.	custom	Oc.	manner	Oc.	be wont	Total
Lk.	2	1:9; 2:42			1	22:39	3
Jn.			1	19:40			1
Ac.	5	6:14; 16:21; 21:21; 26:3; 28:17	2	15:1; 25:16			7
Heb.			1	10:25			1
Total	7		4		1		12

1486. ἔθω, eth′ō

Book	Oc.	be wont	Oc.	as his custom was (with 2596 and 3488)	Oc.	as his manner was (with 2596 and 3488)	Total
Mt.	1	27:15					1
Mk.	1	10:1					1
Lk.			1	4:16			1
Ac.					1	17:2	1
Total	2		1		1		4

1487. εἰ, ei

Book	Oc.	if	Oc.	whether	Oc.	that	Oc.	Not Tr.	Oc.	Misc.	Total
Mt.	33	4:3, 6; 5:29, 30; 6:23, 30; 7:11; 8:31; 10:25; 11:14, 21, 23; 12:7, 26, 27, 28; 14:28; 17:4; 18:8, 9; 19:10, 17, 21; 22:45; 23:30; 24: 24, 43; 26:24, 39, 42; 27:40, 42, 43	2	26:63; 27:49			2	12:10; 19:3			37
Mk.	9	3:26; 9:23; 11:13, 25, 26; 13:22; 14:21, 35; 15:44	2	3:2; 15:36	1	9:42	2	8:12; 10:2	1	14:29	15
Lk.	24	4:3, 9; 6:32; 7:39; 9:23; 10:13; 11:13, 19, 20, 36; 12:26, 28, 39, 49; 16:11, 12, 31; 17:6; 19:42; 22:42; 23:31, 35, 37, 39	4	6:7; 14:28, 31; 23:6	1	17:2	4	13:23; 14:3; 22:49, 67			33
Jn.	32	1:25; 3:12; 4:10; 5:47; 7:4, 23; 8:19, 39, 42, 46; 9:41; 10:24, 35, 37, 38; 11:12, 21, 32; 13:14, 17, 32; 14:7, 28; 15:18, 19, 20, 20; 18:8, 23, 23, 36; 20:15	1	9:25			1	5:46			34
Ac.	16	4:9; 5:39; 8:22, 37; 13:15; 16:15; 17:27; 18:14, 15; 19:38, 39; 20:16; 23:9; 25:11, 11; 27:39	6	4:19; 5:8; 10:18; 17:11; 19:2b; 25: 20	3	26:8, 23, 23	6	1:6; 7:1; 19: 2a; 21:37; 22: 25, 27	1	11:17	32
Ro.	34	3:3, 5, 7; 4:2, 14; 5:10, 15, 17; 6:5, 8; 7:16, 20; 8:9, 10, 11, 13, 13, 17, 25, 31; 9:22; 11:6, 6, 12, 15, 16, 16, 17, 18, 21, 24; 12:18; 14:15; 15:27									34
1 Co.	36	3:12; 6:2; 7:9, 15; 7:36; 8:2, 3, 13; 9:2, 11, 11, 12, 17, 17; 10:27, 30; 11:6, 6, 16, 31, 34; 12:17, 17, 19; 14:35, 38; 15:2, 12, 13, 14, 16, 17, 19, 29, 32, 32	2	7:16, 16			3	2:8; 14:10; 15:37			41
2 Co.	9	2:2, 5; 3:7, 9, 11; 5:14; 8:12; 11:4, 30	2	2:9; 13:5					1	13:4	12
Gal.	15	1:10; 2:14, 17, 18, 21; 3:18, 21, 29; 4:7, 15; 5:11, 15, 18, 25; 6:3									15
Phl.	1	1:22									1
Col.	2	2:20; 3:1									2
1 Th.	1	4:14									1
2 Th.	1	3:14									1
1 Ti.	8	3:5; 5:4, 8, 10, 10, 10, 10, 10									8
2 Ti.	4	2:11, 12, 12, 13									4
Phe.	2	1:17, 18									2
Heb.	12	2:2; 4:3, 5, 8; 7:11; 8:4, 7; 9:13; 11:15; 12:7, 8, 25			1	7:15	1	3:11			14
Jas.	7	1:5, 26; 2:8, 9, 11; 3:14; 4:11									7
1 Pt.	10	1:6, 17; 2:19, 20, 20; 3:17; 4:14, 16, 17, 18									10
2 Pt.	2	2:4, 20									2
1 Jn.	4	2:19; 3:13; 4:11; 5:9	1	4:1							5
Total	262		20		6		19		3		310

Miscellaneous: Mk. 14:29 (with 2532), although; Ac. 11:17, forasmuch; 2 Co. 13:4, though.

1488. εἶ, ei

Book	Oc.	thou art	Oc.	be	Total
Mt.	12	2:6; 5:25; 11:3; 14:33; 16:16, 17, 18, 23; 22:16; 25:24; 26:73; 27:11	5	4:3, 6; 14:28; 26:63; 27:40	17
Mk.	10	1:11, 24; 3:11; 8:29; 12:14, 34; 14:61, 70, 70; 15:2			10
Lk.	12	3:22; 4:34, 41; 7:19, 20; 15:31; 19:21; 22:58, 67, 70; 23:3, 40	4	4:3, 9; 23:37, 39	16
Jn.	24	1:19, 21, 21, 22, 42, 49, 49; 3:10; 4:12, 19; 6:69; 7:52; 8:25, 48, 53; 9:28; 11:27; 18:17, 25, 33, 37; 19:9, 12; 21:12	2	1:25; 10:24	26
Ac.	6	9:5; 13:33; 21:38; 22:8, 27; 26:15			6
Ro.	3	2:1; 9:20; 14:4			3
Gal.	1	4:7			1
Heb.	3	1:5, 12; 5:5			3
Jas.	2	4:11, 12			2
Rev.	8	2:9; 3:1, 15, 16, 17; 4:11; 5:9; 16:5			8
Total	81		11		92

1490a. εἰ δὲ μή, ei de mē

Book	Oc.	or else	Oc.	else	Oc.	if not	Total
Mk.			2	2:21, 22			2
Jn.	1	14:11			1	14:2	2
Rev.	2	2:5, 16					2
Total	3		2		1		6

1490b. εἰ δὲ μήγε, ei de mē′ge

Book	Oc.	else	Oc.	if not	Oc.	if otherwise	Oc.	or else	Oc.	otherwise	Total
Mt.	1	9:17							1	6:1	2
Lk.	1	5:37	2	10:6; 13:9	1	5:36	1	14:32			5
2 Co.					1	11:16					1
Total	2		2		2		1		1		8

Word 1490 has 14 occurrences.

1489. εἴγε, ei′ge

Book	Oc.	if so be that	Oc.	if	Oc.	if yet	Total
2 Co.	1	5:3					1
Gal.					1	3:4	1
Eph.	1	4:21	1	3:2			2
Col.			1	1:23			1
Total	2		2		1		5

1491. εἶδος, ei′dos

Book	Oc.	shape	Oc.	fashion	Oc.	sight	Oc.	appearance	Total
Lk.	1	3:22	1	9:29					2
Jn.	1	5:37							1
2 Co.					1	5:7			1
1 Th.							1	5:22	1
Total	2		1		1		1		5

1492a. εἴδω, ei'dō

Book	Oc.	know	Oc.	cannot tell (with 3656)	Oc.	know how	Oc.	wist	Oc.	Misc.	Total
Mt.	21	6:8, 32; 9:6; 12:25; 15:12; 20:22, 25; 22:16, 29; 24:36, 42, 43; 25:12, 13, 26; 26:2, 70, 72, 74; 27:18; 28:5	1	21:27	1	7:11			1	27:65	24
Mk.	18	1:24, 34; 2:10; 4:13, 27; 5:33; 6:20; 10:19, 38, 42; 12:14, 15a, 24; 13:32, 33, 35; 14:68, 71	1	11:33			2	9:6; 14:40	1	12:28	22
Lk.	19	4:34, 41; 5:24; 6:8; 8:53; 9:33, 55; 11:17; 12:30, 39; 13:25, 27; 18:20; 19:22; 20:21; 22:34, 57, 60; 23:34			1	11:13	1	2:49	3	11:44; 12:56; 20:7	24
Jn.	79	1:26, 31, 33a; 2:9, 9; 3:2, 11; 4:10, 22, 22, 25, 42; 5:32; 6:6, 42, 61, 64; 7:15, 27, 28, 28, 28, 29; 8:14a, 19, 19, 19, 37, 55, 55, 55; 9:12, 20, 21, 21, 24, 25, 25, 29, 29, 30, 31; 10:4, 5; 11:22, 24, 42, 49; 12:35, 50; 13:1, 3, 7, 11, 17, 18; 14:4, 4, 5, 5; 15:15, 21; 16:30b; 18:2, 4, 21; 19:10, 28, 35; 20:2, 9, 13, 14; 21:4, 12, 15, 16, 17, 24	3	3:8; 8:14b; 16:18			1	5:13	2	4:32; 16:30a	85
Ac.	13	2:22, 30; 3:16; 5:7; 7:18; 10:37; 12:11; 16:3; 19:32; 20:22, 25, 29; 26:27					2	12:9; 23:5	3	3:17; 7:40; 24:22	18
Ro.	13	3:19; 5:3; 6:9, 16; 7:7, 14, 18; 8:22, 26, 27, 28; 13:11; 14:14							3	2:2; 11:2; 15:29	16
1 Co.	25	1:16; 2:2, 11, 11, 12; 3:16; 5:6; 6:2, 3, 9, 15, 16, 19; 7:16, 16; 8:1, 2, 4; 9:13, 24; 11:3; 12:2; 14:11; 15:58; 16:15							2	13:2; 14:16	27
2 Co.	13	1:7; 4:14; 5:1, 6, 11, 16; 9:2; 11:11, 31; 12:2a, 2d, 3a, 3c	3	12:2b, 2c, 3b							16
Gal.	3	2:16; 4:8, 13									3
Eph.	4	1:18; 6:8, 9, 21									4
Phl.	4	1:17, 19, 25; 4:15			2	4:12, 12					6
Col.	4	2:1; 3:24; 4:1, 6									4
1 Th.	12	1:4, 5; 2:1, 2, 5, 11; 3:3, 4; 4:2, 5; 5:2, 12			1	4:4					13
2 Th.	3	1:8; 2:6; 3:7									3
1 Ti.	3	1:8, 9; 3:15			1	3:5					4
2 Ti.	5	1:12, 15; 2:23; 3:14, 15									5
Tit.	2	1:16; 3:11									2
Phe.	1	1:21									1
Heb.	2	8:11; 10:30									2
Jas.	3	3:1; 4:4, 17									3
1 Pt.	3	1:18; 3:9; 5:9									3
2 Pt.	2	1:12, 14			1	2:9					3
1 Jn.	15	2:11, 20, 21, 21, 29; 3:2, 5, 14, 15; 5:13, 15, 15, 18, 19, 20									15
3 Jn.	1	1:12									1
Jd.	2	1:5, 10									2
Rev.	11	2:2, 9, 13, 19; 3:1, 8, 15, 17; 7:14; 12:12; 19:12									11
Total	281		8		7		6		15		317

Miscellaneous: Mt. 27:65, can; Mk. 12:28, perceive; Lk. 11:44, be aware; Lk. 12:56, can; Lk. 20:7 (with 3261), cannot tell; Jn. 4:32, know of; Jn. 16:30a, be sure; Ac. 3:17; 7:40, wot; Ac. 24:22, have knowledge; Ro. 2:2, be sure; Ro. 11:2, wot; Ro. 15:29, be sure; 1 Co. 13:2; 14:16, understand.

1492b. εἴδω, ei'dō

Book	Oc.	see	Oc.	behold	Oc.	look	Oc.	perceive	Oc.	Not Tr.	Oc.	Misc.	Total
Mt.	56	2:2, 9, 10, 16; 3:7, 16; 4:16, 18, 21; 5:1, 16; 8:14, 18, 34; 9:2, 8, 9, 11, 22, 23, 36; 11:8, 9; 12:2, 38; 13:15, 17, 17; 14:14, 26; 16:28; 17:8; 18:31; 20:3; 21:15, 19, 20, 32, 38; 22:11; 23:39; 24:15, 33; 25:37, 38, 39, 44; 26:8, 58, 71; 27:3, 24, 49, 54; 28:6, 17					1	13:14			1	9:4	58
Mk.	39	1:10, 16, 19; 2:5, 12, 14, 16; 5:6, 14, 16, 22, 32; 6:33, 34, 38, 48, 49, 50; 7:2; 9:1, 8, 9, 14, 20, 25, 38; 10:14; 11:13, 20; 12:15b, 34; 13:14, 29; 14:67, 69; 15:32, 36, 39; 16:5	1	9:15			1	4:12			1	8:33	42
Lk.	65	1:12, 29; 2:15, 17, 20, 26, 26, 30, 48; 5:2, 8, 12, 20, 26; 7:13, 22, 25, 26, 39; 8:20, 28, 34, 35, 36, 47; 9:9, 27, 32, 49, 54; 10:24, 24, 31, 33; 11:38; 12:54; 13:12, 35; 14:18; 15:20; 17:14, 15, 22; 18:15, 24, 43; 19:3, 4, 5, 7, 37; 20:13, 14; 21:1, 2, 20, 31; 22:49, 58; 23:8, 8, 8, 47; 24:24, 39b	4	19:41; 21:29; 22:56; 24:39a			1	9:47			1	10:32	71
Jn.	36	1:33b, 39, 39, 46, 47, 48, 50; 3:3; 4:29, 48; 5:6; 6:14, 22, 24, 26, 30; 8:56, 56; 9:1; 11:31, 32, 33, 34; 12:9, 21, 40, 41; 18:26; 19:6, 26, 33; 20:8, 20, 25, 29; 21:21	1	20:27	1	7:52							38
Ac.	44	2:27, 31; 3:3, 9, 12; 4:20; 6:15; 7:24, 31, 34b, 55; 8:39; 9:12, 27, 35, 40; 10:3, 17; 11:5, 6, 13, 23; 12:3, 16; 13:12, 35, 36, 37, 45; 14:11; 16:10, 19, 27, 40; 19:21; 21:32; 22:14, 18; 26:13, 16; 28:4, 15, 20, 27	1	13:41			2	14:9; 28:26	1	7:34a	1	15:6	49
Ro.	1	1:11	1	11:22									2
1 Co.	3	2:9; 8:10; 16:7											3
Gal.	4	1:19; 2:7, 14; 6:11											4
Phl.	4	1:27, 30; 2:28; 4:9											4
1 Th.	3	2:17; 3:6, 10											3
1 Ti.	2	6:16, 16											2
2 Ti.	1	1:4											1
Heb.	4	3:9; 11:5, 13, 23											4
Jas.	1	5:11											1
1 Pt.	2	1:8; 3:10											2
1 Jn.	1	5:16	1	3:1									2
3 Jn.	1	1:14											1
Rev.	47	1:2, 12, 17, 19, 20, 20; 4:4; 5:1, 2; 6:1, 2, 9; 7:1, 2; 8:2; 9:1, 17; 10:1, 5; 12:13; 13:1, 2, 3; 14:6; 15:1, 2; 16:13; 17:3, 6, 6, 8, 12, 15, 16, 18; 18:1, 7; 19:11, 17, 19; 20:1, 4, 11, 12; 21:1, 2, 22	7	5:6, 11; 6:5, 12; 7:9; 8:13; 13:11	5	4:1; 6:8; 14:1, 14; 15:5							59
Total	314		16		6		5		1		4		346

Miscellaneous: Mt. 9:4; Mk. 8:33, know; Lk. 10:32, look on; Ac. 15:6, consider.

Word 1492 has 663 occurrences.

1493. εἰδωλεῖον, eidōlei'on

Book	idol's temple	Total
1 Co.	8:10	1

1494. εἰδωλόθυτον, eidōloth'uton

Book	Oc.	things offered unto idols	Oc.	things offered in sacrifice to idols	Oc.	things sacrificed unto idols	Oc.	meats offered to idols	Total
Ac.	1	21:25					1	15:29	2
1 Co.	3	8:1, 7, 10	3	8:4; 10:19, 28					6
Rev.					2	2:14, 20			2
Total	4		3		2		1		10

1495. εἰδωλολατρεία, eidōlolatrei'a

Book	idolatry	Total
1 Co.	10:14	1
Gal.	5:20	1
Col.	3:5	1
1 Pt.	4:3	1
Total		4

1496. εἰδωλολάτρης, eidōlolat'rēs

Book	idolater	Total
1 Co.	5:10, 11; 6:9; 10:7	4
Eph.	5:5	1
Rev.	21:8; 22:15	2
Total		7

1497. εἴδωλον, ei'dōlon

Book	idol	Total
Ac.	7:41; 15:20	2
Ro.	2:22	1
1 Co.	8:4, 7; 10:19; 12:2	4
2 Co.	6:16	1
1 Th.	1:9	1
1 Jn.	5:21	1
Rev.	9:20	1
Total		11

1498. εἴην, ei'ēn

Book	Oc.	should be	Oc.	be	Oc.	meant	Oc.	might be	Oc.	should mean	Oc.	wert	Oc.	Not Tr.	Total
Lk.	2	1:29; 9:46	2	3:15; 22:23	2	15:26; 18:36	1	8:9							7
Jn.	1	13:24													1
Ac.			1	21:33					1	10:17			1	8:20	3
Rev.											1	3:15			1
Total	3		3		2		1		1		1		1		12

1499. εἰ καί, ei kai

Book	Oc.	though	Oc.	if	Oc.	and if	Oc.	if that	Oc.	if also	Total
Mt.	1	26:33									1
Lk.	2	11:8; 18:4	1	11:18							3
1 Co.			2	4:7; 7:21							2
2 Co.	9	4:16; 5:16; 7:8, 8, 8, 12; 11:6; 12:11, 15	1	4:3					1	11:15	11
Phl.					1	2:17	1	3:12			2
Col.	1	2:5									1
Heb.	1	6:9									1
1 Pt.					1	3:14					1
Total	14		4		2		1		1		22

1500. εἰκῆ, eikē'

Book	Oc.	in vain	Oc.	without a cause	Oc.	vainly	Total
Mt.			1	5:22			1
Ro.	1	13:4					1
1 Co.	1	15:2					1
Gal.	3	3:4, 4; 4:11					3
Col.					1	2:18	1
Total	5		1		1		7

1501. εἴκοσι, ei'kosi

Book	twenty	Total
Lk.	14:31	1
Jn.	6:19	1
Ac.	1:15; 27:28	2
1 Co.	10:8	1
Rev.	4:4, 4, 10; 5:8, 14; 11:16; 19:4	7
Total		12

1502. εἴκω, ei'kō

Book	give place	Total
Gal.	2:5	1

1503. εἴκω, ei'kō

Book	be like	Total
Jas.	1:6, 23	2

1504. εἰκών, eikōn'

Book	image	Total
Mt.	22:20	1
Mk.	12:16	1
Lk.	20:24	1
Ro.	1:23; 8:29	2
1 Co.	11:7; 15:49, 49	3
2 Co.	3:18; 4:4	2
Col.	1:15; 3:10	2
Heb.	10:1	1
Rev.	13:14, 15, 15, 15; 14:9, 11; 15:2; 16:2; 19:20; 20:4	10
Total		23

1505. εἰλικρίνεια, eilikri'neia

Book	sincerity	Total
1 Co.	5:8	1
2 Co.	1:12; 2:17	2
Total		3

1506. εἰλικρινής, eilikrinēs'

Book	Oc.	sincere	Oc.	pure	Total
Phl.	1	1:10			1
2 Pt.			1	3:1	1
Total	1		1		2

1507. εἰλίσσω, heilis'sō

Book	roll together	Total
Rev.	6:14	1

1509. εἰ μή τι, ei mē ti

Book	except	Total
Lk.	9:13	1
1 Co.	7:5	1
2 Co.	13:5	1
Total		3

1508. εἰ μή, ei mē

Book	Oc.	but	Oc.	save	Oc.	except	Oc.	if not	Oc.	Not Tr.	Oc.	Misc.	Total
Mt.	12	5:13; 11:27a; 12:4, 24, 39; 14:17; 15:24; 16:4; 17:21; 19:17; 21:19; 24:36	3	11:27b; 13:57; 17:8	2	19:9; 24:22							17
Mk.	7	2:7, 26; 6:4; 9:29; 10:18; 11:13; 13:32	2	5:37; 6:8							4	6:5; 8:14; 9:9; 13:20	13
Lk.	5	5:21; 6:4; 10:22, 22; 11:29	4	4:26; 8:51; 17:18; 18:19							1	4:27	10
Jn.	6	3:13; 10:10; 14:6; 17:12; 18:30; 19:15	2	6:22, 46	1	19:11	4	9:33; 15:22, 24; 18:30					13
Ac.	1	11:19					1	26:32			1	21:25	3
Ro.	5	7:7a; 11:15; 13:1, 8; 14:14			2	7:7b; 9:29							7
1 Co.	6	1:14; 2:11b; 7:17; 8:4; 10:13; 12:3	2	2:2, 11a							2	14:5; 15:2	10
2 Co.	2	2:2; 12:5			1	12:13			1	3:1			4
Gal.	1	1:7	2	1:19; 6:14									3
Eph.	1	4:9											1
Phl.	1	4:15											1
1 Ti.											1	5:19	1
Heb.	1	3:18											1
1 Jn.	2	2:22; 5:5											2
Rev.	4	9:4; 14:3; 19:12; 21:27	1	13:17							1	2:17	6
Total	54		16		6		5		1		10		92

Miscellaneous: Mk. 6:5, save that; Mk. 8:14, more than; Mk. 9:9 (with 3652), till; Mk. 13:20, except that; Lk. 4:27, saving; Ac. 21:25, save only that; 1 Co. 14:5 (with 1623), except; 1 Co. 15:2 (with 1623), unless; 1 Ti. 5:19 (with 1623), but; Rev. 2:17, saving.

1510. εἰμί, eimi′

Book	Oc.	I am (with 1473)	Oc.	am	Oc.	it is I (with 1473)	Oc.	be	Oc.	I was (with 1473)	Oc.	have been	Oc.	Not Tr.	Total
Mt.	5	8:9; 20:15; 22:32; 24:5; 28:20	6	3:11; 8:8; 11:29; 18:20; 27:24, 43	3	14:27; 26:22, 25									14
Mk.	2	13:6; 14:62	1	1:7	1	6:50									4
Lk.	6	1:18, 19; 7:8; 21:8; 22:27, 70	8	3:16; 5:8; 7:6; 15:19, 21; 18:11; 22:33, 58	1	24:39			1	19:22					16
Jn.	35	1:20, 27; 3:28a; 4:26; 6:35, 41, 48, 51; 7:34, 36; 8:12, 18, 23, 23, 24, 28, 58; 9:9; 10:7, 9, 11, 14; 11:25; 12:26; 13:19; 14:3, 6; 15:1, 5; 17:24; 18:5, 6, 8, 35, 37	17	1:21; 3:28b; 7:28, 29, 33; 8:16; 9:5; 10:36; 13:13, 33; 16:32; 17:11, 14, 16; 18:17, 25; 19:21	1	6:20					1	14:9			54
Ac.	11	9:5; 10:21, 26; 13:25a; 18:10; 21:39; 22:3, 8; 23:6; 26:15, 29	2	13:25b; 27:23									1	25:10	14
Ro.	3	7:14; 11:1, 13	1	1:14											4
1 Co.	3	1:12; 3:4; 15:9a	11	9:1, 1, 2b; 12:15, 15, 16, 16; 13:2; 15:9b, 10, 10			1	9:2a							15
2 Co.			1	12:10			1	12:11							2
Phl.			1	4:11											1
Col.			1	2:5											1
1 Ti.	1	1:15													1
1 Pt.	1	1:16													1
Heb.													1	12:21	1
2 Pt.			1	1:13											1
Rev.	7	1:8, 11, 17; 2:23; 21:6; 22:13, 16	5	1:18; 3:17; 18:7; 19:10; 22:9											12
Total	74		55		6		2		1		1		2		141

1511. εἶναι, ei′nai

Book	Oc.	to be	Oc.	be	Oc.	was	Oc.	is	Oc.	am	Oc.	are (art)	Oc.	were	Oc.	Not Tr.	Oc.	Misc.	Total
Mt.	1	17:4	2	19:21; 20:27			1	22:23	2	16:13, 15									6
Mk.	3	9:5, 35; 14:64					1	12:18	2	8:27, 29							1	6:49	7
Lk.	1	9:33	5	2:49; 8:38; 14:26, 27, 33	7	2:4; 4:41; 5:12; 9:18a; 11:1; 19:11; 20:6	4	11:8; 20:27, 41; 23:2	2	9:18b, 20			1	2:6	2	20:20; 22:24	1	2:44	23
Jn.	1	7:4			1	17:5											1	1:46	3
Ac.	3	5:36; 16:15; 17:18	2	13:47; 18:15	6	4:32; 8:9; 18:3, 28; 19:1; 28:6	3	8:37; 17:29; 23:8	1	13:25			1	27:4			4	2:12; 16:13; 17:7, 20	20
Ro.	3	1:22; 6:11; 14:14	6	3:26; 4:11, 13, 16; 8:29; 15:16			1	7:3			3	1:20; 2:19; 3:9	1	9:3	1	16:19			15
1 Co.	6	3:18; 7:25, 26; 11:16; 12:23; 14:37	1	11:19									1	7:7	2	7:32; 10:6			10
2 Co.	1	7:11	2	5:9; 9:5			1	10:7							1	11:16			5
Gal.	4	2:6, 9; 4:21; 6:3																	4
Eph.			3	1:4, 12; 3:6															3
Phl.	3	1:23; 2:6; 4:11													2	3:8, 8			5
1 Th.																	1	2:6	1
1 Ti.	2	1:7; 2:12	1	3:2			1	6:5							1	6:18			5
2 Ti.			1	2:24															1
Tit.	2	3:1, 2	2	1:7; 2:2											2	2:4, 9			6
Heb.	2	5:12; 12:11			1	11:4													3
Jas.	1	1:26	2	1:18; 4:4															3
1 Pt.			1	1:21			1	5:12											2
1 Jn.							1	2:9											1
Rev.											3	2:2, 9; 3:9							3
Total	33		28		15		14		7		6		4		11		8		126

Miscellaneous: Mk. 6:49, had been; Lk. 2:44, to have been; Jn. 1:46, come; Ac. 2:12 (with 2309), mean; Ac. 16:13, be made; Ac. 17:7, there is; Ac. 17:20 (with 2309), mean; 1 Th. 2:6, have been.

1512. εἴ περ, ei per

Book	Oc.	if so be that	Oc.	though	Oc.	seeing	Oc.	if so be	Total
Ro.	2	8:9, 17							2
1 Co.	1	15:15	1	8:5					2
2 Th.					1	1:6			1
1 Pt.							1	2:3	1
Total	3		1		1		1		6

1513. εἴ πως, ei pōs

Book	if by any means	Total
Ac.	27:12	1
Ro.	1:10; 11:14	2
Phl.	3:11	1
Total		4

1514. εἰρηνεύω, eire̱neu´ō

Book	Oc.	have peace	Oc.	live peaceably	Oc.	live in peace	Oc.	be at peace	Total
Mk.	1	9:50							1
Ro.			1	12:18					1
2 Co.					1	13:11			1
2 Th.							1	5:13	1
Total	1		1		1		1		4

1515. εἰρήνη, eire̱´ne̱

Book	Oc.	peace	Oc.	one	Oc.	rest	Oc.	quietness	Total
Mt.	4	10:13, 13, 34, 34							4
Mk.	1	5:34							1
Lk.	14	1:79; 2:14, 29; 7:50; 8:48; 10:5, 6, 6; 11:21; 12:51; 14:32; 19:38, 42; 24:36							14
Jn.	6	14:27, 27; 16:33; 20:19, 21, 26							6
Ac.	4	10:36; 12:20; 15:33; 16:36	1	7:26	1	9:31	1	24:2	7
Ro.	11	1:7; 2:10; 3:17; 5:1; 8:6; 10:15; 14:17, 19; 15:13, 33; 16:20							11
1 Co.	4	1:3; 7:15; 14:33; 16:11							4
2 Co.	2	1:2; 13:11							2
Gal.	3	1:3; 5:22; 6:16							3
Eph.	7	1:2; 2:14, 15, 17; 4:3; 6:15, 23							7
Phl.	3	1:2; 4:7, 9							3
Col.	2	1:2; 3:15							2
1 Th.	3	1:1; 5:3, 23							3
2 Th.	3	1:2; 3:16, 16							3
1 Ti.	1	1:2							1
2 Ti.	2	1:2; 2:22							2
Tit.	1	1:4							1
Phe.	1	1:3							1
Heb.	4	7:2; 11:31; 12:14; 13:20							4
Jas.	3	2:16; 3:18, 18							3
1 Pt.	3	1:2; 3:11; 5:14							3
2 Pt.	2	1:2; 3:14							2
2 Jn.	1	1:3							1
3 Jn.	1	1:14							1
Jd.	1	1:2							1
Rev.	2	1:4; 6:4							2
Total	89		1		1		1		92

1516. εἰρηνικός, eire̱nikos´

Book	peaceable	Total
Heb.	12:11	1
Jas.	3:17	1
Total		2

1517. εἰρηνοποιέω, eire̱nopoie´ō

Book	make peace	Total
Col.	1:20	1

1518. εἰρηνοποιός, eire̱nopoios´

Book	peacemakers	Total
Mt.	5:9	1

See page 105 for Word 1519.

1520. εἷς, heis

Book	Oc.	one	Oc.	a	Oc.	other	Oc.	some	Oc.	Not Tr.	Oc.	Misc.	Total
Mt.	42	5:18, 29, 30; 6:24, 24, 27, 29; 10:29, 42; 12:11; 13: 46; 16:14; 18:5, 6, 10, 12, 14, 16, 24, 28; 19:16, 17; 20:13, 21a; 21:24; 22:35; 23:8, 9, 10, 15; 24:40a; 25:15, 18, 24, 40, 45; 26:14, 21, 47, 51; 27:38a, 48	3	5:41; 27:14, 15	2	20:21b; 24:40b					2	8:19; 27:38b	49
Mk.	25	5:22; 6:15; 8:14, 28; 9:17, 37, 42; 10:17, 18, 21, 37a; 11:29; 12:6, 28, 29, 32; 13:1; 14:10, 18, 20, 43, 47; 15:6, 27a, 36	1	14:51	2	10:37b; 15:27b	6	4:8, 8, 8, 20, 20, 20			1	2:7	35
Lk.	31	4:40; 5:3; 7:41; 9:8; 10:42; 11:46; 12:6, 25, 27, 52; 15:4, 7, 10, 19, 26; 16:5, 13, 13; 17:2, 15, 34, 36; 18:10, 19, 22; 20:3; 22:47, 50; 23:17, 39; 24: 18	1	15:15									32
Jn.	31	1:40; 6:8, 22, 70, 71; 7:21, 50; 8:41; 9:25; 10:16, 30; 11:49, 50, 52; 12:2, 4; 13:21, 23; 17:11, 21, 21, 22, 22, 23; 18:14, 22, 26, 39; 19:34; 20:12a, 24	2	6:9; 20:7	1	20:12b					2	1:3; 21: 25	36
Ac.	9	1:22; 11:28; 17:26, 27; 20:31; 21:26; 23:6, 17; 28:25							1	2:3	4	1:24; 2: 6; 4:32; 21:19	14
Ro.	19	3:10, 12, 30; 5:12, 15, 15, 16, 16, 17, 17, 17, 18, 18, 19, 19; 9:10; 12:4, 5a; 15:6									1	12:5b	20
1 Co.	28	3:8; 4:6, 6; 6:5, 16, 17; 8:4, 6, 6; 9:24; 10:17, 17, 17; 11:5; 12:11, 12, 12, 12, 13, 13, 13, 14, 18, 19, 20, 26, 26; 14:27									1	14:31	29
2 Co.	2	5:14; 11:2											2
Gal.	6	3:16, 20, 20, 28; 4:22a; 5:14			1	4:22b							7
Eph.	10	2:14, 15, 16, 18; 4:4, 4, 5, 5, 6, 7							1	4:16	1	5:33	12
Phl.	3	1:27; 2:2; 3:13											3
Col.	1	3:15									1	4:6	2
1 Th.	2	2:11; 5:11a									1	5:11b	3
2 Th.	1	1:3											1
1 Ti.	3	2:5, 5; 5:9											3
Heb.	2	2:11; 11:12											2
Jas.	3	2:10, 19; 4:12	1	4:13									4
2 Pt.	1	3:8											1
1 Jn.	2	5:7, 8											2
Rev.	8	5:5; 6:1; 7:13; 15:7; 17:1, 10; 21:9, 21b	1	18:21					2	21:21a; 22:2	3	4:8; 8: 13; 19:17	14
Total	229		9		6		6		4		17		271

Miscellaneous: Mt. 8:19, a certain; Mt. 27:38b, another; Mk. 2:7, only; Jn. 1:3, any; Jn. 21:25 (with 2596), every one; Ac. 1:24 (with 3639), whether; Ac. 2: 6, man; Ac. 4:32, any; Ac. 21:19 (with 1538 and 2596), particularly; Ro. 12:5b (with 2596), every man; 1 Co. 14:31 (with 2596), one by one; Eph. 5:33 (with 2596), every one; Col. 4:6, man; 1 Th. 5:11b, another; Rev. 4:8, each; Rev. 8:13; 19:17, an.

1519. εἰς, eis

Book	Oc.	into	Oc.	to	Oc.	unto
Mt.	127	2:11, 12, 13, 14, 20, 21, 22; 3:10, 12; 4:1, 5, 8, 12, 18; 5:1, 20, 25, 29, 30; 6:6, 13a, 26b, 30; 7:19, 21; 8:5, 12, 14, 23, 28b, 31, 32, 32, 33; 9:1, 1, 17, 17, 23, 26, 28, 38; 10:5, 5, 11, 12, 23; 11:7; 12:4, 9, 11, 29, 44; 13:2, 30b, 36, 42, 47, 48, 50, 54; 14:13, 15, 22a, 23, 32, 34, 35; 15:11, 14, 17b, 17c, 21, 29, 39b; 16:13; 17:1, 15, 15, 22, 25; 18:3, 8, 8, 9, 9, 30; 19:1, 17, 23, 24; 20:1, 2, 4, 7; 21:2, 10, 12, 17, 18, 21, 23, 31; 22:10, 13; 24:38; 25:21, 23, 30, 41, 46, 46; 26:18, 30, 32, 41, 45, 52, 71; 27:6, 27, 53; 28:7, 10, 11, 16, 16	22	2:1, 8; 7:13; 8:28a; 9:7, 13; 10:17, 21, 22; 14:19; 16:5; 17:24, 27; 20:17, 18; 21:1b; 22:3, 5, 5, 9; 23:34; 25:10	15	3:11; 7:14; 8:18; 9:6; 12:20; 13:52; 14:22b; 15:24; 16:21; 21:1a; 22:4; 24:13; 26:3, 36; 27:33
Mk.	90	1:12, 14, 21, 21, 29, 35, 38a, 45; 2:1a, 11, 22, 22, 26; 3:1, 13, 19, 27; 4:1, 37; 5:1b, 12, 12, 13, 13, 18; 6:1, 10, 31, 32, 36, 45a, 46, 51, 56; 7:15, 17, 18, 19, 19, 19, 24, 24, 33; 8:10, 10, 13a, 26b, 27; 9:2, 22, 22, 25, 28, 31, 42b, 43, 43, 43, 45, 45, 45, 47, 47; 10:1, 17, 23, 24, 25; 11:2, 2, 11a, 11b, 15b, 23; 12:41, 43; 13:15; 14:13, 16, 26, 28, 38, 41, 54, 68; 16:5, 7, 12, 15, 19	23	2:17; 5:19, 38; 6:41, 45b; 7:30, 34; 8:3, 13b, 22, 26a; 9:33; 10:32, 33, 46; 11:1a, 15a, 27; 13:9a, 12, 14; 14:8, 32	7	4:35; 5:1a, 21; 11:1b, 11c; 13:13; 15:41
Lk.	101	1:9, 39, 39, 40, 79; 2:3, 4a, 15, 27, 39a; 3:3a, 9, 17; 4:1, 5, 14, 16b, 37, 38, 42; 5:3, 4a, 19, 37, 38; 6:4, 6, 12, 38, 39; 7:1b, 11, 24, 36, 44; 8:22a, 29, 30, 31, 32, 33, 33, 37, 41, 51; 9:10, 12, 28, 34, 44, 44, 52; 10:1, 2, 5, 8, 10, 10, 38, 38; 11:4; 12:5, 28, 58; 13:19a; 14:1, 5, 21, 23; 15:13, 15; 16:4, 9, 16, 22, 28; 17:2, 12, 27; 18:10, 24, 25; 19:12, 30, 45; 21:1, 24; 22:3, 10, 10, 33a, 40, 46, 54, 66; 23:19, 25, 46; 24:7, 26, 51	39	1:23, 56; 2:22, 39b, 41, 42, 45, 51; 4:9, 16a, 31; 5:25, 32; 7:10; 8:39; 9:16, 51, 53, 56; 10:7, 30, 34; 14:8a; 15:17; 16:27; 17:11; 18:14, 31; 19:28, 29; 21:12, 21a; 22:33b, 39; 24:5, 13, 33, 50, 52	10	1:26; 2:4b; 4:26; 5:24; 8:22b; 11:24; 17:24; 18:13a, 35; 24:28
Jn.	64	1:9, 43; 3:4, 5, 17, 19, 22, 24; 4:3, 14b, 28, 38, 43, 45a, 46, 47, 54; 5:7, 24a; 6:3, 14, 15, 17a, 21a, 22b; 7:3, 14; 8:2; 9:39b; 10:1, 36, 40; 11:7, 27, 30, 54b; 12:24, 46a; 13:2, 3, 5, 27; 15:6; 16:13, 20, 21, 28; 17:18, 18; 18:1, 11, 15, 28b, 33, 37c; 19:9, 17; 20:6, 11, 25, 25, 27; 21:3, 7	21	2:2, 12, 13; 3:13; 4:5; 5:1; 6:24b; 8:26; 9:11; 11:38, 55, 56; 12:1, 12, 12; 16:32; 17:1; 20:3, 4, 8; 21:9	22	1:11; 4:8, 36, 45b; 5:24b, 29, 29; 6:27; 7:8, 8, 10, 35, 53; 8:1; 11:31, 54a; 12:25, 27; 13:1; 18:28a; 19:27; 20:1
Ac.	88	1:11, 11, 11, 13; 2:20, 20, 34; 3:1, 2, 3, 8; 5:21a; 7:3, 4a, 9, 15, 16, 34, 39, 55; 8:38; 9:6, 8, 17, 39; 10:16, 22, 24; 11:8, 10, 12; 12:17; 13:14b; 14:1, 20a, 22, 25; 16:9, 10, 15, 19, 23, 24a, 34, 37, 40; 17:10b; 18:7, 18, 19b, 27; 19:8, 22a, 29, 31; 20:1, 2, 3, 18; 21:3a, 8b, 11, 26, 28, 29, 34, 37, 38; 22:4, 10, 11, 23, 24; 23:10, 16, 20, 28; 25:23; 27:1, 6a, 17, 30, 38, 39, 41; 28:5, 17, 23	81	1:25; 5:21b, 36; 6:12; 8:3, 5, 25, 27, 40b; 9:2a, 26, 30, 30; 10:5, 8, 32; 11:2, 13, 20, 25; 12:19; 13:4b, 13, 13, 14a, 31, 34, 46, 48; 14:20b, 21, 24, 26a; 15:2, 4, 22, 30, 38; 16:1, 8, 11, 11, 12, 16; 17:1, 5, 20; 18:1, 19a, 22b, 24; 19:1, 21; 20:6, 14b, 15b, 17; 21:4, 7, 12, 15, 17; 22:5a, 17; 23:31, 32, 33; 24:17; 25:1, 3, 9, 20b; 26:12, 14, 18a; 27:5, 12; 28:6, 13, 13, 16	37	1:12; 4:3b; 5:16; 8:26; 9:2b; 11:18, 22, 26, 27; 12:10; 13:4a, 51; 14:6; 15:39; 17:10a; 18:6; 19:3, 3; 20:13, 22, 38; 21:1, 1, 1, 2, 8a; 22:5b, 7, 21; 25:6, 13, 21; 26:7, 11, 17; 27:8, 40a
Ro.	13	1:26b; 5:2, 12a; 6:3, 3, 4; 8:21; 10:6, 7, 18a; 11:24; 15:24, 28	18	1:17, 24, 28; 2:4; 5:16a, 18b; 7:10a; 8:15; 9:22, 31; 11:36a; 12:10; 13:4b, 14; 14:1; 15:7, 16b; 16:26a	26	1:1, 16, 26; 3:7, 22; 5:15, 16b, 18d, 21; 6:16b, 16c, 19, 19, 22; 7:10b; 9:21, 21, 23; 10:10, 10, 12, 18b; 15:25; 16:5, 19, 19
1 Co.	3	12:13, 13; 14:9	4	4:6; 10:31; 14:8; 16:15	6	1:9; 2:7; 10:2; 11:34; 14:36; 16:3
2 Co.	6	1:16a; 2:13; 7:5; 11:13, 14; 12:4	15	2:12a; 3:13, 18; 4:15; 7:9, 10; 8:4, 24a; 9:1, 8b, 11; 10:5; 12:1; 13:10, 10	11	1:23; 2:4, 16, 16; 4:11; 8:2; 9:5, 13, 13, 13; 10:14
Gal.	4	1:17b, 21; 3:27; 4:6	8	1:17a, 18; 2:1, 8a, 11; 4:24; 6:8, 8	6	1:6, 17c; 2:9, 9; 3:23, 24
Eph.	2	4:9, 15	5	1:5b, 6, 12b; 4:19, 32	8	1:5a, 14b, 15; 2:21; 4:13b, 13c, 16, 30
Phl.			3	1:19; 2:11; 4:17	4	1:11, 12; 3:11; 4:16
Col.	1	1:13	4	1:4; 2:2b; 3:9, 15	6	1:6, 10a, 11, 20; 2:2a; 4:11
1 Th.			3	2:16b; 5:9a, 15b	5	1:5; 2:9, 12b; 4:8, 15
2 Th.	2	3:5, 5	2	2:13, 14b		
1 Ti.	7	1:3, 12, 15; 3:6, 7; 6:7, 9a	2	1:16; 5:24	2	1:6; 2:4
2 Ti.	1	3:6	7	2:14, 20, 20, 25; 3:7; 4:10b, 12	6	2:21, 21; 3:15; 4:10a, 10c, 18a
Tit.			1	3:12		
Phe.						
Heb.	21	1:6; 3:11, 18; 4:1, 3, 3, 5, 10, 11; 6:19; 8:10a; 9:6, 7, 12, 24, 24, 25; 10:5, 31; 11:8a; 13:11	3	7:25a; 10:39b; 11:7	7	2:3, 10; 6:6; 9:28b; 10:39a; 11:26; 12:2
Jas.	4	1:25; 4:13; 5:4, 12	3	1:19c; 4:9, 9	1	2:2
1 Pt.	3	1:12; 2:9b; 3:22	4	1:4a; 4:4, 9, 10	10	1:2, 3, 5, 7, 10, 22, 25b; 3:12; 4:7; 5:10
2 Pt.	1	1:11	2	2:22; 3:9b	2	2:4, 9
1 Jn.	2	4:1, 9			1	3:14
2 Jn.	2	1:7, 10				
3 Jn.			2	1:5, 5		
Jd.	1	1:4b	1	1:4a	2	1:6, 21
Rev.	30	2:10, 22, 22; 5:6; 8:5, 8; 12:6, 9, 14, 14; 13:10; 14:19, 19; 15:8; 16:16, 17, 19; 17:3, 8, 11; 18:21; 19:20; 20:3, 10a, 14, 15; 21:24, 26, 27; 22:14	8	9:9; 10:5; 11:6, 12; 12:4; 13:3; 16:14; 20:8	13	1:11b, 11c, 11d, 11e, 11f, 11g, 11h; 6:13; 9:1, 7; 12:13; 19:9, 17
Total	573		281		207	

1519. εἰς, eis (continued)

Book	Oc.	for	Oc.	in	Oc.	on	Oc.	toward	Oc.	against
Mt.	11	5:13; 6:13b, 34; 8:4; 10:10, 18; 21:19; 24:14; 26:13, 28; 27:10	15	2:23; 4:13; 10:9, 27, 41, 41, 42; 12:18; 13:30a, 33; 18:6, 20; 26:67; 27:51; 28:19	1	27:30b	1	28:1	2	18:15, 21
Mk.	7	1:4, 44; 6:8a, 11; 11:14; 13:9c; 14:9b	14	1:9; 2:1b; 5:14, 14, 34; 6:8b; 9:42a; 11:8, 8; 13:9b, 16a; 14:20, 60; 15:38	3	4:8; 8:23; 14:6			1	3:29a
Lk.	15	1:33, 55; 2:34, 34; 3:3b; 5:4b, 14; 9:3, 5, 13, 62b; 12:19; 14:35, 35; 21:13	20	1:20, 44; 2:28; 4:35; 6:8; 7:1a, 50; 8:34, 34, 48; 11:7, 33; 13:11, 21; 14:8b, 10; 16:8; 21:14, 37; 22:19	5	6:20; 8:23; 12:49; 15:22, 22	2	12:21; 13:22	8	7:30; 12:10, 10; 15:18, 21; 17:3, 4; 22:65
Jn.	7	1:7; 6:51, 58; 8:35a; 9:39a; 12:34; 14:16	19	1:18; 2:23; 3:15, 16, 18b; 5:45; 7:5; 9:7; 11:25, 26a, 52; 12:36; 14:1, 1; 17:23; 19:13; 20:7, 19, 26	35	1:12; 2:11; 3:18a, 36; 4:39; 6:29, 35, 40, 47; 7:31, 38, 39, 48; 8:6, 8, 30; 9:35, 36; 10:42; 11:45, 48; 12:11, 37, 42, 44, 44, 44, 46b; 13:22; 14:12; 16:9; 17:20; 19:37; 21:4, 6	1	6:17b	2	12:7; 13:29
Ac.	8	2:38; 7:5, 21; 10:4; 13:2, 47b; 14:26b; 23:30	16	2:27, 31; 4:3a; 8:16, 23; 10:43; 12:4; 13:29; 16:24b; 17:21; 18:21; 19:5, 22b; 23:11a; 24:24; 26:18b	5	6:15; 13:9; 14:23; 19:4, 4	6	1:10; 20:21, 21; 24:15; 27:40b; 28:14	5	6:11; 9:1; 25 8, 8, 8
Ro.	19	1:5, 25; 2:26; 4:3, 5, 9, 22; 8:28; 9:5, 8; 10:4; 11:36b; 13:4a; 15:2, 4, 26, 31; 16:26, 27	3	8:18; 10:14; 11:32	1	16:6	3	1:27; 5:8; 12:16	1	8:7
1 Co.	5	5:5; 11:17, 17; 14:22; 16:1	6	1:13, 15; 8:6; 11:24, 25; 15:54					3	6:18; 8:12, 12
2 Co.	8	5:5; 8:14, 14; 9:9, 10; 10:8, 8; 11:31	9	1:5, 10, 21; 2:9b; 6:1; 8:6b, 22; 10:16a; 11:3	1	11:20	6	1:16b; 2:8; 7:15; 9:8a; 10:1; 13:4		
Gal.	3	1:5; 3:6; 5:13	6	2:2, 16; 3:17a; 5:10; 6:4, 4	1	3:14	1	2:8b		
Eph.	5	2:22; 4:12, 12; 5:2; 6:22	3	1:10; 3:16; 4:13a	1	4:8	1	1:8		
Phl.	3	1:17, 25; 4:20	5	1:5; 2:16b, 16c, 16d; 2:22	1	1:29				
Col.	2	1:16, 25	3	1:10b; 2:5; 3:10						
1 Th.			2	3:5b; 4:17b			4	3:12, 12, 12; 4:10		
2 Th.			1	2:4			1	1:3		
1 Ti.	1	1:17	1	6:9b					1	6:19
2 Ti.	2	4:11, 18b							1	1:12
Tit.	1	3:14								
Phe.			1	1:6			1	1:5		
Heb.	15	1:8; 3:5; 5:6; 6:16, 20; 7:17, 21, 28; 9:9, 15; 10:12, 14; 11:8b; 13:8, 21b	1	11:9			1	6:10	1	12:3
Jas.	1	2:23	1	3:3						
1 Pt.	6	1:4b, 23, 25a; 2:14; 4:11; 5:11	3	1:8, 21, 21			1	3:21		
2 Pt.	2	2:17; 3:18	2	1:8, 17					1	3:7
1 Jn.	1	2:17	1	5:8	3	5:10a, 13, 13				
2 Jn.	1	1:2								
3 Jn.										
Jd.	1	1:13								
Rev.	16	1:6, 18; 4:9, 10; 5:13, 14; 7:12; 9:15; 10:6; 11:15; 14:11; 15:7; 19:3; 20:10b; 22:2, 5	6	1:11a; 6:15, 15; 11:9; 13:6; 17:17	1	13:13				
Total	140		138		58		29		26	

1519. εἰς, eis (continued)

Book	Oc.	to (with 3488)	Oc.	upon	Oc.	at	Oc.	among	Oc.	that . . . might (with 3488)	Oc.	that . . . may (with 3488)	Oc.	that . . . should (with 3488)
Mt.	3	20:19; 26:2; 27:31	2	26:10; 27:30a	2	12:41; 18:29	1	13:22						
Mk.	1	14:55	1	13:3			5	4:7, 18; 8:19, 20; 13:10						
Lk.	1	5:17	2	8:43; 18:13b	3	8:26; 9:61; 11:32	3	8:14; 10:36; 24:47	1	4:29				
Jn.					1	11:32	2	6:9; 21:23						
Ac.			5	3:4; 11:6; 22:13; 27:26, 29	14	4:6; 7:26; 8:40a; 18:22a; 19:27a; 20:14a, 15a, 16; 21:3b, 13; 23:11b; 25:15; 27:3; 28:12	2	2:22; 4:17			1	3:19		
Ro.	3	7:5; 12:3; 15:8	4	5:12b, 18a, 18c; 13:6	1	4:20			5	3:26; 4:11, 11, 18; 8:29	2	12:2; 15:13	3	6:12; 7:4; 15:16a
1 Co.	3	8:10; 11:22, 33	2	10:11; 15:10										
2 Co.	1	7:3	1	1:11			1	11:6			1	1:4		
Gal.			1	4:11									1	3:17b
Eph.											1	1:18	1	1:12a
Phl.	1	1:23									2	1:10a; 3:21		
Col.														
1 Th.	4	2:16a; 3:2, 5a; 4:9					1	5:15a	1	3:10				
2 Th.	1	3:9							2	2:6, 10	1	1:5	1	2:11
1 Ti.														
2 Ti.					1	2:26								
Tit.														
Phe.														
Heb.	6	2:17; 7:25b; 8:3; 9:14, 28a; 13:21a							1	12:10				
Jas.	2	1:19a, 19b											1	1:18
1 Pt.							1	4:8					1	4:2
2 Pt.														
1 Jn.														
2 Jn.														
3 Jn.														
Jd.														
Rev.			6	8:7; 9:3; 16:1, 2, 3, 4a										
Total	26		24		22		16		10		8		8	

1519. εἰς, eis (continued)

Book	Oc.	of	Oc.	throughout	Oc.	whereunto (with 3639)	Oc.	never (with 3264, 165 and 3488)	Oc.	concerning	Oc.	therein (with 846)	Oc.	to meet (with 529)
Mt.	1	5:22	1	4:24									2	25:1, 6
Mk.			3	1:28, 39; 14: 9a							1	10:15		
Lk.											1	18:17		
Jn.							6	4:14a; 8:51, 52; 10: 28; 11:26b; 13:8						
Ac.	1	25:20a	1	26:20					1	2:25	1	27:6b	1	28 15
Ro.									1	16:19c				
1 Co.														
2 Co.	4	10:13, 15a, 16b; 12:6							1	8:23				
Gal.														
Eph.			1	3:21					1	5:32a				
Phl.														
Col.					1	1:29								
1 Th.									1	5:18			1	4:17a
2 Th.					1	2:14a								
1 Ti.					2	2:7; 6:12								
2 Ti.					1	1;11								
Tit.														
Phe.														
Heb.	1	7:14									1	4:6		
Jas.														
1 Pt.	1	1:11b			1	2:8								
2 Pt.														
1 Jn.														
2 Jn.														
3 Jn.														
Jd.														
Rev.														
Total	8		6		6		6		5		4		4	

Miscellaneous: Mt. 5:35, by; Mt. 8:34 (with 4777), to meet; Mt. 14:31 (with 5001), wherefore; Mt. 15:17a, in at; Mt. 15:39a (with 1684), take; Mt. 24:9 (with 2347), to be afflicted; Mt. 26:8 (with 5001), to what purpose; Mt. 27:7 (with 4927), to bury; Mk. 3:3 (with 3219 and 3488), forth; Mk. 3:29b (with 165, 3656, and 3488), never; Mk. 4:22 (with 5218), abroad; Mk. 14:4 (with 5001); 15:34 (with 5001), why; Lk. 1:50, from; Lk. 2:32 (with 602), to lighten; Lk. 8:17 (with 5218), abroad; Lk. 13:9 (with 3195 and 3488), after that; Lk. 18:5 (with 4956), continual; Lk. 20:20 (with 3488), that so . . . might; Lk. 21:4, in unto; Lk. 21:21b (with 846), thereinto; Lk. 24:20 (with 2917), to be condemned; Jn. 6:21 (with 3639), whither; Jn. 6:22a (with 3639), whereinto; Jn. 6:24a (with 1684), take; Jn. 12:13 (with 5122), to meet; Jn. 18:6 (with 3594 and 3488), backward; Jn. 18:37b (with 5024), for this cause; Ac. 2:39 (with 3112), afar off; Ac. 4:30 (with 2392), to heal; Ac. 7:19 (with 3488), to the end . . . might; Ac. 7:53, by; Ac. 8:20 (with 1498 and 684), perish; Ac. 9:21 (with 5024), for that intent; Ac. 13:22, 47a, to be; Ac. 14:14, in among; Ac. 19:27b (with 3049 and 3662), be despised; Ac. 19:30, in unto; Ac. 20:29, in among; Ac. 21:6a (with 1910), take; Ac. 22:30, before; Ac. 25:16 (with 684), to die; Ac. 26:16 (with 5024), for this purpose; Ac. 26:24 (with 3130), mad; Ro. 1:11 (with 3488), to the end . . . may; Ro. 1:20 (with 3488), so that; Ro. 3:25 (with 1732), to declare; Ro. 4:16 (with 3488), to the end . . . might; Ro. 6:16a (with 5118), to obey; Ro. 9:17 (with 846 and 5024), for this same purpose; Ro. 10:1 (with 4891), that (one) might be saved; Ro. 11:11 (with 3488), for to; Ro. 15:18

1519. εἰς, eis (continued)

Book	Oc.	that (with 3488)	Oc.	wherein (with 3639)	Oc.	to this end (with 5024)	Oc.	therefore (with 5024)	Oc.	Not Tr.	Oc.	Misc.	Total
Mt.									4	6:26a; 19:5; 21:42; 22:16	8	5:35; 8:34; 14:31; 15: 17a, 39a; 24:9; 26:8; 27:7	218
Mk.							1	1:38b	5	5:26; 10:8; 12:10, 14; 13:16b	5	3:3, 29b; 4:22; 14:4; 15:34	167
Lk.							1	4:43	10	3:5, 5; 9:4, 62a; 11: 49; 13:19b; 14:31; 15:6; 17:31; 20:17	9	1:50; 2:32; 8:17; 13: 9; 18:5; 20:20; 21: 4, 21b; 24:20	231
Jn.					1	18:37a			3	6:66; 8:35b; 20:14	6	6:21, 22a, 24a; 12:13; 18:6, 37b	190
Ac.			1	7:4b					4	4:11; 11:29; 13:42; 21:6b	17	2:39; 4:30; 7:19, 53; 8:20; 9:21; 13:22, 47a; 14:14; 19:27b, 30; 20: 29; 21:6a; 22:30; 25: 16; 26:16, 24	295
Ro.					1	14:9			6	6:17; 11:9, 9, 9, 9; 14:19	9	1:11, 20; 3:25; 4:16; 6:16a; 9:17; 10:1; 11: 11; 15:18	119
1 Co.	1	9:18							4	4:3; 6:16; 15:45, 45	2	8:13; 10:6	39
2 Co.					1	2:9a			5	3:7; 6:18, 18; 11:10; 13:2	7	2:12b; 4:4, 17; 8:6a, 24b; 10:15b; 13:3	78
Gal.													31
Eph.									3	2:15; 5:31, 32b	5	1:14a, 19; 3:2, 19; 6:18	37
Phl.											4	1:10b; 2:16a; 3:16; 4:15	23
Col.											3	1:12; 2:22; 4:8	20
1 Th.	1	2:12a									3	3:3, 13; 5:9b	26
2 Th.	1	2:2									1	1:11	14
1 Ti.							1	4:10			2	4:3; 6:17	19
2 Ti.													19
Tit.													2
Phe.													2
Heb.									5	1:5, 5; 7:24; 8:10b, 10c	10	1:14; 4:16; 6:8; 7:3; 9:26; 10:1, 19, 24; 11:3, 11	73
Jas.									1	5:3	1	2:6	15
1 Pt.	1	3:7	2	3:20; 5:12					2	1:11a; 2:7	4	2:9a, 21; 3:9; 4:6	40
2 Pt.											2	2:12; 3:9a	12
1 Jn.									1	5:10b	1	3:8	10
2 Jn.													3
3 Jn.													2
Jd.									1	1:25			6
Rev.									2	8:11; 16:4b			82
Total	4		3		3		3		56		99		1773

(with 5118), to make obedient; 1 Co. 8:13, while stands; 1 Co. 10:6 (with 3488), to the intent . . . should; 2 Co. 2:12b, to preach; 2 Co. 4:4 (with 3261 and 3488), lest . . . should; 2 Co. 4:17 (with 5136 and 2596), far more exceeding; 2 Co. 8:6a (with 3488), insomuch that; 2 Co. 8:24b (with 4283), before; 2 Co. 10:15b (with 3950), abundantly; 2 Co. 13:3 (with 5109), to you-ward; Eph. 1:14a, until; Eph. 1:19 (with 2248), to us-ward; Eph. 3:2 (with 5109), to you-ward; Eph. 3:19, with; Eph. 6:18 (with 846 and 5024), thereunto; Phl. 1:10b, till; Phl. 2:16a (with 2745), that . . . rejoice; Phl. 3:16 (with 3639), whereto; Phl. 4:15 (with 3056), as concerning; Col. 1:12 (with 3210 and 3488), to be partakers of; Col. 2:22 (with 5256), to perish; Col. 4:8 (with 846 and 5024), for the same purpose; 1 Th. 3:3 (with 5024), thereunto; 1 Th. 3:13 (with 3488), to the end . . . may; 1 Th. 5:9b (with 3947), to obtain; 2 Th. 1:11 (with 3639), wherefore; 1 Ti. 4:3 (with 3236), to be received; 1 Ti. 6:17 (with 619), to enjoy; Heb. 1:14 (with 1248), to minister; Heb. 4:16 (with 996), to help; Heb. 6:8 (with 2740), to be burned; Heb. 7:3 (with 1336 and 3488), continually; Heb. 9:26 (with 115), to put away; Heb. 10:1 (with 1336 and 3488), continually; Heb. 10:19 (with 1529), to enter into; Heb. 10:24 (with 3848), to provoke unto; Heb. 11:3 (with 3488), so that; Heb. 11:11 (with 2602), to conceive; Jas. 2:6, before; 1 Pt. 2:9a (with 3947), peculiar; 1 Pt. 2:21 (with 5024), hereunto; 1 Pt. 3:9 (with 5024), thereunto; 1 Pt. 4:6 (with 5024), for this cause; 2 Pt. 2:12 (with 259), to be taken; 2 Pt. 3:9a (with 2248), to us-ward; 1 Jn. 3:8 (with 5024), for this purpose.

1521. εἰσάγω, eisag'ō

Book	Oc.	bring in	Oc.	bring	Oc.	lead	Total
Lk.	2	2:27; 14:21	1	22:54			3
Jn.	1	18:16					1
Ac.	1	7:45	3	9:8; 21:28, 29	1	21:37	5
Heb.	1	1:6					1
Total	5		4		1		10

1522. εἰσακούω, eisakou'ō

Book	hear	Total
Mt.	6:7	1
Lk.	1:13	1
Ac.	10:31	1
1 Co.	14:21	1
Heb.	5:7	1
Total		5

1523. εἰσδέχομαι, eisdech'omai

Book	receive	Total
2 Co.	6:17	1

1524. εἴσειμι, eis'eimi

Book	Oc.	go	Oc.	go in	Oc.	enter	Total
Ac.	1	3:3	1	21:18	1	21:26	3
Heb.	1	9:6					1
Total	2		1		1		4

1525. εἰσέρχομαι, eiser'chomai

Book	Oc.	enter	Oc.	go	Oc.	come in	Oc.	go in	Oc.	enter in	Oc.	come	Oc.	arise	Total
Mt.	19	5:20; 6:6; 7:21; 8:5; 10:5, 11; 12: 4, 29; 18:3, 8, 9; 19:17, 23, 24; 23: 13b; 24:38; 25:21, 23; 26:41	4	15:11; 21:12; 26: 58; 27:53	2	22:11, 12	5	7:13b; 9: 25; 23: 13a, 13c; 25:10	2	7:13a; 12:45	4	8:8; 10: 12; 17: 25; 21: 10			36
Mk.	22	1:21, 45; 2:1; 3:1, 27; 5:12, 13; 6: 10; 7:17, 24; 9:25, 43, 45, 47; 10: 15, 23, 24, 25b; 11:11; 13:15; 14: 38; 16:5	4	2:26; 8:26; 10: 25a; 11:15	3	5:39; 6:22, 25	2	14:14; 15:43			1	9:28			32
Lk.	28	1:40; 4:38; 6:6; 7:1, 6, 44; 8:30, 32, 33; 9:4, 34, 52; 10:5, 8, 10, 38; 17:12, 27; 18:17, 24, 25b; 19:1; 21:21; 22:3, 10, 40, 46; 24:26	7	1:9; 4:16; 6:4; 7: 36; 18:25a; 19:7, 45	3	1:28; 7:45; 14:23	4	8:51b; 11: 37; 15:28; 24:29	6	11:26, 52, 52; 13:24, 24; 24:3	3	8:41, 51a; 17:7	1	9:46	52
Jn.	7	3:4, 5; 4:38; 10:1; 13:27; 18:1, 33	3	18:28; 19:9; 20:6			3	10:9b; 20:5, 8	2	10:2, 9a					15
Ac.	12	3:8; 5:21; 9:17; 10:24; 11:8, 12; 14:22; 16:40; 18:19; 21:8; 23: 16; 25:23	4	9:6; 13:14; 14:1; 19:8	6	1:13; 5:7, 10; 9:12; 10:3, 25	4	1:21; 10: 27; 11:3; 17:2	3	19:30; 20: 29; 28:8	4	11:20; 14:20; 16:15; 23:33			33
Ro.	1	5:12			1	11:25									2
1 Co.					2	14:23, 24									2
Heb.	13	3:11, 18; 4:1, 3, 3, 5, 6a, 10, 11; 6:19, 20; 9:24, 25							3	3:19; 4:6b; 9:12	1	10:5			17
Jas.	1	5:4			1	2:2b					1	2:2a			3
2 Jn.	1	1:7													1
Rev.	3	11:11; 15:8; 21:27			1	3:20			1	22:14					5
Total	107		22		19		18		17		14		1		198

1526. εἰσί, eisi'

Book	Oc.	are	Oc.	be	Oc.	were	Oc.	have	Oc.	Not Tr.	Oc.	Misc.	Total
Mt.	17	2:18; 7:15; 10:30; 11:8; 12:5, 48; 13:38, 38, 39, 56; 17:26; 18:20; 19: 6, 12a, 12b; 22:14, 30	6	7:13, 14; 15:14; 16: 28; 19:12c; 20:16									23
Mk.	7	4:15, 16, 18a, 20; 6:3; 10:8; 12:25	1	9:1					1	4:18b	1	4:17	10
Lk.	15	7:25, 31, 32; 8:12, 14, 15, 21; 11:7; 12:38; 13:14, 30, 30; 16:8; 20:36, 36	2	9:27; 21:22	1	18:9	1	9:13					19
Jn.	13	4:35; 5:39; 6:64a; 7:49; 8:10; 10: 8, 12; 11:9; 14:2; 17:9, 11, 14, 16			1	6:64b							14
Ac.	9	2:7, 13; 5:25; 13:31; 16:17; 19:38; 21:20; 23:21; 24:11	1	19:26	2	4:13; 16:38	1	21:23					13
Ro.	10	1:32; 2:14; 8:14; 9:4, 7; 13:1, 3, 6; 15:27; 16:7											10
1 Co.	9	1:11; 3:8, 20; 10:18; 12:4, 5, 6; 14: 22, 37	2	8:5, 5									11
2 Co.	4	11:22, 22, 22, 23											4
Gal.	4	3:7, 10, 10; 4:24	1	1:7									5
Eph.	1	5:16											1
Col.	1	2:3											1
1 Ti.	4	5:24; 6:1, 2, 2											4
2 Ti.	1	3:6											1
Tit.	2	1:10; 3:9											2
Heb.	2	1:10, 14			2	7:23; 11:13					1	7:21	5
2 Pt.	2	2:17; 3:7											2
1 Jn.	5	4:5; 5:3, 7, 7, 8a			1	2:19					1	5:8b	7
Jd.	2	1:12, 16	1	1:19									3
Rev.	27	1:19, 20, 20; 2:2, 9; 3:4, 9; 4:5, 11; 5:6, 8; 7:13, 14, 15; 11:4; 14:4, 4, 4, 5; 16:6, 14; 17:9, 10, 12, 15; 19:9; 21:5									1	9:19	28
Total	135		14		7		2		1		4		163

Miscellaneous: Mk. 4:17, endure; Heb. 7:21 (with 1096), be made; 1 Jn. 5:8b, agree; Rev. 9:19, is.

1527. εἷς καθ' εἷς, heis kath heis

Book	one by one	Total
Mk.	14:19	1
Jn.	8:9	1
Total		2

1529. εἴσοδος, eis'odos

Book	Oc.	coming	Oc.	entering in	Oc.	entrance in	Oc.	to enter into (with 1519)	Oc.	entrance	Total
Ac.	1	13:24									1
1 Th.			1	1:9	1	2:1					2
Heb.							1	10:19			1
2 Pt.									1	1:11	1
Total	1		1		1		1		1		5

1528. εἰσκαλέω, eiskale'ō

Book	call in	Total
Ac.	10:23	1

1532. εἰστρέχω, eistrech'ō

Book	run in	Total
Ac.	12:14	1

1530. εἰσπηδάω, eispe̱da'ō

Book	Oc.	run in	Oc.	spring in	Total
Ac.	1	14:14	1	16:29	2

1533. εἰσφέρω, eispher'ō

Book	Oc.	bring	Oc.	bring in	Oc.	lead	Total
Mt.					1	6:13	1
Lk.			2	5:18, 19	1	11:4	3
Ac.	1	17:20					1
1 Ti.	1	6:7					1
Heb.	1	13:11					1
Total	3		2		2		7

1531. εἰσπορεύομαι, eisporeu'omai

Book	Oc.	enter	Oc.	enter in	Oc.	come in	Oc.	go	Total
Mt.	1	15:17							1
Mk.	5	6:56; 7:15, 18, 19; 11:2	2	4:19; 5:40			1	1:21	8
Lk.	1	19:30	2	8:16; 22:10	1	11:33			4
Ac.	2	3:2; 8:3			2	9:28; 28:30			4
Total	9		4		3		1		17

1534. εἶτα, ei'ta

Book	Oc.	then	Oc.	after that	Oc.	afterward	Oc.	furthermore	Total
Mk.	1	4:28a	2	4:28b; 8:25	1	4:17			4
Lk.	1	8:12							1
Jn.	2	19:27; 20:27	1	13:5					3
1 Co.	4	12:28; 15:5, 7, 24							4
1 Ti.	2	2:13; 3:10							2
Heb.							1	12:9	1
Jas.	1	1:15							1
Total	11		3		1		1		16

1535. εἴτε, ei'te

Book	Oc.	or	Oc.	whether	Oc.	or whether	Oc.	if	Total
Ro.	3	12:7, 7, 8	1	12:6			1	14:27	5
1 Co.	15	3:22b, 22c, 22d, 22e, 22f, 22g, 22h; 8:5b; 10:31b, 31c; 12:13b, 13d, 26b; 14:7b; 15:11b	11	3:22a; 8:5a; 10:31a; 12:13a, 13c, 26a; 13:8, 8, 8; 14:7a; 15:11a					26
2 Co.	4	5:9b, 10b; 8:23b; 12:3b	7	1:6a; 5:9a, 10a, 13a; 8:23a; 12:2a, 3a	3	1:6b; 5:13b; 12:2b			14
Eph.	1	6:8b	1	6:8a					2
Phl.	3	1:18b, 20b, 27b	3	1:18a, 20a, 27a					6
Col.	4	1:16b, 16c, 16d, 20b	2	1:16a, 20a					6
1 Th.	1	5:10b	1	5:10a					2
2 Th.	1	2:15b	1	2:15a					2
1 Pt.	1	2:14	1	2:13					2
Total	33		28		3		1		65

1536. εἴ τις, ei tis

Book	Oc.	if any man	Oc.	if any	Oc.	if a man	Oc.	if any thing	Oc.	if ought	Oc.	whosoever	Oc.	Misc.	Total
Mt.	1	16:24													1
Mk.	3	4:23; 7:16; 9:35					1	9:22	2	8:23; 11:25					6
Lk.	2	9:23; 14:26					1	19:8							3
Ac.			1	24:20					1	24:19			1	25:5	3
Ro.	1	8:9	1	13:9									1	11:17	3
1 Co.	13	3:12, 14, 15, 17, 18; 7:36; 8:2, 3; 11:16, 34; 14:37, 38; 16:22	2	7:12; 10:27									1	1:16	16
2 Co.	2	5:17; 10:7	1	2:5	5	11:20, 20, 20, 20, 20	2	2:10; 7:14							10
Gal.	1	1:9			1	6:3									2
Eph.													1	4:29	1
Phl.	1	3:4	6	2:1, 1, 1, 1; 4:8, 8			1	3:15							8
2 Th.	1	3:14	1	3:10											2
1 Ti.	2	5:16; 6:3	2	5:4, 8	2	3:1, 5	1	1:10							7
Tit.			1	1:6											1
Jas.	2	1:26; 3:2	2	1:5, 23											4
1 Pt.	2	4:11, 11	1	3:1											3
2 Jn.			1	1:10											1
Rev.	4	11:5, 5; 13:9; 14:9									2	14:11; 20:15	2	13:10, 10	8
Total	35		19		8		6		3		2		6		79

Miscellaneous: Ac. 25:5, if any wickedness; Ro. 11:17, if some; 1 Co. 1:16, whether any; Eph. 4:29, that which; Rev. 13:10, 10, he that.

1537. ἐκ or ἐξ, ek or ex

Book	Oc.	of	Oc.	from	Oc.	out of	Oc.	by
Mt.	26	1:3, 5, 5, 6, 16, 18, 20; 3:9; 5:37; 6:27; 7:9; 10:29; 13:47; 18:12; 21:25b, 26, 31; 22:35; 23:25; 25:2, 8; 26:21, 27, 29; 27:29, 48	11	3:17; 12:42; 13:49; 15:18b; 16:1; 17:9; 19:12; 21:25a, 25c; 24:31; 28:2	17	2:6, 15; 7:5, 5; 8:28; 12:34, 35, 35; 13:41, 52; 15:11, 18a, 19; 17:5; 21:16; 24:17; 27:53	4	12:33, 37, 37; 15:5
Mk.	11	9:17; 11:14, 30b, 32; 12:44, 44; 14:18, 20, 23, 25; 16:12	13	1:11; 6:14, 16; 7:31; 9:9, 10; 10:20; 11:20, 30a, 31; 12:25; 13:27; 16:3	17	1:25, 26, 29; 5:2, 2, 8, 30; 6:54; 7:20, 21, 26, 29; 9:7, 25; 13:1, 15; 15:46	1	7:11
Lk.	38	1:5, 5, 27, 35; 2:4b, 35, 36; 3:8; 6:44b, 44c, 45c; 10:11; 11:5, 15, 27; 12:6, 13, 15, 25; 14:28, 33; 15:4, 4; 16:9; 17:7a, 15; 20:4b, 6; 21:4, 4, 18; 22:3, 23, 50, 58; 23:8; 24:13, 22	19	1:15, 71, 71, 78; 3:22; 9:7; 10:7, 18; 11:16, 31; 12:36; 16:31; 17:7b; 20:4a, 5, 35; 23:55; 24:46, 49	15	1:74; 2:4a; 4:22, 35, 38; 5:3, 17; 6:42, 45a, 45b; 8:27a; 9:35; 11:54; 17:24; 19:22	1	6:44a
Jn.	85	1:13, 13, 13, 13, 16, 24, 35, 40; 2:15a; 3:1, 5, 6, 6, 8, 25, 31a, 31c; 4:7, 13, 14, 22, 39; 6:8, 11, 13, 26, 51b, 60, 64a, 65, 70, 71; 7:17, 19, 22, 22, 25, 31, 40, 42, 44, 48, 48, 50, 52a; 8:23c, 23d, 41, 44, 44, 46, 47, 47; 9:6, 16; 10:16, 20, 26; 11:19, 37, 45, 46, 49; 12:4, 9a, 49; 13:21; 15:19a, 19b; 16:5, 14, 15; 17:12, 14, 14, 16, 16; 18:9, 26, 36, 36, 37; 19:2; 20:24; 21:2	38	1:19, 32; 2:22; 3:13, 27, 31d; 5:24; 6:23, 31, 32, 32, 33, 38, 41, 42, 50a, 51a, 58, 64b, 66; 8:23a, 23b, 42; 9:1; 10:32; 12:1, 9b, 17b, 27, 28, 32; 13:4; 17:15b; 18:3; 19:23; 20:1, 9; 21:14	20	1:46; 2:15b; 4:30, 47, 54; 7:38, 41, 52b; 8:59; 10:28, 29, 39; 11:55; 12:17a, 34; 13:1; 15:19b; 17:6, 15a; 20:2	1	3:34
Ac.	26	1:24; 2:30; 3:22; 4:6; 5:38, 39; 6:9; 7:37; 10:1, 45; 11:2, 20, 28; 13:21; 15:2, 21, 22, 23; 17:4, 12, 26; 20:30; 22:14; 23;21, 34; 24:10	27	1:25; 2:2; 3:2, 15; 4:2, 10; 7:3b; 10:41; 11:5, 9b; 12:25; 13:30, 34; 14:8; 15:29; 17:3, 31, 33; 18:1, 2; 22:6; 23:10; 26:4, 17, 23; 27:34; 28:17	19	7:3a, 4, 10, 40; 8:39; 12:11, 17; 13:17, 42; 15:14; 16:40; 19:16, 33; 22:18; 24:7; 27:29, 30, 30; 28:3	1	19:25
Ro.	29	1:3; 2:29, 29; 4:12, 14, 16, 16, 16; 5:16b; 9:5, 6, 11, 11, 21, 24, 24, 30; 10:5, 6; 11:1, 6, 6, 14, 36; 13:3; 14:23, 23; 16:10, 11	13	1:17a; 4:24; 6:4, 9, 13, 17; 7:4, 24; 8:11, 11; 10:7, 9; 11:15	4	2:18; 11:24, 26; 13:11	12	1:4, 17b; 2:27; 3:20, 30; 4:2; 5:1, 16a; 9:10, 32, 32; 10:17
1 Co.	22	1:30; 2:12; 7:7; 8:6; 9:7, 7, 13, 14; 10:4, 17; 11:8, 8, 12, 12, 28, 28; 12:15, 15, 16, 16; 15:6, 47a	5	5:2; 9:19; 15:12, 20, 47b	1	5:10		
2 Co.	9	2:17, 17; 3:5, 5; 4:7; 5:1, 18; 9:7; 12:6	5	1:10; 3:1; 5:2, 8; 6:17	3	2:4; 4:6; 8:11	7	2:2; 7:9; 8:14; 11:26, 26; 13:4b, 4c
Gal.	14	2:12, 15; 3:7, 9, 10, 12, 18, 18; 4:4, 23, 23; 5:8; 6:8, 8	5	1:1, 4, 8, 15; 3:13			15	2:16, 16, 16, 16; 3:2, 2, 5, 5, 11, 21, 22, 24; 4:22, 22; 5:5
Eph.	5	2:8, 9; 3:15; 5:30, 30	4	1:20; 4:16; 5:14; 6:6	1	4:29		
Phl.	7	1:16, 17; 3:5, 5, 9, 9; 4:22	1	3:20				
Col.	1	4:11	5	1:13, 18; 2:12, 19; 4:16	2	2:14; 3:8		
1 Th.	3	2:3, 3, 6	2	1:10, 10				
2 Th.					1	2:7		
1 Ti.					1	1:5		
2 Ti.	2	2:8a; 3:6	1	2:8b	4	2:22, 26; 3:11; 4:17		
Tit.	3	1:10, 12; 2:8					1	3:5
Heb.	6	2:11; 3:13; 4:1; 7:5a, 12; 11:3	4	5:7; 7:6; 11:19; 13:20	4	3:16; 7:5b, 14; 8:9	1	10:38
Jas.	2	2:16; 4:1	2	5:20, 20	2	3:10, 13	6	2:18b, 21, 22, 24, 24, 25
1 Pt.	2	1:23; 4:11	3	1:3, 18, 21	1	2:9	1	2:12
2 Pt.			2	1:18; 2:21	2	2:9; 3:5		
1 Jn.	30	2:16, 16, 19b, 19c, 19d, 21, 29; 3:8, 9, 9, 10, 12, 19; 4:1, 2, 3, 4, 5, 5, 6a, 6b, 7, 7, 13; 5:1, 1, 4, 18, 18, 19	2	2:19a; 3:14			1	3:24
2 Jn.	1	1:4						
3 Jn.	1	1:11			1	1:10		
Jd.					2	1:5, 23		
Rev.	44	1:5; 2:7, 11, 17, 21, 22; 3:9; 5:5, 5; 6:1, 1; 7:4, 5, 5, 5, 6, 6, 6, 7, 7, 7, 8, 8, 8, 9, 13; 8:11; 9:20, 21, 21, 21, 21; 11:9; 14:8, 10; 15:7; 16:11c; 17:1, 11; 18:3a, 4c, 12; 21:6, 21	19	3:10; 8:10; 9:1, 13; 10:1, 4, 8; 11:11, 12; 13:13; 14:2, 13, 13, 18; 15:8, 8; 18:1a, 4a; 20:1	45	1:16; 2:5; 3:5, 12, 16; 4:5; 5:7, 9; 6:14; 7:14; 8:4; 9:2a, 3, 17, 18d; 10:10; 11:5, 7; 12:15, 16; 13:1, 11; 14:15, 17, 20; 15:6; 16:1, 7, 13, 13, 13, 21a; 17:8; 18:4b; 19:5, 15, 21a; 20:7, 9, 12; 21:2, 3, 10; 22:1, 19	3	9:18a, 18b, 18c
Total	367		181		162		55	

1537. ἐκ or ἐξ, ek or ex (continued)

Book	Oc.	on	Oc.	with	Oc.	in	Oc.	one of	Oc.	some of	Oc.	among	Oc.	over	Oc.	Not Tr.	Oc.	Misc.	Total
Mt.	13	20:21, 21, 23, 23; 21: 19; 22:44; 25:33, 33, 34, 41; 26: 64; 27:38, 38	1	27:7			1	26:73	2	23:34, 34	1	12:11			2	26:42, 44	2	19:20; 20:2	80
Mk.	9	10:37, 37, 40, 40; 12: 36; 14:62; 15:27, 27; 16:19	8	12:30, 30, 30, 30, 33, 33, 33, 33			2	14:69, 70					1	15:39	1	14:72	3	6:51; 11:8; 14:31	66
Lk.	5	1:11; 20: 42; 22:69; 23:33, 33	4	10:27, 27, 27, 27	1	11:6			2	11:49; 21: 16					1	8:27b	4	11:13; 18:21; 22:16; 23:7	90
Jn.			2	4:6; 12:3			2	18:17, 25	2	9:40; 16:17	2	12:20, 42			3	1:44; 9: 24; 11:1	7	3:31b; 4:12; 6:39, 50b; 9: 32; 16: 4; 19: 12	162
Ac.	5	2:25, 34; 7:55, 56; 28:4a	2	1:18; 8:37			1	21:8			2	6:3; 27:22			5	9:33; 10: 15; 11:9a; 19:34; 28: 4b	3	3:23; 12:7; 15:24	91
Ro.					1	12:18											2	2:8; 3:26	61
1 Co.			1	7:5	5	12:27; 13: 9, 9, 10, 12											1	5:13	35
2 Co.															2	8:7; 9:2	3	1:11; 9:7; 13:4a	29
Gal.																	1	3:8	35
Eph.																	1	3:20	11
Phl.																	1	1:23	9
Col.							2	4:9, 12									1	3:23	11
1 Th.																	2	3:10; 5:13	7
2 Th.																			1
1 Ti.																	1	6:4	2
2 Ti.																			7
Tit.																			4
Heb.	1	1:13													2	7:4; 9: 28	3	5:1; 11:35; 13:10	21
Jas.																	2	2:18a; 3:11	14
1 Pt.			1	1:22															8
2 Pt.															1	2:8			5
1 Jn.																	1	4:6c	34
2 Jn.																			1
3 Jn.																			2
Jd.																			2
Rev.	1	18:20	6	8:5; 17: 2, 6, 6; 18:1b; 19:21b	1	3:18			1	2:10			4	15:2, 2, 2, 2	1	16:11b	8	8:13; 9: 2b; 16: 10, 11a, 21b; 18: 3b, 19; 19:2	133
Total	34		25		8		8		7		5		5		18		46		921

Miscellaneous: Mt. 19:20, from . . . up; Mt. 20:2, for; Mk. 6:51, beyond; Mk. 11:8, off; Mk. 14:31 (with 3953), vehemently; Lk. 11:13 (with 3672), heavenly; Lk. 18:21, from . . . up; Lk. 22:16 (with 846), thereof; Lk. 23:7, unto; Jn. 3:31b (with 1093 and 3488), earthly; Jn. 4:12 (with 846), thereof; Jn. 6:39 (with 3261 and 846), nothing; Jn. 6:50b (with 846), thereof; Jn. 9:32, since . . . began; Jn. 16:4, at; Jn. 19:12 (with 5027), from thenceforth; Ac. 3:23, from among; Ac. 12:7, off from; Ac. 15:24, out from; Ro. 2:8 (with 2052), contentious; Ro. 3:26 (with 4002), believe; 1 Co. 5:13, from among; 2 Co. 1:11, by the means of; 2 Co. 9:7 (with 3077), grudgingly; 2 Co. 13:4a; Gal. 3:8, through; Eph. 3:20 (with 3953 and 5128), exceeding abundantly above; Phl. 1:23, betwixt; Col. 3:23 (with 5490), heartily; 1 Th. 3:10 (with 3953 and 5128), exceedingly; 1 Th. 5:13 (with 3953 and 5128), very highly; 1 Ti. 6:4 (with 3639), whereof; Heb. 5:1, from among; Heb. 11:35 (with 386), raise to life again; Heb. 13:10 (with 3639), whereof; Jas. 2:18a, without; Jas. 3:11, at; 1 Jn. 4:6c (with 5027), hereby; Rev. 8:13; 9:2b, by reason of; Rev. 16:10, for; Rev. 16:11a, 21b, because of; Rev. 18:3b, through; Rev. 18:19, by reason of; Rev. 19:2, at.

1538. ἕκαστος, hek'astos

Book	Oc.	every man	Oc.	every one	Oc.	every	Oc.	Misc.	Total
Mt.	2	16:27; 25:15	2	18:35; 26:22					4
Mk.	1	13:34							1
Lk.			1	2:3	3	4:40; 6:44; 16:5	1	13:15	5
Jn.	2	7:53; 16:32	1	6:7	1	19:23			4
Ac.	3	2:8; 4:35; 11:29	2	2:38; 3:26	4	2:6; 17:27; 20:31; 21:26	2	2:3; 21:19	11
Ro.	3	2:6; 12:3; 14:5	2	14:12; 15:2					5
1 Co.	15	3:5, 8, 10, 13, 13; 4:5; 7:2a, 7, 17a, 20, 24; 10:24; 12:7, 11; 15:23	5	1:12; 7:17b; 11:21; 14:26; 16:2	2	12:18; 15:38	1	7:2b	23
2 Co.	1	9:7	1	5:10					2
Gal.	2	6:4, 5							2
Eph.	1	4:25	1	5:33	2	4:7, 16	1	6:8	5
Phl.	2	2:4, 4							2
Col.					1	4:6			1
1 Th.			1	4:4	1	2:11			2
2 Th.					1	1:3			1
Heb.	2	8:11, 11	1	6:11			2	3:13; 11:21	5
Jas.	1	1:14							1
1 Pt.	2	1:17; 4:10							2
Rev.	2	20:13; 22:12	3	2:23; 5:8; 6:11	2	21:21; 22:2			7
Total	39		20		17		7		83

Miscellaneous: Lk. 13:15, each one; Ac. 2:3, each; Ac. 21:19 (with 1520 and 2596), particularly; 1 Co. 7:2b, every woman; Eph. 6:8, any man; Heb. 3:13 (with 2596 and 2250), daily; Heb. 11:21 (with 3488), both.

1539. ἑκάστοτε, hekas'tote

Book	always	Total
2 Pt.	1:15	1

1540. ἑκατόν, hekaton'

Book	Oc.	hundred	Oc.	hundredfold	Total
Mt.	2	18:12, 28	2	13:8, 23	4
Mk.	3	4:8, 20; 6:40			3
Lk.	3	15:4; 16:6, 7			3
Jn.	2	19:39; 21:11			2
Ac.	1	1:15			1
Rev.	4	7:4; 14:1, 3; 21:17			4
Total	15		2		17

1541. ἑκατονταέτης hekatontaet'ēs

Book	hundred years old	Total
Ro.	4:19	1

1542. ἑκατονταπλασίων hekatontaplasi'ōn

Book	hundredfold	Total
Mt.	19:29	1
Mk.	10:30	1
Lk.	8:8	1
Total		3

1543a. ἑκατοντάρχης hekatontar'chēs

Book	centurion	Total
Ac.	10:1, 22; 24:23; 27:1, 31	5

Word 1543 has 21 occurrences.

1543b. ἑκατόνταρχος, hekaton'tarchos

Book	centurion	Total
Mt.	8:5, 8, 13; 27:54	4
Lk.	7:2, 6; 23:47	3
Ac.	21:32; 22:25, 26; 23:17, 23; 27:6, 11, 43; 28:16	9
Total		16

1545. ἔκβασις, ek'basis

Book	Oc.	way to escape	Oc.	end	Total
1 Co.	1	10:13			1
Heb.			1	13:7	1
Total	1		1		2

1544. ἐκβάλλω, ekbal'lō

Book	Oc.	cast out	Oc.	cast	Oc	bring forth	Oc.	pull out	Oc.	send forth	Oc.	Misc.	Total
Mt.	18	7:5, 5, 22; 8:12, 16, 31; 9:33, 34; 10:1, 8; 12:24, 26, 27, 27, 28; 15:17; 17:19; 21:12	3	21:39; 22:13; 25: 30	3	12:35, 35; 13:52	1	7:4	2	9:38; 12:20	1	9:25	28
Mk.	11	1:34, 39; 3:15, 22, 23; 6:13; 9: 18, 28, 38; 11:15; 16:17	2	12:8; 16:9							5	1:12, 43; 5:40; 7: 26; 9:47	18
Lk.	13	6:22, 42b; 9:40, 49; 11:14, 15, 18, 19, 19, 20; 13:32; 19:45; 20:12	1	20:15			2	6:42a, 42c	1	10:2	4	4:29; 8: 54; 10: 35; 13:28	21
Jn.			4	6:37; 9:34, 35; 12:31							2	2:15; 10: 4	6
Ac.	1	27:38	1	7:58							3	9:40; 13: 50; 16:37	5
Gal.	1	4:30											1
Jas.											1	2:25	1
3 Jn.	1	1:10											1
Rev.											1	11:2	1
Total	45		11		3		3		3		17		82

Miscellaneous: Mt. 9:25, put forth; Mk. 1:12, drive; Mk. 1:43, send away; Mk. 5:40, put out; Mk. 7:26, cast forth; Mk. 9:47, pluck out; Lk. 4:29, thrust Lk. 8:54, put; Lk. 10:35, take out; Lk. 13:28, thrust; Jn. 2:15, drive out; Jn. 10:4, put forth; Ac. 9:40, put; Ac. 13:50, expel; Ac. 16:37, thrust out; Jas. 2:25, send out; Rev. 11:2, leave.

1546. ἐκβολή, ekbolē'

Book	lighten the ship (with 4060)	Total
Ac.	27:18	1

1547. ἐκγαμίζω, ekgamid'zō

Book	give in marriage	Total
Mt.	22:30; 24:38	2
Lk.	17:27	1
1 Co.	7:38, 38	2
Total		5

1548. ἐκγαμίσκω, ekgamis'kō

Book	give in marriage	Total
Lk.	20:34, 35	2

1549. ἔκγονον, ek'gonon

Book	nephew	Total
1 Ti.	5:4	1

1550. ἐκδαπανάω, ekdapana'ō

Book	spend	Total
2 Co.	12:15	1

1551. ἐκδέχομαι, ekdech'omai

Book	Oc.	wait for	Oc.	look for	Oc.	tarry for	Oc.	expect	Oc.	wait	Total
Jn.	1	5:3									1
Ac.	1	17:16									1
1 Co.			1	16:11	1	11:33					2
Heb.			1	11:10			1	10:13			2
Jas.	1	5:7									1
1 Pt.									1	3:20	1
Total	3		2		1		1		1		8

1552. ἔκδηλος, ek'dēlos

Book	manifest	Total
2 Ti.	3:9	1

1553. ἐκδημέω, ekdēme'ō

Book	be absent	Total
2 Co.	5:6, 8, 9	3

1554. ἐκδίδωμι, ekdid'ōmi

Book	Oc.	let out	Oc.	let forth	Total
Mt.	2	21:33, 41			2
Mk.	1	12:1			1
Lk.			1	20:9	1
Total	3		1		4

1555. ἐκδιηγέομαι, ekdiēge'omai

Book	declare	Total
Ac.	13:41; 15:3	2

1556. ἐκδικέω, ekdike'ō

Book	Oc.	avenge	Oc.	revenge	Total
Lk.	2	18:3, 5			2
Ro.	1	12:19			1
2 Co.			1	10:6	1
Rev.	2	6:10; 19:2			2
Total	5		1		6

1558. ἔκδικος, ek'dikos

Book	Oc.	avenger	Oc.	revenger	Total
1 Th.	1	4:6			1
Ro.			1	13:4	1
Total	1		1		2

1557. ἐκδίκησις, ekdik'ęsis

Book	Oc.	vengeance	Oc.	avenge (with 4060)	Oc.	revenge	Oc.	punishment	Total
Lk.	1	21:22	2	18:7, 8					3
Ac.			1	7:24					1
Ro.	1	12:19							1
2 Co.					1	7:11			1
2 Th.	1	1:8							1
Heb.	1	10:30							1
1 Pt.							1	2:14	1
Total	4		3		1		1		9

1559. ἐκδιώκω, ekdiō'kō

Book	persecute	Total
Lk.	11:49	1
1 Th.	2:15	1
Total		2

1560. ἔκδοτος, ek'dotos

Book	be delivered	Total
Ac.	2:23	1

1561. ἐκδοχή, ekdochę'

Book	look for	Total
Heb.	10:27	1

1562. ἐκδύω, ekdu'ō

Book	Oc.	strip	Oc.	take off from	Oc.	unclothe	Total
Mt.	1	27:28	1	27:31			2
Mk.			1	15:20			1
Lk.	1	10:30					1
2 Co.					1	5:4	1
Total	2		2		1		5

1563. ἐκεῖ, ekei'

Book	Oc.	there	Oc.	thither	Oc.	Not Tr.	Oc.	Misc.	Total
Mt.	25	2:13, 15; 5:24; 6:21; 8:12; 12:45; 13:42, 50, 58; 14:23; 15:29; 18:20; 19:2; 21:17; 22:11, 13; 24:28, 51; 25:30; 26:71; 27:36, 47, 55, 61; 28:7	1	2:22			2	17:20; 26:36	28
Mk.	10	1:13; 2:6; 3:1; 5:11; 6:5, 10; 11:5; 13:21; 14:15; 16:7	1	6:33	1	6:55			12
Lk.	14	2:6; 6:6; 8:32; 9:4; 10:6; 11:26; 12:18, 34; 13:28; 15:13; 17:21, 23; 22:12; 23:33	2	17:37; 21:2					16
Jn.	19	2:1, 6, 12; 3:22, 23; 4:6, 40; 5:5; 6:3, 22, 24; 10:40, 42; 11:15, 31; 12:2, 9, 26; 19:42	3	11:8; 18:2, 3					22
Ac.	7	9:33; 14:28; 16:1; 17:14; 19:21; 25:9, 14							7
Ro.	1	9:26					1	15:24	2
2 Co.	1	3:17							1
Tit.	1	3:12							1
Heb.	1	7:8							1
Jas.	3	2:3; 3:16; 4:13							3
Rev.	4	2:14; 12:6; 21:25; 22:5			1	12:14			5
Total	86		7		2		3		98

Miscellaneous: Mt. 17:20, to yonder place; Mt. 26:36, yonder; Ro. 15:24, thitherward.

1564. ἐκεῖθεν, ekei'then

Book	Oc.	thence	Oc.	from thence	Oc.	from that place	Oc.	there	Total
Mt.	8	5:26; 9:27; 11:1; 12:9; 13:53; 14:13; 15:21; 19:15	4	4:21; 9:9; 12:15; 15:29					12
Mk.	3	1:19; 6:11; 9:30	2	6:1; 7:24	1	6:10			6
Lk.	2	9:4; 12:59	1	16:26					3
Jn.	2	4:43; 11:54							2
Ac.	1	18:7	2	13:4; 16:12			1	20:13	4
Total	16		9		1		1		27

1566. ἐκεῖσε, ekei'se

Book	there	Total
Ac.	21:3; 22:5	2

See page 116 for Word 1565.

1567. ἐκζητέω, ekdzęte'ō

Book	Oc.	require	Oc.	seek after	Oc.	diligently seek	Oc.	seek carefully	Oc.	enquire	Total
Lk.	2	11:50, 51									2
Ac.			1	15:17							1
Ro.			1	3:11							1
Heb.					1	11:6	1	12:17			2
1 Pt.									1	1:10	1
Total	2		2		1		1		1		7

1569. ἔκθαμβος, ek'thambos

Book	greatly wondering	Total
Ac.	3:11	1

1570. ἔκθετος, ek'thetos

Book	cast out	Total
Ac.	7:19	1

1568. ἐκθαμβέω, ekthambe'ō

Book	Oc.	be affrighted	Oc.	sore amazed	Oc.	greatly amazed	Total
Mk.	2	16:5, 6	1	14:33	1	9:15	4

1571. ἐκκαθαίρω, ekkathai'rō

Book	Oc.	purge out	Oc.	purge	Total
1 Co.	1	5:7			1
2 Ti.			1	2:21	1
Total	1		1		2

1572. ἐκκαίω, ekkai'ō

Book	burn	Total
Ro.	1:27	1

1573. ἐκκακέω, ekkake'ō

Book	Oc.	faint	Oc.	be weary	Total
Lk.	1	18:1			1
2 Co.	2	4:1, 16			2
Gal.			1	6:9	1
Eph.	1	3:13			1
2 Th.			1	3:13	1
Total	4		2		6

1574. ἐκκεντέω, ekkente'ō

Book	pierce	Total
Jn.	19:37	1
Rev.	1:7	1
Total		2

1575. ἐκκλάω, ekkla'ō

Book	break off	Total
Ro.	11:17, 19, 20	3

1576. ἐκκλείω, ekklei'ō

Book	exclude	Total
Ro.	3:27	1
Gal.	4:17	1
Total		2

1577. ἐκκλησία, ekklesi'a

Book	Oc.	church	Oc.	assembly	Total
Mt.	3	16:18; 18:17, 17			3
Ac.	21	2:47; 5:11; 7:38; 8:1, 3; 9:31; 11:22, 26; 12:1, 5; 13:1; 14:23, 27; 15:3, 4, 22, 41; 16:5; 18:22; 20:17, 28	3	19:32, 39, 41	24
Ro.	5	16:1, 4, 5, 16, 23			5
1 Co.	22	1:2; 4:17; 6:4; 7:17; 10:32; 11:16, 18, 22; 12:28; 14:4, 5, 12, 19, 23, 28, 33, 34, 35; 15:9; 16:1, 19, 19			22
2 Co.	9	1:1; 8:1, 18, 19, 23, 24; 11:8, 28; 12:13			9
Gal.	3	1:2, 13, 22			3
Eph.	9	1:22; 3:10, 21; 5:23, 24, 25, 27, 29, 32			9
Phl.	2	3:6; 4:15			2
Col.	4	1:18, 24; 4:15, 16			4
1 Th.	2	1:1; 2:14			2
2 Th.	2	1:1, 4			2
1 Ti.	3	3:5, 15; 5:16			3
Phe.	1	1:2			1
Heb.	2	2:12; 12:23			2
Jas.	1	5:14			1
3 Jn.	3	1:6, 9, 10			3
Rev.	20	1:4, 11, 20, 20; 2:1, 7, 8, 11, 12, 17, 18, 23, 29; 3:1, 6, 7, 13, 14, 22; 22:16			20
Total	112		3		115

1578. ἐκκλίνω, ekkli'nō

Book	Oc.	eschew	Oc.	avoid	Oc.	go out of the way	Total
Ro.			1	16:17	1	3:12	2
1 Pt.	1	3:11					1
Total	1		1		1		3

1579. ἐκκολυμβάω, ekkolumba'ō

Book	swim out	Total
Ac.	27:42	1

1580. ἐκκομίζω, ekkomid'zō

Book	carry out	Total
Lk.	7:12	1

1581. ἐκκόπτω, ekkop'tō

Book	Oc.	cut off	Oc.	hewn down	Oc.	cut down	Oc.	cut out	Oc.	be hindered	Total
Mt.	2	5:30; 18:8	2	3:10; 7:19							4
Lk.			1	3:9	2	13:7, 9					3
Ro.	1	11:22					1	11:24			2
2 Co.	1	11:12									1
1 Pt.									1	3:7	1
Total	4		3		2		1		1		11

1582. ἐκκρέμαμαι, ekkrem'amai

Book	be very attentive	Total
Lk.	19:48	1

1583. ἐκλαλέω, eklale'ō

Book	tell	Total
Ac.	23:22	1

1584. ἐκλάμπω, eklam'pō

Book	shine forth	Total
Mt.	13:43	1

1585. ἐκλανθάνομαι eklanthan'omai

Book	forget	Total
Heb.	12:5	1

1586. ἐκλέγομαι, ekleg'omai

Book	Oc.	choose	Oc.	choose out	Oc.	make choice	Total
Mk.	1	13:20					1
Lk.	2	6:13; 10:42	1	14:7			3
Jn.	5	6:70; 13:18; 15: 16, 16, 19					5
Ac.	6	1:2, 24; 6:5; 13: 17; 15:22, 25			1	15:7	7
1 Co.	3	1:27, 27, 28					3
Eph.	1	1:4					1
Jas.	1	2:5					1
Total	19		1		1		21

1587. ἐκλείπω, eklei'pō

Book	fail	Total
Lk.	16:9; 22:32	2
Heb.	1:12	1
Total		3

1565. ἐκεῖνος, ekei'nos

Book	Oc.	that	Oc.	those	Oc.	he	Oc.	the same
Mt.	31	7:22, 25, 27; 8:28; 9:22, 26, 31; 10:14, 15; 11:25; 12:1, 45; 13:44; 14:1, 35, 35; 17:27; 18:7, 27, 32; 22:46; 24:36, 46, 48, 50; 26:24, 24, 29; 27:8, 19, 63	10	3:1; 21:40; 22:7, 10; 24:19, 22, 22, 29; 25:7, 19			5	13:1; 15:22; 18:1, 28; 22:23
Mk.	11	3:24, 25; 6:11, 55; 7:20; 13:11, 24b, 32; 14:21, 21, 25	8	1:9; 2:20; 7:15; 8:1; 12:7; 13:17, 19, 24a			1	4:35
Lk.	23	6:23, 48, 49; 9:5; 10:12, 12, 31; 11:26; 12:43, 45, 46, 47; 14:21; 15:14, 15; 17: 9, 31; 18:3; 19:4; 20:18, 35; 21:34; 22: 22	11	2:1; 4:2; 5:35; 9:36; 12:37, 38; 13: 4; 14:24; 19:27; 20:1; 21:23				
Jn.	14	1:39; 4:39; 6:22; 11:51, 53; 14:20; 16: 23, 26; 18:15; 19:27, 31; 21:3, 7, 23	1	8:10	31	1:8, 18; 2:21; 3:30; 4: 25; 5:19, 35, 38, 46; 6: 29; 7:11; 8:42, 44; 9:9, 11, 12, 25, 36, 37; 13:25, 26, 30; 14:21, 26; 15:26; 16:8, 13, 14; 18:17, 25; 19:21	7	1:33; 4:53; 5:9, 11; 10: 1; 12:48; 20:19
Ac.	8	1:19; 3:23; 8:1, 8; 12:1; 14:21; 19:16; 22:11	6	2:18; 7:41; 9:37; 16:3, 35; 20:2	1	3:13	5	2:41; 12:6; 16:33; 19:23; 28:7
Ro.			1	6:21				
1 Co.								
2 Co.					1	10:18	1	7:8
Eph.	1	2:12						
2 Th.	1	1:10						
2 Ti.	3	1:12, 18; 4:8			1	2:13		
Tit.								
Heb.	4	3:10; 4:11; 8:7; 11:15	2	8:10; 10:16				
Jas.	2	1:7; 4:15						
2 Pt.								
1 Jn.					6	2:6; 3:3, 5, 7, 16; 4:17		
Rev.	1	16:14	1	9:6			1	11:13
Total	99		40		40		20	

1588. ἐκλεκτός, eklektos′

Book	Oc.	elect	Oc.	chosen	Total
Mt.	3	24:22, 24, 31	2	20:16; 22:14	5
Mk.	3	13:20, 22, 27			3
Lk.	1	18:7	1	23:35	2
Ro.	1	8:33	1	16:13	2
Col.	1	3:12			1
1 Ti.	1	5:21			1
2 Ti.	1	2:10			1
Tit.	1	1:1			1
1 Pt.	2	1:2; 2:6	2	2:4, 9	4
2 Jn.	2	1:1, 13			2
Rev.			1	17:14	1
Total	16		7		23

1589. ἐκλογή, ekloge′

Book	Oc.	election	Oc.	chosen	Total
Ac.			1	9:15	1
Ro.	4	9:11; 11:5, 7, 28			4
1 Th.	1	1:4			1
2 Pt.	1	1:10			1
Total	6		1		7

1590. ἐκλύω, eklu′ō

Book	Oc.	faint	Oc.	faint (with 2258)	Total
Mt.	1	15:32	1	9:36	2
Mk.	1	8:3			1
Gal.	1	6:9			1
Heb.	2	12:3, 5			2
Total	5		1		6

1591. ἐκμάσσω, ekmas′sō

Book	wipe	Total
Lk.	7:38, 44	2
Jn.	11:2; 12:3; 13:5	3
Total		5

1592. ἐκμυκτερίζω ekmukterid′zō

Book	deride	Total
Lk.	16:14; 23:35	2

1593. ἐκνεύω, ekneu′ō

Book	convey away	Total
Jn.	5:13	1

1594. ἐκνήφω, ekne′phō

Book	awake	Total
1 Co.	15:34	1

1595. ἑκούσιον, hekou′sion

Book	willingly (with 2596)	Total
Phe.	1:14	1

1596. ἑκουσίως, hekousi′ōs

Book	Oc.	wilfully	Oc.	willingly	Total
Heb.	1	10:26			1
1 Pt.			1	5:2	1
Total	1		1		2

1598. ἐκπειράζω, ekpeirad′zō

Book	tempt	Total
Mt.	4:7	1
Lk.	4:12; 10:25	2
1 Co.	10:9	1
Total		4

1597. ἔκπαλαι, ek′palai

Book	Oc.	of a long time	Oc.	of old	Total
2 Pt.	1	2:3	1	3:5	2

1599. ἐκπέμπω, ekpem′pō

Book	Oc.	send forth	Oc.	send away	Total
Ac.	1	13:4	1	17:10	2

1600. ἐκπετάννυμι, ekpetan′numi

Book	stretch forth	Total
Ro.	10:21	1

1602. ἐκπλέω, ekple′ō

Book	Oc.	sail	Oc.	sail thence	Oc.	sail away	Total
Ac.	1	15:39	1	18:18	1	20:6	3

1603. ἐκπληρόω, ekplero′ō

Book	fulfil	Total
Ac.	13:33	1

1601. ἐκπίπτω, ekpip′tō

Book	Oc.	fall	Oc.	fall off	Oc.	be cast	Oc.	take none effect	Oc.	fall away	Oc.	fail	Total
Mk.	1	13:25											1
Ac.	2	27:17, 29	2	12:7; 27:32	1	27:26							5
Ro.							1	9:6					1
1 Co.											1	13:8	1
Gal.	1	5:4											1
Jas.	1	1:11											1
1 Pt.									1	1:24			1
2 Pt.	1	3:17											1
Rev.	1	2:5											1
Total	7		2		1		1		1		1		13

1565. ἐκεῖνος, ekei′nos (continued)

Book	Oc.	they	Oc.	them	Oc.	his	Oc.	him	Oc.	that same	Oc.	she	Oc.	Misc.	Total
Mt.			1	13:11					2	10:19; 26:55			4	8:13; 15:28; 17:18; 24:43	53
Mk.	1	16:20	2	4:11; 16:13							1	16:10			24
Lk.	1	9:34	1	8:32									1	18:14	37
Jn.	5	5:39; 7:45; 10:6; 11:13; 20:13	1	10:35	2	5:47; 9:28	3	3:28; 5:43; 13:27	2	11:49; 18:13	3	11:29; 20:15, 16	1	13:6	70
Ac.	3	10:9, 10; 21:6													23
Ro.	1	11:23					2	14:14, 15							4
1 Co.	2	9:25; 15:11	1	10:11	1	10:28									4
2 Co.					1	8:9							2	8:14, 14	5
Eph.															1
2 Th.															1
2 Ti.					1	2:26							1	3:9	6
Tit.					1	3:7									1
Heb.	1	12:25	2	4:2; 6:7											9
Jas.															2
2 Pt.					1	1:16									1
1 Jn.													1	5:16	7
Rev.															3
Total	14		8		7		5		4		4		10		251

Miscellaneous: Mt. 8:13, selfsame; Mt. 15:28; 17:18, that very; Mt. 24:43, this; Lk. 18:14, the other; Jn. 13:6, Peter; 2 Co. 8:14, 14; 2 Ti. 3:9, their; 1 Jn. 5:16, it.

1604. ἐκπλήρωσις, ekplẹ′rōsis

Book	accomplishment	Total
Ac.	21:26	1

1605. ἐκπλήσσω, ekplẹs′sō

Book	Oc.	be astonished	Oc.	be amazed	Total
Mt.	3	7:28; 13:54; 22:33	1	19:25	4
Mk.	5	1:22; 6:2; 7:37; 10:26; 11:18			5
Lk.	1	4:32	2	2:48; 9:43	3
Ac.	1	13:12			1
Total	10		3		13

1606. ἐκπνέω, ekpne′ō

Book	give up the ghost	Total
Mk.	15:37, 39	2
Lk.	23:46	1
Total		3

1607. ἐκπορεύομαι, ekporeu′omai

Book	Oc.	proceed	Oc.	go out	Oc.	go	Oc.	come	Oc.	depart	Oc.	go forth	Oc.	Misc.	Total
Mt.	2	4:4; 15:18	2	3:5; 17:21			1	15:11	1	20:29					6
Mk.	1	7:21	2	1:5; 7:19	3	10:46; 11: 19; 13:1	3	7:15, 20, 23	1	6:11	1	10:17			11
Lk.	1	4:22	1	4:37									1	3:7	3
Jn.	1	15:26											1	5:29	2
Ac.			1	9:28					1	25:4					2
Eph.	1	4:29													1
Rev.	4	4:5; 11:5; 19:21; 22:1			2	1:16; 19:15					1	16:14	2	9:17, 18	9
Total	10		6		5		4		3		2		4		34

Miscellaneous: Lk. 3:7; Jn. 5:29, come forth; Rev. 9:17, 18, issue.

1608. ἐκπορνεύω, ekporneu′ō

Book	give (one's) self over to fornication	Total
Jd.	1:7	1

1609. ἐκπτύω, ekptu′ō

Book	reject	Total
Gal.	4:14	1

1610. ἐκριζόω, ekridzo′ō

Book	Oc.	root up	Oc.	pluck up by the root	Total
Mt.	2	13:29; 15:13			2
Lk.			1	17:6	1
Jd.			1	1:12	1
Total	2		2		4

1611. ἔκστασις, ek′stasis

Book	Oc.	trance	Oc.	be amazed (with 2983)	Oc.	amazement	Oc.	astonishment	Total
Mk.			1	16:8			1	5:42	2
Lk.			1	5:26					1
Ac.	3	10:10; 11:5; 22:17			1	3:10			4
Total	3		2		1		1		7

1612. ἐκστρέφω, ekstreph′ō

Book	subvert	Total
Tit.	3:11	1

1613. ἐκταράσσω, ektaras′sō

Book	exceedingly trouble	Total
Ac.	16:20	1

1614. ἐκτείνω, ektei′nō

Book	Oc.	stretch forth	Oc.	put forth	Oc.	stretch out	Oc.	cast	Total
Mt.	4	12:13, 13, 49; 14:31	1	8:3	1	26:51			6
Mk.	1	3:5a	1	1:41	1	3:5b			3
Lk.	2	6:10; 22:53	1	5:13					3
Jn.	1	21:18							1
Ac.	2	4:30; 26:1					1	27:30	3
Total	10		3		2		1		16

1615. ἐκτελέω, ektele′ō

Book	finish	Total
Lk.	14:29, 30	2

1616. ἐκτένεια, ekten′eia

Book	instantly (with 1722)	Total
Ac.	26:7	1

1617. ἐκτενέστερον ektenes′teron

Book	more earnestly	Total
Lk.	22:44	1

1618. ἐκτενής, ektenẹs′

Book	Oc.	without ceasing	Oc.	fervent	Total
Ac.	1	12:5			1
1 Pt.			1	4:8	1
Total	1		1		2

1619. ἐκτενῶς, ektenōs′

Book	fervently	Total
1 Pt.	1:22	1

1620. ἐκτίθημι, ektith′ẹmi

Book	Oc.	expound	Oc.	cast out	Total
Ac.	3	11:4; 18:26; 28:23	1	7:21	4

1621. ἐκτινάσσω, ektinas′sō

Book	Oc.	shake off	Oc.	shake	Total
Mt.	1	10:14			1
Mk.	1	6:11			1
Ac.	1	13:51	1	18:6	2
Total	3		1		4

1622. ἐκτός, ektos′

Book	Oc.	out of	Oc.	outside	Oc.	other than	Oc.	without	Oc.	be excepted	Oc.	except (with 1508)	Oc.	unless (with 1508)	Oc.	but (with 1508)	Total
Mt.			1	23:36													1
Ac.					1	26:22											1
1 Co.							1	6:18	1	15:27	1	14:5	1	15:2			4
2 Co.	2	12:2, 3															2
1 Ti.															1	5:19	1
Total	2		1		1		1		1		1		1		1		9

1623. ἕκτος, hek′tos

Book	sixth	Total
Mt.	20:5; 27:45	2
Mk.	15:33	1
Lk.	1:26, 36; 23:44	3
Jn.	4:6; 19:14	2
Ac.	10:9	1
Rev.	6:12; 9:13, 14; 16:12; 21:20	5
Total		14

1624. ἐκτρέπω, ektrep′ō

Book	Oc.	turn aside	Oc.	avoid	Oc.	turn	Oc.	turn out of the way	Total
1 Ti.	2	1:6; 5:15	1	6:20					3
2 Ti.					1	4:4			1
Heb.							1	12:13	1
Total	2		1		1		1		5

1625. ἐκτρέφω, ektreph'ō

Book	Oc.	nourish	Oc.	bring up	Total
Eph.	1	5:29	1	6:4	2

1626. ἔκτρωμα, ek'trōma

Book	born out of due time	Total
1 Co.	15:8	1

1629. ἐκφοβέω, ekphobe'ō

Book	terrify	Total
2 Co.	10:9	1

1627. ἐκφέρω, ekpher'ō

Book	Oc.	carry out	Oc.	bring forth	Oc.	carry forth	Oc.	bear	Total
Lk.			1	15:22					1
Ac.	2	5:6, 9	1	5:15	1	5:10			4
1 Ti.	1	6:7							1
Heb.							1	6:8	1
Total	3		2		1		1		7

1628. ἐκφεύγω, ekpheu'gō

Book	Oc.	escape	Oc.	flee	Total
Lk.	1	21:36			1
Ac.			2	16:27; 19:16	2
Ro.	1	2:3			1
2 Co.	1	11:33			1
1 Th.	1	5:3			1
Heb.	1	2:3			1
Total	5		2		7

1630. ἔκφοβος, ek'phobos

Book	Oc.	sore afraid	Oc.	exceedingly fear (with 1510)	Total
Mk.	1	9:6			1
Heb.			1	12:21	1
Total	1		1		2

1631. ἐκφύω, ekphu'ō

Book	put forth	Total
Mt.	24:32	1
Mk.	13:28	1
Total		2

1633. ἐκχωρέω, ekchōre'ō

Book	depart out	Total
Lk.	21:21	1

1632a. ἐκχέω, ekche'ō

Book	Oc.	pour out	Oc.	shed	Oc.	shed forth	Oc.	spill	Oc.	run out	Total
Mt.									1	9:17	1
Mk.							1	2:22			1
Jn.	1	2:15									1
Ac.	2	2:17, 18	1	22:20	1	2:33					4
Ro.			1	3:15							1
Tit.			1	3:6							1
Rev.	8	16:1, 2, 3, 4, 8, 10, 12, 17	1	16:6							9
Total	11		4		1		1		1		18

1632b. ἐκχύνω, ekchu'nō

Book	Oc.	shed	Oc.	run greedily	Oc.	shed abroad	Oc.	pour out	Oc.	gush out	Oc.	spill	Total
Mt.	2	23:35; 26:28											2
Mk.	1	14:24											1
Lk.	2	11:50; 22:20									1	5:37	3
Ac.							1	10:45	1	1:18			2
Ro.					1	5:5							1
Jd.			1	1:11									1
Total	5		1		1		1		1		1		10

Word 1632 has 28 occurrences.

1634. ἐκψύχω, ekpsu'chō

Book	Oc.	give up the ghost	Oc.	yield up the ghost	Total
Ac.	2	5:5; 12:23	1	5:10	3

1635. ἑκών, hekōn'

Book	willingly	Total
Ro.	8:20	1
1 Co.	9:17	1
Total		2

1637. ἔλαιον, el'aion

Book	oil	Total
Mt.	25:3, 4, 8	3
Mk.	6:13	1
Lk.	7:46; 10:34; 16:6	3
Heb.	1:9	1
Jas.	5:14	1
Rev.	6:6; 18:13	2
Total		11

1636. ἐλαία, elai'a

Book	Oc.	olives	Oc.	olive tree	Oc.	olive berries	Total
Mt.	3	21:1; 24:3; 26:30					3
Mk.	3	11:1; 13:3; 14:26					3
Lk.	4	19:29, 37; 21:37; 22:39					4
Jn.	1	8:1					1
Ro.			2	11:17, 24			2
Jas.					1	3:12	1
Rev.			1	11:4			1
Total	11		3		1		15

1638. ἐλαιών, elaiōn'

Book	Olivet	Total
Ac.	1:12	1

1639. Ἐλαμίτης, Elami'tes

Book	Elamites	Total
Ac.	2:9	1

1640. ἐλάσσων or ἐλάττων, elas'sōn or elat'tōn

Book	Oc.	worse	Oc.	younger	Oc.	under	Oc.	less	Total
Jn.	1	2:10							1
Ro.			1	9:12					1
1 Ti.					1	5:9			1
Heb.							1	7:7	1
Total	1		1		1		1		4

1641. ἐλαττονέω, elattone'ō

Book	have lack	Total
2 Co.	8:15	1

1642. ἐλαττόω, elatto'ō

Book	Oc.	make lower	Oc.	decrease	Total
Jn.			1	3:30	1
Heb.	2	2:7, 9			2
Total	2		1		3

1643. ἐλαύνω. elau'nō

Book	Oc.	row	Oc.	drive	Oc.	carry	Total
Mk.	1	6:48					1
Lk.			1	8:29			1
Jn.	1	6:19					1
Jas.			1	3:4			1
2 Pt.					1	2:17	1
Total	2		2		1		5

1644. ἐλαφρία, elaphri'a

Book	lightness	Total
2 Co.	1:17	1

1646. ἐλάχιστος, elach'istos

Book	Oc.	least	Oc.	very small	Oc.	smallest	Oc.	very little	Total
Mt.	5	2:6; 5:19, 19; 25:40, 45							5
Lk.	3	12:26; 16:10, 10					1	19:17	4
1 Co.	1	15:9	1	4:3	1	6:2			3
Jas.			1	3:4					1
Total	9		2		1		1		13

1645. ἐλαφρός, elaphros'

Book	light	Total
Mt.	11:30	1
2 Co.	4:17	1
Total		2

1647. ἐλαχιστότερος elachistot'eros

Book	less than the least	Total
Eph.	3:8	1

1648. Ἐλεάζαρ, Elead'zar

Book	Eleazar	Total
Mt.	1:15, 15	2

1652. ἐλεεινός, eleeinos'

Book	miserable	Total
1 Co.	15:19	1
Rev.	3:17	1
Total		2

1649. ἔλεγξις, el'engxis

Book	rebuke (with 2192)	Total
2 Pt.	2:16	1

1650. ἔλεγχος, el'engchos

Book	Oc.	reproof	Oc.	evidence	Total
2 Ti.	1	3:16			1
Heb.			1	11:1	1
Total	1		1		2

1651. ἐλέγχω, eleng'chō

Book	Oc.	reprove	Oc.	rebuke	Oc.	convince	Oc.	tell (one's) fault	Oc.	convict	Total
Mt.							1	18:15			1
Lk.	1	3:19									1
Jn.	2	3:20; 16:8			1	8:46			1	8:9	4
1 Co.					1	14:24					1
Eph.	2	5:11, 13									2
1 Ti.			1	5:20							1
2 Ti.	1	4:2									1
Tit.			2	1:13; 2:15	1	1:9					3
Heb.			1	12:5							1
Jas.					1	2:9					1
Rev.			1	3:19							1
Total	6		5		4		1		1		17

1653. ἐλεέω, elee'ō

Book	Oc.	have mercy on	Oc.	obtain mercy	Oc.	have compassion on	Oc.	shew mercy	Oc.	have compassion	Oc.	have pity on	Oc.	have mercy	Oc.	have mercy upon	Oc.	receive mercy	Total
Mt.	5	9:27; 15:22; 17:15; 20: 30, 31	1	5:7	1	18:33a					1	18:33b							8
Mk.	2	10:47, 48			1	5:19													3
Lk.	4	16:24; 17: 13; 18:38, 39																	4
Ro.	2	9:15a, 18	2	11:30, 31			2	9:16; 12:8					1	9:15b	1	11:32			8
1 Co.			1	7:25															1
2 Co.																	1	4:1	1
Phl.	1	2:27																	1
1 Ti.			2	1:13, 16															2
1 Pt.			2	2:10, 10															2
Jd.									1	1:22									1
Total	14		8		2		2		1		1		1		1		1		31

1654. ἐλεημοσύνη, eleēmosu'nē

Book	Oc.	alms	Oc.	almsdeeds	Total
Mt.	4	6:1, 2, 3, 4			4
Lk.	2	11:41; 12:33			2
Ac.	7	3:2, 3, 10; 10:2, 4, 31; 24:17	1	9:36	8
Total	13		1		14

1655. ἐλεήμων, eleē'mōn

Book	merciful	Total
Mt.	5:7	1
Heb.	2:17	1
Total		2

1656. ἔλεος, el'eos

Book	mercy	Total
Mt.	9:13; 12:7; 23:23	3
Lk.	1:50, 54, 58, 72, 78; 10:37	6
Ro.	9:23; 11:31; 15:9	3
Gal.	6:16	1
Eph.	2:4	1
1 Ti.	1:2	1
2 Ti.	1:2, 16, 18	3
Tit.	1:4; 3:5	2
Heb.	4:16	1
Jas.	2:13, 13; 3:17	3
1 Pt.	1:3	1
2 Jn.	1:3	1
Jd.	1:2, 21	2
Total		28

1657. ἐλευθερία, eleutheri'a

Book	liberty	Total
Ro.	8:21	1
1 Co.	10:29	1
2 Co.	3:17	1
Gal.	2:4; 5:1, 13, 13	4
Jas.	1:25; 2:12	2
1 Pt.	2:16	1
2 Pt.	2:19	1
Total		11

1659. ἐλευθερόω, eleuthero'ō

Book	Oc.	make free	Oc.	deliver	Total
Jn.	2	8:32, 36			2
Ro.	3	6:18, 22; 8:2	1	8:21	4
Gal.	1	5:1			1
Total	6		1		7

1658. ἐλεύθερος, eleu'theros

Book	Oc.	free	Oc.	freewoman	Oc.	at liberty	Oc.	free man	Total
Mt.	1	17:26							1
Jn.	2	8:33, 36							2
Ro.	2	6:20; 7:3							2
1 Co.	5	7:21, 22; 9:1, 19; 12:13			1	7:39			6
Gal.	3	3:28; 4:26, 31	3	4:22, 23, 30					6
Eph.	1	6:8							1
Col.	1	3:11							1
1 Pt.	1	2:16							1
Rev.	2	13:16; 19:18					1	6:15	3
Total	18		3		1		1		23

1660. ἔλευσις, el'eusis

Book	coming	Total
Ac.	7:52	1

1661. ἐλεφάντινος, elephan'tinos

Book	ivory	Total
Rev.	18:12	1

1662. Ἐλιακείμ, Eliakeim'

Book	Eliakim	Total
Mt.	1:13, 13	2
Lk.	3:30	1
Total		3

1666. Ἐλισσαῖος, Elissai'os

Book	Eliseus	Total
Lk.	4:27	1

1670a. ἑλκύω, helku'ō

Book	draw	Total
Jn.	6:44; 12:32; 18:10; 21:6, 11	5
Ac.	16:19	1
Total		6

1670b. ἕλκω, hel'kō

Book	draw	Total
Ac.	21:30	1
Jas.	2:6	1
Total		2

Word 1670 has 8 occurrences.

1671. Ἑλλάς, Hellas'

Book	Greece	Total
Ac.	20:2	1

1675. Ἑλληνιστής, Hellenistes'

Book	Grecians	Total
Ac.	6:1; 9:29; 11:20	3

1663. Ἐλιέζερ, Elied'zer

Book	Eliezer	Total
Lk.	3:29	1

1667. ἑλίσσω, helis'sō

Book	fold them up	Total
Heb.	1:12	1

1664. Ἐλιούδ, Elioud'

Book	Eliud	Total
Mt.	1:14, 15	2

1668. ἕλκος, hel'kos

Book	sore	Total
Lk.	16:21	1
Rev.	16:2, 11	2
Total		3

1665. Ἐλισάβετ, Elisab'et

Book	Elisabeth	Total
Lk.	1:5, 7, 13, 24, 36, 40, 41, 41, 57	9

1669. ἑλκόω, helko'ō

Book	full of sores	Total
Lk.	16:20	1

1673. Ἑλληνικός, Hellenikos'

Book	Greek	Total
Lk.	23:38	1
Rev.	9:11	1
Total		2

1672. Ἕλλην, Hel'len

Book	Oc.	Greek	Oc.	Gentile	Total
Jn.	1	12:20	2	7:35, 35	3
Ac.	10	14:1; 16:1, 3; 17:4; 18:4, 17; 19:10, 17; 20:21; 21:28			10
Ro.	3	1:14, 16; 10:12	3	2:9, 10; 3:9	6
1 Co.	3	1:22, 23, 24	2	10:32; 12:13	5
Gal.	2	2:3; 3:28			2
Col.	1	3:11			1
Total	20		7		27

1674. Ἑλληνίς, Hellenis'

Book	Greek	Total
Mk.	7:26	1
Ac.	17:12	1
Total		2

1676. Ἑλληνιστί, Hellenisti'

Book	Greek	Total
Jn.	19:20	1
Ac.	21:37	1
Total		2

1677. ἐλλογέω, elloge'ō

Book	Oc.	impute	Oc.	put on (one's) account	Total
Ro.	1	5:13			1
Phe.			1	1:18	1
Total	1		1		2

1679. ἐλπίζω, elpid'zō

Book	Oc.	trust	Oc.	hope	Oc.	hope for	Oc.	things hoped for	Total
Mt.	1	12:21							1
Lk.	1	24:21	2	6:34; 23:8					3
Jn.	1	5:45							1
Ac.			2	24:26; 26:7					2
Ro.	2	15:12, 24			2	8:24, 25			4
1 Co.	1	16:7	2	13:7; 15:19					3
2 Co.	4	1:10, 13; 5:11; 13:6	1	8:5					5
Phl.	1	2:19	1	2:23					2
1 Ti.	3	4:10; 5:5; 6:17	1	3:14					4
Phe.	1	1:22							1
Heb.							1	11:1	1
1 Pt.	1	3:5	1	1:13					2
2 Jn.	1	1:12							1
3 Jn.	1	1:14							1
Total	18		10		2		1		31

1678. Ἐλμωδάμ, Elmōdam'

Book	Elmodam	Total
Lk.	3:28	1

1681. Ἐλύμας, Elu'mas

Book	Elymas	Total
Ac.	13:8	1

1682. ἐλωΐ, elōi'

Book	Eloi	Total
Mk.	15:34, 34	2

1680. ἐλπίς, elpis'

Book	Oc.	hope	Oc.	faith	Total
Ac.	8	2:26; 16:19; 23:6; 24:15; 26:6, 7; 27:20; 28:20			8
Ro.	13	4:18, 18; 5:2, 4, 5; 8:20, 24, 24, 24; 12:12; 15:4, 13, 13			13
1 Co.	4	9:10, 10, 10; 13:13			4
2 Co.	3	1:7; 3:12; 10:15			3
Gal.	1	5:5			1
Eph.	3	1:18; 2:12; 4:4			3
Phl.	1	1:20			1
Col.	3	1:5, 23, 27			3
1 Th.	4	1:3; 2:19; 4:13; 5:8			4
2 Th.	1	2:16			1
1 Ti.	1	1:1			1
Tit.	3	1:2; 2:13; 3:7			3
Heb.	4	3:6; 6:11, 18; 7:19	1	10:23	5
1 Pt.	3	1:3, 21; 3:15			3
1 Jn.	1	3:3			1
Total	53		1		54

1683. ἐμαυτοῦ, emautou'

Book	Oc.	myself	Oc.	me	Oc.	mine own self	Oc.	mine own	Oc.	I myself	Total
Mt.			1	8:9							1
Lk.	1	7:7	1	7:8							2
Jn.	14	5:31; 7:17, 28; 18:14, 18, 28, 42, 54; 10:18; 12:49; 14:3, 10, 21; 17:19	1	12:32	1	5:30					16
Ac.	4	20:24; 24:10; 26:2, 9									4
Ro.	1	11:4									1
1 Co.	3	4:4, 6; 9:19			1	4:3	1	10:33	1	7:7	6
2 Co.	4	2:1; 11:7, 9; 12:5									4
Gal.	1	2:18									1
Phl.	1	3:13									1
Phe.			1	1:13							1
Total	29		4		2		1		1		37

1684. ἐμβαίνω, embai'nō

Book	Oc.	enter	Oc.	come	Oc.	get	Oc.	go	Oc.	take (with 1519)	Oc.	go up	Oc.	step in	Total
Mt.	2	8:23; 9:1	1	14:32	1	14:22	1	13;2	1	15:39					6
Mk.	3	4:1; 8:10, 13	1	5:18	1	6:45									5
Lk.	1	5:3					1	8:22			1	8:37			3
Jn.	2	6:17, 22							1	6:24			1	5:4	4
Total	8		2		2		2		2		1		1		18

1685. ἐμβάλλω, embal'lō

Book	cast	Total
Lk.	12:5	1

1686. ἐμβάπτω, embap'tō

Book	dip	Total
Mt.	26:23	1
Mk.	14:20	1
Jn.	13:26	1
Total		3

1687. ἐμβατεύω, embateu'ō

Book	intrude into	Total
Col.	2:18	1

1688. ἐμβιβάζω, embibad'zō

Book	put	Total
Ac.	27:6	1

1689. ἐμβλέπω, emblep'ō

Book	Oc.	behold	Oc.	look upon	Oc.	see	Oc.	gaze up	Oc.	can see	Total
Mt.	2	6:26; 19:26									2
Mk.	1	10:21	2	10:27; 14:67	1	8:25					4
Lk.	1	20:17	1	22:61							2
Jn.	1	1:42	1	1:36							2
Ac.							1	1:11	1	22:11	2
Total	5		4		1		1		1		12

1690. ἐμβριμάομαι, embrima'omai

Book	Oc.	straitly charge	Oc.	groan	Oc.	murmur against	Total
Mt.	1	9:30					1
Mk.	1	1:43			1	14:5	2
Jn.			2	11:33, 38			2
Total	2		2		1		5

1692. ἐμέω, eme'ō

Book	spue	Total
Rev.	3:16	1

1693. ἐμμαίνομαι, emmai'nomai

Book	mad against	Total
Ac.	26:11	1

1691. ἐμέ, eme'

Book	Oc.	me	Oc.	I	Oc.	my	Oc.	myself	Total
Mt.	9	10:37, 37, 40, 40; 18:5, 6, 21; 26:10, 11							9
Mk.	6	9:37, 37, 37, 42; 14:6, 7							6
Lk.	8	4:18; 9:48, 48; 10:16, 16; 22:53; 23:28; 24:39							8
Jn.	38	6:35, 37, 47, 57; 7:7, 38; 8:19, 19, 42; 11:25, 26; 12:8, 30, 44, 44, 45, 46, 48; 13:18, 20, 20; 14: 1, 9, 12; 15:18, 20, 23, 24; 16:3, 9, 14, 23, 27, 32; 17:18, 20, 23; 18:8	2	3:30; 9:4					40
Ac.	6	3:22; 7:37; 8:24; 13:25; 22:6; 26:18							6
Ro.	4	1:15; 10:20, 20; 15:3							4
1 Co.	2	9:3; 15:10							2
2 Co.	4	2:5; 11:10; 12:6, 9							4
Eph.					1	6:21			1
Phl.	3	1:12; 2:23, 27							3
Col.					1	4:7			1
2 Ti.	1	1:8							1
Phe.	1	1:17a					1	1:17b	2
Rev.	1	1:17							1
Total	83		2		2		1		88

1694. Ἐμμανουήλ, Emmanouel'

Book	Emmanuel	Total
Mt.	1:23	1

1695. Ἐμμαούς, Emmaous'

Book	Emmaus	Total
Lk.	24:13	1

1696. ἐμμένω, emmen'ō

Book	continue	Total
Ac.	14:22	1
Gal.	3:10	1
Heb.	8:9	1
Total		3

1697. Ἐμμόρ, Emmor'

Book	Emmor	Total
Ac.	7:16	1

1698. ἐμοί, emoi'

Book	Oc.	me	Oc.	I	Oc.	mine	Oc.	my	Total
Mt.	7	10:32; 11:6; 18:26, 29; 25:40, 45; 26:31							7
Mk.	1	14:27	1	5:7					2
Lk.	5	4:6; 7:23; 12:8; 15:29; 22:37	1	8:28					6
Jn.	26	5:46; 6:56; 7:23; 8:12; 10:38, 38; 12:26, 26, 26; 14:10, 10, 11, 20, 30; 15:2, 4, 4, 5, 6, 7; 16: 33; 17:6, 21, 23; 18:35; 19:10	1	2:4					27
Ac.	6	10:28; 11:12; 22:9; 24:20; 26:13; 28:18							6
Ro.	7	7:8, 13, 17, 18, 20, 21b; 14:11	1	7:21a	1	12:19			9
1 Co.	5	4:3; 9:15; 14:11; 15:10; 16:4							5
2 Co.	4	1:17; 9:4; 11:10; 13:3							4
Gal.	9	1:2, 16, 24; 2:3, 6, 8, 9, 20; 6:14b	1	6:14a					10
Eph.	1	3:8							1
Phl.	9	1:7, 21, 26, 30, 30; 2:22; 3:1; 4:9, 21	1	2:16					10
Col.	1	1:29							1
1 Ti.	1	1:16							1
2 Ti.	1	4:8							1
Phe.	2	1:11, 16			1	1:18			3
Heb.	1	10:30					1	13:6	2
Total	86		6		2		1		95

1699. ἐμός, emos'

Book	Oc.	my	Oc.	mine	Oc.	mine own	Oc.	of me	Oc.	I	Total
Mt.	1	18:20	1	20:23	2	20:15; 25:27					4
Mk.	1	8:38	1	10:40							2
Lk.	1	9:26					1	22:19	1	15:31	3
Jn.	31	3:29; 4:34; 5:30a, 47; 7:6, 8, 16a; 8:16, 31, 37, 43, 43, 51, 56; 10:14a, 26, 27; 12:26; 13:35; 14:15, 27; 15:8, 9, 11, 12; 17:13, 24; 18:36, 36, 36, 36	8	7:16b; 10:14b; 14:24; 16:14, 15, 15; 17:10, 10	2	5:30b; 6:38					41
Ro.	2	3:7; 10:1									2
1 Co.	4	5:4; 7:40; 11:25a; 16:18	2	9:2, 3	2	1:15; 16:21	2	11:24, 25b			10
2 Co.	3	1:23; 2:3; 8:23									3
Gal.	1	1:13			1	6:11					2
Phl.	1	1:26			1	3:9					2
Col.							1	4:18			1
2 Th.					1	3:17					1
2 Ti.	1	4:6									1
Phe.	1	1:10			2	1:12, 19					3
2 Pt.	1	1:15									1
3 Jn.	1	1:4									1
Rev.	1	2:20									1
Total	50		12		11		4		1		78

1700. ἐμοῦ, emou′

Book	Oc.	me	Oc.	my	Oc.	mine	Total
Mt.	14	7:23; 11:29; 12:30, 30, 30; 15:5, 8; 17:27; 25:41; 26:23, 38, 39, 40, 42	4	5:11; 10:18, 39; 16:25			18
Mk.	5	7:6, 11; 14:18, 20, 36	3	8:35; 10:29; 13:9			8
Lk.	17	5:8; 8:46; 10:16; 11:7, 23, 23, 23; 12:13; 13:27; 15:31; 16:3; 22:21, 28, 37, 42; 23:43; 24:44	1	9:24			18
Jn.	24	4:9; 5:7, 32, 32, 36, 37, 39, 46; 8:18, 29; 10:8, 9, 18, 25; 13:8, 18; 14:6; 15:5, 26, 27; 16:32; 17:24; 18:34; 19:11	1	13:38			25
Ac.	6	8:24; 11:5; 20:34; 22:18; 23:11; 25:9					6
Ro.	4	1:12; 15:18, 30; 16:7	2	11:27; 16:2	1	16:13	7
2 Co.	5	1:19; 2:2; 7:7; 12:6, 8					5
Gal.	3	1:11, 17; 2:20					3
Eph.	1	6:19					1
Phl.	1	4:10					1
2 Ti.	4	1:13; 2:2; 4:11, 17					4
Tit.	1	3:15					1
Heb.	1	10:7					1
Rev.	11	1:12; 3:4, 18, 20, 21; 4:1; 10:8; 17:1; 21:9, 15; 22:12					11
Total	97		11		1		109

1701. ἐμπαιγμός, empaigmos′

Book	mocking	Total
Heb.	11:36	1

1702. ἐμπαίζω, empaid′zō

Book	mock	Total
Mt.	2:16; 20:19; 27:29, 31, 41	5
Mk.	10:34; 15:20, 31	3
Lk.	14:29; 18:32; 22:63; 23:11, 36	5
Total		13

1703. ἐμπαίκτης, empaik′tęs

Book	Oc.	mockers	Oc.	scoffers	Total
2 Pt.			1	3:3	1
Jd.	1	1:18			1
Total	1		1		2

1704. ἐμπεριπατέω, emperipate′ō

Book	walk in	Total
2 Co.	6:16	1

1705a. ἐμπιπλάω, empipla′ō

Book	fill	Total
Ac.	14:17	1

1705b. ἐμπίπλημι, empip′lęmi

Book	Oc.	fill	Oc.	be full	Total
Lk.	1	1:53	1	6:25	2
Jn.	1	6:12			1
Ro.	1	15:24			1
Total	3		1		4

Word 1705 has 5 occurrences.

1706. ἐμπίπτω, empip′tō

Book	fall	Total
Mt.	12:11	1
Lk.	10:36; 14:5	2
1 Ti.	3:6, 7; 6:9	3
Heb.	10:31	1
Total		7

1707. ἐμπλέκω, emplek′ō

Book	Oc.	entangle (one's) self with	Oc.	entangle therein (with 5025)	Total
2 Ti.	1	2:4			1
2 Pt.			1	2:20	1
Total	1		1		2

1708. ἐμπλοκή, emploke′

Book	plaiting	Total
1 Pt.	3:3	1

1709. ἐμπνέω, empne′ō

Book	breathe out	Total
Ac.	9:1	1

1710. ἐμπορεύομαι, emporeu′omai

Book	Oc.	buy and sell	Oc.	make merchandise	Total
Jas.	1	4:13			1
2 Pt.			1	2:3	1
Total	1		1		2

1711. ἐμπορία, empori′a

Book	merchandise	Total
Mt.	22:5	1

1712. ἐμπόριον, empor′ion

Book	merchandise	Total
Jn.	2:16	1

1713. ἔμπορος, em′poros

Book	merchant	Total
Mt.	13:45	1
Rev.	18:3, 11, 15, 23	4
Total		5

1714. ἐμπρήθω, emprę′thō

Book	burn up	Total
Mt.	22:7	1

1715. ἔμπροσθεν, em′prosthen

Book	Oc.	before	Oc.	in (one's) sight	Oc.	of	Oc.	against	Oc.	in the sight of	Oc.	in the presence of	Oc.	at	Total
Mt.	15	5:16, 24; 6:1, 2; 7:6; 10:32, 32, 33, 33; 11:10; 17:2; 25:32; 26:70; 27:11, 29	1	11:26	1	18:14	1	23:13							18
Mk.	2	1:2; 9:2													2
Lk.	9	5:19; 7:27; 12:8, 8; 14:2; 19.4, 27, 28; 21:36	1	10:21											10
Jn.	6	1:15, 27, 30; 3:28; 10:4; 12:37													6
Ac.	1	18:17													1
2 Co.	1	5:10													1
Gal.	1	2:14													1
Phl.	1	3:13													1
1 Th.	2	3:9, 13							1	1:3	1	2:19			4
1 Jn.	1	3:19													1
Rev.	2	4:6; 22:8											1	19:10	3
Total	41		2		1		1		1		1		1		48

1716. ἐμπτύω, emptu′ō

Book	Oc.	spit upon	Oc.	spit on	Oc.	spit	Total
Mt.					2	26:67; 27:30	2
Mk.	2	10:34; 15:19	1	14:65			3
Lk.			1	18:32			1
Total	2		2		2		6

1717. ἐμφανής, emphanęs′

Book	Oc.	shew openly (with 1325 and 1096)	Oc.	manifest	Total
Ac.	1	10:40			1
Ro.			1	10:20	1
Total	1		1		2

1718. ἐμφανίζω, emphanid′zō

Book	Oc.	inform	Oc.	be manifest	Oc.	appear	Oc.	signify	Oc.	shew	Oc.	declare plainly	Total
Mt.					1	27:53							1
Jn.			2	14:21, 22									2
Ac.	3	24:1; 25:2, 15					1	23:15	1	23:22			5
Heb.					1	9:24					1	11:14	2
Total	3		2		2		1		1		1		10

1719. ἔμφοβος, em′phobos

Book	Oc.	afraid	Oc.	affrighted	Oc.	tremble (with 1096)	Total
Lk.	1	24:5	1	24:37			2
Ac.	2	10:4; 22:9			1	24:25	3
Rev.			1	11:13			1
Total	3		2		1		6

1720. ἐμφυσάω, emphusa′ō

Book	breathe on	Total
Jn.	20:22	1

1721. ἔμφυτος, em′phutos

Book	engrafted	Total
Jas.	1:21	1

1722. ἐν, en

Book	Oc.	in	Oc.	by
Mt.	211	1:20; 2:1, 1, 2, 5, 9, 16, 16, 18, 19; 3:1, 1, 3, 6, 12, 17; 4:13, 16, 16, 21, 23a; 5:12, 15, 16, 19, 19, 25, 28, 45, 48; 6: 1, 2, 2, 4a, 4b, 5, 5, 6a, 6b, 9, 10, 18a, 18b, 20, 23, 29; 7:3, 3, 4, 11, 15, 21, 22; 8:10, 11, 13, 24, 32; 9:4, 10, 31, 33, 35a; 10:11, 15, 16, 17, 19, 20, 23, 27, 27, 28, 32c, 33; 11:1, 2, 6, 8, 8, 11b, 16, 21, 21, 21, 23, 23, 24; 12:5, 5, 19, 21, 32, 32, 36, 40, 40, 41, 42, 50; 13:3, 10, 13, 19, 21, 24, 27, 30, 31, 32, 34, 35, 40, 43, 44, 54, 57, 57, 57; 14:2. 3 10, 33; 15:32, 33; 16:17, 19, 19, 27, 28; 17:5, 22; 18:1b, 2, 4, 6, 10, 10, 14, 18, 18, 19, 20; 19:21, 28; 20:3, 17, 21; 21:8, 8, 9, 9, 12, 14, 15, 22, 28, 32, 33, 41, 42, 42; 22:15, 16, 28, 30, 30, 36, 43; 23:6b. 7. 9, 30, 30, 34, 39; 24:14, 15, 16, 18, 19b, 26, 26, 30, 38, 40, 45, 48, 50, 50; 25:4, 18, 25, 31, 36, 39, 43, 44; 26:6, 6, 13, 23, 29, 55, 55, 69; 27:5, 40, 60, 60; 28:18	26	5:34, 35, 36; 12:24, 27, 27, 28; 14:13; 17:21; 21:23, 24, 27; 22:1; 23:16, 16, 18, 18, 20, 20, 20, 21, 21, 21, 22, 22, 22
Mk.	95	1:2, 3, 4, 5, 9, 11, 13, 19, 20, 23a, 39, 45; 2:6, 8b, 15b, 20; 3:23; 4:1, 2b, 11, 15, 17, 28, 36; 5:5, 5, 13, 20, 27, 30, 30; 6:2, 4a, 4c, 11, 14, 17, 27, 29, 47, 48, 51, 56; 8:1, 14, 26, 38, 38; 9:33a, 36, 41, 50b; 10:10, 21, 30, 30, 32, 37, 52; 11:9, 10, 10, 15, 23, 25, 26, 27; 12:11, 23, 25, 26, 35, 38, 38, 38, 39a; 13:11, 14, 17b, 24, 25, 26, 32; 14:3, 3, 25, 30, 49, 66; 15:7, 29, 41, 46; 16:12, 17	15	3:22; 4:2a; 5:21; 8:3, 27; 9: 29, 29, 33b, 34; 11:28, 29, 33; 12:1, 36; 14:1
Lk.	229	1:5, 6, 7, 8b, 17a, 18, 21b, 22, 25a, 26, 31, 36, 39, 41, 44a, 66, 69, 75, 79, 80; 2:1, 7, 7, 8, 11, 12, 14a, 16, 19, 21, 23, 24, 25, 29, 34, 38, 43b, 44a, 46, 46, 51; 3:1, 2, 4, 4, 15, 17, 20, 22; 4:2, 5, 14, 15, 20, 21, 23, 23, 24, 25, 25, 27, 28, 33, 44; 5:7, 12b, 22, 29, 35; 6:12, 12, 23, 23, 41, 41, 42, 42, 42; 7:9, 21, 23, 25a, 25c, 28b, 32, 37, 37; 8:10, 13, 15b, 27, 27; 9:12, 26, 31a, 36b, 57; 10:7, 12, 13, 13, 13, 20, 20, 21, 26; 11:1b, 2, 2, 21, 31, 32, 35, 43, 43; 12:1, 3, 3, 3, 12, 15, 27, 28, 33, 38, 38, 42, 45, 46a, 52, 58; 13:4, 4, 6a, 10a, 14, 14, 19, 26, 28, 29, 35; 14:15; 15:4, 7, 25; 16:10, 10, 10, 10, 11, 12, 23, 23, 23, 24, 25; 17:6, 24, 26, 26, 28, 31, 31, 31, 36; 18:2, 3, 22, 30, 30; 19:17, 20, 30, 36, 38, 38, 38, 42, 44b, 47; 20:1b, 33, 42, 46a, 46b, 46c; 21:6, 19, 21, 21, 21, 23b, 25a, 27, 37, 38; 22:16, 20, 28, 30, 37, 44, 53, 55a; 23:4, 9, 14, 19, 22, 29, 31, 31, 40, 43, 53; 24:4b, 6, 18a, 18c, 19, 27, 35, 35, 36, 38, 44, 49, 53	8	1:77; 2:27a; 4:1; 11:19, 19; 20:2, 8; 24:32b
Jn.	170	1:1, 2, 4, 5, 10, 23, 28, 45, 47; 2:1, 11, 14, 19, 20, 23a, 23c, 25; 3:13, 14, 21, 23; 4:14, 20, 20, 21a, 23, 24, 31, 44, 53b; 5:3, 13, 14, 26, 26, 28, 35, 38, 39, 42, 43, 43; 6:10, 31, 45, 49, 53, 56, 56, 59, 59, 61; 7:1, 1, 4a, 9, 10, 18, 28, 37; 8:3, 3, 5, 9, 12, 17, 20, 20, 21, 24, 24, 31, 35, 37, 44, 44; 9:3, 5, 34; 10:23, 23, 25, 34, 38, 38; 11:6, 9, 10, 10, 17, 20, 24a, 30, 31, 38, 56; 12:13, 25, 35, 46, 48; 13:1, 31, 32, 32; 14:2, 10, 10, 10, 11, 11, 13, 13, 14, 17, 20b, 20c, 20d, 26, 30; 15:2, 4, 4, 4, 4, 5, 5, 6, 7, 7, 9, 10, 10, 11, 16, 25; 16:23, 23, 24, 25, 25, 26b, 33, 33; 17:10, 11a, 11b, 12, 12, 13, 13; 17:21, 21, 21, 23, 23, 26, 26; 18:20, 20, 20, 26, 38; 19:4, 6, 41a, 41b; 20:12, 25, 30	2	13:35a; 16:30
Ac.	167	1:7, 8, 8, 10, 15, 15, 20a; 2:17, 18, 19, 22, 46a; 3:6, 26; 4:7a, 12a, 24; 5:4, 4, 12b, 18, 20, 22, 25, 25, 34, 37, 42; 6: 1, 1, 7, 15; 7:2, 2, 4, 5, 6, 7, 12, 16, 17, 20, 20, 22, 22, 29b, 30, 30, 34, 35b, 36, 36, 36, 38, 38, 38, 41, 41, 42, 42, 44b, 48; 8:8, 9, 21, 33; 9:10b, 11, 12, 17, 20, 21, 25, 27a, 27c, 29, 37, 37, 43; 10:1, 3, 17, 30, 30, 32, 35, 39, 39, 48; 11:5, 5, 13, 22, 26b, 27, 29; 12:5, 7a; 13:5b, 17b, 18, 19, 33, 35, 40, 41; 14:1, 16, 25; 15:21, 35; 16:3, 6, 12, 18, 32, 36; 17:11, 16b, 17, 17, 22, 24b, 28, 31a, 31b; 18:4, 9, 10, 18, 24, 26; 19:9, 16, 21, 39; 20:8, 10, 16; 21:27, 29; 22:3, 3, 17, 17; 23:6, 9, 35: 24:12, 12, 14, 18b, 20; 25:5b; 26:10, 21, 26; 27:21, 27, 31, 37; 28:7, 9, 11, 11, 18, 30	11	1:3; 4:7b, 7c, 10, 10, 30; 7: 35a; 13:39, 39; 17:31c; 20:19
Ro.	96	1:2, 7, 9b, 18, 19, 21, 27a, 27c, 28; 2:12, 15, 16, 19, 20, 28c, 29b; 3:4a, 16, 24, 25a; 4:10, 10, 10, 10; 5:3, 5, 11, 13, 17; 6:4, 12, 12; 7:5, 5, 6b, 8, 17, 18, 18, 20, 23, 23; 8:1, 2, 3, 3, 3, 4, 8, 9, 9, 9, 10, 11, 11, 37, 39; 9:1, 1, 7, 17a, 25, 26, 28, 33; 10:6, 8, 8, 9b; 12:4, 5; 13:9a, 13; 14:5, 17, 18, 22; 15:13a, 13b, 23, 27, 29, 30, 31; 16:2, 2, 3, 7b, 8. 9, 10, 11, 12, 12, 13, 22	8	1:10; 5:9, 10, 15; 10:5; 14:14; 15:16, 19b
1 Co.	110	1:2b, 2c, 5a, 5c, 6, 7, 8, 10b, 10c, 21, 30, 31; 2:3, 3, 3, 4b, 5, 5, 7, 11, 13a; 3:1, 16, 18b, 19, 21; 4:2, 6, 10, 15, 15, 17, 17, 17, 20, 20, 21b; 5:4, 5. 9; 6:4, 11a, 19, 20, 20; 7:15a, 17, 18, 20a, 22, 37, 37, 39; 8:4, 5, 7, 10; 9:1, 2, 9, 18, 24; 10:2, 2, 5b, 8, 25; 11:11, 13, 18a, 21, 22, 25; 12:6, 18, 25, 28; 14:10, 19, 19, 21a, 25, 28, 33, 34, 35b; 15:17, 18, 19, 19, 22, 22, 23a, 28, 31, 41, 42, 42, 43, 43, 43, 43, 52a, 52b, 58, 58; 16:11, 13, 19, 24	17	1:4, 5b; 3:13; 6:2, 11b; 7:14, 14; 12:3, 3, 9, 9, 13; 14:6, 6, 6, 6; 16:7
2 Co.	123	1:1b, 4, 6, 8, 9, 12a, 12d, 14, 19b, 20, 20, 22; 2:1, 10, 14, 14, 15, 15, 17; 3:2, 3, 3, 7b, 9, 10, 14; 4:2, 4, 6, 6, 7, 10, 10, 11, 12, 12; 5:1, 2, 4, 6, 11, 12, 17, 19a, 21; 6:2, 3, 4, 4, 4, 4, 4, 5, 5, 5, 5, 5, 5, 12, 12, 16; 7:1, 3, 9, 11, 11, 14, 16, 16; 8:2, 7a, 7c, 18, 20, 22; 9:3, 4, 8, 11; 10:3, 6, 14, 16, 17; 11:6b, 9, 10, 10, 17b, 23, 23, 23, 23, 25, 26a, 26b, 26c, 27, 27, 27, 27, 27, 32, 33; 12:2, 2, 3, 5, 9, 9, 10, 10, 10, 10, 10, 12b, 12c, 19; 13:3, 3, 4, 5, 5	14	1:12c; 6:6, 6, 6, 6, 6, 6, 7, 7; 7:6, 7, 7; 10:12, 15b
Gal.	31	1:13, 14, 14, 16a, 22, 24; 2:4, 20a, 20b; 3:8, 10, 10, 12, 19, 26, 28; 4:14, 18a, 19, 25; 5:6, 14, 14; 6:1, 1, 6, 12, 13, 14, 15, 17	4	2:17, 20c; 3:11; 5:4
Eph.	89	1:1b, 3b, 3c, 4, 4, 6b, 7, 8, 9, 10, 10, 10, 11, 12, 13, 13, 15, 17, 18, 20a, 20c, 21, 21, 23; 2:2b, 3b, 4, 6, 6, 7a, 7b, 10, 10, 11, 11, 12b, 13a, 15, 15, 15, 16a, 21, 21, 22a; 3:3, 4, 5a, 6, 9, 10, 11, 12a, 15, 17, 17, 20, 21a; 4:2, 3, 4, 6, 15, 16, 16, 17, 17, 18, 21b, 24; 5:2, 5, 8, 9, 19, 20, 21, 24; 6:1, 4, 5, 9, 10, 10, 12, 13, 18b, 20a, 21, 24	7	2:13b, 18; 3:5b, 21b; 4:14a, 21a; 5:26
Phl.	56	1:1a, 4, 6, 7, 7, 8, 9, 13, 13, 14, 20a, 20c, 22, 24, 26a, 27, 28, 30, 30; 2:1, 5, 5, 6, 7, 12, 12, 13, 15a, 15c, 19, 24, 29; 3:1, 3, 3, 4, 4, 6, 9, 14, 19, 20; 4:1, 2, 3, 3, 4, 6, 9, 10, 11, 12b, 15, 16, 19a, 21	1	4:19b
Col.	68	1:2a, 4, 5, 5, 6, 6, 6, 8, 9, 10, 12, 14, 16b, 18, 19, 20, 22, 24, 24, 27b, 28, 28, 29a; 2:1b, 2, 3, 6, 7a, 7b, 9, 10, 11a, 11b, 12a, 13, 15b, 16, 16, 16, 18, 20, 23, 23; 3:3, 4, 7, 7, 11, 15, 15, 16a, 16b, 16d, 17a, 17c, 18, 22b; 4:1, 2a, 5, 7, 12, 12, 13, 13, 15, 16, 17	4	1:16a, 17, 21; 2:11c
1 Th.	29	1:1, 5a, 5b, 5c, 5d, 6, 7, 8, 8; 2:2b, 3, 13, 14, 14; 3:2, 8, 13a; 4:4, 5, 6, 10, 16d, 17; 5:2, 4, 12b, 13a, 18, 18	3	3:3; 4:1, 15
2 Th.	17	1:1, 4, 4, 4, 8, 10, 10, 10, 12, 12; 2:6, 10b, 12, 17; 3:4, 6, 17	1	3:16
1 Ti.	36	1:2, 4, 13, 14, 16; 2:2, 2, 7, 7, 9a, 11a, 12, 14, 15; 3:4, 9, 11, 13, 13, 15, 16a, 16b, 16d; 4:1, 2, 12, 12, 12, 12, 12, 12, 14; 5:17; 6:17, 17, 18	1	1:18
2 Ti.	25	1:1, 3b, 5, 5, 5, 6, 9, 13, 13, 14, 15, 17, 18a; 2:1, 1, 7, 10, 20, 25; 3:1, 12, 14, 15, 16; 4:5		
Tit.	9	1:5, 13; 2:3, 7, 9, 10, 12; 3:3, 15	1	1:9
Phe.	9	1:6b, 8, 10, 13, 16, 16, 20, 20, 23	1	1:6a
Heb.	45	2:8, 12, 18; 3:2, 5, 8, 8, 11, 12, 12, 15b, 17; 4:3, 5, 7; 5:6, 7; 6:18; 7:10; 8:1b, 5, 9, 9, 13; 9:23; 10:3, 7, 22, 32, 34, 34, 38; 11:9, 18, 19, 26, 34, 37b, 38; 12:23; 13:3, 4, 18, 21, 21	5	1:1, 2; 10:10, 19; 11:2
Jas.	22	1:6, 8, 9, 10, 11, 23, 25, 27; 2:2, 2, 4, 5, 10, 16; 3:2, 14, 18; 4:1b, 5. 16; 5:5, 14b		
1 Pt.	26	1:4, 5b, 11, 14, 15, 17, 22; 2:6, 6, 12c, 22, 24; 3:4, 15, 15, 16b, 19b, 20; 4:1, 2, 3, 11, 19; 5:6, 9, 14b	3	1:5a; 3:19a; 5:10
2 Pt.	19	1:4a, 12, 13a, 18, 19, 19; 2:10, 12b, 13a, 18b; 3:1a, 10a, 10b, 11, 14, 16, 16, 16, 18	1	1:13b
1 Jn.	65	1:5, 6, 7, 7, 8, 10; 2:4, 5, 5, 6, 8, 8, 9, 9, 10, 10, 11, 11, 14, 15, 15, 16, 24, 24, 24, 24, 27, 27, 28a; 3:5, 6, 9, 10, 14, 15, 17, 24, 24, 24; 4:2, 3, 3, 4, 4, 9a, 12, 12, 13, 13, 15, 15, 16b, 16c, 16d, 17, 17, 18, 18; 5:7, 8, 10, 11, 19, 20, 20	3	5:2, 6, 6
2 Jn.	8	1:1, 2, 3, 4, 6, 7, 9, 9		
3 Jn.	3	1:1, 3, 4		
Jd.	5	1:10, 12, 18, 20, 21	1	1:1
Rev.	111	1:4, 5, 9, 9, 9, 10a, 11, 13, 15, 16, 16; 2:1, 1, 7, 12, 13a, 18, 24; 3:1, 4, 4, 5, 7, 12, 21, 21; 4:1, 2, 2, 4, 6; 5:3, 6, 6, 13a, 13c; 6:5, 6; 7:9, 14, 15; 8:1, 9; 9:6, 10, 11, 17, 19a, 19b; 10:2, 7, 8, 9, 10; 11:6, 12, 13b, 15, 19, 19; 12:1, 3, 7, 8, 10, 12: 13:16, 8; 14:5, 6, 13, 14, 17; 15:1, 1, 5; 16:3: 17:3, 4; 18:6, 7, 8a. 10. 19b, 22, 22, 22, 23a, 23b, 24; 19: 1, 11, 14, 17, 17; 20:6, 8, 12, 13, 13, 15; 21:8, 10, 14, 23, 24, 27; 22:2, 3, 18, 19	4	5:9; 9:20; 10:6a; 18:23c
Total	1874		141	

1722. ἐν, en (continued)

Book	Oc.	with	Oc.	among	Oc.	at	Oc.	on	Oc.	through	Oc.	to
Mt.	10	3:11, 11; 7:2, 2; 20:15; 22:37, 37, 37; 25:16; 26:52	12	2:6; 4:23b; 9:35b; 11:11a; 16:7, 8; 20:26, 26, 27; 21:38; 26:5b; 27:56	9	8:6; 11:22, 25; 12:1; 13:49; 14:1; 18:1a; 23:6a; 24:41	3	22:40; 24:20; 26:5a	1	9:34		
Mk.	7	1:8, 8, 23b; 4:24, 30; 5:2; 9:1	5	5:3; 6:4b; 10:43, 43; 15:40	2	6:3; 12:39b	4	2:23, 24; 14:2; 16:5				
Lk.	10	1:51; 3:16; 4:32, 36; 8:15c; 11:20; 14:31; 21:25b, 34; 22:49	16	1:1, 25b, 28, 42; 2:44b; 7:16, 28; 8:7; 9:46, 48; 10:3; 16:15; 22:24, 26, 27, 55b	12	4:18; 9:31b; 10:14; 12:46b; 13:1; 14:14; 19:5; 20:10, 46d; 23:7, 7, 12b	17	1:59; 4:16, 31; 5:17; 6:1, 2, 6, 7; 8:15a, 22, 32; 9:37; 12:51; 13:7, 10b; 14:5; 20:1a	3	10:17; 11:15, 18	1	1:17b
Jn.	4	1:26, 31, 33, 33	7	1:14; 7:12, 43; 9:16; 10:19; 11:54; 15:24	16	2:23b; 4:21b, 45, 45, 46, 53a; 5:2; 6:39; 7:11; 10:22; 11:24b; 12:20; 14:20a; 16:26a; 18:39; 21:20	7	5:9, 16; 7:22, 23, 23; 13:23; 19:31	4	17:11c, 17, 19; 20:31	1	13:35b
Ac.	6	1:5; 2:29, 46b; 5:23; 11:16, 26a	21	4:12a, 34; 5:12; 6:8; 12:18; 13:26; 15:7, 12, 22; 17:34; 18:11; 20:25, 32; 21:19, 34; 24:21; 25:5a, 6; 26:4a, 18; 28:29	30	1:6; 2:5; 7:13, 29a; 8:1, 1, 14; 9:10a, 13, 19, 22, 27b, 28, 36; 11:15b; 13:1, 5a, 27; 14:8; 16:2, 4; 17:13, 16a; 19:1b; 20:5, 15; 21:11; 25:4a, 24; 26:4b			1	4:2	2	12:11; 24:11
Ro.	12	1:4, 9a, 12a, 27b; 9:22; 10:9a; 12:8b, 8c, 8d, 21; 15:32; 16:16	10	1:5, 6, 13, 13; 2:24; 8:29; 11:17; 12:3; 15:9; 16:7a	6	1:15; 3:26; 8:34; 11:5; 15:26; 16:1	3	12:7, 7, 8a	8	1:24a; 3:7, 25b; 6:11, 23; 15:13c, 17, 19a		
1 Co.	10	1:17; 2:4a; 4:21a; 5:8, 8, 8; 10:5a; 14:21b; 16:14, 20	15	1:10a, 11; 2:2, 6; 3:3, 18a; 5:1, 1; 6:5, 7; 11:18b, 19, 19, 30; 15:12	7	1:2; 11:34; 14:35a; 15:23b, 32, 52c; 16:8					1	7:15b
2 Co.	3	1:12b; 7:8; 13:12	4	1:19a; 10:1; 11:26d; 12:12a	2	1:1a; 8:14	3	4:8; 7:5; 8:1	1	11:3	2	4:3; 8:7b
Gal.			4	1:16b; 2:2; 3:1, 5					2	3:14; 5:10		
Eph.	8	1:3a; 3:12b; 4:19; 5:18b; 6:2, 14, 15, 18c	3	2:3a; 3:8; 5:3	4	1:1a, 20b; 2:12a; 3:13			2	2:7c, 22b		
Phl.	1	1:20b	1	2:15b	2	1:1b; 2:10			2	4:7, 13		
Col.	7	1:11; 2:4, 7d; 3:16c, 22a; 4:2b, 6	1	1:27a	2	1:2b; 2:1a	1	3:1			1	1:23
1 Th.	7	2:2c, 17; 4:16a, 16b, 16c, 18; 5:26	4	1:5e; 2:7; 5:12a, 13b	4	2:2a, 19; 3:1, 13b						
2 Th.	4	1:11; 2:9, 10a; 3:8	2	3:7, 11					2	2:13, 16		
1 Ti.	3	2:9b, 11b; 5:2			1	1:3					2	4:15, 15
2 Ti.	2	1:3a; 4:2			9	1:18b; 3:11, 11, 11; 4:8, 13, 16, 20, 20						
Tit.									1	1:3		
Phe.												
Heb.	3	9:22, 25; 11:37a			1	12:2	4	1:3, 3; 8:1a; 10:12	1	13:20		
Jas.	3	1:21; 2:1; 3:13b	6	1:26; 3:6, 13a; 4:1a; 5:13, 14a								
1 Pt.	4	1:12; 2:18; 3:2; 5:14a	3	2:12a; 5:1, 2	3	1:7, 13; 5:13	2	3:22; 4:16	2	1:2, 6b		
2 Pt.	2	2:13b, 16	3	2:1, 1, 8					6	1:1, 2, 4b; 2:3, 18a, 20	7	1:5, 5, 6, 6, 6, 7, 7
1 Jn.					1	2:28b					1	4:16a
2 Jn.												
3 Jn.												
Jd.	3	1:14, 23, 24										
Rev.	25	2:16, 23, 27; 6:8, 8, 8; 9:19c; 12:5; 13:10, 10; 14:2, 7, 9, 10b, 15; 16:8; 17:16; 18:8b, 16; 19:2, 15, 15, 20, 20, 21					2	1:10b; 5:13b	1	8:13		
Total	134		117		111		46		37		18	

1722. ἐν, en (continued)

Book	Oc.	within	Oc.	into	Oc.	of	Oc.	unto	Oc.	for	Oc.	through-out	Oc.	upon	Oc.	because of	Oc.	toward
Mt.	3	3:9; 9:3, 21					1	17:12	1	6:7			1	12:2	2	26:31a, 33		
Mk.	1	2:8a	1	1:16											1	14:27a		
Lk.	8	3:8; 7:39, 49; 12:17; 16:3; 18:4; 19:44a; 24:32a	2	5:16; 23:42	1	1:61			1	1:44b	3	1:65; 7:17, 17	1	21:23c			1	2:14b
Jn.			2	3:35; 5:4														
Ac.			1	7:45	1	26:20							1	20:7				
Ro.	1	8:23	2	1:23, 25	3	2:17, 23; 11:2	1	5:21			2	1:8; 9:17b					1	15:5
1 Co.							2	9:15; 14:11										
2 Co.			1	8:16	2	2:12; 10:15a	1	5:19b										
Gal.			1	1:6	1	4:20												
Eph.					1	4:1												
Phl.									1	1:26b								
Col.																		
1 Th.							2	4:7; 5:23										
2 Th.																		
1 Ti.			1	3:16e			1	3:16c	1	5:10								
2 Ti.																		
Tit.					1	3:5												
Phe.																		
Heb.																		
Jas.					1	5:19			1	5:3			1	4:3				
1 Pt.									1	4:14								
2 Pt.					1	2:12a												
1 Jn.																	1	4:9b
2 Jn.																		
3 Jn.																		
Jd.																		
Rev.			1	14:10a														
Total	13		12		12		8		6		5		4		3		3	

1722. ἐν, en (continued)

	(with 3488 and the infinitive)								(with 3639)					
Book	Oc.	as	Oc.	when	Oc.	while	Oc.	that	Oc.	wherein	Oc.	whereby	Oc.	Misc.
Mt.			2	13:4; 27:12	1	13:25			2	11:20; 25:13				
Mk.	2	2:15a; 4:4											1	2:19
Lk.	18	2:43a; 5:1; 8:5, 42; 9: 18, 29, 33, 34; 10:38; 11:1a, 27, 37; 14:1; 17: 11, 14; 18:35; 24:4a, 30	8	2:27b; 3:21; 5:12a; 8:40; 9:36a, 51; 10: 35; 19:15	4	1:8a; 2:6; 24:15, 51	1	1:21a			1	1:78	2	5:34; 22:7
Jn.									1	19:41c			2	4:52; 5:7
Ac.	2	9:3; 11:15a	1	2:1	1	19:1a			2	2:8; 10:12	2	4:12c; 11:14	6	4:31; 7:33; 11:11; 15:36; 24:18a; 26: 12
Ro.			1	3:4b					3	2:1; 5:2; 7:6a	2	8:15; 14:21		
1 Co.									2	7:24; 15:1				
2 Co.									1	11:12			1	11:21a
Gal.			1	4:18b										
Eph.									3	1:6a; 2:2a; 5:18a	1	4:30	1	6:16
Phl.														
Col.									1	2:12b				
1 Th.														
2 Th.														
1 Ti.														
2 Ti.									1	2:9				
Tit.														
Phe.														
Heb.					1	3:15a			3	6:17; 9:2, 4			2	10:29; 13:9
Jas.														
1 Pt.									2	1:6a; 4:4			2	2:12b; 3:16a
2 Pt.									1	3:13				
1 Jn.														
2 Jn.														
3 Jn.														
Jd.														
Rev.									2	2:13b; 18:19a				
Total	22		13		7		1		24		6		17	

Miscellaneous with 3639: Mk. 2:19; Lk. 5:34, while; Lk. 22:7; Jn. 4:52, when; Jn. 5:7, while; Ac. 4:31; 7:33; 11:11; 15:36, where; Ac. 24:18a; 26:12, whereupon; 2 Co. 11:21a (with 302), whereinsoever; Eph. 6:16; Heb. 10:29, wherewith; Heb. 13:9, therein; 1 Pt. 2:12b; 3:16a, whereas.

1722. εν, en (continued)

	(with 846)										(with 5001)				(with 1064 and 2192)			
Book	Oc.	therein (with 846e)	Oc.	therein (with 846o)	Oc.	thereon (with 846e)	Oc.	there (with 846e)	Oc.	Misc.	Oc.	where-with	Oc.	by what means	Oc.	be with child	Oc.	with child
Mt.					1	21:19					1	5:13			2	1:23; 24:19a	1	1:18
Mk.					1	11:13					1	9:50a			1	13:17a		
Lk.	1	10:9	1	19:45	1	13:6b	1	24:18b			1	14:34			1	21:23a		
Jn.																		
Ac.	1	1:20b	1	17:24a			2	9:38; 20:22	1	14:15			1	4:9				
Ro.	1	6:2	1	1:17														
1 Co.																		
2 Co.																		
Gal.																		
Eph.			1	6:20b					1	2:16b								
Phl.																		
Col.	1	2:7c																
1 Th.																	1	5:3
2 Th.																		
1 Ti.																		
2 Ti.																		
Tit.																		
Phe.																		
Heb.																		
Jas.									2	3:9, 9								
1 Pt.									1	2:2								
2 Pt.	1	3:10c																
1 Jn.																		
2 Jn.																		
3 Jn.																		
Jd.																		
Rev.	5	1:3; 10:6c, 6d; 13:12; 21:22	2	10:6b; 11:1											1	12:2		
Total	10		6		3		3		5		3		1		5		2	

Miscellaneous with 846: Ac. 14:15, therein; Eph. 2:16b, thereby; Jas. 3:9, 9, therewith; 1 Pt. 2:2, thereby.

Miscellaneous: Mt. 7:6, under; Mt. 14:6 (with 3219 and 3488), before them; Mk. 5:25 (with 5507), which had; Mk. 9:50c (with 240), one with another; Lk. 2:36 (with 4160 and 2250), be of age; Lk. 2:49, about; Lk. 7:25b (with 2441 and 1741), gorgeously apparalled; Lk. 8:1 (with 2517 and 3488), afterward; Lk. 8:43 (with 5507), having; Lk. 18:8 (with 4934), speedily; Lk. 21:36 (with 3856 and 2540), always; Ac. 5:27, before; Ac. 17:23 (with 3639), with;

1722. ἐν, en (continued)

Book	Oc.	shortly (with 4934)	Oc.	openly (with 5218)	Oc.	when	Oc.	openly (with 3854)	Oc.	quickly (with 4934)	Oc.	Not Tr.	Oc.	Misc.	Total
Mt.			3	6:4c, 6c, 18c							6	10:32a, 32b; 13:1; 22:23; 26:31b, 34	2	7:6; 14:6	301
Mk.											3	1:15; 4:35; 14:27b	2	5:25; 9:50c	142
Lk.											9	2:44c; 7:11; 10:31; 12:8, 8; 13:31; 20:19; 23:12a; 24:13	7	2:36, 49; 7:25b; 8:1, 43; 18:8; 21:36	369
Jn.							1	7:4b			2	5:5; 21:3			219
Ac.	1	25:4b			1	13:17a			2	12:7b; 22:18	9	1:21, 21; 7:14, 44a; 8:6; 13:15; 16:33; 20:26; 27:7	7	5:27; 17:23; 20:28; 26:7, 28, 29a, 29b	281
Ro.	1	16:20									5	1:12b; 2:28b; 4:11, 12; 15:6	6	1:24b; 2:5, 28a, 29a; 3:19; 13:9b	173
1 Co.											4	2:13b; 11:23; 14:21c; 15:3	1	13:12	169
2 Co.											4	3:7a, 7c, 8, 11	3	11:6a, 17a, 21b	165
Gal.															44
Eph.											1	4:14b	4	4:32; 6:18a, 19a, 19b	126
Phl.													1	4:12a	65
Col.							1	2:15a			1	3:17b	1	1:29b	89
1 Th.											2	2:5, 5	1	2:6	53
2 Th.					1	1:7									27
1 Ti.											1	2:8			47
2 Ti.															37
Tit.											1	1:6			13
Phe.															10
Heb.											2	4:4; 11:37c	1	4:11	68
Jas.											2	1:1, 4			38
1 Pt.					1	4:13					1	4:12			51
2 Pt.													2	2:7; 3:1b	43
1 Jn.															71
2 Jn.															8
3 Jn.															3
Jd.															9
Rev.	2	1:1; 22:6									3	2:14; 11:13a; 13:3	1	18:2	160
Total	4		3		3		2		2		56		39		2781

Ac. 20:28, over; Ac. 26:7 (with 1616), instantly; Ac. 26:28, 29a (with 3541), almost; Ac. 26:29b (with 4083), altogether; Ro. 1:24b, between; Ro. 2:5, against; Ro. 2:28a (with 5218), outwardly; Ro. 2:29a (with 2927), inwardly; Ro. 3:19, under; Ro. 13:9b (with 3488), namely; 1 Co. 13:12 (with 135), darkly; 2 Co. 11:6a (with 3856), throughly; 2 Co. 11:17a (with 877); 2 Co. 11:21b (with 877), foolishly; Eph. 4:32, for . . . sake; Eph. 6:18a (with 3856 and 2540), always; Eph. 6:19a (with 457), that (one) may open; Eph. 6:19b (with 3854), boldly; Phl. 4:12a (with 3856), every where; Col. 1:29b (with 1411), mightily; 1 Th. 2:6 (with 922), burdensome; Heb. 4:11, after; 2 Pt. 2:7 (with 766), filthy; 2 Pt. 3:1b, by way of; Rev. 18:2 (with 2479), mightily.

1723. ἐναγκαλίζομαι, enangkalid'zomai

Book	Oc.	take in (one's) arms	Oc.	take up in (one's) arms	Total
Mk.	1	9:36	1	10:16	2

1724. ἐνάλιος, enal'ios

Book	things in the sea	Total
Jas.	3:7	1

1725. ἔναντι, en'anti

Book	before	Total
Lk.	1:8	1

1726. ἐναντίον, enanti'on

Book	Oc.	before	Oc.	in the sight of	Total
Mk.	1	2:12			1
Lk.	2	20:26; 24:19			2
Ac.	1	8:32	1	7:10	2
Total	4		1		5

1727. ἐναντίος, enanti'os

Book	Oc.	contrary	Oc.	against	Total
Mt.	1	14:24			1
Mk.	1	6:48	1	15:39	2
Ac.	2	26:9; 27:4	1	28:17	3
1 Th.	1	2:15			1
Tit.	1	2:8			1
Total	6		2		8

1728. ἐνάρχομαι, enar'chomai

Book	begin	Total
Gal.	3:3	1
Phl.	1:6	1
Total		2

1729. ἐνδεής, endeēs'

Book	lack	Total
Ac.	4:34	1

1730. ἔνδειγμα, en'deigma

Book	manifest token	Total
2 Th.	1:5	1

1731. ἐνδείκνυμι, endeik'numi

Book	Oc.	shew	Oc.	shew forth	Oc.	do	Total
Ro.	3	2:15; 9:17, 22					3
2 Co.	1	8:24					1
Eph.	1	2:7					1
1 Ti.			1	1:16			1
2 Ti.					1	4:14	1
Tit.	2	2:10; 3:2					2
Heb.	2	6:10, 11					2
Total	9		1		1		11

1732. ἔνδειξις, en'deixis

Book	Oc.	to declare (with 1519)	Oc.	to declare (with 4214)	Oc.	proof	Oc.	evident token	Total
Ro.	1	3:25	1	3:26					2
2 Co.					1	8:24			1
Phl.							1	1:28	1
Total	1		1		1		1		4

1733. ἕνδεκα, hen'deka

Book	eleven	Total
Mt.	28:16	1
Mk.	16:14	1
Lk.	24:9, 33	2
Ac.	1:26; 2:14	2
Total		6

1734. ἑνδέκατος, hendek'atos

Book	eleventh	Total
Mt.	20:6, 9	2
Rev.	21:20	1
Total		3

1735. ἐνδέχεται, endech'etai

Book	it can be	Total
Lk.	13:33	1

1736. ἐνδημέω, endēme'ō

Book	Oc.	be at home	Oc.	be present	Oc.	present	Total
2 Co.	1	5:6	1	5:8	1	5:9	3

1737. ἐνδιδύσκω, endidus'kō

Book	Oc.	wear	Oc.	clothe in	Total
Lk.	1	8:27	1	16:19	2

1738. ἔνδικος, en'dikos

Book	just	Total
Ro.	3:8	1
Heb.	2:2	1
Total		2

1739. ἐνδόμησις, endom'ēsis

Book	building	Total
Rev.	21:18	1

1740. ἐνδοξάζω, endoxad'zō

Book	glorify	Total
2 Th.	1:10, 12	2

1741. ἔνδοξος, en'doxos

Book	Oc.	glorious	Oc.	gorgeously	Oc.	honourable	Total
Lk.	1	13:17	1	7:25			2
1 Co.					1	4:10	1
Eph.	1	5:27					1
Total	2		1		1		4

1742. ἔνδυμα, en'duma

Book	Oc.	raiment	Oc.	garment	Oc.	clothing	Total
Mt.	4	3:4; 6:25, 28; 28:3	2	22:11, 12	1	7:15	7
Lk.	1	12:23					1
Total	5		2		1		8

1743. ἐνδυναμόω, endunamo'ō

Book	Oc.	be strong	Oc.	strengthen	Oc.	increase in strength	Oc.	enable	Oc.	be made strong	Total
Ac.					1	9:22					1
Ro.	1	4:20									1
Eph.	1	6:10									1
Phl.			1	4:13							1
1 Ti.							1	1:12			1
2 Ti.	1	2:1	1	4:17							2
Heb.									1	11:34	1
Total	3		2		1		1		1		8

1744. ἐνδύνω, endu'nō

Book	creep	Total
2 Ti.	3:6	1

1745. ἔνδυσις, en'dusis

Book	put on	Total
1 Pt.	3:3	1

1746. ἐνδύω, endu'ō

Book	Oc.	put on	Oc.	clothed with	Oc.	clothed in	Oc.	have on	Oc.	clothe with	Oc.	be endued with	Oc.	arrayed in	Oc.	be clothed	Total
Mt.	2	6:25; 27:31					1	22:11									3
Mk.	2	6:9; 15:20	1	1:6					1	15:17							4
Lk.	2	12:22; 15:22									1	24:49					3
Ac.													1	12:21			1
Ro.	2	13:12, 14															2
1 Co.	4	15:53, 53, 54, 54															4
2 Co.															1	5:3	1
Gal.	1	3:27															1
Eph.	2	4:24; 6:11					1	6:14									3
Col.	2	3:10, 12															2
1 Th.	1	5:8															1
Rev.			1	1:13	2	15:6; 19:14											3
Total	18		2		2		2		1		1		1		1		28

1747. ἐνέδρα, ened'ra

Book	laying wait (with 4060)	Total
Ac.	25:3	1

1748. ἐνεδρεύω, enedreu'ō

Book	Oc.	lie in wait for	Oc.	lay wait for	Total
Lk.			1	11:54	1
Ac.	1	23:21			1
Total	1		1		2

1749. ἔνεδρον, en'edron

Book	lying in wait	Total
Ac.	23:16	1

1750. ἐνειλέω, eneile'ō

Book	wrap in	Total
Mk.	15:46	1

1751. ἔνειμι, en'eimi

Book	such things as (one) has (with 3488)	Total
Lk.	11:41	1

1752. ἕνεκα, ἕνεκεν, εἵνεκεν, hen′eka, hen′eken, hei′neken

Book	Oc.	for . . . sake	Oc.	for . . . cause	Oc.	for	Oc.	because (with 3639)	Oc.	wherefore (with 5001)	Oc.	by reason of	Oc.	that . . . might (with infinitive)	Total
Mt.	6	5:10, 11; 10:18, 39; 16:25; 19:29	1	19:5											7
Mk.	3	8:35; 10:29; 13:9	1	10:7											4
Lk.	4	6:22; 9:24; 18: 29; 21:12					1	4:18							5
Ac.			1	26:21	1	28:20			1	19:32					3
Ro.	1	8:36			1	14:20									2
2 Co.			2	7:12a, 12b							1	3:10	1	7:12c	4
Total	14		5		2		1		1		1		1		25

1753. ἐνέργεια, energ′eia

Book	Oc.	working	Oc.	effectual working	Oc.	operation	Oc.	strong	Total
Eph.	1	1:19	2	3:7; 4:16					3
Phl.	1	3:21							1
Col.	1	1:29			1	2:12			2
2 Th.	1	2:9					1	2:11	2
Total	4		2		1		1		8

1754. ἐνεργέω, energe′ō

Book	Oc.	work	Oc.	shew forth (one's) self	Oc.	wrought	Oc.	be effec-tual	Oc.	effec-tually work	Oc.	effec-tual fervent	Oc.	work effec-tually in	Oc.	be mighty in	Oc.	to do	Total
Mt.			1	14:2															1
Mk.			1	6:14															1
Ro.	1	7:5																	1
1 Co.	2	12:6, 11																	2
2 Co.	1	4:12					1	1:6											2
Gal.	2	3:5; 5:6											1	2:8a	1	2:8b			4
Eph.	3	1:11; 2: 2; 3:20			1	1:20													4
Phl.	1	2:13a															1	2:13b	2
Col.	1	1:29																	1
1 Th.									1	2:13									1
2 Th.	1	2:7																	1
Jas.											1	5:16							1
Total	12		2		1		1		1		1		1		1		1		21

1755. ἐνέργημα, energ′ẹma

Book	Oc.	operation	Oc.	working	Total
1 Co.	1	12:6	1	12:10	2

1756. ἐνεργής, energẹs′

Book	Oc.	effectual	Oc.	powerful	Total
1 Co.	1	16:9			1
Phe.	1	1:6			1
Heb.			1	4:12	1
Total	2		1		3

1757. ἐνευλογέω, eneuloge′ō

Book	bless	Total
Ac.	3:25	1
Gal.	3:8	1
Total		2

1758. ἐνέχω, enech′ō

Book	Oc.	have a quarrel against	Oc.	urge	Oc.	entangle with	Total
Mk.	1	6:19					1
Lk.			1	11:53			1
Gal.					1	5:1	1
Total	1		1		1		3

1759. ἐνθάδε, enthad′e

Book	Oc.	hither	Oc.	here	Oc.	there	Total
Lk.			1	24:41			1
Jn.	2	4:15, 16					2
Ac.	2	17:6; 25:17	2	16:28; 25:24	1	10:18	5
Total	4		3		1		8

1760. ἐνθυμέομαι, enthume′omai

Book	think	Total
Mt.	1:20; 9:4	2
Ac.	10:19	1
Total		3

1761. ἐνθύμησις, enthu′mẹsis

Book	Oc.	thought	Oc.	device	Total
Mt.	2	9:4; 12:25			2
Ac.			1	17:29	1
Heb.	1	4:12			1
Total	3		1		4

1762. ἔνι, en′i

Book	Oc.	there is	Oc.	is	Total
Gal.	3	3:28, 28, 28			3
Col.	1	3:11			1
Jas.			1	1:17	1
Total	4		1		5

1763. ἐνιαυτός, eniautos′

Book	year	Total
Lk.	4:19	1
Jn.	11:49, 51; 18:13	3
Ac.	11:26; 18:11	2
Gal.	4:10	1
Heb.	9:7, 25; 10:1, 3	4
Jas.	4:13; 5:17	2
Rev.	9:15	1
Total		14

1764. ἐνίστημι, enis′tẹmi

Book	Oc.	present	Oc.	things present	Oc.	be at hand	Oc.	come	Total
Ro.			1	8:38					1
1 Co.	1	7:26	1	3:22					2
Gal.	1	1:4							1
2 Th.					1	2:2			1
2 Ti.							1	3:1	1
Heb.	1	9:9							1
Total	3		2		1		1		7

1765. ἐνισχύω, enischu′ō

Book	strengthen	Total
Lk.	22:43	1
Ac.	9:19	1
Total		2

1766. ἔνατος, en′natos

Book	ninth	Total
Mt.	20:5; 27:45, 46	3
Mk.	15:33, 34	2
Lk.	23:44	1
Ac.	3:1; 10:3, 30	3
Rev.	21:20	1
Total		10

1767. ἐννέα, enne′a

Book	nine	Total
Lk.	17:17	1

1768. ἐννενηκονταεννέα ennenẹkontaenne′a

Book	ninety nine	Total
Mt.	18:12, 13	2
Lk.	15:4, 7	2
Total		4

1769. ἐννεός, enneos′

Book	speechless	Total
Ac.	9:7	1

1770. ἐννεύω, enneu′ō

Book	make signs	Total
Lk.	1:62	1

1771. ἔννοια, en'noia

Book	Oc.	intent	Oc.	mind	Total
Heb.	1	4:12			1
1 Pt.			1	4:1	1
Total	1		1		2

1772. ἔννομος, en'nomos

Book	Oc.	lawful	Oc.	under law	Total
Ac.	1	19:39			1
1 Co.			1	9:21	1
Total	1		1		2

1773. ἔννυχον, en'nuchon

Book	a great while before day (with 3029)	Total
Mk.	1:35	1

1774. ἐνοικέω, enoike'ō

Book	dwell in	Total
Ro.	8:11	1
2 Co.	6:16	1
Col.	3:16	1
2 Ti.	1:5, 14	2
Total		5

1775. ἑνότης, henot'ēs

Book	unity	Total
Eph.	4:3, 13	2

1776. ἐνοχλέω, enochle'ō

Book	trouble	Total
Heb.	12:15	1

1777. ἔνοχος, en'ochos

Book	Oc.	in danger of	Oc.	guilty of	Oc.	subject to	Total
Mt.	4	5:21, 22, 22, 22	1	26:66			5
Mk.	1	3:29	1	14:64			2
1 Co.			1	11:27			1
Heb.					1	2:15	1
Jas.			1	2:10			1
Total	5		4		1		10

1778. ἔνταλμα, en'talma

Book	commandment	Total
Mt.	15:9	1
Mk.	7:7	1
Col.	2:22	1
Total		3

1779. ἐνταφιάζω, entaphiad'zō

Book	Oc.	burial	Oc.	bury	Total
Mt.	1	26:12			1
Jn.			1	19:40	1
Total	1		1		2

1780. ἐνταφιασμός entaphiasmos'

Book	burying	Total
Mk.	14:8	1
Jn.	12:7	1
Total		2

1781. ἐντέλλομαι, entel'lomai

Book	Oc.	command	Oc.	give commandment	Oc.	give charge	Oc.	enjoin	Oc.	charge	Total
Mt.	3	15:4; 19:7; 28:20			1	4:6			1	17:9	5
Mk.	3	10:3; 11:6; 13:34									3
Lk.					1	4:10					1
Jn.	3	8:5; 15:14, 17	1	14:31							4
Ac.	1	13:47	1	1:2							2
Heb.			1	11:22			1	9:20			2
Total	10		3		2		1		1		17

1782. ἐντεῦθεν, enteu'then

Book	Oc.	hence	Oc.	on either side (with 2532)	Oc.	from hence	Total
Mt.	1	17:20					1
Lk.	1	13:31			2	4:9; 16:26	3
Jn.	3	2:16; 7:3; 14:31	2	19:18, 18	1	18:36	6
Jas.	1	4:1					1
Rev.			2	22:2, 2			2
Total	6		4		3		13

1783. ἔντευξις, ent'euxis

Book	Oc.	intercession	Oc.	prayer	Total
1 Ti.	1	2:1	1	4:5	2

1784. ἔντιμος, en'timos

Book	Oc.	precious	Oc.	dear	Oc.	more honour-able	Oc.	in reputa-tion	Total
Lk.			1	7:2	1	14:8			2
Phl.							1	2:29	1
1 Pt.	2	2:4, 6							2
Total	2		1		1		1		5

1785. ἐντολή, entolē'

Book	Oc.	commandment	Oc.	precept	Total
Mt.	7	5:19; 15:3, 6; 19:17; 22:36, 38, 40			7
Mk.	7	7:8, 9; 10:19; 12:28, 29, 30, 31	1	10:5	8
Lk.	4	1:6; 15:29; 18:20; 23:56			4
Jn.	10	10:18; 11:57; 12:49, 50; 13:34; 14:15, 21; 15:10, 10, 12			10
Ac.	1	17:15			1
Ro.	7	7:8, 9, 10, 11, 12, 13; 13:9			7
1 Co.	2	7:19; 14:37			2
Eph.	2	2:15; 6:2			2
Col.	1	4:10			1
1 Ti.	1	6:14			1
Tit.	1	1:14			1
Heb.	3	7:5, 16, 18	1	9:19	4
2 Pt.	2	2:21; 3:2			2
1 Jn.	14	2:3, 4, 7, 7, 7, 8; 3:22, 23, 23, 24; 4:21; 5:2, 3, 3			14
2 Jn.	4	1:4, 5, 6, 6			4
Rev.	3	12:17; 14:12; 22:14			3
Total	69		2		71

1786. ἐντόπιος, entop'ios

Book	of that place	Total
Ac.	21:12	1

1787. ἐντός, entos'

Book	within	Total
Mt.	23:26	1
Lk.	17:21	1
Total		2

1788. ἐντρέπω, entrep'ō

Book	Oc.	reverence	Oc.	regard	Oc.	be ashamed	Oc.	shame	Total
Mt.	1	21:37							1
Mk.	1	12:6							1
Lk.	1	20:13	2	18:2, 4					3
1 Co.							1	4:14	1
2 Th.					1	3:14			1
Tit.					1	2:8			1
Heb.	1	12:9							1
Total	4		2		2		1		9

1789. ἐντρέφω, entreph'ō

Book	nourish up in	Total
1 Ti.	4:6	1

1792. ἐντρυφάω, entrupha'ō

Book	sport (one's) self	Total
2 Pt.	2:13	1

1790. ἔντρομος, en'tromos

Book	Oc.	tremble (with 1096)	Oc.	trembling	Oc.	quake	Total
Ac.	1	7:32	1	16:29			2
Heb.					1	12:21	1
Total	1		1		1		3

1791. ἐντροπή, entropē'

Book	shame	Total
1 Co.	6:5; 15:34	2

1795. ἐντυπόω, entupo'ō

Book	engrave	Total
2 Co.	3:7	1

1793. ἐντυγχάνω, entungchan'ō

Book	Oc.	make intercession	Oc.	deal	Total
Ac.			1	25:24	1
Ro.	3	8:27, 34; 11:2			3
Heb.	1	7:25			1
Total	4		1		5

1794. ἐντυλίσσω, entulis'sō

Book	Oc.	wrap in	Oc.	wrap together	Total
Mt.	1	27:59			1
Lk.	1	23:53			1
Jn.			1	20:7	1
Total	2		1		3

1796. ἐνυβρίζω, enubrid'zō

Book	do despite unto	Total
Heb.	10:29	1

1797. ἐνυπνιάζομαι, enupniad'zomai

Book	Oc.	dream	Oc.	filthy dreamer	Total
Ac.	1	2:17			1
Jd.			1	1:8	1
Total	1		1		2

1798. ἐνύπνιον, enup'nion

Book	dream	Total
Ac.	2:17	1

1799. ἐνώπιον, enō'pion

Book	Oc.	before	Oc.	in the sight of	Oc.	in the presence of	Oc.	in (one's) sight	Oc.	in (one's) presence	Oc.	to	Oc.	Not Tr.	Total
Lk.	13	1:6, 17, 75; 5:18, 25; 8: 47; 12:6, 9, 9; 15:18; 16: 15a; 23:14; 24:43	2	1:15; 16:15b	3	1:19; 14:10; 15: 10	1	15:21	1	13:26	1	24:11	1	4:7	22
Jn.					1	20:30									1
Ac.	10	2:25; 4:10; 6:6; 7:46; 9: 15; 10:4, 30, 33; 19:9, 19	3	4:19; 8:21; 10:31	1	27:35							1	6:5	15
Ro.	1	14:22	1	12:17			1	3:20							3
1 Co.									1	1:29					1
2 Co.			4	4:2; 7:12; 8: 21, 21											4
Gal.	1	1:20													1
1 Ti.	4	5:4, 20, 21; 6:12	2	2:3; 6:13											6
2 Ti.	2	2:14; 4:1													2
Heb.							2	4:13; 13:21							2
Jas.			1	4:10											1
1 Pt.			1	3:4											1
1 Jn.							1	3:22							1
3 Jn.	1	1:6													1
Rev.	32	1:4; 2:14; 3:2, 5, 5, 8, 9; 4:5, 6, 10, 10; 5:8; 7:9, 9, 11, 15; 8:2, 3, 4; 9:13; 11:4, 16; 12:4, 10; 13:12; 14:3, 3, 5; 15:4; 16:19; 19:20; 20:12	2	13:13, 14	2	14:10, 10									36
Total	64		16		7		5		2		1		2		97

1800. Ἐνώς, Enōs'

Book	Enos	Total
Lk.	3:38	1

1801. ἐνωτίζομαι, enōtid'zomai

Book	hearken to	Total
Ac.	2:14	1

1802. Ἐνώχ, Enōch'

Book	Enoch	Total
Lk.	3:37	1
Heb.	11:5	1
Jd.	1:14	1
Total		3

1803. ἕξ, hex

Book	six	Total
Mt.	17:1	1
Mk.	9:2	1
Lk.	4:25; 13:14	2
Jn.	2:6, 20; 12:1	3
Ac.	11:12; 18:11; 27:37	3
Jas.	5:17	1
Rev.	4:8; 13:18	2
Total		13

1804. ἐξαγγέλλω, exanggel'lō

Book	shew forth	Total
1 Pt.	2:9	1

1805. ἐξαγοράζω, exagorad'zō

Book	redeem	Total
Gal.	3:13; 4:5	2
Eph.	5:16	1
Col.	4:5	1
Total		4

1806. ἐξάγω, exag'ō

Book	Oc.	lead out	Oc.	bring out	Oc.	bring forth	Oc.	fetch out	Total
Mk.	2	8:23; 15:20							2
Lk.	1	24:50							1
Jn.	1	10:3							1
Ac.	1	21:38	5	7:36, 40; 12:17; 13: 17; 16:39	1	5:19	1	16:37	8
Heb.	1	8:9							1
Total	6		5		1		1		13

1807. ἐξαιρέω, exaire'ō

Book	Oc.	deliver	Oc.	pluck out	Oc.	rescue	Total
Mt.			2	5:29; 18:9			2
Ac.	4	7:10, 34; 12:11; 26:17			1	23:27	5
Gal.	1	1:4					1
Total	5		2		1		8

1808. ἐξαίρω, exai'rō

Book	Oc.	take away	Oc.	put away	Total
1 Co.	1	5:2	1	5:13	2

1809. ἐξαιτέομαι, exaite'omai

Book	desire	Total
Lk.	22:31	1

1810. ἐξαίφνης, exaiph'nēs

Book	suddenly	Total
Mk.	13:36	1
Lk.	2:13; 9:39	2
Ac.	9:3; 22:6	2
Total		5

1811. ἐξακολουθέω exakolouthe'ō

Book	follow	Total
2 Pt.	1:16; 2:2, 15	3

1812. ἑξακόσιοι, hexakos'ioi

Book	six hundred	Total
Rev.	13:18; 14:20	2

1813. ἐξαλείφω, exalei'phō

Book	Oc.	blot out	Oc.	wipe away	Total
Ac.	1	3:19			1
Col.	1	2:14			1
Rev.	1	3:5	2	7:17; 21:4	3
Total	3		2		5

1814. ἐξάλλομαι, exal'lomai

Book	leap up	Total
Ac.	3:8	1

1815. ἐξανάστασις, exanas'tasis

Book	resurrection	Total
Phl.	3:11	1

1816. ἐξανατέλλω, exanatel'lō

Book	spring up	Total
Mt.	13:5	1
Mk.	4:5	1
Total		2

1817. ἐξανίστημι, exanis'tēmi

Book	Oc.	raise up	Oc.	rise up	Total
Mk.	1	12:19			1
Lk.	1	20:28			1
Ac.			1	15:5	1
Total	2		1		3

1818. ἐξαπατάω, exapata'ō

Book	Oc.	deceive	Oc.	beguile	Total
Ro.	2	7:11; 16:18			2
1 Co.	1	3:18			1
2 Co.			1	11:3	1
2 Th.	1	2:3			1
Total	4		1		5

1819. ἐξάπινα, exap'ina

Book	suddenly	Total
Mk.	9:8	1

1821. ἐξαποστέλλω, exapostel'lō

Book	Oc.	send away	Oc.	send forth	Oc.	send	Oc.	send out	Total
Lk.	3	1:53; 20:10, 11							3
Ac.	1	17:14	2	9:30; 11:22	2	12:11; 22:21	1	7:12	6
Gal.			2	4:4, 6					2
Total	4		4		2		1		11

1820. ἐξαπορέομαι, exapore'omai

Book	Oc.	despair	Oc.	in despair	Total
2 Co.	1	1:8	1	4:8	2

1822. ἐξαρτίζω, exartid'zō

Book	Oc.	accomplish (with 1096)	Oc.	throughly furnish	Total
Ac.	1	21:5			1
2 Ti.			1	3:17	1
Total	1		1		2

1823. ἐξαστράπτω, exastrap'tō

Book	glistering	Total
Lk.	9:29	1

1824. ἐξαύτης, exau'tēs

Book	Oc.	immediately	Oc.	by and by	Oc.	straightway	Oc.	presently	Total
Mk.			1	6:25					1
Ac.	3	10:33; 11:11; 21:32			1	23:30			4
Phl.							1	2:23	1
Total	3		1		1		1		6

1825. ἐξεγείρω, exegei'rō

Book	raise up	Total
Ro.	9:17	1
1 Co.	6:14	1
Total		2

1826. ἔξειμι, ex'eimi

Book	Oc.	depart	Oc.	go out	Oc.	get	Total
Ac.	2	17:15; 20:7	1	13:42	1	27:43	4

1827. ἐξελέγχω, exeleng'chō

Book	convince	Total
Jd.	1:15	1

1828. ἐξέλκω, exel'kō

Book	draw away	Total
Jas.	1:14	1

1829. ἐξέραμα, exer'ama

Book	vomit	Total
2 Pt.	2:22	1

1830. ἐξερευνάω, exereuna'ō

Book	search diligently	Total
1 Pt.	1:10	1

1831. ἐξέρχομαι, exer'chomai

Book	Oc.	go out	Oc.	come	Oc.	depart	Oc.	go	Oc.	go forth	Oc.	come out	Oc.	come forth	Oc.	Misc.	Total
Mt.	15	9:32; 11:7, 8, 9; 12: 14; 18:28; 20:1, 3, 5, 6; 22:10; 24:1; 25:6; 26:30, 71	5	2:6; 8:28; 15: 22; 24:27; 27: 53	3	9:31; 17: 18; 28:8	5	12:43; 13:1; 15: 21; 21: 17; 26:75	4	13:3; 14:14; 24:26; 25:1	6	5:26; 8: 32, 34; 12:44; 25:55; 27:32	2	13:49; 15:18	4	9:26; 10:11, 14; 15: 19	44
Mk.	13	1:35, 45; 3:21; 4:3; 5: 13, 14; 6:1, 12; 7:30; 8:27; 11:11; 14:26; 16:8	8	1:25, 26, 29; 5:2, 8; 6:54; 9:25; 11:12	3	6:10; 7: 31; 9:30	3	5:30; 7: 29; 14: 68	6	2:12, 13; 3: 6; 6: 24; 14: 16; 16: 20	3	6:34; 9 26; 14: 48	3	1:38; 8:11; 9:29	1	1:28	40
Lk.	14	2:1; 4:14; 6:12; 7:24, 25, 26; 8:5, 35a; 10: 10; 11:14; 14:21, 23; 21:37; 22: 62	4	4:35, 35, 41; 8:29	8	4:42; 5:8; 8:35b, 38; 9:4, 6; 10: 35; 12:59	8	6:19; 8: 2, 33, 46; 9:5; 11: 24a; 14: 18; 17: 29	3	5:27; 7: 17; 8: 27	6	1:22; 4: 36; 11: 24b; 15: 28; 22: 39, 52			1	13:31	44
Jn.	7	8:9; 11:31; 13:30, 31; 18:16, 29, 38	2	13:3; 19:5	1	4:43	2	4:30; 8: 59	8	1:43; 12:13; 18:1, 4; 19:4, 17; 20: 3; 21:3	3	16:27; 17:8; 19:34	3	11:44; 16:28, 30	4	8:42; 10:9, 39; 21: 23	30
Ac.	4	12:9, 10; 15:24; 19: 12	4	7:4; 16:18a; 28:3. 15	12	11:25; 12: 17; 14:20; 15:40; 16: 36, 40b; 17:33; 18: 23; 20:1, 11; 21:5, 8	4	16:10, 13, 19, 40a	1	16:3	2	8:7; 16: 18b	1	7:7	5	1:21; 7: 3; 10: 23; 16: 39; 22: 18	33
Ro.							1	10:18									1
1 Co.							1	5:10			1	14:36					2
2 Co.							1	8:17			1	6:17			1	2:13	3
Phl.					1	4:15											1
1 Th.															1	1:8	1
Heb.	2	11:8, 8	2	3:16; 7:5					1	13:13	1	11:15					6
Jas.															1	3:10	1
1 Jn.	2	2:19; 4:1															2
3 Jn.									1	1:7							1
Rev.	3	3:12; 6:4; 20:8	9	9:3; 14:15, 17, 18, 20; 15:6; 16:17; 18:4; 19:5					1	6:2							13
Total	60		34		28		25		25		23		9		18		222

Miscellaneous: Mt. 9:26, go abroad; Mt. 10:11, go thence; Mt. 10:14, depart out; Mt. 15:19, proceed; Mk. 1:28, spread abroad; Lk. 13:31, get out; Jn. 8:42, proceed forth; Jn. 10:9, out: Jn. 10:39, escape; Jn. 21:23, go abroad; Ac. 1:21, out; Ac. 7:3, get; Ac. 10:23, go away; Ac. 16:39, depart out; Ac. 22:18, get; 2 Co. 2:13, go from thence; 1 Th. 1:8, spread abroad; Jas. 3:10, proceed.

1832. ἔξεστι, ex'esti

Book	Oc.	be lawful	Oc.	may	Oc.	let	Total
Mt.	9	12:2, 4, 10, 12; 14:4; 19:3; 20: 15; 22:17; 27:6					9
Mk.	6	2:24, 26; 3:4; 6:18; 10:2; 12: 14					6
Lk.	5	6:2, 4, 9; 14:3; 20:22					5
Jn.	2	5:10; 18:31					2
Ac.	2	16:21; 22:25	2	8:37; 21:37	1	2:29	5
1 Co.	4	6:12, 12; 10:23, 23					4
2 Co.	1	12:4					1
Total	29		2		1		32

1833. ἐξετάζω, exetad'zō

Book	Oc.	search	Oc.	enquire	Oc.	ask	Total
Mt.	1	2:8	1	10:11			2
Jn.					1	21:12	1
Total	1		1		1		3

1834. ἐξηγέομαι, exẹge'omai

Book	Oc.	declare	Oc.	tell	Total
Lk.			1	24:35	1
Jn.	1	1:18			1
Ac.	4	10:8; 15:12, 14; 21:19			4
Total	5		1		6

1835. ἑξήκοντα, hexẹ'konta

Book	Oc.	threescore	Oc.	sixty	Oc.	sixtyfold	Total
Mt.			1	13:23	1	13:8	2
Mk.			2	4:8, 20			2
Lk.	1	24:13					1
1 Ti.	1	5:9					1
Rev.	3	11:3; 12:6; 13:18					3
Total	5		3		1		9

1837. ἐξηχέομαι, exẹche'omai

Book	sound out	Total
1 Th.	1:8	1

1838. ἕξις, hex'is

Book	use	Total
Heb.	5:14	1

1836. ἑξῆς, hexẹs'

Book	Oc.	next	Oc.	next day	Oc.	day after	Oc.	day following	Oc.	morrow	Total
Lk.	1	9:37			1	7:11					2
Ac.			1	27:18			1	21:1	1	25:17	3
Total	1		1		1		1		1		5

1839. ἐξίστημι, exis'tẹmi

Book	Oc.	be amazed	Oc.	be astonished	Oc.	bewitch	Oc.	be beside (one's) self	Oc.	make astonished	Oc.	wonder	Total
Mt.	1	12:23											1
Mk.	2	2:12; 6:51	1	5:42			1	3:21					4
Lk.			2	2:47; 8:56					1	24:22			3
Ac.	3	2:7, 12; 9:21	2	10:45; 12:16	2	8:9, 11					1	8:13	8
2 Co.							1	5:13					1
Total	6		5		2		2		1		1		17

1840. ἐξισχύω, exischu'ō

Book	be able	Total
Eph.	3:18	1

1841. ἔξοδος, ex'odos

Book	Oc.	decease	Oc.	departing	Total
Lk.	1	9:31			1
Heb.			1	11:22	1
2 Pt.	1	1:15			1
Total	2		1		3

1842. ἐξολοθρεύω, exolothreu'ō

Book	destroy	Total
Ac.	3:23	1

1843. ἐξομολογέω, exomologe'ō

Book	Oc.	confess	Oc.	thank	Oc.	promise	Total
Mt.	1	3:6	1	11:25			2
Mk.	1	1:5					1
Lk.			1	10:21	1	22:6	2
Ac.	1	19:18					1
Ro.	2	14:11; 15:9					2
Phl.	1	2:11					1
Jas.	1	5:16					1
Rev.	1	3:5					1
Total	8		2		1		11

1844. ἐξορκίζω, exorkid'zō

Book	adjure	Total
Mt.	26:63	1

1845. ἐξορκιστής, exorkistẹs'

Book	exorcist	Total
Ac.	19:13	1

1846. ἐξορύσσω, exorus'sō

Book	Oc.	break up	Oc.	pluck out	Total
Mk.	1	2:4			1
Gal.			1	4:15	1
Total	1		1		2

1847. ἐξουδενόω, exoudeno'ō

Book	be set at nought	Total
Mk.	9:12	1

1848. ἐξουθενέω, exouthene'ō

Book	Oc.	despise	Oc.	set at nought	Oc.	esteem least	Oc.	contemptible	Total
Lk.	1	18:9	1	23:11					2
Ac.			1	4:11					1
Ro.	1	14:3	1	14:10					2
1 Co.	2	1:28; 16:11			1	6:4			3
2 Co.							1	10:10	1
Gal.	1	4:14							1
1 Th.	1	5:20							1
Total	6		3		1		1		11

1849. ἐξουσία, exousi'a

Book	Oc.	power	Oc.	authority	Oc.	right	Oc.	liberty	Oc.	jurisdiction	Oc.	strength	Total
Mt.	4	9:6, 8; 10:1; 28:18	6	7:29; 8:9; 21:23, 23, 24, 27									10
Mk.	3	2:10; 3:15; 6:7	7	1:22, 27; 11:28, 28, 29, 33; 13:34									10
Lk.	7	4:6, 32; 5:24; 10:19; 12:5, 11; 22:53	8	4:36; 7:8; 9:1; 19:17; 20:2, 2, 8, 20					1	23:7			16
Jn.	7	1:12; 10:18, 18; 17:2; 19:10, 10, 11	1	5:27									8
Ac.	4	1:7; 5:4; 8:19; 26:18	3	9:14; 26:10, 12									7
Ro.	6	9:21; 13:1, 1, 1, 2, 3											6
1 Co.	8	7:37; 9:4, 5, 6, 12, 12, 18; 11: 10	1	15:24			1	8:9					10
2 Co.	1	13:10	1	10:8									2
Eph.	4	1:21; 2:2; 3:10; 6:12											4
Col.	4	1:13, 16; 2:10, 15											4
2 Th.	1	3:9											1
Tit.	1	3:1											1
Heb.					1	13:10							1
1 Pt.			1	3:22									1
Jd.	1	1:25											1
Rev.	18	2:26; 6:8; 9:3, 3, 10, 19; 11:6, 6; 12:10; 13:4, 5, 7, 12; 14:18; 16:9; 17:12; 18:1; 20:6	1	13:2	1	22:14					1	17:13	21
Total	69		29		2		1		1		1		103

1850. ἐξουσιάζω, exousiad'zō

Book	Oc.	have power of	Oc.	exercise authority upon	Oc.	bring under the power	Total
Lk.			1	22:25			1
1 Co.	2	7:4, 4			1	6:12	3
Total	2		1		1		4

1851. ἐξοχή, exochē'

Book	principal (with 2596)	Total
Ac.	25:23	1

1852. ἐξυπνίζω, exupnid'zō

Book	awake out of sleep	Total
Jn.	11:11	1

1853. ἔξυπνος, ex'upnos

Book	awake out of sleep (with 1096)	Total
Ac.	16:27	1

1854. ἔξω, ex'ō

Book	Oc.	without	Oc.	out	Oc.	out of	Oc.	forth	Oc.	outward	Oc.	strange	Oc.	away	Total
Mt.	3	12:46, 47; 26:29	2	5:13; 26:75	2	21:17, 39							1	13:48	8
Mk.	5	1:45; 3:31, 32; 4:11; 11:4	1	14:68	4	5:10; 8:23; 11:19; 12:8									10
Lk.	3	1:10; 8:20; 13:25	5	8:54; 13:28; 14:35; 22:62; 24:50	3	4:29; 13:33; 20:15									11
Jn.	2	18:16; 20:11	4	6:37; 9:34, 35; 12:31			6	11:43; 15:6; 19:4, 4, 5, 13							12
Ac.	1	5:23	1	16:30	6	4:15; 7:58; 14:19; 16:13; 21:5, 30	2	5:34; 9:40			1	26:11			11
1 Co.	2	5:12, 13													2
2 Co.									1	4:16					1
Col.	1	4:5													1
1 Th.	1	4:12													1
Heb.	3	13:11, 12, 13													3
1 Jn.			1	4:18											1
Rev.	2	14:20; 22:15	2	3:12; 11:2											4
Total	23		16		15		8		1		1		1		65

1855. ἔξωθεν, ex'ōthen

Book	Oc.	without	Oc.	outside	Oc.	from without	Oc.	outward	Oc.	outwardly	Total
Mt.			1	23:25			1	23:27	1	23:28	3
Mk.					2	7:15, 18					2
Lk.	1	11:40	1	11:39							2
2 Co.	1	7:5									1
1 Ti.	1	3:7									1
1 Pt.							1	3:3			1
Rev.	1	11:2									1
Total	4		2		2		2		1		11

1856. ἐξωθέω, exōthe'ō

Book	Oc.	drive out	Oc.	thrust in	Total
Ac.	1	7:45	1	27:39	2

1857. ἐξώτερος, exō'teros

Book	outer	Total
Mt.	8:12; 22:13; 25:30	3

1858. ἑορτάζω, heortad'zō

Book	keep the feast	Total
1 Co.	5:8	1

1859. ἑορτή, heortē'

Book	Oc.	feast	Oc.	holy day	Total
Mt.	2	26:5; 27:15			2
Mk.	2	14:2; 15:6			2
Lk.	4	2:41, 42; 22:1; 23:17			4
Jn.	17	2:23; 4:45, 45; 5:1; 6:4; 7:2, 8, 8, 10, 11, 14, 37; 11:56; 12:12, 20; 13:1, 29			17
Ac.	1	18:21			1
Col.			1	2:16	1
Total	26		1		27

1860. ἐπαγγελία, epanggeli'a

Book	Oc.	promise	Oc.	message	Total
Lk.	1	24:29			1
Ac.	8	1:4; 2:33, 39; 7:17; 13:23, 32; 23:21; 26:6			8
Ro.	8	4:13, 14, 16, 20; 9:4, 8, 9; 15:8			8
2 Co.	2	1:20; 7:1			2
Gal.	10	3:14, 16, 17, 18, 18, 21, 22, 29; 4:23, 28			10
Eph.	4	1:13; 2:12; 3:6; 6:2			4
1 Ti.	1	4:8			1
2 Ti.	1	1:1			1
Heb.	14	4:1; 6:12, 15, 17; 7:6; 8:6; 9:15; 10:36; 11:9, 9, 13, 17, 33, 39			14
2 Pt.	2	3:4, 9			2
1 Jn.	1	2:25	1	1:5	2
Total	52		1		53

1861. ἐπαγγέλλω, epanggel'lō

Book	Oc.	promise	Oc.	profess	Oc.	make promise	Total
Mk.	1	14:11					1
Ac.	1	7:5					1
Ro.	1	4:21					1
Gal.					1	3:19	1
1 Ti.			2	2:10; 6:21			2
Tit.	1	1:2					1
Heb.	3	10:23; 11:11; 12:26			1	6:13	4
Jas.	2	1:12; 2:5					2
2 Pt.	1	2:19					1
1 Jn.	1	2:25					1
Total	11		2		2		15

1862. ἐπάγγελμα, epang'gelma

Book	promise	Total
2 Pt.	1:4; 3:13	2

1864. ἐπαγωνίζομαι epagōnid'zomai

Book	earnestly contend for	Total
Jd.	1:3	1

1863. ἐπάγω, epag'ō

Book	Oc.	bring	Oc.	bring upon	Oc.	bring in upon	Total
Ac.	1	5:28					1
2 Pt.			1	2:1	1	2:5	2
Total	1		1		1		3

1865. ἐπαθροίζω, epathroid'zō

Book	gather thick together	Total
Lk.	11:29	1

1866. Ἐπαίνετος, Epai'netos

Book	Epenetus	Total
Ro.	16:5	1

1867. ἐπαινέω, epaine'ō

Book	Oc.	praise	Oc.	laud	Oc.	commend	Total
Lk.					1	16:8	1
Ro.			1	15:11			1
1 Co.	4	11:2, 17, 22, 22					4
Total	4		1		1		6

1868. ἔπαινος, ep'ainos

Book	praise	Total
Ro.	2:29; 13:3	2
1 Co.	4:5	1
2 Co.	8:18	1
Eph.	1:6, 12, 14	3
Phl.	1:11; 4:8	2
1 Pt.	1:7; 2:14	2
Total		11

1869. ἐπαίρω, epai'rō

Book	Oc.	lift up	Oc.	exalt (one's) self	Oc.	take up	Oc.	hoise up	Total
Mt.	1	17:8							1
Lk.	6	6:20; 11:27; 16:23; 18:13; 21:28; 24:50							6
Jn.	4	4:35; 6:5; 13:18; 17:1							4
Ac.	3	2:14; 14:11; 22:22			1	1:9	1	27:40	5
2 Co.			2	10:5; 11:20					2
1 Ti.	1	2:8							1
Total	15		2		1		1		19

1870. ἐπαισχύνομαι epaischu'nomai

Book	be ashamed	Total
Mk.	8:38, 38	2
Lk.	9:26, 26	2
Ro.	1:16; 6:21	2
2 Ti.	1:8, 12, 16	3
Heb.	2:11; 11:16	2
Total		11

1871. ἐπαιτέω, epaite'ō

Book	to beg	Total
Lk.	16:3	1

1872. ἐπακολουθέω, epakolouthe'ō

Book	Oc.	follow	Oc.	follow after	Total
Mk.	1	16:20			1
1 Ti.	1	5:10	1	5:24	2
1 Pt.	1	2:21			1
Total	3		1		4

1873. ἐπακούω, epakou'ō

Book	hear	Total
2 Co.	6:2	1

1874. ἐπακροάομαι epakroa'omai

Book	hear	Total
Ac.	16:25	1

1875. ἐπάν, epan'

Book	when	Total
Mt.	2:8	1
Lk.	11:22, 34	2
Total		3

1876. ἐπάναγκες, epan'angkes

Book	necessary	Total
Ac.	15:28	1

1877. ἐπανάγω, epanag'ō

Book	Oc.	return	Oc.	thrust out	Oc.	launch out	Total
Mt.	1	21:18					1
Lk.			1	5:3	1	5:4	2
Total	1		1		1		3

1878. ἐπαναμιμνήσκω epanamimnẹs'kō

Book	put in mind	Total
Ro.	15:15	1

1879. ἐπαναπαύομαι, epanapau'omai

Book	Oc.	rest	Oc.	rest in	Total
Lk.	1	10:6			1
Ro.			1	2:17	1
Total	1		1		2

1881. ἐπανίσταμαι, epanis'tamai

Book	rise up against	Total
Mt.	10:21	1
Mk.	13:12	1
Total		2

1880. ἐπανέρχομαι, epaner'chomai

Book	Oc.	come again	Oc.	return	Total
Lk.	1	10:35	1	19:15	2

1882. ἐπανόρθωσις, epanor'thōsis

Book	correction	Total
2 Ti.	3:16	1

1884. ἐπαρκέω, eparke'ō

Book	relieve	Total
1 Ti.	5:10, 16, 16	3

1883. ἐπάνω, epan'ō

Book	Oc.	over	Oc.	on	Oc.	thereon (with 846)	Oc.	upon	Oc.	above	Oc.	more than	Total
Mt.	2	2:9; 27:37	2	5:14; 21:7a	3	21:7b; 23:20, 22	2	23:18; 28:2					9
Mk.											1	14:5	1
Lk.	4	4:39; 11:44; 19:17, 19	1	10:19									5
Jn.									2	3:31, 31			2
1 Co.									1	15:6			1
Rev.			1	6:8			1	20:3					2
Total	6		4		3		3		3		1		20

1885. ἐπαρχία, eparchi'a

Book	province	Total
Ac.	23:34; 25:1	2

1886. ἔπαυλις, ep'aulis

Book	habitation	Total
Ac.	1:20	1

1888. ἐπαυτοφώρῳ, epautophō'rō

Book	in the very act	Total
Jn.	8:4	1

1889. Ἐπαφρᾶς, Epaphras'

Book	Epaphras	Total
Col.	1:7; 4:12	2
Phe.	1:23	1
Total		3

1887. ἐπαύριον, epau'rion

Book	Oc.	morrow	Oc.	next day	Oc.	day following	Oc.	next day after	Oc.	morrow after	Total
Mt.			1	27:62							1
Mk.	1	11:12									1
Jn.			2	1:29; 12:12	2	1:43; 6:22	1	1:35			5
Ac.	6	10:9, 23; 20:7; 22:30; 23:32; 25:23	3	14:20; 21:8; 25:6					1	10:24	10
Total	7		6		2		1		1		17

1890. ἐπαφρίζω, epaphrid'zō

Book	foam out	Total
Jd.	1:13	1

1891. Ἐπαφρόδιτος Epaphrod'itos

Book	Epaphroditus	Total
Phl.	2:25; 4:18	2

1892. ἐπεγείρω, epegei'rō

Book	Oc.	raise	Oc.	stir up	Total
Ac.	1	13:50	1	14:2	2

1893. ἐπεί, epei′

Book	Oc.	because	Oc.	otherwise	Oc.	for then	Oc.	else	Oc.	seeing	Oc.	foras-much as	Oc.	for that	Oc.	Misc.	Total
Mt.	2	18:32; 27:6															2
Mk.	1	15:42															1
Lk.									1	1:34					1	7:1	2
Jn.	2	13:29; 19:31															2
Ro.			3	11:6, 6, 22	1	3:6											4
1 Co.							3	7:14; 14:16; 15:29			1	14:12			1	5:10	5
2 Co.															2	11:18; 13:3	2
Heb.	2	6:13; 11:11	1	9:17	2	9:26; 10:2			2	4:6; 5:11	1	2:14	1	5:2			9
Total	7		4		3		3		3		2		1		4		27

Miscellaneous: Lk. 7:1, when; 1 Co. 5:10, for; 2 Co. 11:18, seeing that; 2 Co. 13:3, since.

1894. ἐπειδή, epeidẹ′

Book	Oc.	for	Oc.	because	Oc.	seeing	Oc.	forasmuch as	Oc.	after that	Oc.	since	Oc.	for that	Total
Mt.			1	21:46											1
Lk.	1	11:6													1
Ac.			1	14:12	1	13:46	1	15:24							3
1 Co.	1	1:22			1	14:16			1	1:21	1	15:21			4
2 Co.													1	5:4	1
Phl.	1	2:26													1
Total	3		2		2		1		1		1		1		11

1895. ἐπειδήπερ, epeidẹ′per

Book	forasmuch as	Total
Lk.	1:1	1

1896. ἐπεῖδον, epei′don

Book	Oc.	look on	Oc.	behold	Total
Lk.	1	1:25			1
Ac.			1	4:29	1
Total	1		1		2

1897. ἐπείπερ, epei′per

Book	seeing	Total
Ro.	3:30	1

1898. ἐπεισαγωγή, epeisagōgẹ′

Book	bringing in	Total
Heb.	7:19	1

1899. ἔπειτα, ep′eita

Book	Oc.	then	Oc.	after that	Oc.	afterward(s)	Total
Mk.	1	7:5					1
Lk.	1	16:7					1
Jn.	1	11:7					1
1 Co.			3	12:28; 15:6, 7	2	15:23, 46	5
Gal.	2	1:18; 2:1			1	1:21	3
1 Th.	1	4:17					1
Heb.	1	7:27	1	7:2			2
Jas.	2	3:17; 4:14					2
Total	9		4		3		16

1900. ἐπέκεινα, epek′eina

Book	beyond	Total
Ac.	7:43	1

1901. ἐπεκτείνομαι epektei′nomai

Book	reach forth unto	Total
Phl.	3:13	1

1902. ἐπενδύομαι, ependu′omai

Book	be clothed upon	Total
2 Co.	5:2, 4	2

1903. ἐπενδύτης, ependu′tẹs

Book	fisher's coat	Total
Jn.	21:7	1

1904. ἐπέρχομαι, eper′chomai

Book	Oc.	come	Oc.	come upon	Oc.	come on	Oc.	come thither	Total
Lk.	2	1:35; 21:35	1	11:22	1	21:26			4
Ac.	3	1:8; 8:24; 13:40					1	14:19	4
Eph.	1	2:7							1
Jas.			1	5:1					1
Total	6		2		1		1		10

1906. ἐπερώτημα, eperō′tẹma

Book	answer	Total
1 Pt.	3:21	1

1905. ἐπερωτάω, eperōta′ō

Book	Oc.	ask	Oc.	demand	Oc.	desire	Oc.	ask question	Oc.	question	Oc.	ask after	Total
Mt.	7	12:10; 17:10; 22:23, 35, 41, 46; 27:11			1	16:1							8
Mk.	25	5:9; 7:5, 17; 8:5, 23, 27; 9:11, 16, 21, 28, 32, 33; 10:2, 10, 17; 11:29; 12:18, 28, 34; 13:3; 14:60, 61; 15:2, 4, 44											25
Lk.	14	3:10; 6:9; 8:9, 30; 9:18; 18:18, 40; 20:21, 27, 40; 21:7; 22:64; 23:3, 6	2	3:14; 17:20			1	2:46	1	23:9			18
Jn.	3	18:7, 21, 21											3
Ac.	3	1:6; 5:27; 23:34											3
Ro.											1	10:20	1
1 Co.	1	14:35											1
Total	53		2		1		1		1		1		59

1907. ἐπέχω, epech′ō

Book	Oc.	mark	Oc.	give heed unto	Oc.	stay	Oc.	hold forth	Oc.	take heed unto	Total
Lk.	1	14:7									1
Ac.			1	3:5	1	19:22					2
Phl.							1	2:16			1
1 Ti.									1	4:16	1
Total	1		1		1		1		1		5

1908. ἐπηρεάζω, epẹread′zō

Book	Oc.	despitefully use	Oc.	falsely accuse	Total
Mt.	1	5:44			1
Lk.	1	6:28			1
1 Pt.			1	3:16	1
Total	2		1		3

1909a. ἐπί, epi′ (with genitive)

Book	Oc.	on	Oc.	in	Oc.	upon	Oc.	before	Oc.	over	Oc.	of	Oc.	at	Oc.	to	Oc.	Not Tr.	Oc.	Misc.	Total
Mt.	11	9:2, 6; 14:25; 16:19, 19; 18:18, 18, 19; 24: 17; 26: 12; 27:19	10	2:22; 4: 6; 6:10; 18:16; 19:28a; 21:19a; 23:2; 24:30; 26:64; 28:18	6	6:19; 10:27; 23:9, 35b; 24:3; 25:31			3	24:45; 25: 21b, 23b					1	28:14			1	1:11	32
Mk.	8	2:10; 4:1; 6:47; 8:6; 9:3, 20; 13:15; 14:35	6	4:31, 31; 8: 4; 11: 4; 12: 14, 26	3	6:48, 49; 7: 30	1	13:9									1	12:32	3	2:26; 4: 26; 14: 51	22
Lk.	6	2:14; 8: 13, 16; 18:8; 22: 21, 30b	6	4:11; 5: 18; 6: 17; 11: 2; 17: 34; 21: 23	4	5:24; 12:3; 17:31; 21:25			1	12:42	2	4:25a; 22:59	3	20:37; 22: 30a, 40					4	3:2a; 4:27, 29; 20: 21	26
Jn.	4	6:2, 19; 17:4; 19: 19	1	19:13	1	19:31							2	6:21; 21:1	1	21:11			1	20:7	10
Ac.	9	2:30; 5: 15, 30; 10:39; 21:23, 40; 25:6, 17; 27: 44b	3	2:19; 8: 28; 20: 9a	1	12:21	7	23:30; 24:19, 20; 25: 9, 26, 26; 26: 2	1	6:3	2	4:27a; 10:34	1	25:10	1	10:11b	1	12:20	2	8:27; 11:28b	28
Ro.			1	1:9	1	9:28			1	9:5											3
1 Co.	1	11:10	1	8:5			3	6:1, 1, 6													5
2 Co.			1	13:1			1	7:14													2
Gal.	1	3:13									2	3:16, 16									3
Eph.	2	1:10; 6:3	1	1:16													1	3:15	1	4:6	5
Col.	1	3:2	2	1:16, 20	1	3:5															4
1 Th.			1	1:2																	1
1 Ti.			1	6:17			2	5:19; 6:13													3
Phe.			1	1:4																	1
Heb.	3	8:4; 11: 13; 12:25	3	1:2; 8: 10; 10: 16b	1	6:7													1	10:16a	8
Jas.	2	5:5, 17																			2
1 Pt.			1	1:20																	1
2 Pt.			1	3:3																	1
Rev.	24	4:2, 9, 10; 5:1b, 10; 6:10, 16b; 7:1b, 1c, 15a; 9: 17; 11: 10c; 13: 14, 14; 14:6, 14b, 15; 17: 8a, 9; 19: 4, 18, 19; 20:6, 11	12	1:20; 5: 3, 13a; 7:3; 9: 4; 11:8; 13:16, 16; 14: 1b, 9a; 18:17; 22:4	19	3:10, 10; 5: 7, 13b; 7:10; 10:1, 5, 5, 8, 8; 11: 10a; 12:1; 13:1b, 8; 16: 18; 17:1; 18:24; 19:21; 21:5			5	2:26; 9:11; 11:6; 14:18; 17:18	1	8:13					1	21:16			62
Total	72		52		37		14		11		7		6		3		4		13		219

Miscellaneous: Mt. 1:11, about the time; Mk. 2:26, in the days of; Mk. 4:26, into; Mk. 14:51, about; Lk. 3:2a, being; Lk. 4:27, in the time of; Lk. 4:29 (with 3639), whereon; Lk. 20:21 (with 225), truly; Jn. 20:7, about; Ac. 8:27 (with 2258), had the charge of; Ac. 11:28b, in the days of; Eph. 4:6, above; Heb. 10:16a, into.

1909b. ἐπί, epi′ (with dative)

Book	Oc.	in	Oc.	at	Oc.	for	Oc.	upon	Oc.	over
Mt.	5	13:14; 14:8, 11; 18:5; 24:5	3	7:28; 22:33; 24:33	1	19:9	1	16:18	1	24:47
Mk.	9	4:38a; 5:33; 6:25, 28, 55: 9:37, 39; 10:24b; 13:6	6	1:22; 10:22, 24a; 11:18; 12:17; 13:29	1	3:5	3	6:39; 11:7; 13:2		
Lk.	6	1:47; 9:48, 49; 18:9; 21:8; 24:47	11	1:14, 29; 2:33, 47; 4:22, 32; 5:5, 9; 9:43, 43; 20:26	2	2:20; 13:17	2	19:44; 21:6	6	12:44; 15:7, 7, 10; 19:41; 23:38
Jn.			1	8:7			2	4:27; 11:38		
Ac.	8	2:26, 38; 3:11; 4:17b, 18; 5:28a, 40; 14:3	5	3:10, 10, 12; 5:9; 13:12	5	4:21; 15:14, 31; 20:38; 26:6	1	8:16	1	8:2
Ro.	4	4:18; 5:2; 8:20; 15:12			1	5:12				
1 Co.	3	9:10, 10; 13:6	1	14:16	1	1:4				
2 Co.	8	1:4, 9, 9; 3:14; 7:4, 7, 13a; 9:14			3	7:13b; 9:13, 15				
Gal.										
Eph.							2	2:20; 4:26		
Phl.					2	1:5; 3:12	3	1:3; 2:17, 27		
Col.										
1 Th.	1	3:7b			1	3:9			1	3:7a
1 Ti.	1	4:10								
2 Ti.										
Tit.	1	1:2								
Phe.	1	1:7								
Heb.	3	2:13; 9:10, 26					1	8:6		
Jas.					2	5:1, 7				
1 Pt.										
1 Jn.	1	3:3								
3 Jn.										
Rev.	2	9:14; 22:16	1	21:12	1	18:9	1	19:14	2	11:10b; 18:11
Total	53		28		20		16		11	

Miscellaneous: Mt. 9:16, unto; Mt. 25:20, 22, beside; Mt. 26:50a (with 3639), wherefore; Mk. 2:4 (with 3639), wherein; Mk. 6:34, toward; Lk. 1:59, after; Lk. 3:20, above; Lk. 5:25 (with 3639), whereon; Lk. 11:22 (with 3639), wherein; Lk. 16:26, beside; Ac. 3:16, through; Ac. 5:35, as touching; Ac. 9:33 (with 2621), keep; Ac. 11:19, about; Ro. 5:14b, after; Ro. 6:21 (with 3639), whereof; Ro. 16:19, on (one's) behalf; 1 Co. 8:11, through; 2 Co. 9:6, 6 (with

1909c. ἐπί, epi′ (with accusative)

Book	Oc.	on	Oc.	upon	Oc.	unto	Oc.	to	Oc.	against	Oc.	over	Oc.	in
Mt.	23	4:5; 5:15, 39, 45, 45; 10:29, 34; 13:2; 14:19, 26, 28, 29; 15:32, 35; 17:6; 21:44, 44; 23:4; 26:7, 39, 50b; 27:25, 25	16	3:16; 7:24, 25, 26; 9:18; 10:13; 11:29; 12:18; 13:5; 19:28b; 21:5; 23:35a, 36; 24:2; 27:29a, 35	3	6:27; 12:28; 27:27	5	3:7, 13; 5:23; 13:48; 21:19b	5	10:21; 12:26; 24:7, 7; 26:55	3	25:21a, 23a; 27:45	2	27:29b, 43
Mk.	9	4:5, 16, 20, 21, 38b; 8:2; 9:22; 14:46; 16:18	4	1:10; 8:25; 10:16; 15:24	4	5:21; 15:22, 46; 16:2	1	11:13	8	3:24, 25, 26; 10:11; 13:8, 8, 12; 14:48	1	15:33	1	15:1
Lk.	18	1:65; 4:9; 5:12; 6:29, 48a; 8:8; 10:34, 35; 11:33; 15:5, 20; 17:16; 20:18b, 19; 21:12a, 35, 35; 23:30	20	1:12, 35; 2:25, 40; 3:22; 4:18; 5:19, 36; 6:48b, 49; 8:6; 9:38; 10:6a; 11:20; 13:4; 19:35, 43; 20:18a; 21:34; 24:49	8	3:2b; 6:35; 10:9, 11; 12:11; 23:1; 24:1, 12	15	1:16, 17; 5:11; 8:27; 9:62; 10:6b; 12:25, 58; 17:4; 19:5; 22:44, 52a; 23:33, 48; 24:24	11	9:5; 11:17, 17, 18; 12:53e, 53f; 14:31; 21:10, 10; 22:52b, 53	8	1:33; 2:8; 9:1; 10:19; 12:14; 19:14, 27; 23:44		
Jn.	7	1:33b; 3:36; 7:30, 44; 12:15; 13:25; 21:20	5	1:32, 33a, 51; 9:15; 18:4	1	6:16	1	19:33	1	13:18				
Ac.	26	2:18, 18; 4:5, 22; 5:5, 18; 7:54; 8:17; 9:17; 10:44, 45; 11:15, 15, 17; 13:11b; 14:10; 16:31; 17:26; 19:6, 16, 17; 20:37; 21:5, 27; 22:19; 28:3	18	1:8, 26; 2:3, 17; 4:33; 5:11, 11, 28b; 7:57; 8:24; 10:9; 13:11a, 40; 15:10, 17a; 18:6; 21:35; 26:16	17	8:26, 36; 9:21; 10:11a; 11:11, 21; 12:10; 14:13, 15; 16:19; 17:6, 19; 19:12; 21:32; 24:8; 25:12; 26:18	11	8:32; 9:4, 35; 12:12; 15:19; 17:14; 18:12; 20:13; 26:20; 27:43, 44c	4	4:27b; 8:1; 13:50, 51	4	7:10, 11, 27; 19:13	3	2:1; 9:42; 27:20
Ro.	6	4:5, 24; 9:23; 11:22a; 12:20; 15:3	5	2:9; 3:22; 4:9, 9; 15:20					2	1:18; 2:2	1	5:14a		
1 Co.	1	14:25	1	3:12										
2 Co.			3	1:23; 3:15; 12:9					1	10:2	1	3:13	1	2:3
Gal.	1	6:16a	1	6:16b			1	4:9						
Eph.			1	5:6										
Phl.														
Col.	1	3:6												
1 Th.			1	2:16										
2 Th.					1	2:1								
1 Ti.	1	1:18											1	5:5
2 Ti.					2	2:16; 4:4								
Tit.	1	3:6												
Heb.			1	11:21	1	6:1a					3	2:7; 3:6; 10:21		
Jas.			1	2:21			1	2:3			1	5:14		
1 Pt.	1	2:24	2	4:14; 5:7	1	2:25			1	3:12b	1	3:12a	1	3:5
2 Pt.							1	2:22						
Rev.	19	3:3a; 4:4b; 6:16a; 7:1a, 1d, 11, 16; 9:7; 10:2b; 11:16a; 14:1a, 16, 16; 15:2; 18:19; 19:12, 16, 16; 20:9	27	1:17; 2:24; 3:3b, 12; 4:4a; 8:3b, 10, 10; 10:2a; 11:11b, 11c, 16b; 12:3; 13:1a, 1c; 14:14a; 16:2, 8, 10, 12, 21; 17:3, 5, 16; 19:11; 20:4a, 4b	3	7:17; 16:14; 22:18	2	21:10; 22:14			4	6:8; 13:7; 16:9; 18:20	6	2:17; 5:1a; 14:9b; 17:8b; 20:1, 4c
Total	114		106		41		38		33		27		15	

Miscellaneous: Mt. 10:18, before; Mt. 18:6, about; Mt. 25:40, 45 (with 3645), inasmuch as; Mk. 9:12, 13, of; Mk. 11:2 (with 3639), whereon; Lk. 4:25c, throughout; Lk. 15:4, after; Lk. 19:30 (with 3639), whereon; Lk. 21:12b, before; Jn. 12:14 (with 846), thereon; Ac. 4:17a (with 4019), further; Ac. 10:10,

1909b. ἐπί, epi′ (with dative) (continued)

Book	Oc.	on	Oc.	of	Oc.	by	Oc.	with	Oc.	against	Oc.	Not Tr.	Oc.	Misc.	Total
Mt.			2	18:13, 13	2	4:4, 4	2	18:26, 29					4	9:16; 25:20, 22; 26:50a	21
Mk.	1	2:21	1	6:52									2	2:4; 6:34	23
Lk.	1	7:13			2	4:4, 4	1	18:7	6	12:52, 52, 53a, 53b, 53c, 53d	1	24:25	5	1:59; 3:20; 5:25; 11:22; 16:26	43
Jn.	1	4:6	1	12:16	1	5:2									6
Ac.	1	27:44a	1	4:9			2	21:24; 28:14					4	3:16; 5:35; 9:33; 11:19	28
Ro.	2	9:33; 10:11			2	10:19, 19							3	5:14b; 6:21; 16:19	12
1 Co.			1	16:17									1	8:11	7
2 Co.			1	12:21									2	9:6, 6	14
Gal.													1	5:13	1
Eph.													2	2:10; 6:16	4
Phl.					1	3:9							1	4:10	7
Col.													1	3:14	1
1 Th.													1	4:7	4
1 Ti.	1	1:16													2
2 Ti.													1	2:14	1
Tit.															1
Phe.															1
Heb.			2	8:1; 11:4									4	7:11; 9:15, 17; 10:28	10
Jas.															2
1 Pt.	1	2:6													1
1 Jn.															1
3 Jn.													1	1:10	1
Rev.	2	6:2, 5					1	12:17					2	6:4; 10:11	12
Total	10		9		8		6		6		1		35		203

2129), bountifully; Gal. 5:13; Eph. 2:10, unto; Eph. 6:16, above; Phl. 4:10 (with 3639), wherein; Col. 3:14, above; 1 Th. 4:7, unto; 2 Ti. 2:14, to; Heb. 7:11; 9:15, under; Heb. 9:17, after; Heb. 10:28, under; 3 Jn. 1:10 (with 5025), therewith; Rev. 6:4 (with 846), thereon; Rev. 10:11, before.

1909c. ἐπί, epi′ (with accusative) (continued)

Book	Oc.	into	Oc.	for	Oc.	at	Oc.	toward	Oc.	together (with 846)	Oc.	among	Oc.	Not Tr.	Oc.	Misc.	Total
Mt.	6	13:8, 20, 23; 18:12; 22:9; 24:16			1	9:9	2	12:49; 14:14	1	22:34	1	13:7	1	9:15	4	10:18; 18:6; 25:40, 45	73
Mk.	1	6:53			1	2:14									3	9:12, 13; 11:2	33
Lk.	2	19:4, 23	4	7:44; 18:4; 23:28, 28, 28	2	5:27; 24:22			1	17:35			3	1:48; 4:25b, 36	4	4:25c; 15:4; 19:30; 21:12b	96
Jn.			1	19:24	1	8:59							1	9:6	1	12:14	19
Ac.	2	7:23; 9:11			1	10:25			4	1:15; 2:44; 3:1; 4:26	1	1:21	12	4:29; 10:16; 11:10; 13:31; 15:17b; 16:18; 17:2; 18:20; 20:9b, 11; 24:4; 28:6	7	4:17a; 10:10, 17; 11:28a; 19:8, 10, 34	110
Ro.							1	11:22b					1	7:1	1	11:13	17
1 Co.	3	2:9; 11:20; 14:23					1	7:36					2	7:5, 39			8
2 Co.																	6
Gal.													1	4:1			4
Eph.							1	2:7									2
Phl.			1	3:14													1
Col.																	1
1 Th.																	1
2 Th.											1	1:10			2	2:4; 3:4	4
1 Ti.																	2
2 Ti.													2	3:9, 13			4
Tit.																	1
Heb.			1	12:10			1	6:1b					1	11:30	3	7:13; 8:8, 8	11
Jas.															1	2:7	4
1 Pt.			1	1:13													8
2 Pt.													1	1:13			2
Rev.	1	11:11a			2	3:20; 8:3a					1	7:15b			1	1:7	66
Total	15		8		8		6		6		4		25		27		473

into; Ac. 10:17, before; Ac. 11:28a, throughout; Ac. 19:8, for the space of; Ac. 19:10, by the space of; Ac. 19:34, the space of; Ro. 11:13 (with 3645), inasmuch as; 2 Th. 2:4, above; 2 Th. 3:4, touching; Heb. 7:13, of; Heb. 8:8, 8, with; Jas. 2:7, by; Rev. 1:7, because of.

Word 1909 has 895 occurrences.

1910. ἐπιβαίνω, epibai′nō

Book	Oc.	sit	Oc.	come	Oc.	go aboard	Oc.	take (with 1519)	Oc.	come into	Oc.	enter into	Total
Mt.	1	21:5											1
Ac.			1	20:18	1	21:2	1	21:6	1	25:1	1	27:2	5
Total	1		1		1		1		1		1		6

1911. ἐπιβάλλω, epibal′lō

Book	Oc.	lay	Oc.	put	Oc.	lay on	Oc.	beat	Oc.	cast on	Oc.	think thereon	Oc.	fall	Oc.	stretch forth	Oc.	cast upon	Total
Mt.	1	26:50	1	9:16															2
Mk.	1	14:46					1	4:37	1	11:7	1	14:72							4
Lk.	2	20:19; 21:12	2	5:36; 9:62									1	15:12					5
Jn.	2	7:30, 44																	2
Ac.	2	5:18; 21:27			1	4:3									1	12:1			4
1 Co.																	1	7:35	1
Total	8		3		1		1		1		1		1		1		1		18

1912. ἐπιβαρέω, epibare′ō

Book	Oc.	overcharge	Oc.	be chargeable unto	Oc.	be chargeable to	Total
2 Co.	1	2:5					1
1 Th.			1	2:9			1
2 Th.					1	3:8	1
Total	1		1		1		3

1913. ἐπιβιβάζω, epibibad′zō

Book	Oc.	set on	Oc.	set thereon	Total
Lk.	1	10:34	1	19:35	2
Ac.	1	23:24			1
Total	2		1		3

1914. ἐπιβλέπω, epiblep′ō

Book	Oc.	regard	Oc.	look	Oc.	have respect to	Total
Lk.	1	1:48	1	9:38			2
Jas.					1	2:3	1
Total	1		1		1		3

1915. ἐπίβλημα, epib′lēma

Book	piece	Total
Mt.	9:16	1
Mk.	2:21	1
Lk.	5:36, 36	2
Total		4

1916. ἐπιβοάω, epiboa′ō

Book	cry	Total
Ac.	25:24	1

1917. ἐπιβουλή, epiboulē′

Book	Oc.	lying in wait	Oc.	lay wait for (with 1096)	Oc.	lay wait (with 3195 and 2071)	Oc.	laying await	Total
Ac.	1	20:19	1	20:3	1	23:30	1	9:24	4

1918. ἐπιγαμβρεύω epigambreu′ō

Book	marry	Total
Mt.	22:24	1

1919. ἐπίγειος, epig′eios

Book	Oc.	earthly	Oc.	terrestrial	Oc.	in earth	Total
Jn.	1	3:12					1
1 Co.			2	15:40, 40			2
2 Co.	1	5:1					1
Phl.	1	3:19			1	2:10	2
Jas.	1	3:15					1
Total	4		2		1		7

1920. ἐπιγίνομαι, epigin′omai

Book	blow	Total
Ac.	28:13	1

1922. ἐπίγνωσις, epig′nōsis

Book	Oc.	knowledge	Oc.	acknowledging	Oc.	acknowledgement	Total
Ro.	3	1:28; 3:20; 10:2					3
Eph.	2	1:17; 4:13					2
Phl.	1	1:9					1
Col.	3	1:9, 10; 3:10			1	2:2	4
1 Ti.	1	2:4					1
2 Ti.	1	3:7	1	2:25			2
Tit.			1	1:1			1
Phe.			1	1:6			1
Heb.	1	10:26					1
2 Pt.	4	1:2, 3, 8; 2:20					4
Total	16		3		1		20

1923. ἐπιγραφή, epigraphē′

Book	superscription	Total
Mt.	22:20	1
Mk.	12:16; 15:26	2
Lk.	20:24; 23:38	2
Total		5

1921. ἐπιγινώσκω, epiginōs′kō

Book	Oc.	know	Oc.	acknowledge	Oc.	perceive	Oc.	take knowledge of	Oc.	have knowledge of	Oc.	know well	Total
Mt.	5	7:16, 20; 11:27, 27; 17:12							1	14:35			6
Mk.	3	5:30; 6:33, 54			1	2:8							4
Lk.	5	1:4; 7:37; 23:7; 24:16, 31			2	1:22; 5:22							7
Ac.	9	3:10; 9:30; 12:14; 19:34; 22:24, 29; 25:10; 27:39; 28:1					2	4:13; 24:8					11
Ro.	1	1:32											1
1 Co.	2	13:12, 12	2	14:37; 16:18									4
2 Co.	1	13:5	3	1:13, 13, 14							1	6:9	5
Col.	1	1:6											1
1 Ti.	1	4:3											1
2 Pt.	2	2:21, 21											2
Total	30		5		3		2		1		1		42

1924. ἐπιγράφω, epigraph′ō

Book	Oc.	write	Oc.	write over	Oc.	write thereon	Oc.	with this inscription (with 1722 and 3639)	Total
Mk.			1	15:26					1
Ac.							1	17:23	1
Heb.	2	8:10; 10:16							2
Rev.					1	21:12			1
Total	2		1		1		1		5

1925. ἐπιδείκνυμι, epideik′numi

Book	shew	Total
Mt.	16:1; 22:19; 24:1	3
Lk.	17:14; 20:24; 24:40	3
Ac.	9:39; 18:28	2
Heb.	6:17	1
Total		9

1926. ἐπιδέχομαι, epidech′omai

Book	receive	Total
3 Jn.	1:9, 10	2

1927. ἐπιδημέω, epidēme′ō

Book	Oc.	be there	Oc.	stranger	Total
Ac.	1	17:21	1	2:10	2

1928. ἐπιδιατάσσομαι epidiatas′somai

Book	add thereto	Total
Gal.	3:15	1

1929. ἐπιδίδωμι, epidid'ōmi

Book	Oc.	give	Oc.	deliver	Oc.	offer	Oc.	let drive (with 5242)	Oc.	deliver unto	Total
Mt.	2	7:9, 10									2
Lk.	4	11:11, 11; 24:30, 42			1	11:12			1	4:17	6
Jn.	1	13:26									1
Ac.			1	15:30			1	27:15			2
Total	7		1		1		1		1		11

1930. ἐπιδιορθόω, epidiortho'ō

Book	set in order	Total
Tit.	1:5	1

1931. ἐπιδύω, epidu'ō

Book	go down	Total
Eph.	4:26	1

1932. ἐπιείκεια, epiei'keia

Book	Oc.	clemency	Oc.	gentleness	Total
Ac.	1	24:4			1
2 Co.			1	10:1	1
Total	1		1		2

1933. ἐπιεικής, epieikẹs'

Book	Oc.	gentle	Oc.	patient	Oc.	moderation	Total
Phl.					1	4:5	1
1 Ti.			1	3:3			1
Tit.	1	3:2					1
Jas.	1	3:17					1
1 Pt.	1	2:18					1
Total	3		1		1		5

1936. ἐπίθεσις, epith'esis

Book	Oc.	laying on	Oc.	putting on	Total
Ac.	1	8:18			1
1 Ti.	1	4:14			1
2 Ti.			1	1:6	1
Heb.	1	6:2			1
Total	3		1		4

1935. ἐπιθανάτιος, epithanat'ios

Book	appoint to death	Total
1 Co.	4:9	1

1934. ἐπιζητέω, epidzẹte'ō

Book	Oc.	seek after	Oc.	seek	Oc.	desire	Oc.	seek for	Oc.	enquire	Total
Mt.	3	6:32; 12:39; 16:4									3
Mk.	1	8:12									1
Lk.	1	12:30	1	11:29							2
Ac.					1	13:7	1	12:19	1	19:39	3
Ro.							1	11:7			1
Phl.					2	4:17, 17					2
Heb.			2	11:14; 13:14							2
Total	5		3		3		2		1		14

1938. ἐπιθυμητής, epithumẹtẹs'

Book	lust after (with 1510)	Total
1 Co.	10:6	1

1940. ἐπικαθίζω, epikathid'zō

Book	set	Total
Mt.	21:7	1

1937. ἐπιθυμέω, epithume'ō

Book	Oc.	desire	Oc.	covet	Oc.	lust	Oc.	lust after	Oc.	fain	Total
Mt.	1	13:17					1	5:28			2
Lk.	3	16:21; 17:22; 22:15							1	15:16	4
Ac.			1	20:33							1
Ro.			2	7:7; 13:9							2
1 Co.					1	10:6					1
Gal.					1	5:17					1
1 Ti.	1	3:1									1
Heb.	1	6;11									1
Jas.					1	4:2					1
1 Pt.	1	1:12									1
Rev.	1	9:6									1
Total	8		3		3		1		1		16

1939. ἐπιθυμία, epithumi'a

Book	Oc.	lust	Oc.	concupiscence	Oc.	desire	Oc.	lust after	Total
Mk.	1	4:19							1
Lk.					1	22:15			1
Jn.	1	8:44							1
Ro.	4	1:24; 6:12; 7:7; 13:14	1	7:8					5
Gal.	2	5:16, 24							2
Eph.	2	2:3; 4:22							2
Phl.					1	1:23			1
Col.			1	3:5					1
1 Th.			1	4:5	1	2:17			2
1 Ti.	1	6:9							1
2 Ti.	3	2:22; 3:6; 4:3							3
Tit.	2	2:12; 3:3							2
Jas.	2	1:14, 15							2
1 Pt.	4	1:14; 2:11; 4:2, 3							4
2 Pt.	4	1:4; 2:10, 18; 3:3							4
1 Jn.	3	2:16, 16, 17							3
Jd.	2	1:16, 18							2
Rev.							1	18:14	1
Total	31		3		3		1		38

1941. ἐπικαλέομαι, epikale'omai

Book	Oc.	call on	Oc.	be (one's) surname	Oc.	be surnamed	Oc.	call upon	Oc.	call	Oc.	appeal unto	Oc.	appeal to	Oc.	appeal	Total
Mt.			1	10:3													1
Lk.					1	22:3											1
Ac.	4	2:21; 9:14, 21; 22:16	5	10:5, 32; 11: 13 12:12, 25	4	1:23; 4:36; 10:18; 15:22	1	7:59	1	15:17	4	25:11, 12; 26: 32; 28:19	1	25:25	1	25:21	21
Ro.	1	10:14					2	10:12, 13									3
1 Co.							1	1:2									1
2 Co.									1	1:23							1
2 Ti.	1	2:22															1
Heb.									1	11:16							1
Jas.									1	2:7							1
1 Pt.	1	1:17															1
Total	7		6		5		4		4		4		1		1		32

1942. ἐπικάλυμα, epikal′uma

Book	cloke	Total
1 Pt.	2:16	1

1943. ἐπικαλύπτω, epikalup′tō

Book	cover	Total
Ro.	4:7	1

1944. ἐπικατάρατος epikatar′atos

Book	cursed	Total
Jn.	7:49	1
Gal.	3:10, 13	2
Total		3

1946. Ἐπικούρειος, Epikou′reios

Book	Epicurean	Total
Ac.	17:18	1

1947. ἐπικουρία, epikouri′a

Book	help	Total
Ac.	26:22	1

1948. ἐπικρίνω epikri′nō

Book	give sentence	Total
Lk.	23:24	1

1945. ἐπίκειμαι, epik′eimai

Book	Oc.	press upon	Oc.	be instant	Oc.	lie	Oc.	be laid thereon	Oc.	lie on	Oc.	be laid upon	Oc.	be imposed on	Total
Lk.	1	5:1	1	23:23											2
Jn.					1	11:38	1	21:9							2
Ac.									1	27:20					1
1 Co.											1	9:16			1
Heb.													1	9:10	1
Total	1		1		1		1		1		1		1		7

1949. ἐπιλαμβάνομαι, epilamban′omai

Book	Oc.	take	Oc.	take by	Oc.	catch	Oc.	take on	Oc.	lay hold on	Oc.	take hold of	Oc.	lay hold upon	Total
Mt.					1	14:31									1
Mk.			1	8:23											1
Lk.	2	9:47; 14:4									2	20:20, 26	1	23:26	5
Ac.	5	9:27; 17:19; 18: 17; 21:30, 33	1	23:19	1	16:19									7
1 Ti.									2	6:12, 19					2
Heb.			1	8:9			2	2:16, 16							3
Total	7		3		2		2		2		2		1		19

1950. ἐπιλανθάνομαι, epilanthan′omai

Book	Oc.	forget	Oc.	be forgetful	Total
Mt.	1	16:5			1
Mk.	1	8:14			1
Lk.	1	12:6			1
Phl.	1	3:13			1
Heb.	2	6:10; 13:16	1	13:2	3
Jas.	1	1:24			1
Total	7		1		8

1951. ἐπιλέγομαι, epileg′omai

Book	Oc.	be called	Oc.	choose	Total
Jn.	1	5:2			1
Ac.			1	15:40	1
Total	1		1		2

1952. ἐπιλείπω, epilei′pō

Book	fail	Total
Heb.	11:32	1

1953. ἐπιλησμονή, epilẹsmonẹ′

Book	forgetful	Total
Jas.	1:25	1

1954. ἐπίλοιπος, epil′oipos

Book	rest	Total
1 Pt.	4:2	1

1955. ἐπίλυσις, epil′usis

Book	interpretation	Total
2 Pt.	1:20	1

1956. ἐπιλύω, epilu′ō

Book	Oc.	expound	Oc.	determine	Total
Mk.	1	4:34			1
Ac.			1	19:39	1
Total	1		1		2

1957. ἐπιμαρτυρέω, epimarture′ō

Book	testify	Total
1 Pt.	5:12	1

1958. ἐπιμέλεια, epimel′eia

Book	refresh (one's) self (with 5077)	Total
Ac.	27:3	1

1959. ἐπιμελέομαι, epimele′omai

Book	take care of	Total
Lk.	10:34, 35	2
1 Ti.	3:5	1
Total		3

1960. ἐπιμελῶς, epimelōs′

Book	diligently	Total
Lk.	15:8	1

1961. ἐπιμένω, epimen′ō

Book	Oc.	tarry	Oc.	continue in	Oc.	continue	Oc.	abide	Oc.	abide in	Oc.	abide still	Total
Jn.					1	8:7							1
Ac.	5	10:48; 21:4, 10; 28: 12, 14	1	13:43	1	12:16					1	15:34	8
Ro.			2	6:1; 11:22					1	11:23			3
1 Co.	2	16:7, 8											2
Gal.							1	1:18					1
Phl.							1	1:24					1
Col.			1	1:23									1
1 Ti.			1	4:16									1
Total	7		5		2		2		1		1		18

1962. ἐπινεύω, epineu′ō

Book	consent	Total
Ac.	18:20	1

1963. ἐπίνοια, epin′oia

Book	thought	Total
Ac.	8:22	1

1964. ἐπιορκέω, epiorke′ō

Book	forswear (one's) self	Total
Mt.	5:33	1

1965. ἐπίορκος, epi′orkos

Book	perjured person	Total
1 Ti.	1:10	1

1966. ἐπιοῦσα, epiou′sa

Book	Oc.	next day	Oc.	following	Oc.	next	Total
Ac.	2	16:11; 20:15	2	21:18; 23:11	1	7:26	5

1967. ἐπιούσιος, epiou′sios

Book	daily	Total
Mt.	6:11	1
Lk.	11:3	1
Total		2

1968. ἐπιπίπτω, epipip′tō

Book	Oc.	fall	Oc.	fall on	Oc.	press	Oc.	lie	Total
Mk.					1	3:10			1
Lk.	2	1:12; 15:20							2
Jn.							1	13:25	1
Ac.	7	8:16; 10:10, 44; 11: 15; 13:11; 19:17; 20:37	1	20:10					8
Ro.	1	15:3							1
Total	10		1		1		1		13

1969. ἐπιπλήσσω, epiplẹs′sō

Book	rebuke	Total
1 Ti.	5:1	1

1970. ἐπιπνίγω, epipni′gō

Book	choke	Total
Lk.	8:7	1

1971. ἐπιποθέω, epipothe'ō

Book	Oc.	greatly desire	Oc.	long	Oc.	earnestly desire	Oc.	long after	Oc.	greatly long after	Oc.	lust	Oc.	desire	Oc.	longed after (with 2258)	Total
Ro.			1	1:11													1
2 Co.					1	5:2	1	9:14									2
Phl.									1	1:8					1	2:26	2
1 Th.	1	3:6															1
2 Ti.	1	1:4															1
Jas.											1	4:5					1
1 Pt.													1	2:2			1
Total	2		1		1		1		1		1		1		1		9

1972. ἐπιπόθησις, epipoth'ēsis

Book	Oc.	earnest desire	Oc.	vehement desire	Total
2 Co.	1	7:7	1	7:11	2

1973. ἐπιπόθητος, epipoth'ētos

Book	longed for	Total
Phl.	4:1	1

1974. ἐπιποθία, epipothi'a

Book	great desire	Total
Ro.	15:23	1

1975. ἐπιπορεύομαι, epiporeu'omai

Book	come	Total
Lk.	8:4	1

1976. ἐπιῤῥάπτω, epirhrap'tō

Book	sew	Total
Mk.	2:21	1

1977. ἐπιῤῥίπτω, epirhrip'tō

Book	cast	Total
Lk.	19:35	1
1 Pt.	5:7	1
Total		2

1979. ἐπισιτισμός, episitismos'

Book	victuals	Total
Lk.	9:12	1

1978. ἐπίσημος, epis'ēmos

Book	Oc.	notable	Oc.	of note	Total
Mt.	1	27:16			1
Ro.			1	16:7	1
Total	1		1		2

1980. ἐπισκέπτομαι, episkep'tomai

Book	Oc.	visit	Oc.	look out	Total
Mt.	2	25:36, 43			2
Lk.	3	1:68, 78; 7:16			3
Ac.	3	7:23; 15:14, 36	1	6:3	4
Heb.	1	2:6			1
Jas.	1	1:27			1
Total	10		1		11

1982. ἐπισκιάζω, episkiad'zō

Book	overshadow	Total
Mt.	17:5	1
Mk.	9:7	1
Lk.	1:35; 9:34	2
Ac.	5:15	1
Total		5

1981. ἐπισκηνόω, episkēno'ō

Book	rest	Total
2 Co.	12:9	1

1983. ἐπισκοπέω, episkope'ō

Book	Oc.	look diligently	Oc.	take the oversight	Total
Heb.	1	12:15			1
1 Pt.			1	5:2	1
Total	1		1		2

1984. ἐπισκοπή, episkopē'

Book	Oc.	visitation	Oc.	bishoprick	Oc.	office of a bishop	Total
Lk.	1	19:44					1
Ac.			1	1:20			1
1 Ti.					1	3:1	1
1 Pt.	1	2:12					1
Total	2		1		1		4

1985. ἐπίσκοπος, epis'kopos

Book	Oc.	bishop	Oc.	overseer	Total
Ac.			1	20:28	1
Phl.	1	1:1			1
1 Ti.	1	3:2			1
Tit.	1	1:7			1
1 Pt.	1	2:25			1
Total	4		1		5

1986. ἐπισπάομαι, epispa'omai

Book	become uncircumcised	Total
1 Co.	7:18	1

1988. ἐπιστάτης, epistat'ēs

Book	Master (Christ)	Total
Lk.	5:5; 8:24, 24, 45; 9:33, 49; 17:13	7

1987. ἐπίσταμαι, epis'tamai

Book	Oc.	know	Oc.	understand	Total
Mk.			1	14:68	1
Ac.	9	10:28; 15:7; 18:25; 19:15, 25; 20:18; 22:19; 24:10; 26:26			9
1 Ti.	1	6:4			1
Heb.	1	11:8			1
Jas.	1	4:14			1
Jd.	1	1:10			1
Total	13		1		14

1989. ἐπιστέλλω, epistel'lō

Book	Oc.	write	Oc.	write unto	Oc.	write a letter unto	Total
Ac.	1	21:25	1	15:20			2
Heb.					1	13:22	1
Total	1		1		1		3

1990. ἐπιστήμων, epistē'mōn

Book	endued with knowledge	Total
Jas.	3:13	1

1993. ἐπιστομίζω, epistomid'zō

Book	stop the mouth	Total
Tit.	1:11	1

1992. ἐπιστολή, epistolē'

Book	Oc.	epistle	Oc.	letter	Total
Ac.	2	15:30; 23:33	3	9:2; 22:5; 23:25	5
Ro.	1	16:22			1
1 Co.	1	5:9	1	16:3	2
2 Co.	4	3:1, 2, 3; 7:8b	4	7:8a; 10:9, 10, 11	8
Col.	1	4:16			1
1 Th.	1	5:27			1
2 Th.	3	2:15; 3:14, 17	1	2:2	4
2 Pt.	2	3:1, 16			2
Total	15		9		24

1991. ἐπιστηρίζω, epistērid'zō

Book	Oc.	confirm	Oc.	strengthen	Total
Ac.	3	14:22; 15:32, 41	1	18:23	4

1994. ἐπιστρέφω, epistreph'ō

Book	Oc.	turn	Oc.	be converted	Oc.	return	Oc.	turn about	Oc.	turn again	Oc.	Misc.	Total
Mt.			1	13:15	3	10:13; 12:44; 24:18	1	9:22					5
Mk.			1	4:12			2	5:30; 8:33	1	13:16			4
Lk.	2	1:16, 17	1	22:32	2	2:20; 17:31			1	17:4	1	8:55	7
Jn.			1	12:40			1	21:20					2
Ac.	8	9:35, 40; 11:21; 14:15; 15:19; 16:18; 26:18, 20	2	3:19; 28:27							1	15:36	11
2 Co.	1	3:16											1
Gal.	1	4:9											1
1 Th.	1	1:9											1
Jas.											2	5:19, 20	2
1 Pt.					1	2:25							1
2 Pt.	1	2:21							1	2:22			2
Rev.	2	1:12, 12											2
Total	16		6		6		4		3		4		39

Miscellaneous: Lk. 8:55, come again; Ac. 15:36, go again; Jas. 5:19, 20, convert.

1995. ἐπιστροφή, epistrophē′

Book	conversion	Total
Ac.	15:3	1

1998. ἐπισυντρέχω, episuntrech′ō

Book	come running together	Total
Mk.	9:25	1

1996. ἐπισυνάγω, episunag′ō

Book	Oc.	gather together	Oc.	gather	Total
Mt.	1	24:31	2	23:37, 37	3
Mk.	2	1:33; 13:27			2
Lk.	2	12:1; 13:34			2
Total	5		2		7

2000. ἐπισφαλής, episphalēs′

Book	dangerous	Total
Ac.	27:9	1

2001. ἐπισχύω, epischu′ō

Book	be more fierce	Total
Lk.	23:5	1

1997. ἐπισυναγωγή, episunagōgē′

Book	Oc.	gathering together	Oc.	assembling together	Total
2 Th.	1	2:1			1
Heb.			1	10:25	1
Total	1		1		2

2002. ἐπισωρεύω, episōreu′ō

Book	heap	Total
2 Ti.	4:3	1

2006. ἐπιτήδειος, epitē′deios

Book	things which are needful	Total
Jas.	2:16	1

1999. ἐπισύστασις, episu′stasis

Book	Oc.	that which comes upon	Oc.	a raising up (with 4060)	Total
2 Co.	1	11:28			1
Ac.			1	24:12	1
Total	1		1		2

2003. ἐπιταγή, epitagē′

Book	Oc.	commandment	Oc.	authority	Total
Ro.	1	16:26			1
1 Co.	2	7:6, 25			2
2 Co.	1	8:8			1
1 Ti.	1	1:1			1
Tit.	1	1:3	1	2:15	2
Total	6		1		7

2004. ἐπιτάσσω, epitas′sō

Book	Oc.	command	Oc.	charge	Oc.	enjoin	Total
Mk.	3	1:27; 6:27, 39	1	9:25			4
Lk.	4	4:36; 8:25, 31; 14:22					4
Ac.	1	23:2					1
Phe.					1	1:8	1
Total	8		1		1		10

2005. ἐπιτελέω, epitele′ō

Book	Oc.	perform	Oc.	perfect	Oc.	accomplish	Oc.	finish	Oc.	performance	Oc.	make	Oc.	do	Total
Lk.													1	13:32	1
Ro.	1	15:28													1
2 Co.	1	8:11a	1	7:1			1	8:6	1	8:11b					4
Gal.			1	3:3											1
Phl.	1	1:6													1
Heb.					1	9:6					1	8:5			2
1 Pt.					1	5:9									1
Total	3		2		2		1		1		1		1		11

2007. ἐπιτίθημι, epitith′ēmi

Book	Oc.	lay on	Oc.	lay	Oc.	put	Oc.	lay upon	Oc.	put on	Oc.	put upon	Oc.	set	Oc.	Not Tr.	Oc.	Misc.	Total
Mt.	1	19:15	2	9:18; 23:4	2	21:7; 27:29			1	19:13							1	27:37	7
Mk.	1	5:23	1	16:18	1	8:25	1	6:5			2	7:32; 8:23	1	4:21	1	10:30	2	3:16, 17	10
Lk.	3	4:40; 13:13; 23:26	1	15:5									1	8:16					5
Jn.					1	9:15			1	19:2									2
Ac.	4	6:6; 8:19; 13:3; 28:8	2	8:17; 28:3	2	9:17; 15:10	3	15:28; 16:23; 19:6	1	9:12							2	18:10; 28:10	14
1 Ti.	1	5:22																	1
Rev.			1	1:17													2	22:18, 18	3
Total	10		7		6		4		3		2		2		1		7		42

Miscellaneous: Mt. 27:37, set up; Mk. 3:16, 17 (with 3586), surname; Ac. 18:10, set on; Ac. 28:10, lade with; Rev. 22:18, 18, add.

2008. ἐπιτιμάω, epitima′ō

Book	Oc.	rebuke	Oc.	charge	Oc.	straightly charge	Total
Mt.	5	8:26; 16:22; 17:18; 19:13; 20:31	1	12:16			6
Mk.	6	1:25; 4:39; 8:32, 33; 9:25; 10:13	3	3:12; 8:30; 10:48			9
Lk.	11	4:35, 39, 41; 8:24; 9:42, 55; 17:3; 18:15, 39; 19:39; 23:40			1	9:21	12
2 Ti.	1	4:2					1
Jd.	1	1:9					1
Total	24		4		1		29

2009. ἐπιτιμία, epitimi′a

Book	punishment	Total
2 Co.	2:6	1

2010. ἐπιτρέπω, epitrep′ō

Book	Oc.	suffer	Oc.	permit	Oc.	give leave	Oc.	give liberty	Oc.	give license	Oc.	let	Total
Mt.	3	8:21, 31; 19:8											3
Mk.	1	10:4			1	5:13							2
Lk.	3	8:32, 32; 9:59									1	9:61	4
Jn.					1	19:38							1
Ac.	2	21:39; 28:16	1	26:1			1	27:3	1	21:40			5
1 Co.			2	14:34; 16:7									2
1 Ti.	1	2:12											1
Heb.			1	6:3									1
Total	10		4		2		1		1		1		19

2011. ἐπιτροπή, epitropē′

Book	commission	Total
Ac.	26:12	1

2012. ἐπίτροπος, epit′ropos

Book	Oc.	steward	Oc.	tutor	Total
Mt.	1	20:8			1
Lk.	1	8:3			1
Gal.			1	4:2	1
Total	2		1		3

2013. ἐπιτυγχάνω, epitungchan′ō

Book	obtain	Total
Ro.	11:7, 7	2
Heb.	6:15; 11:33	2
Jas.	4:2	1
Total		5

2014. ἐπιφαίνω, epiphai'nō

Book	Oc.	appear	Oc.	give light	Total
Lk.			1	1:79	1
Ac.	1	27:20			1
Tit.	2	2:11; 3:4			2
Total	3		1		4

2015. ἐπιφάνεια, epiphan'eia

Book	Oc.	appearing	Oc.	brightness	Total
2 Th.			1	2:8	1
1 Ti.	1	6:14			1
2 Ti.	3	1:10; 4:1, 8			3
Tit.	1	2:13			1
Total	5		1		6

2016. ἐπιφανής, epiphanēs'

Book	notable	Total
Ac.	2:20	1

2017. ἐπιφαύω, epiphau'ō

Book	give light	Total
Eph.	5:14	1

2018. ἐπιφέρω, epipher'ō

Book	Oc.	bring	Oc.	take	Oc.	add	Oc.	bring against	Total
Ac.	2	19:12; 25:18							2
Ro.			1	3:5					1
Phl.					1	1:16			1
Jd.							1	1:9	1
Total	2		1		1		1		5

2019. ἐπιφωνέω, epiphōne'ō

Book	Oc.	cry	Oc.	give a shout	Oc.	cry against	Total
Lk.	1	23:21					1
Ac.			1	12:22	1	22:24	2
Total	1		1		1		3

2020. ἐπιφώσκω, epiphōs'kō

Book	Oc.	begin to dawn	Oc.	draw on	Total
Mt.	1	28:1			1
Lk.			1	23:54	1
Total	1		1		2

2021. ἐπιχειρέω, epicheire'ō

Book	Oc.	take in hand	Oc.	go about	Oc.	take upon	Total
Lk.	1	1:1					1
Ac.			1	9:29	1	19:13	2
Total	1		1		1		3

2025. ἐπιχρίω, epichri'ō

Book	Oc.	anoint	Oc.	anoint (with 1909)	Total
Jn.	1	9:11	1	9:6	2

2022. ἐπιχέω, epiche'ō

Book	pour in	Total
Lk.	10:34	1

2023. ἐπιχορηγέω, epichorēge'ō

Book	Oc.	minister	Oc.	minister nourishment	Oc.	add	Oc.	minister unto	Total
2 Co.	1	9:10							1
Gal.	1	3:5							1
Col.			1	2:19					1
2 Pt.					1	1:5	1	1:11	2
Total	2		1		1		1		5

2024. ἐπιχορηγία, epichorēgi'a

Book	supply	Total
Eph.	4:16	1
Phl.	1:19	1
Total		2

2027. ἐποκέλλω, epokel'lō

Book	run aground	Total
Ac.	27:41	1

2026. ἐποικοδομέω, epoikodome'ō

Book	Oc.	build up	Oc.	build thereupon	Oc.	build	Oc.	build thereon	Total
Ac.	1	20:32							1
1 Co.			2	3:10b, 14	1	3:12	1	3:10a	4
Eph.					1	2:20			1
Col.	1	2:7							1
Jd.	1	1:20							1
Total	3		2		2		1		8

2028. ἐπονομάζω, eponomad'zō

Book	call	Total
Ro.	2:17	1

2029. ἐποπτεύω, epopteu'ō

Book	behold	Total
1 Pt.	2:12; 3:2	2

2032. ἐπουράνιος, epouran'ios

Book	Oc.	heavenly	Oc.	celestial	Oc.	in heaven	Oc.	high	Total
Mt.	1	18:35							1
Jn.	1	3:12	2	15:40, 40					3
1 Co.	3	15:48, 48, 49							3
Eph.	4	1:3, 20; 2:6; 3:10					1	6:12	5
Phl.					1	2:10			1
2 Ti.	1	4:18							1
Heb.	6	3:1; 6:4; 8:5; 9:23; 11:16; 12:22							6
Total	16		2		1		1		20

2030. ἐπόπτης, epop'tēs

Book	eyewitness	Total
2 Pt.	1:16	1

2031. ἔπος, e'pos

Book	say (with 2036)	Total
Heb.	7:9	1

2034. ἑπτακίς, heptakis'

Book	seven times	Total
Mt.	18:21, 22	2
Lk.	17:4, 4	2
Total		4

2035. ἑπτακισχίλιοι heptakischil'ioi

Book	seven thousand	Total
Ro.	11:4	1

2033. ἑπτά, hepta'

Book	Oc.	seven	Oc.	seventh	Total
Mt.	8	12:45; 15:34, 36, 37; 16:10; 18:22; 22:25, 28	1	22:26	9
Mk.	9	8:5, 6, 8, 20, 20; 12:20, 22, 23; 16:9			9
Lk.	6	2:36; 8:2; 11:26; 20:29, 31, 33			6
Ac.	8	6:3; 13:19; 19:14; 20:6; 21:4, 8, 27; 28:14			8
Heb.	1	11:30			1
Rev.	54	1:4, 4, 11, 12, 13, 16, 20, 20, 20, 20, 20, 20; 2:1, 1; 3:1, 1; 4:5, 5; 5:1, 5, 6, 6, 6; 8:2, 2, 6, 6; 10:3, 4, 4; 11:13; 12:3, 3; 13:1; 15:1, 1, 6, 6, 7, 7, 8, 8; 16:1; 17:1, 1, 3, 7, 9, 9, 10, 11; 21:9, 9, 9			54
Total	86		1		87

2036. ἔπω, ep'ō

Book	Oc.	say	Oc.	speak	Oc.	tell	Oc.	command	Oc.	bid	Oc.	Misc.	Total
Mt.	161	2:5, 8; 3:7, 15; 4:3a, 4; 5:11, 22, 22; 8:10, 13, 19, 21, 22, 32; 9:2, 3, 4, 5, 5, 11, 12, 15, 22; 11:3, 4, 25; 12:2, 3, 11, 24, 25, 39, 47, 48a, 49; 13:10, 11, 27, 28, 37, 52, 57; 14:2, 16, 18, 28, 29; 15:3, 5, 10, 12, 13, 15, 16, 24, 26, 27, 28, 32, 34; 16:2, 6, 8, 14, 16, 17, 23, 24; 17:4, 7, 11, 17, 19, 20, 22, 24; 18:3, 21; 19:4, 5, 11, 14, 16, 17, 18, 23, 26, 27, 28; 20:4, 13, 17, 21a, 22, 25, 32; 21:3, 16, 21, 21, 24a, 25, 26, 27, 28, 29, 30, 30, 38; 22:13, 18, 24, 29, 37, 44; 23:39; 24:2, 4, 23, 26, 48; 25:8, 12, 22, 24, 26; 26:1, 10, 15, 18, 18, 21, 23, 25, 25, 26, 33, 35, 44, 49, 50, 55, 61, 62, 63a, 64, 66, 73; 27:4, 6, 17, 21, 21, 25, 43, 63, 64; 28:5, 6, 13	7	8:8; 10:27; 12:32, 32; 16:11; 17:13; 22:1	13	8:4; 12:48b; 16:20; 17:9; 18:17; 21:5, 24b; 22:4, 17; 24:3; 26:63b; 28:7, 7	1	4:3b	2	16:12; 23:3	2	2:13; 20:21b	186
Mk.	83	1:17, 44; 2:8, 9, 9, 19; 3:32; 4:39, 40; 5:7, 34; 6:16, 22, 24, 24, 31, 37; 7:6, 10, 11, 27, 29; 8:5, 20, 34; 9:17, 21, 23, 29, 36, 39; 10:3, 4, 5, 14, 18, 20, 21, 29, 36, 37, 38, 39, 39, 51, 52; 11:3, 3, 6, 14, 23, 23, 29, 31, 32; 12:7, 15, 16, 17, 24, 32, 32, 34, 36, 36; 13:2, 21; 14:6, 14, 16, 18, 20, 22, 24, 48, 62, 72; 15:2, 12, 39; 16:7b, 8, 15	6	1:42; 3:9; 9:18; 12:12, 26; 14:39	6	5:33; 7:36; 8:26; 9:12; 13:4; 16:7a	3	5:43; 8:7; 10:49					98
Lk.	277	1:13, 18, 19, 28, 30, 34, 35, 38, 42, 46, 60, 61; 2:10, 15, 28, 34, 48, 49; 3:12, 13, 14; 4:3a, 6, 8, 9, 12, 23, 24, 43; 5:4, 5, 10, 13, 20, 22, 23, 23, 24, 27, 31, 33, 34; 6:2, 3, 8, 9, 10; 7:7, 9, 13, 14, 20, 22, 31, 40a, 40b, 43, 43, 48, 50; 8:10, 21, 22, 25, 28, 30, 45, 45, 46, 48, 52; 9:3, 9, 12, 13, 13, 14, 19, 20, 20, 22, 33, 41, 43, 48, 49, 50, 54a, 55, 57, 58, 59, 59, 60, 61, 62; 10:10, 18, 21, 23, 26, 27, 28, 29, 30, 35, 37, 37, 40a, 41; 11:1, 2, 5, 5, 7, 15, 17, 27, 28, 39, 46, 49; 12:11, 12, 13a 14, 15, 18, 20, 22, 41, 42, 45; 13:2, 7, 12, 15, 20, 23, 23, 32a, 35; 14:5, 10, 15, 16, 17, 18, 19, 20, 21, 22, 23, 25; 15:11, 12, 17, 21, 22, 27, 29, 31; 16:2, 3, 6, 6, 7, 7, 15, 24, 25, 27, 30, 31; 17:1, 5, 6, 14, 17, 19, 20, 22, 37; 18:4, 6, 16, 19, 21, 22, 24, 26, 27, 28, 29, 31, 41, 42; 19:5, 8, 9, 12, 13, 17, 19, 24, 25, 30, 32, 33, 34, 39, 40; 20:3a, 5, 6, 8, 13, 16, 17, 23, 24, 25, 34, 39, 39, 41, 42, 45; 21:3, 5, 8; 22:8, 9, 10, 15, 17, 25, 31, 33, 34, 35, 35, 36, 38, 38, 40, 46, 48, 49, 51, 52, 56, 58, 60, 61, 67b, 70, 71; 23:4, 14, 22, 28, 43, 46, 46; 24:5, 17, 18, 19, 19, 24, 25, 32, 38, 41, 44, 46	16	6:26, 39; 7:39; 8:4; 12:3, 13b, 16; 14:3; 15:3; 18:9; 19:11, 28; 20:2a, 19; 21:29; 24:40	8	5:14; 7:42; 8:56; 9:21; 13:32b; 20:2b; 22:67a, 67c	3	4:3b; 9:54b; 19:15	1	10:40b	2	20:3b; 7:40c	307
Jn.	182	1:22, 23, 25, 30, 33, 38, 42, 46, 48, 50, 50; 2:16, 18, 19, 20, 22; 3:2, 3, 7, 9, 10, 26, 27, 28; 4:10, 13, 17, 17, 27, 32, 48, 52, 53; 5:11, 12, 14, 19; 6:10, 25, 26, 28, 29, 30, 32, 34, 35, 36, 41, 43, 53, 59, 60, 61, 67; 7:3, 9, 16, 20, 21, 33, 35, 36, 38, 42, 45, 52; 8:7, 10, 11, 11, 13, 14, 21, 23, 24, 25, 28, 39, 41, 42, 48, 52, 55, 57, 58; 9:7, 11, 11, 12, 15, 17, 20, 23, 24, 25, 26, 28, 30, 34, 35, 36, 37, 39, 40, 41; 10:7, 26, 34, 36; 11:4, 11, 12, 14, 16, 21, 25, 28, 28, 34, 37, 40, 41, 42, 49; 12:6, 7, 19, 27, 30, 35, 39, 41, 44, 49; 13:7, 11, 12, 21, 21, 33; 14:23, 26, 28, 28; 15:20; 16:4b, 15, 17, 19, 19; 17:1; 18:4, 6, 7, 11, 21, 22b, 25, 25, 29, 30, 31, 31, 33, 37, 38; 19:21, 24, 30; 20:14, 17, 20, 21, 22, 25, 26, 28; 21:6, 17, 17, 20, 23	19	1:15; 4:50; 7:39; 9:6, 22; 10:6, 41; 11:43, 51; 12:38; 13:28; 18:1, 9 16, 22a, 32; 20:18; 21:19, 19	13	3:12, 12; 4:29, 39; 9:27; 10:24, 25; 11:46; 14:2; 16:4a; 18:8, 34; 20:15					1	10:35	215
Ac.	121	1:7, 11, 15, 24; 2:34, 37; 3:4, 6, 22; 4:8, 19, 23, 24, 25; 5:3, 8b, 9, 19, 29, 35; 6:2; 7:1, 3, 7, 26, 27, 33, 35, 37, 40, 56, 60; 8:20, 24, 29, 30, 31, 34, 37, 37; 9:5, 5, 6, 10, 10, 15, 17, 34, 40; 10:3, 4, 4, 14, 19, 21, 22, 34; 11:8, 13; 12:8, 11, 15, 17; 13:2, 10, 16, 22, 46; 14:10; 15:7, 36; 16:18, 20, 31; 17:32; 18:6, 14, 21; 19:2, 2, 3, 3, 4, 15, 21, 25; 20:10, 18, 35; 21:11, 14, 20, 39; 22:8, 10, 10, 13, 14, 19, 21, 25, 27; 23:1, 3, 4, 11, 14, 20, 23; 24:20, 22; 25:9, 10; 26:15, 15, 29; 27:21, 31; 28:21, 26, 29	9	1:9; 2:29; 18:9; 19:41; 20:36; 21:37; 26:30; 27:35; 28:25	1	5:8a	2	11:12; 22:24					133
Ro.	1	10:6											1
1 Co.	9	1:15; 10:28; 11:22, 24; 12:3, 15, 16, 21; 15:27											9
2 Co.	1	6:16					1	4:6					2
Gal.	1	2:14											1
Col.	1	4:17											1
Tit.	1	1:12											1
Heb.	5	1:5; 3:10; 10:7, 30; 12:21									1	7:9	6
Jas.	5	2:3, 3, 11, 11, 16											5
1 Jn.	4	1:6, 8, 10; 4:20											4
Jd.	1	1:9											1
Rev.	6	7:14; 17:7; 21:5, 6; 22:6, 17											6
Total	859		57		41		8		5		6		976

Miscellaneous: Mt. 2:13, bring word; Mt. 20:21b, grant; Lk. 20:3b, answer; Lk. 7:40c, say on; Jn. 10:35, call; Heb. 7:9 (with 2031), say.

2037. Ἔραστος, Er'astos

Book	Erastus	Total
Ac.	19:22	1
Ro.	16:23	1
2 Ti.	4:20	1
Total		3

2038. ἐργάζομαι, ergad′zomai

Book	Oc.	work	Oc.	wrought	Oc.	do	Oc.	minister about	Oc.	forbear working (with 3261)	Oc.	labour for	Oc.	labour	Oc.	commit	Oc.	trade by	Oc.	trade	Total
Mt.	2	7:23; 21:28	1	26:10															1	25:16	4
Mk.			1	14:6																	1
Lk.	1	13:14																			1
Jn.	6	5:17, 17; 6:28, 30; 9:4, 4	1	3:21							1	6:27									8
Ac.	2	10:35; 13:41	1	18:3																	3
Ro.	4	2:10; 4:4, 5; 13:10																			4
1 Co.	2	4:12; 16:10					1	9:13	1	9:6											4
Gal.					1	6:10															1
Eph.	1	4:28																			1
Col.					1	3:23															1
1 Th.	1	4:11											1	2:9							2
2 Th.	3	3:10, 11, 12	1	3:8																	4
Heb.			1	11:33																	1
Jas.															1	2:9					1
2 Jn.			1	1:8																	1
3 Jn.					1	1:5															1
Rev.																	1	18:17			1
Total	22		7		3		1		1		1		1		1		1		1		39

2039. ἐργασία, ergasi′a

Book	Oc.	gain	Oc.	craft	Oc.	diligence	Oc.	work	Total
Lk.					1	12:58			1
Ac.	3	16:16, 19; 19:24	1	19:25					4
Eph.							1	4:19	1
Total	3		1		1		1		6

2040. ἐργάτης, ergat′ēs

Book	Oc.	labourer	Oc.	workman	Oc.	worker	Total
Mt.	5	9:37, 38; 20:1, 2, 8	1	10:10			6
Lk.	3	10:2, 2, 7			1	13:27	4
Ac.			1	19:25			1
2 Co.					1	11:13	1
Phl.					1	3:2	1
1 Ti.	1	5:18					1
2 Ti.			1	2:15			1
Jas.	1	5:4					1
Total	10		3		3		16

2041. ἔργον, er′gon

Book	Oc.	work	Oc.	deed	Oc.	doing	Oc.	labour	Total
Mt.	5	5:16; 11:2; 23:3, 5; 26:10							5
Mk.	2	13:34; 14:6							2
Lk.			2	11:48; 24:19					2
Jn.	23	4:34; 5:20, 36, 36; 6:28, 29; 7:3, 7, 21; 8:39; 9:3, 4; 10:25, 32, 32, 33, 37, 38; 14:10, 11, 12; 15:24; 17:4	4	3:19, 20, 21; 8:41					27
Ac.	10	5:38; 7:41; 9:36; 13:2, 41, 41; 14:26; 15:18, 38; 26:20	1	7:22					11
Ro.	13	2:15; 3:27; 4:2, 6; 9:11, 32; 11:6, 6, 6, 6; 13:3, 12; 14:20	4	2:6; 3:20, 28; 15:18	1	2:7			18
1 Co.	7	3:13, 13, 14, 15; 9:1; 15:58; 16:10	1	5:2					8
2 Co.	2	9:8; 11:15	1	10:11					3
Gal.	8	2:16, 16, 16; 3:2, 5, 10; 5:19; 6:4							8
Eph.	4	2:9, 10; 4:12; 5:11							4
Phl.	2	1:6; 2:30					1	1:22	3
Col.	2	1:10, 21	1	3:17					3
1 Th.	2	1:3; 5:13							2
2 Th.	2	1:11; 2:17							2
1 Ti.	6	2:10; 3:1; 5:10, 10, 25; 6:18							6
2 Ti.	6	1:9; 2:21; 3:17; 4:5, 14, 18							6
Tit.	8	1:16, 16; 2:7, 14; 3:1, 5, 8, 14							8
Heb.	11	1:10; 2:7; 3:9; 4:3, 4, 10; 6:1, 10; 9:14; 10:24; 13:21							11
Jas.	15	1:4, 25; 2:14, 17, 18, 18, 18, 20, 21, 22, 22, 24, 25, 26; 3:13							15
1 Pt.	2	1:17; 2:12							2
2 Pt.	1	3:10	1	2:8					2
1 Jn.	2	3:8, 12	1	3:18					3
2 Jn.			1	1:11					1
3 Jn.			1	1:10					1
Jd.			1	1:15					1
Rev.	19	2:2, 5, 9, 13, 19, 19, 23, 26; 3:1, 2, 8, 15; 9:20; 14:13; 15:3; 18:6; 20:12, 13; 22:12	3	2:6, 22; 16:11					22
Total	152		22		1		1		176

2042. ἐρεθίζω, erethid′zō

Book	provoke	Total
2 Co.	9:2	1
Col.	3:21	1
Total		2

2043. ἐρείδω, erei′dō

Book	stick fast	Total
Ac.	27:41	1

2044. ἐρεύγομαι, ereug′omai

Book	utter	Total
Mt.	13:35	1

2045. ἐρευνάω, ereuna′ō

Book	search	Total
Jn.	5:39; 7:52	2
Ro.	8:27	1
1 Co.	2:10	1
1 Pt.	1:11	1
Rev.	2:23	1
Total		6

2046. ἐρέω, ere′ō

Book	Oc.	say	Oc.	speak	Oc.	tell	Oc.	speak of	Oc.	call	Total
Mt.	10	7:4, 22; 13:30; 17:20; 21:3, 25; 25:34, 40, 41; 26:75			1	21:24					11
Mk.	1	11:31			1	11:29					2
Lk.	17	2:24; 4:12, 23; 12:19; 13:25, 27; 14:9; 15:18; 17:7, 8, 21, 23; 19:31; 20:5; 22:11, 13; 23:29	1	12:10							18
Jn.	3	4:18; 6:65; 12:50	1	11:13	1	14:29			1	15:15	6
Ac.	2	13:34; 17:28	3	2:16; 8:24; 20:38			2	13:40; 23:5			7
Ro.	10	3:5; 4:1; 6:1; 7:7; 8:31; 9:14, 19, 20, 30; 11:19	1	4:18							11
1 Co.	3	14:16, 23; 15:35									3
2 Co.	2	12:6, 9									2
Phl.	1	4:4									1
Heb.	5	1:13; 4:3, 7; 10:9; 13:5	1	4:4							6
Jas.	1	2:18									1
Rev.	2	7:14; 19:3			1	17:7					3
Total	57		7		4		2		1		71

2047. ἐρημία, ere̱mi′a

Book	Oc.	wilderness	Oc.	desert	Total
Mt.	1	15:33			1
Mk.	1	8:4			1
2 Co.	1	11:26			1
Heb.			1	11:38	1
Total	3		1		4

2048a. ἔρημος, er′e̱mos (substantive)

Book	Oc.	wilderness	Oc.	desert	Total
Mt.	4	3:1, 3; 4:1; 11:7	1	24:26	5
Mk.	4	1:3, 4, 12, 13			4
Lk.	7	3:2, 4; 4:1; 5:16; 7:24; 8:29; 15:4	1	1:80	8
Jn.	4	1:23; 3:14; 6:49; 11:54	1	6:31	5
Ac.	7	7:30, 36, 38, 42, 44; 13:18; 21:38			7
1 Co.	1	10:5			1
Heb.	2	3:8, 17			2
Rev.	3	12:6, 14; 17:3			3
Total	32		3		35

2049. ἐρημόω, ere̱mo′ō

Book	Oc.	bring to desolation	Oc.	desolate	Oc.	come to nought	Oc.	make desolate	Total
Mt.	1	12:25							1
Lk.	1	11:17							1
Rev.			1	17:16	1	18:17	1	18:19	3
Total	2		1		1		1		5

2048b. ἔρημος, er′e̱mos (adjective)

Book	Oc.	desert	Oc.	desolate	Oc.	solitary	Total
Mt.	2	14:13, 15	1	23:38			3
Mk.	4	1:45; 6:31, 32, 35			1	1:35	5
Lk.	3	4:42; 9:10, 12	1	13:35			4
Ac.	1	8:26	1	1:20			2
Gal.			1	4:27			1
Total	10		4		1		15

Word 2048 has 50 occurrences.

2050. ἐρήμωσις, ere̱′mōsis

Book	desolation	Total
Mt.	24:15	1
Mk.	13:14	1
Lk.	21:20	1
Total		3

2051. ἐρίζω, erid′zō

Book	strive	Total
Mt.	12:19	1

2052. ἐριθεία, erithei′a

Book	Oc.	strife	Oc.	contention	Oc.	contentious (with 1537)	Total
Ro.					1	2:8	1
2 Co.	1	12:20					1
Gal.	1	5:20					1
Phl.	1	2:3	1	1:16			2
Jas.	2	3:14, 16					2
Total	5		1		1		7

2053. ἔριον, er′ion

Book	wool	Total
Heb.	9:19	1
Rev.	1:14	1
Total		2

2054. ἔρις, er′is

Book	Oc.	strife	Oc.	debate	Oc.	contention	Oc.	variance	Total
Ro.	1	13:13	1	1:29					2
1 Co.	1	3:3			1	1:11			2
2 Co.			1	12:20					1
Gal.							1	5:20	1
Phl.	1	1:15							1
1 Ti.	1	6:4							1
Tit.					1	3:9			1
Total	4		2		2		1		9

2055. ἐρίφιον, eriph′ion

Book	goat	Total
Mt.	25:33	1

2056. ἔριφος, er′iphos

Book	Oc.	goat	Oc.	kid	Total
Mt.	1	25:32			1
Lk.			1	15:29	1
Total	1		1		2

2057. Ἑρμᾶς, Hermas′

Book	Hermas	Total
Ro.	16:14	1

2058. ἑρμηνεία, herme̱nei′a

Book	interpretation	Total
1 Co.	12:10; 14:26	2

2059. ἑρμηνεύω, herme̱neu′ō

Book	Oc.	by interpretation	Oc.	being interpreted	Total
Jn.	2	1:42; 9:7	1	1:38	3
Heb.	1	7:2			1
Total	3		1		4

2060. Ἑρμῆς, Herme̱s′

Book	Oc.	Mercurius (in mythology)	Oc.	Hermes (a Christian)	Total
Ac.	1	14:12			1
Ro.			1	16:14	1
Total	1		1		2

2061. Ἑρμογένης, Hermogen′e̱s

Book	Hermogenes	Total
2 Ti.	1:15	1

2062. ἑρπετόν, herpeton′

Book	Oc.	creeping thing	Oc.	serpent	Total
Ac.	2	10:12; 11:6			2
Ro.	1	1:23			1
Jas.			1	3:7	1
Total	3		1		4

2063. ἐρυθρός, eruthros′

Book	Red	Total
Ac.	7:36	1
Heb.	11:29	1
Total		2

2064. ἔρχομαι, er'chomai

Book	Oc.	come	Oc.	go	Oc.	Misc.	Total
Mt.	114	2:2, 8, 9, 11, 21, 23; 3:7, 11, 14; 4:13; 5:17, 17, 24; 6:10; 7:15, 25, 27; 8:2, 7, 9, 9, 14, 28, 29; 9:1, 10,13, 15, 18, 18, 23, 28; 10:13, 23, 34, 34, 35; 11:3, 14, 18, 19; 12:42, 44; 13:4, 19, 25, 32, 54; 14:28, 29a, 33, 34; 15:25, 29, 39; 16:5, 13, 24, 27, 28; 17:10, 11, 12, 14, 24; 18:7, 7, 11, 31; 19:1, 14; 20:9, 10, 28; 21:1, 5, 9, 19, 23, 32, 40; 22:3; 23:35, 39; 24:5, 30, 39, 42, 43, 44, 46, 48; 25:6, 10, 11, 13, 19, 27, 31, 36, 39; 26:36, 40, 43, 45, 47, 64; 27:33, 49, 57, 64; 28:1, 11, 13	4	12:9; 13:36; 14:12, 29b	1	3:16	119
Mk.	78	1:7, 9, 14, 24, 40, 45; 2:3, 17, 18, 20; 3:8, 31; 4:4, 15, 22; 5:1, 15, 22, 23, 27, 33, 35, 38; 6:1, 29, 31, 48, 53; 7:1, 25, 31; 8:10, 22, 34, 38; 9:1, 7, 11, 12, 13, 14, 33; 10:1, 14, 30, 45, 46, 50; 11:9, 10, 13, 13, 15, 27, 27; 12:9, 14, 18, 42; 13:6, 26, 35, 36; 14:3, 16, 17, 32, 37, 41, 41, 45, 62, 66; 15:21, 36, 43; 16:1, 2	1	3:19	4	1:29; 2:13; 4:21; 5:26	83
Lk.	99	1:43, 59; 2:16, 27, 51; 3:3, 12, 16; 4:16, 34, 42; 5:7, 7, 17, 32, 35; 6:17, 47; 7:3, 7, 8, 8, 19, 20, 33, 34; 8:12, 17, 35, 41, 47, 49; 9:23, 26, 56; 10:1, 32, 33; 11:2, 25, 31; 12:36, 37, 38, 38, 39, 40, 43, 45, 49, 54; 13:6, 7, 14, 35; 14:9, 10, 17, 20, 26, 27, 31; 15:6, 17, 20, 25, 30; 16:21, 28; 17:1, 1, 20, 20, 22, 27; 18:3, 5, 8, 16, 30; 19:5, 10, 13, 18, 20, 23, 38; 20:16; 21:6, 8, 27; 22:7, 18, 45; 23:26, 29, 42; 24:1, 23	2	2:44; 14:1			101
Jn.	152	1:7, 9, 11, 15, 27, 29, 30, 31, 39, 39, 46, 47; 3:2, 2, 8, 19, 20, 21, 22, 26, 26, 31, 31; 4:5, 7, 15, 16, 21, 23, 25, 25, 27, 30, 35, 40, 45a, 46, 54; 5:7, 24, 25, 28, 40, 43, 43; 6:5, 14, 15, 17b, 23, 24, 35, 37, 44, 45, 65; 7:27, 28, 30, 31, 34, 36, 37, 41, 42, 45, 50; 8:2, 14, 14, 20, 21, 22, 42; 9:4, 7, 39; 10:8, 10, 10, 12; 11:17, 19, 20, 27, 29, 30, 32, 34, 38, 45, 48, 56; 12:1, 9, 12, 12, 13, 15, 22, 23, 27, 28, 46, 47; 13: 1,6,33; 14:3, 6, 18, 23, 28, 30; 15:22, 26; 16:2, 4, 7, 8, 13, 13, 21, 25, 28, 32, 32; 17:1, 11, 13; 18:3, 4, 37; 19:32, 33, 38, 39, 39; 20:1, 2, 3, 4, 6, 8, 18, 19, 24, 26; 21:8, 13, 22, 23	3	4:45b; 6:17a; 21:3	1	10:41	156
Ac.	46	1:11; 2:20; 3:19; 7:11; 8:27, 36, 40; 9:17, 21; 10:29; 11:5; 12:10, 12; 13:13, 25, 51; 14:24; 15:30; 16:7, 37, 39; 17:1, 13, 15; 18:1, 2, 21; 19:1, 4, 6, 18; 20:2, 6, 14, 15; 21:1, 8, 11, 12; 22:11, 13; 24: 8; 25:23; 27:8; 28:13, 16	2	4:23; 28:14	6	5:15; 11:12; 13:44; 18:7; 19:27; 22:30	54
Ro.	11	1:10, 13; 3:8; 7:9; 9:9; 15:22, 23, 24, 29, 29, 32					11
1 Co.	18	2:1, 1; 4:5, 18, 19, 21; 11:26, 34; 13:10; 14:6; 15:35; 16:2, 5, 10, 11, 12, 12, 12					18
2 Co.	16	1:15, 16, 23; 2:1, 3, 12; 7:5; 9:4; 11:4, 9; 12:1, 14, 20, 21; 13:1, 2					16
Gal.	8	1:21; 2:11, 12, 12; 3:19, 23, 25; 4:4					8
Eph.	2	2:17; 5:6					2
Phl.	2	1:27; 2:24			1	1:12	3
Col.	2	3:6; 4:10					2
1 Th.	4	1:10; 2:18; 3:6; 5:2					4
2 Th.	2	1:10; 2:3					2
1 Ti.	4	1:15; 2:4; 3:14; 4:13					4
2 Ti.	4	3:7; 4:9, 13, 21					4
Tit.	1	3:12					1
Heb.	4	6:7; 8:8; 10:37; 13:23	1	11:8			5
2 Pt.	1	3:3					1
1 Jn.	5	2:18; 4:2, 3, 3; 5:6					5
2 Jn	3	1:7, 10, 12					3
3 Jn.	2	1:3, 10					2
Jd.	1	1:14					1
Rev.	37	1:4, 7, 8; 2:5, 16; 3:10, 11; 4:8; 5:7; 6:1, 3, 5, 7, 17; 7:13, 14; 8:3; 9:12; 11:14, 17, 18; 14:7, 15; 16: 15; 17:1, 10, 10; 18:10; 19:7; 21:9; 22:7, 12, 17, 17, 17, 20, 20					37
Total	616		13		13		642

Miscellaneous: Mt. 3:16, light; Mk. 1:29, enter; Mk. 2:13, resort; Mk. 4:21, bring; Mk. 5:26, grow; Jn. 10:41, resort; Ac. 5:15, pass by; Ac. 11:12 (with 4762), accompany; Ac. 13:44, next; Ac. 18:7, enter; Ac. 19:27, to be set; Ac. 22:30, appear; Phl. 1:12, fall out.

2065. ἐρωτάω, erōta'ō

Book	Oc.	ask	Oc.	beseech	Oc.	pray	Oc.	desire	Oc.	intreat	Total
Mt.	2	16:13; 21:24	1	15:23							3
Mk.	1	4:10	1	7:26							2
Lk.	4	9:45; 19:31; 20:3; 22:68	4	4:38; 7:3; 8:37; 11:37	4	5:3; 14:18, 19; 16:27	2	7:36; 14:32			14
Jn.	15	1:19, 21, 25; 5:12; 8:7; 9:2, 15, 19, 21, 23; 16:5, 19, 23, 30; 18:19	4	4:40, 47; 19:31, 38	7	4:31; 14:16; 16:26; 17:9, 9, 15, 20	1	12:21			27
Ac.	1	3:3			2	10:48; 23:18	3	16:39; 18: 20; 23:20			6
Phl.									1	4:3	1
1 Th.			2	4:1; 5:12							2
2 Th.			1	2:1							1
1 Jn.					1	5:16					1
2 Jn.			1	1:5							1
Total	23		14		14		6		1		58

2066. ἐσθής, esthēs'

Book	Oc.	apparel	Oc.	clothing	Oc.	robe	Oc.	raiment	Total
Lk.					1	23:11			1
Ac.	2	1:10; 12:21	1	10:30					3
Jas.	1	2:2a	1	2:3			1	2:2b	3
Total	3		2		1		1		7

2067. ἔσθησις, es'thēsis

Book	garment	Total
Lk.	24:4	1

2068. ἐσθίω, esthi'ō

Book	Oc.	eat	Oc.	live	Oc.	devour	Total
Mt.	11	9:11; 11:18, 19; 12:1; 14:21; 15:2, 27, 38; 24:49; 26:21, 26					11
Mk.	11	1:6; 2:16, 16; 7:2, 3, 4, 5, 28; 14:18, 18, 22					11
Lk.	12	5:30, 33; 6:1; 7:33, 34; 10:7, 8; 12:45; 15:16; 17:27, 28; 22: 30					12
Ac.	1	27:35					1
Ro.	10	14:2, 3, 3, 3, 3, 6, 6, 6, 6, 20					10
1 Co.	16	8:7, 10; 9:7, 7; 10:18, 25, 27, 28, 31; 11:22, 26, 27, 28, 29, 29, 34	1	9:13			17
2 Th.	2	3:10, 12					2
Heb.					1	10:27	1
Total	63		1		1		65

2069. Ἐσλί, Esli'

Book	Esli	Total
Lk.	3:25	1

2070. ἐσμέν, esmen′

Book	Oc.	are	Oc.	have hope (with 1679)	Oc.	was	Oc.	be	Oc.	have our being	Total
Mk.	1	5:9									1
Lk.	2	9:12; 17:10									2
Jn.	4	9:28, 40; 10:30; 17:22					1	8:33			5
Ac.	8	2:32; 3:15; 5:32; 10:39; 14:15; 16:28; 17: 28b; 23:15							1	17:28a	9
Ro.	5	6:15; 8:12, 16; 12:5; 14:8									5
1 Co.	4	3:9; 10:17, 22; 15:19b	1	15:19a							5
2 Co.	7	1:14, 24; 2:15, 17; 3:5; 10:11; 13:6									7
Gal.	3	3:25; 4:28, 31									3
Eph.	3	2:10; 4:25; 5:30									3
Phl.	1	3:3									1
1 Th.	1	5:5									1
Heb.	3	3:6; 10:10, 39			1	4:2					4
1 Jn.	7	2:5; 3:2, 19; 4:6, 17; 5:19, 20									7
Total	49		1		1		1		1		53

2071. ἔσομαι, es′omai

Book	Oc.	shall be	Oc.	will be	Oc.	be	Oc.	shall have	Oc.	shall come to pass	Oc.	shall	Oc.	Not Tr.	Oc.	Misc.	Total
Mt.	44	5:21, 22, 22, 22; 6: 5, 22, 23; 8:12; 10: 15, 22; 11:22, 24; 12:11, 27, 40, 45; 13:40, 42, 49, 50; 16:19, 19, 22; 17: 17; 18:18, 18; 19: 5, 30; 20:16, 26; 22: 13, 28; 23:11; 24:3, 7, 9, 21, 27, 37, 39, 40, 51; 25:30; 27:64	1	6:21	1	5:48	1	19:27									47
Mk.	15	6:11; 9:19, 35; 10:8, 31, 43, 43, 44; 12:7, 23; 13:4, 8, 8, 13, 19			1	14:2	2	11:23, 24			1	13:25					19
Lk.	41	1:15, 20, 32, 33, 34, 45, 66; 2:10; 4:7; 6: 35, 35, 40; 9:41, 48; 10:12, 14; 11:19, 30, 36; 12:20, 52; 13:28, 30, 30; 14:14; 15:7; 17:24, 26, 30, 31, 34, 35, 36; 21:7, 11, 11, 17, 23, 24, 25; 23:43	2	12:34, 55			2	1:14; 14:10			2	5:10; 22:69			2	3:5; 22:49	49
Jn.	6	6:45; 8:36, 55; 12: 26; 14:17; 19:24															6
Ac.	5	1:8; 13:11; 22:15; 27:22, 25	1	27:10	2	11:28; 24:15			3	2:17, 21; 3:23					3	7:6; 23: 30; 24:25	14
Ro.	3	4:18; 6:5; 15:12					1	9:9	1	9:26							5
1 Co.	3	6:16; 11:27; 14:11									1	14:9					4
2 Co.	6	3:8; 6:16b, 18b; 11: 15; 12:6; 13:11	2	6:16a, 18a													8
Eph.	1	5:31													1	6:3	2
Phl.	1	4:9															1
Col.													1	2:8			1
1 Th.	1	4:17															1
1 Ti.	1	4:6															1
2 Ti.	4	2:2, 21; 3:2, 9													1	4:3	5
Heb.	2	1:5b; 8:10b	3	1:5a; 8: 10a, 12	1	3:12									1	2:13	7
Jas.	2	1:25; 5:3															2
2 Pt.	1	2:1															1
1 Jn.	2	3:2, 2															2
2 Jn.	1	1:2			1	1:3											2
Jd.					1	1:18											1
Rev.	12	10:9; 20:6; 21:3, 3, 4, 4, 7b, 25; 22:3, 3, 5, 12	1	21:7a	1	10:6									1	22:14	15
Total	151		10		8		6		4		4		1		9		193

Miscellaneous: Lk. 3:5, shall be made; Lk. 22:49, what would follow; Ac. 7:6, should; Ac. 23:30 (with 1917 and 3195), lay wait; Ac. 24:25 (with 3195), to come; Eph. 6:3, mayest; 2 Ti. 4:3, will come; Heb. 2:13, will; Rev. 22:14, may have.

2072. ἔσοπτρον, es′optron

Book	glass	Total
1 Co.	13:12	1
Jas.	1:23	1
Total		2

2073. ἑσπέρα, hesper′a

Book	Oc.	evening	Oc.	eventide	Total
Lk.	1	24:29			1
Ac.	1	28:23	1	4:3	2
Total	2		1		3

2074. Ἐσρώμ, Esrōm′

Book	Esrom	Total
Mt.	1:3, 3	2
Lk.	3:33	1
Total		3

2075. ἐστέ, este'

Book	Oc.	are	Oc.	be	Oc.	is	Oc.	belong to	Oc.	have been	Oc.	Not Tr.	Total
Mt.	8	5:11, 13, 14; 8:26; 15:16; 23:8, 28, 31			1	10:20							9
Mk.	2	4:40; 7:18			1	13:11	1	9:41					4
Lk.	10	6:22; 9:55; 11:44; 13:25, 27; 16:15; 22:28; 24:17, 38, 48											10
Jn.	15	8:23, 23, 31, 37, 44, 47; 10:26, 34; 13:10, 11, 17, 35; 15:3, 14, 19							1	15:27			16
Ac.	4	3:25; 7:26; 19:15; 22:3											4
Ro.	5	1:6; 6:14, 16; 8:9; 15:14											5
1 Co.	17	1:30; 3:3, 3, 4, 9, 16, 17; 4:8; 5:2, 7; 6:2, 19; 9:1, 2; 12:27; 14:12; 15:17											17
2 Co.	4	1:7; 3:2; 6:16; 7:3	4	2:9; 3:3; 13:5, 5									8
Gal.	6	3:3, 26, 28, 29; 4:6; 5:18											6
Eph.	3	2:5, 8, 19									1	5:5	4
Col.	1	2:10											1
1 Th.	4	2:20; 4:9; 5:4, 5											4
Heb.	1	12:8b	1	12:8a									2
1 Jn.	2	2:14; 4:4											2
Total	82		5		2		1		1		1		92

See page 154 for Word 2076.

2077. ἔστω, es'tō

Book	Oc.	let be	Oc.	be	Oc.	Not Tr.	Total
Mt.	4	5:37; 18:17; 20:26, 27					4
Lk.	1	12:35					1
Ac.			4	2:14; 4:10; 13:38; 28:28	1	1:20	5
2 Co.			1	12:16			1
Gal.	2	1:8, 9					2
1 Ti.	1	3:12					1
Jas.	1	1:19					1
1 Pt.	1	3:3					1
Total	10		5		1		16

2079. ἐσχάτως, eschat'ōs

Book	lie at the point of death (with 2192)	Total
Mk.	5:23	1

2078. ἔσχατος, es'chatos

Book	Oc.	last	Oc.	lowest	Oc.	uttermost	Oc.	last state	Oc.	ends	Oc.	latter end	Total
Mt.	8	19:30, 30; 20:8, 12, 14, 16, 16; 27:64			1	5:26	1	12:45					10
Mk.	5	9:35; 10:31, 31; 12:6, 22											5
Lk.	3	12:59; 13:30, 30	2	14:9, 10			1	11:26					6
Jn.	8	6:39, 40, 44, 54; 7:37; 8:9; 11:24; 12:48											8
Ac.	1	2:17			1	1:8			1	13:47			3
1 Co.	5	4:9; 15:8, 26, 45, 52											5
2 Ti.	1	3:1											1
Heb.	1	1:2											1
Jas.	1	5:3											1
1 Pt.	2	1:5, 20											2
2 Pt.	1	3:3									1	2:20	2
1 Jn.	2	2:18, 18											2
Jd.	1	1:18											1
Rev.	7	1:11, 17; 2:8, 19; 15:1; 21:9; 22:13											7
Total	46		2		2		2		1		1		54

2080. ἔσω, es'ō

Book	Oc.	within	Oc.	in	Oc.	into	Oc.	inward	Oc.	inner	Oc.	Not Tr.	Total
Mt.			1	26:58									1
Mk.					1	15:16					1	14:54	2
Jn.	1	20:26											1
Ac.	1	5:23											1
Ro.							1	7:22					1
1 Co.	1	5:12											1
Eph.									1	3:16			1
Total	3		1		1		1		1		1		8

2081. ἔσωθεν, es'ōthen

Book	Oc.	within	Oc.	from within	Oc.	inward part	Oc.	inwardly	Oc.	inward man	Oc.	without	Total
Mt.	3	23:25, 27, 28					1	7:15					4
Mk.			2	7:21, 23									2
Lk.	1	11:40	1	11:7	1	11:39							3
2 Co.	1	7:5							1	4:16			2
Rev.	2	4:8; 5:1									1	11:2	3
Total	7		3		1		1		1		1		14

2082. ἐσώτερος, esō'teros

Book	Oc.	inner	Oc.	within	Total
Ac.	1	16:24			1
Heb.			1	6:19	1
Total	1		1		2

2083. ἑταῖρος, hetai'ros

Book	Oc.	friend	Oc.	fellow	Total
Mt.	3	20:13; 22:12; 26:50	1	11:16	4

2076. ἐστί, esti′

Book	Oc.	is	Oc.	are	Oc.	was	Oc.	be	Oc.	have	Oc.	Not Tr.	Oc.	Misc.	Total
Mt.	105	1:20, 23; 2:2; 3:3, 11, 17; 5:3, 10, 34, 35, 35, 48; 6:13, 21, 22, 25; 7:9, 12; 8: 27; 9:5, 15; 10:10, 11, 24, 26, 37, 37, 38; 11:6, 10, 11, 14, 16, 30; 12:6, 8, 23, 30, 48, 50; 13:19, 20, 22, 23, 31, 32, 32, 33, 37, 38, 39, 39, 44, 45, 47, 52, 55, 57; 14:2, 15, 26; 15:26; 17:4, 5; 18:1, 4, 8, 9, 14; 19:14, 24, 26a; 20:1, 15, 23; 21: 10, 11, 38, 42; 22:8, 32, 38, 42, 45; 23:8, 9, 10, 16, 17, 18; 24:6, 26, 33, 45; 26:18, 26, 28, 38, 48, 66, 68; 27:6, 33, 37; 28:6	3	10:2; 15: 20; 19:26b	1	16:20	5	6:23; 18:7; 19:10; 26:39; 27:42			1	3:15	5	5:37; 9: 13; 12: 7; 13:21; 27:62	120
Mk.	61	1:27; 2:9, 19, 28; 3:17, 29, 33, 35; 4: 22, 26, 31, 41; 5:41; 6:3, 4, 15, 15, 16, 35; 7:15a, 27, 34; 9:5, 7, 21, 39, 40, 40, 42, 43, 45, 47; 10:14, 24, 25, 29, 40; 12:7, 11, 27, 28, 29, 31, 32, 32, 33, 35, 37; 13:28, 29, 33; 14:14, 22, 24, 34, 44, 69; 15:22, 34, 42; 16:6	2	7:15b; 10:27	4	2:1; 5: 14; 6:55; 10:47	1	7:4					5	7:11; 9: 10; 12: 42; 14: 35; 15: 16	73
Lk.	87	1:36, 61, 63; 2:11; 4:22, 24; 5:21, 23, 34, 39; 6:5, 20, 35, 36, 40, 47, 48, 49; 7: 23, 27, 28, 28, 39, 49; 8:11, 11, 17, 25, 25, 26, 30; 9:9, 33, 35, 38, 50, 50, 62; 10:7, 22, 22, 29, 42; 11:23, 29, 34, 34; 12:1, 2, 6, 23, 34, 42; 13:18, 19, 21; 14: 22, 35; 15:31; 16:10, 10, 15, 17; 17:1, 21; 18:16, 25, 29; 19:9, 46; 20:2, 14, 17, 38, 44; 21:30, 31; 22:11, 19, 38, 53, 59, 64; 23:15, 38; 24:6, 29	4	11:21, 41; 14:17; 18: 27	2	7:4; 19:3	4	11:35; 14:31; 20:6; 23:35	4	6:32, 33, 34; 12: 24	1	6:43	4	12:15; 23:6, 7; 24:21	106
Jn.	135	1:19, 27, 30, 33, 34, 42, 47; 3:6, 6, 8, 19, 29, 31, 31, 31, 33; 4:10, 11, 18, 20, 22, 23, 29, 34, 37, 42; 5:2, 10, 12, 25, 27, 30, 31, 32, 32, 45; 6:9a, 14, 29, 31, 33, 39, 40, 42, 45, 50, 51, 55, 55, 58, 60, 63a, 70; 7:6, 11, 12, 16, 18, 18, 22, 25, 26, 27, 27, 28, 36, 40, 41; 8:13, 14, 16, 17, 19, 26, 29, 34, 39, 44, 44, 50, 54, 54, 54; 9:4, 8, 9, 9, 12, 16, 17, 19, 20, 24, 29, 30, 30, 36, 37; 10:1, 2, 13, 29, 34; 11:4, 10; 12:14, 31, 34, 35, 50; 13:10, 16, 25, 26; 14:21, 24, 28; 15:1, 12, 20; 16:17, 18, 32; 17:3, 17; 18:36, 36, 38; 19:35, 40; 20:31; 21:7a, 20, 24, 24	13	3:21; 4: 35; 6:9b, 63b, 63c; 7:7; 10: 16, 21; 16: 15; 17:7, 10; 20:30; 21:25	10	2:9, 17; 5:13, 15; 6:24; 12: 9; 20:14; 21:4, 7b, 12	3	7:17; 9:25; 20:15	1	18:39	2	6:64; 14:10	2	11:39, 57	166
Ac.	42	1:7, 12; 2:15, 16, 25, 29, 39; 4:11, 12, 12, 36; 6:2; 7:33, 37, 38; 8:10, 21b, 26; 9:15, 20, 21, 22; 10:4, 6, 28, 34, 35, 36, 42; 12:15; 16:12; 17:3; 19:35; 20:10, 35; 21:22, 28; 22:26; 23:19; 25:14, 16; 28:4	2	15:18; 21:24	9	9:26, 38; 12:9; 19: 34; 22:29; 23:5, 27, 34: 26:26	6	4:19; 5:39; 18:15; 19:2; 25:5, 11	4	8:21a; 13:15; 18:10; 19:25	3	12:3; 21: 33; 28:22	3	19:36; 21:11;, 23:6	69
Ro.	36	1:9, 12, 16, 19, 25; 2:2, 11, 28; 3:8, 10, 11, 11, 12, 18, 22; 4:15, 16; 5:14; 7:3, 14; 8:9, 24, 34; 10:1, 8, 12; 11:6, 6, 23; 13:1, 4, 4; 14:4, 17, 23; 16:5			1	4:21			1	9:2					38
1 Co.	61	1:18, 18, 25, 25; 3:5, 7, 11, 13, 17, 19; 4:3, 4, 17; 6:5, 7, 16, 17, 18, 19; 7:8, 9, 19, 19, 22, 22, 39, 40; 9:3, 16b, 18; 10: 16, 16, 19, 19, 28; 11:3, 5, 7, 8, 13, 14, 15, 20, 24, 25; 12:6, 12a, 14, 15, 16; 14: 14, 15, 25, 26, 33, 35; 15:12, 44, 44, 58; 16:15	9	2:14; 3: 21, 22; 6: 15, 20; 7: 14b; 12: 12b, 22; 14:10			1	15:13	1	9:16a	1	7:29	1	7:14a	74
2 Co.	12	1:12; 2:2, 3; 3:17; 4:3b, 4; 7:15; 9:1; 10:18; 11:10; 12:13; 13:5					1	4:3a			1	9:12			14
Gal.	15	1:7, 11; 3:12, 16, 20, 20; 4:1, 2, 24b, 25, 26, 26; 5:3, 22, 23	3	4:24a; 5: 19, 19											18
Eph.	22	1:14,18,23; 2:14; 3:13; 4:9,10,15,21; 5: 5,10,12,13,18, 23, 23,32; 6:1, 2.9, 9,17									1	6:12			23
Phl.	4	1:7, 8, 28; 2:13	1	4:8											5
Col.	13	1:7, 15, 17, 18, 18, 24, 27; 2:10; 3:5, 14, 20, 25; 4:9	2	2:17, 22							3	1:6; 2: 23; 3:1			18
1 Th.	2	2:13; 4:3													2
2 Th.	5	1:3; 2:4, 9; 3:3, 17													5
1 Ti.	10	1:5, 20; 3:15,16; 4:8b,10; 5:4, 8; 6:6,10	1	5:25									1	4:8a	12
2 Ti.	5	1:6, 12; 2:17; 4:11, 11	2	1:15; 2:20											7
Tit.	1	1:13	1	3:8			1	1:6							3
Heb.	10	2:6; 4:13; 5:13; 7:2, 15; 8:6; 9:15; 11: 1, 6; 12:7											2	5:14; 9:5	12
Jas.	15	1:17, 27; 2:17, 19, 20, 26, 26; 3:5, 17; 4: 4, 12, 14, 16, 17; 5:11					1	1:23			1	3:15	1	1:13	18
1 Pt.	4	1:25; 2:15; 3:4, 22					2	1:6; 4:11							6
2 Pt.	3	1:9, 17; 3:4	1	3:16									1	1:14	5
1 Jn.	72	1:5, 5, 5, 7, 8, 9, 10; 2:2, 4, 4, 7, 8, 9, 10, 11, 15, 16, 16, 18, 18, 21, 22, 22, 22, 25, 27, 27, 29; 3:2, 3, 4, 5, 7, 7, 8, 10b, 11, 15, 20, 23; 4:2, 3, 3, 3, 4, 6, 7, 8, 10, 12, 15, 16, 17, 18, 20; 5:1, 3, 4, 5, 5, 6, 6, 6, 9, 9, 11, 11, 14, 16, 17, 17, 20	2	3:10a; 4:1											74
2 Jn.	3	1:6, 6, 7													3
3 Jn.	2	1:11, 12													2
Rev.	26	2:7; 5:2, 12, 13a; 13:10, 18, 18; 14:12; 17:8, 8, 8, 10, 11, 11, 11, 14, 18; 19:8, 10; 20:2, 12, 14; 21:8, 16a, 17; 22:10	5	1:4; 5:13b; 21:12, 16b, 22	2	16:21; 21:1									33
Total	751		51		29		25		11		14		25		906

Miscellaneous: Mt. 5:37, come; Mt. 9:13; 12:7, mean; Mt. 13:21, dure; Mt. 27:62 (with 3226), follow; Mk. 7:11, is to say; Mk. 9:10, mean; Mk. 12: 42, make; Mk. 14:35, were; Mk. 15:16, call; Lk. 12:15, consist; Lk. 23:6, were; Lk. 23:7, belong; Lk. 24:21, had been; Jn. 11:39, has been; Jn. 11:57, were; Ac. 19:36 (with 1163), ought; Ac. 21:11, own; Ac. 23:6, were; 1 Co. 7:14a, were; 1 Ti. 4:8a (with 5524), profiteth; Heb. 5:14, belong; Heb. 9:5 (with 3656), cannot; Jas. 1:13 (with 551), cannot be tempted; 2 Pt. 1:14, must.

2084. ἑτερόγλωσσος heterog'lōssos

Book	other tongue	Total
1 Co.	14:21	1

2085. ἑτεροδιδασκαλέω, heterodidaskale'ō

Book	Oc.	teach other doctrine	Oc.	teach otherwise	Total
1 Ti.	1	1:3	1	6:3	2

2086. ἑτεροζυγέω, heterodzuge'ō

Book	be unequally yoked together with	Total
2 Co.	6:14	1

2087. ἕτερος, het'eros

Book	Oc.	another	Oc.	other	Oc.	other thing	Oc.	some	Oc.	next day	Oc.	Misc.	Total
Mt.	2	8:21; 11:3	5	6:24, 24; 12:45; 15:30; 16:14									7
Mk.	1	16:12											1
Lk.	12	6:6; 9:56, 59, 61; 14:19, 20, 31; 16:7, 18; 19:20; 20:11; 22:58	16	4:43; 5:7; 7:41; 8:3, 8; 10:1; 11:16, 26; 16:13, 13; 17:34, 35, 36; 18:10; 23:32, 40	2	3:18; 22:65	2	8:6, 7			1	9:29	33
Jn.	1	19:37											1
Ac.	4	1:20; 7:18; 12:17; 17:7	9	2:4, 13, 40; 4:12; 8:34; 15:35; 17:34; 23:6; 27:1					2	20:15; 27:3	3	13:35; 17:21; 19:39	18
Ro.	7	2:1, 21; 7:3, 3, 4, 23; 13:8	2	8:39; 13:9									9
1 Co.	7	3:4; 4:6; 6:1; 10:24; 12:9, 10; 15:40b	4	8:4; 10:29; 14:17, 21							1	15:40a	12
2 Co.	2	11:4, 4	1	8:8									3
Gal.	2	1:6; 6:4	1	1:19									3
Eph.			1	3:5									1
Phl.			1	2:4									1
1 Ti.					1	1:10							1
2 Ti.			1	2:2									1
Heb.	3	7:11, 13, 15	1	11:36							1	5:6	5
Jas.	2	2:25; 4:12											2
Jd.											1	1:7	1
Total	43		42		3		2		2		7		99

Miscellaneous: Lk. 9:29 (with 1096), be altered; Ac. 13:35, another Psalm; Ac. 17:21, else; Ac. 19:39, other matter; 1 Co. 15:40a, one; Heb. 5:6, another place; Jd. 1:7, strange.

2088. ἑτέρως, heter'ōs

Book	otherwise	Total
Phl.	3:15	1

2091. ἑτοιμασία, hetoimasi'a

Book	preparation	Total
Eph.	6:15	1

2090. ἑτοιμάζω, hetoimad'zō

Book	Oc.	prepare	Oc.	make ready	Oc.	provide	Total
Mt.	6	3:3; 20:23; 22:4; 25:34, 41; 26:17	1	26:19			7
Mk.	3	1:3; 10:40; 14:12	2	14:15, 16			5
Lk.	8	1:76; 2:31; 3:4; 12:47; 22:8, 9; 23:56; 24:1	5	1:17; 9:52; 17:8; 22:12, 13	1	12:20	14
Jn.	2	14:2, 3					2
Ac.			1	23:23			1
1 Co.	1	2:9					1
2 Ti.	1	2:21					1
Phe.	1	1:22					1
Heb.	1	11:16					1
Rev.	6	8:6; 9:7, 15; 12:6; 16:12; 21:2	1	19:7			7
Total	29		10		1		40

2089. ἔτι, et'i

Book	Oc.	yet	Oc.	more	Oc.	any more	Oc.	still	Oc.	further	Oc.	longer	Oc.	Misc.	Total
Mt.	5	12:46; 17:5; 19:20; 26:47; 27:63	1	18:16					1	26:65			1	5:13	8
Mk.	4	5:35a; 8:17; 12:6; 14:43							1	5:35b			1	14:63	6
Lk.	12	8:49; 9:42; 14:22, 32; 15:20; 18:22; 22:37, 47, 60; 24:6, 41, 44			1	20:36					1	16:2	4	1:15; 14:26; 20:40; 22:71	18
Jn.	7	4:35; 7:33; 12:35; 13:33; 14:19a; 16:12; 20:1	6	11:54; 14:19b; 16:10, 21, 25; 17:11									2	14:30; 21:6	15
Ac.	3	9:1; 10:44; 18:18							1	21:28			1	2:26	5
Ro.	4	3:7; 5:6, 8; 9:19	8	6:9, 9; 7:17, 20; 11:6, 6, 6, 6									2	6:2; 14:15	14
1 Co.	4	3:2, 3; 12:31; 15:17													4
2 Co.	1	1:10	1	5:16b									1	5:16a	3
Gal.	4	1:10; 2:20; 5:11, 11	2	3:18; 4:7							1	3:25			7
Phl.	1	1:9													1
2 Th.	1	2:5													1
Heb.	5	7:10, 15; 9:8; 10:37; 11:4	6	8:12; 10:2, 17, 18, 26; 11:32					1	7:11			3	11:36; 12:26, 27	15
Rev.	1	6:11	12	3:12; 7:16a; 9:12; 18:21, 22a, 22c, 23, 23; 20:3; 21:1, 4a; 22:3	4	7:16b; 12:8; 18:22b; 21:4b	4	22:11, 11, 11, 11			1	10:6			22
Total	52		36		5		4		4		3		15		119

Miscellaneous: Mt. 5:13, thenceforth; Mk. 14:63, any further; Lk. 1:15, even; Lk. 14:26, yea; Lk. 20:40, after that; Lk. 22:71, any further; Jn. 14:30, hereafter; Jn. 21:6, now; Ac. 2:26, moreover; Ro. 6:2, any longer; Ro. 14:15, now; 2 Co. 5:16a, henceforth; Heb. 11:36, moreover; Heb. 12:26, 27, yet more.

2092. ἕτοιμος, het'oimos

Book	Oc.	ready	Oc.	prepared	Oc.	readiness	Oc.	made ready to (one's) hand	Total
Mt.	4	22:4, 8; 24:44; 25:10							4
Mk.			1	14:15					1
Lk.	3	12:40; 14:17; 22:33							3
Jn.	1	7:6							1
Ac.	2	23:15, 21							2
2 Co.	1	9:5			1	10:6	1	10:16	3
Tit.	1	3:1							1
1 Pt.	2	1:5; 3:15							2
Total	14		1		1		1		17

2093. ἑτοίμως, hetoi'mōs

Book	ready	Total
Ac.	21:13	1
2 Co.	12:14	1
1 Pt.	4:5	1
Total		3

2096. Εὔα, Eu'a

Book	Eve	Total
2 Co.	11:3	1
1 Ti.	2:13	1
Total		2

2094. ἔτος, et'os

Book	year	Total
Mt.	9:20	1
Mk.	5:25, 42	2
Lk.	2:36, 37, 41, 42; 3:1, 23; 4:25; 8:42, 43; 12:19; 13:7, 8, 11, 16; 15:29	15
Jn.	2:20; 5:5; 8:57	3
Ac.	4:22; 7:6, 30, 36, 42; 9:33; 13:20, 21; 19:10; 24:10, 17	11
Ro.	15:23	1
2 Co.	12:2	1
Gal.	1:18; 2:1; 3:17	3
1 Ti.	5:9	1
Heb.	1:12; 3:9, 17	3
2 Pt.	3:8, 8	2
Rev.	20:2, 3, 4, 5, 6, 7	6
Total		49

2095. εὖ, eu

Book	Oc.	well	Oc.	well done	Oc.	good	Total
Mt.			2	25:21, 23			2
Mk.					1	14:7	1
Lk.	1	19:17					1
Ac.	1	15:29					1
Eph.	1	6:3					1
Total	3		2		1		6

2097. εὐαγγελίζω, euanggelid'zō

Book	Oc.	preach	Oc.	preach the Gospel	Oc.	bring good tidings	Oc.	shew glad tidings	Oc.	bring glad tidings	Oc.	declare	Oc.	declare glad tidings	Oc.	Misc.	Total
Mt.			1	11:5													1
Lk.	3	3:18; 4:43; 16:16	4	4:18; 7:22; 9:6; 20:1	1	2:10	2	1:19; 8:1									10
Ac.	10	5:42; 8:4, 12, 35, 40; 10:36; 11:20; 14:15; 15:35; 17:18	3	8:25; 14:21; 16:10									1	13:32	1	14:7	15
Ro.			3	1:15; 10:15a; 15:20					1	10:15b							4
1 Co.	2	15:1, 2	4	1:17; 9:16, 16, 18													6
2 Co.	1	11:7	1	10:16													2
Gal.	3	1:8b, 16, 23	3	1:8a, 9; 4:13											1	1:11	7
Eph.	2	2:17; 3:8															2
1 Th.					1	3:6											1
Heb.	1	4:6	1	4:2													2
1 Pt.			2	1:12; 4:6											1	1:25	3
Rev.	1	14:6									1	10:7					2
Total	23		22		2		2		1		1		1		3		55

Miscellaneous: Ac. 14:7 (with 2258), preached the gospel; Gal. 1:11, be preached; 1 Pt. 1:25, be preached by the gospel.

2098a. εὐαγγέλιον, euanggel'ion

Book	gospel	Total
Mt.	4:23; 9:35; 24:14; 26:13	4
Mk.	1:1, 14, 15; 8:35; 10:29; 13:10; 14:9; 16:15	8
Ac.	15:7; 20:24	2
Ro.	1:1, 9, 16; 2:16; 10:16; 11:28; 15:16, 19, 29; 16:25	10
1 Co.	4:15; 9:12, 14, 14, 18, 18, 23; 15:1	8
2 Co.	2:12; 4:3, 4; 8:18; 9:13; 10:14; 11:4, 7	8
Gal.	1:6, 7, 11; 2:2, 5, 7, 14	7
Eph.	1:13; 3:6; 6:15, 19	4
Phl.	1:5, 7, 12, 17, 27, 27; 2:22; 4:3, 15	9
Col.	1:5, 23	2
1 Th.	1:5; 2:2, 4, 8, 9; 3:2	6
2 Th.	1:8; 2:14	2
1 Ti.	1:11	1
2 Ti.	1:8, 10; 2:8	3
Phe.	1:13	1
1 Pt.	4:17	1
Rev.	14:6	1
Total		77

2098b. εὐαγγέλιον, euanggel'ion

Arranged according to various titles

Book	Oc.	gospel	Oc.	gospel of Christ	Oc.	gospel of God	Oc.	gospel of the Kingdom	Oc.	Misc.	Total
Mt.	1	26:13					3	4:23; 9:25; 24:14			4
Mk.	6	1:15; 8:35; 10:29; 13:10; 14:9; 16:15							2	1:1, 14	8
Ac.	1	15:7							1	20:24	2
Ro.	4	2:16; 10:16; 11:28; 16:25	3	1:16; 15:19, 29	2	1:1; 15:16			1	1:9	10
1 Co.	6	4:15; 9:14, 14, 18b, 23; 15:1	2	9:12, 18a							8
2 Co.	3	4:3; 8:18; 11:4	3	2:12; 9:13; 10:14	1	11:7			1	4:4	8
Gal.	6	1:6, 11; 2:2, 5, 7, 14	1	1:7							7
Eph.	2	3:6; 6:19							2	1:13; 6:15	4
Phl.	8	1:5, 7, 12, 17, 27b; 2:22; 4:3, 15	1	1:27a							9
Col.	2	1:5, 23									2
1 Th.	2	1:5; 2:4	1	3:2	3	2:2, 8, 9					6
2 Th.	1	2:14							1	1:8	2
1 Ti.									1	1:11	1
2 Ti.	3	1:8, 10; 2:8									3
Phe.	1	1:13									1
1 Pt.					1	4:17					1
Rev.									1	14:6	1
Total	46		11		7		3		10		77

Miscellaneous: Mk. 1:1, Gospel of Jesus Ghrist; Mk. 1:14, Gospel of the Kingdom of God; Ac. 20:24, Gospel of the grace of God; Ro. 1:9, Gospel of His Son; 2 Co. 4:4, glorious Gospel of Christ; Eph. 1:13, Gospel of your salvation; Eph. 6:15, Gospel of peace; 2 Th. 1:8, Gospel of our Lord Jesus Christ; 1 Ti. 1:11, glorious Gospel of the blessed God; Rev. 14:6, everlasting Gospel.

2099. εὐαγγελιστής euanggelistes'

Book	evangelist	Total
Ac.	21:8	1
Eph.	4:11	1
2 Ti.	4:5	1
Total		3

2100. εὐαρεστέω, euareste'ō

Book	Oc.	please	Oc.	be well pleased	Total
Heb.	2	11:5, 6	1	13:16	3

2101. εὐάρεστος, euar'estos

Book	Oc.	acceptable	Oc.	well pleasing	Oc.	please well (with 1510)	Oc.	accepted	Total
Ro.	3	12:1, 2; 14:18							3
2 Co.							1	5:9	1
Eph.	1	5:10							1
Phl.			1	4:18					1
Col.			1	3:20					1
Tit.					1	2:9			1
Heb.			1	13:21					1
Total	4		3		1		1		9

2102. εὐαρέστως, euares'tōs

Book	acceptably	Total
Heb.	12:28	1

2103. Εὔβουλος, Eu'boulos

Book	Eubulus	Total
2 Ti.	4:21	1

2104. εὐγένης, eugen′ēs

Book	Oc.	nobleman (with 444)	Oc.	more noble	Oc.	noble	Total
Lk.	1	19:12					1
Ac.			1	17:11			1
1 Co.					1	1:26	1
Total	1		1		1		3

2105. εὐδία, eudi′a

Book	fair weather	Total
Mt.	16:2	1

2106. εὐδοκέω, eudoke′ō

Book	Oc.	be well pleased	Oc.	please	Oc.	have pleasure	Oc.	be willing	Oc.	be (one's) good pleasure	Oc.	take pleasure	Oc.	think good	Total
Mt.	3	3:17; 12:18; 17:5													3
Mk.	1	1:11													1
Lk.	1	3:22							1	12:32					2
Ro.			2	15:26, 27											2
1 Co.	1	10:5	1	1:21											2
2 Co.							1	5:8			1	12:10			2
Gal.			1	1:15											1
Col.			1	1:19											1
1 Th.							1	2:8					1	3:1	2
2 Th.					1	2:12									1
Heb.					3	10:6, 8, 38									3
2 Pt.	1	1:17													1
Total	7		5		4		2		1		1		1		21

2107. εὐδοκία, eudoki′a

Book	Oc.	good pleasure	Oc.	good will	Oc.	seem good (with 1096)	Oc.	desire	Total
Mt.					1	11:26			1
Lk.			1	2:14	1	10:21			2
Ro.							1	10:1	1
Eph.	2	1:5, 9							2
Phl.	1	2:13	1	1:15					2
2 Th.	1	1:11							1
Total	4		2		2		1		9

2109. εὐεργετέω, euergete′ō

Book	doing good	Total
Ac.	10:38	1

2110. εὐεργέτης, euerget′ēs

Book	benefactor	Total
Lk.	22:25	1

2108. εὐεργεσία, euergesi′a

Book	Oc.	good deed done	Oc.	benefit	Total
Ac.	1	4:9			1
1 Ti.			1	6:2	1
Total	1		1		2

2111. εὔθετος, eu′thetos

Book	Oc.	fit	Oc.	meet	Total
Lk.	2	9:62; 14:35			2
Heb.			1	6:7	1
Total	2		1		3

2112. εὐθέως, euthe′ōs

Book	Oc.	immediately	Oc.	straightway	Oc.	forthwith	Oc.	Misc.	Total
Mt.	6	4:22; 8:3; 14:31; 20:34; 24:29; 26:74	7	4:20; 14:22, 27; 21:2, 3; 25:15; 27:48	2	13:5; 26:49			15
Mk.	15	1:31, 42; 2:8, 12; 4:5, 15, 16, 17, 29; 5:2, 30; 6:27, 50; 10:52; 14:43	19	1:10, 18, 20, 21; 2:2; 3:6; 5:29, 42; 6:25, 45, 54; 7:35; 8:10; 9:15, 20, 24; 11:3; 14:45; 15:1	3	1:29, 43; 5:13	3	1:30; 5:36; 11:2	40
Lk.	3	5:13; 6:49; 12:36	3	5:39; 12:54; 14:5			2	17:7; 21:9	8
Jn.	4	5:9; 6:21; 13:30; 18:27							4
Ac.	5	9:18, 34; 16:10; 17:10, 14	2	9:20; 22:29	2	12:10; 21:30			9
Gal.	1	1:16							1
Jas.			1	1:24					1
3 Jn.							1	1:14	1
Rev.	1	4:2							1
Total	35		32		7		6		80

Miscellaneous: Mk. 1:30, anon; Mk. 5:36; 11:2, as soon as; Lk. 17:7; 21:9, by and by; 3 Jn. 1:14, shortly.

2113. εὐθυδρομέω, euthudrome′ō

Book	come with a straight course	Total
Ac.	16:11; 21:1	2

2114. εὐθυμέω, euthume′ō

Book	Oc.	be of good cheer	Oc.	be merry	Total
Ac.	2	27:22, 25			2
Jas.			1	5:13	1
Total	2		1		3

2118. εὐθύτης, euthu′tēs

Book	righteousness	Total
Heb.	1:8	1

2115. εὔθυμος, eu′thumos

Book	Oc.	of good cheer	Oc.	more cheerfully	Total
Ac.	1	27:36	1	24:10	2

2116. εὐθύνω, euthu′nō

Book	Oc.	make straight	Oc.	governor (with 3488)	Total
Jn.	1	1:23			1
Jas.			1	3:4	1
Total	1		1		2

2117a. εὐθύς, euthus′ (adjective)

Book	Oc.	straight	Oc.	right	Total
Mt.	1	3:3			1
Mk.	1	1:3			1
Lk.	2	3:4, 5			2
Ac.	1	9:11	2	8:21; 13:10	3
2 Pt.			1	2:15	1
Total	5		3		8

2119. εὐκαιρέω, eukaire′ō

Book	Oc.	have leisure	Oc.	spend time	Oc.	have convenient time	Total
Mk.	1	6:31					1
Ac.			1	17:21			1
1 Co.					1	16:12	1
Total	1		1		1		3

2117b. εὐθύς, euthus (adverb)

Book	Oc.	immediately	Oc.	straightway	Oc.	anon	Oc.	by and by	Oc.	forthwith	Total
Mt.			1	3:16	1	13:20	1	13:21			3
Mk.	2	1:12, 28									2
Jn.	1	21:3	1	13:32					1	19:34	3
Total	3		2		1		1		1		8

Word 2117 has 16 occurrences.

2120. εὐκαιρία, eukairi′a

Book	opportunity	Total
Mt.	26:16	1
Lk.	22:6	1
Total		2

2121. εὔκαιρος, eu′kairos

Book	Oc.	convenient	Oc.	in time of need	Total
Mk.	1	6:21			1
Heb.			1	4:16	1
Total	1		1		2

2122. εὐκαίρως, eukai′rōs

Book	Oc.	conveniently	Oc.	in season	Total
Mk.	1	14:11			1
2 Ti.			1	4:2	1
Total	1		1		2

2123. εὐκοπώτερος, eukopō′teros

Book	easier	Total
Mt.	9:5; 19:24	2
Mk.	2:9; 10:25	2
Lk.	5:23; 16:17; 18:25	3
Total		7

2124. εὐλάβεια, eulab′eia

Book	Oc.	godly fear	Oc.	fear	Total
Heb.	1	12:28	1	5:7	2

2126. εὐλαβής, eulabẹs′

Book	devout	Total
Lk.	2:25	1
Ac.	2:5; 8:2	2
Total		3

2125. εὐλαβέομαι, eulabe′omai

Book	Oc.	fearing	Oc.	moved with fear	Total
Ac.	1	23:10			1
Heb.			1	11:7	1
Total	1		1		2

2127. εὐλογέω, euloge′ō

Book	Oc.	bless	Oc.	praise	Total
Mt.	6	5:44; 14:19; 21:9; 23:39; 25:34; 26:26			6
Mk.	6	6:41; 8:7; 10:16; 11:9, 10; 14:22			6
Lk.	13	1:28, 42, 42; 2:28, 34; 6:28; 9:16; 13: 35; 19:38; 24:30, 50, 51, 53	1	1:64	14
Jn.	1	12:13			1
Ac.	1	3:26			1
Ro.	2	12:14, 14			2
1 Co.	3	4:12; 10:16; 14:16			3
Gal.	1	3:9			1
Eph.	1	1:3			1
Heb.	7	6:14, 14; 7:1, 6, 7; 11:20, 21			7
Jas.	1	3:9			1
1 Pt.	1	3:9			1
Total	43		1		44

2128. εὐλογητός, eulogẹtos′

Book	blessed (said of God)	Total
Mk.	14:61	1
Lk.	1:68	1
Ro.	1:25; 9:5	2
2 Co.	1:3; 11:31	2
Eph.	1:3	1
1 Pt.	1:3	1
Total		8

2130. εὐμετάδοτος, eumetad′otos

Book	ready to distribute	Total
1 Ti.	6:18	1

2131. Εὐνίκη, Euni′kẹ

Book	Eunice	Total
2 Ti.	1:5	1

2129. εὐλογία, eulogi′a

Book	Oc.	blessing	Oc.	bounty	Oc.	bountifully (with 1909)	Oc.	fair speech	Total
Ro.	1	15:29					1	16:18	2
1 Co.	1	10:16							1
2 Co.			2	9:5, 5	2	9:6, 6			4
Gal.	1	3:14							1
Eph.	1	1:3							1
Heb.	2	6:7; 12:17							2
Jas.	1	3:10							1
1 Pt.	1	3:9							1
Rev.	3	5:12, 13; 7:12							3
Total	11		2		2		1		16

2132. εὐνοέω, eunoe′ō

Book	agree	Total
Mt.	5:25	1

2134. εὐνουχίζω, eunouchid′zō

Book	make eunuchs	Total
Mt.	19:12, 12	2

2133. εὔνοια, eu′noia

Book	Oc.	benevolence	Oc.	good will	Total
1 Co.	1	7:3			1
Eph.			1	6:7	1
Total	1		1		2

2135. εὐνοῦχος, eunou′chos

Book	eunuch	Total
Mt.	19:12, 12, 12	3
Ac.	8:27, 34, 36, 38, 39	5
Total		8

2136. Εὐοδία, Euodi′a

Book	Euodias	Total
Phl.	4:2	1

2137. εὐοδόω, euodo′ō

Book	Oc.	prosper	Oc.	have a prosporous journey	Total
Ro.			1	1:10	1
1 Co.	1	16:2			1
3 Jn.	2	1:2, 2			2
Total	3		1		4

2138. εὐπειθής, eupeithẹs′

Book	easy to be intreated	Total
Jas.	3:17	1

2139. εὐπερίστατος euperis′tatos

Book	which doth so easily beset	Total
Heb.	12:1	1

2140. εὐποιΐα, eupoii′a

Book	to do good	Total
Heb.	13:16	1

2141. εὐπορέω, eupore′ō

Book	his ability (with 5000)	Total
Ac.	11:29	1

2142. εὐπορία, eupori′a

Book	wealth	Total
Ac.	19:25	1

2143. εὐπρέπεια, euprep′eia

Book	grace	Total
Jas.	1:11	1

2144. εὐπρόσδεκτος, eupros′dektos

Book	Oc.	accepted	Oc.	acceptable	Total
Ro.	1	15:31	1	15:16	2
2 Co.	2	6:2; 8:12			2
1 Pt.			1	2:5	1
Total	3		2		5

2145. εὐπρόσεδρος, eupros′edros

Book	that (one) may attend upon (with 4214 and 3488)	Total
1 Co.	7:35	1

2146. εὐπροσωπέω, euprosōpe′ō

Book	make a fair show	Total
Gal.	6:12	1

2147. εὑρίσκω, heuris′kō

Book	Oc.	find	Oc.	Misc.	Total
Mt.	28	1:18; 2:8; 7:7, 8, 14; 8:10; 10:39, 39; 11:29; 12:43, 44; 13:44, 46; 16:25; 17:27; 18:13, 28; 20:6; 21:2, 19; 22:9, 10; 24: 46; 26:40, 43, 60, 60; 27:32	1	2:11	29
Mk.	11	1:37; 7:30; 11:2, 4, 13, 13; 13:36; 14:16, 37, 40, 55			11
Lk.	44	1:30; 2:12, 45, 46; 4:17; 5:19; 6:7; 7:9, 10; 8:35; 9:36; 11:9, 10, 24, 25; 12:37, 38, 43; 13:6, 7; 15:4, 5, 6, 8, 9, 9, 24, 32; 17:18; 18:8; 19:30, 32, 48; 22:13, 45; 23:2, 4, 14, 22; 24:2, 3, 23, 24, 33	1	9:12	45
Jn.	19	1:41, 41, 43, 45, 45; 2:14; 5:14; 6:25; 7:34, 35, 36; 9:35; 10:9; 11:17; 12:14; 18:38; 19:4, 6; 21:6			19
Ac.	34	4:21; 5:10, 22, 23, 23, 39; 7:11, 46, 46; 8:40; 9:2, 33; 10:27; 11:26; 12:19; 13:6, 22, 28; 17:6, 23, 27; 18:2; 19:1, 19; 21: 2; 23:9; 24:5, 12, 18, 20; 27:6, 28, 28; 28:14	1	23:29	35
Ro.	5	4:1; 7:10, 18, 21; 10:20			5
1 Co.	2	4:2; 15:15			2
2 Co.	6	2:13; 5:3; 9:4; 11:12; 12:20, 20			6
Gal.	1	2:17			1
Phl.	2	2:8; 3:9			2
2 Ti.	2	1:17, 18			2
Heb.	3	4:16; 11:5; 12:17	1	9:12	4
1 Pt.	2	1:7; 2:22			2
2 Pt.	1	3:14			1
2 Jn.	1	1:4			1
Rev.	13	2:2; 3:2; 5:4; 9:6; 12:8; 14:5; 16:20; 18:14, 21, 22, 24; 20:11, 15			13
Total	174		4		178

Miscellaneous: Mt. 2:11, see; Lk. 9:12, get; Ac. 23:29, perceive; Heb. 9:12, obtain.

2148. Εὐροκλύδων, Euroklu′dōn

Book	Euroclydon	Total
Ac.	27:14	1

2149. εὐρύχωρος, euru′chōros

Book	broad	Total
Mt.	7:13	1

2150. εὐσέβεια, euseb′eia

Book	Oc.	godliness	Oc.	holiness	Total
Ac.			1	3:12	1
1 Ti.	8	2:2; 3:16; 4:7, 8; 6:3, 5, 6, 11			8
2 Ti.	1	3:5			1
Tit.	1	1:1			1
2 Pt.	4	1:3, 6, 7; 3:11			4
Total	14		1		15

2151. εὐσεβέω, eusebe′ō

Book	Oc.	worship	Oc.	shew piety	Total
Ac.	1	17:23			1
1 Ti.			1	5:4	1
Total	1		1		2

2152. εὐσεβής, eusebe̱s′

Book	Oc.	devout	Oc.	godly	Total
Ac.	3	10:2, 7; 22:12			3
2 Pt.			1	2:9	1
Total	3		1		4

2153. εὐσεβῶς, eusebōs′

Book	godly	Total
2 Ti.	3:12	1
Tit.	2:12	1
Total		2

2154. εὔσημος, eu′se̱mos

Book	easy to be understood	Total
1 Co.	14:9	1

2155. εὔσπλαγχνος, eu′splangchnos

Book	Oc.	tenderhearted	Oc.	pitiful	Total
Eph.	1	4:32			1
1 Pt.			1	3:8	1
Total	1		1		2

2156. εὐσχημόνως, eusche̱mon′ōs

Book	Oc.	honestly	Oc.	decently	Total
Ro.	1	13:13			1
1 Co.			1	14:40	1
1 Th.	1	4:12			1
Total	2		1		3

2157. εὐσχημοσύνη euscheмosu′ne̱

Book	comeliness	Total
1 Co.	12:23	1

2158. εὐσχήμων, eusche̱′mōn

Book	Oc.	honourable	Oc.	comely	Total
Mk.	1	15:43			1
Ac.	2	13:50; 17:12			2
1 Co.			2	7:35; 12:24	2
Total	3		2		5

2159. εὐτόνως, euton′ōs

Book	Oc.	vehemently	Oc.	mightily	Total
Lk.	1	23:10			1
Ac.			1	18:28	1
Total	1		1		2

2160. εὐτραπελία, eutrapeli′a

Book	jesting	Total
Eph.	5:4	1

2161. Εὔτυχος, Eu′tuchos

Book	Eutychus	Total
Ac.	20:9	1

2162. εὐφημία, euphe̱mi′a

Book	good report	Total
2 Co.	6:8	1

2163. εὔφημος, eu′phe̱mos

Book	of good report	Total
Phl.	4:8	1

2164. εὐφορέω, euphore′ō

Book	bring forth plentifully	Total
Lk.	12:16	1

2165. εὐφραίνω, euphrai′nō

Book	Oc.	rejoice	Oc.	be merry	Oc.	make merry	Oc.	fare	Oc.	make glad	Total
Lk.			3	12:19; 15:23, 24	2	15:29, 32	1	16:19			6
Ac.	2	2:26; 7:41									2
Ro.	1	15:10									1
2 Co.									1	2:2	1
Gal.	1	4:27									1
Rev.	2	12:12; 18:20			1	11:10					3
Total	6		3		3		1		1		14

2166. Εὐφράτης, Euphrat′e̱s

Book	Euphrates	Total
Rev.	9:14; 16:12	2

2167. εὐφροσύνη, euphrosu′ne̱

Book	Oc.	joy	Oc.	gladness	Total
Ac.	1	2:28	1	14:17	2

2168. εὐχαριστέω, eucharis te′ō

Book	Oc.	give thanks	Oc.	thank	Oc.	be thankful	Total
Mt.	2	15:36; 26:27					2
Mk.	2	8:6; 14:23					2
Lk.	3	17:16; 22:17, 19	1	18:11			4
Jn.	2	6:11, 23	1	11:41			3
Ac.	1	27:35	1	28:15			2
Ro.	3	14:6, 6; 16:4	2	1:8; 7:25	1	1:21	6
1 Co.	3	10:30; 11:24; 14:17	3	1:4, 14; 14:18			6
2 Co.	1	1:11					1
Eph.	2	1:16; 5:20					2
Phl.			1	1:3			1
Col.	3	1:3, 12; 3:17					3
1 Th.	2	1:2; 5:18	1	2:13			3
2 Th.	1	2:13	1	1:3			2
Phe.			1	1:4			1
Rev.	1	11:17					1
Total	26		12		1		39

2169. εὐχαριστία, eucharisti′a

Book	Oc.	thanksgiving	Oc.	giving of thanks	Oc.	thanks	Oc.	thankfulness	Total
Ac.							1	24:3	1
1 Co.			1	14:16					1
2 Co.	3	4:15; 9:11, 12							3
Eph.			1	5:4					1
Phl.	1	4:6							1
Col.	2	2:7; 4:2							2
1 Th.					1	3:9			1
1 Ti.	2	4:3, 4	1	2:1					3
Rev.	1	7:12			1	4:9			2
Total	9		3		2		1		15

2170. εὐχάριστος, euchar̠′istos

Book	thankful	Total
Col.	3:15	1

2171. εὐχή, euche̱′

Book	Oc.	vow	Oc.	prayer	Total
Ac.	2	18:18; 21:23			2
Jas.			1	5:15	1
Total	2		1		3

2172. εὔχομαι, eu′chomai

Book	Oc.	wish	Oc.	pray	Oc.	can wish	Oc.	I would	Total
Ac.	1	27:29					1	26:29	2
Ro.					1	9:3			1
2 Co.	1	13:9	1	13:7					2
Jas.			1	5:16					1
3 Jn.	1	1:2							1
Total	3		2		1		1		7

2173. εὔχρηστος, eu′chre̱stos

Book	Oc.	profitable	Oc.	meet for use	Total
2 Ti.	1	4:11	1	2:21	2
Phe.	1	1:11			1
Total	2		1		3

2174. εὐψυχέω, eupsuche′ō

Book	be of good comfort	Total
Phl.	2:19	1

2175. εὐωδία, euōdi'a

Book	Oc.	sweet savour	Oc.	sweet smelling	Oc.	sweet smell	Total
2 Co.	1	2:15					1
Eph.			1	5:2			1
Phl.					1	4:18	1
Total	1		1		1		3

2176. εὐώνυμος, euō'numos

Book	Oc.	left	Oc.	on the left hand	Oc.	left foot	Total
Mt.	4	20:21, 23; 25: 33; 27:38	1	25:41			5
Mk.	1	15:27	2	10:37, 40			3
Ac.			1	21:3			1
Rev.					1	10:2	1
Total	5		4		1		10

2177. ἐφάλλομαι, ephal'lomai

Book	leap	Total
Ac.	19:16	1

2178. ἐφάπαξ, ephap'ax

Book	once	Total
Ro.	6:10	1
1 Co.	15:6	1
Heb.	7:27; 9:12; 10:10	3
Total		5

2179. Ἐφεσῖνος, Ephesi'nos

Book	of Ephesus	Total
Rev.	2:1	1

2180. Ἐφέσιος, Ephes'ios

Book	Oc.	Ephesian	Oc.	of Ephesus	Total
Ac.	4	19:28, 34, 35b; 21:29	1	19:35a	5

2181. Ἔφεσος, Eph'esos

Book	Ephesus	Total
Ac.	18:19, 21, 24; 19:1, 17, 26; 20:16, 17	8
1 Co.	15:32; 16:8	2
Eph.	1:1	1
1 Ti.	1:3	1
2 Ti.	1:18; 4:12	2
Rev.	1:11	1
Total		15

2182. ἐφευρέτης, epheuret'ēs

Book	inventor	Total
Ro.	1:30	1

2183. ἐφημερία, ephēmeri'a

Book	course	Total
Lk.	1:5, 8	2

2184. ἐφήμερος, ephē'meros

Book	daily	Total
Jas.	2:15	1

2185. ἐφικνέομαι, ephikne'omai

Book	reach	Total
2 Co.	10:13, 14	2

2192. ἔχω, ech'ō

Book	Oc.	have	Oc.	be	Oc.	need (with 5432)
Mt.	60	3:4, 9, 14; 5:23, 46; 6:1, 8; 7:29; 8:9, 20, 20; 9:6, 36; 11:15, 18; 12:10, 11; 13:5, 5, 6, 9, 12, 12, 12, 21, 27, 43, 44, 46; 14:4, 17; 15:30, 32, 34; 17:20; 18:8, 9, 25, 25; 19:16, 21, 22; 21:3, 21, 28; 22:12, 24, 25, 28; 25:25, 28, 29, 29, 29; 26:7, 11, 11, 65; 27:16, 65	3	8:16; 9:12b; 14:35	2	9:12a; 14:16
Mk.	60	1:22; 2:10, 17a, 19, 25; 3:1, 3, 10, 15, 22, 26, 29, 30; 4:5, 5, 6, 9, 17, 23, 25, 25, 25, 40; 5:3, 15; 6: 18, 34, 36, 38; 7:16, 25; 8:1, 2, 5, 7, 14, 16, 17, 17, 18, 18; 9:17, 43, 45, 47, 50; 10:21, 21, 22, 23; 11:3, 13, 22, 25; 12:6, 23, 44; 14:3, 7, 7	4	1:32, 34; 2: 17b; 6:55		
Lk.	64	3:8, 11, 11, 11; 4:33, 40; 5:24; 6:8; 7:8, 33, 40, 42; 8:8, 13, 18, 18, 18, 27; 9:3, 11, 58, 58; 11:5, 6, 36; 12:4, 5, 17, 19, 50; 13:6, 11; 14:18b, 19, 35; 15:4, 8, 11; 16:1, 28, 29; 17:6, 7; 18:22, 22, 24; 19:17, 24, 25, 26, 26, 26, 31, 34; 20:24, 28, 33; 21:4; 22:36, 36, 37; 24:39, 39, 41	2	5:31b; 7:2	2	5:31a; 15:7
Jn.	79	2:3; 3:15, 16, 29, 36; 4:11, 11, 17, 17, 18, 18, 32, 44; 5:2, 5, 7, 24, 26, 26, 36, 38, 39, 40, 42; 6:9, 40, 47, 53, 54, 68; 7:20; 8:6, 12, 26, 41, 48, 49, 52; 9:41; 10:10, 10, 16, 18, 18, 20; 11:17; 12:6, 8, 8, 35, 36, 48; 13:8, 29, 29, 35; 14:21, 30; 15:13, 22, 22, 24; 16:12, 15, 21, 22, 33, 33; 17:5, 13; 18:10; 19:7, 10, 10, 11, 11, 15; 20:31; 21:5	3	5:6; 9:21, 23	3	2:25; 13:10; 16:30
Ac.	29	2:44, 45, 47; 3:6; 4:35; 9:14, 31; 13:5; 14:9; 15:21; 18:18; 19:13, 38; 21:23; 23:17, 18, 19, 29; 24:15, 16, 19, 23; 25:16, 19, 26, 26; 28:9, 19, 29	5	7:1; 12:15; 17: 11; 21:13; 24:9		
Ro.	24	1:13; 2:14, 14, 20; 4:2; 5:1, 2; 6:21, 22; 8:9, 23; 9:10, 21; 10:2; 12:4, 4, 6; 13:3; 14:22, 22; 15: 4, 17, 23, 23				
1 Co.	48	2:16; 4:7, 15; 5:1; 6:1, 4, 19; 7:2, 2, 7, 12, 13, 25, 28, 29, 29, 37, 37, 40; 8:1, 10; 9:4, 5, 6, 17; 11: 4, 10, 16, 22, 22; 12:12, 21, 21, 23, 24, 30; 13:1, 2, 2, 2, 3; 14:26, 26, 26, 26, 26; 15:31, 34				
2 Co.	21	1:9, 15; 2:3, 4, 13; 3:4, 12; 4:1, 7, 13; 5:1, 12; 6:10; 7:1, 5; 8:11, 12, 12; 9:8; 10:6, 15	1	12:14		
Gal.	5	2:4; 4:22, 27; 6:4, 10				
Eph.	7	1:7; 2:12, 18; 3:12; 4:28a; 5:5, 27			1	4:28b
Phl.	9	1:7, 23, 30; 2:2, 20, 27; 3:4, 9, 17				
Col.	6	1:14; 2:1, 23; 3:13; 4:1, 13				
1 Th.	5	1:9; 3:6; 4:12, 13; 5:1			2	1:8; 4:9
2 Th.	1	3:9				
1 Ti.	9	3:4, 7; 4:8; 5:4, 12, 16; 6:2, 8, 16	1	5:25		
2 Ti.	3	1:3b; 2:19; 3:5				
Tit.	2	1:6; 2:8				
Phe.	2	1:5, 7	1	1:8		
Heb.	33	2:14; 3:3; 4:14, 15; 5:12, 12, 14; 6:18, 19; 7:3, 5, 6, 24, 28; 8:1, 3; 9:1, 4, 4; 10:1, 2, 19, 34, 35, 36; 11:10, 15; 12:9, 28; 13:10, 10, 14, 18	1	9:8		
Jas.	10	1:4; 2:1, 14, 14, 17, 18, 18; 3:14; 4:2, 2				
1 Pt.	3	2:12; 3:16; 4:8	1	4:5		
2 Pt.	3	1:19; 2:14, 14				
1 Jn.	26	1:3, 6, 7, 8; 2:1, 7, 20, 23, 28; 3:3, 15, 17, 17, 21; 4:16, 17, 18, 21; 5:10, 12, 12, 12, 12, 13, 14, 15			1	2:27
2 Jn.	4	1:5, 9, 9, 12				
3 Jn.	2	1:4, 13				
Jd.	1	1:19				
Rev.	96	1:16, 18; 2:3, 4, 6, 7, 10, 11, 12, 14, 14, 15, 17, 18, 20, 24, 25, 29; 3:1, 1, 4, 6, 7, 8, 11, 13, 17, 22; 4:4, 7, 8a; 5:6, 8; 6:2, 5; 7:2; 8:3, 6, 9; 9:3, 4, 8, 9, 10, 11, 11, 14, 17, 19; 10:2; 11:6, 6; 12:3, 6, 12, 12, 17; 13:1, 9, 11, 14, 17, 18; 14:1, 6, 11, 14, 17, 18, 18; 15:1, 2, 6; 16:2, 9; 17:1, 3, 4, 7, 9, 13; 18:1, 19; 19:10, 12, 16; 20:1, 6, 6; 21:9, 11, 12, 12, 14, 15, 23			1	22:5
Total	612		22		12	

2186. ἐφίστημι, ephis'tēmi

Book	Oc.	come upon	Oc.	come	Oc.	stand	Oc.	stand by	Oc.	Misc.	Total
Lk.	2	2:9; 20:1	2	10:40; 21:34	1	4:39	1	24:4	1	2:38	7
Ac.	3	4:1; 6:12; 12:7	2	11:11; 23:27	2	10:17; 22:13	2	22:20; 23:11	2	17:5; 28:2	11
1 Th.	1	5:3									1
2 Ti.									2	4:2, 6	2
Total	6		4		3		3		5		21

Miscellaneous: Lk. 2:38, come in; Ac. 17:5, assault; Ac. 28:2, present; 2 Ti. 4:2, be instant; 2 Ti. 4:6, be at hand.

2187. Ἐφραΐμ, Ephraim'

Book	Ephraim	Total
Jn.	11:54	1

2188. ἐφφαθά, ephphatha'

Book	Ephphatha	Total
Mk.	7:34	1

2191. ἔχιδνα, ech'idna

Book	viper	Total
Mt.	3:7; 12:34; 23:33	3
Lk.	3:7	1
Ac.	28:3	1
Total		5

2190. ἐχθρός, echthros'

Book	Oc.	enemy	Oc.	foe	Total
Mt.	6	5:43, 44; 13:25, 28, 39; 22:44	1	10:36	7
Mk.	1	12:36			1
Lk.	8	1:71, 74; 6:27, 35; 10:19; 19:27, 43; 20:43			8
Ac.	1	13:10	1	2:35	2
Ro.	3	5:10; 11:28; 12:20			3
1 Co.	2	15:25, 26			2
Gal.	1	4:16			1
Phl.	1	3:18			1
Col.	1	1:21			1
2 Th.	1	3:15			1
Heb.	2	1:13; 10:13			2
Jas.	1	4:4			1
Rev.	2	11:5, 12			2
Total	30		2		32

2189. ἔχθρα, ech'thra

Book	Oc.	enmity	Oc.	hatred	Total
Lk.	1	23:12			1
Ro.	1	8:7			1
Gal.			1	5:20	1
Eph.	2	2:15, 16			2
Jas.	1	4:4			1
Total	5		1		6

2192. ἔχω, ech'ō (continued)

Book	Oc.	be with child (with 1722 and 1064)	Oc.	hold	Oc.	count	Oc.	can	Oc.	next	Oc.	thank (with 5385)	Oc.	Not Tr.	Oc.	Misc.	Total
Mt.	2	1:23; 24:19	1	21:26	1	14:5									3	1:18; 4:24; 21:46	72
Mk.	1	13:17			1	11:32	1	14:8	1	1:38			1	14:63	3	5:23; 16:8, 18	72
Lk.	1	21:23									1	17:9	1	22:71	7	8:6; 13:33; 14:14, 18a, 28; 19:20; 23:17	78
Jn.															2	4:52; 8:57	87
Ac.					1	20:24	1	4:14	2	20:15; 21:26			2	1:12; 11:3	5	8:7; 15:36; 16:16; 24:25; 27:39	45
Ro.															1	1:28	25
1 Co.															1	6:7	49
2 Co.																	22
Gal.																	5
Eph.																	8
Phl.			1	2:29													10
Col.																	6
1 Th.															1	5:3	8
2 Th.																	1
1 Ti.			2	1:19; 3:9							1	1:12			1	5:20	14
2 Ti.											1	1:3a			2	1:13; 2:17	6
Tit.																	2
Phe.					1	1:17											4
Heb.							1	6:13							4	6:9; 7:27; 11:25; 12:1	39
Jas.																	10
1 Pt.															1	2:16	5
2 Pt.															2	1:15; 2:16	5
1 Jn.																	27
2 Jn.																	4
3 Jn.																	2
Jd.															1	1:3	2
Rev.	1	12:2	1	6:9											2	4:8b; 17:18	101
Total	5		5		4		3		3		3		4		36		709

Miscellaneous: Mt. 1:18 (with 1722 and 1064), with child; Mt. 4:24 (with 2560), sick people; Mt. 21:46, take; Mk. 5:23, lie; Mk. 16:8 (with 5056), tremble; Mk. 16:18 (with 2573), recover; Lk. 8:6 (with 3261), lack; Lk. 13:33, following; Lk. 14:14 (with 3656), cannot; Lk. 14:18a, must; Lk. 14:28, have sufficient; Lk. 19:20, keep; Lk. 23:17, must; Jn. 4:52 (with 2866), begin to amend; Jn. 8:57, be old; Ac. 8:7, be possessed with; Ac. 15:36, do; Ac. 16:16, be possessed with; Ac. 24:25 (with 3468 and 3488), for this time; Ac. 27:39, with; Ro. 1:28, retain; 1 Co. 6:7 (with 2917), go to law; 1 Th. 5:3 (with 1722 and 1064), with child; 1 Ti. 5:20 (with 5301), may fear; 2 Ti. 1:13, hold fast; 2 Ti. 2:17 (with 3442), eat; Heb. 6:9, accompany; Heb. 7:27 (with 318), need; Heb. 11:25 (with 619), enjoy; Heb. 12:1 (with 3929), be compassed about with; 1 Pt. 2:16, use; 2 Pt. 1:15, be able; 2 Pt. 2:16 (with 1649), rebuke; Jd. 1:3, be needful; Rev. 4:8b (with 372), rest; Rev. 17:18 (with 932), reign.

2193. ἕως, he'ōs

Book	Oc.	till	Oc.	unto	Oc.	until	Oc.	to	Oc.	till (with 3639)	Oc.	how long (with 4119)	Oc.	until (with 3639)	Oc.	while
Mt.	12	2:9; 5:18, 18, 26; 10:11, 23; 12:20; 16:28; 18:21; 22:44; 23:39; 24:34	9	1:17c; 11: 23a; 20:8; 22:26; 23: 35; 26:58; 27:8, 45; 28:20	10	1:17b; 2: 13, 15; 11:12, 13; 18:22, 22; 24:39; 26:29; 27:64	5	1:17a; 11: 23b; 24: 21, 31; 27:51	4	1:25; 13:33; 18:30, 34	2	17:17, 17	1	17:9		
Mk.	3	6:10; 9:1; 12:36	3	6:23; 13:19; 14:34	2	14:25; 15:33	2	13:27; 15:38			2	9:19, 19			2	6:45; 14:32
Lk.	6	1:80; 9:27; 17:8; 19:13; 20:43; 21:32	3	4:29, 42; 11:51	4	13:35; 15:4; 16: 16; 23: 44	3	10:15, 15; 23: 5	3	12:50, 59; 13:21	1	9:41	1	24:49		
Jn.	2	21:22, 23	1	8:9	1	2:10			1	13:38	1	10:24			3	9:4; 12: 35, 36
Ac.	3	8:40; 21:5; 28:23	5	1:8, 22; 7: 45; 13:47; 17:15	2	2:35; 13:20	3	8:10; 9: 38; 23:23	3	23:12, 21; 25:21			2	21:26; 23: 14		
Ro.			1	11:8												
1 Co.			4	1:8; 4:13; 8:7; 15:6	2	4:5; 16:8										
2 Co.							2	1:13; 12:2								
2 Th.					1	2:7										
1 Ti.	1	4:13														
Heb.	1	10:13			1	1:13	1	8:11								
Jas.			1	5:7a	1	5:7b										
2 Pt.													1	1:19		
1 Jn.																
Rev.					1	20:5					1	6:10	1	6:11		
Total	28		27		25		16		11		7		6		5	

2194. Ζαβουλών, Dzaboulōn'

Book	Zabulon	Total
Mt.	4:13, 15	2
Rev.	7:8	1
Total		3

2195. Ζακχαῖος, Dzakchai'os

Book	Zacchaeus	Total
Lk.	19:2, 5, 8	3

2196. Ζαρά, Dzara'

Book	Zara	Total
Mt.	1:3	1

2197. Ζαχαρίας, Dzachari'as

Book	Oc.	Zacharias (father of John the Baptist)	Oc.	Zacharias (son of Barachias)	Total
Mt.			1	23:35	1
Lk.	9	1:5, 12, 13, 18, 21, 40, 59, 67; 3:2	1	11:51	10
Total	9		2		11

2198. ζάω, dza'ō

Book	Oc.	live	Oc.	be alive	Oc.	alive	Oc.	quick	Oc.	lively	Oc.	Not Tr.	Oc.	Misc.	Total
Mt.	5	4:4; 9:18; 16:16; 22:32; 26:63	1	27:63											6
Mk.	2	5:23; 12:27	1	16:11											3
Lk.	7	2:36; 4:4; 10:28; 15:13; 20:38, 38; 24:5	1	24:23											8
Jn.	18	4:10, 11, 50, 51, 53; 5:25; 6:51, 51, 57, 57, 57, 58, 69; 7:38; 11:25, 26; 14:19, 19													18
Ac.	6	14:15; 17:28; 22:22; 25:24; 26:5; 28:4	1	25:19	3	1:3; 9:41; 20:12	1	10:42	1	7:38					12
Ro.	19	1:17; 6:2, 10, 10; 7:1, 2, 3; 8:12, 13, 13; 9:26; 10:5; 12:1; 14:7; 14:8, 8, 8, 9, 11	2	6:13; 7:9	1	6:11									22
1 Co.	3	7:39; 9:14; 15:45													3
2 Co.	8	3:3; 4:11; 5:15, 15; 6:9, 16; 13:4, 4											1	1:8	9
Gal.	8	2:14, 19, 20b, 20c, 20d; 3:11, 12; 5:25									1	2:20a			9
Phl.	2	1:21, 22													2
Col.	2	2:20; 3:7													2
1 Th.	3	1:9; 3:8; 5:10	2	4:15, 17											5
1 Ti.	4	3:15; 4:10; 5:6; 6:17													4
2 Ti.	1	3:12					1	4:1							2
Tit.	1	2:12													1
Heb.	10	3:12; 7:8, 25; 9:14, 17; 10:20, 31, 38; 12:9, 22					1	4:12					1	2:15	12
Jas.	1	4:15													1
1 Pt.	4	1:23; 2:4, 24; 4:6					1	4:5	2	1:3; 2:5					7
1 Jn.	1	4:9													1
Rev.	12	1:18a; 3:1; 4:9, 10; 5:14; 7:2, 17; 10:6; 13:14; 15:7; 16:3; 20:4	1	2:8	2	1:18b; 19: 20									15
Total	117		9		6		4		3		1		2		142

Miscellaneous: 2 Co. 1:8, life; Heb. 2:15, lifetime.

2199. Ζεβεδαῖος, Dzebadai'os

Book	Zebedee	Total
Mt.	4:21, 21; 10:2; 20:20; 26:37; 27:56	6
Mk.	1:19, 20; 3:17; 10:35	4
Lk.	5:10	1
Jn.	21:2	1
Total		12

2200. ζεστός, dzestos'

Book	hot	Total
Rev.	3:15, 15, 16	3

2201. ζεῦγος, dzeu'gos

Book	Oc.	pair	Oc.	yoke	Total
Lk.	1	2:24	1	14:19	2

2193. ἕως, he'ōs (continued)

Book	Oc.	even unto	Oc.	until (with 3655)	Oc.	as far as	Oc.	while (with 3639)	Oc.	hitherto (with 737)	Oc.	till (with 3655)	Oc.	Not Tr.	Oc.	Misc.	Total
Mt.	2	24:27; 26:38					2	14:22; 26:36							1	5:25	48
Mk.															1	14:54	15
Lk.	1	2:15	2	22:16, 18	1	24:50					2	13:8; 15:8			1	22:51	28
Jn.			1	9:18					2	5:17; 16:24					1	2:7	13
Ac.					2	11:19, 22							1	26:11			21
Ro.													1	3:12			2
1 Co.																	6
2 Co.	1	3:15															3
2 Th.																	1
1 Ti.																	1
Heb.																	3
Jas.																	2
2 Pt.																	1
1 Jn.															1	2:9	1
Rev.																	3
Total	4		3		3		2		2		2		2		5		148

Miscellaneous: Mt. 5:25 (with 3655), whiles; Mk. 14:54, even; Lk. 22:51, far; Jn. 2:7, up to; 1 Jn. 2:9, even until.

2202. ζευκτηρία, dzeukte̱ri'a

Book	band	Total
Ac.	27:40	1

2203. Ζεύς, Dzeus'

Book	Jupiter	Total
Ac.	14:12, 13	2

2204. ζέω, dze'ō

Book	Oc.	be fervent	Oc.	fervent	Total
Ac.	1	18:25			1
Ro.			1	12:11	1
Total	1		1		2

2205. ζῆλος, dze̱'los

Book	Oc.	zeal	Oc.	envying	Oc.	indignation	Oc.	envy	Oc.	fervent mind	Oc.	jealousy	Oc.	emulation	Total
Jn.	1	2:17													1
Ac.					1	5:17	1	13:45							2
Ro.	1	10:2	1	13:13											2
1 Co.			1	3:3											1
2 Co.	2	7:11; 9:2	1	12:20					1	7:7	1	11:2			5
Gal.													1	5:20	1
Phl.	1	3:6													1
Col.	1	4:13													1
Heb.					1	10:27									1
Jas.			2	3:14, 16											2
Total	6		5		2		1		1		1		1		17

2206. ζηλόω, dze̱lo'ō

Book	Oc.	zealously affect	Oc.	move with envy	Oc.	envy	Oc.	be zealous	Oc.	affect	Oc.	desire	Oc.	covet	Oc.	covet earnestly	Oc.	Misc.	Total
Ac.			2	7:9; 17:5															2
1 Co.					1	13:4					1	14:1	1	14:39	1	12:31			4
2 Co.																	1	11:2	1
Gal.	2	4:17a, 18							1	4:17b									3
Jas.																	1	4:2	1
Rev.							1	3:19											1
Total	2		2		1		1		1		1		1		1		2		12

Miscellaneous: 2 Co. 11:2, be jealous over; Jas. 4:2, desire to have.

2207. ζηλωτής, dze̱lōte̱s'

Book	zealous	Total
Ac.	21:20; 22:3	2
1 Co.	14:12	1
Gal.	1:14	1
Tit.	2:14	1
Total		5

2208. Ζηλωτής, Dze̱lōte̱s'

Book	Zelotes	Total
Lk.	6:15	1
Ac.	1:13	1
Total		2

2209. ζημία, dze̱mi'a

Book	Oc.	loss	Oc.	damage	Total
Ac.	1	27:21	1	27:10	2
Phl.	2	3:7, 8			2
Total	3		1		4

2210. ζημιόω, dze̱mio'ō

Book	Oc.	lose	Oc.	suffer loss	Oc.	be cast away	Oc.	receive damage	Total
Mt.	1	16:26							1
Mk.	1	8:36							1
Lk.					1	9:25			1
1 Co.			1	3:15					1
2 Co.							1	7:9	1
Phl.			1	3:8					1
Total	2		2		1		1		6

2211. Ζηνᾶς, Dze̱nas'

Book	Zenas	Total
Tit.	3:13	1

2212. ζητέω, dze̱te′ō

Book	Oc.	seek	Oc.	seek for	Oc.	go about	Oc.	desire	Oc.	Misc.	Total
Mt.	12	2:13, 20; 6:33; 7:7, 8; 12:43; 13:45; 18:12; 21:46; 26:16, 59; 28:5					2	12:46, 47			14
Mk.	6	8:11; 11:18; 12:12; 14:1, 11; 16:6	3	1:37; 3:32; 14:55							9
Lk.	25	2:45, 48, 49; 4:42; 5:18; 6:19; 11:9, 10, 16, 24, 54; 12:29, 31; 13:6, 7, 24; 15:8; 17:33; 19:3, 10, 47; 20:19; 22:2, 6; 24:5					1	9:9	1	12:48	27
Jn.	31	1:38; 4:23, 27; 5:16, 18, 30, 44; 6:26; 7:1, 4, 11, 18, 18, 25, 30, 34, 36; 8:21, 37, 40, 50, 50; 10:39; 11:8, 56; 13:33; 18:4, 7, 8; 19:12; 20:15	1	6:24	2	7:19, 20			1	16:19	35
Ac.	6	10:19, 21; 13:8, 11; 17:5, 27			1	21:31			3	9:11; 16:10; 27:30	10
Ro.	2	10:20; 11:3	1	2:7	1	10:3					4
1 Co.	6	7:27, 27; 10:24, 33; 13:5; 14:12							2	1:22; 4:2	8
2 Co.	2	12:14; 13:3									2
Gal.	2	1:10; 2:17									2
Phl.	1	2:21									1
Col.	1	3:1									1
1 Th.	1	2:6									1
2 Ti.	1	1:17									1
Heb.	1	8:7									1
1 Pt.	2	3:11; 5:8									2
Rev.	1	9:6									1
Total	100		5		4		3		7		119

Miscellaneous: Lk. 12:48, require; Jn. 16:19, enquire; Ac. 9:11, enquire for; Ac. 16:10, endeavour; Ac. 27:30, be about; 1 Co. 1:22, seek after; 1 Co. 4:2, require.

2213. ζήτημα, dze̱′te̱ma

Book	question	Total
Ac.	15:2; 18:15; 23:29; 25:19; 26:3	5

2214. ζήτησις, dze̱′te̱sis

Book	question	Total
Jn.	3:25	1
Ac.	25:20	1
1 Ti.	1:4; 6:4	2
2 Ti.	2:23	1
Tit.	3:9	1
Total		6

2215. ζιζάνιον, dzidzan′ion

Book	tares	Total
Mt.	13:25, 26, 27, 29, 30, 36, 38, 40	8

2216. Ζοροβάβελ, Dzorobab′el

Book	Zorobabel	Total
Mt.	1:12, 13	2
Lk.	3:27	1
Total		3

2217. ζόφος, dzoph′os

Book	Oc.	darkness	Oc.	mist	Oc.	blackness	Total
2 Pt.	1	2:4	1	2:17			2
Jd.	1	1:6			1	1:13	2
Total	2		1		1		4

2218. ζυγός, dzugos′

Book	Oc.	yoke	Oc.	pair of balances	Total
Mt.	2	11:29, 30			2
Ac.	1	15:10			1
Gal.	1	5:1			1
1 Ti.	1	6:1			1
Rev.			1	6:5	1
Total	5		1		6

2219. ζύμη, dzu′me̱

Book	leaven	Total
Mt.	13:33; 16:6, 11, 12	4
Mk.	8:15, 15	2
Lk.	12:1; 13:21	2
1 Co.	5:6, 7, 8, 8	4
Gal.	5:9	1
Total		13

2220. ζυμόω, dzumo′ō

Book	leaven	Total
Mt.	13:33	1
Lk.	13:21	1
1 Co.	5:6	1
Gal.	5:9	1
Total		4

2221. ζωγρέω, dzōgre′ō

Book	Oc.	catch	Oc.	take captive	Total
Lk.	1	5:10			1
2 Ti.			1	2:26	1
Total	1		1		2

2222. ζωή, dzōe̱′

Book	Oc.	life	Oc.	lifetime	Total
Mt.	7	7:14; 18:8, 9; 19:16, 17, 29; 25:46			7
Mk.	4	9:43, 45; 10:17, 30			4
Lk.	5	1:75; 10:25; 12:15; 18:18, 30	1	16:25	6
Jn.	36	1:4, 4; 3:15, 16, 36, 36; 4:14, 36; 5:24, 24, 26, 26, 29, 39, 40; 6:27, 33, 35, 40, 47, 48, 51, 53, 54, 63, 68; 8:12; 10:10, 28; 11:25; 12:25, 50; 14:6; 17:2, 3; 20:31			36
Ac.	8	2:28; 3:15; 5:20; 8:33; 11:18; 13:46, 48; 17:25			8
Ro.	14	2:7; 5:10, 17, 18, 21; 6:4, 22, 23; 7:10; 8:2, 6, 10, 38; 11:15			14
1 Co.	2	3:22; 15:19			2
2 Co.	6	2:16, 16; 4:10, 11, 12; 5:4			6
Gal.	1	6:8			1
Eph.	1	4:18			1
Phl.	3	1:20; 2:16; 4:3			3
Col.	2	3:3, 4			2
1 Ti.	4	1:16; 4:8; 6:12, 19			4
2 Ti.	2	1:1, 10			2
Tit.	2	1:2; 3:7			2
Heb.	2	7:3, 16			2
Jas.	2	1:12; 4:14			2
1 Pt.	2	3:7, 10			2
2 Pt.	1	1:3			1
1 Jn.	13	1:1, 2, 2; 2:25; 3:14, 15; 5:11, 11, 12, 12, 13, 16, 20			13
Jd.	1	1:21			1
Rev.	15	2:7, 10; 3:5; 11:11; 13:8; 17:8; 20:12, 15; 21:6, 27; 22:1, 2, 14, 17, 19			15
Total	133		1		134

2223. ζώνη, dzō′ne̱

Book	Oc.	girdle	Oc.	purse	Total
Mt.	1	3:4	1	10:9	2
Mk.	1	1:6	1	6:8	2
Ac.	2	21:11, 11			2
Rev.	2	1:13; 15:6			2
Total	6		2		8

2224. ζώννυμι, dzōn′numi

Book	gird	Total
Jn.	21:18, 18	2

2225. ζωογονέω, dzōogone′ō

Book	Oc.	preserve	Oc.	live	Total
Lk.	1	17:33			1
Ac.			1	7:19	1
Total	1		1		2

2226. ζῶον, dzō′on

Book	beast	Total
Heb.	13:11	1
2 Pt.	2:12	1
Jd.	1:10	1
Rev.	4:6, 7, 7, 7, 7, 8, 9; 5:6, 8, 11, 14; 6:1, 3, 5, 6, 7; 7:11; 14:3; 15:7; 19:4	20
Total		23

2227. ζωοποιέω, dzōopoie′ō

Book	Oc.	quicken	Oc.	give life	Oc.	make alive	Total
Jn.	3	5:21, 21; 6:63					3
Ro.	2	4:17; 8:11					2
1 Co.	2	15:36, 45			1	15:22	3
2 Co.			1	3:6			1
Gal.			1	3:21			1
1 Ti.	1	6:13					1
1 Pt.	1	3:18					1
Total	9		2		1		12

2228. ἤ, e̱

Book	Oc.	or	Oc.	than	Oc.	either	Oc.	or else	Oc.	nor	Oc.	Not Tr.	Oc.	Misc.	Total
Mt.	52	5:17, 18, 36; 6:31, 31; 7:4, 9, 16; 9:5; 10:11, 14, 19, 37, 37; 11:3; 12:5, 25; 13:21; 15:4, 5, 6; 16:14, 26; 17:25, 25; 18: 8a, 8b, 8d, 16, 16, 20; 19:29, 29, 29, 29, 29, 29, 29; 21:25; 22:17; 23:17, 19; 24:23; 25: 37, 38, 39, 44, 44, 44, 44, 44; 27:17	6	10:15; 11:22, 24; 18:13; 19: 24; 26:53b	2	6:24a; 12:33a	3	6:24b; 12: 29, 33b			4	1:18; 20:15, 15; 26:53a	2	18:8c, 9	69
Mk.	27	2:9; 3:4, 4, 33; 4:21, 30; 6: 15, 56, 56; 7:10, 11, 12; 8:37; 10:29, 29, 29, 29, 29, 29, 29; 11:30; 12:14, 15; 13:21, 35, 35, 35	5	6:11b; 9:43, 45, 47; 10:25							1	14:30	1	6:11a	34
Lk.	31	2:24; 5:23; 6:9, 9; 7:19, 20; 8:16; 9:25; 11:12; 12:11, 11, 14, 29, 41; 13:4, 15; 14:5, 12, 31; 17:7, 21, 23; 18:11, 29, 29, 29, 29; 20:2, 4, 22; 22:27	7	10:12, 14; 15: 7; 16:17; 17: 2; 18:14, 25	3	6:42; 15: 8; 16:13a	1	16:13b	1	22:68	1	2:26	3	9:13; 12: 51; 22: 34	47
Jn.	9	2:6; 4:27; 6:19; 7:17, 48; 9: 2, 21; 13:29; 18:34	2	3:19; 4:1									1	13:10	12
Ac.	25	1:7; 3:12, 12; 4:7, 34; 5:38; 7:49; 8:34; 10:14, 28, 28; 11: 8; 17:29, 29; 18:14; 19:12; 20:33, 33; 23:9, 29; 24:23; 26:31; 28:6, 17, 21	5	4:19; 5:29; 20:35; 25:6; 27:11			1	24:20			2	2:20; 7:2	5	17:21; 24:11, 12, 21; 25: 16	38
Ro.	22	2:4, 15; 3:1; 4:9, 10, 13; 6:16; 8:35, 35, 35, 35, 35, 35; 9:11; 10:7; 11:34, 35; 14:4, 10, 13, 21, 21	1	13:11							5	3:29; 6:3; 7:1; 9:21; 11:2	1	1:21	29
1 Co.	36	1:13; 2:1; 4:3, 21; 5:10, 10, 10; 5:11b, 11c, 11d, 11e, 11f; 7:11, 15, 16; 9:6, 7, 8, 10; 10:19; 11:4, 5, 6, 22; 13:1; 14:6b, 6c, 6d, 7, 23, 24, 27, 29, 36b, 37; 15:37	4	7:9; 9:15; 14:5, 19	1	14:6a			1	12:21	5	3:5; 5:11a; 6:9; 10:22; 11:14	5	6:16, 19; 11:27; 14:36a; 16:6	52
2 Co.	9	1:13b, 17; 3:1; 6:15; 9:7; 10: 12; 11:4, 4; 12:6	1	1:13a							2	11:7; 13:5			12
Gal.	7	1:8, 10, 10; 2:2; 3:2, 5, 15	1	4:27											8
Eph.	4	3:20; 5:3, 27, 27							3	5:4, 5, 5					7
Phl.	1	2:3			1	3:12									2
Col.	5	2:16, 16, 16, 16; 3:17													5
1 Th.	2	2:19a, 19b									1	2:19c			3
2 Th.	1	2:4													1
1 Ti.	6	2:9, 9, 9; 5:4, 16, 19	1	1:4											7
2 Ti.			1	3:4											1
Tit.	2	1:6; 3:12													2
Phe.	1	1:18													1
Heb.	4	2:6; 10:28; 12:16, 20	1	11:25											5
Jas.	3	2:3, 15; 4:15			1	3:12					1	4:5	1	1:17	6
1 Pt.	6	1:11; 3:3, 9; 4:15, 15, 15	1	3:17									1	1:18	8
2 Pt.			1	2:21											1
1 Jn.			1	4:4											1
Rev.	6	3:15; 13:16, 17, 17, 17; 14:9													6
Total	259		38		8		5		5		22		20		357

Miscellaneous: Mt. 18:8c, 9, rather than; Mk. 6:11a, and; Lk. 9:13, but; Lk. 12:51, rather; Lk. 22:34, that; Jn. 13:10, save; Ac. 17:21, but either; Ac. 24:11, but; Ac. 24:12, neither; Ac. 24:21, except it be; Ac. 25:16, that; Ro. 1:21, neither; 1 Co. 6:16, 19, what; 1 Co. 11:27, and; 1 Co. 14:36a, what; 1 Co. 16:6, yea; Jas. 1:17, neither; 1 Pt. 1:18, and.

2229. ἦ, e̱

Book	surely (with 3275)	Total
Heb.	6:14	1

2230. ἡγεμονεύω, he̱gemoneu′ō

Book	be governor	Total
Lk.	2:2; 3:1	2

2231. ἡγεμονία, he̱gemoni′a

Book	reign	Total
Lk.	3:1	1

2234. ἡδέως, he̱de′ōs

Book	gladly	Total
Mk.	6:20; 12:37	2
2 Co.	11:19	1
Total		3

2232. ἡγεμών, he̱gemōn′

Book	Oc.	governor	Oc.	ruler	Oc.	prince	Total
Mt.	10	10:18; 27:2, 11, 11, 14, 15, 21, 23, 27; 28:14			1	2:6	11
Mk.			1	13:9			1
Lk.	1	20:20	1	21:12			2
Ac.	7	23:24, 26, 33, 34; 24:1, 10; 26:30					7
1 Pt.	1	2:14					1
Total	19		2		1		22

2233. ἡγέομαι, he̱ge′omai

Book	Oc.	count	Oc.	think	Oc.	esteem	Oc.	have the rule over	Oc.	be governor	Oc.	Misc.	Total
Mt.									1	2:6			1
Lk.											1	22:26	1
Ac.			1	26:2					1	7:10	2	14:12; 15:22	4
2 Co.			1	9:5									1
Phl.	3	3:7, 8, 8	1	2:6	1	2:3					1	2:25	6
1 Th.					1	5:13							1
2 Th.	1	3:15											1
1 Ti.	2	1:12; 6:1											2
Heb.	1	10:29			1	11:26	3	13:7, 17, 24			1	11:11	6
Jas.	1	1:2											1
2 Pt.	2	2:13; 3:9	1	1:13							1	3:15	4
Total	10		4		3		3		2		6		28

Miscellaneous: Lk. 22:26, be chief; Ac. 14:12 (with 3056 and 3488), chief speaker; Ac. 15:22, chief; Phl. 2:25, suppose; Heb. 11:11, judge; 2 Pt. 3:15, account.

2235. ἤδη, e̱'de̱

Book	Oc.	now	Oc.	already	Oc.	yet	Oc.	even now	Oc.	by this time	Oc.	now already	Total
Mt.	4	3:10; 14:15, 24; 15:32	2	5:28; 17:12	1	24:32							7
Mk.	6	4:37; 6:35, 35; 8:2; 11:11; 15:42	1	15:44	1	13:28							8
Lk.	6	3:9; 7:6; 11:7; 14:17; 21: 30, 30	1	12:49			1	19:37					8
Jn.	9	4:51; 5:6; 6:17; 7:14; 13:2; 15:3; 19:28; 21:4, 14	6	3:18; 4:35; 9:22, 27; 11:17; 19:33					1	11:39			16
Ac.	2	4:3; 27:9a									1	27:9b	3
Ro.	3	1:10; 4:19; 13:11											3
1 Co.	3	4:8, 8; 6:7	1	5:3									4
Phl.	1	4:10	2	3:12, 12									3
2 Th.			1	2:7									1
1 Ti.			1	5:15									1
2 Ti.	1	4:6	1	2:18									2
2 Pt.	1	3:1											1
1 Jn.	1	2:8	1	4:3									2
Total	37		17		2		1		1		1		59

2236. ἥδιστα, he̱'dista

Book	Oc.	most gladly	Oc.	very gladly	Total
2 Co.	1	12:9	1	12:15	2

2237. ἡδονή, he̱done̱'

Book	Oc.	pleasure	Oc.	lust	Total
Lk.	1	8:14			1
Tit.	1	3:3			1
Jas.			2	4:1, 3	2
2 Pt.	1	2:13			1
Total	3		2		5

2238. ἡδύοσμον, he̱du'osmon

Book	mint	Total
Mt.	23:23	1
Lk.	11:42	1
Total		2

2239. ἦθος, e̱'thos

Book	manners	Total
1 Co.	15:33	1

2240. ἥκω, he̱'kō

Book	come	Total
Mt.	8:11; 23:36; 24:14, 50	4
Mk.	8:3	1
Lk.	12:46; 13:29, 35; 15: 27; 19:43	5
Jn.	2:4; 4:47; 6:37; 8:42	4
Ac.	28:23	1
Ro.	11:26	1
Heb.	10:7, 9, 37	3
2 Pt.	3:10	1
1 Jn.	5:20	1
Rev.	2:25; 3:3, 3, 9; 15:4; 18:8	6
Total		27

2241. Ἠλί, E̱li'

Book	Eli	Total
Mt.	27:46, 46	2

2242. Ἡλί, He̱li'

Book	Heli	Total
Lk.	3:23	1

2243. Ἡλίας, He̱li'as

Book	Elias	Total
Mt.	11:14; 16:14; 17:3, 4, 10, 11, 12; 27:47, 49	9
Mk.	6:15; 8:28; 9:4, 5, 11, 12, 13; 15:35, 36	9
Lk.	1:17; 4:25, 26; 9:8, 19, 30, 33, 54	8
Jn.	1:21, 25	2
Ro.	11:2	1
Jas.	5:17	1
Total		30

2244. ἡλικία, he̱liki'a

Book	Oc.	stature	Oc.	age	Total
Mt.	1	6:27			1
Lk.	3	2:52; 12:25; 19:3			3
Jn.			2	9:21, 23	2
Eph.	1	4:13			1
Heb.			1	11:11	1
Total	5		3		8

2245. ἡλίκος, he̱li'kos

Book	Oc.	what great	Oc.	how great	Total
Col.	1	2:1			1
Jas.			1	3:5	1
Total	1		1		2

2246. ἥλιος, he̱'lios

Book	Oc.	sun	Oc.	east	Total
Mt.	5	5:45; 13:6, 43; 17:2; 24:29			5
Mk.	4	1:32; 4:6; 13:24; 16:2			4
Lk.	3	4:40; 21:25; 23:45			3
Ac.	4	2:20; 13:11; 26:13; 27:20			4
1 Co.	1	15:41			1
Eph.	1	4:26			1
Jas.	1	1:11			1
Rev.	11	1:16; 6:12; 7:16; 8:12; 9:2; 10:1; 12:1; 16:8; 19:17; 21:23; 22:5	2	7:2; 16:12	13
Total	30		2		32

2247. ἧλος, he̱'los

Book	nail	Total
Jn.	20:25, 25	2

2248. ἡμᾶς, he̱mas'

Book	Oc.	us	Oc.	we	Oc.	our	Oc.	usward (with 1519)	Oc.	Not Tr.	Total
Mt.	13	6:13, 13; 8:25, 29, 31; 9:27; 13:56; 17:4; 20:7, 30, 31; 27:4, 25									13
Mk.	5	1:24; 5:12; 6:3; 9:5, 22									5
Lk.	18	1:71, 78; 4:34; 7:20; 9:33; 11:1, 4, 4, 45; 12:41; 16:26; 17:13; 19:14; 20:6; 23:30, 30, 39; 24:22									18
Jn.	2	1:22; 9:34									2
Ac.	21	1:21; 3:4; 5:28; 7:27, 40; 11:15; 14:11; 16:10, 15, 37, 37, 37; 20:5; 21:5b, 11, 17; 27:6, 7; 28: 2, 7, 10	8	4:12; 6:2; 14:22; 21:1, 5a; 27:1, 20, 26							29
Ro.	9	4:24; 5:8; 8:18, 35, 37, 39; 9:24; 15:7; 16:6	3	3:8; 6:6; 7:6					1	13:11	13
1 Co.	5	4:1, 9; 6:14; 7:15; 8:8	1	10:6	2	9:10, 10					8
2 Co.	18	1:4a, 5, 10, 11, 14, 21, 21, 22; 2:14; 3:6; 4:14; 5:5, 14, 18; 7:2, 6; 8:20; 10:2	5	1:4b, 8; 5:10; 8:4, 6							23
Gal.	5	1:4, 23; 2:4; 3:13; 5:1									5
Eph.	8	1:3, 4a, 5, 6, 8; 2:4, 7; 5:2	3	1:4b, 12; 2:5			1	1:19			12
Phl.	1	3:17									1
Col.	2	1:12, 13									2
1 Th.	9	1:10; 2:15, 16, 18; 3:6, 6; 4:7, 8; 5:9	1	1:8							10
2 Th.	3	2:16; 3:7, 9	1	1:4							4
2 Ti.	2	1:9; 2:12									2
Tit.	5	2:12, 14; 3:5, 6, 15									5
Heb.	1	2:3	2	2:1; 13:6							3
Jas.	1	1:18a	1	1:18b							2
1 Pt.	4	1:3; 3:18, 21; 5:10									4
2 Pt.	1	1:3					1	3:9			2
1 Jn.	6	1:7, 9; 3:1; 4:10, 11, 19									6
3 Jn.	2	1:9, 10									2
Rev.	7	1:5, 5, 6; 5:9, 10; 6:16, 16									7
Total	148		25		2		2		1		178

2249. ἡμεῖς, he̱meis′

Book	Oc.	we	Oc.	us	Oc.	we ourselves	Total
Mt.	5	6:12; 9:14; 17:19; 19:27; 28:14					5
Mk.	3	9:28; 10:28; 14:58					3
Lk.	5	3:14; 9:13; 18:28; 23:41; 24:21					5
Jn.	17	1:16; 4:22; 6:42, 69; 7:35; 8:41, 48; 9:21, 24, 28, 29, 40; 12:34; 17:11, 22; 19:7; 21:3	1	11:16			18
Ac.	21	2:8, 32; 3:15; 4:9, 20; 5:32; 6:4; 10:33, 39, 47; 13:32; 14:15; 15:10; 20:6, 13; 21:7, 12, 25; 23:15; 24:8; 28:21					21
Ro.	3	6:4; 8:23; 15:1					3
1 Co.	17	1:23; 2:12, 16; 4:8, 10, 10, 10; 8:6, 6; 9:11, 11, 12, 25; 11:16; 12:13; 15:30, 52					17
2 Co.	16	1:6; 3:18; 4:11, 13; 5:16, 21; 9:4; 10:7, 13; 11:12, 21; 13:4, 6, 7, 7, 9					16
Gal.	7	1:8; 2:9, 15, 16; 4:3, 28; 5:5					7
Eph.	1	2:3					1
Phl.	1	3:3					1
Col.	2	1:9, 28					2
1 Th.	6	2:13, 17; 3:6, 12; 4:15, 17	1	5:8			7
2 Th.	1	2:13					1
Tit.	1	3:5			1	3:3	2
Heb.	5	2:3; 3:6; 10:39; 12:1a, 25	1	12:1b			6
2 Pt.	1	1:18					1
1 Jn.	9	3:14, 16; 4:6, 10, 11, 14, 16, 17, 19					9
3 Jn.	2	1:8, 12					2
Total	123		3		1		127

2250. ἡμέρα, he̱mer′a

Book	Oc.	day	Oc.	daily (with 2596)	Oc.	time	Oc.	Not Tr.	Oc.	Misc.	Total
Mt.	41	2:1; 3:1; 4:2; 6:34; 7:22; 9:15; 10:15; 11:12, 22, 24; 12:36, 40, 40; 13:1; 15:32; 16:21; 17:1, 23; 20:2, 6, 12, 19; 22:23, 46; 23:30; 24:19, 22, 22, 29, 36, 37, 38, 38, 50; 25:13; 26:2, 29, 61; 27:40, 63, 64	1	26:55					1	28:20	43
Mk.	27	1:9, 13; 2:1, 20, 20; 4:27, 35; 5:5; 6:11, 21; 8:1, 2, 31; 9:2, 31; 10:34; 13:17, 19, 20, 20, 24, 32; 14:1, 12, 25, 58; 15:29	1	14:49							28
Lk.	75	1:5, 20, 23, 24, 25, 39, 59, 75, 80; 2:1, 6, 21, 22, 37, 43, 44, 46; 4:2, 2, 16, 25, 42; 5:17, 35, 35; 6:12, 13, 23; 8:22; 9:12, 22, 28, 36, 37; 10:12; 12:46; 13:14, 14, 16, 31; 14:5; 15:13; 16:19; 17:4, 4, 22, 22, 24, 26, 26, 27, 28, 29, 30, 31; 18:7, 33; 19:42, 43; 20:1; 21:6, 22, 23, 34; 22:7, 66; 23:12, 29, 54; 24:7, 13, 18, 21, 29, 46	3	9:23; 19:47; 22:53	2	9:51; 23:7			5	1:7, 18; 2:36; 11:3; 21:37	85
Jn.	30	1:39; 2:1, 12, 19, 20; 4:40, 43; 5:9; 6:39, 40, 44, 54; 7:37; 8:56; 9:4; 11:6, 9, 9, 17, 24, 53; 12:1, 7, 48; 14:20; 16:23, 26; 19:31; 20:19, 26									30
Ac.	81	1:2, 3, 5, 15, 22; 2:1, 15, 17, 18, 20, 29, 41; 3:24; 5:36, 37; 6:1; 7:8, 26, 41, 45; 9:9, 19, 23, 24, 37, 43; 10:3, 30, 40, 48; 11:27; 12:3, 18, 21; 13:14, 31, 41; 15:36; 16:12, 18, 35; 17:31; 20:6, 6, 6, 16, 18, 26, 31; 21:4, 5, 7, 10, 15, 26, 26, 27, 38; 23:1, 12; 24:1, 11, 24; 25:1, 6, 13, 14; 26:7, 22; 27:7, 20, 29, 33, 33, 39; 28:7, 12, 13, 14, 17, 23	6	2:46, 47; 3:2; 16:5; 17:11; 19:9	1	8:1	1	16:13	5	5:42; 15:7; 17:17; 18:18; 26:13	94
Ro.	11	2:5, 16; 8:36; 10:21; 11:8; 13:12, 13; 14:5, 5, 6, 6					1	14:5			12
1 Co.	5	1:8; 3:13; 5:5; 10:8; 15:4	1	15:31					1	4:3	7
2 Co.	5	1:14; 4:16, 16; 6:2, 2	1	11:28							6
Gal.	2	1:18; 4:10									2
Eph.	3	4:30; 5:16; 6:13									3
Phl.	4	1:5, 6, 10; 2:16									4
Col.	2	1:6, 9									2
1 Th.	6	2:9; 3:10; 5:2, 4, 5, 8									6
2 Th.	3	1:10; 2:2; 3:8									3
1 Ti.	1	5:5									1
2 Ti.	5	1:3, 12, 18; 3:1; 4:8									5
Heb.	15	1:2; 3:8; 4:4, 7, 8; 5:7; 7:3; 8:8, 9, 10; 10:16, 25, 32; 11:30; 12:10	2	7:27; 10:11					1	3:13	18
Jas.	2	5:3, 5									2
1 Pt.	3	2:12; 3:10, 20									3
2 Pt.	11	1:19; 2:8, 8, 9, 13; 3:3, 7, 8, 8, 10, 12							1	3:18	12
1 Jn.	1	4:17									1
Jd.	1	1:6									1
Rev.	21	1:10; 2:10, 13; 4:8; 6:17; 7:15; 8:12; 9:6, 15; 10:7; 11:3, 6, 9, 11; 12:6, 10; 14:11; 16:14; 18:8; 20:10; 21:25									21
Total	355		15		3		2		14		389

Miscellaneous: Mt. 28:20 (with 3856 and 3488), alway; Lk. 1:7, 18, year; Lk. 2:36, age; Lk. 11:3 (with 2596), day by day; Lk. 21:37, day time; Ac. 5:42 (with 3856), daily; Ac. 15:7, while; Ac. 17:17 (with 2596 and 3856), daily; Ac. 18:18, while; Ac. 26:13 (with 3219), midday; 1 Co. 4:3, judgment; Heb. 3:13 (with 2596 and 1538), daily; 2 Pt. 3:18 (with 165 and 1519), forever.

2251. ἡμέτερος, he̱met′eros

Book	Oc.	our	Oc.	your	Total
Ac.	3	2:11; 24:6; 26:5			3
Ro.	1	15:4			1
1 Co.			1	15:31	1
2 Ti.	1	4:15			1
Tit.	1	3:14			1
1 Jn.	2	1:3; 2:2			2
Total	8		1		9

2253. ἡμιθανής, he̱mithane̱s′

Book	half dead	Total
Lk.	10:30	1

2252. ἤμην, e̱′me̱n

Book	Oc.	was	Oc.	I imprisoned (with 1473 and 5339)	Oc.	I was (with 1473)	Oc.	should be	Total
Mt.	3	25:35, 36, 43							3
Mk.	1	14:49							1
Jn.	3	11:15; 16:4; 17:12							3
Ac.	4	10:30; 11:11, 17; 22:20	1	22:19	1	11:5			6
1 Co.	1	13:11							1
Gal.	1	1:22					1	1:10	2
Total	13		1		1		1		16

2254. ἡμῖν, he̱min′

Book	Oc.	us	Oc.	we	Oc.	our	Oc.	for us	Total
Mt.	16	3:15; 6:11, 12; 8:31; 13:36; 15:15; 20:12; 21:25; 22:17, 25; 24:3; 25:8, 9, 11; 26: 63, 68	3	8:29; 15:33; 19:27					19
Mk.	9	9:22, 38, 38; 10:35, 37; 12:19; 13:4; 14:15; 16:3	1	1:24					10
Lk.	23	1:1, 2, 74; 2:15, 48; 7:5, 16; 10:11, 17; 11:3, 4, 4; 13:25; 20:2, 22, 28; 22:8, 67; 23: 18; 24:24, 32, 32, 32	2	4:34; 9:13	1	17:5	1	1:69	27
Jn.	16	1:14; 2:18; 4:12, 25; 6:34, 52; 8:5; 10:24; 11:50; 14:8, 8, 9, 22; 16:17; 17:21; 18:31							16
Ac.	31	1:17, 21, 22; 2:29; 3:12; 6:14; 7:38, 40; 10:41, 42; 11:13, 17; 13:33, 47; 14:17; 15:7, 8, 25, 28; 16:9, 16, 17, 17, 21; 20:14; 21:16, 18; 25:24; 27:2; 28:2, 15	2	21:23; 28:22	1	19:27			34
Ro.	5	5:5; 8:4, 32; 9:29; 12:6							5
1 Co.	7	1:18, 30; 2:10, 12; 4:6; 8:6; 15:57							7
2 Co.	12	1:8; 4:12, 17; 5:5, 18, 19; 6:12; 7:7; 8:5, 7; 10:8, 13							12
Eph.	2	1:9; 3:20	1	6:12					3
Col.	3	1:8; 2:14; 4:3							3
1 Th.	2	2:8; 3:6							2
1 Ti.	1	6:17							1
2 Ti.	3	1:7, 9, 14							3
Heb.	5	1:2; 7:26; 10:15, 20; 12:1b	3	4:13; 5:11; 12:1a					8
Jas.	2	3:3; 4:5	1	5:17					3
1 Pt.	3	1:12; 2:21; 4:3							3
2 Pt.	3	1:1, 3, 4							3
1 Jn.	17	1:2, 8, 9, 10; 2:25; 3:1, 23, 24, 24; 4:9, 12, 12, 13, 13, 16; 5:11, 20							17
2 Jn.	1	1:2							1
Total	161		13		2		1		177

2255. ἥμισυ, he̱′misu

Book	half	Total
Mk.	6:23	1
Lk.	19:8	1
Rev.	11:9, 11; 12:14	3
Total		5

2256. ἡμιώριον, he̱miō′rion

Book	half	Total
Rev.	8:1	1

See page 169 for Word 2258.

2259. ἡνίκα, he̱ni′ka

Book	when	Total
2 Co.	3:15, 16	2

2257. ἡμῶν, he̱mōn′

Book	Oc.	our	Oc.	us	Oc.	we	Oc.	Not Tr.	Oc.	Misc.	Total
Mt.	10	6:9, 11, 12, 12; 8:17; 20:33; 21:42; 23:30; 25:8; 27:25	2	1:23; 15:23	1	28:13					13
Mk.	5	9:40b; 11:10; 12:7, 11, 29	1	9:40a							6
Lk.	16	1:55, 71, 72, 73, 74, 75, 78, 79; 7:5; 11:2, 3, 4; 13:26; 20:14; 24:20, 32	5	9:49, 50, 50; 16:26; 24:29					1	24:22	22
Jn.	12	3:11; 4:12, 20; 6:31; 7:51; 8:39, 53; 9:20; 11:11, 48; 12:38; 19:7							1	10:24	13
Ac.	31	2:8, 39; 3:13, 25; 5:30; 7:2, 11, 12, 15, 19, 19, 38, 39, 44, 45, 45; 13:17; 14:17; 15:10, 25, 26, 36; 16:20; 17: 20; 19:25; 20:21; 22:14; 24:7; 26:7; 27:10; 28:25	7	1:22; 7:40; 15:9, 24; 17:27; 24:4; 28:15	6	16:16; 21:10, 17; 26:14; 27: 18, 27					44
Ro.	30	1:3, 7; 3:5; 4:1, 12, 24, 25, 25; 5:1, 5, 11, 21; 6:6, 11, 23; 7:5, 25; 8:16, 23, 26a, 39; 9:10; 10:16; 13:11; 15: 6; 16:1, 9, 18, 20, 24	10	4:16; 5:8b; 8:26b, 31, 31, 32, 34; 14:7, 12; 15:2	2	5:6, 8a	1	15:30			43
1 Co.	22	1:2, 2, 3, 7, 8, 9, 10; 2:7; 5:4, 4, 7a; 6:11; 9:1; 10:1, 6, 11; 12:23, 24; 15:3, 14, 31, 57	2	4:8; 5:7b							24
2 Co.	40	1:2, 3, 4, 5, 7, 8, 11b, 12, 12, 14, 18, 22; 3:2, 2, 5; 4:3, 6, 10, 11, 16, 17; 5:1, 2, 12; 6:11, 11; 7:3, 4, 5b, 12, 14; 8:9, 22, 23, 24; 9:3; 10:4, 8, 15; 11:31	14	1:11a, 19, 20; 2:14; 3:3; 4:7; 5:20, 21; 7:9; 8:4, 19, 19, 20; 9:11	2	4:18; 7:5a					56
Gal.	7	1:3, 4, 4; 2:4; 3:24; 6:14, 18	2	3:13; 4:26							9
Eph.	11	1:2, 3, 14, 17; 2:3, 14; 3:11, 14; 5:20; 6:22, 24	2	4:7; 5:2							13
Phl.	5	1:2; 3:20, 21; 4:20, 23									5
Col.	4	1:2, 3, 7; 3:4	2	2:14; 4:3							6
1 Th.	26	1:1, 2, 3, 3, 5; 2:1, 2, 3, 4, 9, 19, 19, 20; 3:2, 2, 5, 7, 9, 11, 11, 11, 13, 13; 5:9, 23, 28	7	1:6, 9; 2:13; 3:6; 4: 1; 5:10, 25							33
2 Th.	18	1:1, 2, 8, 10, 11, 12, 12; 2:1, 1, 14, 14, 15, 16, 16; 3:6a, 12, 14, 18	4	1:7; 2:2; 3:1, 6b							22
1 Ti.	9	1:1, 1, 2, 2, 12, 14; 2:3; 6:3, 14									9
2 Ti.	4	1:2, 8, 9, 10									4
Tit.	6	1:3, 4; 2:10, 13; 3:4, 6	1	2:14							7
Phe.	4	1:1, 2, 3, 25									4
Heb.	7	1:3; 3:1; 4:15; 7:14; 12:9, 29; 13:20	5	6:20; 9:24; 11:40, 40; 13:18	1	10:26					13
Jas.	3	2:1, 21; 3:6									3
1 Pt.	2	1:3; 2:24	3	2:21; 4:1, 17							5
2 Pt.	9	1:1, 2, 8, 11, 14, 16; 3:15, 15, 18	1	3:2							10
1 Jn.	11	1:1, 1, 9; 2:2; 3:5, 19, 20b, 21a; 4:10, 17; 5:4	13	1:3; 2:19, 19, 19, 19, 19; 3:16, 20a, 21b; 4: 6, 6; 5:14, 15							24
2 Jn.	1	1:12	1	1:2							2
3 Jn.	1	1:12									1
Jd.	5	1:4, 4, 17, 21, 25									5
Rev.	14	1:5; 5:10; 6:10; 7:3, 10, 12; 11:8, 15; 12:10, 10, 10; 19:1, 5; 22:21									14
Total	313		82		12		1		2		410

Miscellaneous: Lk. 24:22, our company; Jn. 10:24 (with 5490), us.

2260. ἤπερ, e̱′per

Book	than	Total
Jn.	12:43	1

2261. ἤπιος, e̱′pios

Book	gentle	Total
1 Th.	2:7	1
2 Ti.	2:24	1
Total		2

2262. Ἤρ, E̱r

Book	Er	Total
Lk.	3:28	1

2263. ἤρεμος, e̱′remos

Book	quiet	Total
1 Ti.	2:2	1

2264. Ἡρώδης, Hērō'dēs

Book	Oc.	Herod, Antipas	Oc.	Herod, the Great	Oc.	Herod, Agrippa	Total
Mt.	4	14:1, 3, 6, 6	9	2:1, 3, 7, 12, 13, 15, 16, 19, 22			13
Mk.	8	6:14, 16, 17, 18, 20, 21, 22; 8:15					8
Lk.	13	3:1, 19, 19; 8:3; 9:7, 9; 13:31; 23:7, 7, 8, 11, 12, 15	1	1:5			14
Ac.	2	4:27; 13:1	1	23:35	6	12:1, 6, 11, 19, 20, 21	9
Total	27		11		6		44

2265. Ἡρωδιανοί, Hērōdianoi'

Book	Herodians	Total
Mt.	22:16	1
Mk.	3:6; 12:13	2
Total		3

2258. ἦν, ēn

Book	Oc.	was	Oc.	were	Oc.	had been	Oc.	had (with dative)	Oc.	had	Oc.	taught (with 1321)	Oc.	stood (with 2476)	Oc.	Misc.	Total
Mt.	20	1:18; 2:9, 15; 3:4; 7:27; 8:30; 12:4, 10, 40; 14:23, 24, 24; 21:25, 33; 26:69, 71; 27:54, 56, 61; 28:3	9	4:18; 14:21; 15:38; 22:8, 25; 24:38; 25:2; 26:43; 27:55	2	23:30a; 26:24					1	7:29			5	9:36; 19:22; 23:30b; 25:21, 23	37
Mk.	34	1:6, 13, 13, 23, 33, 45; 2:4; 3:1; 4:1, 36a, 38; 5:5, 11, 21, 40, 42; 6:47, 48, 52; 7:26; 11:13, 30, 32; 14:1, 67; 15:7, 25, 26, 39, 40b, 41, 42, 46 16:4	17	1:16; 2:6, 15; 4:36b; 5:13; 6:31, 34, 44; 8:9; 9:4, 6; 10:32a; 12:20; 14:4, 21, 40; 15:40a							1	1:22			8	1:39; 2:18; 10:22, 32b; 14:54, 56, 59; 15:43	60
Lk.	62	1:7b, 66, 80; 2:7, 25, 25, 26, 36, 40, 51; 4:17, 32, 33, 38; 5:3, 17a, 17d, 18, 29a; 6:6, 6; 7:2, 12, 37; 8:32; 9:45, 53; 11:14, 14; 13:10, 11, 11; 14:2; 15:24, 24, 25, 25, 32, 32; 16:1, 19, 20; 17:16; 18:2, 3, 23, 34; 19:2, 2, 3; 20:4; 21:37; 22:56, 59; 23:8, 19, 38, 44, 47, 53, 54; 24:10	16	1:6, 7c, 10; 2:8; 4:25, 27; 5:10, 17b, 17c; 7:39; 8:40; 9:14, 30, 32; 20:29; 24:53	2	4:16; 8:2	4	1:7a; 7:41; 8:42; 10:39			2	4:31; 19:47	1	5:1	15	1:21, 22; 2:33; 3:23; 4:20, 44; 5:16, 29b; 6:12; 14:1; 15:1; 23:51, 55; 24:13, 32	102
Jn.	85	1:1, 1, 1, 2, 4, 4, 8, 9, 10, 15, 15, 28, 30, 39, 40, 44; 2:1, 13, 23, 25; 3:1, 23, 23, 24, 26; 4:6, 6, 46; 5:1, 5, 9, 35; 6:4, 10, 22, 62; 7:2, 12, 39, 42; 8:44; 9:8, 14, 16, 24; 10:22; 11:1, 2, 6, 15, 18, 30, 32a, 38, 41, 55; 12:1, 2, 6; 13:5, 23, 30; 18:1, 10, 13, 13, 14, 15, 16, 18a, 28, 40; 19:14, 19, 20, 20, 23, 31, 31, 41, 42; 20:7, 24; 21:7, 18	20	1:24; 2:6; 3:19; 8:39, 42; 9:33, 41; 10:6, 41; 12:16, 20; 15:19; 17:6; 18:30, 36; 19:11; 20:19, 26; 21:2, 8	3	9:18; 11:21, 32b							2	18:18b, 25	1	10:40	111
Ac.	37	1:17; 2:24; 3:10; 4:3, 22, 33; 7:9, 20, 22; 8:1, 16, 28, 32; 9:9, 10, 28, 33, 36, 36; 10:1, 38; 11:21, 24; 12:5, 6, 18, 20; 13:7, 46; 14:12; 16:1; 17:1; 18:25; 19:16, 32; 21:3; 27:8	25	1:15; 2:1, 2, 5, 44; 4:6, 31, 32a; 5:12; 11:20; 12:3, 12; 13:1, 48; 16:12; 17:11; 18:3, 14; 19:7, 14; 20:8, 8, 16; 23:13; 27:37	2	4:13; 14:26	3	4:32b; 7:44; 21:9	3	20:13; 21:29; 22:29			1	16:9	10	1:10, 13, 14; 2:42; 8:13, 27; 10:24; 14:4, 7; 18:7	81
Ro.	1	5:13	4	6:17, 20, 20; 7:5													5
1 Co.	2	10:4; 16:12	4	6:11; 10:1; 12:2, 19													6
2 Co.	1	5:19															1
Gal.	1	2:11	3	2:6; 4:3, 3					1	1:23					2	3:21; 4:15	7
Eph.			3	2:3, 12; 5:8													3
Phl.			1	3:7											1	2:26	2
Col.	1	2:14															1
1 Th.			1	3:4													1
2 Th.			1	3:10													1
Tit.			1	3:3													1
Heb.	3	7:10; 11:38; 12:21	3	2:15; 7:11; 8:4a	1	8:7									1	8:4b	8
Jas.	2	1:24; 5:17															2
1 Pt.			1	2:25													1
2 Pt.			1	3:5	1	2:21											2
1 Jn.	3	1:1, 2; 3:12a	2	2:19a; 3:12b	1	2:19b											6
Rev.	13	1:4, 8; 4:3, 8; 10:10; 11:17; 13:2; 16:5; 17:8, 8, 11; 21:18, 21	3	9:8, 10; 18:23													16
Total	265		115		12		7		4		4		4		43		454

Miscellaneous: Mt. 9:36 (with 1590), fainted; Mt. 19:22 (with 2192), had; Mt. 23:30b, would have been; Mt. 25:21, 23, hast been; Mk. 1:39 (with 2784), preached; Mk. 2:18, used; Mk. 10:22 (with 2192), had; Mk. 10:32b (with 4154), went before; Mk. 14:54 (with 4675), sat; Mk. 14:56, 59 (with 2470), agreed together; Mk. 15:43 (with 4227), waited for; Lk. 1:21 (with 4228), waited for; Lk. 1:22 (with 1269), beckoned; Lk. 2:33 (with 2296), marvelled; Lk. 3:23, began to be; Lk. 4:20 (with 816), be fastened on; Lk. 4:44 (with 2784), preached; Lk. 5:16 (with 5198), withdrew himself; Lk. 5:29b (with 2621), sat down; Lk. 6:12 (with 1273), continued all night; Lk. 14:1 (with 3806), watched; Lk. 15:1 (with 1448), drew near; Lk. 23:51 (with 4684), consented; Lk. 23:55 (with 4805), came with; Lk. 24:13 (with 4098), went; Lk. 24:32 (with 2545), did burn; Jn. 10:40 (with 907), baptized; Ac. 1:10 (with 816), looked steadfastly; Ac. 1:13 (with 2650), abode; Ac. 1:14; 2:42; 8:13 (with 4242), continued; Ac. 8:27 (with 1909), had charge of; Ac. 10:24 (with 4228), waited for; Ac. 14:4, held; Ac. 14:7 (with 2097), preached the gospel; Ac. 18:7 (with 4827), joined hard; Gal. 3:21, should have been; Gal. 4:15, is; Phl. 2:26 (with 1971), longed after; Heb. 8:4b, should be.

2266. Ἡρωδιάς, He̱rōdias'

Book	Herodias	Total
Mt.	14:3, 6	2
Mk.	6:17, 19, 22	3
Lk.	3:19	1
Total		6

2267. Ἡρωδίων, He̱rōdi'ōn

Book	Herodian	Total
Ro.	16:11	1

2269. Ἠσαῦ, E̱sau'

Book	Esau	Total
Ro.	9:13	1
Heb.	11:20; 12:16	2
Total		3

2268. Ἡσαΐας, He̱sai'as

Book	Esaias	Total
Mt.	3:3; 4:14; 8:17; 12:17; 13:14; 15:7	6
Mk.	7:6	1
Lk.	3:4; 4:17	2
Jn.	1:23; 12:38, 39, 41	4
Ac	8:28, 30; 28:25	3
Ro.	9:27, 29; 10:16, 20; 15:12	5
Total		21

2270. ἡσυχάζω, he̱suchad'zō

Book	Oc.	hold (one's) peace	Oc.	rest	Oc.	cease	Oc.	be quiet	Total
Lk.	1	14:4	1	23:56					2
Ac.	1	11:18			1	21:14			2
1 Th.							1	4:11	1
Total	2		1		1		1		5

2273. ἤτοι, e̱'toi

Book	whether	Total
Ro.	6:16	1

2271. ἡσυχία, he̱suchi'a

Book	Oc.	silence	Oc.	quietness	Total
Ac.	1	22:2			1
2 Th.			1	3:12	1
1 Ti.	2	2:11, 12			2
Total	3		1		4

2272. ἡσύχιος, he̱su'chios

Book	Oc.	quiet	Oc.	peaceable	Total
1 Ti.			1	2:2	1
1 Pt.	1	3:4			1
Total	1		1		2

2274. ἡττάω, he̱tta'ō

Book	Oc.	overcome	Oc.	be inferior	Total
2 Co.			1	12:13	1
2 Pt.	2	2:19, 20			2
Total	2		1		3

2275. ἥττημα, he̱t'te̱ma

Book	Oc.	diminishing	Oc.	fault	Total
Ro.	1	11:12			1
1 Co.			1	6:7	1
Total	1		1		2

2276. ἧττον, he̱t'ton

Book	Oc.	worse	Oc.	less	Total
1 Co.	1	11:17			1
2 Co.			1	12:15	1
Total	1		1		2

2277. ἤτω, e̱'tō

Book	be	Total
1 Co.	16:22	1
Jas.	5:12	1
Total		2

2280. Θαδδαῖος, Thaddai'os

Book	Thaddaeus	Total
Mt.	10:3	1
Mk.	3:18	1
Total		2

2278. ἠχέω, e̱che'ō

Book	Oc.	roaring	Oc.	sounding	Total
Lk.	1	21:25			1
1 Co.			1	13:1	1
Total	1		1		2

2279. ἦχος, e̱'chos

Book	Oc.	sound	Oc.	fame	Total
Lk.			1	4:37	1
Ac.	1	2:2			1
Heb.	1	12:19			1
Total	2		1		3

2281. θάλασσα, thal'assa

Book	sea	Total
Mt.	4:15, 18, 18; 8:24, 26, 27, 32; 13:1, 47; 14:24, 25, 26; 15:29; 17:27; 18:6; 21:21; 23:15	17
Mk.	1:16, 16; 2:13; 3:7; 4:1, 1, 1, 39, 41; 5:1, 13, 13, 21; 6:47, 48, 49; 7:31; 9:42; 11:23	19
Lk.	17:2, 6; 21:25	3
Jn.	6:1, 16, 17, 18, 19, 22, 25; 21:1, 7	9
Ac.	4:24; 7:36; 10:6, 32; 14:15; 17:14; 27:30, 38, 40; 28:4	10
Ro.	9:27	1
1 Co.	10:1, 2	2
2 Co.	11:26	1
Heb	11:12, 29	2
Jas.	1:6	1
Jd.	1:13	1
Rev.	4:6; 5:13; 7:1, 2, 3; 8:8, 8, 9; 10:2, 5, 6, 8; 12:12; 13:1, 1; 14:7; 15:2, 2; 16:3, 3; 18:17, 19, 21; 20:8, 13; 21:1	26
Total		92

2282. θάλπω, thal'pō

Book	cherish	Total
Eph.	5:29	1
1 Th.	2:7	1
Total		2

2283. Θάμαρ, Tham'ar

Book	Thamar	Total
Mt.	1:3	1

2284. θαμβέω, thambe'ō

Book	Oc.	be amazed	Oc.	be astonished	Total
Mk.	2	1:27; 10:32	1	10:24	3
Ac.			1	9:6	1
Total	2		2		4

2285. θάμβος, tham'bos

Book	Oc.	be amazed (with 1096)	Oc.	be astonished (with 3923)	Oc.	wonder	Total
Lk.	1	4:36	1	5:9			2
Ac.					1	3:10	1
Total	1		1		1		3

2286. θανάσιμος, thanas'imos

Book	deadly	Total
Mk.	16:18	1

2287. θανατηφόρος, thanate̱'phoros

Book	deadly	Total
Jas.	3:8	1

2288. θάνατος, than'atos

Book	Oc.	death	Oc.	deadly	Total
Mt.	7	4:16; 10:21; 15:4; 16:28; 20:18; 26:38, 66			7
Mk.	6	7:10; 9:1; 10:33; 13:12; 14:34, 64			6
Lk.	7	1:79; 2:26; 9:27; 22:33; 23:15, 22; 24:20			7
Jn.	8	5:24; 8:51, 52; 11:4, 13; 12:33; 18:32; 21:19			8
Ac.	8	2:24; 13:28; 22:4; 23:29; 25:11, 25; 26:31; 28:18			8
Ro.	22	1:32; 5:10, 12, 12, 14, 17, 21; 6:3, 4, 5, 9, 16, 21, 23; 7:5, 10, 13, 13, 24; 8:2, 6, 38			22
1 Co.	7	3:22; 11:26; 15:21, 26, 54, 55, 56			7
2 Co.	9	1:9, 10; 2:16, 16; 3:7; 4:11, 12; 7:10; 11:23			9
Phl.	6	1:20; 2:8, 8, 27, 30; 3:10			6
Col.	1	1:22			1
2 Ti.	1	1:10			1
Heb.	10	2:9, 9, 14, 14, 15; 5:7; 7:23; 9:15, 16; 11:5			10
Jas.	2	1:15; 5:20			2
1 Jn.	6	3:14, 14; 5:16, 16, 16, 17			6
Rev.	17	1:18; 2:10, 11, 23; 6:8, 8; 9:6, 6; 12:11; 13:3a; 18:8; 20:6, 13, 14, 14; 21:4, 8	2	13:3b, 12	19
Total	117		2		119

2289. θανατόω, thanato'ō

Book	Oc.	put to death	Oc.	cause to be put to death	Oc.	kill	Oc.	become dead	Oc.	mortify	Total
Mt.	2	26:59; 27:1	1	10:21							3
Mk.	1	14:55	1	13:12							2
Lk.			1	21:16							1
Ro.					1	8:36	1	7:4	1	8:13	3
2 Co.					1	6:9					1
1 Pt.	1	3:18									1
Total	4		3		2		1		1		11

2290. θάπτω, thap'tō

Book	bury	Total
Mt.	8:21, 22; 14:12	3
Lk.	9:59, 60; 16:22	3
Ac.	2:29; 5:6, 9, 10	4
1 Co.	15:4	1
Total		11

2291. Θάρα, Thar'a

Book	Thara	Total
Lk.	3:34	1

2292. θαῤῥέω, tharhre'ō

Book	Oc.	be bold	Oc.	be confident	Oc.	confident	Oc.	have confidence	Oc.	boldly	Total
2 Co.	2	10:1, 2	1	5:8	1	5:6	1	7:16			5
Heb.									1	13:6	1
Total	2		1		1		1		1		6

2293. θαρσέω, tharse'ō

Book	Oc.	be of good cheer	Oc.	be of good comfort	Total
Mt.	2	9:2; 14:27	1	9:22	3
Mk.	1	6:50	1	10:49	2
Lk.			1	8:48	1
Jn.	1	16:33			1
Ac.	1	23:11			1
Total	5		3		8

2294. θάρσος, thar'sos

Book	courage	Total
Ac.	28:15	1

2295. θαῦμα, thau'ma

Book	admiration	Total
Rev.	17:6	1

2296. θαυμάζω, thaumad'zō

Book	Oc.	marvel	Oc.	wonder	Oc.	have in admiration	Oc.	admire	Oc.	marvelled (with 2258)	Total
Mt.	7	8:10, 27; 9:8, 33; 21:20; 22:22; 27:14	1	15:31							8
Mk.	5	5:20; 6:6; 12:17; 15:5, 44	1	6:51							6
Lk.	5	1:21, 63; 7:9; 11:38; 20:26	7	2:18; 4:22; 8:25; 9:43; 11:14; 24:12, 41					1	2:33	13
Jn.	6	3:7; 4:27; 5:20, 28; 7:15, 21									6
Ac.	3	2:7; 3:12; 4:13	2	7:31; 13:41							5
Gal.	1	1:6									1
2 Th.							1	1:10			1
1 Jn.	1	3:13									1
Jd.					1	1:16					1
Rev.	1	17:7	3	13:3; 17:6, 8							4
Total	29		14		1		1		1		46

2297. θαυμάσιος, thaumas'ios

Book	wonderful	Total
Mt.	21:15	1

2298. θαυμαστός, thaumastos'

Book	Oc.	marvelous	Oc.	marvel	Oc.	marvellous thing	Total
Mt.	1	21:42					1
Mk.	1	12:11					1
Jn.					1	9:30	1
2 Co.			1	11:14			1
1 Pt.	1	2:9					1
Rev.	2	15:1, 3					2
Total	5		1		1		7

2299. θεά, thea'

Book	goddess	Total
Ac.	19:27, 35, 37	3

2300. θεάομαι, thea'omai

Book	Oc.	see	Oc.	behold	Oc.	look	Oc.	look upon	Total
Mt.	4	6:1; 11:7; 22:11; 23:5							4
Mk.	2	16:11, 14							2
Lk.	2	5:27; 7:24	1	23:55					3
Jn.	5	1:32, 38; 6:5; 8:10; 11:45	1	1:14	1	4:35			7
Ac.	4	1:11; 8:18; 21:27; 22:9							4
Ro.	1	15:24							1
1 Jn.	2	4:12, 14					1	1:1	3
Total	20		2		1		1		24

2301. θεατρίζω, theatrid'zō

Book	make a gazingstock	Total
Heb.	10:33	1

2302. θέατρον, the'atron

Book	Oc.	theatre	Oc.	spectacle	Total
Ac.	2	19:29, 31			2
1 Co.			1	4:9	1
Total	2		1		3

2303. θεῖον, thei'on

Book	brimstone	Total
Lk.	17:29	1
Rev.	9:17, 18; 14:10; 19:20; 20:10; 21:8	6
Total		7

2304. θεῖος, thei'os

Book	Oc.	divine	Oc.	Godhead	Total
Ac.			1	17:29	1
2 Pt.	2	1:3, 4			2
Total	2		1		3

2305. θειότης, theiot'ēs

Book	Godhead	Total
Ro.	1:20	1

2306. θειώδης, theiō'dēs

Book	brimstone	Total
Rev.	9:17	1

2307. θέλημα, thel'ēma

Book	Oc.	will	Oc.	desire	Oc.	pleasure	Total
Mt.	6	6:10; 7:21; 12:50; 18:14; 21:31; 26:42					6
Mk.	1	3:35					1
Lk.	5	11:2; 12:47, 47; 22:42; 23:25					5
Jn.	11	1:13, 13; 4:34; 5:30, 30; 6:38, 38, 39, 40; 7:17; 9:31					11
Ac.	3	13:22; 21:14; 22:14					3
Ro.	4	1:10; 2:18; 12:2; 15:32					4
1 Co.	3	1:1; 7:37; 16:12					3
2 Co.	2	1:1; 8:5					2
Gal.	1	1:4					1
Eph.	6	1:1, 5, 9, 11; 5:17; 6:6	1	2:3			7
Col.	3	1:1, 9; 4:12					3
1 Th.	2	4:3; 5:18					2
2 Ti.	2	1:1; 2:26					2
Heb.	5	10:7, 9, 10, 36; 13:21					5
1 Pt.	5	2:15; 3:17; 4:2, 3, 19					5
2 Pt.	1	1:21					1
1 Jn.	2	2:17; 5:14					2
Rev.					1	4:11	1
Total	62		1		1		64

2308. θέλησις, thel'ēsis

Book	will	Total
Heb.	2:4	1

2310. θεμέλιος, themel'ios

Book	foundation	Total
Lk.	6:48, 49; 14:29	3
Ac.	16:26	1
Ro.	15:20	1
1 Co.	3:10, 11, 12	3
Eph.	2:20	1
1 Ti.	6:19	1
2 Ti.	2:19	1
Heb.	6:1; 11:10	2
Rev.	21:14, 19, 19	3
Total		16

2309. θέλω, thel'ō

Book	Oc.	will (would)	Oc.	will (would) have	Oc.	desire	Oc.	desirous	Oc.	list	Oc.	to will	Oc.	Misc.	Total
Mt.	38	1:19; 2:18; 5:40, 42; 7:12; 8:2, 3; 11:14; 12:38; 13:28; 14:5; 15:28, 32; 16:24, 25; 17:4; 18:23, 30; 19:17, 21; 20:14, 15, 21, 26, 27, 32; 21:29; 22:3; 23:4, 37, 37; 26:15, 17, 39; 27:15, 17, 21, 34	3	9:13; 12:7; 27:43					1	17:12					42
Mk.	21	1:40, 41; 3:13; 6:19, 22, 25, 26, 48; 8:34, 35; 9:30; 10:35, 36, 43, 44, 51; 14:7, 12, 36; 15:9, 12	1	7:24	1	9:35			1	9:13			1	12:38	25
Lk.	20	4:6; 5:12, 13; 6:31; 9:23, 24, 54; 10:29; 12:49; 13:31, 34, 34; 15:28; 16:26; 18:4, 13, 41; 19:27; 22:9; 23:20	2	1:62; 19:14	4	5:39; 8:20; 10:24; 20:46	1	23:8					1	14:28	28
Jn.	19	1:43; 5:6, 21, 40; 6:11, 67; 7:1, 17, 44; 8:44; 9:27, 27; 12:21; 15:7; 17:24; 21:18, 18, 22, 23					1	16:19	1	3:8			2	5:35; 6:21	23
Ac.	12	7:28, 39; 10:10; 14:13; 17:18; 18:21; 19:33; 24:6, 27; 25:9, 9; 26:5	2	9:6; 16:3									2	2:12; 17:20	16
Ro.	12	7:15, 16, 19, 19, 20, 21; 9:16, 18, 18, 22; 11:25; 13:3	2	1:13; 16:19							1	7:18			15
1 Co.	10	4:19, 21; 7:7, 36, 39; 10:1, 20; 14:5, 35; 16:7	3	7:32; 11:3; 12:1									4	10:27; 12:18; 14:19; 15:38	17
2 Co.	4	5:4; 8:11; 12:20, 20	1	1:8	2	11:12; 12:6	1	11:32					1	8:10	9
Gal.	4	1:7; 3:2; 4:17; 5:17			5	4:9, 20, 21; 6:12, 13									9
Phl.											1	2:13			1
Col.	2	1:27; 2:1											1	2:18	3
1 Th.	1	2:18	1	4:13											2
2 Th.	1	3:10													1
1 Ti.	1	5:11	1	2:4	1	1:7									3
2 Ti.	1	3:12													1
Phe.	1	1:14													1
Heb.	4	10:5, 8; 12:17; 13:18													4
Jas.	2	2:20; 4:15													2
1 Pt.	1	3:10											1	3:17	2
2 Pt.													1	3:5	1
3 Jn.	1	1:13													1
Rev.	3	11:5, 6; 22:17													3
Total	158		16		13		3		3		2		4		209

Miscellaneous: Mk. 12:38, love; Lk. 14:28, intend; Jn. 5:35, be willing; Jn. 6:21, willingly; Ac. 2:12; 17:20, mean; 1 Co. 10:27, be disposed; 1 Co. 12:18, please; 1 Co. 14:19, have rather; 1 Co. 15:38, please; 2 Co. 8:10, be forward; Col. 2:18, voluntary; 1 Pt. 3:17, be so; 2 Pt. 3:5, willingly.

2311. θεμελίοω, themelio'ō

Book	Oc.	found	Oc.	ground	Oc.	lay the foundation	Oc.	settle	Total
Mt.	1	7:25							1
Lk.	1	6:48							1
Eph.			1	3:17					1
Col.			1	1:23					1
Heb.					1	1:10			1
1 Pt.							1	5:10	1
Total	2		2		1		1		6

2312. θεοδίδακτος, theodid'aktos

Book	taught of God	Total
1 Th.	4:9	1

2313. θεομαχέω, theomache'ō

Book	fight against God	Total
Ac.	23:9	1

2314. θεόμαχος, theom'achos

Book	to fight against God	Total
Ac.	5:39	1

2315. θεόπνευστος, theop'neustos

Book	given by inspiration of God	Total
2 Ti.	3:16	1

2316. Θεός, Theos′

Book	Oc.	God	Oc.	god	Oc.	godly	Oc.	God-ward (with 4214)	Oc.	Misc.	Total
Mt.	55	1:23; 3:9, 16; 4:3, 4, 6, 7, 10; 5:8, 9, 34; 6:24, 30, 33; 8:29; 9:8; 12:4, 28, 28; 14:33; 15:3, 4, 6, 31; 16:16, 23; 19:6, 17, 24, 26; 21:12, 31, 43; 22:16, 21, 21, 29, 30, 31, 32, 32, 32, 32, 32, 37; 23:22; 26:61, 63, 63; 27:40, 43, 43, 46, 46, 54									55
Mk.	52	1:1, 14, 15, 24; 2:7, 12, 26; 3:11, 35; 4:11, 26, 30; 5:7, 7; 7:8, 9, 13; 8:33; 9:1, 47; 10:6, 9, 14, 15, 18, 23, 24, 25, 27, 27; 11:22; 12:14, 17, 17, 24, 26, 26, 26, 26, 27, 27, 29, 30, 32, 34; 13:19; 14:25; 15:34, 34, 39, 43; 16:19									52
Lk.	124	1:6, 8, 16, 19, 26, 30, 32, 35, 37, 47, 64, 68, 78; 2:13, 14, 20, 28, 40, 52; 3: 2, 6, 8, 38; 4:3, 4, 8, 9, 12, 34, 41, 43; 5:1, 21, 25, 26; 6:4, 12, 20; 7:16, 16, 28, 29, 30; 8:1, 10, 11, 21, 28, 39; 9:2, 11, 20, 27, 43, 60, 62; 10:9, 11, 27; 11:20, 20, 28, 42, 49; 12:6, 8, 9, 20, 21, 24, 28, 31; 13:13, 18, 20, 28, 29; 14:15; 15:10; 16:13, 15, 15, 16; 17:15, 18, 20, 20, 21; 18:2, 4, 7, 11, 13, 16, 17, 19, 24, 25, 27, 29, 43, 43; 19:11, 37; 20:21, 25, 25, 36, 37, 37, 37, 38; 21:4, 31; 22:16, 18, 69, 70; 23:35, 40, 47, 51; 24:19, 53									124
Jn.	82	1:1, 1, 2, 6, 12, 13, 18, 29, 34, 36, 49, 51; 3:2, 2, 3, 5, 16, 17, 18, 21, 33, 34, 34, 34, 36; 4:10, 24; 5:18, 18, 25, 42, 44; 6:27, 28, 29, 33, 45, 46, 69; 7:17; 8:40, 41, 42, 42, 47, 47, 47, 54; 9:3, 16, 24, 29, 31, 33, 35; 10:33, 35b, 36; 11:4, 4, 22, 22, 27, 40, 52; 12:43; 13:3, 3, 31, 32, 32; 14:1; 16:2, 27, 30; 17:3; 19:7; 20:17, 17, 28, 31; 21:19	2	10:34, 35a							84
Ac.	165	1:3; 2:11, 17, 22, 22, 23, 24, 30, 32, 33, 36, 39, 47; 3:8, 9, 13, 13, 15, 18, 21, 22, 25, 26; 4:10, 19, 19, 21, 24, 24, 31; 5:4, 29, 30, 31, 32, 39; 6:2, 7, 11; 7:2, 6, 7, 9, 17, 25, 32, 32, 32, 32, 35, 37, 42, 45, 46, 46, 55, 55, 56; 8:10, 12, 14, 20, 21, 22, 37; 9:20; 10:2, 2, 3, 4, 15, 22, 28, 31, 33, 33, 34, 38, 38, 40, 41, 42, 46; 11:1, 9, 17, 17, 18, 18, 23; 12:5, 23, 24; 13:5, 7, 16, 17, 21, 23, 26, 30, 33, 36, 37, 43, 44, 46; 14:15, 22, 26, 27; 15:4, 7, 8, 10, 12, 14, 18, 19, 40; 16:14, 17, 25, 34; 17:13, 23, 24, 29, 30; 18:7, 11, 13, 21, 26; 19:8, 11; 20:21, 24, 25, 27, 28, 32; 21:19; 22:3, 14; 23:1, 3, 4; 24:14, 15, 16; 26:6, 8, 18, 20, 22, 29; 27:23, 24, 25, 35; 28:15, 23, 28, 31	6	7:40, 43; 12: 22; 14: 11; 19: 26; 28: 6					1	7:20	172
Ro.	153	1:1, 4, 7, 7, 8, 9, 10, 16, 17, 18, 19, 19, 21, 21, 23, 24, 25, 26, 28, 28, 32; 2:2, 3, 4, 5, 11, 13, 16, 17, 23, 24, 29; 3:2, 3, 4, 5, 5, 6, 7, 11, 18, 19, 21, 22, 23, 25, 25, 29, 30; 4:2, 3, 6, 17, 20, 20; 5:1, 2, 5, 8, 10, 11, 15; 6:10, 11, 13, 13, 17, 22, 23; 7:4, 22, 25, 25; 8:3, 7, 7, 8, 9, 14, 14, 16, 17, 19, 21, 27, 28, 31, 33, 33, 34, 39; 9:5, 6, 8, 11, 14, 16, 20, 22, 26; 10:1, 2, 3, 3, 9, 17; 11:1, 2, 2, 8, 21, 22, 23, 29, 30, 32, 33; 12:1, 1, 2, 3; 13:1, 1, 2, 4, 4, 6; 14:3, 4, 6, 6, 11, 12, 17, 18, 20, 22; 15:5, 6, 7, 8, 9, 13, 15, 16, 17, 19, 30, 32, 33; 16:20, 26, 27									153
1 Co.	104	1:1, 2, 3, 4, 4, 9, 14, 18, 20, 21, 21, 21, 24, 24, 25, 25, 27, 27, 28, 30; 2:1, 5, 7, 7, 9, 10, 10, 11, 11, 12, 12, 14; 3:6, 7, 9, 9, 9, 10, 16, 16, 17, 17, 17, 19, 23; 4:1, 5, 9, 20; 5:13; 6:9, 10, 11, 13, 14, 19, 20, 20; 7:7, 15, 17, 19, 24, 40; 8:3, 4, 6, 8; 9:9, 21; 10:5, 13, 20, 31, 32; 11:3, 7, 12, 13, 16, 22; 12:3, 6, 18, 24, 28; 14:2, 18, 25, 25, 28, 33, 36; 15:9, 10, 10, 15, 15, 24, 28, 34, 38, 50, 57	2	8:5, 5							106
2 Co.	72	1:1, 1, 2, 3, 3, 4, 9, 12b, 18, 19, 20, 20, 21, 23; 2:14, 15, 17, 17, 17; 3:3, 5; 4:2, 2, 4b, 6, 6, 7, 15; 5:1, 5, 11, 13, 18, 19, 20, 20, 21; 6:1, 4, 7, 16, 16, 16, 16; 7:1, 6, 12; 8:1, 5, 16; 9:7, 8, 11, 12, 13, 14, 15; 10:4, 5, 13; 11:7, 11, 31; 12:2, 3, 19, 21; 13:4, 4, 7, 11, 14	1	4:4a	2	1:12a; 11:2	1	3:4	3	7:9, 10, 11	79
Gal.	30	1:1, 3, 4, 10, 13, 15, 20, 24; 2:6, 19, 20, 21; 3:6, 8, 11, 17, 18, 20, 21, 26; 4: 4, 6, 7, 8a, 9, 9, 14; 5:21; 6:7, 16	1	4:8b							31
Eph.	32	1:1, 2, 3, 17; 2:4, 8, 10, 16, 19, 22; 3:2, 7, 9, 10, 19; 4:6, 13, 18, 24, 30, 32; 5:1, 2, 5, 6, 20, 21; 6:6, 11, 13, 17, 23									32
Phl.	22	1:2, 3, 8, 11, 28; 2:6, 6, 9, 11, 13, 15, 27; 3:3, 9, 14, 15; 4:6, 7, 9, 18, 19, 20	1	3:19							23
Col.	22	1:1, 2, 3, 6, 10, 15, 25, 25, 27; 2:2, 12, 19; 3:1, 3, 6, 12, 15, 17, 22; 4:3, 11, 12									22
1 Th.	36	1:1, 1, 2, 3, 4, 9, 9; 2:2, 2, 4, 4, 5, 8, 9, 10, 12, 13, 13, 13, 14, 15; 3:2, 9, 9, 11, 13; 4:1, 3, 5, 7, 8, 14, 16; 5:9, 18, 23					1	1:8			37
2 Th.	19	1:1, 2, 3, 4, 5, 5, 6, 8, 11, 12; 2:4, 4, 4, 4, 11, 13, 13, 16; 3:5									19
1 Ti.	22	1:1, 2, 11, 17; 2:3, 5, 5; 3:5, 15, 15, 16; 4:3, 4, 5, 10; 5:4, 5, 21; 6:1, 11, 13, 17			1	1:4					23
2 Ti.	12	1:1, 2, 3, 6, 7, 8; 2:9, 15, 19, 25; 3:17; 4:1									12
Tit.	13	1:1, 1, 2, 3, 4, 7, 16; 2:5, 10, 11, 13; 3:4, 8									13
Phe.	2	1:3, 4									2
Heb.	69	1:1, 6, 8, 9, 9; 2:4, 9, 13, 17; 3:4, 12; 4:4, 9, 10, 12, 14; 5:1, 4, 10, 12; 6:1, 3, 5, 6, 7, 10, 13, 17, 18; 7:1, 3, 19, 25; 8:10; 9:14, 14, 20, 24; 10:7, 9, 12, 21, 29, 31, 36; 11:3, 4, 4, 5, 5, 6, 10, 16, 16, 19, 25, 40; 12:2, 7, 15, 22, 23, 28, 29; 13:4, 7, 15, 16, 20									69
Jas.	17	1:1, 5, 13, 13, 20, 27; 2:5, 19, 23, 23; 3:9, 9; 4:4, 4, 6, 7, 8									17
1 Pt.	39	1:2, 3, 5, 21, 21, 23; 2:4, 5, 10, 12, 15, 16, 17, 19, 20; 3:4, 5, 15, 17, 18, 20, 21, 22; 4:2, 6, 10, 11, 11, 11, 14, 16, 17, 17, 19; 5:2, 5, 6, 10, 12									39
2 Pt.	7	1:1, 2, 7, 21; 2:4; 3:5, 12									7
1 Jn.	63	1:5; 2:5, 14, 17; 3:1, 2, 8, 9, 9, 10, 10; 3:17, 20, 21; 4:1, 2, 2, 3, 4, 6, 6, 6, 7, 7, 7, 8, 8, 9, 9, 10, 11, 12, 12, 15, 15, 15, 16, 16, 16, 16, 20, 20, 21; 5:1, 2, 2, 3, 4, 5, 9, 9, 10, 10, 10, 11, 12, 13, 13, 18, 18, 19, 20, 20									63
2 Jn.	2	1:3, 9									2
3 Jn.	2	1:11, 11							1	1:6	3
Jd.	5	1:1, 4, 4, 21, 25									5
Rev.	99	1:1, 2, 6, 9; 2:7, 18; 3:1, 2, 12, 12, 12, 12, 14; 4:5, 8; 5:6, 9, 10; 6:9; 7:2, 3, 10, 11, 12, 15, 17; 8:2, 4; 9:4, 13; 10:7; 11:1, 4, 11, 13, 16, 16, 17, 19; 12:5, 6, 10, 10, 17; 13:6; 14:4, 5, 7, 10, 12, 19; 15:1, 2, 3, 3, 7, 8; 16:1, 7, 9, 11, 14, 19, 21; 17:17, 17; 18:5, 8, 20; 19:1, 4, 5, 6, 9, 10, 13, 15, 17; 20: 4, 6, 9, 12; 21:2, 3, 3, 3, 4, 7, 10, 11, 22, 23; 22:1, 3, 5, 6, 9, 18, 19									99
Total	1320		13		3		2		5		1343

Miscellaneous: Ac. 7:20, exceeding; 2 Co. 7:9 (with 2596), after a godly manner; 2 Co. 7:10 (with 2596), godly; 2 Co. 7:11 (with 2596); 3 Jn. 1:6 (with 516), after a godly sort.

2317. θεοσέβεια, theoseb′eia

Book	godliness	Total
1 Ti.	2:10	1

2318. θεοσεβής, theosebẹs′

Book	worshipper of God	Total
Jn.	9:31	1

2319. θεοστυγής, theostugẹs′

Book	hater of God	Total
Ro.	1:30	1

2320. θεότης, theot′ẹs

Book	Godhead	Total
Col.	2:9	1

2321. Θεόφιλος, Theoph′ilos

Book	Theophilus	Total
Lk.	1:3	1
Ac.	1:1	1
Total		2

2322. θεραπεία, therapei′a

Book	Oc.	household	Oc.	healing	Total
Mt.	1	24:45			1
Lk.	1	12:42	1	9:11	2
Rev.			1	22:2	1
Total	2		2		4

2324. θεράπων, therap′ōn

Book	servant	Total
Heb.	3:5	1

2323. θεραπεύω, therapeu′ō

Book	Oc.	heal	Oc.	cure	Oc.	worship	Total
Mt.	14	4:23, 24; 8:7, 16; 9:35; 10:1, 8; 12:10, 15, 22; 14:14; 15:30; 19:2; 21:14	2	17:16, 18			16
Mk.	6	1:34; 3:2, 10, 15; 6:5, 13					6
Lk.	12	4:23, 40; 5:15; 6:7, 18; 8:2, 43; 9:6; 10:9; 13:14, 14; 14:3	2	7:21; 9:1			14
Jn.			1	5:10			1
Ac.	4	4:14; 5:16; 8:7; 28:9			1	17:25	5
Rev.	2	13:3, 12					2
Total	38		5		1		44

2325. θερίζω, therid′zō

Book	reap	Total
Mt.	6:26; 25:24, 26	3
Lk.	12:24; 19:21, 22	3
Jn.	4:36, 36, 37, 38	4
1 Co.	9:11	1
2 Co.	9:6, 6	2
Gal.	6:7, 8, 8, 9	4
Jas.	5:4	1
Rev.	14:15, 15, 16	3
Total		21

2326. θερισμός, therismos′

Book	harvest	Total
Mt.	9:37, 38, 38; 13:30, 30, 39	6
Mk.	4:29	1
Lk.	10:2, 2, 2	3
Jn.	4:35, 35	2
Rev.	14:15	1
Total		13

2327. θεριστής, theristẹs′

Book	reaper	Total
Mt.	13:30, 39	2

2328. θερμαίνω, thermai′nō

Book	Oc.	warm (one's) self	Oc.	be warmed	Total
Mk.	2	14:54, 67			2
Jn.	3	18:18, 18, 25			3
Jas.			1	2:16	1
Total	5		1		6

2329. θέρμη, ther′mẹ

Book	heat	Total
Ac.	28:3	1

2330. θέρος, ther′os

Book	summer	Total
Mt.	24:32	1
Mk.	13:28	1
Lk.	21:30	1
Total		3

2331. Θεσσαλονικεύς, Thessalonikeus′

Book	Oc.	Thessalonian	Oc.	of Thessalonica	Total
Ac.	1	20:4	1	27:2	2
1 Th.	1	1:1			1
2 Th.	1	1:1			1
Total	3		1		4

2332. Θεσσαλονίκη Thessaloni′kẹ

Book	Thessalonica	Total
Ac.	17:1, 11, 13	3
Phl.	4:16	1
2 Ti.	4:10	1
Total		5

2333. Θευδᾶς, Theudas′

Book	Theudas	Total
Ac.	5:36	1

2335. θεωρία, theōri′a

Book	sight	Total
Lk.	23:48	1

2336. θήκη, thẹ′kẹ

Book	sheath	Total
Jn.	18:11	1

2339. θήρα, thẹ′ra

Book	trap	Total
Ro.	11:9	1

2334. θεωρέω, theōre′ō

Book	Oc.	see	Oc.	behold	Oc.	perceive	Oc.	consider	Oc.	look on	Total
Mt.	1	28:1	1	27:55							2
Mk.	4	3:11; 5:15, 38; 16:4	2	12:41; 15:47					1	15:40	7
Lk.	2	24:37, 39	5	10:18; 14:29; 21:6; 23:35, 48							7
Jn.	20	2:23; 6:19, 40, 62; 7:3; 8:51; 9:8; 10:12; 12:45, 45; 14:17, 19, 19; 16:10, 16, 17, 19; 20:6, 12, 14	1	17:24	2	4:19; 12:19					23
Ac.	11	3:16; 4:13; 7:56; 9:7; 10:11; 17:16; 19:26; 20:38; 21:20; 25:24; 28:6	1	8:13	2	17:22; 27:10					14
Heb.							1	7:4			1
1 Jn.	1	3:17									1
Rev.	1	11:11	1	11:12							2
Total	40		11		4		1		1		57

2337. θηλάζω, thẹlad′zō

Book	Oc.	give suck	Oc.	suck	Oc.	suckling	Total
Mt.	1	24:19			1	21:16	2
Mk.	1	13:17					1
Lk.	2	21:23; 23:29	1	11:27			3
Total	4		1		1		6

2338a. θήλεια, thẹ′leia

Book	woman	Total
Ro.	1:26, 27	2

2338b. θῆλυ, thẹ′lu

Book	female	Total
Mt.	19:4	1
Mk.	10:6	1
Gal.	3:28	1
Total		3

Word 2338 has 5 occurrences.

2340. θηρεύω, thẹreu′ō

Book	catch	Total
Lk.	11:54	1

2341. θηριομαχέω thẹriomache′ō

Book	fight with beasts	Total
1 Co.	15:32	1

2342. θηρίον, thẹri′on

Book	Oc.	beast	Oc.	wild beast	Oc.	venemous beast	Total
Mk.			1	1:13			1
Ac.	1	28:5	2	10:12; 11:6	1	28:4	4
Tit.	1	1:12					1
Heb.	1	12:20					1
Jas.	1	3:7					1
Rev.	38	6:8; 11:7; 13:1, 2, 3, 4, 4, 4, 11, 12, 12, 14, 14, 15, 15, 15, 17, 18; 14:9, 11; 15:2; 16:2, 10, 13; 17:3, 7, 8, 8, 11, 12, 13, 16, 17; 19:19, 20, 20; 20:4, 10					38
Total	42		3		1		46

2343. θησαυρίζω, thẹsaurid′zō

Book	Oc.	lay up	Oc.	in store	Oc.	lay up treasure	Oc.	treasure up	Oc.	heap treasure together	Oc.	keep in store	Total
Mt.	2	6:19, 20											2
Lk.					1	12:21							1
Ro.							1	2:5					1
1 Co.			1	16:2									1
2 Co.	1	12:14											1
Jas.									1	5:3			1
2 Pt.											1	3:7	1
Total	3		1		1		1		1		1		8

2344. θησαυρός, thẹsauros′

Book	treasure	Total
Mt.	2:11; 6:19, 20, 21; 12:35, 35; 13:44, 52; 19:21	9
Mk.	10:21	1
Lk.	6:45, 45; 12:33, 34; 18:22	5
2 Co.	4:7	1
Col.	2:3	1
Heb.	11:26	1
Total		18

2345. θιγγάνω, thinggan′ō

Book	Oc.	touch	Oc.	handle	Total
Col.			1	2:21	1
Heb.	2	11:28; 12:20			2
Total	2		1		3

2346. θλίβω, thli′bō

Book	Oc.	trouble	Oc.	afflict	Oc.	narrow	Oc.	throng	Oc.	suffer tribulation	Total
Mt.					1	7:14					1
Mk.							1	3:9			1
2 Co.	2	4:8; 7:5	1	1:6							3
1 Th.									1	3:4	1
2 Th.	2	1:6, 7									2
1 Ti.			1	5:10							1
Heb.			1	11:37							1
Total	4		3		1		1		1		10

2347. θλίψις, thlip′sis

Book	Oc.	tribulation	Oc.	affliction	Oc.	trouble	Oc.	anguish	Oc.	persecution	Oc.	burdened	Oc.	to be afflicted (with 1519)	Total
Mt.	3	13:21; 24:21, 29											1	24:9	4
Mk.	1	13:24	2	4:17; 13:19											3
Jn.	1	16:33					1	16:21							2
Ac.	1	14:22	3	7:10, 11; 20:23					1	11:19					5
Ro.	5	2:9; 5:3, 3; 8:35; 12:12													5
1 Co.					1	7:28									1
2 Co.	2	1:4a; 7:4	4	2:4; 4:17; 6:4; 8:2	2	1:4b, 8					1	8:13			9
Eph.	1	3:13													1
Phl.			2	1:16; 4:14											2
Col.			1	1:24											1
1 Th.			3	1:6; 3:3, 7											3
2 Th.	2	1:4, 6													2
Heb.			1	10:33											1
Jas.			1	1:27											1
Rev.	5	1:9; 2:9, 10, 22; 7:14													5
Total	21		17		3		1		1		1		1		45

2348. θνήσκω, thnẹ′skō

Book	Oc.	be dead	Oc.	die	Oc.	dead man	Oc.	dead	Total
Mt.	1	2:20							1
Mk.	1	15:44							1
Lk.	1	8:49			1	7:12			2
Jn.	4	11:39, 44; 12:1; 19:33	1	11:21			1	11:41	6
Ac.	2	14:19; 25:19							2
1 Ti.	1	5:6							1
Total	10		1		1		1		13

2349. θνητός, thnẹtos′

Book	Oc.	mortal	Oc.	mortality (with 3488)	Total
Ro.	2	6:12; 8:11			2
1 Co.	2	15:53, 54			2
2 Co.	1	4:11	1	5:4	2
Total	5		1		6

2352. θραύω, thrau′ō

Book	bruise	Total
Lk.	4:18	1

2350. θορυβέω, thorube′ō

Book	Oc.	make ado	Oc.	make a noise	Oc.	set on an uproar	Oc.	trouble (one's) self	Total
Mt.			1	9:23					1
Mk.	1	5:39							1
Ac.					1	17:5	1	20:10	2
Total	1		1		1		1		4

2353. θρέμμα, threm′ma

Book	cattle	Total
Jn.	4:12	1

2351. θόρυβος, thor′ubos

Book	Oc.	tumult	Oc.	uproar	Total
Mt.	1	27:24	1	26:5	2
Mk.	1	5:38	1	14:2	2
Ac.	2	21:34; 24:18	1	20:1	3
Total	4		3		7

2354. θρηνέω, thrẹne′ō

Book	Oc.	mourn	Oc.	lament	Total
Mt.	1	11:17			1
Lk.	1	7:32	1	23:27	2
Jn.			1	16:20	1
Total	2		2		4

2355. θρῆνος, thre'nos

Book	lamentation	Total
Mt.	2:18	1

2356. θρησκεία, threskei'a

Book	Oc.	religion	Oc.	worshipping	Total
Ac.	1	26:5			1
Col.			1	2:18	1
Jas.	2	1:26, 27			2
Total	3		1		4

2357. θρῆσκος, thres'kos

Book	religious	Total
Jas.	1:26	1

2358. θριαμβεύω, thriambeu'ō

Book	Oc.	cause to triumph	Oc.	triumph over	Total
2 Co.	1	2:14			1
Col.			1	2:15	1
Total	1		1		2

2359. θρίξ, thrix

Book	hair	Total
Mt.	3:4; 5:36; 10:30	3
Mk.	1:6	1
Lk.	7:38, 44; 12:7; 21:18	4
Jn.	11:2; 12:3	2
Ac.	27:34	1
1 Pt.	3:3	1
Rev.	1:14; 9:8, 8	3
Total		15

2360. θροέω, throe'ō

Book	trouble	Total
Mt.	24:6	1
Mk.	13:7	1
2 Th.	2:2	1
Total		3

2361. θρόμβος, throm'bos

Book	great drop	Total
Lk.	22:44	1

2362. θρόνος, thron'os

Book	Oc.	throne	Oc.	seat	Total
Mt.	5	5:34; 19:28, 28; 23:22; 25:31			5
Lk.	2	1:32; 22:30	1	1:52	3
Ac.	2	2:30; 7:49			2
Col.	1	1:16			1
Heb.	4	1:8; 4:16; 8:1; 12:2			4
Rev.	40	1:4; 3:21, 21; 4:2, 2, 3, 4a, 5, 5, 6, 6, 6, 9, 10, 10; 5:1, 6, 7, 11, 13; 6: 16; 7:9, 10, 11, 11, 15, 15, 17; 8:3; 12:5; 14:3, 5; 16:17; 19:4, 5; 20: 4, 11; 21:5; 22:1, 3	6	2:13; 4:4b, 4c; 11:16; 13:2; 16:10	46
Total	54		7		61

2363. Θυάτειρα, Thuat'eira

Book	Thyatira	Total
Ac.	16:14	1
Rev.	1:11; 2:18, 24	3
Total		4

2364. θυγάτηρ, thugat'er

Book	daughter	Total
Mt.	9:18, 22; 10:35, 37; 14: 6; 15:22, 28; 21:5	8
Mk.	5:34, 35; 6:22; 7:26, 29, 30	6
Lk.	1:5; 2:36; 8:42, 48, 49; 12:53, 53; 13:16; 23:28	9
Jn.	12:15	1
Ac.	2:17; 7:21; 21:9	3
2 Co.	6:18	1
Heb.	11:24	1
Total		29

2365. θυγάτριον, thugat'rion

Book	Oc.	little daughter	Oc.	young daughter	Total
Mk.	1	5:23	1	7:25	2

2366. θύελλα, thu'ella

Book	tempest	Total
Heb.	12:18	1

2367. θύϊνος, thu'inos

Book	thyine	Total
Rev.	18:12	1

2368. θυμίαμα, thumi'ama

Book	Oc.	incense	Oc.	odour	Total
Lk.	2	1:10, 11			2
Rev.	2	8:3, 4	2	5:8; 18:13	4
Total	4		2		6

2369. θυμιαστήριον thumiaste'rion

Book	censer	Total
Heb.	9:4	1

2370. θυμιάω, thumia'ō

Book	burn incense	Total
Lk.	1:9	1

2371. θυμομαχέω, thumomache'ō

Book	highly displeased	Total
Ac.	12:20	1

2372. θυμός, thumos'

Book	Oc.	wrath	Oc.	fierceness	Oc.	indignation	Total
Lk.	1	4:28					1
Ac.	1	19:28					1
Ro.					1	2:8	1
2 Co.	1	12:20					1
Gal.	1	5:20					1
Eph.	1	4:31					1
Col.	1	3:8					1
Heb.	1	11:27					1
Rev.	8	12:12; 14:8, 10, 19; 15:1, 7; 16:1; 18:3	2	16:19; 19:15			10
Total	15		2		1		18

2373. θυμόω, thumo'ō

Book	be wroth	Total
Mt.	2:16	1

2374. θύρα, thu'ra

Book	Oc.	door	Oc.	gate	Total
Mt.	5	6:6; 24:33; 25:10; 27:60; 28:2			5
Mk.	6	1:33; 2:2; 11:4; 13:29; 15:46; 16:3			6
Lk.	3	11:7; 13:25, 25			3
Jn.	7	10:1, 2, 7, 9; 18:16; 20:19, 26			7
Ac.	9	5:9, 19, 23; 12:6, 13; 14:27; 16:26, 27; 21:30	1	3:2	10
1 Co.	1	16:9			1
2 Co.	1	2:12			1
Col.	1	4:3			1
Jas.	1	5:9			1
Rev.	4	3:8, 20, 20; 4:1			4
Total	38		1		39

2375. θυρεός, thureos'

Book	shield	Total
Eph.	6:16	1

2376. θυρίς, thuris'

Book	window	Total
Ac.	20:9	1
2 Co.	11:33	1
Total		2

2377. θυρωρός, thurōros'

Book	Oc.	porter	Oc.	that keeps the door (with 3488)	Total
Mk.	1	13:34			1
Jn.	1	10:3	2	18:16, 17	3
Total	2		2		4

2378. θυσία, thusi'a

Book	sacrifice	Total
Mt.	9:13; 12:7	2
Mk.	9:49; 12:33	2
Lk.	2:24; 13:1	2
Ac.	7:41, 42	2
Ro.	12:1	1
1 Co.	10:18	1
Eph.	5:2	1
Phl.	2:17; 4:18	2
Heb.	5:1; 7:27; 8:3; 9:9, 23, 26; 10:1, 5, 8, 11, 12, 26; 11:4; 13:15, 16	15
1 Pt.	2:5	1
Total		29

2379. θυσιαστήριον thusiaste'rion

Book	altar	Total
Mt.	5:23, 24; 23:18, 19, 20, 35	6
Lk.	1:11; 11:51	2
Ro.	11:3	1
1 Co.	9:13, 13; 10:18	3
Heb.	7:13; 13:10	2
Jas.	2:21	1
Rev.	6:9; 8:3, 3, 5; 9:13; 11: 1; 14:18; 16:7	8
Total		23

2380. θύω, thu'ō

Book	Oc.	kill	Oc.	sacrifice	Oc.	do sacrifice	Oc.	slay	Total
Mt.	1	22:4							1
Mk.	1	14:12							1
Lk.	4	15:23, 27, 30; 22:7							4
Jn.	1	10:10							1
Ac.	1	10:13			2	14:13, 18	1	11:7	4
1 Co.			3	5:7; 10: 20, 20					3
Total	8		3		2		1		14

2381. Θωμᾶς, Thōmas'

Book	Thomas	Total
Mt.	10:3	1
Mk.	3:18	1
Lk.	6:15	1
Jn.	11:16; 14:5; 20:24, 26, 27, 28, 29; 21:2	8
Ac.	1:13	1
Total		12

2382. θώραξ, thō'rax

Book	breastplate	Total
Eph.	6:14	1
1 Th.	5:8	1
Rev.	9:9, 9, 17	3
Total		5

2383. Ἰάειρος, Iae'iros

Book	Jairus	Total
Mk.	5:22	1
Lk.	8:41	1
Total		2

2384. ʼΙακώβ, Iakōbʹ

Book	Oc.	Jacob (son of Isaac)	Oc.	Jacob (father of Joseph)	Total
Mt.	4	1:2, 2; 8:11; 22:32	2	1:15, 16	6
Mk.	1	12:26			1
Lk.	4	1:33; 3:34; 13:28; 20:37			4
Jn.	3	4:5, 6, 12			3
Ac.	8	3:13; 7:8, 8, 12, 14, 15, 32, 46			8
Ro.	2	9:13; 11:26			2
Heb.	3	11:9, 20, 21			3
Total	25		2		27

2386. ἴαμα, iʹama

Book	healing	Total
1 Co.	12:9, 28, 30	3

2387. ʼΙαμβρῆς, Iambrēsʹ

Book	Jambres	Total
2 Ti.	3:8	1

2388. ʼΙαννά, Iannaʹ

Book	Janna	Total
Lk.	3:24	1

2389. ʼΙαννῆς, Iannēsʹ

Book	Jannes	Total
2 Ti.	3:8	1

2385. ʼΙάκωβος, Iakʹōbos

Book	Oc.	James (son of Zebedee)	Oc.	James (son of Alphaeus)	Oc.	James (brother of Jesus)	Total
Mt.	3	4:21; 10:2; 17:1	2	10:3; 27:56	1	13:55	6
Mk.	11	1:19, 29; 3:17, 17; 5:37, 37; 9:2; 10:35, 41; 13:3; 14:33	2	3:18; 16:1	2	6:3; 15:40	15
Lk.	5	5:10; 6:14; 8:51; 9:28, 54	3	6:15, 16; 24:10			8
Ac.	2	1:13; 12:2	5	1:13, 13; 12:17; 15:13; 21:18			7
1 Co.			1	15:7			1
Gal.			2	2:9, 12	1	1:19	3
Jas.			1	1:1			1
Jd.					1	1:1	1
Total	21		16		5		42

2390. ἰάομαι, iaʹomai

Book	Oc.	heal	Oc.	make whole	Total
Mt.	3	8:8, 13; 13:15	1	15:28	4
Mk.	1	5:29			1
Lk.	12	4:18; 5:17; 6:17, 19; 7:7; 8:47; 9:2, 11, 42; 14:4; 17:15; 22:51			12
Jn.	3	4:47; 5:13; 12:40			3
Ac.	4	3:11; 10:38; 28:8, 27	1	9:34	5
Heb.	1	12:13			1
Jas.	1	5:16			1
1 Pt.	1	2:24			1
Total	26		2		28

2391. ʼΙάρεδ, Iarʹed

Book	Jared	Total
Lk.	3:37	1

2393. ἴασπις, iʹaspis

Book	jasper	Total
Rev.	4:3; 21:11, 18, 19	4

2392. ἴασις, iʹasis

Book	Oc.	cure	Oc.	to heal (with 1519)	Oc.	healing	Total
Lk.	1	13:32					1
Ac.			1	4:30	1	4:22	2
Total	1		1		1		3

2394. ʼΙάσων, Iasʹōn

Book	Jason	Total
Ac.	17:5, 6, 7, 9	4
Ro.	16:21	1
Total		5

2395. ἰατρός, iatrosʹ

Book	physician	Total
Mt.	9:12	1
Mk.	2:17; 5:26	2
Lk.	4:23; 5:31; 8:43	3
Col.	4:14	1
Total		7

2397. ἰδέα, ideʹa

Book	countenance	Total
Mt.	28:3	1

2396. ἴδε, idʹe

Book	Oc.	behold	Oc.	lo	Oc.	look	Oc.	see	Total
Mt.	3	25:20, 22; 26:65	1	25:25					4
Mk.	5	2:24; 3:34; 11:21; 15:4; 16:6					1	13:1	6
Jn.	12	1:29, 36, 47; 3:26; 5:14; 11:3, 36; 12:19; 18:21; 19:4, 5, 14	2	7:26; 16:29	1	7:52			15
Ro.	1	2:17							1
Gal.	1	5:2							1
Total	22		3		1		1		27

2399. ἰδιώτης, idiōʹtēs

Book	Oc.	unlearned	Oc.	ignorant	Oc.	rude	Total
Ac.			1	4:13			1
1 Co.	3	14:16, 23, 24					3
2 Co.					1	11:6	1
Total	3		1		1		5

See page 178 for Word 2398.

2400. ἰδού, idouʹ

Book	Oc.	behold	Oc.	lo	Oc.	see	Total
Mt.	55	1:20, 23; 2:1, 13, 19; 4:11; 7:4; 8:2, 24, 29, 32, 34; 9:2, 3, 10, 18, 20, 32; 10:16; 11:8, 10, 19; 12:2, 10, 18, 41, 42, 46, 47, 49; 13:3; 15:22; 17:3, 5, 5; 19:16, 27; 20:18, 30; 21:5; 22:4; 23:34, 38; 24:25, 26, 26; 25:6; 26:45, 46, 51; 27:51; 28:2, 7a, 9, 11	7	2:9; 3:16, 17; 24:23; 26:47; 28:7b, 20			62
Mk.	8	1:2; 3:32; 4:3; 5:22; 10:33; 13:23; 14:41; 15:35	4	10:28; 13:21, 21; 14:42			12
Lk.	48	1:20, 31, 36, 38, 48; 2:10, 25, 34, 48; 5:12, 18; 6:23; 7:12, 25, 27, 34, 37; 8:41; 9:30, 38; 10:3, 19, 25; 11:31, 32, 41; 13:7, 11, 30, 32, 35; 14:2; 17:21c; 18:31; 19:2, 8, 20; 22:10, 21, 31, 38, 47; 23:14, 29, 50; 24:4, 13, 49	9	1:44; 2:9; 9:39; 13:16; 15:29; 17:21a, 21b; 18:28; 23:15	2	17:23, 23	59
Jn.	5	4:35; 12:15; 16:32; 19:26, 27					5
Ac.	20	1:10; 2:7; 5:9, 25, 28; 7:56; 8:27; 9:10, 11; 10:17, 19, 21, 30; 11:11; 12:7; 13:11, 25; 16:1; 20:22, 25	2	13:46; 27:24	1	8:36	23
Ro.	1	9:33					1
1 Co.	1	15:51					1
2 Co.	6	5:17; 6:2, 2, 9; 7:11; 12:14					6
Gal.	1	1:20					1
Heb.	2	2:13; 8:8	2	10:7, 9			4
Jas.	7	3:3, 4, 5; 5:4, 7, 9, 11					7
1 Pt.	1	2:6					1
Jd.	1	1:14					1
Rev.	25	1:7, 18; 2:10, 22; 3:8, 9, 9, 11, 20; 4:1, 2; 5:5; 6:2, 8; 9:12; 11:14; 12:3; 14:14; 15:5; 16:15; 19:11; 21:3, 5; 22:7, 12	5	5:6; 6:5, 12; 7:9; 14:1			30
Total	181		29		3		213

2401. ʼΙδουμαία, Idoumaiʹa

Book	Idumaea	Total
Mk.	3:8	1

2402. ἱδρώς, hidrōsʹ

Book	sweat	Total
Lk.	22:44	1

2403. ʼΙεζαβήλ, Iedzabēlʹ

Book	Jezebel	Total
Rev.	2:20	1

2404. ʽΙεράπολις, Hierapʹolis

Book	Hierapolis	Total
Col.	4:13	1

2405. ἱερατεία, hieratei'a

Book	Oc.	priest's office	Oc.	office of the priesthood	Total
Lk.	1	1:9			1
Heb.			1	7:5	1
Total	1		1		2

2406. ἱεράτευμα, hierat'euma

Book	priesthood	Total
1 Pt.	2:5, 9	2

2407. ἱερατεύω, hierateu'ō

Book	execute the priest's office	Total
Lk.	1:8	1

2408. Ἱερεμίας, Hieremi'as

Book	Oc.	Jeremias	Oc.	Jeremy	Total
Mt.	1	16:14	2	2:17; 27:9	3

2409. ἱερεύς, hiereus'

Book	Oc.	priest	Oc.	high priest	Total
Mt.	3	8:4; 12:4, 5			3
Mk.	2	1:44; 2:26			2
Lk.	5	1:5; 5:14; 6:4; 10:31; 17:14			5
Jn.	1	1:19			1
Ac.	3	4:1; 6:7; 14:13	1	5:24	4
Heb.	14	5:6; 7:1, 3, 11, 15, 17, 21, 21, 23; 8: 4, 4; 9:6; 10:11, 21			14
Rev.	3	1:6; 5:10; 20:6			3
Total	31		1		32

2410. Ἱεριχώ, Hierichō'

Book	Jericho	Total
Mt.	20:29	1
Mk.	10:46, 46	2
Lk.	10:30; 18:35; 19:1	3
Heb.	11:30	1
Total		7

2411. ἱερόν, hieron'

Book	temple	Total
Mt.	4:5; 12:5, 6; 21:12, 12, 14, 15, 23; 24:1, 1; 26: 55	11
Mk.	11:11, 15, 15, 16, 27; 12:35; 13:1, 3; 14:49	9
Lk.	2:27, 37, 46; 4:9; 18: 10; 19:45, 47; 20:1; 21: 5, 37, 38; 22:52, 53; 24:53	14
Jn.	2:14, 15; 5:14; 7:14, 28; 8:2, 20, 59; 10:23; 11: 56; 18:20	11
Ac.	2:46; 3:1, 2, 2, 3, 8, 10; 4:1; 5:20, 21, 24, 25, 42; 19:27; 21:26, 27, 28, 29, 30; 22:17; 24:6, 12, 18; 25:8; 26:21	25
1 Co.	9:13	1
Total		71

2412. ἱεροπρεπής, hieroprepēs'

Book	as becometh holiness	Total
Tit.	2:3	1

2413. ἱερός, hieros'

Book	holy	Total
1 Co.	9:13	1
2 Ti.	3:15	1
Total		2

2414. Ἱεροσόλυμα, Hierosol'uma

Book	Jerusalem	Total
Mt.	2:1, 3; 3:5; 4:25; 5:35; 15:1; 16:21; 20:17, 18; 21:1, 10	11
Mk.	3:8, 22; 7:1; 10:32, 33; 11:11, 15, 27; 15:41	9
Lk.	2:22, 42; 18:31; 19:28; 23:7	5
Jn.	1:19; 2:13, 23; 4:20, 21, 45; 5:1, 2; 10:22; 11:18, 55; 12:12	12
Ac.	1:4; 8:1, 14; 11:2, 22, 27; 13:13; 18:21; 20:16; 21:17; 25:1, 7, 9, 15, 24; 26:4, 10, 20; 28:17	19
Gal.	1:17, 18; 2:1	3
Total		59

2415. Ἱεροσολυμίτης Hierosolumi'tēs

Book	of Jerusalem	Total
Mk.	1:5	1
Jn.	7:25	1
Total		2

2417. ἱερόσυλος, hieros'ulos

Book	robber of churches	Total
Ac.	19:37	1

2416. ἱεροσυλέω, hierosule'ō

Book	commit sacrilege	Total
Ro.	2:22	1

2418. ἱερουργέω, hierourge'ō

Book	minister	Total
Ro.	15:16	1

2419. Ἱερουσαλήμ, Hierousalēm'

Book	Jerusalem	Total
Mt.	23:37, 37	2
Mk.	11:1	1
Lk.	2:25, 38, 41, 43, 45; 4:9; 5:17; 6:17; 9:31, 51, 53; 10:30; 13:4, 22, 33, 34, 34; 17:11; 19:11; 21:20, 24; 23:28; 24:13, 18, 33, 47, 49, 52	28
Ac.	1:8, 12, 12, 19; 2:5, 14; 4:6, 16; 5:16, 28; 6:7; 8:25, 26, 27; 9:2, 13, 21, 26, 28; 10:39; 12:25; 13:27, 31; 15:2, 4; 16:4; 19:21; 20:22; 21:4, 11, 12, 13, 15, 31; 22:5, 17, 18; 23:11; 24:11; 25:3, 20	41
Ro.	15:19, 25, 26, 31	4
1 Co.	16:3	1
Gal.	4:25, 26	2
Heb.	12:22	1
Rev.	3:12; 21:2, 10	3
Total		83

2398. ἴδιος, id'ios

Book	Oc.	his own	Oc.	their own	Oc.	privately	Oc.	apart	Oc.	your own	Oc.	his	Oc.	own	Oc.	Not Tr.	Oc.	Misc.	Total
Mt.	2	9:1; 25:14			1	24:3	5	14:13, 23; 17: 1, 19; 20:17			1	22:5					1	25:15	10
Mk.	1	15:20			3	6:32; 9: 28; 13:3	2	6:31; 9:2									2	4:34; 7:33	8
Lk.	3	2:3; 6:44; 10:34			2	9:10; 10: 23											1	6:41	6
Jn.	13	1:11, 11, 41; 4:44; 5:43; 7:18; 8:44; 10:3, 4; 13: 1; 15:19; 16: 32; 19:27									1	5:18	1	10:12					15
Ac.	7	1:7, 25; 2:6; 4:32; 13:36; 20:28; 28:30	2	4:23; 25:19	1	23:19							1	2:8			4	1:19; 3: 12; 21: 6; 24:23	15
Ro.	3	8:32; 14:4, 5	2	10:3; 11:24															5
1 Co.	9	3:8, 8; 6:18; 7:4b, 37; 9: 7; 11:21; 15: 23, 38															6	4:12; 7: 2, 4a, 7; 12:11; 14:35	15
Gal.	1	6:5			1	2:2											1	6:9	3
Eph.			1	5:24					1	5:22									2
Col.									1	3:18									1
1 Th.			1	2:15					2	2:14; 4:11b							1	4:11a	4
1 Ti.	3	3:4, 5; 5:8	2	3:12; 6:1							1	6:15			1	5:4	2	2:6; 4:2	9
2 Ti.	1	1:9	1	4:3															2
Tit.			2	2:5, 9									1	1:12			1	1:3	4
Heb.	3	7:27; 9:12; 13:12									1	4:10							4
Jas.	1	1:14																	1
1 Pt.			1	3:5					1	3:1									2
2 Pt.	1	2:22							1	3:17	1	2:16	2	3:3, 16			1	1:20	6
Jd.			1	1:6															1
Total	48		13		8		7		6		5		5		1		20		113

Miscellaneous: Mt. 25:15, his several; Mk. 4:34, when . . . alone; Mk. 7:33, aside; Lk. 6:41, thine own; Ac. 1:19 (one's) proper; Ac. 3:12, our own; Ac. 21:6, home; Ac. 24:23, his acquaintance; 1 Co. 4:12, our own; 1 Co. 7:2, 4a, her own; 1 Co. 7:7 (one's) proper; 1 Co. 12:11, severally; 1 Co. 14:35, their; Gal. 6:9, due; 1 Th. 4:11a, your own business; 1 Ti. 2:6, due; 1 Ti. 4:2, their; Tit. 1:3, due; 2 Pt. 1:20, private.

2420. ἱερωσύνη, hierōsu'ne̱

Book	priesthood	Total
Heb.	7:11, 12, 14, 24	4

2421. Ἰεσσαί, Iessai'

Book	Jesse	Total
Mt.	1:5, 6	2
Lk.	3:32	1
Ac.	13:22	1
Ro.	15:12	1
Total		5

2422. Ἰεφθάε, Iephtha'e

Book	Jephthae	Total
Heb.	11:32	1

2423. Ἰεχονίας, Iechoni'as

Book	Jechonias	Total
Mt.	1:11, 12	2

2424. Ἰησοῦς, Ie̱sous'

Book	Oc.	Jesus	Oc.	Jesus (Joshua)	Oc.	Jesus (Justus)	Total
Mt.	172	1:1, 16, 18, 21, 25; 2:1; 3:13, 15, 16; 4:1, 7, 10, 12, 17, 18, 23; 7:28; 8:3, 4, 5, 7, 10, 13, 14, 18, 20, 22, 29, 34; 9:2, 4, 9, 10, 12, 15, 19, 22, 23, 27, 28, 30, 35; 10:5; 11:1, 4, 7, 25; 12:1, 15, 25; 13:1, 34, 36, 51, 53, 57; 14:1, 12, 13, 14, 16, 22, 25, 27, 29, 31; 15:1, 16, 21, 28, 29, 30, 32, 34; 16:6, 8, 13, 17, 20, 21, 24; 17:1, 4, 7, 8, 9, 11, 17, 18, 19, 20, 22, 25, 26; 18:1, 2, 22; 19:1, 14, 18, 21, 23, 26, 28; 20:17, 22, 25, 30, 32, 34; 21:1, 6, 11, 12, 16, 21, 24, 27, 31, 42; 22:1, 18, 29, 37, 41; 23:1; 24:1, 2, 4; 26:1, 4, 6, 10, 17, 19, 26, 31, 34, 36, 49, 50, 50, 51, 52, 55, 57, 59, 63, 64, 69, 71, 75; 27:1, 11, 11, 17, 20, 22, 26, 27, 37, 46, 50, 54, 55, 57, 58; 28:5, 9, 10, 16, 18					172
Mk.	93	1:1, 9, 14, 17, 24, 25, 41; 2:5, 8, 15, 17, 19; 3:7; 5:6, 7, 13, 15, 19, 20, 21, 27, 30, 36; 6:4, 30, 34; 7:27; 8:1, 17, 27; 9:2, 4, 5, 8, 23, 25, 27, 39; 10:5, 14, 18, 21, 23, 24, 27, 29, 32, 38, 39, 42, 47, 47, 49, 50, 51, 52, 52; 11: 6, 7, 11, 14, 15, 22, 29, 33, 33; 12:17, 24, 29, 34, 35, 41; 13:2, 5; 14:6, 18, 22, 27, 30, 48, 53, 55, 60, 62, 67, 72; 15:1, 5, 15, 34, 37, 43; 16:6					93
Lk.	98	1:31; 2:21, 27, 43, 52; 3:21, 23; 4:1, 4, 8, 12, 14, 34, 35; 5:8, 10, 12, 19, 22, 31; 6:3, 9, 11; 7:3, 4, 6, 9, 19, 22, 40; 8:28, 28, 30, 35, 35, 38, 39, 40, 41, 45, 46, 50; 9:33, 36, 41, 42, 43, 47, 50, 58, 60, 62; 10:21, 29, 30, 37, 39, 41; 13:2, 12, 14; 14:3; 17:13, 17; 18:16, 19, 22, 24, 37, 38, 40, 42; 19:3, 5, 9, 35, 35; 20:8, 34; 22:47, 48, 51, 52, 63; 23:8, 20, 25, 26, 28, 34, 42, 43, 46, 52; 24:3, 15, 19, 36					98
Jn.	254	1:17, 29, 36, 37, 38, 42, 42, 43, 45, 47, 48, 50; 2:1, 2, 3, 4, 7, 11, 13, 19, 22, 24; 3:2, 3, 5, 10, 22; 4:1, 2, 6, 7, 10, 13, 16, 17, 21, 26, 34, 44, 46, 47, 48, 50, 50, 53, 54; 5:1, 6, 8, 13, 14, 15, 16, 17, 19; 6:1, 3, 5, 10, 11, 14, 15, 17, 19, 22, 24, 24, 26, 29, 32, 35, 42, 43, 53, 61, 64, 67, 70; 7:1, 6, 14, 16, 21, 28, 33, 37, 39; 8:1, 6, 9, 10, 11, 12, 14, 19, 20, 21, 25, 28, 31, 34, 39, 42, 49, 54, 58, 59; 9:3, 11, 14, 35, 37, 39, 41; 10:6, 7, 23, 25, 32, 34; 11: 4, 5, 9, 13, 14, 17, 20, 21, 23, 25, 30, 32, 33, 35, 38, 39, 40, 41, 44, 45, 46, 51, 54, 56; 12:1, 3, 7, 9, 11, 12, 14, 16, 21, 22, 23, 30, 35, 36, 44; 13:1, 3, 7, 8, 10, 21, 23, 23, 25, 26, 27, 29, 31, 36, 38; 14:6, 9, 23; 16:19, 31; 17: 1, 3; 18:1, 2, 4, 5, 5, 7, 8, 11, 12, 15, 15, 19, 20, 22, 23, 28, 32, 33, 34, 36, 37; 19:1, 5, 9, 9, 11, 13, 16, 18, 19, 20, 23, 25, 26, 28, 30, 33, 38, 38, 38, 39, 40, 42; 20:2, 12, 14, 14, 15, 16, 17, 19, 21, 24, 26, 29, 30, 31; 21:1, 4, 4, 5, 7, 10, 12, 13, 14, 15, 17, 20, 21, 22, 23, 25					254
Ac.	67	1:1, 11, 14, 16, 21; 2:22, 32, 36, 38; 3:6, 13, 20, 26; 4:2, 10, 13, 18, 27, 30, 33; 5:30, 40, 42; 6:14; 7:55, 59; 8: 12, 16, 35, 37; 9:5, 17, 27, 29, 34; 10:36, 38; 11:17, 20; 13:23, 33; 15:11, 26; 16:18, 31; 17:3, 7, 18; 18:5, 28; 19:4, 5, 10, 13, 13, 15, 17; 20:21, 24, 35; 21:13; 22:8; 25:19; 26:9, 15; 28:23, 31	1	7:45			68
Ro.	38	1:1, 3, 6, 7, 8; 2:16; 3:22, 24, 26; 4:24; 5:1, 11, 15, 17, 21; 6:3, 11, 23; 7:25; 8:1, 2, 11, 39; 10:9; 13:14; 14: 14; 15:5, 6, 8, 16, 17, 30; 16:3, 18, 20, 24, 25, 27					38
1 Co.	27	1:1, 2, 2, 3, 4, 7. 8, 9, 10, 30; 2:2; 3:11; 4:15; 5:4, 4, 5; 6:11; 8:6; 9:1; 11:23; 12:3, 3; 15:31, 57; 16:22, 23, 24					27
2 Co.	20	1:1, 2, 3, 14, 19; 4:5, 5, 6, 10, 10, 11, 11, 14, 14; 5:18; 8:9; 11:4, 31; 13:5, 14					20
Gal.	17	1:1, 3, 12; 2:4, 16, 16; 3:1, 14, 22, 26, 28; 4:14; 5:6; 6:14, 15, 17, 18					17
Eph.	21	1:1, 1, 2, 3, 5, 15, 17; 2:6, 7, 10, 13, 20; 3:1, 9, 11, 14, 21; 4:21; 5:20; 6:23, 24					21
Phl.	22	1:1, 1, 2, 6, 8, 11, 19, 26; 2:5, 10, 11, 19, 21; 3:3, 8, 12, 14, 20; 4:7, 19, 21, 23					22
Col.	7	1:1, 2, 3, 4, 28; 2:6; 3:17			1	4:11	8
1 Th.	17	1:1, 1, 3, 10; 2:14, 15, 19; 3:11, 13; 4:1, 2, 14, 14; 5:9, 18, 23, 28					17
2 Th.	12	1:1, 2, 7, 8, 12, 12; 2:1, 14, 16; 3:6, 12, 18					12
1 Ti.	14	1:1, 1, 2, 12, 14, 15, 16; 2:5; 3:13; 4:6; 5:21; 6:3, 13, 14					14
2 Ti.	14	1:1, 1, 2, 9, 10, 13; 2:1, 3, 8, 10; 3:12, 15; 4:1, 22					14
Tit.	4	1:1, 4; 2:13; 3:6					4
Phe.	7	1:1, 3, 5, 6, 9, 23, 25					7
Heb.	13	2:9; 3:1; 4:14; 6:20; 7:22; 10:10, 19; 12:2, 24; 13:8, 12, 20, 21	1	4:8			14
Jas.	2	1:1; 2:1					2
1 Pt.	11	1:1, 2, 3, 3, 7, 13; 2:5; 3:21; 4:11; 5:10, 14					11
2 Pt.	9	1:1, 1, 2, 8, 11, 14, 16; 2:20; 3:18					9
1 Jn.	12	1:3, 7; 2:1, 22; 3:23; 4:2, 3, 15; 5:1, 5, 6, 20					12
2 Jn.	2	1:3, 7					2
Jd.	5	1:1, 1, 4, 17, 21					5
Rev.	14	1:1, 2, 5, 9, 9; 12:17; 14:12; 17:6; 19:10, 10; 20:4; 22:16, 20, 21					14
Total	972		2		1		975

2425. ἱκανός, hikanos'

Book	Oc.	many	Oc.	much	Oc.	worthy	Oc.	long	Oc.	sufficient	Oc.	Misc.	Total
Mt.					2	3:11; 8:8					1	28:12	3
Mk.					1	1:7					2	10:46; 15:15	3
Lk.	3	7:11; 8:32; 23:9	1	7:12	2	3:16; 7:6	2	8:27; 20:9			2	22:38; 23:8	10
Ac.	7	9:23, 43; 12:12; 14:21; 19: 19; 20:8; 27:7	5	5:37; 11:24, 26; 19:26; 27:9			2	8:11; 14:3			5	17:9; 18:18; 20: 11, 37; 22:6	19
1 Co.	1	11:30									1	15:9	2
2 Co.									3	2:6, 16; 3:5			3
2 Ti.											1	2:2	1
Total	11		6		5		4		3		12		41

Miscellaneous: Mt. 28:12, large; Mk. 10:46, great number of; Mk. 15:15 (with 4060), to content; Lk. 22:38, enough; Lk. 23:8, a long season; Ac. 17:9, security; Ac. 18:18, good; Ac. 20:11, long while; Ac. 20:37, sore; Ac. 22:6, great; 1 Co. 15:9, meet; 2 Ti. 2:2, able.

2426. ἱκανότης, hikanot'e̱s

Book	sufficiency	Total
2 Co.	3:5	1

2427. ἱκανόω, hikano'ō

Book	Oc.	make able	Oc.	make meet	Total
2 Co.	1	3:6			1
Col.			1	1:12	1
Total	1		1		2

2430. Ἰκόνιον, Ikon'ion

Book	Iconium	Total
Ac.	13:51; 14:1, 19, 21; 16:2	5
2 Ti.	3:11	1
Total		6

2428. ἱκετηρία, hikete̱ri'a

Book	supplication	Total
Heb.	5:7	1

2431. ἱλαρός, hilaros'

Book	cheerful	Total
2 Co.	9:7	1

2432. ἱλαρότης, hilarot'e̱s

Book	cheerfulness	Total
Ro.	12:8	1

2429. ἰκμάς, hikmas'

Book	moisture	Total
Lk.	8:6	1

2433. ἱλάσκομαι, hilas'komai

Book	Oc.	be merciful	Oc.	make reconciliation for	Total
Lk.	1	18:13			1
Heb.			1	2:17	1
Total	1		1		2

2434. ἱλασμός, hilasmos'

Book	propitiation	Total
1 Jn.	2:2; 4:10	2

2435. ἱλαστήριον, hilastḗrion

Book	Oc.	propitiation	Oc.	mercyseat	Total
Ro.	1	3:25			1
Heb.			1	9:5	1
Total	1		1		2

2436. ἵλεως, hil'eōs

Book	Oc.	be it far	Oc.	merciful	Total
Mt.	1	16:22			1
Heb.			1	8:12	1
Total	1		1		2

2437. Ἰλλυρικόν, Illurikon'

Book	Illyricum	Total
Ro.	15:19	1

2438. ἱμάς, himas'

Book	Oc.	latchet	Oc.	thong	Total
Mk.	1	1:7			1
Lk.	1	3:16			1
Jn.	1	1:27			1
Ac.			1	22:25	1
Total	3		1		4

2439. ἱματίζω, himatid'zō

Book	clothe	Total
Mk.	5:15	1
Lk.	8:35	1
Total		2

2440. ἱμάτιον, himat'ion

Book	Oc.	garment	Oc.	raiment	Oc.	clothes	Oc.	cloke	Oc.	robe	Oc.	vesture	Oc.	apparel	Total
Mt.	9	9:16, 16, 20, 21; 14:36; 21:8; 23:5; 27:35, 35	3	11:8; 17:2; 27:31	3	21:7; 24:18; 26:65	1	5:40							16
Mk.	8	2:21; 5:27; 6:56; 10:50; 11:7, 8; 13:16; 15:24	1	9:3	3	5:28, 30; 15:20									12
Lk.	4	5:36; 8:44; 19:35; 22:36	2	7:25; 23:34	2	8:27; 19:36	1	6:29							9
Jn.	3	13:4, 12; 19:23	1	19:24					2	19:2, 5					6
Ac.	2	9:39; 12:8	2	18:6; 22:20	4	7:58; 14:14; 16:22; 22:23									8
Heb.	1	1:11													1
Jas.	1	5:2													1
1 Pt.													1	3:3	1
Rev.	2	3:4; 16:15	3	3:5, 18; 4:4							2	19:13, 16			7
Total	30		12		12		2		2		2		1		61

2441. ἱματισμός, himatismos'

Book	Oc.	vesture	Oc.	apparel	Oc.	raiment	Oc.	array	Total
Mt.	1	27:35							1
Lk.			1	7:25	1	9:29			2
Jn.	1	19:24							1
Ac.			1	20:33					1
1 Ti.							1	2:9	1
Total	2		2		1		1		6

2444. ἱνατί, hinati'

Book	Oc.	why	Oc.	wherefore	Total
Mt.	1	27:46	1	9:4	2
Lk.	1	13:7			1
Ac.	2	4:25; 7:26			2
1 Co.	1	10:29			1
Total	5		1		6

2442. ἱμείρομαι, himei'romai

Book	be affectionately desirous	Total
1 Th.	2:8	1

See page 181 for Word 2443.

2445. Ἰόππη, Iop'pē

Book	Joppa	Total
Ac.	9:36, 38, 42, 43; 10:5, 8, 23, 32; 11:5, 13	10

2446. Ἰορδάνης, Iordan'ēs

Book	Jordan	Total
Mt.	3:5, 6, 13; 4:15, 25; 19:1	6
Mk.	1:5, 9; 3:8; 10:1	4
Lk.	3:3; 4:1	2
Jn.	1:28; 3:26; 10:40	3
Total		15

2447. ἰός, ios'

Book	Oc.	poison	Oc.	rust	Total
Ro.	1	3:13			1
Jas.	1	3:8	1	5:3	2
Total	2		1		3

2449. Ἰουδαία, Ioudai'a

Book	Oc.	Judaea	Oc.	Jewry	Total
Mt.	8	2:1, 5, 22; 3:1, 5; 4:25; 19:1; 24:16			8
Mk.	4	1:5; 3:7; 10:1; 13:14			4
Lk.	8	1:5, 65; 2:4; 3:1; 5:17; 6:17; 7:17; 21:21	1	23:5	9
Jn.	6	3:22; 4:3, 47, 54; 7:3; 11:7	1	7:1	7
Ac.	12	1:8; 2:9; 8:1; 9:31; 10:37; 11:1, 29; 12:19; 15:1; 21:10; 26:20; 28:21			12
Ro.	1	15:31			1
2 Co.	1	1:16			1
Gal.	1	1:22			1
1 Th.	1	2:14			1
Total	42		2		44

2448. Ἰουδά, Iouda'

Book	Juda	Total
Lk.	1:39	1

2450. Ἰουδαΐζω, Ioudaid'zō

Book	to live as do the Jews	Total
Gal.	2:14	1

2451. Ἰουδαϊκός, Ioudaikos'

Book	Jewish	Total
Tit.	1:14	1

2452. Ἰουδαϊκώς, Ioudaikōs'

Book	as do the Jews	Total
Gal.	2:14	1

2453. Ἰουδαῖος, Ioudai'os

Book	Oc.	Jew	Oc.	of Judea	Oc.	Jewess	Total
Mt.	5	2:2; 27:11, 29, 37; 28:15					5
Mk.	6	7:3; 15:2, 9, 12, 18, 26	1	1:5			7
Lk.	5	7:3; 23:3, 37, 38, 51					5
Jn.	70	1:19; 2:6, 13, 18, 20; 3:1, 25; 4:9, 9, 22; 5:1, 10, 15, 16, 18; 6:4, 41, 52; 7:1, 2, 11, 13, 15, 35; 8:22, 31, 48, 52, 57; 9:18, 22, 22; 10:19, 24, 31, 33; 11:8, 19, 31, 33, 36, 45, 54, 55; 12:9, 11; 13:33; 18:12, 14, 20, 31, 33, 35, 36, 38, 39; 19:3, 7, 12, 14, 19, 20, 21, 21, 21, 31, 38, 40, 42; 20:19	1	3:22			71
Ac.	79	2:5, 10; 9:22, 23; 10:22, 28, 39; 11:19; 12:3, 11; 13:5, 6, 42, 43, 45, 50; 14:1, 1, 2, 4, 5, 19; 16:3, 20; 17:1, 5, 10, 13, 17; 18:2, 2, 4, 5, 12, 14, 14, 19, 24, 28; 19:10, 13, 14, 17, 33, 34; 20:3, 19, 21; 21:11, 20, 21, 27, 39; 22:3, 12, 30; 23:12, 20, 27, 30; 24:5, 9, 18, 27; 25:2, 7, 8, 9, 10, 15, 24; 26:2, 3, 4, 7, 21; 28:17, 19, 29	1	2:14	2	16:1; 24:24	82
Ro.	11	1:16; 2:9, 10, 17, 28, 29; 3:1, 9, 29; 9:24; 10:12					11
1 Co.	8	1:22, 23, 24; 9:20, 20, 20; 10:32; 12:13					8
2 Co.	1	11:24					1
Gal.	4	2:13, 14, 15; 3:28					4
Col.	1	3:11					1
1 Th.	1	2:14					1
Rev.	2	2:9; 3:9					2
Total	193		3		2		198

2454. Ἰουδαϊσμός, Ioudaismos′

Book	Jews' religion	Total
Gal.	1:13, 14	2

2456. Ἰουλία, Iouli′a

Book	Julia	Total
Ro.	16:15	1

2457. Ἰούλιος, Iou′lios

Book	Julius	Total
Ac.	27:1, 3	2

2458. Ἰουνίας, Iouni′as

Book	Junia	Total
Ro.	16:7	1

2455. Ἰουδάς, Ioudas′

			(Son of Jacob)						(Brother of James)										
Book	Oc.	Judas (Iscariot)	Oc.	Juda	Oc.	Judah	Oc.	Judas	Oc.	Judas	Oc.	Jude	Oc.	Judas (Barsabas)	Oc.	Juda (Ancestors of Jesus)	Oc.	Misc.	Total
Mt.	5	10:4; 26: 14, 25, 47; 27:3	2	2:6, 6			2	1:2, 3									1	13:55	10
Mk.	3	3:19; 14: 10, 43															1	6:3	4
Lk.	4	6:16b; 22: 3, 47, 48	2	1:39; 3:33					1	6:16a					2	3:26, 30			9
Jn.	8	6:71; 12: 4; 13:2, 26, 29; 18: 2, 3, 5							1	14:22									9
Ac.	2	1:16, 25							1	1:13			3	15:22, 27, 32			2	5:37; 9:11	8
Heb.			1	7:14	1	8:8													2
Jd.											1	1:1							1
Rev.			2	5:5; 7:5															2
Total	22		7		1		2		3		1		3		2		4		45

Miscellaneous: Mt. 13:55; Mk. 6:3, Judas (brother ot Jesus); Ac. 5:37, Judas (of Galilee); Ac. 9:11, Judas (of Damascus).

2443. ἵνα, hin′a

Book	Oc.	that	Oc.	to	Oc.	lest	Oc.	for to	Oc.	Not Tr.	Oc.	Misc.	Total
Mt.	33	1:22; 2:15; 4:3, 14; 5:29, 30; 7:1, 12; 8:8; 9:6; 10: 25; 12:10, 16; 14:15, 36; 16:20; 18:6, 14, 16; 19:13, 16; 20:21, 33; 21:4; 23:26; 24:20; 26:4, 41, 56, 63; 27:20, 35; 28:10	3	26:16; 27:26, 32	2	17:27; 26:5					1	20:31	39
Mk.	43	1:38; 2:10; 3:2, 9a, 12, 14, 14; 4:12, 22; 5:10, 12, 18, 43; 6:8, 12, 25, 36, 56; 7:9, 26, 36; 8:30; 9:9, 12, 18, 30; 10:13, 17, 35, 37, 48, 51; 11:16, 25; 12:2, 15, 19; 13:18; 14:12, 35; 15:11, 32; 16:1	14	4:21, 21; 6:41; 7: 32; 8:6, 22; 9:22; 11:28; 12:13; 13: 34; 14:10; 15:15, 20, 21	2	3:9b; 14:38	1	3:10	1	5:23	1	14:49	62
Lk.	39	1:4, 43; 4:3; 5:24; 6:7, 31; 7:6, 36; 8:10, 16, 31, 32; 9:12, 45; 10:40; 11:33, 50, 54; 12:36; 14:10, 23; 15: 29; 16:4, 9, 24, 27; 17:2; 18:15, 39, 41; 19:15; 20: 10, 14, 20, 28; 21:36; 22:8, 30, 32	3	6:34; 9:40; 19:4	5	8:12; 14: 29; 16: 28; 18: 5; 22:46							47
Jn.	113	1:7b, 22, 31; 2:25; 3:15, 16, 17b, 21; 4:15, 36, 47; 5: 20, 23, 34, 40; 6:5, 7, 12, 28, 29, 30, 39, 40, 50; 7:3, 23; 8:6; 9:2, 3, 22, 36, 39; 10:10b, 17, 38; 11:4, 11, 16, 37, 42, 50, 52, 57; 12:9, 10, 23, 36, 38, 40, 46; 13: 1, 15, 18, 19, 29, 34, 34; 14:3, 13, 16, 29, 31; 15:2, 8, 11, 12, 13, 16, 16, 17, 25; 16:1, 2, 4, 7, 24, 30, 32, 33; 17:1, 2, 3, 11, 12, 13, 15, 15, 19, 21, 21, 21, 22, 23, 23, 24, 24, 26; 18:9, 28b, 32, 36, 37, 39; 19:4, 24, 28, 31, 31, 35, 36, 38; 20:31, 31	24	1:7a, 8, 19, 27; 3: 17a; 4:8, 34; 5:7, 36; 6:15, 38; 7:32; 8:56, 59; 10:31; 11:19, 31, 55; 12: 20, 47, 47; 13:2; 17:4; 19:16	5	3:20; 5: 14; 12: 35, 42; 18:28a	2	10:10a; 11:53			1	11:15	145
Ac.	10	2:25; 4:17; 5:15; 8:19; 9:21; 19:4; 21:24; 22:24; 23:24; 24:4	3	16:30, 36; 27:42	1	5:26	2	17:15; 22:5					16
Ro.	29	1:11, 13; 3:8, 19; 4:16; 5:20, 21; 6:1, 4, 6; 7:4, 13, 13; 8:4, 17; 9:11, 23; 11:11, 19, 31, 32; 14:9; 15:4, 6, 16, 31, 31, 32; 16:2			2	11:25; 15:20							31
1 Co.	47	1:10, 31; 2:5, 12; 3:18; 4:2, 3, 6, 6, 8; 5:2, 5, 7; 7: 5, 5, 29, 34, 35; 9:15, 15, 18, 19, 20, 20, 21, 22, 22, 23, 24; 10:33; 11:19, 32, 34; 12:25; 14:1, 5, 5, 12, 13, 19, 31; 15:28; 16:2, 6, 10, 11, 16	7	1:27, 27, 28; 9:25; 13:3; 16:12, 12	4	1:15, 17; 8:13; 9: 12							58
2 Co.	37	1:9, 11, 15, 17; 2:4, 4, 5, 9; 4:7, 10, 11, 15; 5:4, 10, 12, 15, 21; 6:3; 7:9; 8:6, 7, 9, 13, 14; 9:3b, 4, 5, 8; 10:9; 11:7, 12, 12, 16; 12:8, 9; 13:7, 7	1	12:7b	6	2:3, 11; 9:3a; 12: 7a, 7c; 13:10							44
Gal.	14	1:16; 2:4, 5, 9, 10, 16, 19; 3:14, 14, 22, 24; 4:5b, 17; 6:13	1	4:5a	1	6:12					1	5:17	17
Eph.	20	1:17; 2:7, 10; 3:16, 17, 19; 4:10, 14, 28, 29; 5:26, 27, 27, 33; 6:3, 13, 19, 20, 21, 22			1	2;9	1	2:15			1	3:10	23
Phl.	10	1:9, 10, 26, 27; 2:2, 10, 15, 19, 28; 3:8	1	2:30	1	2:27							12
Col.	11	1:9, 18, 28; 2:2; 4:3, 4, 8, 12, 16, 16, 17			2	2:4; 3:21							13
1 Th.	6	2:16; 4:1, 12, 13; 5:4, 10											6
2 Th.	6	1:11; 2:12; 3:1, 2, 12, 14	1	3:9									7
1 Ti.	13	1:3, 16, 18, 20; 2:2; 3:15; 4:15; 5:7, 16, 20, 21; 6: 1, 19			2	3:6, 7							15
2 Ti.	5	1:4; 2:4, 10; 3:17; 4:17											5
Tit.	13	1:5, 9, 13; 2:4, 5, 8, 10, 12, 14; 3:7, 8, 13, 14											13
Phe.	3	1:13, 14, 15									1	1:19	4
Heb.	15	2:14, 17; 4:16; 5:1; 6:12, 18; 9:25; 10:9, 36; 11:35, 40; 12:27; 13:12, 17, 19			5	3:13; 4: 11; 11: 28; 12:3, 13							20
Jas.	2	1:4; 4:3			2	5:9, 12							4
1 Pt.	13	1:7; 2:2, 12, 21, 24; 3:1, 9, 16, 18; 4:6, 11, 13; 5:6											13
2 Pt.	1	1:4			1	3:17							2
1 Jn.	18	1:3, 4; 2:1, 19, 27, 28; 3:1, 8, 11, 23; 4:9, 17, 21; 5:3, 13, 13, 16, 20	2	1:9; 3:5									20
2 Jn.	5	1:5, 6, 6, 8, 12											5
3 Jn.	1	1:8	1	1:4									2
Rev.	29	2:10; 3:11, 18, 18, 18; 6:4, 11; 7:1; 8:3; 9:4, 5, 5, 20; 11:6; 12:6, 14, 15; 13:15, 15, 17; 14:13; 16:12; 18:4, 4; 19:8, 15, 18; 20:3; 22:14	8	2:21; 3:9; 6:2; 8:6; 13:12, 16; 21:15, 23	1	16:15	2	9:15; 12:4			2	8:12; 13:13	42
Total	536		69		43		8		1		8		665

Miscellaneous: Mt. 20:31, because; Mk. 14:49 (irregular), must; Jn. 11:15, to the intent; Gal. 5:17, so that; Eph. 3:10, to the intent that; Phe. 1:19, albeit; Rev. 8:12, so as; Rev. 13:13, so that.

2459. Ἰοῦστος, Ious′tos

Book	Oc.	Justus (of Corinth)	Oc.	Justus (surname of Barsabas)	Oc.	Justus (Jesus, a fellow worker of Paul)	Total
Ac.	1	18:7	1	1:23			2
Col.					1	4:11	1
Total	1		1		1		3

2460. ἱππεύς, hippeus′

Book	horseman	Total
Ac.	23:23, 32	2

2461. ἱππικόν, hippikon′

Book	horseman	Total
Rev.	9:16	1

2462. ἵππος, hip′pos

Book	horse	Total
Jas.	3:3	1
Rev.	6:2, 4, 5, 8; 9:7, 9, 17, 17; 14:20; 18:13; 19:11, 14, 18, 19, 21	15
Total		16

2463. ἶρις, i′ris

Book	rainbow	Total
Rev.	4:3; 10:1	2

2464. Ἰσαάκ, Isaak′

Book	Isaac	Total
Mt.	1:2, 2; 8:11; 22:32	4
Mk.	12:26	1
Lk.	3:34; 13:28; 20:37	3
Ac.	3:13; 7:8, 8, 32	4
Ro.	9:7, 10	2
Gal.	4:28	1
Heb.	11:9, 17, 18, 20	4
Jas.	2:21	1
Total		20

2465. ἰσάγγελος, isang′gelos

Book	equal unto the angels	Total
Lk.	20:36	1

2466. Ἰσαχάρ, Isachar′

Book	Issachar	Total
Rev.	7:7	1

2467. ἴσημι, is′ęmi

Book	know	Total
Ac.	26:4	1
Heb.	12:17	1
Total		2

2469. Ἰσκαριώτης, Iskariō′tęs

Book	Iscariot	Total
Mt.	10:4; 26:14	2
Mk.	3:19; 14:10	2
Lk.	6:16; 22:3	2
Jn.	6:71; 12:4; 13:2, 26; 14:22	5
Total		11

2468. ἴσθι, is′thi

Book	Oc.	be thou	Oc.	be	Oc.	agree (with 2132)	Oc.	give thyself wholly to (with 1722)	Oc.	Not Tr.	Total
Mt.	1	2:13			1	5:25					2
Mk.			1	5:34							1
Lk.									1	19:17	1
1 Ti.							1	4:15			1
Total	1		1		1		1		1		5

2470. ἴσος, i′sos

Book	Oc.	equal	Oc.	agree together (with 2258)	Oc.	as much	Oc.	like	Total
Mt.	1	20:12							1
Mk.			2	14:56, 59					2
Lk.					1	6:34			1
Jn.	1	5:18							1
Ac.							1	11:17	1
Phl.	1	2:6							1
Rev.	1	21:16							1
Total	4		2		1		1		8

2471. ἰσότης, isot′ęs

Book	Oc.	equality	Oc.	equal	Total
2 Co.	2	8:14, 14			2
Col.			1	4:1	1
Total	2		1		3

2472. ἰσότιμος, isot′imos

Book	like precious	Total
2 Pt.	1:1	1

2473. ἰσόψυχος, isop′suchos

Book	likeminded	Total
Phl.	2:20	1

2474. Ἰσραήλ, Israęl′

Book	Israel	Total
Mt.	2:6, 20, 21; 8:10; 9:33; 10:6, 23; 15:24, 31; 19:28; 27:9, 42	12
Mk.	12:29; 15:32	2
Lk.	1:16, 54, 68, 80; 2:25, 32, 34; 4:25, 27; 7:9; 22:30; 24:21	12
Jn.	1:31, 49; 3:10; 12:13	4
Ac.	1:6; 2:36; 4:8, 10, 27; 5:21, 31; 7:23, 37, 42; 9:15; 10:36; 13:17, 23, 24; 28:20	16
Ro.	9:6, 6, 27, 27, 31; 10:1, 19, 21; 11:2, 7, 25, 26	12
1 Co.	10:18	1
2 Co.	3:7, 13	2
Gal.	6:16	1
Eph.	2:12	1
Phl.	3:5	1
Heb.	8:8, 10; 11:22	3
Rev.	2:14; 7:4; 21:12	3
Total		70

2475. Ἰσραηλίτης, Israęli′tęs

Book	Oc.	Israel	Oc.	Israelite	Total
Jn.			1	1:47	1
Ac.	5	2:22; 3:12; 5:35; 13:16; 21:28			5
Ro.			2	9:4; 11:1	2
2 Co.			1	11:22	1
Total	5		4		9

2477. ἱστορέω, historeʹō

Book	see	Total
Gal.	1:18	1

2476. ἵστημι, his′tęmi

Book	Oc.	stand	Oc.	set	Oc.	establish	Oc.	stand still	Oc.	stand by	Oc.	Misc.	Total
Mt.	14	2:9; 6:5; 12:25, 26, 46, 47; 13:2; 16:28; 20:3, 6, 6; 24:15; 27:11, 47	3	4:5; 18:2; 25:33	1	18:16	1	20:32	1	26:73	1	26:15	21
Mk.	7	3:24, 25, 26, 31; 9:1; 11:5; 13:14	1	9:36			1	10:49			1	13:9	10
Lk.	19	1:11; 5:1, 2; 6:17; 7:38; 8:20; 9:27; 11:18; 13:25; 17:12; 18:11, 13, 40; 19:8; 21:36; 23:10, 35, 49; 24:36	2	4:9; 9:47			1	7:14			3	6:8, 8; 8:44	25
Jn.	18	1:26, 35; 3:29; 6:22; 7:37; 8:9; 11:56; 18:5, 16, 18, 18, 25; 19:25; 20:11, 14, 19, 26; 21:4	1	8:3					1	12:29	1	8:44	21
Ac.	21	1:11; 3:8; 4:14; 5:20, 23, 25; 7:33, 55, 56; 9:7; 10:30; 11:13; 12:14; 16:9; 17:22; 21:40; 24:20, 21; 25:10; 26:6, 16	4	4:7; 5:27; 6:6; 22:30			1	8:38	1	22:25	8	1:23; 2:14; 6:13; 7:60; 17:31; 25:18; 26:22; 27:21	35
Ro.	2	5:2; 11:20			2	3:31; 10:3					2	14:4a, 4b	6
1 Co.	3	7:37; 10:12; 15:1											3
2 Co.	1	1:24			1	13:1							2
Eph.	3	6:11, 13, 14											3
Col.	1	4:12											1
2 Ti.	1	2:19											1
Heb.	1	10:11			1	10:9							2
Jas.	2	2:3; 5:9											2
1 Pt.	1	5:12											1
Jd.											1	1:24	1
Rev.	21	3:20; 5:6; 6:17; 7:1, 9, 11; 8:2, 3; 10:5, 8; 11:4, 11; 12:4; 13:1; 14:1; 15:2; 18:10, 15, 17; 19:17; 20:12											21
Total	115		11		5		4		3		17		155

Miscellaneous: Mt. 26:15, covenant; Mk. 13:9, bring; Lk. 6:8, 8, stand forth; Lk. 8:44, stanch; Jn. 8:44, abide; Ac. 1:23, appoint; Ac. 2:14, stand up; Ac. 6:13, set up; Ac. 7:60, lay; Ac. 17:31, appoint; Ac. 25:18, stand up; Ac. 26:22, continue; Ac. 27:21, stand forth; Ro. 14:4a, hold up; Ro. 14:4b, make stand; Jd. 1:24, present.

2478. ἰσχυρός, ischuros′

Book	Oc.	mighty	Oc.	strong	Oc.	strong man	Oc.	boisterous	Oc.	powerful	Oc.	valiant	Total
Mt.	1	3:11			2	12:29, 29	1	14:30					4
Mk.	1	1:7			2	3:27, 27							3
Lk.	2	3:16; 15:14	1	11:22	1	11:21							4
1 Co.	1	1:27	3	1:25; 4:10; 10:22									4
2 Co.									1	10:10			1
Heb.			2	5:7; 6:18							1	11:34	3
1 Jn.			1	2:14									1
Rev.	5	10:1; 18:10, 21; 19:6, 18	2	5:2; 18:8									7
Total	10		9		5		1		1		1		27

2479. ἰσχύς, ischus′

Book	Oc.	strength	Oc.	power	Oc.	might	Oc.	ability	Oc.	mightily (with 1722)	Oc.	mighty	Total
Mk.	2	12:30, 33											2
Lk.	1	10:27											1
Eph.					1	6:10					1	1:19	2
2 Th.			1	1:9									1
1 Pt.							1	4:11					1
2 Pt.			1	2:11									1
Rev.	1	5:12			1	7:12			1	18:2			3
Total	4		2		2		1		1		1		11

2480. ἰσχύω, ischu′ō

Book	Oc.	can (could)	Oc.	be able	Oc.	avail	Oc.	prevail	Oc.	be whole	Oc.	cannot (with 3656)	Oc.	can do	Oc.	may	Oc.	Misc.	Total
Mt.	1	26:40							1	9:12					1	8:28	1	5:13	4
Mk.	3	5:4; 9:18; 14:37							1	2:17									4
Lk.	4	6:48; 8:43; 14:6; 20:26	3	13:24; 14: 29, 30							1	16:3							8
Jn.			1	21:6															1
Ac.	1	25:7	2	6:10; 15: 10			2	19:16, 20									1	27:16	6
Gal.					2	5:6; 6:15													2
Phl.													1	4:13					1
Heb.																	1	9:17	1
Jas.					1	5:16													1
Rev.							1	12:8											1
Total	9		6		3		3		2		1		1		1		3		29

Miscellaneous: Mt. 5:13, be good; Ac. 27:16 (with 3333), have much work; Heb. 9:17, be of strength.

2481. ἴσως, I′sōs

Book	it may be	Total
Lk.	20:13	1

2482. Ἰταλία, Itali′a

Book	Italy	Total
Ac.	18:2; 27:1, 6	3
Heb.	13:24	1
Total		4

2483. Ἰταλικός, Italikos′

Book	Italian	Total
Ac.	10:1	1

2484. Ἰτουραῖα, Itourai′a

Book	Ituraea	Total
Lk.	3:1	1

2485. ἰχθύδιον, ichthu′dion

Book	Oc.	little fish	Oc.	small fish	Total
Mt.	1	15:34			1
Mk.			1	8:7	1
Total	1		1		2

2486. ἰχθύς, ichthus′

Book	fish	Total
Mt.	7:10; 14:17, 19; 15:36; 17:27	5
Mk.	6:38, 41, 41, 43	4
Lk.	5:6, 9; 9:13, 16; 11:11, 11; 24:42	7
Jn.	21:6, 8, 11	3
1 Co.	15:39	1
Total		20

2487. ἴχνος, ich′nos

Book	step	Total
Ro.	4:12	1
2 Co.	12:18	1
1 Pt.	2:21	1
Total		3

2488. Ἰωάθαμ, Iōath′am

Book	Joatham	Total
Mt.	1:9	1

2489. Ἰωάννα, Iōan′na

Book	Joanna	Total
Lk.	8:3; 24:10	2

2490. Ἰωαννᾶς, Iōannas′

Book	Joanna	Total
Lk.	3:27	1

2492. Ἰώβ, Iōb′

Book	Job	Total
Jas.	5:11	1

2491. Ἰωάννης, Iōan′nes

Book	Oc.	John (the Baptist)	Oc.	John (the apostle)	Oc.	John (Mark)	Oc.	John (chief priest)	Total
Mt.	23	3:1, 4, 13, 14; 4:12; 9:14; 11:2, 4, 7, 11, 12, 13, 18; 14:2, 3, 4, 8, 10; 16:14; 17:13; 21:25, 26, 32	3	4:21; 10:2; 17:1					26
Mk.	16	1:4, 6, 9, 14; 2:18, 18; 6:14, 16, 17, 18, 20, 24, 25; 8:28; 11:30, 32	10	1:19, 29; 3:17; 5:37; 9:2, 38; 10:35, 41; 13:3; 14:33					26
Lk.	24	1:13, 60, 63; 3:2, 15, 16, 20; 5:33; 7:18, 19, 20, 22, 24, 24, 28, 29, 33; 9:7, 9, 19; 11:1; 16:16; 20:4, 6	7	5:10; 6:14; 8:51; 9:28, 49, 54; 22:8					31
Jn.	20	1:6, 15, 19, 26, 28, 29, 32, 35, 40; 3:23, 24, 25, 26, 27; 4: 1; 5:33, 36; 10:40, 41, 41							20
Ac.	9	1:5, 22; 10:37; 11:16; 13:24, 25; 18:25; 19:3, 4	10	1:13; 3:1, 3, 4, 11; 4:13, 19; 8:14; 12:2, 12	4	12:25; 13:5, 13; 15:37	1	4:6	24
Gal.			1	2:9					1
Rev.			5	1:1, 4, 9; 21:2; 22:8					5
Total	92		36		4		1		133

2493. Ἰωήλ, Iōel′

Book	Joel	Total
Ac.	2:16	1

2494. Ἰωνάν, Iōnan′

Book	Jonan	Total
Lk.	3:30	1

2495. Ἰωνᾶς, Iōnas′

Book	Oc.	Jonas (the prophet)	Oc.	Jona (father of Peter)	Total
Mt.	5	12:39, 40, 41, 41; 16:4			5
Lk.	4	11:29, 30, 32, 32			4
Jn.			4	1:42; 21:15, 16, 17	4
Total	9		4		13

2496. Ἰωράμ, Iōram′

Book	Joram	Total
Mt.	1:8, 8	2

2497. Ἰωρείμ, Iōreim′

Book	Jorim	Total
Lk.	3:29	1

2498. Ἰωσαφάτ, Iōsaphat′

Book	Josaphat	Total
Mt.	1:8, 8	2

2499. Ἰωσή, Iōsẹ′

Book	Jose (son of Eliezer)	Total
Lk.	3:29	1

2500. Ἰωσῆς, Iōsẹs′

Book	Oc.	Joses (Brother of James)	Oc.	Joses (Brother of Jesus)	Oc.	Joses (Barnabas)	Total
Mt.	1	27:56	1	13:55			2
Mk.	2	15:40, 47	1	6:3			3
Ac.					1	4:36	1
Total	3		2		1		6

2502. Ἰωσίας, Iōsi′as

Book	Josias	Total
Mt.	1:10, 11	2

2503. ἰῶτα, iō′ta

Book	jot	Total
Mt.	5:18	1

2501. Ἰωσήφ, Iōsẹph′

Book	Oc.	Joseph (husband of Mary)	Oc.	Joseph (son of Jacob)	Oc.	Joseph (of Arimathaea)	Oc.	Joseph (Barsabas)	Oc.	Joseph (son of Judas)	Oc.	Joseph (son of Jonan)	Oc.	Joseph (son of Mattathias)	Total
Mt.	7	1:16, 18, 19, 20, 24; 2:13, 19			2	27:57, 59									9
Mk.					2	15:43, 45									2
Lk.	7	1:27; 2:4, 16, 33, 43; 3:23; 4:22			1	23:50			1	3:26	1	3:30	1	3:24	11
Jn.	2	1:45; 6:42	1	4:5	1	19:38									4
Ac.			5	7:9, 13, 13, 14, 18			1	1:23							6
Heb.			2	11:21, 22											2
Rev.			1	7:8											1
Total	16		9		6		1		1		1		1		35

2504. καγώ, kagō′

Book	Oc.	and I	Oc.	I also	Oc.	so I	Oc.	I	Oc.	even I	Oc.	me also (with dative)	Oc.	Misc.	Total
Mt.	2	11:28; 26:15	5	2:8; 10:32, 33; 16:18; 21:24a									1	21:24b	8
Mk.			1	11:29											1
Lk.	4	2:48; 11:9; 16:9; 22:29	1	20:3							1	1:3			6
Jn.	17	1:31, 33, 34; 5:17; 6:56, 57; 8:26; 10:27, 28, 38; 12:32; 14:20; 15:4, 5; 17:21, 26; 20:15			1	15:9							4	7:28; 10:15; 17:18; 20:21	22
Ac.	2	22:13, 19	1	10:26			1	26:29			1	8:19			5
Ro.	1	11:3	1	3:7											2
1 Co.	1	2:1	2	7:40; 16:4					2	7:8; 10:33	1	15:8	1	11:1	7
2 Co.	2	6:17; 12:20	2	11:18, 21	3	11:22, 22, 22	1	11:16							8
Gal.	1	6:14					1	4:12							2
Eph.			1	1:15											1
Phl.	1	2:28	1	2:19											2
1 Th.							1	3:5							1
Heb.	1	8:9													1
Jas.	2	2:18, 18													2
Rev.			2	2:6; 3:10					1	2:27			1	3:21	4
Total	34		17		4		4		3		3		7		72

Miscellaneous: Mt. 21:24b, I in likewise; Jn. 7:28 (with accusative), both me; Jn. 10:15, even so I; Jn. 17:18, even so I also; Jn. 20:21, even so I; 1 Co. 11:1; Rev. 3:21, even I also.

2505. καθά, katha′

Book	as	Total
Mt.	27:10	1

2506. καθαίρεσις, kathai′resis

Book	Oc.	destruction	Oc.	pulling down	Total
2 Co.	2	10:8; 13:10	1	10:4	3

2508. καθαίρω, kathai′rō

Book	purge	Total
Jn.	15:2	1
Heb.	10:2	1
Total		2

2507. καθαιρέω, kathaire′ō

Book	Oc.	take down	Oc.	destroy	Oc.	put down	Oc.	pull down	Oc.	cast down	Total
Mk.	2	15:36, 46									2
Lk.	1	23:53			1	1:52	1	12:18			3
Ac.	1	13:29	2	13:19; 19:27							3
2 Co.									1	10:5	1
Total	4		2		1		1		1		9

2509. καθάπερ, kathap′er

Book	Oc.	as	Oc.	even as	Oc.	as well as	Total
Ro.	1	12:4	1	4:6			2
1 Co.	1	12:12					1
2 Co.	2	3:13; 8:11	2	1:14; 3:18			4
1 Th.	2	2:11; 3:6	2	3:12; 4:5			4
Heb.	1	5:4			1	4:2	2
Total	7		5		1		13

2510. καθάπτω, kathap′tō

Book	fasten on	Total
Ac.	28:3	1

2511. καθαρίζω, katharid′zō

Book	Oc.	cleanse	Oc.	make clean	Oc.	be clean	Oc.	purge	Oc.	purify	Total
Mt.	4	8:3b; 10:8; 11:5; 23:26	2	8:2; 23:25	1	8:3a					7
Mk.	1	1:42	1	1:40	1	1:41	1	7:19			4
Lk.	4	4:27; 7:22; 17:14, 17	2	5:12; 11:39	1	5:13					7
Ac.	2	10:15; 11:9							1	15:9	3
2 Co.	1	7:1									1
Eph.	1	5:26									1
Tit.									1	2:14	1
Heb.							2	9:14, 22	1	9:23	3
Jas.	1	4:8									1
1 Jn.	2	1:7, 9									2
Total	16		5		3		3		3		30

2512. καθαρισμός, katharismos′

Book	Oc.	cleansing	Oc.	purifying	Oc.	be purged	Oc.	purge (with 4060)	Oc.	purification	Total
Mk.	1	1:44									1
Lk.	1	5:14							1	2:22	2
Jn.			2	2:6; 3:25							2
Heb.							1	1:3			1
2 Pt.					1	1:9					1
Total	2		2		1		1		1		7

2513. καθαρός, katharos′

Book	Oc.	pure	Oc.	clean	Oc.	clear	Total
Mt.	1	5:8	2	23:26; 27:59			3
Lk.			1	11:41			1
Jn.			4	13:10, 10, 11; 15:3			4
Ac.	1	20:26	1	18:6			2
Ro.	1	14:20					1
1 Ti.	2	1:5; 3:9					2
2 Ti.	2	1:3; 2:22					2
Tit.	3	1:15, 15, 15					3
Heb.	1	10:22					1
Jas.	1	1:27					1
1 Pt.	1	1:22					1
Rev.	4	15:6; 21:18a, 21; 22:1	2	19:8, 14	1	21:18b	7
Total	17		10		1		28

2514. καθαρότης, katharot′ēs

Book	purifying	Total
Heb.	9:13	1

2515. καθέδρα, kathed′ra

Book	seat	Total
Mt.	21:12; 23:2	2
Mk.	11:15	1
Total		3

2516. καθέζομαι, kathed′zomai

Book	sit	Total
Mt.	26:55	1
Lk.	2:46	1
Jn.	4:6; 11:20; 20:12	3
Ac.	6:15	1
Total		6

2517. καθεξῆς, kathexēs′

Book	Oc.	in order	Oc.	afterward	Oc.	after	Oc.	by order	Total
Lk.	1	1:3	1	8:1					2
Ac.	1	18:23			1	3:24	1	11:4	3
Total	2		1		1		1		5

2518. καθεύδω, katheu′dō

Book	sleep	Total
Mt.	8:24; 9:24; 13:25; 25:5; 26:40, 43, 45	7
Mk.	4:27, 38; 5:39; 13:36; 14:37, 37, 40, 41	8
Lk.	8:52; 22:46	2
Eph.	5:14	1
1 Th.	5:6, 7, 7, 10	4
Total		22

2519. καθηγητής, kathēgētēs′

Book	master	Total
Mt.	23:8, 10, 10	3

2520. καθήκω, kathē′kō

Book	Oc.	fit	Oc.	convenient	Total
Ac.	1	22:22			1
Ro.			1	1:28	1
Total	1		1		2

2521. κάθημαι, kath′ēmai

Book	Oc.	sit	Oc.	sit down	Oc.	sit by	Oc.	be set down	Oc.	dwell	Total
Mt.	15	4:16, 16; 9:9; 11:16; 13:1, 2; 20:30; 22:44; 23:22; 24:3; 26:58, 64, 69; 27:61; 28:2	2	15:29; 27:36			1	27:19			18
Mk.	11	2:6, 14; 3:32, 34; 4:1; 5:15; 10:46; 12:36; 13:3; 14:62; 16:5									11
Lk.	9	1:79; 5:27; 7:32; 8:35; 10:13; 18:35; 20:42; 22:56, 69	1	22:55	1	5:17			1	21:35	12
Jn.	4	2:14; 6:3; 9:8; 12:15									4
Ac.	7	2:2, 34; 3:10; 8:28; 14:8; 20:9; 23:3									7
1 Co.					1	14:30					1
Col.	1	3:1									1
Heb.	1	1:13									1
Jas.	2	2:3, 3									2
Rev.	32	4:2, 3, 4, 9, 10; 5:1, 7, 13; 6:2, 4, 5, 8, 16; 7:10, 15; 9:17; 11:16; 14:14, 15, 16; 17:1, 3, 9, 15; 18:7; 19:4, 11, 18, 19, 21; 20:11; 21:5									32
Total	82		3		2		1		1		89

2522. καθημερινός, kathēmerinos′

Book	daily	Total
Ac.	6:1	1

2523. καθίζω, kathid′zō

Book	Oc.	sit	Oc.	sit down	Oc.	set	Oc.	be set	Oc.	be set down	Oc.	continue	Oc.	tarry	Total
Mt.	7	19:28, 28; 20:21, 23; 23:2; 25:31; 26:36	1	13:48			1	5:1							9
Mk.	7	10:37, 40; 11:2, 7; 12:41; 14:32; 16:19	1	9:35											8
Lk.	2	19:30; 22:30	5	4:20; 5:3; 14:28, 31; 16:6									1	24:49	8
Jn.	1	12:14	2	8:2; 19:13											3
Ac.	6	2:3, 30; 8:31; 12:21; 25:6, 17	2	13:14; 16:13							1	18:11			9
1 Co.			1	10:7	1	6:4									2
Eph.					1	1:20									1
2 Th.	1	2:4													1
Heb.			2	1:3; 10:12			1	8:1	1	12:2					4
Rev.	2	3:21a; 20:4							1	3:21b					3
Total	26		14		2		2		2		1		1		48

2524. καθίημι, kathi′ēmi

Book	let down	Total
Lk.	5:19	1
Ac.	9:25; 10:11; 11:5	3
Total		4

2525. καθίστημι, kathis′tēmi

Book	Oc.	make	Oc.	make ruler	Oc.	ordain	Oc.	be	Oc.	appoint	Oc.	conduct	Oc.	set	Total
Mt.			4	24:45, 47; 25:21, 23											4
Lk.	1	12:14	2	12:42, 44											3
Ac.	3	7:10, 27, 35							1	6:3	1	17:15			5
Ro.	2	5:19, 19													2
Tit.					1	1:5									1
Heb.	1	7:28			2	5:1; 8:3							1	2:7	4
Jas.							2	3:6; 4:4							2
2 Pt.	1	1:8													1
Total	8		6		3		2		1		1		1		22

2526. καθό, katho′

Book	Oc.	according to	Oc.	as	Oc.	inasmuch as	Total
Ro.			1	8:26			1
2 Co.	2	8:12, 12					2
1 Pt.					1	4:13	1
Total	2		1		1		4

2527. καθόλου, kathol′ou

Book	at all	Total
Ac.	4:18	1

2528. καθοπλίζω, kathoplid′zō

Book	arm	Total
Lk.	11:21	1

2529. καθοράω, kathora′ō

Book	clearly see	Total
Ro.	1:20	1

2530. καθότι, kathot′i

Book	Oc.	because	Oc.	forsomuch as	Oc.	as	Oc.	according as	Total
Lk.	1	1:7	1	19:9					2
Ac.	1	2:24			1	2:45	1	4:35	3
Total	2		1		1		1		5

2531. καθώς, kathōs′

Book	Oc.	as	Oc.	even as	Oc.	according as	Oc.	when	Oc.	according to	Oc.	how	Oc.	as well as (with 2532)	Total
Mt.	3	21:6; 26:24; 28:6													3
Mk.	6	4:33; 9:13; 14:16, 21; 15:8; 16:7	1	11:6											7
Lk.	13	1:55, 70; 2:20, 23; 5:14; 6:31, 36; 11:1, 30; 17:26; 22:13, 29; 24:39	3	1:2; 19:32; 24:24											16
Jn.	26	1:23; 3:14; 5:30; 6:31, 57, 58; 7:38; 8:28; 10:15, 26; 12:14; 13:15, 33, 34; 14:27, 31; 15:4, 9, 12; 17:2, 11, 18, 21, 23; 19:40; 20:21	6	5:23; 12:50; 15:10; 17:14, 16, 22											32
Ac.	8	2:4, 22; 7:42, 44, 48; 15:8, 15; 22:3					1	7:17	1	11:29	1	15:14	1	10:47	12
Ro.	17	1:17; 2:24; 3:4, 8, 8, 10; 4:17; 8:36; 9:13, 29, 33; 10:15; 11:26; 15:3, 7, 9, 21	2	1:13, 28	1	11:8									20
1 Co.	15	2:9; 4:17; 5:7; 8:2; 10:6, 7, 8, 9, 10; 11:2; 12:11, 18; 14:34; 15:38, 49	4	1:6; 10:33; 11:1; 13:12	1	1:31									20
2 Co.	11	1:5, 14; 4:1; 6:16; 8:5, 6, 15; 9:3, 9; 10:7; 11:12			1	9:7									12
Gal.	2	2:7; 5:21	1	3:6											3
Eph.	5	3:3; 4:17, 21; 5:2, 3	4	4:4, 32; 5:25, 29	1	1:4									10
Phl.	2	2:12; 3:17	1	1:7											3
Col.	4	1:6, 6, 7; 2:7	1	3:13											5
1 Th.	8	1:5; 2:2, 4, 5, 13; 4:1, 6, 11	4	2:14; 3:4; 4:13; 5:11											12
2 Th.	1	1:3	1	3:1											2
1 Ti.	1	1:3													1
Heb.	8	3:7; 4:3, 7; 5:3, 6; 8:5; 10:25; 11:12													8
1 Pt.	1	4:10													1
2 Pt.			2	1:14; 3:15											2
1 Jn.	5	2:18; 3:2, 12, 23; 4:17	4	2:6, 27; 3:3, 7											9
2 Jn.	2	1:4, 6													2
3 Jn.			2	1:2, 3											2
Total	138		36		4		1		1		1		1		182

See page 188 for Word 2532.

2533. Καϊάφας, Kaiaph′as

Book	Caiaphas	Total
Mt.	26:3, 57	2
Lk.	3:2	1
Jn.	11:49; 18:13, 14, 24, 28	5
Ac.	4:6	1
Total		9

2534. καίγε, kai′ge

Book	at least	Total
Lk.	19:42	1

2535. Κάϊν, Ka′in

Book	Cain	Total
Heb.	11:4	1
1 Jn.	3:12	1
Jd.	1:11	1
Total		3

2536. Καϊνάν, Kainan′

Book	Oc.	Cainan (son of Enos)	Oc.	Cainan (son of Arphaxad)	Total
Lk.	1	3:37	1	3:36	2

2539. καίπερ, kai′per

Book	Oc.	though	Oc.	and yet	Total
Phl.	1	3:4			1
Heb.	3	5:8; 7:5; 12:17			3
2 Pt.	1	1:12			1
Rev.			1	17:8	1
Total	5		1		6

2538. καινότης, kainot′ēs

Book	newness	Total
Ro.	6:4; 7:6	2

2537. καινός, kainos′

Book	new	Total
Mt.	9:17; 13:52; 26:28, 29; 27:60	5
Mk.	1:27; 2:21, 22; 14:24, 25; 16:17	6
Lk.	5:36, 36, 36, 38; 22:20	5
Jn.	13:34; 19:41	2
Ac.	17:19, 21	2
1 Co.	11:25	1
2 Co.	3:6; 5:17, 17	3
Gal.	6:15	1
Eph.	2:15; 4:24	2
Heb.	8:8, 13; 9:15	3
2 Pt.	3:13, 13	2
1 Jn.	2:7, 8	2
2 Jn.	1:5	1
Rev.	2:17; 3:12, 12; 5:9; 14:3; 21:1, 1, 2, 5	9
Total		44

2540. καιρός, kairos′

Book	Oc.	time	Oc.	season	Oc.	opportunity	Oc.	due time	Oc.	always (with 1722 and 3856)	Oc.	Not Tr.	Oc.	Misc.	Total
Mt.	8	8:29; 11:25; 12:1; 13:30; 14:1; 16:3; 21:34; 26:18	2	21:41; 24:45											10
Mk.	4	1:15; 10:30; 11:13; 13:33	1	12:2											5
Lk.	6	8:13b; 12:56; 18:30; 19:44; 21:8, 24	4	1:20; 4:13; 13:1; 20:10					1	21:36			2	8:13a; 12:42	13
Jn.	3	7:6, 6, 8	1	5:4											4
Ac.	5	3:19; 7:20; 12:1; 17:26; 19:23	3	1:7; 13:11; 14:17									1	24:25	9
Ro.	5	3:26; 8:18; 9:9; 11:5; 13:11					1	5:6							6
1 Co.	3	4:5; 7:5, 29													3
2 Co.	3	6:2, 2; 8:14													3
Gal.	1	4:10	1	6:9	1	6:10									3
Eph.	3	1:10; 2:12; 5:16							1	6:18					4
Col.	1	4:5													1
1 Th.	1	2:17	1	5:1											2
2 Th.	1	2:6													1
1 Ti.	3	2:6; 4:1; 6:15													3
2 Ti.	3	3:1; 4:3, 6													3
Tit.	1	1:3													1
Heb.	2	9:9, 10			1	11:15					1	11:11			4
1 Pt.	3	1:5, 11; 4:17					1	5:6							4
Rev.	7	1:3; 11:18; 12:12, 14, 14, 14; 22:10													7
Total	63		13		2		2		2		1		3		86

Miscellaneous: Lk. 8:13a, while; Lk. 12:42, due season; Ac. 24:25, convenient season.

2541. Καῖσαρ, Kai′sar

Book	Caesar	Total
Mt.	22:17, 21, 21, 21	4
Mk.	12:14, 16, 17, 17	4
Lk.	2:1; 3:1; 20:22, 24, 25, 25; 23:2	7
Jn.	19:12, 12, 15	3
Ac.	11:28; 17:7; 25:8, 10, 11, 12, 12, 21; 26:32; 27:24; 28:19	11
Phl.	4:22	1
Total		30

2542. Καισάρεια, Kaisar′eia

Book	Oc.	Caesarea (of Palestine)	Oc.	Caesarea (Philippi)	Total
Mt.			1	16:13	1
Mk.			1	8:27	1
Ac.	15	8:40; 9:30; 10:1, 24; 11:11; 12:19; 18:22; 21:8, 16; 23:23, 33; 25:1, 4, 6, 13			15
Total	15		2		17

2543. καίτοι, kai′toi

Book	although	Total
Heb.	4:3	1

2544. καίτοιγε, kai′toige

Book	Oc.	though	Oc.	nevertheless	Total
Jn.	1	4:2			1
Ac.	1	17:27	1	14:17	2
Total	2		1		3

2545. καίω, kai′ō

Book	Oc.	burn	Oc.	did burn (with 2258)	Oc.	light	Total
Mt.					1	5:15	1
Lk.	1	12:35	1	24:32			2
Jn.	2	5:35; 15:6					2
1 Co.	1	13:3					1
Heb.	1	12:18					1
Rev.	5	4:5; 8:8, 10; 19:20; 21:8					5
Total	10		1		1		12

2546. κἀκεῖ, kakei′

Book	Oc.	and there	Oc.	there also	Oc.	thither also	Total
Mt.	3	5:23; 10:11; 28:10					3
Mk.	1	1:35	1	1:38			2
Jn.	1	11:54					1
Ac.	4	14:7; 22:10; 25:20; 27:6			1	17:13	5
Total	9		1		1		11

2547. κἀκεῖθεν, kakei′then

Book	Oc.	and from thence	Oc.	and thence	Oc.	and afterward	Oc.	thence also	Total
Mk.	1	10:1							1
Ac.	4	7:4; 21:1; 27:4; 28:15	2	14:26; 20:15	1	13:21	1	27:12	8
Total	5		2		1		1		9

2548. κἀκεῖνος, kakei′nos

Book	Oc.	and he	Oc.	and they	Oc.	he also	Oc.	and them	Oc.	and the other	Oc.	and him	Oc.	they also	Oc.	him also	Oc.	Misc.	Total
Mt.			1	15:18			1	20:4	1	23:23									3
Mk.			2	16:11, 13							2	12:4, 5							4
Lk.	2	11:7; 22:12							1	11:42					1	20:11			4
Jn.	2	7:29; 19:35			1	14:12							1	17:24			2	6:57; 10:16	6
Ac.					1	5:37	1	18:19									1	15:11	3
1 Co.													1	10:6					1
2 Ti.					1	2:12													1
Heb.																	1	4:2	1
Total	4		3		3		2		2		2		2		1		4		23

Miscellaneous: Jn. 6:57, even he; Jn. 10:16, them also; Ac. 15:11, they; Heb. 4:2, them.

2532. καί, kai

Occurrences rendered other than "and" or "not translated"

Book	Oc.	also	Oc.	even	Oc.	both	Oc.	then	Oc.	so	Oc.	likewise
Mt.	38	3:10; 5:39, 40; 6:14, 21; 10:4; 12:45; 13:26; 15:3, 16; 16:1; 17:12; 18:33, 35; 19:3, 28; 20: 4, 7; 22:26, 27; 23:26, 28; 24:27, 37, 39, 44; 25: 11, 17, 22, 41, 44; 26:13, 35, 69, 71, 73; 27:44, 57	9	5:46, 47; 7:12; 8:27; 12:8; 13: 12; 18:33; 20: 14; 25:29	2	10:28; 12:22	5	15:21; 16:22; 22:35; 23:32; 27:25	3	22:10; 25: 20; 27: 64	3	18:35; 20: 10; 24:33
Mk.	18	2:15, 21, 26, 28; 3:19; 7:18; 8:7, 38; 11:25; 12: 6, 22; 14:9, 31, 67; 15:31, 40, 41, 43	6	1:27; 4:25, 41; 6:2; 10:45; 13: 22			3	7:1; 10: 28; 12: 18	1	13:29		
Lk.	81	1:35, 36; 2:4, 35; 3:9, 12; 4:23, 41, 43; 5:10, 36, 39; 6:4, 5, 6, 13, 14, 16, 29, 29, 31, 32, 33, 34, 36; 7:8, 49; 8:36; 9:61; 10:1, 39; 11:1, 4, 18, 30, 34, 34, 40, 45, 46, 49; 12:8, 34, 40, 54; 13:8; 14:12, 12, 26; 16:1, 10, 10, 14, 22, 28; 17: 24, 26, 28; 18:15; 19:9; 20:12, 31, 32; 21:2; 22: 20, 24, 39, 56, 58, 59, 68; 23:7, 27, 32, 35, 36, 38, 51, 55; 24:22, 23	14	6:33; 8:18, 25; 9:54; 10:11, 17; 12:7, 41, 57; 18: 11; 19:26, 42; 20:37; 24:24	4	2:46; 5:36; 21:16; 22:33	7	2:28; 7: 22; 8:37; 18:26; 19:15, 23; 20: 44	4	11:2; 14: 21; 16:5; 20:15	4	3:14; 17:10; 19:19; 21:31
Jn.	47	3:23; 5:18, 19, 27; 6:24, 36, 67; 7:3, 10, 47, 52; 8:19; 9:15, 27, 40; 11:16, 33, 52; 12:9, 10, 18, 26, 42; 13:9, 14, 32, 34; 14:1, 3, 7, 19; 15:20, 20, 23; 17:1, 19, 20, 21; 18:5, 17, 25; 19:23, 39; 20:8; 21:3, 20, 25	4	5:21; 8:25; 11: 22, 37	8	2:2; 4:36; 7: 28; 9:37; 11: 48, 57; 12: 28; 15:24			3	6:57; 13: 33; 15:8		
Ac.	57	1:3, 11; 2:22, 26; 3:17; 5:2, 16; 7:45; 8:13; 9: 32; 10:45; 11:1, 18, 30; 12:3; 13:5, 9, 22, 23, 35; 14:5, 15; 15:27, 32, 35c; 17:6, 12, 28, 28; 19:17, 21, 27; 20:30; 21:13, 16, 24, 28; 22:5, 5, 20, 29; 23:11, 30, 33, 35; 24:6, 9, 15, 26; 25: 22; 26:10, 26, 29; 27:10, 36; 28:9, 10	3	5:39; 15:8; 26:11	3	2:29, 36; 26: 29			1	7:51	1	3:24
Ro.	52	1:13, 16, 24, 27; 2:9, 10, 12; 3:29, 29; 4:6, 9, 11, 12, 16, 21, 24; 5:3, 11, 15; 6:4, 5, 8, 11; 7: 4; 8:11, 17, 21, 23, 26, 29, 30, 30, 30, 34; 9:10, 24, 25; 11:1, 5, 16, 22, 31; 13:5, 6; 15:7, 14, 14, 14, 22, 27; 16:2, 4	10	1:13; 5:14, 18, 21; 8:23, 34; 9: 24; 11:5; 15:3, 6	3	11:33; 14:9, 9			1	11:16	1	16:5
1 Co.	37	1:8, 16; 2:13; 4:8; 5:12; 6:14; 7:3, 4, 22; 9:8; 10:9, 10, 13; 11:6, 12, 19, 23, 25; 12:12; 13:12; 14:15, 15, 19, 34; 15:1, 2, 3, 14, 18, 21, 28, 40, 42, 48, 48, 49; 16:10	10	2:11; 3:5; 5:7; 7: 7; 9:14; 11:5; 14: 12; 15:22, 24; 16:1	6	4:5, 11; 6:13, 14; 7:29, 34					1	14:9
2 Co.	34	1:5, 6, 7, 11, 14, 14, 22; 2:9, 10; 3:6; 4:10, 11, 13, 14; 5:5, 11; 6:1, 13; 8:6, 6, 7, 10, 11, 14, 19, 21; 9:6, 6, 12; 10:11, 14; 11:15; 13:4, 9	8	1:3, 8, 13; 3:10; 7:14; 10:7, 13; 11:12	1	9:10	1	2:2				
Gal.	8	2:1, 10, 13, 17; 5:21, 25; 6:1, 7	4	2:16; 4:3, 29; 5: 12			1	4:7	1	1:9	1	2:13
Eph.	12	1:11, 13, 13, 21; 2:3, 22; 4:9, 10; 5:2, 25; 6:9, 21	7	2:3, 5; 4:4, 32; 5: 12, 23, 29								
Phl.	15	1:15, 20, 29; 2:4, 5, 9, 18, 27; 3:4, 12, 20; 4:3, 3, 10, 15	5	1:15; 3:15, 18, 21; 4:16	4	2:13; 4:9, 12, 12			1	1:20		
Col.	15	1:6, 7, 8, 9, 29; 2:11, 12; 3:4, 7, 8, 13, 15; 4:3, 3, 16	1	3:13							1	4:16
1 Th.	12	1:5, 8; 2:8, 10, 13, 14; 3:6; 4:6, 8, 14; 5:11, 24	8	2:2, 14, 19; 3:4, 12, 13; 4:5, 13	2	2:15; 5:15						
2 Th.	2	1:5, 11	3	2:16; 3:1, 10								
1 Ti.	5	2:9; 5:13, 20, 25; 6:12			2	4:10, 16						
2 Ti.	12	1:5, 12; 2:2, 5, 10, 11, 12, 20; 3:8, 9; 4:8, 15										
Tit.			1	1:15	1	1:9						
Phe.	2	1:21, 22	1	1:19	1	1:16						
Heb.	23	1:2; 2:14; 3:2; 4:10; 5:2, 3, 5, 6; 7:2, 2, 9, 12, 25; 8:3, 6; 9:1; 10:15; 11:11, 19; 12:1, 26; 13:3, 12	3	7:4; 11:12, 19	1	9:21			1	3:19		
Jas.	8	1:11; 2:2, 19, 25, 26; 3:2, 4; 5:8	2	2:17; 3:5			1	2:4				
1 Pt.	14	2:5, 6, 8, 18, 21; 3:1, 5, 18, 19, 21; 4:6, 13; 5: 1, 1							1	1:15	1	4:1
2 Pt.	6	1:19; 2:1; 3:10, 15, 16, 16	3	1:14; 2:1, 1	1	3:18						
1 Jn.	9	1:3; 2:2, 6, 23, 24; 3:4; 4:11, 21; 5:1	1	2:18			1	1:5	1	4:17		
2 Jn.	1	1:1			1	1:9						
3 Jn.	1	1:12										
Jd.	2	1:8, 14	1	1:23	1	1:25						
Rev.	5	1:9; 2:15; 6:11; 11:8; 14:17	4	2:13d; 3:4; 17: 11; 18:6	2	13:15; 19:18	1	22:9				
Total	516		108		43		20		18		13	

2532. καί, kai (continued)

Book	Oc.	or	Oc.	and also	Oc.	yea	Oc.	that	Oc.	but	Oc.	yet	Oc.	for	Oc.	Misc.	Total
Mt.	1	7:10			1	26:60b			1	26:60a							63
Mk.			1	5:16			1	9:39							2	9:13; 13:29	32
Lk.	2	11:12; 12:38					3	5:1; 8:1; 10:38			1	3:20	1	6:32	3	9:5; 12:7; 19:15	124
Jn.					1	16:32			1	1:20	1	8:16					65
Ac.	3	9:2; 17:21; 25:11			2	3:16; 7:43			1	16:7					1	25:27	72
Ro.			2	2:10; 16:2c									1	11:27	1	2:15	71
1 Co.					1	2:10									1	4:7	56
2 Co.	1	13:1													1	8:11	46
Gal.											1	3:4			1	2:8	17
Eph.																	19
Phl.															1	2:27	26
Col.																	17
1 Th.			1	2:10													23
2 Th.																	5
1 Ti.															1	5:13	8
2 Ti.																	12
Tit.																	2
Phe.																	4
Heb.																	28
Jas.															1	2:4	12
1 Pt.			1	5:1b													17
2 Pt.																	10
1 Jn.									1	2:27			1	3:4	1	4:3	15
2 Jn.																	2
3 Jn.																	1
Jd.																	4
Rev.	2	20:4; 21:27													1	14:11	15
Total	9		5		5		4		4		3		3		15		766

Miscellaneous: Mk. 9:13, indeed; Mk. 13:29, in like manner; Lk. 9:5, very; Lk. 12:7, even very; Lk. 19:15, then; Ac. 25:27, withal; Ro. 2:15, else; 1 Co. 4:7, now; 2 Co. 8:11, therefore; Gal. 2:8, the same; Phl. 2:27, indeed; 1 Ti. 5:13, withal; Jas. 2:4, then; 1 Jn. 4:3, and even; Rev. 14:11, nor.

2549. κακία, kaki'a

Book	Oc.	malice	Oc.	maliciousness	Oc.	evil	Oc.	wickedness	Oc.	naughtiness	Total
Mt.					1	6:34					1
Ac.							1	8:22			1
Ro.			1	1:29							1
1 Co.	2	5:8; 14:20									2
Eph.	1	4:31									1
Col.	1	3:8									1
Tit.	1	3:3									1
Jas.									1	1:21	1
1 Pt.	1	2:1	1	2:16							2
Total	6		2		1		1		1		11

2550. κακοήθεια, kakoe'theia

Book	malignity	Total
Ro.	1:29	1

2552. κακοπάθεια, kakopath'eia

Book	suffering affliction	Total
Jas.	5:10	1

2551. κακολογέω, kakologe'ō

Book	Oc.	curse	Oc.	speak evil of	Total
Mt.	1	15:4			1
Mk.	1	7:10	1	9:39	2
Ac.			1	19:9	1
Total	2		2		4

2553. κακοπαθέω, kakopathe'ō

Book	Oc.	endure hardness	Oc.	suffer trouble	Oc.	endure affliction	Oc.	be afflicted	Total
2 Ti.	1	2:3	1	2:9	1	4:5			3
Jas.							1	5:13	1
Total	1		1		1		1		4

2554. κακοποιέω, kakopoie'ō

Book	Oc.	do evil	Oc.	evil doing	Total
Mk.	1	3:4			1
Lk.	1	6:9			1
1 Pt.			1	3:17	1
3 Jn.	1	1:11			1
Total	3		1		4

2555. κακοποιός, kakopoios'

Book	Oc.	evildoer	Oc.	malefactor	Total
Jn.			1	18:30	1
1 Pt.	4	2:12, 14; 3:16; 4:15			4
Total	4		1		5

2556. κακός, kakos'

Book	Oc.	evil	Oc.	evil things	Oc.	harm	Oc.	that which is evil (with 3488)	Oc.	wicked	Oc.	ill	Oc.	bad	Oc.	noisome	Total
Mt.	2	24:48; 27:23							1	21:41							3
Mk.	2	7:21; 15:14															2
Lk.	1	23:22	1	16:25													2
Jn.	1	18:23															1
Ac.	2	9:13; 23:9			2	16:28; 28:5											4
Ro.	13	2:9; 3:8; 7:19, 21; 9: 11; 12:17, 17, 21, 21; 13:3, 4b; 14:20; 16:19	1	1:30			1	13:4a			1	13:10					16
1 Co.	2	13:5; 15:33	1	10:6													3
2 Co.	1	13:7											1	5:10			2
Phl.	1	3:2															1
Col.	1	3:5															1
1 Th.	2	5:15, 15															2
1 Ti.	1	6:10															1
2 Ti.	1	4:14															1
Tit.	1	1:12															1
Heb.	1	5:14															1
Jas.	2	1:13; 3:8															2
1 Pt.	5	3:9, 9, 10, 11, 12															5
3 Jn.							1	1:11									1
Rev.	1	2:2													1	16:2	2
Total	40		3		2		2		1		1		1		1		51

2557. κακοῦργος, kakour'gos

Book	Oc.	malefactor	Oc.	evil doer	Total
Lk.	3	23:32, 33, 39			3
2 Ti.			1	2:9	1
Total	3		1		4

2558. κακουχέω, kakouche'ō

Book	Oc.	torment	Oc.	suffer adversity	Total
Heb.	1	11:37	1	13:3	2

2559. κακόω, kako'ō

Book	Oc.	entreat evil	Oc.	make evil affected	Oc.	vex	Oc.	hurt	Oc.	harm	Total
Ac.	2	7:6, 19	1	14:2	1	12:1	1	18:10			5
1 Pt.									1	3:13	1
Total	2		1		1		1		1		6

2560. κακῶς, kakōs'

Book	Oc.	be sick (with 2192)	Oc.	be diseased (with 2192)	Oc.	evil	Oc.	grievously	Oc.	sore	Oc.	miserably	Oc.	amiss	Oc.	sick people (with 2192)	Total
Mt.	2	8:16; 9:12	1	14:35			1	15:22	1	17:15	1	21:41			1	4:24	7
Mk.	3	1:34; 2:17; 6: 55	1	1:32													4
Lk.	2	5:31; 7:2															2
Jn.					1	18:23											1
Ac.					1	23:5											1
Jas.													1	4:3			1
Total	7		2		2		1		1		1		1		1		16

2561. κάκωσις, kak'ōsis

Book	affliction	Total
Ac.	7:34	1

2562. καλάμη, kalam'ē

Book	stubble	Total
1 Co.	3:12	1

2563. κάλαμος, kal'amos

Book	Oc.	reed	Oc.	pen	Total
Mt.	5	11:7; 12:20; 27:29, 30, 48			5
Mk.	2	15:19, 36			2
Lk.	1	7:24			1
3 Jn.			1	1:13	1
Rev.	3	11:1; 21:15, 16			3
Total	11		1		12

2565. καλλιέλαιος, kalliel'aios

Book	good olive tree	Total
Ro.	11:24	1

2566. καλλίον, kalli'on

Book	very well	Total
Ac.	25:10	1

2564. καλέω, kale'ō

Book	Oc.	call	Oc.	bid	Oc.	be so named	Oc.	named (with 3586)	Oc.	Misc.	Total
Mt.	23	1:21, 23, 25; 2:7, 15, 23; 4:21; 5:9, 19, 19; 9:13; 10:25; 20:8; 21:13; 22:3a, 43, 45; 23:7, 8, 9, 10; 25:14; 27:8	4	22:3b, 4, 8, 9							27
Mk.	3	1:20; 2:17; 11:17									3
Lk.	29	1:13, 31, 32, 35, 36, 59, 60, 61, 62, 76; 2:4, 21a, 23; 5:32; 6:15, 46; 7:11; 8:2; 9:10; 10:39; 14:13; 15:19, 21; 19:13, 29; 20:44; 21:37; 22:25; 23:33	11	7:39; 14:7, 8, 8, 9, 10, 10, 12, 16, 17, 24	1	2:21b	1	19:2			42
Jn.	3	1:42; 2:2; 10:3									3
Ac.	13	1:12, 19, 23; 3:11; 4:18; 9:11; 10:1; 13:1; 14:12; 27:8, 14, 16; 28:1							3	7:58; 15:37; 24:2	16
Ro.	8	4:17; 8:30, 30; 9:7, 11, 24, 25, 26									8
1 Co.	11	1:9; 7:15, 17, 18, 18, 20, 21, 22, 22, 24; 15:9	1	10:27							12
Gal.	4	1:6, 15; 5:8, 13									4
Eph.	2	4:1, 4									2
Col.	1	3:15									1
1 Th.	3	2:12; 4:7; 5:24									3
2 Th.	1	2:14									1
1 Ti.	1	6:12									1
2 Ti.	1	1:9									1
Heb.	6	2:11; 3:13; 5:4; 9:15; 11:8, 18									6
Jas.	1	2:23									1
1 Pt.	6	1:15; 2:9, 21; 3:6, 9; 5:10									6
2 Pt.	1	1:3									1
1 Jn.	1	3:1									1
Rev.	7	1:9; 11:8; 12:9; 16:16; 19:9, 11, 13									7
Total	125		16		1		1		3		146

Miscellaneous: Ac. 7:58, be (one's) name; Ac. 15:37, be (one's) surname; Ac. 24:2, call forth.

2567. καλοδιδάσκαλος kalodidas'kalos

Book	teacher of good things	Total
Tit.	2:3	1

2568. Καλοὶ, Λιμένες Kaloi' Limen'es

Book	fair havens	Total
Ac.	27:8	1

2569. καλοποιέω, kalopoie'ō

Book	well doing	Total
2 Th.	3:13	1

2571. κάλυμα, kal'uma

Book	vail	Total
2 Co.	3:13, 14, 15, 16	4

2570. καλός, kalos'

Book	Oc.	good	Oc.	better	Oc.	honest	Oc.	meet	Oc.	goodly	Oc.	Misc.	Total
Mt.	17	3:10; 5:16; 7:17, 18, 19; 12:33, 33; 13:8, 23, 24, 27, 37, 38, 48; 17:4; 26:10, 24	2	18:8, 9			1	15:26	1	13:45			21
Mk.	6	4:8, 20; 9:5, 50; 14:6, 21	4	9:42, 43, 45, 47			1	7:27					11
Lk.	7	3:9; 6:38, 43, 43; 8:15a; 9:33; 14:34			1	8:15b			1	21:5			9
Jn.	7	2:10, 10; 10:11, 11, 14, 32, 33											7
Ac.											1	27:8	1
Ro.	4	7:16, 18, 21; 14:21			1	12:17							5
1 Co.	5	5:6; 7:1, 8, 26, 26	1	9:15									6
2 Co.					2	8:21; 13:7							2
Gal.	2	4:18, 18									1	6:9	3
1 Th.	1	5:21											1
1 Ti.	17	1:8, 18; 2:3; 3:1, 7, 13; 4:4, 6, 6; 5:4, 10, 25; 6:12, 12, 13, 18, 19											17
2 Ti.	3	1:14; 2:3; 4:7											3
Tit.	5	2:7, 14; 3:8, 8, 14											5
Heb.	5	5:14; 6:5; 10:24; 13:9, 18											5
Jas.	2	3:13; 4:17									1	2:7	3
1 Pt.	2	2:12b; 4:10			1	2:12a							3
Total	83		7		5		2		2		3		102

Miscellaneous: Ac. 27:8, fair; Gal. 6:9, well; Jas. 2:7, worthy.

2572. καλύπτω, kalup'tō

Book	Oc.	cover	Oc.	hide	Total
Mt.	2	8:24; 10:26			2
Lk.	2	8:16; 23:30			2
2 Co.			2	4:3, 3	2
Jas.			1	5:20	1
1 Pt.	1	4:8			1
Total	5		3		8

2573. καλώς, kalōs'

Book	Oc.	well	Oc.	good	Oc.	full well	Oc.	very well	Oc.	Misc.	Total
Mt.	2	12:12; 15:7	1	5:44							3
Mk.	4	7:6, 37; 12:28, 32			1	7:9			1	16:18	6
Lk.	2	6:26; 20:39	1	6:27							3
Jn.	4	4:17; 8:48; 13:13; 18:23									4
Ac.	2	10:33; 28:25					1	25:10			3
Ro.	1	11:20									1
1 Co.	3	7:37, 38; 14:17									3
2 Co.	1	11:4									1
Gal.	2	4:17; 5:7									2
Phl.	1	4:14									1
1 Ti.	4	3:4, 12, 13; 5:17									4
Heb.									1	13:18	1
Jas.	2	2:8, 19							1	2:3	3
2 Pt.	1	1:19									1
3 Jn.	1	1:6									1
Total	30		2		1		1		3		37

Miscellaneous: Mk. 16:18 (with 2192), recover; Heb. 13:18, honestly; Jas. 2:3, in a good place.

2574. κάμηλος, kam'ēlos

Book	camel	Total
Mt.	3:4; 19:24; 23:24	3
Mk.	1:6; 10:25	2
Lk.	18:25	1
Total		6

2575. κάμινος, kam'inos

Book	furnace	Total
Mt.	13:42, 50	2
Rev.	1:15; 9:2	2
Total		4

2576. καμμύω, kammu'ō

Book	close	Total
Mt.	13:15	1
Ac.	28:27	1
Total		2

2577. κάμνω, kam'nō

Book	Oc.	be wearied	Oc.	sick	Oc.	faint	Total
Heb.	1	12:3					1
Jas.			1	5:15			1
Rev.					1	2:3	1
Total	1		1		1		3

2578. κάμπτω, kamp'tō

Book	bow	Total
Ro.	11:4; 14:11	2
Eph.	3:14	1
Phl.	2:10	1
Total		4

2579. κἄν, kan

Book	Oc.	though	Oc.	and if	Oc.	if but	Oc.	also if	Oc.	at the least	Oc.	and if so much as	Oc.	yet	Total
Mt.	1	26:35					1	21:21							2
Mk.			1	16:18	2	5:28; 6:56									3
Lk.			1	13:9											1
Jn.	3	8:14; 10:38; 11:25													3
Ac.									1	5:15					1
2 Co.													1	11:16	1
Heb.											1	12:20			1
Jas.			1	5:15											1
Total	4		3		2		1		1		1		1		13

2580. Κανᾶ, Kana'

Book	Cana	Total
Jn.	2:1, 11; 4:46; 21:2	4

2581. Κανανίτης, Kanani'tēs

Book	Canaanite	Total
Mt.	10:4	1
Mk.	3:18	1
Total		2

2582. Κανδάκη, Kandak'ē

Book	Candace	Total
Ac.	8:27	1

2583. κανών, kanōn'

Book	Oc.	rule	Oc.	line	Total
2 Co.	2	10:13, 15	1	10:16	3
Gal.	1	6:16			1
Phl.	1	3:16			1
Total	4		1		5

2584. Καπερναούμ Kapernaoum'

Book	Capernaum	Total
Mt.	4:13; 8:5; 11:23; 17:24	4
Mk.	1:21; 2:1; 9:33	3
Lk.	4:23, 31; 7:1; 10:15	4
Jn.	2:12; 4:46; 6:17, 24, 59	5
Total		16

2585. καπηλεύω, kapēleu'ō

Book	corrupt	Total
2 Co.	2:17	1

2586. καπνός, kapnos'

Book	smoke	Total
Ac.	2:19	1
Rev.	8:4; 9:2, 2, 2, 3, 17, 18; 14:11; 15:8; 18:9, 18; 19:3	12
Total		13

2587. Καππαδοκία, Kappadoki'a

Book	Cappadocia	Total
Ac.	2:9	1
1 Pt.	1:1	1
Total		2

2588. καρδία, kardi'a

Book	Oc.	heart	Oc.	broken hearted (with 4837)	Total
Mt.	17	5:8, 28; 6:21; 9:4; 11:29; 12:34, 35, 40; 13:15, 15, 19; 15:8, 18, 19; 18:35; 22:37; 24:48			17
Mk.	12	2:6, 8; 3:5; 4:15; 6:52; 7:6, 19, 21; 8:17; 11:23; 12:30, 33			12
Lk.	23	1:17, 51, 66; 2:19, 35, 51; 3:15; 5:22; 6:45, 45, 45; 8:12, 15; 9:47; 10:27; 12:34, 45; 16:15; 21:14, 34; 24:25, 32, 38	1	4:18	24
Jn.	7	12:40, 40; 13:2; 14:1, 27; 16:6, 22			7
Ac.	21	2:26, 37, 46; 4:32; 5:3, 4; 7:23, 39, 51, 54; 8:21, 22, 37; 11:23; 13:22; 14:17; 15:9; 16:14; 21:13; 28:27, 27			21
Ro.	15	1:21, 24; 2:5, 15, 29; 5:5; 6:17; 8:27; 9:2; 10:1, 6, 8, 9, 10; 16:18			15
1 Co.	5	2:9; 4:5; 7:37, 37; 14:25			5
2 Co.	11	1:22; 2:4; 3:2, 3, 15; 4:6; 5:12; 6:11; 7:3; 8:16; 9:7			11
Gal.	1	4:6			1
Eph.	5	3:17; 4:18; 5:19; 6:5, 22			5
Phl.	2	1:7; 4:7			2
Col.	5	2:2; 3:15, 16, 22; 4:8			5
1 Th.	3	2:4, 17; 3:13			3
2 Th.	2	2:17; 3:5			2
1 Ti.	1	1:5			1
2 Ti.	1	2:22			1
Heb.	11	3:8, 10, 12, 15; 4:7, 12; 8:10; 10:16, 22, 22; 13:9			11
Jas.	5	1:26; 3:14; 4:8; 5:5, 8			5
1 Pt.	3	1:22; 3:4, 15			3
2 Pt.	2	1:19; 2:14			2
1 Jn.	4	3:19, 20, 20, 21			4
Rev.	3	2:23; 17:17; 18:7			3
Total	159				160

2589. καρδιογνώστης kardiognōs'tēs

Book	which knows the hearts	Total
Ac.	1:24; 15:8	2

2590. καρπός, karpos'

Book	fruit	Total
Mt.	3:8, 10; 7:16, 17, 17, 18, 18, 19, 20; 12:33, 33, 33; 13:8, 26; 21:19, 34, 34, 41, 43	19
Mk.	4:7, 8, 29; 11:14; 12:2	5
Lk.	1:42; 3:8, 9; 6:43, 43, 44; 8:8; 12:17; 13:6, 7, 9; 20:10	12
Jn.	4:36; 12:24; 15:2, 2, 2, 4, 5, 8, 16, 16	10
Ac.	2:30	1
Ro.	1:13; 6:21, 22; 15:28	4
1 Co.	9:7	1
Gal.	5:22	1
Eph.	5:9	1
Phl.	1:11, 22; 4:17	3
2 Ti.	2:6	1
Heb.	12:11; 13:15	2
Jas.	3:17, 18; 5:7, 18	4
Rev.	22:2, 2	2
Total		66

2591. Κάρπος, Kar'pos

Book	Carpus	Total
2 Ti.	4:13	1

2592. καρποφορέω, karpophore'ō

Book	Oc.	bring forth fruit	Oc.	bear fruit	Oc.	be fruitful	Total
Mt.			1	13:23			1
Mk.	2	4:20, 28					2
Lk.	1	8:15					1
Ro.	2	7:4, 5					2
Col.	1	1:6			1	1:10	2
Total	6		1		1		8

2593. καρποφόρος, karpophor'os

Book	fruitful	Total
Ac.	14:17	1

2594. καρτερέω, kartere'ō

Book	endure	Total
Heb.	11:27	1

2595. κάρφος, kar'phos

Book	mote	Total
Mt.	7:3, 4, 5	3
Lk.	6:41, 42, 42	3
Total		6

2596a. κατά, kata′ (with accusative)

Book	Oc.	according to	Oc.	after	Oc.	in	Oc.	by	Oc.	daily (with 2250)	Oc.	as	Oc.	of	Oc.	every
Mt.	4	2:16; 9:29; 16:27; 25:15	1	23:3	6	1:20; 2:12, 13, 19, 22; 27:19			1	26:55						
Mk.	1	7:5							1	14:49						
Lk.	7	1:9, 38; 2:22, 24, 29, 39; 23:56	2	2:27, 42	2	6:23; 15:14	3	10:4, 31; 11:3	3	9:23; 19:47; 22:53	3	4:16; 22:22, 39			3	2:41; 8:1; 16:19
Jn.	2	7:24; 18:31	1	8:15			2	10:3; 19:7							1	21:25
Ac.	6	2:30; 7:44; 13:23; 22:3, 12; 24:6	4	13:22; 23:3; 24:14a; 26:5	12	3:13, 22; 11:1; 13:1; 15:23, 36; 17:22; 24:12, 14b; 25:3b; 26:11, 13	2	27:2; 28:16	6	2:46a, 47; 3:2; 16:5; 17:11; 19:9	2	17:2; 23:31	2	24:22; 27:5	1	8:3
Ro.	18	1:3, 4; 2:2, 6, 16; 4:18; 8:27, 28; 9:3, 11; 10:2; 11:5; 12:6, 6; 15:5; 16:25, 25, 26	10	2:5; 7:22; 8:1, 1, 4, 4, 5, 5, 12, 13	3	1:15; 5:6; 16:5	3	2:7; 4:16; 11:24a			1	3:5	2	4:4, 4		
1 Co.	4	3:8, 10; 15:3, 4	3	1:26; 7:40; 10:18	2	14:40; 16:19	4	7:6a; 12:8; 14:27, 31	1	15:31	2	3:3; 9:8	1	7:6b		
2 Co.	6	1:17; 10:2, 13, 15; 11:15; 13:10	8	5:16, 16; 7:9, 11; 10:3, 7; 11:17, 18	1	10:1	1	8:8	1	11:28						
Gal.	2	1:4; 3:29	4	1:11; 4:23, 29, 29			1	2:2a			1	4:28				
Eph.	15	1:5, 7, 9, 11a, 19; 2:2, 2; 3:7a, 11, 16, 20; 4:7, 16, 22b; 6:5	2	1:11b; 4:24			2	3:3, 7b							1	5:33
Phl.	3	1:20; 3:21; 4:19														
Col.	4	1:11, 25, 29; 3:22b	5	2:8, 8, 8, 22; 3:10	3	3:20, 22a; 4:15										
2 Th.	1	1:12	2	2:9; 3:6			1	2:3								
1 Ti.	3	1:11, 18; 6:3					2	1:1; 5:21								
2 Ti.	6	1:1, 8, 9, 9; 2:8; 4:14	1	4:3												
Tit.	4	1:1a, 3; 3:5, 7	2	1:1b, 4							1	1:9				
Phe.					1	1:2							1	1:14a		
Heb.	6	2:4; 7:5; 8:4, 5, 9; 9:19	11	5:6, 10; 6:20; 7:11, 11, 15, 16, 16, 17, 21; 12:10	6	1:10; 2:17; 3:8; 4:15a; 9:9a; 11:13	5	7:22; 9:22; 10:1, 8; 11:7	2	7:27; 10:11					2	9:25; 10:3
Jas.	1	2:8	1	3:9												
1 Pt.	7	1:2, 3, 17; 3:7; 4:6, 6, 19									1	1:15				
2 Pt.	2	3:13, 15	1	3:3												
1 Jn.	1	5:14														
2 Jn.			1	1:6												
3 Jn.							1	1:14								
Jd.			2	1:16, 18												
Rev.	4	2:23; 18:6; 20:12, 13											1	4:8	1	22:2
Total	107		61		36		27		15		11		7		9	

Word 2596 continued on next page

2596b. κατά, kata′ (with genitive)

Book	Oc.	against	Oc.	throughout	Oc.	by	Oc.	down	Oc.	of	Oc.	Not Tr.	Oc.	Misc.	Total
Mt.	14	5:11, 23; 10:35, 35, 35; 12:14, 25, 25, 30, 32, 32; 20:11; 26:59; 27:1			1	26:63	1	8:32							16
Mk.	6	3:6; 9:40; 11:25; 14:55, 56, 57					1	5:13					1	14:3	8
Lk.	2	9:50; 11:23	1	23:5			1	8:33			1	23:14	1	4:14	6
Jn.	2	18:29; 19:11													2
Ac.	14	4:26, 26; 6:13; 14:2; 16:22; 19:16; 21:28; 24:1; 25:2, 3a, 7, 15, 27; 27:14	3	9:31, 42; 10:37											17
Ro.	2	8:31; 11:2							1	8:33					3
1 Co.	1	4:6							1	15:15			1	11:4	3
2 Co.	2	10:5; 13:8									1	8:2			3
Gal.	4	3:21; 5:17, 17, 23													4
Col.	1	2:14													1
1 Ti.	1	5:19													1
Heb.					3	6:13, 13, 16									3
Jas.	2	3:14; 5:9													2
1 Pt.	1	2:11													1
2 Pt.	1	2:11													1
Jd.	1	1:15b											1	1:15a	2
Rev.	4	2:4, 14, 20; 12:7													4
Total	58		4		4		3		2		2		4		77

Miscellaneous: Mk. 14:3, on; Lk. 4:14, through; 1 Co. 11:4, covered; Jd. 1:15a, upon.

Word 2596 has 481 occurrences.

2596a. κατά, kata′ (with accusative) (continued)

Book	Oc.	at	Oc.	privately (with 2398)	Oc.	apart (with 2398)	Oc.	to	Oc.	in every	Oc.	through	Oc.	concerning	Oc.	toward	Oc.	with
Mt.	1	27:15	1	24:3	5	14:13, 23; 17:1, 19; 20:17												
Mk.	1	15:6	3	6:32; 9:28; 13:3	2	6:31; 9:2											1	1:27
Lk.	2	10:32; 23:17	2	9:10; 10:23							2	9:6; 13:22						
Jn.	1	5:4																
Ac.	1	16:25	1	23:19			2	16:7a; 25:16	5	5:42; 14:23; 15:21a; 20:23; 22:19	1	3:17			2	8:26; 27:12a		
Ro.	1	9:9					1	14:22					2	9:5; 11:28a				
1 Co.																	1	2:1
2 Co.							1	8:3					1	11:21				
Gal.			1	2:2b			1	2:11										
Eph.																	1	6:6
Phl.											1	2:3			1	3:14		
Col.																		
2 Th.																		
1 Ti.																		
2 Ti.	1	4:1																
Tit.									1	1:5								
Phe.																		
Heb.																		
Jas.																		
1 Pt.																		
2 Pt.																		
1 Jn.																		
2 Jn.																		
3 Jn.																		
Jd.																		
Rev.																		
Total	8		8		7		5		6		4		3		3		3	

2597. καταβαίνω, katabai′nō

Book	Oc.	come down	Oc.	descend	Oc.	go down	Oc.	fall down	Oc.	step down	Oc.	get down	Oc.	fall	Total
Mt.	6	8:1; 14:29; 17:9; 24:17; 27:40, 42	4	3:16; 7:25, 27; 28:2											10
Mk.	3	3:22; 9:9; 15:30	2	1:10; 15:32	1	13:15									6
Lk.	7	6:17; 8:23; 9:54; 10:31; 17:31; 19:5, 6	1	3:22	3	2:51; 10:30; 18:14	1	22:44							12
Jn.	10	3:13; 4:47, 49; 6:33, 38, 41, 42, 50, 51, 58	3	1:32, 33, 51	4	2:12; 4:51; 5:4; 6:16			1	5:7					18
Ac.	6	7:34; 8:15; 14:11; 16:8; 24:22; 25:7	3	10:11; 11:5; 24:1	9	7:15; 8:26, 38; 10:21; 14:25; 18:22; 20:10; 23:10; 25:6					1	10:20			19
Ro.			1	10:7											1
Eph.			2	4:9, 10											2
1 Th.			1	4:16											1
Jas.	1	1:17													1
Rev.	8	3:12; 10:1; 12:12; 13:13; 18:1; 20:1, 9; 21:2	1	21:10									1	16:21	10
Total	41		18		17		1		1		1		1		80

2598. καταβάλλω, katabal′lō

Book	Oc.	cast down	Oc.	lay	Total
2 Co.	1	4:9			1
Heb.			1	6:1	1
Rev.	1	12:10			1
Total	2		1		3

2599. καταβαρέω, katabare′ō

Book	burden	Total
2 Co.	12:16	1

2600. κατάβασις, katab′asis

Book	descent	Total
Lk.	19:37	1

2596a. κατά, kata′ (with accusative) (continued)

Book	Oc.	in diver's	Oc.	about	Oc.	throughout	Oc.	after the manner of	Oc.	your (with 5109)	Oc.	Not Tr.	Oc.	Misc.	Total
Mt.	1	24:7											1	19:3	21
Mk.	1	13:8											2	4:34; 7:33	12
Lk.	1	21:11			1	8:39							6	1:18; 2:31; 6:26; 8:4; 10:33; 17:30	37
Jn.							1	2:6							8
Ac.			3	2:10; 12:1; 27:27	2	8:1; 24:5			2	18:15; 24:22	5	13:27; 15:21b; 18:4; 19:23; 27:12b	20	2:46b; 5:15; 8:36; 14:1; 15:11; 16:7b; 17:17, 25, 28; 18:14; 19:20; 20:20; 21:19, 21; 25:14, 23; 26:3; 27:7, 7, 25	79
Ro.											1	3:2	7	4:1; 7:13; 11:21, 24b, 28b; 12:5; 14:15	49
1 Co.							1	15:32					2	12:31; 16:2	21
2 Co.											1	1:8	3	4:13, 17; 7:10	23
Gal.							1	3:15					2	1:13; 3:1	13
Eph.									1	1:15			2	4:22a; 6:21	24
Phl.													5	1:12; 3:5, 6a, 6b; 4:11	10
Col.													1	4:7	13
2 Th.															4
1 Ti.															5
2 Ti.															8
Tit.															8
Phe.													1	1:14b	3
Heb.													7	3:3, 13; 4:15b; 7:20; 9:5, 9b, 27	39
Jas.													1	2:17	3
1 Pt.													2	4:14, 14	10
2 Pt.															3
1 Jn.															1
2 Jn.															1
3 Jn.															1
Jd.															2
Rev.															6
Total	3		3		3		3		3		7		62		404

Miscellaneous: Mt. 19:3, for; Mk. 4:34 (with 2398), when . . . alone; Mk. 7:33, aside; Lk. 1:18 (with 5001), whereby; Lk. 2:31, before; Lk. 6:26 (with 4923), so; Lk. 8:4, out of every; Lk. 10:33 (with 846), where he was; Lk. 17:30 (with 4923), even thus; Ac. 2:46b (with 3524), from house to house; Ac. 5:15, into; Ac. 8:36, on; Ac. 14:1 (with 846 and 3488), together; Ac. 15:11, even as; Ac. 16:7b, into; Ac. 17:17 (with 2250 and 3856), daily; Ac. 17:25, and; Ac. 17:28 (with 5109), your own; Ac. 18:14 (with 3056), reason would; Ac. 19:20 (with 2904), mightily; Ac. 20:20 (with 3524), from house to house; Ac. 21:19 (with 1520 and 1538), particularly; Ac. 21:21, among; Ac. 25:14 (with 3488), cause; Ac. 25:23 (with 1851), principal; Ac. 26:3, among; Ac. 27:7, 7, over against; Ac. 27:25, even as; Ro. 4:1, as pertaining to; Ro. 7:13 (with 5136), exceeding; Ro. 11:21, 24b, natural; Ro. 11:28b, as touching; Ro. 12:5 (as an adverb with 1520), every man; Ro. 14:15 (with 26), charitably; 1 Co. 12:31 (with 5136), more excellent; 1 Co. 16:2, upon; 2 Co. 4:13, according as; 2 Co. 4:17 (with 5136), far more; 2 Co. 7:10 (with 2316), godly; Gal. 1:13 (with 5136), beyond measure; Gal. 3:1, before; Eph. 4:22a, as concerning; Eph. 6:21, my; Phl. 1:12, unto; Phl. 3:5, as touching; Phl. 3:6a, as concerning; Phl. 3:6b, touching; Phl. 4:11, in respect of; Col. 4:7, my; Phe. 1:14b (with 1595), willingly; Heb. 3:3 (with 3645), inasmuch as; Heb. 3:13 (with 2250 and 1538), daily; Heb. 4:15b; like as; Heb. 7:20 (with 3645), inasmuch as; Heb. 9:5 (with 3213), particularly; Heb. 9:9b, as pertaining to; Heb. 9:27 (with 3645), as; Jas. 2:17 (with 1438), being alone; 1 Pt. 4:14, 14, on (one's) part.

2601. καταβιβάζω, katabibad′zō

Book	Oc.	bring down	Oc.	thrust down	Total
Mt.	1	11:23			1
Lk.			1	10:15	1
Total	1		1		2

2602. καταβολή, katabolē′

Book	Oc.	foundation	Oc.	to conceive (with 1519)	Total
Mt.	2	13:35; 25:34			2
Lk.	1	11:50			1
Jn.	1	17:24			1
Eph.	1	1:4			1
Heb.	2	4:3; 9:26	1	11:11	3
1 Pt.	1	1:20			1
Rev.	2	13:8; 17:8			2
Total	10		1		11

2603. καταβραβεύω katabrabeu′ō

Book	beguile of (one's) reward	Total
Col.	2:18	1

2604. καταγγελεύς katanggeleus′

Book	setter forth	Total
Ac.	17:18	1

2605. καταγγέλλω, katanggel′lō

Book	Oc.	preach	Oc.	shew	Oc.	declare	Oc.	teach	Oc.	speak of	Total
Ac.	6	4:2; 13:5, 38; 15:36; 17:3, 13	2	16:17; 26:23	1	17:23	1	16:21			10
Ro.									1	1:8	1
1 Co.	1	9:14	1	11:26	1	2:1					3
Phl.	2	1:16, 18									2
Col.	1	1:28									1
Total	10		3		2		1		1		17

2606. καταγελάω, katagela′ō

Book	laugh to scorn	Total
Mt.	9:24	1
Mk.	5:40	1
Lk.	8:53	1
Total		3

2607. καταγινώσκω, katagino̅'sko̅

Book	Oc.	condemn	Oc.	blame	Total
Gal.			1	2:11	1
1 Jn.	2	3:20, 21			2
Total	2		1		3

2608. κατάγνυμι, katag'numi

Book	break	Total
Mt.	12:20	1
Jn.	19:31, 32, 33	3
Total		4

2610. καταγωνίζομαι katago̅nid'zomai

Book	subdue	Total
Ro.	11:33	1

2609. κατάγω, katag'o̅

Book	Oc.	bring down	Oc.	land	Oc.	bring	Oc.	bring forth	Oc.	touch	Total
Lk.					1	5:11					1
Ac.	4	9:30; 22:30; 23:15, 20	2	21:3; 28:12			1	23:28	1	27:3	8
Ro.	1	10:6									1
Total	5		2		1		1		1		10

2611. καταδέω, katade'o̅

Book	bind up	Total
Lk.	10:34	1

2612. κατάδηλος, katad'e̱los

Book	evident	Total
Heb.	7:15	1

2613. καταδικάζω, katadikad'zo̅

Book	condemn	Total
Mt.	12:7, 37	2
Lk.	6:37, 37	2
Jas.	5:6	1
Total		5

2614. καταδιώκω, katadio̅'ko̅

Book	follow after	Total
Mk.	1:36	1

2615. καταδουλόω, katadoulo'o̅

Book	bring into bondage	Total
2 Co.	11:20	1
Gal.	2:4	1
Total		2

2616. καταδυναστεύω katadunasteu'o̅

Book	oppress	Total
Ac.	10:38	1
Jas.	2:6	1
Total		2

2617. καταισχύνω, kataischu'no̅

Book	Oc.	ashamed	Oc.	confound	Oc.	dishonour	Oc.	shame	Total
Lk.	1	13:17							1
Ro.	3	5:5; 9:33; 10:11							3
1 Co.			2	1:27, 27	2	11:4, 5	1	11:22	5
2 Co.	2	7:14; 9:4							2
1 Pt.	1	3:16	1	2:6					2
Total	7		3		2		1		13

2618. κατακαίω, katakai'o̅

Book	Oc.	burn	Oc.	burn up	Oc.	burn utterly	Total
Mt.	2	13:30, 40	1	3:12			3
Lk.	1	3:17					1
Ac.	1	19:19					1
1 Co.	1	3:15					1
Heb.	1	13:11					1
2 Pt.			1	3:10			1
Rev.	1	17:16	2	8:7, 7	1	18:8	4
Total	7		4		1		12

2619. κατακαλύπτω katakalup'to̅

Book	cover	Total
1 Co.	11:6, 6, 7	3

2620. κατακαυχάομαι, katakaucha'omai

Book	Oc.	boast against	Oc.	rejoice against	Oc.	glory	Oc.	boast	Total
Ro.	1	11:18a					1	11:18b	2
Jas.			1	2:13	1	3:14			2
Total	1		1		1		1		4

2621. κατάκειμαι, katak'eimai

Book	Oc.	lie	Oc.	sit at meat	Oc.	keep	Oc.	sat down (with 2258)	Total
Mk.	2	1:30; 2:4	2	2:15; 14:3					4
Lk.	1	5:25					1	5:29	2
Jn.	2	5:3, 6							2
Ac.	1	28:8			1	9:33			2
1 Co.			1	8:10					1
Total	6		3		1		1		11

2622. κατακλάω, katakla'o̅

Book	break	Total
Mk.	6:41	1
Lk.	9:16	1
Total		2

2623. κατακλείω, kataklei'o̅

Book	shut up	Total
Lk.	3:20	1
Ac.	26:10	1
Total		2

2624. κατακληροδοτέω katakle̱rodote'o̅

Book	divide by lot	Total
Ac.	13:19	1

2625. κατακλίνω, katakli'no̅

Book	Oc.	sit down	Oc.	sit at meat	Oc.	make sit down	Total
Lk.	1	14:8	1	24:30	1	9:14	3

2626. κατακλύζω, katak lud'zo̅

Book	overflow	Total
2 Pt.	3:6	1

2627. κατακλυσμός, kataklusmos'

Book	flood	Total
Mt.	24:38, 39	2
Lk.	17:27	1
2 Pt.	2:5	1
Total		4

2628. κατακολουθέω, katakolouthe'o̅

Book	Oc.	follow after	Oc.	follow	Total
Lk.	1	23:55			1
Ac.			1	16:17	1
Total	1		1		2

2629. κατακόπτω, katakop'to̅

Book	cut	Total
Mk.	5:5	1

2630. κατακρημνίζω katakre̱mnid'zo̅

Book	cast down headlong	Total
Lk.	4:29	1

2631. κατάκριμα, katak'rima

Book	condemnation	Total
Ro.	5:16, 18; 8:1	3

2632. κατακρίνω, katakri'no̅

Book	Oc.	condemn	Oc.	damn	Total
Mt.	4	12:41, 42; 20:18; 27:3			4
Mk.	2	10:33; 14:64	1	16:16	3
Lk.	2	11:31, 32			2
Jn.	2	8:10, 11			2
Ro.	3	2:1; 8:3, 34	1	14:23	4
1 Co.	1	11:32			1
Heb.	1	11:7			1
Jas.	1	5:9			1
2 Pt.	1	2:6			1
Total	17		2		19

2633. κατάκρισις, katak'risis

Book	Oc.	condemnation	Oc.	condemn	Total
2 Co.	1	3:9	1	7:3	2

2634. κατακυριεύω, katakurieu'o̅

Book	Oc.	exercise dominion over	Oc.	overcome	Oc.	be lord over	Oc.	exercise lordship over	Total
Mt.	1	20:25							1
Mk.							1	10:42	1
Ac.			1	19:16					1
1 Pt.					1	5:3			1
Total	1		1		1		1		4

2637. κατάλαλος, katal'alos

Book	backbiter	Total
Ro.	1:30	1

2635. καταλαλέω, katalale'o̅

Book	Oc.	speak evil of	Oc.	speak against	Total
Jas.	3	4:11, 11, 11			3
1 Pt.	1	3:16	1	2:12	2
Total	4		1		5

2636. καταλαλία, katalali'a

Book	Oc.	backbiting	Oc.	evil speaking	Total
2 Co.	1	12:20			1
1 Pt.			1	2:1	1
Total	1		1		2

2638. καταλαμβάνω, katalamban'ō

Book	Oc.	take	Oc.	apprehend	Oc.	comprehend	Oc.	perceive	Oc.	come upon	Oc.	overtake	Oc.	find	Oc.	attain	Oc.	obtain	Total
Mk.	1	9:18																	1
Jn.	2	8:3, 4			1	1:5			1	12:35									4
Ac.							2	4:13; 10:34					1	25:25					3
Ro.															1	9:30			1
1 Co.																	1	9:24	1
Eph.					1	3:18													1
Phl.			3	3:12, 12, 13															3
1 Th.											1	5:4							1
Total	3		3		2		2		1		1		1		1		1		15

2639. καταλέγω, kataleg'ō

Book	take into the number	Total
1 Ti.	5:9	1

2640. κατάλειμμα, katal'eimma

Book	remnant	Total
Ro.	9:27	1

2642. καταλιθάζω, katalithad'zō

Book	stone	Total
Lk.	20:6	1

2644. καταλλάσσω, katallas'sō

Book	reconcile	Total
Ro.	5:10, 10	2
1 Co.	7:11	1
2 Co.	5:18, 19, 20	3
Total		6

2641. καταλείπω, katalei'pō

Book	Oc.	leave	Oc.	forsake	Oc.	reserve	Total
Mt.	4	4:13; 16:4; 19:5; 21:17					4
Mk.	3	10:7; 12:19; 14:52					3
Lk.	4	5:28; 10:40; 15:4; 20:31					4
Jn.	1	8:9					1
Ac.	6	2:31; 6:2; 18:19; 21:3; 24:27; 25:14					6
Ro.					1	11:4	1
Eph.	1	5:31					1
1 Th.	1	3:1					1
Tit.	1	1:5					1
Heb.	1	4:1	1	11:27			2
2 Pt.			1	2:15			1
Total	22		2		1		25

2643. καταλλαγή, katallage'

Book	Oc.	reconciliation	Oc.	atonement	Oc.	reconciling	Total
Ro.			1	5:11	1	11:15	2
2 Co.	2	5:18, 19					2
Total	2		1		1		4

2646. κατάλυμα, katal'uma

Book	Oc.	guestchamber	Oc.	inn	Total
Mk.	1	14:14			1
Lk.	1	22:11	1	2:7	2
Total	2		1		3

2645. κατάλοιπος, katal'oipos

Book	residue	Total
Ac.	15:17	1

2648. καταμανθάνω katamanthan'ō

Book	consider	Total
Mt.	6:28	1

2649. καταμαρτυρέω katamarture'ō

Book	witness against	Total
Mt.	26:62; 27:13	2
Mk.	14:60; 15:4	2
Total		4

2650. καταμένω, katamen'ō

Book	abode (with 2258)	Total
Ac.	1:13	1

2647. καταλύω, katalu'ō

Book	Oc.	destroy	Oc.	throw down	Oc.	lodge	Oc.	guest	Oc.	come to nought	Oc.	overthrow	Oc.	dissolve	Total
Mt.	4	5:17, 17; 26:61; 27:40	1	24:2											5
Mk.	2	14:58; 15:29	1	13:2											3
Lk.			1	21:6	1	9:12	1	19:7							3
Ac.	1	6:14							1	5:38	1	5:39			3
Ro.	1	14:20													1
2 Co.													1	5:1	1
Gal.	1	2:18													1
Total	9		3		1		1		1		1		1		17

2651. καταμόνας, katamon'as

Book	alone	Total
Mk.	4:10	1
Lk.	9:18	1
Total		2

2652. κατανάθεμα, katanath'ema

Book	curse	Total
Rev.	22:3	1

2653. καταναθεματίζω katanathematid'zō

Book	curse	Total
Mt.	26:74	1

2654. καταναλίσκω, katanalis'kō

Book	consume	Total
Heb.	12:29	1

2655. καταναρκάω, katanarka'ō

Book	Oc.	be burdensome	Oc.	be chargeable	Total
2 Co.	2	12:13, 14	1	11:9	3

2656. κατανεύω, kataneu'ō

Book	beckon	Total
Lk.	5:7	1

2657. κατανοέω, katanoe'ō

Book	Oc.	consider	Oc.	behold	Oc.	perceive	Oc.	discover	Total
Mt.	1	7:3							1
Lk.	2	12:24, 27			2	6:41; 20:23			4
Ac.	1	11:6	2	7:31, 32			1	27:39	4
Ro.	1	4:19							1
Heb.	2	3:1; 10:24							2
Jas.			2	1:23, 24					2
Total	7		4		2		1		14

2658. καταντάω, katanta'ō

Book	Oc.	come	Oc.	attain	Total
Ac.	8	16:1; 18:19, 24; 20:15; 21:7; 25:13; 26:7; 28:13	1	27:12	9
1 Co.	2	10:11; 14:36			2
Eph.	1	4:13			1
Phl.			1	3:11	1
Total	11		2		13

2661. καταξιόω, kataxio'ō

Book	Oc.	count worthy	Oc.	account worthy	Total
Lk.			2	20:35; 21:36	2
Ac.	1	5:41			1
2 Th.	1	1:5			1
Total	2		2		4

2659. κατάνυξις, katan'uxis

Book	slumber	Total
Ro.	11:8	1

2660. κατανύσσω, katanus'sō

Book	prick	Total
Ac.	2:37	1

2662. καταπατέω, katapate'ō

Book	Oc.	tread underfoot	Oc.	trample	Oc.	tread down	Oc.	tread	Total
Mt.	1	5:13	1	7:6					2
Lk.					1	8:5	1	12:1	2
Heb.	1	10:29							1
Total	2		1		1		1		5

2663. κατάπαυσις, katap'ausis

Book	rest	Total
Ac.	7:49	1
Heb.	3:11, 18; 4:1, 3, 3, 5, 10, 11	8
Total		9

2664. καταπαύω, katapau'ō

Book	Oc.	restrain	Oc.	rest	Oc.	give rest	Oc.	cease	Total
Ac.	1	14:18							1
Heb.			1	4:4	1	4:8	1	4:10	3
Total	1		1		1		1		4

2665. καταπέτασμα katapet'asma

Book	veil	Total
Mt.	27:51	1
Mk.	15:38	1
Lk.	23:45	1
Heb.	6:19; 9:3; 10:20	3
Total		6

2666. καταπίνω, katapi'nō

Book	Oc.	swallow up	Oc.	swallow	Oc.	drown	Oc.	devour	Total
Mt.			1	23:24					1
1 Co.	1	15:54							1
2 Co.	2	2:7; 5:4							2
Heb.					1	11:29			1
1 Pt.							1	5:8	1
Rev.	1	12:16							1
Total	4		1		1		1		7

2667. καταπίπτω, katapip'tō

Book	Oc.	fall	Oc.	fall down	Total
Ac.	1	26:14	1	28:6	2

2672. καταράομαι katara'omai

Book	curse	Total
Mt.	5:44; 25:41	2
Mk.	11:21	1
Lk.	6:28	1
Ro.	12:14	1
Jas.	3:9	1
Total		6

2668. καταπλέω, katapleʹō

Book	arrive	Total
Lk.	8:26	1

2669. καταπονέω, kataponeʹō

Book	Oc.	oppress	Oc.	vex	Total
Ac.	1	7:24			1
2 Pt.			1	2:7	1
Total	1		1		2

2670. καταποντίζω, katapontid'zō

Book	Oc.	sink	Oc.	drown	Total
Mt.	1	14:30	1	18:6	2

2671. κατάρα, katar'a

Book	Oc.	curse	Oc.	cursing	Oc.	cursed	Total
Gal.	3	3:10, 13, 13					3
Heb.			1	6:8			1
Jas.			1	3:10			1
2 Pt.					1	2:14	1
Total	3		2		1		6

2673. καταργέω, katarge'ō

Book	Oc.	destroy	Oc.	do away	Oc.	abolish	Oc.	cumber	Oc.	loose	Oc.	cease	Oc.	fail	Oc.	deliver	Oc.	Misc.	Total
Lk.							1	13:7											1
Ro.	1	6:6							1	7:2					1	7:6	3	3:3, 31; 4:14	6
1 Co.	2	6:13; 15:26	1	13:10									1	13:8a			5	1:28; 2:6; 13:8b, 11; 15:24	9
2 Co.			2	3:11, 14	1	3:13											1	3:7	4
Gal.											1	5:11					2	3:17; 5:4	3
Eph.					1	2:15													1
2 Th.	1	2:8																	1
2 Ti.					1	1:10													1
Heb.	1	2:14																	1
Total	5		3		3		1		1		1		1		1		11		27

Miscellaneous: Ro. 3:3, make without effect; Ro. 3:31, make void; Ro. 4:14, make of none effect; 1 Co. 1:28, bring to nought; 1 Co. 2:6, come to nought; 1 Co. 13:8b, vanish away; 1 Co. 13:11, put away; 1 Co. 15:24, put down; 2 Co. 3:7, be to be done away; Gal. 3:17, make of none effect; Gal. 5:4, become of no effect.

2674. καταριθμέω, katarithme'ō

Book	number	Total
Ac.	1:17	1

2676. κατάρτισις, katar'tisis

Book	perfection	Total
2 Co.	13:9	1

2677. καταρτισμός, katartismos'

Book	perfecting	Total
Eph.	4:12	1

2678. κατασείω, katasei'ō

Book	beckon	Total
Ac.	12:17; 13:16; 19:33; 21:40	4

2675. καταρτίζω, katartid'zō

Book	Oc.	perfect	Oc.	make perfect	Oc.	mend	Oc.	be perfect	Oc.	fit	Oc.	frame	Oc.	prepare	Oc.	restore	Oc.	perfectly joined together	Total
Mt.	1	21:16			1	4:21													2
Mk.					1	1:19													1
Lk.							1	6:40											1
Ro.									1	9:22									1
1 Co.																	1	1:10	1
2 Co.							1	13:11											1
Gal.															1	6:1			1
1 Th.	1	3:10																	1
Heb.			1	13:21							1	11:3	1	10:5					3
1 Pt.			1	5:10															1
Total	2		2		2		2		1		1		1		1		1		13

2679. κατασκάπτω, kataskap'tō

Book	Oc.	ruin	Oc.	dig down	Total
Ac.	1	15:16			1
Ro.			1	11:3	1
Total	1		1		2

2680. κατασκευάζω, kataskeuad'zō

Book	Oc.	prepare	Oc.	build	Oc.	make	Oc.	ordain	Total
Mt.	1	11:10							1
Mk.	1	1:2							1
Lk.	2	1:17; 7:27							2
Heb.	1	11:7	3	3:3, 4, 4	1	9:2	1	9:6	6
1 Pt.	1	3:20							1
Total	6		3		1		1		11

2681. κατασκηνόω, kataskeno'ō

Book	Oc.	lodge	Oc.	rest	Total
Mt.	1	13:32			1
Mk.	1	4:32			1
Lk.	1	13:19			1
Ac.			1	2:26	1
Total	3		1		4

2682. κατασκήνωσις kataske'nōsis

Book	nest	Total
Mt.	8:20	1
Lk.	9:58	1
Total		2

2683. κατασκιάζω, kataskiad'zō

Book	shadow	Total
Heb.	9:5	1

2684. κατασκοπέω, kataskope'ō

Book	spy out	Total
Gal.	2:4	1

2685. κατάσκοπος, katas'kopos

Book	spy	Total
Heb.	11:31	1

2686. κατασοφίζομαι, katasophid'zomai

Book	deal subtilly with	Total
Ac.	7:19	1

2687. καταστέλλω, katastel'lō

Book	Oc.	appease	Oc.	quiet	Total
Ac.	1	19:35	1	19:36	2

2688. κατάστημα, katas'tema

Book	behaviour	Total
Tit.	2:3	1

2689. καταστολή, katastolē'

Book	apparel	Total
1 Ti.	2:9	1

2690. καταστρέφω, katastreph'ō

Book	overthrow	Total
Mt.	21:12	1
Mk.	11:15	1
Total		2

2691. καταστρηνιάω, katastrēnia'ō

Book	begin to wax wanton against	Total
1 Ti.	5:11	1

2692. καταστροφή, katastrophē'

Book	Oc.	subverting	Oc.	overthrow	Total
2 Ti.	1	2:14			1
2 Pt.			1	2:6	1
Total	1		1		2

2693. καταστρώννυμι, katastrōn'numi

Book	overthrow	Total
1 Co.	10:5	1

2694. κατασύρω, katasu'rō

Book	hale	Total
Lk.	12:58	1

2695. κατασφάττω, katasphat'tō

Book	slay	Total
Lk.	19:27	1

2696. κατασφραγίζω, katasphragid'zō

Book	seal	Total
Rev.	5:1	1

2697. κατάσχεσις, katas'chesis

Book	possession	Total
Ac.	7:5, 45	2

2699. κατατομή, katatomē'

Book	concision	Total
Phl.	3:2	1

2698. κατατίθημι, katatith'ēmi

Book	Oc.	lay	Oc.	shew	Oc.	do	Total
Mk.	1	15:46					1
Ac.			1	24:27	1	25:9	2
Total	1		1		1		3

2700. κατατοξεύω, katatoxeu'ō

Book	thrust through	Total
Heb.	12:20	1

2701. κατατρέχω, katatrech'ō

Book	run down	Total
Ac.	21:32	1

2702. καταφάγω, kataphag'ō

Book	Oc.	devour	Oc.	eat up	Oc.	devour up	Total
Mt.					1	13:4	1
Mk.	2	8:5; 15:30			1	4:4	3
Jn.			1	2:17			1
Rev.	2	12:4; 20:9	2	10:9, 10			4
Total	4		3		2		9

2703. καταφέρω, katapher'ō

Book	Oc.	fall	Oc.	sink down	Oc.	give	Total
Ac.	1	20:9a	1	20:9b	1	26:10	3

2704. καταφεύγω, katapheu'gō

Book	flee	Total
Ac.	14:6	1
Heb.	6:18	1
Total		2

2705. καταφθείρω, kataphthei'rō

Book	Oc.	corrupt	Oc.	utterly perish	Total
2 Ti.	1	3:8			1
2 Pt.			1	2:12	1
Total	1		1		2

2706. καταφιλέω, kataphile'ō

Book	kiss	Total
Mt.	26:49	1
Mk.	14:45	1
Lk.	7:38, 45; 15:20	3
Ac.	20:37	1
Total		6

2707. καταφρονέω, kataphrone'ō

Book	despise	Total
Mt.	6:24; 18:10	2
Lk.	16:13	1
Ro.	2:4	1
1 Co.	11:22	1
1 Ti.	4:12; 6:2	2
Heb.	12:2	1
2 Pt.	2:10	1
Total		9

2708. καταφροντής, kataphrontēs'

Book	despiser	Total
Ac.	13:41	1

2710. καταχθόνιος, katachthon'ios

Book	under the earth	Total
Phl.	2:10	1

2712. καταψύχω, katapsu'chō

Book	cool	Total
Lk.	16:24	1

2709. καταχέω, katache'ō

Book	pour	Total
Mt.	26:7	1
Mk.	14:3	1
Total		2

2711. καταχράομαι, katachra'omai

Book	abuse	Total
1 Co.	7:31; 9:18	2

2713. κατείδωλος, katei'dōlos

Book	wholly given to idolatry	Total
Ac.	17:16	1

2714. κατέναντι, katen'anti

Book	Oc.	over against	Oc.	before	Total
Mk.	3	11:2; 12:41; 13:3			3
Lk.	1	19:30			1
Ro.			1	4:17	1
Total	4		1		5

2715. κατενώπιον, katenō'pion

Book	Oc.	before	Oc.	in the sight of	Oc.	in (one's) sight	Oc.	before the presence of	Total
2 Co.	1	12:19	1	2:17					2
Eph.	1	1:4							1
Col.					1	1:22			1
Jd.							1	1:24	1
Total	2		1		1		1		5

2716. κατεξουσιάζω, katexousiad'zō

Book	exercise authority upon	Total
Mt.	20:25	1
Mk.	10:42	1
Total		2

2718. κατέρχομαι, kater'chomai

Book	Oc.	come down	Oc.	come	Oc.	go down	Oc.	depart	Oc.	land	Oc.	descend	Total
Lk.	2	4:31; 9:37											2
Ac.	3	9:32; 15:1; 21:10	3	11:27; 18:5; 27:5	2	8:5; 12:19	1	13:4	1	18:22			10
Jas.											1	3:15	1
Total	5		3		2		1		1		1		13

2717. κατεργάζομαι, katergad'zomai

Book	Oc.	work	Oc.	do	Oc.	do deed	Oc.	to perform	Oc.	cause	Oc.	work out	Total
Ro.	6	1:27; 4:15; 5:3; 7:8, 13; 15:18	4	2:9; 7:15, 17, 20			1	7:18					11
1 Co.					1	5:3							1
2 Co.	6	4:17; 5:5; 7:10, 10, 11; 12:12							1	9:11			7
Eph.			1	6:13									1
Phl.											1	2:12	1
Jas.	2	1:3, 20											2
1 Pt.	1	4:3											1
Total	15		5		1		1		1		1		24

2719. κατεσθίω, katesthi'ō

Book	devour	Total
Mt.	23:14	1
Mk.	12:40	1
Lk.	20:47	1
2 Co.	11:20	1
Gal.	5:15	1
Rev.	11:5	1
Total		6

2720. κατευθύνω, kateuthu'nō

Book	Oc.	direct	Oc.	guide	Total
Lk.			1	1:79	1
1 Th.	1	3:11			1
2 Th.	1	3:5			1
Total	2		1		3

2721. κατεφίστημι, katephis'tēmi

Book	make insurrection against	Total
Ac.	18:12	1

2722. κατέχω, katech'ō

Book	Oc.	hold	Oc.	hold fast	Oc.	keep	Oc.	possess	Oc.	stay	Oc.	take	Oc.	have	Oc.	make	Oc.	Misc.	Total
Mt.																	1	21:38	1
Lk.					1	8:15			1	4:42	1	14:9							3
Jn.													1	5:4					1
Ac.															1	27:40			1
Ro.	2	1:18; 7:6																	2
1 Co.					1	11:2	1	7:30									1	15:2	3
2 Co.							1	6:10											1
1 Th.			1	5:21															1
2 Th.																	2	2:6, 7	2
Phe.																	1	1:13	1
Heb.	1	3:14	2	3:6; 10:23															3
Total	3		3		2		2		1		1		1		1		5		19

Miscellaneous: Mt. 21:38, seize on; 1 Co. 15:2, keep in memory; 2 Th. 2:6, withhold; 2 Th. 2:7, let; Phe. 1:13, retain.

2723. κατηγορέω, katēgore'ō

Book	Oc.	accuse	Oc.	object	Total
Mt.	2	12:10; 27:12			2
Mk.	2	3:2; 15:3			2
Lk.	4	11:54; 23:2, 10, 14			4
Jn.	3	5:45, 45; 8:6			3
Ac.	8	22:30; 24:2, 8, 13; 25:5, 11, 16; 28:19	1	24:19	9
Ro.	1	2:15			1
Rev.	1	12:10			1
Total	21		1		22

2724. κατηγορία, katēgori'a

Book	Oc.	accusation	Oc.	accused	Total
Lk.	1	6:7			1
Jn.	1	18:29			1
1 Ti.	1	5:19			1
Tit.			1	1:6	1
Total	3		1		4

2725. κατήγορος, katē'goros

Book	accuser	Total
Jn.	8:10	1
Ac.	23:30, 35; 24:8; 25:16, 18	5
Rev.	12:10	1
Total		7

2726. κατήφεια, katē'pheia

Book	heaviness	Total
Jas.	4:9	1

2727. κατηχέω, katēche'ō

Book	Oc.	instruct	Oc.	teach	Oc.	inform	Total
Lk.	1	1:4					1
Ac.	1	18:25			2	21:21, 24	3
Ro.	1	2:18					1
1 Co.			1	14:19			1
Gal.			2	6:6, 6			2
Total	3		3		2		8

2728. κατιόω, katio'ō

Book	canker	Total
Jas.	5:3	1

2729. κατισχύω, katischu'ō

Book	Oc.	prevail against	Oc.	prevail	Total
Mt.	1	16:18			1
Lk.			1	23:23	1
Total	1		1		2

2731. κατοίκησις, katoi'kēsis

Book	dwelling	Total
Mk.	5:3	1

2732. κατοικητήριον katoikēte'rion

Book	habitation	Total
Eph.	2:22	1
Rev.	18:2	1
Total		2

2730. κατοικέω, katoike'ō

Book	Oc.	dwell	Oc.	dweller	Oc.	inhabiter	Oc.	inhabitant	Total
Mt.	4	2:23; 4:13; 12:45; 23:21							4
Lk.	2	11:26; 13:4							2
Ac.	18	1:20; 2:5, 14; 4:16; 7:2, 4, 4, 48; 9:22, 32, 35; 11:29; 13:27; 17:24, 26; 19:10, 17; 22:12	2	1:19; 2:9					20
Eph.	1	3:17							1
Col.	2	1:19; 2:9							2
Heb.	1	11:9							1
Jas.	1	4:5							1
2 Pt.	1	3:13							1
Rev.	12	2:13, 13; 3:10; 6:10; 11:10, 10; 13:8, 12, 14, 14; 14:6; 17:8			2	8:13; 12:12	1	17:2	15
Total	42		2		2		1		47

2733. κατοικία, katoiki'a

Book	habitation	Total
Ac.	17:26	1

2734. κατοπτρίζομαι katoptrid'zomai

Book	behold as in a glass	Total
2 Co.	3:18	1

2735. κατόρθωμα, kator'thōma

Book	very worthy deed	Total
Ac.	24:2	1

2736a. κάτω, kat'ō

Book	Oc.	down	Oc.	beneath	Oc.	bottom	Total
Mt.	1	4:6			1	27:51	2
Mk.			1	14:66	1	15:38	2
Lk.	1	4:9					1
Jn.	2	8:6, 8	1	8:23			3
Ac.	1	20:9	1	2:19			2
Total	5		3		2		10

2736b. κατωτέρο, katōter'o

Book	under	Total
Mt.	2:16	1

Word 2736 has 11 occurrences.

2737. κατώτερος, katō'teros

Book	lower	Total
Eph.	4:9	1

2738. καῦμα, kau'ma

Book	heat	Total
Rev.	7:16; 16:9	2

2739. καυματίζω, kaumatid'zō

Book	scorch	Total
Mt.	13:6	1
Mk.	4:6	1
Rev.	16:8, 9	2
Total		4

2740. καῦσις, kau'sis

Book	to be burned (with 1519)	Total
Heb.	6:8	1

2741. καυσόω, kauso'ō

Book	with fervent heat	Total
2 Pt.	3:10, 12	2

2742. καύσων, kau'sōn

Book	Oc.	heat	Oc.	burning heat	Total
Mt.	1	20:12			1
Lk.	1	12:55			1
Jas.			1	1:11	1
Total	2		1		3

2743. καυτηριάζω, kauteriad'zō

Book	sear with a hot iron	Total
1 Ti.	4:2	1

2744. καυχάομαι, kaucha'omai

Book	Oc.	glory	Oc.	boast	Oc.	rejoice	Oc.	make boast	Oc.	joy	Total
Ro.	1	5:3			1	5:2	2	2:17, 23	1	5:11	5
1 Co.	5	1:29, 31, 31; 3:21; 4:7									5
2 Co.	14	5:12; 10:17, 17; 11:12, 18, 18, 30, 30; 12:1, 5, 5, 6, 9, 11	7	7:14; 9:2; 10:8, 13, 15, 16; 11:16							21
Gal.	2	6:13, 14									2
Eph.			1	2:9							1
Phl.					1	3:3					1
2 Th.	1	1:4									1
Jas.					2	1:9; 4:16					2
Total	23		8		4		2		1		38

2745. καύχημα, kau'chēma

Book	Oc.	rejoicing	Oc.	to glory	Oc.	glorying	Oc.	boasting	Oc.	rejoice	Total
Ro.			1	4:2							1
1 Co.			1	9:16	2	5:6; 9:15					3
2 Co.	1	1:14	1	5:12			1	9:3			3
Gal.	1	6:4									1
Phl.	1	1:26							1	2:16	2
Heb.	1	3:6									1
Total	4		3		2		1		1		11

2747. Κεγχρεαί, Kengchreai'

Book	Cenchrea	Total
Ac.	18:18	1
Ro.	16:1	1
Total		2

2746. καύχησις, kau'chēsis

Book	Oc.	boasting	Oc.	rejoicing	Oc.	glorying	Oc.	whereof I may glory	Total
Ro.	1	3:27					1	15:17	2
1 Co.			1	15:31					1
2 Co.	5	7:14; 8:24; 9:4; 11:10, 17	1	1:12	1	7:4			7
1 Th.			1	2:19					1
Jas.			1	4:16					1
Total	6		4		1		1		12

2748. Κεδρών, Kedrōn'

Book	Cedron	Total
Jn.	18:1	1

2749. κεῖμαι, kei'mai

Book	Oc.	lie	Oc.	be laid	Oc.	be set	Oc.	be appointed	Oc.	be	Oc.	be made	Oc.	laid up	Oc.	there	Total
Mt.	1	28:6	1	3:10	1	5:14											3
Lk.	2	2:12, 16	3	3:9; 23:53; 24:12	1	2:34							1	12:19			7
Jn.	4	20:5, 6, 7, 12	1	11:41	2	2:6; 19:29									1	21:9	8
1 Co.			1	3:11													1
2 Co.									1	3:15							1
Phl.					1	1:17											1
1 Th.							1	3:3									1
1 Ti.											1	1:9					1
1 Jn.	1	5:19															1
Rev.	1	21:16			1	4:2											2
Total	9		6		6		1		1		1		1		1		26

2750. κειρία, keiri'a

Book	graveclothes	Total
Jn.	11:44	1

2751. κείρω, kei'rō

Book	Oc.	shear	Oc.	shearer	Total
Ac.	1	18:18	1	8:32	2
1 Co.	2	11:6, 6			2
Total	3		1		4

2752. κέλευμα, kel'euma

Book	shout	Total
1 Th.	4:16	1

2753. κελεύω, keleu'ō

Book	Oc.	command	Oc.	at (one's) commandment	Oc.	give commandment	Oc.	bid	Total
Mt.	6	14:9, 19; 15:35; 18:25; 27:58, 64			1	8:18	1	14:28	8
Lk.	1	18:40							1
Ac.	17	4:15; 5:34; 8:38; 12:19; 16:22; 21:33, 34; 22:24, 30; 23:3, 10, 35; 24:8; 25:6, 17, 21; 27:43	1	25:23					18
Total	24		1		1		1		27

2754. κενοδοξία, kenodoxi'a

Book	vainglory	Total
Phl.	2:3	1

2755. κενόδοξος, kenod'oxos

Book	desirous of vain glory	Total
Gal.	5:26	1

2756. κενός, kenos'

Book	Oc.	vain	Oc.	in vain	Oc.	empty	Oc.	vain things	Total
Mk.					1	12:3			1
Lk.					3	1:53; 20:10, 11			3
Ac.							1	4:25	1
1 Co.	2	15:14, 14	2	15:10, 58					4
2 Co.	1	6:1							1
Gal.	1	2:2							1
Eph.	1	5:6							1
Phl.	2	2:16, 16							2
Col.	1	2:8							1
1 Th.	1	3:5	1	2:1					2
Jas.			1	2:20					1
Total	9		4		4		1		18

2757. κενοφωνία, kenophōni'a

Book	vain babblings	Total
1 Ti.	6:20	1
2 Ti.	2:16	1
Total		2

2760. κεντυρίων, kenturi'ōn

Book	centurion	Total
Mk.	15:39, 44, 45	3

2758. κενόω, keno'ō

Book	Oc.	make void	Oc.	make of none effect	Oc.	make of no reputation	Oc.	be in vain	Total
Ro.	1	4:14							1
1 Co.	1	9:15	1	1:17					2
2 Co.							1	9:3	1
Phl.					1	2:7			1
Total	2		1		1		1		5

2759. κέντρον, ken'tron

Book	Oc.	sting	Oc.	prick	Total
Ac.			2	9:5; 26:14	2
1 Co.	2	15:55, 56			2
Rev.	1	9:10			1
Total	3		2		5

2761. κενῶς, kenōs'

Book	in vain	Total
Jas.	4:5	1

2762. κεραία, kerai'a

Book	tittle	Total
Mt.	5:18	1
Lk.	16:17	1
Total		2

2763. κεραμεύς, kerameus'

Book	potter	Total
Mt.	27:7, 10	2
Ro.	9:21	1
Total		3

2764. κεραμικός, keramikos'

Book	of a potter	Total
Rev.	2:27	1

2765. κεράμιον, keram'ion

Book	pitcher	Total
Mk.	14:13	1
Lk.	22:10	1
Total		2

2766. κέραμος, ker'amos

Book	tiling	Total
Lk.	5:19	1

2767. κεράννυμι, keran'numi

Book	Oc.	fill	Oc.	pour out	Total
Rev.	2	18:6, 6	1	14:10	3

2768. κέρας, ker'as

Book	horn	Total
Lk.	1:69	1
Rev.	5:6; 9:13; 12:3; 13:1, 1, 11; 17:3, 7, 12, 16	10
Total		11

2769. κεράτιον, kerat'ion

Book	husk	Total
Lk.	15:16	1

2770. κερδαίνω, kerdai'nō

Book	Oc.	gain	Oc.	win	Oc.	get gain	Total
Mt.	5	16:26; 18:15; 25:17, 20, 22					5
Mk.	1	8:36					1
Lk.	1	9:25					1
Ac.	1	27:21					1
1 Co.	5	9:19, 20, 20, 21, 22					5
Phl.			1	3:8			1
Jas.					1	4:13	1
1 Pt.			1	3:1			1
Total	13		2		1		16

2771. κέρδος, ker'dos

Book	Oc.	gain	Oc.	lucre	Total
Phl.	2	1:21; 3:7			2
Tit.			1	1:11	1
Total	2		1		3

2772. κέρμα, ker'ma

Book	money	Total
Jn.	2:15	1

2773. κερματιστής, kermatistẹs'

Book	changer of money	Total
Jn.	2:14	1

2774. κεφάλαιον, kephal'aion

Book	sum	Total
Ac.	22:28	1
Heb.	8:1	1
Total		2

2775. κεφαλαιόω, kephalaio'ō

Book	wound in the head	Total
Mk.	12:4	1

2776. κεφαλή, kephalẹ'

Book	head	Total
Mt.	5:36; 6:17; 8:20; 10:30; 14:8, 11; 21:42; 26:7; 27:29, 30, 37, 39	12
Mk.	6:24, 25, 27, 28; 12:10; 14:3; 15:19, 29	8
Lk.	7:38, 44, 46; 9:58; 12:7; 20:17; 21:18, 28	8
Jn.	13:9; 19:2, 30; 20:7, 12	5
Ac.	4:11; 18:6, 18; 21:24; 27:34	5
Ro.	12:20	1
1 Co.	11:3, 3, 3, 4, 4, 5, 5, 7, 10; 12:21	10
Eph.	1:22; 4:15; 5:23, 23	4
Col.	1:18; 2:10, 19	3
1 Pt.	2:7	1
Rev.	1:14; 4:4; 9:7, 17, 17, 19; 10:1; 12:1, 3, 3; 13:1, 1, 3; 14:14; 17:3, 7, 9; 18:19; 19:12	19
Total		76

2777. κεφαλίς, kephalis'

Book	volume	Total
Heb.	10:7	1

2778. κῆνσος, kẹn'sos

Book	tribute	Total
Mt.	17:25; 22:17, 19	3
Mk.	12:14	1
Total		4

2779. κῆπος, kẹ'pos

Book	garden	Total
Lk.	13:19	1
Jn.	18:1, 26; 19:41, 41	4
Total		5

2780. κηπουρός, kẹpouros'

Book	gardener	Total
Jn.	20:15	1

2781. κηρίον, kẹri'on

Book	honeycomb (with 3193)	Total
Lk.	24:42	1

2782. κήρυγμα, kẹ'rugma

Book	preaching	Total
Mt.	12:41	1
Lk.	11:32	1
Ro.	16:25	1
1 Co.	1:21; 2:4; 15:14	3
2 Ti.	4:17	1
Tit.	1:3	1
Total		8

2783. κήρυξ, kẹ'rux

Book	preacher	Total
1 Ti.	2:7	1
2 Ti.	1:11	1
2 Pt.	2:5	1
Total		3

2785. κῆτος, kẹ'tos

Book	whale	Total
Mt.	12:40	1

2784. κηρύσσω, kẹrus'sō

Book	Oc.	preach	Oc.	publish	Oc.	proclaim	Oc.	preached (with 2258)	Oc.	preacher	Total
Mt.	9	3:1; 4:17, 23; 9:35; 10:7, 27; 11:1; 24:14; 26:13									9
Mk.	9	1:4, 7, 14, 38; 3:14; 6:12; 14:9; 16:15, 20	4	1:45; 5:20; 7:36; 13:10			1	1:39			14
Lk.	6	3:3; 4:18, 19; 8:1; 9:2; 24:47	1	8:39	1	12:3	1	4:44			9
Ac.	8	8:5; 9:20; 10:37, 42; 15:21; 19:13; 20:25; 28:31									8
Ro.	3	2:21; 10:8, 15							1	10:14	4
1 Co.	4	1:23; 9:27; 15:11, 12									4
2 Co.	4	1:19; 4:5; 11:4, 4									4
Gal.	2	2:2; 5:11									2
Phl.	1	1:15									1
Col.	1	1:23									1
1 Th.	1	2:9									1
1 Ti.	1	3:16									1
2 Ti.	1	4:2									1
1 Pt.	1	3:19									1
Rev.					1	5:2					1
Total	51		5		2		2		1		61

2786. Κηφᾶς, Kẹphas'

Book	Cephas	Total
Jn.	1:42	1
1 Co.	1:12; 3:22; 9:5; 15:5	4
Gal.	2:9	1
Total		6

2787. κιβωτός, kibōtos'

Book	ark	Total
Mt.	24:38	1
Lk.	17:27	1
Heb.	9:4; 11:7	2
1 Pt.	3:20	1
Rev.	11:19	1
Total		6

2788. κιθάρα, kithar'a

Book	harp	Total
1 Co.	14:7	1
Rev.	5:8; 14:2; 15:2	3
Total		4

2789. κιθαρίζω, kitharid'zō

Book	to harp	Total
1 Co.	14:7	1
Rev.	14:2	1
Total		2

2790. κιθαρῳδός, kitharōdos'

Book	harper	Total
Rev.	14:2; 18:22	2

2791. Κιλικία, Kiliki'a

Book	Cilicia	Total
Ac.	6:9; 15:23, 41; 21:39; 22:3; 23:34; 27:5	7
Gal.	1:21	1
Total		8

2792. κινάμωμον, kinam'ōmon

Book	cinnamon	Total
Rev.	18:13	1

2794. κίνδυνος, kin'dunos

Book	peril	Total
Ro.	8:35	1
2 Co.	11:26, 26, 26, 26, 26, 26, 26, 26	8
Total		9

2793. κινδυνεύω, kinduneu'ō

Book	Oc.	be in danger	Oc.	be in jeopardy	Oc.	stand in jeopardy	Total
Lk.			1	8:23			1
Ac.	2	19:27, 40					2
1 Co.					1	15:30	1
Total	2		1		1		4

2795. κινέω, kine'ō

Book	Oc.	move	Oc.	wag	Oc.	remove	Oc.	mover	Total
Mt.	1	23:4	1	27:39					2
Mk.			1	15:29					1
Ac.	2	17:28; 21:30					1	24:5	3
Rev.	1	6:14			1	2:5			2
Total	4		2		1		1		8

2796. κίνησις, kin'ēsis

Book	moving	Total
Jn.	5:3	1

2797. Κίς, Kis

Book	Cis	Total
Ac.	13:21	1

2799. κλαίω, klai'ō

Book	Oc.	weep	Oc.	bewail	Total
Mt.	2	2:18; 26:75			2
Mk.	4	5:38, 39; 14:72; 16:10			4
Lk.	11	6:21, 25; 7:13, 32, 38; 8:52, 52; 19:41; 22:62; 23:28, 28			11
Jn.	8	11:31, 33, 33; 16:20; 20:11, 11, 13, 15			8
Ac.	2	9:39; 21:13			2
Ro.	2	12:15, 15			2
1 Co.	2	7:30, 30			2
Phl.	1	3:18			1
Jas.	2	4:9; 5:1			2
Rev.	5	5:4, 5; 18:11, 15, 19	1	18:9	6
Total	39		1		40

2798. κλάδος, klad'os

Book	branch	Total
Mt.	13:32; 21:8; 24:32	3
Mk.	4:32; 13:28	2
Lk.	13:19	1
Ro.	11:16, 17, 18, 19, 21	5
Total		11

2800. κλάσις, klas'is

Book	breaking	Total
Lk.	24:35	1
Ac.	2:42	1
Total		2

2801. κλάσμα, klas'ma

Book	Oc.	fragment	Oc.	broken meat	Total
Mt.	1	14:20	1	15:37	2
Mk.	3	6:43; 8:19, 20	1	8:8	4
Lk.	1	9:17			1
Jn.	2	6:12, 13			2
Total	7		2		9

2802. Κλαύδη, Klau'dē

Book	Clauda	Total
Ac.	27:16	1

2803. Κλαυδία, Klaudi'a

Book	Claudia	Total
2 Ti.	4:21	1

2804. Κλαύδιος, Klau'dios

Book	Oc.	Claudius (Caesar)	Oc.	Claudius (Lysias)	Total
Ac.	2	11:28; 18:2	1	23:26	3

2805. κλαυθμός, klauthmos'

Book	Oc.	weeping	Oc.	wailing	Oc.	weep	Total
Mt.	5	2:18; 8:12; 22:13; 24:51; 25:30	2	13:42, 50			7
Lk.	1	13:28					1
Ac.					1	20:37	1
Total	6		2		1		9

2806. κλάω, kla'ō

Book	break	Total
Mt.	14:19; 15:36; 26:26	3
Mk.	8:6, 19; 14:22	3
Lk.	22:19; 24:30	2
Ac.	2:46; 20:7, 11; 27:35	4
1 Co.	10:16; 11:24, 24	3
Total		15

2807. κλείς, kleis

Book	key	Total
Mt.	16:19	1
Lk.	11:52	1
Rev.	1:18; 3:7; 9:1; 20:1	4
Total		6

2811. κλέος, kle'os

Book	glory	Total
1 Pt.	2:20	1

2808. κλείω, klei'ō

Book	Oc.	shut	Oc.	shut up	Total
Mt.	2	6:6; 25:10	1	23:13	3
Lk.	1	11:7	1	4:25	2
Jn.	2	20:19, 26			2
Ac.	2	5:23; 21:30			2
1 Jn.			1	3:17	1
Rev.	5	3:7, 7, 8; 11:6; 21:25	1	20:3	6
Total	12		4		16

2809. κλέμμα, klem'ma

Book	theft	Total
Rev.	9:21	1

2810. Κλεόπας, Kleop'as

Book	Cleopas	Total
Lk.	24:18	1

2812. κλέπτης, klep'tēs

Book	thief	Total
Mt.	6:19, 20; 24:43	3
Lk.	12:33, 39	2
Jn.	10:1, 8, 10; 12:6	4
1 Co.	6:10	1
1 Th.	5:2, 4	2
1 Pt.	4:15	1
2 Pt.	3:10	1
Rev.	3:3; 16:15	2
Total		16

2813. κλέπτω, klep'tō

Book	steal	Total
Mt.	6:19, 20; 19:18; 27:64; 28:13	5
Mk.	10:19	1
Lk.	18:20	1
Jn.	10:10	1
Ro.	2:21, 21; 13:9	3
Eph.	4:28	1
Total		12

2814. κλῆμα, klē'ma

Book	branch	Total
Jn.	15:2, 4, 5, 6	4

2815. Κλήμης, Klē'mēs

Book	Clement	Total
Phl.	4:3	1

2816. κληρονομέω, klēronome'ō

Book	Oc.	inherit	Oc.	be heir	Oc.	obtain by inheritance	Total
Mt.	3	5:5; 19:29; 25:34					3
Mk.	1	10:17					1
Lk.	2	10:25; 18:18					2
1 Co.	4	6:9, 10; 15:50, 50					4
Gal.	1	5:21	1	4:30			2
Heb.	2	6:12; 12:17	1	1:14	1	1:4	4
1 Pt.	1	3:9					1
Rev.	1	21:7					1
Total	15		2		1		18

2817. κληρονομία, klēronomi'a

Book	inheritance	Total
Mt.	21:38	1
Mk.	12:7	1
Lk.	12:13; 20:14	2
Ac.	7:5; 20:32	2
Gal.	3:18	1
Eph.	1:14, 18; 5:5	3
Col.	3:24	1
Heb.	9:15; 11:8	2
1 Pt.	1:4	1
Total		14

2818. κληρονόμος, klēronom'os

Book	heir	Total
Mt.	21:38	1
Mk.	12:7	1
Lk.	20:14	1
Ro.	4:13, 14; 8:17, 17	4
Gal.	3:29; 4:1, 7	3
Tit.	3:7	1
Heb.	1:2; 6:17; 11:7	3
Jas.	2:5	1
Total		15

2819. κλῆρος, klē'ros

Book	Oc.	lot	Oc.	part	Oc.	inheritance	Oc.	heritage	Total
Mt.	2	27:35, 35							2
Mk.	1	15:24							1
Lk.	1	23:34							1
Jn.	1	19:24							1
Ac.	3	1:26, 26; 8:21	2	1:17, 25	1	26:18			6
Col.					1	1:12			1
1 Pt.							1	5:3	1
Total	8		2		2		1		13

2821. κλῆσις, klē'sis

Book	Oc.	calling	Oc.	vocation	Total
Ro.	1	11:29			1
1 Co.	2	1:26; 7:20			2
Eph.	2	1:18; 4:4	1	4:1	3
Phl.	1	3:14			1
2 Th.	1	1:11			1
2 Ti.	1	1:9			1
Heb.	1	3:1			1
2 Pt.	1	1:10			1
Total	10		1		11

2820. κληρόω, klērō'ō

Book	obtain an inheritance	Total
Eph.	1:11	1

2824. κλίμα, kli'ma

Book	Oc.	region	Oc.	part	Total
Ro.			1	15:23	1
2 Co.	1	11:10			1
Gal.	1	1:21			1
Total	2		1		3

2826. κλινίδιον, klinid'ion

Book	couch	Total
Lk.	5:19, 24	2

2822. κλητός, klētos'

Book	called	Total
Mt.	20:16; 22:14	2
Ro.	1:1, 6, 7; 8:28	4
1 Co.	1:1, 2, 24	3
Jd.	1:1	1
Rev.	17:14	1
Total		11

2828. κλισία, klisi'a

Book	company	Total
Lk.	9:14	1

2825. κλίνη, kli'nē

Book	Oc.	bed	Oc.	table	Total
Mt.	2	9:2, 6			2
Mk.	2	4:21; 7:30	1	7:4	3
Lk.	3	5:18; 8:16; 17:34			3
Ac.	1	5:15			1
Rev.	1	2:22			1
Total	9		1		10

2823. κλίβανος, klib'anos

Book	oven	Total
Mt.	6:30	1
Lk.	12:28	1
Total		2

2829. κλοπή, klopē'

Book	theft	Total
Mt.	15:19	1
Mk.	7:22	1
Total		2

2827. κλίνω, kli'nō

Book	Oc.	lay	Oc.	bow	Oc.	bow down	Oc.	be far spent	Oc.	turn to flight	Oc.	wear away	Total
Mt.	1	8:20											1
Lk.	1	9:58			1	24:5	1	24:29			1	9:12	4
Jn.			1	19:30									1
Heb.									1	11:34			1
Total	2		1		1		1		1		1		7

2830. κλύδων, klu'dōn

Book	Oc.	raging	Oc.	wave	Total
Lk.	1	8:24			1
Jas.			1	1:6	1
Total	1		1		2

2831. κλυδονίζομαι kludonid'zomai

Book	toss to and fro	Total
Eph.	4:14	1

2832. Κλωπᾶς, Klōpas'

Book	Cleophas	Total
Jn.	19:25	1

2833. κνήθω, knē'thō

Book	have itching	Total
2 Ti.	4:3	1

2835. κοδράντης, kodran'tēs

Book	farthing	Total
Mt.	5:26	1
Mk.	12:42	1
Total		2

2836. κοιλία, koili'a

Book	Oc.	womb	Oc.	belly	Total
Mt.	1	19:12	2	12:40; 15:17	3
Mk.			1	7:19	1
Lk.	7	1:15, 41, 42, 44; 2:21; 11:27; 23:29	1	15:16	8
Jn.	1	3:4	1	7:38	2
Ac.	2	3:2; 14:8			2
Ro.			1	16:18	1
1 Co.			2	6:13, 13	2
Gal.	1	1:15			1
Phl.			1	3:19	1
Rev.			2	10:9, 10	2
Total	12		11		23

2834. Κνίδος, Kni'dos

Book	Cnidus	Total
Ac.	27:7	1

2838. κοίμησις, koi'mēsis

Book	taking of rest	Total
Jn.	11:13	1

2837. κοιμάω, koima'ō

Book	Oc.	sleep	Oc.	fall asleep	Oc.	be asleep	Oc.	fall on sleep	Oc.	be dead	Total
Mt.	2	27:52; 28:13									2
Lk.	1	22:45									1
Jn.	2	11:11, 12									2
Ac.	1	12:6	1	7:60			1	13:36			3
1 Co.	3	11:30; 15:20, 51	2	15:6, 18					1	7:39	6
1 Th.	1	4:14			2	4:13, 15					3
2 Pt.			1	3:4							1
Total	10		4		2		1		1		18

2839. κοινός, koinos'

Book	Oc.	common	Oc.	unclean	Oc.	defiled	Oc.	unholy	Total
Mk.					1	7:2			1
Ac.	5	2:44; 4:32; 10:14, 28; 11:8							5
Ro.			3	14:14, 14, 14					3
Tit.	1	1:4							1
Heb.							1	10:29	1
Jd.	1	1:3							1
Total	7		3		1		1		12

2840. κοινόω, koino'ō

Book	Oc.	defile	Oc.	call common	Oc.	pollute	Oc.	unclean	Total
Mt.	5	15:11, 11, 18, 20, 20							5
Mk.	5	7:15, 15, 18, 20, 23							5
Ac.			2	10:15; 11:9	1	21:28			3
Heb.							1	9:13	1
Rev.	1	21:27							1
Total	11		2		1		1		15

2841. κοινωνέω, koinōne'ō

Book	Oc.	be partaker	Oc.	communicate	Oc.	distribute	Total
Ro.	1	15:27			1	12:13	2
Gal.			1	6:6			1
Phl.			1	4:15			1
1 Ti.	1	5:22					1
Heb.	1	2:14					1
1 Pt.	1	4:13					1
2 Jn.	1	1:11					1
Total	5		2		1		8

2843. κοινωνικός, koinōnikos'

Book	willing to communicate	Total
1 Ti.	6:18	1

2846. κοιτών, koitōn'

Book	chamberlain (with 1909)	Total
Ac.	12:20	1

2842. κοινωνία. koinōni'a

Book	Oc.	fellowship	Oc.	communion	Oc.	distribution	Oc.	contribution	Oc.	communication	Oc.	to communicate	Total
Ac.	1	2:42											1
Ro.							1	15:26					1
1 Co.	1	1:9	2	10:16, 16									3
2 Co.	1	8:4	2	6:14; 13:14	1	9:13							4
Gal.	1	2:9											1
Eph.	1	3:9											1
Phl.	3	1:5; 2:1; 3:10											3
Phe.									1	1:6			1
Heb.											1	13:16	1
1 Jn.	4	1:3, 3, 6, 7											4
Total	12		4		1		1		1		1		20

2844. κοινωνός, koinōnos'

Book	Oc.	partaker	Oc.	partner	Oc.	fellowship	Oc.	companion	Total
Mt.	1	23:30							1
Lk.			1	5:10					1
1 Co.	1	10:18			1	10:20			2
2 Co.	1	1:7	1	8:23					2
Phe.			1	1:17					1
Heb.							1	10:33	1
1 Pt.	1	5:1							1
2 Pt.	1	1:4							1
Total	5		3		1		1		10

2845. κοίτη, koi'tē

Book	Oc.	bed	Oc.	conceive	Oc.	chambering	Total
Lk.	1	11:7					1
Ro.			1	9:10	1	13:13	2
Heb.	1	13:4					1
Total	2		1		1		4

2847. κόκκινος, kok'kinos

Book	Oc.	scarlet	Oc.	scarlet color	Oc.	scarlet colored	Total
Mt.	1	27:28					1
Heb.	1	9:19					1
Rev.	2	18:12, 16	1	17:4	1	17:3	4
Total	4		1		1		6

2848. κόκκος, kok'kos

Book	Oc.	grain	Oc.	corn	Total
Mt.	2	13:31; 17:20			2
Mk.	1	4:31			1
Lk.	2	13:19; 17:6			2
Jn.			1	12:24	1
1 Co.	1	15:37			1
Total	6		1		7

2849. κολάζω, kolad'zō

Book	punish	Total
Ac.	4:21	1
2 Pt.	2:9	1
Total		2

2850. κολακεία, kolakei'a

Book	flattering	Total
1 Th.	2:5	1

2851. κόλασις, kol'asis

Book	Oc.	punishment	Oc.	torment	Total
Mt.	1	25:46			1
1 Jn.			1	4:18	1
Total	1		1		2

2852. κολαφίζω, kolaphid'zō

Book	buffet	Total
Mt.	26:67	1
Mk.	14:65	1
1 Co.	4:11	1
2 Co.	12:7	1
1 Pt.	2:20	1
Total		5

2854. κολλούριον, kollou'rion

Book	eyesalve	Total
Rev.	3:18	1

2853. κολλάω, kolla'ō

Book	Oc.	join (one's) self	Oc.	cleave	Oc.	be joined	Oc.	keep company	Total
Lk.	1	15:15	1	10:11					2
Ac.	3	5:13; 8:29; 9:26	1	17:34			1	10:28	5
Ro.			1	12:9					1
1 Co.					2	6:16, 17			2
Total	4		3		2		1		10

2855. κολλυβιστής, kollubistēs'

Book	Oc.	money-changer	Oc.	changer	Total
Mt.	1	21:12			1
Mk.	1	11:15			1
Jn.			1	2:15	1
Total	2		1		3

2856. κολοβόω, kolobo'ō

Book	shorten	Total
Mt.	24:22, 22	2
Mk.	13:20, 20	2
Total		4

2857. Κολοσσαί, Kolossai'

Book	Colosse	Total
Col.	1:2	1

2858. Κολοσσαεύς, Kolossaeus'

Book	Colossian	Total
Col.	subscript	1

2859. κόλπος, kol'pos

Book	Oc.	bosom	Oc.	creek	Total
Lk.	3	6:38; 16:22, 23			3
Jn.	2	1:18; 13:23			2
Ac.			1	27:39	1
Total	5		1		6

2860. κολυμβάω, kolumba'ō

Book	swim	Total
Ac.	27:43	1

2861. κολυμβήθρα, kolumbē'thra

Book	pool	Total
Jn.	5:2, 4, 7; 9:7, 11	5

2862. κολωνία, kolōni'a

Book	colony	Total
Ac.	16:12	1

2863. κομάω, koma'ō

Book	have long hair	Total
1 Co.	11:14, 15	2

2864. κόμη, ko'mē

Book	hair	Total
1 Co.	11:15	1

2865. κομίζω, komid'zō

Book	Oc.	receive	Oc.	bring	Total
Mt.	1	25:27			1
Lk.			1	7:37	1
2 Co.	1	5:10			1
Eph.	1	6:8			1
Col.	1	3:25			1
Heb.	3	10:36; 11:19, 39			3
1 Pt.	2	1:9; 5:4			2
2 Pt.	1	2:13			1
Total	10		1		11

2866. κομψότερον, kompsot'eron

Book	begin to amend (with 2192)	Total
Jn.	4:52	1

2867. κονιάω, konia'ō

Book	whited	Total
Mt.	23:27	1
Ac.	23:3	1
Total		2

2868. κονιορτός, koniortos'

Book	dust	Total
Mt.	10:14	1
Lk.	9:5; 10:11	2
Ac.	13:51; 22:23	2
Total		5

2869. κοπάζω, kopad'zō

Book	cease	Total
Mt.	14:32	1
Mk.	4:39; 6:51	2
Total		3

2870. κοπετός, kopetos'

Book	lamentation	Total
Ac.	8:2	1

2871. κοπή, kopē'

Book	slaughter	Total
Heb.	7:1	1

2872. κοπιάω, kopia'ō

Book	Oc.	labour	Oc.	bestow labour	Oc.	toil	Oc.	be wearied	Total
Mt.	1	11:28			1	6:28			2
Lk.					2	5:5; 12:27			2
Jn.	1	4:38b	1	4:38a			1	4:6	3
Ac.	1	20:35							1
Ro.	2	16:12, 12	1	16:6					3
1 Co.	3	4:12; 15:10; 16:16							3
Gal.			1	4:11					1
Eph.	1	4:28							1
Phl.	1	2:16							1
Col.	1	1:29							1
1 Th.	1	5:12							1
1 Ti.	2	4:10; 5:17							2
2 Ti.	1	2:6							1
Rev.	1	2:3							1
Total	16		3		3		1		23

2873. κόπος, kop'os

Book	Oc.	labour	Oc.	trouble (with 3830)	Oc.	weariness	Total
Mt.			1	26:10			1
Mk.			1	14:6			1
Lk.			2	11:7; 18:5			2
Jn.	1	4:38					1
1 Co.	2	3:8; 15:58					2
2 Co.	3	6:5; 10:15; 11:23			1	11:27	4
Gal.			1	6:17			1
1 Th.	3	1:3; 2:9; 3:5					3
2 Th.	1	3:8					1
Heb.	1	6:10					1
Rev.	2	2:2; 14:13					2
Total	13		5		1		19

2874. κοπρία, kopri'a

Book	Oc.	dunghill	Oc.	dung (with 906)	Total
Lk.	1	14:35	1	13:8	2

2875. κόπτω, kop'tō

Book	Oc.	bewail	Oc.	lament	Oc.	cut down	Oc.	wail	Oc.	mourn	Total
Mt.			1	11:17	1	21:8			1	24:30	3
Mk.					1	11:8					1
Lk.	2	8:52; 23:27									2
Rev.			1	18:9			1	1:7			2
Total	2		2		2		1		1		8

2876. κόραξ, kor'ax

Book	raven	Total
Lk.	12:24	1

2877. κοράσιον, koras'ion

Book	Oc.	damsel	Oc.	maid	Total
Mt.	1	14:11	2	9:24, 25	3
Mk.	5	5:41, 42; 6:22, 28, 28			5
Total	6		2		8

2878a. κορβᾶν, korban'

Book	treasury	Total
Mt.	27:6	1

2878b. κορβανᾶς, korbanas'

Book	corban	Total
Mk.	7:11	1

Word 2878 has 2 occurrences.

2879. Κορέ, Kore'

Book	Core	Total
Jd.	1:11	1

2880. κορέννυμι, koren'numi

Book	Oc.	eat enough	Oc.	full	Total
Ac.	1	27:38			1
1 Co.			1	4:8	1
Total	1		1		2

2881. Κορίνθιος, Korin'thios

Book	Corinthian	Total
Ac.	18:8	1
2 Co.	6:11	1
Total		2

2882. Κόρινθος, Kor'inthos

Book	Corinth	Total
Ac.	18:1; 19:1	2
1 Co.	1:2	1
2 Co.	1:1, 23	2
2 Ti.	4:20	1
Total		6

2883. Κορνήλιος, Kornē'lios

Book	Cornelius	Total
Ac.	10:1, 3, 7, 17, 21, 22, 24, 25, 30, 31	10

2884. κόρος, kor'os

Book	measure	Total
Lk.	16:7	1

2885. κοσμέω, kosme'ō

Book	Oc.	adorn	Oc.	garnish	Oc.	trim	Total
Mt.			2	12:44; 23:29	1	25:7	3
Lk.	1	21:5	1	11:25			2
1 Ti.	1	2:9					1
Tit.	1	2:10					1
1 Pt.	1	3:5					1
Rev.	1	21:2	1	21:19			2
Total	5		4		1		10

2886. κοσμικός, kosmikos'

Book	worldly	Total
Tit.	2:12	1
Heb.	9:1	1
Total		2

2887. κόσμιος, kos'mios

Book	Oc.	modest	Oc.	of good behaviour	Total
1 Ti.	1	2:9	1	3:2	2

2888. κοσμοκράτωρ kosmokrat'ōr

Book	ruler	Total
Eph.	6:12	1

2889. κόσμος, kos'mos

Book	Oc.	world	Oc.	adorning	Total
Mt.	9	4:8; 5:14; 13:35, 38; 16:26; 18:7; 24:21; 25:34; 26:13			9
Mk.	3	8:36; 14:9; 16:15			3
Lk.	3	9:25; 11:50; 12:30			3
Jn.	79	1:9, 10, 10, 10, 29; 3:16, 17, 17, 17, 19; 4:42; 6:14, 33, 51; 7:4, 7; 8:12, 23, 23, 26; 9:5, 5, 39; 10:36; 11:9, 27; 12:19, 25, 31, 31, 46, 47, 47; 13:1, 1; 14:17, 19, 22, 27, 30, 31; 15:18, 19, 19, 19, 19, 19; 16:8, 11, 20, 21, 28, 28, 33, 33; 17:5, 6, 9, 11, 11, 12, 13, 14, 14, 14, 15, 16, 16, 18, 18, 21, 23, 24, 25; 18:20, 36, 36, 37; 21:25			79
Ac.	1	17:24			1
Ro.	9	1:8, 20; 3:6, 19; 4:13; 5:12, 13; 11:12, 15			9
1 Co.	21	1:20, 21, 27, 27, 28; 2:12; 3:19, 22; 4:9, 13; 5:10, 10; 6:2, 2; 7:31, 31, 33, 34; 8:4; 11:32; 14:10			21
2 Co.	3	1:12; 5:19; 7:10			3
Gal.	3	4:3; 6:14, 14			3
Eph.	3	1:4; 2:2, 12			3
Phl.	1	2:15			1
Col.	4	1:6; 2:8, 20, 20			4
1 Ti.	3	1:15; 3:16; 6:7			3
Heb.	5	4:3; 9:26; 10:5; 11:7, 38			5
Jas.	5	1:27; 2:5; 3:6; 4:4, 4			5
1 Pt.	2	1:20; 5:9	1	3:3	3
2 Pt.	5	1:4; 2:5, 5, 20; 3:6			5
1 Jn.	23	2:2, 15, 15, 15, 16, 16, 17; 3:1, 13, 17; 4:1, 3, 4, 5, 5, 5, 9, 14, 17; 5:4, 4, 5, 19			23
2 Jn.	1	1:7			1
Rev.	3	11:15; 13:8; 17:8			3
Total	186		1		187

2890. Κούαρτος, Kou′artos

Book	Quartus	Total
Ro.	16:23	1

2891. κοῦμι, kou′mi

Book	cumi	Total
Mk.	5:41	1

2892. κουστωδία, koustō̄di′a

Book	watch	Total
Mt.	27:65, 66; 28:11	3

2893. κουφίζω, kouphid′zō

Book	lighten	Total
Ac.	27:38	1

2894. κόφινος, koph′inos

Book	basket	Total
Mt.	14:20; 16:9	2
Mk.	6:43; 8:19	2
Lk.	9:17	1
Jn.	6:13	1
Total		6

2895. κράββατος, krab′batos

Book	Oc.	bed	Oc.	couch	Total
Mk.	5	2:4, 9, 11, 12; 6:55			5
Jn.	5	5:8, 9, 10, 11, 12			5
Ac.	1	9:33	1	5:15	2
Total	11		1		12

2897. κραιπάλη, kraipal′e̱

Book	surfeiting	Total
Lk.	21:34	1

2896. κράζω, krad′zō

Book	Oc.	cry	Oc.	cry out	Total
Mt.	7	9:27; 14:30; 15:23; 20:31; 21:9, 15; 27:50	4	8:29; 14:26; 20:30; 27: 23	11
Mk.	7	1:26; 3:11; 5:5, 7; 9:26; 10:48; 11:9	5	9:24; 10:47; 15:13, 14, 39	12
Lk.	1	18:39	3	4:41; 9:39; 19:40	4
Jn.	5	1:15; 7:28, 37; 12:13, 44	1	19:12	6
Ac.	5	7:60; 16:17; 19:32; 21:36; 24:21	6	7:57; 14:14; 19:28, 34; 21:28; 23:6	11
Ro.	2	8:15; 9:27			2
Gal.	1	4:6			1
Jas.	1	5:4			1
Rev.	11	6:10; 7:2, 10; 10:3, 3; 12: 2; 14:15; 18:2, 18, 19; 19: 17			11
Total	40		19		59

2898. κρανίον, krani′on

Book	Oc.	skull	Oc.	calvary	Total
Mt.	1	27:33			1
Mk.	1	15:22			1
Lk.			1	23:33	1
Jn.	1	19:17			1
Total	3		1		4

2899. κράσπεδον, kras′pedon

Book	Oc.	border	Oc.	hem	Total
Mt.	1	23:5	2	9:20; 14:36	3
Mk.	1	6:56			1
Lk.	1	8:44			1
Total	3		2		5

2900. κραταιός, krataios′

Book	mighty	Total
1 Pt.	5:6	1

2901. κραταιόω, krataio′ō

Book	Oc.	wax strong	Oc.	strengthen	Oc.	be strong	Total
Lk.	2	1:80; 2:40					2
1 Co.					1	16:13	1
Eph.			1	3:16			1
Total	2		1		1		4

2902. κρατέω, krate′ō

Book	Oc.	hold	Oc.	take	Oc.	lay hold on	Oc.	hold fast	Oc.	take by	Oc.	lay hold upon	Oc.	lay hand on	Oc.	Misc.	Total
Mt.			3	22:6; 26: 4, 50	4	12:11; 14:3; 26:55, 57	1	26:48	1	9:25			2	18:28; 21:46	1	28:9	12
Mk.	3	7:3, 4, 8	5	9:27; 14:1, 44, 46, 49	3	3:21; 12:12; 14:51			2	1:31; 5:41	1	6:17			1	9:10	15
Lk.	1	24:16							1	8:54							2
Jn.															2	20:23, 23	2
Ac.	2	2:24; 3:11	1	24:6											1	27:13	4
Col.	1	2:19															1
2 Th.	1	2:15															1
Heb.							1	4:14			1	6:18					2
Rev.	4	2:1, 14, 15; 7:1			1	20:2	3	2:13, 25; 3:11									8
Total	12		9		8		5		4		2		2		5		47

Miscellaneous: Mt. 28:9, hold by; Mk. 9:10, keep; Jn. 20:23, 23, retain; Ac. 27:13, obtain.

2903. κράτιστος, krat′istos

Book	Oc.	most excellent	Oc.	most noble	Total
Lk.	1	1:3			1
Ac.	1	23:26	2	24:3; 26:25	3
Total	2		2		4

2904. κράτος, krat′os

Book	Oc.	power	Oc.	dominion	Oc.	strength	Oc.	mightily (with 2596)	Total
Lk.					1	1:51			1
Ac.							1	19:20	1
Eph.	2	1:19; 6:10							2
Col.	1	1:11							1
1 Ti.	1	6:16							1
Heb.	1	2:14							1
1 Pt.			2	4:11; 5:11					2
Jd.			1	1:25					1
Rev.	1	5:13	1	1:6					2
Total	6		4		1		1		12

2905. κραυγάζω, kraugad′zō

Book	Oc.	cry	Oc.	cry out	Total
Mt.	2	12:19; 15:22			2
Jn.	2	11:43; 18:40	2	19:6, 15	4
Ac.			1	22:23	1
Total	4		3		7

2906. κραυγή, krauge̱′

Book	Oc.	cry	Oc.	crying	Oc.	clamour	Total
Mt.	1	25:6					1
Ac.	1	23:9					1
Eph.					1	4:31	1
Heb.			1	5:7			1
Rev.	1	14:18	1	21:4			2
Total	3		2		1		6

2907. κρέας, kre′as

Book	flesh	Total
Ro.	14:21	1
1 Co.	8:13	1
Total		2

2908. κρεῖσσον, kreis′son

Book	better	Total
1 Co.	7:38	1

2909. κρείττων or κρείσσων, kreit′tōn or kreis′sōn

Book	Oc.	better	Oc.	best	Total
1 Co.	2	7:9; 11:17	1	12:31	3
Phl.	1	1:23			1
Heb.	13	1:4; 6:9; 7:7, 19, 22; 8:6, 6; 9:23; 10:34; 11:16, 35, 40; 12:24			13
1 Pt.	1	3:17			1
2 Pt.	1	2:21			1
Total	18		1		19

2910. κρεμάννυμι, kreman′numi

Book	hang	Total
Mt.	18:6; 22:40	2
Lk.	23:39	1
Ac.	5:30; 10:39; 28:4	3
Gal.	3:13	1
Total		7

2911. κρημνός, kre̱mnos′

Book	steep place	Total
Mt.	8:32	1
Mk.	5:13	1
Lk.	8:33	1
Total		3

2912. Κρής, Kres

Book	Oc.	Cretes	Oc.	Cretians	Total
Ac.	1	2:11			1
Tit.			1	1:12	1
Total	1		1		2

2913. Κρήσκης, Kres'kes

Book	Crescens	Total
2 Ti.	4:10	1

2914. Κρήτη, Kre'te

Book	Crete	Total
Ac.	27:7, 12, 13, 21	4
Tit.	1:5	1
Total		5

2915. κριθή, krithe'

Book	barley	Total
Rev.	6:6	1

2916. κρίθινος, kri'thinos

Book	barley	Total
Jn.	6:9, 13	2

2918. κρίνον, kri'non

Book	lily	Total
Mt.	6:28	1
Lk.	12:27	1
Total		2

2917. κρίμα, kri'ma

Book	Oc.	judgment	Oc.	damnation	Oc.	condemnation	Oc.	be condemned	Oc.	go to law (with 2192)	Oc.	avenge (with 2919)	Total
Mt.	1	7:2	1	23:14									2
Mk.			1	12:40									1
Lk.			1	20:47	1	23:40	1	24:20					3
Jn.	1	9:39											1
Ac.	1	24:25											1
Ro.	4	2:2, 3; 5:16; 11:33	2	3:8; 13:2									6
1 Co.			1	11:29	1	11:34			1	6:7			3
Gal.	1	5:10											1
1 Ti.			1	5:12	1	3:6							2
Heb.	1	6:2											1
Jas.					1	3:1							1
1 Pt.	1	4:17											1
2 Pt.	1	2:3											1
Jd.					1	1:4							1
Rev.	2	17:1; 20:4									1	18:20	3
Total	13		7		5		1		1		1		28

2919. κρίνω, kri'nō

Book	Oc.	judge	Oc.	determine	Oc.	condemn	Oc.	go to law	Oc.	call in question	Oc.	esteem	Oc.	Misc.	Total
Mt.	5	7:1, 1, 2, 2; 19:28											1	5:40	6
Lk.	6	6:37, 37; 7:43; 12:57; 19:22, 30													6
Jn.	16	5:22, 30; 7:24, 24, 51; 8:15, 15, 16, 26, 50; 12:47, 47, 48, 48; 16:11; 18:31			3	3:17, 18, 18									19
Ac.	11	4:19; 7:7; 13:46; 16:15; 17:31; 23:3; 24:6; 25:9, 10, 20; 26:6	4	3:13; 20:16; 25:25; 27:1	1	13:27			2	23:6; 24:21			4	15:19; 16:4; 21:25; 26:8	22
Ro.	15	2:1, 1, 1, 3, 12, 16, 27; 3:4, 6, 7; 14:3, 4, 10, 13, 13			1	14:22					2	14:5, 5			18
1 Co.	13	4:5; 5:3, 12, 12, 13; 6:2, 2, 3; 10:15, 29; 11:13, 31, 32	1	2:2			2	6:1, 6					1	7:37	17
2 Co.	1	5:14	1	2:1											2
Col.	1	2:16													1
2 Th.													1	2:12	1
2 Ti.	1	4:1													1
Tit.			1	3:12											1
Heb.	2	10:30; 13:4													2
Jas.	5	2:12; 4:11, 11, 11, 12													5
1 Pt.	4	1:17; 2:23; 4:5, 6													4
Rev.	8	6:10; 11:18; 16:5; 18:8; 19:2, 11; 20:12, 13											1	18:20	9
Total	88		7		5		2		2		2		8		114

Miscellaneous: Mt. 5:40, sue at the law; Ac. 15:19, sentence is; Ac. 16:4, ordain; Ac. 21:25, conclude; Ac. 26:8, think; 1 Co. 7:37, decree; 2 Th. 2:12, damn; Rev. 18:20 (with 2917), avenge.

2920. κρίσις, kri'sis

Book	Oc.	judgment	Oc.	damnation	Oc.	accusation	Oc.	condemnation	Total
Mt.	11	5:21, 22; 10:15; 11:22, 24; 12:18, 20, 36, 41, 42; 23:23	1	23:33					12
Mk.	1	6:11	1	3:29					2
Lk.	4	10:14; 11:31, 32, 42							4
Jn.	8	5:22, 27, 30; 7:24; 8:16; 12:31; 16:8, 11	1	5:29			2	3:19; 5:24	11
Ac.	1	8:33							1
2 Th.	1	1:5							1
1 Ti.	1	5:24							1
Heb.	2	9:27; 10:27							2
Jas.	2	2:13, 13							2
2 Pt.	3	2:4, 9; 3:7			1	2:11			4
1 Jn.	1	4:17							1
Jd.	2	1:6, 15			1	1:9			3
Rev.	4	14:7; 16:7; 18:10; 19:2							4
Total	41		3		2		2		48

2921. Κρίσπος, Kris'pos

Book	Crispus	Total
Ac.	18:8	1
1 Co.	1:14	1
Total		2

2924. κριτικός, kritikos'

Book	discerner	Total
Heb.	4:12	1

2922. κριτήριον, krite'rion

Book	Oc.	to judge	Oc.	judgment	Oc.	judgment seat	Total
1 Co.	1	6:2	1	6:4			2
Jas.					1	2:6	1
Total	1		1		1		3

2923. κριτής, krites'

Book	Oc.	judge	Oc.	Judge	Total
Mt.	3	5:25, 25; 12:27			3
Lk.	5	11:19; 12:58, 58; 18:2, 6			5
Ac.	3	13:20; 18:15; 24:10	1	10:42	4
2 Ti.	1	4:8			1
Heb.			1	12:23	1
Jas.	3	2:4; 4:11; 5:9			3
Total	15		2		17

2925. κρούω, krou′ō

Book	knock	Total
Mt.	7:7, 8	2
Lk.	11:9, 10; 12:36; 13:25	4
Ac.	12:13, 16	2
Rev.	3:20	1
Total		9

2926. κρυπτή, krupte̱′

Book	secret place	Total
Lk.	11:33	1

2927. κρυπτός, kruptos′

Book	Oc.	secret	Oc.	hid	Oc.	hidden	Oc.	inwardly	Total
Mt.	6	6:4, 4, 6, 6, 18, 18	1	10:26					7
Mk.			1	4:22					1
Lk.	1	8:17	1	12:2					2
Jn.	3	7:4, 10; 18:20							3
Ro.	1	2:16					1	2:29	2
1 Co.	1	14:25			1	4:5			2
2 Co.					1	4:2			1
1 Pt.					1	3:4			1
Total	12		3		3		1		19

2928. κρύπτω, krup′tō

Book	Oc.	hide	Oc.	hide (one's) self	Oc.	keep secret	Oc.	secretly	Oc.	hidden	Total
Mt.	4	5:14; 13:44, 44; 25:25			1	13:35					5
Lk.	2	18:34; 19:42									2
Jn.			2	8:59; 12:36			1	19:38			3
Col.	1	3:3									1
1 Ti.	1	5:25									1
Heb.	1	11:23									1
Rev.	2	6:15, 16							1	2:17	3
Total	11		2		1		1		1		16

2929. κρυσταλλίζω krustallid′zō

Book	clear as crystal	Total
Rev.	21:11	1

2930. κρύσταλλος, krus′tallos

Book	crystal	Total
Rev.	4:6; 22:1	2

2931. κρυφῇ, kruphe̱′

Book	in secret	Total
Eph.	5:12	1

2932. κτάομαι, kta′omai

Book	Oc.	possess	Oc.	purchase	Oc.	provide	Oc.	obtain	Total
Mt.					1	10:9			1
Lk.	2	18:12; 21:19							2
Ac.			2	1:18; 8:20			1	22:28	3
1 Th.	1	4:4							1
Total	3		2		1		1		7

2933. κτῆμα, kte̱′ma

Book	possession	Total
Mt.	19:22	1
Mk.	10:22	1
Ac.	2:45; 5:1	2
Total		4

2934. κτῆνος, kte̱′nos

Book	beast	Total
Lk.	10:34	1
Ac.	23:24	1
1 Co.	15:39	1
Rev.	18:13	1
Total		4

2935. κτήτωρ, kte̱′tōr

Book	possessor	Total
Ac.	4:34	1

2936. κτίζω, ktid′zō

Book	Oc.	create	Oc.	Creator	Oc.	make	Total
Mk.	1	13:19					1
Ro.			1	1:25			1
1 Co.	1	11:9					1
Eph.	3	2:10; 3:9; 4:24			1	2:15	4
Col.	3	1:16, 16; 3:10					3
1 Ti.	1	4:3					1
Rev.	3	4:11, 11; 10:6					3
Total	12		1		1		14

2937. κτίσις, ktis′is

Book	Oc.	creature	Oc.	creation	Oc.	building	Oc.	ordinance	Total
Mk.	1	16:15	2	10:6; 13:19					3
Ro.	5	1:25; 8:19, 20, 21, 39	2	1:20; 8:22					7
2 Co.	1	5:17							1
Gal.	1	6:15							1
Col.	2	1:15, 23							2
Heb.	1	4:13			1	9:11			2
1 Pt.							1	2:13	1
2 Pt.			1	3:4					1
Rev.			1	3:14					1
Total	11		6		1		1		19

2938. κτίσμα, ktis′ma

Book	creature	Total
1 Ti.	4:4	1
Jas.	1:18	1
Rev.	5:13; 8:9	2
Total		4

2939. κτιστής, ktiste̱s′

Book	Creator	Total
1 Pt.	4:19	1

2940. κυβεία, kubei′a

Book	sleight	Total
Eph.	4:14	1

2941. κυβέρνησις, kuber′ne̱sis

Book	government	Total
1 Co.	12:28	1

2942. κυβερνήτης, kuberne̱′te̱s

Book	Oc.	master	Oc.	shipmaster	Total
Ac.	1	27:11			1
Rev.			1	18:17	1
Total	1		1		2

2943. κυκλόθεν, kukloth′en

Book	Oc.	round about	Oc.	about	Total
Rev.	3	4:3, 4; 5:11	1	4:8	4

2944. κυκλόω, kuklo′ō

Book	Oc.	compass about	Oc.	compass	Oc.	come round about	Oc.	stand round about	Total
Lk.			1	21:20					1
Jn.					1	10:24			1
Ac.							1	14:20	1
Heb.	1	11:30							1
Rev.	1	20:9							1
Total	2		1		1		1		5

2945. κύκλῳ, ku′klō

Book	Oc.	round about	Oc.	round	Total
Mk.	2	3:34; 6:36	1	6:6	3
Lk.	1	9:12			1
Ro.	1	15:19			1
Rev.	2	4:6; 7:11			2
Total	6		1		7

2946. κύλισμα, ku′lisma

Book	wallowing	Total
2 Pt.	2:22	1

2947. κυλιόω, kulio′ō

Book	wallow	Total
Mk.	9:20	1

2948. κυλλός, kullos′

Book	maimed	Total
Mt.	15:30, 31; 18:8	3
Mk.	9:43	1
Total		4

2949. κῦμα, ku′ma

Book	wave	Total
Mt.	8:24; 14:24	2
Mk.	4:37	1
Ac.	27:41	1
Jd.	1:13	1
Total		5

2950. κύμβαλον, kum′balon

Book	cymbal	Total
1 Co.	13:1	1

2951. κύμινον, ku′minon

Book	cummin	Total
Mt.	23:23	1

2952. κυνάριον, kunar'ion

Book	dog	Total
Mt.	15:26, 27	2
Mk.	7:27, 28	2
Total		4

2953. Κύπριος, Ku'prios

Book	Cyprus	Total
Ac.	4:36; 11:20; 21:16	3

2954. Κύπρος, Ku'pros

Book	Cyprus	Total
Ac.	11:19; 13:4; 15:39; 21:3; 27:4	5

2960. κυριακός, kuriakos'

Book	Lord's	Total
1 Co.	11:20	1
Rev.	1:10	1
Total		2

2955. κύπτω, kup'tō

Book	Oc.	stoop	Oc.	stoop down	Total
Mk.			1	1:7	1
Jn.	2	8:6, 8			2
Total	2		1		3

2956. Κυρηναῖος, Kurēnai'os

Book	Oc.	Cyrene	Oc.	Cyrenian	Total
Mt.	1	27:32			1
Mk.			1	15:21	1
Lk.			1	23:26	1
Ac.	2	11:20; 13:1	1	6:9	3
Total	3		3		6

2957. Κυρήνη, Kurē'nē

Book	Cyrene	Total
Ac.	2:10	1

2958. Κυρήνιος, Kurē'nios

Book	Cyrenius	Total
Lk.	2:2	1

2959. Κυρία, Kuri'a

Book	lady	Total
2 Jn.	1:1, 5	2

2961. κυριεύω, kurieu'ō

Book	Oc.	have dominion over	Oc.	exercise lordship over	Oc.	be Lord of	Oc.	lords	Total
Lk.			1	22:25					1
Ro.	3	6:9, 14; 7:1			1	14:9			4
2 Co.	1	1:24							1
1 Ti.							1	6:15	1
Total	4		1		1		1		7

2962. κύριος, ku'rios

Book	Oc.	Lord	Oc.	lord	Oc.	master	Oc.	sir	Oc.	Sir	Oc.	Misc.	Total
Mt.	52	1:20, 22, 24; 2:13, 15, 19; 3:3; 4:7, 10; 5:33; 7:21, 21, 22, 22; 8:2, 6, 8, 21, 25; 9:28, 38; 11:25; 12:8; 13:51; 14:28, 30; 15:22, 25, 27a; 16:22; 17:4, 15; 18:21; 20:30, 31, 33; 21:3, 9, 42; 22:37, 43, 44, 44, 45; 23:39; 24:42; 25:37, 44; 26:22; 27:10; 28:2, 6	26	10:24, 25; 18:25, 26, 27, 31, 32, 34; 20:8; 21:40; 24:45, 46, 48, 50; 25:11, 11, 18, 19, 20, 21, 21, 22, 23, 23, 24, 26	2	6:24; 15:27b	3	13:27; 21:30; 27:63					83
Mk.	18	1:3; 2:28; 5:19; 7:28; 9:24; 11:3, 9, 10; 12:11, 29, 29, 30, 36, 36, 37; 13:20; 16:19, 20	1	12:9	1	13:35							20
Lk.	87	1:6, 9, 11, 15, 16, 17, 25, 28, 32, 38, 43, 45, 46, 58, 66, 68, 76; 2:9, 9, 11, 15, 22, 23, 23, 24, 26, 38, 39; 3:4; 4:8, 12, 18, 19; 5:8, 12, 17; 6:5, 46, 46; 7:6, 13, 31; 9:54, 57, 59, 61; 10:1, 2, 17, 21, 27, 40; 11:1, 39; 12:41, 42a; 13:8, 15, 23, 35; 17:5, 6, 37; 18:6, 41; 19:8, 8, 16, 18, 20, 25, 31, 34, 38; 20:37, 42, 42, 44; 22:31, 33, 38, 49, 61, 61; 23:42; 24:3, 34	18	12:36, 37, 42b, 43, 45, 46, 47; 13:25, 25; 14:21, 22, 23; 16:3, 5, 5, 8; 20:13, 15	1	16:13					1	19:33	107
Jn.	43	1:23; 4:1; 6:23, 34, 68; 8:11; 9:36, 38; 11:2, 3, 12, 21, 27, 32, 34, 39; 12:13, 38, 38; 13:6, 9, 13, 14, 25, 36, 37; 14:5, 8, 22; 20:2, 13, 18, 20, 25, 28; 21:7, 7, 12, 15, 16, 17, 20, 21	3	13:16; 15:15, 20			1	12:21	6	4:11, 15, 19, 49; 5:7; 20:15			53
Ac.	108	1:6, 21, 24; 2:20, 21, 25, 34, 34, 36, 39, 47; 3:19, 22; 4:26, 29, 33; 5:9, 14, 19; 7:30, 31, 33, 37, 49, 59, 60; 8:16, 24, 25, 26, 39; 9:1, 5, 5, 6, 6, 10, 10, 11, 13, 15, 17, 27, 29, 31, 35, 42; 10:4, 14, 36, 48; 11:8, 16, 17, 20, 21, 21, 23, 24; 12:7, 11, 17, 23; 13:2, 10, 11, 12, 47, 48, 49; 14:3, 23; 15:11, 17, 17, 26, 35, 36; 16:10, 14, 15, 31, 32; 17:24, 27; 18:8, 9, 25, 25; 19:5, 10, 13, 17; 20:19, 21, 24, 35; 21:13, 14, 20; 22:8, 10, 10, 16, 19; 23:11; 26:15; 28:31	1	25:26	2	16:16, 19	1	16:30			1	19:20	113
Ro.	44	1:3, 7; 4:8, 24; 5:1, 11, 21; 6:11, 23; 7:25; 8:39; 9:28, 29; 10:9, 12, 13, 16; 11:3, 34; 12:11, 19; 13:14; 14:6, 6, 6, 8, 8, 8, 11, 14; 15:6, 11, 30; 16:2, 8, 11, 12, 12, 13, 18, 20, 22, 24			1	14:4							45
1 Co.	68	1:2, 3, 7, 8, 9, 10, 31; 2:8, 16; 3:5, 20; 4:4, 5, 17, 19; 5:4, 4, 5; 6:11, 13, 13, 14, 17; 7:10, 12, 17, 22, 22, 25, 25, 32, 32, 34, 35, 39; 8:6; 9:1, 1, 2, 5, 14; 10:21, 21, 22, 26, 28; 11:11, 23, 23, 26, 27, 27, 29, 32; 12:3, 5; 14:21, 37; 15:31, 47, 57, 58, 58; 16:7, 10, 19, 22, 23	1	8:5									69
2 Co.	30	1:2, 3, 14; 2:12; 3:16, 17, 17, 18, 18; 4:5, 10, 14; 5:6, 8, 11; 6:17, 18; 8:5, 9, 19, 21; 10:8, 17, 18; 11:17, 31; 12:1, 8; 13:10, 14											30
Gal.	6	1:3, 19; 5:10; 6:14, 17, 18	1	4:1									7
Eph.	25	1:2, 3, 15, 17; 2:21; 3:11, 14; 4:1, 5, 17; 5:8, 10, 17, 19, 20, 22, 29; 6:1, 4, 7, 8, 10, 21, 23, 24			2	6:5, 9a					1	6:9b	28
Phl.	15	1:2, 14; 2:11, 19, 24, 29; 3:1, 8, 20; 4:1, 2, 4, 5, 10, 23											15
Col.	13	1:2, 3, 10; 2:6; 3:16, 17, 18, 20, 23, 24, 24; 4:7, 17			2	3:22; 4:1a					1	4:1b	16
1 Th.	25	1:1, 1, 3, 6, 8; 2:15, 19; 3:8, 11, 12, 13; 4:1, 2, 6, 15, 15, 16, 17, 17; 5:2, 9, 12, 23, 27, 28											25
2 Th.	21	1:1, 2, 7, 8, 9, 12, 12; 2:1, 8, 13, 14, 16; 3:1, 3, 4, 5, 6, 12, 16, 16, 18											21
1 Ti.	8	1:1, 2, 12, 14; 5:21; 6:3, 14, 15a	1	6:15b									9
2 Ti.	17	1:2, 8, 16, 18, 18; 2:7, 14, 19, 22, 24; 3:11; 4:1, 8, 14, 17, 18, 22											17
Tit.	1	1:4											1
Phe.	6	1:3, 5, 16, 20, 20, 25											6
Heb.	17	1:10; 2:3; 7:14, 21; 8:2, 8, 9, 10, 11; 10:16, 30, 30; 12:5, 6, 14; 13:6, 20											17
Jas.	14	1:1, 7, 12; 2:1; 4:10, 15; 5:4, 7, 8, 10, 11, 11, 14, 15											14
1 Pt.	7	1:3, 25; 2:3, 13; 3:12, 12, 15	1	3:6									8
2 Pt.	14	1:2, 8, 11, 14, 16; 2:9, 11, 20; 3:2, 8, 9, 10, 15, 18											14
2 Jn.	1	1:3											1
Jd.	6	1:4, 5, 9, 14, 17, 21											6
Rev.	21	1:8; 4:8, 11; 11:8, 15, 17; 14:13; 15:3, 4; 16:5, 7; 17:14a; 18:8; 19:1, 6, 16a; 21:22; 22:5, 6, 20, 21	2	17:14b; 19:16b			1	7:14					24
Total	667		55		11		6		6		4		749

Miscellaneous: Lk. 19:33, owner; Ac. 19:20, God; Eph. 6:9b; Col. 4:1b, master.

2963. κυριότης, kuriot'ēs

Book	Oc.	dominion	Oc.	government	Total
Eph.	1	1:21			1
Col.	1	1:16			1
2 Pt.			1	2:10	1
Jd.	1	1:8			1
Total	3		1		4

2964. κυρόω, kuro'ō

Book	confirm	Total
2 Co.	2:8	1
Gal.	3:15	1
Total		2

2965. κύων, ku'ōn

Book	dog	Total
Mt.	7:6	1
Lk.	16:21	1
Phl.	3:2	1
2 Pt.	2:22	1
Rev.	22:15	1
Total		5

2966. κῶλον, kō'lon

Book	carcase	Total
Heb.	3:17	1

2967. κωλύω, kōlu'ō

Book	Oc.	forbid	Oc.	hinder	Oc.	withstand	Oc.	keep from	Oc.	let	Oc.	not suffer	Total
Mt.	1	19:14											1
Mk.	3	9:38, 39; 10:14											3
Lk.	5	6:29; 9:49, 50; 18:16; 23:2	1	11:52									6
Ac.	3	10:47; 16:6; 24:23	1	8:36	1	11:17	1	27:43					6
Ro.									1	1:13			1
1 Co.	1	14:39											1
1 Th.	1	2:16											1
1 Ti.	1	4:3											1
Heb.											1	7:23	1
2 Pt.	1	2:16											1
3 Jn.	1	1:10											1
Total	17		2		1		1		1		1		23

2968. κώμη, kō'mē

Book	Oc.	village	Oc.	town	Total
Mt.	3	9:35; 14:15; 21:2	1	10:11	4
Mk.	4	6:6, 36, 56; 11:2	4	8:23, 26, 26, 27	8
Lk.	9	8:1; 9:52, 56; 10:38; 13:22; 17:12; 19:30; 24:13, 28	3	5:17; 9:6, 12	12
Jn.			3	7:42; 11:1, 30	3
Ac.	1	8:25			1
Total	17		11		28

2969. κωμόπολις, kōmop'olis

Book	town	Total
Mk.	1:38	1

2971. κώνωψ, kō'nōps

Book	gnat	Total
Mt.	23:24	1

2972. Κῶς, Kōs

Book	Coos	Total
Ac.	21:1	1

2973. Κωσάμ, Kōsam'

Book	Cosam	Total
Lk.	3:28	1

2970. κῶμος, kō'mos

Book	Oc.	revelling	Oc.	rioting	Total
Ro.			1	13:13	1
Gal.	1	5:21			1
1 Pt.	1	4:3			1
Total	2		1		3

2974. κωφός, kōphos'

Book	Oc.	dumb	Oc.	deaf	Oc.	speechless	Total
Mt.	6	9:32, 33; 12:22, 22; 15:30, 31	1	11:5			7
Mk.			3	7:32, 37; 9:25			3
Lk.	2	11:14, 14	1	7:22	1	1:22	4
Total	8		5		1		14

2975. λαγχάνω, langchan'ō

Book	Oc.	obtain	Oc.	be (one's) lot	Oc.	cast lots	Total
Lk.			1	1:9			1
Jn.					1	19:24	1
Ac.	1	1:17					1
2 Pt.	1	1:1					1
Total	2		1		1		4

2976. Λάζαρος, Lad'zaros

Book	Oc.	Lazarus (of Bethany)	Oc.	Lazarus (of the parable)	Total
Lk.			4	16:20, 23, 24, 25	4
Jn.	11	11:1, 2, 5, 11, 14, 43; 12:1, 2, 9, 10, 17			11
Total	11		4		15

2977. λάθρα, lath'ra

Book	Oc.	privily	Oc.	secretly	Total
Mt.	2	1:19; 2:7			2
Jn.			1	11:28	1
Ac.	1	16:37			1
Total	3		1		4

2978. λαῖλαψ, lai'laps

Book	Oc.	storm	Oc.	tempest	Total
Mk.	1	4:37			1
Lk.	1	8:23			1
2 Pt.			1	2:17	1
Total	2		1		3

2979. λακτίζω, laktid'zō

Book	kick	Total
Ac.	9:5; 26:14	2

See page 212 for Word 2980.

2981. λαλιά, lalia'

Book	Oc.	speech	Oc.	saying	Total
Mt.	1	26:73			1
Mk.	1	14:70			1
Jn.	1	8:43	1	4:42	2
Total	3		1		4

2982. λαμά, lama'

Book	lama	Total
Mt.	27:46	1
Mk.	15:34	1
Total		2

2983. λαμβάνω, lamban'ō

Book	Oc.	receive	Oc.	take	Oc.	have	Oc.	catch	Oc.	Not Tr.	Oc.	Misc.	Total
Mt.	20	7:8; 10:8, 41, 41; 13:20; 17:24; 19:29; 20:7, 9, 10, 10, 11; 21:22, 34; 23:14; 25:16, 18, 20, 22, 24	31	8:17; 10:38; 13:31, 33; 14:19; 15:26, 36; 16:5, 7; 17:25, 27; 21:35; 22:15; 25:1, 3, 3, 4; 26: 26, 26, 27, 52; 27:1, 6, 7, 9, 24, 30, 48, 59; 28:12, 15			1	21:39			5	5:40; 12:14; 16:8, 9, 10	57
Mk.	6	4:16; 10:30; 11:24; 12:2, 40; 15: 23	12	6:41; 7:27; 8:6, 14; 9:36; 12: 8, 19, 20, 21; 14:22, 22, 23	1	12:22	1	12:3					20
Lk.	4	11:10; 19:12, 15; 20:47	14	5:5; 6:4; 9:16, 39; 13:19, 21; 20:28, 29, 30, 31; 22:17, 19; 24:30, 43							3	5:26; 7:16; 20:21	21
Jn.	29	1:12, 16; 3:11, 27, 32, 33; 4:36; 5: 34, 41, 43, 43, 44; 6:21; 7:23, 39; 10:18b; 12:48; 13:20, 20, 20, 20, 30; 14:17; 16:14, 24; 17:8; 18:3; 19:30; 20:22	16	6:7, 11; 10:17, 18a; 12:3, 13; 13:4, 12; 16:15; 18:31; 19:1, 6, 23, 27, 40; 21:13									45
Ac.	18	1:8; 2:33, 38; 3:5; 7:53; 8:15, 17, 19; 9:19; 10:43, 47; 16:24; 17: 15; 19:2; 20:24, 35; 26:10, 18	9	1:20, 25; 2:23; 9:25; 15:14; 16:3; 17:9; 27:35; 28:15	1	25:16			1	3:3	1	24:27	30
Ro.	7	1:5; 4:11; 5:11, 17; 8:15, 15; 13:2	2	7:8, 11									9
1 Co.	8	2:12; 3:8, 14; 4:7, 7, 7; 9:24; 14:5	3	10:13; 11:23, 24							1	9:25	12
2 Co.	3	11:4, 4, 24	2	11:8, 20			1	12:16					6
Gal.	2	3:2, 14									1	2:6	3
Phl.			1	2:7							1	3:12	2
Col.	1	4:10											1
1 Ti.	1	4:4											1
2 Ti.											1	1:5	1
Heb.	10	2:2; 7:5, 8, 9; 9:15; 10:26; 11:8, 11, 13, 35	3	5:1, 4; 9:19	1	11:36					3	2:3; 4:16; 11:29	17
Jas.	5	1:7, 12; 3:1; 4:3; 5:7	1	5:10									6
1 Pt.	1	4:10											1
2 Pt.	1	1:17									1	1:9	2
1 Jn.	3	2:27; 3:22; 5:9											3
2 Jn.	2	1:4, 10											2
3 Jn.			1	1:7									1
Rev.	12	2:17, 27; 3:3; 4:11; 5:12; 14:9, 11; 17:12, 12; 8:4; 19:20; 20:4	11	3:11; 5:7, 8, 9; 6:4; 8:5; 10:8, 9, 10; 11:17; 22:17									23
Total	133		106		3		3		1		17		263

Miscellaneous: Mt. 5:40, take away; Mt. 12:14, hold; Mt. 16:8, bring; Mt. 16:9, 10, take up; Lk. 5:26 (with 1611), be amazed; Lk. 7:16, come on; Lk. 20: 21, accept; Ac. 24:27 (with 1240), come into (one's) room; 1 Co. 9:25, obtain; Gal. 2:6, accept; Phl. 3:12, attain; 2 Ti. 1:5, call to; Heb. 2:3, begin; Heb. 4:16, obtain; Heb. 11:29 (with 3884), assay to do; 2 Pt. 1:9 (with 3024), forget.

2980. λαλέω, lale'ō

Book	Oc.	speak	Oc.	say	Oc.	tell	Oc.	talk	Oc.	preach	Oc.	utter	Oc.	Misc.	Total
Mt.	24	9:18, 33; 10:19, 19, 20, 20; 12:22, 34, 34, 36, 46b, 47; 13:3, 10, 13, 33, 34, 34; 14:27; 15:31; 17:5; 23:1; 26:47; 28:18			1	26:13	1	12:46a							26
Mk.	15	1:34; 2:7; 4:33, 34; 5:35, 36; 7:35, 37; 8:32; 13:11, 11, 11; 14:43; 16:17, 19	1	9:6			1	6:50	1	2:2			1	14:9	19
Lk.	25	1:19, 20, 22, 55, 64, 70; 2:33, 38, 50; 4: 41; 5:4, 21; 6:45; 7:15; 8:49; 9:11; 11: 14, 37; 12:3; 22:47, 60; 24:6, 25, 36, 44			4	1:45; 2: 17, 18, 20							1	24:32	30
Jn.	47	1:37; 3:11, 31, 34; 4:26; 6:63; 7:13, 17, 18, 26, 46; 8:12, 20, 28, 30, 38, 44, 44; 9:21, 29; 10:6; 12:29, 36, 41, 48, 49, 49, 50, 50; 14:10, 10, 25; 15:3, 11, 22; 16: 1, 13, 13, 25, 25, 29, 33; 17:1, 13; 18: 20a, 23; 19:10	6	8:25, 26; 16: 6, 18; 18: 20b, 21	2	8:40; 16:4	4	4:27, 27; 9: 37; 14: 30							59
Ac.	47	2:4, 6, 7, 11, 31; 3:21, 24; 4:1, 17, 20, 29, 31; 5:20, 40; 6:10, 11, 13; 7:6, 38, 44; 8:26; 9:27, 29; 10:7, 32, 44, 46; 11: 15, 20; 13:46; 14:1, 9; 16:13, 14, 32; 17:19; 18:9, 25; 19:6; 20:30; 21:39; 22:9; 23:9; 26:14, 26; 28:21, 25	4	3:22; 23:7, 18; 26:22	5	9:6; 10: 6; 11: 14; 22: 10; 27: 25	1	26:31	5	8:25; 11: 19; 13: 42; 14: 25; 16:6					62
Ro.	2	7:1; 15:18	1	3:19											3
1 Co.	32	2:6, 7, 13; 3:1; 12:3, 30; 13:1, 11; 14: 2, 2, 2, 3, 4, 5, 5, 6, 6, 9, 9, 11, 11, 13, 18, 19, 21, 23, 27, 28, 29, 34, 35, 39	1	9:8											33
2 Co.	9	2:17; 4:13, 13; 7:14; 11:17, 17, 23; 12: 19; 13:3									1	12:4			10
Eph.	3	4:25; 5:19; 6:20													3
Phl.	1	1:14													1
Col.	2	4:3, 4													2
1 Th.	4	1:8; 2:2, 4, 16													4
1 Ti.	1	5:13													1
Tit.	2	2:1, 15													2
Heb.	13	1:1, 2; 2:2, 3, 5; 4:8; 6:9; 7:14; 9:19; 11:4; 12:24, 25; 13:7	2	5:5; 11:18									1	3:5	16
Jas.	3	1:19; 2:12; 5:10													3
1 Pt.	2	3:10; 4:11													2
2 Pt.	2	1:21; 3:16													2
1 Jn.	1	4:5													1
2 Jn.	1	1:12													1
3 Jn.	1	1:14													1
Jd.	2	1:15, 16													2
Rev.	5	1:12; 10:8; 13:5, 11, 15					4	4:1; 17: 1; 21:9, 15			3	10:3, 4, 4			12
Total	244		15		12		11		6		4		3		295

Miscellaneous: Mk. 14:9, speak of; Lk. 24:32, talk with; Heb. 3:5, speak after.

2984. Λάμεχ, Lam'ech

Book	Lamech	Total
Lk.	3:36	1

2985. λαμπάς, lampas'

Book	Oc.	lamp	Oc.	torch	Oc.	light	Total
Mt.	5	25:1, 3, 4, 7, 8					5
Jn.			1	18:3			1
Ac.					1	20:8	1
Rev.	2	4:5; 8:10					2
Total	7		1		1		9

2988. λαμπρῶς, lamprōs'

Book	sumptuously	Total
Lk.	16:19	1

2987. λαμπρότης, lamprot'ēs

Book	brightness	Total
Ac.	26:13	1

2991. λαξευτός, laxeutos'

Book	hewn in stone	Total
Lk.	23:53	1

2986. λαμπρός, lampros'

Book	Oc.	bright	Oc.	goodly	Oc.	white	Oc.	gorgeous	Oc.	gay	Oc.	clear	Total
Lk.							1	23:11					1
Ac.	1	10:30											1
Jas.			1	2:2					1	2:3			2
Rev.	1	22:16	1	18:14	2	15:6; 19:8					1	22:1	5
Total	2		2		2		1		1		1		9

2989. λάμπω, lam'pō

Book	Oc.	shine	Oc.	give light	Total
Mt.	2	5:16; 17:2	1	5:15	3
Lk.	1	17:24			1
Ac.	1	12:7			1
2 Co.	2	4:6, 6			2
Total	6		1		7

2990. λανθάνω, lanthan'ō

Book	Oc.	be hid	Oc.	be ignorant of	Oc.	unawares	Total
Mk.	1	7:24					1
Lk.	1	8:47					1
Ac.	1	26:26					1
Heb.					1	13:2	1
2 Pt.			2	3:5, 8			2
Total	3		2		1		6

2992. λαός, laos'

Book	people	Total
Mt.	1:21; 2:4, 6; 4:16, 23; 9:35; 13:15; 15:8; 21:23; 26:3, 5, 47; 27:1, 25, 64	15
Mk.	7:6; 11:32; 14:2	3
Lk.	1:10, 17, 21, 68, 77; 2:10, 31, 32; 3:15, 18, 21; 6:17; 7:1, 16, 29; 8:47; 9:13; 18:43; 19:47, 48; 20:1, 6, 9, 19, 26, 45; 21:23, 38; 22:2, 66; 23:5, 13, 14, 27, 35; 24:19	36
Jn.	8:2; 11:50; 18:14	3
Ac.	2:47; 3:9, 11, 12, 23; 4:1, 2, 8, 10, 17, 21, 25, 27; 5:12, 13, 20, 25, 26, 34, 37; 6:8, 12; 7:17, 34; 10:2, 41, 42; 12:4, 11; 13:15, 17, 17, 24, 31; 15:14; 18:10; 19:4; 21:28, 30, 36, 39, 40; 23:5; 26:17, 23; 28:17, 26, 27	48
Ro.	9:25, 25, 26; 10:21; 11:1, 2; 15:10, 11	8
1 Co.	10:7; 14:21	2
2 Co.	6:16	1
Tit.	2:14	1
Heb.	2:17; 4:9; 5:3; 7:5, 11, 27; 8:10; 9:7, 19, 19; 10:30; 11:25; 13:12	13
1 Pt.	2:9, 10, 10	3
2 Pt.	2:1	1
Jd.	1:5	1
Rev.	5:9; 7:9; 10:11; 11:9; 14:6; 17:15; 18:4; 21:3	8
Total		143

2993. Λαοδίκεια, Laodik'eia

Book	Laodicea	Total
Col.	2:1; 4:13, 15, 16	4
Rev.	1:11	1
Total		5

2996. Λασαία, Lasai'a

Book	Lasea	Total
Ac.	27:8	1

2994. Λαοδικεύς, Laodikeus'

Book	Laodiceans	Total
Col.	4:16	1
Rev.	3:14	1
Total		2

2997. λάσχω, las'chō

Book	burst asunder	Total
Ac.	1:18	1

2998. λατομέω, latome'ō

Book	hew	Total
Mt.	27:60	1
Mk.	15:46	1
Total		2

2995. λάρυγξ, lar'ungx

Book	throat	Total
Ro.	3:13	1

2999. λατρεία, latrei'a

Book	Oc.	service	Oc.	divine service	Total
Jn.	1	16:2			1
Ro.	2	9:4; 12:1			2
Heb.	1	9:6	1	9:1	2
Total	4		1		5

3001. λάχανον, lach'anon

Book	herb	Total
Mt.	13:32	1
Mk.	4:32	1
Lk.	11:42	1
Ro.	14:2	1
Total		4

3002. Λεββαῖος, Lebbai'os

Book	Lebbaeus	Total
Mt.	10:3	1

3003. λεγεών, legeōn'

Book	legion	Total
Mt.	26:53	1
Mk.	5:9, 15	2
Lk.	8:30	1
Total		4

3000. λατρεύω, latreu'ō

Book	Oc.	serve	Oc.	worship	Oc.	do the service	Oc.	worshipper	Total
Mt.	1	4:10							1
Lk.	3	1:74; 2:37; 4:8							3
Ac.	3	7:7; 26:7; 27:23	2	7:42; 24:14					5
Ro.	2	1:9, 25							2
Phl.			1	3:3					1
2 Ti.	1	1:3							1
Heb.	4	8:5; 9:14; 12:28; 13:10			1	9:9	1	10:2	6
Rev.	2	7:15; 22:3							2
Total	16		3		1		1		21

See page 214 for Word 3004.

3005. λεῖμμα, leim'ma

Book	remnant	Total
Ro.	11:5	1

3007. λείπω, lei'pō

Book	Oc.	lack	Oc.	be wanting	Oc.	want (with 1722)	Oc.	be destitute	Total
Lk.	1	18:22							1
Tit.			2	1:5; 3:13					2
Jas.	1	1:5			1	1:4	1	2:15	3
Total	2		2		1		1		6

3006. λεῖος, lei'os

Book	smooth	Total
Lk.	3:5	1

3008. λειτουργέω, leitourge'ō

Book	minister	Total
Ac.	13:2	1
Ro.	15:27	1
Heb.	10:11	1
Total		3

3009. λειτουργία, leitourgi'a

Book	Oc.	service	Oc.	ministry	Oc.	ministration	Total
Lk.					1	1:23	1
2 Co.	1	9:12					1
Phl.	2	2:17, 30					2
Heb.			2	8:6; 9:21			2
Total	3		2		1		6

3010. λειτουργικός, leitourgikos'

Book	ministering	Total
Heb.	1:14	1

3004. λέγω, leg´ō

Book	Oc.	say	Oc.	speak	Oc.	call	Oc.	tell	Oc.	Misc.	Total
Mt.	275	1:20, 22; 2:2, 13, 15, 17, 20; 3:2, 3, 9, 9, 14, 17; 4:6, 9, 10, 14, 17, 19; 5:2, 18, 20, 22, 26, 28, 32, 34, 39, 44; 6:2, 5, 16, 25, 29, 31; 7:21; 8:2, 3, 4, 6, 7, 9, 10, 11, 17, 20, 25, 26, 27, 29, 31; 9: 6, 9b, 14, 18, 21, 24, 27, 28, 28, 29, 30, 33, 34, 37; 10:5, 7, 15, 23, 42; 11:7, 9, 11, 17, 18, 19, 22, 24; 12:6, 10, 13, 17, 23, 31, 36, 38, 44; 13:3, 14, 17, 24, 31, 35, 36, 51, 51, 54; 14:4, 15, 17, 26, 27, 30, 31, 33; 15:1, 4, 5, 7, 22, 23, 25, 33, 34; 16:2, 7, 13, 13, 15, 15, 18, 22, 28; 17:5, 9, 10, 10, 12, 14, 20, 25, 25, 26; 18: 1, 3, 10,13, 18, 19, 22,22, 26, 28,29, 32; 19:3, 7, 8, 9, 10, 18, 20, 23, 24, 25, 28; 20:6, 7, 7, 8, 12, 21, 22, 23, 30, 31, 33; 21:2, 4, 9, 10, 11, 13, 15, 16, 16, 19, 20, 21, 23, 25, 31, 31, 31, 37, 41, 42, 43; 22:1, 4, 8, 12, 16, 20, 21, 21, 23, 24, 31, 35, 42, 42, 43, 43; 23:2, 3, 16, 30, 36, 39; 24:2, 3, 5, 34, 47; 25:9, 11, 12, 20, 37, 40, 44, 45, 45; 26:5, 8, 13, 17, 18, 21, 22, 25, 27, 29, 31, 34, 35, 36b, 38, 39, 40, 42, 45, 48, 52, 64, 64, 65, 68, 69, 70, 70. 71; 27:4, 9, 11, 11, 13, 19, 22a, 22c, 23, 24, 29, 40, 41, 46, 47, 49, 54, 63; 28:9, 10, 13, 18	1	21:45	13	1:16; 2:23; 4: 18; 10:2; 13: 55; 19:17; 26: 3, 14, 36a; 27: 16, 17, 22b, 33a	2	10:27; 21: 27	2	9:9a; 27:33b	293
Mk.	196	1:7, 15, 24, 25, 27, 37, 38, 40, 41, 44; 2:5, 10, 11, 12, 14, 16, 17, 18, 24, 25, 27; 3:3, 4, 5, 11, 21, 22, 23, 28, 30, 33, 34; 4:2, 9, 11, 13, 21, 24, 26, 30, 35, 38, 41; 5:8, 9, 12, 19, 23, 28, 30, 31, 31, 35, 36, 39, 41, 41; 6:2, 4, 10, 11, 14, 15, 15, 18, 25, 35, 37, 38, 38, 50; 7:9, 11, 14, 18, 20, 28, 34, 37; 8:1, 12, 12, 15, 16, 17, 19, 21, 24, 26, 27, 27, 29, 29, 29, 33; 9:1, 1, 5, 7, 11, 11, 13, 19, 24, 25, 26, 31, 35, 38, 41; 10:11, 15, 23, 24, 26, 27, 28, 29, 35, 42, 47, 49, 51; 11:2, 5, 9, 17, 21, 22, 23, 23, 24, 28, 31, 33a, 33b; 12:6, 14, 16, 18, 18, 26, 35, 35, 38, 43, 43; 13:1, 5, 6, 30, 37, 37; 14:2, 4, 9, 12, 13, 14, 18, 19, 25, 27, 30, 30, 31b, 32, 34, 36, 37, 41, 44, 45, 57, 58, 60, 61, 63, 65, 67, 68, 68, 69, 70; 15: 2, 4, 9, 14, 28, 29, 31, 34, 35, 36; 16:3, 6	3	12:1; 14:31a, 71	3	10:18; 12:37; 15:12	4	1:30; 8: 30; 10:32; 11:33c	1	15:7	207
Lk.	195	1:24, 63, 66, 67; 2:13; 3:4, 7, 8, 8, 10, 11, 14, 16, 22; 4:4, 21, 22, 24, 34, 35, 36, 41; 5:8, 12, 21, 24, 26, 30, 39; 6:5, 20, 27, 42, 46; 7:4, 6, 8, 9, 14, 16, 19, 20, 26, 28, 32, 33, 34, 39, 47, 49; 8:8, 9, 20, 24, 25, 30, 38, 45, 49, 50, 54; 9:7, 18, 18, 20, 23, 33, 35, 38; 10:2, 5, 9, 12, 17, 25; 11:2, 8, 9, 18, 24, 29, 45, 45, 51, 53; 12:1, 4, 5, 8, 16, 17, 22, 27, 37, 44, 54, 54, 55; 13:8, 14, 17, 18, 24, 25, 26, 31, 35; 14:3, 7b, 12, 24, 30; 15:2, 3, 6, 7, 9, 10; 16:1, 5, 7, 9, 29; 17:4, 6, 10, 13, 37; 18:2, 3, 6, 13, 17, 18, 29, 38, 41; 19:7, 14, 16, 18, 20, 22, 26, 38, 42, 46; 20:2, 5, 14, 21, 21, 28, 41, 42; 21:3, 7, 8, 10, 32; 22:11, 16, 18, 19, 20, 37, 42, 57, 59, 60, 64, 66, 70; 23:2, 2, 3, 3, 5, 18, 21, 30, 34, 35, 37, 39, 40, 42, 43, 47; 24:7, 23, 23, 29, 34, 36	12	5:36; 7:24; 9:31, 34; 11:27; 12: 41; 13:6; 18:1, 34; 20:9; 21:5; 22:65	4	18:19; 20:37; 22:1, 47	15	4:25; 9: 27; 10:24; 12:51, 59; 13:3, 5, 27; 17:34; 18:8, 14; 19:40; 20: 8; 22:34; 24:10	1	14:7a	227
Jn.	239	1:15, 21, 22, 26, 29, 32, 36, 38a, 39, 41, 43, 45, 46, 47, 48, 49, 51, 51; 2:3, 4, 5, 5, 7, 8, 10, 22; 3:3, 4, 5, 11; 4:7, 9, 10, 11, 15, 16, 17, 19, 20, 21, 25a, 26, 28, 31, 33, 34, 35, 35, 42, 49, 50, 51; 5:6, 8, 10, 18, 19, 24, 25, 34; 6:5, 6, 8, 12, 14, 20, 26, 32, 42, 42, 47, 52, 53, 65; 7:6, 11, 12, 12, 15, 25, 26, 28, 31, 37, 40, 41, 41, 50; 8:4, 5, 6, 12, 19, 22, 22, 25, 31, 33, 34, 39, 46, 48, 51, 52, 54, 58; 9:2, 8, 9, 9, 10, 12, 16, 16, 17, 17, 19, 19, 41; 10:1, 7, 20, 21, 24, 33, 36, 41; 11:3, 7, 8, 11, 23, 24, 27, 31, 32, 34, 36, 39, 39, 40, 44, 47; 12:4, 21, 23, 24, 29, 29, 33, 34; 13:6, 8, 9, 10, 13, 16, 20, 21, 25, 27, 29, 31, 33, 36, 37, 38; 14:5, 6, 8, 9, 9, 12, 22; 16:12, 17, 18, 18, 20, 23, 26, 29a; 18:5, 17, 17, 26, 34, 37, 38, 38, 40; 19:3, 4, 5, 6, 6, 9, 10, 12, 14, 15, 21, 24, 26, 27, 28,35, 37; 20:2, 13,13,15,15,16a,16b,17,19, 22,25,27, 29; 21:3, 3, 5, 7,10,12,15,15,15,16,16,16,17, 17, 18, 19, 21, 22	10	2:21; 6:71; 8:26, 27; 11:13, 56; 13:18, 22, 24; 16:29b	11	4:5, 25b; 9:11; 11:16, 54; 15: 15; 19:13, 17, 17; 20:24; 21:2	5	8:45; 12: 22, 22; 13: 19; 16:7	2	1:38b; 20:16c	267
Ac.	83	1:6; 2:7, 12, 13, 17, 34, 40; 3:25; 4:16, 32; 5:23, 25, 28, 38; 6:11, 13, 14; 7:48, 49, 59; 8:10, 19, 26; 9:4, 21; 10:26; 11:3, 4, 7, 16, 18; 12:7, 8, 15; 13:15a, 25, 35; 14:11; 15:5, 13, 17, 24; 16:9, 15, 17, 28, 35; 17:7, 18, 18, 19; 18:13; 19:4, 13, 26, 28; 20:23; 21:4, 11, 21, 23, 37, 40; 22:7, 18, 22, 26; 23:8, 9, 12, 30; 24:2; 25:14; 26:14,22, 31; 27:10, 24,33; 28:4, 6,17, 26	9	1:3; 2:25; 8:6, 34; 13:45; 24:10; 26:1; 27:11; 28: 24	5	3:2; 6:9; 9:36; 10:28; 24:14	2	17:21; 22: 27	6	5:36; 8:9; 13: 15b; 14: 15, 18; 25:20	105
Ro.	30	2:22; 3:8, 19; 4:3, 9; 7:7; 9:1, 15, 17, 25; 10:8, 11, 16, 18, 19, 19, 20, 21; 11:1, 2, 2, 4, 9, 11; 12:3, 19; 14:11; 15:8, 10, 12	4	3:5; 6:19; 10:6; 11:13					1	4:6	35
1 Co.	12	1:12, 12; 3:4; 7:8; 9:8, 10; 10:29; 11:25; 14:16, 21, 34; 15:12	7	1:10; 6:5; 7:6, 12, 35; 10:15; 15:34	2	8:5; 12:3			1	15:51	22
2 Co.	6	6:2, 17, 18; 9:3, 4; 11:16	5	6:13; 7:3; 8:8; 11:21, 21							11
Gal.	7	1:9; 3:16, 17; 4:1, 30; 5:2, 16	1	3:15			1	4:21			9
Eph.	3	4:8, 17; 5:14	2	5:12, 32	2	2:11, 11					7
Phl.			1	4:11			2	3:18, 18			3
Col.	1	2:4			1	4:11					2
1 Th.	2	4:15; 5:3									2
2 Th.					1	2:4	1	2:5			2
1 Ti.	2	1:7; 5:18	2	2:7; 4:1							4
2 Ti.	2	2:7, 18									2
Tit.	1	2:8									1
Phe.	2	1:19, 21									2
Heb.	25	1:6, 7; 2:6, 12; 3:7, 15; 4:7; 5:6; 6:14; 7:21; 8:8, 8, 9, 10, 11, 13; 9:20; 10:5, 8, 16, 30; 11:14, 32; 12:26; 13:6	3	7:13; 8:1; 9:5	4	7:11; 9:2, 3; 11:24			1	5:11	33
Jas.	7	1:13; 2:14, 23; 4:5, 6, 13, 15									7
2 Pt.	1	3:4									1
1 Jn.	4	2:4, 6, 9; 5:16									4
2 Jn.									2	1:10, 11	2
Jd.	1	1:14					1	1:18			2
Rev.	90	1:8, 11, 17; 2:1, 7, 8, 9, 11, 12, 17, 18, 24a, 29; 3:1, 6, 7, 9, 13, 14, 17, 22; 4:1, 8, 10; 5:5, 9, 12, 13, 14; 6:1, 3, 5, 6, 7, 10, 16; 7:3, 10, 12, 13; 8:13; 9:14; 10:4, 8, 9, 9, 11; 11:1, 12, 15, 17; 12:10; 13:4, 14; 14:7, 8, 9, 13, 13, 18; 15:3; 16:1, 5, 7, 17; 17: 1, 15; 18:2, 4, 7, 10, 16, 18, 19, 21; 19:1, 4, 5, 6, 9, 9, 10, 17; 21:3, 5, 9; 22:9, 10, 17, 20	1	2:24b	2	2:20; 8:11					93
Total	1184		61		48		33		17		1343

Miscellaneous: Mt. 9:9a, name; Mt. 27:33b, to say; Mk. 15:7, name; Lk. 14:7a, put forth; Jn. 1:38b; 20:16c, be to say; Ac. 5:36, boast; Ac. 8:9, give out Ac. 13:15b, say on; Ac. 14:15, saying; Ac. 14:18 (with 4923), with these sayings; Ac. 25:20, ask; Ro. 4:6, describe; 1 Co. 15:51, shew; Heb. 5:11, to say; 2 Jn. 1:10, 11, bid.

3011. λειτουργός, leitourgos′

Book	Oc.	minister	Oc.	he that ministers	Total
Ro.	2	13:6; 15:16			2
Phl.			1	2:25	1
Heb.	2	1:7; 8:2			2
Total	4		1		5

3012. λέντιον, len′tion

Book	towel	Total
Jn.	13:4, 5	2

3013. λεπίς, lepis′

Book	scale	Total
Ac.	9:18	1

3014. λέπρα, lep′ra

Book	leprosy	Total
Mt.	8:3	1
Mk.	1:42	1
Lk.	5:12, 13	2
Total		4

3015. λεπρός, lepros′

Book	leper	Total
Mt.	8:2; 10:8; 11:5; 26:6	4
Mk.	1:40; 14:3	2
Lk.	4:27; 7:22; 17:12	3
Total		9

3016. λεπτόν, lepton′

Book	mite	Total
Mk.	12:42	1
Lk.	12:59; 21:2	2
Total		3

3017. Λευΐ, Leui′

Book	Oc.	Levi (Son of Jacob)	Oc.	Levi (Son of Melchi)	Oc.	Levi (Son of Simeon)	Total
Lk.			1	3:24	1	3:29	2
Heb.	2	7:5, 9					2
Rev.	1	7:7					1
Total	3		1		1		5

3018. Λευΐς, Leuis′

Book	Levi	Total
Mk.	2:14	1
Lk.	5:27, 29	2
Total		3

3019. Λευΐτης, Leui′tes

Book	Levite	Total
Lk.	10:32	1
Jn.	1:19	1
Ac.	4:36	1
Total		3

3021. λευκαίνω, leukai′nō

Book	Oc.	white	Oc.	make white	Total
Mk.	1	9:3			1
Rev.			1	7:14	1
Total	1		1		2

3022. λευκός, leukos′

Book	white	Total
Mt.	5:36; 17:2; 28:3	3
Mk.	9:3; 16:5	2
Lk.	9:29	1
Jn.	4:35; 20:12	2
Ac.	1:10	1
Rev.	1:14, 14; 2:17; 3:4, 5, 18; 4:4; 6:2, 11; 7:9, 13; 14:14; 19:11, 14, 14; 20:11	16
Total		25

3020. Λευϊτικός, Leuitikos′

Book	Levitical	Total
Heb.	7:11	1

3025. ληνός, lenos′

Book	Oc.	winepress	Oc.	winepress (with 3531)	Total
Mt.	1	21:33			1
Rev.	3	14:19, 20, 20	1	19:15	4
Total	4		1		5

3023. λεών, leōn′

Book	lion	Total
2 Ti.	4:17	1
Heb.	11:33	1
1 Pt.	5:8	1
Rev.	4:7; 5:5; 9:8, 17; 10:3; 13:2	6
Total		9

3024. λήθη, le′the

Book	forget (with 2983)	Total
2 Pt.	1:9	1

3026. λῆρος, le′ros

Book	idle tales	Total
Lk.	24:11	1

3028. λῆψις, lep′sis

Book	receiving	Total
Phl.	4:15	1

3031. λιβανωτός, libanōtos′

Book	censer	Total
Rev.	8:3, 5	2

3027. λῃστής, lestes′

Book	Oc.	thief	Oc.	robber	Total
Mt.	4	21:13; 26:55; 27:38, 44			4
Mk.	3	11:17; 14:48; 15:27			3
Lk.	4	10:30, 36; 19:46; 22:52			4
Jn.			3	10:1, 8; 18:40	3
2 Co.			1	11:26	1
Total	11		4		15

3030. λίβανος, lib′anos

Book	frankincense	Total
Mt.	2:11	1
Rev.	18:13	1
Total		2

3032. Λιβερτῖνος, Liberti′nos

Book	Libertine	Total
Ac.	6:9	1

3029. λίαν, li′an

Book	Oc.	exceeding	Oc.	greatly	Oc.	very chiefest (with 5128)	Oc.	great	Oc.	sore	Oc.	very	Total
Mt.	3	2:16; 4:8; 8:28	1	27:14									4
Mk.	1	9:3					1	1:35	1	6:51	1	16:2	4
Lk.	1	23:8											1
2 Co.					2	11:5; 12:11							2
2 Ti.			1	4:15									1
2 Jn.			1	1:4									1
3 Jn.			1	1:3									1
Total	5		4		2		1		1		1		14

3033. Λιβύη, Libu′e

Book	Libya	Total
Ac.	2:10	1

3035. λίθινος, lith′inos

Book	of stone	Total
Jn.	2:6	1
2 Co.	3:3	1
Rev.	9:20	1
Total		3

3034. λιθάζω, lithad′zō

Book	stone	Total
Jn.	10:31, 32, 33; 11:8	4
Ac.	5:26; 14:19	2
2 Co.	11:25	1
Heb.	11:37	1
Total		8

3036. λιθοβολέω, lithobole′ō

Book	Oc.	stone	Oc.	cast stone	Total
Mt.	2	21:35; 23:37			2
Mk.			1	12:4	1
Lk.	1	13:34			1
Jn.	1	8:5			1
Ac.	3	7:58, 59; 14:5			3
Heb.	1	12:20			1
Total	8		1		9

3037. λίθος, li′thos

Book	Oc.	stone	Oc.	one stone	Oc.	another	Oc.	stumbling stone (with 4248)	Oc.	mill stone (with 3357)	Total
Mt.	9	3:9; 4:3, 6; 7:9; 21:42, 44; 27:60, 66; 28:2	1	24:2a	1	24:2b					11
Mk.	6	5:5; 12:10; 13:1; 15:46; 16:3, 4	1	13:2a	1	13:2b			1	9:42	9
Lk.	10	3:8; 4:3, 11; 11:11; 19:40; 20:17, 18; 21:5; 22:41; 24:2	2	19:44a; 21:6a	2	19:44b; 21:6b					14
Jn.	7	8:7, 59; 10:31; 11:38, 39, 41; 20:1									7
Ac.	2	4:11; 17:29									2
Ro.							2	9:32, 33			2
1 Co.	1	3:12									1
2 Co.	1	3:7									1
1 Pt.	5	2:4, 5, 6, 7, 8									5
Rev.	8	4:3; 17:4; 18:12, 16, 21; 21:11, 11, 19									8
Total	49		4		4		2		1		60

3038. λιθόστρωτος, lithos'trōtos

Book	Pavement	Total
Jn.	19:13	1

3039. λικμάω, likma'ō

Book	grind to powder	Total
Mt.	21:44	1
Lk.	20:18	1
Total		2

3040. λιμήν, limēn'

Book	Oc.	haven	Oc.	the fair havens (with 2570)	Total
Ac.	2	27:12, 12	1	27:8	3

3042. λιμός, limos'

Book	Oc.	famine	Oc.	hunger	Oc.	dearth	Total
Mt.	1	24:7					1
Mk.	1	13:8					1
Lk.	3	4:25; 15:14; 21:11	1	15:17			4
Ac.					2	7:11; 11:28	2
Ro.	1	8:35					1
2 Co.			1	11:27			1
Rev.	1	18:8	1	6:8			2
Total	7		3		2		12

3041. λίμνη, lim'nē

Book	lake	Total
Lk.	5:1, 2; 8:22, 23, 33	5
Rev.	19:20; 20:10, 14, 15; 21:8	5
Total		10

3045. λιπαρός, liparos'

Book	dainty	Total
Rev.	18:14	1

3046. λίτρα, li'tra

Book	pound	Total
Jn.	12:3; 19:39	2

3044. Λῖνος, Li'nos

Book	Linus	Total
2 Ti.	4:21	1

3047. λίψ, lips

Book	south west	Total
Ac.	27:12	1

3043. λίνον, li'non

Book	Oc.	flax	Oc.	linen	Total
Mt.	1	12:20			1
Rev.			1	15:6	1
Total	1		1		2

3048. λογία, logi'a

Book	Oc.	collection	Oc.	gatherings	Total
1 Co.	1	16:1	1	16:2	2

3049. λογίζομαι, logid'zomai

Book	Oc.	think	Oc.	impute	Oc.	reckon	Oc.	count	Oc.	account	Oc.	suppose	Oc.	reason	Oc.	number	Oc.	Misc.	Total
Mk.													1	11:31	1	15:28			2
Lk.					1	22:37													1
Ac.																	1	19:27	1
Ro.	1	2:3	6	4:6, 8, 11, 22, 23, 24	5	4:4, 9, 10; 6:11; 8:18	4	2:26; 4:3, 5; 9:8	1	8:36							2	3:28; 14:14	19
1 Co.	2	13:5, 11							1	4:1									3
2 Co.	6	3:5; 10:2, 2, 7, 11;	1	5:19							1	11:5							8
Gal.		12:6							1	3:6									1
Phl.							1	3:13									1	4:8	2
2 Ti.																	1	4:16	1
Heb.									1	11:19									1
Jas.			1	2:23															1
1 Pt.											1	5:12							1
Total	9		8		6		5		4		2		1		1		5		41

Miscellaneous: Ac. 19:27 (with 1519 and 3662), despise; Ro. 3:28, conclude; Ro. 14:14, esteem; Phl. 4:8, think on; 2 Ti. 4:16, lay to (one's) charge.

3050. λογικός, logikos'

Book	Oc.	reasonable	Oc.	of the word	Total
Ro.	1	12:1			1
1 Pt.			1	2:2	1
Total	1		1		2

3053. λογισμός, logismos'

Book	Oc.	thought	Oc.	imagination	Total
Ro.	1	2:15			1
2 Co.			1	10:5	1
Total	1		1		2

3051. λόγιον, log'ion

Book	oracle	Total
Ac.	7:38	1
Ro.	3:2	1
Heb.	5:12	1
1 Pt.	4:11	1
Total		4

3052. λόγιος, log'ios

Book	eloquent	Total
Ac.	18:24	1

3054. λογομαχέω, logomache'ō

Book	strive about words	Total
2 Ti.	2:14	1

3055. λογομαχία, logomachi'a

Book	strife of words	Total
1 Ti.	6:4	1

See page 217 for Word 3056.

3058. λοιδορέω, loidore'ō

Book	revile	Total
Jn.	9:28	1
Ac.	23:4	1
1 Co.	4:12	1
1 Pt.	2:23	1
Total		4

3059. λοιδορία, loidori'a

Book	Oc.	railing	Oc.	to speak reproachfully (with 5384)	Total
1 Ti.			1	5:14	1
1 Pt.	2	3:9, 9			2
Total	2		1		3

3057. λόγχη, long'chē

Book	spear	Total
Jn.	19:34	1

3061. λοιμός, loimos'

Book	Oc.	pestilence	Oc.	pestilent	Total
Mt.	1	24:7			1
Lk.	1	21:11			1
Ac.			1	24:5	1
Total	2		1		3

3060. λοίδορος, loi'doros

Book	Oc.	railer	Oc.	reviler	Total
1 Co.	1	5:11	1	6:10	2

3062. λοιποί, loipoi'

Book	Oc.	other	Oc.	rest	Oc.	others	Oc.	remnant	Oc.	residue	Oc.	which remain	Oc.	other things	Total
Mt.	1	25:11	1	27:49			1	22:6							3
Mk.									1	16:13			1	4:19	2
Lk.	2	18:11; 24:10	2	12:26; 24:9	2	8:10; 18:9									6
Ac.	1	17:9	3	2:37; 5:13; 27:44	1	28:9									5
Ro.	1	1:13	1	11:7											2
1 Co.	2	9:5; 15:37	2	7:12; 11:34											4
2 Co.	2	12:13; 13:2													2
Gal.	1	2:13													1
Eph.	1	4:17			1	2:3									2
Phl.	2	1:13; 4:3													2
1 Th.					2	4:13; 5:6									2
1 Ti.					1	5:20									1
2 Pt.	1	3:16													1
Rev.	1	8:13	3	2:24; 9:20; 20:5			3	11:13; 12:17; 19:21			1	3:2			8
Total	15		12		7		4		1		1		1		41

3056. λόγος, log'os

Book	Oc.	word	Oc.	saying	Oc.	account	Oc.	speech	Oc.	Word (Christ)	Oc.	thing	Oc.	Not Tr.	Oc.	Misc.	Total
Mt.	16	8:8, 16; 10:14; 12: 32, 37, 37; 13:19, 20, 21, 22, 22, 23; 15:23; 22:46; 24: 35; 26:44	9	7:24, 26, 28; 15:12; 19:1, 11, 22; 26:1; 28:15	2	12:36; 18:23					1	21:24			4	5:32, 37; 22:15; 25:19	32
Mk.	18	2:2; 4:14, 15, 15, 16, 17, 18, 19, 20, 33; 5:36; 7:13; 8: 38; 10:24; 12:13; 13:31; 14:39; 16: 20	4	7:29; 8:32; 9:10; 10:22											2	1:45; 11:29	24
Lk.	23	1:2, 20; 3:4; 4:22, 32, 36; 5:1; 7:7; 8: 11, 12, 13, 15, 21; 9:26; 10:39; 11:28; 12:10; 20:20; 21: 33; 22:61; 23:9; 24:19, 44	4	1:29; 6:47; 9:28, 44	1	16:2					2	1:4; 20:3			3	5:15; 7: 17; 24: 17	33
Jn.	19	2:22; 4:41, 50; 5: 24, 38; 8:31, 37, 43; 10:35; 12:48; 14:23, 24b; 15:3, 20a, 25; 17:6, 14, 17, 20	17	4:37, 39; 6: 60; 7:36, 40; 8:51, 52, 55; 10:19; 12:38; 14:24a; 15: 20b; 18:9, 32; 19:8, 13; 21: 23					4	1:1, 1, 1, 14							40
Ac.	47	2:22, 40, 41; 4:4, 29, 31; 5:5; 6:2, 4, 7; 7:22; 8:4, 14, 25; 10:36, 44; 11: 1, 19; 12:24; 13:5, 7, 15, 26, 44, 46, 48, 49; 14:3, 25; 15:7, 15, 24, 32, 35, 36; 16:6, 32; 17: 11, 13; 18:11, 15; 19:10, 20; 20:32, 35, 38; 22:22	3	6:5; 7:29; 16:36	1	19:40	1	20:7			1	5:24	1	20:2	10	1:1; 8: 21; 10: 29; 11: 22; 14: 12; 15: 6, 27; 18:14; 19:38; 20:24	64
Ro.	3	9:6, 9; 15:18	2	3:4; 13:9	1	14:12									2	9:28, 28	8
1 Co.	10	1:17; 2:4b, 13; 4: 20; 12:8, 8; 14:9, 19, 19, 36	1	15:54			3	2:1, 4a; 4:19					1	15:2	2	1:5, 18	17
2 Co.	6	1:18; 2:17; 4:2; 5: 19; 6:7; 10:11					2	10:10; 11:6							1	8:7	9
Gal.	2	5:14; 6:6															2
Eph.	2	1:13; 5:6													2	4:29; 6:19	4
Phl.	2	1:14; 2:16			1	4:17									1	4:15	4
Col.	4	1:5, 25; 3:16, 17					1	4:6							2	2:23; 4:3	7
1 Th.	9	1:5, 6, 8; 2:5, 13, 13, 13; 4:15, 18															9
2 Th.	5	2:2, 15, 17; 3:1, 14															5
1 Ti.	5	4:5, 6, 12; 5:17; 6:3	3	1:15; 3:1; 4:9													8
2 Ti.	6	1:13; 2:9, 15, 17; 4:2, 15	1	2:11													7
Tit.	3	1:3, 9; 2:5	1	3:8			1	2:8									5
Heb.	8	2:2; 4:2, 12; 5:13; 7:28; 12:19; 13:7, 22			1	13:17					1	5:11			2	4:13; 6:1	12
Jas.	5	1:18, 21, 22, 23; 3:2															5
1 Pt.	4	1:23; 2:8; 3:1, 1			1	4:5									1	3:15	6
2 Pt.	4	1:19; 2:3; 3:5, 7															4
1 Jn.	5	1:10; 2:5, 7, 14; 3:18							2	1:1; 5:7							7
3 Jn.	1	1:10															1
Rev.	11	1:2, 3, 9; 3:8, 10; 6:9; 12:11; 20:4; 21:5; 22:18, 19	5	19:9; 22: 6, 7, 9, 10					1	19:13							17
Total	218		50		8		8		7		5		2		32		330

Miscellaneous: Mt. 5:32, cause; Mt. 5:37, communication; Mt. 22:15, talk; Mt. 25:19 (with 4768), reckon; Mk. 1:45, matter; Mk. 11:29, question; Lk. 5: 15, fame; Lk. 7:17, rumour; Lk. 24:17, communication; Ac. 1:1, treatise; Ac. 8:21, matter; Ac. 10:29, intent; Ac. 11:22, tidings; Ac. 14:12, speaker; Ac. 15:6, matter; Ac. 15:27. mouth; Ac. 18:14 (with 2596), reason would; Ac. 19:38, matter; Ac. 20:24, these things; Ro. 9:28, 28, work; 1 Co. 1:5, utterance; 1 Co. 1:18, preaching; 2 Co. 8:7, utterance; Eph. 4:29, communication; Eph. 6:19, utterance; Phl. 4:15 (with 1519), as concerning; Col. 2:23, shew; Col. 4:3, utterance; Heb. 4:13 (with 2254 and 3488), have to do; Heb. 6:1, doctrine; 1 Pt. 3:15, reason.

3063. λοιπόν, loipon′

Book	Oc.	finally	Oc.	now	Oc.	then	Oc.	besides	Oc.	moreover (with 1161 and 3639)	Oc.	it remains (with 2076)	Oc.	furthermore	Oc.	henceforth	Oc.	from henceforth	Total
Mt.			1	26:45															1
Mk.			1	14:41															1
Ac.					1	27:20													1
1 Co.							1	1:16	1	4:2	1	7:29							3
2 Co.	1	13:11																	1
Eph.	1	6:10																	1
Phl.	2	3:1; 4:8																	2
1 Th.													1	4:1					1
2 Th.	1	3:1																	1
2 Ti.															1	4:8			1
Heb.																	1	10:13	1
Total	5		2		1		1		1		1		1		1		1		14

3064. λοιποῦ, loipou′

Book	from henceforth	Total
Gal.	6:17	1

3065. Λουκᾶς, Loukas′

Book	Oc.	Luke	Oc.	Lucas	Total
Col.	1	4:14			1
2 Ti.	1	4:11			1
Phe.			1	1:24	1
Total	2		1		3

3066. Λούκιος, Lou′kios

Book	Lucius	Total
Ac.	13:1	1
Ro.	16:21	1
Total		2

3067. λουτρόν. loutron′

Book	washing	Total
Eph.	5:26	1
Tit.	3:5	1
Total		2

3068. λούω, lou′ō

Book	wash	Total
Jn.	13:10	1
Ac.	9:37; 16:33	2
Heb.	10:22	1
2 Pt.	2:22	1
Rev.	1:5	1
Total		6

3069. Λύδδα, Lud′da

Book	Lydda	Total
Ac.	9:32, 35, 38	3

3070. Λυδία, Ludi′a

Book	Lydia	Total
Ac.	16:14, 40	2

3071. Λυκαονία, Lukaoni′a

Book	Lycaonia	Total
Ac.	14:6	1

3072. Λυκαονιστί, Lukaonisti′

Book	speech of Lycaonia	Total
Ac.	14:11	1

3073. Λυκία, Luki′a

Book	Lycia	Total
Ac.	27:5	1

3074. λύκος, lu′kos

Book	wolf	Total
Mt.	7:15; 10:16	2
Lk.	10:3	1
Jn.	10:12, 12	2
Ac.	20:29	1
Total		6

3075. λυμαίνομαι, lumai′nomai

Book	make havoc	Total
Ac.	8:3	1

3076. λυπέω, lupe′ō

Book	Oc.	be sorrowful	Oc.	grieve	Oc.	make sorry	Oc.	be sorry	Oc.	sorrow	Oc.	cause grief	Oc.	be in heaviness	Total
Mt.	3	19:22; 26:22, 37					3	14:9; 17:23; 18:31							6
Mk.	1	14:19	1	10:22											2
Jn.	1	16:20	1	21:17											2
Ro.			1	14:15											1
2 Co.	1	6:10	2	2:4, 5b	6	2:2, 2; 7:8, 8, 9a, 9c			2	7:9b, 11	1	2:5a			12
Eph.			1	4:30											1
1 Th.									1	4:13					1
1 Pt.													1	1:6	1
Total	6		6		6		3		3		1		1		26

3077. λύπη, lu′pe

Book	Oc.	sorrow	Oc.	heaviness	Oc.	grievous	Oc.	grudgingly (with 1537)	Oc.	grief	Total
Lk.	1	22:45									1
Jn.	4	16:6, 20, 21, 22									4
Ro.			1	9:2							1
2 Co.	4	2:3, 7; 7:10, 10	1	2:1			1	9:7			6
Phl.	2	2:27, 27									2
Heb.					1	12:11					1
1 Pt.									1	2:19	1
Total	11		2		1		1		1		16

3078. Λυσανίας, Lusani′as

Book	Lysanias	Total
Lk.	3:1	1

3082. Λύστρα, Lus′tra

Book	Lystra	Total
Ac.	14:6, 8, 21; 16:1, 2	5
2 Ti.	3:11	1
Total		6

3079. Λυσίας, Lusi′as

Book	Lysias	Total
Ac.	23:26; 24:7, 22	3

3080. λύσις, lu′sis

Book	to be loosed	Total
1 Co.	7:27	1

3081. λυσιτελεῖ, lusitelei′

Book	it is better	Total
Lk.	17:2	1

3083. λύτρον, lu′tron

Book	ransom	Total
Mt.	20:28	1
Mk.	10:45	1
Total		2

3084. λυτρόω, lutro′ō

Book	redeem	Total
Lk.	24:21	1
Tit.	2:14	1
1 Pt.	1:18	1
Total		3

3085. λύτρωσις, lu′trōsis

Book	Oc.	redemption	Oc.	redeem (with 4060)	Total
Lk.	1	2:38	1	1:68	2
Heb.	1	9:12			1
Total	2		1		3

3086. λυτρωτής, lutrōtes′

Book	deliverer	Total
Ac.	7:35	1

3087. λυχνία, luchni'a

Book	candlestick	Total
Mt.	5:15	1
Mk.	4:21	1
Lk.	8:16; 11:33	2
Heb.	9:2	1
Rev.	1:12, 13, 20, 20; 2:1, 5; 11:4	7
Total		12

3088. λύχνος, luch'nos

Book	Oc.	candle	Oc.	light	Total
Mt.	1	5:15	1	6:22	2
Mk.	1	4:21			1
Lk.	4	8:16; 11:33, 36; 15:8	2	11:34; 12:35	6
Jn.			1	5:35	1
2 Pt.			1	1:19	1
Rev.	2	18:23; 22:5	1	21:23	3
Total	8		6		14

3090. Λωΐς, Lōis'

Book	Lois	Total
2 Ti.	1:5	1

3091. Λώτ, Lōt

Book	Lot	Total
Lk.	17:28, 29, 32	3
2 Pt.	2:7	1
Total		4

3089. λύω, lu'ō

Book	Oc.	loose	Oc.	break	Oc.	unloose	Oc.	destroy	Oc.	dissolve	Oc.	put off	Oc.	melt	Oc.	break up	Oc.	break down	Total
Mt.	5	16:19, 19; 18:18, 18; 21:2	1	5:19															6
Mk.	4	7:35; 11: 2, 4, 5			1	1:7													5
Lk.	6	13:15, 16; 19:30, 31, 33, 33			1	3:16													7
Jn.	1	11:44	3	5:18; 7: 23; 10: 35	1	1:27	1	2:19											6
Ac.	4	2:24; 13: 25; 22: 30; 24:26	1	27:41							1	7:33			1	13:43			7
1 Co.	1	7:27																	1
Eph.																	1	2:14	1
2 Pt.									2	3:11, 12			1	3:10					3
1 Jn.							1	3:8											1
Rev.	6	5:2, 5; 9: 14, 15; 20:3, 7																	6
Total	27		5		3		2		2		1		1		1		1		43

3092. Μαάθ, Maath'

Book	Maath	Total
Lk.	3:26	1

3093. Μαγδαλά, Magdala'

Book	Magdala	Total
Mt.	15:39	1

3094. Μαγδαληνή, Magdalene'

Book	Magdalene	Total
Mt.	27:56, 61; 28:1	3
Mk.	15:40, 47; 16:1, 9	4
Lk.	8:2; 24:10	2
Jn.	19:25; 20:1, 18	3
Total		12

3095. μαγεία, magei'a

Book	sorcery	Total
Ac.	8:11	1

3096. μαγεύω, mageu'ō

Book	use sorcery	Total
Ac.	8:9	1

3098. Μαγώγ, Magōg'

Book	Magog	Total
Rev.	20:8	1

3099. Μαδιάν, Madian'

Book	Madian	Total
Ac.	7:29	1

3097. μάγος, mag'os

Book	Oc.	wise man	Oc.	sorcerer	Total
Mt.	4	2:1, 7, 16, 16			4
Ac.			2	13:6, 8	2
Total	4		2		6

3100. μαθητεύω, matheteu'ō

Book	Oc.	teach	Oc.	instruct	Oc.	be disciple	Total
Mt.	1	28:19	1	13:52	1	27:57	3
Ac.	1	14:21					1
Total	2		1		1		4

3101. μαθητής, mathetes'

Book	disciple	Total
Mt.	5:1; 8:21, 23, 25; 9:10, 11, 14, 14, 19, 37; 10:1, 24, 25, 42; 11:1, 2; 12:1, 2, 49; 13:10, 36; 14:12, 15, 19, 19, 22, 26; 15:2, 12, 23, 32, 33, 36, 36; 16:5, 13, 20, 21, 24; 17:6, 10, 13, 16, 19; 18:1; 19:10, 13, 23, 25; 20:17; 21:1, 6, 20; 22:16; 23:1; 24:1, 3; 26:1, 8, 17, 18, 19, 26, 35, 36, 40, 45, 56; 27:64; 28:7, 8, 9, 13, 16	74
Mk.	2:15, 16, 18, 18, 18, 23; 3:7, 9; 4:34; 5:31; 6:1, 29, 35, 41, 45; 7:2, 5, 17; 8:1, 4, 6, 10, 27, 27, 33, 34; 9:14, 18, 28, 31; 10:10, 13, 23, 24, 46; 11:1, 14; 12:43; 13:1; 14:12, 13, 14, 16, 32; 16:7	45
Lk.	5:30, 33; 6:1, 13, 17, 20, 40; 7:11, 18, 19; 8:9, 22; 9:1, 14, 16, 18, 40, 43, 54; 10:23; 11:1, 1; 12:1, 22; 14:26, 27, 33; 16:1; 17:1, 22; 18:15; 19:29, 37, 39; 20:45; 22:11, 39, 45	38
Jn.	1:35, 37; 2:2, 11, 12, 17, 22; 3:22, 25; 4:1, 2, 8, 27, 31, 33; 6:3, 8, 11, 11, 12, 16, 22, 22, 22, 24, 60, 61, 66; 7:3; 8:31; 9:2, 27, 28, 28; 11:7, 8, 12, 54; 12:4, 16; 18:5, 22, 23, 35; 15:8; 16:17, 29; 18:1, 1, 2, 15, 15, 16, 17, 19, 25; 19:26, 27, 27, 38; 20:2, 3, 4, 8, 10, 18, 19, 20, 25, 26, 30; 21:1, 2, 4, 7, 8, 12, 14, 20, 23, 24	81
Ac.	1:15; 6:1, 2, 7; 9:1, 10, 19, 25, 26, 26, 38; 11:26, 29; 13:52; 14:20, 22, 28; 15:10; 16:1; 18:23, 27; 19:1, 9, 30; 20:1, 7, 30; 21:4, 16, 16	30
Total		268

3102. μαθήτρια, mathe'tria

Book	disciple	Total
Ac.	9:36	1

3103. Μαθουσάλα, Mathousal'a

Book	Mathusala	Total
Lk.	3:37	1

3105. μαίνομαι, mai'nomai

Book	Oc.	be mad	Oc.	be beside (one's) self	Total
Jn.	1	10:20			1
Ac.	2	12:15; 26:25	1	26:24	3
1 Co.	1	14:23			1
Total	4		1		5

3106. μακαρίζω, makarid'zō

Book	Oc.	call blessed	Oc.	count happy	Total
Lk.	1	1:48			1
Jas.			1	5:11	1
Total	1		1		2

3107. μακάριος, makar'ios

Book	Oc.	blessed	Oc.	happy	Oc.	happier	Total
Mt.	13	5:3, 4, 5, 6, 7, 8, 9, 10, 11; 11:6; 13:16; 16:17; 24:46					13
Lk.	15	1:45; 6:20, 21, 21, 22; 7:23; 10:23; 11:27, 28; 12:37, 38, 43; 14:14, 15; 23:29					15
Jn.	1	20:29	1	13:17			2
Ac.	1	20:35	1	26:2			2
Ro.	2	4:7, 8	1	14:22			3
1 Co.					1	7:40	1
1 Ti.	2	1:11; 6:15					2
Tit.	1	2:13					1
Jas.	2	1:12, 25					2
1 Pt.			2	3:14; 4:14			2
Rev.	7	1:3; 14:13; 16:15; 19:9; 20:6; 22:7, 14					7
Total	44		5		1		50

3104. Μαϊνάν, Mainan'

Book	Menan	Total
Lk.	3:31	1

3108. μακαρισμός, makarismos'

Book	blessedness	Total
Ro.	4:6, 9	2
Gal.	4:15	1
Total		3

3109. Μακεδονία, Makedoni′a

Book	Macedonia	Total
Ac.	16:9, 10, 12; 18:5; 19:21, 22; 20:1, 3	8
Ro.	15:26	1
1 Co.	16:5, 5	2
2 Co.	1:16, 16; 2:13; 7:5; 8:1; 11:9	6
Phl.	4:15	1
1 Th.	1:7, 8; 4:10	3
1 Ti.	1:3	1
Total		22

3110. Μακεδών, Makedōn′

Book	Oc.	of Macedonia	Oc.	Macedonian	Total
Ac.	2	16:9; 19:29	1	27:2	3
2 Co.	2	9:2, 4			2
Total	4		1		5

3111. μάκελλον, mak′ellon

Book	shambles	Total
1 Co.	10:25	1

3112. μακράν, makran′

Book	Oc.	far	Oc.	afar off	Oc.	good way off	Oc.	far hence	Oc.	great way off	Oc.	far off	Total
Mt.					1	8:30							1
Mk.	1	12:34											1
Lk.	1	7:6							1	15:20			2
Jn.	1	21:8											1
Ac.	1	17:27	1	2:39			1	22:21					3
Eph.			1	2:17							1	2:13	2
Total	4		2		1		1		1		1		10

3113. μακρόθεν, makroth′en

Book	Oc.	afar off	Oc.	from far	Total
Mt.	2	26:58; 27:55			2
Mk.	4	5:6; 11:13; 14:54; 15:40	1	8:3	5
Lk.	4	16:23; 18:13; 22:54; 23:49			4
Rev.	3	18:10, 15, 17			3
Total	13		1		14

3115. μακροθυμία, makrothumi′a

Book	Oc.	longsuffering	Oc.	patience	Total
Ro.	2	2:4; 9:22			2
2 Co.	1	6:6			1
Gal.	1	5:22			1
Eph.	1	4:2			1
Col.	2	1:11; 3:12			2
1 Ti.	1	1:16			1
2 Ti.	2	3:10; 4:2			2
Heb.			1	6:12	1
Jas.			1	5:10	1
1 Pt.	1	3:20			1
2 Pt.	1	3:15			1
Total	12		2		14

3116. μακροθυμώς makrothumōs′

Book	patiently	Total
Ac.	26:3	1

3118. μακροχρόνιος makrochron′ios

Book	live long	Total
Eph.	6:3	1

3114. μακροθυμέω, makrothume′ō

Book	Oc.	be patient	Oc.	have patience	Oc.	have long patience	Oc.	bear long	Oc.	suffer long	Oc.	be long suffering	Oc.	patiently endure	Total
Mt.			2	18:26, 29											2
Lk.							1	18:7							1
1 Co.									1	13:4					1
1 Th.	1	5:14													1
Heb.													1	6:15	1
Jas.	2	5:7a, 8			1	5:7b									3
2 Pt.											1	3:9			1
Total	3		2		1		1		1		1		1		10

3117. μακρός, makros′

Book	Oc.	long	Oc.	far	Total
Mt.	1	23:14			1
Mk.	1	12:40			1
Lk.	1	20:47	2	15:13; 19:12	3
Total	3		2		5

3120. μαλακός, malakos′

Book	Oc.	soft	Oc.	effeminate	Total
Mt.	2	11:8, 8			2
Lk.	1	7:25			1
1 Co.			1	6:9	1
Total	3		1		4

3119. μαλακία, malaki′a

Book	disease	Total
Mt.	4:23; 9:35; 10:1	3

3121. Μαλελεήλ, Maleleēl′

Book	Maleleel	Total
Lk.	3:37	1

3122. μάλιστα, mal′ista

Book	Oc.	specially	Oc.	especially	Oc.	chiefly	Oc.	most of all	Total
Ac.	1	25:26	1	26:3			1	20:38	3
Gal.			1	6:10					1
Phl.					1	4:22			1
1 Ti.	2	4:10; 5:8	1	5:17					3
2 Ti.			1	4:13					1
Tit.	1	1:10							1
Phe.	1	1:16							1
2 Pt.					1	2:10			1
Total	5		4		2		1		12

3123. μᾶλλον, mal′lon

Book	Oc.	more	Oc.	rather	Oc.	the more	Oc.	better (with 2570)	Oc.	Misc.	Total
Mt.	4	6:30; 7:11; 10:25; 18:13	4	10:6, 28; 25:9; 27:24					1	6:26	9
Mk.			2	5:26; 15:11	3	7:36; 10:48; 14:31	1	9:42			6
Lk.	3	11:13; 12:24, 28	1	10:20	1	18:39			1	5:15	6
Jn.	1	12:43	1	3:19	2	5:18; 19:8					4
Ac.	3	4:19; 20:35; 27:11	1	5:29	3	5:14; 9:22; 22:2					7
Ro.	6	5:9, 10, 15, 17; 11:12, 24	2	8:35; 14:13							8
1 Co.	2	12:22; 14:18	7	5:2; 6:7, 7; 7:21; 9:12; 14:1, 5			1	9:15			10
2 Co.	2	3:9, 11	4	2:7; 3:8; 5:8; 12:9	2	7:7, 13					8
Gal.	1	4:27	1	4:9							2
Eph.			3	4:28; 5:4, 11							3
Phl.	4	1:9, 9; 2:12; 3:4	1	1:12					1	1:23	6
1 Th.	4	4:1, 1, 10, 10									4
1 Ti.			2	1:4; 6:2							2
2 Ti.	1	3:4									1
Phe.	1	1:16	1	1:9							2
Heb.	2	9:14; 12:25	3	11:25; 12:9, 13	1	10:25					6
2 Pt.									1	1:10	1
Total	34		33		12		2		4		85

Miscellaneous: Mt. 6:26 (with 1308), be much better; Lk. 5:15, so much the more; Phl. 1:23 (with 4083), far; 2 Pt. 1:10, the rather.

3124. Μάλχος, Mal'chos

Book	Malchus	Total
Jn.	18:10	1

3125. μάμμη, mam'mē

Book	grandmother	Total
2 Ti.	1:5	1

3126. μαμμωνᾶς or μαμωνᾶς Mammōnas' or Mamōnas'

Book	mammon	Total
Mt.	6:24	1
Lk.	16:9, 11, 13	3
Total		4

3127. Μαναήν, Manaēn'

Book	Manaen	Total
Ac.	13:1	1

3128. Μανασσῆς, Manassēs'

Book	Oc.	Manasses (king of Judah)	Oc.	Manasses (son of Joseph)	Total
Mt.	2	1:10, 10			2
Rev.			1	7:6	1
Total	2		1		3

3129. μανθάνω, manthan'ō

Book	Oc.	learn	Oc.	understand	Total
Mt.	3	9:13; 11:29; 24:32			3
Mk.	1	13:28			1
Jn.	2	6:45; 7:15			2
Ac.			1	23:27	1
Ro.	1	16:17			1
1 Co.	3	4:6; 14:31, 35			3
Gal.	1	3:2			1
Eph.	1	4:20			1
Phl.	2	4:9, 11			2
Col.	1	1:7			1
1 Ti.	3	2:11; 5:4, 13			3
2 Ti.	3	3:7, 14, 14			3
Tit.	1	3:14			1
Heb.	1	5:8			1
Rev.	1	14:3			1
Total	24		1		25

3130. μανία, mani'a

Book	mad	Total
Ac.	26:24	1

3131. μάννα, man'na

Book	manna	Total
Jn.	6:31, 49, 58	3
Heb.	9:4	1
Rev.	2:17	1
Total		5

3132. μαντεύομαι, manteu'omai

Book	by soothsaying	Total
Ac.	16:16	1

3133. μαραίνω, marai'nō

Book	fade away	Total
Jas.	1:11	1

3134. μαρὰν ἀθά, maran' atha'

Book	Maran-atha	Total
1 Co.	16:22	1

3135. μαργαρίτης, margari'tēs

Book	pearl	Total
Mt.	7:6; 13:45, 46	3
1 Ti.	2:9	1
Rev.	17:4; 18:12, 16; 21: 21, 21	5
Total		9

3136. Μάρθα, Mar'tha

Book	Martha	Total
Lk.	10:38, 40, 41, 41	4
Jn.	11:1, 5, 19, 20, 21, 24, 30, 39; 12:2	9
Total		13

3139. μάρμαρος, mar'maros

Book	marble	Total
Rev.	18:12	1

3138. Μάρκος, Mar'kos

Book	Oc.	Mark	Oc.	Marcus	Total
Ac.	4	12:12, 25; 15:37, 39			4
Col.			1	4:10	1
2 Ti.	1	4:11			1
Phe.			1	1:24	1
1 Pt.			1	5:13	1
Total	5		3		8

3137. Μαρία or Μαριάμ, Mari'a or Mariam'

Book	Oc.	Mary (mother of Jesus)	Oc.	Mary (Magdalene)	Oc.	Mary (sister of Martha)	Oc.	Mary (mother of James)	Oc.	Mary (mother of John)	Oc.	Mary (of Rome)	Total
Mt.	5	1:16, 18, 20; 2:11; 13:55	3	27:56a, 61a; 28:1a			3	27:56b, 61b; 28:1b					11
Mk.	1	6:3	3	15:40a, 47a; 16:1a			4	15:40b, 47b; 16:1b, 9					8
Lk.	12	1:27, 30, 34, 38, 39, 41, 46, 56; 2:5, 16, 19, 34	2	8:2; 24:10a	2	10:39, 42	1	24:10b					17
Jn.			5	19:25b; 20:1, 11, 16, 18	9	11:1, 2, 19, 20, 28, 31, 32, 45; 12:3	1	19:25a					15
Ac.	1	1:14							1	12:12			2
Ro.											1	16:6	1
Total	19		13		11		9		1		1		54

3140. μαρτυρέω, marture'ō

Book	Oc.	bear witness	Oc.	testify	Oc.	bear record	Oc.	witness	Oc.	be a witness	Oc.	give testimony	Oc.	have good report	Oc.	Misc.	Total
Mt.									1	23:31							1
Lk.	2	4:22; 11:48															2
Jn.	16	1:7, 8, 15; 3:26, 28; 5:31, 32a, 33, 36, 37; 8:18, 18; 10:25; 15:27; 18: 23, 37	10	2:25; 3:11, 32; 4:39, 44; 5:39; 7:7; 13: 21; 15:26; 21:24	6	1:32, 34; 8:13, 14; 12:17; 19:35	1	5:32b									33
Ac.	3	15:8; 22:5; 23:11	1	26:5			1	26:22			2	13:22; 14:3	1	22:12	4	6:3; 10: 22, 43; 16:2	12
Ro.					1	10:2	1	3:21									2
1 Co.			1	15:15													1
2 Co.					1	8:3											1
Gal.					1	4:15											1
Col.					1	4:13											1
1 Th.															1	2:11	1
1 Ti.							1	6:13							1	5:10	2
Heb.			2	7:17; 11:4b			1	7:8	1	10:15					4	11:2, 4a, 5, 39	8
1 Jn.	3	1:2; 5:6, 8	2	4:14; 5:9	1	5:7									1	5:10	7
3 Jn.	1	1:6	1	1:3	1	1:12b							1	1:12a			4
Rev.			2	22:16, 20	1	1:2											3
Total	25		19		13		5		2		2		2		11		79

Miscellaneous: Ac. 6:3, of honest report; Ac. 10:22, of good report; Ac. 10:43, give witness; Ac. 16:2, be well reported of; 1 Th. 2:11, charge; 1 Ti. 5:10, be well reported of; Heb. 11:2, obtain good report; Heb. 11:4a, obtain witness; Heb. 11:5, have testimony; Heb. 11:39, obtain good report; 1 Jn. 5:10, give.

3141. μαρτυρία, marturi′a

Book	Oc.	witness	Oc.	testimony	Oc.	record	Oc.	report	Total
Mk.	3	14:55, 56, 59							3
Lk.	1	22:71							1
Jn.	5	1:7; 3:11; 5:31, 32, 36	5	3:32, 33; 5:34; 8:17; 21:24	4	1:19; 8:13, 14; 19:35			14
Ac.			1	22:18					1
1 Ti.							1	3:7	1
Tit.	1	1:13							1
1 Jn.	4	5:9, 9, 9, 10a			2	5:10b, 11			6
3 Jn.					1	1:12			1
Rev.	1	20:4	8	1:2, 9; 6:9; 11:7; 12:11, 17; 19:10, 10					9
Total	15		14		7		1		37

3142. μαρτύριον, martu′rion

Book	Oc.	testimony	Oc.	witness	Oc.	to be testified	Total
Mt.	2	8:4; 10:18	1	24:14			3
Mk.	3	1:44; 6:11; 13:9					3
Lk.	3	5:14; 9:5; 21:13					3
Ac.			2	4:33; 7:44			2
1 Co.	2	1:6; 2:1					2
2 Co.	1	1:12					1
2 Th.	1	1:10					1
1 Ti.					1	2:6	1
2 Ti.	1	1:8					1
Heb.	1	3:5					1
Jas.			1	5:3			1
Rev.	1	15:5					1
Total	15		4		1		20

3143. μαρτύρομαι, martu′romai

Book	Oc.	testify	Oc.	take to record	Total
Ac.			1	20:26	1
Gal.	1	5:3			1
Eph.	1	4:17			1
Total	2		1		3

3144. μάρτυς, mar′tus

Book	Oc.	witness	Oc.	martyr	Oc.	record	Total
Mt.	2	18:16; 26:65					2
Mk.	1	14:63					1
Lk.	1	24:48					1
Ac.	12	1:8, 22; 2:32; 3:15; 5:32; 6:13; 7:58; 10:39, 41; 13:31; 22:15; 26:16	1	22:20			13
Ro.	1	1:9					1
2 Co.	1	13:1			1	1:23	2
Phl.					1	1:8	1
1 Th.	2	2:5, 10					2
1 Ti.	2	5:19; 6:12					2
2 Ti.	1	2:2					1
Heb.	2	10:28; 12:1					2
1 Pt.	1	5:1					1
Rev.	3	1:5; 3:14; 11:3	2	2:13; 17:6			5
Total	29		3		2		34

3145. μασσάομαι, massa′omai

Book	gnaw	Total
Rev.	16:10	1

3146. μαστιγόω, mastigo′ō

Book	scourge	Total
Mt.	10:17; 20:19; 23:34	3
Mk.	10:34	1
Lk.	18:33	1
Jn.	19:1	1
Heb.	12:6	1
Total		7

3147. μαστίζω, mastid′zō

Book	to scourge	Total
Ac.	22:25	1

3148. μάστιξ, mas′tix

Book	Oc.	plague	Oc.	scourging	Total
Mk.	3	3:10; 5:29, 34			3
Lk.	1	7:21			1
Ac.			1	22:24	1
Heb.			1	11:36	1
Total	4		2		6

3149. μαστός, mastos′

Book	pap	Total
Lk.	11:27; 23:29	2
Rev.	1:13	1
Total		3

3150. ματαιολογία mataiologi′a

Book	vain jangling	Total
1 Ti.	1:6	1

3151. ματαιολόγος mataiolog′os

Book	vain talker	Total
Tit.	1:10	1

3152. μάταιος, mat′aios

Book	Oc.	vain	Oc.	vanities	Total
Ac.			1	14:15	1
1 Co.	2	3:20; 15:17			2
Tit.	1	3:9			1
Jas.	1	1:26			1
1 Pt.	1	1:18			1
Total	5		1		6

3153. ματαιότης, mataiot′ēs

Book	vanity	Total
Ro.	8:20	1
Eph.	4:17	1
2 Pt.	2:18	1
Total		3

3154. ματαιόω, mataio′ō

Book	become vain	Total
Ro.	1:21	1

3155. μάτην, mat′ēn

Book	in vain	Total
Mt.	15:9	1
Mk.	7:7	1
Total		2

3156. Ματθαῖος, Matthai′os

Book	Matthew	Total
Mt.	9:9; 10:3	2
Mk.	3:18	1
Lk.	6:15	1
Ac.	1:13	1
Total		5

3157. Ματθάν, Matthan′

Book	Matthan	Total
Mt.	1:15, 15	2

3158. Ματθάτ, Matthat′

Book	Matthat	Total
Lk.	3:24, 29	2

3159. Ματθίας, Matthi′as

Book	Matthias	Total
Ac.	1:23, 26	2

3160. Ματταθά, Mattatha′

Book	Mattatha	Total
Lk.	3:31	1

3161. Ματταθίας, Mattathi′as

Book	Mattathias	Total
Lk.	3:25, 26	2

3162. μάχαιρα, mach′aira

Book	sword	Total
Mt.	10:34; 26:47, 51, 52, 52, 52, 55	7
Mk.	14:43, 47, 48	3
Lk.	21:24; 22:36, 38, 49, 52	5
Jn.	18:10, 11	2
Ac.	12:2; 16:27	2
Ro.	8:35; 13:4	2
Eph.	6:17	1
Heb.	4:12; 11:34, 37	3
Rev.	6:4; 13:10, 10, 14	4
Total		29

3163. μάχη, mach′ē

Book	Oc.	fighting	Oc.	strife	Oc.	striving	Total
2 Co.	1	7:5					1
2 Ti.			1	2:23			1
Tit.					1	3:9	1
Jas.	1	4:1					1
Total	2		1		1		4

3164. μάχομαι, mach′omai

Book	Oc.	strive	Oc.	fight	Total
Jn.	1	6:52			1
Ac.	1	7:26			1
2 Ti.	1	2:24			1
Jas.			1	4:2	1
Total	3		1		4

3165. μέ, me

Book	Oc.	me	Oc.	I	Oc.	my	Oc.	Not Tr.	Total
Mt.	33	3:14; 8:2; 10:33, 40; 11:28; 14:28, 30; 15:8, 9, 22; 18:32; 19:14, 17; 22:18; 23:39; 25:35, 35, 36, 36, 36, 42, 43, 43, 43; 26:21, 23, 34, 46, 55, 55, 75; 27:46; 28:10	4	16:13, 15; 26:32, 35	1	26:12			38
Mk.	22	1:40; 5:7; 6:22, 23; 7:6, 7; 8:38; 9:19, 37, 39; 10:14, 18, 47, 48; 12:15; 14:18, 30, 42, 48, 49, 72; 15:34	5	8:27, 29; 10:36; 14:28, 31					27
Lk.	34	1:43, 48; 2:49a; 4:18, 18; 5:12; 6:46, 47; 8:28; 9:26, 48; 10:16, 40; 11:6; 12:9, 14; 13:35; 14:18, 19, 26; 15:19; 16:4, 24; 18:3, 5, 16, 19, 38, 39; 20:23; 22:21, 34, 61; 24:39	10	2:49b; 4:43; 9:18, 20; 10:35; 11:18; 13:33; 19:5, 27; 22:15					44
Jn.	100	1:33, 48; 2:17; 4:34; 5:7, 11, 24, 30, 36, 37, 40, 43; 6:26, 35, 36, 37, 38, 39, 40, 44, 44, 45, 57, 57, 65; 7:16, 19, 28, 29, 33, 34, 36, 37; 8:16, 18, 21, 26, 28, 29, 29, 37, 40, 42, 46, 49, 54; 9:4; 10:15, 17, 32; 11:42; 12:27, 44, 45, 49; 13:13, 20, 21, 33, 38; 14:7, 9, 15, 19, 19, 21, 21, 23, 24, 24, 28; 15:9, 16, 21, 25; 16:5, 5, 10, 16, 16, 17, 17, 19, 19; 17:5, 8, 21, 23, 24, 25, 26; 18:21, 23; 19:11; 20:21, 29; 21:15, 16, 17, 17	1	10:16					101
Ac.	32	2:28; 7:28; 8:31, 36; 9:4, 6, 17; 10:29; 11:11; 12:11; 16:15; 20:23; 22:7, 8, 10, 13, 21; 23:3, 3, 18, 22; 24:12, 18, 19; 25:11; 26:5, 13, 14, 14, 21, 28; 28:18	8	11:15; 13:25; 16:30; 18:21; 19:21, 21; 22:17; 25:10			1	24:13	41
Ro.	5	7:11, 23, 24; 8:2; 9:20	2	15:16, 19					7
1 Co.	4	1:17; 4:4; 16:6, 11							4
2 Co.	8	2:2; 11:16, 16, 32; 12:6, 7, 11, 21	3	2:3, 13; 7:7					11
Gal.	4	1:15; 2:20; 4:12, 14	1	4:18					5
Eph.			1	6:20					1
Phl.	2	2:30; 4:13	1	1:7					3
Col.			1	4:4					1
1 Ti.	2	1:12, 12							2
2 Ti.	8	1:15, 16, 17; 3:11; 4:9, 16, 17, 18							8
Tit.	1	3:12							1
Heb.	4	3:9, 9; 8:11; 11:32							4
Rev.	3	17:3; 21:9, 10							3
Total	262		37		1		1		301

3166. μεγαλαυχέω megalauche'ō

Book	boast great things	Total
Jas.	3:5	1

3167. μεγαλεῖος, megalei'os

Book	Oc.	great thing	Oc.	wonderful work	Total
Lk.	1	1:49			1
Ac.			1	2:11	1
Total	1		1		2

3169. μεγαλοπρεπής megaloprepęs'

Book	excellent	Total
2 Pt.	1:17	1

3168. μεγαλειότης, megaleiot'ęs

Book	Oc.	mighty power	Oc.	magnificence	Oc.	majesty	Total
Lk.	1	9:43					1
Ac.			1	19:27			1
2 Pt.					1	1:16	1
Total	1		1		1		3

3170. μεγαλύνω, megalu'nō

Book	Oc.	magnify	Oc.	enlarge	Oc.	shew great	Total
Mt.			1	23:5			1
Lk.	1	1:46			1	1:58	2
Ac.	3	5:13; 10:46; 19:17					3
2 Co.			1	10:15			1
Phl.	1	1:20					1
Total	5		2		1		8

3171. μεγάλως, megal'ōs

Book	greatly	Total
Phl.	4:10	1

3172. μεγαλωσύνη, megalōsu'nę

Book	Oc.	Majesty (said of God)	Oc.	majesty	Total
Heb.	2	1:3; 8:1			2
Jd.			1	1:25	1
Total	2		1		3

3174. μέγεθος, meg'ethos

Book	greatness	Total
Eph.	1:19	1

3173. μέγας, meg'as

Book	Oc.	great	Oc.	loud	Oc.	Misc.	Total
Mt.	18	2:10; 4:16; 5:19, 35; 7:27; 8:24, 26; 15:28; 20:25, 26; 22:36, 38; 24:21, 24, 31; 27:60; 28:2, 8	2	27:46, 50			20
Mk.	9	4:32, 37, 39; 5:11, 42; 10:42, 43; 13:2; 16:4	4	1:26; 5:7; 15:34, 37	2	4:41; 14:15	15
Lk.	17	1:15, 32; 2:10; 4:25, 38; 5:29; 6:49; 7:16; 8:37; 9:48; 13:19; 14:16; 16:26; 21:11, 11, 23; 24:52	7	1:42; 4:33; 8:28; 17:15; 19:37; 23:23, 46	2	2:9; 22:12	26
Jn.	3	6:18; 7:37; 21:11	1	11:43	1	19:31	5
Ac.	23	2:20; 4:33, 33; 5:5, 11; 6:8; 7:11; 8:1, 2, 8, 9, 10b; 10:11; 11:5, 28; 15:3; 16:26; 19:27, 28, 34, 35; 23:9; 26:22	6	7:57, 60; 8:7; 14:10; 16:28; 26:24	2	8:10a, 13	31
Ro.	1	9:2					1
1 Co.	2	9:11; 16:9					2
2 Co.	1	11:15					1
Eph.	1	5:32					1
1 Ti.	2	3:16; 6:6					2
2 Ti.	1	2:20					1
Tit.	1	2:13					1
Heb.	3	4:14; 10:35; 13:20			3	8:11; 10:21; 11:24	6
Jd.	1	1:6					1
Rev.	67	1:10; 2:22; 6:4, 12, 17; 7:14; 8:8, 10; 9:2, 14; 11:8, 11, 12, 13, 15, 17, 18, 19; 12:1, 3, 9, 12, 14; 13:2, 5, 13, 16; 14:2, 8, 19; 15:1, 3; 16:1, 9, 12, 14, 17, 18, 18, 19, 19, 21, 21; 17:1, 5, 6, 18; 18:1, 2b, 10, 16, 18, 19, 21, 21; 19:1, 2, 5, 17b, 18; 20:1, 11, 12; 21:3, 10, 10, 12	13	5:2, 12; 6:10; 7:2, 10; 8:13; 10:3; 12:10; 14:7, 9, 15, 18; 19:17a	2	6:13; 18:2a	82
Total	150		33		12		195

Miscellaneous: Mk. 4:41 (with 5301), exceedingly; Mk. 14:15, large; Lk. 2:9 (with 5301), sore; Lk. 22:12, large; Jn. 19:31, high; Ac. 8:10a, greatest; Ac. 8:13 (with 1411), sign; Heb. 8:11, greatest; Heb. 10:21, high; Heb. 11:24, to years; Rev. 6:13, mighty; Rev. 18:2a, strong.

3175. μεγιστᾶνες, megistan'es

Book	Oc.	great men	Oc.	lords	Total
Mk.			1	6:21	1
Rev.	2	6:15; 18:23			2
Total	2		1		3

3176. μέγιστος, meg'istos

Book	exceeding great	Total
2 Pt.	1:4	1

3178. μέθη, meth'ḙ

Book	drunkenness	Total
Lk.	21:34	1
Ro.	13:13	1
Gal.	5:21	1
Total		3

3177. μεθερμηνεύω, methermḙneu'ō

Book	Oc.	being interpreted	Oc.	be by interpretation	Total
Mt.	1	1:23			1
Mk.	3	5:41; 15:22, 34			3
Jn.	1	1:41			1
Ac.	1	4:36	1	13:8	2
Total	6		1		7

3179. μεθίστημι or μεθιστάνω, methis'tḙmi or methistan'ō

Book	Oc.	remove	Oc.	put out	Oc.	turn away	Oc.	translate	Total
Lk.			1	16:4					1
Ac.	1	13:22			1	19:26			2
1 Co.	1	13:2							1
Col.							1	1:13	1
Total	2		1		1		1		5

3180. μεθοδεία, methodei'a

Book	Oc.	lie in wait	Oc.	wile	Total
Eph.	1	4:14	1	6:11	2

3181. μεθόριος, methor'ios

Book	border	Total
Mk.	7:24	1

3183. μέθυσος, meth'usos

Book	drunkard	Total
1 Co.	5:11; 6:10	2

3182. μεθύσκω, methus'kō

Book	Oc.	be drunken	Oc.	be drunk	Total
Lk.	1	12:45			1
Eph.			1	5:18	1
1 Th.	1	5:7			1
Total	2		1		3

3184. μεθύω, methu'ō

Book	Oc.	be drunken	Oc.	have well drunk	Oc.	be made drunk	Total
Mt.	1	24:49					1
Jn.			1	2:10			1
Ac.	1	2:15					1
1 Co.	1	11:21					1
1 Th.	1	5:7					.1
Rev.	1	17:6			1	17:2	2
Total	5		1		1		7

3185. μεῖζον, meid'zon

Book	the more	Total
Mt.	20:31	1

3187. μείζων, meid'zōn

Book	Oc.	greater	Oc.	greatest	Oc.	elder	Oc.	more	Total
Mt.	5	11:11, 11; 12:6; 23:17, 19	4	13:32; 18:1, 4; 23:11					9
Mk.	2	4:32; 12:31	1	9:34					3
Lk.	4	7:28, 28; 12:18; 22:27	3	9:46; 22:24, 26					7
Jn.	13	1:50; 4:12; 5:20, 36; 8:53; 10:29; 13:16, 16; 14:12, 28; 15:13, 20; 19:11							13
Ro.					1	9:12			1
1 Co.	1	14:5	1	13:13					2
Heb.	4	6:13, 16; 9:11; 11:26							4
Jas.	1	3:1					1	4:6	2
2 Pt.	1	2:11							1
1 Jn.	3	3:20; 4:4; 5:9							3
Total	34		9		1		1		45

3186. μειζότερος, meidzot'eros

Book	greater	Total
3 Jn.	1:4	1

3188. μέλαν, mel'an

Book	ink	Total
2 Co.	3:3	1
2 Jn.	1:12	1
3 Jn.	1:13	1
Total		3

3189. μέλας, mel'as

Book	black	Total
Mt.	5:36	1
Rev.	6:5, 12	2
Total		3

3190. Μελεᾶς, Meleas'

Book	Melea	Total
Lk.	3:3	1

3192. μέλι, mel'i

Book	honey	Total
Mt.	3:4	1
Mk.	1:6	1
Rev.	10:9, 10	2
Total		4

3191. μελετάω, meleta'ō

Book	Oc.	premeditate	Oc.	imagine	Oc.	meditate	Total
Mk.	1	13:11					1
Ac.			1	4:25			1
1 Ti.					1	4:15	1
Total	1		1		1		3

3193. μελίσσιος, melis'sios

Book	honeycomb (with 2781)	Total
Lk.	24:42	1

3194. Μελίτη, Meli'tḙ

Book	Melita	Total
Ac.	28:1	1

See page 225 for Word 3195.

3197. Μελχί, Melchi'

Book	Melchi	Total
Lk.	3:24, 28	2

3199. μέλω, mel'ō

Book	Oc.	care	Oc.	take care	Total
Mt.	1	22:16			1
Mk.	2	4:38; 12:14			2
Lk.	1	10:40			1
Jn.	2	10:13; 12:6			2
Ac.	1	18:17			1
1 Co.	1	7:21	1	9:9	2
1 Pt.	1	5:7			1
Total	9		1		10

3198. Μελχισεδέκ, Melchisedek'

Book	Melchisedec	Total
Heb.	5:6, 10; 6:20; 7:1, 10, 11, 15, 17, 21	9

3196. μέλος, mel'os

Book	member	Total
Mt.	5:29, 30	2
Ro.	6:13, 13, 19, 19; 7:5, 23, 23; 12:4, 4, 5	10
1 Co.	6:15, 15, 15; 12:12, 12, 14, 18, 19, 20, 22, 25, 26, 26, 26, 26, 27	16
Eph.	4:25; 5:30	2
Col.	3:5	1
Jas.	3:5, 6; 4:1	3
Total		34

3200. μεμβράνα, membran'a

Book	parchment	Total
2 Ti.	4:13	1

3201. μέμφομαι, mem'phomai

Book	find fault	Total
Mk.	7:2	1
Ro.	9:19	1
Heb.	8:8	1
Total		3

3202. μεμψίμοιρος mempsim'oiros

Book	complainer	Total
Jd.	1:16	1

3203. μέν, men

Book	Oc.	indeed	Oc.	verily	Oc.	truly	Oc.	Not Tr.	Oc.	Misc.	Total
Mt.	5	3:11; 13:32; 20:23; 23:27; 26:41			2	9:37; 17:11	13	10:13; 13:4, 8, 23; 16:3, 14; 21:35; 22:5, 8; 23:28; 25:15, 33; 26:24			20
Mk.	3	1:8; 10:39; 14:21	1	9:12	1	14:38	2	4:4; 12:5	1	16:19	8
Lk.	4	3:16; 11:48; 23:33, 41			2	10:2; 22:22	6	3:18; 8:5; 10:6; 13:9; 23:33, 56			12
Jn.					1	20:30	7	7:12; 10:41; 11:6; 16:9, 22; 19:24, 32			8
Ac.	3	4:16; 11:16; 22:9	3	19:4; 22:3; 26:9	3	1:5; 3:22; 5: 23	41	1:1, 6, 18; 2:41; 3:21; 5:41; 8:4, 25; 9:7, 31; 11:19; 12:5; 13:4, 36; 14:3, 4, 12; 15: 3, 30; 16:5; 17:12, 17, 30, 32; 18:14; 19: 32, 38; 21:39; 23:8, 18, 22, 31; 25:4, 11; 26: 4; 27:21, 41, 44; 28:5, 22, 24			50
Ro.	2	6:11; 14:20	1	2:25			17	1:8; 2:7, 8; 3:2; 5:16; 7:12, 25; 8:10, 17; 9: 21; 10:1; 11:13, 22, 28; 14:2, 5; 16:19			20
1 Co.	1	11:7	2	5:3; 14:17			19	1:12, 18, 23; 2:15; 3:4; 6:4, 7; 7:7; 9:24, 25; 11:14, 18, 21; 12:8, 20, 28; 15:39, 40, 51			22
2 Co.	1	8:17			1	12:12	6	2:16; 4:12; 9:1; 10:1, 10; 11:4			8
Gal.							3	4:8, 23, 24			3
Eph.									1	4:11	1
Phl.	2	1:15; 3:1					4	1:16, 28; 2:23; 3:13			6
Col.	1	2:23									1
1 Th.									1	2:18	1
2 Ti.							3	1:10; 2:20; 4:4	1	2:19	4
Tit.							1	1:15			1
Heb.			6	3:5; 6:16; 7: 5, 18; 9:1; 12:10	2	7:23; 11:15	12	1:7; 7:2, 8, 11, 21; 8:4; 9:6, 23; 10:11, 33; 12:9, 11			20
Jas.							1	3:17			1
1 Pt.	1	2:4	1	1:20			4	2:14; 3:18; 4:6, 14			6
Jd.							3	1:8, 10, 22			3
Total	23		14		12		142		4		195

Miscellaneous: Mk. 16:19, so; Eph. 4:11, some; 1 Th. 2:18, even; 2 Ti. 2:19 (with 5004), nevertheless.

3204. μενοῦνγε, menoun'ge

Book	Oc.	yea rather	Oc.	nay but	Oc.	yes verily	Oc.	yea doubtless	Total
Lk.	1	11:28							1
Ro.			1	9:20	1	10:18			2
Phl.							1	3:8	1
Total	1		1		1		1		4

3205. μέντοι, men'toi

Book	Oc.	yet	Oc.	nevertheless	Oc.	howbeit	Oc.	but	Oc.	Not Tr.	Total
Jn.	2	4:27; 20:5	1	12:42	1	7:13	1	21:4			5
2 Ti.			1	2:19							1
Jas.									1	2:8	1
Jd.									1	1:8	1
Total	2		2		1		1		2		8

3195. μέλλω, mel'lō

Book	Oc.	shall	Oc.	should	Oc.	would	Oc.	to come	Oc.	will	Oc.	things to come	Oc.	Not Tr.	Oc.	Misc.	Total
Mt.	5	16:27; 17:12, 22; 20:22; 24:6					2	3:7; 12:32	1	2:13					1	11:14	9
Mk.	1	13:4													1	10:32	2
Lk.	3	9:44; 21:7, 36	4	9:31; 19: 11; 22:23; 24:21	1	10:1	1	3:7							3	7:2; 13:9; 19:4	12
Jn.			6	6:71; 7:39; 11:51; 12: 4, 33; 18: 32	2	6:6, 15			3	7:35, 35; 14:22					1	4:47	12
Ac.	3	23:3; 24:15; 26:2	8	11:28; 19: 27; 20:38; 22:29; 23: 27; 26:22, 23; 28:6	6	12:6; 16:27; 23:15, 20; 25: 4; 27: 30	1	24:25	2	17:31; 27:10			3	13:34; 22:26; 23:30	12	3:3; 5:35; 18:14; 20: 3, 7, 13a, 13b; 21:27, 37; 22:16; 27:2, 33	35
Ro.	3	4:24; 8:13, 18									1	8:38			1	5:14	5
1 Co.											1	3:22					1
Gal.															1	3:23	1
Eph.															1	1:21	1
Col.											1	2:17					1
1 Th.			1	3:4													1
1 Ti.															3	1:16; 4:8; 6:19	3
2 Ti.	1	4:1															1
Heb.	2	1:14; 10:27					5	2:5; 6:5; 9:11; 10:1; 13:14			1	11:20			2	8:5; 11:8	10
Jas.	1	2:12															1
1 Pt.	1	5:1															1
2 Pt.															1	2:6	1
Rev.	5	1:19; 2:10, 10; 3:10; 17:8	1	6:11					1	3:16					6	3:2; 8:13; 10:4, 7; 12: 4, 5	13
Total	25		20		9		9		7		4		3		33		110

Miscellaneous: Mt. 11:14, be; Mk. 10:32 (with 3488), what things should; Lk. 7:2, be ready; Lk. 13:9 (with 1519), after that; Lk. 19:4, be; Jn. 4:47, be at the point of; Ac. 3:3, about; Ac. 5:35, intend; Ac. 18:14; Ac. 20:3, be about; Ac. 20:7, ready; Ac. 20:13a, intend; Ac. 20:13b, mind; Ac. 21:27, be almost; Ac. 21:37, be; Ac. 22:16, tarry; Ac. 27:2, mean; Ac. 27:33 (with 1096), be coming; Ro. 5:14, be to come; Gal. 3:23, should afterwards; Eph. 1:21, be to come; 1 Ti. 1:16, should hereafter; 1 Ti. 4:8, be to come; 1 Ti. 6:19, time to come; Heb. 8:5, be about; Heb. 11:8, should after; 2 Pt. 2:6, after should; Rev. 3:2, be ready; Rev. 8:13, be yet; Rev. 10:4, be about; Rev. 10:7, begin; Rev. 12:4, be ready; Rev. 12:5, be.

3206. μένω, men′ō

Book	Oc.	abide	Oc.	remain	Oc.	dwell	Oc.	continue	Oc.	tarry	Oc.	endure	Oc.	Misc.	Total
Mt.	1	10:11	1	11:23					1	26:38					3
Mk.	1	6:10							1	14:34					2
Lk.	5	1:56; 8:27; 9:4; 19:5; 24:29a	1	10:7					1	24:29b					7
Jn.	23	1:32, 39b; 3:36; 4:40b; 5:38; 7:9; 8:35, 35; 10:40; 11:6; 12: 24, 34, 46; 14:16; 15:4, 4, 4, 5, 6, 7, 7, 10, 10	5	1:33; 9:41; 15:11, 16; 19:31	5	1:38, 39a; 6:56; 14: 10, 17	3	2:12; 8: 31; 15:9	3	4:40a; 21:22, 23	1	6:27	1	14:25	41
Ac.	6	16:15; 18:3; 20:23; 21:7, 8; 27:31	1	27:41	2	28:16, 30			3	9:43; 18: 20; 20: 15			3	5:4a, 4b; 20:5	15
Ro.													1	9:11	1
1 Co.	6	3:14; 7:8, 20, 24, 40; 13:13	2	7:11; 15:6											8
2 Co.			3	3:11, 14; 9:9											3
Phl.	1	1:25													1
1 Ti.							1	2:15							1
2 Ti.	2	2:13; 4:20					1	3:14							3
Heb.	1	7:3	1	12:27			3	7:24; 13: 1, 14			1	10:34			6
1 Pt.	1	1:23									1	1:25			2
1 Jn.	12	2:6, 10, 14, 17, 24a, 27, 27, 28; 3:6, 14, 15, 24b	2	2:24b; 3:9	7	3:17, 24a; 4:12, 13, 15, 16, 16	2	2:19, 24c							23
2 Jn.	2	1:9, 9			1	1:2									3
Rev.							1	17:10							1
Total	61		16		15		11		9		3		5		120

Miscellaneous: Jn. 14:25, be present; Ac. 5:4a, whiles . . . remain; Ac. 5:4b (with 4571), be (one's) own; Ac. 20:5, tarry for; Ro. 9:11, stand.

3207. μερίζω, merid′zō

Book	Oc.	divide	Oc.	distribute	Oc.	deal	Oc.	be difference between	Oc.	give part	Total
Mt.	3	12:25, 25, 26									3
Mk.	4	3:24, 25, 26; 6:41									4
Lk.	1	12:13									1
Ro.					1	12:3					1
1 Co.	1	1:13	1	7:17			1	7:34			3
2 Co.			1	10:13							1
Heb.									1	7:2	1
Total	9		2		1		1		1		14

3208. μέριμνα, mer′imna

Book	care	Total
Mt.	13:22	1
Mk.	4:19	1
Lk.	8:14; 21:34	2
2 Co.	11:28	1
1 Pt.	5:7	1
Total		6

3209. μεριμνάω, merimna′ō

Book	Oc.	take thought	Oc.	care	Oc.	be careful	Oc.	have care	Total
Mt.	7	6:25, 27, 28, 31, 34, 34; 10:19							7
Lk.	4	12:11, 22, 25, 26			1	10:41			5
1 Co.			4	7:32, 33, 34, 34			1	12:25	5
Phl.			1	2:20	1	4:6			2
Total	11		5		2		1		19

3210. μερίς, meris′

Book	Oc.	part	Oc.	to be partaker (with 1519)	Total
Lk.	1	10:42			1
Ac.	2	8:21; 16:12			2
2 Co.	1	6:15			1
Col.			1	1:12	1
Total	4		1		5

3211. μερισμός, merismos′

Book	Oc.	gift	Oc.	dividing asunder	Total
Heb.	1	2:4	1	4:12	2

3212. μεριστής, meristes′

Book	divider	Total
Lk.	12:14	1

3214. μεσημβρία, mesembri′a

Book	Oc.	south	Oc.	noon	Total
Ac.	1	8:26	1	22:6	2

3215. μεσιτεύω, mesiteu′ō

Book	confirm	Total
Heb.	6:17	1

3213. μέρος, mer′os

Book	Oc.	part	Oc.	portion	Oc.	coast	Oc.	behalf	Oc.	respect	Oc.	Misc.	Total
Mt.	1	2:22	1	24:51	2	15:21; 16:13							4
Mk.	1	8:10											1
Lk.	1	11:36	2	12:46; 15:12							1	24:42	4
Jn.	3	13:8; 19:23, 23									1	21:6	4
Ac.	5	2:10; 5:2; 20:2; 23:6, 9			1	19:1					1	19:27	7
Ro.	1	11:25									2	15:15, 24	3
1 Co.	4	13:9, 9, 10, 12									3	11:18; 12:27; 14:27	7
2 Co.	2	1:14; 2:5					1	9:3	1	3:10			4
Eph.	2	4:9, 16											2
Col.									1	2:16			1
Heb.											1	9:5	1
1 Pt.							1	4:16					1
Rev.	4	16:19; 20:6; 21:8; 22:19											4
Total	24		3		3		2		2		9		43

Miscellaneous: Lk. 24:42, piece; Jn. 21:6, side; Ac. 19:27, craft; Ro. 15:15, some sort; Ro. 15:24, somewhat; 1 Co. 11:18 (with 5000), partly; 1 Co. 12: 27, particular; 1 Co. 14:27, course; Heb. 9:5 (with 2596), particularly.

3216. μεσίτης, mesi'tes

Book	mediator	Total
Gal.	3:19, 20	2
1 Ti.	2:5	1
Heb.	8:6; 9:15; 12:24	3
Total		6

3217. μεσονύκτιον, mesonuk'tion

Book	midnight	Total
Mk.	13:35	1
Lk.	11:5	1
Ac.	16:25; 20:7	2
Total		4

3218. Μεσοποταμία Mesopotami'a

Book	Mesopotamia	Total
Ac.	2:9; 7:2	2

3220. μεσότοιχον, mesot'oichon

Book	middle wall between	Total
Eph.	2:14	1

3221. μεσουράνημα mesouran'ema

Book	midst of heaven	Total
Rev.	8:13; 14:6; 19:17	3

3222. μεσόω, meso'ō

Book	about the midst	Total
Jn.	7:14	1

3219. μέσος, mes'os

Book	Oc.	midst	Oc.	among	Oc.	from among (with 1537)	Oc.	out of the way (with 1537)	Oc.	midnight (with 3471)	Oc.	Misc.	Total
Mt.	4	10:16; 14:24; 18:2, 20			1	13:49			1	25:6	2	13:25; 14:6	8
Mk.	4	6:47; 7:31; 9:36; 14:60									1	3:3	5
Lk.	10	2:46; 4:30, 35; 5:19; 6:8; 17:11; 21:21; 22:55a; 23:45; 24:36	4	8:7; 10:3; 22:27, 55b									14
Jn.	6	8:3, 9, 59; 19:18; 20:19, 26	1	1:26									7
Ac.	6	1:15, 18; 2:22; 4:7; 17:22; 27:21			2	17:33; 23:10			1	27:27	1	26:13	10
1 Co.					1	5:2					1	6:5	2
2 Co.					1	6:17							1
Phl.	1	2:15											1
Col.							1	2:14					1
1 Th.			1	2:7									1
2 Th.							1	2:7					1
Heb.	1	2:12											1
Rev.	9	1:13; 2:1, 7; 4:6; 5:6, 6; 6:6; 7:17; 22:2											9
Total	41		6		5		2		2		5		61

Miscellaneous: Mt. 13:25 (with 303b), among; Mt. 14:6 (with 1722 and 3488), before them; Mk. 3:3 (with 1519 and 3488), forth; Ac. 26:13 (with 2250), mid-day; 1 Co. 6:5 (with 303b), between.

3223. Μεσσίας, Messi'as

Book	Messias	Total
Jn.	1:41; 4:25	2

3225. μεστόω, mesto'ō

Book	fill	Total
Ac.	2:13	1

3224. μεστός, mestos'

Book	full	Total
Mt.	23:28	1
Jn.	19:29; 21:11	2
Ro.	1:29; 15:14	2
Jas.	3:8, 17	2
2 Pt.	2:14	1
Total		8

3227. μεταβαίνω, metabai'nō

Book	Oc.	depart	Oc.	remove	Oc.	pass	Oc.	go	Total
Mt.	4	8:34; 11:1; 12:9; 15:29	2	17:20, 20					6
Lk.							1	10:7	1
Jn.	2	7:3; 13:1			1	5:24			3
Ac.	1	18:7							1
1 Jn.					1	3:14			1
Total	7		2		2		1		12

3226a. μετά, meta' (with genitive)

Book	Oc.	with	Oc.	among	Oc.	against	Oc.	Not Tr.	Oc.	Misc.	Total
Mt.	59	1:23; 2:3, 11; 4:21; 5:25, 41; 8:11; 9:11, 15; 12:3, 4, 30, 30, 41, 42, 45; 13:20; 14:7; 15:30; 16:27; 17:3, 17; 18:16; 19:10; 20:2, 20; 21:2; 22:16; 24:30, 31, 49, 51; 25:3, 4, 10, 19b, 31; 26:11, 18, 20, 23, 29, 36, 38, 40, 47, 47, 51, 55, 58, 69, 71, 72; 27:34, 41, 54; 28:8, 12, 20							2	18:23; 27:66	61
Mk.	44	1:13, 20, 29, 36; 2:16, 16, 19, 19, 25; 3:5, 6, 7, 14; 4:16, 36; 5:18, 24, 40; 6:25, 50; 8:10, 14, 38; 9:8, 24; 10:30; 11:11; 13:26; 14:7, 14, 17, 18, 20, 33, 43, 43, 48, 54, 67; 15:1, 7, 28, 31; 16:10							1	14:62	45
Lk.	45	1:28, 39, 66; 2:36, 51; 5:29, 30, 34; 6:3, 4, 17; 7:36; 8:13, 45; 9:49; 10:17; 11:7, 23, 23, 31, 32; 12:13, 46, 58; 13:1; 14:9, 31; 15:29, 30, 31; 17:15, 20; 21:27; 22:11, 15, 21, 28, 33, 52, 53, 59; 23:43; 24:29, 30, 52	2	22:37; 24:5					5	1:58, 72; 9:39; 10:37; 23:12	52
Jn.	38	3:2, 22b, 26; 4:27, 27; 6:3, 66; 7:33; 8:29; 9:37, 40; 11:16, 31, 54; 12:8, 17, 35; 13:8, 18, 33; 14:9, 16, 30; 15:27; 16:4, 32; 17:12, 24; 18:2, 3, 5, 18, 26; 19:18, 40; 20:7, 24, 26b	3	6:43; 11:56; 16:19					1	3:25	42
Ac.	35	1:26; 2:28; 4:29, 31; 7:9, 38, 45; 9:19, 28, 39; 10:38; 11:21; 13:17; 14:23, 27; 15:4, 35; 17:11; 18:10; 20:18, 19, 24, 31, 34; 24:1b, 3, 7, 18, 18; 25:12, 23; 26:12; 27:10, 24; 28:31							3	2:29; 5:26; 15:33	38
Ro.	7	12:15, 15, 18; 15:10, 33; 16:20, 24									7
1 Co.	8	6:6, 7; 7:12, 13; 16:11, 12, 23, 24									8
2 Co.	7	6:15, 16; 7:15; 8:4, 18; 13:11, 14									7
Gal.	5	2:1, 12; 4:25, 30; 6:18									5
Eph.	7	4:2, 2, 25; 6:5, 7, 23, 24									7
Phl.	7	1:4; 2:12, 29; 4:3, 6, 9, 23									7
Col.	2	1:11; 4:18									2
1 Th.	3	1:6; 3:13; 5:28									3
2 Th.	5	1:7, 7; 3:12, 16, 18									5
1 Ti.	9	1:14; 2:9, 15; 3:4; 4:3, 4, 14; 6:6, 21									9
2 Ti.	6	2:10, 22; 4:11, 11, 22, 22									6
Tit.	3	2:15; 3:15, 15									3
Phe.	1	1:25									1
Heb.	12	5:7; 7:21; 9:19; 10:22; 11:9, 31; 12:14, 17, 28; 13:17, 23, 25							2	4:16; 10:34	14
1 Pt.	1	3:15									1
1 Jn.	6	1:3, 3, 3, 6, 7; 2:19							1	4:17	7
2 Jn.	2	1:2, 3									2
Rev.	33	1:7, 12; 2:22; 3:4, 20, 20, 21, 21; 4:1b; 6:8; 12:9, 17; 13:4, 7; 14:1, 4; 17:1, 2, 12, 14, 14; 18:3, 9; 19:20; 20:4, 6; 21:3, 3, 3, 9, 15; 22:12, 21			4	2:16; 11:7; 19:19, 19	1	14:13	1	10:8	39
Total	345		5		4		1		16		371

Miscellaneous: Mt. 18:23, of; Mt. 27:66, and setting; Mk. 14:62, in; Lk. 1:58, upon; Lk. 1:72, to; Lk. 9:39 (with 876), that (one) foameth again; Lk. 10:37, on; Lk. 23:12 (with 240), together; Jn. 3:25, and; Ac. 2:29 (with 3854), freely; Ac. 5:26 (with 3656), without; Ac. 15:33, in; Heb. 4:16 (with 3854), boldly; Heb. 10:34 (with 5379), joyfully; 1 Jn. 4:17 (with 2257), our; Rev. 10:8, unto.

See page 228 for Word 3226b.

3226b. μετά, meta′ (with accusative)

Book	Oc.	after	Oc.	hereafter (with 4923)	Oc.	afterward (with 4923)	Oc.	Misc.	Total
Mt.	9	1:12; 17:1; 24:29; 25:19a; 26:2, 32, 73; 27:53, 63					1	27:62	10
Mk.	9	1:14; 8:31; 9:2; 13:24; 14:1, 28, 70; 16:12, 19							9
Lk.	10	1:24; 2:46; 5:27; 9:28; 10:1; 12:4, 5; 15:13; 22:20, 58			2	17:8; 18:4			12
Jn.	14	2:12; 3:22a; 4:43; 5:1, 4; 6:1; 7:1; 11:7, 11; 13:27; 19:28, 38; 20:26a; 21:1	1	13:7	1	5:14			16
Ac.	27	1:3; 5:37; 7:5, 7; 10:37, 41; 12:4; 13:15, 20, 25; 15:13, 16, 36; 18:1; 19:4, 21; 20:1, 6, 29; 21:15; 24:1a, 24; 25:1; 27:14; 28:11, 13, 17					2	1:5; 7:4	29
1 Co.							1	11:25	1
Gal.	2	1:18; 3:17							2
Tit.	1	3:10							1
Heb.	7	4:7; 8:10; 9:3, 27; 10:15, 16, 26			1	4:8	1	7:28	9
1 Pt.							1	1:11	1
2 Pt.	1	1:15							1
Rev.	8	4:1a; 7:1, 9; 11:11; 15:5; 18:1; 19:1; 20:3	3	1:19; 4:1c; 9:12					11
Total	88		4		4		6		102

Miscellaneous: Mt. 27:62 (with 2076), follow; Ac. 1:5, hence; Ac. 7:4; 1 Co. 11:25, when; Heb. 7:28, since; 1 Pt. 1:11 (with 4923), follow.

Word 3226 has 473 occurrences.

3228. μεταβάλλω, metabal′lō

Book	change (one's) mind	Total
Ac.	28:6	1

3229. μετάγω, metag′ō

Book	turn about	Total
Jas.	3:3, 4	2

3230. μεταδίδωμι, metadid′ōmi

Book	Oc.	impart	Oc.	give	Total
Lk.	1	3:11			1
Ro.	1	1:11	1	12:8	2
Eph.			1	4:28	1
1 Th.	1	2:8			1
Total	3		2		5

3232. μεταίρω, metai′rō

Book	depart	Total
Mt.	13:53; 19:1	2

3234. μετακινέω, metakine′ō

Book	move away	Total
Col.	1:23	1

3231. μετάθεσις, metath′esis

Book	Oc.	change	Oc.	translation	Oc.	removing	Total
Heb.	1	7:12	1	11:5	1	12:27	3

3233. μετακαλέω, metakale′ō

Book	Oc.	call	Oc.	call for	Oc.	call hither	Oc.	call to (one's self)	Total
Ac.	1	20:17	1	24:25	1	10:32	1	7:14	4

3235. μεταλαμβάνω, metalamban′ō

Book	Oc.	be partaker	Oc.	eat	Oc.	have	Oc.	take	Oc.	receive	Total
Ac.			1	2:46	1	24:25	1	27:33			3
2 Ti.	1	2:6									1
Heb.	1	12:10							1	6:7	2
Total	2		1		1		1		1		6

3236. μετάληψις, metal′epsis

Book	to be received (with 1519)	Total
1 Ti.	4:3	1

3237. μεταλλάσσω, metallas′sō

Book	change	Total
Ro.	1:25, 26	2

3238. μεταμέλλομαι, metamel′lomai

Book	Oc.	repent	Oc.	repent (one's) self	Total
Mt.	2	21:29, 32	1	27:3	3
2 Co.	2	7:8, 8			2
Heb.	1	7:21			1
Total	5		1		6

3239. μεταμορφόω, metamorpho′ō

Book	Oc.	transfigure	Oc.	transform	Oc.	change	Total
Mt.	1	17:2					1
Mk.	1	9:2					1
Ro.			1	12:2			1
2 Co.					1	3:18	1
Total	2		1		1		4

3240. μετανοέω, metanoe′ō

Book	repent	Total
Mt.	3:2; 4:17; 11:20, 21; 12:41	5
Mk.	1:15; 6:12	2
Lk.	10:13; 11:32; 13:3, 5; 15:7, 10; 16:30; 17:3, 4	9
Ac.	2:38; 3:19; 8:22; 17:30; 26:20	5
2 Co.	12:21	1
Rev.	2:5, 5, 16, 21, 21, 22; 3:3, 19; 9:20, 21; 16:9, 11	12
Total		34

3241. μετάνοια, metan′oia

Book	repentance	Total
Mt.	3:8, 11; 9:13	3
Mk.	1:4; 2:17	2
Lk.	3:3, 8; 5:32; 15:7; 24:47	5
Ac.	5:31; 11:18; 13:24; 19:4; 20:21; 26:20	6
Ro.	2:4	1
2 Co.	7:9, 10	2
2 Ti.	2:25	1
Heb.	6:1, 6; 12:17	3
2 Pt.	3:9	1
Total		24

3243. μεταπέμπω, metapemp′ō

Book	Oc.	send for	Oc.	call for	Total
Ac.	6	10:22, 29, 29; 24:24, 26; 25:3	2	10:5; 11:13	8

3244. μεταστρέφω, metastreph′ō

Book	Oc.	turn	Oc.	pervert	Total
Ac.	1	2:20			1
Gal.			1	1:7	1
Jas.	1	4:9			1
Total	2		1		3

3242. μεταξύ, metaxu′

Book	Oc.	between	Oc.	meanwhile	Oc.	next	Total
Mt.	2	18:15; 23:35					2
Lk.	2	11:51; 16:26					2
Jn.			1	4:31			1
Ac.	2	12:6; 15:9			1	13:42	3
Ro.			1	2:15			1
Total	6		2		1		9

3245. μετασχηματίζω, metaschēmatid′zō

Book	Oc.	trans-form	Oc.	trans-fer in a figure	Oc.	transform (one's) self	Oc.	change	Total
1 Co.			1	4:6					1
2 Co.	2	11:14, 15			1	11:13			3
Phl.							1	3:21	1
Total	2		1		1		1		5

3246. μετατίθημι, metatith′ēmi

Book	Oc.	translate	Oc.	carry over	Oc.	remove	Oc.	change	Oc.	turn	Total
Ac.			1	7:16							1
Gal.					1	1:6					1
Heb.	2	11:5, 5					1	7:12			3
Jd.									1	1:4	1
Total	2		1		1		1		1		6

3247. μετέπειτα, metep′eita

Book	afterward	Total
Heb.	12:17	1

3248. μετέχω, metech′ō

Book	Oc.	be partaker	Oc.	take part	Oc.	use	Oc.	pertain	Total
1 Co.	5	9:10, 12; 10:17, 21, 30							5
Heb.			1	2:14	1	5:13	1	7:13	3
Total	5		1		1		1		8

3249. μετεωρίζω, meteōrid′zō

Book	be of doubtful mind	Total
Lk.	12:29	1

3250. μετοικεσία, metoikesi′a

Book	Oc.	carrying away into	Oc.	carried away to	Oc.	be brought to	Total
Mt.	2	1:17, 17	1	1:11	1	1:12	4

3251. μετοικίζω, metoikid′zō

Book	Oc.	remove into	Oc.	carry away	Total
Ac.	1	7:4	1	7:43	2

3252. μετοχή, metoche̱′

Book	fellowship	Total
2 Co.	6:14	1

3255. μετρητής, metre̱te̱s′

Book	firkin	Total
Jn.	2:6	1

3254. μετρέω, metre′ō

Book	Oc.	measure	Oc.	mete	Total
Mt.			1	7:2	1
Mk.	1	4:24b	1	4:24a	2
Lk.			1	6:38	1
2 Co.	1	10:12			1
Rev.	5	11:1, 2; 21:15, 16, 17			5
Total	7		3		10

3253. μέτοχος, met′ochos

Book	Oc.	partaker	Oc.	partner	Oc.	fellow	Total
Lk.			1	5:7			1
Heb.	4	3:1, 14; 6:4; 12:8			1	1:9	5
Total	4		1		1		6

3257. μετρίως, metri′ōs

Book	a little	Total
Ac.	20:12	1

3259. μέτωπον, met′ōpon

Book	forehead	Total
Rev.	7:3; 9:4; 13:16; 14:1, 9; 17:5; 20:4; 22:4	8

3256. μετριοπαθέω metriopathe′ō

Book	have compassion on	Total
Heb.	5:2	1

3258. μέτρον, met′ron

Book	measure	Total
Mt.	7:2; 23:32	2
Mk.	4:24	1
Lk.	6:38, 38	2
Jn.	3:34	1
Ro.	12:3	1
2 Co.	10:13, 13	2
Eph.	4:7, 13, 16	3
Rev.	21:17	1
Total		13

3260. μέχρι or μεχρίς, mech′ri or mechris′

Book	Oc.	unto	Oc.	until	Oc.	till	Oc.	to	Oc.	till (with 3639)	Total
Mt.			3	11:23; 13:30; 28:15							3
Mk.									1	13:30	1
Ac.			2	10:30; 20:7							2
Ro.	1	15:19					1	5:14			2
Eph.					1	4:13					1
Phl.	2	2:8, 30									2
1 Ti.			1	6:14							1
2 Ti.	1	2:9									1
Heb.	3	3:6, 14; 12:4	1	9:10							4
Total	7		7		1		1		1		17

See page 230 for Word 3261.

3262. ἐὰν μή, ean′ me̱

Book	Oc.	except	Oc.	if not	Oc.	whosoever not (with 3639)	Oc.	but	Oc.	if no	Oc.	not	Oc.	before	Total
Mt.	4	5:20; 12:29; 18:3; 26:42	4	6:15; 10:13b; 18:16, 35	2	10:14; 11:6									10
Mk.	3	3:27; 7:3, 4			1	10:15	1	10:30			1	4:22			6
Lk.	2	13:3, 5			2	7:23; 18:17									4
Jn.	12	3:2, 3, 5, 27; 4:48; 6:44, 53, 65; 12:24; 15:4, 4; 20:25	5	8:24; 12:47; 13:8; 15:6; 16:7a			1	5:19					1	7:51	19
Ac.	3	8:31; 15:1; 27:31													3
Ro.	1	10:15	1	11:23											2
1 Co.	4	14:6, 7, 9; 15:36	3	8:8b; 9:16b; 14:11					1	14:28					8
Gal.							1	2:16							1
2 Th.	1	2:3													1
2 Ti.	1	2:5													1
Jas.			1	2:17											1
1 Jn.			1	3:21											1
Rev.	2	2:5, 22	1	3:3											3
Total	33		16		5		3		1		1		1		60

3263. ἵνα μή, hin′a me̱

Book	Oc.	that not	Oc.	lest	Oc.	that . . . no	Oc.	that nothing (with 5000)	Oc.	albeit not	Oc.	so that not	Total
Mt.	4	7:1; 12:16; 24:20; 26:41	2	17:27; 26:5									6
Mk.	3	3:12; 5:10; 13:18	2	3:9; 14:38									5
Lk.	3	8:31; 9:45; 22:32	5	8:12; 14:29; 16:28; 18:5; 22:46									8
Jn.	9	3:15; 4:15; 6:50; 7:23; 12:40, 46; 16:1; 18:36; 19:31	5	3:20; 5:14; 12:35, 42; 18:28			1	6:12					15
Ac.	2	2:25; 24:4	1	5:26	1	4:17							4
Ro.			2	11:25; 15:20									2
1 Co.	3	7:5; 11:32, 34	4	1:15, 17; 8:13; 9:12	3	4:6; 12:25; 16: 2							10
2 Co.	5	1:9; 2:5; 6:3; 9:4; 10:9	6	2:3, 11; 9:3; 12:7, 7; 13:10									11
Gal.			1	6:12							1	5:17	2
Eph.			1	2:9									1
Phl.			1	2:27									1
Col.			2	2:4; 3:21									2
1 Th.	1	4:13											1
1 Ti.	1	6:1	2	3:6, 7									3
Tit.	2	2:5; 3:14											2
Phe.	1	1:14							1	1:19			2
Heb.	2	6:12; 11:40	5	3:13; 4:11; 11:28; 12:3, 13									7
Jas.			2	5:9, 12									2
2 Pt.			1	3:17									1
1 Jn.	1	2:1											1
2 Jn.	1	1:8											1
Rev.	7	7:1; 9:4, 5, 20; 11:6; 18:4, 4	1	16:15	2	13:17; 20:3							10
Total	45		43		6		1		1		1		97

3264. οὐ μή, ou me̱

Book	Oc.	not	Oc.	in no wise	Oc.	no	Oc.	never (with 1519. 165, and 3488)	Oc.	no more at all (with 2089)	Oc.	Not Tr.	Oc.	Misc.	Total
Mt.	14	10:23; 13:14, 14; 15:6; 16:22, 28; 18:3; 23:39; 24:2, 2, 34, 35; 26:29, 35	2	5:18; 10:42									3	5:20, 26; 24:21	19
Mk.	8	9:1, 41; 10:15; 13:2, 2, 30, 31; 16:18									1	14:25	2	13:19; 14:31	11
Lk.	15	6:37, 37; 9:27; 12:59; 13:35; 18:7, 30; 21:18, 32, 33; 22:16, 18, 34, 67, 68	1	18:17									2	1:15; 10:19	18
Jn.	6	4:48; 8:12; 10:5; 11:56; 13:38; 20:25	1	6:37			6	4:14; 8:51, 52; 10:28; 11:26; 13:8					2	6:35, 35	15
Ac.	2	28:26, 26	1	13:41											3
Ro.	1	4:8													1
1 Co.					1	8:13									1
Gal.	2	4:30; 5:16													2
1 Th.	2	4:15; 5:3													2
Heb.	1	8:11			2	8:12; 10:17							2	13:5a, 5b	5
1 Pt.	1	2:6													1
2 Pt.													1	1:10	1
Rev.	4	2:11; 3:3, 5; 15:4	1	21:27	3	3:12; 18:7, 22b			5	18:21, 22a, 22c, 23, 23			2	18:14; 21:25	15
Total	56		6		6		6		5		1		14		94

Miscellaneous: Mt. 5:20, in no case; Mt. 5:26, by no means; Mt. 24:21, nor ever; Mk. 13:19, neither; Mk. 14:31, not . . . in any wise; Lk. 1:15, neither; Lk. 10:19, by any means; Jn. 6:35, 35; Heb. 13:5a, never; Heb. 13:5b (with 3661), nor; 2 Pt. 1:10 (with 4118), never; Rev. 18:14, at all; Rev. 21:25, not at all.

3261. μή, me̱

Book	Oc.	not	Oc.	no	Oc.	that not	Oc.	God forbid (with 1096)	Oc.	lest
Mt.	53	1:19, 20; 2:12; 3:9, 10; 5:17, 29, 30, 34, 39, 42; 6:2, 3, 7, 8, 13, 16, 18, 19; 7:1, 6, 19, 26; 10:5, 5, 26, 28, 28, 31, 34; 12:30, 30; 13:19; 14:27; 17:7; 18:13, 25; 19:6, 14; 21:21; 22:12, 29; 23:3, 8, 23; 24:17, 23, 26, 26; 25:29; 26:5; 28:5, 10	11	6:25, 31, 34; 9:36; 10:19; 13:5, 6; 22:23, 24, 25; 23:9	3	6:1; 18:10; 24:6				
Mk.	26	2:4; 3:20; 4:12, 12; 5:36; 6:9, 11, 34, 50; 9:39; 10:9, 14, 19, 19, 19, 19, 19; 11:23; 12:15, 24; 13:7, 15, 16, 21; 14:2; 16:6	8	4:5, 6; 6:8, 8, 8; 12:18, 19; 13:11	1	5:7			2	13:5, 36
Lk.	72	1:13, 20, 30; 2:10, 26; 2:45; 3:8, 9; 4:42; 5:10, 19; 6:29, 30, 37, 37, 49; 7:6, 13, 30; 8:10, 10, 18, 28, 49, 50, 52; 9:5, 33, 50; 10:7, 10, 20; 11:4, 7, 23, 23, 35, 42; 12:4a, 7, 21, 29a, 32, 33, 47, 48; 13:14; 14:8, 12, 29; 17:23, 31, 31; 18:1, 2a, 16, 20, 20, 20, 20; 19:26, 27; 20:7; 21:8b, 9, 14, 21; 22:40, 42; 23:28; 24:16, 23	6	11:36; 12:4b, 11, 22; 13:11; 22:36	1	21:8a	1	20:16		
Jn.	36	2:16; 3:7, 16, 18, 18; 5:23, 28, 45; 6:20, 27, 43, 64; 7:24, 49; 9:39; 10:1, 37, 38; 11:37, 50; 12:15, 47, 48; 13:9; 14:1, 24, 27; 15:2; 18:17, 25, 40; 19:21, 24; 20:17, 27, 29								
Ac.	32	3:23; 4:18; 5:7; 7:19, 60; 9:26; 10:15, 47; 11:9; 12:19; 13:11; 14:18; 15:19, 38, 38; 17:6; 18:9, 9; 20:10, 16, 22, 29; 21:12, 14, 34; 23:9, 21; 25:27; 27:7, 15, 21, 24	2	1:20; 23:8	8	1:4; 5:28, 40; 9:38; 19:31; 21:4, 21; 25:24			4	13:40; 23:10; 27:17, 42
Ro.	47	1:28; 2:14, 14, 21, 22; 3:8; 4:5, 17, 19; 5:14; 6:12; 8:1, 4; 9:30; 10:6, 20, 20; 11:8, 8, 10, 18, 20; 12:2, 3, 11, 14, 16, 16, 19, 21; 13:3, 13, 13, 13, 14; 14:1, 3, 3, 3, 6, 6, 15, 16, 20, 22; 15:1	2	5:13; 7:3			10	3:4, 6, 31; 6:2, 15; 7:7, 13; 9:14b; 11:1b, 11b		
1 Co.	39	1:28; 2:5; 4:7, 18; 5:8, 9, 11; 6:9; 7:1, 5, 10, 11, 12, 13, 18, 18, 21, 23, 27, 27, 30, 30, 30, 31, 38; 9:18, 21; 10:6, 28, 33; 11:22, 29; 13:1, 2, 3; 14:20, 39; 15:33, 34	3	1:29; 4:6; 7:37			1	6:15	1	10:12
2 Co.	19	2:1, 13; 3:7, 13; 4:2, 7, 18, 18, 18; 5:19; 6:1, 9, 14, 17; 9:5, 7; 10:2, 14; 12:21b	2	5:21; 8:20					3	12:6, 21a; 13:10
Gal.	8	4:18; 5:1, 7, 13, 26; 6:7, 9, 9	1	4:8	2	3:1; 5:15	3	2:17; 3:21; 6:14	1	6:1
Eph.	10	4:26, 26, 30; 5:7, 15, 17, 18, 27; 6:4, 6	3	2:12; 4:29; 5:11	1	3:13				
Phl.	3	2:4, 12; 3:9								
Col.	8	1:23; 2:18, 21; 3:2, 9, 19, 21, 22							1	2:8
1 Th.	8	1:8; 2:9, 15; 4:5, 5; 5:6, 19, 20	1	4:13						
2 Th.	8	1:8, 8; 2:2, 12; 3:6, 8, 13, 15	1	3:14						
1 Ti.	17	1:20; 2:9; 3:3a, 3c, 6, 8, 8, 8, 11; 4:14; 5:1, 9, 13, 16, 19; 6:2, 3	1	3:3b	1	6:17				
2 Ti.	1	1:8			2	2:14; 4:16				
Tit.	11	1:6, 7a. 7b, 7c, 7e, 11, 14; 2:3, 3, 9, 10	1	1:7d						
Heb.	20	3:8, 15; 4:2, 7; 6:1; 7:6; 9:9; 10:25, 35; 11:3, 5, 8, 13, 27; 12:5, 19; 13:2, 9, 16, 17			2	3:18; 12:25			3	12:15, 15, 16
Jas.	18	1:5, 7, 16, 22, 26; 2:1, 11, 11, 14a, 16; 3:1, 14; 4:2, 11, 17; 5:9, 12, 17	1	2:13						
1 Pt.	11	1:8, 14; 2:16; 3:6, 7, 9, 14; 4:4, 12, 16; 5:2	1	3:10						
2 Pt.	3	2:21; 3:8, 9								
1 Jn.	17	2:4, 15, 28; 3:10, 10, 13, 14, 18, 21; 4:1, 3, 8, 20; 5:10, 12, 16, 16								
2 Jn.	3	1:7, 9, 10a								
3 Jn.	2	1:10, 11								
Jd.	3	1:5, 6, 19								
Rev.	12	1:17; 3:18; 5:5; 6:6; 7:3; 8:12; 10:4; 11:2; 13:15; 19:10; 22:9, 10								
Total	487		44		21		15		15	

3265. μηδαμῶς, mēdamōs′

Book	not so	Total
Ac.	10:14; 11:8	2

3266. μηδέ, mēde′

Book	Oc.	neither	Oc.	nor	Oc.	not	Oc.	nor yet	Oc.	not once	Oc.	no not	Oc.	not so much as	Total
Mt.	5	7:6; 10:10a, 10b; 23:10; 24:20	5	10:9, 9, 10c, 14; 22:29			1	6:25							11
Mk.	4	8:26a; 12:24; 13:11, 15	2	6:11; 8:26b									1	2:2	7
Lk.	5	3:14; 12:22, 47; 14:12b; 16:26	4	10:4; 14:12a, 12c; 17:23											9
Jn.	2	4:15; 14:27													2
Ac.	2	21:21; 23:8	1	4:18											3
Ro.	2	6:13; 9:11	2	14:21, 21											4
1 Co.	5	5:8; 10:7, 8, 9, 10									1	5:11			6
2 Co.			1	4:2											1
Eph.									1	5:3					1
Col.					2	2:21, 21									2
2 Th.	1	3:10													1
1 Ti.	2	1:4; 5:22	1	6:17											3
2 Ti.			1	1:8											1
Heb.			1	12:5											1
1 Pt.	2	3:14; 5:3			1	5:2									3
1 Jn.	2	2:15; 3:18													2
Total	32		18		3		1		1		1		1		57

3261. μή, mē (continued)

Book	Oc.	neither	Oc.	no man (with 5000)	Oc.	but	Oc.	none	Oc.	Not Tr. (as an interrogative)	Oc.	Not Tr.	Oc.	Misc.	Total
Mt.	2	10:9; 24:18	2	8:28; 24:4					3	7:9, 10; 9:15			1	10:10	75
Mk.									1	2:19			1	8:1	39
Lk.	3	10:4a; 12:29b; 18:2b			1	17:1	2	3:11; 11:24	6	5:34; 11:11, 11, 12; 17:9; 22:35	1	22:34	5	7:42; 8:6; 10:4b; 16:26; 20:27	98
Jn.									12	3:4; 4:12; 6:67; 7:35, 41, 47, 51, 52; 8:53; 9:27, 40; 10:21			2	6:39; 7:15	50
Ac.					2	4:20; 20:20			2	7:28, 42	1	20:27	1	9:9	52
Ro.	1	14:21							6	3:3, 5; 9:14a, 20; 11:1a, 11a			1	14:13	67
1 Co.			1	16:11			1	7:29	11	1:13; 9:8, 9; 10:22; 12:29, 29, 29, 29, 30, 30, 30	1	1:7	3	1:10; 4:5; 9:6	61
2 Co.			1	11:16					1	12:17	1	13:7	2	3:14; 4:4	29
Gal.															15
Eph.															14
Phl.											1	1:28			4
Col.			1	2:16											10
1 Th.													2	4:6; 5:15	11
2 Th.			1	2:3											10
1 Ti.											1	1:7	1	1:3	21
2 Ti.															3
Tit.															12
Heb.													2	4:15; 12:27	27
Jas.									2	2:14b; 3:12					21
1 Pt.													1	4:15	13
2 Pt.													1	1:9	4
1 Jn.															17
2 Jn.	1	1:10b													4
3 Jn.															2
Jd.															3
Rev.											1	7:16			13
Total	7		6		3		3		44		7		23		675

Miscellaneous: Mt. 10:10, nor; Mk. 8:1 (with 5000), nothing; Lk. 7:42, nothing; Lk. 8:6 (with 2192), lack; Lk. 10:4b, nor; Lk. 16:26 (with 1410), cannot; Lk. 20:27, any; Jn. 6:39, nothing; Jn. 7:15, never; Ac. 9:9, without; Ro. 14:13, that no man; 1 Co. 1:10, that no; 1 Co. 4:5 (with 5000), nothing; 1 Co. 9:6 (with 2038), forbear working; 2 Co. 3:14 (with 343), untaken away; 2 Co. 4:4 (with 1519 and 3488), lest; 1 Th. 4:6, that no man; 1 Th. 5:15, that none; 1 Ti. 1:3, that no; Heb. 4:15 (with 1410), cannot; Heb. 12:27 (with 4431 and 3488), those things which cannot be shaken; 1 Pt. 4:15 (with 5000), none; 2 Pt. 1:9 (with 3818), lack.

3267. μηδείς, mēdeis′

Book	Oc.	no man	Oc.	nothing	Oc.	no	Oc.	none	Oc.	not	Oc.	anything	Oc.	Misc.	Total
Mt.	4	8:4; 9:30; 16:20; 17:9	1	27:19											5
Mk.	5	5:43; 7:36; 8:30; 9:9; 11:14	3	1:44a; 5:26; 6:8									1	1:44b	9
Lk.	5	3:14; 5:14; 8:56; 9:21; 10:4	2	6:35; 9:3	1	3:13			1	4:35					9
Jn.							1	8:10							1
Ac.	2	9:7; 23:22	8	4:21; 10:20; 11:12; 19:36; 23:14, 29; 25:25; 27:33	8	4:17; 13:28; 15:28; 16:28; 19:40; 21:25; 28:6, 18	3	8:24; 11:19; 24:23	1	8:28			2	10:28; 25:17	24
Ro.	2	12:17; 13:8a									1	13:8b			3
1 Co.	3	3:18, 21; 10:24			3	1:7; 10:25, 27									6
2 Co.			2	6:10; 7:9	2	6:3a; 13:7					1	6:3b	1	11:5	6
Gal.	1	6:17	1	6:3											2
Eph.	1	5:6													1
Phl.			3	1:28; 2:3; 4:6											3
Col.	1	2:18													1
1 Th.	1	3:3	1	4:12											2
2 Th.													2	2:3; 3:11	2
1 Ti.	2	4:12; 5:22	2	5:21; 6:4			1	5:14							5
Tit.	2	2:15; 3:2	1	3:13	1	2:8									4
Heb.					1	10:2									1
Jas.	1	1:13	2	1:4, 6											3
1 Pt.													1	3:6	1
1 Jn.	1	3:7													1
3 Jn.			1	1:7											1
Rev.	1	3:11					1	2:10							2
Total	32		27		16		6		2		2		7		92

Miscellaneous: Mk. 1:44b, any man; Ac. 10:28, not any man; Ac. 25:17 (with 4060), without any; 2 Co. 11:5, not a whit; 2 Th. 2:3, any; 2 Th. 3:11, not at all; 1 Pt. 3:6, any.

3268. μηδέποτε, mēdep′ote

Book	never	Total
2 Ti.	3:7	1

3269. μηδέπω, mēdep′ō

Book	not as yet	Total
Heb.	11:7	1

3270. Μῆδος, Mē′dos

Book	Mede	Total
Ac.	2:9	1

3272. μῆκος, mē′kos

Book	length	Total
Eph.	3:18	1
Rev.	21:16, 16	2
Total		3

3271. μηκέτι, mēket′i

Book	Oc.	no more	Oc.	no longer	Oc.	henceforth not	Oc.	no	Oc.	no . . . henceforward	Oc.	hereafter	Oc.	Misc.	Total
Mt.									1	21:19					1
Mk.	2	1:45; 9:25					1	2:2			1	11:14			4
Jn.	2	5:14; 8:11													2
Ac.	1	13:34											2	4:17; 25:24	3
Ro.	1	15:23			1	6:6							1	14:13	3
2 Co.													1	5:15	1
Eph.	1	4:28			1	4:17							1	4:14	3
1 Th.			2	3:1, 5											2
1 Ti.			1	5:23											1
1 Pt.			1	4:2											1
Total	7		4		2		1		1		1		5		21

Miscellaneous: Ac. 4:17, henceforth; Ac. 25:24, any longer; Ro. 14:13, not any more; 2 Co. 5:15, not henceforth; Eph. 4:14, henceforth no more.

3273. μηκύνω, mēku′nō

Book	grow up	Total
Mk.	4:27	1

3274. μηλωτή, mēlōtē′

Book	sheepskin	Total
Heb.	11:37	1

3275. μήν, mēn

Book	surely (with 2229)	Total
Heb.	6:14	1

3276. μήν, mēn

Book	month	Total
Lk.	1:24, 26, 36, 56; 4:25	5
Ac.	7:20; 18:11; 19:8; 20:3; 28:11	5
Gal.	4:10	1
Jas.	5:17	1
Rev.	9:5, 10, 15; 11:2; 13:5; 22:2	6
Total		18

3277. μηνύω, mēnu′ō

Book	Oc.	shew	Oc.	tell	Total
Lk.	1	20:37			1
Jn.	1	11:57			1
Ac.			1	23:30	1
1 Co.	1	10:28			1
Total	3		1		4

3278a. μὴ οὐκ, mē ouk

Book	not	Total
Ro.	10:18, 19	2
1 Co.	9:4, 5; 11:22	3
Total		5

3278b. οὐ μή, ou mē

Book	not	Total
Jn.	18:11	1

Word 3278 has 6 occurrences.

3279. μήποτε or μή ποτε, mē′pote or mē pot′e

Book	Oc.	lest	Oc.	lest at any time	Oc.	whether or not	Oc.	lest haply (with 2443)	Oc.	lest haply	Oc.	if peradventure	Oc.	no . . . at all	Oc.	Not Tr.	Total
Mt.	5	7:6; 13:29; 15:32; 25:9; 27:64	3	4:6; 5:25; 13:15													8
Mk.	1	14:2	1	4:12													2
Lk.	3	12:58; 14:8, 12	2	4:11; 21:34	1	3:15	1	14:29									7
Jn.															1	7:26	1
Ac.	1	28:27							1	5:39							2
2 Ti.											1	2:25					1
Heb.	2	3:12; 4:1	1	2:1									1	9:17			4
Total	12		7		1		1		1		1		1		1		25

3280. μήπω, me̱′pō

Book	not yet	Total
Ro.	9:11	1
Heb.	9:8	1
Total		2

3281. μήπως or μή πως, me̱′pōs or me̱ pōs

Book	Oc.	lest	Oc.	lest by any means	Oc.	lest perhaps	Oc.	lest haply	Oc.	lest by some means	Oc.	lest that by any means	Total
Ac.	1	27:29											1
Ro.	1	11:21											1
1 Co.			1	8:9							1	9:27	2
2 Co.	2	12:20, 20	1	11:3	1	2:7	1	9:4					5
Gal.	1	4:11	1	2:2									2
1 Th.									1	3:5			1
Total	5		3		1		1		1		1		12

3282. μηρός, me̱ros′

Book	thigh	Total
Rev.	19:16	1

3283. μήτε, me̱′te

Book	Oc.	neither	Oc.	nor	Oc.	so much as	Oc.	or	Total
Mt.	4	5:34, 35b, 36; 11:18a	2	5:35a; 11:18b					6
Mk.					1	3:20			1
Lk.	5	7:33a; 9:3a, 3c, 3d, 3e	2	7:33b; 9:3b					7
Ac.	3	23:12a, 21a; 27:20a	4	23:8, 12b, 21b; 27:20b					7
Eph.	1	4:27							1
2 Th.	1	2:2b	2	2:2c, 2d			1	2:2a	4
1 Ti.	1	1:7a	1	1:7b					2
Heb.	1	7:3a	1	7:3b					2
Jas.	3	5:12, 12, 12							3
Rev.	1	7:3a	3	7:1, 1, 3b					4
Total	20		15		1		1		37

3284. μήτηρ, me̱′te̱r

Book	mother	Total
Mt.	1:18; 2:11, 13, 14, 20, 21; 10:35, 37; 12:46, 47, 48, 49, 50; 13:55; 14:8, 11; 15:4, 4, 5, 6; 19:5, 12, 19, 29; 20:20; 27:56, 56	27
Mk.	3:31, 32, 33, 34, 35; 5:40; 6:24, 28; 7:10, 10, 11, 12; 10:7, 19. 29, 30; 15:40	17
Lk.	1:15, 43, 60; 2:33, 34, 43, 48, 51; 7:12, 15; 8:19, 20, 21, 51; 12:53, 53; 14:26; 18:20	18
Jn.	2:1, 3, 5, 12; 3:4; 6:42; 19:25, 25, 26, 26, 27	11
Ac.	1:14; 3:2; 12:12; 14:8	4
Ro.	16:13	1
Gal.	1:15; 4:26	2
Eph.	5:31; 6:2	2
1 Ti.	5:2	1
2 Ti.	1:5	1
Rev.	17:5	1
Total		85

3285. μήτι, me̱′ti

Book	Oc.	not	Oc.	Not Tr.	Total
Mt.	1	12:23	3	7:16; 26:22, 25	4
Mk.			3	4:21; 14:19, 19	3
Lk.			1	6:39	1
Jn.	1	4:29	3	7:31; 8:22; 18:35	4
Ac.			1	10:47	1
2 Co.			1	1:17	1
Jas.			1	3:11	1
Total	2		13		15

3286. μήτιγε, me̱′tige

Book	how much more	Total
1 Co.	6:3	1

3288. μήτρα, me̱′tra

Book	womb	Total
Lk.	2:23	1
Ro.	4:19	1
Total		2

3287. μήτις or μή τις, me̱′tis or me̱ tis

Book	Oc.	any	Oc.	any man	Oc.	Not Tr.	Total
Jn.	2	7:48; 21:5	1	4:33			3
2 Co.					1	12:18	1
Total	2		1		1		4

3289. μητραλῴας, me̱tralō′as

Book	murderer of a mother	Total
1 Ti.	1:9	1

3290. μητρόπολις, me̱trop′olis

Book	chiefest city	Total
1 Ti.	subscript	1

3292. μιαίνω, miai′nō

Book	defile	Total
Jn.	18:28	1
Tit.	1:15, 15	2
Heb.	12:15	1
Jd.	1:8	1
Total		5

3293. μίασμα, mi′asma

Book	pollution	Total
2 Pt.	2:20	1

3291. μία, mi′a

Book	Oc.	one	Oc.	first	Oc.	a certain	Oc.	a	Oc.	the other	Oc.	agree (with 4060 and 1106)	Total
Mt.	11	5:18, 19, 36; 17:4, 4, 4; 19:5, 6; 20:12; 24:41a; 26:40	1	28:1			2	21:19; 26:69	1	24:41b			15
Mk.	7	9:5, 5, 5; 10:8, 8; 14:37, 66	1	16:2	1	12:42							9
Lk.	13	9:33, 33, 33; 13:10; 14:18; 15:8; 16:17; 17:22, 34, 35, 36; 20:1; 22:59	1	24:1	3	5:12, 17; 8:22							17
Jn.	1	10:16	2	20:1, 19									3
Ac.	6	4:32; 12:10; 19:34; 21:7; 24:21; 28:13	1	20:7									7
1 Co.	2	6:16; 10:8	1	16:2									3
2 Co.	1	11:24											1
Gal.	1	4:24											1
Eph.	3	4:4, 5; 5:31											3
Phl.	1	1:27											1
1 Ti.	2	3:2, 12											2
Tit.	1	1:6	1	3:10									2
Heb.	3	10:12, 14; 12:16											3
2 Pt.	2	3:8, 8											2
Rev.	9	6:1; 9:12; 13:3; 17:12, 13; 18:8, 10, 17, 19					1	9:13			1	17:17	11
Total	63		8		4		3		1		1		80

3294. μιασμός, miasmos′

Book	uncleanness	Total
2 Pt.	2:10	1

3295. μίγμα, mig′ma

Book	mixture	Total
Jn.	19:39	1

3296. μίγνυμι, mig′numi

Book	mingle	Total
Mt.	27:34	1
Lk.	13:1	1
Rev.	8:7; 15:2	2
Total		4

3297. μικρόν, mikron′

Book	Oc.	a little while	Oc.	a little	Oc.	a while	Total
Mt.			1	26:39	1	26:73	2
Mk.			2	14:35, 70			2
Jn.	9	13:33; 14:19; 16:16, 16, 16, 17, 17, 18, 19, 19					9
2 Co.			2	11:1, 16			2
Heb.			1	10:37			1
Total	9		6		1		16

3298. μικρός or μικρότερος, mikros' or mikrot'eros

Book	Oc.	little	Oc.	least	Oc.	small	Oc.	less	Total
Mt.	4	10:42; 18:6, 10, 14	2	11:11; 13:32					6
Mk.	1	9:42					2	4:31; 15:40	3
Lk.	3	12:32; 17:2; 19:3	2	7:28; 9:48					5
Jn.	2	7:33; 12:35							2
Ac.			1	8:10	1	26:22			2
1 Co.	1	5:6							1
Gal.	1	5:9							1
Heb.			1	8:11					1
Jas.	1	3:5							1
Rev.	3	3:8; 6:11; 20:3			5	11:18; 13:16; 19:5, 18; 20:12			8
Total	16		6		6		2		30

3300. μίλιον, mil'ion

Book	mile	Total
Mt.	5:41	1

3301. μιμέομαι, mime'omai

Book	follow	Total
2 Th.	3:7, 9	2
Heb.	13:7	1
3 Jn.	1:11	1
Total		4

3305. μισθαποδοσία misthapodosi'a

Book	recompence of reward	Total
Heb.	2:2; 10:35; 11:26	3

3306. μισθαποδότης misthapodot'ẹs

Book	rewarder	Total
Heb.	11:6	1

3299. Μίλητος, Mil'ẹtos

Book	Oc.	Miletus	Oc.	Miletum	Total
Ac.	2	20:15, 17			2
2 Ti.			1	4:20	1
Total	2		1		3

3302. μιμητής, mimẹtẹs'

Book	follower	Total
1 Co.	4:16; 11:1	2
Eph.	5:1	1
1 Th.	1:6; 2:14	2
Heb.	6:12	1
1 Pt.	3:13	1
Total		7

3303. μιμνήσκω, mimnẹs'kō

Book	Oc.	be mindful	Oc.	remember	Total
Heb.	1	2:6	1	13:3	2

3304. μισέω, mise'ō

Book	Oc.	hate	Oc.	hateful	Total
Mt.	6	5:43, 44; 6:24; 10:22; 24:9, 10			6
Mk.	1	13:13			1
Lk.	7	1:71; 6:22, 27; 14:26; 16:13; 19:14; 21:17			7
Jn.	12	3:20; 7:7, 7; 12:25; 15:18, 18, 19, 23, 23, 24, 25; 17:14			12
Ro.	2	7:15; 9:13			2
Eph.	1	5:29			1
Tit.	1	3:3			1
Heb.	1	1:9			1
1 Jn.	5	2:9, 11; 3:13, 15; 4:20			5
Jd.	1	1:23			1
Rev.	4	2:6, 6, 15; 17:16	1	18:2	5
Total	41		1		42

3308. μισθός, misthos'

Book	Oc.	reward	Oc.	hire	Oc.	wages	Total
Mt.	9	5:12, 46; 6:1, 2, 5, 16; 10:41, 41, 42	1	20:8			10
Mk.	1	9:41					1
Lk.	2	6:23, 35	1	10:7			3
Jn.					1	4:36	1
Ac.	1	1:18					1
Ro.	1	4:4					1
1 Co.	4	3:8, 14; 9:17, 18					4
1 Ti.	1	5:18					1
Jas.			1	5:4			1
2 Pt.	1	2:13			1	2:15	2
2 Jn.	1	1:8					1
Jd.	1	1:11					1
Rev.	2	11:18; 22:12					2
Total	24		3		2		29

3307. μίσθιος, mis'thios

Book	hired servant	Total
Lk.	15:17, 19	2

3309. μισθόω, mistho'ō

Book	hire	Total
Mt.	20:1, 7	2

3310. μίσθωμα, mis'thōma

Book	hired house	Total
Ac.	28:30	1

3312. Μιτυλήνη, Mitulẹ'nẹ

Book	Mitylene	Total
Ac.	20:14	1

3311. μισθωτός, misthōtos'

Book	Oc.	hireling	Oc.	hired servant	Total
Mk.			1	1:20	1
Jn.	3	10:12, 13, 13			3
Total	3		1		4

3313. Μιχαήλ, Michaẹl'

Book	Michael	Total
Jd.	1:9	1
Rev.	12:7	1
Total		2

3314. μνᾶ, mna

Book	pound	Total
Lk.	19:13, 16, 16, 18, 18, 20, 24, 24, 25	9

3315. μνάομαι, mna'omai

Book	Oc.	remember	Oc.	be mindful	Oc.	be had in remembrance	Oc.	in remembrance	Oc.	come in remembrance	Total
Mt.	3	5:23; 26:75; 27:63									3
Lk.	5	1:72; 16:25; 23:42; 24:6, 8					1	1:54			6
Jn.	3	2:17, 22; 12:16									3
Ac.	1	11:16			1	10:31					2
1 Co.	1	11:2									1
2 Ti.			1	1:4							1
Heb.	2	8:12; 10:17									2
2 Pt.			1	3:2							1
Jd.	1	1:17									1
Rev.									1	16:19	1
Total	16		2		1		1		1		21

3317. μνεία, mnei'a

Book	Oc.	mention	Oc.	remembrance	Total
Ro.	1	1:9			1
Eph.	1	1:16			1
Phl.			1	1:3	1
1 Th.	1	1:2	1	3:6	2
2 Ti.			1	1:3	1
Phe.	1	1:4			1
Total	4		3		7

3318. μνῆμα, mnẹ'ma

Book	Oc.	sepulchre	Oc.	tomb	Oc.	grave	Total
Mk.			1	5:5			1
Lk.	2	23:53; 24:1	1	8:27			3
Ac.	2	2:29; 7:16					2
Rev.					1	11:9	1
Total	4		2		1		7

3316. Μνάσων, Mna'sōn

Book	Mnason	Total
Ac.	21:16	1

3320. μνήμη, mnẹ'mẹ

Book	remembrance	Total
2 Pt.	1:15	1

3319. μνημεῖον, mnẹmei'on

Book	Oc.	sepulchre	Oc.	grave	Oc.	tomb	Total
Mt.	3	23:29; 27:60b; 28:8	2	27:52, 53	2	8:28; 27:60a	7
Mk.	6	15:46, 46; 16:2, 3, 5, 8			3	5:2, 3; 6:29	9
Lk.	8	11:47, 48; 23:55; 24:2, 9, 12, 22, 24	1	11:44			9
Jn.	11	19:41, 42; 20:1, 1, 2, 3, 4, 6, 8, 11, 11	5	5:28; 11:17, 31, 38; 12:17			16
Ac.	1	13:29					1
Total	29		8		5		42

3321. μνημονεύω, mne̱moneu'ō

Book	Oc.	remember	Oc.	be mindful	Oc.	make mention	Total
Mt.	1	16:9					1
Mk.	1	8:18					1
Lk.	1	17:32					1
Jn.	3	15:20; 16:4, 21					3
Ac.	2	20:31, 35					2
Gal.	1	2:10					1
Eph.	1	2:11					1
Col.	1	4:18					1
1 Th.	2	1:3; 2:9					2
2 Th.	1	2:5					1
2 Ti.	1	2:8					1
Heb.	1	13:7	1	11:15	1	11:22	3
Rev.	3	2:5; 3:3; 18:5					3
Total	19		1		1		21

3322. μνημόσυνον mne̱mos'unon

Book	memorial	Total
Mt.	26:13	1
Mk.	14:9	1
Ac.	10:4	1
Total		3

3323. μνηστεύω, mne̱steu'ō

Book	espouse	Total
Mt.	1:18	1
Lk.	1:27; 2:5	2
Total		3

3324. μογιλάλος, mogilal'os

Book	having an impediment in (one's) speech	Total
Mk.	7:32	1

3325. μόγις, mog'is

Book	hardly	Total
Lk.	9:39	1

3326. μόδιος, mod'ios

Book	bushel	Total
Mt.	5:15	1
Mk.	4:21	1
Lk.	11:33	1
Total		3

3327. μοί, moi

Book	Oc.	me	Oc.	my	Oc.	I	Oc.	mine	Total
Mt.	31	2:8; 4:9; 7:21, 22; 8:21, 22; 9:9; 11:27; 14:8, 18; 15:8, 25, 32; 16:24; 17:17; 18:28; 19:21, 28; 20:13, 15; 21:2, 24; 22:19; 25:20, 22, 35, 42; 26:15, 53; 27:10; 28:18							31
Mk.	8	2:14; 6:25; 8:2, 34; 10:21; 11:29, 30; 12:15	1	5:9					9
Lk.	27	1:25, 38, 43, 49; 4:23; 5:27; 7:45; 9:23, 59, 59, 61; 10:22, 40; 11:5, 7; 15:6, 9, 12; 17:8; 18:5, 13, 22; 20:3, 24; 22:29, 68; 23:14					1	9:38	28
Jn.	41	1:33, 43; 3:28; 4:7, 10, 15, 21, 29, 39; 5:11, 36; 6:37, 39; 8:45, 46; 9:11; 10:27, 29, 37; 12:49, 50; 13:36, 36; 14:11, 11, 31; 17:4, 6, 7, 8, 9, 11, 12, 22, 24, 24; 18:9, 11; 20:15; 21:19, 22							41
Ac.	29	1:8; 2:28; 5:8; 7:7, 42, 49b; 9:15; 11:7, 9, 12; 12:8; 13:2; 20:19, 22; 21:39; 22:5, 7, 9, 11, 13, 18, 27; 23:19, 30; 25:24, 27; 27:21, 23, 25	1	7:49a	6	3:6; 18:10; 21:37; 22:6, 17; 24:11			36
Ro.	7	7:13, 18; 9:1, 19; 12:3; 15:15, 30			2	7:10; 9:2			9
1 Co.	12	1:11; 3:10; 6:12, 12; 7:1; 9:15, 16b, 16c; 10:23, 23; 15:32; 16:9	1	9:18	3	5:12; 9:16a, 16d			16
2 Co.	7	2:12; 9:1; 12:1, 7, 9, 13; 13:10	4	6:16, 18; 7:4, 4					11
Gal.	5	2:6, 9; 4:15, 21; 6:17							5
Eph.	4	3:2, 3, 7; 6:19							4
Phl.	4	2:18; 3:7; 4:3, 15	3	1:19, 22; 4:16					7
Col.	2	1:25; 4:11							2
2 Ti.	7	3:11; 4:8, 8, 11, 14, 16, 17							7
Phe.	3	1:13, 19, 22							3
Heb.	5	1:5; 2:13; 8:10; 10:5; 13:6							5
Jas.	1	2:18							1
2 Pt.	1	1:14							1
Rev.	24	1:17; 5:5; 7:13, 14; 10:4, 9, 9, 11; 11:1; 14:13; 17:1, 7, 15; 19:9, 9, 10; 21:5, 6, 10; 22:1, 6, 8, 9, 10	1	21:7					25
Total	218		11		11		1		241

3328. μοιχαλίς, moichalis'

Book	Oc.	adulterous	Oc.	adulteress	Oc.	adultery	Total
Mt.	2	12:39; 16:4					2
Mk.	1	8:38					1
Ro.			2	7:3, 3			2
Jas.			1	4:4			1
2 Pt.					1	2:14	1
Total	3		3		1		7

3329. μοιχάω, moicha'ō

Book	commit adultery	Total
Mt.	5:32, 32; 19:9, 9	4
Mk.	10:11, 12	2
Total		6

3330. μοιχεία, moichei'a

Book	adultery	Total
Mt.	15:19	1
Mk.	7:21	1
Jn.	8:3	1
Gal.	5:19	1
Total		4

3331. μοιχεύω, moicheu'ō

Book	Oc.	commit adultery	Oc.	in adultery	Total
Mt.	3	5:27, 28; 19:18			3
Mk.	1	10:19			1
Lk.	3	16:18, 18; 18:20			3
Jn.			1	8:4	1
Ro.	3	2:22, 22; 13:9			3
Jas.	2	2:11, 11			2
Rev.	1	2:22			1
Total	13		1		14

3332. μοιχός, moichos'

Book	adulterer	Total
Lk.	18:11	1
1 Co.	6:9	1
Heb.	13:4	1
Jas.	4:4	1
Total		4

3335. μολύνω, molu'nō

Book	defile	Total
1 Co.	8:7	1
Rev.	3:4; 14:4	2
Total		3

3334. Μολόχ, Moloch'

Book	Moloch	Total
Ac.	7:43	1

3336. μολυσμός, molusmos'

Book	filthiness	Total
2 Co.	7:1	1

3333. μόλις, mol'is

Book	Oc.	scarce	Oc.	scarcely	Oc.	hardly	Oc.	have much work (with 2480)	Total
Ac.	2	14:18; 27:7			1	27:8	1	27:16	4
Ro.			1	5:7					1
1 Pt.			1	4:18					1
Total	2		2		1		1		6

3337. μομφή, momphe̱'

Book	quarrel	Total
Col.	3:13	1

3338. μονή, mone̱'

Book	Oc.	mansion	Oc.	abode	Total
Jn.	1	14:2	1	14:23	2

3339. μονογενής, monogene̱s'

Book	Oc.	only begotten	Oc.	only	Oc.	only child	Total
Lk.			2	7:12; 8:42	1	9:38	3
Jn.	4	1:14, 18; 3:16, 18					4
Heb.	1	11:17					1
1 Jn.	1	4:9					1
Total	6		2		1		9

3340. μόνον, mon'on

Book	Oc.	only	Oc.	alone	Oc.	but	Total
Mt.	6	5:47; 8:8; 10:42; 14:36; 21: 19, 21			1	9:21	7
Mk.	2	5:36; 6:8					2
Lk.	1	8:50					1
Jn.	4	5:18; 11:52; 12:9; 13:9	1	17:20			5
Ac.	7	8:16; 11:19; 18:25; 19:27; 21: 13; 26:29; 27:10	1	19:26			8
Ro.	10	1:32; 3:29; 4:12, 16; 5:3, 11; 8:23; 9:10, 24; 13:5	1	4:23			11
1 Co.	2	7:39; 15:19					2
2 Co.	5	7:7; 8:10, 19, 21; 9:12					5
Gal.	6	1:23; 2:10; 3:2; 4:18; 5:13; 6: 12					6
Eph.	1	1:21					1
Phl.	4	1:27, 29; 2:12, 27					4
1 Th.	3	1:5, 8; 2:8					3
2 Th.	1	2:7					1
1 Ti.	1	5:13					1
2 Ti.	2	2:20; 4:8					2
Heb.	2	9:10; 12:26					2
Jas.	2	1:22; 2:24					2
1 Pt.	1	2:18					1
1 Jn.	2	2:2; 5:6					2
Total	62		3		1		66

3341. μόνος, mon'os

Book	Oc.	only	Oc.	alone	Oc.	by (one's) self	Total
Mt.	4	4:10; 12:4; 17:8; 24:36	3	4:4; 14:23; 18: 15			7
Mk.	1	9:8	1	6:47	1	9:2	3
Lk.	2	4:8; 24:18	5	4:4; 5:21; 6:4; 9:36; 10:40	1	24:12	8
Jn.	2	5:44; 17:3	8	6:15, 22; 8:9, 16, 29; 12:24; 16:32, 32			10
Ro.	2	16:4, 27	1	11:3			3
1 Co.	2	9:6; 14:36					2
Gal.			1	6:4			1
Phl.	1	4:15					1
Col.	1	4:11					1
1 Th.			1	3:1			1
1 Ti.	3	1:17; 6:15, 16					3
2 Ti.	1	4:11					1
Heb.			1	9:7			1
2 Jn.	1	1:1					1
Jd.	2	1:4, 25					2
Rev.	2	9:4; 15:4					2
Total	24		21		2		47

3342. μονόφθαλμος monoph'thalmos

Book	with one eye	Total
Mt.	18:9	1
Mk.	9:47	1
Total		2

3343. μονόω, mono'ō

Book	be desolate	Total
1 Ti.	5:5	1

3344. μορφή, morphē'

Book	form	Total
Mk.	16:12	1
Phl.	2:6, 7	2
Total		3

3345. μορφόω, morpho'ō

Book	form	Total
Gal.	4:19	1

3346. μόρφωσις, mor'phōsis

Book	form	Total
Ro.	2:20	1
2 Ti.	3:5	1
Total		2

3347. μοσχοποιέω, moschopoie'ō

Book	make a calf	Total
Ac.	7:41	1

3348. μόσχος, mos'chos

Book	calf	Total
Lk.	15:23, 27, 30	3
Heb.	9:12, 19	2
Rev.	4:7	1
Total		6

3349. μόχθος, moch'thos

Book	Oc.	travail	Oc.	painfulness	Total
2 Co.			1	11:27	1
1 Th.	1	2:9			1
2 Th.	1	3:8			1
Total	2		1		3

3350. μοῦ, mou

Book	Oc.	my	Oc.	me	Oc.	mine	Oc.	I	Oc.	mine own	Total
Mt.	79	2:6, 15; 3:17; 7:21; 8:6, 8, 8, 9, 21; 9:18; 10:22, 32, 33; 11:10, 27, 29, 30, 30; 12:18, 18, 18, 18, 44, 48, 48, 49, 49, 50, 50; 13:30, 35; 15:13, 22; 16:17, 18; 17:5, 15; 18:5, 10, 19, 21, 35; 19:20, 29; 20:21, 23, 23, 23, 23; 21:13, 28, 37; 22:4, 4, 44, 44; 24:5, 9, 35, 36, 48; 25:27, 34, 40; 26:12, 18, 18, 26, 28, 29, 38, 39, 42, 53; 27: 35, 35, 46, 46; 28:10	9	3:11a; 4:19; 10:37, 37, 38, 38; 16:23, 23, 24	2	7:24, 26	1	3:11b			91
Mk.	34	1:2, 11; 3:33, 33, 34, 34, 35, 35; 5:23, 30; 6:23; 9:7, 17, 37, 39, 41; 10:20, 40, 40; 11:17; 12:6, 36, 36; 13:6, 13, 31; 14:8, 14, 22, 24, 34; 15:34, 34; 16:17	6	1:7b, 17; 5:31; 7:14; 8:33, 34	1	9:24	1	1:7a			42
Lk.	77	1:18, 20, 25, 43, 44b, 46, 47, 47; 2:49; 3:22; 6:47; 7:6, 7, 8, 27, 44, 44, 45, 46, 46; 8:21, 21; 9:35, 38, 48, 59, 61; 10:22, 29, 40; 11: 7, 24; 12:4, 13, 17, 18, 18, 18, 19, 45; 14:23, 24, 26, 27b, 33; 15: 6, 17, 18, 24, 29; 16:3, 5, 24, 27; 18:21; 19:8, 23, 46; 20:13, 42, 42; 21:8, 12, 17, 33; 22:11, 19, 20, 28, 29, 30, 30, 42; 23:46; 24: 39, 39, 49	9	4:7, 8; 8:45, 45, 46; 9: 23; 14:27a; 19:27b; 23:42	5	1:44a; 2: 30; 11:6; 18:3; 19: 27a	2	3:16; 22:53			93
Jn.	93	2:16; 4:49; 5:17, 24, 31, 43; 6:32, 51, 54, 54, 55, 55, 56, 56, 65; 8:14, 19, 19, 28, 31, 38, 49, 52, 54, 54; 10:15, 16, 17, 18, 25, 27, 28, 29, 29, 32, 37; 11:21, 32; 12:7, 27, 47, 48; 13:6, 8, 9, 37; 14: 2, 7, 12, 13, 14, 20, 21, 21, 23, 23, 24, 26, 28a; 15:1, 7, 8, 10, 10, 10, 14, 15, 16, 20, 21, 23, 24; 16:10, 23, 24, 26; 18:37; 19:24, 24; 20:13, 17b, 17c, 17d, 17e, 25, 25, 27, 27, 28, 28; 21:15, 16, 17	11	1:15, 15, 15, 27, 27, 30, 30, 30; 11:41, 42; 20: 17a	4	2:4; 9:11, 15, 30	1	14:28b	1	8:50	110
Ac.	36	2:14, 17, 18, 18, 18, 25, 25, 26, 26, 26, 27, 34, 34; 7:34, 49, 49, 50, 59; 9:15, 16; 10:30a; 11:8; 13:22b, 33; 15:7, 17; 16:15; 20:24, 24, 25, 29, 34; 22:1; 24:17; 26:4a; 28:19	7	1:4; 10:30b; 15:13; 24: 13; 25:11; 26:3, 29	1	21:13	3	22:17; 24:20; 25:15	2	13: 22a; 26:4b	49
Ro.	35	1:8, 9, 9, 9; 2:16; 7:4, 18, 23, 23, 23; 9:1, 2, 3, 3, 17, 17, 25, 25, 26; 10:21; 11:3, 14; 15:14, 31; 16:3, 4, 5, 7, 7, 8, 9, 11, 21, 21, 25			2	11:13; 16:23					37
1 Co.	25	1:4, 11; 2:4, 4; 4:14, 17, 17; 8:13, 13; 9:1, 15, 18, 27; 10:14, 29; 11:24, 33; 13:3, 3; 14:14, 14, 18, 19; 15:58; 16:24	4	4:16; 11:1, 2; 14:21			1	4:18			30
2 Co.	6	2:13, 13; 12:9, 9, 9, 21	4	11:1, 1, 9, 28	2	11:30; 12:5					12
Gal.	7	1:14b, 15; 4:14, 14, 19, 20; 6:17							1	1:14a	8
Eph.	6	1:16; 3:4, 13, 14; 6:10, 19									6
Phl.	21	1:3, 7, 7, 8, 13, 14, 16, 20, 20; 2:2, 12, 12, 12, 25, 25; 3:1, 8; 4:1, 3, 14, 19	1	3:17	1	1:4					23
Col.	5	1:24, 24; 2:1; 4:10, 18									5
2 Ti.	7	1:3, 6, 16; 2:1, 8; 3:10; 4:16					1	1:12			8
Phe.	6	1:4, 4, 10, 20, 23, 24									6
Heb.	17	1:5, 13; 2:12; 3:9, 10, 11, 11; 4:3, 3, 5; 5:5; 8:9b, 10; 10:16, 34, 38; 12:5					1	8:9a			18
Jas.	14	1:2, 16, 19; 2:1, 3, 5, 14, 18, 18; 3:1, 10, 12; 5:10, 12									14
1 Pt.	1	5:13									1
2 Pt.	2	1:14, 17									2
1 Jn.	3	2:1; 3:13, 18									3
Rev.	26	1:20; 2:3, 13, 13, 13, 13, 16, 26, 27; 3:5, 8, 8, 10, 12, 12, 12, 12, 12, 16, 20, 21, 21; 10:10, 10; 11:3; 18:4; 22:12	1	1:10	1	22:16					28
Total	500		52		19		11		4		586

3351. μουσικός, mousikos′

Book	musician	Total
Rev.	18:22	1

3352. μυελός, muelos′

Book	marrow	Total
Heb.	4:12	1

3353. μυέω, mue′ō

Book	instruct	Total
Phl.	4:12	1

3355. μυκάομαι, muka′omai

Book	roar	Total
Rev.	10:3	1

3354. μῦθος, mu′thos

Book	fable	Total
1 Ti.	1:4; 4:7	2
2 Ti.	4:4	1
Tit.	1:14	1
2 Pt.	1:16	1
Total		5

3356. μυκτηρίζω, mukte̱rid′zō

Book	mock	Total
Gal.	6:7	1

3357. μυλικός, mulikos′

Book	millstone (with 3037)	Total
Mk.	9:42	1

3358. μύλος, mu′los

Book	Oc.	millstone (with 3584)	Oc.	millstone	Total
Mt.	1	18:6			1
Lk.	1	17:2			1
Rev.			2	18:21, 22	2
Total	2		2		4

3359. μύλων, mu′lōn

Book	mill	Total
Mt.	24:41	1

3360. Μύρα, Mu′ra

Book	Myra	Total
Ac.	27:5	1

3361. μυρίας, muri′as

Book	Oc.	ten thousand times ten thousand	Oc.	two hundred thousand thousand (with 1417)	Oc.	innumerable multitude	Oc.	ten thousand	Oc.	innumerable company	Oc.	fifty thousand (with 3902)	Oc.	thousands	Total
Lk.					1	12:1									1
Ac.											1	19:19	1	21:20	2
Heb.									1	12:22					1
Jd.							1	1:14							1
Rev.	2	5:11, 11	2	9:16, 16											4
Total	2		2		1		1		1		1		1		9

3362. μυρίζω, murid′zō

Book	anoint	Total
Mk.	14:8	1

3363. μύριοι, mu′rioi

Book	ten thousand	Total
Mt.	18:24	1
1 Co.	4:15; 14:19	2
Total		3

3364. μύρον, mu′ron

Book	ointment	Total
Mt.	26:7, 9, 12	3
Mk.	14:3, 4	2
Lk.	7:37, 38, 46; 23:56	4
Jn.	11:2; 12:3, 3, 5	4
Rev.	18:13	1
Total		14

3365. Μυσία, Musi′a

Book	Mysia	Total
Ac.	16:7, 8	2

3366. μυστήριον, muste̱′rion

Book	mystery	Total
Mt.	13:11	1
Mk.	4:11	1
Lk.	8:10	1
Ro.	11:25; 16:25	2
1 Co.	2:7; 4:1; 13:2; 14:2; 15:51	5
Eph.	1:9; 3:3, 4, 9; 5:32; 6:19	6
Col.	1:26, 27; 2:2; 4:3	4
2 Th.	2:7	1
1 Ti.	3:9, 16	2
Rev.	1:20; 10:7; 17:5, 7	4
Total		27

3367. μυωπάζω, muōpad′zō

Book	cannot see afar off	Total
2 Pt.	1:9	1

3368. μώλωψ, mō′lōps

Book	stripe	Total
1 Pt.	2:24	1

3369. μωμάομαι, mōma′omai

Book	blame	Total
2 Co.	6:3; 8:20	2

3370. μῶμος, mō′mos

Book	blemish	Total
2 Pt.	2:13	1

3371. μωραίνω, mōrai′nō

Book	Oc.	lose savour	Oc.	become a fool	Oc.	make foolish	Total
Mt.	1	5:13					1
Lk.	1	14:34					1
Ro.			1	1:22			1
1 Co.					1	1:20	1
Total	2		1		1		4

3372. μωρία, mōri′a

Book	foolishness	Total
1 Co.	1:18, 21, 23; 2:14; 3:19	5

3373. μωρολογία, mōrologi′a

Book	foolish talking	Total
Eph.	5:4	1

3374. μωρός, mōros′

Book	Oc.	foolish	Oc.	fool	Oc.	foolishness	Total
Mt.	4	7:26; 25:2, 3, 8	3	5:22; 23:17, 19			7
1 Co.	1	1:27	2	3:18; 4:10	1	1:25	4
2 Ti.	1	2:23					1
Tit.	1	3:9					1
Total	7		5		1		13

3376. Νaασσών, Naassōn′

Book	Naasson	Total
Mt.	1:4, 4	2
Lk.	3:32	1
Total		3

3377. Ναγγαί, Nanggai′

Book	Nagge	Total
Lk.	3:25	1

3378. Ναζαρέθ or Ναζαρέτ Nadzareth′ or Nadzaret′

Book	Nazareth	Total
Mt.	2:23; 4:13; 21:11	3
Mk.	1:9	1
Lk.	1:26; 2:4, 39, 51; 4:16	5
Jn.	1:45, 46	2
Ac.	10:38	1
Total		12

3375. Μωσεύς, Μωσῆς, Μωϋσεύς, or Μωϋσῆς, Mōseus′, Mōse̱s′, Mōuseus′, or Mōuse̱s′

Book	Oc.	Moses	Oc.	Moses	Oc.	Moses	Oc.	Moses	Total
Mt.	1	23:2	6	8:4; 17:3, 4; 19:7, 8; 22:24					7
Mk.	3	9:4, 5; 12:26	5	1:44; 7:10; 10:3, 4; 12:19					8
Lk.	6	2:22; 9:33; 16:29,31; 24:27,44	4	5:14; 9:30; 20:28, 37					10
Jn.	4	1:17; 7:22, 23; 9:28	9	1:45; 3:14; 5:45, 46; 6:32; 7:19, 22; 8:5; 9:29					13
Ac.	3	13:39; 21:21; 28:23	11	3:22; 6:11; 7:20, 22, 29, 31, 32, 40, 44; 15:21; 26:22	2	15:1, 5	3	6:14; 7:35, 37	19
Ro.	1	5:14	3	9:15; 10:5, 19					4
1 Co.	1	9:9	1	10:2					2
2 Co.	1	3:7	2	3:13, 15					3
2 Ti.					1	3:8			1
Heb.	2	3:16; 10:28	8	3:2, 3, 5; 7:14; 8:5; 11:23, 24; 12:21	1	9:19			11
Jd.	1	1:9							1
Rev.	1	15:3							1
Total	24		49		4		3		80

3379. Ναζαρηνός, Nadzare̱nos′

Book	Nazareth, of	Total
Mk.	1:24; 14:67; 16:6	3
Lk.	4:34	1
Total		4

3380. Ναζωραῖος, Nadzōrai′os

Book	Oc.	Nazareth, of	Oc.	Nazarene	Total
Mt.	1	26:71	1	2:23	2
Mk.	1	10:47			1
Lk.	2	18:37; 24:19			2
Jn.	3	18:5, 7; 19:19			3
Ac.	6	2:22; 3:6; 4:10; 6:14; 22:8; 26:9	1	24:5	7
Total	13		2		15

3381. Ναθάν, Nathan′

Book	Nathan	Total
Lk.	3:31	1

3382. Ναθαναήλ, Nathanae̱l′

Book	Nathanael	Total
Jn.	1:45, 46, 47, 48, 49; 21:2	6

3383. ναί, nai

Book	Oc.	yea	Oc.	even so	Oc.	yes	Oc.	truth	Oc.	verily	Oc.	surely	Total
Mt.	6	5:37, 37; 9:28; 11:9; 13:51; 21:16	1	11:26	1	17:25	1	15:27					9
Mk.					1	7:28							1
Lk.	2	7:26; 12:5	1	10:21					1	11:51			4
Jn.	3	11:27; 21:15, 16											3
Ac.	2	5:8; 22:27											2
Ro.					1	3:29							1
2 Co.	6	1:17, 17, 18, 19, 19, 20											6
Phe.	1	1:20											1
Jas.	2	5:12, 12											2
Rev.	1	14:13	3	1:7; 16:7; 22:20b							1	22:20a	5
Total	23		5		3		1		1		1		34

3384. Ναΐν, Nain'

Book	Nain	Total
Lk.	7:11	1

3385. ναός, naos'

Book	Oc.	temple	Oc.	shrine	Total
Mt.	9	23:16, 16, 17, 21, 35; 26:61; 27:5, 40, 51			9
Mk.	3	14:58; 15:29, 38			3
Lk.	4	1:9, 21, 22; 23:45			4
Jn.	3	2:19, 20, 21			3
Ac.	2	7:48; 17:24	1	19:24	3
1 Co.	4	3:16, 17, 17; 6:19			4
2 Co.	2	6:16, 16			2
Eph.	1	2:21			1
2 Th.	1	2:4			1
Rev.	16	3:12; 7:15; 11:1, 2, 19, 19; 14:15, 17; 15: 5, 6, 8, 8; 16:1, 17; 21:22, 22			16
Total	45		1		46

3386. Ναούμ, Naoum'

Book	Naum	Total
Lk.	3:25	1

3387. νάρδος, nar'dos

Book	spikenard (with 4001)	Total
Mk.	14:3	1
Jn.	12:3	1
Total		2

3388. Νάρκισσος, Nar'kissos

Book	Narcissus	Total
Ro.	16:11	1

3389. ναυαγέω, nauage'ō

Book	Oc.	suffer shipwreck	Oc.	make shipwreck	Total
2 Co.	1	11:25			1
1 Ti.			1	1:19	1
Total	1		1		2

3390. ναύκληρος, nau'klēros

Book	owner of a ship	Total
Ac.	27:11	1

3391. ναῦς, naus

Book	ship	Total
Ac.	27:41	1

3392. ναύτης, nau'tēs

Book	Oc.	shipman	Oc.	sailor	Total
Ac.	2	27:27, 30			2
Rev.			1	18:17	1
Total	2		1		3

3393. Ναχώρ, Nachōr'

Book	Nachor	Total
Lk.	3:34	1

3394. νεανίας, neani'as

Book	young man	Total
Ac.	7:58; 20:9; 23:17, 18, 22	5

3395. νεανίσκος, neanis'kos

Book	young man	Total
Mt.	19:20, 22	2
Mk.	14:51, 51; 16:5	3
Lk.	7:14	1
Ac.	2:17; 5:10	2
1 Jn.	2:13, 14	2
Total		10

3396. Νεάπολις, Neap'olis

Book	Neapolis	Total
Ac.	16:11	1

3397. Νεεμάν, Neeman'

Book	Naaman	Total
Lk.	4:27	1

3398. νεκρός, nekros'

Book	dead	Total
Mt.	8:22, 22; 10:8; 11:5; 14: 2; 17:9; 22:31, 32; 23: 27; 27:64; 28:4, 7	12
Mk.	6:14, 16; 9:9, 10, 26; 12:25, 26, 27	8
Lk.	7:15, 22; 9:7, 60, 60; 15:24, 32; 16:30, 31; 20:35, 37, 38; 24:5, 46	14
Jn.	2:22; 5:21, 25; 12:1, 9, 17; 20:9; 21:14	8
Ac.	3:15; 4:2, 10; 5:10; 10: 41, 42; 13:30, 34; 17:3, 31, 32; 20:9; 23:6; 24: 15, 21; 26:8, 23; 28:6	18
Ro.	1:4; 4:17, 24; 6:4, 9, 11, 13; 7:4, 8; 8:10, 11, 11; 10:7, 9; 11:15; 14:9	16
1 Co.	15:12, 12, 13, 15, 16, 20, 21, 29, 29, 29, 32, 35, 42, 52	14
2 Co.	1:9	1
Gal.	1:1	1
Eph.	1:20; 2:1, 5; 5:14	4
Phl.	3:11	1
Col.	1:18; 2:12, 13	3
1 Th.	1:10; 4:16	2
2 Ti.	2:8; 4:1	2
Heb.	6:1, 2; 9:14, 17; 11:19, 35; 13:20	7
Jas.	2:17, 20, 26, 26	4
1 Pt.	1:3, 21; 4:5, 6	4
Rev.	1:5, 17, 18; 2:8; 3:1; 11:18; 14:13; 16:3; 20:5, 12, 12, 13, 13	13
Total		132

3399. νεκρόω, nekro'ō

Book	Oc.	be dead	Oc.	mortify	Total
Ro.	1	4:19			1
Col.			1	3:5	1
Heb.	1	11:12			1
Total	2		1		3

3400. νέκρωσις, nek'rōsis

Book	Oc.	deadness	Oc.	dying	Total
Ro.	1	4:19			1
2 Co.			1	4:10	1
Total	1		1		2

3401a. νέος, ne'os

Book	Oc.	new	Oc.	new man	Oc.	young woman	Total
Mt.	2	9:17, 17					2
Mk.	3	2:22, 22, 22					3
Lk.	4	5:37, 37, 38, 39					4
1 Co.	1	5:7					1
Col.			1	3:10			1
Tit.					1	2:4	1
Heb.	1	12:24					1
Total	11		1		1		13

3401b. νεώτερος, neō'teros

Book	Oc.	younger	Oc.	young man	Oc.	younger man	Oc.	young	Total
Lk.	3	15:12, 13; 22:26							3
Jn.							1	21:18	1
Ac.			1	5:6					1
1 Ti.	3	5:2, 11, 14			1	5:1			4
Tit.			1	2:6					1
1 Pt.	1	5:5							1
Total	7		2		1		1		11

Word 3401 has 24 occurrences.

3402. νεοσσός, neossos'

Book	young	Total
Lk.	2:24	1

3403. νεότης, neot'ēs

Book	youth	Total
Mt.	19:20	1
Mk.	10:20	1
Lk.	18:21	1
Ac.	26:4	1
1 Ti.	4:12	1
Total		5

3404. νεόφυτος, neoph'utos

Book	novice	Total
1 Ti.	3:6	1

3405. Νέρων, Ner'ōn

Book	Nero	Total
2 Ti.	subscript	1

3406. νεύω, neu'ō

Book	beckon	Total
Jn.	13:24	1
Ac.	24:10	1
Total		2

3407. νεφέλη, nephel'ē

Book	cloud	Total
Mt.	17:5, 5; 24:30; 26:64	4
Mk.	9:7, 7; 13:26; 14:62	4
Lk.	9:34, 34, 35; 12:54; 21:27	5
Ac.	1:9	1
1 Co.	10:1, 2	2
1 Th.	4:17	1
2 Pt.	2:17	1
Jd.	1:12	1
Rev.	1:7; 10:1; 11:12; 14: 14, 14, 15, 16	7
Total		26

3408. Νεφθαλείμ, Nephthaleim'

Book	Nephthalim	Total
Mt.	4:13, 15	2
Rev.	7:6	1
Total		3

3409. νέφος, neph'os

Book	cloud	Total
Heb.	12:1	1

3410. νεφρός, nephros'

Book	reins	Total
Rev.	2:23	1

3411. νεωκόρος, neōkor'os

Book	worshipper	Total
Ac.	19:35	1

3412. νεωτερικός, neōterikos'

Book	youthful	Total
2 Ti.	2:22	1

3413. νή, nē

Book	I protest by	Total
1 Co.	15:31	1

3414. νήθω, nē'thō

Book	spin	Total
Mt.	6:28	1
Lk.	12:27	1
Total		2

3415. νηπιάζω, nēpiad'zō

Book	be a child	Total
1 Co.	14:20	1

3416. νήπιος, nē'pios

Book	Oc.	child	Oc.	babe	Oc.	childish	Total
Mt.			2	11:25; 21:16			2
Lk.			1	10:21			1
Ro.			1	2:20			1
1 Co.	4	13:11a, 11b, 11c, 11d	1	3:1	1	13:11e	6
Gal.	2	4:1, 3					2
Eph.	1	4:14					1
Heb.			1	5:13			1
Total	7		6		1		14

3417. Νηρεύς, Nēreus'

Book	Nereus	Total
Ro.	16:15	1

3418. Νηρί, Nēri'

Book	Neri	Total
Lk.	3:27	1

3419. νησίον, nēsi'on

Book	island	Total
Ac.	27:16	1

3420. νῆσος, nē'sos

Book	Oc.	island	Oc.	isle	Total
Ac.	4	27:26; 28:1, 7, 9	2	13:6; 28:11	6
Rev.	2	6:14; 16:20	1	1:9	3
Total	6		3		9

3421. νηστεία, nēstei'a

Book	Oc.	fasting	Oc.	fast	Total
Mt.	1	17:21			1
Mk.	1	9:29			1
Lk.	1	2:37			1
Ac.	1	14:23	1	27:9	2
1 Co.	1	7:5			1
2 Co.	2	6:5; 11:27			2
Total	7		1		8

3422. νηστεύω, nēsteu'ō

Book	fast	Total
Mt.	4:2; 6:16, 16, 17, 18; 9:14, 14, 15	8
Mk.	2:18, 18, 18, 19, 19, 20	6
Lk.	5:33, 34, 35; 18:12	4
Ac.	10:30; 13:2, 3	3
Total		21

3423. νῆστις, nēs'tis

Book	fasting	Total
Mt.	15:32	1
Mk.	8:3	1
Total		2

3424a. νηφάλεος, nēphal'eos

Book	Oc.	vigilant	Oc.	sober	Total
1 Ti.	1	3:2	1	3:11	2

3424b. νηφάλιος, nēphal'ios

Book	sober	Total
Tit.	2:2	1

Word 3424 has 3 occurrences.

3425. νήφω, nē'phō

Book	Oc.	be sober	Oc.	watch	Total
1 Th.	2	5:6, 8			2
2 Ti.			1	4:5	1
1 Pt.	2	1:13; 5:8	1	4:7	3
Total	4		2		6

3426. Νίγερ, Nig'er

Book	Niger	Total
Ac.	13:1	1

3427. Νικάνωρ, Nikan'ōr

Book	Nicanor	Total
Ac.	6:5	1

3428. νικάω, nika'ō

Book	Oc.	overcome	Oc.	conquer	Oc.	prevail	Oc.	get the victory	Total
Lk.	1	11:22							1
Jn.	1	16:33							1
Ro.	3	3:4; 12:21, 21							3
1 Jn.	6	2:13, 14; 4:4; 5:4, 4, 5							6
Rev.	13	2:7, 11, 17, 26; 3:5, 12, 21, 21; 11:7; 12:11; 13:7; 17:14; 21:7	2	6:2, 2	1	5:5	1	15:2	17
Total	24		2		1		1		28

3429. νίκη, ni'kē

Book	victory	Total
1 Jn.	5:4	1

3430. Νικόδημος, Nikod'ēmos

Book	Nicodemus	Total
Jn.	3:1, 4, 9; 7:50; 19:39	5

3431. Νικολαΐτης, Nikolai'tēs

Book	Nicolaitane	Total
Rev.	2:6, 15	2

3432. Νικόλαος, Nikol'aos

Book	Nicolas	Total
Ac.	6:5	1

3433. Νικόπολις, Nikop'olis

Book	Nicopolis	Total
Tit.	3:12	1

3434. νῖκος, ni'kos

Book	victory	Total
Mt.	12:20	1
1 Co.	15:54, 55, 57	3
Total		4

3435. Νινευΐ, Nineui'

Book	Nineve	Total
Lk.	11:32	1

3436. Νινευΐτης, Nineui'tēs

Book	Oc.	Nineveh	Oc.	Ninevites	Total
Mt.	1	12:41			1
Lk.			1	11:30	1
Total	1		1		2

3437. νιπτήρ, niptēr'

Book	bason	Total
Jn.	13:5	1

3438. νίπτω, nip'tō

Book	wash	Total
Mt.	6:17; 15:2	2
Mk.	7:3	1
Jn.	9:7, 7, 11, 11, 15; 13:5, 6, 8, 8, 10, 12, 14, 14	13
1 Ti.	5:10	1
Total		17

3439. νοιέω, noie'ō

Book	Oc.	understand	Oc.	perceive	Oc.	consider	Oc.	think	Total
Mt.	4	15:17; 16:9, 11; 24:15							4
Mk.	1	13:14	2	7:18; 8:17					3
Jn.	1	12:40							1
Ro.	1	1:20							1
Eph.	1	3:4					1	3:20	2
1 Ti.	1	1:7							1
2 Ti.					1	2:7			1
Heb.	1	11:3							1
Total	10		2		1		1		14

3440. νόημα, no'ēma

Book	Oc.	mind	Oc.	device	Oc.	thought	Total
2 Co.	3	3:14; 4:4; 11:3	1	2:11	1	10:5	5
Phl.	1	4:7					1
Total	4		1		1		6

3441. νόθος, noth'os

Book	bastard	Total
Heb.	12:8	1

3442. νομή, nome̱′

Book	Oc.	pasture	Oc.	eat (with 2192)	Total
Jn.	1	10:9			1
2 Ti.			1	2:17	1
Total	1		1		2

3443. νομίζω, nomid′zō

Book	Oc.	suppose	Oc.	think	Oc.	be wont	Total
Mt.	1	20:10	2	5:17; 10:34			3
Lk.	2	2:44; 3:23					2
Ac.	4	7:25; 14:19; 16:27; 21:29	2	8:20; 17:29	1	16:13	7
1 Co.	1	7:26	1	7:36			2
1 Ti.	1	6:5					1
Total	9		5		1		15

3444. νομικός, nomikos′

Book	Oc.	lawyer	Oc.	about the law	Total
Mt.	1	22:35			1
Lk.	6	7:30; 10:25; 11:45, 46, 52; 14:3			6
Tit.	1	3:13	1	3:9	2
Total	8		1		9

3445. νομίμως, nomim′ōs

Book	lawfully	Total
1 Ti.	1:8	1
2 Ti.	2:5	1
Total		2

3446. νόμισμα, nom′isma

Book	money	Total
Mt.	22:19	1

3447. νομοδιδάσκαλος, nomodidas′kalos

Book	Oc.	doctor of the law	Oc.	teacher of the law	Total
Lk.	1	5:17			1
Ac.	1	5:34			1
1 Ti.			1	1:7	1
Total	2		1		3

3448. νομοθεσία, nomothesi′a

Book	giving of the law	Total
Ro.	9:4	1

3449. νομοθετέω, nomothete′ō

Book	Oc.	receive the law	Oc.	establish	Total
Heb.	1	7:11	1	8:6	2

3450. νομοθέτης, nomothet′e̱s

Book	lawgiver	Total
Jas.	4:12	1

3451. νόμος, nom′os

Book	law	Total
Mt.	5:17, 18; 7:12; 11:13; 12:5; 22:36, 40; 23:23	8
Lk.	2:22, 23, 24, 27, 39; 10:26; 16:16, 17; 24:44	9
Jn.	1:17, 45; 7:19, 19, 23, 49, 51; 8:5, 17; 10:34; 12:34; 15:25; 18:31; 19:7, 7	15
Ac.	6:13; 7:53; 13:15, 39; 15:5, 24; 18:13, 15; 21:20, 24, 28; 22:3, 12; 23:3, 29; 24:6, 14; 25:8; 28:23	19
Ro.	2:12, 12, 13, 13, 14, 14, 14, 14, 15, 17, 18, 20, 23, 23, 25, 25, 26, 27, 27; 3:19, 19, 20, 20, 21, 21, 27, 27, 28, 31, 31; 4:13, 14, 15, 15, 16; 5:13, 13, 20; 6:14, 15; 7:1, 1, 2, 2, 3, 4, 5, 6, 7, 7, 7, 8, 9, 12, 14, 16, 21, 22, 23, 23, 23, 25, 25; 8:2, 2, 3, 4, 7; 9:31, 31, 32; 10:4, 5; 13:8, 10	75
1 Co.	7:39; 9:8, 9, 20, 20, 20; 14:21, 34; 15:56	9
Gal.	2:16, 16, 16, 19, 19, 21; 3:2, 5, 10, 10, 11, 12, 13, 17, 18, 19, 21, 21, 21, 23, 24; 4:4, 5, 21, 21; 5:3, 4, 14, 18, 23; 6:2, 13	32
Eph.	2:15	1
Phl.	3:5, 6, 9	3
1 Ti.	1:8, 9	2
Heb.	7:5, 12, 16, 19, 28, 28; 8:4, 10; 9:19, 22; 10:1, 8, 16, 28	14
Jas.	1:25; 2:8, 9, 10, 11, 12; 4:11, 11, 11, 11	10
Total		197

3452. νοσέω, nose′ō

Book	dote	Total
1 Ti.	6:4	1

3453. νόσημα, nos′e̱ma

Book	disease	Total
Jn.	5:4	1

3454. νόσος, nos′os

Book	Oc.	disease	Oc.	sickness	Oc.	infirmity	Total
Mt.	1	4:24	4	4:23; 8:17; 9:35; 10:1			5
Mk.	1	1:34	1	3:15			2
Lk.	3	4:40; 6:17; 9:1			1	7:21	4
Ac.	1	19:12					1
Total	6		5		1		12

3455. νοσσιά, nossia′

Book	brood	Total
Lk.	13:34	1

3456. νοσσίον, nossi′on

Book	chicken	Total
Mt.	23:37	1

3457. νοσφίζομαι, nosphid′zomai

Book	Oc.	keep back	Oc.	purloin	Total
Ac.	2	5:2, 3			2
Tit.			1	2:10	1
Total	2		1		3

3458. νότος, not′os

Book	Oc.	south	Oc.	south wind	Total
Mt.	1	12:42			1
Lk.	2	11:31; 13:29	1	12:55	3
Ac.			2	27:13; 28:13	2
Rev.	1	21:13			1
Total	4		3		7

3459. νουθεσία, nouthesi′a

Book	admonition	Total
1 Co.	10:11	1
Eph.	6:4	1
Tit.	3:10	1
Total		3

3460. νουθετέω, nouthete′ō

Book	Oc.	warn	Oc.	admonish	Total
Ac.	1	20:31			1
Ro.			1	15:14	1
1 Co.	1	4:14			1
Col.	1	1:28	1	3:16	2
1 Th.	1	5:14	1	5:12	2
2 Th.			1	3:15	1
Total	4		4		8

3461. νουμηνία, noume̱ni′a

Book	new moon	Total
Col.	2:16	1

3462. νουνεχῶς, nounechōs′

Book	discreetly	Total
Mk.	12:34	1

3463. νοῦς, nous

Book	Oc.	mind	Oc.	understanding	Total
Lk.			1	24:45	1
Ro.	6	1:28; 7:23, 25; 11:34; 12:2; 14:5			6
1 Co.	7	1:10; 2:16, 16; 14:14, 15, 15, 19			7
Eph.	2	4:17, 23			2
Phl.			1	4:7	1
Col.	1	2:18			1
2 Th.	1	2:2			1
1 Ti.	1	6:5			1
2 Ti.	1	3:8			1
Tit.	1	1:15			1
Rev.	1	17:9	1	13:18	2
Total	21		3		24

3464. Νυμφᾶς, Numphas′

Book	Nymphas	Total
Col.	4:15	1

3465. νύμφη, num′phe̱

Book	Oc.	bride	Oc.	daughter in law	Total
Mt.			1	10:35	1
Lk.			2	12:53, 53	2
Jn.	1	3:29			1
Rev.	4	18:23; 21:2, 9; 22:17			4
Total	5		3		8

3466. νυμφίος, numphi′os

Book	bridegroom	Total
Mt.	9:15, 15; 25:1, 5, 6, 10	6
Mk.	2:19, 19, 20	3
Lk.	5:34, 35	2
Jn.	2:9; 3:29, 29, 29	4
Rev.	18:23	1
Total		16

3467. νυμφών, numphōn′

Book	bridechamber.	Total
Mt.	9:15	1
Mk.	2:19	1
Lk.	5:34	1
Total		3

3468. νῦν, nun

Book	Oc.	now	Oc.	present	Oc.	henceforth	Oc.	this (with 3488)	Oc.	this time	Oc.	Misc.	Total
Mt.	3	26:65; 27:42, 43							1	24:21			4
Mk.	2	10:30; 15:32							1	13:19			3
Lk.	8	2:29; 6:21, 21, 25; 11:39; 16:25; 19:42; 22:36			3	1:48; 5:10; 12:52					1	22:69	12
Jn.	27	2:8; 4:18, 23; 5:25; 8:40, 52; 9:21, 41; 11:22; 12:27, 31, 31; 13:31, 36; 14:29; 15:22, 24; 16:5, 22, 29, 30, 32; 17:5, 7, 13; 18:36; 21:10									1	11:8	28
Ac.	21	2:33; 3:17; 7:4, 34, 52; 10:5, 33; 12:11; 13:11; 15:10; 16:36, 37; 20:22, 25; 22:1, 16; 23:15, 21; 24:13; 26:6, 17			1	18:6					1	24:25	23
Ro.	11	3:21; 5:9, 11; 6:19, 21; 8:1, 22; 11:30, 31; 13:11; 16:26	2	8:18; 11:5			1	3:26					14
1 Co.	3	3:2; 7:14; 12:20									1	16:12	4
2 Co.	5	5:16b; 6:2, 2; 7:9; 13:2					1	8:14			1	5:16a	7
Gal.	6	1:23; 2:20; 3:3; 4:9, 25, 29											6
Eph.	4	2:2; 3:5, 10; 5:8											4
Phl.	5	1:5, 20, 30; 2:12; 3:18											5
Col.	1	1:24											1
1 Th.	1	3:8											1
2 Th.	1	2:6											1
1 Ti.	1	4:8					1	6:17					2
2 Ti.	1	1:10	1	4:10									2
Tit.			1	2:12									1
Heb.	5	2:8; 9:5, 24, 26; 12:26											5
Jas.	3	4:13, 16; 5:1											3
1 Pt.	5	1:12; 2:10, 10, 25; 3:21											5
2 Pt.	2	3:7, 18											2
1 Jn.	4	2:18, 28; 3:2; 4:3											4
2 Jn.	1	1:5											1
Jd.	1	1:25											1
Total	121		4		4		3		2		5		139

Miscellaneous: Lk. 22:69 (with 575 and 3488), hereafter; Jn. 11:8, of late; Ac. 24:25 (with 2192 and 3488), for this time; 1 Co. 16:12, at this time; 2 Co. 5:16a (with 575 and 3488), henceforth.

3469. τανῦν or τὰ νῦν, tanun′ or ta nun

Book	Oc.	now	Oc.	but now	Total
Ac.	4	4:29; 5:38; 20:32; 27:22	1	17:30	5

3471. νύξ, nux

Book	Oc.	night	Oc.	midnight (with 3219)	Total
Mt.	9	2:14; 4:2; 12:40, 40; 14:25; 26:31, 34; 27:64; 28:13	1	25:6	10
Mk.	5	4:27; 5:5; 6:48; 14:27, 30			5
Lk.	7	2:8, 37; 5:5; 12:20; 17:34; 18:7; 21:37			7
Jn.	7	3:2; 7:50; 9:4; 11:10; 13:30; 19:39; 21:3			7
Ac.	15	5:19; 9:24, 25; 12:6; 16:9, 33; 17:10; 18:9; 20:31; 23:11, 23, 31; 26:7; 27:23, 27a	1	27:27b	16
Ro.	1	13:12			1
1 Co.	1	11:23			1
1 Th.	6	2:9; 3:10; 5:2, 5, 7, 7			6
2 Th.	1	3:8			1
1 Ti.	1	5:5			1
2 Ti.	1	1:3			1
2 Pt.	1	3:10			1
Rev.	8	4:8; 7:15; 8:12; 12:10; 14:11; 20:10; 21:25; 22:5			8
Total	63		2		65

3470. νυνί, nuni′

Book	now	Total
Ro.	6:22; 7:6, 17; 15:23, 25	5
1 Co.	5:11; 12:18; 13:13; 14:6; 15:20	5
2 Co.	8:11, 22	2
Eph.	2:13	1
Col.	1:21, 26; 3:8	3
Phe.	1:9, 11	2
Heb.	8:6; 11:16	2
Total		20

3472. νύσσω, nus′sō

Book	pierce	Total
Jn.	19:34	1

3473. νυστάζω, nustad′zō

Book	slumber	Total
Mt.	25:5	1
2 Pt.	2:3	1
Total		2

3474. νυχθήμερον nuchthe′meron

Book	a night and a day	Total
2 Co.	11:25	1

3475. Νῶε, Nō′e

Book	Oc.	Noe	Oc.	Noah	Total
Mt.	2	24:37, 38			2
Lk.	3	3:36; 17:26, 27			3
Heb.			1	11:7	1
1 Pt.			1	3:20	1
2 Pt.			1	2:5	1
Total	5		3		8

3476. νωθρός, nōthros′

Book	Oc.	dull	Oc.	slothful	Total
Heb.	1	5:11	1	6:12	2

3477. νῶτος, nō′tos

Book	back	Total
Ro.	11:10	1

3478. ξενία, xeni′a

Book	lodging	Total
Ac.	28:23	1
Phe.	1:22	1
Total		2

3479. ξενίζω, xenid′zō

Book	Oc.	lodge	Oc.	think it strange	Oc.	strange	Oc.	entertain	Total
Ac.	6	10:6, 18, 23, 32; 21:16; 28:7			1	17:20			7
Heb.							1	13:2	1
1 Pt.			2	4:4, 12					2
Total	6		2		1		1		10

3481. ξένος, xen′os

Book	Oc.	stranger	Oc.	strange	Oc.	host	Total
Mt.	5	25:35, 38, 43, 44; 27:7					5
Ac.	1	17:21	1	17:8			2
Ro.					1	16:23	1
Eph.	2	2:12, 19					2
Heb.	1	11:13	1	13:9			2
1 Pt.			1	4:12			1
3 Jn.	1	1:5					1
Total	10		3		1		14

3480. ξενοδοχέω, xenodoche′ō

Book	lodge strangers	Total
1 Ti.	5:10	1

3482. ξέστης, xes′tes

Book	pot	Total
Mk.	7:4, 8	2

3483. ξηραίνω, xerai′nō

Book	Oc.	wither away	Oc.	wither	Oc.	dry up	Oc.	pine away	Oc.	be ripe	Total
Mt.	3	13:6; 21:19, 20									3
Mk.	2	4:6; 11:21	2	3:1, 3	2	5:29; 11:20	1	9:18			7
Lk.	1	8:6									1
Jn.			1	15:6							1
Jas.			1	1:11							1
1 Pt.			1	1:24							1
Rev.					1	16:12			1	14:15	2
Total	6		5		3		1		1		16

3484. ξηρός, xe̱ros′

Book	Oc.	withered	Oc.	dry	Oc.	dry land	Oc.	land	Total
Mt.	1	12:10					1	23:15	2
Lk.	2	6:6, 8	1	23:31					3
Jn.	1	5:3							1
Heb.					1	11:29			1
Total	4		1		1		1		7

3485. ξύλινος, xu′linos

Book	of wood	Total
2 Ti.	2:20	1
Rev.	9:20	1
Total		2

3486. ξύλον, xu′lon

Book	Oc.	tree	Oc.	staff	Oc.	wood	Oc.	stocks	Total
Mt.			2	26:47, 55					2
Mk.			2	14:43, 48					2
Lk.	1	23:31	1	22:52					2
Ac.	3	5:30; 10: 39; 13:29					1	16:24	4
1 Co.					1	3:12			1
Gal.	1	3:13							1
1 Pt.	1	2:24							1
Rev.	4	2:7; 22:2, 2, 14			2	18:12, 12			6
Total	10		5		3		1		19

3487. ξυράω, xura′ō

Book	shave	Total
Ac.	21:24	1
1 Co.	11:5, 6	2
Total		3

3488. ὁ, ἡ, τό, ho, he̱, to

Renderings other than "the."

Book	Oc.	which	Oc.	who	Oc.	the things	Oc.	the son	Oc.	Misc.	Total
Mt.	73	1:22a; 2:15b, 17a, 20c, 23a; 4:13b, 14a, 16b, 16c; 5: 6a, 12d, 16e, 44d, 45b, 46a, 48b; 6:1e, 4d, 6d, 6g, 9a, 18c, 18f; 7:6a, 11c, 13f, 14c; 9:8c; 10:20d, 28a, 28d, 32c, 33c; 11:14, 21b, 23a, 23d; 12:17a, 50d; 13:14b, 19d, 35a; 15:18a, 20a, 27d; 16:17c; 18:6b, 10e, 11c, 12c, 13b, 14b, 19c; 19:4b, 9b, 28b; 20:12b; 21:4a; 22: 23b, 31c; 23:9c, 16a; 26:25, 28d, 75c; 27:3a, 9a, 17b, 22b, 35b, 44b, 52b; 28:5c	6	1:16c; 10:2c, 4b; 13:9, 43e; 26:3g	2	6:34c; 16: 23c	3	4:21a; 10:2e, 3b	4	1:6e; 22:21a, 21b; 25:17a	88
Mk.	14	3:22b, 34a; 6:26c; 11:25b, 26b; 12:25a, 38c; 13:32d; 14:18b, 24d; 15:28b, 39b, 41b; 16:6c					3	1:19a; 3: 17a, 18a	3	12:17b, 17c; 16:1c	20
Lk.	44	1:2a, 70b; 2:15f, 17b, 18b, 21d; 4:22c; 5:7b; 6:3b, 8c, 27a, 27c; 7:39b, 47b; 8:21b; 10:11b, 13b, 15a; 10: 23c; 11:2a, 33c, 35b, 40b, 40c, 44, 50c, 51c; 12:47b; 13:34a; 14:24b; 15:6e, 30b; 16:21b; 18:7d, 9a; 19: 26a, 27b; 20:27b, 46b; 21:22b; 22:19b, 20f; 23:33b; 24:44b	1	1:36b			1	6:15a	4	5:33c; 19: 42b; 20:25b, 25c	50
Jn.	45	1:18b, 24a, 29f, 40c; 2:9d; 3:13f, 29e; 4:25b; 5:2c, 12b, 15c, 23f; 6:22c, 27b, 27d, 33c, 39b, 40c, 41c, 44b, 46b, 50b, 51c, 58b; 8:31b; 9:40b; 11:2a, 16a, 27c, 31b, 37a, 42b, 45b; 12:1c, 4b; 13:1h; 14:24d; 18:2a, 5c, 14a; 19:24b, 32e, 39a; 20:8b; 21:24b	2	7:49b; 13:11			1	21:2d	1	19:25f	49
Ac.	49	1:11c, 16d; 2:7; 3:2c, 10a; 4:11b, 11d, 24d; 5:17c; 6: 9b; 7:34c, 35c, 37b, 38e, 52c; 8:1d, 14a; 9:7b, 11c, 21c, 22b, 32b; 10:7b, 17d, 18, 21b, 42b; 11:22d; 12:9a; 13:27e; 14:3b, 13c; 15:16b, 19a, 23d; 16:3c, 4f; 17: 12a, 21; 19:26c; 20:19b, 32d; 21:20c; 22:29a; 23:13a; 24:14c; 25:24b; 26:4c; 28:9b	6	4:25a, 36a; 13:9; 15: 17f, 38a; 21:37d					1	7:16c	56
Ro.	17	1:3b; 2:14a, 21a; 4:11c; 5:5e, 15i; 7:5d, 10b, 23f; 9: 6c, 30, 30; 10:5b; 15:26c, 31d; 16:1c, 11d			3	2:14b; 8: 5b, 5e			7	13:7b, 7e, 7h, 7k; 14:19a; 16:10b, 11b	27
1 Co.	13	1:2c, 4d, 24, 28c; 2:11e, 12d; 3:10c; 4:17b; 8:10a; 11:24b; 12:6b; 15:10b, 57b			5	2:11a, 11f, 14a; 7:34d, 34g			5	1:11; 7:32b, 33b; 10:33b; 15:23	23
2 Co.	19	1:1d, 1f, 6b, 8b, 9d; 2:6c; 3:7g; 4:11a, 17a; 5:2b; 7: 14b; 8:16b, 19c, 20b, 22b; 10:2c; 11:28b, 31c; 12:21b	7	1:4a, 19c, 22a; 4:6b; 5:5b, 18c, 21a					3	8:15a, 15c; 11:30a	29
Gal.	6	1:11b, 22d; 3:10a, 21d; 4:25c; 6:1a	6	1:1, 4a, 15b; 2:3, 9c, 20d					1	5:24a	13
Eph.	9	1:10e, 10g; 2:11c, 17a; 3:2d, 9c; 4:22c, 24b; 5:4	8	1:3c, 12c, 19c; 2:11b, 13a, 14b; 3:9f; 4:6							17
Phl.	10	1:11; 2:9b, 13b; 3:3b, 6b, 9a, 9b, 9c; 4:7b, 13	1	3:19f	1	2:4b			1	2:21c	13
Col.	12	1:4c, 5b, 6a, 12b, 23d, 25c, 26b, 29b; 3:5b, 10b; 4:9b, 11a	3	1:8a; 2:12e; 4:11b							15
1 Th.	11	1:10c; 2:14c; 4:5b, 10b, 13c, 15a, 15e, 17a; 5:12, 15, 21	1	5:10							12
2 Th.	1	2:16c	2	2:4a, 12a							3
1 Ti.	5	1:1, 4, 14c; 3:13b; 5:13b	8	1:12a, 13; 2:6a; 6:13b, 13d, 15a, 16, 17e							13
2 Ti.	7	1:1, 9, 13, 14; 2:10; 3:15, 15	2	1:9; 4:1							9
Tit.	1	1:1									1
Phe.	2	1:6c, 11									2
Heb.	6	4:3b; 6:7a; 7:28d; 9:3b; 11:3c, 12d	6	2:9a; 6:18a; 7:1d, 5c, 9; 10:29a							12
Jas.	3	1:21b; 3:9c; 5:4e	2	4:12b; 5:4c					1	4:14a	6
1 Pt.	6	1:3c, 11a, 25d; 2:7a, 10, 10	7	1:5, 10a, 17a, 21a; 3:5b; 5:1b, 10b							13
2 Pt.									1	2:22a	1
2 Jn.	1	1:2b	1	1:7b							2
3 Jn.			1	1:9b							1
Jd.	1	1:17b	1	1:4a							2
Rev.	58	1:4b, 4e, 4f, 4g, 8d, 8e, 8f, 11f; 2:9e, 20b, 23c; 3:9b, 10e, 12i, 12j; 4:8c; 7:10b, 13b, 17b; 8:3f, 6b, 9c, 13f; 9:13e, 14d, 15b, 18g; 10:8d, 8f; 11:2b, 16b, 17c; 12: 4h, 9g, 10j, 17e; 14:3f, 4a, 10d, 13c, 17b; 16:2e, 5c, 9d; 17:1b, 7f, 9b, 18d; 18:14d, 15b; 19:14b, 21e; 20: 8b, 13b, 13e; 21:8d, 9b; 22:8d	8	1:9a; 2:1f, 18e; 4:9d; 14:11c; 15:7e; 18:8c, 9c							66
Total	413		79		11		8		32		543

Miscellaneous: Mt. 1:6e, her . . . wife; Mt. 22:21a, the things which are; Mt. 22:21b, the things that are; Mt. 25:17a, he . . . received; Mk. 12:17b, 17c, the things that are; Mk. 16:1c, the mother; Lk. 5:33c, the disciples; Lk. 19:42b, things which belong; Lk. 20:25b, 25c, the things which be; Jn. 19:25f, the wife; Ac. 7:16c, the father; Ro. 13:7b, 7e, 7h, 7k, to whom; Ro. 14:19a, the things which make for; Ro. 16:10b, 11b, them . . . of (one's) household; 1 Co. 1:11, them . . . of the house; 1 Co. 7:32b, the things that belong to; 1 Co. 7:33b, the things that are; 1 Co. 10:33b, the profit; 1 Co. 15:23, they that are; 2 Co. 8:15a, 15c, he that gathered; 2 Co. 11:30a, the things which concern; Gal. 5:24a, they that are; Phl. 2:21c, the things which are; Jas. 4:14a, what on; 2 Pt. 2:22a, according to.

3489. ὀγδοήκοντα, ogdoẹ'konta

Book	fourscore	Total
Lk.	2:37; 16:7	2

3490. ὄγδοος, og'doos

Book	eighth	Total
Lk.	1:59	1
Ac.	7:8	1
2 Pt.	2:5	1
Rev.	17:11; 21:20	2
Total		5

3491. ὄγκος, ong'kos

Book	weight	Total
Heb.	12:1	1

3493. ὁδεύω, hodeu'ō

Book	journey	Total
Lk.	10:33	1

3492. ὅδε, ἥδε, τόδε, ho'de, hẹ'de, tod'e

Book	Oc.	these things	Oc.	thus	Oc.	after this manner	Oc.	he	Oc.	she	Oc.	such	Total
Lk.							1	16:25	1	10:39			2
Ac.			1	21:11	1	15:23							2
Jas.											1	4:13	1
Rev.	7	2:1, 8, 12, 18; 3:1, 7, 14											7
Total	7		1		1		1		1		1		12

3494. ὁδηγέω, hodẹgẹ'ō

Book	Oc.	lead	Oc.	guide	Total
Mt.	1	15:14			1
Lk.	1	6:39			1
Jn.			1	16:13	1
Ac.			1	8:31	1
Rev.	1	7:17			1
Total	3		2		5

3495. ὁδηγός, hodẹgos'

Book	Oc.	guide	Oc.	leader	Total
Mt.	2	23:16, 24	1	15:14	3
Ac.	1	1:16			1
Ro.	1	2:19			1
Total	4		1		5

3496. ὁδοιπορέω, hodoipore'ō

Book	go on (one's) journey	Total
Ac.	10:9	1

3497. ὁδοιπορία, hodoipori'a

Book	Oc.	journey	Oc.	journeyings	Total
Jn.	1	4:6			1
2 Co.			1	11:26	1
Total	1		1		2

3499. ὀδούς, odous'

Book	tooth	Total
Mt.	5:38, 38; 8:12; 13:42, 50; 22:13; 24:51; 25:30	8
Mk.	9:18	1
Lk.	13:28	1
Ac.	7:54	1
Rev.	9:8	1
Total		12

3498. ὁδός, hodos'

Book	Oc.	way	Oc.	way side	Oc.	journey	Oc.	highway	Oc.	Misc.	Total
Mt.	16	2:12; 3:3; 4:15; 5:25; 7:13, 14; 8:28; 10:5; 11:10; 15:32; 20:17; 21: 8, 8, 19, 32; 22:16	3	13:4, 19; 20:30	1	10:10	2	22:9, 10			22
Mk.	12	1:2, 3; 8:3, 27; 9:33, 34; 10:17, 32, 52; 11:8, 8; 12:14	2	4:4, 15	1	6:8			2	2:23; 10:46	17
Lk.	13	1:76, 79; 3:4, 5; 7:27; 9:57; 10:4, 31; 12:58; 19:36; 20:21; 24:32, 35	3	8:5, 12; 18: 35	3	2:44; 9:3; 11:6	1	14:23			20
Jn.	4	1:23; 14:4, 5, 6									4
Ac.	19	2:28; 8:26, 36, 39; 9:2, 17, 27; 13:10; 14:16; 16:17; 18:25, 26; 19:9, 23; 22:4; 24:14, 22; 25:3; 26:13			1	1:12					20
Ro.	3	3:16, 17; 11:33									3
1 Co.	2	4:17; 12:31									2
1 Th.	1	3:11									1
Heb.	3	3:10; 9:8; 10:20									3
Jas.	3	1:8; 2:25; 5:20									3
2 Pt.	4	2:2, 15, 15, 21									4
Jd.	1	1:11									1
Rev.	2	15:3; 16:12									2
Total	83		8		6		3		2		102

Miscellaneous: Mk. 2:23 (with 4060), go; Mk. 10:46, highway side.

3500. ὀδυνάω, oduna'ō

Book	Oc.	sorrow	Oc.	torment	Total
Lk.	1	2:48	2	16:24, 25	3
Ac.	1	20:38			1
Total	2		2		4

3501. ὀδύνη, odu'nẹ

Book	sorrow	Total
Ro.	9:2	1
1 Ti.	6:10	1
Total		2

3502. ὀδυρμός, odurmos'

Book	mourning	Total
Mt.	2:18	1
2 Co.	7:7	1
Total		2

3504. Ὀζίας, Odzi'as

Book	Ozias	Total
Mt.	1:8, 9	2

3503. ὅ εστι, ho esti'

Book	Oc.	which is	Oc.	that is	Oc.	that is to say	Oc.	which make	Oc.	called	Total
Mk.	1	3:17	2	7:34; 15:42	1	7:11	1	12:42	1	15:16	6
Eph.	1	6:17									1
Col.	1	1:24									1
Heb.	1	7:2									1
Rev.	1	21:8	1	21:17							2
Total	5		3		1		1		1		11

3505. ὄζω, od'zō

Book	stink	Total
Jn.	11:39	1

3506. ὅθεν, hoth'en

Book	Oc.	wherefore	Oc.	from whence	Oc.	whereupon	Oc.	where	Oc.	whence	Oc.	from thence	Oc.	whereby	Total
Mt.			1	12:44	1	14:7	2	25:24, 26							4
Lk.									1	11:24					1
Ac.			1	14:26	1	26:19					1	28:13			3
Heb.	4	2:17; 3:1; 7:25; 8:3	1	11:19	1	9:18									6
1 Jn.													1	2:18	1
Total	4		3		3		2		1		1		1		15

3507. ὀθόνη, othon'e̱

Book	sheet	Total
Ac.	10:11; 11:5	2

3508. ὀθόνιον, othon'ion

Book	linen clothes	Total
Lk.	24:12	1
Jn.	19:40; 20:5, 6, 7	4
Total		5

3509. οἰκεῖος, oikei'os

Book	Oc.	of the household	Oc.	of (one's) own house	Total
Gal.	1	6:10			1
Eph.	1	2:19			1
1 Ti.			1	5:8	1
Total	2		1		3

3510. οἰκέτης, oiket'e̱s

Book	Oc.	servant	Oc.	household servant	Total
Lk.	1	16:13			1
Ac.			1	10:7	1
Ro.	1	14:4			1
1 Pt.	1	2:18			1
Total	3		1		4

3511. οἰκέω, oike'ō

Book	dwell	Total
Ro.	7:17, 18, 20; 8:9, 11	5
1 Co.	3:16; 7:12, 13	3
1 Ti.	6:16	1
Total		9

3512. οἴκημα, oi'ke̱ma

Book	prison	Total
Ac.	12:7	1

3513. οἰκητήριον, oike̱te̱'rion

Book	Oc.	house	Oc.	habitation	Total
2 Co.	1	5:2			1
Jd.			1	1:6	1
Total	1		1		2

3515. οἰκιακός, oikiakos'

Book	of (one's) household	Total
Mt.	10:25, 36	2

3516. οἰκοδεσποτέω oikodespote'ō

Book	guide the house	Total
1 Ti.	5:14	1

3514. οἰκία, oiki'a

Book	Oc.	house	Oc.	at home (with 1722)	Oc.	household	Oc.	from house to house	Total
Mt.	25	2:11; 5:15; 7:24, 25, 26, 27; 8:14; 9:10, 23, 28; 10:12, 13, 14; 12:25, 29, 29; 13:1, 36, 57; 17:25; 19:29; 23:14; 24:17, 43; 26:6	1	8:6					26
Mk.	19	1:29; 2:15; 3:25, 25, 27, 27; 6:4, 10; 7:24; 9:33; 10:10, 29, 30; 12:40; 13:15, 15, 34, 35; 14:3							19
Lk.	24	4:38; 5:29; 6:48, 48, 49, 49; 7:6, 36, 37, 44; 8:27, 51; 9:4; 10:5, 7, 7, 7; 15:8, 25; 17:31; 18:29; 20:47; 22:10, 11							24
Jn.	5	4:53; 8:35; 11:31; 12:3; 14:2							5
Ac.	12	4:34; 9:11, 17; 10:6, 17, 32; 11:11; 12:12; 16:32; 17:5; 18:7, 7							12
1 Co.	2	11:22; 16:15							2
2 Co.	2	5:1, 1							2
Phl.					1	4:22			1
1 Ti.							1	5:13	1
2 Ti.	2	2:20; 3:6							2
2 Jn.	1	1:10							1
Total	92		1		1		1		95

3517. οἰκοδεσπότης, oikodespot'e̱s

Book	Oc.	householder	Oc.	goodman of the house	Oc.	master of the house	Oc.	goodman	Total
Mt.	4	13:27, 52; 20:1; 21:33	2	20:11; 24:43	1	10:25			7
Mk.			1	14:14					1
Lk.			1	12:39	2	13:25; 14:21	1	22:11	4
Total	4		4		3		1		12

3518. οἰκοδομέω, oikodome'ō

Book	Oc.	build	Oc.	edify	Oc.	builder	Oc.	build up	Oc.	be in building	Oc.	embolden	Total
Mt.	7	7:24, 26; 16:18; 21:33; 23:29; 26:61; 27:40			1	21:42							8
Mk.	3	12:1; 14:58; 15:29			1	12:10							4
Lk.	10	4:29; 6:48, 49; 7:5; 11:47, 48; 12:18; 14:28, 30; 17:28			1	20:17							11
Jn.									1	2:20			1
Ac.	2	7:47, 49	1	9:31	1	4:11							4
Ro.	1	15:20											1
1 Co.			5	8:1; 10:23; 14:4, 4, 17							1	8:10	6
Gal.	1	2:18											1
1 Th.			1	5:11									1
1 Pt.					1	2:7	1	2:5					2
Total	24		7		5		1		1		1		39

3519. οἰκοδομή, oikodome̱'

Book	Oc.	edifying	Oc.	building	Oc.	edification	Oc.	wherewith (one) may edify	Total
Mt.			1	24:1					1
Mk.			2	13:1, 2					2
Ro.					1	15:2	1	14:19	2
1 Co.	3	14:5, 12, 26	1	3:9	1	14:3			5
2 Co.	1	12:19	1	5:1	2	10:8; 13:10			4
Eph.	3	4:12, 16, 29	1	2:21					4
Total	7		6		4		1		18

3520. οἰκοδομία, oikodomi'a

Book	edifying	Total
1 Ti.	1:4	1

3521. οἰκονομέω, oikonome'ō

Book	be steward	Total
Lk.	16:2	1

3522. οἰκονομία, oikonomi'a

Book	Oc.	dispensation	Oc.	stewardship	Total
Lk.			3	16:2, 3, 4	3
1 Co.	1	9:17			1
Eph.	2	1:10; 3:2			2
Col.	1	1:25			1
Total	4		3		7

3523. οἰκονόμος, oikonom'os

Book	Oc.	steward	Oc.	chamberlain	Oc.	governor	Total
Lk.	4	12:42; 16:1, 3, 8					4
Ro.			1	16:23			1
1 Co.	2	4:1, 2					2
Gal.					1	4:2	1
Tit.	1	1:7					1
1 Pt.	1	4:10					1
Total	8		1		1		10

3524. οἶκος, oi'kos

Book	Oc.	house	Oc.	household	Oc.	home (with 1519)	Oc.	at home (with 1722)	Oc.	Misc.	Total
Mt.	10	9:6, 7; 10:6; 11:8; 12:4, 44; 15:24; 21:13, 13; 23:38									10
Mk.	12	2:1, 11, 26; 3:19; 5:38; 7:17, 30; 8:3, 26; 9:28; 11:17, 17			1	5:19					13
Lk.	31	1:23, 27, 33, 40, 56, 69; 2:4; 5:24, 25; 6:4; 7:10; 8:39, 41; 10:5, 38; 11:17, 17, 24; 12:39, 52; 13:35; 14:1, 23; 16:4, 27; 18:14; 19: 5, 9, 46, 46; 22:54			1	15:6			2	9:61; 11:51	34
Jn.	5	2:16, 16, 17; 7:53; 11:20									5
Ac.	23	2:2, 36, 46; 5:42; 7:10, 20, 42, 47, 49; 8:3; 10:2, 22, 30; 11:12, 13, 14; 16:15b, 31, 34; 18:8; 19:16; 20:20; 21:8	1	16:15a							24
Ro.	1	16:5									1
1 Co.	1	16:19	1	1:16			2	11:34; 14: 35			4
Col.	1	4:15									1
1 Ti.	4	3:4, 5, 12, 15							1	5:4	5
2 Ti.	1	1:16	1	4:19							2
Tit.	1	1:11									1
Phe.	1	1:2									1
Heb.	11	3:2, 3, 4, 5, 6, 6; 8:8, 8, 10; 10:21; 11:7									11
1 Pt.	2	2:5; 4:17									2
Total	104		3		2		2		3		114

Miscellaneous: Lk. 9:61, at home at (one's) house; Lk. 11:51, temple; 1 Ti. 5:4 (with 2398), at home.

3525. οἰκουμένη, oikoumen'ē

Book	Oc.	world	Oc.	earth	Total
Mt.	1	24:14			1
Lk.	2	2:1; 4:5	1	21:26	3
Ac.	5	11:28; 17:6, 31; 19:27; 24:5			5
Ro.	1	10:18			1
Heb.	2	1:6; 2:5			2
Rev.	3	3:10; 12:9; 16:14			3
Total	14		1		15

3526. οἰκουρός, oikouros'

Book	keeper at home	Total
Tit.	2:5	1

3527. οἰκτείρω or οἰκτερέω, oiktei'rō or oiktere'ō

Book	Oc.	have compassion on	Oc.	have compassion	Total
Ro.	1	9:15a	1	9:15b	2

3528. οἰκτιρμός, oiktirmos'

Book	mercy	Total
Ro.	12:1	1
2 Co.	1:3	1
Phl.	2:1	1
Col.	3:12	1
Heb.	10:28	1
Total		5

3529. οἰκτίρμων, oiktir'mōn

Book	Oc.	merciful	Oc.	of tender mercy	Total
Lk.	2	6:36, 36			2
Jas.			1	5:11	1
Total	2		1		3

3530. οἰνοπότης, oinopot'ēs

Book	winebibber	Total
Mt.	11:19	1
Lk.	7:34	1
Total		2

3531. οἶνος, oi'nos

Book	Oc.	wine	Oc.	winepress (with 3025)	Total
Mt.	3	9:17, 17, 17			3
Mk.	5	2:22, 22, 22, 22; 15:23			5
Lk.	6	1:15; 5:37, 37, 38; 7:33; 10:34			6
Jn.	6	2:3, 3, 9, 10, 10; 4:46			6
Ro.	1	14:21			1
Eph.	1	5:18			1
1 Ti.	2	3:8; 5:23			2
Tit.	1	2:3			1
Rev.	7	6:6; 14:8, 10; 16:19; 17:2; 18:3, 13	1	19:15	8
Total	32		1		33

3533a. οἶμαι, oi'mai

Book	Oc.	suppose	Oc.	think	Total
Phl.	1	1:16			1
Jas.			1	1:7	1
Total	1		1		2

3532. οἰνοφλυγία, oinophlugi'a

Book	excess of wine	Total
1 Pt.	4:3	1

3533b. οἴομαι, oi'omai

Book	suppose	Total
Jn.	21:25	1

Words 3533 has 3 occurrences.

3534. οἷος, hoi'os

Book	Oc.	such as	Oc.	as	Oc.	which	Oc.	what manner	Oc.	so as	Oc.	what manner of man	Oc.	what	Total
Mt.	1	24:21													1
Mk.	1	13:19							1	9:3					2
Lk.							1	9:55							1
Ro.			1	9:6											1
1 Co.			2	15:48, 48											2
2 Co.	3	10:11; 12: 20, 20													3
Phl.					1	1:30									1
1 Th.											1	1:5			. 1
2 Ti.					1	3:11a							1	3:11b	2
Rev.	1	16:18													1
Total	6		3		2		1		1		1		1		15

3535. ὀκνέω, okne′ō

Book	delay	Total
Ac.	9:38	1

3536. ὀκνηρός, okneros′

Book	Oc.	slothful	Oc.	grievous	Total
Mt.	1	25:26			1
Ro.	1	12:11			1
Phl.			1	3:1	1
Total	2		1		3

3537. ὀκταήμερος, oktae′meros

Book	the eighth day	Total
Phl.	3:5	1

3538. ὀκτώ, oktō′

Book	Oc.	eight	Oc.	eighteen (with 1176 and 2532)	Total
Lk.	2	2:21; 9:28	3	13:4, 11, 16	5
Jn.	2	5:5; 20:26			2
Ac.	1	9:33			1
1 Pt.	1	3:20			1
Total	6		3		9

3539. ὄλεθρος, ol′ethros

Book	destruction	Total
1 Co.	5:5	1
1 Th.	5:3	1
2 Th.	1:9	1
1 Ti.	6:9	1
Total		4

3540. ὀλιγόπιστος, oligop′istos

Book	of little faith	Total
Mt.	6:30; 8:26; 14:31; 16:8	4
Lk.	12:28	1
Total		5

3541. ὀλίγος, oli′gos

Book	Oc.	few	Oc.	(a) little	Oc.	small	Oc.	few things	Oc.	almost (with 1722)	Oc.	a while	Oc.	Misc.	Total
Mt.	5	7:14; 9:37; 15:34; 20:16; 22:14					2	25:21, 23							7
Mk.	2	6:5; 8:7	1	1:19							1	6:31			4
Lk.	2	10:2; 13:23	3	5:3; 7:47, 47									1	12:48	6
Ac.	2	17:4, 12			5	12:18; 15:2; 19:23, 24; 27:20			2	26:28, 29			1	14:28	10
2 Co.			1	8:15											1
Eph.													1	3:3	1
1 Ti.			1	5:23									1	4:8	2
Heb.	1	12:10													1
Jas.			1	3:5									1	4:14	2
1 Pt.	1	3:20									1	5:10	2	1:6; 5:12	4
Rev.	1	3:4					2	2:14, 20					2	12:12; 17:10	5
Total	14		7		5		4		2		2		9		43

Miscellaneous: Lk. 12:48, few stripes; Ac. 14:28 (with 3656), long; Eph. 3:3 (with 1722), in few words; 1 Ti. 4:8 (with 4214), little; Jas. 4:14 (with 4214), for a little time; 1 Pt. 1:6, for a season; 1 Pt. 5:12 (with 1223), briefly; Rev. 12:12, short; Rev. 17:10, a short space.

3542. ὀλιγόψυχος, oligop′suchos

Book	feebleminded	Total
1 Th.	5:14	1

3543. ὀλιγωρέω, oligōre′ō

Book	despise	Total
Heb.	12:5	1

3544. ὀλοθρευτής, olothreutes′

Book	destroyer	Total
1 Co.	10:10	1

3545. ὀλοθρεύω, olothreu′ō

Book	destroy	Total
Heb.	11:28	1

3546. ὁλοκαύτωμα holokau′tōma

Book	burnt offering	Total
Mk.	12:33	1
Heb.	10:6, 8	2
Total		3

3547. ὁλοκληρία, holokleri′a

Book	perfect soundness	Total
Ac.	3:16	1

3548. ὁλόκληρος, holok′leros

Book	Oc.	whole	Oc.	entire	Total
1 Th.	1	5:23			1
Jas.			1	1:4	1
Total	1		1		2

3549. ὀλολύζω, ololud′zō

Book	howl	Total
Jas.	5:1	1

3551. ὁλοτελής, holoteles′

Book	wholly	Total
1 Th.	5:23	1

3552. Ὀλυμπᾶς, Olumpas′

Book	Olympas	Total
Ro.	16:15	1

3553. ὄλυνθος, ol′unthos

Book	untimely fig	Total
Rev.	6:13	1

3550. ὅλος, hol′os

Book	Oc.	all	Oc.	whole	Oc.	every whit	Oc.	altogether	Oc.	throughout (with 1223)	Total
Mt.	15	1:22; 4:23, 24; 9:26, 31; 14:35; 20:6; 21:4; 22:37, 37, 37, 40; 24:14; 26:56, 59	8	5:29, 30; 6:22, 23; 13:33; 16:26; 26:13; 27:27							23
Mk.	13	1:28, 33, 39; 12:30, 30, 30, 30, 33, 33, 33, 33, 44; 14:55	6	6:55; 8:36; 14:9; 15:1, 16, 33							19
Lk.	11	1:65; 4:14; 5:5; 7:17; 8:43; 10:27, 27, 27, 27; 23:5, 44	6	8:39; 9:25; 11:34, 36, 36; 13:21							17
Jn.			2	4:53; 11:50	2	7:23; 13:10	1	9:34	1	19:23	6
Ac.	17	2:2, 47; 5:11; 7:10, 11; 8:37; 9:31, 42; 10:22, 37; 11:28; 13:49; 18:8; 19:27; 21:30, 31; 22:30	4	11:26; 15:22; 19:29; 28:30							21
Ro.	2	8:36; 10:21	2	1:8; 16:23							4
1 Co.			4	5:6; 12:17, 17; 14:23							4
2 Co.	1	1:1									1
Gal.			2	5:3, 9							2
Phl.	1	1:13									1
1 Th.	1	4:10									1
Tit.			1	1:11							1
Heb.	2	3:2, 5									2
Jas.			4	2:10; 3:2, 3, 6							4
1 Jn.			2	2:2; 5:19							2
Rev.	2	3:10; 13:3	2	12:9; 16:14							4
Total	65		43		2		1		1		112

3554. ὅλως, hol'ōs

Book	Oc.	at all	Oc.	commonly	Oc.	utterly	Total
Mt.	1	5:34					1
1 Co.	1	15:29	1	5:1	1	6:7	3
Total	2		1		1		4

3556. ὁμιλέω, homile'ō

Book	Oc.	talk	Oc.	commune with	Oc.	commune together	Total
Lk.	1	24:14	1	24:15			2
Ac.	1	20:11			1	24:26	2
Total	2		1		1		4

3555. ὄμβρος, om'bros

Book	shower	Total
Lk.	12:54	1

3557. ὁμιλία, homili'a

Book	communication	Total
1 Co.	15:33	1

3558. ὅμιλος, hom'ilos

Book	company	Total
Rev.	18:17	1

3559. ὄμμα, om'ma

Book	eye	Total
Mk.	8:23	1

3560. ὄμνυμι or ὀμνύω, om'numi or omnu'ō

Book	swear	Total
Mt.	5:34, 36; 23:16, 16, 18, 18, 20, 20, 21, 21, 22, 22; 26:74	13
Mk.	6:23; 14:71	2
Lk.	1:73	1
Ac.	2:30; 7:17	2
Heb.	3:11, 18; 4:3; 6:13, 13, 16; 7:21	7
Jas.	5:12	1
Rev.	10:6	1
Total		27

3561. ὁμοθυμαδόν, homothumadon'

Book	Oc.	with one accord	Oc.	with one mind	Total
Ac.	11	1:14; 2:1, 46; 4:24; 5:12; 7:57; 8:6; 12:20; 15:25; 18:12; 19:29			11
Ro.			1	15:6	1
Total	11		1		12

3562. ὁμοιάζω, homoiad'zō

Book	agree thereto	Total
Mk.	14:70	1

3563. ὁμοιοπαθής, homoiopathēs'

Book	Oc.	of like passions	Oc.	subject to like passions	Total
Ac.	1	14:15			1
Jas.			1	5:17	1
Total	1		1		2

3564. ὅμοιος, hom'oios

Book	like	Total
Mt.	11:16; 13:31, 33, 44, 45, 47, 52; 20:1; 22:39	9
Mk.	12:31	1
Lk.	6:47, 48, 49; 7:31, 32; 12:36; 13:18, 19, 21	9
Jn.	8:55; 9:9	2
Ac.	17:29	1
Gal.	5:21	1
1 Jn.	3:2	1
Jd.	1:7	1
Rev.	1:13, 15; 2:18; 4:3, 3, 6, 7, 7, 7; 9:7, 7, 10, 19; 11:1; 13:2, 4, 11; 14:14; 16:13; 18:18; 21:11, 18	22
Total		47

3565. ὁμοιότης, homoiot'ēs

Book	Oc.	like as (with 2596)	Oc.	similitude	Total
Heb.	1	4:15	1	7:15	2

3566. ὁμοιόω, homoio'ō

Book	Oc.	liken	Oc.	make like	Oc.	be like	Oc.	in the likeness of	Oc.	resemble	Total
Mt.	6	7:24, 26; 11:16; 13:24; 18:23; 25:1			2	6:8; 22:2					8
Mk.	1	4:30									1
Lk.	2	7:31; 13:20							1	13:18	3
Ac.							1	14:11			1
Ro.			1	9:29							1
Heb.			1	2:17							1
Total	9		2		2		1		1		15

3567. ὁμοίωμα, homoi'ōma

Book	Oc.	likeness	Oc.	made like to	Oc.	similitude	Oc.	shape	Total
Ro.	2	6:5; 8:3	1	1:23	1	5:14			4
Phl.	1	2:7							1
Rev.							1	9:7	1
Total	3		1		1		1		6

3568. ὁμοίως, homoi'ōs

Book	Oc.	likewise	Oc.	moreover (with 1161)	Oc.	so	Total
Mt.	3	22:26; 26:35; 27:41					3
Mk.	2	4:16; 15:31					2
Lk.	10	3:11; 5:33; 6:31; 10:32, 37; 13:5; 16:25; 17:28, 31; 22:36			1	5:10	11
Jn.	3	5:19; 6:11; 21:13					3
Ro.	1	1:27					1
1 Co.	3	7:3, 4, 22					3
Heb.			1	9:21			1
Jas.	1	2:25					1
1 Pt.	3	3:1, 7; 5:5					3
Jd.	1	1:8					1
Rev.	1	8:12					1
Total	28		1		1		30

3569. ὁμοίωσις, homoi'ōsis

Book	similitude	Total
Jas.	3:9	1

3570. ὁμολογέω, homologe'ō

Book	Oc.	confess	Oc.	profess	Oc.	promise	Oc.	give thanks	Oc.	confession is made	Total
Mt.	2	10:32, 32	1	7:23	1	14:7					4
Lk.	2	12:8, 8									2
Jn.	4	1:20, 20; 9:22; 12:42									4
Ac.	2	23:8; 24:14									2
Ro.	1	10:9							1	10:10	2
1 Ti.			1	6:12							1
Tit.			1	1:16							1
Heb.	1	11:13					1	13:15			2
1 Jn.	4	1:9; 4:2, 3, 15									4
2 Jn.	1	1:7									1
Total	17		3		1		1		1		23

3571. ὁμολογία, homologi'a

Book	Oc.	profession	Oc.	confession	Oc.	professed	Total
2 Co.					1	9:13	1
1 Ti.	1	6:12	1	6:13			2
Heb.	3	3:1; 4:14; 10:23					3
Total	4		1		1		6

3572. ὁμολογουμένως homologoumen'ōs

Book	without controversy	Total
1 Ti.	3:16	1

3573. ὁμότεχνος, homot'echnos

Book	of the same craft	Total
Ac.	18:3	1

3574. ὁμοῦ, homou′

Book	together	Total
Jn.	4:36; 20:4; 21:2	3

3575. ὁμόφρων, homoph′rōn

Book	of one mind	Total
1 Pt.	3:8	1

3576. ὅμως, hom′ōs

Book	Oc.	nevertheless	Oc.	and even	Oc.	though it be but	Total
Jn.	1	12:42					1
1 Co.			1	14:7			1
Gal.					1	3:15	1
Total	1		1		1		3

3577. ὄναρ, on′ar

Book	dream	Total
Mt.	1:20; 2:12, 13, 19, 22; 27:19	6

3578. ὀνάριον, onar′ion

Book	young ass	Total
Jn.	12:14	1

3579. ὀνειδίζω, oneidid′zō

Book	Oc.	upbraid	Oc.	reproach	Oc.	revile	Oc.	cast in (one's) teeth	Oc.	suffer reproach	Total
Mt.	1	11:20			1	5:11	1	27:44			3
Mk.	1	16:14			1	15:32					2
Lk.			1	6:22							1
Ro.			1	15:3							1
1 Ti.									1	4:10	1
Jas.	1	1:5									1
1 Pt.			1	4:14							1
Total	3		3		2		1		1		10

3580. ὀνειδισμός, oneidismos′

Book	reproach	Total
Ro.	15:3	1
1 Ti.	3:7	1
Heb.	10:33; 11:26; 13:13	3
Total		5

3581. ὄνειδος, on′eidos

Book	reproach	Total
Lk.	1:25	1

3582. Ὀνήσιμος, Onē′simos

Book	Onesimus	Total
Col.	4:9	1
Phe.	1:10	1
Total		2

3583. Ὀνησίφορος, Onēsiph′oros

Book	Onesiphorus	Total
2 Ti.	1:16; 4:19	2

3585. ὀνίνημι, onin′ēmi

Book	have joy	Total
Phe.	1:20	1

3584. ὀνικός, onikos′

Book	millstone (with 3358)	Total
Mt.	18:6	1
Lk.	17:2	1
Total		2

3586. ὄνομα, on′oma

Book	Oc.	name	Oc.	named	Oc.	called	Oc.	surname (with 2007)	Oc.	named (with 2564)	Oc.	Not Tr.	Total
Mt.	22	1:21, 23, 25; 6:9; 7:22, 22, 22; 10:2, 22, 41, 41, 42; 12:21; 18:5, 20; 19:29; 21:9; 23:39; 24:5, 9; 27:32; 28:19	1	27:57									23
Mk.	13	5:9, 9, 22; 6:14; 9:37, 38, 39, 41; 11:9, 10; 13:6, 13; 16:17	1	14:32			2	3:16, 17					16
Lk.	25	1:5b, 13, 27, 27, 31, 49, 59, 61, 63; 2:21, 25; 6:22; 8:30; 9:48, 49; 10:17, 20; 11:2; 13:35; 19:38; 21:8, 12, 17; 24:18, 47	7	1:5a, 26; 5:27; 8:41; 10:38; 16:20; 23:50	1	24:13			1	19:2			34
Jn.	24	1:6, 12; 2:23; 3:18; 5:43, 43; 10:3, 25; 12:13, 28; 14:13, 14, 26; 15:16, 21; 16:23, 24, 26; 17:6, 11, 12, 26; 18:10; 20:31	1	3:1									25
Ac.	39	1:15; 2:21, 38; 3:6, 16, 16; 4:7, 10, 12, 17, 18, 30; 5:28, 40, 41; 8:12, 16; 9:14, 15, 16, 21, 27, 29; 10:43, 48; 13:6, 8; 15:14, 17, 26; 16:18; 18:15; 19:5, 13, 17; 21:13; 22:16; 26:9; 28:7	18	5:1, 34; 9:10, 12, 33, 36; 11:28; 12:13; 16:1, 14; 17:34; 18:2, 7, 24; 19:24; 20:9; 21:10; 27:1	3	8:9; 9:11; 10:1							60
Ro.	5	1:5; 2:24; 9:17; 10:13; 15:9											5
1 Co.	6	1:2, 10, 13, 15; 5:4; 6:11											6
Eph.	2	1:21; 5:20											2
Phl.	4	2:9, 9, 10; 4:3											4
Col.	1	3:17											1
2 Th.	2	1:12; 3:6											2
1 Ti.	1	6:1											1
2 Ti.	1	2:19											1
Heb.	4	1:4; 2:12; 6:10; 13:15											4
Jas.	3	2:7; 5:10, 14											3
1 Pt.	1	4:14											1
1 Jn.	4	2:12; 3:23; 5:13, 13											4
3 Jn.	2	1:7, 14											2
Rev.	35	2:3, 13, 17; 3:1, 4, 5, 5, 8, 12, 12, 12; 6:8; 8:11; 9:11, 11; 11:18; 13:1, 6, 8, 17, 17; 14:1, 11; 15:2, 4; 16:9; 17:3, 5, 8; 19:12, 13, 16; 21:12, 14; 22:4									1	11:13	36
Total	194		28		4		2		1		1		230

3587. ὀνομάζω, onomad′zō

Book	Oc.	name	Oc.	call	Total
Lk.	2	6:13, 14			2
Ac.			1	19:13	1
Ro.	1	15:20			1
1 Co.	1	5:1	1	5:11	2
Eph.	3	1:21; 3:15; 5:3			3
2 Ti.	1	2:19			1
Total	8		2		10

3588. ὄνος, on′os

Book	ass	Total
Mt.	21:2, 5, 7	3
Lk.	13:15; 14:5	2
Jn.	12:15	1
Total		6

3590. ὄξος, ox′os

Book	vinegar	Total
Mt.	27:34, 48	2
Mk.	15:36	1
Lk.	23:36	1
Jn.	19:29, 29, 30	3
Total		7

3589. ὄντως, on′tōs

Book	Oc.	indeed	Oc.	certainly	Oc.	of a truth	Oc.	verily	Oc.	clean	Total
Mk.	1	11:32									1
Lk.	1	24:34	1	23:47							2
Jn.	1	8:36									1
1 Co.					1	14:25					1
Gal.							1	3:21			1
1 Ti.	3	5:3, 5, 16									3
2 Pt.									1	2:18	1
Total	6		1		1		1		1		10

3591. ὀξύς, oxus′

Book	Oc.	sharp	Oc.	swift	Total
Ro.			1	3:15	1
Rev.	7	1:16; 2:12; 14:14, 17, 18, 18; 19:15			7
Total	7		1		8

3592. ὀπή, opē′

Book	Oc.	cave	Oc.	place	Total
Heb.	1	11:38			1
Jas.			1	3:11	1
Total	1		1		2

3593. ὄπισθεν, op′isthen

Book	Oc.	behind	Oc.	after	Oc.	backside	Total
Mt.	1	9:20	1	15:23			2
Mk.	1	5:27					1
Lk.	1	8:44	1	23:26			2
Rev.	1	4:6			1	5:1	2
Total	4		2		1		7

3595. ὁπλίζω, hoplid′zō

Book	arm (one's) self with	Total
1 Pt.	4:1	1

3596. ὅπλον, hop′lon

Book	Oc.	weapon	Oc.	instrument	Oc.	armour	Total
Jn.	1	18:3					1
Ro.			2	6:13, 13	1	13:12	3
2 Co.	1	10:4			1	6:7	2
Total	2		2		2		6

3594. ὀπίσω, opis′ō

Book	Oc.	after	Oc.	behind	Oc.	back (with 1519 and 3488)	Oc.	back	Oc.	follow	Oc.	backward (with 1519 and 3488)	Total
Mt.	3	3:11; 10:38; 16:24	1	16:23			1	24:18	1	4:19			6
Mk.	4	1:7, 17, 20; 8:34	1	8:33	1	13:16							6
Lk.	4	9:23; 14:27; 19:14; 21:8	2	4:8; 7:38	2	9:62; 17:31							8
Jn.	4	1:15, 27, 30; 12:19			2	6:66; 20:14					1	18:6	7
Ac.	2	5:37; 20:30											2
Phl.			1	3:13									1
1 Ti.	1	5:15											1
2 Pt.	1	2:10											1
Jd.	1	1:7											1
Rev.	2	12:15; 13:3	1	1:10									3
Total	22		6		5		1		1		1		36

3597. ὁποῖος, hopoi′os

Book	Oc.	what manner of	Oc.	such as	Oc.	of what sort	Oc.	whatsoever (with 4118)	Oc.	what manner of man	Total
Ac.			1	26:29							1
1 Co.					1	3:13					1
Gal.							1	2:6			1
1 Th.	1	1:9									1
Jas.									1	1:24	1
Total	1		1		1		1		1		5

3598. ὁπότε, hopot′e

Book	when	Total
Lk.	6:3	1

3600. ὀπτασία, optasi′a

Book	vision	Total
Lk.	1:22; 24:23	2
Ac.	26:19	1
2 Co.	12:1	1
Total		4

3599. ὅπου, hop′ou

Book	Oc.	where	Oc.	whither	Oc.	whithersoever (with 302)	Oc.	wheresoever (with 302)	Oc.	wheresoever (with 1437)	Oc.	whereas	Oc.	Not Tr.	Oc.	Misc.	Total
Mt.	10	6:19, 19, 20, 20, 21; 13:5; 25:24, 26; 26:57; 28:6							2	24:28; 26:13					1	8:19	13
Mk.	11	2:4; 4:5, 15; 5:40; 6:55; 9:44, 46, 48; 13:14; 14:14b; 16:6			1	6:56	3	9:18; 14:9, 14a							1	6:10	16
Lk.	3	12:33, 34; 22:11			1	9:57									1	17:37	5
Jn.	22	1:28; 3:8; 4:20, 46; 6:23, 62; 7:34, 36, 42; 10:40; 11:30, 32; 12:1, 26; 14:3; 17:24; 18:1; 19:18, 20, 41; 20:12, 19	8	8:21, 22; 13:33, 36; 14:4; 18:20; 21:18, 18													30
Ac.	1	17:1															1
Ro.	1	15:20															1
1 Co.											1	3:3					1
Col.	1	3:11															1
Heb.	2	9:16; 10:18	1	6:20													3
Jas.	1	3:16			1	3:4											2
2 Pt.											1	2:11					1
Rev.	6	2:13, 13; 11:8; 12:6, 14; 20:10			1	14:4							1	17:9			8
Total	58		9		4		3		2		2		1		3		82

Miscellaneous: Mt. 8:19 (with 1437), whithersoever; Mk. 6:10 (with 1437), in what place soever; Lk. 17:37, wheresoever.

3601. ὄπτομαι, op'tomai

Book	Oc.	see	Oc.	appear	Oc.	look	Oc.	shew (one's) self	Oc.	being seen	Total
Mt.	7	5:8; 24:30; 26:64; 27:4, 24; 28:7, 10	1	17:3							8
Mk.	3	13:26; 14:62; 16:7	1	9:4							4
Lk.	4	3:6; 13:28; 17:22; 21:27	4	1:11; 9:31; 22:43; 24:34							8
Jn.	8	1:50, 51; 3:36; 11:40; 16:16, 17, 19, 22			1	19:37					9
Ac.	3	2:17; 13:31; 20:25	8	2:3; 7:2, 30, 35; 9:17; 16:9; 26:16, 16	1	18:15	1	7:26	1	1:3	14
Ro.	1	15:21									1
1 Co.	4	15:5, 6, 7, 8									4
1 Ti.	1	3:16									1
Heb.	2	12:14; 13:23	1	9:28							3
1 Jn.	1	3:2									1
Rev.	3	1:7; 11:19; 22:4	2	12:1, 3							5
Total	37		17		2		1		1		58

3602. ὀπτός, optos'

Book	broiled	Total
Lk.	24:42	1

3603. ὀπώρα, opō'ra

Book	fruit	Total
Rev.	18:14	1

3605. ὅραμα, hor'ama

Book	Oc.	vision	Oc.	sight	Total
Mt.	1	17:9			1
Ac.	10	9:10, 12; 10:3, 17, 19; 11:5; 12:9; 16: 9, 10; 18:9	1	7:31	11
Total	11		1		12

3604. ὅπως, hop'ōs

Book	Oc.	that	Oc.	how	Oc.	to	Oc.	so that	Oc.	when	Oc.	because	Total
Mt.	15	2:8, 23; 5:16, 45; 6:2, 4, 5, 16, 18; 8:17, 34; 9:38; 12: 17; 13:35; 23:35	2	12:14; 22: 15	1	26:59							18
Mk.	1	5:23	1	3:6									2
Lk.	4	2:35; 7:3; 10:2; 16:28	1	24:20	1	11:37	1	16:26					7
Jn.	1	11:57											1
Ac.	11	8:15, 24; 9:2, 12, 17; 15:17; 23:15, 20; 24:26; 25:3, 26			2	9:24; 23: 23			1	3:19	1	20:16	15
Ro.	3	3:4; 9:17, 17											3
1 Co.	1	1:29											1
2 Co.	2	8:11, 14											2
Gal.	1	1:4											1
2 Th.	1	1:12											1
Phe.	1	1:6											1
Heb.	2	2:9; 9:15											2
Jas.	1	5:16											1
1 Pt.	1	2:9											1
Total	45		4		4		1		1		1		56

3606. ὅρασις, hor'asis

Book	Oc.	vision	Oc.	in sight	Oc.	look upon	Total
Ac.	1	2:17					1
Rev.	1	9:17	1	4:3b	1	4:3a	3
Total	2		1		1		4

3607. ὁρατός, horatos'

Book	visible	Total
Col.	1:16	1

3608. ὁράω, hora'ō

Book	Oc.	see	Oc.	take heed	Oc.	behold	Oc.	perceive	Oc.	Not Tr.	Total
Mt.	3	8:4; 9:30; 24:6	2	16:6; 18:10							5
Mk.	1	1:44	1	8:15					1	8:24	3
Lk.	4	1:22; 9:36; 16:23; 24:23	1	12:15	1	23:49					6
Jn.	22	1:18, 34; 3:11, 32; 4:45; 5:37; 6:2, 36, 46, 46; 8:38, 38, 57; 9:37; 14: 7, 9, 9; 15:24; 19:35; 20:18, 25, 29									22
Ac.	2	7:44; 22:15	1	22:26			1	8:23			4
1 Co.	1	9:1									1
Col.	2	2:1, 18									2
1 Th.	1	5:15									1
Heb.	3	2:8; 8:5; 11:27									3
Jas.	1	2:24									1
1 Pt.	1	1:8									1
1 Jn.	6	1:1, 2, 3; 3:6; 4:20, 20									6
3 Jn.	1	1:11									1
Rev.	3	18:18; 19:10; 22:9									3
Total	51		5		1		1		1		59

3609. ὀργή, orgē'

Book	Oc.	wrath	Oc.	anger	Oc.	vengeance	Oc.	indignation	Total
Mt.	1	3:7							1
Mk.			1	3:5					1
Lk.	2	3:7; 21:23							2
Jn.	1	3:36							1
Ro.	11	1:18; 2:5, 5, 8; 4:15; 5:9; 9:22, 22; 12:19; 13:4, 5			1	3:5			12
Eph.	2	2:3; 5:6	1	4:31					3
Col.	1	3:6	1	3:8					2
1 Th.	3	1:10; 2:16; 5:9							3
1 Ti.	1	2:8							1
Heb.	2	3:11; 4:3							2
Jas.	2	1:19, 20							2
Rev.	5	6:16, 17; 11:18; 16:19; 19:15					1	14:10	6
Total	31		3		1		1		36

3610. ὀργίζω, orgid'zō

Book	Oc.	be angry	Oc.	be wroth	Total
Mt.	1	5:22	2	18:34; 22:7	3
Lk.	2	14:21; 15:28			2
Eph.	1	4:26			1
Rev.	1	11:18	1	12:17	2
Total	5		3		8

3613. ὀρέγομαι, oreg'omai

Book	Oc.	desire	Oc.	covet after	Total
1 Ti.	1	3:1	1	6:10	2
Heb.	1	11:16			1
Total	2		1		3

3611. ὀργίλος, orgi'los

Book	soon angry	Total
Tit.	1:7	1

3612. ὀργυιά, orguia'

Book	fathom	Total
Ac.	27:28, 28	2

3614. ὀρεινός, oreinos'

Book	hill	Total
Lk.	1:39, 65	2

3615. ὄρεξις, or'exis

Book	lust	Total
Ro.	1:27	1

3616. ὀρθοποδέω, orthopode'ō

Book	walk uprightly	Total
Gal.	2:14	1

3617. ὀρθός, orthos'

Book	Oc.	upright	Oc.	straight	Total
Ac.	1	14:10			1
Heb.			1	12:13	1
Total	1		1		2

3618. ὀρθοτομέω, orthotome'ō

Book	rightly divide	Total
2 Ti.	2:15	1

3619. ὀρθρίζω, orthrid'zō

Book	come early in the morning	Total
Lk.	21:38	1

3620. ὀρθρινός, orthrinos'

Book	morning	Total
Rev.	22:16	1

3621. ὄρθριος, or'thrios

Book	early	Total
Lk.	24:22	1

3622. ὄρθρος, or'thros

Book	early in the morning	Total
Lk.	24:1	1
Jn.	8:2	1
Ac.	5:21	1
Total		3

3623. ὀρθῶς, orthōs'

Book	Oc.	rightly	Oc.	plain	Oc.	right	Total
Mk.			1	7:35			1
Lk.	2	7:43; 20:21			1	10:28	3
Total	2		1		1		4

3625. ὅριον, hor'ion

Book	Oc.	coast	Oc.	border	Total
Mt.	5	2:16; 8:34; 15:22, 39; 19:1	1	4:13	6
Mk.	4	5:17; 7:31, 31; 10:1			4
Ac.	1	13:50			1
Total	10		1		11

3624. ὁρίζω, horid'zō

Book	Oc.	determine	Oc.	ordain	Oc.	as it was determined (with 2596 and 3488)	Oc.	declare	Oc.	limit	Oc.	determinate	Total
Lk.					1	22:22							1
Ac.	2	11:29; 17:26	2	10:42; 17:31							1	2:23	5
Ro.							1	1:4					1
Heb.									1	4:7			1
Total	2		2		1		1		1		1		8

3626. ὁρκίζω, horkid'zō

Book	Oc.	adjure	Oc.	charge	Total
Mk.	1	5:7			1
Ac.	1	19:13			1
1 Th.			1	5:27	1
Total	2		1		3

3627. ὅρκος, hor'kos

Book	oath	Total
Mt.	5:33; 14:7, 9; 26:72	4
Mk.	6:26	1
Lk.	1:73	1
Ac.	2:30	1
Heb.	6:16, 17	2
Jas.	5:12	1
Total		10

3628. ὁρκωμοσία, horkōmosi'a

Book	oath	Total
Heb.	7:20, 21, 21, 28	4

3631. ὅρμημα, hor'mẹma

Book	violence	Total
Rev.	18:21	1

3629. ὁρμάω, horma'ō

Book	Oc.	run violently	Oc.	run	Oc.	rush	Total
Mt.	1	8:32					1
Mk.	1	5:13					1
Lk.	1	8:33					1
Ac.			1	7:57	1	19:29	2
Total	3		1		1		5

3630. ὁρμή, hormẹ'

Book	Oc.	assault	Oc.	Not Tr.	Total
Ac.	1	14:5			1
Jas.			1	3:4	1
Total	1		1		2

3632. ὄρνεον, or'neon

Book	Oc.	fowl	Oc.	bird	Total
Rev.	2	19:17, 21	1	18:2	3

3633. ὄρνις, or'nis

Book	hen	Total
Mt.	23:37	1
Lk.	13:34	1
Total		2

3634. ὁροθεσία, horothesi'a

Book	bound	Total
Ac.	17:26	1

3635. ὄρος, or'os

Book	Oc.	mountain	Oc.	mount	Oc.	hill	Total
Mt.	12	4:8; 5:1; 8:1; 14:23; 15:29; 17:1, 9, 20; 18:12; 21:21; 24:16; 28:16	3	21:1; 24:3; 26:30	1	5:14	16
Mk.	8	3:13; 5:5, 11; 6:46; 9:2, 9; 11:23; 13:14	3	11:1; 13:3; 14:26			11
Lk.	7	3:5; 4:5; 6:12; 8:32; 9:28; 21:21; 23:30	4	19:29, 37; 21:37; 22:39	2	4:29; 9:37	13
Jn.	4	4:20, 21; 6:3, 15	1	8:1			5
Ac.			3	1:12; 7:30, 38			3
1 Co.	1	13:2					1
Gal.			2	4:24, 25			2
Heb.	2	11:38; 12:20	3	8:5; 12:18, 22			5
2 Pt.			1	1:18			1
Rev.	7	6:14, 15, 16; 8:8; 16:20; 17:9; 21:10	1	14:1			8
Total	41		21		3		65

3636. ὀρύσσω, orus'sō

Book	dig	Total
Mt.	21:33; 25:18	2
Mk.	12:1	1
Total		3

3638. ὀρχέομαι, orche'omai

Book	dance	Total
Mt.	11:17; 14:6	2
Mk.	6:22	1
Lk.	7:32	1
Total		4

3637. ὀρφανός, orphanos'

Book	Oc.	comfortless	Oc.	fatherless	Total
Jn.	1	14:18			1
Jas.			1	1:27	1
Total	1		1		2

3639a. ὅς, ἥ, ὅ, hos, hẹ, ho

Book	Oc.	which	Oc.	whom	Oc.	that	Oc.	who	Oc.	whose	Oc.	what
Mt.	22	1:23; 2:9, 16; 11:4, 10b; 12:2, 4; 13:17, 17, 23, 31, 32, 33a, 44, 48; 15:13; 18:23, 28; 21:24, 42; 27:56, 60	16	1:16; 3:17; 7:9; 11:10a; 12:18, 18; 17:5; 18:7; 19:11; 20:23b; 23:35; 24:45, 46; 26:24; 27:9, 15	13	8:4; 10:26; 12:11; 13:12; 19:29; 20:22, 22, 23a; 21:15; 24:2, 50b; 26:13; 27:33	2	13:46; 27:57	2	3:11, 12	6	7:2, 2; 10:27, 27; 19:6; 20:15
Mk.	19	1:2, 44; 2:26; 3:17; 4:31; 5:41; 7:4, 13; 9:39; 11:21, 23b; 12:10, 42; 13:19; 14:32; 15:22, 34, 43, 46	10	1:11; 3:13; 6:16; 10:40; 13:20; 14:21, 71; 15:12, 40; 16:9	12	7:11a, 15, 34; 10:29, 38, 38, 39, 39; 13:2; 14:9, 72; 15:42	3	4:16; 5:3; 15:41	2	1:7; 7:25	5	4:24; 5:33; 10:9; 13:37; 14:8
Lk.	60	1:73; 2:11, 15, 31, 37, 50; 3:19; 5:3, 9, 10, 17, 18, 21; 6:2, 4, 16, 17, 46, 49; 7:27b; 8:2, 13, 13, 27; 9:27, 31b, 36, 43; 10:24, 24, 30, 39; 11:27; 12:20, 24; 13:14, 19, 21a, 30, 30; 15:9; 16:1, 20; 17:12, 31; 19:20, 30a; 20:17, 47; 21:6a, 6b, 15; 23:27, 29a, 29c; 24:1, 10, 19, 23, 44	21	6:13, 14, 34; 7:4, 27a, 43, 47b; 8:2, 35, 38; 9:9; 12:37, 42, 43, 48b; 13:4, 16; 17:1; 19:15; 22:22; 23:25	24	1:61; 2:20; 5:29; 6:38; 7:49; 8:17, 17; 10:23; 12:2, 2; 14:15, 33; 15:16; 18:29; 19:21, 21, 22, 22, 26, 37; 21:6c; 23:29b; 24:17, 25	4	7:2; 9:31a; 18:30; 23:51	6	1:27; 2:25; 3:16, 17; 13:1; 24:18	6	6:3; 7:22; 8:47; 9:33; 12:12; 22:60
Jn.	53	1:9, 13, 30b, 38, 41, 42; 2:22, 23; 4:12, 29, 53; 5:28, 32, 36a; 6:2, 9, 13, 27, 39, 51b; 7:31, 39; 8:26, 38, 38, 40b; 9:7; 10:6, 16, 29; 12:38; 14:24; 15:3, 24, 26b; 17:4, 5, 6, 8, 22, 24b; 18:1, 9, 9, 11, 13, 16, 32; 19:17; 20:16, 30; 21:10, 20b	32	1:26, 30a, 45, 47; 3:26b; 4:18; 5:21, 38, 45; 6:29; 7:25, 28; 8:54; 10:35, 36; 11:3; 12:1, 9; 13:18, 23, 24, 26;14:17, 26a; 15:26a; 17:3, 11, 24a; 19:26; 20:2; 21:7, 20a	31	1:3; 3:2, 11, 11; 4:5, 14b, 14c, 32, 45, 50; 5:20, 36b; 6:14, 37, 51a, 63, 64; 7:3; 8:40a; 9:24; 10:25; 12:48; 13:27, 29; 14:10, 12; 15:15, 20; 16:17, 18; 20:7	1	9:19	6	1:27b; 4:46; 6:42; 10:12; 11:2; 18:26	7	3:32; 4:22, 22; 11:46; 13:7; 18:21; 19:22
Ac.	54	1:4, 7, 11a, 12, 16, 25; 2:22, 33; 3:18, 21b, 25; 4:36; 6:14; 7:17, 18b, 20a, 40b, 43, 45a; 8:6, 24, 32; 9:36, 36; 10:17, 36, 37, 39a; 11:6, 30; 13:7, 22b; 14:15, 26; 15:10, 29; 16:2; 17:31a, 34; 20:24, 28, 28, 38; 22:10; 24:14, 15; 25:7; 26:7, 7, 10, 16, 16; 27:17, 39	61	1:2b, 3; 2:24, 36; 3:2, 13, 15a, 16, 21a; 4:10, 10, 22, 27; 5:25, 30, 32, 36a; 6:3, 6; 7:35, 39, 45b, 52; 8:10; 9:5; 10:39b; 13:22a, 37; 14:23; 15:17, 24; 17:3, 7, 23b, 31b; 19:13, 16, 25, 27; 20:25; 21:16, 29; 22:5, 8; 23:29; 24:6b, 8a; 25:15, 16, 18, 19, 24, 26; 26:15, 17, 26; 27:23b; 28:4, 8, 15, 23	8	1:22; 7:16, 44; 19:35; 21:11, 23, 26; 24:21	20	1:23; 3:3; 5:36b; 7:38, 46; 8:27a; 10:32b, 38; 11:14a, 23; 14:8, 9, 16; 16:24; 18:27; 21:32; 24:6a, 19; 28:7, 10	8	10:5, 6, 32a; 13:6, 25; 16:14; 18:7; 27:23a	6	8:30; 10:15; 11:9; 14:11; 22:15; 28:22
Ro.	11	1:2, 27; 3:30; 6:17; 7:15, 16, 19b; 9:23; 10:8; 11:2; 16:17	25	1:5, 6, 9; 3:25; 4:6, 8, 17, 24; 5:2a, 11; 6:16, 16; 8:29, 30, 30, 30; 9:4, 5b, 18, 18, 24; 10:14, 14; 14:15; 16:4	9	2:23; 5:12; 6:10, 10; 7:19a, 20; 8:3, 25, 32	10	1:25; 2:6; 4:16, 18, 25; 5:14; 8:34, 34; 16:5, 7	6	2:29; 3:8, 14; 4:7, 7; 9:5a	4	4:21; 7:15, 15; 8:24
1 Co.	15	2:7, 8, 9, 13; 3:11, 14; 6:19; 10:16, 16, 20; 12:23; 15:1a, 1b, 2, 31	9	1:9; 3:5; 7:39; 8:6, 6, 11; 10:11; 15:6, 15	6	2:16; 4:7; 6:5; 10:13b; 14:37; 15:9	6	1:8, 30; 4:5, 17, 17; 10:13a			3	7:36; 10:15; 15:10
2 Co.	12	1:6; 2:4; 9:2; 10:8, 13; 11:4, 4, 17; 12:4, 21; 13:3, 10	9	1:10b; 2:3, 10, 10; 4:4a; 8:22; 10:18; 11:4a; 12:17	2	1:17; 5:10	4	1:10a; 3:6; 4:4b; 10:1	2	8:18; 11:15	2	1:13; 11:12a
Gal.	10	1:7, 20, 23; 2:2, 4, 10, 18, 20; 3:16; 5:21	5	1:5; 2:5; 3:19b; 4:19b; 6:14	2	1:9; 3:10			1	3:1		
Eph.	9	1:9, 14, 20; 2:10; 3:5, 11; 4:15; 6:17, 20	11	1:7, 11, 13, 13; 2:3, 21, 22; 3:12, 15; 4:16; 6:22	1	3:20	1	5:5				
Phl.	3	2:5; 3:12; 4:9	3	2:15; 3:8, 18			2	2:6; 3:21	3	3:19, 19; 4:3		
Col.	13	1:23a, 24, 27b; 2:10, 14, 17, 19, 22; 3:7, 15, 25; 4:3, 17	7	1:14, 27a, 28; 2:3, 11; 4:8, 10			5	1:7, 13, 15, 18; 4:9				
1 Th.	1	2:13	1	1:10			1	5:24				
2 Th.	4	1:5; 2:15; 3:6, 17	1	2:8	1	1:4	1	3:3	1	2:9		
1 Ti.	8	1:11, 19; 2:10; 4:3, 14; 6:10, 15, 21	5	1:15, 20, 20; 6:16, 16			2	2:4; 4:10			1	1:7
2 Ti.	4	1:6b, 12a, 13; 4:8	6	1:3, 12b, 15; 2:17; 4:15, 18	1	4:13					1	2:7
Tit.	4	1:2, 3; 3:5, 6					1	2:14	1	1:11		
Phe.	1	1:5	3	1:10, 12, 13								
Heb.	25	2:11, 13; 6:10, 18, 19; 7:2b, 13b, 14, 19; 8:2; 9:5, 7, 9, 20; 10:1, 10, 20, 32; 11:4, 7, 8, 29; 12:14, 19; 13:9	17	1:2, 2; 2:10, 10; 4:13; 5:11; 6:7; 7:2a, 4, 13a; 11:18, 38; 12:6, 6, 7; 13:21, 23	4	2:18; 8:9, 10; 10:16	9	1:3; 5:7; 7:16, 27; 8:1; 9:14; 11:33; 12:2, 16	7	3:6, 17; 6:8; 11:10; 12:26; 13:7, 11		
Jas.	2	1:12b; 2:5	1	1:17	3	1:12a; 4:5, 12	1	5:10				
1 Pt.	7	1:10, 12b; 2:7, 8a; 3:4, 19; 4:11a	6	1:8, 8, 12a; 2:4; 4:11b; 5:9			5	2:22, 23, 24a; 3:22; 4:5	3	2:24b; 3:3, 6		
2 Pt.	4	3:1, 10, 16, 16	4	1:17; 2:2, 17, 19			1	2:15	1	2:3		
1 Jn.	11	1:1b, 1c, 1d, 5; 2:7, 7, 8, 24a, 27; 3:24; 5:9	2	4:20, 20	7	3:11; 4:2, 3a, 16; 5:10, 14, 15b						
2 Jn.			1	1:1								
3 Jn.	2	1:6a, 10	2	1:1, 6b								
Jd.	2	1:15, 15	1	1:13								
Rev.	39	1:1a, 4, 20, 20; 2:6, 7, 8, 17; 3:4; 4:1a, 5; 5:6, 8, 13a; 6:9; 7:9; 8:2; 9:14, 20, 20; 10:4, 5, 8; 12:16; 13:2, 4, 14, 14; 14:4; 17:12, 15, 16, 18; 18:6; 19:20; 20:2, 12; 21:8, 12	3	7:2; 17:2; 20:8	5	3:2; 17:8a, 11; 19:12; 21:17	5	1:2; 2:13b, 14; 10:6; 12:5	4	13:8, 12; 17:8b; 20:11	1	1:11
Total	395		262		129		84		53		42	

3639a. ὅς, ἥ, ὅ, hos, hę, ho (continued)

Book	Oc.	that which	Oc.	whereof	Oc.	the things which	Oc.	wherewith	Oc.	he that	Oc.	whereunto	Oc.	when	Oc.	those things which	Oc.	wherein
Mt.	1	25:29							1	10:38			1	24:50a				
Mk.	2	2:24; 4:25c							2	4:25b; 9:40								
Lk.	3	8:18c; 12:3b; 17:10	1	23:14					1	9:50			3	12:40, 46, 46			1	1:25
Jn.					1	11:45	2	13:5; 17:26	1	3:26a								
Ac.			6	2:32; 3:15b; 21:24; 24:8b; 25:11; 26:2	1	4:20					2	13:2; 27:8	2	9:39; 12:4	1	26:22		
Ro.	1	11:7													1	15:18		
1 Co.	5	4:6; 11:23a; 15:3, 36, 37															1	7:20
2 Co.	1	12:6					3	1:4; 7:7; 10:2									1	12:13
Gal.	1	1:8					1	5:1			1	4:9						
Eph.			1	3:7			2	2:4; 4:1									1	1:8
Phl.																		
Col.			3	1:5, 23b, 25											1	2:18		
1 Th.							1	3:9										
2 Th.					1	3:4												
1 Ti.											1	4:6						
2 Ti.					1	3:14												
Tit.					1	2:1												
Phe.																		
Heb.			1	12:8	1	5:8												
Jas.																		
1 Pt.											1	3:21						
2 Pt.									1	1:9	1	1:19a						
1 Jn.	3	1:1a, 3; 2:24b	1	4:3b					1	4:6								
2 Jn.	1	1:5													1	1:8		
3 Jn.																		
Jd.																		
Rev.	2	2:25a; 3:11			4	1:19, 19, 19; 22:6									1	2:10		
Total	20		13		10		9		7		6		6		5		4	

3639a. ὅς, ἥ, ὅ, hos, hē, ho (continued)

Book	Oc.	and	Oc.	such as	Oc.	what things	Oc.	and he	Oc.	whence	Oc.	things which	Oc.	Not Tr.	Oc.	Misc.	Total
Mt.			1	24:44	1	6:8									1	23:37	67
Mk.					1	9:9	1	9:38							1	15:16	58
Lk.	1	6:48											6	1:26; 8:41; 11:6; 17:7; 23:41; 24:13	7	7:45; 12:1, 10, 48a; 13:34; 17:29, 30	144
Jn.													1	1:27a	10	1:15; 3:34; 4:38; 5:4; 12:50; 14:26b; 17:2, 9, 12; 19:37	145
Ac.	3	7:20b; 8:27b; 9:33	1	3:6	1	21:19	1	13:31							9	1:11b, 24; 6:10; 7:28, 40a; 9:17; 10:21a; 13:39; 22:4	184
Ro.													1	16:27	4	14:22, 23; 15:21a, 21b	72
1 Co.															3	4:2; 10:30; 11:23b	48
2 Co.													1	4:6			37
Gal.																	21
Eph.																	26
Phl.									1	3:20					1	4:11	13
Col.															3	1:6, 9; 3:6	32
1 Th.																	4
2 Th.																	9
1 Ti.															1	1:6	18
2 Ti.															2	2:2; 3:8	15
Tit.																	7
Phe.																	4
Heb.									1	11:15					1	8:3	66
Jas.																	7
1 Pt.															1	1:12c	23
2 Pt.															1	2:12	13
1 Jn.																	25
2 Jn.																	3
3 Jn.																	4
Jd.																	3
Rev.			1	5:13b							2	1:1b; 4:1b			1	2:15	68
Total	4		3		3		2		2		2		9		46		1116

Miscellaneous: Mt. 23:37 (with 5058), even as; Mk. 15:16 (with 2076), called; Lk. 7:45, the time; Lk. 12:1, the meantime; Lk. 12:10 (with 3856), whosoever; Lk. 12:48a (with 3856), whomsoever; Lk. 13:34 (with 5058), as; Lk. 17:29, the same; Lk. 17:30 (with 2250), in the day when; Jn. 1:15, he of whom; Jn. 3:34, he whom; Jn. 4:38, that whereon; Jn. 5:4 (with 1221), whatsoever; Jn. 12:50, whatsoever; Jn. 14:26b (with 3856), whatsoever; Jn. 17:2 (with 3856), as many as; Jn. 17:9, them which; Jn. 17:12, those that; Jn. 19:37, him whom; Ac. 1:11b (with 5058), in like manner; Ac. 1:24 (with 1520), whether; Ac. 6:10, by which; Ac. 7:28 (with 5058), as; Ac. 7:40a, to; Ac. 9:17, as; Ac. 10:21a, he whom; Ac. 13:39, from which; Ac. 22:4, and I; Ro. 14:22, that thing which; Ro. 14:23 (with 3856), whatsoever; Ro. 15:21a, to whom; Ro. 15:21b, they that; 1 Co. 4:2 (with 1161 and 3062), moreover; 1 Co. 10:30, that for which; 1 Co. 11:23b, in which; Phl. 4:11, whatsoever state; Col. 1:6, 9, the; Col. 3:6, which things; 1 Ti. 1:6, from which; 2 Ti. 2:2, the things that; 2 Ti. 3:8 (with 5058), as; Heb. 8:3, somewhat; 1 Pt. 1:12c, which things; 2 Pt. 2:12, the things that; Rev. 2:15, which thing.

3639b. ὅς, ἥ, ὅ, hos, hẹ, ho (with 302)

							with 302 not translated										
Book	Oc.	whosoever	Oc.	whatsoever	Oc.	whomsoever	Oc.	whoso	Oc.	whom	Oc.	till (with 891)	Oc.	he that	Oc.	Misc.	Total
Mt.	15	5:19b, 21, 22, 22, 31, 32a; 12:32, 32; 15:5a; 16:25, 25; 19:9; 23:16, 16, 18b	1	10:11	2	21:44; 26:48	1	18:6									19
Mk.	8	3:35; 8:35, 35, 38; 9:41, 42; 10:44; 11:23a			1	14:44							2	3:29; 4:25a			11
Lk.	6	8:18a, 18b; 9:24, 24, 26; 12:8	4	9:4; 10:5, 8, 10	1	20:18									1	13:25	12
Jn.	1	4:14a							1	1:33					1	5:19	3
Ac.	1	2:21			1	8:19									1	7:3	3
Ro.	1	10:13	1	16:2					2	9:15, 15							4
1 Co.	1	11:27									2	11:26; 15:25					3
2 Co.															1	11:21	1
Gal.															1	5:17	1
Jas.	1	4:4															1
1 Jn.	1	4:15	1	5:15a			2	2:5; 3:17									4
Rev.											1	2:25					1
Total	35		7		5		3		3		3		2		5		63

Miscellaneous: Lk. 13:25 (with 302 not tr. and 575), when once; Jn. 5:19, what things soever; Ac. 7:3 (with 302 not tr.), which; 2 Co. 11:21 (with 1722), wherein soever; Gal. 5:17 (with 302 not tr.), that.

3639c. ὅς, ἥ, ὅ, hos, hẹ, ho (with 1437)

							with 1437 not translated									
Book	Oc.	whosoever	Oc.	whatsoever	Oc.	whom-soever	Oc.	that	Oc.	whom	Oc.	whoso	Oc.	which	Oc.	what	Total
Mt.	8	5:19a, 32b; 10:14, 42; 11:6; 20:26, 27; 23:18a	6	14:7; 15:5b; 16:19, 19; 20:4, 7	1	11:27	2	12:36; 18:19	1	7:9	1	18:5					19
Mk.	5	9:37, 37; 10:11, 15, 43	6	6:22, 23; 7:11b; 10:35; 11:23c; 13:11									1	4:22			12
Lk.	6	7:23; 9:48, 48; 17:33, 33; 18:17			1	4:6			1	10:22							8
Jn.															1	15:7	1
Ac.									1	7:7							1
1 Co.					1	16:3	1	6:18									2
Gal.			1	6:7													1
Eph.			1	6:8													1
1 Jn.			1	3:22													1
3 Jn.			1	1:5													1
Total	19		16		3		3		3		1		1		1		47

3639d. ὅς, ἥ, ὅ, hos, hẹ, ho (as a demonstrative)

Book	Oc.	some	Oc.	one	Oc.	another	Oc.	other	Total
Mt.	4	13:4, 8, 8, 8	2	21:35a; 25:15a	4	21:35b, 35c; 25:15b, 15c			10
Mk.	1	4:4							1
Lk.	1	8:5	1	23:33a			1	23:33b	3
Ac.	2	27:44, 44							2
Ro.			3	9:21a; 14:2, 5a	2	9:21b; 14:5b			5
1 Co.	1	12:28	3	7:7a; 11:21a; 12:8	2	7:7b; 11:21b			6
2 Co.			1	2:16a			1	2:16b	2
2 Ti.	2	2:20, 20							2
Jd.	1	1:22					1	1:23	2
Total	12		10		8		3		33

3639e. ὅς, ἥ, ὅ, hos, hē, ho (with prepositions)

Book	Oc.	wherein (with 1722)	Oc.	(with 1519)	Oc.	(with 1909)	Oc.	(with 1223)	Oc.	(with 3912)	Oc.	whereby (with 1722)	Oc.	(with 1223)	Oc.	(with 3912)	Oc.	(with 4214)
Mt.	2	11:20; 25:13																
Mk.					1	2:4												
Lk.					1	11:22			1	1:4	1	1:78						
Jn.	1	19:41																
Ac.	2	2:8; 10:12	1	7:4							2	4:12; 11:14b			1	19:40		
Ro.	3	2:1; 5:2b; 7:6									2	8:15; 14:21						
1 Co.	2	7:24; 15:1c																
2 Co.	1	11:12b																
Gal.																		
Eph.	3	1:6; 2:2; 5:18									1	4:30					1	3:4
Phl.					1	4:10												
Col.	1	2:12																
2 Th.																		
1 Ti.																		
2 Ti.	1	2:9																
Tit.																		
Phe.																		
Heb.	3	6:17; 9:2, 4											1	12:28				
1 Pt.	2	1:6; 4:4	2	3:20; 5:12														
2 Pt.	1	3:13					1	3:12					2	1:4; 3:6				
Rev.	2	2:13a; 18:19																
Total	24		3		3		1		1		6		3		1		1	

3639e. ὅς, ἥ, ὅ, hos, hē, ho (with prepositions) (continued)

Book	Oc.	wherefore (with 1223 & 156)	Oc.	(with 1223)	Oc.	(with 1519)	Oc.	(with 1909)	Oc.	(with 5384)	Oc.	whereof (with 3912)	Oc.	(with 1537)	Oc.	(with 1909)
Mt.							1	26:50								
Mk.																
Lk.									1	7:47a						
Jn.																
Ac.	1	22:24	2	10:21; 23:28							1	24:13				
Ro.															1	6:21
1 Co.											1	7:1				
2 Co.																
Gal.																
Eph.																
Phl.																
Col.																
2 Th.					1	1:11										
1 Ti.													1	6:4		
2 Ti.	1	1:6a														
Tit.	1	1:13														
Phe.																
Heb.											1	2:5	1	13:10		
1 Pt.																
2 Pt.																
Rev.																
Total	3		2		1		1		1		3		2		1	

3639e. ὅς, ἥ, ὅ, hos, hē, ho (with prepositions) (continued)

Book	Oc.	till (with 2193)	Oc.	whereunto (with 1519)	Oc.	until (with 2193)	Oc.	where (with 1722)	Oc.	whereon (with 1909)	Oc.	since (with 575)	Oc.	because (with 473)	Oc.	till (with 891)	Oc.	while (with 1722)
Mt.	4	1:25; 13:33b; 18:30, 34			1	17:9												
Mk.									1	11:2							1	2:19
Lk.	3	12:50, 59; 13:21b			1	24:49			3	4:29; 5:25; 19:30b	1	24:21	2	1:20b; 19:44			1	5:34
Jn.	1	13:38					1	11:6									1	5:7
Ac.	3	23:12, 21; 25:21			1	23:14	4	4:31; 7:33; 11:11; 15:36			1	24:11	1	12:23	1	7:18a		
Ro.																		
1 Co.																		
2 Co.																		
Gal.															1	3:19a		
Eph.																		
Phl.																		
Col.			1	1:29														
2 Th.			1	2:14									1	2:10				
1 Ti.			2	2:7; 6:12														
2 Ti.			1	1:11														
Tit.																		
Phe.																		
Heb.																		
1 Pt.			1	2:8b														
2 Pt.					1	1:19b					1	3:4						
Rev.					1	6:11					1	16:18			1	7:3		
Total	11		6		5		5		4		4		4		3		3	

3639e. ὅς, ἥ, ὅ, hos, hē, ho (with prepositions) (continued)

Book	Oc.	until the day that (with 891 & 2250)	Oc.	whereas (with 1722)	Oc.	whereupon (with 1722)	Oc.	wherewith (with 1722)	Oc.	until (with 891)	Oc.	while (with 891)	Oc.	while (with 2193)	Oc.	when (with 1722)	Oc.	Misc.	Total
Mt.	1	24:38											2	14:22; 26:36					11
Mk.																	1	13:30	4
Lk.	2	1:20a; 17:27													1	22:7	2	4:18; 12:3a	20
Jn.															1	4:52	2	6:21, 22	7
Ac.					2	24:18; 26:12					1	27:33					6	1:2a, 21; 15:11; 17:23a; 20:18; 27:25	30
Ro.									1	11:25							1	12:3	8
1 Co.																			3
2 Co.																			1
Gal.									1	4:19a									2
Eph.							1	6:16											6
Phl.																	1	3:16	2
Col.																			2
2 Th.																			3
1 Ti.																			3
2 Ti.																			3
Tit.																			1
Phe.																	1	1:21	1
Heb.							1	10:29			1	3:13							8
1 Pt.			2	2:12; 3:16															7
2 Pt.																			6
Rev.																	1	2:15	6
Total	3		2		2		2		2		2		2		2		15		134

Miscellaneous: Mk. 13:30 (with 3260), till; Lk. 4:18 (with 1752), because; Lk. 12:3a (with 473), therefore; Jn. 6:21 (with 1519), whither; Jn. 6:22 (with 1519), whereinto; Ac. 1:2a (with 891 and 2250), until the day in which; Ac. 1:21 (with 1722), that; Ac. 15:11 (with 2596 and 5058), even as; Ac. 17:23a (with 1722), with; Ac. 20:18 (with 575), that; Ac. 27:25 (with 2596), even as; Ro. 12:3 (with 3744), more than; Phl. 3:16 (with 1519), whereto; Phe. 1:21 (with 5128), more than; Rev. 2:15, which thing.

Word 3639 has 1393 occurrences.

3640. ὁσάκις, hosak'is

Book	Oc.	as often as (with 302)	Oc.	as often as (with 1437)	Oc.	as oft as (with 302)	Total
1 Co.	1	11:26			1	11:25	2
Rev.			1	11:6			1
Total	1		1		1		3

3641. ὅσιος, hos'ios

Book	Oc.	holy	Oc.	Holy One	Oc.	mercies	Oc.	shall be	Total
Ac.			2	2:27; 13:35	1	13:34			3
1 Ti.	1	2:8							1
Tit.	1	1:8							1
Heb.	1	7:26							1
Rev.	1	15:4					1	16:5	2
Total	4		2		1		1		8

3642. ὁσιότης, hosiot'ēs

Book	holiness	Total
Lk.	1:75	1
Eph.	4:24	1
Total		2

See page 258 for Word 3645.

3643. ὁσίως, hosi'ōs

Book	holily	Total
1 Th.	2:10	1

3646. ὅσπερ, hos'per

Book	whomsoever	Total
Mk.	15:6	1

See page 263 for Word 3648.

3644. ὀσμή, osmē'

Book	Oc.	savour	Oc.	odour	Total
Jn.			1	12:3	1
2 Co.	3	2:14, 16, 16			3
Eph.	1	5:2			1
Phl.			1	4:18	1
Total	4		2		6

3650. ὄσφρησις, os'phrēsis

Book	smelling	Total
1 Co.	12:17	1

3651. ὀσφύς, osphus'

Book	loins	Total
Mt.	3:4	1
Mk.	1:6	1
Lk.	12:35	1
Ac.	2:30	1
Eph.	6:14	1
Heb.	7:5, 10	2
1 Pt.	1:13	1
Total		8

3647. ὀστέον, oste'on

Book	bone	Total
Mt.	23:27	1
Lk.	24:39	1
Jn.	19:36	1
Eph.	5:30	1
Heb.	11:22	1
Total		5

3649. ὀστράκινος, ostra'kinos

Book	Oc.	earthen	Oc.	of earth	Total
2 Co.	1	4:7			1
2 Ti.			1	2:20	1
Total	1		1		2

3652. ὅταν, hot'an

Book	Oc.	when	Oc.	as soon as	Oc.	as long as	Oc.	that	Oc.	whensoever	Oc.	while	Oc.	till (with 1508)	Total
Mt.	19	5:11; 6:2, 5, 6, 16; 9:15; 10:19, 23; 12:43; 13:32; 15:2; 19:28; 21:40; 23:15; 24:15, 32, 33; 25:31; 26:29													19
Mk.	17	2:20; 3:11; 4:15, 16, 29, 31, 32; 8:38; 11:25; 12:23, 25; 13:4, 7, 11, 14, 28, 29					1	14:25	1	14:7			1	9:9	20
Lk.	29	5:35; 6:22, 22, 26; 8:13; 9:26; 11:2, 21, 24, 34, 36; 12:11, 54, 55; 13:28; 14:8, 10, 10, 12, 13; 16:4, 9; 17:10; 21:7, 9, 20, 30, 31; 23:42													29
Jn.	15	2:10; 4:25; 5:7; 7:27, 31; 8:28, 44; 10:4; 13:19; 14:29; 15:26; 16:4, 13, 21a; 21:18	1	16:21b	1	9:5									17
Ac.	2	23:35; 24:22													2
Ro.	2	2:14; 11:27													2
1 Co.	11	13:10; 14:26; 15:24, 24, 27, 28, 54; 16:2, 3, 5, 12									1	3:4			12
2 Co.	2	10:6; 12:10; 13:9													3
Col.	2	3:4; 4:16													2
1 Th.	1	5:3													1
2 Th.	1	1:10													1
1 Ti.	1	5:11													1
Tit.	1	3:12													1
Heb.	1	1:6													1
Jas.	1	1:2													1
1 Jn.	2	2:28; 5:2													2
Rev.	7	4:9; 9:5; 10:7; 11:7; 17:10; 18:9; 20:7	1	12:4											8
Total	115		2		1		1		1		1		1		122

3653. ὅτε, hot'e

Book	Oc.	when	Oc.	while	Oc.	as soon as	Oc.	after that	Oc.	after	Oc.	that	Total
Mt.	12	7:28; 9:25; 11:1; 12:3; 13:26, 48, 53; 17:25; 19:1; 21:1, 34; 26:1					1	27:31					13
Mk.	11	1:32; 2:25; 4:10; 7:17; 8:19, 20; 11:1, 19; 14:12; 15:20, 41									1	6:21	12
Lk.	10	2:21, 22, 42; 4:25; 6:13; 13:35; 17:22; 22:14, 35; 23:33			1	15:30							11
Jn.	21	1:19; 2:22; 4:21, 23, 45; 5:25; 6:24; 9:4, 14; 12:16, 17, 41; 13:31; 16:25; 19:6, 8, 23, 30; 20:24; 21:15, 18	1	17:12					1	13:12			23
Ac.	10	1:13; 8:12, 39; 11:2; 12:6; 21:5, 35; 22:20; 27:39; 28:16											10
Ro.	4	2:16; 6:20; 7:5; 13:11											4
1 Co.	2	13:11, 11											2
Gal.	6	1:15; 2:11, 12, 14; 4:3, 4											6
Phl.	1	4:15											1
Col.	1	3:7											1
1 Th.	1	3:4											1
2 Th.	1	3:10											1
2 Ti.	1	4:3											1
Tit.							1	3:4					1
Heb.	1	7:10	1	9:17									2
1 Pt.	1	3:20											1
Jd.	1	1:9											1
Rev.	13	1:17; 5:8; 6:1, 3, 5, 7, 9, 12; 8:1; 10:3, 4; 12:13; 22:8			1	10:10							14
Total	97		2		2		2		1		1		105

See page 260 for Word 3654.

3655. ὅτου, hot'ou

Book	Not Tr.	Total
Mt.	5:25	1
Lk.	13:8; 15:8; 22:16, 18	4
Jn.	9:18	1
Total		6

See page 264 for Word 3656.

3658. οὐά, oua'

Book	ah	Total
Mk.	15:29	1

3657. οὗ, hou

Book	Oc.	where	Oc.	whither	Oc.	when	Oc.	wherein	Oc.	whithersoever (with 1437)	Total
Mt.	3	2:9; 18:20; 28:16									3
Lk.	3	4:16, 17; 22:10	2	10:1; 24:28			1	23:53			6
Jn.	1	11:41									1
Ac.	9	1:13; 2:2; 7:29; 12:12; 16:13; 20:6, 8; 25:10; 28:14									9
Ro.	3	4:15; 5:20; 9:26									3
1 Co.									1	16:6	1
2 Co.	1	3:17									1
Col.	1	3:1									1
Heb.					1	3:9					1
Rev.	1	17:15									1
Total	22		2		1		1		1		27

3645. ὅσος, hos'os

Book	Oc.	as many as	Oc.	whatsoever	Oc.	that	Oc.	whatsoever things	Oc.	whatsoever (with 302)	Oc.	as long as	Oc.	how great things	Oc.	what	Oc.	as
Mt.	2	14:36; 22:10	2	17:12; 28:20	3	13:44, 46; 18:25			3	7:12; 21:22; 23:3	1	9:15						
Mk.	1	3:10	2	9:13; 10:21	1	12:44							2	5:19, 20	2	6:30, 30		
Lk.	1	11:8	2	4:23; 12:3	3	4:40; 18:12, 22							2	8:39, 39				
Jn.	1	1:12	2	15:14; 17:7	2	10:41; 16:15			3	11:22; 16:13, 23								
Ac.	7	3:24; 4:6, 34; 5:36, 37; 10:45; 13:48	1	4:28					1	3:22			1	9:16	1	15:12		
Ro.	3	2:12, 12; 8:14					2	3:19; 15:4			1	7:1						
1 Co.											1	7:39						
2 Co.																		
Gal.	4	3:10, 27; 6:12, 16									1	4:1						
Phl.	1	3:15					6	4:8, 8, 8, 8, 8, 8										
Col.	1	2:1																
1 Ti.	1	6:1																
2 Ti.																		
Heb.																	3	1:4; 9:27; 10:25
2 Pt.											1	1:13						
Jd.															1	1:10b		
Rev.	2	2:24; 18:17															1	21:16
Total	24		9		9		8		7		5		5		4		4	

3659. οὐαί, ouai′

Book	Oc.	woe	Oc.	alas	Total
Mt.	14	11:21, 21; 18:7, 7; 23:13, 14, 15, 16, 23, 25, 27, 29; 24:19; 26:24			14
Mk.	2	13:17; 14:21			2
Lk.	15	6:24, 25, 25, 26; 10:13, 13; 11:42, 43, 44, 46, 47, 52; 17:1; 21: 23; 22:22			15
1 Co.	1	9:16			1
Jd.	1	1:11			1
Rev.	8	8:13, 13, 13; 9:12, 12; 11:14, 14; 12:12	6	18:10, 10, 16, 16, 19, 19	14
Total	41		6		47

3660. οὐδαμῶς, oudamōs′

Book	not	Total
Mt.	2:6	1

3661. οὐδέ, oude′

Book	Oc.	neither	Oc.	nor	Oc.	not	Oc.	no not	Oc.	not so much as	Oc.	then not	Oc.	Not Tr.	Oc.	Misc.	Total
Mt.	15	5:15; 6:15, 26a, 28; 7: 18; 9:17; 11:27; 12:4, 19b; 13:13; 16:9, 10; 21:27; 22:46; 23:13	6	6:20, 26b; 10:24; 12: 19a; 24:21; 25:13	1	25:45	2	8:10; 24: 36							2	6:29; 27:14	26
Mk.	9	4:22; 8:17; 11:26, 33; 12:21; 13:32b; 14:59, 68; 16:13			1	12:10	1	13:32a							1	6:31	12
Lk.	8	6:43; 7:7; 8:17; 11:33; 12:33; 16:31; 17:21; 20:8	4	6:44; 12: 24, 24; 21: 15	3	12:27, 27; 23: 40	1	7:9	1	6:3					2	18:13; 23:15	19
Jn.	6	6:24; 7:5; 8:11, 42; 13: 16; 14:17	4	1:13, 13; 11:50; 16:3	1	1:3							1	5:22	2	15:4; 21:25	14
Ac.	7	2:27, 31; 4:32, 34; 16: 21; 17:25; 20:24	3	8:21; 9:9; 24:18			1	7:5							1	19:2	12
Ro.	3	2:28; 8:7; 9:7	1	9:16			1	3:10							2	4:15; 11:21	7
1 Co.	2	11:16; 15:50	1	2:6	2	4:3; 14: 21	1	6:5	1	5:1	2	15:13, 16			1	11:14	10
2 Co.			1	7:12											1	3:10	2
Gal.	5	1:1, 12, 17; 2:3; 6:13	3	3:28, 28; 4: 14			1	2:5									9
Phl.	1	2:16															1
1 Th.			2	2:3; 5:5													2
2 Th.	1	3:8															1
1 Ti.			2	2:12; 6:16											1	6:7	3
Heb.	3	9:12, 18; 10:8	1	13:5	1	8:4									1	9:25	6
1 Pt.	1	2:22															1
2 Pt.			1	1:8													1
1 Jn.	1	3:6			1	2:23											2
Rev.	7	5:3b, 3c; 7:16a, 16b; 9:4, 4; 21:23	2	5:3a; 7: 16c													9
Total	69		31		10		8		2		2		1		14		137

Miscellaneous: Mt. 6:29, even not; Mt. 27:14, never; Mk. 6:31, no . . . so much as; Lk. 18:13, so much as; Lk. 23:15, no nor; Jn. 15:4, no more; Jn. 21:25, even not; Ac. 19:2 (with 235), not so much as; Ro. 4:15, no; Ro. 11:21, also not; 1 Co. 11:14, not even; 2 Co. 3:10, no; 1 Ti. 6:7 (with 5000), nothing; Heb. 9:25, nor yet.

3645. ὅσος, hos′os (continued)

Book	Oc.	as many as (with 302)	Oc.	in as much as (with 1909)	Oc.	how much	Oc.	that ever	Oc.	all that	Oc.	in as much as (with 2596)	Oc.	all things that	Oc.	Not Tr.	Oc.	Misc.	Total
Mt.	1	22:9	2	25:40, 45													2	18:18, 18	16
Mk.	1	6:56															6	2:19; 3:8, 28; 6:11; 7:36; 11:24	15
Lk.									1	9:10							1	9:5	10
Jn.							3	4:29, 39; 10:8									2	6:11; 21:25	13
Ac.	1	2:39			1	9:13			2	4:23; 14:27			1	15:4			1	9:39	17
Ro.			1	11:13													1	6:3	8
1 Co.																			1
2 Co.																	1	1:20	1
Gal.																			5
Phl.																			7
Col.																			1
1 Ti.																			1
2 Ti.																	1	1:18	1
Heb.					1	8:6					2	3:3; 7:20			1	10:37b	2	2:15; 10:37a	9
2 Pt.																			1
Jd.																	1	1:10a	2
Rev.	1	13:15			1	18:7							1	1:2			1	3:19	7
Total	4		3		3		3		3		2		2		1		16		115

Miscellaneous: Mt. 18:18, 18 (with 1437), whatsoever; Mk. 2:19 (with 5450), as long as; Mk. 3:8, what great things; Mk. 3:28 (with 302), wherewith soever; Mk. 6:11 (with 302), whosoever; Mk. 7:36, the more; Mk. 11:24 (with 302), which things soever; Lk. 9:5 (with 302), whosoever; Jn. 6:11, as much as; Jn. 21:25, which; Ac. 9:39, which; Ro. 6:3, so many as; 2 Co. 1:20, all; 2 Ti. 1:18, how many things; Heb. 2:15, who; Heb. 10:37a, while; Jd. 1:10a, those things which; Rev. 3:19 (with 1437), as many as.

3662a. οὐδείς, oudeis′

Book	Oc.	no man	Oc.	nothing	Oc.	none	Oc.	no	Oc.	neither any man	Oc.	Misc.	Total
Mt.	7	6:24; 9:16; 11:27; 17:8; 20:7; 22:46; 24:36	9	5:13; 10:26; 17:20; 21:19; 23:16, 18; 26:62; 27:12, 24	1	19:17							17
Mk.	7	2:21, 22; 5:3; 7:24; 9:39; 10:29; 13:32	5	7:15; 9:29; 11:13; 14:61; 15:4	1	10:18			1	5:4	1	11:2	15
Lk.	9	5:36, 37, 39; 8:16; 9:62; 10:22; 11:33; 15:16; 18:29	6	5:5; 12:2; 22:35; 23:9, 15, 41	6	1:61; 4:26, 27; 14:24; 18:19, 34	5	4:24; 16:13; 23:4, 14, 22			2	7:28; 19:30	28
Jn.	23	1:18; 3:2, 13, 32; 4:27; 5:22; 6:44, 65; 7:4, 13, 27, 30, 44; 8:10, 11, 20; 9:4; 10:18, 29; 13:28; 14:6; 15:13; 16:22	7	3:27; 5:30; 7:26; 8:28, 54; 18:20; 21:3	5	7:19; 15:24; 16:5; 17:12; 21:12	5	10:41; 16:29; 18:38; 19:4, 11			1	8:33	41
Ac.	6	5:13, 23; 9:8; 18:10; 20:33; 25:11b	6	4:14; 17:21; 20:20; 21:24; 26:31; 28:17	6	8:16; 18:17; 20:24; 25:11a, 18; 26:22	5	15:9; 23:9; 25:10; 27:22; 28:5			4	5:36; 19:27; 26:26; 27:34	27
Ro.	1	14:7b	1	14:14	1	14:7a	1	8:1					4
1 Co.	6	2:11, 15; 3:11; 12:3, 3; 14:2	6	4:4; 7:19, 19; 8:4a; 13:2, 3	5	1:14; 2:8; 8:4b; 9:15; 14:10							17
2 Co.	4	5:16; 7:2, 2, 2	2	12:11, 11			1	7:5					7
Gal.	2	3:11, 15	3	2:6b; 4:1; 5:2	1	5:10	1	2:6a			1	4:12	8
Eph.	1	5:29											1
Phl.	1	2:20	1	1:20			1	4:15					3
1 Ti.	1	6:16	2	4:4; 6:7									3
2 Ti.	2	2:4; 4:16					1	2:14					3
Tit.			1	1:15									1
Phe.			1	1:14									1
Heb.	2	7:13; 12:14	3	2:8; 7:14, 19			1	6:13					6
Jas.	1	3:8					1	3:12	1	1:13			3
1 Jn.	1	4:12											1
Rev.	10	2:17; 3:7, 7, 8; 5:3, 4; 7:9; 14:3; 15:8; 19:12	1	3:17									11
Total	84		54		27		22		2		8		197

Miscellaneous: Mk. 11:2, never; Lk. 7:28, not a; Lk. 19:30 (with 4355), yet never; Jn. 8:33, any man; Ac. 5:36, nought; Ac. 19:27 (with 1519 and 3049), be despised; Ac. 26:26 (with 3656 and 5000), none; Ac. 27:34, not . . . any; Gal. 4:12, not at all.

3654a. ὅτι, hot′i (as a demonstrative)

Book	Oc.	that	Oc.	for	Oc.	because	Oc.	how that
Mt.	65	2:16, 22; 3:9; 4:12; 5:17, 20, 21, 22, 23, 27, 28, 32, 33, 38, 43; 6:7, 29, 32; 8:11, 27; 9:6, 28; 10:34; 11:24; 12:6, 36; 13:17; 15:12, 17; 16:17, 18, 20; 17:10, 12, 13; 18:10, 19; 19:4, 23, 28; 20:10, 25, 30; 21:31, 45; 22:16, 34; 23:31; 24:32, 33, 43, 47; 25:24, 26; 26:2, 21, 34, 53, 54; 27:3, 18, 24, 63; 28:5, 7	1	6:26	1	11:25	3	12:5; 16:12, 21
Mk.	40	2:1, 8, 10, 16; 4:38, 41; 5:29; 6:2, 14, 15, 15; 7:18; 8:31; 9:1, 11b, 13, 25; 10:42, 47; 11:3, 23, 23, 24, 32; 12:12, 14, 26, 28, 34, 35, 43; 13:28, 29, 30; 14:30; 15:10, 39; 16:4, 7, 11	2	1:27; 12:32				
Lk.	57	1:22; 2:49, 49; 3:8; 4:4; 5:24; 6:5; 7:4, 16, 16, 37, 43; 8:47, 53; 9:7, 8, 8, 19; 10:11, 12, 20a, 21a, 24, 40; 11:38; 12:30, 37, 39, 44, 51; 13:2a, 4; 14:24; 15:7; 16:25; 17:15; 18:8, 9, 11, 37; 19:7, 22, 26, 40; 20:19, 21, 37; 21:3, 20, 30, 31; 22:37, 70; 23:7; 24:21, 39a, 44	8	1:45, 48; 4:36; 7:39; 8:25; 12:24; 15:6, 9	5	10:20b; 16:8a; 17:9; 19:11, 31	1	7:22
Jn.	129	1:34; 2:17, 18, 22; 3:2, 7, 19, 21, 28, 28, 33; 4:1b, 19, 20, 25, 27, 42b, 44, 47, 53a; 5:6, 15, 32, 36, 42, 45; 6:15, 22, 22, 24, 36, 46, 61, 65, 69; 7:7b, 26, 35, 42; 8:17, 24, 24, 27, 28, 37a, 48, 52, 54; 9:8, 17a, 18, 20, 20, 24, 25, 29, 30, 31, 32, 35; 10:38; 11:6, 13, 15, 20, 22, 24, 27, 31a, 40, 41, 42, 42, 50, 51, 56; 12:9, 12, 16, 34a, 50; 13:1, 3, 3, 19, 21, 29, 35; 14:10, 11, 20, 22, 31; 15:18; 16:4a, 15, 19a, 20, 21b, 26, 27b, 30, 30; 17:7, 8b, 8c, 21, 23, 25; 18:8, 14, 37; 19:4, 10, 21, 28, 35; 20:9, 14, 18, 31; 21:4, 7, 12, 15, 16, 17b, 23a, 24	4	4:35b; 5:28; 7:52; 14:17b	5	7:23; 8:45; 14:28b; 16:17; 21:17a		
Ac.	73	2:29, 30, 31, 36; 3:10, 17; 4:10, 13, 13, 16; 5:9, 41; 6:14; 7:6; 8:14, 18; 9:20, 22, 26, 27, 38; 10:34, 42; 11:1; 12:9, 11; 13:38; 14:9, 22; 15:5, 24; 16:3, 10, 19, 38; 17:3, 3, 13; 19:25, 26, 26, 34; 20:23, 23, 25, 26, 29, 31, 34, 38; 21:21, 22, 24, 29, 31; 22:2, 19, 29a; 23:5, 6, 22, 27, 34; 24:11, 14, 26; 26:5, 27; 27:10, 25; 28:1, 22, 28	2	8:33; 22:15	1	22:29b	4	7:25; 13:32; 15:7; 20:35a
Ro.	38	1:8, 13, 32; 2:2, 3, 4; 3:2, 19; 4:9, 21, 23; 5:3; 6:3, 6, 8, 9, 16, 17; 7:14, 16, 18, 21; 8:16, 18, 22, 28, 38; 9:2, 30; 10:2, 5, 9, 9; 11:25; 13:11; 14:14; 15:14, 29			2	8:21; 14:23	1	7:1
1 Co.	44	1:5, 11, 12, 14, 15; 3:16, 20; 4:9a; 5:6; 6:2, 3, 9, 15, 16, 19; 7:26; 8:1, 4, 4; 9:10, 13, 24; 10:19a, 20; 11:2, 3, 14, 17, 23; 12:2, 3; 14:23, 25, 37; 15:4, 4, 5, 12, 12, 15b, 27b, 50, 58; 16:15	1	16:17	1	6:7	3	1:26; 10:1; 15:3
2 Co.	28	1:7, 8, 10, 12, 14, 23; 2:3; 3:5; 4:14; 5:1, 6, 14, 19; 7:3, 8b, 9, 9, 16; 8:9; 9:2; 10:7, 11; 11:31; 12:13, 19; 13:2, 6, 6	5	1:5; 2:15; 7:14; 8:3; 9:12	2	7:13; 11:7	3	8:2; 12:4; 13:5
Gal.	15	1:6, 11, 23; 2:7, 14, 16; 3:7, 8a, 11a; 4:15, 22; 5:2, 3, 10, 21	1	4:27			1	1:13
Eph.	6	2:11, 12; 4:9; 5:5; 6:8, 9	1	2:18			1	3:3
Phl.	14	1:6, 12, 17, 19, 20, 25, 27; 2:11, 16, 22, 24, 26; 4:10, 15	1	4:16				
Col.	3	3:24; 4:1, 13						
1 Th.	7	2:1; 3:3, 4, 6; 4:14, 15; 5:2	1	1:5	1	2:13		
2 Th.	5	2:2, 4, 5; 3:4, 10	1	3:7	1	2:13		
1 Ti.	4	1:8, 9, 15; 4:1						
2 Ti.	6	1:5, 12, 15; 2:23; 3:1, 15						
Tit.	1	3:11						
Phe.	2	1:21, 22						
Heb.	10	2:6, 6; 3:19; 7:8, 14; 11:6, 13, 14, 18, 19					1	12:17
Jas.	9	1:3, 7; 2:19, 20; 3:1; 4:4, 5; 5:11, 20					1	2:24
1 Pt.	4	1:12, 18; 2:3; 3:9						
2 Pt.	5	1:14, 20; 3:3, 5, 8						
1 Jn.	35	1:5, 6, 8, 10; 2:3, 5, 18, 18, 19, 22, 29, 29; 3:2a, 5, 14a, 15, 19, 24; 4:3, 10, 10, 13a, 14, 15; 5:1, 2, 5, 11, 13, 14, 15, 15, 18, 19, 20	3	3:2b, 20a; 4:8	4	3:16; 4:13b, 17; 5:6		
2 Jn.	1	1:4						
3 Jn.	1	1:12						
Jd.							2	1:5, 18a
Rev.	10	2:6, 23; 3:1, 1, 9, 15, 17c; 10:6; 12:12b, 13	3	18:20; 19:7; 21:5	5	2:4, 14, 20; 3:17a; 11:17		
Total	612		34		28		21	

3662b. οὐδείς, oudeis′ (double negative passages)

Book	Oc.	nothing	Oc.	no man	Oc.	any man	Oc.	any	Oc.	no	Oc.	man	Oc.	Misc.	Total
Mt.					1	22:16									1
Mk.	2	14:60; 15:5	5	3:27; 5:37; 9:8; 12:14, 34	1	16:8b			1	6:5			2	7:12; 16:8a	11
Lk.	2	4:2; 10:19	2	8:51; 9:36a			2	8:43; 9:36b			1	23:53	1	20:40	8
Jn.	8	5:19; 6:63; 9:33; 12:19; 14:30; 15:5; 16:23, 24	1	8:15	1	18:31					1	19:41	2	11:49; 18:9	13
Ac.							1	4:12							1
1 Co.	1	8:2													1
2 Co.			1	11:9											1
1 Jn.									1	1:5					1
Rev.			1	18:11											1
Total	13		10		3		3		2		2		5		38

Miscellaneous: Mk. 7:12, ought; Mk. 16:8a, neither . . . anything; Lk. 20:40, not any at all; Jn. 11:49, nothing at all; Jn. 18:9, none.

Word 3662 has 235 occurrences.

3663. οὐδέποτε, oudep′ote

Book	Oc.	never	Oc.	neither at any time	Oc.	nothing at any time (with 3856)	Total
Mt.	5	7:23; 9:33; 21:16, 42; 26:33					5
Mk.	2	2:12, 25					2
Lk.	1	15:29b	1	15:29a			2
Jn.	1	7:46					1
Ac.	2	10:4; 14:8			1	11:8	3
1 Co.	1	13:8					1
Heb.	2	10:1, 11					2
Total	14		1		1		16

3654a. ὅτι, hot′i (as a demonstrative) (continued)

Book	Oc.	how	Oc.	because that	Oc.	why	Oc.	though	Oc.	as though	Oc.	for that	Oc.	Not Tr.	Total
Mt.													25	2:23; 4:6; 5:31; 6:5b, 16; 7:23; 9:18, 33; 10:7; 14:26; 18:13; 19:8, 9; 20:12; 21:3, 16, 43; 26:29, 65, 72, 74, 75; 27:43, 47; 28:13	95
Mk.					2	9:11a, 28							39	1:15, 37, 40; 2:12; 3:11, 21, 22, 22, 28; 5:23, 28, 35; 6:4, 16, 18, 23, 35, 55; 7:6, 20; 8:24; 9:26, 31; 10:33; 11:17; 12:6, 7, 19, 29; 13:6; 14:14, 18, 25, 27a, 58, 58, 69, 71, 72	83
Lk.	2	1:58; 21:5	1	13:14									34	1:25, 61; 2:23; 4:10, 11, 12, 21, 24, 41a, 43a; 5:26, 36; 8:49; 9:22; 12:55; 13:35; 14:30; 15:2, 27a; 17:10a; 18:29; 19:9, 42; 20:5; 21:8, 32; 22:16, 18, 61; 23:5, 40; 24:7, 34, 46	108
Jn.	3	4:1a; 12:19; 14:28a											43	1:20, 32; 2:25; 3:11; 4:17, 21, 35a, 37, 39, 42a, 51, 52, 53b; 5:24, 25; 6:5, 14, 42; 7:12, 31; 8:33, 34, 55; 9:9, 9, 9, 17b, 19, 23, 41; 10:7, 36a, 41; 11:31b; 12:34b; 13:33; 15:25; 16:19b, 23; 18:6, 9; 20:15; 21:23b	184
Ac.	2	14:27; 20:35b	2	2:6; 10:45									20	2:13; 3:22; 5:4, 23, 25; 6:11; 11:3; 12:3; 13:34b; 15:1; 16:36; 17:6; 18:13; 19:21; 23:20; 24:21; 25:8, 16; 26:31; 28:25	104
Ro.							1	9:6					7	3:8, 10; 4:17; 8:36; 9:12, 17; 14:11	49
1 Co.													3	10:19b; 14:21; 15:27a	52
2 Co.							1	11:21					5	1:13, 18; 3:3; 6:16; 11:10	44
Gal.	1	4:13											2	1:20; 3:8b	20
Eph.															8
Phl.									1	3:12					16
Col.															3
1 Th.															9
2 Th.			1	1:3											8
1 Ti.											1	1:12	1	6:7	6
2 Ti.															6
Tit.															1
Phe.	1	1:19													3
Heb.													3	7:17; 10:8; 13:18	14
Jas.	1	2:22											1	1:13	12
1 Pt.															4
2 Pt.															5
1 Jn.			1	4:9									2	3:20b; 4:20	45
2 Jn.															1
3 Jn.															1
Jd.													1	1:18b	3
Rev.	1	2:2											1	3:17b	20
Total	11		5		2		2		1		1		187		904

3664. οὐδέπω, oudep'ō

	with another negative										
Book	Oc.	never before	Oc.	never yet	Oc.	nothing yet	Oc.	not yet	Oc.	as yet not	Total
Lk.	1	23:53									1
Jn.			1	19:41			1	7:39	1	20:9	3
1 Co.					1	8:2					1
Total	1		1		1		1		1		5

3665a. οὐκέτι, ouket'i (combined as one word)

Book	Oc.	no more	Oc.	henceforth not	Oc.	not as yet	Oc.	now . . . not	Oc.	not now	Total
Mt.	1	19:6									1
Mk.	1	10:8									1
Lk.	2	15:19, 21									2
Jn.	1	6:66	1	15:15			1	4:42			3
Ac.	2	20:25, 38									2
2 Co.					1	1:23					1
Eph.	1	2:19									1
Phe.									1	1:16	1
Total	8		1		1		1		1		12

3654b. ὅτι, hot'i (causal)

Book	Oc.	for	Oc.	because	Oc.	because that	Oc.	that	Oc.	for that	Oc.	Not Tr.	Oc.	Misc.	Total
Mt.	37	5:3, 4, 5, 6, 7, 8, 9, 10, 12, 34, 35, 35, 45; 6:5a, 13; 7:13; 11:21, 23, 26, 29; 12:42; 13:16, 16; 15:23; 16:17, 23; 17:15; 23:13, 14, 15, 23, 25, 27; 24:42, 44; 25:8, 13	15	2:18; 5:36; 7:14; 9:36: 11:20; 12:41; 13:11, 13; 14:5; 15:32; 16:7, 8; 20: 7, 15; 23:29											52
Mk.	4	5:9; 6:17; 8:33; 14:27b	12	1:34; 3:30; 4:29; 6:34; 7:19; 8:2, 16, 17; 9:38, 41; 11:18; 16:14											16
Lk.	57	1:37, 49, 68; 2:11, 30; 4:6, 32, 41b, 43b; 5:8; 6:19, 20, 21, 21, 24, 25, 25, 35; 7:47; 8:37, 42; 9: 12, 38; 10:13, 21b; 11:31, 32, 42, 43, 44, 46, 47, 48, 52; 12:15, 32, 40; 13:24, 31, 33; 14:11, 14, 17; 15:24, 32; 16:3, 8b, 15, 24; 18: 14; 19:4, 43; 21:22; 23:29, 31; 24:29, 39b	10	8:30; 9:49, 53; 11:18; 12:17; 13:2b; 15:27b; 19:3, 17, 21							1	17:10b			68
Jn.	30	1:15, 17, 30; 4:22; 5:38, 39; 6: 38; 7:8, 29; 8:14, 16, 20, 29, 44b; 10:4, 5; 11:47; 12:49; 14:28c; 15:5, 15, 15; 16:14; 17:8a, 9, 24; 18:2, 18; 19:20, 42	48	1:50; 3:18, 23; 5:16, 18, 27, 30; 6:2, 26, 26, 41; 7:1, 7a, 22, 30; 8:22, 37b, 43, 44a, 47; 9:16, 22; 10: 13, 17, 36b; 11:9, 10; 12: 6b; 14:12, 17a, 19; 15:19, 21, 27; 16:3, 4b, 6, 9, 10, 11, 16, 21a, 27a, 32; 17: 14; 19:7; 20:13, 29	4	7:39; 10: 33; 12: 11, 39	1	12:6a	1	12:18	1	2:25			85
Ac.	12	1:5, 17; 2:25; 4:21; 5:38; 9:15; 10:14, 38; 11:8, 24; 13:41; 22: 21	4	2:27; 6:1; 8:20; 17:18									1	13:34a	17
Ro.	2	8:29; 11:36	6	5:5; 6:15; 8:27; 9:7, 28, 32									1	5:8	9
1 Co.	3	4:9b; 10:17; 11:15	6	1:25; 2:14; 3:13; 12:15, 16; 15:15a											9
2 Co.	4	4:6; 7:8a; 8:17; 10:10	1	11:11					1	1:24					6
Gal.	4	3:11b; 4:12, 20; 6:8	2	2:11; 4:6											6
Eph.	4	4:25; 5:23, 30; 6:12	1	5:16											5
Phl.	1	1:29	2	2:30; 4:17			1	4:11							4
Col.	3	1:16, 19; 2:9													3
1 Th.	4	2:14; 3:8; 4:16; 5:9													4
2 Th.	1	2:3	2	1:10; 3:9											3
1 Ti.	1	4:4	5	1:13; 4:10; 5:12; 6:2, 2											6
2 Ti.	1	1:16													1
Phe.			1	1:7											1
Heb.	3	8:10, 11, 12	1	8:9											4
Jas.	3	1:12, 23; 5:8	1	1:10											4
1 Pt.	10	1:16; 2:15; 3:12, 18; 4:1, 8, 14, 17; 5:5, 7	2	2:21; 5:8											12
1 Jn.	8	2:16; 3:8, 9a, 11; 4:7; 5:4, 7, 9	19	2:8, 12, 13, 13, 13, 14, 14, 21a, 21b; 3:1, 9b, 12, 14b, 22; 4:1, 4, 18, 19; 5:10	1	2:11	1	2:21c							29
2 Jn.	1	1:7													1
Jd.	1	1:11													1
Rev.	36	3:4, 8; 4:11; 5:9; 6:17; 7:17; 11: 2; 12:10, 12a; 14:7, 15, 15, 18; 15:1, 4, 4, 4; 16:6, 21; 17:14; 18: 3, 5, 7, 8, 10, 11, 17, 19, 23, 23; 19:2, 2, 6; 21:4; 22:5, 10	7	3:10, 16; 5:4; 8:11; 11: 10; 14:8; 16:5											43
Total	230		145		5		3		2		2		2		389

Miscellaneous: Ac. 13:34a, as concerning that; Ro. 5:8, in that.

Word 3654 has 1293 occurrences.

3665b. οὐκέτι or οὐκ ἔτι, ouket'i or ouk et'i (with another negative)

Book	Oc.	any more	Oc.	no more	Oc.	not any more	Oc.	after that	Oc.	yet	Oc.	no more at all	Oc.	after that . . . not	Total
Mt.	1	22:46													1
Mk.	1	9:8	2	7:12; 14:25	1	22:16	1	12:34	1	15:5					6
Lk.	1	22:16											1	20:40	2
Ac.			1	8:39											1
Rev.	1	18:11									1	18:14			2
Total	4		3		1		1		1		1		1		12

3665c. οὐκ ἔτι, ouk et'i (as two separate words)

Book	Oc.	no more	Oc.	now not	Oc.	now no more	Oc.	yet not	Oc.	no longer	Oc.	hereafter not	Total
Jn.	5	11:54; 14:19; 16:10, 21, 25	1	21:6	1	17:11					1	14:30	8
Ro.	8	6:9, 9; 7:17, 20; 11:6, 6, 6, 6	1	14:15									9
2 Co.	1	5:16											1
Gal.	2	3:18; 4:7					1	2:20	1	3:25			4
Heb.	2	10:18, 26											2
Total	18		2		1		1		1		1		24

Word 3665 has 48 occurrences.

3648. ὅστις, ἥτις, ὅτι, hos'tis, hę'tis, hot'i

Book	Oc.	which	Oc.	who	Oc.	whosoever	Oc.	that	Oc.	what-soever (with 302)	Oc.	who-soever (with 302)	Oc.	whatsoever (with 3856 and 302)	Oc.	Misc.	Total
Mt.	15	7:15, 24b, 26; 13:52; 16:28; 19:12, 12, 12; 20:1; 21:33, 41; 22:2; 23:27; 25:1; 27:55			8	5:39, 41; 7:24a; 10:32; 13:12, 12; 18:4; 23:12a	3	2:6; 18:28; 27:62			2	10:33; 12:50			2	23:12b; 25:3	30
Mk.	2	9:1; 12:18	1	15:7	1	8:34									1	4:20	5
Lk.	13	1:20; 2:4, 10; 7:37; 8:3, 15, 26, 43; 9:30; 10:42; 12:1; 15:7; 23:55	1	23:19	1	14:27	1	7:39	1	10:35							17
Jn.	2	8:53; 21:25					1	8:25	3	2:5; 14:13; 15:16							6
Ac.	8	10:47; 11:20, 28; 12:10; 16:12, 16, 17; 23:21	10	7:53; 8:15; 10:41; 13:31, 43; 17:10; 21:4; 23:33; 24:1; 28:18											5	3:23; 5:16; 9:35; 17:11; 23:14	23
Ro.	2	2:15; 16:12	7	1:25, 32; 9:4; 11:4; 16:4, 6, 7			1	6:2									10
1 Co.	3	3:17; 6:20; 7:13													2	5:1; 16:2	5
2 Co.	2	3:14; 9:11	1	8:10													3
Gal.	4	4:24, 24, 26; 5:19	1	2:4	1	5:4					1	5:10					7
Eph.	3	1:23; 3:13; 6:2	1	4:19													4
Phl.	2	1:28; 4:3	1	2:20											1	3:7	4
Col.	4	2:23; 3:5, 14; 4:11											2	3:17, 23			6
2 Th.			1	1:9													1
1 Ti.	3	1:4; 3:15; 6:9															3
2 Ti.	1	1:5	2	2:2, 18													3
Tit.			1	1:11													1
Heb.	8	2:3; 8:6; 9:2, 9; 10:8, 11, 35; 12:5	2	8:5; 13:7													10
Jas.					1	2:10									1	4:14	2
1 Pt.	1	2:11															1
2 Pt.			1	2:1													1
1 Jn.	1	1:2															1
Rev.	7	2:24; 9:4; 11:8; 12:13; 17:12; 19:2; 20:4					2	1:12; 17:8							1	1:7	10
Total	81		30		12		8		4		3		2		13		153

Miscellaneous: Mt. 23:12b, he that; Mt. 25:3, they that; Mk. 4:20, such as; Ac. 3:23 (with 302), which; Ac. 5:16, and they; Ac. 9:35, and; Ac. 17:11, in that they; Ac. 23:14, and they; 1 Co. 5:1 (with 302), as; 1 Co. 16:2 (with 302), as; Phl. 3:7, what things; Jas. 4:14, whereas ye; Rev. 1:7, they which.

3656. οὐ, οὐκ, or οὐχ, ou, ouk, or ouch

Book	Oc.	not	Oc.	no	Oc.	not (used interrogatively expecting affirmative answer)	Oc.	cannot (with 1410)
Mt.	142	1:25; 2:18, 18; 3:11; 4:4, 7; 5:17, 21, 27, 33, 36; 6:5, 20, 26a, 28; 7: 3, 21, 25, 29; 8:8, 20; 9:12, 13, 13, 14, 24; 10:20, 24, 26, 26, 29, 34, 37, 37, 38, 38; 11:11, 17, 17, 20; 12:2, 4, 7, 7, 19, 20, 20, 24, 25, 31, 32; 13:5, 11, 12, 13, 13, 17, 17, 21, 34, 57, 58; 14:4, 16; 15:2, 11, 13, 20, 23, 24, 26, 32b; 16:3, 11, 11, 12, 17, 18, 23; 17:12, 16, 19, 21; 18: 14, 22, 30; 19:8, 10, 11, 18b, 18c, 18d; 20:22, 23, 26, 28; 21:21, 25, 29, 30, 32, 32; 22:3, 8, 11, 16b, 17, 32; 23:3, 4, 30, 37; 24:21, 29, 39, 42, 43, 44, 50, 50; 25:9, 12, 24, 24, 26, 26, 43, 43, 43, 44, 45; 26:11, 24, 39, 40, 42, 70, 72, 74; 27:6, 34; 28:6	11	6:1; 12:39; 16:4, 7, 8; 19:18a; 20:13; 25:3, 42, 42; 26:55	13	6:26b, 30; 7:22; 12:3, 5; 13:55; 17:24; 18: 33; 19:4; 20:15; 22: 31; 24:2; 27:13	6	5:14; 6:24; 7:18; 21:27; 26:53; 27: 42
Mk.	70	1:7, 22, 34; 2:17b, 18, 24, 26, 27; 4:5, 25, 27, 34; 5:19, 39; 6:4, 18, 19, 26, 52; 7:3, 4, 5, 19, 24, 27; 8:21, 33; 9:6, 18, 28, 30, 37, 38, 38, 40, 44, 44, 46, 46, 48, 48; 10:27, 38, 40, 43, 45; 11:13, 16, 26, 31; 12:14b, 14c, 27, 34; 13:11, 14, 19, 24, 33, 35; 14:7, 29, 36, 49, 56, 68, 71; 15:23; 16:6, 14	9	2:17a; 4:7, 17, 40; 8:16, 17; 9:3; 12: 20, 22	13	4:13, 21, 38; 6:3, 3; 7:18a; 8:18, 18, 18; 11:17; 12:24, 26; 14:37	7	2:19; 3:24, 25, 26; 7:18b; 11:33; 15: 31
Lk.	109	1:20, 22, 34; 2:37, 43, 50; 3:16; 4:4, 12, 41; 5:31, 32, 36; 6:2, 4, 40, 41, 42, 43, 44, 46, 48; 7:6, 6, 32, 32, 45b, 46; 8:17b, 17c, 19, 47, 52; 9:40, 49, 50, 53, 55, 56, 58; 10:24, 24, 42; 11:8, 38, 44, 46, 52; 12:2, 2, 6, 10, 15, 27, 39, 40, 46, 46, 56, 57; 13:24, 25, 27, 34; 14:6, 26a, 27a, 30, 33a; 15:13, 28; 16:11, 12, 31; 17:9, 18, 20, 22; 18:4a, 4b, 11; 19: 3, 14, 21, 21, 22, 22, 23, 44, 44, 48; 20:5, 26, 38; 21:6, 6, 9, 15; 22:26, 57, 58, 60; 23:34, 51; 24:3, 6, 18, 24, 39	17	1:7, 33; 2:7; 7:44, 45a; 8:13, 14; 8: 27a; 9:13; 11:29; 12:17, 33; 15:7; 16:2; 20:22, 31; 22:53	8	2:49; 4:22; 10:40; 11:40; 13:15, 16; 14:5; 15:4	9	11:7; 13:33; 14:14, 20, 26b, 27b, 33b; 16:3, 13
Jn.	195	1:5, 8, 10, 11, 13, 20, 20, 21a, 25, 26, 27, 31, 33; 2:9, 12, 24, 25; 3:8, 10, 11, 12, 17, 18, 28, 34, 36; 4:2, 18, 22, 32; 5:10, 13, 18, 23, 24, 30b, 31, 34, 38, 38, 40, 41, 42, 43, 44, 47; 6:7, 17, 22b, 24, 26, 32, 36, 38, 46, 58, 64; 7:1, 10, 16, 22, 28, 28, 34a, 35, 36a, 45; 8:13, 16, 23, 27, 29, 35, 40, 41, 43a, 44a, 45, 46, 47, 47, 49, 50, 55, 55; 9:12, 16, 16, 18, 21, 21, 25, 27, 29, 30, 31, 32; 10:5, 6, 8, 10, 12, 12, 13, 16, 21, 25, 26, 26, 33, 37; 11:4, 9, 15, 21, 32, 51, 52; 12:5, 6, 8, 9, 16, 30, 35, 37, 39, 42, 44, 47, 47, 49; 13:7, 10, 16, 18, 36; 14:5, 9, 10b, 17b, 18, 22, 24, 24, 27; 15:15, 16, 19, 20, 21, 22a, 24; 16:3, 4, 7, 9, 13, 16, 17, 19, 26, 30, 32; 17:9, 14, 14, 15, 16, 16, 25; 18:17, 25, 28, 30, 31, 36, 36; 19: 12, 33, 36; 20:2, 5, 7, 13, 14, 24, 30; 21:4, 8, 11, 18, 23, 23, 23	22	1:21b, 47; 2:3: 4:9, 17, 17, 38, 44; 5: 7; 6:53; 7:18, 52; 8:37, 44b; 9:41; 11:10; 13:8; 15: 22b; 19:6, 9, 15; 21:5	14	4:35; 6:42, 70; 7:19, 25; 8:48; 9:8; 10:34; 11:37, 40; 14:10a; 18:26; 19:10, 10	16	3:3, 5; 7:7, 34b, 36b; 8:14, 21, 22, 43b; 10:35; 13:33, 37; 14:17a; 15:4; 16:12, 18
Ac.	68	1:5, 7; 2:15, 24, 27, 31, 34; 5:4, 22, 42; 6:2, 10, 13; 7:18, 25, 32, 39, 40, 48, 52, 53; 8:21b, 32; 10:41; 12:9, 14, 22, 23; 13:25, 25, 35, 39; 14:17; 16:7, 21; 17:4, 12, 24, 27, 29; 18:20; 19:26a, 27, 30, 32, 35; 20:12, 27, 31; 21:13; 22:9, 11, 18, 22; 23:5, 5; 25:7, 11, 16; 26:19, 25, 26b, 29; 27:10, 14, 39; 28:4, 19	15	7:5b, 11; 10:34; 12:18; 13:37; 15: 2, 24; 18:15; 19: 23, 24, 26b; 21:39; 25:26; 27:20; 28:2	5	2:7; 5:28; 9:21; 13: 10; 21:38	5	4:16, 20; 5:39; 15: 1; 27:31
Ro.	101	1:13, 16, 21, 28, 32; 2:13, 21, 28, 29, 29; 3:17; 4:2, 4, 10, 12, 13, 16, 19, 20, 23; 5:3, 5, 11, 13, 15, 16; 6:14, 14, 15; 7:6, 7, 7, 7, 15, 15, 16, 18b, 19, 19, 20; 8:7, 9a, 9b, 12, 15, 18, 20, 23, 24, 25, 26, 32; 9:1, 6, 6, 8, 10, 11, 16, 24, 25, 25, 26, 31, 32, 33; 10:2, 3, 11, 14, 14, 16, 19a; 11: 2a, 4, 7, 18, 21, 25; 12:4; 13:3, 4, 5, 9, 9, 9, 9, 9; 14:6, 6, 17, 23, 23; 15:3, 18, 18, 20, 21, 21; 16:4, 18	11	2:11; 3:9, 12b, 18, 22; 4:15; 7:18a; 10:12, 19b; 13:1, 10	3	6:16; 9:21; 11:2b	1	8:8
1 Co.	107	1:16, 17, 17, 21, 26, 26, 26; 2:1, 2, 4, 6, 8, 9a, 12, 13, 14a; 3:1, 2; 4: 4, 7, 14, 15, 19, 20; 5:6a, 10; 6:5, 9b, 12, 12, 13, 19b; 7:4, 4, 6, 10, 12, 15, 28, 28, 35, 36; 8:7, 8; 9:2, 7a, 9, 12b, 26, 26; 10:1, 5, 13b, 20, 20, 23, 23; 11:6, 7, 8, 17, 17, 20, 22, 31; 12:1, 14, 15, 15, 15, 16, 16, 16, 24; 13:4, 4, 4, 5a, 5b, 5c, 6; 14:2, 16, 17, 22, 22, 33, 34; 15:9, 10, 10, 14, 15, 15, 16, 17, 29, 32, 36, 37, 39, 46, 51, 58; 16:7, 12, 22	9	7:25; 10:13a; 11: 16; 12:21b, 21c, 24; 13:5d; 15:12, 13	17	3:16; 5:6b; 6:2, 3, 9a, 15, 16, 19a; 9:1, 1, 1, 6, 7b, 12a, 13, 24	4	10:21, 21; 12:21a; 15:50
2 Co.	76	1:8, 12, 18a, 19a, 24; 2:4, 5, 11, 17; 3:3, 3, 5, 6, 13; 4:1, 5, 8, 8, 9, 9, 16; 5:3, 4, 7, 12, 12; 6:12; 7:3, 7, 8, 9, 12, 14; 8:5, 8, 10, 12, 13, 19, 21; 9:12; 10:3, 4, 8, 8, 12, 12, 14, 15, 16, 18; 11:4, 4, 4, 6, 11, 17, 29, 29, 31; 12:1, 4, 5, 6, 13, 14, 14, 14, 16, 20, 20; 13:2, 3, 6, 7, 10	4	2:13; 8:15b; 11: 14, 15	3	12:18, 18; 13:5	3	12:2, 2, 3
Gal.	28	1:1, 7, 10, 11, 16, 20; 2:14, 14, 15, 16a, 16b, 21; 3:10, 12, 16, 20; 4:8, 14, 17, 21, 27, 27, 31; 5:8, 18, 21; 6:4, 7	2	2:6; 5:23				
Eph.	9	1:16, 21; 2:8, 9; 3:5; 4:20; 5:4; 6:7, 12						
Phl.	12	1:16, 22, 29; 2:6, 16, 21, 27; 3:1, 12, 13; 4:11, 17	1	3:3				
Col.	6	1:9; 2:1, 8, 19, 23; 3:23	1	3:25				
1 Th.	15	1:5, 8; 2:1, 3, 4, 8, 13, 17; 4:7, 8, 9, 13; 5:4, 5, 9	1	5:1				
2 Th.	7	2:5, 10; 3:2, 7, 9, 10, 14						
1 Ti.	8	1:9; 2:7, 12, 14; 3:5; 5:8, 13, 18					1	5:25
2 Ti.	11	1:7, 9, 12, 16; 2:5, 9, 20, 24; 3:9; 4:3, 8	1	3:9			1	2:13
Tit.	1	3:5						
Heb.	50	1:12; 2:5, 11, 16; 3:10, 16, 19; 4:2, 6, 8, 15; 5:5, 12; 6:10; 7:11, 16, 20, 21, 27; 8:2, 9, 9; 9:7, 11, 11, 24; 10:1, 2, 5, 8, 37, 39; 11:1, 5, 16, 23, 31, 35, 38, 39; 12:7, 8, 9, 18, 20, 25, 26; 13:6, 9, 9	8	5:4; 8:7; 9:22; 10:6, 38; 12:17; 13:10, 14				
Jas.	14	1:20, 23, 25; 2:24; 3:2, 10, 15; 4:2a, 2c, 3, 11, 14; 5:6, 17	2	1:17; 2:11	8	2:4, 5, 6, 7, 21, 25; 4:1, 4	1	4:2b
1 Pt.	11	1:8, 12, 18, 23; 2:10, 10, 18, 23, 23; 3:3, 21	1	2:22				
2 Pt.	10	1:12, 16, 21; 2:3, 3, 4, 5, 10, 11; 3:9						
1 Jn.	35	1:6, 8b, 10, 10; 2:2, 4, 11, 15, 16, 19, 19, 21a, 21b, 27a; 3:1, 6, 6, 9a, 10, 12; 4:3, 6, 6, 8, 10, 18b, 20; 5:3, 6, 10, 12, 16, 17, 18, 18	5	1:8a; 2 7, 27b; 3:5; 4:18a			1	3:9b
2 Jn.	5	1:1, 5, 9, 10, 12						
3 Jn.	3	1:9, 11, 13	1	1:4				
Jd.	2	1:9, 10						
Rev.	35	2:2, 2, 3, 9, 13, 21, 24a, 24b; 3:2, 4, 8, 9, 17; 4:8; 6:10; 9:4, 6, 20; 11:9; 12:8, 11; 13:8; 14:4; 16:9, 11, 18, 20; 17:8, 8, 8, 11; 20:4a, 5, 15	15	7:16; 10:6; 14:5, 11; 18:7; 20:6, 11; 21:1, 4a, 22, 23, 25; 22:3, 5, 5				
Total	1130		136		84		55	

3656. οὐ, οὐκ, or οὐχ, ou, ouk, or ouch (continued)

Book	Oc.	no (with 3856)	Oc.	cannot tell (with 1492)	Oc.	nor	Oc.	never	Oc.	nothing	Oc.	nothing (with 5001)	Oc.	cannot	Oc.	nothing (with 5000)	Oc.	Misc.	Total
Mt.	1	24:22	1	21:27							1	15:32	1	19:11					176
Mk.	1	13:20	1	11:33			1	14:21			2	6:36; 8:2			1	4:22	1	3:29	106
Lk.					1	18:4c	2	23:29, 29	1	8:17a							5	1:37; 11:6; 13:33; 14:14; 16:3	152
Jn.			2	8:14; 16:18															249
Ac.																	6	5:26; 13:46; 14:28; 19:11; 24:11; 26:26a	99
Ro.	1	3:20																	117
1 Co.					3	2:9b; 6:10a, 10b			1	9:16							1	7:9	142
2 Co.			3	12:2, 2, 3					1	8:15a					1	13:8	1	11:10	92
Gal.	1	2:16											1	3:17					32
Eph.	1	5:5																	10
Phl.																			13
Col.																			7
1 Th.																			16
2 Th.																			7
1 Ti.																			9
2 Ti.																			13
Tit.																			1
Heb.	1	12:11															1	9:5	60
Jas.																			25
1 Pt.																			12
2 Pt.	1	1:20																	11
1 Jn.	2	2:21; 3:15b																	43
2 Jn.																			5
3 Jn.																			4
Jd.																			2
Rev.																			50
Total	9		7		4		3		3		3		2		2		15		1453

Miscellaneous: Mk. 3:29 (with 1519, 3488, and 165), never; Lk. 1:37 (with 4387 and 3856), nothing; Lk. 11:6 (with 2192), nothing; Lk. 13:33 (with 1735), cannot be; Lk. 14:14 (with 2192), cannot; Lk. 16:3 (with 2480), cannot; Ac. 5:26 (with 970 and 3226), without violence; Ac. 13:46 (with 514), unworthy; Ac. 14:28 (with 3541), long; Ac. 19:11 (with 5077 and 3488), special; Ac. 24:11 (with 4019), yet but; Ac. 26:26a (with 5000 and 3662), none; 1 Co. 7:9 (with 1467), cannot contain; 2 Co. 11:10, no man; Heb. 9:5 (with 2076), cannot.

3666. οὐκοῦν, oukoun

Book	then	Total
Jn.	18:37	1

See page 267 for Word 3667.

3669. οὐρά, oura'

Book	tail	Total
Rev.	9:10, 10, 19, 19; 12:4	5

3670. οὐράνιος, ouran'ios

Book	heavenly	Total
Mt.	6:14, 26, 32; 15:13	4
Lk.	2:13	1
Ac.	26:19	1
Total		6

3668. οὔπω, ou'pō

Book	Oc.	not yet	Oc.	hitherto . . . not	Oc.	as yet (with negative)	Oc.	no . . . as yet	Total
Mt.	3	15:17; 16:9; 24:6							3
Mk.	2	8:17; 13:7							2
Jn.	11	2:4; 3:24; 7:6, 8, 8, 30, 39; 8:20, 57; 11: 30; 20:17							11
Ac.					1	8:16			1
1 Co.			1	3:2					1
Heb.	2	2:8; 12:4							2
1 Jn.	1	3:2							1
Rev.	1	17:10					1	17:12	2
Total	20		1		1		1		23

3671. οὐρανόθεν, ouranoth'en

Book	from heaven	Total
Ac.	14:17; 26:13	2

3672. οὐρανός, ouranos'

Book	Oc.	heaven	Oc.	air	Oc.	sky	Oc.	heavenly (with 1537)	Total
Mt.	78	3:2, 16, 17; 4:17; 5:3, 10, 12, 16, 18, 19, 19, 20, 34, 45, 48; 6:1, 9, 10, 20; 7:11, 21, 21; 8:11; 10:7, 32, 33; 11:11, 12, 23, 25; 12:50; 13:11, 24, 31, 33, 44, 45, 47, 52; 14:19; 16:1, 17, 19, 19, 19; 18:1, 3, 4, 10, 10, 14, 18, 18, 19, 23; 19:12, 14, 21, 23; 20:1; 21:25, 25; 22:2, 30; 23:9, 13, 22; 24:29, 29, 30, 30, 31, 35, 36; 25:1; 26:64; 28:2, 18	3	6:26; 8:20; 13:32	3	16:2, 3, 3			84
Mk.	18	1:10, 11; 6:41; 7:34; 8:11; 10:21; 11:25, 26, 30, 31; 12:25; 13:25, 25, 27, 31, 32; 14: 62; 16:19	2	4:4, 32					20
Lk.	32	2:15; 3:21, 22; 4:25; 6:23; 9:16, 54; 10:15, 18, 20, 21; 11:2, 2, 16; 12:33; 15:7, 18, 21; 16:17; 17:24, 24, 29; 18:13, 22; 19:38; 20:4, 5; 21:11, 26, 33; 22:43; 24:51	3	8:5; 9:58; 13:19	1	12:56	1	11:13	37
Jn.	19	1:32, 51; 3:13, 13, 13, 27, 31; 6:31, 32, 32, 33, 38, 41, 42, 50, 51, 58; 12:28; 17:1							19
Ac.	24	1:10, 11, 11, 11; 2:2, 5, 19, 34; 3:21; 4:12, 24; 7:42, 49, 55, 56; 9:3; 10:11, 16; 11:5, 9, 10; 14:15; 17:24; 22:6	2	10:12; 11: 6					26
Ro.	2	1:18; 10:6							2
1 Co.	2	8:5; 15:47							2
2 Co.	3	5:1, 2; 12:2							3
Gal.	1	1:8							1
Eph.	4	1:10; 3:15; 4:10; 6:9							4
Phl.	1	3:20							1
Col.	5	1:5, 16, 20, 23; 4:1							5
1 Th.	2	1:10; 4:16							2
2 Th.	1	1:7							1
Heb.	10	1:10; 4:14; 7:26; 8:1; 9:23, 24; 10:34; 12:23, 25, 26			1	11:12			11
Jas.	2	5:12, 18							2
1 Pt.	3	1:4, 12; 3:22							3
2 Pt.	6	1:18; 3:5, 7, 10, 12, 13							6
1 Jn.	1	5:7							1
Rev.	54	3:12; 4:1, 2; 5:3, 13; 6:13, 14; 8:1, 10; 9:1; 10:1, 4, 5, 6, 8; 11:6, 12, 12, 13, 15, 19; 12: 1, 3, 4, 7, 8, 10, 12; 13:6, 13; 14:2, 7, 13, 17; 15:1, 5; 16:11, 17, 21; 18:1, 4, 5, 20; 19:1, 11, 14; 20:1, 9, 11; 21:1, 1, 2, 3, 10							54
Total	268		10		5		1		284

3673. Οὐρβανός, Ourbanos'

Book	Urbane	Total
Ro.	16:9	1

3674. Οὐρίας, Ouri'as

Book	Urias	Total
Mt.	1:6	1

3675. οὖς, ous

Book	ear	Total
Mt.	10:27; 11:15; 13:9, 15, 15, 16, 43	7
Mk.	4:9, 23; 7:16, 33; 8:18	5
Lk.	1:44; 4:21; 8:8; 9:44; 12:3; 14:35; 22:50	7
Ac.	7:51, 57; 11:22; 28:27, 27	5
Ro.	11:8	1
1 Co.	2:9; 12:16	2
Jas.	5:4	1
1 Pt.	3:12	1
Rev.	2:7, 11, 17, 29; 3:6, 13, 22; 13:9	8
Total		37

3676. οὐσία, ousia

Book	Oc.	goods	Oc.	substance	Total
Lk.	1	15:12	1	15:13	2

3677. οὔτε, ou'te

Book	Oc.	neither	Oc.	nor	Oc.	nor yet	Oc.	no not	Oc.	not	Oc.	yet not	Oc.	Misc.	Total
Mt.	4	6:20a; 12:32, 32; 22:30a	2	6:20b; 22:30b											6
Mk.	1	12:25a	1	12:25b			1	5:3							3
Lk.	3	14:35a; 20:35a, 36	1	20:35b	1	14:35b			1	12:26					6
Jn.	5	1:25b; 4:21a; 5:37a; 8:19a; 9:3a	4	1:25a; 5:37b; 8:19b; 9:3b	1	4:21b							1	4:11	11
Ac.	9	15:10a; 19:37a; 24:12a, 12b, 13; 25:8a, 8b; 28:21, 21	2	15:10b; 24:12c	2	19:37b; 25:8c							1	4:12	14
Ro.	1	8:38a	9	8:38b, 38c, 38d, 38e, 38f, 38g, 39, 39, 39											10
1 Co.	7	3:7, 7; 6:9a; 8:8, 8; 11:11, 11	7	6:9b, 9c, 9d, 9e, 10, 10, 10									1	3:2	15
Gal.	3	1:12; 5:6a; 6:15a	2	5:6b; 6:15b											5
1 Th.	2	2:5a, 6b	4	2:3, 5b, 6a, 6c											6
3 Jn.	1	1:10													1
Rev.	8	3:15a, 16a; 5:4; 9:20b; 12:8; 20: 4; 21:4a, 4c	8	3:15b, 16b; 9:20c, 20d, 21, 21, 21; 21:4b							1	9:20a			17
Total	44		40		4		1		1		1		3		94

Miscellaneous: Jn. 4:11 (with 502), nothing to draw with; Ac. 4:12, none; 1 Co. 3:2 (with 235), neither.

3667. οὖν, oun

Book	Oc.	therefore	Oc.	then	Oc.	so	Oc.	and	Oc.	now	Oc.	wherefore	Oc.	but	Oc.	Not Tr.	Oc.	Misc.	Total
Mt.	39	3:8, 10; 5:19, 23, 48; 6:2, 8, 9, 22, 23, 31, 34; 7:12, 24; 9:38; 10:16, 26, 31, 32; 13:18, 40; 18:4, 26; 19:6; 21:40; 22:9, 17, 21, 28; 23:3, 20; 24:15, 42; 25:13, 27, 28; 27:17, 64; 28:19	13	7:11; 12:12, 26; 13:27, 28, 56; 17:10; 19:7; 21:25; 22:43, 45; 26:54; 27:22	1	1:17	1	18:29			1	24:26							55
Mk.	7	10:9; 12:6, 9, 23, 27, 37; 13:35	3	3:31; 11:31; 15:12													1	16:19	11
Lk.	29	3:8, 9; 4:7; 6:36; 7:42; 8:18; 10:2, 2, 40; 11:34, 35, 36; 12:7, 40; 13:14; 15:28; 16:11, 27; 19:12; 20:15, 29, 33, 44; 21:8, 14, 36; 23:16, 20, 22	12	3:7, 10; 6:9; 7:31; 10:37; 11:13; 12:26; 13:15; 20:5, 17; 22:36, 70			1	3:18	1	10:36			1	21:7			1	14:33	45
Jn.	64	2:22; 3:29; 4:1, 6, 33; 5:10; 6:13, 15, 24, 30a, 43, 45, 52, 60; 7:3, 40; 8:13, 24, 36; 9:7, 8, 10, 16, 41; 10:19, 39; 11:3, 6, 33, 38, 54; 12:9, 17, 19, 21, 29, 50; 13:24, 31; 16:18, 22; 18:4, 8, 25, 31b, 37, 39; 19:1, 4, 6, 8, 13, 16, 24, 24, 26, 30, 31, 38, 42; 20:3, 25; 21:6, 7a	116	1:21, 22, 25; 2:18, 20; 3:25; 4:5, 9, 11, 28, 30, 45, 48, 52; 5:4, 12, 19; 6:5, 14, 21, 28, 30b, 32, 34, 41, 42, 53, 67, 68; 7:6, 11, 25, 28, 30, 33, 35, 45, 47; 8:12, 19, 21, 22, 25, 28, 31, 41, 48, 52, 57, 59; 9:12, 15, 19, 24, 28; 10:7, 24, 31; 11:12, 14, 16, 17, 20, 21, 31, 32, 36, 41, 45, 47, 53, 56; 12:1, 3, 4, 7, 28, 35; 13:6, 14, 22, 27, 30; 16:17; 18:3, 6, 7, 10, 11, 12, 16, 17, 19, 27, 28, 29, 31a, 33, 40; 19:5, 10, 20, 21, 23, 32, 40; 20:2, 6, 10, 19, 20, 21; 21:5, 9, 13, 23	8	4:40, 46, 53; 6:10, 19; 7:43; 13:12; 21:15	2	6:62; 20:11	3	16:19; 19:29; 21:7b			2	8:5; 9:18	6	5:18; 8:38, 42; 9:25; 12:2; 20:8	1	20:30	202
Ac.	34	1:6; 2:30, 33, 36; 3:19; 8:4, 22; 10:29, 32, 33, 33; 12:5; 13:38, 40; 14:3; 15:2, 10, 27; 16:11, 36; 17:12, 17, 20, 23; 19:32; 20:28; 21:22, 23; 23:15; 25:5, 17; 26:22; 28:20, 28	9	2:41; 9:31; 10:23; 11:17; 17:29; 19:3, 36; 22:29; 23:31	5	13:4; 15:30; 23:18, 22; 28:9	7	5:41; 8:25; 15:3, 39; 17:30; 25:23; 28:5	3	1:18; 11:19; 25:1	3	1:21; 6:3; 19:38	2	23:21; 25:4	2	18:14; 26:4	2	16:5; 26:9	67
Ro.	21	2:21, 26; 3:28; 5:1, 18; 6:4, 12; 8:12; 9:18; 11:22; 12:1, 20; 13:7, 10, 12; 14:8, 13, 19; 15:17, 28; 16:19	24	3:1, 9, 27, 31; 4:1, 9, 10; 5:9; 6:1, 15, 21; 7:7, 13; 8:31; 9:14, 19, 30; 10:14; 11:1, 5, 7, 11, 19; 14:16	4	7:3, 25; 9:16; 14:12													49
1 Co.	11	5:7; 6:7; 7:26; 8:4; 10:31; 11:20; 14:11, 23; 15:11; 16:11, 18	7	3:5; 6:4, 15; 9:18; 10:19; 14:15, 26					1	9:25	1	4:16							20
2 Co.	7	1:17; 5:6, 11; 7:1; 9:5; 11:15; 12:9	1	3:12							1	8:24					1	5:20	10
Gal.	3	3:5; 5:1; 6:10	3	3:19, 21; 4:15															6
Eph.	5	4:1, 17; 5:1, 7; 6:14	1	5:15					1	2:19									7
Phl.	5	2:1, 23, 28, 29; 3:15																	5
Col.	4	2:6, 16; 3:5, 12	1	3:1							1	2:20							6
1 Th.	1	5:6	1	4:1															2
2 Th.	1	2:15																	1
1 Ti.	3	2:1, 8; 5:14	1	3:2															4
2 Ti.	5	1:8; 2:1, 3, 21; 4:1																	5
Phe.	1	1:17																	1
Heb.	9	4:1, 6, 11, 16; 7:11; 9:23; 10:19, 35; 13:15	3	2:14; 4:14; 9:1															12
Jas.	4	4:4, 7, 17; 5:7																	4
1 Pt.	3	2:7; 4:7; 5:6	1	4:1							1	2:1			1	2:13			6
2 Pt.	1	3:17	1	3:11															2
1 Jn.	1	2:24																	1
3 Jn.	1	1:8																	1
Rev.	4	2:5; 3:3, 3, 19																	4
Total	263		197		18		11		9		8		5		9		6		526

Miscellaneous: Mk. 16:19, so then; Lk. 14:33, likewise; Jn. 20:30, and . . . truly; Ac. 16:5, and so; Ac. 26:9, verily; 2 Co. 5:20, now then.

3678a. οὗτος, hou'tos (nominative masculine singular)

Book	Oc.	this	Oc.	he	Oc.	the same	Oc.	this man	Oc.	this fellow	Oc.	Not Tr.	Oc.	Misc.	Total
Mt.	17	3:3, 17; 7:12; 8:27; 11:10; 12:23; 13:19, 55; 14:2; 15:8; 17:5; 21:10, 11, 38; 27:37, 54; 28:15	3	13:22, 23; 27:58	6	5:19; 13:20; 18:4; 21:42; 24:13; 26:23	2	9:3; 27:47	3	12:24; 26:61, 71	1	10:22			32
Mk.	7	4:41; 6:3; 7:6; 9:7; 12:7; 14:69; 15:39			3	3:35; 8:35; 13:13	1	2:7			1	12:10	1	6:16	13
Lk.	20	1:29, 36; 4:22, 36; 5:21; 7:17, 27, 49; 8:25; 9:9, 35; 14:30; 15:24, 30, 32; 17:18; 18:11; 20:14; 23:38, 47	6	1:32; 19:2; 20:28, 30; 23:22, 35	6	2:25; 9:24, 48; 16:1; 20:17; 23:51	6	7:39; 15:2; 18:14; 22:56; 23:41, 52	1	22:59			1	2:34	40
Jn.	28	1:15, 30, 34; 2:20; 4:29, 42; 6:14, 42a, 50, 58, 60; 7:25, 26, 36, 40, 41, 46, 49; 9:8, 9, 16, 19, 20, 24; 11:47; 12:34; 21:23, 24	6	1:41; 4:47; 6:42b, 46; 7:35; 18:30	7	1:2, 7, 33; 3:2, 26; 7:18; 15:5	9	6:52; 7:15, 31; 9:2, 3, 33; 11:37, 37; 21:21					1	6:71	51
Ac.	16	4:11; 6:13, 14; 7:37, 38, 40; 9:21, 22; 17:3, 18; 19:26; 21:28; 22:26; 26:31, 32; 28:4	11	3:10; 4:9; 7:36; 9:15, 20; 10:6, 6, 32, 36; 17:24; 18:26	2	7:19; 14:9	4	1:18; 4:10; 8:10; 18:25	1	18:13			2	1:11; 13:7	36
Ro.	2	4:9; 9:9	1	8:9											3
1 Co.					1	8:3									1
Heb.	1	7:1					2	3:3; 7:4							3
Jas.			2	1:23, 25a	1	3:2	1	1:25b							4
1 Pt.					1	2:7									1
2 Pt.	1	1:17													1
1 Jn.	2	5:6, 20	1	2:22											3
2 Jn.	1	1:7	1	1:9											2
Rev.	1	20:14			1	3:5									2
Total	96		31		28		25		5		2		5		192

Miscellaneous: Mk. 6:16, it; Lk. 2:34, this child; Jn. 6:71, he it was that; Ac. 1:11, this same; Ac. 13:7, who.

3678b. οὗτοι, hou'toi (nominative masculine plural)

Book	Oc.	these	Oc.	they	Oc.	the same	Oc.	such as	Oc.	Not Tr.	Total
Mt.	6	4:3; 20:12, 21; 21:16; 25:46; 26:62							1	13:38	7
Mk.	6	4:15, 16, 18a, 20; 12:40; 14:60					1	4:18b			7
Lk.	7	8:13, 21; 13:2; 19:40; 21:4; 24:17, 44	3	8:14, 15; 13:4	1	20:47					11
Jn.	3	6:5; 17:11, 25	1	18:21	1	12:21					5
Ac.	13	1:14; 2:7, 15; 11:12; 16:17, 20; 17:6, 7, 11; 20:5; 24:20; 25:11; 27:31	2	13:4; 24:15							15
Ro.	3	2:14; 11:24, 31	2	8:14; 9:6							5
1 Co.			1	16:17							1
Gal.			1	6:12	1	3:7					2
Col.	1	4:11									1
1 Ti.	1	3:10									1
2 Ti.	1	3:8									1
Heb.	2	11:13, 39									2
2 Pt.	2	2:12, 17									2
1 Jn.	1	5:7									1
Jd.	5	1:8, 10, 12, 16, 19									5
Rev.	14	7:13, 14; 11:4, 6, 10; 14:4, 4, 4; 17:13, 14, 16; 19:9; 21:5; 22:6									14
Total	65		10		3		1		1		80

3678c. αὕτη, haut'ē (nominative feminine singular)

Book	Oc.	this	Oc.	she	Oc.	this woman	Oc.	which	Oc.	the same	Oc.	hereof	Oc.	Not Tr.	Total
Mt.	6	13:54; 21:42; 22:20, 38; 24:34; 26:8	1	26:12	1	26:13					1	9:26			9
Mk.	9	1:27; 8:12; 12:11, 16, 30, 31, 43; 13:30; 14:4	3	12:44; 14:8, 9											12
Lk.	8	2:2; 4:21; 8:9, 11; 11:29; 21:3, 32; 22:53	7	2:36, 37, 38; 7:12, 44; 8:42; 21:4	2	7:45, 46									17
Jn.	8	1:19; 3:19, 29; 8:4; 11:4; 12:30; 15:12; 17:3													8
Ac.	5	5:38; 8:32; 9:36; 17:19; 21:11			1	9:36	1	8:26	1	16:17					8
Ro.	1	11:27	1	16:2									1	7:10	3
1 Co.	2	8:9; 9:3													2
2 Co.	3	1:12; 2:6; 11:10													3
Eph.	1	3:8													1
Tit.	1	1:13													1
Heb.	2	8:10; 10:16													2
Jas.	2	1:27; 3:15													2
1 Jn.	10	1:5; 2:25; 3:11, 23; 5:3, 4, 9, 11, 11, 14													10
2 Jn.	2	1:6, 6													2
Rev.	1	20:5													1
Total	61		12		4		1		1		1		1		81

3678d. αὗται, hau'tai (nominative feminine plural)

Book	these	Total
Lk.	21:22	1
Ac.	20:34	1
Gal.	4:24	1
Total		3

Word 3678 has 356 occurrences.

3679. οὕτω, οὕτως, hou'tō, hou'tōs

Book	Oc.	so	Oc.	thus	Oc.	even so	Oc	on this wise	Oc.	likewise	Oc.	after this manner	Oc.	Misc.	Total
Mt.	22	5:12, 16, 19, 47; 6:30; 7:12; 9:33; 11:26; 12:40; 13:40, 49; 18:35; 19:8, 10, 12; 20:16, 26; 24:27, 33, 37, 39, 46	3	2:5; 3:15; 26:54	4	7:17; 12:45; 18:14; 23:28	1	1:18	1	17:12	1	6:9	1	26:40	33
Mk.	7	2:8; 4:26, 40; 7:18; 10:43; 14:59; 15:39	1	2:7									2	2:12; 13:29	10
Lk.	16	6:10; 9:15; 10:21; 11:30; 12:21, 28, 38, 43, 54; 14:33; 17:10, 24, 26; 21:31; 22:26; 24:24	5	1:25; 2:48; 19:31; 24:46, 46					2	15:7, 10					23
Jn.	7	3:8, 16; 5:21, 26; 8:59; 12:50; 18:22	2	4:6; 11:48	2	3:14; 14:31	1	21:1					2	7:46; 15:4	14
Ac.	23	1:11; 3:18; 7:1, 8; 8:32; 12:8; 13:8, 47; 14:1; 17:11, 33; 19:20; 20:11, 13, 35; 21:11; 22:24; 23:11; 24:9, 14; 27:17, 44; 28:14			1	12:15	2	7:6; 13:34					1	27:25	27
Ro.	13	1:15; 4:18; 5:12, 15, 18, 19, 21; 6:4; 11:5, 26, 31; 12:5; 15:20	1	9:20	1	6:19	1	10:6	1	6:11					17
1 Co.	28	2:11; 3:15; 4:1; 5:3; 6:5; 7:17, 17, 26, 36, 40; 8:12; 9:14, 15, 24, 26, 26; 11:12, 28; 12:12; 14:9, 12, 25b; 15:11, 11, 22, 42, 45; 16:1	1	14:25a							1	7:7a	2	7:7b; 14:21	32
2 Co.	8	1:5, 7; 7:14; 8:6, 11; 9:5; 10:7; 11:3													8
Gal.	5	1:6; 3:3; 4:3, 29; 6:2													5
Eph.	4	4:20; 5:24, 28, 33													4
Phl.	2	3:17; 4:1													2
Col.	1	3:13													1
1 Th.	4	2:8; 4:14, 17; 5:2			1	2:4									5
2 Th.	1	3:17													1
2 Ti.	1	3:8													1
Heb.	6	5:3, 5; 6:15; 9:28; 10:33; 12:21	2	6:9; 9:6			1	4:4							9
Jas.	9	1:11; 2:12, 12, 17, 26; 3:5, 6, 10, 12													9
1 Pt.	1	2:15									1	3:5			2
2 Pt.	1	1:11											1	3:4	2
1 Jn.	2	2:6; 4:11													2
Rev.	3	2:15; 3:16; 16:18	2	9:17; 18:21									1	11:5	6
Total	164		17		9		6		4		3		10		213

Miscellaneous: Mt. 26:40, what; Mk. 2:12, on this fashion; Mk. 13:29, so in like manner; Jn. 7:46 (with 5513), like; Jn. 15:4, no more; Ac. 27:25, even; 1 Co. 7:7b, after that; 1 Co. 14:21, for all that; 2 Pt. 3:4, as they were; Rev. 11:5, in this manner.

3680. οὐχί, ouchi'

Book	Oc.	not (as an interrogative)	Oc.	nay	Oc.	not	Oc.	not so	Total
Mt.	10	5:46, 47; 6:25; 10:29; 12:11; 13:27, 55, 56; 18:12; 20:13							10
Lk.	10	6:39; 12:6; 14:28, 31; 15:8; 17:8, 17; 22:27; 24:26, 32	4	12:51; 13:3, 5; 16:30			1	1:60	15
Jn.	3	7:42; 11:9; 14:22			2	13:10, 11			5
Ac.	2	5:4; 7:50							2
Ro.	3	2:26; 3:29; 8:32	1	3:27					4
1 Co.	14	1:20; 3:3, 4; 5:2, 12; 6:1, 7, 7; 8:10; 9:1, 8; 10:16, 16, 18			1	10:29			15
2 Co.	1	3:8			1	10:13			2
1 Th.	1	2:19							1
Heb.	2	1:14; 3:17							2
Total	46		5		4		1		56

3683. ὀφείλημα, ophei'lēma

Book	debt	Total
Mt.	6:12	1
Ro.	4:4	1
Total		2

3681. ὀφειλέτης, opheilet'ēs

Book	Oc.	debtor	Oc.	sinner	Oc.	which owed	Total
Mt.	1	6:12			1	18:24	2
Ro.	3	1:14; 8:12; 15:27					3
Lk.			1	13:4			1
Gal.	1	5:3					1
Total	5		1		1		7

3682. ὀφειλή, opheilē'

Book	Oc.	debt	Oc.	dues	Total
Mt.	1	18:32			1
Ro.			1	13:7	1
Total	1		1		2

3684. ὀφείλω or ὀφειλέω, ophei'lō or opheile'ō

Book	Oc.	ought	Oc.	owe	Oc.	be bound	Oc.	be (one's) duty	Oc.	be a debtor	Oc.	be guilty	Oc.	be indebted	Oc.	Misc.	Total
Mt.			2	18:28, 28					1	23:16	1	23:18			2	18:30, 34	6
Lk.			3	7:41; 16:5, 7			1	17:10					1	11:4			5
Jn.	2	13:14; 19:7															2
Ac.	1	17:29															1
Ro.	1	15:1	1	13:8			1	15:27									3
1 Co.	2	11:7, 10													4	5:10; 7:3, 36; 9:10	6
2 Co.	2	12:11, 14															2
Eph.	1	5:28															1
2 Th.					2	1:3; 2:13											2
Phe.			1	1:18													1
Heb.	2	5:3, 12													1	2:17	3
1 Jn.	3	2:6; 3:16; 4:11															3
3 Jn.	1	1:8															1
Total	15		7		2		2		1		1		1		7		36

Miscellaneous: Mt. 18:30, debt; Mt. 18:34, be due; 1 Co. 5:10, must needs; 1 Co. 7:3, due; 1 Co. 7:36, need; 1 Co. 9:10, should; Heb. 2:17, behoove.

3685. ὄφελον, oph'elon

Book	Oc.	I would	Oc.	I would to God	Oc.	would to God	Total
1 Co.			1	4:8			1
2 Co.					1	11:1	1
Gal.	1	5:12					1
Rev.	1	3:15					1
Total	2		1		1		4

3686. ὄφελος, oph'elos

Book	Oc.	it profiteth	Oc.	it advantageth	Total
1 Co.			1	15:32	1
Jas.	2	2:14, 16			2
Total	2		1		3

3687. ὀφθαλμοδουλεία ophthalmodoulei′a

Book	eyeservice	Total
Eph.	6:6	1
Col.	3:22	1
Total		2

3688. ὀφθαλμός, ophthalmos′

Book	Oc.	eye	Oc.	sight	Total
Mt.	26	5:29, 38, 38; 6:22, 22, 23; 7:3, 3, 4, 4, 5, 5; 9:29, 30; 13:15, 15, 16; 17:8; 18:9, 9; 20:15, 33, 34, 34; 21:42; 26:43			26
Mk.	7	7:22; 8:18, 25; 9:47, 47; 12:11; 14:40			7
Lk.	17	2:30; 4:20; 6:20, 41, 41, 42, 42, 42, 42; 10: 23; 11:34, 34; 16:23; 18:13; 19:42; 24:16, 31			17
Jn.	18	4:35; 6:5; 9:6, 10, 11, 14, 15, 17, 21, 26, 30, 32; 10:21; 11:37, 41; 12:40, 40; 17:1			18
Ac.	6	9:8, 18, 40; 26:18; 28:27, 27	1	1:9	7
Ro.	3	3:18; 11:8, 10			3
1 Co.	5	2:9; 12:16, 17, 21; 15:52			5
Gal.	2	3:1; 4:15			2
Eph.	1	1:18			1
Heb.	1	4:13			1
1 Pt.	1	3:12			1
2 Pt.	1	2:14			1
1 Jn.	3	1:1; 2:11, 16			3
Rev.	10	1:7, 14; 2:18; 3:18; 4:6, 8; 5:6; 7:17; 19: 12; 21:4			10
Total	101		1		102

3689. ὄφις, oph′is

Book	serpent	Total
Mt.	7:10; 10:16; 23:33	3
Mk.	16:18	1
Lk.	10:19; 11:11	2
Jn.	3:14	1
1 Co.	10:9	1
2 Co.	11:3	1
Rev.	9:19; 12:9, 14, 15; 20:2	5
Total		14

3690. ὀφρύς, ophrus′

Book	brow	Total
Lk.	4:29	1

3691. ὀχλέω, ochle′ō

Book	vex	Total
Lk.	6:18	1
Ac.	5:16	1
Total		2

3692. ὀχλοποιέω, ochlopoie′ō

Book	gather a company	Total
Ac.	17:5	1

3694. ὀχύρωμα, ochu′rōma

Book	strong hold	Total
2 Co.	10:4	1

3697. ὄψιμος, op′simos

Book	latter	Total
Jas.	5:7	1

3693. ὄχλος, och′los

Book	Oc.	people	Oc.	multitude	Oc.	press	Oc.	company	Oc.	number of people	Oc.	number	Total
Mt.	8	7:28; 9:23, 25; 12:23, 46; 14:13; 21:26; 27:15	42	4:25; 5:1; 8:1, 18; 9:8, 33, 36; 11:7; 12:15; 13: 2, 2, 34, 36; 14:5, 14, 15, 19, 19, 22, 23; 15: 10, 30, 31, 32, 33, 35, 36, 39; 17:14; 19:2; 20: 29, 31; 21:8, 9, 11, 46; 22:33; 23:1; 26:47, 55; 27:20, 24									50
Mk.	19	5:21, 24; 6:33, 34, 45; 7:14, 17; 8:6, 6, 34; 9:15, 25; 10:1; 11:18; 12:12, 37, 41; 15:11, 15	15	2:13; 3:9, 20, 32; 4:1, 1, 36; 5:31; 7:33; 8:1, 2; 9:14, 17; 14:43; 15:8	3	2:4; 5:27, 30			1	10:46			38
Lk.	22	3:10; 4:42; 5:1, 3; 7:9, 11, 12, 24; 8:4, 40, 42; 9:11, 18, 37; 11:14, 29; 12:1, 54; 13:14, 17; 23:4, 48	12	3:7; 5:15, 19; 6:19; 8: 45; 9:12, 16; 14:25; 18: 36; 19:39; 22:6, 47	2	8:19; 19:3	5	5:29; 6:17; 9:38; 11: 27; 12:13					41
Jn.	17	6:22, 24; 7:12, 12, 20, 31, 32, 40, 43, 49; 11:42; 12:9, 12, 17, 18, 29, 34	2	5:13; 6:2			1	6:5					20
Ac.	15	8:6; 11:24, 26; 14:11, 13, 14, 18, 19; 17: 8, 13; 19:26, 35; 21:27, 35; 24:12	5	13:45; 16:22; 19:33; 21:34; 24:18			1	6:7			1	1:15	22
Rev.	1	19:1	3	7:9; 17:15; 19:6									4
Total	82		79		5		7		1		1		175

3695. ὀψάριον, opsar′ion

Book	Oc.	fish	Oc.	small fish	Total
Jn.	4	6:11; 21:9, 10, 13	1	6:9	5

3696. ὀψέ, opse′

Book	Oc.	in the end	Oc.	even	Oc.	at even	Total
Mt.	1	28:1					1
Mk.			1	11:19	1	13:35	2
Total	1		1		1		3

3698. ὄψιος, op′sios

Book	Oc.	even	Oc.	evening	Oc.	in the evening (with 1096)	Oc.	eventide (with 5510)	Oc.	at even (with 1096)	Total
Mt.	4	8:16; 20:8; 26:20; 27:57	3	14:15, 23; 16:2							7
Mk.	3	4:35; 6:47; 15:42			1	14:17	1	11:11	1	1:32	6
Jn.	1	6:16	1	20:19							2
Total	8		4		1		1		1		15

3699. ὄψις, op′sis

Book	Oc.	appearance	Oc.	face	Oc.	countenance	Total
Jn.	1	7:24	1	11:44			2
Rev.					1	1:16	1
Total	1		1		1		3

3700. ὀψώνιον, opsō′nion

Book	Oc.	wage	Oc.	charges	Total
Lk.	1	3:14			1
Ro.	1	6:23			1
1 Co.			1	9:7	1
2 Co.	1	11:8			1
Total	3		1		4

3701. ὁ ὢν καὶ ὁ ἦν καὶ ὁ ἐρχόμενος, ho ōn kai ho ẹn kai ho erchom′enos

Book	Oc.	which is	Oc.	and which was	Oc.	and which is to come	Oc.	which art	Oc.	and wast	Oc.	which was	Oc.	and is	Oc.	and is to come	Oc.	and art to come	Oc.	and shall be	Total
Rev.	2	1:4a, 8a	2	1:4b, 8b	2	1:4c, 8c	2	11:17a; 16:5a	2	11:17b; 16:5b	1	4:8a	1	4:8b	1	4:8c	1	11:17c	1	16:5c	15

3702. παγιδεύω, pagideu′ō

Book	entangle	Total
Mt.	22:15	1

3703. παγίς, pagis′

Book	snare	Total
Lk.	21:35	1
Ro.	11:9	1
1 Ti.	3:7; 6:9	2
2 Ti.	2:26	1
Total		5

3704. πάθημα, path′ẹma

Book	Oc.	suffering	Oc.	affliction	Oc.	affection	Oc.	motion	Total
Ro.	1	8:18					1	7:5	2
2 Co.	3	1:5, 6, 7							3
Gal.					1	5:24			1
Phl.	1	3:10							1
Col.	1	1:24							1
2 Ti.			1	3:11					1
Heb.	2	2:9, 10	1	10:32					3
1 Pt.	3	1:11; 4:13; 5:1	1	5:9					4
Total	11		3		1		1		16

3705. παθητός, pathētos′

Book	suffer	Total
Ac.	26:23	1

3706. πάθος, path′os

Book	Oc.	inordinate affection	Oc.	affection	Oc.	lust	Total
Ro.			1	1:26			1
Col.	1	3:5					1
1 Th.					1	4:5	1
Total	1		1		1		3

3712. παιδιόθεν, paidioth′en

Book	of a child	Total
Mk.	9:21	1

3707. παιδαγωγός, paidagōgos′

Book	Oc.	schoolmaster	Oc.	instructor	Total
1 Co.			1	4:15	1
Gal.	2	3:24, 25			2
Total	2		1		3

3708. παιδάριον, paidar′ion

Book	Oc.	child	Oc.	lad	Total
Mt.	1	11:16			1
Jn.			1	6:9	1
Total	1		1		2

3709. παιδεία, paidei′a

Book	Oc.	chastening	Oc.	nurture	Oc.	instruction	Oc.	chastisement	Total
Eph.			1	6:4					1
2 Ti.					1	3:16			1
Heb.	3	12:5, 7, 11					1	12:8	4
Total	3		1		1		1		6

3710. παιδευτής, paideutēs′

Book	Oc.	instructor	Oc.	which corrected	Total
Ro.	1	2:20			1
Heb.			1	12:9	1
Total	1		1		2

3711. παιδεύω, paideu′ō

Book	Oc.	chasten	Oc.	chastise	Oc.	learn	Oc.	teach	Oc.	instruct	Total
Lk.			2	23:16, 22							2
Ac.					1	7:22	1	22:3			2
1 Co.	1	11:32									1
2 Co.	1	6:9									1
1 Ti.					1	1:20					1
2 Ti.									1	2:25	1
Tit.							1	2:12			1
Heb.	3	12:6, 7, 10									3
Rev.	1	3:19									1
Total	6		2		2		2		1		13

3713. παιδίον, paidi′on

Book	Oc.	child	Oc.	little child	Oc.	young child	Oc.	damsel	Total
Mt.	2	14:21; 15:38	6	18:2, 3, 4, 5; 19:13, 14	9	2:8, 9, 11, 13, 13, 14, 20, 20, 21			17
Mk.	4	7:28; 9:24, 36, 37	2	10:14, 15	1	10:13	4	5:39, 40, 40, 41	11
Lk.	12	1:59, 66, 76, 80; 2:17, 21, 27, 40; 7:32; 9:47, 48; 11:7	2	18:16, 17					14
Jn.	3	4:49; 16:21; 21:5							3
1 Co.	1	14:20							1
Heb.	3	2:13, 14; 11:23							3
1 Jn.			2	2:13, 18					2
Total	25		12		10		4		51

3714. παιδίσκη, paidis′kē

Book	Oc.	damsel	Oc.	bondwoman	Oc.	maid	Oc.	maiden	Oc.	bondmaid	Total
Mt.	1	26:69									1
Mk.					2	14:66, 69					2
Lk.					1	22:56	1	12:45			2
Jn.	1	18:17									1
Ac.	2	12:13; 16:16									2
Gal.			4	4:23, 30, 30, 31					1	4:22	5
Total	4		4		3		1		1		13

3716. παῖς, pais

Book	Oc.	servant	Oc.	child	Oc.	son (Christ)	Oc.	son	Oc.	man-servant	Oc.	maid	Oc.	maiden	Oc.	young man	Total
Mt.	5	8:6, 8, 13; 12:18; 14:2	3	2:16; 17:18; 21:15													8
Lk.	4	1:54, 69; 7:7; 15:26	2	2:43; 9:42					1	12:45	1	8:51	1	8:54			9
Jn.							1	4:51									1
Ac.	1	4:25	2	4:27, 30	2	3:13, 26									1	20:12	6
Total	10		7		2		1		1		1		1		1		24

3717. παίω, pai′ō

Book	Oc.	smite	Oc.	strike	Total
Mt.	1	26:68			1
Mk.	1	14:47			1
Lk.	1	22:64			1
Jn.	1	18:10			1
Rev.			1	9:5	1
Total	4		1		5

3715. παίζω, paid′zō

Book	play	Total
1 Co.	10:7	1

3718. Πακατιανή, Pakatianē′

Book	Pacatiana	Total
1 Ti.	subscript	1

3719. πάλαι, pal′ai

Book	Oc.	long ago	Oc.	any while	Oc.	a great while ago	Oc.	old	Oc.	in time past	Oc.	of old	Total
Mt.	1	11:21											1
Mk.			1	15:44									1
Lk.					1	10:13							1
Heb.									1	1:1			1
2 Pt.							1	1:9					1
Jd.											1	1:4	1
Total	1		1		1		1		1		1		6

3720. παλαιός, palaios′

Book	Oc.	old	Oc.	old wine	Total
Mt.	3	9:16, 17; 13:52			3
Mk.	3	2:21, 21, 22			3
Lk.	4	5:36, 36, 37, 39b	1	5:39a	5
Ro.	1	6:6			1
1 Co.	2	5:7, 8			2
2 Co.	1	3:14			1
Eph.	1	4:22			1
Col.	1	3:9			1
1 Jn.	2	2:7, 7			2
Total	18		1		19

3721. παλαιότης, palaiot′ēs

Book	oldness	Total
Ro.	7:6	1

3723. πάλη, pal′ē

Book	wrestle	Total
Eph.	6:12	1

3722. παλαιόω, palaio′ō

Book	Oc.	wax old	Oc.	make old	Oc.	decay	Total
Lk.	1	12:33					1
Heb.	1	1:11	1	8:13a	1	8:13b	3
Total	2		1		1		4

3724. παλιγγενεσία palinggenesi′a

Book	regeneration	Total
Mt.	19:28	1
Tit.	3:5	1
Total		2

3725. πάλιν, pal′in

Book	again	Total
Mt.	4:7, 8; 5:33; 13:44, 45, 47; 18:19; 19:24; 20:5; 21:36; 22:1, 4; 26:42, 43, 44, 72; 27:50	17
Mk.	2:1, 13; 3:1, 20; 4:1; 5:21; 7:31; 8:13, 25; 10:1, 1, 10, 24, 32; 11:27; 12:4, 5; 14:39, 40, 61, 69, 70, 70; 15:4, 12, 13	26
Lk.	13:20; 23:20	2
Jn.	1:35; 4:3, 13, 46, 54; 6:15; 8:2, 8, 12, 21; 9:15, 17, 26, 27; 10:7, 17, 18, 19, 31, 39, 40; 11:7, 8, 38; 12:22, 28, 39; 13:12; 14:3; 16:16, 17, 19, 22, 28; 18:7, 27, 33, 38, 40; 19:4, 9, 37; 20:10, 21, 26; 21:1, 16	47
Ac.	10:15, 16; 11:10; 17:32; 18:21; 27:28	6
Ro.	8:15; 11:23; 15:10, 11, 12	5
1 Co.	3:20; 7:5; 12:21	3
2 Co.	1:16; 2:1; 3:1; 5:12; 10:7; 11:16; 12:19, 21; 13:2	9
Gal.	1:9, 17; 2:1, 18; 4:9, 9, 19; 5:1, 3	9
Phl.	1:26; 2:28; 4:4	3
Heb.	1:5, 6; 2:13, 13; 4:5, 7; 5:12; 6:1, 6; 10:30	10
Jas.	5:18	1
2 Pt.	2:20	1
1 Jn.	2:8	1
Rev.	10:8, 11	2
Total		142

3729. πανδοχεῖον, pandochei′on

Book	inn	Total
Lk.	10:34	1

3730. πανδοχεύς, pandocheus′

Book	host	Total
Lk.	10:35	1

3731. πανήγυρις, panē′guris

Book	general assembly	Total
Heb.	12:23	1

3732. πανοικί, panoiki′

Book	with all (one's) house	Total
Ac.	16:34	1

3735. πανοῦργος, panour′gos

Book	crafty	Total
2 Co.	12:16	1

3726. παμπληθεί, pamplēthei′

Book	all at once	Total
Lk.	23:18	1

3727. πάμπολυς, pam′polus

Book	very great	Total
Mk.	8:1	1

3728. Παμφυλία, Pamphuli′a

Book	Pamphylia	Total
Ac.	2:10; 13:13; 14:24; 15:38; 27:5	5

3733. πανοπλία, panopli′a

Book	Oc.	whole armour	Oc.	all . . . armour	Total
Lk.			1	11:22	1
Eph.	2	6:11, 13			2
Total	2		1		3

3734. πανουργία, panourgi′a

Book	Oc.	craftiness	Oc.	subtility	Oc.	cunning craftiness	Total
Lk.	1	20:23					1
1 Co.	1	3:19					1
2 Co.	1	4:2	1	11:3			2
Eph.					1	4:14	1
Total	3		1		1		5

3736. πανταχόθεν, pantachoth′en

Book	from every quarter	Total
Mk.	1:45	1

3739. πάντη, pan′tē

Book	always	Total
Ac.	24:3	1

3737. πανταχοῦ, pantachou′

Book	Oc.	every where	Oc.	in all places	Total
Mk.	1	16:20			1
Lk.	1	9:6			1
Ac.	3	17:30; 21:28; 28:22	1	24:3	4
1 Co.	1	4:17			1
Total	6		1		7

3738. παντελής, pantelēs′

Book	Oc.	in no wise (with 1519 and 3488)	Oc.	uttermost	Total
Lk.	1	13:11			1
Heb.			1	7:25	1
Total	1		1		2

3740. πάντοθεν, pan′tothen

Book	Oc.	on every side	Oc.	always	Oc.	round about	Total
Lk.	1	19:43					1
Jn.			1	18:20			1
Heb.					1	9:4	1
Total	1		1		1		3

3741. παντοκράτωρ, pantokrat′ōr

Book	Oc.	Almighty	Oc.	omnipotent	Total
2 Co.	1	6:18			1
Rev.	8	1:8; 4:8; 11:17; 15:3; 16:7, 14; 19:15; 21:22	1	19:6	9
Total	9		1		10

3742. πάντοτε, pan′tote

Book	Oc.	always	Oc.	ever	Oc.	alway	Oc.	evermore	Total
Mt.	2	26:11, 11							2
Mk.	2	14:7, 7							2
Lk.		18:1	1	15:31					2
Jn.	5	8:29; 11:42; 12:8, 8; 18:20b	1	18:20a	1	7:6	1	6:34	8
Ro.	1	1:9							1
1 Co.	2	1:4; 15:58							2
2 Co.	4	2:14; 4:10; 5:6; 9:8							4
Gal.	1	4:18							1
Eph.	1	5:20							1
Phl.	3	1:4, 20; 2:12			1	4:4			4
Col.	2	1:3; 4:12			1	4:6			3
1 Th.	2	1:2; 3:6	2	4:17; 5:15	1	2:16	1	5:16	6
2 Th.	2	1:3, 11			1	2:13			3
2 Ti.			1	3:7					1
Phe.	1	1:4							1
Heb.			1	7:25					1
Total	29		6		5		2		42

3743. πάντως, pan′tōs

Book	Oc.	by all means	Oc.	altogether	Oc.	surely	Oc.	must needs (with 1163)	Oc.	no doubt	Oc.	in no wise	Oc.	at all	Total
Lk.					1	4:23									1
Ac.	1	18:21					1	21:22	1	28:4					3
Ro.											1	3:9			1
1 Co.	1	9:22	2	5:10; 9:10									1	16:12	4
Total	2		2		1		1		1		1		1		9

3744a. παρά, para' (with genitive)

Book	Oc.	of	Oc.	from	Oc.	the Lord's doing (with 2962)	Oc.	Not Tr.	Oc.	Misc.	Total
Mt.	5	2:4, 7, 16; 18:19; 20:20			1	21:42					6
Mk.	1	8:11	2	12:2; 14:43	1	12:11			2	3:21; 5:26	6
Lk.	4	6:19, 34; 11:16; 12:48	3	1:45; 2:1; 8:49					1	10:7	8
Jn.	13	1:14; 4:9, 52; 5:44a; 6:45, 46; 8:26, 40; 9:16, 33; 10:18; 15:15; 17:7	10	1:6; 5:34, 41, 44b; 7:29; 15:26, 26; 16:27, 28; 17:8			2	1:40; 7:51			25
Ac.	12	2:33; 3:2, 5; 7:16; 9:2; 10:22; 17:9; 20:24; 22:30; 24:8; 26:22; 28:22	4	9:14; 22:5; 26:10, 12							16
Ro.							1	11:27			1
Gal.	1	1:12									1
Eph.	1	6:8									1
Phl.	1	4:18a	1	4:18b							2
1 Th.	2	2:13; 4:1									2
2 Th.	1	3:6					1	3:8			2
2 Ti.	4	1:13, 18; 2:2; 3:14									4
Jas.	2	1:5, 7									2
2 Pt.			1	1:17							1
1 Jn.	2	3:22; 5:15									2
2 Jn.			3	1:3, 3, 4							3
Rev.	2	2:27; 3:18									2
Total	51		24		2		4		3		84

Miscellaneous: Mk. 3:21 (with 3488), (one's) friends; Mk. 5:26 (with 1438), that (one) has; Lk. 10:7 (with 846), as they give.

3744b. παρά, para' (with dative)

Book	Oc.	with	Oc.	among	Oc.	by	Oc.	before	Oc.	of	Oc.	in	Oc.	in the sight of	Total
Mt.	4	19:26, 26; 21:25; 22:25	1	28:15					1	6:1					6
Mk.	3	10:27, 27, 27													3
Lk.	7	1:30, 37; 2:52; 11:37; 18:27, 27; 19:7			1	9:47									8
Jn.	9	1:39; 4:40; 8:38, 38; 14:17, 23, 25; 17:5, 5			1	19:25									10
Ac.	8	9:43; 10:6a; 18:3, 20; 21:7, 8, 16; 26:8													8
Ro.	2	2:11; 9:14					1	2:13			2	11:25; 12:16			5
1 Co.	2	3:19; 7:24			1	16:2									3
2 Co.	1	1:17													1
Gal.													1	3:11	1
Eph.	1	6:9													1
Col.			1	4:16											1
2 Th.	1	1:6													1
2 Ti.	1	4:13													1
Jas.	1	1:17					1	1:27							2
1 Pt.	1	2:20							1	2:4					2
2 Pt.	1	3:8					1	2:11							2
Rev.			1	2:13											1
Total	42		3		3		3		2		2		1		56

3744c. παρά, para' (with accusative)

Book	Oc.	by . . . side	Oc.	at	Oc.	than	Oc.	by	Oc.	above	Oc.	contrary to	Oc.	against	Oc.	Misc.	Total
Mt.	4	13:1, 4, 19; 20:30	1	15:30			1	4:18							1	15:29	7
Mk.	5	2:13; 4:1, 4, 15; 10:46					1	1:16							1	5:21	7
Lk.	3	8:5, 12; 18:35	5	7:38; 8:35, 41; 10:39; 17:16	1	3:13	2	5:1, 2	2	13:2, 4							13
Ac.	3	10:6b, 32; 16:13	6	4:35, 37; 5:2, 10; 7:58; 22:3							1	18:13					10
Ro.									1	14:5	2	11:24; 16:17	2	1:26; 4:18	2	1:25; 12:3	7
1 Co.					1	3:11									2	12:15, 16	3
2 Co.															1	11:24	1
Gal.					2	1:8, 9											2
Heb.					7	1:4; 2:7, 9; 3:3; 9:23; 11:4; 12:24	1	11:12	1	1:9					1	11:11	10
Total	15		12		11		5		4		3		2		8		60

Miscellaneous: Mt. 15:29, and; Mk. 5:21, nigh unto; Ro. 1:25, more than; Ro. 12:3 (with 3639), more than; 1 Co. 12:15, 16 (with 5024), therefore; 2 Co. 11:24, save; Heb. 11:11, past.

Word 3744 has 200 occurrences.

3745. παραβαίνω, parabai'nō

Book	Oc.	transgress	Oc.	fall by transgression	Total
Mt.	2	15:2, 3			2
Ac.			1	1:25	1
2 Jn.	1	1:9			1
Total	3		1		4

3746. παραβάλλω, parabal'lō

Book	Oc.	compare	Oc.	arrive	Total
Mk.	1	4:30			1
Ac.			1	20:15	1
Total	1		1		2

3747. παράβασις, parab'asis

Book	Oc.	transgression	Oc.	breaking	Total
Ro.	2	4:15; 5:14	1	2:23	3
Gal.	1	3:19			1
1 Ti.	1	2:14			1
Heb.	2	2:2; 9:15			2
Total	6		1		7

3748. παραβάτης, parabat'ēs

Book	Oc.	transgressor	Oc.	breaker	Oc.	transgress	Total
Ro.			1	2:25	1	2:27	2
Gal.	1	2:18					1
Jas.	2	2:9, 11					2
Total	3		1		1		5

3749. παραβιάζομαι
parabiad´zomai

Book	constrain	Total
Lk.	24:29	1
Ac.	16:15	1
Total		2

3750. παραβολή, parabolē´

Book	Oc.	parable	Oc.	figure	Oc.	comparison	Oc.	proverb	Total
Mt.	17	13:3, 10, 13, 18, 24, 31, 33, 34, 34, 35, 36, 53; 15:15; 21:33, 45; 22:1; 24:32							17
Mk.	12	3:23; 4:2, 10, 11, 13, 13, 33, 34; 7:17; 12: 1, 12; 13:28			1	4:30			13
Lk.	17	5:36; 6:39; 8:4, 9, 10, 11; 12:16, 41; 13: 6; 14:7; 15:3; 18:1, 9; 19:11; 20:9, 19; 21:29					1	4:23	18
Heb.			2	9:9; 11: 19					2
Total	46		2		1		1		50

3751. παραβουλεύομαι
parabouleu´omai

Book	regard not	Total
Phl.	2:30	1

3753. παραγγέλλω, paranggel´lō

Book	Oc.	command	Oc.	charge	Oc.	give commandment	Oc.	give charge	Oc.	declare	Oc.	give in charge	Total
Mt.	1	10:5											1
Mk.	2	6:8; 8:6											2
Lk.	2	8:29; 9:21	2	5:14; 8:56									4
Ac.	8	1:4; 4:18; 5:28, 40; 10:42; 15: 5; 16:18; 17:30	2	16:23; 23:22	1	23:30							11
1 Co.	1	7:10											1
1 Th.	1	4:11							1	11:17			2
2 Th.	4	3:4, 6, 10, 12											4
1 Ti.	1	4:11	2	1:3; 6:17			1	6:13			1	5:7	5
Total	20		6		1		1		1		1		30

3752. παραγγελία, paranggeli´a

Book	Oc.	commandment	Oc.	charge	Oc.	straitly	Total
Ac.			1	16:24	1	5:28	2
1 Th.	1	4:2					1
1 Ti.	1	1:5	1	1:18			2
Total	2		2		1		5

3754. παραγίνομαι, paragin´omai

Book	Oc.	come	Oc.	be present	Oc.	go	Total
Mt.	3	2:1; 3:1, 13					3
Mk.	1	14:43					1
Lk.	8	7:4, 20; 8:19; 11:6; 12: 51; 14:21; 19:16; 22:52					8
Jn.	2	3:23; 8:2					2
Ac.	19	5:21, 22, 25; 9:26, 39; 10: 32, 33; 11:23; 13:14; 14: 27; 15:4; 17:10; 18:27; 20:18; 23:35; 24:17, 24; 25:7; 28:21	1	21:18	1	23:16	21
1 Co.	1	16:3					1
Heb.	1	9:11					1
Total	35		1		1		37

3756. παραδειγματίζω, paradeigmatid´zō

Book	Oc.	make a public example	Oc.	put to an open shame	Total
Mt.	1	1:19			1
Heb.			1	6:6	1
Total	1		1		2

3755. παράγω, parag´ō

Book	Oc.	pass by	Oc.	pass away	Oc.	pass forth	Oc.	depart	Oc.	pass	Total
Mt.	1	20:30			1	9:9	1	9:27			3
Mk.	2	2:14; 15:21									2
Jn.	2	8:59; 9:1									2
1 Co.			1	7:31							1
1 Jn.			1	2:17					1	2:8	2
Total	5		2		1		1		1		10

3757. παράδεισος, parad´eisos

Book	paradise	Total
Lk.	23:43	1
2 Co.	12:4	1
Rev.	2:7	1
Total		3

3758. παραδέχομαι, paradech´omai

Book	receive	Total
Mk.	4:20	1
Ac.	16:21; 22:18	2
1 Ti.	5:19	1
Heb.	12:6	1
Total		5

3759. παραδιατριβή, paradiatribē´

Book	perverse disputing	Total
1 Ti.	6:5	1

3761. παράδοξος, parad´oxos

Book	strange	Total
Lk.	5:26	1

3760. παραδίδωμι, paradid´ōmi

Book	Oc.	deliver	Oc.	betray	Oc.	deliver up	Oc.	give	Oc.	give up	Oc.	give over	Oc.	commit	Oc.	Misc.	Total
Mt.	12	5:25, 25; 11:27; 18: 34; 20:19; 25:14, 20, 22; 26:15; 27:2, 18, 26	15	10:4; 17:22; 20:18; 24:10; 26:2, 16, 21, 23, 24, 25, 45, 46, 48; 27:3, 4	4	10:17, 19, 21; 24:9									1	4:12	32
Mk.	7	7:13; 9:31; 10:33, 33; 15:1, 10, 15	9	3:19; 13:12; 14:10, 11, 18, 21, 41, 42, 44	2	13:9, 11									2	1:14; 4:29	20
Lk.	11	1:2; 4:6; 9:44; 10: 22; 12:58; 18:32; 20:20; 21:12; 23: 25; 24:7, 20	6	21:16; 22:4, 6, 21, 22, 48													17
Jn.	4	18:35, 36; 19:11, 16	9	6:64, 71; 12:4; 13:2, 11, 21; 18:2, 5; 21:20	1	18:30			1	19:30							15
Ac.	8	6:14; 12:4; 16:4; 21:11; 22:4; 27:1; 28:16, 17			1	3:13			1	7:42			1	8:3	3	14:26; 15:26, 40	14
Ro.	2	4:25; 6:17			1	8:32			2	1:24, 26	1	1:28					6
1 Co.	4	5:5; 11:2, 23a; 15:3	1	11:23b	1	15:24	1	13:3									7
2 Co.	1	4:11															1
Gal.							1	2:20									1
Eph.							2	5:2, 25			1	4:19					3
1 Ti.	1	1:20															1
1 Pt.													1	2:23			1
2 Pt.	2	2:4, 21															2
Jd.	1	1:3															1
Total	53		40		10		4		4		2		2		6		121

Miscellaneous: Mt. 4:12, cast into prison; Mk. 1:14, put in prison; Mk. 4:29, bring forth; Ac. 14:26, recommend; Ac. 15:26, hazard; Ac. 15:40, recommend.

3762. παράδοσις, parad'osis

Book	Oc.	tradition	Oc.	ordinance	Total
Mt.	3	15:2, 3, 6			3
Mk.	5	7:3, 5, 8, 9, 13			5
1 Co.			1	11:2	1
Gal.	1	1:14			1
Col.	1	2:8			1
2 Th.	2	2:15; 3:6			2
Total	12		1		13

3763. παραζηλόω, paradze̱lo'ō

Book	Oc.	provoke to jealousy	Oc.	provoke to emulation	Total
Ro.	2	10:19; 11:11	1	11:14	3
1 Co.	1	10:22			1
Total	3		1		4

3764. παραθαλάσσιος parathalas'sios

Book	upon the sea coast	Total
Mt.	4:13	1

3765. παραθεωρέω, paratheōre'ō

Book	neglect	Total
Ac.	6:1	1

3766. παραθήκη, parathe̱'ke̱

Book	that . . . committed (with 3488)	Total
2 Ti.	1:12	1

3767. παραινέω, paraine'ō

Book	Oc.	admonish	Oc.	exhort	Total
Ac.	1	27:9	1	27:22	2

3769. παρακαθίζω parakathid'zō

Book	sit	Total
Lk.	10:39	1

3768. παραιτέομαι, paraite'omai

Book	Oc.	refuse	Oc.	excuse	Oc.	make excuse	Oc.	avoid	Oc.	reject	Oc.	intreat	Total
Lk.			2	14:18b, 19	1	14:18a							3
Ac.	1	25:11											1
1 Ti.	2	4:7; 5:11											2
2 Ti.							1	2:23					1
Tit.									1	3:10			1
Heb.	2	12:25, 25									1	12:19	3
Total	5		2		1		1		1		1		11

3770. παρακαλέω, parakale'ō

Book	Oc.	beseech	Oc.	comfort	Oc.	exhort	Oc.	desire	Oc.	pray	Oc.	intreat	Oc.	Misc.	Total
Mt.	5	8:5, 31, 34; 14:36; 18:29	2	2:18; 5:4			1	18:32	1	26:53					9
Mk.	7	1:40; 5:10, 12, 23; 6:56; 7:32; 8:22							2	5:17, 18					9
Lk.	4	7:4; 8:31, 32, 41	1	16:25							1	15:28	1	3:18	7
Ac.	6	13:42; 16:15, 39; 21:12; 25:2; 27:33	2	16:40; 20:12	4	2:40; 11:23; 14: 22; 15:32	4	8:31; 9: 38; 19: 31; 28: 14	3	16:9; 24: 4; 27:34			2	20:2; 28:20	21
Ro.	3	12:1; 15:30; 16:17			1	12:8									4
1 Co.	3	1:10; 4:16; 16:15	1	14:31			1	16:12			1	4:13			6
2 Co.	5	2:8; 5:20; 6:1; 10:1; 12: 8	9	1:4, 4, 4, 6; 2:7; 7: 6, 6, 7, 13	1	9:5	2	8:6; 12: 18					1	13:11	18
Eph.	1	4:1	1	6:22											2
Phl.	2	4:2, 2													2
Col.			2	2:2; 4:8											2
1 Th.	1	4:10	4	3:2, 7; 4:18; 5:11	3	2:11; 4:1; 5:14									8
2 Th.			1	2:17	1	3:12									2
1 Ti.	1	1:3			2	2:1; 6:2					1	5:1			4
2 Ti.					1	4:2									1
Tit.					3	1:9; 2:6, 15									3
Phe.	2	1:9, 10													2
Heb.	2	13:19, 22			2	3:13; 10:25									4
1 Pt.	1	2:11			2	5:1, 12									3
Jd.					1	1:3									1
Total	43		23		21		8		6		3		4		108

Miscellaneous: Lk. 3:18, in (one's) exhortation; Ac. 20:2, give exhortation; Ac. 28:20, call for; 2 Co. 13:11, be of good comfort.

3771. παρακαλύπτω parakalup'tō

Book	hide	Total
Lk.	9:45	1

3772. παρακαταθήκη, parakatathe̱'ke̱

Book	Oc.	that committed to (one's) trust (with 3488)	Oc.	that committed (with 3488)	Total
1 Ti.	1	6:20			1
2 Ti.			1	1:14	1
Total	1		1		2

3773. παράκειμαι, parak'eimai

Book	be present	Total
Ro.	7:18, 21	2

3774. παράκλησις, parak'le̱sis

Book	Oc.	consolation	Oc.	exhortation	Oc.	comfort	Oc.	intreaty	Total
Lk.	2	2:25; 6:24							2
Ac.	2	4:36; 15:31	1	13:15	1	9:31			4
Ro.	1	15:5	1	12:8	1	15:4			3
1 Co.			1	14:3					1
2 Co.	5	1:5, 6, 6, 7; 7:7	1	8:17	4	1:3, 4; 7:4, 13	1	8:4	11
Phl.	1	2:1							1
1 Th.			1	2:3					1
2 Th.	1	2:16							1
1 Ti.			1	4:13					1
Phe.	1	1:7							1
Heb.	1	6:18	2	12:5; 13:22					3
Total	14		8		6		1		29

3776. παρακοή, parakoe̱'

Book	disobedience	Total
Ro.	5:19	1
2 Co.	10:6	1
Heb.	2:2	1
Total		3

3778. παρακούω, parakou'ō

Book	neglect to hear	Total
Mt.	18:17, 17	2

3777. παρακολουθέω, parakoloutheʹō

Book	Oc.	follow	Oc.	have under-standing	Oc.	attain	Oc.	fully know	Total
Mk.	1	16:17							1
Lk.			1	1:3					1
1 Ti.					1	4:6			1
2 Ti.							1	3:10	1
Total	1		1		1		1		4

3775. παράκλητος, parak'le̱tos

Book	Oc.	comforter	Oc.	advocate	Total
Jn.	4	14:16, 26; 15:26; 16:7			4
1 Jn.			1	2:1	1
Total	4		1		5

3779. παρακύπτω, parakup′tō

Book	Oc.	stoop down	Oc.	look	Total
Lk.	1	24:12			1
Jn.	2	20:5, 11			2
Jas.			1	1:25	1
1 Pt.			1	1:12	1
Total	3		2		5

3780. παραλαμβάνω, paralamban′ō

Book	Oc.	take	Oc.	receive	Oc.	take unto	Oc.	take up	Oc.	take with	Total
Mt.	11	2:13, 14, 20, 21; 12:45; 17:1; 18:16; 20:17; 24: 40, 41; 27:27			2	1:20, 24	2	4:5, 8	1	26:37	16
Mk.	5	4:36; 5:40; 9:2; 10:32; 14:33	1	7:4							6
Lk.	7	9:10, 28; 11:26; 17:34, 35, 36; 18:31									7
Jn.	1	19:16	2	1:11; 14:3							3
Ac.	6	15:39; 16:33; 21:24, 26, 32; 23:18									6
1 Co.			3	11:23; 15:1, 3							3
Gal.			2	1:9, 12							2
Phl.			1	4:9							1
Col.			2	2:6; 4:17							2
1 Th.			2	2:13; 4:1							2
2 Th.			1	3:6							1
Heb.			1	12:28							1
Total	30		15		2		2		1		50

3781. παραλέγομαι, paraleg′omai

Book	Oc.	pass	Oc.	sail by	Total
Ac.	1	27:8	1	27:13	2

3782. παράλιος, paral′ios

Book	sea coast	Total
Lk.	6:17	1

3783. παραλλαγή, parallagẹ′

Book	variableness	Total
Jas.	1:17	1

3784. παραλογίζομαι, paralogid′zomai

Book	Oc.	beguile	Oc.	deceive	Total
Col.	1	2:4			1
Jas.			1	1:22	1
Total	1		1		2

3785. παραλυτικός, paralutikos′

Book	Oc.	sick of the palsy	Oc.	(one) that has the palsy	Total
Mt.	4	8:6; 9:2, 2, 6	1	4:24	5
Mk.	5	2:3, 4, 5, 9, 10			5
Total	9		1		10

3786. παραλύω, paralu′ō

Book	Oc.	sick of the palsy	Oc.	taken with palsy	Oc.	feeble	Total
Lk.	1	5:24	1	5:18			2
Ac.	1	9:33	1	8:7			2
Heb.					1	12:12	1
Total	2		2		1		5

3787. παραμένω, paramen′ō

Book	Oc.	continue	Oc.	abide	Total
1 Co.			1	16:6	1
Heb.	1	7:23			1
Jas.	1	1:25			1
Total	2		1		3

3788. παραμυθέομαι
paramuthe′omai

Book	comfort	Total
Jn.	11:19, 31	2
1 Th.	2:11; 5:14	2
Total		4

3789. παραμυθία, paramuthi′a

Book	comfort	Total
1 Co.	14:3	1

3790. παραμύθιον, paramu′thion

Book	comfort	Total
Phl.	2:1	1

3791. παρανομέω, paranome′ō

Book	contrary to the law	Total
Ac.	23:3	1

3792. παρανομία, paranomi′a

Book	iniquity	Total
2 Pt.	2:16	1

3793. παραπικραίνω
parapikrai′nō

Book	provoke	Total
Heb.	3:16	1

3794. παραπικρασμός
parapikrasmos′

Book	provocation	Total
Heb.	3:8, 15	2

3795. παραπίπτω, parapip′tō

Book	fall away	Total
Heb.	6:6	1

3796. παραπλέω, paraple′ō

Book	sail by	Total
Ac.	20:16	1

3797. παραπλήσιον, paraplẹ′sion

Book	nigh unto	Total
Phl.	2:27	1

3798. παραπλησίως, paraplẹsi′ōs

Book	likewise	Total
Heb.	2:14	1

3799. παραπορεύομαι, paraporeu′omai

Book	Oc.	pass by	Oc.	go	Oc.	pass	Total
Mt.	1	27:39					1
Mk.	2	11:20; 15:29	1	2:23	1	9:30	4
Total	3		1		1		5

3800. παράπτωμα, parap′tōma

Book	Oc.	trespass	Oc.	offence	Oc.	sin	Oc.	fall	Oc.	fault	Total
Mt.	4	6:14, 15, 15; 18:35									4
Mk.	2	11:25, 26									2
Ro.			7	4:25; 5:15, 15, 16, 17, 18, 20			2	11:11, 12			9
2 Co.	1	5:19									1
Gal.									1	6:1	1
Eph.	1	2:1			2	1:7; 2:5					3
Col.	1	2:13b			1	2:13a					2
Jas.									1	5:16	1
Total	9		7		3		2		2		23

3801. παραῤῥυέω, pararhrue′ō

Book	let slip	Total
Heb.	2:1	1

3802. παράσημος, paras′ẹmos

Book	sign	Total
Ac.	28:11	1

3803. παρασκευάζω, paraskeuad′zō

Book	Oc.	make ready	Oc.	prepare oneself	Oc.	be ready	Oc.	ready	Total
Ac.	1	10:10							1
1 Co.			1	14:8					1
2 Co.					1	9:2	1	9:3	2
Total	1		1		1		1		4

3804. παρασκευή, paraskeuẹ′

Book	preparation	Total
Mt.	27:62	1
Mk.	15:42	1
Lk.	23:54	1
Jn.	19:14, 31, 42	3
Total		6

3805. παρατείνω, paratei′nō

Book	continue	Total
Ac.	20:7	1

3806. παρατηρέω, paratẹre′ō

Book	Oc.	watched	Oc.	observe	Oc.	watched (with 2258)	Total
Mk.	1	3:2					1
Lk.	2	6:7; 20:20			1	14:1	3
Ac.	1	9:24					1
Gal.			1	4:10			1
Total	4		1		1		6

3807. παρατήρησις, paratẹ′rẹsis

Book	observation	Total
Lk.	17:20	1

3808. παρατίθημι, paratith'ęmi

Book	Oc.	set before	Oc.	commit	Oc.	commend	Oc.	put forth	Oc.	commit the keeping of	Oc.	allege	Total
Mt.							2	13:24, 31					2
Mk.	4	6:41; 8:6, 6, 7											4
Lk.	3	9:16; 10:8; 11:6	1	12:48	1	23:46							5
Ac.	1	16:34			2	14:23; 20:32					1	17:3	4
1 Co.	1	10:27											1
1 Ti.			1	1:18									1
2 Ti.			1	2:2									1
1 Pt.									1	4:19			1
Total	9		3		3		2		1		1		19

3809. παρατυγχάνω paratungchan'ō

Book	meet with	Total
Ac.	17:17	1

3810. παραυτίκα, parauti'ka

Book	but for a moment	Total
2 Co.	4:17	1

3811. παραφέρω, parapher'ō

Book	Oc.	take away	Oc.	remove	Total
Mk.	1	14:36			1
Lk.			1	22:42	1
Total	1		1		2

3812. παραφρονέω paraphrone'ō

Book	as a fool	Total
2 Co.	11:23	1

3813. παραφρονία, paraphroni'a

Book	madness	Total
2 Pt.	2:16	1

3814. παραχειμάζω paracheimad'zo

Book	winter	Total
Ac.	27:12; 28:11	2
1 Co.	16:6	1
Tit.	3:12	1
Total		4

3815. παραχειμασία paracheimasi'a

Book	winter in	Total
Ac.	27:12	1

3816. παραχρῆμα, parachrę'ma

Book	Oc.	immediately	Oc.	straight way	Oc.	forthwith	Oc.	presently	Oc.	soon	Total
Mt.							1	21:19	1	21:20	2
Lk.	9	1:64; 4:39; 5:25; 8:44, 47; 13:13; 18:43; 19:11; 22:60	1	8:55							10
Ac.	4	3:7; 12:23; 13:11; 16:26	2	5:10; 16:33	1	9:18					7
Total	13		3		1		1		1		19

3817. πάρδαλις, par'dalis

Book	leopard	Total
Rev.	13:2	1

3819. παρεισάγω, pareisag'ō

Book	privily bring in	Total
2 Pt.	2:1	1

3820. παρείσακτος, pareis'aktos

Book	brought in unawares	Total
Gal.	2:4	1

3821. παρεισδύνω, pareisdu'nō

Book	creep in unawares	Total
Jd.	1:4	1

3818. πάρειμι, par'eimi

Book	Oc.	be present	Oc.	come	Oc.	present	Oc.	be here present	Oc.	be here	Oc.	such things as one hath (with 3488)	Oc.	he that lacketh (with 3261 and 3639)	Total
Mt.			1	26:50											1
Lk.	1	13:1													1
Jn.			2	7:6; 11:28											2
Ac.			3	10:21; 12:20; 17:6			1	10:33	1	24:19					5
1 Co.	1	5:3b			1	5:3a									2
2 Co.	5	10:2, 11; 11:9; 13:2, 10													5
Gal.	2	4:18, 20													2
Col.			1	1:6											1
Heb.					1	12:11					1	13:5			2
2 Pt.					1	1:12							1	1:9	2
Total	9		7		3		1		1		1		1		23

3822. παρεισέρχομαι, pareiser'chomai

Book	Oc.	enter	Oc.	come in privily	Total
Ro.	1	5:20			1
Gal.			1	2:4	1
Total	1		1		2

3824. παρεκτός, parektos'

Book	Oc.	saving	Oc.	except	Oc.	be without	Total
Mt.	1	5:32					1
Ac.			1	26:29			1
2 Co.					1	11:28	1
Total	1		1		1		3

3823. παρεισφέρω, pareispher'ō

Book	give	Total
2 Pt.	1:5	1

3826. παρενοχλέω, parenochle'ō

Book	trouble	Total
Ac.	15:19	1

3825. παρεμβολή, parembolę'

Book	Oc.	castle	Oc.	camp	Oc.	army	Total
Ac.	6	21:34, 37; 22:24; 23:10, 16, 32					6
Heb.			2	13:11, 13	1	11:34	3
Rev.			1	20:9			1
Total	6		3		1		10

3827. παρεπίδημος, parepid'ęmos

Book	Oc.	pilgrim	Oc.	stranger	Total
Heb.	1	11:13			1
1 Pt.	1	2:11	1	1:1	2
Total	2		1		3

3828. παρέρχομαι, parer'chomai

Book	Oc.	pass away	Oc.	pass	Oc.	pass by	Oc.	pass over	Oc.	trans-gress	Oc.	past	Oc.	go	Oc.	come forth	Oc.	come	Total
Mt.	3	24:35, 35; 26:42	6	5:18, 18; 8:28; 14:15; 24:34; 26:39															9
Mk.	2	13:31, 31	2	13:30; 14:35	1	6:48													5
Lk.	3	21:32, 33, 33	1	16:17	1	18:37	1	11:42	1	15:29			1	17:7	1	12:37			9
Ac.			1	27:9	1	16:8											1	24:7	3
2 Co.	1	5:17																	1
Jas.	1	1:10																	1
1 Pt.											1	4:3							1
2 Pt.	1	3:10																	1
Rev.	1	21:1																	1
Total	12		10		3		1		1		1		1		1		1		31

3830. παρέχω, parech'ō

Book	Oc.	trouble (with 2873)	Oc.	give	Oc.	bring	Oc.	shew	Oc.	do for	Oc.	keep	Oc.	minister	Oc.	offer	Total
Mt.	1	26:10															1
Mk.	1	14:6															1
Lk.	2	11:7; 18:5							1	7:4					1	6:29	4
Ac.			1	17:31	2	16:16; 19:24	1	28:2			1	22:2					5
Gal.	1	6:17															1
Col.			1	4:1													1
1 Ti.			1	6:17									1	1:4			2
Tit.							1	2:7									1
Total	5		3		2		2		1		1		1		1		16

3829. πάρεσις, par'esis

Book	remission	Total
Ro.	3:25	1

3831. παρηγορία, paregori'a

Book	comfort	Total
Col.	4:11	1

3832. παρθενία, partheni'a

Book	virginity	Total
Lk.	2:36	1

3834. Πάρθος, Par'thos

Book	Parthian	Total
Ac.	2:9	1

3833. παρθένος, parthen'os

Book	virgin	Total
Mt.	1:23; 25:1, 7, 11	4
Lk.	1:27, 27	2
Ac.	21:9	1
1 Co.	7:25, 28, 34, 36, 37	5
2 Co.	11:2	1
Rev.	14:4	1
Total		14

3835. παρίημι, pari'emi

Book	hang down	Total
Heb.	12:12	1

3836a. παρίστημι, paris'temi

Book	yield	Total
Ro.	6:13a, 16	2

3836b. παρίστημι, paris'temi

Book	Oc.	stand by	Oc.	present	Oc.	yield	Oc.	shew	Oc.	stand	Oc.	Misc.	Total
Mt.											1	26:53	1
Mk.	4	14:47, 69, 70; 15:35							1	15:39	1	4:29	6
Lk.	1	19:24	1	2:22					1	1:19			3
Jn.	2	18:22; 19:26											2
Ac.	5	1:10; 9:39; 23:2, 4; 27:23	2	9:41; 23:33			1	1:3			5	4:10, 26; 23:24; 24:13; 27:24	13
Ro.			1	12:1	3	6:13b, 19, 19					2	14:10; 16:2	6
1 Co.											1	8:8	1
2 Co.			2	4:14; 11:2									2
Eph.			1	5:27									1
Col.			2	1:22, 28									2
2 Ti.							1	2:15			1	4:17	2
Total	12		9		3		2		2		11		39

Miscellaneous: Mt. 26:53, give presently; Mk. 4:29, come; Ac. 4:10, stand here; Ac. 4:26, stand up; Ac. 23:24, provide; Ac. 24:13, prove; Ac. 27:24, bring before; Ro. 14:10, stand before; Ro. 16:2, assist; 1 Co. 8:8, commend; 2 Ti. 4:17, stand with.

Word 3836 has 41 occurrences.

3837. Παρμενᾶς, Parmenas'

Book	Parmenas	Total
Ac.	6:5	1

3838. πάροδος, par'odos

Book	way	Total
1 Co.	16:7	1

3839. παροικέω, paroike'ō

Book	Oc.	be a stranger	Oc.	sojourn	Total
Lk.	1	24:18			1
Heb.			1	11:9	1
Total	1		1		2

3840. παροικία, paroiki'a

Book	Oc.	dwell as strangers	Oc.	sojourning here	Total
Ac.	1	13:17			1
1 Pt.			1	1:17	1
Total	1		1		2

3841. πάροικος, par'oikos

Book	Oc.	stranger	Oc.	sojourn	Oc.	foreigner	Total
Ac.	1	7:29	1	7:6			2
Eph.					1	2:19	1
1 Pt.	1	2:11					1
Total	2		1		1		4

3842. παροιμία, paroimi'a

Book	Oc.	proverb	Oc.	parable	Total
Jn.	3	16:25, 25, 29	1	10:6	4
2 Pt.	1	2:22			1
Total	4		1		5

3843. πάροινος, par'oinos

Book	given to wine	Total
1 Ti.	3:3	1
Tit.	1:7	1
Total		2

3844. παροίχομαι, paroi'chomai

Book	past	Total
Ac.	14:16	1

3845. παρομοιάζω, paromoiad'zō

Book	be like unto	Total
Mt.	23:27	1

3846. παρόμοιος, parom'oios

Book	like thing	Total
Mk.	7:8, 13	2

3847. παροξύνω, paroxu'nō

Book	Oc.	stir	Oc.	easily provoked	Total
Ac.	1	17:16			1
1 Co.			1	13:5	1
Total	1		1		2

3848. παροξυσμός, paroxusmos'

Book	Oc.	contention . . . so sharp	Oc.	to provoke unto (with 1519)	Total
Ac.	1	15:39			1
Heb.			1	10:24	1
Total	1		1		2

3849. παροργίζω, parorgid'zō

Book	Oc.	anger	Oc.	provoke to wrath	Total
Ro.	1	10:19			1
Eph.			1	6:4	1
Total	1		1		2

3850. παροργισμός
parorgismos´

Book	wrath	Total
Eph.	4:26	1

3851. παροτρύνω, parotru´nō

Book	stir up	Total
Ac.	13:50	1

3852. παρουσία, parousi´a

Book	Oc.	coming	Oc.	presence	Total
Mt.	4	24:3, 27, 37, 39			4
1 Co.	2	15:23; 16:17			2
2 Co.	2	7:6, 7	1	10:10	3
Phl.	1	1:26	1	2:12	2
1 Th.	4	2:19; 3:13; 4:15; 5:23			4
2 Th.	3	2:1, 8, 9			3
Jas.	2	5:7, 8			2
2 Pt.	3	1:16; 3:4, 12			3
1 Jn.	1	2:28			1
Total	22		2		24

3853. παροψίς, paropsis´

Book	platter	Total
Mt.	23:25, 26	2

3854. παῤῥησία, parhrẹsi´a

Book	Oc.	boldness	Oc.	confidence	Oc.	openly	Oc.	plainly	Oc.	openly (with 1722)	Oc.	boldly (with 1722)	Oc.	Misc.	Total
Mk.					1	8:32									1
Jn.					3	7:13; 11:54; 18:20	4	10:24; 11: 14; 16:25, 29	1	7:4			1	7:26	9
Ac.	3	4:13, 29, 31	1	28:31									1	2:29	5
2 Co.													2	3:12; 7:4	2
Eph.	1	3:12									1	6:19			2
Phl.	1	1:20													1
Col.									1	2:15					1
1 Ti.	1	3:13													1
Phe.													1	1:8	1
Heb.	1	10:19	2	3:6; 10:35									1	4:16	4
1 Jn.	1	4:17	3	2:28; 3:21; 5:14											4
Total	8		6		4		4		2		1		6		31

Miscellaneous: Jn. 7:26, boldly; Ac. 2:29 (with 3226), freely; 2 Co. 3:12, plainness of speech; 2 Co. 7:4, boldness of speech; Phe. 1:8, bold; Heb. 4:16 (with 3226), boldly.

3855. παῤῥησιάζομαι, parhrẹsiad´zomai

Book	Oc.	speak boldly	Oc.	preach boldly	Oc.	be bold	Oc.	wax bold	Oc.	boldly	Oc.	freely	Total
Ac.	3	14:3; 18:26; 19:8	1	9:27			1	13:46	1	9:29	1	26:26	7
Eph.	1	6:20											1
1 Th.					1	2:2							1
Total	4		1		1		1		1		1		9

See page 280 for Word 3856.

3857. πάσχα, pas´cha

Book	Oc.	Passover	Oc.	Easter	Total
Mt.	4	26:2, 17, 18, 19			4
Mk.	5	14:1, 12, 12, 14, 16			5
Lk.	7	2:41; 22:1, 7, 8, 11, 13, 15			7
Jn.	10	2:13, 23; 6:4; 11:55, 55; 12:1; 13:1; 18: 28, 39; 19:14			10
Ac.			1	12:4	1
1 Co.	1	5:7			1
Heb.	1	11:28			1
Total	28		1		29

3858. πάσχω, πάθω, or πένθω, pas´chō, path´ō, or pen´thō

Book	Oc.	suffer	Oc.	be vexed	Oc.	passion (with 3488)	Oc.	feel	Total
Mt.	3	16:21; 17: 12; 27:19	1	17:15					4
Mk.	3	5:26; 8:31; 9:12							3
Lk.	6	9:22; 13:2; 17:25; 22: 15; 24:26, 46							6
Ac.	3	3:18; 9:16; 17:3			1	1:3	1	28:5	5
1 Co.	1	12:26							1
2 Co.	1	1:6							1
Gal.	1	3:4							1
Phl.	1	1:29							1
1 Th.	1	2:14							1
2 Th.	1	1:5							1
2 Ti.	1	1:12							1
Heb.	4	2:18; 5:8; 9:26; 13:12							4
1 Pt.	12	2:19, 20, 21, 23; 3: 14, 17, 18; 4:1, 1, 15, 19; 5:10							12
Rev.	1	2:10							1
Total	39		1		1		1		42

3859. Πάταρα, Pat´ara

Book	Patara	Total
Ac.	21:1	1

3860. πατάσσω, patas´sō

Book	Oc.	smite	Oc.	strike	Total
Mt.	1	26:31	1	26:51	2
Mk.	1	14:27			1
Lk.	2	22:49, 50			2
Ac.	3	7:24; 12:7, 23			3
Rev.	2	11:6; 19:15			2
Total	9		1		10

3861. πατέω, pate´ō

Book	Oc.	tread	Oc.	tread down	Oc.	tread under feet	Total
Lk.	1	10:19	1	21:24			2
Rev.	2	14:20; 19: 15			1	11:2	3
Total	3		1		1		5

3856. πᾶς, pas

Book	Oc.	all	Oc.	all things	Oc.	every	Oc.	all men
Mt.	78	1:17; 2:3, 4, 16, 16; 3:5, 5, 15; 4:8, 9, 24; 5:15, 18; 6:29, 32, 33; 8:16; 9:35a; 10:30; 11:13, 28; 12:15, 23; 13:32, 34, 44, 46, 51, 56, 56; 14:20, 35; 15:37; 18:25, 26, 29, 31, 32, 34; 19:20, 27; 21:10, 12, 26; 22:10, 27, 28; 23:3, 5, 8, 27, 35, 36; 24:2, 8, 9, 14, 30, 33, 34, 47; 25:5, 7, 31, 32; 26:1, 27, 31, 35, 52, 56, 70; 27:1, 22, 25, 45; 28:18, 19	9	7:12; 11:27; 13:41; 17: 11; 19:26; 21:22; 22:4; 23:20; 28:20a	14	3:10; 4:4; 7:17, 19; 9:35b, 35c; 12:25, 25, 36; 13: 47, 52; 15:13; 18:16; 19:3	3	10:22; 19:11; 26:33
Mk.	49	1:5, 5, 27, 32; 2:12, 12, 13; 3:28; 4:13, 31, 32; 5:12, 26, 33; 6:33, 39, 41, 42, 50; 7:3, 14a, 19, 23; 9:15, 35, 35; 10:20, 28, 44; 11:17, 18; 12: 22, 28, 29, 33, 43, 44, 44; 13:4, 10, 30, 37; 14:23, 27, 29, 31, 50, 53, 64	9	4:34; 6:30; 7:37; 9:12, 23; 10:27; 11:11; 13: 23; 14:36	2	9:49b; 16:15	3	1:37; 5:20; 13:13
Lk.	110	1:6, 48, 63, 65, 65, 66, 71, 75; 2:1, 3, 10, 18, 19, 31, 38, 47, 51; 3:3, 6, 19, 20; 4:5, 7, 13, 15, 20, 22, 25, 28, 36, 40; 5:9; 6:10, 17, 19b, 26; 7:1, 17, 18, 29, 35; 8:40, 45, 47, 52, 54; 9:1, 7, 13, 17, 23, 43a, 48; 10:19; 11:50; 12:7, 18, 27, 30, 31, 41, 44; 13:2, 3, 4, 5, 17, 17, 17, 27, 28; 14: 18, 29, 33b; 15:1, 14, 31; 16:14, 26; 17:10; 18:12, 21, 22, 28, 43; 19: 37; 20:6, 32, 38, 45; 21:3, 15, 24, 29, 32, 35a, 36b, 38; 22:70; 23:48, 49; 24:9, 9, 14, 19, 21, 25, 27, 27, 47	9	1:3; 2:20; 9:43c; 10:22; 11:41; 14:17; 18:31; 21: 22; 24:44	9	2:23; 3:5, 5, 9; 4:4, 37; 5:17; 10: 1; 11:17	2	3:15; 21:17
Jn.	23	1:16; 2:15; 3:31, 31; 4:39; 5:22, 28; 6:37, 39; 6:45a; 7:21; 8:2; 10:8, 29; 13:10, 11, 18; 15:21; 16:13; 17:2a, 10, 21; 18:40	17	1:3; 3:35; 4:25, 29, 45; 5:20; 10:41; 13:3; 14:26, 26; 15:15; 16:15, 30; 17: 7; 18:4; 19:28; 21:17	3	1:9; 2:10; 15:2a	7	1:7; 2:24; 3: 26; 5:23; 11: 48; 12:32; 13: 35
Ac.	127	1:1, 8, 14, 18, 19, 21; 2:7, 7, 12, 17, 32, 36, 39, 44; 3:9, 11, 16, 18, 21b, 24, 25; 4:10, 10, 16, 24, 29, 33; 5:5, 17, 20, 21, 23, 34, 36, 37; 7:10, 14, 22, 50; 8:1, 10, 27, 40; 9:14, 21, 26, 35, 39, 40; 10:2, 33a, 36, 38, 41, 43a, 44; 11:14, 23; 12:11; 13:10, 10, 10, 22, 24, 39a; 14:16; 15:3, 12, 17, 17, 18; 16:26a, 32, 33; 17:7, 11, 21, 25a, 26, 26, 30; 18:2, 17, 23; 19:7, 10, 17, 17, 26, 34; 20:18, 19, 25, 27, 28, 32, 36, 37; 21:5, 18, 20, 21, 24, 27; 22:3, 5, 12, 15; 23:1; 24:3, 5, 8; 25:24, 24; 26:3, 4, 14, 20, 29; 27:20, 24, 35, 36, 37, 44; 28:30, 31	13	3:21a, 22; 10:33b, 39; 13: 39b; 14:15; 17:22, 24, 25b; 20:35; 22:10; 24:14; 26:2	9	2:5, 43; 3:23; 10: 35; 13:27; 15:21, 36; 18:4; 26:11	7	1:24; 2:45; 4: 21; 17:31; 19: 19; 20:26; 21: 28
Ro.	45	1:5, 7, 8, 18, 29; 3:9, 12, 19b, 22, 22, 23; 4:11, 16, 16; 5:12, 12, 18, 18; 8:32a, 37; 9:5, 6, 7, 17; 10:12, 12, 16, 18; 11:26, 32, 32; 12:4, 17, 18; 13:7; 14:10; 15:11, 11, 13, 14, 33; 16:4, 15, 24, 26	5	8:28, 32b; 11:36; 14:2, 20	8	2:9; 3:2, 4, 19a; 13:1; 14:5, 11, 11	1	16:19
1 Co.	64	1:2a, 5b, 5c, 10; 3:22; 7:7, 17; 8:1; 9:19b, 24; 10:1, 1, 2, 3, 4, 11, 17, 31; 12:6, 6, 11, 12, 13, 13, 19, 26, 26, 29, 29, 29, 29, 30, 30, 30; 13:2, 2, 2, 3; 14:5, 18, 23, 24, 24, 24, 31, 31, 31, 33; 15:7, 8, 10, 19, 22, 22, 24, 24, 25, 28c, 28d, 39, 51, 51; 16:20, 24	31	2:10, 15; 3:21; 4:13; 6: 12, 12, 12; 8:6, 6; 9:12, 22a, 25b; 10:23, 23, 23, 23, 33b; 11:2, 12; 13:7, 7, 7, 7; 14:26, 40; 15:27, 27, 27, 28a, 28b; 16:14	7	1:2b; 4:17; 6:18; 11:3, 4, 5; 15:30	3	9:19a, 22b; 10:33a
2 Co.	27	1:1, 3, 4a; 2:3, 3, 5; 3:2, 18; 5:10, 14, 14, 15; 7:1, 4, 13, 15; 8:7b, 18; 9:8a, 8b, 11b; 10:6; 11:28; 12:12; 13:2, 13, 14	13	2:9; 4:15; 5:17, 18; 6:4, 10; 7:11, 14, 16; 9:8c; 11:6b, 9; 12:19	6	2:14; 4:2; 9:8d; 10:5, 5; 13:1	1	9:13
Gal.	10	1:2; 2:14; 3:8, 22, 26, 28; 4:1, 26; 5:14; 6:6	1	3:10b	1	5:3	1	6:10
Eph.	31	1:3, 8, 15, 21a, 23, 23; 2:3, 21; 3:8, 18, 19, 20, 21; 4:2, 6, 6, 6, 6, 10a, 13, 19, 31, 31; 5:3, 9; 6:16, 16, 18b, 18c, 18d, 24	10	1:10, 11, 22, 22; 3:9b; 4: 10b, 15; 5:13a, 20; 6:21	3	1:21b; 4:14, 16b	1	3:9a
Phl.	19	1:1, 4b, 7, 7, 8, 9, 13, 20, 25; 2:17, 21, 26, 29; 4:5, 7, 18, 19, 22, 23	6	2:14; 3:8, 8, 21; 4:12b, 13	7	1:3, 4a, 18; 2:9, 10, 11; 4:21		
Col.	23	1:4, 6, 9, 10a, 11, 11, 19, 28c; 2:2, 3, 9, 10, 13, 19, 22; 3:8, 11, 11, 14, 16, 17b; 4:7, 12	9	1:16, 16, 17, 17, 18, 20; 3:20, 22; 4:9	6	1:10b, 15, 23, 28a, 28b, 28d		
1 Th.	12	1:2, 7; 2:15; 3:7, 9, 13; 4:6, 10; 5:5, 22, 26, 27	1	5:21	1	1:8	3	3:12; 5:14, 15
2 Th.	11	1:3, 4, 10, 11; 2:4, 9, 10, 12; 3:16b, 16c, 18			3	2:17; 3:6, 17	1	3:2
1 Ti.	17	1:15, 16; 2:1, 1, 2, 2, 4, 6, 11; 3:4; 4:9, 10, 15; 5:2, 20; 6:1, 10	4	3:11; 4:8; 6:13, 17	3	2:8; 4:4; 5:10		
2 Ti.	9	1:15; 3:11, 12, 16, 17; 4:2, 8, 17, 21	3	2:7, 10; 4:5	2	2:21; 4:18	3	2:24; 3:9; 4:16
Tit.	8	2:10a, 11, 14, 15; 3:2, 2, 15, 15	4	1:15; 2:7, 9, 10b	2	1:16; 3:1		
Phe.	1	1:5			1	1:6		
Heb.	24	1:6, 11, 14; 2:8b, 11, 15; 3:16; 4:4; 5:9; 6:16; 7:2, 7; 8:11; 9:19b, 19c, 21; 11:13, 39; 12:8, 23; 13:4, 24, 24, 25	12	1:2, 3; 2:8a, 8c, 10, 10, 17; 3:4b; 4:13; 8:5; 9: 22; 13:18	9	2:2; 3:4a; 5:1; 8: 3; 9:19a; 10:11; 12:1, 6; 13:21	1	12:14
Jas.	5	1:2, 8, 21; 2:10; 4:16	1	5:12	5	1:17, 17, 19; 3:7, 16	1	1:5
1 Pt.	10	1:24, 24; 2:1, 1, 1, 18; 3:8; 5:7, 10, 14	3	4:7, 8, 11	1	2:13	1	2:17
2 Pt.	4	1:5; 3:9, 11, 16	2	1:3; 3:4				
1 Jn.	5	1:7, 9; 2:16, 19; 5:17	3	2:20, 27; 3:20	3	4:1, 2, 3		
2 Jn.	1	1:1						
3 Jn.			1	1:2			1	1:12
Jd.	5	1:3, 15, 15, 15, 15						
Rev.	30	1:7b; 2:23; 5:6, 13b; 7:4, 9, 11, 17; 8:3, 7; 11:6; 12:5; 13:7, 8, 12, 16; 14:8; 15:4; 18:3, 12a, 17b, 19, 23, 24; 19:5, 17, 21; 21:4, 8; 22:21	4	4:11; 18:14; 21:5, 7	12	1:7a; 5:9, 13a; 6:14, 15, 15; 14: 6; 16:3, 20; 18: 2, 2, 17a	1	19:18
Total	748		170		117		41	

3856. πᾶς, pas (continued)

Book	Oc.	whosoever	Oc.	everyone	Oc.	whole	Oc.	every man	Oc.	all manner of	Oc.	no (with 3656)	Oc.	every thing	Oc.	any
Mt.	2	5:22, 28	5	7:8, 21, 26; 19:29; 25:29	3	8:32, 34; 13:2			6	4:23, 23; 5:11; 10:1, 1; 12:31	1	24:22	1	8:33	1	18:19
Mk.			1	9:49a	1	4:1					1	13:20				
Lk.	6	6:47; 14:11, 33a; 16:18, 18; 20:18	6	6:40; 9:43b; 11:4, 10; 18:14; 19:26	3	1:10; 6:19a; 21:35b	2	6:30; 16:16	1	11:42						
Jn.	8	3:15, 16; 4:13; 8:34; 11:26; 12:46; 16:2; 19:12	4	3:8, 20; 6:40; 18:37			1	6:45b								
Ac.	1	10:43b	2	16:26b; 28:2	2	6:5; 13:44			1	10:12						
Ro.	3	2:1; 9:33; 10:11	2	1:16; 10:4	1	8:22	2	2:10; 12:3	1	7:8	1	3:20				
1 Co.			1	16:16			2	8:7; 9:25a					1	1:5a		
2 Co.													2	8:7a; 9:11a	1	1:4b
Gal.			2	3:10a, 13							1	2:16				
Eph.					2	3:15; 4:16a					1	5:5	1	5:24		
Phl.													1	4:6		
Col.																
1 Th.													1	5:18		
2 Th.																
1 Ti.																
2 Ti.			1	2:19												
Tit.																
Phe.																
Heb.			1	5:13			1	2:9			1	12:11			1	4:12
Jas.																
1 Pt.							1	3:15	1	1:15						
2 Pt.											1	1:20				
1 Jn.	9	2:23; 3:4, 6, 6, 9, 10, 15a; 5:1a, 18	3	2:29; 4:7; 5:1b			1	3:3			2	2:21; 3:15b				
2 Jn.	1	1:9														
3 Jn.																
Jd.																
Rev.	1	22:15					1	22:18	1	21:19					4	7:1, 16; 9:4 4
Total	31		28		12		11		11		9		7		7	

3856. πᾶς, pas (continued)

Book	Oc.	what-soever	Oc.	whosoever (with 3639 and 302)	Oc.	always (with 1223)	Oc.	daily (with 2250)	Oc.	any thing	Oc.	no (with 3261)	Oc.	Not Tr.	Oc.	Misc.	Total
Mt.	1	15:17			1	18:10							2	7:24; 10:32	3	13:19; 24:6; 28:20b	130
Mk.													1	11:24	3	4:11; 7: 14b, 18	70
Lk.			1	12:8											4	1:37; 12:10, 48; 21:36a	153
Jn.															2	15:2b; 17: 2b	65
Ac.			1	2:21	1	2:25	2	5:42; 17:17	1	10:14					3	5:11; 9:32; 11:8	170
Ro.			1	10:13											1	14:23	71
1 Co.	2	10:25, 27									1	1:29					112
2 Co.															3	4:8; 7:5; 11:6a	53
Gal.																	16
Eph.	1	5:13b									1	4:29			1	6:18a	52
Phl.															1	4:12a	34
Col.													2	3:17a, 23			40
1 Th.																	18
2 Th.					1	3:16a											16
1 Ti.																	24
2 Ti.																	18
Tit.																	14
Phe.																	2
Heb.															1	4:15	51
Jas.																	12
1 Pt.															1	5:5	18
2 Pt.																	7
1 Jn.	1	5:4															27
2 Jn.																	2
3 Jn.																	2
Jd.													1	1:25			6
Rev.	1	18:22b							1	21:27			1	22:3	3	18:12b, 12c, 22a	60
Total	6		3		3		2		2		2		7		26		1243

Miscellaneous: Mt. 13:19, any one; Mt. 24:6, all these things; Mt. 28:20b (with 2250 and 3488), alway; Mk. 4:11 (with 3488), all these things; Mk. 7:14b, every one of you; Mk. 7:18, whatsoever thing; Lk. 1:37 (with 4387 and 3656), nothing; Lk. 12:10 (with 3639), whosoever; Lk. 12:48 (with 3639), whomsoever; Lk. 21:36a (with 1722 and 2540), always; Jn. 15:2b, every branch; Jn. 17:2b (with 3639), as many as; Ac. 5:11, as many as; Ac. 9:32, all quarters; Ac. 11:8 (with 3663), nothing; Ro. 14:23 (with 3639), whatsoever; 2 Co. 4:8, every side; 2 Co. 7:5, every side; 2 Co. 11:6a, thoroughly; Eph. 6:18a (with 1722 and 2540), always; Phl. 4:12a (with 1722), every where; Heb. 4:15, all points; 1 Pt. 5:5, all of you; Rev. 18:12b, 12c, all manner; Rev. 18:22a (with 3264), no.

3862. πατήρ, patẹr′

Book	Oc.	Father	Oc.	father	Oc.	parent	Total
Mt.	44	5:16, 45, 48; 6:1, 4, 6, 6, 8, 9, 14, 15, 18, 18, 26, 32; 7:11, 21; 10:20, 29, 32, 33; 11:25, 26, 27, 27, 27; 12:50; 13:43; 15:13; 16:17, 27; 18:10, 14, 19, 35; 20:23; 23:9b; 24:36; 25:34; 26:29, 39, 42, 53; 28:19	19	2:22; 3:9; 4:21, 22; 8:21; 10:21, 35, 37; 15:4, 4, 5, 6; 19:5, 19, 29; 21:31; 23:9a, 30, 32			63
Mk.	5	8:38; 11:25, 26; 13:32; 14:36	14	1:20; 5:40; 7:10, 10, 11, 12; 9:21, 24; 10:7, 19, 29; 11:10; 13:12; 15:21			19
Lk.	17	2:49; 6:36; 9:26; 10:21, 21, 22, 22, 22; 11:2, 13; 12:30, 32; 22:29, 42; 23:34, 46; 24:49	38	1:17, 32, 55, 59, 62, 67, 72, 73; 2:48; 3:8; 6:23, 26; 8:51; 9:42, 59; 11:11, 47, 48; 12:53, 53; 14:26; 15: 12, 12, 17, 18, 18, 20, 20, 21, 22, 27, 28, 29; 16:24, 27, 27, 30; 18:20			55
Jn.	122	1:14, 18; 2:16; 3:35; 4:21, 23, 23; 5:17, 18, 19, 20, 21, 22, 23, 23, 26, 30, 36, 36, 37, 43, 45; 6:27, 32, 37, 39, 44, 45, 46, 46, 57, 57, 65; 8: 16, 18, 19, 19, 19, 27, 28, 29, 38a, 41b, 42, 49, 54; 10:15, 15, 17, 18, 25, 29, 29, 30, 32, 36, 37, 38; 11:41; 12:26, 27, 28, 49, 50; 13:1, 3; 14:2, 6, 7, 8, 9, 9, 10, 10, 10, 11, 11, 12, 13, 16, 20, 21, 23, 24, 26, 28, 28, 31, 31; 15:1, 8, 9, 10, 15, 16, 23, 24, 26, 26; 16:3, 10, 15, 16, 17, 23, 25, 26, 27, 28, 28, 32; 17:1, 5, 11, 21, 24, 25; 18:11; 20:17, 17, 17, 21	16	4:12, 20, 53; 6:31, 42, 49, 58; 7:22; 8:38b, 39, 41a, 44, 44, 44, 53, 56			138
Ac.	3	1:4, 7; 2:33	32	3:13, 22, 25; 5:30; 7:2, 2, 4, 11, 12, 14, 15, 19, 20, 32, 38, 39, 44, 45, 45, 51, 52; 13:17, 32, 36; 15: 10; 16:1, 3; 22:1, 14; 26:6; 28:8, 25			35
Ro.	4	1:7; 6:4; 8:15; 15:6	11	4:1, 11, 12, 12, 16, 17, 18; 9:5, 10; 11:28; 15:8			15
1 Co.	3	1:3; 8:6; 15:24	3	4:15; 5:1; 10:1			6
2 Co.	5	1:2, 3, 3; 6:18; 11:31					5
Gal.	4	1:1, 3, 4; 4:6	1	4:2			5
Eph.	8	1:2, 3, 17; 2:18; 3:14; 4:6; 5:20; 6:23	3	5:31; 6:2, 4			11
Phl.	3	1:2; 2:11; 4:20	1	2:22			4
Col.	6	1:2, 3, 12; 2:2; 3:17, 21					6
1 Th.	5	1:1, 1, 3; 3:11, 13	1	2:11			6
2 Th.	3	1:1, 2; 2:16					3
1 Ti.	1	1:2	1	5:1			2
2 Ti.	1	1:2					1
Tit.	1	1:4					1
Phe.	1	1:3					1
Heb.	2	1:5; 12:9b	6	1:1; 3:9; 7:10; 8:9; 12:7, 9a	1	11:23	9
Jas.	3	1:17, 27; 3:9	1	2:21			4
1 Pt.	3	1:2, 3, 17					3
2 Pt.	1	1:17	1	3:4			2
1 Jn.	12	1:2, 3; 2:1, 13b, 15, 16, 22, 23, 24; 3:1; 4:14; 5:7	2	2:13a, 14			14
2 Jn.	4	1:3, 3, 4, 9					4
Jd.	1	1:1					1
Rev.	5	1:6; 2:27; 3:5, 21; 14:1					5
Total	267		150		1		418

3863. Πάτμος, Pat′mos

Book	Patmos	Total
Rev.	1:9	1

3864. πατραλῴας, patralō′as

Book	murder of a father	Total
1 Ti.	1:9	1

3865. πατριά, patria′

Book	Oc.	lineage	Oc.	kindred	Oc.	family	Total
Lk.	1	2:4					1
Ac.			1	3:25			1
Eph.					1	3:15	1
Total	1		1		1		3

3866. πατριάρχης, patriarch′ẹs

Book	patriarch	Total
Ac.	2:29; 7:8, 9	3
Heb.	7:4	1
Total		4

3867. πατρικός, patrikos′

Book	of (one's) fathers	Total
Gal.	1:14	1

3868. πατρίς, patris′

Book	Oc.	(one's) own country	Oc.	country	Total
Mt.	2	13:54, 57			2
Mk.	2	6:1, 4			2
Lk.	1	4:24	1	4:23	2
Jn.			1	4:44	1
Heb.			1	11:14	1
Total	5		3		8

3869. Πατρόβας, Patrob′as

Book	Patrobas	Total
Ro.	16:14	1

3870. πατροπαράδοτος patroparad′otos

Book	received by tradition from (one's) fathers	Total
1 Pt.	1:18	1

3871. πατρῷος, patrō′os

Book	Oc.	of (one's) fathers	Oc.	of the fathers	Total
Ac.	2	24:14; 28:17	1	22:3	3

3872. Παῦλος, Pau′los

Book	Oc.	Paul	Oc.	Paulus (the deputy)	Total
Ac.	132	13:9, 13, 16, 43, 45, 46, 50; 14:9, 11, 12, 14, 19; 15:2, 2, 12, 22, 25, 35, 36, 38, 40; 16:3, 9, 14, 17, 18, 19, 25, 28, 29, 36, 37; 17:2, 4, 10, 13, 14, 15, 16, 22, 33; 18:1, 5, 9, 12, 14, 18; 19:1, 4, 6, 11, 13, 15, 21, 26, 29, 30; 20:1, 7, 9, 10, 13, 16, 37; 21:4, 8, 11, 13, 18, 26, 29, 30, 32, 37, 39, 40; 22:25, 28, 30; 23:1, 3, 5, 6, 10, 11, 12, 14, 16, 16, 17, 18, 20, 24, 31, 33; 24:1, 10, 23, 24, 26, 27; 25:2, 4, 6, 7, 9, 10, 14, 19, 21, 23; 26:1, 1, 24, 28, 29; 27:1, 3, 9, 11, 21, 24, 31, 33, 43; 28:3, 8, 15, 16, 17, 25, 30	1	13:7	133
Ro.	1	1:1			1
1 Co.	8	1:1, 12, 13, 13; 3:4, 5, 22; 16:21			8
2 Co.	2	1:1; 10:1			2
Gal.	2	1:1; 5:2			2
Eph.	2	1:1; 3:1			2
Phl.	1	1:1			1
Col.	3	1:1, 23; 4:18			3
1 Th.	2	1:1; 2:18			2
2 Th.	2	1:1; 3:17			2
1 Ti.	1	1:1			1
2 Ti.	1	1:1			1
Tit.	1	1:1			1
Phe.	3	1:1, 9, 19			3
2 Pt.	1	3:15			1
Total	162		1		163

3873. παύω, pau′ō

Book	Oc.	cease	Oc.	leave	Oc.	refrain	Total
Lk.	2	8:24; 11:1	1	5:4			3
Ac.	5	5:42; 6:13; 13:10; 20:1, 31	1	21:32			6
1 Co.	1	13:8					1
Eph.	1	1:16					1
Col.	1	1:9					1
Heb.	1	10:2					1
1 Pt.	1	4:1			1	3:10	2
Total	12		2		1		15

3874. Πάφος, Paph'os

Book	Paphos	Total
Ac.	13:6, 13	2

3875. παχύνω, pachu'nō

Book	wax gross	Total
Mt.	13:15	1
Ac.	28:27	1
Total		2

3876. πέδη, ped'ẹ

Book	fetter	Total
Mk.	5:4, 4	2
Lk.	8:29	1
Total		3

3877. πεδινός, pedinos'

Book	plain (with 5017)	Total
Lk.	6:17	1

3878. πεζεύω, pedzeu'ō

Book	go afoot	Total
Ac.	20:13	1

3879. πεζῇ, pedzẹ'

Book	Oc.	on foot	Oc.	afoot	Total
Mt.	1	14:13			1
Mk.			1	6:33	1
Total	1		1		2

3881. πειθός, peithos'

Book	enticing	Total
1 Co.	2:4	1

3880. πειθαρχέω, peitharche'ō

Book	Oc.	obey	Oc.	hearken unto	Oc.	obey a magistrate	Total
Ac.	2	5:29, 32	1	27:21			3
Tit.					1	3:1	1
Total	2		1		1		4

3884. πεῖρα, pei'ra

Book	Oc.	assay (with 2983)	Oc.	trial	Total
Heb.	1	11:29	1	11:36	2

3882. πείθω, pei'thō

Book	Oc.	persuade	Oc.	trust	Oc.	obey	Oc.	have confidence	Oc.	believe	Oc.	be confident	Oc.	Misc.	Total
Mt.	2	27:20; 28:14	1	27:43											3
Mk.			1	10:24											1
Lk.	2	16:31; 20:6	2	11:22; 18:9											4
Ac.	9	13:43; 14:19; 18:4; 19:8, 26; 21:14; 26:26, 28; 28:23			2	5:36, 37			3	17:4; 27:11; 28:24			3	5:40; 12:20; 23:21	17
Ro.	3	8:38; 14:14; 15:14			1	2:8					1	2:19			5
2 Co.	1	5:11	2	1:9; 10:7			1	2:3							4
Gal.	1	1:10			2	3:1; 5:7	1	5:10							4
Phl.			1	2:24			2	1:25; 3:3			1	1:6	2	1:14; 3:4	6
2 Th.							1	3:4							1
2 Ti.	2	1:5, 12													2
Phe.							1	1:21							1
Heb.	2	6:9; 11:13	1	13:18	1	13:17							1	2:13	5
Jas.					1	3:3									1
1 Jn.													1	3:19	1
Total	22		8		7		6		3		2		7		55

Miscellaneous: Ac. 5:40, agree to; Ac. 12:20, make (one's) friend; Ac. 23:21, yield unto; Phl. 1:14, wax confident; Phl. 3:4, have whereof (one) might trust; Heb. 2:13 (with 1510), put (one's) trust; 1 Jn. 3:19, assure.

3883. πεινάω, peina'ō

Book	Oc.	hunger	Oc.	be an hungred	Oc.	be hungry	Oc.	hungry	Total
Mt.	2	5:6; 21:18	7	4:2; 12:1, 3; 25:35, 37, 42, 44					9
Mk.			1	2:25	1	11:12			2
Lk.	3	4:2; 6:21, 25	1	6:3			1	1:53	5
Jn.	1	6:35							1
Ro.	1	12:20							1
1 Co.	2	4:11; 11:34			1	11:21			3
Phl.					1	4:12			1
Rev.	1	7:16							1
Total	10		9		3		1		23

3885. πειράζω, peirad'zō

Book	Oc.	tempt	Oc.	try	Oc.	tempter	Oc.	prove	Oc.	assay	Oc.	examine	Oc.	go about	Total
Mt.	5	4:1; 16:1; 19:3; 22:18, 35			1	4:3									6
Mk.	4	1:13; 8:11; 10:2; 12:15													4
Lk.	3	4:2; 11:16; 20:23													3
Jn.	1	8:6					1	6:6							2
Ac.	2	5:9; 15:10							1	16:7			1	24:6	4
1 Co.	3	7:5; 10:9, 13													3
2 Co.											1	13:5			1
Gal.	1	6:1													1
1 Th.	1	3:5b			1	3:5a									2
Heb.	5	2:18, 18; 3:9; 4:15; 11:37	1	11:17											6
Jas.	4	1:13, 13, 13, 14													4
Rev.			3	2:2, 10; 3:10											3
Total	29		4		2		1		1		1		1		39

3886. πειρασμός, peirasmos'

Book	Oc.	temptation	Oc.	temptations	Oc.	try	Total
Mt.	2	6:13; 26:41					2
Mk.	1	14:38					1
Lk.	6	4:13; 8:13; 11:4; 22:28, 40, 46					6
Ac.	1	20:19					1
1 Co.	2	10:13, 13					2
Gal.	1	4:14					1
1 Ti.	1	6:9					1
Heb.	1	3:8					1
Jas.	2	1:2, 12					2
1 Pt.	1	1:6			1	4:12	2
2 Pt.			1	2:9			1
Rev.	1	3:10					1
Total	19		1		1		21

3887. πειράω, peira'ō

Book	Oc.	assay	Oc.	go about	Total
Ac.	1	9:26	1	26:21	2

3888. πεισμονή, peismonẹ'

Book	persuasion	Total
Gal.	5:8	1

3889. πέλαγος, pel'agos

Book	Oc.	depth	Oc.	sea	Total
Mt.	1	18:6			1
Ac.			1	27:5	1
Total	1		1		2

3890. πελεκίζω, pelekid′zō

Book	behead	Total
Rev.	20:4	1

3891. πέμπτος, pemp′tos

Book	fifth	Total
Rev.	6:9; 9:1; 16:10; 21:20	4

3892. πέμπω, pem′pō

Book	Oc.	send	Oc.	thrust in	Oc.	again send	Total
Mt.	4	2:8; 11:2; 14:10; 22:7					4
Mk.	1	5:12					1
Lk.	8	4:26; 7:6, 10, 19; 15:15; 16:24, 27; 20:13			2	20:11, 12	10
Jn.	33	1:22, 33; 4:34; 5:23, 24, 30, 37; 6:38, 39, 40, 44; 7:16, 18, 28, 33; 8:16, 18, 26, 29; 9:4; 12:44, 45, 49; 13:16, 20, 20; 14:24, 26; 15:21, 26; 16:5, 7; 20:21					33
Ac.	12	10:5, 32, 33; 11:29; 15:22, 25; 19:31; 20:17; 23:30; 25:21, 25, 27					12
Ro.	1	8:3					1
1 Co.	2	4:17; 16:3					2
2 Co.	1	9:3					1
Eph.	1	6:22					1
Phl.	5	2:19, 23, 25, 28; 4:16					5
Col.	1	4:8					1
1 Th.	2	3:2, 5					2
2 Th.	1	2:11					1
Tit.	1	3:12					1
1 Pt.	1	2:14					1
Rev.	3	1:11; 11:10; 22:16	2	14:15, 18			5
Total	77		2		2		81

3893. πένης, pen′ęs

Book	poor	Total
2 Co.	9:9	1

3894. πενθερά, penthera′

Book	Oc.	mother-in-law	Oc.	wife's mother	Total
Mt.	1	10:35	1	8:14	2
Mk.			1	1:30	1
Lk.	2	12:53, 53	1	4:38	3
Total	3		3		6

3895. πενθερός, pentheros′

Book	father-in-law	Total
Jn.	18:13	1

3896. πενθέω, penthe′ō

Book	Oc.	mourn	Oc.	wail	Oc.	bewail	Total
Mt.	2	5:4; 9:15					2
Mk.	1	16:10					1
Lk.	1	6:25					1
1 Co.	1	5:2					1
2 Co.					1	12:21	1
Jas.	1	4:9					1
Rev.	1	18:11	2	18:15, 19			3
Total	7		2		1		10

3897. πένθος, pen′thos

Book	Oc.	sorrow	Oc.	mourning	Total
Jas.			1	4:9	1
Rev.	3	18:7, 7; 21:4	1	18:8	4
Total	3		2		5

3898. πεντιχρός, pentichros′

Book	poor	Total
Lk.	21:2	1

3899. πεντακίς, pentakis′

Book	five times	Total
2 Co.	11:24	1

3900. πεντακισχίλιοι pentakischil′ioi

Book	five thousand	Total
Mt.	14:21; 16:9	2
Mk.	6:44; 8:19	2
Lk.	9:14	1
Jn.	6:10	1
Total		6

3901. πεντακόσιοι, pentakos′ioi

Book	five hundred	Total
Lk.	7:41	1
1 Co.	15:6	1
Total		2

3902. πέντε, pen′te

Book	Oc.	five	Oc.	three score and fifteen (with 1440)	Oc.	fifty thousand (with 3361)	Total
Mt.	12	14:17, 19; 16:9; 25:2, 2, 15, 16, 16, 20, 20, 20, 20					12
Mk.	3	6:38, 41; 8:19					3
Lk.	9	1:24; 9:13, 16; 12:6, 52; 14:19; 16:28; 19:18, 19					9
Jn.	5	4:18; 5:2; 6:9, 13, 19					5
Ac.	3	4:4; 20:6; 24:1	1	7:14	1	19:19	5
1 Co.	1	14:19					1
Rev.	3	9:5, 10; 17:10					3
Total	36		1		1		38

3903. πεντεκαιδέκατος pentekaidek′atos

Book	fifteenth	Total
Lk.	3:1	1

3904. πεντήκοντα, pentę′konta

Book	fifty	Total
Mk.	6:40	1
Lk.	7:41; 9:14; 16:6	3
Jn.	8:57; 21:11	2
Ac.	13:20	1
Total		7

3905. πεντηκοστή, pentękostę′

Book	Pentecost	Total
Ac.	2:1; 20:16	2
1 Co.	16:8	1
Total		3

3906. πεποίθησις, pepoi′thęsis

Book	Oc.	confidence	Oc.	trust	Total
2 Co.	3	1:15; 8:22; 10:2	1	3:4	4
Eph.	1	3:12			1
Phl.	1	3:4			1
Total	5		1		6

3907. περ, per

Book	Oc.	whomsoever (with 3639)	Oc.	Not Tr.	Total
Mk.	1	15:6			1
Heb.			3	3:6, 14; 6:3	3
Total	1		3		4

3908. πέραν, per′an

Book	Oc.	other side	Oc.	beyond	Oc.	over	Oc.	on the other side	Oc.	farther side	Total
Mt.	4	8:18, 28; 14:22; 16:5	3	4:15, 25; 19:1							7
Mk.	5	4:35; 5:1, 21; 6:45; 8:13	1	3:8					1	10:1	7
Lk.	1	8:22									1
Jn.			3	1:28; 3:26; 10:40	3	6:1, 17; 18:1	2	6:22, 25			8
Total	10		7		3		2		1		23

3909. πέρας, per′as

Book	Oc.	end	Oc.	utmost part	Oc.	uttermost part	Total
Mt.					1	12:42	1
Lk.			1	11:31			1
Ro.	1	10:18					1
Heb.	1	6:16					1
Total	2		1		1		4

3910. Πέργαμος, Per′gamos

Book	Pergamos	Total
Rev.	1:11; 2:12	2

3911. Πέργη, Perg′ę

Book	Perga	Total
Ac.	13:13, 14; 14:25	3

3912a. περί, peri′ (with genitive)

Book	Oc.	of	Oc.	for	Oc.	concerning	Oc.	as touching	Oc.	about	Oc.	touching	Oc.	whereof (with 3639)	Oc.	Not Tr.	Oc.	Misc.	Total
Mt.	7	11:10; 15:7; 17:13; 21:45; 22:42; 24:36; 26:24	4	2:8; 6:28; 22:16; 26:28	3	4:6; 11:7; 16:11	2	18:19; 22:31									3	9:36; 12:36; 20:24	19
Mk.	8	1:30; 5:27; 7:6, 25; 8:30; 10:10; 13:32; 14:21	3	1:44; 12:14; 14:24	2	5:16; 7:17	1	12:26									1	10:41	15
Lk.	20	1:1; 2:33, 38; 3:15; 4:14, 37; 5:15; 7:3, 17, 18, 27; 9:9, 11, 45; 11:53; 13:1; 16:2; 21:5; 23:8; 24:14	8	2:27; 3:19, 19; 4:38; 5:14; 12:26; 19:37; 22:32	6	2:17b; 7:24; 22:37; 24:19, 27, 44									1	2:17a	4	1:4; 2:18; 4:10; 24:4	39
Jn.	48	1:7, 8, 15, 22, 30, 47; 2:21, 25; 5:31, 32, 32, 36, 37, 39, 46; 7:7, 13, 17, 39; 8:13, 14, 18, 18, 26, 46; 9:17; 10:25, 41; 11:13, 13; 12:41; 13:18, 22, 24; 15:26; 16:8, 8, 8, 9, 10, 11, 19, 25; 18:19, 19, 23, 34; 21:24	13	9:21; 10:13, 33, 33; 12:6; 15:22; 16:26; 17:9, 9, 9, 20, 20; 19:24	4	7:12, 32; 9:18; 11:19b			1	3:25							2	6:41, 61	68
Ac.	32	1:1; 2:29, 31; 5:24; 7:52; 8:34, 34, 34; 9:13; 11:22; 13:29; 15:6; 17:32; 18:15, 25; 21:21; 22:10; 23:6, 11, 20, 29; 24:8, 22, 25; 25:9, 19, 19, 20b, 26; 26:26; 28:15, 21b	4	8:15; 19:40a; 24:10, 21a	11	1:16; 8:12; 19:8, 39; 21:24; 22:18; 23:15; 24:24; 25:16; 28:21a, 23	1	21:25	4	15:2; 19:23; 25:15, 24	2	24:21b; 26:2	1	24:13			8	1:3; 10:19; 19:40b; 25:18, 20a; 26:7; 28:22, 31	63
Ro.	3	14:12; 15:14, 21	1	8:3	1	1:3													5
1 Co.	1	1:11			3	7:25; 12:1; 16:1	2	8:1; 16:12					1	7:1			3	1:4; 7:37; 8:4	10
2 Co.	1	10:8					1	9:1											2
Eph.			1	6:18													1	6:22	2
Phl.																	3	1:27; 2:19, 20	3
Col.			3	1:3; 2:1; 4:3							1	4:10					1	4:8	5
1 Th.	3	1:9; 4:6; 5:1	3	1:2; 3:9; 5:25	2	3:2; 4:13	1	4:9											9
2 Th.			4	1:3, 11; 2:13; 3:1															4
1 Ti.																	1	1:7	1
2 Ti.	1	1:3																	1
Tit.	1	2:8													1	3:8			2
Phe.			1	1:10															1
Heb.	9	4:4, 8; 5:11; 6:9; 9:5; 10:7; 11:7, 22a, 32	9	5:3, 3; 10:6, 8, 18, 26; 11:40; 13:11, 18	3	7:14; 11:20, 22b							1	2:5					22
1 Pt.	3	1:10, 10; 3:15	2	3:18; 5:7															5
2 Pt.	2	1:12; 3:16																	2
1 Jn.	4	1:1; 2:27; 5:9, 10	5	2:2, 2, 2; 4:10; 5:16	1	2:26													10
3 Jn.																	1	1:2	1
Jd.	3	1:3, 15, 15							1	1:9									4
Total	146		61		36		8		6		3		3		2		28		293

Miscellaneous: Mt. 9:36, on; Mt. 12:36 (with 846), thereof; Mt. 20:24, against; Mk. 10:41, with; Lk. 1:4 (with 3639), wherein; Lk. 2:18, at; Lk. 4:10, over Lk. 24:4 (with 5027), thereabout; Jn. 6:41, 61, at; Ac. 1:3, pertaining to; Ac. 10:19, on; Ac. 19:40b (with 3639), whereby; Ac. 25:18, against; Ac. 25:20a (with 5027), such manner of; Ac. 26:7, for . . . sake; Ac. 28:22, as concerning; Ac. 28:31, which concern; 1 Co. 1:4, on (one's) behalf; 1 Co. 7:37, over; 1 Co. 8:4, as concerning; Eph. 6:22 (with 3488), (one's) affairs; Phl. 1:27 (with 3488), (one's) affairs; Phl. 2:19, 20 (with 3488), (one's) state; Col. 4:8, (with 3488), (one's) estate; 1 Ti. 1:7 (with 5001), whereof; 3 Jn. 1:2, above.

3912b. περί, peri′ (with accusative)

Book	Oc.	about	Oc.	concerning	Oc.	of	Oc.	Not Tr.	Oc.	Misc.	Total
Mt.	7	3:4; 8:18; 20:3, 5, 6, 9; 27:46									7
Mk.	8	1:6; 3:8, 32, 34; 4:10; 6:48; 9:14, 42			1	4:19					9
Lk.	5	10:40, 41; 13:8; 17:2; 22:49									5
Jn.							1	11:19a			1
Ac.	3	10:9; 22:6, 6			1	19:25	1	28:7	2	13:13; 21:8	7
Phl.									1	2:23	1
1 Ti.	1	6:4	2	1:19; 6:21							3
2 Ti.			2	2:18; 3:8							2
Tit.									1	2:7	1
Jd.	1	1:7									1
Rev.									1	15:6	1
Total	25		4		2		2		5		38

Miscellaneous: Ac. 13:13, (one's) company; Ac. 21:8, of (one's) company; Phl. 2:23 (with 3488), how it will go with; Tit. 2:7, in; Rev. 15:6, having.

Word 3912 has 331 occurrences.

3913. περιάγω, periag'ō

Book	Oc.	go about	Oc.	lead about	Oc.	compass	Total
Mt.	2	4:23; 9:35			1	23:15	3
Mk.	1	6:6					1
Ac.	1	13:11					1
1 Co.			1	9:5			1
Total	4		1		1		6

3914. περιαιρέω, periaire'ō

Book	Oc.	take away	Oc.	take up	Total
Ac.	1	27:20	1	27:40	2
2 Co.	1	3:16			1
Heb.	1	10:11			1
Total	3		1		4

3915. περιαστράπτω, periastrap'tō

Book	Oc.	shine round	Oc.	shine round about	Total
Ac.	1	22:6	1	9:3	2

3916. περιβάλλω, peribal'lō

Book	Oc.	clothe	Oc.	clothed with	Oc.	array	Oc.	array in	Oc.	clothe in	Oc.	cast about	Oc.	put on	Total
Mt.	4	6:31; 25:36, 38, 43			1	6:29									5
Mk.									1	16:5	1	14:51			2
Lk.					1	12:27	1	23:11			1	19:43			3
Jn.													1	19:2	1
Ac.											1	12:8			1
Rev.	3	3:5, 18; 4:4	4	7:9; 10:1; 12:1; 19:13	1	17:4	2	7:13; 19:8	2	11:3; 18:16					12
Total	7		4		3		3		3		3		1		24

3917. περιβλέπω, periblep'ō

Book	Oc.	look round about	Oc.	look round about upon	Oc.	look round about on	Total
Mk.	3	5:32; 9:8; 10:23	1	11:11	2	3:5, 34	6
Lk.			1	6:10			1
Total	3		2		2		7

3918. περιβόλαιον, peribol'aion

Book	Oc.	covering	Oc.	vesture	Total
1 Co.	1	11:15			1
Heb.			1	1:12	1
Total	1		1		2

3919. περιδέω, peride'ō

Book	bind about	Total
Jn.	11:44	1

3920. περιεργάζομαι periergad'zomai

Book	be a busybody	Total
2 Th.	3:11	1

3921. περίεργος, peri'ergos

Book	Oc.	curious arts	Oc.	busybody	Total
Ac.	1	19:19			1
1 Ti.			1	5:13	1
Total	1		1		2

3922. περιέρχομαι, perier'chomai

Book	Oc.	wander about	Oc.	vagabond	Oc.	fetch a compass	Total
Ac.			1	19:13	1	28:13	2
1 Ti.	1	5:13					1
Heb.	1	11:37					1
Total	2		1		1		4

3923. περιέχω, periech'ō

Book	Oc.	be astonished (with 2285)	Oc.	after this manner (with 5026 and 5079)	Oc.	be contained	Total
Lk.	1	5:9					1
Ac.			1	23:25			1
1 Pt.					1	2:6	1
Total	1		1		1		3

3924. περιζώννυμι, peridzōn'numi

Book	Oc.	gird (one's) self	Oc.	be girded about	Oc.	have . . . girded	Oc.	have . . . girt about	Oc.	be girt	Total
Lk.	2	12:37; 17:8	1	12:35							3
Ac.	1	12:8									1
Eph.							1	6:14			1
Rev.					1	15:6			1	1:13	2
Total	3		1		1		1		1		7

3925. περίθεσις, perith'esis

Book	wearing	Total
1 Pt.	3:3	1

3926. περιΐστημι, periis'tēmi

Book	Oc.	shun	Oc.	avoid	Oc.	stand by	Oc.	stand round about	Total
Jn.					1	11:42			1
Ac.							1	25:7	1
2 Ti.	1	2:16							1
Tit.			1	3:9					1
Total	1		1		1		1		4

3927. περικάθαρμα perikath'arma

Book	filth	Total
1 Co.	4:13	1

3928. περικαλύπτω, perikalup'tō

Book	Oc.	cover	Oc.	blindfold	Oc.	overlay	Total
Mk.	1	14:65					1
Lk.			1	22:64			1
Heb.					1	9:4	1
Total	1		1		1		3

3929. περίκειμαι, perik'eimai

Book	Oc.	be hanged	Oc.	be bound with	Oc.	be compas-sed with	Oc.	be compas-sed about with (with 2192)	Total
Mk.	1	9:42							1
Lk.	1	17:2							1
Ac.			1	28:20					1
Heb.					1	5:2	1	12:1	2
Total	2		1		1		1		5

3930. περικεφαλαία perikephalai'a

Book	helmet	Total
Eph.	6:17	1
1 Th.	5:8	1
Total		2

3931. περικρατής, perikratēs'

Book	come by	Total
Ac.	27:16	1

3932. περικρύπτω, perikrup'tō

Book	hide	Total
Lk.	1:24	1

3933. περικυκλόω, perikuklo'ō

Book	compass round	Total
Lk.	19:43	1

3934. περιλάμπω, perilam'pō

Book	shine round about	Total
Lk.	2:9	1
Ac.	26:13	1
Total		2

3935. περιλείπω, perilei'pō

Book	remain	Total
1 Th.	4:15, 17	2

3936. περίλυπος, peril'upos

Book	Oc.	exceeding sorrowful	Oc.	very sorrowful	Oc.	exceeding sorry	Total
Mt.	1	26:38					1
Mk.	1	14:34			1	6:26	2
Lk.			2	18:23, 24			2
Total	2		2		1		5

3937. περιμένω, perimen'ō

Book	wait for	Total
Ac.	1:4	1

3938. πέριξ, per'ix

Book	round about	Total
Ac.	5:16	1

3939. περιοικέω, perioike'ō

Book	dwell round about	Total
Lk.	1:65	1

3940. περίοικος, peri'oikos

Book	neighbour	Total
Lk.	1:58	1

3941. περιούσιος, periou'sios

Book	peculiar	Total
Tit.	2:14	1

3942. περιοχή, perioche'

Book	place	Total
Ac.	8:32	1

3943. περιπατέω, peripate'ō

Book	Oc.	walk	Oc.	go	Oc.	walk about	Oc.	be occupied	Total
Mt.	7	4:18; 9:5; 11:5; 14:25, 26, 29; 15:31							7
Mk.	9	1:16; 2:9; 5:42; 6:48, 49; 7:5; 8:24; 11:27; 16:12	1	12:38					10
Lk.	5	5:23; 7:22; 11:44; 20:46; 24:17							5
Jn.	17	1:36; 5:8, 9, 11, 12; 6:19, 66; 7:1, 1; 8:12; 10:23; 11:9, 10, 54; 12:35, 35; 21:18							17
Ac.	8	3:6, 8, 8, 9, 12; 14:8, 10; 21:21							8
Ro.	5	6:4; 8:1, 4; 13:13; 14:15							5
1 Co.	2	3:3; 7:17							2
2 Co.	5	4:2; 5:7; 10:2, 3; 12:18							5
Gal.	1	5:16							1
Eph.	8	2:2, 10; 4:1, 17, 17; 5:2, 8, 15							8
Phl.	2	3:17, 18							2
Col.	4	1:10; 2:6; 3:7; 4:5							4
1 Th.	3	2:12; 4:1, 12							3
2 Th.	2	3:6, 11							2
Heb.							1	13:9	1
1 Pt.					1	5:8			1
1 Jn.	5	1:6, 7; 2:6, 6, 11							5
2 Jn.	3	1:4, 6, 6							3
3 Jn.	2	1:3, 4							2
Rev.	5	2:1; 3:4; 9:20; 16:15; 21:24							5
Total	93		1		1		1		96

3944. περιπείρω, peripei'rō

Book	pierce through	Total
1 Ti.	6:10	1

3945. περιπίπτω, peripip'tō

Book	Oc.	fall into	Oc.	fall among	Total
Lk.			1	10:30	1
Ac.	1	27:41			1
Jas.	1	1:2			1
Total	2		1		3

3946. περιποιέομαι peripoie'omai

Book	purchase	Total
Ac.	20:28	1
1 Ti.	3:13	1
Total		2

3947. περιποίησις, peripoi'ęsis

Book	Oc.	purchased possession	Oc.	to obtain (with 1519)	Oc.	obtaining	Oc.	saving	Oc.	peculiar (with 1519)	Total
Eph.	1	1:14									1
1 Th.			1	5:9							1
2 Th.					1	2:14					1
Heb.							1	10:39			1
1 Pt.									1	2:9	1
Total	1		1		1		1		1		5

3948. περιῤῥήγνυμι perirhręg'numi

Book	rend off	Total
Ac.	16:22	1

3949. περισπάω, perispa'ō

Book	cumber	Total
Lk.	10:40	1

3950. περισσεία, perissei'a

Book	Oc.	abundance	Oc.	abundantly (with 1519)	Oc.	superfluity	Total
Ro.	1	5:17					1
2 Co.	1	8:2	1	10:15			2
Jas.					1	1:21	1
Total	2		1		1		4

3951. περίσσευμα, peris'seuma

Book	Oc.	abundance	Oc.	that was left	Total
Mt.	1	12:34			1
Mk.			1	8:8	1
Lk.	1	6:45			1
2 Co.	2	8:14, 14			2
Total	4		1		5

3952. περισσεύω, perisseu'ō

Book	Oc.	abound	Oc.	abundance	Oc.	remain	Oc.	exceed	Oc.	increase	Oc.	be left	Oc.	redound	Oc.	Misc.	Total
Mt.					1	14:20	1	5:20			1	15:37			2	13:12; 25:29	5
Mk.			1	12:44													1
Lk.			2	12:15; 21:4	1	9:17									1	15:17	4
Jn.					1	6:12									1	6:13	2
Ac.									1	16:5							1
Ro.	2	5:15; 15:13													1	3:7	3
1 Co.	1	15:58													2	8:8; 14:12	3
2 Co.	6	1:5, 5; 8:2, 7, 7; 9:8b					1	3:9					1	4:15	2	9:8a, 12	10
Eph.	1	1:8															1
Phl.	4	1:9; 4:12, 12, 18													1	1:26	5
Col.	1	2:7															1
1 Th.	2	3:12; 4:1							1	4:10							3
Total	17		3		3		2		2		1		1		10		39

Miscellaneous: Mt. 13:12, have more abundance; Mt. 25:29, have abundance; Lk. 15:17, have enough and to spare; Jn. 6:13, remain over and above; Ro. 3:7, abound more; 1 Co. 8:8, be the better; 1 Co. 14:12, excel; 2 Co. 9:8a, make abound; 2 Co. 9:12, abundant; Phl. 1:26, be more abundant.

3953. περισσός, perissos′

Book	Oc.	more	Oc.	beyond measure	Oc.	vehemently (with 1537)	Oc.	more abundantly	Oc.	advantage	Oc.	superfluous	Oc.	very highly (with 5128 and 1537)	Oc.	exceeding abundantly above (with 5128 and 1537)	Oc.	exceedingly (with 5128 and 1537)	Total
Mt.	2	5:37, 47																	2
Mk.			1	6:51	1	14:31													2
Jn.							1	10:10											1
Ro.									1	3:1									1
2 Co.											1	9:1							1
Eph.															1	3:20			1
1 Th.													1	5:13			1	3:10	2
Total	2		1		1		1		1		1		1		1		1		10

3954. περισσότερον, perissot′eron

Book	Oc.	more abundantly	Oc.	a great deal	Oc.	far more	Total
Mk.			1	7:36			1
1 Co.	1	15:10					1
Heb.	1	6:17			1	7:15	2
Total	2		1		1		4

3957. περισσῶς, perissōs′

Book	Oc.	the more	Oc.	out of measure	Oc.	exceedingly	Total
Mt.	1	27:23					1
Mk.			1	10:26			1
Ac.					1	26:11	1
Total	1		1		1		3

3955. περισσότερος, perissot′eros

Book	Oc.	more	Oc.	greater	Oc.	more abundant	Oc.	much more	Oc.	overmuch	Total
Mt.	1	11:9	1	23:14							2
Mk.			1	12:40							1
Lk.	2	12:4, 48	1	20:47			1	7:26			4
1 Co.					3	12:23, 23, 24					3
2 Co.	1	10:8							1	2:7	2
Total	4		3		3		1		1		12

3956. περισσοτέρως, perissoter′ōs

Book	Oc.	more abundantly	Oc.	more exceedingly	Oc.	more abundant	Oc.	much more	Oc.	more frequent	Oc.	the rather	Oc.	exceedingly	Oc.	the more earnest	Total
Mk.			1	15:14													1
2 Co.	3	1:12; 2:4; 12:15			2	7:15; 11:23a			1	11:23b			1	7:13			7
Gal.			1	1:14													1
Phl.							1	1:14									1
1 Th.	1	2:17															1
Heb.											1	13:19			1	2:1	2
Total	4		2		2		1		1		1		1		1		13

3958. περιστερά, peristera′

Book	Oc.	dove	Oc.	pigeon	Total
Mt.	3	3:16; 10:16; 21:12			3
Mk.	2	1:10; 11:15			2
Lk.	1	3:22	1	2:24	2
Jn.	3	1:32; 2:14, 16			3
Total	9		1		10

3959. περιτέμνω, peritem′nō

Book	circumcise	Total
Lk.	1:59; 2:21	2
Jn.	7:22	1
Ac.	7:8; 15:1, 5, 24; 16:3; 21:21	6
1 Co.	7:18, 18	2
Gal.	2:3; 5:2, 3; 6:12, 13, 13	6
Col.	2:11	1
Total		18

3962. περιτρέπω, peritrep′ō

Book	make mad (with 3130 and 1519)	Total
Ac.	26:24	1

3963. περιτρέχω, peritrech′ō

Book	run through	Total
Mk.	6:55	1

3960. περιτίθημι, perítith′ēmi

Book	Oc.	put on	Oc.	put upon	Oc.	set about	Oc.	put about	Oc.	bestow upon	Oc.	hedge round about (with 5318)	Total
Mt.	2	27:28, 48									1	21:33	3
Mk.	1	15:36			1	12:1	1	15:17					3
Jn.			1	19:29									1
1 Co.									1	12:23			1
Total	3		1		1		1		1		1		8

3961. περιτομή, peritomē′

Book	Oc.	circumcision	Oc.	circumcised	Total
Jn.	2	7:22, 23			2
Ac.	3	7:8; 10:45; 11:2			3
Ro.	15	2:25, 25, 26, 27, 28, 29; 3:1, 30; 4:9, 10, 10, 11, 12, 12; 15:8			15
1 Co.	1	7:19			1
Gal.	7	2:7, 8, 9, 12; 5:6, 11; 6:15			7
Eph.	1	2:11			1
Phl.	1	3:3	1	3:5	2
Col.	4	2:11, 11; 3:11; 4:11			4
Tit.	1	1:10			1
Total	35		1		36

3964. περιφέρω, peripher′ō

Book	Oc.	carry about	Oc.	bear about	Total
Mk.	1	6:55			1
2 Co.			1	4:10	1
Eph.	1	4:14			1
Heb.	1	13:9			1
Jd.	1	1:12			1
Total	4		1		5

3965. περιφρονέω, periphrone′ō

Book	despise	Total
Tit.	2:15	1

3966. περίχωρος, perich′ōros

Book	Oc.	region round about	Oc.	country round about	Oc.	country about	Oc.	region that lieth round about	Total
Mt.	1	3:5	1	14:35					2
Mk.	2	1:28; 6:55							2
Lk.	2	4:14; 7:17	2	4:37; 8:37	1	3:3			5
Ac.							1	14:6	1
Total	5		3		1		1		10

3967. περίψωμα, perip'sōma

Book	offscouring	Total
1 Co.	4:13	1

3968. περπερεύομαι, perpereu'omai

Book	vaunt itself	Total
1 Co.	13:4	1

3969. Περσίς, Persis'

Book	Persis	Total
Ro.	16:12	1

3970. πέρυσι, per'usi

Book	a year ago (with 575)	Total
2 Co.	8:10; 9:2	2

3971. πετεινόν, peteinon'

Book	Oc.	fowl	Oc.	bird	Total
Mt.	2	6:26; 13:4	2	8:20; 13:32	4
Mk.	2	4:4, 32			2
Lk.	3	8:5; 12:24; 13:19	1	9:58	4
Ac.	2	10:12; 11:6			2
Ro.			1	1:23	1
Jas.			1	3:7	1
Total	9		5		14

3972. πέτομαι or πετάομαι, pet'omai or peta'omai

Book	Oc.	fly	Oc.	flying	Total
Rev.	3	12:14; 14:6; 19:17	2	4:7; 8:13	5

3973. πέτρα, pet'ra

Book	rock	Total
Mt.	7:24, 25; 16:18; 27:51, 60	5
Mk.	15:46	1
Lk.	6:48, 48; 8:6, 13	4
Ro.	9:33	1
1 Co.	10:4, 4	2
1 Pt.	2:8	1
Rev.	6:15, 16	2
Total		16

3974. Πέτρος, Pet'ros

Book	Oc.	Peter	Oc.	stone	Total
Mt.	24	4:18; 8:14; 10:2; 14:28, 29; 15:15; 16:16, 18, 22, 23; 17:1, 4, 24, 26; 18:21; 19:27; 26:33, 35, 37, 40, 58, 69, 73, 75			24
Mk.	19	3:16; 5:37; 8:29, 32, 33; 9:2, 5; 10:28; 11:21; 13:3; 14:29, 33, 37, 54, 66, 67, 70, 72; 16:7			19
Lk.	20	5:8; 6:14; 8:45, 51; 9:20, 28, 32, 33; 12:41; 18:28; 22:8, 34, 54, 55, 58, 60, 61, 61, 62; 24:12			20
Jn.	33	1:40, 44; 6:8, 68; 13:6, 8, 9, 24, 36, 37; 18:10, 11, 15, 16, 16, 17, 18, 25, 26, 27; 20:2, 3, 4, 6; 21:2, 3, 7, 7, 11, 15, 17, 20, 21	1	1:42	34
Ac.	58	1:13, 15; 2:14, 37, 38; 3:1, 3, 4, 6, 11, 12; 4:8, 13, 19; 5:3, 8, 9, 15, 29; 8:14, 20; 9:32, 34, 38, 39, 40, 40; 10:5, 9, 13, 14, 17, 18, 19, 21, 23, 25, 26, 32, 34, 44, 45, 46; 11:2, 4, 7, 13; 12:3, 5, 6, 7, 11, 13, 14, 14, 16, 18; 15:7			58
Gal.	5	1:18; 2:7, 8, 11, 14			5
1 Pt.	1	1:1			1
2 Pt.	1	1:1			1
Total	161		1		162

3975. πετρώδης, petrō'dēs

Book	Oc.	stony place	Oc.	stony ground	Total
Mt.	2	13:5, 20			2
Mk.			2	4:5, 16	2
Total	2		2		4

3976. πήγανον, pē'ganon

Book	rue	Total
Lk.	11:42	1

3977. πηγή, pēgē'

Book	Oc.	fountain	Oc.	well	Total
Mk.	1	5:29			1
Jn.			3	4:6, 6, 14	3
Jas.	2	3:11, 12			2
2 Pt.			1	2:17	1
Rev.	5	7:17; 8:10; 14:7; 16:4; 21:6			5
Total	8		4		12

3978. πήγνυμι, pēg'numi

Book	pitch	Total
Heb.	8:2	1

3979. πηδάλιον, pēdal'ion

Book	Oc.	rudder	Oc.	helm	Total
Ac.	1	27:40			1
Jas.			1	3:4	1
Total	1		1		2

3980. πηλίκος, pēli'kos

Book	Oc.	how great	Oc.	how large	Total
Gal.			1	6:11	1
Heb.	1	7:4			1
Total	1		1		2

3981. πηλός, pēlos'

Book	clay	Total
Jn.	9:6, 6, 11, 14, 15	5
Ro.	9:21	1
Total		6

3982. πήρα, pē'ra

Book	scrip	Total
Mt.	10:10	1
Mk.	6:8	1
Lk.	9:3; 10:4; 22:35, 36	4
Total		6

3983. πῆχυς, pē'chus

Book	cubit	Total
Mt.	6:27	1
Lk.	12:25	1
Jn.	21:8	1
Rev.	21:17	1
Total		4

3984. πιάζω, piad'zō

Book	Oc.	take	Oc.	catch	Oc.	apprehend	Oc.	lay hand on	Total
Jn.	5	7:30, 32, 44; 10:39; 11:57	2	21:3, 10			1	8:20	8
Ac.	1	3:7			1	12:4			2
2 Co.					1	11:32			1
Rev.	1	19:20							1
Total	7		2		2		1		12

3985. πιέζω, pied'zō

Book	press down	Total
Lk.	6:38	1

3986. πιθανολογία, pithanologi'a

Book	enticing words	Total
Col.	2:4	1

3987. πικραίνω, pikrai'nō

Book	Oc.	make bitter	Oc.	be bitter	Total
Col.			1	3:19	1
Rev.	2	8:11; 10:9	1	10:10	3
Total	2		2		4

3988. πικρία, pikri'a

Book	bitterness	Total
Ac.	8:23	1
Ro.	3:14	1
Eph.	4:31	1
Heb.	12:15	1
Total		4

3989. πικρός, pikros'

Book	bitter	Total
Jas.	3:11, 14	2

3990. πικρῶς, pikrōs'

Book	bitterly	Total
Mt.	26:75	1
Lk.	22:62	1
Total		2

3991. Πιλάτος, Pilat'os

Book	Pilate	Total
Mt.	27:2, 13, 17, 22, 24, 58, 58, 62, 65	9
Mk.	15:1, 2, 4, 5, 9, 12, 14, 15, 43, 44	10
Lk.	3:1; 13:1; 23:1, 3, 4, 6, 11, 12, 13, 20, 24, 52	12
Jn.	18:29, 31, 33, 35, 37, 38; 19:1, 4, 6, 8, 10, 12, 13, 15, 19, 21, 22, 31, 38, 38	20
Ac.	3:13; 4:27; 13:28	3
1 Ti.	6:13	1
Total		55

3992. πίμπρημι or πρέω, pim'prēmi or pre'ō

Book	swollen	Total
Ac.	28:6	1

3993. πινακίδιον, pinakid'ion

Book	writing table	Total
Lk.	1:63	1

3994. πίναξ, pin'ax

Book	Oc.	charger	Oc.	platter	Total
Mt.	2	14:8, 11			2
Mk.	2	6:25, 28			2
Lk.			1	11:39	1
Total	4		1		5

3995. πίνω or πίω, pi'nō or pi'ō

Book	Oc.	drink	Oc.	drink of	Total
Mt.	12	6:25, 31; 11:18, 19; 24:38, 49; 26:27, 29, 29, 42; 27:34, 34	3	20:22, 22, 23	15
Mk.	6	2:16; 14:23, 25, 25; 15:23; 16:18	4	10:38, 38, 39, 39	10
Lk.	17	1:15; 5:30, 33, 39; 7:33, 34; 10:7; 12: 19, 29, 45; 13:26; 17:8, 8, 27, 28; 22: 18, 30			17
Jn.	11	4:7, 9, 10, 12, 13, 14; 6:53, 54, 56; 7: 37; 18:11			11
Ac.	3	9:9; 23:12, 21			3
Ro.	1	14:21			1
1 Co.	14	9:4; 10:4, 4, 7, 21, 31; 11:22, 25, 26, 27, 28, 29, 29; 15:32			14
Heb.	1	6:7			1
Rev.	3	14:10; 16:6; 18:3			3
Total	68		7		75

3996. πιότης, piot'ēs

Book	fatness	Total
Ro.	11:17	1

3997. πιπράσκω or πράω pipras'kō or pra'ō

Book	sell	Total
Mt.	13:46; 18:25; 26:9	3
Mk.	14:5	1
Jn.	12:5	1
Ac.	2:45; 4:34; 5:4	3
Ro.	7:14	1
Total		9

3999. Πισιδία, Pisidi'a

Book	Pisidia	Total
Ac.	13:14; 14:24	2

4001. πιστικός, pistikos'

Book	spikenard (with 3387)	Total
Mk.	14:3	1
Jn.	12:3	1
Total		2

3998. πίπτω, pip'tō

Book	Oc.	fall	Oc.	fall down	Oc.	light	Oc.	fail	Total
Mt.	15	7:25, 27; 10:29; 13:4, 5, 7, 8; 15:14, 27; 17:6, 15; 21:44, 44; 24:29; 26: 39	4	2:11; 4:9; 18:26, 29					19
Mk.	7	4:4, 5, 7, 8; 5:22; 9:20; 14:35							7
Lk.	16	5:12; 6:39, 49; 8:5, 6, 7, 8, 14; 10:18; 11:17; 13:4; 16:21; 20:18, 18; 21: 24; 23:30	2	8:41; 17:16			1	16:17	19
Jn.	2	12:24; 18:6	1	11:32					3
Ac.	4	1:26; 9:4; 22:7; 27:34	5	5:5, 10; 10:25; 15:16; 20:9					9
Ro.	3	11:11, 22; 14:4							3
1 Co.	2	10:8, 12	1	14:25					3
Heb.	2	3:17; 4:11	1	11:30					3
Jas.	1	5:12							1
Rev.	17	1:17; 6:13, 16; 7:11; 8:10, 10; 9:1; 11:11, 13, 16; 14:8, 8; 16:19; 17:10; 18:2, 2; 19:10	5	4:10; 5:8, 14; 19:4; 22:8	1	7:16			23
Total	69		19		1		1		90

4000. πιστεύω, pisteu'ō

Book	Oc.	believe	Oc.	commit unto	Oc.	commit to (one's) trust	Oc.	be committed to (one's) trust	Oc.	be committed unto	Oc.	be put in trust with	Oc.	believer	Total
Mt.	11	8:13; 9:28; 18:6; 21:22, 25, 32, 32, 32; 24:23, 26; 27:42													11
Mk.	15	1:15; 5:36; 9:23, 23, 24, 42; 11: 23, 24, 31; 13:21; 15:32; 16:13, 14, 16, 17													15
Lk.	8	1:20, 45; 8:12, 13, 50; 20:5; 22:67; 24:25			1	16:11									9
Jn.	99	1:7, 12, 50; 2:11, 22, 23; 3:12, 12, 15, 16, 18, 18, 18, 36; 4:21, 39, 41, 42, 48, 50, 53; 5:24, 38, 44, 46, 46, 47, 47; 6:29, 30, 35, 36, 40, 47, 64, 64, 69; 7:5, 31, 38, 39, 48; 8:24, 30, 31, 45, 46; 9:18, 35, 36, 38; 10:25, 26, 37, 38, 38, 38, 42; 11:15, 25, 26, 26, 27, 40, 42, 45, 48; 12:11, 36, 37, 38, 39, 42, 44, 44, 46, 47; 13:19; 14:1, 1, 10, 11, 11, 12, 29; 16:9, 27, 30, 31; 17:8, 20, 21; 19:35; 20:8, 25, 29, 29, 31, 31	1	2:24											100
Ac.	38	2:44; 4:4, 32; 8:12, 13, 37, 37; 9: 26, 42; 10:43; 11:17, 21; 13:12, 39, 41, 48; 14:1, 23; 15:5, 7, 11; 16:31, 34; 17:12, 34; 18:8, 8, 27; 19:2, 4, 18; 21:20, 25; 22:19; 24: 14; 26:27, 27; 27:25											1	5:14	39
Ro.	20	1:16; 3:22; 4:3, 5, 11, 17, 18, 24; 6:8; 9:33; 10:4, 9, 10, 11, 14, 14, 16; 13:11; 14:2; 15:13	1	3:2											21
1 Co.	8	1:21; 3:5; 11:18; 13:7; 14:22, 22; 15:2, 11	1	9:17											9
2 Co.	2	4:13, 13													2
Gal.	3	2:16; 3:6, 22	1	2:7											4
Eph.	2	1:13, 19													2
Phl.	1	1:29													1
1 Th.	4	1:7; 2:10, 13; 4:14									1	2:4			5
2 Th.	4	1:10, 10; 2:11, 12													4
1 Ti.	2	1:16; 3:16					1	1:11							3
2 Ti.	1	1:12													1
Tit.	1	3:8							1	1:3					2
Heb.	2	4:3; 11:6													2
Jas.	3	2:19, 19, 23													3
1 Pt.	4	1:8, 21; 2:6, 7													4
1 Jn.	10	3:23; 4:1, 16; 5:1, 5, 10, 10, 10, 13, 13													10
Jd.	1	1:5													1
Total	239		4		1		1		1		1		1		248

4002. πίστις, pis'tis

Book	Oc.	faith	Oc.	assurance	Oc.	believe (with 1537)	Oc.	belief	Oc.	them that believe	Oc.	fidelity	Total
Mt.	8	8:10; 9:2, 22, 29; 15:28; 17:20; 21:21; 23:23											8
Mk.	5	2:5; 4:40; 5:34; 10:52; 11:22											5
Lk.	11	5:20; 7:9, 50; 8:25, 48; 17:5, 6, 19; 18:8, 42; 22:32											11
Ac.	15	3:16, 16; 6:5, 7, 8; 11:24; 13:8; 14:9, 22, 27; 15:9; 16:5; 20:21; 24:24; 26:18	1	17:31									16
Ro.	39	1:5, 8, 12, 17, 17, 17; 3:3, 22, 25, 27, 28, 30, 30, 31; 4:5, 9, 11, 12, 13, 14, 16, 16, 19, 20; 5:1, 2; 9:30, 32; 10:6, 8, 17; 11:20; 12:3, 6; 14:1, 22, 23, 23; 16:26			1	3:26							40
1 Co.	7	2:5; 12:9; 13:2, 13; 15:14, 17; 16:13											7
2 Co.	7	1:24, 24; 4:13; 5:7; 8:7; 10:15; 13:5											7
Gal.	22	1:23; 2:16, 16, 20; 3:2, 5, 7, 8, 9, 11, 12, 14, 22, 23, 23, 24, 25, 26; 5:5, 6, 22; 6:10											22
Eph.	8	1:15; 2:8; 3:12, 17; 4:5, 13; 6:16, 23											8
Phl.	5	1:25, 27; 2:17; 3:9, 9											5
Col.	5	1:4, 23; 2:5, 7, 12											5
1 Th.	8	1:3, 8; 3:2, 5, 6, 7, 10; 5:8											8
2 Th.	4	1:3, 4, 11; 3:2					1	2:13					5
1 Ti.	19	1:2, 4, 5, 14, 19, 19; 2:7, 15; 3:9, 13; 4:1, 6, 12; 5: 8, 12; 6:10, 11, 12, 21											19
2 Ti.	8	1:5, 13; 2:18, 22; 3:8, 10, 15; 4:7											8
Tit.	5	1:1, 4, 13; 2:2; 3:15									1	2:10	6
Phe.	2	1:5, 6											2
Heb.	31	4:2; 6:1, 12; 10:22, 38; 11:1, 3, 4, 5, 6, 7, 7, 8, 9, 11, 13, 17, 20, 21, 22, 23, 24, 27, 28, 29, 30, 31, 33, 39; 12:2; 13:7							1	10:39			32
Jas.	16	1:3, 6; 2:1, 5, 14, 14, 17, 18, 18, 18, 20, 22, 22, 24, 26; 5:15											16
1 Pt.	5	1:5, 7, 9, 21; 5:9											5
2 Pt.	2	1:1, 5											2
1 Jn.	1	5:4											1
Jd.	2	1:3, 20											2
Rev.	4	2:13, 19; 13:10; 14:12											4
Total	239		1		1		1		1		1		244

4003. πιστός, pistos'

Book	Oc.	faithful	Oc.	believe	Oc.	believing	Oc.	true	Oc.	faithfully	Oc.	believer	Oc.	sure	Total
Mt.	5	24:45; 25:21, 21, 23, 23													5
Lk.	6	12:42; 16:10, 10, 11, 12; 19:17													6
Jn.					1	20:27									1
Ac.	1	16:15	2	10:45; 16:1									1	13:34	4
1 Co.	5	1:9; 4:2, 17; 7:25; 10:13													5
2 Co.			1	6:15			1	1:18							2
Gal.	1	3:9													1
Eph.	2	1:1; 6:21													2
Col.	4	1:2, 7; 4:7, 9													4
1 Th.	1	5:24													1
2 Th.	1	3:3													1
1 Ti.	5	1:12, 15; 3:11; 4:9; 6:2b	3	4:3, 10; 5:16	1	6:2a	1	3:1			1	4:12			11
2 Ti.	3	2:2, 11, 13													3
Tit.	3	1:6, 9; 3:8													3
Heb.	5	2:17; 3:2, 5; 10:23; 11:11													5
1 Pt.	2	4:19; 5:12													2
1 Jn.	1	1:9													1
3 Jn.									1	1:5					1
Rev.	8	1:5; 2:10, 13; 3:14; 17:14; 19: 11; 21:5; 22:6													8
Total	53		6		2		2		1		1		1		66

4005. πλανάω, plana'ō

Book	Oc.	deceive	Oc.	err	Oc.	go astray	Oc.	seduce	Oc.	wander	Oc.	be out of the way	Total
Mt.	4	24:4, 5, 11, 24	1	22:29	3	18:12, 12, 13							8
Mk.	2	13:5, 6	2	12:24, 27									4
Lk.	1	21:8											1
Jn.	2	7:12, 47											2
1 Co.	2	6:9; 15:33											2
Gal.	1	6:7											1
2 Ti.	2	3:13, 13											2
Tit.	1	3:3											1
Heb.			1	3:10					1	11:38	1	5:2	3
Jas.			2	1:16; 5:19									2
1 Pt.					1	2:25							1
2 Pt.					1	2:15							1
1 Jn.	2	1:8; 3:7					1	2:26					3
Rev.	7	12:9; 13:14; 18:23; 19:20; 20:3, 8, 10					1	2:20					8
Total	24		6		5		2		1		1		39

4004. πιστόω, pisto'ō

Book	be assured of	Total
2 Ti.	3:14	1

4007. πλανήτης, planē'tēs

Book	wandering	Total
Jd.	1:13	1

4008. πλάνος, plan'os

Book	Oc.	deceiver	Oc.	seducing	Total
Mt.	1	27:63			1
2 Co.	1	6:8			1
1 Ti.			1	4:1	1
2 Jn.	2	1:7, 7			2
Total	4		1		5

4006. πλάνη, plan'ē

Book	Oc.	error	Oc.	to deceive	Oc.	deceit	Oc.	delusion	Total
Mt.	1	27:64							1
Ro.	1	1:27							1
Eph.			1	4:14					1
1 Th.					1	2:3			1
2 Th.							1	2:11	1
Jas.	1	5:20							1
2 Pt.	2	2:18; 3:17							2
1 Jn.	1	4:6							1
Jd.	1	1:11							1
Total	7		1		1		1		10

4009. πλάξ, plax

Book	table	Total
2 Co.	3:3, 3	2
Heb.	9:4	1
Total		3

4010. πλάσμα, plas′ma

Book	thing formed	Total
Ro.	9:20	1

4011. πλάσσω, plas′sō

Book	form	Total
Ro.	9:20	1
1 Ti.	2:13	1
Total		2

4012. πλαστός, plastos′

Book	feigned	Total
2 Pt.	2:3	1

4013. πλατεῖα, platei′a

Book	street	Total
Mt.	6:5; 12:19	2
Lk.	10:10; 13:26; 14:21	3
Ac.	5:15	1
Rev.	11:8; 21:21; 22:2	3
Total		9

4014. πλάτος, plat′os

Book	breadth	Total
Eph.	3:18	1
Rev.	20:9; 21:16, 16	3
Total		4

4015. πλατύνω, platu′nō

Book	Oc.	enlarge	Oc.	make broad	Total
Mt.			1	23:5	1
2 Co.	2	6:11, 13			2
Total	2		1		3

4016. πλατύς, platus′

Book	wide	Total
Mt.	7:13	1

4017. πλέγμα, pleg′ma

Book	broidered hair	Total
1 Ti.	2:9	1

4018. πλεῖστος, pleis′tos

Book	Oc.	most	Oc.	very great	Total
Mt.	1	11:20	1	21:8	2
1 Co.	1	14:27			1
Total	2		1		3

4019. πλείων, πλεῖον, or πλέον, plei′ōn, plei′on, or ple′on

Book	Oc.	more	Oc.	many	Oc.	greater	Oc.	further (with 1909)	Oc.	most	Oc.	more part	Oc.	Not Tr.	Oc.	Misc.	Total
Mt.	4	6:25; 20:10; 21:36; 26:53			2	12:41, 42							1	5:20			7
Mk.	2	12:33, 43															2
Lk.	4	3:13; 9:13; 12:23; 21:3			2	11:31, 32			2	7:42, 43					1	11:53	9
Jn.	5	4:1, 41; 7:31; 15:2; 21:15															5
Ac.	3	23:13, 21; 25:6	7	2:40; 13:31; 21:10; 24:17; 25:14; 27:20; 28:23	1	15:28	2	4:17; 24:4			2	19:32; 27:12			4	4:22; 18:20; 20:9; 24:11	19
1 Co.	1	9:19	1	10:5											1	15:6	3
2 Co.			2	2:6; 4:15											1	9:2	3
Phl.			1	1:14													1
2 Ti.	1	2:16					1	3:9									2
Heb.	2	3:3, 3	1	7:23											1	11:4	4
Rev.	1	2:19															1
Total	23		12		5		3		2		2		1		8		56

Miscellaneous: Lk. 11:53, many things; Ac. 4:22, above; Ac. 18:20, longer; Ac. 20:9 (with 1909), long; Ac. 24:11 (with 3656), yet but; 1 Co. 15:6, greater part; 2 Co. 9:2, very many; Heb. 11:4, more excellent.

4020. πλέκω, plek′ō

Book	plait	Total
Mt.	27:29	1
Mk.	15:17	1
Jn.	19:2	1
Total		3

4021. πλεονάζω, pleonad′zō

Book	Oc.	abound	Oc.	abundant	Oc.	have over	Oc.	make to increase	Total
Ro.	3	5:20, 20; 6:1							3
2 Co.			1	4:15	1	8:15			2
Phl.	1	4:17							1
1 Th.							1	3:12	1
2 Th.	1	1:3							1
2 Pt.	1	1:8							1
Total	6		1		1		1		9

4022. πλεονεκτέω, pleonekte′ō

Book	Oc.	make a gain	Oc.	defraud	Oc.	get an advantage	Total
2 Co.	2	12:17, 18	1	7:2	1	2:11	4
1 Th.			1	4:6			1
Total	2		2		1		5

4023. πλεονέκτης, pleonek′tẹs

Book	covetous	Total
1 Co.	5:10, 11; 6:10	3
Eph.	5:5	1
Total		4

4024. πλεονεξία, pleonexi′a

Book	Oc.	covetousness	Oc.	greediness	Oc.	covetous practice	Total
Mk.	1	7:22					1
Lk.	1	12:15					1
Ro.	1	1:29					1
2 Co.	1	9:5					1
Eph.	1	5:3	1	4:19			2
Col.	1	3:5					1
1 Th.	1	2:5					1
2 Pt.	1	2:3			1	2:14	2
Total	8		1		1		10

4025. πλευρά, pleura′

Book	side	Total
Jn.	19:34; 20:20, 25, 27	4
Ac.	12:7	1
Total		5

4026. πλέω or πλεύω ple′ō or pleu′ō

Book	sail	Total
Lk.	8:23	1
Ac.	21:3; 27:2, 6, 24	4
Total		5

4027. πληγή, plẹgẹ′

Book	Oc.	plague	Oc.	stripe	Oc.	wound	Total
Lk.			1	12:48	1	10:30	2
Ac.			2	16:23, 33			2
2 Co.			2	6:5; 11:23			2
Rev.	12	9:20; 11:6; 15:1, 6, 8; 16:9, 21, 21; 18:4, 8; 21:9; 22:18			3	13:3, 12, 14	15
Total	12		5		4		21

4028. πλῆθος, plẹ′thos

Book	Oc.	multitude	Oc.	company	Oc.	bundle	Total
Mk.	2	3:7, 8					2
Lk.	7	1:10; 2:13; 5:6; 6:17; 8:37; 19:37; 23:1	1	23:27			8
Jn.	2	5:3; 21:6					2
Ac.	16	2:6; 4:32; 5:14, 16; 6:2, 5; 14:1, 4; 15:12, 30; 17:4; 19:9; 21:22, 36; 23:7; 25:24			1	28:3	17
Heb.	1	11:12					1
Jas.	1	5:20					1
1 Pt.	1	4:8					1
Total	30		1		1		32

4029. πληθύνω, plẹthu′nō

Book	Oc.	multiply	Oc.	abound	Total
Mt.			1	24:12	1
Ac.	5	6:1, 7; 7:17; 9:31; 12:24			5
2 Co.	1	9:10			1
Heb.	2	6:14, 14			2
1 Pt.	1	1:2			1
2 Pt.	1	1:2			1
Jd.	1	1:2			1
Total	11		1		12

4030. πλήθω, plḗ'thō

Book	Oc.	fill	Oc.	accomplish	Oc.	furnish	Oc.	full . . . come	Total
Mt.	1	27:48			1	22:10			2
Lk.	7	1:15, 41, 67; 4:28; 5:7, 26; 6:11	4	1:23; 2:6, 21, 22			1	1:57	12
Jn.	1	19:29							1
Ac.	9	2:4; 3:10; 4:8, 31; 5:17; 9:17; 13:9, 45; 19:29							9
Total	18		4		1		1		24

4031. πλήκτης, plḗk'tēs

Book	striker	Total
1 Ti.	3:3	1
Tit.	1:7	1
Total		2

4032. πλημμύρα, plēmmu'ra

Book	flood	Total
Lk.	6:48	1

4033. πλήν, plēn

Book	Oc.	but	Oc.	nevertheless	Oc.	notwithstanding	Oc.	but rather	Oc.	except	Oc.	than	Oc.	save	Total
Mt.	3	11:22, 24; 18:7	2	26:39, 64											5
Mk.	1	12:32													1
Lk.	7	6:24, 35; 10:14; 19:27, 22:21, 22; 23:28	3	13:33; 18:8; 22:42	2	10:11, 20	2	11:41; 12:31							14
Jn.	1	8:10													1
Ac.	1	27:22							1	8:1	1	15:28	1	20:23	4
1 Co.			1	11:11											1
Eph.			1	5:33											1
Phl.			1	3:16	2	1:18; 4:14									3
Rev.	1	2:25													1
Total	14		8		4		2		1		1		1		31

4034. πλήρης, plḗ'rēs

Book	full	Total
Mt.	14:20; 15:37	2
Mk.	4:28; 6:43; 8:19	3
Lk.	4:1; 5:12	2
Jn.	1:14	1
Ac.	6:3, 5, 8; 7:55; 9:36; 11:24; 13:10; 19:28	8
2 Jn.	1:8	1
Total		17

4035. πληροφορέω, plērophore'ō

Book	Oc.	be fully persuaded	Oc.	be most surely believed	Oc.	be fully known	Oc.	make full proof of	Total
Lk.			1	1:1					1
Ro.	2	4:21; 14:5							2
2 Ti.					1	4:17	1	4:5	2
Total	2		1		1		1		5

4039. πλησίον, plēsi'on

Book	Oc.	neighbor	Oc.	near	Total
Mt.	3	5:43; 19:19; 22:39			3
Mk.	2	12:31, 33			2
Lk.	3	10:27, 29, 36			3
Jn.			1	4:5	1
Ac.	1	7:27			1
Ro.	3	13:9, 10; 15:2			3
Gal.	1	5:14			1
Eph.	1	4:25			1
Heb.	1	8:11			1
Jas.	1	2:8			1
Total	16		1		17

4036. πληροφορία, plērophori'a

Book	Oc.	full assurance	Oc.	assurance	Total
Col.	1	2:2			1
1 Th.			1	1:5	1
Heb.	2	6:11; 10:22			2
Total	3		1		4

4037. πληρόω, plēro'ō

Book	Oc.	fulfill	Oc.	fill	Oc.	be full	Oc.	complete	Oc.	end	Oc.	Misc.	Total
Mt.	15	1:22; 2:15, 17, 23; 3:15; 4:14; 5:17; 8:17; 12:17; 13:35; 21:4; 26:54, 56; 27:9, 35			1	13:48					1	23:32	17
Mk.	3	1:15; 14:49; 15:28											3
Lk.	6	1:20; 4:21; 21:22, 24; 22:16; 24:44	2	2:40; 3:5					1	7:1	1	9:31	10
Jn.	10	3:29; 12:38; 13:18; 15:25; 17:12, 13; 18:9, 32; 19:24, 36	2	12:3; 16:6	2	15:11; 16:24					1	7:8	15
Ac.	7	1:16; 3:18; 9:23; 12:25; 13:25, 27; 14:26	4	2:2; 5:3, 28; 13:52	1	7:23			1	19:21	3	2:28; 7:30; 24:27	16
Ro.	2	8:4; 13:8	3	1:29; 15:13, 14							1	15:19	6
2 Co.	1	10:6	1	7:4									2
Gal.	1	5:14											1
Eph.			4	1:23; 3:19; 4:10; 5:18									4
Phl.	1	2:2	1	1:11	1	4:18					1	4:19	4
Col.	2	1:25; 4:17	1	1:9			2	2:10; 4:12					5
2 Th.	1	1:11											1
2 Ti.			1	1:4									1
Jas.	1	2:23											1
1 Jn.					1	1:4							1
2 Jn.					1	1:12							1
Rev.	1	6:11									1	3:2	2
Total	51		19		7		2		2		9		90

Miscellaneous: Mt. 23:32, fill up; Lk. 9:31, accomplish; Jn. 7:8, be full come; Ac. 2:28, make full; Ac. 7:30, expire; Ac. 24:27, after; Ro. 15:19, fully preach; Phl. 4:19, supply; Rev. 3:2, perfect.

4038. πλήρωμα, plḗ'rōma

Book	Oc.	fulness	Oc.	full	Oc.	fulfilling	Oc.	which is put in to fill up	Oc.	piece that filled up	Total
Mt.							1	9:16			1
Mk.			1	8:20					1	2:21	2
Jn.	1	1:16									1
Ro.	3	11:12, 25; 15:29			1	13:10					4
1 Co.	2	10:26, 28									2
Gal.	1	4:4									1
Eph.	4	1:10, 23; 3:19; 4:13									4
Col.	2	1:19; 2:9									2
Total	13		1		1		1		1		17

4040. πλησμονή, plęsmonę′

Book	satisfying	Total
Col.	2:23	1

4041. πλήσσω, plęs′sō

Book	smite	Total
Rev.	8:12	1

4042. πλοιάριον, ploiar′ion

Book	Oc.	boat	Oc.	little ship	Oc.	small ship	Total
Mk.			1	4:36	1	3:9	2
Jn.	3	6:22, 22, 23	1	21:8			4
Total	3		2		1		6

4043. πλοῖον, ploi′on

Book	Oc.	ship	Oc.	shipping	Total
Mt.	13	4:21, 22; 8:23, 24; 9:1; 13:2; 14:13, 22, 24, 29, 32, 33; 15:39			13
Mk.	16	1:19, 20; 4:1, 36, 37; 5:2, 18, 21; 6:32, 45, 47, 51, 54; 8:10, 13, 14			16
Lk.	8	5:2, 3, 3, 7, 7, 11; 8:22, 37			8
Jn.	6	6:17, 19, 21, 21; 21:3, 6	1	6:24	7
Ac.	19	20:13, 38; 21:2, 3, 6; 27:2, 6, 10, 15, 17, 19, 22, 30, 31, 37, 38, 39, 44; 28:11			19
Jas.	1	3:4			1
Rev.	3	8:9; 18:17, 19			3
Total	66		1		67

4044. πλόος, plo′os

Book	Oc.	course	Oc.	sailing	Oc.	voyage	Total
Ac.	1	21:7	1	27:9	1	27:10	3

4045. πλούσιος, plou′sios

Book	rich	Total
Mt.	19:23, 24; 27:57	3
Mk.	10:25; 12:41	2
Lk.	6:24; 12:16; 14:12; 16:1, 19, 21, 22; 18:23, 25; 19:2; 21:1	11
2 Co.	8:9	1
Eph.	2:4	1
1 Ti.	6:17	1
Jas.	1:10, 11; 2:5, 6; 5:1	5
Rev.	2:9; 3:17; 6:15; 13:16	4
Total		28

4046. πλουσίως, plousi′ōs

Book	Oc.	richly	Oc.	abundantly	Total
Col.	1	3:16			1
1 Ti.	1	6:17			1
Tit.			1	3:6	1
2 Pt.			1	1:11	1
Total	2		2		4

4047. πλουτέω, ploute′ō

Book	Oc.	be rich	Oc.	be made rich	Oc.	rich	Oc.	wax rich	Oc.	be increased with goods	Total
Lk.	1	12:21			1	1:53					2
Ro.	1	10:12									1
1 Co.	1	4:8									1
2 Co.	1	8:9									1
1 Ti.	2	6:9, 18									2
Rev.	1	3:18	2	18:15, 19			1	18:3	1	3:17	5
Total	7		2		1		1		1		12

4048. πλουτίζω, ploutid′zō

Book	Oc.	enrich	Oc.	make rich	Total
1 Co.	1	1:5			1
2 Co.	1	9:11	1	6:10	2
Total	2		1		3

4049. πλοῦτος, plou′tos

Book	riches	Total
Mt.	13:22	1
Mk.	4:19	1
Lk.	8:14	1
Ro.	2:4; 9:23; 11:12, 12, 33	5
2 Co.	8:2	1
Eph.	1:7, 18; 2:7; 3:8, 16	5
Phl.	4:19	1
Col.	1:27; 2:2	2
1 Ti.	6:17	1
Heb.	11:26	1
Jas.	5:2	1
Rev.	5:12; 18:17	2
Total		22

4050. πλύνω, plu′nō

Book	wash	Total
Rev.	7:14	1

See page 296 for Word 4051.

4052. πνευματικός pneumatikos′

Book	spiritual	Total
Ro.	1:11; 7:14; 15:27	3
1 Co.	2:13, 13, 15; 3:1; 9:11; 10:3, 4, 4; 12:1; 14:1, 37; 15:44, 44, 46, 46	15
Gal.	6:1	1
Eph.	1:3; 5:19; 6:12	3
Col.	1:9; 3:16	2
1 Pt.	2:5, 5	2
Total		26

4053. πνευματικῶς pneumatikōs′

Book	spiritually	Total
1 Co.	2:14	1
Rev.	11:8	1
Total		2

4054. πνέω, pne′ō

Book	Oc.	blow	Oc.	wind	Total
Mt.	2	7:25, 27			2
Lk.	1	12:55			1
Jn.	2	3:8; 6:18			2
Ac.			1	27:40	1
Rev.	1	7:1			1
Total	6		1		7

4056. πνικτός, pniktos′

Book	strangled	Total
Ac.	15:20, 29; 21:25	3

4055. πνίγω, pni′gō

Book	Oc.	take by the throat	Oc.	choke	Total
Mt.	1	18:28			1
Mk.			1	5:13	1
Total	1		1		2

4057. πνοή, pnoę′

Book	Oc.	wind	Oc.	breath	Total
Ac.	1	2:2	1	17:25	2

4058. ποδήρης, podę′ręs

Book	garment down to the foot	Total
Rev.	1:13	1

See page 298 for Word 4060.

4059. πόθεν, poth′en

Book	whence	Total
Mt.	13:27, 54, 56; 15:33; 21:25	5
Mk.	6:2; 8:4; 12:37	3
Lk.	1:43; 13:25, 27; 20:7	4
Jn.	1:48; 2:9; 3:8; 4:11; 6:5; 7:27, 27, 28; 8:14, 14; 9:29, 30; 19:9	13
Jas.	4:1	1
Rev.	2:5; 7:13	2
Total		28

4061. ποίημα, poi′ęma

Book	Oc.	thing that is made	Oc.	workmanship	Total
Ro.	1	1:20			1
Eph.			1	2:10	1
Total	1		1		2

4062. ποίησις, poi′ęsis

Book	deed	Total
Jas.	1:25	1

4063. ποιητής, poiętęs′

Book	Oc.	doer	Oc.	poet	Total
Ac.			1	17:28	1
Ro.	1	2:13			1
Jas.	4	1:22, 23, 25; 4:11			4
Total	5		1		6

4064. ποικίλος, poiki′los

Book	Oc.	divers	Oc.	manifold	Total
Mt.	1	4:24			1
Mk.	1	1:34			1
Lk.	1	4:40			1
2 Ti.	1	3:6			1
Tit.	1	3:3			1
Heb.	2	2:4; 13:9			2
Jas.	1	1:2			1
1 Pt.			2	1:6; 4:10	2
Total	8		2		10

4065. ποιμαίνω, poimai′nō

Book	Oc.	feed	Oc.	rule	Oc.	feed cattle	Total
Mt.			1	2:6			1
Lk.					1	17:7	1
Jn.	1	21:16					1
Ac.	1	20:28					1
1 Co.	1	9:7					1
1 Pt.	1	5:2					1
Jd.	1	1:12					1
Rev.	1	7:17	3	2:27; 12:5; 19:15			4
Total	6		4		1		11

4066. ποιμήν, poimēn′

Book	Oc.	shepherd	Oc.	Shepherd	Oc.	pastor	Total
Mt.	3	9:36; 25:32; 26:31					3
Mk.	2	6:34; 14:27					2
Lk.	4	2:8, 15, 18, 20					4
Jn.	6	10:2, 11, 11, 12, 14, 16					6
Eph.					1	4:11	1
Heb.			1	13:20			1
1 Pt.			1	2:25			1
Total	15		2		1		18

4067. ποίμνη, poim′nē

Book	Oc.	flock	Oc.	fold	Total
Mt.	1	26:31			1
Lk.	1	2:8			1
Jn.			1	10:16	1
1 Co.	2	9:7, 7			2
Total	4		1		5

4068. ποίμνιον, poim′nion

Book	flock	Total
Lk.	12:32	1
Ac.	20:28, 29	2
1 Pt.	5:2, 3	2
Total		5

4051. πνεῦμα, pneu′ma

Book	Oc.	Spirit	Oc.	Holy Ghost	Oc.	Spirit (of God)	Oc.	Spirit (of the Lord)	Oc.	(My) Spirit	Oc.	Spirit (of truth)	Oc.	Spirit (of Christ)	Oc.	Misc.
Mt.	2	4:1; 22:43	5	1:18, 20; 3:11; 12:32; 28:19	2	3:16; 12:28			1	12:18					2	10:20; 12:31
Mk.	2	1:10, 12	4	1:8; 3:29; 12:36; 13:11												
Lk.	3	2:27; 4:1b, 14	11	1:15, 35, 41, 67; 2:25, 26; 3:16, 22; 4:1a; 12:10, 12			1	4:18							1	11:13
Jn.	9	1:32, 33a; 3:5, 6a, 8b, 34; 4:24a; 6:63a; 7:39a	4	1:33b; 7:39b; 14:26; 20:22							3	14:17; 15:26; 16:13				
Ac.	8	2:4b; 6:10; 8:29; 10:19; 11:12, 28; 16:7; 21:4	42	1:2, 5, 8, 16; 2:4a, 33, 38; 4:8, 31; 5:3, 32; 6:3, 5; 7:51, 55; 8:15, 17, 18, 19; 9:17, 31; 10:38, 44, 45, 47; 11:15, 16, 24; 13:2, 4, 9, 52; 15:8, 28; 16:6; 19:2, 2, 6; 20:23, 28; 21:11; 28:25			2	5:9; 8:39	2	2:17, 18						
Ro.	14	8:1, 4, 5, 5, 9a, 10, 11a, 13, 16a, 23, 26, 26, 27; 15:30	5	5:5; 9:1; 14:17; 15:13, 16	3	8:9b, 14; 15:19							1	8:9c	5	1:4; 8:2, 6, 11b, 15b
1 Co.	12	2:4, 10b, 12b; 12:4, 7, 8, 8, 9, 9, 11, 13, 13	3	2:13; 6:19; 12:3b	6	2:11b, 14; 3:16; 6:11; 7:40; 12:3a									1	2:10a
2 Co.	6	1:22; 3:6b, 8, 17a; 5:5; 12:18	2	6:6; 13:14	1	3:3	2	3:17b, 18								
Gal.	15	3:2, 3, 5, 14; 4:29; 5:5, 16, 17, 17, 18, 22, 25, 25; 6:8, 8													1	4:6
Eph.	10	2:18, 22; 3:5, 16; 4:3, 4; 5:9, 18; 6:17, 18													2	1:13; 4:30
Phl.	1	2:1													1	1:19
Col.	1	1:8														
1 Th.	1	5:19	2	1:5, 6											1	4:8
2 Th.	1	2:13														
1 Ti.	2	3:16; 4:1a														
2 Ti.			1	1:14												
Tit.			1	3:5												
Phe.																
Heb.			5	2:4; 3:7; 6:4; 9:8; 10:15											2	9:14; 10:29
Jas.	1	4:5														
1 Pt.	3	1:2, 22; 3:18	1	1:12									1	1:11	1	4:14
2 Pt.			1	1:21												
1 Jn.	5	3:24; 4:13; 5:6, 6, 8	1	5:7	1	4:2a										
Jd.	1	1:19	1	1:20												
Rev.	14	1:10; 2:7, 11, 17, 29; 3:6, 13, 22; 4:2; 14:13; 17:3; 19:10; 21:10; 22:17													1	11:11
Total	111		89		13		5		3		3		2		18	

Miscellaneous: Mt. 10:20, Spirit (of your Father); Mt. 12:31, (Holy) Ghost; Lk. 11:13, (Holy) Spirit; Ro. 1:4, Spirit (of holiness); Ro. 8:2, Spirit (of life); Ro. 8:6 (with 5327), spiritually minded; Ro. 8:11b, (His) Spirit; Ro. 8:15b, Spirit (of adoption); 1 Co. 2:10a, (His) Spirit; Gal. 4:6, Spirit (of His Son); Eph. 1:13, (Holy) Spirit (of promise); Eph. 4:30, (Holy) Spirit (of God); Phl. 1:19, Spirit (of Jesus Christ); 1 Th. 4:8 (Holy) Spirit; Heb. 9:14, (eternal) Spirit; Heb. 10:29, Spirit (of grace); 1 Pt. 4:14, Spirit (of glory and of God); Rev. 11:11, Spirit (of life).

4069. ποῖος, poi'os

Book	Oc.	what	Oc.	which	Oc.	what things	Oc.	what way	Oc.	what manner of	Total
Mt.	5	21:23, 24, 27; 24:42, 43	2	19:18; 22:36							7
Mk.	4	4:30; 11:28, 29, 33	1	12:28							5
Lk.	6	6:32, 33, 34; 12:39; 20:2, 8			1	24:19	1	5:19			8
Jn.	3	12:33; 18:32; 21:19	1	10:32							4
Ac.	4	4:7, 7; 7:49; 23:34									4
Ro.	1	3:27									1
1 Co.	1	15:35									1
Jas.	1	4:14									1
1 Pt.	1	2:20							1	1:11	2
Rev.	1	3:3									1
Total	27		4		1		1		1		34

4051. πνεῦμα, pneu'ma (continued)

Book	Oc.	(human) spirit	Oc.	(evil) spirit	Oc.	spirit (general)	Oc.	spirit	Oc.	(Jesus' own) spirit	Oc.	(Jesus' own) ghost	Oc.	Misc.	Total
Mt.	2	5:3; 26:41	4	8:16; 10:1; 12:43, 45							1	27:50			19
Mk.	1	14:38	14	1:23, 26, 27; 3:11, 30; 5:2, 8, 13; 6:7; 7:25; 9:17, 20, 25, 25					2	2:8; 8:12					23
Lk.	6	1:17, 47, 80; 8:55; 9:55; 23:46	12	4:33, 36; 6:18; 7:21; 8:2, 29; 9:39, 42; 10:20; 11:24, 26; 13:11	2	24:37, 39			2	2:40; 10:21					38
Jn.	2	4:23, 24b			2	3:6b; 6:63b			2	11:33; 13:21	1	19:30	1	3:8a	24
Ac.	6	7:59; 17:16; 18:5, 25; 19:21; 20:22	8	5:16; 8:7; 16:16, 18; 19:12, 13, 15, 16	2	23:8, 9									70
Ro.	5	1:9; 2:29; 7:6; 8:16b; 12:11			2	8:15a; 11:8									35
1 Co.	13	2:11a; 5:3, 4, 5; 6:20; 7:34; 14:2, 14, 15, 15, 16, 32; 16:18	1	2:12a	4	4:21; 6:17; 12:10; 15:45							1	14:12	41
2 Co.	4	2:13; 3:6a; 7:1, 13	1	11:4	1	4:13									17
Gal.	1	6:18			1	6:1									18
Eph.			1	2:2	2	1:17; 4:23									15
Phl.	1	3:3			1	1:27									4
Col.	1	2:5													2
1 Th.	1	5:23													5
2 Th.					2	2:2, 8									3
1 Ti.			1	4:1b	1	4:12									4
2 Ti.	1	4:22			1	1:7									3
Tit.															1
Phe.	1	1:25													1
Heb.	2	4:12; 12:23					3	1:7, 14; 12:9							12
Jas.	1	2:26													2
1 Pt.	1	4:6	1	3:19	1	3:4									9
2 Pt.															1
1 Jn.			1	4:3	4	4:1, 1, 6, 6	1	4:2b							13
Jd.															2
Rev.			3	16:13, 14; 18:2			4	1:4; 3:1; 4:5; 5:6					1	13:15	23
Total	49		47		26		8		6		2		3		385

Miscellaneous: Jn. 3:8a, wind; 1 Co. 14:12, spiritual gift; Rev. 13:15, life.

4070. πολεμέω, poleme'o

Book	Oc.	make war	Oc.	fight	Oc.	war	Total
Jas.					1	4:2	1
Rev.	3	13:4; 17:14; 19:11	3	2:16; 12:7, 7			6
Total	3		3		1		7

4071. πόλεμος, pol'emos

Book	Oc.	war	Oc.	battle	Oc.	fight	Total
Mt.	2	24:6, 6					2
Mk.	2	13:7, 7					2
Lk.	2	14:31; 21:9					2
1 Co.			1	14:8			1
Heb.					1	11:34	1
Jas.	1	4:1					1
Rev.	5	11:7; 12:7, 17; 13:7; 19:19	4	9:7, 9; 16:14; 20:8			9
Total	12		5		1		18

4073. πολιτάρχης, politar'chēs

Book	ruler of the city	Total
Ac.	17:6, 8	2

4072. πόλις, pol'is

Book	city	Total
Mt.	2:23; 4:5; 5:14, 35; 8:33, 34; 9:1, 35; 10:5, 11, 14, 15, 23, 23; 11:1, 20; 12:25; 14:13; 21:10, 17, 18; 22:7; 23:34, 34; 26:18; 27:53; 28:11	27
Mk.	1:33, 45; 5:14; 6:11, 33, 56; 11:19; 14:13, 16	9
Lk.	1:26, 39; 2:3, 4, 4, 11, 39; 4:29, 29, 31, 43; 5:12; 7:11, 12, 12, 37; 8:1, 4, 27, 34, 39; 9:5, 10; 10:1, 8, 10, 11, 12; 13:22; 14:21; 18:2, 3; 19:17, 19, 41; 22:10; 23:19, 51; 24:49	39
Jn.	1:44; 4:5, 8, 28, 30, 39; 11:54; 19:20	8
Ac.	5:16; 7:58; 8:5, 8, 9, 40; 9:6; 10:9; 11:5; 12:10; 13:44, 50; 14:4, 6, 13, 19, 20, 21; 15:21, 36; 16:4, 12, 12, 13, 14, 20, 39; 17:5, 16; 18:10; 19:29, 35; 20:23; 21:5, 29, 30, 39; 22:3; 24:12; 25:23; 26:11; 27:8	42
Ro.	16:23	1
2 Co.	11:26, 32	2
Tit.	1:5	1
Heb.	11:10, 16; 12:22; 13:14	4
Jas.	4:13	1
2 Pt.	2:6	1
Jd.	1:7	1
Rev.	3:12; 11:2, 8, 13; 14:8, 20; 16:19, 19; 17:18; 18:10, 10, 16, 18, 19, 21; 20:9; 21:2, 10, 14, 15, 16, 16, 18, 19, 21, 23; 22:14, 19	28
Total		164

4060. ποιέω, poie'ō

Book	Oc.	do	Oc.	make	Oc.	bring forth	Oc.	commit	Oc.	cause	Oc.	work
Mt.	59	1:24; 5:19, 44, 46, 47, 47; 6:1, 2, 2, 3, 3; 7:12, 12, 21, 22, 24, 26; 8:9, 9; 9:28; 12:2, 2, 3, 12, 50; 13:28, 41, 58, 17:12; 18:35; 19:16; 20:5, 15, 32; 21:6, 15, 21, 23, 24, 27, 31, 36, 40; 23:3, 3, 3, 5, 23; 24:46; 25:40, 40, 45, 45; 26:12, 13, 19; 27:22, 23; 28:15	15	3:3; 4:19; 5:36; 12:16, 33, 33; 17:4; 19:4, 4; 20:12b; 21:13; 22:2; 23:15, 15; 25:16	10	3:8, 10; 7:17, 17, 18, 18, 19; 13:23, 26; 21:43			1	5:32	1	20:12a
Mk.	33	2:24, 25; 3:8, 35; 5:19, 20, 32; 6:5, 20, 30; 7:8, 12, 13, 37a; 9:13, 39; 10:17, 35, 36, 51; 11:3, 5, 28, 28, 29, 33; 12:9; 14:7, 8, 9; 15:8, 12, 14	9	1:3, 17; 3:12; 6:21; 7:37b; 8:25; 9:5; 10:6; 11:17			1	15:7				
Lk.	60	1:49; 2:27; 3:10, 11, 12, 14, 19; 4:23; 5:6; 6:2, 2, 3, 10, 11, 23, 26, 27, 31, 31, 33, 43b, 46, 47, 49; 7:8, 8; 8:21, 39, 39; 9:10, 15, 43, 54; 10:25, 28, 37b; 11:42; 12:4, 17, 18, 43, 47; 16:3, 4, 8; 17:9, 10, 10, 10; 18:18, 41; 19:48; 20:2, 8, 13, 15; 22:19; 23:22, 31, 34	13	3:4; 5:29, 33, 34; 9:33; 11:40, 40; 14:12, 13, 16; 15:19; 16:9; 19:46	4	3:8, 9; 6:43a, 43c	1	12:48				
Jn.	81	2:5, 11, 18, 23; 3:2, 2, 21; 4:29, 34, 39, 45, 54; 5:16, 19, 19, 19, 19, 20, 29, 30, 36; 6:2, 6, 14, 28, 38; 7:3, 4, 4, 17, 21, 31, 31, 51; 8:28, 29, 38, 39, 40, 41, 44; 9:16, 26, 31, 33; 10:25, 37, 38, 41; 11:45, 46, 47, 47; 12:16, 18, 37; 13:7, 12, 15, 15, 17, 27; 14:10, 12, 12, 12, 13, 14, 31; 15:5, 14, 15, 21, 24, 24; 16:3; 17:4; 18:35; 19:24; 20:30; 21:25	21	2:15, 16; 4:1, 46; 5:11, 15, 18; 6:10, 15; 7:23; 8:53; 9:6, 11, 14; 10:33; 12:2; 14:23; 18:18; 19:7, 12, 23			1	8:34	1	11:37		
Ac.	31	1:1b; 2:22, 37; 4:7, 16, 28; 6:8; 8:6; 9:6, 6, 13, 36; 10:6, 33, 39; 11:30; 12:8; 14:11, 15a, 27; 15:4, 17; 16:18, 30; 19:14; 21:23, 33; 22:10, 10, 26; 26:10	15	1:1a; 2:36; 3:12; 4:24; 7:40, 43, 44, 50; 8:2; 9:39; 14:15b; 17:24, 26; 19:24; 23:13			1	28:17	1	15:3	3	15:12; 19:11; 21:19
Ro.	15	1:28, 32; 2:3, 14; 3:8, 12; 7:15, 16, 19, 20, 21; 10:5; 12:20; 13:3, 4	6	1:9; 9:20, 21, 28; 13:14; 15:26					1	16:17		
1 Co.	13	5:2; 6:18; 7:36, 37, 38, 38; 9:23; 10:31, 31; 11:24, 25; 15:29; 16:1	2	6:15; 10:13								
2 Co.	6	8:10, 11; 11:12, 12; 13:7, 7	1	5:21			1	11:7				
Gal.	6	2:10; 3:10, 12; 5:3, 17; 6:9										
Eph.	4	3:20; 6:6, 8, 9	4	1:16; 2:14, 15; 4:16								
Phl.	2	2:14; 4:14	1	1:4								
Col.	2	3:17, 23							1	4:16		
1 Th.	3	4:10; 5:11, 24	1	1:2								
2 Th.	2	3:4, 4										
1 Ti.	3	1:13; 4:16; 5:21	1	2:1								
2 Ti.	1	4:5										
Tit.	1	3:5										
Phe.	2	1:14, 21	1	1:4								
Heb.	9	6:3; 7:27; 10:7, 9, 36; 13:6, 17, 19, 21a	6	1:2, 7; 8:5, 9; 12:13, 27							1	13:21b
Jas.	6	2:8, 12, 19; 4:15, 17, 17	1	3:18			I	5:15				
1 Pt.	3	2:22; 3:11, 12										
2 Pt.	2	1:10b, 19	1	1:10a								
1 Jn.	6	1:6; 2:17, 29; 3:7, 10, 22	2	1:10; 5:10			3	3:4a, 8, 9				
3 Jn.	3	1:5, 6, 10										
Jd.												
Rev.	4	2:5; 13:13a, 14a; 22:14	14	1:6; 3:9, 12; 5:10; 11:7; 12:17; 13:7, 13b, 14b; 14:7; 17:16; 19:19; 21:5; 22:15					4	12:15; 13:12b, 15, 16	3	16:14; 19:20; 21:27
Total	357		114		14		9		9		8	

4074. πολιτεία, politei'a

Book	Oc.	freedom	Oc.	commonwealth	Total
Ac.	1	22:28			1
Eph.			1	2:12	1
Total	1		1		2

4076. πολιτεύομαι, politeu'omai

Book	Oc.	live	Oc.	let (one's) conversation be	Total
Ac.	1	23:1			1
Phl.			1	1:27	1
Total	1		1		2

4075. πολίτευμα, polit'euma

Book	conversation	Total
Phl.	3:20	1

4077. πολίτης, poli'tes

Book	citizen	Total
Lk.	15:15; 19:14	2
Ac.	21:39	1
Total		3

4078. πολλάκις, pollak'is

Book	Oc.	often	Oc.	oft	Oc.	ofttimes	Oc.	oftentimes	Total
Mt.			1	17:15b	1	17:15a			2
Mk.	1	5:4			1	9:22			2
Jn.					1	18:2			1
Ac.			1	26:11					1
Ro.							1	1:13	1
2 Co.	3	11:26, 27, 27	1	11:23			1	8:22	5
Phl.	1	3:18							1
2 Ti.			1	1:16					1
Heb.	2	9:25, 26	1	6:7			1	10:11	4
Total	7		5		3		3		18

4079. πολλαπλασίων pollaplasi'ōn

Book	manifold more	Total
Lk.	18:30	1

4080. πολυλογία, polulogi'a

Book	much speaking	Total
Mt.	6:7	1

4081. πολυμέρως, polumer'ōs

Book	at sundry times	Total
Heb.	1:1	1

4082. πολυποίκιλος polupoi'kilos

Book	manifold	Total
Eph.	3:10	1

4060. ποιέω, poie'ō (continued)

Book	Oc.	shew	Oc.	bear	Oc.	keep	Oc.	fulfill	Oc.	deal	Oc.	perform	Oc.	Not Tr.	Oc.	Misc.	Total
Mt.					1	26:18									2	26:73; 28:14	89
Mk.													1	2:23	5	3:6, 14; 4:32; 15:1, 15	49
Lk.	2	1:51; 10:37a	2	8:8; 13:9					2	1:25; 2:48	1	1:72			6	1:68; 12:33; 13:22; 18:7, 8; 19:18	91
Jn.	1	6:30			1	7:19									2	5:27; 16:2	108
Ac.	1	7:36			1	18:21	1	13:22					1	7:19	15	5:34; 7:24; 10:2; 15:33; 16:21; 18:23; 20:3, 24; 21:13; 23:12; 24:12, 17; 25:3, 17; 27:18	70
Ro.											1	4:21					23
1 Co.																	15
2 Co.															1	11:25	9
Gal.																	6
Eph.							1	2:3							1	3:11	10
Phl.																	3
Col.																	3
1 Th.																	4
2 Th.																	2
1 Ti.																	4
2 Ti.																	1
Tit.																	1
Phe.																	3
Heb.					1	11:28									2	1:3; 3:2	19
Jas.	1	2:13	1	3:12a											2	3:12b; 4:13	12
1 Pt.																	3
2 Pt.															1	1:15	4
1 Jn.															1	3:4b	12
3 Jn.																	3
Jd.															2	1:3, 15	2
Rev.			1	22:2			1	17:17a							3	13:5, 12a; 17:17b	30
Total	5		4		4		3		2		2		2		43		576

Miscellaneous: Mt. 26:73 (with 1212), bewray; Mt. 28:14 (with 275), secure; Mk. 3:6, take; Mk. 3:14, ordain; Mk. 4:32, shoot out; Mk. 15:1, hold; Mk. 15:15 (with 2425), content; Lk. 1:68 (with 3085), redeem; Lk. 12:33, provide; Lk. 13:22 (with 4097), journeying; Lk. 18:7, 8 (with 1557), avenge; Lk. 19:18, gain; Jn. 5:27, execute; Jn. 16:2 (with 656), put out of the synagogue; Ac. 5:34, put; Ac. 7:24 (with 1557), avenge; Ac. 10:2, give; Ac. 15:33, tarry; Ac. 16:21, observe; Ac. 18:23, spend; Ac. 20:3, abide; Ac. 20:24, move; Ac. 21:13, mean; Ac. 23:12 (with 4863), band together; Ac. 24:12 (with 1999), raise up; Ac. 24:17, bring; Ac. 25:3 (with 1747), lay wait; Ac. 25:17 (with 311 and 3267), without any delay; Ac. 27:18 (with 1546), lighten the ship; 2 Co. 11:25, be; Eph. 3:11, purpose; Heb. 1:3 (with 2512), have purged; Heb. 3:2, appoint; Jas. 3:12b, yield; Jas. 4:13, continue; 2 Pt. 1:15, have; 1 Jn. 3:4b (with 458), transgress the law; Jd. 1:3, give; Jd. 1:15, execute; Rev. 13:5, continue; Rev. 13:12a, exercise; Rev. 17:17b (with 3291 and 1106), agree.

4083. πολύς, polus′

Book	Oc.	many	Oc.	much	Oc.	great	Oc.	Misc.	Total
Mt.	32	3:7; 7:13, 22, 22; 8:11, 16, 30; 9:10; 10:31; 13:3, 17, 58; 15:30b; 16:21; 19:30; 20:16, 28; 22:14; 24:5, 5, 10, 11, 11, 12; 25:21, 23; 26:28, 60; 27:19, 52, 53, 55	3	6:30; 13:5; 26:9	14	2:18; 4:25; 5:12; 8:1, 18; 12:15; 13:2; 14:14; 15:30a; 19:2, 22; 20:29; 24:30; 26:47	3	9:14, 37; 25:19	52
Mk.	36	1:34, 34; 2:2, 15, 15; 3:10; 4:2, 33; 5:9, 26, 26; 6:2, 13, 13, 20, 31, 33, 34b; 7:4, 8, 13; 8:31; 9:12, 26b; 10:31, 45, 48a; 11:8; 12:5, 41a; 13:6, 6; 14:24, 56; 15:3, 41	7	1:45; 4:5; 5:10, 21, 24; 6:34a; 12:41b	7	3:7, 8; 4:1; 9:14; 10:22; 13:26; 14:43	10	3:12; 5:23, 38, 43; 6:35a, 35b; 9:26a; 10:48b; 12:27, 37	60
Lk.	27	1:1, 14, 16; 2:34, 35; 3:18; 4:25, 27, 41; 7:21, 21, 47a; 8:3, 30; 9:22; 10:24, 41; 12:7, 19b, 47; 13:24; 14:16; 15:13; 17:25; 21:8; 22:65; 23:8	11	7:11, 47b; 8:4; 9:37; 10:40; 12:19a, 48, 48, 48; 16:10, 10	11	2:36; 5:6, 15, 29; 6:17, 23, 35; 10:2; 14:25; 21:27; 23:27	2	8:29; 18:39	51
Jn.	25	2:12, 23; 4:39, 41; 6:60, 66; 7:31, 40; 8:26, 30; 10:20, 32, 41, 42; 11:19, 45, 47, 55; 12:11, 42; 14:2; 16:12; 19:20; 20:30; 21:25	9	3:23; 6:10; 7:12; 12:9, 12, 24; 14:30; 15:5, 8	3	5:3; 6:2, 5	1	5:6	38
Ac.	25	1:3, 5; 2:43; 4:4; 5:12; 8:7, 7, 25; 9:13, 42; 10:27; 13:43; 15:32, 35; 16:18, 23; 17:12; 18:8; 19:18; 20:19; 24:10; 25:7; 26:9, 10; 28:10	9	10:2; 14:22; 15:7; 16:16; 18:10, 27; 20:2; 26:24; 27:10	11	6:7; 11:21; 14:1; 17:4; 21:40; 22:28; 23:10; 24:2, 7; 25:23; 28:29	4	26:29; 27:14, 21; 28:6	49
Ro.	12	4:17, 18; 5:15a, 15c, 16, 19, 19; 8:29; 12:4, 5; 15:23; 16:2	9	3:2; 5:9, 10, 15b, 17; 9:22; 15:22; 16:6, 12					21
1 Co.	14	1:26, 26, 26; 4:15; 8:5, 5; 10:17, 33; 11:30; 12:12, 12, 14, 20; 16:9	3	2:3; 12:22; 16:19			1	16:12	18
2 Co.	9	1:11, 11; 2:4b, 17; 6:10; 8:22a; 9:12; 11:18; 12:21	7	2:4a; 3:9, 11; 6:4; 8:4, 15, 22b	5	3:12; 7:4, 4; 8:2, 22c			21
Gal.	3	1:14; 3:16; 4:27							3
Eph.					1	2:4			1
Phl.	1	3:18	1	2:12			1	1:23	3
Col.					1	4:13			1
1 Th.			3	1:5, 6; 2:2	1	2:17			4
1 Ti.	3	6:9, 10, 12	1	3:8	1	3:13			5
2 Ti.	1	2:2	1	4:14					2
Tit.	1	1:10	1	2:3					2
Phe.			1	1:8	1	1:7			2
Heb.	4	2:10; 5:11; 9:28; 12:15	2	12:9, 25	1	10:32			7
Jas.	2	3:1, 2	1	5:16					3
1 Pt.			1	1:7			1	1:3	2
2 Pt.	1	2:2							1
1 Jn.	2	2:18; 4:1							2
2 Jn.	2	1:7, 12							2
3 Jn.	1	1:13							1
Rev.	9	1:15; 5:11; 8:11; 9:9; 10:11; 14:2; 17:1; 19:6b, 12	3	5:4; 8:3; 19:1	2	7:9; 19:6a			14
Total	210		73		59		23		365

Miscellaneous: Mt. 9:14, oft; Mt. 9:37, plenteous; Mt. 25:19, long; Mk. 3:12, straitly; Mk. 5:23, 38, greatly; Mk. 5:43, straitly; Mk. 6:35a, far spent; Mk. 6:35b, far passed; Mk. 9:26a, sore; Mk. 10:48b, a great deal; Mk. 12:27, greatly; Mk. 12:37, common; Lk. 8:29, oftentimes; Lk. 18:39, so much; Jn. 5:6, long; Ac. 26:29, altogether; Ac. 27:14, 21, long; Ac. 28:6, a great while; 1 Co. 16:12, greatly; Phl. 1:23, far; 1 Pt. 1:3, abundant.

4085. πολυτελής, poluteles′

Book	Oc.	very precious	Oc.	costly	Oc.	of great price	Total
Mk.	1	14:3					1
1 Ti.			1	2:9			1
1 Pt.					1	3:4	1
Total	1		1		1		3

4084. πολύσπλαγχνος polu′splangchnos

Book	very pitiful	Total
Jas.	5:11	1

4087. πολυτρόπως, polutrop′ōs

Book	in divers manners	Total
Heb.	1:1	1

4088. πόμα, pom′a

Book	drink	Total
1 Co.	10:4	1
Heb.	9:10	1
Total		2

4086. πολύτιμος, polut′imos

Book	Oc.	of great price	Oc.	very costly	Total
Mt.	1	13:46			1
Jn.			1	12:3	1
Total	1		1		2

4089. πονηρία, poneri′a

Book	Oc.	wickedness	Oc.	iniquity	Total
Mt.	1	22:18			1
Mk.	1	7:22			1
Lk.	1	11:39			1
Ac.			1	3:26	1
Ro.	1	1:29			1
1 Co.	1	5:8			1
Eph.	1	6:12			1
Total	6		1		7

4090. πονηρός, poneros′

Book	Oc.	evil	Oc.	wicked	Oc.	wicked one	Oc.	evil things	Oc.	Misc.	Total
Mt.	16	5:11, 37, 39, 45; 6:13, 23; 7:11, 17, 18; 9:4; 12:34, 35a, 35b, 39; 15:19; 20:15	5	12:45; 13:49; 16:4; 18:32; 25:26	2	13:19, 38	1	12:35c	1	22:10	25
Mk.	1	7:22					1	7:23			2
Lk.	12	3:19; 6:22, 35, 45, 45, 45; 7:21; 8:2; 11:4, 13, 29, 34	1	19:22							13
Jn.	3	3:19; 7:7; 17:15									3
Ac.	4	19:12, 13, 15, 16	1	18:14					2	17:5; 28:21	7
Ro.	1	12:9									1
1 Co.									1	5:13	1
Gal.	1	1:4									1
Eph.	2	5:16; 6:13	1	6:16							3
Col.			1	1:21							1
1 Th.	1	5:22									1
2 Th.	1	3:3	1	3:2							2
1 Ti.	1	6:4									1
2 Ti.	2	3:13; 4:18									2
Heb.	2	3:12; 10:22									2
Jas.	2	2:4; 4:16									2
1 Jn.	1	3:12b			4	2:13, 14; 3:12a; 5:18			1	5:19	6
2 Jn.	1	1:11									1
3 Jn.									1	1:10	1
Rev.									1	16:2	1
Total	51		10		6		2		7		76

Miscellaneous: Mt. 22:10, bad; Ac. 17:5, lewd; Ac. 28:21, harm; 1 Co. 5:13, wicked person; 1 Jn. 5:19, wickedness; 3 Jn. 1:10, malicious; Rev. 16:2, grievous.

4091. πονηρότερος, ponērot'eros

Book	more wicked	Total
Mt.	12:45	1
Lk.	11:26	1
Total		2

4092. πόνος, pon'os

Book	pain	Total
Rev.	16:10, 11; 21:4	3

4093. Ποντικός, Pontikos'

Book	born in Pontus	Total
Ac.	18:2	1

4094. Πόντιος, Pon'tios

Book	Pontius	Total
Mt.	27:2	1
Lk.	3:1	1
Ac.	4:27	1
1 Ti.	6:13	1
Total		4

4095. Πόντος, Pon'tos

Book	Pontus	Total
Ac.	2:9	1
1 Pt.	1:1	1
Total		2

4096. Πόπλιος, Pop'lios

Book	Publius	Total
Ac.	28:7, 8	2

4097. πορεία, porei'a

Book	Oc.	journeying (with 4060)	Oc.	way	Total
Lk.	1	13:22			1
Jas.			1	1:11	1
Total	1		1		2

4098. πορεύομαι, poreu'omai

Book	Oc.	go	Oc.	depart	Oc.	walk	Oc.	go (one's) way	Oc.	Misc.	Total
Mt.	23	2:8, 20; 8:9, 9; 9:13; 10:6, 7; 11:4; 12:1, 45; 17:27; 18:12; 21:2, 6; 22:9, 15; 25:9, 16; 26:14; 27:66; 28:7, 9, 19	5	2:9; 11:7; 19:15; 24:1; 25:41					2	28:11, 16	30
Mk.	3	16:10, 12, 15									3
Lk.	41	1:39; 2:3, 41; 4:42a; 5:24; 7:6, 8, 8, 11, 50; 8:48; 9:13, 51, 52, 53, 56, 57; 10:37, 38; 11:5, 26; 13:32; 14:10, 19, 31; 15:4, 15, 18; 16:30; 17:11, 14; 19:12, 28, 36; 21:8; 22:8, 22, 33, 39; 24:28, 28	2	4:42b; 13:31	2	1:6; 13:33	3	4:30; 7:22; 17:19	2	8:14; 24:13	50
Jn.	13	7:35, 35, 53; 8:1, 11; 10:4; 11:11; 14:2, 3, 12, 28; 16:28; 20:17	1	16:7			2	4:50, 50			16
Ac.	27	1:11, 25; 5:20; 8:26, 27, 36, 39; 9:11; 10:20; 12:17; 16:7, 16, 36; 17:14; 18:6; 19:21; 20:1, 22; 22:5, 10; 23:23, 32; 25:12, 20; 26:12; 27:3; 28:26	2	5:41; 22:21	2	9:31; 14:16	3	9:15; 21:5; 24:25	4	1:10; 9:3; 22:6; 26:13	38
Ro.	1	15:25							1	15:24	2
1 Co.	4	10:27; 16:4, 4, 6									4
1 Ti.	1	1:3									1
2 Ti.			1	4:10							1
Jas.	1	4:13									1
1 Pt.	2	3:19, 22			1	4:3					3
2 Pt.					2	2:10; 3:3					2
Jd.	1	1:11			2	1:16, 18					3
Total	117		11		9		8		9		154

Miscellaneous: Mt. 28:11, be going; Mt. 28:16, go away; Lk. 8:14, go forth; Lk. 24:13 (with 2258), went; Ac. 1:10, go up; Ac. 9:3, journey; Ac. 22:6, make (one's) journey; Ac. 26:13, journey; Ro. 15:24, take (one's) journey.

4099. πορθέω, porthe'ō

Book	Oc.	destroy	Oc.	waste	Total
Ac.	1	9:21			1
Gal.	1	1:23	1	1:13	2
Total	2		1		3

4100. πορισμός, porismos'

Book	gain	Total
1 Ti.	6:5, 6	2

4101. Πόρκιος, Por'kios

Book	Porcius	Total
Ac.	24:27	1

4102. πορνεία, pornei'a

Book	fornication	Total
Mt.	5:32; 15:19; 19:9	3
Mk.	7:21	1
Jn.	8:41	1
Ac.	15:20, 29; 21:25	3
Ro.	1:29	1
1 Co.	5:1, 1; 6:13, 18; 7:2	5
2 Co.	12:21	1
Gal.	5:19	1
Eph.	5:3	1
Col.	3:5	1
1 Th.	4:3	1
Rev.	2:21; 9:21; 14:8; 17:2, 4; 18:3; 19:2	7
Total		26

4103. πορνεύω, porneu'ō

Book	Oc.	commit fornication	Oc.	commit	Total
1 Co.	2	6:18; 10:8a	1	10:8b	3
Rev.	5	2:14, 20; 17:2; 18:3, 9			5
Total	7		1		8

4104. πόρνη, por'nē

Book	Oc.	harlot	Oc.	whore	Total
Mt.	2	21:31, 32			2
Lk.	1	15:30			1
1 Co.	2	6:15, 16			2
Heb.	1	11:31			1
Jas.	1	2:25			1
Rev.	1	17:5	4	17:1, 15, 16; 19:2	5
Total	8		4		12

4105. πόρνος, por'nos

Book	Oc.	fornicator	Oc.	whoremonger	Total
1 Co.	4	5:9, 10, 11; 6:9			4
Eph.			1	5:5	1
1 Ti.			1	1:10	1
Heb.	1	12:16	1	13:4	2
Rev.			2	21:8; 22:15	2
Total	5		5		10

4106. πόῤῥω, por'hrō

Book	Oc.	far	Oc.	a great way off	Total
Mt.	1	15:8			1
Mk.	1	7:6			1
Lk.			1	14:32	1
Total	2		1		3

4107. πόῤῥωθεν, por'hrōthen

Book	afar off	Total
Lk.	17:12	1
Heb.	11:13	1
Total		2

4108. ποῤῥωτέρω, porhrōter'ō

Book	further	Total
Lk.	24:28	1

4109. πορφύρα, porphu'ra

Book	purple	Total
Mk.	15:17, 20	2
Lk.	16:19	1
Rev.	17:4; 18:12	2
Total		5

4110. πορφυροῦς, porphurous'

Book	purple	Total
Jn.	19:2, 5	2
Rev.	18:16	1
Total		3

4111. πορφυρόπωλις porphurop'ōlis

Book	seller of purple	Total
Ac.	16:14	1

4112. ποσάκις, posak'is

Book	Oc.	how often	Oc.	how oft	Total
Mt.	1	23:37	1	18:21	2
Lk.	1	13:34			1
Total	2		1		3

4113. πόσις, pos'is

Book	drink	Total
Jn.	6:55	1
Ro.	14:17	1
Col.	2:16	1
Total		3

4114. πόσος, pos′os

Book	Oc.	how much	Oc.	how many	Oc.	how many things	Oc.	what	Oc.	how long	Oc.	how great	Total
Mt.	3	7:11; 10:25; 12:12	3	15:34; 16:9, 10	1	27:13					1	6:23	8
Mk.			4	6:38; 8:5, 19, 20	1	15:4			1	9:21			6
Lk.	5	11:13; 12:24, 28; 16:5, 7	1	15:17									6
Ac.			1	21:20									1
Ro.	2	11:12, 24											2
2 Co.							1	7:11					1
Phe.	1	1:16											1
Heb.	2	9:14; 10:29											2
Total	13		9		2		1		1		1		27

4115. ποταμός, potamos′

Book	Oc.	river	Oc.	flood	Oc.	stream	Oc.	water	Total
Mt.			2	7:25, 27					2
Mk.	1	1:5							1
Lk.					2	6:48, 49			2
Jn.	1	7:38							1
Ac.	1	16:13							1
2 Co.							1	11:26	1
Rev.	6	8:10; 9:14; 16:4, 12; 22:1, 2	2	12:15, 16					8
Total	9		4		2		1		16

4117. ποταπός, potapos′

Book	Oc.	what manner of	Oc.	what	Oc.	what manner of man	Oc.	what manner of person	Total
Mt.					1	8:27			1
Mk.	1	13:1a	1	13:1b					2
Lk.	2	1:29; 7:39							2
2 Pt.							1	3:11	1
1 Jn.	1	3:1							1
Total	4		1		1		1		7

4118. ποτέ, pote′

Book	Oc.	in time past	Oc.	at any time	Oc.	in times past	Oc.	sometimes	Oc.	sometime	Oc.	once	Oc.	Not Tr.	Oc.	Misc.	Total
Lk.															1	22:32	1
Jn.															1	9:13	1
Ac.													1	28:27			1
Ro.					1	11:30					1	7:9			1	1:10	3
1 Co.															1	9:7	1
Gal.	1	1:13			1	1:23a					1	1:23b	1	2:6			4
Eph.	2	2:2, 11			1	2:3	2	2:13; 5:8							1	5:29	6
Phl.															1	4:10	1
Col.									2	1:21; 3:7							2
1 Th.			1	2:5													1
Tit.							1	3:3									1
Phe.	1	1:11															1
Heb.			3	1:5, 13; 2:1									1	4:1			4
1 Pt.	1	2:10							1	3:20					1	3:5	3
2 Pt.															2	1:10, 21	2
Total	5		4		3		3		3		2		3		9		32

Miscellaneous: Lk. 22:32, when; Jn. 9:13, aforetime; Ro. 1:10, at length; 1 Co. 9:7, any time; Eph. 5:29, ever yet; Phl. 4:10, at the last; 1 Pt. 3:5, in the old time; 2 Pt. 1:10 (with 3264), never; 2 Pt. 1:21, in old time.

4116. ποταμοφόρητος potamophor′ētos

Book	carried away of the flood	Total
Rev.	12:15	1

4120. πότερον, pot′eron

Book	whether	Total
Jn.	7:17	1

4119. πότε, pot′e

Book	Oc.	when	Oc.	how long (with 2193)	Total
Mt.	5	24:3; 25:37, 38, 39, 44	2	17:17, 17	7
Mk.	3	13:4, 33, 35	2	9:19, 19	5
Lk.	3	12:36; 17:20; 21:7	1	9:41	4
Jn.	1	6:25	1	10:24	2
Rev.			1	6:10	1
Total	12		7		19

4121. ποτήριον, potē′rion

Book	cup	Total
Mt.	10:42; 20:22, 23; 23:25, 26; 26:27, 39, 42	8
Mk.	7:4, 8; 9:41; 10:38, 39; 14:23, 36	7
Lk.	11:39; 22:17, 20, 20, 42	5
Jn.	18:11	1
1 Co.	10:16, 21, 21; 11:25, 25, 26, 27, 28	8
Rev.	14:10; 16:19; 17:4; 18:6	4
Total		33

4122. ποτίζω, potid′zō

Book	Oc.	give to drink	Oc.	give drink	Oc.	water	Oc.	make to drink	Oc.	watering	Oc.	feed	Total
Mt.	2	10:42; 27:48	3	25:35, 37, 42									5
Mk.	2	9:41; 15:36											2
Lk.									1	13:15			1
Ro.			1	12:20									1
1 Co.					3	3:6, 7, 8	1	12:13			1	3:2	5
Rev.							1	14:8					1
Total	4		4		3		2		1		1		15

4123. Ποτίολοι, Poti′oloi

Book	Puteoli	Total
Ac.	28:13	1

4125. πού, pou

Book	Oc.	a certain place	Oc.	about	Total
Ro.			1	4:19	1
Heb.	2	2:6; 4:4			2
Total	2		1		3

4126. ποῦ, pou

Book	Oc.	where	Oc.	whither	Total
Mt.	4	2:2, 4; 8:20; 26:17			4
Mk.	3	14:12, 14; 15:47			3
Lk.	7	8:25; 9:58; 12:17; 17:17, 37; 22:9, 11			7
Jn.	11	1:38, 39; 7:11; 8:10, 19; 9:12; 11:34, 57; 20:2, 13, 15	8	3:8; 7:35; 8:14, 14; 12:35; 13:36; 14:5; 16:5	19
Ro.	1	3:27			1
1 Co.	8	1:20, 20, 20; 12:17, 17, 19; 15:55, 55			8
Heb.			1	11:8	1
1 Pt.	1	4:18			1
2 Pt.	1	3:4			1
1 Jn.			1	2:11	1
Rev.	1	2:13			1
Total	37		10		47

4124. πότος, pot′os

Book	banqueting	Total
1 Pt.	4:3	1

4127. Πούδης, Pou′dēs

Book	Pudens	Total
2 Ti.	4:21	1

4128. πούς, pous

Book	Oc.	foot	Oc.	footstool (with 5186)	Total
Mt.	9	4:6; 7:6; 10:14; 15:30; 18:8, 8, 29; 22: 13; 28:9	2	5:35; 22:44	11
Mk.	5	5:22; 6:11; 7:25; 9:45, 45	1	12:36	6
Lk.	17	1:79; 4:11; 7:38, 38, 38, 44, 44, 45, 46; 8:35, 41; 9:5; 10:39; 15:22; 17:16; 24: 39, 40	1	20:43	18
Jn.	14	11:2, 32, 44; 12:3, 3; 13:5, 6, 8, 9, 10, 12, 14, 14; 20:12			14
Ac.	17	4:35, 37; 5:2, 9, 10; 7:5, 33, 58; 10:25; 13:25, 51; 14:8, 10; 16:24; 21:11; 22: 3; 26:16	2	2:35; 7:49	19
Ro.	3	3:15; 10:15; 16:20			3
1 Co.	4	12:15, 21; 15:25, 27			4
Eph.	2	1:22; 6:15			2
1 Ti.	1	5:10			1
Heb.	2	2:8; 12:13	2	1:13; 10:13	4
Rev.	11	1:15, 17; 2:18; 3:9; 10:1, 2; 11:11; 12: 1; 13:2; 19:10; 22:8			11
Total	85		8		93

4129. πρᾶγμα, prag'ma

Book	Oc.	thing	Oc.	matter	Oc.	business	Oc.	work	Total
Mt.	1	18:19							1
Lk.	1	1:1							1
Ac.	1	5:4							1
Ro.					1	16:2			1
1 Co.			1	6:1					1
2 Co.			1	7:11					1
1 Th.			1	4:6					1
Heb.	3	6:18; 10: 1; 11:1							3
Jas.							1	3:16	1
Total	6		3		1		1		11

4131. πραγματεύομαι pragmateu'omai

Book	occupy	Total
Lk.	19:13	1

4130. πραγματεία, pragmatei'a

Book	affair	Total
2 Ti.	2:4	1

4133. πράκτωρ, prak'tōr

Book	officer	Total
Lk.	12:58, 58	2

4132. πραιτώριον, praitō'rion

Book	Oc.	judgment hall	Oc.	hall of judgment	Oc.	common hall	Oc.	praetorium	Oc.	palace	Total
Mt.					1	27:27					1
Mk.							1	15:16			1
Jn.	3	18:28b, 33; 19:9	1	18:28a							4
Ac.	1	23:35									1
Phl.									1	1:13	1
Total	4		1		1		1		1		8

4136. πρᾳότης, praot'ẹs

Book	meekness	Total
1 Co.	4:21	1
2 Co.	10:1	1
Gal.	5:23; 6:1	2
Eph.	4:2	1
Col.	3:12	1
1 Ti.	6:11	1
2 Ti.	2:25	1
Tit.	3:2	1
Total		9

4134. πρᾶξις, prax'is

Book	Oc.	deed	Oc.	work	Oc.	office	Total
Mt.			1	16:27			1
Lk.	1	23:51					1
Ac.	1	19:18					1
Ro.	1	8:13			1	12:4	2
Col.	1	3:9					1
Total	4		1		1		6

4135. πρᾷος, pra'os

Book	meek	Total
Mt.	11:29	1

4137. πρασιά, prasia'

Book	in ranks	Total
Mk.	6:40	1

4139. πραΰς, praus'

Book	meek	Total
Mt.	5:5; 21:5	2
1 Pt.	3:4	1
Total		3

4138. πράσσω, pras'sō

Book	Oc.	do	Oc.	commit	Oc.	exact	Oc.	require	Oc.	deed	Oc.	keep	Oc.	use arts	Total
Lk.	3	22:23; 23:15, 41b			1	3:13	1	19:23	1	23:41a					6
Jn.	2	3:20; 5:29													2
Ac.	10	3:17; 5:35; 15:29; 16:28; 17:7; 19: 36; 26:9, 20, 26, 31	2	25:11, 25									1	19:19	13
Ro.	7	1:32b; 2:1, 3; 7:15, 19; 9:11; 13:4	2	1:32a; 2:2							1	2:25			10
1 Co.	1	9:17													1
2 Co.	1	5:10	1	12:21											2
Gal.	1	5:21													1
Eph.	1	6:21													1
Phl.	1	4:9													1
1 Th.	1	4:11													1
Total	28		5		1		1		1		1		1		38

4140. πραΰτης, prau'tẹs

Book	meekness	Total
Jas.	1:21; 3:13	2
1 Pt.	3:15	1
Total		3

4143. πρεσβεύω, presbeu'ō

Book	ambassador	Total
2 Co.	5:20	1
Eph.	6:20	1
Total		2

4142. πρεσβεία, presbei'a

Book	Oc.	ambassage	Oc.	message	Total
Lk.	1	14:32	1	19:14	2

4141. πρέπω, prep'ō

Book	Oc.	become	Oc.	comely	Total
Mt.	1	3:15			1
1 Co.			1	11:13	1
Eph.	1	5:3			1
1 Ti.	1	2:10			1
Tit.	1	2:1			1
Heb.	2	2:10; 7:26			2
Total	6		1		7

4144. πρεσβυτέριον, presbuter'ion

Book	Oc.	elders	Oc.	estate of elders	Oc.	presbytery	Total
Lk.	1	22:66					1
Ac.			1	22:5			1
1 Ti.					1	4:14	1
Total	1		1		1		3

4146. πρεσβύτης, presbu'tẹs

Book	Oc.	old man	Oc.	aged man	Oc.	aged	Total
Lk.	1	1:18					1
Tit.			1	2:2			1
Phe.					1	1:9	1
Total	1		1		1		3

4145a. πρεσβύτερος, presbu'teros

Book	Oc.	elder	Oc.	old man	Oc.	eldest	Total
Mt.	13	15:2; 16:21; 21:23; 26:3, 47, 57, 59; 27:1, 3, 12, 20, 41; 28:12					13
Mk.	7	7:3, 5; 8:31; 11:27; 14:43, 53; 15:1					7
Lk.	5	7:3; 9:22; 15:25; 20:1; 22:52					5
Jn.					1	8:9	1
Ac.	17	4:5, 8, 23; 6:12; 11:30; 14:23; 15:2, 4, 6, 22, 23; 16:4; 20:17; 21:18; 23:14; 24:1; 25:15	1	2:17			18
1 Ti.	3	5:1, 17, 19					3
Tit.	1	1:5					1
Heb.	1	11:2					1
Jas.	1	5:14					1
1 Pt.	2	5:1, 5					2
2 Jn.	1	1:1					1
3 Jn.	1	1:1					1
Rev.	12	4:4, 10; 5:5, 6, 8, 11, 14; 7:11, 13; 11:16; 14:3; 19:4					12
Total	64		1		1		66

4145b. πρεσβύτερα, presbu'tera

Book	elder woman	Total
1 Ti.	5:2	1

Word 4145 has 67 occurrences

4147. πρεσβῦτις, presbu'tis

Book	aged woman	Total
Tit.	2:3	1

4148. πρηνής, prẹnẹs'

Book	headlong	Total
Ac.	1:18	1

4149. πρίζω, prid'zō

Book	saw asunder	Total
Heb.	11:37	1

4151. Πρίσκα, Pris'ka

Book	Prisca	Total
2 Ti.	4:19	1

4152. Πρίσκιλλα, Pris'killa

Book	Priscilla	Total
Ac.	18:2, 18, 26	3
Ro.	16:3	1
1 Co.	16:19	1
Total		5

4153. πρό, pro

Book	Oc.	before	Oc.	above	Oc.	ago	Oc.	or ever	Total
Mt.	5	5:12; 6:8; 8:29; 11:10; 24:38							5
Mk.	1	1:2							1
Lk.	8	1:76; 2:21; 7:27; 9:52; 10:1; 11:38; 21:12; 22:15							8
Jn.	9	1:48; 5:7; 10:8; 11:55; 12:1; 13:1, 19; 17:5, 24							9
Ac.	7	5:23, 36; 12:6, 14; 13:24; 14:13; 21:38					1	23:15	8
Ro.	1	16:7							1
1 Co.	2	2:7; 4:5							2
2 Co.			1	12:2a	1	12:2b			2
Gal.	3	1:17; 2:12; 3:23							3
Eph.	1	1:4							1
Col.	1	1:17							1
2 Ti.	2	1:9; 4:21							2
Tit.	1	1:2							1
Heb.	1	11:5							1
Jas.	1	5:9	1	5:12					2
1 Pt.	1	1:20	1	4:8					2
Total	44		3		1		1		49

4150a. πρίν, prin

Book	Oc.	before	Oc.	ere	Total
Mt.	2	26:34, 75			2
Mk.	1	14:72			1
Lk.	1	22:61			1
Jn.	2	8:58; 14:29	1	4:49	3
Total	6		1		7

4150b. πρὶν ἤ, prin ẹ

Book	Oc.	before	Oc.	before that	Total
Mt.	1	1:18			1
Mk.	1	14:30			1
Lk.	1	2:26	1	22:34	2
Ac.	2	2:20; 7:2	1	25:16	3
Total	5		2		7

Word 4150 has 14 occurrences.

4154. προάγω, proag'ō

Book	Oc.	go before	Oc.	bring forth	Oc.	went before (with 2258)	Oc.	bring out	Total
Mt.	6	2:9; 14:22; 21:9, 31; 26:32; 28:7							6
Mk.	4	6:45; 11:9; 14:28; 16:7			1	10:32			5
Lk.	1	18:39							1
Ac.			2	12:6; 25:26			1	16:30	3
1 Ti.	2	1:18; 5:24							2
Heb.	1	7:18							1
Total	14		2		1		1		18

4155. προαιρέομαι, proaire'omai

Book	purpose	Total
2 Co.	9:7	1

4156. προαιτιάομαι proaitia'omai

Book	prove before	Total
Ro.	3:9	1

4157. προακούω, proakou'ō

Book	hear before	Total
Col.	1:5	1

4158. προαμαρτάνω, proamartan'ō

Book	Oc.	sin already	Oc.	sin heretofore	Total
2 Co.	1	12:21	1	13:2	2

4159. προαύλιον, proau'lion

Book	porch	Total
Mk.	14:68	1

4160. προβαίνω, probai'nō

Book	Oc.	be well stricken	Oc.	go on	Oc.	go farther	Oc.	be of . . . age (with 2250 and 1722)	Total
Mt.			1	4:21					1
Mk.					1	1:19			1
Lk.	2	1:7, 18					1	2:36	3
Total	2		1		1		1		5

4162. προβατικός, probatikos'

Book	sheep market	Total
Jn.	5:2	1

4161. προβάλλω, probal'lō

Book	Oc.	shoot forth	Oc.	put forward	Total
Lk.	1	21:30			1
Ac.			1	19:33	1
Total	1		1		2

4163. πρόβατον, prob'aton

Book	Oc.	sheep	Oc.	sheepfold (with 833)	Total
Mt.	11	7:15; 9:36; 10:6, 16; 12:11, 12; 15:24; 18:12; 25:32, 33; 26:31			11
Mk.	2	6:34; 14:27			2
Lk.	2	15:4, 6			2
Jn.	20	2:14, 15; 10:2, 3, 3, 4, 4, 7, 8, 11, 12, 12, 12, 13, 15, 16, 26, 27; 21:16, 17	1	10:1	21
Ac.	1	8:32			1
Ro.	1	8:36			1
Heb.	1	13:20			1
1 Pt.	1	2:25			1
Rev.	1	18:13			1
Total	40		1		41

4164. προβιβάζω, probibad'zō

Book	Oc.	instruct before	Oc.	draw	Total
Mt.	1	14:8			1
Ac.			1	19:33	1
Total	1		1		2

4165. προβλέπω, problep'ō

Book	provide	Total
Heb.	11:40	1

4166. προγίνομαι, progin'omai

Book	be past	Total
Ro.	3:25	1

4167. προγινώσκω, proginōs'kō

Book	Oc.	foreknow	Oc.	fore-ordain	Oc.	know	Oc.	know before	Total
Ac.					1	26:5			1
Ro.	2	8:29; 11:2							2
1 Pt.			1	1:20					1
2 Pt.							1	3:17	1
Total	2		1		1		1		5

4169. πρόγονος, prog'onos

Book	Oc.	parent	Oc.	forefather	Total
1 Ti.	1	5:4			1
2 Ti.			1	1:3	1
Total	1		1		2

4168. πρόγνωσις, prog'nōsis

Book	foreknowledge	Total
Ac.	2:23	1
1 Pt.	1:2	1
Total		2

4170. προγράφω, prograph'ō

Book	Oc.	write	Oc.	write aforetime	Oc.	write afore	Oc.	evidently set forth	Oc.	before ordain	Total
Ro.	1	15:4b	1	15:4a							2
Gal.							1	3:1			1
Eph.					1	3:3					1
Jd.									1	1:4	1
Total	1		1		1		1		1		5

4171. πρόδηλος, prod'ẹlos

Book	Oc.	evident	Oc.	manifest beforehand	Oc.	open beforehand	Total
1 Ti.			1	5:25	1	5:24	2
Heb.	1	7:14					1
Total	1		1		1		3

4173. προδότης, prodot'ẹs

Book	Oc.	traitor	Oc.	betrayer	Total
Lk.	1	6:16			1
Ac.			1	7:52	1
2 Ti.	1	3:4			1
Total	2		1		3

4172. προδίδωμι, prodid'ōmi

Book	first give	Total
Ro.	11:35	1

4174. πρόδρομος, prod'romos

Book	forerunner	Total
Heb.	6:20	1

4175. προείδω, proei'dō

Book	Oc.	see before	Oc.	foresee	Total
Ac.	1	2:31			1
Gal.			1	3:8	1
Total	1		1		2

4176. προελπίζω, proelpid'zō

Book	first trust	Total
Eph.	1:12	1

4178. προενάρχομαι, proenar'chomai

Book	Oc.	begin	Oc.	begin before	Total
2 Co.	1	8:6	1	8:10	2

4179. προεπαγγέλλομαι proepanggel'lomai

Book	promise afore	Total
Ro.	1:2	1

4177. προέπω, proep'ō

Book	Oc.	speak before	Oc.	tell in time past	Oc.	forewarn	Total
Ac.	1	1:16					1
Gal.			1	5:21			1
1 Th.					1	4:6	1
Total	1		1		1		3

4182. προετοιμάζω, proetoimad'zō

Book	Oc.	prepare afore	Oc.	before ordain	Total
Ro.	1	9:23			1
Eph.			1	2:10	1
Total	1		1		2

4180. προερέω, proere'ō

Book	Oc.	say before	Oc.	tell before	Oc.	speak before	Oc.	foretell	Total
Mt.			1	24:25					1
Mk.							1	13:23	1
Ro.	1	9:29							1
2 Co.	1	7:3	1	13:2					2
Gal.	1	1:9							1
Heb.	1	10:15							1
2 Pt.					1	3:2			1
Jd.					1	1:17			1
Total	4		2		2		1		9

4183. προευαγγελίζομαι proeuanggelid'zomai

Book	preach before the gospel	Total
Gal.	3:8	1

4184. προέχομαι, proech'omai

Book	be better	Total
Ro.	3:9	1

4181. προέρχομαι, proer'chomai

Book	Oc.	go before	Oc.	go farther	Oc.	go forward	Oc.	outgo	Oc.	pass on	Total
Mt.			1	26:39							1
Mk.					1	14:35	1	6:33			2
Lk.	2	1:17; 22:47									2
Ac.	2	20:5, 13							1	12:10	3
2 Co.	1	9:5									1
Total	5		1		1		1		1		9

4185. προηγέομαι, proege'omai

Book	prefer	Total
Ro.	12:10	1

4186. πρόθεσις, proth'esis

Book	Oc.	purpose	Oc.	shewbread (with 740)	Total
Mt.			1	12:4	1
Mk.			1	2:26	1
Lk.			1	6:4	1
Ac.	2	11:23; 27:13			2
Ro.	2	8:28; 9:11			2
Eph.	2	1:11; 3:11			2
2 Ti.	2	1:9; 3:10			2
Heb.			1	9:2	1
Total	8		4		12

4187. προθέσμιος, prothes'mios

Book	time appointed	Total
Gal.	4:2	1

4190. προθύμως, prothu'mōs

Book	of a ready mind	Total
1 Pt.	5:2	1

4189. πρόθυμος, proth'umos

Book	Oc.	ready	Oc.	willing	Total
Mt.			1	26:41	1
Mk.	1	14:38			1
Ro.	1	1:15			1
Total	2		1		3

4188. προθυμία, prothumi'a

Book	Oc.	forwardness of mind	Oc.	readiness	Oc.	readiness of mind	Oc.	ready mind	Oc.	willing mind	Total
Ac.					1	17:11					1
2 Co.	1	9:2	1	8:11			1	8:19	1	8:12	4
Total	1		1		1		1		1		5

4192. προκαλέομαι prokale'omai

Book	provoke	Total
Gal.	5:26	1

4191. προΐστημι, prois'tẹmi

Book	Oc.	rule	Oc.	maintain	Oc.	be over	Total
Ro.	1	12:8					1
1 Th.					1	5:12	1
1 Ti.	4	3:4, 5, 12; 5:17					4
Tit.			2	3:8, 14			2
Total	5		2		1		8

4193. προκαταγγέλλω, prokatanggel'lō

Book	Oc.	shew before	Oc.	foretell	Oc.	have notice before	Total
Ac.	2	3:18; 7:52	1	3:24			3
2 Co.					1	9:5	1
Total	2		1		1		4

4194. προκαταρτίζω, prokatartid'zō

Book	make up beforehand	Total
2 Co.	9:5	1

4195. πρόκειμαι, prok'eimai

Book	Oc.	be set before	Oc.	be first	Oc.	be set forth	Total
2 Co.			1	8:12			1
Heb.	3	6:18; 12:1, 2					3
Jd.					1	1:7	1
Total	3		1		1		5

4196. προκηρύσσω, prokẹrus'sō

Book	Oc.	preach before	Oc.	preach first	Total
Ac.	1	3:20	1	13:24	2

4197. προκοπή, prokopē′

Book	Oc.	furtherance	Oc.	profit	Total
Phl.	2	1:12, 25			2
1 Ti.			1	4:15	1
Total	2		1		3

4201. προλαμβάνω, prolamban′ō

Book	Oc.	come aforehand	Oc.	take before	Oc.	overtake	Total
Mk.	1	14:8					1
1 Co.			1	11:21			1
Gal.					1	6:1	1
Total	1		1		1		3

4198. προκόπτω, prokop′tō

Book	Oc.	increase	Oc.	be far spent	Oc.	profit	Oc.	proceed	Oc.	wax	Total
Lk.	1	2:52									1
Ro.			1	13:12							1
Gal.					1	1:14					1
2 Ti.	1	2:16					1	3:9	1	3:13	3
Total	2		1		1		1		1		6

4199. πρόκριμα, prok′rima

Book	prefer one before another	Total
1 Ti.	5:21	1

4200. προκυρόω, prokuro′ō

Book	confirm before	Total
Gal.	3:17	1

4202. προλέγω, proleg′ō

Book	Oc.	tell before	Oc.	foretell	Total
2 Co.			1	13:2	1
Gal.	1	5:21			1
1 Th.	1	3:4			1
Total	2		1		3

4206. προνοέω, pronoe′ō

Book	Oc.	provide for	Oc.	provide	Total
Ro.			1	12:17	1
2 Co.	1	8:21			1
1 Ti.	1	5:8			1
Total	2		1		3

4203. προμαρτύρομαι promartu′romai

Book	testify beforehand	Total
1 Pt.	1:11	1

4204. προμελετάω, promeleta′ō

Book	meditate before	Total
Lk.	21:14	1

4205. προμεριμνάω promerimna′ō

Book	take thought beforehand	Total
Mk.	13:11	1

4210. προπάσχω, propas′chō

Book	suffer before	Total
1 Th.	2:2	1

4207. πρόνοια, pron′oia

Book	Oc.	providence	Oc.	provision	Total
Ac.	1	24:2			1
Ro.			1	13:14	1
Total	1		1		2

4209. προορίζω, proorid′zō

Book	Oc.	predestinate	Oc.	determine before	Oc.	ordain	Total
Ac.			1	4:28			1
Ro.	2	8:29, 30					2
1 Co.					1	2:7	1
Eph.	2	1:5, 11					2
Total	4		1		1		6

4208. προοράω, proora′ō

Book	Oc.	foresee	Oc.	see before	Total
Ac.	1	2:25	1	21:29	2

4211. προπέμπω, propem′pō

Book	Oc.	bring on (one's) way	Oc.	bring (forward) on (one's) journey	Oc.	conduct forth	Oc.	accompany	Total
Ac.	2	15:3; 21:5					1	20:38	3
Ro.	1	15:24							1
1 Co.			1	16:6	1	16:11			2
2 Co.	1	1:16							1
Tit.			1	3:13					1
3 Jn.			1	1:6					1
Total	4		3		1		1		9

4212. προπετής, propetēs′

Book	Oc.	rashly	Oc.	heady	Total
Ac.	1	19:36			1
2 Ti.			1	3:4	1
Total	1		1		2

4213. προπορεύομαι, proporeu′omai

Book	Oc.	go	Oc.	go before	Total
Lk.	1	1:76			1
Ac.			1	7:40	1
Total	1		1		2

4215. προσάββατον prosab′baton

Book	day before the sabbath	Total
Mk.	15:42	1

4216. προσαγορεύω prosagoreu′ō

Book	call	Total
Heb.	5:10	1

See page 308 for word 4214.

4217. προσάγω, prosag′ō

Book	Oc.	bring	Oc.	draw near	Total
Lk.	1	9:41			1
Ac.	1	16:20	1	27:27	2
1 Pt.	1	3:18			1
Total	3		1		4

4218. προσαγωγή, prosagōgē′

Book	access	Total
Ro.	5:2	1
Eph.	2:18; 3:12	2
Total		3

4219. προσαιτέω, prosaite′ō

Book	beg	Total
Mk.	10:46	1
Lk.	18:35	1
Jn.	9:8	1
Total		3

4220. προσαναβαίνω prosanabai′nō

Book	go up	Total
Lk.	14:10	1

4221. προσαναλίσκω prosanalis′kō

Book	spend	Total
Lk.	8:43	1

4222. προσαναπληρόω prosanaplēro′ō

Book	supply	Total
2 Co.	9:12; 11:9	2

4224. προσαπειλέω, prosapeile′ō

Book	threaten further	Total
Ac.	4:21	1

4223. προσανατίθημι, prosanatith′ēmi

Book	Oc.	confer	Oc.	add in conference	Total
Gal.	1	1:16	1	2:6	2

4225. προσδαπανάω prosdapana′ō

Book	spend more	Total
Lk.	10:35	1

4226. προσδέομαι, prosde′omai

Book	need	Total
Ac.	17:25	1

4227. προσδέχομαι, prosdech′omai

Book	Oc.	look for	Oc.	wait for	Oc.	receive	Oc.	waited for (with 2258)	Oc.	allow	Oc.	take	Oc.	accept	Total
Mk.							1	15:43							1
Lk.	1	2:38	3	2:25; 12:36; 23:51	1	15:2									5
Ac.	1	23:21							1	24:15					2
Ro.					1	16:2									1
Phl.					1	2:29									1
Tit.	1	2:13													1
Heb.											1	10:34	1	11:35	2
Jd.	1	1:21													1
Total	4		3		3		1		1		1		1		14

4228. προσδοκάω, prosdoka′ō

Book	Oc.	look for	Oc.	waited for (with 2258)	Oc.	expect	Oc.	be in expectation	Oc.	look	Oc.	look when	Oc.	waiting for	Oc.	tarry	Total
Mt.	2	11:3; 24:50															2
Lk.	3	7:19, 20; 12:46	1	1:21			1	3:15					1	8:40			6
Ac.			1	10:24	1	3:5			1	28:6b	1	28:6a			1	27:33	5
2 Pt.	3	3:12, 13, 14															3
Total	8		2		1		1		1		1		1		1		16

4229. προσδοκία, prosdoki′a

Book	Oc.	looking after	Oc.	expectation	Total
Lk.	1	21:26			1
Ac.			1	12:11	1
Total	1		1		2

4230. προσεάω, prosea′ō

Book	suffer	Total
Ac.	27:7	1

4231. προσεγγίζω, prosenggid′zō

Book	come nigh	Total
Mk.	2:4	1

4234. προσέρχομαι, proser′chomai

Book	Oc.	come	Oc.	come to	Oc.	come unto	Oc.	go to	Oc.	go unto	Oc.	draw near	Oc.	Misc.	Total
Mt.	20	4:11; 8:19; 9:20; 13:10, 27; 14:12; 15:12, 23; 16:1; 17:7; 19:16; 25: 20, 22, 24; 26:50, 60, 60; 28:2, 9, 18	18	4:3; 8:25; 9:14, 28; 14: 15; 15:1; 17:14, 19, 24; 18:21; 20:20; 21:14, 28, 30; 22:23; 24:1; 26: 17, 49	11	5:1; 8:5; 13:36; 15:30; 18:1; 19:3; 21:23; 24: 3; 26:7, 69, 73	1	27:58							50
Mk.	2	1:31; 12:28	1	10:2	1	6:35	1	14:45							5
Lk.	4	7:14; 8:44; 9:12; 13:31	3	8:24; 20:27; 23:36			1	10:34	1	23:52			1	9:42	10
Jn.			1	12:21											1
Ac.	3	12:13; 22:27; 28:9	1	23:14	3	10:28; 18:2; 24:23			1	9:1	1	7:31	2	8:29; 22:26	11
1 Ti.													1	6:3	1
Heb.			1	11:6	4	4:16; 7:25; 12: 18, 22					1	10:22	1	10:1	7
1 Pt.	1	2:4													1
Total	30		25		19		3		2		2		5		86

Miscellaneous: Lk. 9:42, be a coming; Ac. 8:29, go near; Ac. 22:26, go; 1 Ti. 6:3, consent to; Heb. 10:1, comer thereunto.

4232. προσεδρεύω, prosedreu′ō

Book	wait at	Total
1 Co.	9:13	1

4233. προσεργάζομαι, prosergad′zomai

Book	gain	Total
Lk.	19:16	1

4235. προσευχή, proseuchē′

Book	Oc.	prayer	Oc.	pray earnestly	Total
Mt.	3	17:21; 21:13, 22			3
Mk.	2	9:29; 11:17			2
Lk.	3	6:12; 19:46; 22:45			3
Ac.	9	1:14; 2:42; 3:1; 6:4; 10:4, 31; 12:5; 16: 13, 16			9
Ro.	3	1:9; 12:12; 15:30			3
1 Co.	1	7:5			1
Eph.	2	1:16; 6:18			2
Phl.	1	4:6			1
Col.	2	4:2, 12			2
1 Th.	1	1:2			1
1 Ti.	2	2:1; 5:5			2
Phe.	2	1:4, 22			2
Jas.			1	5:17	1
1 Pt.	2	3:7; 4:7			2
Rev.	3	5:8; 8:3, 4			3
Total	36		1		37

4236. προσεύχομαι, proseu′chomai

Book	Oc.	pray	Oc.	make prayer	Oc.	pray for	Total
Mt.	15	5:44; 6:5, 5, 6, 6, 7, 9; 14:23; 19:13; 24:20; 26:36, 39, 41, 42, 44	1	23:14			16
Mk.	10	1:35; 6:46; 11:24, 25; 13:18, 33; 14:32, 35, 38, 39	1	12:40			11
Lk.	18	1:10; 3:21; 5:16; 6:12, 28; 9: 18, 28, 29; 11:1, 1, 2; 18:1, 10, 11; 22:40, 41, 44, 46	1	20:47			19
Ac.	16	1:24; 6:6; 8:15; 9:11, 40; 10: 9, 30; 11:5; 12:12; 13:3; 14: 23; 16:25; 20:36; 21:5; 22:17; 28:8					16
Ro.					1	8:26	1
1 Co.	8	11:4, 5, 13; 14:13, 14, 14, 15, 15					8
Eph.	1	6:18					1
Phl.	1	1:9					1
Col.	3	1:3, 9; 4:3					3
1 Th.	2	5:17, 25					2
2 Th.	2	1:11; 3:1					2
1 Ti.	1	2:8					1
Heb.	1	13:18					1
Jas.	4	5:13, 14, 17, 18					4
Jd.	1	1:20					1
Rev.	83		3		1		87

4237. προσέχω, prosech′ō

Book	Oc.	beware	Oc.	give heed to	Oc.	take heed to	Oc.	give heed unto	Oc.	take heed	Oc.	take heed unto	Oc.	take heed whereunto (with 3639)	Oc.	Misc.	Total
Mt.	5	7:15; 10:17; 16:6, 11, 12							1	6:1							6
Lk.	2	12:1; 20:46			2	17:3; 21:34											4
Ac.			1	8:10	1	5:35	1	8:6			1	20:28			2	8:11; 16:14	6
1 Ti.			2	1:4; 4:1											2	3:8; 4: 13	4
Tit.			1	1:14													1
Heb.			1	2:1											1	7:13	2
2 Pt.													1	1:19			1
Total	7		5		3		1		1		1		1		5		24

Miscellaneous: Ac. 8:11, have regard to; Ac. 16:14, attend unto; 1 Ti. 3:8, be given to; 1 Ti. 4:13, give attendance to; Heb. 7:13, give attendance at.

4238. προσηλόω, prose̤lo'ō

Book	nail to	Total
Col.	2:14	1

4239. προσήλυτος, prose̤'lutos

Book	proselyte	Total
Mt.	23:15	1
Ac.	2:10; 6:5; 13:43	3
Total		4

4240. πρόσκαιρος, pros'kairos

Book	Oc.	for a while	Oc.	for a time	Oc.	temporal	Oc.	for a season	Total
Mt.	1	13:21							1
Mk.			1	4:17					1
2 Co.					1	4:18			1
Heb.							1	11:25	1
Total	1		1		1		1		4

4214. πρός, pros

Book	Oc.	unto	Oc.	to	Oc.	with	Oc.	for	Oc.	against	Oc.	among	Oc.	at
Mt.	19	3:10, 13, 15; 11:28; 13:2; 14:25, 28; 19:14; 21:1, 32, 37; 23:34, 37; 25:36, 39; 26:14, 40; 27:19, 62	18	2:12; 3:5, 14; 5:28; 6:1; 7:15; 10:6, 13; 13:30; 14:29; 17:14; 21:34; 25:9; 26:18a, 45, 57; 27:4, 14	2	13:56; 26:55	2	23:5; 26:12	1	4:6			1	26:18b
Mk.	27	1:5, 32; 2:3, 13; 3:8, 13, 31; 4:1a; 6:25, 30, 33, 45, 48, 51; 7:1, 31; 9:17, 19b, 20; 10:1, 14; 12:4, 6, 13, 18; 14:10; 15:43	14	1:40, 45; 3:7; 4:41; 5:15, 19; 9:14; 10:7, 50; 11:7, 27; 12:2; 13:22; 14:53	6	6:3; 9:10, 16, 19a; 11:31; 14:49	1	10:5	1	12:12	8	1:27; 8:16; 9:33, 34; 10:26; 12:7; 15:31; 16:3	5	1:33; 5:22; 7:25; 11:1; 14:54
Lk.	100	1:13, 18, 19, 28, 34, 61, 80; 2:20, 34, 48, 49; 3:9, 12, 13, 14; 4:21, 23, 26, 26, 40, 43; 5:4, 10, 22, 31, 33, 34, 36; 6:9; 7:3, 7, 20, 20, 24, 40; 8:21, 22; 9:3, 13, 33, 43, 50, 57, 59, 62; 10:2, 23, 26, 29; 11:1, 5, 5, 39, 53; 12:1, 15, 16, 22, 41a; 13:7, 23, 34; 14:3, 7b, 23, 25; 15:3; 16:1, 30; 17:1, 22; 18:3, 7, 9, 16, 31, 40; 19:5, 8, 9, 13, 33, 39, 42; 20:2, 3, 23, 41; 22:15, 52, 70; 23:14, 22, 28; 24:5, 10, 17a, 18, 25, 44	39	1:27, 43, 55, 73; 2:15; 6:47; 7:4, 6, 19, 44, 50; 8:4, 19, 25, 35; 9:14, 23; 11:6; 12:41b, 58; 14:6, 7a, 26, 28; 15:18, 20, 22; 16:26, 26; 19:35; 20:9, 10; 21:38; 22:45; 23:4, 7, 15; 24:17b, 32	4	6:11; 9:41; 18:11; 20:5	1	8:13	3	4:11; 5:30; 20:19	3	4:36; 20:14; 22:23	2	16:20; 19:29
Jn.	47	1:29; 2:3; 3:4, 26a; 4:15, 30, 40, 47, 48, 49; 5:33; 6:5, 5, 28, 34, 45, 65; 7:3, 33, 37, 50a; 8:2, 3, 7, 57; 10:35, 41; 11:3, 4, 15, 21, 29; 12:32; 13:1; 14:3, 6, 12, 23, 28, 28; 16:7, 7; 18:24, 29, 38; 20:10, 17c	41	1:42, 47; 3:2, 20, 21, 26b; 4:33, 35; 5:40, 45; 6:17, 35, 37, 37, 44, 68; 7:45, 50b; 8:31; 9:13; 11:19, 45, 46; 13:3, 6; 14:18; 16:5, 10, 16, 17b, 28; 17:11, 13; 18:13; 19:39; 20:2, 2, 17a, 17b; 21:22, 23	2	1:1, 2	1	5:35			5	6:52; 7:35; 12:19; 16:17a; 19:24	1	20:11
Ac.	81	1:7; 2:29, 37, 38; 3:11, 12, 22, 22, 25b; 4:1, 8, 19, 23b; 5:9, 35; 7:3, 31; 8:14, 20, 26; 9:6, 11, 15, 38; 10:15, 21b, 28; 11:11, 20; 12:5, 8, 15, 21; 13:15a, 31, 32, 36; 15:2b, 7, 25, 33, 36; 16:37; 17:2, 15a; 18:6, 14, 21; 19:2, 2, 3, 31; 20:6; 21:11, 18, 37, 39; 22:1, 5, 8, 10, 13, 15, 21, 25; 23:3, 15, 17, 18b, 24; 25:22; 26:1, 6, 14a, 28; 27:3; 28:17, 21, 25b, 26, 30	30	2:7, 12; 4:23a, 24; 8:24; 9:2, 10, 27, 32, 40; 10:3, 13, 21a, 33; 11:3, 30; 12:20; 14:11; 16:36; 17:15b; 20:18; 23:18a, 22, 30a; 25:16, 21; 26:9; 27:12; 28:8, 23	6	2:47; 3:25a; 11:2; 15:2a; 17:17; 24:12	2	3:10; 13:15b	8	6:1; 9:5, 29; 19:38; 23:30b; 24:19; 25:19; 26:14b	3	4:15; 28:4, 25a	1	3:2
Ro.	6	1:10, 13; 10:21b; 15:23, 29, 32	8	8:31; 10:1, 21a; 15:2, 17, 22, 24, 30	2	5:1; 8:18								
1 Co.	7	4:21; 12:2; 14:6, 26; 16:5, 11, 12	8	2:1; 4:18, 19; 6:5; 12:7; 13:12; 14:12; 15:34	4	2:3; 16:6, 7, 10	4	7:5, 35, 35; 10:11	1	6:1				
2 Co.	7	1:15, 16, 20; 6:11; 7:12; 8:17; 12:17	13	2:1; 3:1, 16; 4:2, 6; 5:12; 7:3; 8:19; 10:4; 11:8; 12:14; 13:1, 7	4	5:8; 6:14, 15; 11:9	2	2:16; 7:8			1	12:21		
Gal.	2	6:10, 10	1	1:17	4	1:18; 2:5b; 4:18, 20	1	2:5a						
Eph.	5	2:18; 3:14; 5:31; 6:9, 22	1	4:29			1	4:12	6	6:11b, 12, 12, 12, 12, 12				
Phl.	1	4:6	2	1:26; 2:25										
Col.	2	4:8, 10	1	2:23					2	3:13, 19				
1 Th.	6	1:9a; 2:1, 2, 18; 3:6, 11	1	1:9b	1	3:4	1	2:17						
2 Th.					3	2:5; 3:1, 10								
1 Ti.	3	3:14; 4:7, 8b					1	1:16						
2 Ti.	3	2:24; 3:17; 4:9					4	3:16, 16, 16, 16						
Tit.	4	1:16; 3:2, 12, 12	1	3:1										
Phe.					1	1:13	1	1:15						
Heb.	6	1:8; 5:5, 7; 7:21; 9:20; 13:13	6	1:13; 2:17; 5:1, 14; 6:11; 9:13	2	4:13; 10:16	2	12:10, 11	1	12:4				
Jas.			1	4:5			1	4:14						
1 Pt.			2	2:4; 3:15										
2 Pt.	2	1:3; 3:16												
1 Jn.	4	5:16, 16, 16, 17			2	1:2; 2:1								
2 Jn.	2	1:10, 12a	1	1:12b										
3 Jn.			1	1:14										
Rev.	5	10:9; 12:5, 12; 21:9; 22:18	1	3:20					1	13:6			1	1:17
Total	339		190		43		25		24		20		11	

4241. προσκαλέομαι, proskale'omai

Book	Oc.	call unto	Oc.	call	Oc.	call for	Oc.	call to	Total
Mt.	4	10:1; 15:32; 18:2; 20:25	2	15:10; 18:32					6
Mk.	8	3:13, 23; 6:7; 7:14; 8:1, 34; 12:43; 15:44					1	10:42	9
Lk.	3	7:19; 16:5; 18:16	1	15:26					4
Ac.	5	6:2; 20:1; 23:17, 18, 23	4	2:39; 5:40; 13:2; 16:10	1	13:7			10
Jas.					1	5:14			1
Total	20		7		2		1		30

4214. πρός, pros (continued)

Book	Oc.	toward	Oc.	that	Oc.	by	Oc.	at (with dative)	Oc.	in	Oc.	according to	Oc.	of	Oc.	Not Tr.	Oc.	Misc.	Total
Mt.																	1	19:8	44
Mk.					2	4:1b; 11:4											3	2:2; 5:11; 14:4	67
Lk.	1	24:29	1	18:1	1	22:56	1	19:37	2	12:3; 24:12	1	12:47	1	14:32	4	2:18; 4:4; 6:3; 14:5	2	23:12; 24:14	166
Jn.							3	18:16; 20:12, 12									1	13:28	101
Ac.	1	24:16			1	5:10									1	11:14	4	26:26, 31; 27:34; 28:10	138
Ro.																	2	3:26; 4:2	18
1 Co.																			24
2 Co.	2	1:18; 7:4	1	3:13							1	5:10					2	1:12; 3:4	33
Gal.											1	2:14							9
Eph.			1	6:11a													2	3:4; 4:14	16
Phl.	1	2:30																	4
Col.	1	4:5																	6
1 Th.	2	4:12; 5:14															2	1:8; 2:9	13
2 Th.			1	3:8															4
1 Ti.															1	4:8a			5
2 Ti.																			7
Tit.																			5
Phe.	1	1:5																	3
Heb.													2	1:7; 11:18					19
Jas.			1	3:3															3
1 Pt.																	1	4:12	3
2 Pt.																			2
1 Jn.	1	3:21							1	5:14									8
2 Jn.																			3
3 Jn.																			1
Rev.																	1	1:13	9
Total	10		5		4		4		3		3		3		6		21		711

Miscellaneous: Mt. 19:8, because of; Mk. 2:2, about; Mk. 5:11, nigh unto; Mk. 14:4, within; Lk. 23:12, between; Lk. 24:14 (with 240), together; Jn. 13:28 (with 5001), for what intent; Ac. 26:26, before; Ac. 26:31, between; Ac. 27:34 (with genitive), for; Ac. 28:10 (with 5432), necessary; Ro. 3:26 (with 1732), to declare; Ro. 4:2, before; 2 Co. 1:12 (with 5109), to you-ward; 2 Co. 3:4 (with 2316), to God-ward; Eph. 3:4 (with 3639), whereby; Eph. 4:14 (with 3180), whereby (one) lies in wait; 1 Th. 1:8 (with 2316), to God-ward; 1 Th. 2:9, because; 1 Pt. 4:12 (with 3886), to try; Rev. 1:13 (with dative), about.

4242. προσκαρτερέω, proskartere´ō

Book	Oc.	continue	Oc.	continue instant	Oc.	continue steadfastly	Oc.	attend continually	Oc.	give (one's) self continually	Oc.	wait on	Oc.	wait on continually	Total
Mk.											1	3:9			1
Ac.	3	1:14; 2:46; 8:13			1	2:42			1	6:4			1	10:7	6
Ro.			1	12:12			1	13:6							2
Col.	1	4:2													1
Total	4		1		1		1		1		1		1		10

4243. προσκαρτέρησις proskarter´ẹsis

Book	perseverance	Total
Eph.	6:18	1

4244. προσκεφάλαιον proskephal´aion

Book	pillow	Total
Mk.	4:38	1

4245. προσκληρόω, prosklẹro´ō

Book	consort with	Total
Ac.	17:4	1

4246. πρόσκλισις, pros´klisis

Book	partiality	Total
1 Ti.	5:21	1

4247. προσκολλάω, proskolla´ō

Book	Oc.	cleave	Oc.	be joined	Oc.	join (one's) self	Total
Mt.	1	19:5					1
Mk.	1	10:7					1
Ac.					1	5:36	1
Eph.			1	5:31			1
Total	2		1		1		4

4248. πρόσκομμα, pros´komma

Book	Oc.	stumbling stone (with 3037)	Oc.	stumbling block	Oc.	stumbling	Oc.	offence	Total
Ro.	2	9:32, 33	1	14:13			1	14:20	4
1 Co.			1	8:9					1
1 Pt.					1	2:8			1
Total	2		2		1		1		6

4249. προσκοπή, proskopẹ´

Book	offence	Total
2 Co.	6:3	1

4250. προσκόπτω, proskop´tō

Book	Oc.	stumble	Oc.	stumble at	Oc.	dash	Oc.	beat upon	Total
Mt.					1	4:6	1	7:27	2
Lk.					1	4:11			1
Jn.	2	11:9, 10							2
Ro.	1	14:21	1	9:32					2
1 Pt.			1	2:8					1
Total	3		2		2		1		8

4251. προσκυλίω, proskuli´ō

Book	roll	Total
Mt.	27:60	1
Mk.	15:46	1
Total		2

4252. προσκυνέω, proskune´ō

Book	worship	Total
Mt.	2:2, 8, 11; 4:9, 10; 8:2; 9:18; 14:33; 15:25; 18:26; 20:20; 28:9, 17	13
Mk.	5:6; 15:19	2
Lk.	4:7, 8; 24:52	3
Jn.	4:20, 20, 21, 22, 22, 23, 23, 24, 24; 9:38; 12:20	11
Ac.	7:43; 8:27; 10:25; 24:11	4
1 Co.	14:25	1
Heb.	1:6; 11:21	2
Rev.	3:9; 4:10; 5:14; 7:11; 9:20; 11:1, 16; 13:4, 4, 8, 12, 15; 14:7, 9, 11; 15:4; 16:2; 19:4, 10, 10, 20; 20:4; 22:8, 9	24
Total		60

4253. προσκυνητής proskunẹtẹs´

Book	worshipper	Total
Jn.	4:23	1

4256. πρόσληψις, pros´lẹpsis

Book	receiving	Total
Ro.	11:15	1

4254. προσλαλέω, proslale´ō

Book	Oc.	speak to	Oc.	speak with	Total
Ac.	1	13:43	1	28:20	2

4255. προσλαμβάνω, proslamban´ō

Book	Oc.	receive	Oc.	take	Oc.	take unto	Total
Mt.			1	16:22			1
Mk.			1	8:32			1
Ac.	1	28:2	3	27:33, 34, 36	2	17:5; 18:26	6
Ro.	4	14:1, 3; 15:7, 7					4
Phe.	2	1:12, 17					2
Total	7		5		2		14

4258. προσορμίζω, prosormid´zō

Book	draw to the shore	Total
Mk.	6:53	1

4260. προσοχθίζω prosochthid´zō

Book	be grieved with	Total
Heb.	3:10, 17	2

4259. προσοφείλω, prosophei´lō

Book	owe besides	Total
Phe.	1:19	1

4261. πρόσπεινος, pros´peinos

Book	very hungry	Total
Ac.	10:10	1

4257. προσμένω, prosmen´ō

Book	Oc.	continue with	Oc.	continue in	Oc.	be with	Oc.	cleave unto	Oc.	tarry	Oc.	abide still	Total
Mt.	1	15:32											1
Mk.					1	8:2							1
Ac.							1	11:23	1	18:18			2
1 Ti.			1	5:5							1	1:3	2
Total	1		1		1		1		1		1		6

4262. προσπήγνυμι prospẹg´numi

Book	crucify	Total
Ac.	2:23	1

4264. προσποιέομαι prospoie´omai

Book	make as though	Total
Lk.	24:28	1

4263. προσπίπτω, prospip´tō

Book	Oc.	fall down before	Oc.	beat upon	Oc.	fall down at	Oc.	fall	Total
Mt.			1	7:25					1
Mk.	2	3:11; 5:33					1	7:25	3
Lk.	2	8:28, 47			1	5:8			3
Ac.	1	16:29							1
Total	5		1		1		1		8

4266. προσρήγνυμι, prosrẹg´numi

Book	Oc.	beat vehemently upon	Oc.	beat vehemently against	Total
Lk.	1	6:48	1	6:49	2

4265. προσπορεύομαι prosporeu´omai

Book	come unto	Total
Mk.	10:35	1

4268. προστάτις, prostat´is

Book	succourer	Total
Ro.	16:2	1

4267. προστάσσω, prostas´sō

Book	Oc.	command	Oc.	bid	Total
Mt.	2	8:4; 21:6	1	1:24	3
Mk.	1	1:44			1
Lk.	1	5:14			1
Ac.	2	10:33, 48			2
Total	6		1		7

4269. προστίθημι, prostith'ēmi

Book	Oc.	add	Oc.	again send (with 3892)	Oc.	give more	Oc.	increase	Oc.	proceed further	Oc.	lay unto	Oc.	speak to any more	Total
Mt.	2	6:27, 33													2
Mk.					1	4:24									1
Lk.	4	3:20; 12:25, 31; 19:11	2	20:11, 12			1	17:5							7
Ac.	4	2:41, 47; 5:14; 11:24							1	12:3	1	13:36			6
Gal.	1	3:19													1
Heb.													1	12:19	1
Total	11		2		1		1		1		1		1		18

4270. προστρέχω, prostrech'ō

Book	Oc.	run to	Oc.	run	Oc.	run thither to	Total
Mk.	1	9:15	1	10:17			2
Ac.					1	8:30	1
Total	1		1		1		3

4271. προσφάγιον, prosphag'ion

Book	meat	Total
Jn.	21:5	1

4272. πρόσφατος, pros'phatos

Book	new	Total
Heb.	10:20	1

4273. προσφάτως, prosphat'ōs

Book	lately	Total
Ac.	18:2	1

4275. προσφιλής, prosphilēs'

Book	lovely	Total
Phl.	4:8	1

4276. προσφορά, prosphora'

Book	Oc.	offering	Oc.	offering up	Total
Ac.	2	21:26; 24:17			2
Ro.			1	15:16	1
Eph.	1	5:2			1
Heb.	5	10:5, 8, 10, 14, 18			5
Total	8		1		9

4274. προσφέρω, prospher'ō

Book	Oc.	offer	Oc.	bring unto	Oc.	bring to	Oc.	bring	Oc.	offer up	Oc.	offer unto	Oc.	offer to	Oc.	Misc.	Total
Mt.	2	5:24; 8:4	7	4:24; 8:16; 12:22; 14:35; 18:24; 19:13; 22:19	3	9:2, 32; 17:16	2	5:23; 25:20							1	2:11	15
Mk.	1	1:44			1	10:13a	1	10:13b									3
Lk.	2	5:14; 23:36	3	12:11; 18:15; 23:14													5
Jn.															2	16:2; 19:29	2
Ac.	2	8:18; 21:26											1	7:42			3
Heb.	15	5:1, 3; 8:3, 3, 4; 9:7, 9, 14, 25, 28; 10:1, 2, 8, 11, 12							3	5:7; 11:17, 17	1	11:4			1	12:7	20
Total	22		10		4		3		3		1		1		4		48

Miscellaneous: Mt. 2:11, present unto; Jn. 16:2, do; Jn. 19:29, put to; Heb. 12:7, deal with.

4277. προσφωνέω, prosphōne'ō

Book	Oc.	call	Oc.	call unto	Oc.	call to	Oc.	speak	Oc.	speak to	Oc.	speak unto	Total
Mt.			1	11:16									1
Lk.	2	6:13; 13:12			1	7:32			1	23:20			4
Ac.							1	22:2			1	21:40	2
Total	2		1		1		1		1		1		7

4278. πρόσχυσις, pros'chusis

Book	sprinkling	Total
Heb.	11:28	1

4279. προσψαύω, prospsau'ō

Book	touch	Total
Lk.	11:46	1

4280. προσωποληπτέω prosōpolēpte'ō

Book	have respect to persons	Total
Jas.	2:9	1

4281. προσωπολήπτης prosōpolēp'tēs

Book	respecter of persons	Total
Ac.	10:34	1

4282. προσωποληψία prosōpolēpsi'a

Book	respect of persons	Total
Ro.	2:11	1
Eph.	6:9	1
Col.	3:25	1
Jas.	2:1	1
Total		4

4284. προτάσσω, protas'sō

Book	appoint before	Total
Ac.	17:26	1

4285. προτείνω, protei'nō

Book	bind	Total
Ac.	22:25	1

4283. πρόσωπον, pros'ōpon

Book	Oc.	face	Oc.	person	Oc.	presence	Oc.	countenance	Oc.	Not Tr.	Oc.	Misc.	Total
Mt.	9	6:16, 17; 11:10; 16:3; 17:2, 6; 18:10; 26:39, 67	1	22:16									10
Mk.	2	1:2; 14:65	1	12:14									3
Lk.	13	1:76; 2:31; 5:12; 7:27; 9:51, 52, 53; 10:1; 12:56; 17:16; 21:35; 22:64; 24:5	1	20:21			1	9:29					15
Ac.	6	6:15, 15; 7:45; 17:26; 20:25, 38			3	3:13, 19; 5:41	1	2:28	1	13:24	1	25:16	12
1 Co.	3	13:12, 12; 14:25											3
2 Co.	5	3:7a, 13, 18; 4:6; 11:20	2	1:11; 2:10	1	10:1	1	3:7b			3	5:12; 8:24; 10:7	12
Gal.	2	1:22; 2:11	1	2:6									3
Col.	1	2:1											1
1 Th.	2	2:17b; 3:10			1	2:17a							3
2 Th.					1	1:9							1
Heb.					1	9:24							1
Jas.	1	1:23									1	1:11	2
1 Pt.	1	3:12											1
Jd.			1	1:16									1
Rev.	10	4:7; 6:16; 7:11; 9:7, 7; 10:1; 11:16; 12:14; 20:11; 22:4											10
Total	55		7		7		3		1		5		78

Miscellaneous: Ac. 25:16 (with 2596), face to face; 2 Co. 5:12, appearance; 2 Co. 8:24 (with 1519), before; 2 Co. 10:7, outward appearance; Jas. 1:11, fashion.

4286. πρότερον, prot'eron

Book	Oc.	before (with 3488)	Oc.	first	Oc.	former	Oc.	before	Oc.	at the first (with 3488)	Total
Jn.	2	6:62; 9:8					1	7:51			3
2 Co.							1	1:15			1
Gal.									1	4:13	1
1 Ti.	1	1:13									1
Heb.			2	4:6; 7:27	1	10:32					3
1 Pt.					1	1:14					1
Total	3		2		2		2		1		10

4287. πρότερος, prot'eros

Book	former	Total
Eph.	4:22	1

4289. προτρέπομαι, protrep'omai

Book	exhort	Total
Ac.	18:27	1

4288. προτίθεμαι, protith'emai

Book	Oc.	purpose	Oc.	set forth	Total
Ro.	1	1:13	1	3:25	2
Eph.	1	1:9			1
Total	2		1		3

4290. προτρέχω, protrech'ō

Book	Oc.	run before	Oc.	outrun	Total
Lk.	1	19:4			1
Jn.			1	20:4	1
Total	1		1		2

4291. προϋπάρχω, proupar'chō

Book	Oc.	be before	Oc.	be beforetime	Total
Lk.	1	23:12			1
Ac.			1	8:9	1
Total	1		1		2

4293. προφέρω, propher'ō

Book	bring forth	Total
Lk.	6:45, 45	2

4292. πρόφασις, proph'asis

Book	Oc.	pretence	Oc.	cloke	Oc.	shew	Oc.	colour	Total
Mt.	1	23:14							1
Mk.	1	12:40							1
Lk.					1	20:47			1
Jn.			1	15:22					1
Ac.							1	27:30	1
Phl.	1	1:18							1
1 Th.			1	2:5					1
Total	3		2		1		1		7

4294. προφητεία, prophẹtei'a

Book	Oc.	prophecy	Oc.	prophesying	Total
Mt.	1	13:14			1
Ro.	1	12:6			1
1 Co.	3	12:10; 13:2, 8	2	14:6, 22	5
1 Th.			1	5:20	1
1 Ti.	2	1:18; 4:14			2
2 Pt.	2	1:20, 21			2
Rev.	7	1:3; 11:6; 19:10; 22:7, 10, 18, 19			7
Total	16		3		19

4297. προφητικός, prophẹtikos'

Book	Oc.	of the prophets	Oc.	of prophecy	Total
Ro.	1	16:26			1
2 Pt.			1	1:19	1
Total	1		1		2

4295. προφητεύω, prophẹteu'ō

Book	prophesy	Total
Mt.	7:22; 11:13; 15:7; 26: 68	4
Mk.	7:6; 14:65	2
Lk.	1:67; 22:64	2
Jn.	11:51	1
Ac.	2:17, 18; 19:6; 21:9	4
1 Co.	11:4, 5; 13:9; 14:1, 3, 4, 5, 5, 24, 31, 39	11
1 Pt.	1:10	1
Jd.	1:14	1
Rev.	10:11; 11:3	2
Total		28

4298. προφῆτις, prophẹ'tis

Book	prophetess	Total
Lk.	2:36	1
Rev.	2:20	1
Total		2

4299. προφθάνω, prophthan'ō

Book	prevent	Total
Mt.	17:25	1

4301. προχειροτονέω procheirotone'ō

Book	choose before	Total
Ac.	10:41	1

4296. προφήτης, prophẹ'tẹs

Book	prophet	Total
Mt.	1:22; 2:5, 15, 17, 23; 3:3; 4:14; 5:12, 17; 7:12; 8:17; 10:41, 41, 41; 11:9, 9, 13; 12:17, 39; 13:17, 35, 57; 14:5; 16:4, 14; 21:4, 11, 26, 46; 22:40; 23:29, 30, 31, 34, 37; 24:15; 26:56; 27:9, 35	39
Mk.	1:2; 6:4, 15, 15; 8:28; 11:32; 13:14	7
Lk.	1:70, 76; 3:4; 4:17, 24, 27; 6:23; 7:16, 26, 26, 28, 39; 9:8, 19; 10: 24; 11:29, 47, 49, 50; 13:28, 33, 34; 16:16, 29, 31; 18:31; 20:6; 24: 19, 25, 27, 44	31
Jn.	1:21, 23, 25, 45; 4:19, 44; 6:14, 45; 7:40, 52; 8:52, 53; 9:17; 12:38	14
Ac.	2:16, 30; 3:18, 21, 22, 23, 24, 25; 7:37, 42, 48, 52; 8:28, 30, 34; 10: 43; 11:27; 13:1, 15, 20, 27, 40; 15:15, 32; 21:10; 24:14; 26:22, 27; 28:23, 25	30
Ro.	1:2; 3:21; 11:3	3
1 Co.	12:28, 29; 14:29, 32, 32, 37	6
Eph.	2:20; 3:5; 4:11	3
1 Th.	2:15	1
Tit.	1:12	1
Heb.	1:1; 11:32	2
Jas.	5:10	1
1 Pt.	1:10	1
2 Pt.	2:16; 3:2	2
Rev.	10:7; 11:10, 18; 16:6; 18:20, 24; 22:6, 9	8
Total		149

4300. προχειρίζομαι, procheirid'zomai

Book	Oc.	choose	Oc.	make	Total
Ac.	1	22:14	1	26:16	2

4302. Πρόχορος, Proch'oros

Book	Prochorus	Total
Ac.	6:5	1

4306. πρώϊμος, prō'imos

Book	early	Total
Jas.	5:7	1

4304. πρωΐ, prōi'

Book	Oc.	in the morning	Oc.	early in the morning	Oc.	early	Oc.	morning	Total
Mt.	1	16:3	1	20:1					2
Mk.	4	1:35; 11: 20; 13:35; 15:1	1	16:2	1	16:9			6
Jn.					1	20:1			1
Ac.							1	28:23	1
Total	5		2		2		1		10

4303. πρύμνα, prum'na

Book	Oc.	hinder part of the ship	Oc.	stern	Oc.	hinder part	Total
Mk.	1	4:38					1
Ac.			1	27:29	1	27:41	2
Total	1		1		1		3

4305. πρωΐα, prōi'a

Book	Oc.	morning	Oc.	early	Total
Mt.	2	21:18; 27:1			2
Jn.	1	21:4	1	18:28	2
Total	3		1		4

4307. πρωϊνος, prōinos'

Book	morning	Total
Rev.	2:28	1

4308. πρώρα, prō'ra

Book	Oc.	forepart	Oc.	foreship	Total
Ac.	1	27:41	1	27:30	2

4309. πρωτεύω, prōteu'ō

Book	have the preeminence	Total
Col.	1:18	1

4310. πρωτοκαθεδρία, prōtokathedri'a

Book	Oc.	chief seat	Oc.	uppermost seat	Oc.	highest seat	Total
Mt.	1	23:6					1
Mk.	1	12:39					1
Lk.			1	11:43	1	20:46	2
Total	2		1		1		4

4311. πρωτοκλισία, prōtoklisi'a

Book	Oc.	uppermost room	Oc.	chief room	Oc.	highest room	Total
Mt.	1	23:6					1
Mk.	1	12:39					1
Lk.			2	14:7; 20:46	1	14:8	3
Total	2		2		1		5

4312. πρῶτον, prō´ton

Book	Oc.	first	Oc.	at the first (with 3488)	Oc.	first of all	Oc.	Misc.	Total
Mt.	9	5:24; 6:33; 7:5; 8:21; 12:29; 13:30; 17:10, 11; 23:26							9
Mk.	7	3:27; 4:28; 7:27; 9:11, 12; 13:10; 16:9							7
Lk.	9	6:42; 9:59, 61; 10:5; 11:38; 14:28, 31; 17:25; 21:9			1	12:1			10
Jn.	1	18:13	2	12:16; 19:39			3	2:10; 10:40; 15:18	6
Ac.	5	3:26; 7:12; 11:26; 13:46; 26:20					1	15:14	6
Ro.	5	1:8, 16; 2:9, 10; 15:24					1	3:2	6
1 Co.	2	12:28; 15:46			1	11:18			3
2 Co.	1	8:5							1
Eph.	1	4:9							1
1 Th.	1	4:16							1
2 Th.	1	2:3							1
1 Ti.	3	2:1; 3:10; 5:4							3
2 Ti.	1	1:5							1
Heb.	1	7:2							1
Jas.	1	3:17							1
1 Pt.	1	4:17							1
2 Pt.	2	1:20; 3:3							2
Total	51		2		2		5		60

Miscellaneous: Jn. 2:10, at the beginning; Jn. 10:40, at first; Jn. 15:18, before; Ac. 15:14, at the first; Ro. 3:2, chiefly.

4313. πρῶτος, prō´tos

Book	Oc.	first	Oc.	chief	Oc.	first day	Oc.	former	Oc.	Misc.	Total
Mt.	15	10:2; 12:45; 17:27; 19:30, 30; 20:8, 10, 16, 16; 21:28, 31, 36; 22:25, 38; 27:64	1	20:27	1	26:17					17
Mk.	8	9:35; 10:31, 31; 12:20, 28, 29, 30; 14:12			1	16:9			2	6:21; 10:44	11
Lk.	8	2:2; 11:26; 13:30, 30; 14:18; 16:5; 19:16; 20:29	1	19:47					1	15:22	10
Jn.	6	1:41; 5:4; 8:7; 19:32; 20:4, 8							2	1:15, 30	8
Ac.	4	12:10; 20:18; 26:23; 27:43	6	13:50; 16:12; 17:4; 25:2; 28:7, 17			1	1:1			11
Ro.	1	10:19									1
1 Co.	3	14:30; 15:45, 47							1	15:3	4
Eph.	1	6:2									1
Phl.	1	1:5									1
1 Ti.	3	1:16; 2:13; 5:12	1	1:15							4
2 Ti.	2	2:6; 4:16									2
Heb.	9	8:7, 13; 9:1, 2, 6, 8, 15, 18; 10:9									9
2 Pt.									1	2:20	1
1 Jn.	1	4:19									1
Rev.	18	1:11, 17; 2:4, 5, 8, 19; 4:1, 7; 8:7; 13:12, 12; 16:2; 20:5, 6; 21:1, 1, 19; 22:13					1	21:4			19
Total	80		9		2		2		7		100

Miscellaneous: Mk. 6:21, chief estate; Mk. 10:44, chiefest; Lk. 15:22, best; Jn. 1:15, 30, before; 1 Co. 15:3, first of all; 2 Pt. 2:20, beginning.

4314. πρωτοστάτης, prōtostat´ęs

Book	ringleader	Total
Ac.	24:5	1

4315. πρωτοτόκια, prōtotok´ia

Book	birthright	Total
Heb.	12:16	1

4316. πρωτοτόκος, prōtotok´os

Book	Oc.	firstborn	Oc.	firstbegotten	Total
Mt.	1	1:25			1
Lk.	1	2:7			1
Ro.	1	8:29			1
Col.	2	1:15, 18			2
Heb.	2	11:28; 12:23	1	1:6	3
Rev.			1	1:5	1
Total	7		2		9

4317. πταίω, ptai´ō

Book	Oc.	offend	Oc.	stumble	Oc.	fall	Total
Ro.			1	11:11			1
Jas.	3	2:10; 3:2, 2					3
2 Pt.					1	1:10	1
Total	3		1		1		5

4318. πτέρνα, pter´na

Book	heel	Total
Jn.	13:18	1

4319. πτερύγιον, pterug´ion

Book	pinnacle	Total
Mt.	4:5	1
Lk.	4:9	1
Total		2

4320. πτέρυξ, pter´ux

Book	wing	Total
Mt.	23:37	1
Lk.	13:34	1
Rev.	4:8; 9:9; 12:14	3
Total		5

4321. πτηνον, ptęnon´

Book	bird	Total
1 Co.	15:39	1

4322. πτοέω, ptoe´ō

Book	terrify	Total
Lk.	21:9; 24:37	2

4323. πτόησις, pto´ęsis

Book	amazement	Total
1 Pt.	3:6	1

4324. Πτολεμαΐς, Ptolemais´

Book	Ptolemais	Total
Ac.	21:7	1

4325. πτύον, ptu´on

Book	fan	Total
Mt.	3:12	1
Lk.	3:17	1
Total		2

4326. πτύρω, ptu´rō

Book	terrify	Total
Phl.	1:28	1

4327. πτύσμα, ptus´ma

Book	spittle	Total
Jn.	9:6	1

4328. πτύσσω, ptus´sō

Book	close	Total
Lk.	4:20	1

4329. πτύω, ptu´ō

Book	spit	Total
Mk.	7:33; 8:23	2
Jn.	9:6	1
Total		3

4330. πτῶμα, ptō´ma

Book	Oc.	dead body	Oc.	carcase	Oc.	corpse	Total
Mt.			1	24:28			1
Mk.					1	6:29	1
Rev.	3	11:8, 9, 9					3
Total	3		1		1		5

4331. πτῶσις, ptō´sis

Book	fall	Total
Mt.	7:27	1
Lk.	2:34	1
Total		2

4332. πτωχεία, ptōchei´a

Book	poverty	Total
2 Co.	8:2, 9	2
Rev.	2:9	1
Total		3

4333. πτωχεύω, ptōcheu´ō

Book	become poor	Total
2 Co.	8:9	1

4334. πτωχός, ptōchos´

Book	Oc.	poor	Oc.	beggar	Oc.	poor man	Oc.	beggarly	Total
Mt.	5	5:3; 11:5; 19:21; 26:9, 11							5
Mk.	5	10:21; 12:42, 43; 14:5, 7							5
Lk.	8	4:18; 6:20; 7:22; 14:13, 21; 18:22; 19:8; 21:3	2	16:20, 22					10
Jn.	4	12:5, 6, 8; 13:29							4
Ro.	1	15:26							1
2 Co.	1	6:10							1
Gal.	1	2:10					1	4:9	2
Jas.	3	2:3, 5, 6			1	2:2			4
Rev.	2	3:17; 13:16							2
Total	30		2		1		1		34

4335. πυγμή, pugmē'

Book	oft	Total
Mk.	7:3	1

4336. Πύθων, Pu'thōn

Book	divination	Total
Ac.	16:16	1

4337. πυκνός, puknos'

Book	Oc.	often	Oc.	oftener	Total
Lk.	1	5:33			1
Ac.			1	24:26	1
1 Ti.	1	5:23			1
Total	2		1		3

4338. πυκτέω, pukte'ō

Book	fight	Total
1 Co.	9:26	1

4339. πύλη, pu'lē

Book	gate	Total
Mt.	7:13, 13, 14; 16:18	4
Lk.	7:12; 13:24	2
Ac.	3:10; 9:24; 12:10	3
Heb.	13:12	1
Total		10

4340. πυλών, pulōn'

Book	Oc.	gate	Oc.	porch	Total
Mt.			1	26:71	1
Lk.	1	16:20			1
Ac.	5	10:17; 12:13, 14, 14; 14:13			5
Rev.	11	21:12, 12, 13, 13, 13, 13, 15, 21, 21, 25; 22:14			11
Total	17		1		18

4341. πυνθάνομαι, punthan'omai

Book	Oc.	ask	Oc.	demand	Oc.	enquire	Oc.	understand	Total
Mt.			1	2:4					1
Lk.	2	15:26; 18:36							2
Jn.	1	13:24			1	4:52			2
Ac.	4	4:7; 10:18, 29; 23:19	1	21:33	1	23:20	1	23:34	7
Total	7		2		2		1		12

4342. πῦρ, pur

Book	Oc.	fire	Oc.	fiery	Total
Mt.	12	3:10, 11, 12; 5:22; 7:19; 13:40, 42, 50; 17:15; 18:8, 9; 25:41			12
Mk.	8	9:22, 43, 44, 45, 46, 47, 48, 49			8
Lk.	7	3:9, 16, 17; 9:54; 12:49; 17:29; 22:55			7
Jn.	1	15:6			1
Ac.	4	2:3, 19; 7:30; 28:5			4
Ro.	1	12:20			1
1 Co.	3	3:13, 13, 15			3
2 Th.	1	1:8			1
Heb.	4	1:7; 11:34; 12:18, 29	1	10:27	5
Jas.	3	3:5, 6; 5:3			3
1 Pt.	1	1:7			1
2 Pt.	1	3:7			1
Jd.	2	1:7, 23			2
Rev.	25	1:14; 2:18; 3:18; 4:5; 8:5, 7, 8; 9:17, 18; 10:1; 11:5; 13:13; 14:10, 18; 15:2; 16:8; 17:16; 18:8; 19:12, 20; 20:9, 10, 14, 15; 21:8			25
Total	73		1		74

4343. πυρά, pura'

Book	fire	Total
Ac.	28:2, 3	2

4344. πύργος, pur'gos

Book	tower	Total
Mt.	21:33	1
Mk.	12:1	1
Lk.	13:4; 14:28	2
Total		4

4345. πυρέσσω, pures'sō

Book	be sick of a fever	Total
Mt.	8:14	1
Mk.	1:30	1
Total		2

4346. πυρετός, puretos'

Book	fever	Total
Mt.	8:15	1
Mk.	1:31	1
Lk.	4:38, 39	2
Jn.	4:52	1
Ac.	28:8	1
Total		6

4347. πύρινος, pu'rinos

Book	of fire	Total
Rev.	9:17	1

4348. πυρόω, puro'ō

Book	Oc.	burn	Oc.	fiery	Oc.	be on fire	Oc.	try	Total
1 Co.	1	7:9							1
2 Co.	1	11:29							1
Eph.			1	6:16					1
2 Pt.					1	3:12			1
Rev.	1	1:15					1	3:18	2
Total	3		1		1		1		6

4349. πυῤῥάζω, purhrad'zō

Book	be red	Total
Mt.	16:2, 3	2

4350. πυῤῥός, purhros, purhros'

Book	red	Total
Rev.	6:4; 12:3	2

4351. πύρωσις, pu'rōsis

Book	Oc.	burning	Oc.	fiery trial	Total
1 Pt.			1	4:12	1
Rev.	2	18:9, 18			2
Total	2		1		3

4352. -πω, -pō

An enclitic particle meaning "even," "yet." Used only in composition. See words 3269, 3280, 3664, 3668.

4353. πωλέω, pōle'ō

Book	Oc.	sell	Oc.	be sold	Total
Mt.	6	10:29; 13:44; 19:21; 21:12, 12; 25:9			6
Mk.	3	10:21; 11:15, 15			3
Lk.	6	12:6, 33; 17:28; 18:22; 19:45; 22:36			6
Jn.	2	2:14, 16			2
Ac.	3	4:34, 37; 5:1			3
1 Co.			1	10:25	1
Rev.	1	13:17			1
Total	21		1		22

4354. πῶλος, pō'los

Book	colt	Total
Mt.	21:2, 5, 7	3
Mk.	11:2, 4, 5, 7	4
Lk.	19:30, 33, 33, 35	4
Jn.	12:15	1
Total		12

4355. πώποτε, pō'pote

Book	Oc.	at any time	Oc.	yet never (with 3662)	Oc.	never	Oc.	never (with 3264)	Total
Lk.			1	19:30					1
Jn.	2	1:18; 5:37			1	8:33	1	6:35	4
1 Jn.	1	4:12							1
Total	3		1		1		1		6

4356. πωρόω, pōro'ō

Book	Oc.	harden	Oc.	blind	Total
Mk.	2	6:52; 8:17			2
Jn.	1	12:40			1
Ro.			1	11:7	1
2 Co.			1	3:14	1
Total	3		2		5

4357. πώρωσις, pō'rōsis

Book	Oc.	blindness	Oc.	hardness	Total
Mk.			1	3:5	1
Ro.	1	11:25			1
Eph.	1	4:18			1
Total	2		1		3

4358. -πως, -pōs

Book	Oc.	by any means	Oc.	by some means	Oc.	perhaps	Oc,	haply	Oc.	Not Tr.	Total
Ac.	1	27:12							1	27:29	2
Ro.	2	1:10; 11:14							1	11:21	3
1 Co.	2	8:9; 9:27									2
2 Co.	1	11:3			1	2:7	1	9:4	2	12:20, 20	5
Gal.	1	2:2							1	4:11	2
Phl.	1	3:11									1
1 Th.			1	3:5							1
Total	8		1		1		1		5		16

4359. πῶς, pōs

Book	Oc.	how	Oc.	by what means	Oc.	after what manner	Oc.	that	Total
Mt.	14	6:28; 7:4; 10:19; 12:4, 26, 29, 34; 16:11; 21:20; 22:12, 43, 45; 23:33; 26:54							14
Mk.	14	2:26; 3:23; 4:13, 40; 5:16; 8:21; 9:12; 10:23, 24; 11:18; 12:35, 41; 14:1, 11							14
Lk.	15	1:34; 6:42; 8:18; 10:26; 11:18; 12:11, 27, 50, 56; 14:7; 18:24; 20:41, 44; 22:2, 4	1	8:36					16
Jn.	19	3:4, 9, 12; 4:9; 5:44, 47; 6:42, 52; 7:15; 8:33; 9:10, 15, 16, 19, 26; 11:36; 12:34; 14:5, 9	1	9:21					20
Ac.	8	2:8; 4:21; 8:31; 9:27, 27; 11:13; 12:17; 15:36			1	20:18			9
Ro.	8	3:6; 4:10; 6:2; 8:32; 10:14, 14, 14, 15							8
1 Co.	9	3:10; 7:32, 33, 34; 14:7, 9, 16; 15:12, 35							9
2 Co.	1	3:8							1
Gal.	1	4:9							1
Eph.							1	5:15	1
Col.	1	4:6							1
1 Th.	2	1:9; 4:1							2
2 Th.	1	3:7							1
1 Ti.	2	3:5, 15							2
Heb.	1	2:3							1
1 Jn.	2	3:17; 4:20							2
Rev.	1	3:3							1
Total	99		2		1		1		103

4360. Ῥαάβ, Hraab′

Book	Rahab	Total
Heb.	11:31	1
Jas.	2:25	1
Total		2

4361. ῥαββί, hrabbi′

Book	Oc.	Master (Christ)	Oc.	Rabbi (Christ)	Oc.	rabbi	Total
Mt.	2	26:25, 49			3	23:7, 7, 8	5
Mk.	4	9:5; 11:21; 14:45, 45					4
Jn.	3	4:31; 9:2; 11:8	5	1:38, 49; 3:2, 26; 6:25			8
Total	9		5		3		17

4362. ῥαββονί or ῥαββουνί, hrabboni′ or hrabbouni′

Book	Oc.	Lord (Christ)	Oc.	Rabboni (Christ)	Total
Mk.	1	10:51			1
Jn.			1	20:16	1
Total	1		1		2

4363. ῥαβδίζω, hrabdid′zō

Book	Oc.	beat	Oc.	beat with rods	Total
Ac.	1	16:22			1
2 Co.			1	11:25	1
Total	1		1		2

4364. ῥάβδος, hrab′dos

Book	Oc.	rod	Oc.	staff	Oc.	sceptre	Total
Mt.			1	10:10			1
Mk.			1	6:8			1
Lk.			1	9:3			1
1 Co.	1	4:21					1
Heb.	1	9:4	1	11:21	2	1:8, 8	4
Rev.	4	2:27; 11:1; 12:5; 19:15					4
Total	6		4		2		12

4365. ῥαβδοῦχος, hrabdou′chos

Book	serjeant	Total
Ac.	16:35, 38	2

4366. Ῥαγαῦ, Hragau′

Book	Ragau	Total
Lk.	3:35	1

4367. ῥᾳδιούργημα hradiourg′ēma

Book	lewdness	Total
Ac.	18:14	1

4368. ῥᾳδιουργία, hradiourgi′a

Book	mischief	Total
Ac.	13:10	1

4369. ῥακά, hraka′

Book	Raca	Total
Mt.	5:22	1

4370. ῥάκος, hrak′os

Book	cloth	Total
Mt.	9:16	1
Mk.	2:21	1
Total		2

4371. Ῥαμά, Hrama′

Book	Rama	Total
Mt.	2:18	1

4372. ῥαντίζω, hrantid′zō

Book	sprinkle	Total
Heb.	9:13, 19, 21; 10:22	4

4373. ῥαντισμός, hrantismos′

Book	sprinkling	Total
Heb.	12:24	1
1 Pt.	1:2	1
Total		2

4374. ῥαπίζω, hrapid′zō

Book	Oc.	smite	Oc.	smite with the palm of (one's) hand	Total
Mt.	1	5:39	1	26:67	2

4375. ῥάπισμα, hrap′isma

Book	Oc.	strike with the palm of (one's) hand (with 906)	Oc.	strike with the palm of (one's) hand (with 1325)	Oc.	smite with (one's) hand (with 1325)	Total
Mk.	1	14:65					1
Jn.			1	18:22	1	19:3	2
Total	1		1		1		3

4376. ῥαφίς, hraphis′

Book	needle	Total
Mt.	19:24	1
Mk.	10:25	1
Lk.	18:25	1
Total		3

4377. Ῥαχάβ, Hrachab′

Book	Rachab	Total
Mt.	1:5	1

4378. Ῥαχήλ, Hrachēl′

Book	Rachel	Total
Mt.	2:18	1

4379. Ῥεβέκκα, Hrebek′ka

Book	Rebecca	Total
Ro.	9:10	1

4380. ῥέδα, hred′a

Book	chariot	Total
Rev.	18:13	1

4381. Ῥεμφάν, Hremphan′

Book	Remphan	Total
Ac.	7:43	1

4382. ῥέω or ῥεύω, hre′ō or hreu′ō

Book	flow	Total
Jn.	7:38	1

4383. ῥέω, hre′ō

Book	Oc.	speak	Oc.	say	Oc.	speak of	Oc.	command	Oc.	make	Total
Mt.	12	1:22; 2:15, 17, 23; 4:14; 8:17; 12:17; 13:35; 21:4; 22:31; 27:9, 35	6	5:21, 27, 31, 33, 38, 43	2	3:3; 24:15					20
Mk.					1	13:14					1
Ro.			2	9:12, 26							2
Gal.									1	3:16	1
Rev.			1	6:11			1	9:4			2
Total	12		9		3		1		1		26

4384. Ῥήγιον, Hreg'ion

Book	Rhegium	Total
Ac.	28:13	1

4385. ῥῆγμα, hreg'ma

Book	ruin	Total
Lk.	6:49	1

4386a. ῥήγνυμι, hreg'numi

Book	Oc.	rend	Oc.	break	Oc.	break forth	Oc.	burst	Oc.	throw down	Total
Mt.	1	7:6	1	9:17							2
Lk.							1	5:37	1	9:42	2
Gal.					1	4:27					1
Total	1		1		1		1		1		5

4386b. ῥήσσω, hres'sō

Book	Oc.	burst	Oc.	tear	Total
Mk.	1	2:22	1	9:18	2

Word 4386 has 7 occurrences.

4388. Ῥησά, Hresa'

Book	Rhesa	Total
Lk.	3:27	1

4387. ῥῆμα, hre'ma

Book	Oc.	word	Oc.	saying	Oc.	thing	Oc.	no thing (with 3656)	Oc.	Not Tr.	Total
Mt.	5	4:4; 12:36; 18:16; 26:75; 27:14							1	5:11	6
Mk.	1	14:72	1	9:32							2
Lk.	8	1:38; 2:29; 3:2; 4:4; 5:5; 20:26; 24:8, 11	8	1:65; 2:17, 50, 51; 7:1; 9:45, 45; 18:34	2	2:15, 19	1	1:37			19
Jn.	12	3:34; 5:47; 6:63, 68; 8:20, 47; 10:21; 12:47, 48; 14:10; 15:7; 17:8									12
Ac.	13	2:14; 5:20; 6:11, 13; 10:22, 37, 44; 11:14, 16; 13:42; 16:38; 26:25; 28:25			1	5:32					14
Ro.	4	10:8, 8, 17, 18									4
2 Co.	2	12:4; 13:1									2
Eph.	2	5:26; 6:17									2
Heb.	4	1:3; 6:5; 11:3; 12:19									4
1 Pt.	2	1:25, 25									2
2 Pt.	1	3:2									1
Jd.	1	1:17									1
Rev.	1	17:17									1
Total	56		9		3		1		1		70

4389. ῥήτωρ, hre'tōr

Book	orator	Total
Ac.	24:1	1

4390. ῥητῶς, hretōs'

Book	expressly	Total
1 Ti.	4:1	1

4391. ῥίζα, hrid'za

Book	root	Total
Mt.	3:10; 13:6, 21	3
Mk.	4:6, 17; 11:20	3
Lk.	3:9; 8:13	2
Ro.	11:16, 17, 18, 18; 15:12	5
1 Ti.	6:10	1
Heb.	12:15	1
Rev.	5:5; 22:16	2
Total		17

4392. ῥιζόω, hridzo'ō

Book	root	Total
Eph.	3:17	1
Col.	2:7	1
Total		2

4393. ῥιπή, hripe'

Book	twinkling	Total
1 Co.	15:52	1

4394. ῥιπίζω, hripid'zō

Book	toss	Total
Jas.	1:6	1

4395. ῥιπτέω, hripte'ō

Book	cast off	Total
Ac.	22:23	1

4396. ῥίπτω, hrip'tō

Book	Oc.	cast down	Oc.	cast	Oc.	scatter abroad	Oc.	cast out	Oc.	throw	Total
Mt.	2	15:30; 27:5			1	9:36					3
Lk.			1	17:2					1	4:35	2
Ac.			1	27:29			1	27:19			2
Total	2		2		1		1		1		7

4397. Ῥοβοάμ, Hroboam'

Book	Roboam	Total
Mt.	1:7, 7	2

4398. Ῥόδη, Hrod'e

Book	Rhoda	Total
Ac.	12:13	1

4399. Ῥόδος, Hrod'os

Book	Rhodes	Total
Ac.	21:1	1

4400. ῥοιζηδόν, hroidzedon'

Book	with a great noise	Total
2 Pt.	3:10	1

4401. ῥομφαία, hromphai'a

Book	sword	Total
Lk.	2:35	1
Rev.	1:16; 2:12, 16; 6:8; 19:15, 21	6
Total		7

4402. Ῥουβήν, Hrouben'

Book	Reuben	Total
Rev.	7:5	1

4403. Ῥούθ, Hrouth

Book	Ruth	Total
Mt.	1:5	1

4404. Ῥοῦφος, Hrou'phos

Book	Rufus	Total
Mk.	15:21	1
Ro.	16:13	1
Total		2

4407. ῥυπαρία, hrupari'a

Book	filthiness	Total
Jas.	1:21	1

4405. ῥύμη, hru'me

Book	Oc.	street	Oc.	lane	Total
Mt.	1	6:2			1
Lk.			1	14:21	1
Ac.	2	9:11; 12:10			2
Total	3		1		4

4406. ῥύομαι, hru'omai

Book	Oc.	deliver	Oc.	Deliverer	Total
Mt.	2	6:13; 27:43			2
Lk.	2	1:74; 11:4			2
Ro.	2	7:24; 15:31	1	11:26	3
2 Co.	3	1:10, 10, 10			3
Col.	1	1:13			1
1 Th.	1	1:10			1
2 Th.	1	3:2			1
2 Ti.	3	3:11; 4:17, 18			3
2 Pt.	2	2:7, 9			2
Total	17		1		18

4408. ῥυπαρός, hruparos'

Book	vile	Total
Jas.	2:2	1

4409. ῥύπος, hru'pos

Book	filth	Total
1 Pt.	3:21	1

4410. ῥυπόω, hrupo'ō

Book	filthy	Total
Rev.	22:11, 11	2

4411. ῥύσις, hru'sis

Book	issue	Total
Mk.	5:25	1
Lk.	8:43, 44	2
Total		3

4412. ῥυτίς, hrutis'

Book	wrinkle	Total
Eph.	5:27	1

4413. Ῥωμαϊκός, Hrōmaikos'

Book	Latin	Total
Lk.	23:38	1

4414. Ῥωμαῖος, Hrōmai'os

Book	Oc.	Roman	Oc.	of Rome	Total
Jn.	1	11:48			1
Ac.	10	16:21, 37, 38; 22:25, 26, 27, 29; 23:27; 25:16; 28:17	1	2:10	11
Total	11		1		12

4415. Ῥωμαϊστί, Hrōmaisti'

Book	Latin	Total
Jn.	19:20	1

4416. Ῥώμη, Hrō'me̱

Book	Rome	Total
Ac.	18:2; 19:21; 23:11; 28:14, 16	5
Ro.	1:7, 15	2
2 Ti.	1:17	1
Total		8

4417. ῥώννυμι, hrōn'numi

Book	farewell	Total
Ac.	15:29; 23:30	2

4418. σαβαχθανί, sabachthani'

Book	sabacthani	Total
Mt.	27:46	1
Mk.	15:34	1
Total		2

4419. Σαβαώθ, Sabaōth'

Book	sabaoth	Total
Ro.	9:29	1
Jas.	5:4	1
Total		2

4420. σαββατισμός, sabbatismos'

Book	rest	Total
Heb.	4:9	1

4421. σάββατον, sab'baton

Book	Oc.	sabbath day	Oc.	sabbath	Oc.	week	Total
Mt.	8	12:1, 2, 5a, 8, 10, 11, 12; 24:20	2	12:5b; 28:1a	1	28:1b	11
Mk.	6	1:21; 2:23, 24; 3:2, 4; 6:2	4	2:27, 27, 28; 16:1	2	16:2, 9	12
Lk.	8	4:31; 6:2, 7, 9; 13:14a; 14:1, 3; 23:56	10	4:16; 6:1, 5, 6; 13:10, 14b, 15, 16; 14:5; 23:54	2	18:12; 24:1	20
Jn.	9	5:10, 16; 7:22, 23, 23; 9:14, 16; 19:31, 31	2	5:9, 18	2	20:1, 19	13
Ac.	5	1:12; 13:27, 44; 15:21; 17:2	4	13:14, 42; 16:13; 18:4	1	20:7	10
1 Co.					1	16:2	1
Col.	1	2:16					1
Total	37		22		9		68

4422. σαγήνη, sage̱'ne̱

Book	net	Total
Mt.	13:47	1

4423. Σαδδουκαῖος, Saddoukai'os

Book	Sadducees	Total
Mt.	3:7; 16:1, 6, 11, 12; 22:23, 34	7
Mk.	12:18	1
Lk.	20:27	1
Ac.	4:1; 5:17; 23:6, 7, 8	5
Total		14

4424. Σαδώκ, Sadōk'

Book	Sadoc	Total
Mt.	1:14, 14	2

4425. σαίνω, sai'nō

Book	move	Total
1 Th.	3:3	1

4426. σάκκος, sak'kos

Book	sackcloth	Total
Mt.	11:21	1
Lk.	10:13	1
Rev.	6:12; 11:3	2
Total		4

4427. Σαλά, Sala'

Book	Sala	Total
Lk.	3:35	1

4428. Σαλαθιήλ, Salathie̱l'

Book	Salathiel	Total
Mt.	1:12, 12	2
Lk.	3:27	1
Total		3

4429. Σαλαμίς, Salamis'

Book	Salamis	Total
Ac.	13:5	1

4430. Σαλείμ, Saleim'

Book	Salim	Total
Jn.	3:23	1

4431. σαλεύω, saleu'ō

Book	Oc.	shake	Oc.	move	Oc.	shake together	Oc.	that are shaken	Oc.	which cannot be shaken (with 3261)	Oc.	stir up	Total
Mt.	2	11:7; 24:29											2
Mk.	1	13:25											1
Lk.	3	6:48; 7:24; 21:26			1	6:38							4
Ac.	2	4:31; 16:26	1	2:25							1	17:13	4
2 Th.	1	2:2											1
Heb.	1	12:26					1	12:27a	1	12:27b			3
Total	10		1		1		1		1		1		15

4432. Σαλήμ, Sale̱m'

Book	Salem	Total
Heb.	7:1, 2	2

4433. Σαλμών, Salmōn'

Book	Salmon	Total
Mt.	1:4, 5	2
Lk.	3:32	1
Total		3

4434. Σαλμώνη, Salmō'ne̱

Book	Salmone	Total
Ac.	27:7	1

4435. σάλος, sal'os

Book	wave	Total
Lk.	21:25	1

4436. σάλπιγξ, sal'pingx

Book	Oc.	trumpet	Oc.	trump	Total
Mt.	1	24:31			1
1 Co.	1	14:8	1	15:52	2
1 Th.			1	4:16	1
Heb.	1	12:19			1
Rev.	6	1:10; 4:1; 8:2, 6, 13; 9:14			6
Total	9		2		11

4437. σαλπίζω, salpid'zō

Book	Oc.	sound	Oc.	sound a trumpet	Oc.	trumpet sounds	Total
Mt.			1	6:2			1
1 Co.					1	15:52	1
Rev.	10	8:6, 7, 8, 10, 12, 13; 9:1, 13; 10:7; 11:15					10
Total	10		1		1		12

4438. σαλπιστής, salpiste̱s'

Book	trumpeter	Total
Rev.	18:22	1

4439. Σαλώμη, Salō'me̱

Book	Salome	Total
Mk.	15:40; 16:1	2

4440. Σαμάρεια, Samar'eia

Book	Samaria	Total
Lk.	17:11	1
Jn.	4:4, 5, 7	3
Ac.	1:8; 8:1, 5, 9, 14; 9:31; 15:3	7
Total		11

4441. Σαμαρείτης, Samarei'te̱s

Book	Samaritans	Total
Mt.	10:5	1
Lk.	9:52; 10:33; 17:16	3
Jn.	4:9, 39, 40; 8:48	4
Ac.	8:25	1
Total		9

4442. Σαμαρεῖτις, Samarei'tis

Book	Samaria	Total
Jn.	4:9, 9	2

4443. Σαμοθράκη, Samothrak'e̱

Book	Samothracia	Total
Ac.	16:11	1

4444. Σάμος, Sam'os

Book	Samos	Total
Ac.	20:15	1

4445. Σαμουήλ, Samoue̱l'

Book	Samuel	Total
Ac.	3:24; 13:20	2
Heb.	11:32	1
Total		3

4446. Σαμψών, Sampsōn'

Book	Samson	Total
Heb.	11:32	1

4447. σανδάλιον, sandal'ion

Book	sandal	Total
Mk.	6:9	1
Ac.	12:8	1
Total		2

4448. σανίς, sanis'

Book	board	Total
Ac.	27:44	1

4449. Σαούλ, Saoul'

Book	Oc.	Saul (Paul)	Oc.	Saul (son of Cis)	Total
Ac.	8	9:4, 4, 17; 22:7, 7, 13; 26:14, 14	1	13:21	9

4450. σαπρός, sapros'

Book	Oc.	corrupt	Oc.	bad	Total
Mt.	4	7:17, 18; 12:33, 33	1	13:48	5
Lk.	2	6:43, 43			2
Eph.	1	4:29			1
Total	7		1		8

4451. Σαπφείρη, Sapphei're̱

Book	Sapphira	Total
Ac.	5:1	1

4452. σάπφειρος, sap'pheiros

Book	sapphire	Total
Rev.	21:19	1

4453. σαργάνη, sargan'ē

Book	basket	Total
2 Co.	11:33	1

4454. Σάρδεις, Sar'deis

Book	Sardis	Total
Rev.	1:11; 3:1, 4	3

4455. σάρδινος, sar'dinos

Book	sardine	Total
Rev.	4:3	1

4456. σάρδιος, sar'dios

Book	sardius	Total
Rev.	21:20	1

4457. σαρδόνυξ, sardon'ux

Book	sardonyx	Total
Rev.	21:20	1

4458. Σάρεπτα, Sar'epta

Book	Sarepta	Total
Lk.	4:26	1

4459. σαρκικός, sarkikos'

Book	Oc.	carnal	Oc.	fleshly	Total
Ro.	2	7:14; 15:27			2
1 Co.	5	3:1, 3, 3, 4; 9:11			5
2 Co.	1	10:4	1	1:12	2
Heb.	1	7:16			1
1 Pt.			1	2:11	1
Total	9		2		11

4460. σάρκινος, sar'kinos

Book	fleshly	Total
2 Co.	3:3	1

4461. σάρξ, sarx

Book	Oc.	flesh	Oc.	carnal	Oc.	carnally minded (with 5327)	Oc.	fleshly	Total
Mt.	5	16:17; 19:5, 6; 24:22; 26:41							5
Mk.	4	10:8, 8; 13:20; 14:38							4
Lk.	2	3:6; 24:39							2
Jn.	13	1:13, 14; 3:6, 6; 6:51, 52, 53, 54, 55, 56, 63; 8:15; 17:2							13
Ac.	4	2:17, 26, 30, 31							4
Ro.	25	1:3; 2:28; 3:20; 4:1; 6:19; 7:5, 18, 25; 8:1, 3, 3, 3, 4, 5, 5, 8, 9, 12, 12, 13; 9:3, 5, 8; 11:14; 13:14	1	8:7	1	8:6			27
1 Co.	11	1:26, 29; 5:5; 6:16; 7:28; 10:18; 15:39, 39, 39, 39, 50							11
2 Co.	11	1:17; 4:11; 5:16, 16; 7:1, 5; 10:2, 3, 3; 11:18; 12:7							11
Gal.	18	1:16; 2:16, 20; 3:3; 4:13, 14, 23, 29; 5:13, 16, 17, 17, 19, 24; 6:8, 8, 12, 13							18
Eph.	10	2:3, 3, 11, 11, 15; 5:29, 30, 31; 6:5, 12							10
Phl.	5	1:22, 24; 3:3, 4, 4							5
Col.	8	1:22, 24; 2:1, 5, 11, 13, 23; 3:22					1	2:18	9
1 Ti.	1	3:16							1
Phe.	1	1:16							1
Heb.	5	2:14; 5:7; 9:13; 10:20; 12:9	1	9:10					6
Jas.	1	5:3							1
1 Pt.	7	1:24; 3:18, 21; 4:1, 1, 2, 6							7
2 Pt.	2	2:10, 18							2
1 Jn.	3	2:16; 4:2, 3							3
2 Jn.	1	1:7							1
Jd.	3	1:7, 8, 23							3
Rev.	7	17:16; 19:18, 18, 18, 18, 18, 21							7
Total	147		2		1		1		151

4462. Σαρούχ, Sarouch'

Book	Saruch	Total
Lk.	3:35	1

4463. σαρόω, saro'ō

Book	sweep	Total
Mt.	12:44	1
Lk.	11:25; 15:8	2
Total		3

4464. Σάῤῥα, Sar'hra

Book	Oc.	Sarah	Oc.	Sara	Total
Ro.	2	4:19; 9:9			2
Heb.			1	11:11	1
1 Pt.			1	3:6	1
Total	2		2		4

4465. Σάρων, Sar'ōn

Book	Saron	Total
Ac.	9:35	1

4466. Σατάν, Satan'

Book	Satan	Total
2 Co.	12:7	1

4467. Σατανᾶς, Satanas'

Book	Satan	Total
Mt.	4:10; 12:26, 26; 16:23	4
Mk.	1:13; 3:23, 23, 26; 4:15; 8:33	6
Lk.	4:8; 10:18; 11:18; 13:16; 22:3, 31	6
Jn.	13:27	1
Ac.	5:3; 26:18	2
Ro.	16:20	1
1 Co.	5:5; 7:5	2
2 Co.	2:11; 11:14	2
1 Th.	2:18	1
2 Th.	2:9	1
1 Ti.	1:20; 5:15	2
Rev.	2:9, 13, 13, 24; 3:9; 12:9; 20:2, 7	8
Total		36

4468. σάτον, sat'on

Book	measure	Total
Mt.	13:33	1
Lk.	13:21	1
Total		2

4469. Σαῦλος, Sau'los

Book	Saul	Total
Ac.	7:58; 8:1, 3; 9:1, 8, 11, 19, 22, 24, 26; 11:25, 30; 12:25; 13:1, 2, 7, 9	17

4470. σβέννυμι, sben'numi

Book	Oc.	quench	Oc.	go out	Total
Mt.	1	12:20	1	25:8	2
Mk.	3	9:44, 46, 48			3
Eph.	1	6:16			1
1 Th.	1	5:19			1
Heb.	1	11:34			1
Total	7		1		8

4471. σέ, se

Book	Oc.	thee	Oc.	thou	Oc.	thy house	Oc.	Not Tr.	Total
Mt.	27	4:6; 5:25, 25, 29, 30, 39, 41, 42; 9:22; 14:28; 18:8, 9, 15, 33b; 20:13; 25:21, 23, 24, 37, 38, 39, 39, 44; 26:35, 63, 68, 73	2	18:33a; 25:27	1	26:18			30
Mk.	13	1:24; 3:32; 5:7, 19, 31, 34; 9:17, 43, 45, 47; 10:49, 52; 14:31							13
Lk.	38	1:19, 35; 2:48; 4:10, 11, 34; 6:29, 30; 7:7, 20, 50; 8:20, 45, 48; 11:27, 36; 12:58, 58, 58; 13:31; 14:9, 10, 12, 18, 19; 16:27; 17:3, 4, 4, 19; 18:42; 19:21, 22, 43, 43, 43, 44; 22:64							38
Jn.	29	1:48, 48, 50; 7:20; 8:10, 11; 10:33; 11:8, 28; 13:8; 16:30; 17:1, 3, 4, 11, 13, 25, 25; 18:26, 35; 19:10, 10; 21:15, 16, 17, 18, 20, 22, 23							29
Ac.	29	5:9; 7:27, 34, 35; 9:34; 10:19, 22, 33; 11:14; 13:11, 33, 47a; 18:10; 21:37; 22:14, 19, 21; 23:3, 18, 20, 30; 24:4a, 8, 25; 26:3, 16, 17, 17, 24	9	8:23; 9:6; 10:6; 13:47b; 23:11; 24:4b, 10; 26:29; 27:24			2	4:30; 5:3	40
Ro.	7	2:4, 27; 4:17; 9:17; 11:18, 22; 15:3	1	3:4					8
1 Co.	2	4:7; 8:10							2
Phl.	1	4:3							1
1 Ti.	3	1:3, 18; 3:14	1	6:14					4
2 Ti.	4	1:4, 6; 3:15; 4:21							4
Tit.	3	1:5; 3:12, 15	1	3:8					4
Phe.	3	1:10, 18, 23							3
Heb.	8	1:5, 9; 2:12; 5:5; 6:14, 14; 13:5, 5							8
2 Jn.	2	1:5, 13							2
3 Jn.	2	1:14, 14	1	1:2					3
Rev.	6	3:3, 3, 9, 10, 16; 15:4	1	10:11					7
Total	177		16		1		2		196

4472. σεαυτοῦ, -τῷ, -τόν or σαυτοῦ, -τῷ, -τόν, seautou', -tō', -ton', or sautou', -tō', ton'

Book	Oc.	thyself	Oc.	thine own self	Oc.	thou thyself	Oc.	thee	Oc.	thy	Total
Mt.	5	4:6; 8:4; 19:19; 22:39; 27:40									5
Mk.	3	1:44; 12:31; 15:30									3
Lk.	6	4:9, 23; 5:14; 10:27; 23:37, 39									6
Jn.	7	1:22; 7:4; 8:13, 53; 10:33; 14:22; 21:18	1	17:5							8
Ac.	2	16:28; 26:1							1	9:34	3
Ro.	4	2:1, 5, 21; 14:22			1	2:19					5
Gal.	1	6:1									1
1 Ti.	4	4:7, 16, 16; 5:22									4
2 Ti.	1	2:15					1	4:11			2
Tit.	1	2:7									1
Phe.			1	1:19							1
Jas.	1	2:8									1
Total	35		2		1		1		1		40

4473. σεβάζομαι, sebad'zomai

Book	worship	Total
Ro.	1:25	1

4475. Σεβαστός, Sebastos'

Book	Oc.	Augustus	Oc.	Augustus (adj.)	Total
Ac.	2	25:21, 25	1	27:1	3

4477. σειρά, seira'

Book	chain	Total
2 Pt.	2:4	1

4474. σέβασμα, seb'asma

Book	Oc.	devotion	Oc.	that is worshipped	Total
Ac.	1	17:23			1
2 Th.			1	2:4	1
Total	1		1		2

4476. σέβομαι, seb'omai

Book	Oc.	worship	Oc.	devout	Oc.	religious	Total
Mt.	1	15:19					1
Mk.	1	7:7					1
Ac.	4	16:14; 18:7, 13; 19:27	3	13:50; 17:4, 17	1	13:43	8
Total	6		3		1		10

4478. σεισμός, seismos'

Book	Oc.	earthquake	Oc.	tempest	Total
Mt.	3	24:7; 27:54; 28:2	1	8:24	4
Mk.	1	13:8			1
Lk.	1	21:11			1
Ac.	1	16:26			1
Rev.	7	6:12; 8:5; 11:13, 13, 19; 16:18, 18			7
Total	13		1		14

4479. σείω, sei'ō

Book	Oc.	shake	Oc.	move	Oc.	quake	Total
Mt.	1	28:4	1	21:10	1	27:51	3
Heb.	1	12:26					1
Rev.	1	6:13					1
Total	3		1		1		5

4480. Σεκοῦνδος, Sekoun'dos

Book	Secundus	Total
Ac.	20:4	1

4481. Σελεύκεια, Seleuk'eia

Book	Seleucia	Total
Ac.	13:4	1

4482. σελήνη, sele'ne

Book	moon	Total
Mt.	24:29	1
Mk.	13:24	1
Lk.	21:25	1
Ac.	2:20	1
1 Co.	15:41	1
Rev.	6:12; 8:12; 12:1; 21:23	4
Total		9

4483. σεληνιάζομαι seleniad'zomai

Book	be lunatick	Total
Mt.	4:24; 17:15	2

4485. σεμίδαλις, semid'alis

Book	fine flour	Total
Rev.	18:13	1

4484. Σεμεΐ, Semei'

Book	Semei	Total
Lk.	3:26	1

4488. Σέργιος, Serg'ios

Book	Sergius	Total
Ac.	13:7	1

4486. σεμνός, semnos'

Book	Oc.	grave	Oc.	honest	Total
Phl.			1	4:8	1
1 Ti.	2	3:8, 11			2
Tit.	1	2:2			1
Total	3		1		4

4487. σεμνότης, semnot'es

Book	Oc.	gravity	Oc.	honesty	Total
1 Ti.	1	3:4	1	2:2	2
Tit.	1	2:7			1
Total	2		1		3

4489. Σήθ, Seth

Book	Seth	Total
Lk.	3:38	1

4490. Σήμ, Sem

Book	Sem	Total
Lk.	3:36	1

4491. σημαίνω, semai'nō

Book	signify	Total
Jn.	12:33; 18:32; 21:19	3
Ac.	11:28; 25:27	2
Rev.	1:1	1
Total		6

4493. σημειόω, semeio'ō

Book	note	Total
2 Th.	3:14	1

4492. σημεῖον, semei'on

Book	Oc.	sign	Oc.	miracle	Oc.	wonder	Oc.	token	Total
Mt.	13	12:38, 39, 39, 39; 16:1, 3, 4, 4, 4; 24:3, 24, 30; 26:48							13
Mk.	7	8:11, 12, 12; 13:4, 22; 16:17, 20							7
Lk.	10	2:12, 34; 11:16, 29, 29, 29, 30; 21:7, 11, 25	1	23:8					11
Jn.	4	2:18; 4:48; 6:30; 20:30	13	2:11, 23; 3:2; 4:54; 6:2, 14, 26; 7:31; 9:16; 10:41; 11:47; 12:18, 37					17
Ac.	7	2:19, 22, 43; 4:30; 5:12; 7:36; 14:3	6	4:16, 22; 6:8; 8:6, 13; 15:12					13
Ro.	2	4:11; 15:19							2
1 Co.	2	1:22; 14:22							2
2 Co.	2	12:12, 12							2
2 Th.	1	2:9					1	3:17	2
Heb.	1	2:4							1
Rev.	1	15:1	3	13:14; 16:14; 19:20	3	12:1, 3; 13:13			7
Total	50		23		3		1		77

4494. σήμερον, sē'meron

Book	Oc.	this day	Oc.	to day	Oc.	this (with 3488)	Total
Mt.	5	6:11; 11:23; 27:8, 19; 28:15	3	6:30; 16:3; 21:28			8
Mk.	1	14:30					1
Lk.	4	2:11; 4:21; 19:9; 22:34	7	5:26; 12:28; 13:32, 33; 19:5; 23:43; 24:21			11
Ac.	9	4:9; 13:33; 19:40; 20:26; 22:3; 24:21; 26:2, 29; 27:33					9
Ro.					1	11:8	1
2 Co.	2	3:14, 15					2
Heb.	1	1:5	7	3:7, 13, 15; 4:7, 7; 5:5; 13:8			8
Jas.			1	4:13			1
Total	22		18		1		41

4495. σήπω, sē'pō

Book	be corrupted	Total
Jas.	5:2	1

4496. σηρικός, sērikos'

Book	silk	Total
Rev.	18:12	1

4497. σής, sēs

Book	moth	Total
Mt.	6:19, 20	2
Lk.	12:33	1
Total		3

4498. σητόβρωτος, sētob'rōtos

Book	motheaten	Total
Jas.	5:2	1

4499. σθενόω, stheno'ō

Book	strengthen	Total
1 Pt.	5:10	1

4500. σιαγών, siagōn'

Book	cheek	Total
Mt.	5:39	1
Lk.	6:29	1
Total		2

4501. σιγάω, siga'ō

Book	Oc.	hold (one's) peace	Oc.	keep silence	Oc.	keep close	Oc.	keep secret	Total
Lk.	1	20:26			1	9:36			2
Ac.	2	12:17; 15:13	1	15:12					3
Ro.							1	16:25	1
1 Co.	1	14:30	2	14:28, 34					3
Total	4		3		1		1		9

4502. σιγή, sigē'

Book	silence	Total
Ac.	21:40	1
Rev.	8:1	1
Total		2

4503. σιδήρεος, sidē'reos

Book	Oc.	of iron	Oc.	iron	Total
Ac.			1	12:10	1
Rev.	4	2:27; 9:9; 12:5; 19:15			4
Total	4		1		5

4504. σίδηρος, sid'ēros

Book	iron	Total
Rev.	18:12	1

4505. Σιδών, Sidōn'

Book	Sidon	Total
Mt.	11:21, 22; 15:21	3
Mk.	3:8; 7:24, 31	3
Lk.	4:26; 6:17; 10:13, 14	4
Ac.	27:3	1
Total		11

4506. Σιδώνιος, Sidō'nios

Book	Sidon	Total
Ac.	12:20	1

4507. σικάριος, sikar'ios

Book	murderer	Total
Ac.	21:38	1

4508. σίκερα, sik'era

Book	strong drink	Total
Lk.	1:15	1

4509. Σίλας, Si'las

Book	Silas	Total
Ac.	15:22, 27, 32, 34, 40; 16:19, 25, 29; 17:4, 10, 14, 15; 18:5	13

4510. Σιλουανός, Silouanos'

Book	Silvanus	Total
2 Co.	1:19	1
1 Th.	1:1	1
2 Th.	1:1	1
1 Pt.	5:12	1
Total		4

4511. Σιλωάμ, Silōam'

Book	Siloam	Total
Lk.	13:4	1
Jn.	9:7, 11	2
Total		3

4512. σιμικίνθιον, simikin'thion

Book	apron	Total
Ac.	19:12	1

4513. Σίμων, Si'mōn

Book	Oc.	Simon (Peter)	Oc.	Simon (Zelotes)	Oc.	Simon (father of Judas)	Oc.	Simon (Magus)	Oc.	Simon (the tanner)	Oc.	Simon (the Pharisee)	Oc.	Simon (of Cyrene)	Oc.	Simon (brother of Jesus)	Oc.	Simon (the leper)	Total
Mt.	5	4:18; 10:2; 16:16, 17; 17:25	1	10:4									1	27:32	1	13:55	1	26:6	9
Mk.	6	1:16, 29, 30, 36; 3:16; 14:37	1	3:18									1	15:21	1	6:3	1	14:3	10
Lk.	12	4:38, 38; 5:3, 4, 5, 8, 10, 10; 6:14; 22:31, 31; 24:34	1	6:15							3	7:40, 43, 44	1	23:26					17
Jn.	22	1:40, 41, 42; 6:8, 68; 13:6, 9, 24, 36; 18:10, 15, 25; 20:2, 6; 21:2, 3, 7, 11, 15, 15, 16, 17			4	6:71; 12:4; 13:2, 26													26
Ac.	4	10:5, 18, 32a; 11:13	1	1:13			4	8:9, 13, 18, 24	4	9:43; 10:6, 17, 32b									13
2 Pt.	1	1:1																	1
Total	50		4		4		4		4		3		3		2		2		76

4514. Σινᾶ, Sina'

Book	Oc.	Sina	Oc.	Sinai	Total
Ac.	2	7:30, 38			2
Gal.			2	4:24, 25	2
Total	2		2		4

4516. σινδών, sindōn'

Book	Oc.	linen cloth	Oc.	linen	Oc.	fine linen	Total
Mt.	1	27:59					1
Mk.	2	14:51, 52	1	15:46b	1	15:46a	4
Lk.			1	23:53			1
Total	3		2		1		6

4515. σίναπι, sin'api

Book	mustard seed	Total
Mt.	13:31; 17:20	2
Mk.	4:31	1
Lk.	13:19; 17:6	2
Total		5

4517. σινιάζω, siniad'zō

Book	sift	Total
Lk.	22:31	1

4518. σιτευτός, siteutos'

Book	fatted	Total
Lk.	15:23, 27, 30	3

4519. σιτιστός, sitistos'

Book	fatling	Total
Mt.	22:4	1

4522. Σιών, Siōn'

Book	Sion	Total
Mt.	21:5	1
Jn.	12:15	1
Ro.	9:33; 11:26	2
Heb.	12:22	1
1 Pt.	2:6	1
Rev.	14:1	1
Total		7

4520. σιτόμετρον, sitom'etron

Book	portion of meat	Total
Lk.	12:42	1

4521. σῖτος, si'tos

Book	Oc.	wheat	Oc.	corn	Total
Mt.	4	3:12; 13:25, 29, 30			4
Mk.			1	4:28	1
Lk.	3	3:17; 16:7; 22:31			3
Jn.	1	12:24			1
Ac.	1	27:38	1	7:12	2
1 Co.	1	15:37			1
Rev.	2	6:6; 18:13			2
Total	12		2		14

4523. σιωπάω, siōpa'ō

Book	Oc	hold (one's) peace	Oc.	peace	Oc.	dumb	Total
Mt.	2	20:31; 26:63					2
Mk.	4	3:4; 9:34; 10:48; 14:61	1	4:39			5
Lk.	2	18:39; 19:40			1	1:20	3
Ac.	1	18:9					1
Total	9		1		1		11

4524. σκανδαλίζω, skandalid'zō

Book	Oc.	offend	Oc.	make to offend	Total
Mt.	14	5:29, 30; 11:6; 13:21, 57; 15:12; 17:27; 18:6, 8, 9; 24:10; 26:31, 33, 33			14
Mk.	8	4:17; 6:3; 9:42, 43, 45, 47; 14:27, 29			8
Lk.	2	7:23; 17:2			2
Jn.	2	6:61; 16:1			2
Ro.	1	14:21			1
1 Co.			2	8:13, 13	2
2 Co.	1	11:29			1
Total	28		2		30

4526. σκάπτω, skap'tō

Book	dig	Total
Lk.	6:48; 13:8; 16:3	3

4528. σκέλος, skel'os

Book	leg	Total
Jn.	19:31, 32, 33	3

4527. σκάφη, skaph'e̱

Book	boat	Total
Ac.	27:16, 30, 32	3

4529. σκέπασμα, skep'asma

Book	raiment	Total
1 Ti.	6:8	1

4525. σκάνδαλον, skan'dalon

Book	Oc.	offence	Oc.	stumbling block	Oc.	occasion of stumbling	Oc.	occasion to fall	Oc.	thing that offends	Total
Mt.	4	16:23; 18:7, 7, 7							1	13:41	5
Lk.	1	17:1									1
Ro.	2	9:33; 16:17	1	11:9			1	14:13			4
1 Co.			1	1:23							1
Gal.	1	5:11									1
1 Pt.	1	2:8									1
1 Jn.					1	2:10					1
Rev.			1	2:14							1
Total	9		3		1		1		1		15

4530. Σκευᾶς, Skeuas'

Book	Sceva	Total
Ac.	19:14	1

4531. σκευή, skeue̱'

Book	tackling	Total
Ac.	27:19	1

4532. σκεῦος, skeu'os

Book	Oc.	vessel	Oc.	goods	Oc.	stuff	Oc.	sail	Total
Mt.			1	12:29					1
Mk.	1	11:16	1	3:27					2
Lk.	1	8:16			1	17:31			2
Jn.	1	19:29							1
Ac.	4	9:15; 10: 11, 16; 11: 5					1	27:17	5
Ro.	3	9:21, 22, 23							3
2 Co.	1	4:7							1
1 Th.	1	4:4							1
2 Ti.	2	2:20, 21							2
Heb.	1	9:21							1
1 Pt.	1	3:7							1
Rev.	3	2:27; 18: 12, 12							3
Total	19		2		1		1		23

4533. σκηνή, ske̱ne̱'

Book	Oc.	tabernacle	Oc.	habitation	Total
Mt.	1	17:4			1
Mk.	1	9:5			1
Lk.	1	9:33	1	16:9	2
Ac.	3	7:43, 44; 15:16			3
Heb.	10	8:2, 5; 9:2, 3, 6, 8, 11, 21; 11:9; 13: 10			10
Rev.	3	13:6; 15:5; 21:3			3
Total	19		1		20

4534. σκηνοπηγία, ske̱nope̱gi'a

Book	tabernacles	Total
Jn.	7:2	1

4535. σκηνοποιός, ske̱nopoios'

Book	tentmaker	Total
Ac.	18:3	1

4536. σκῆνος, ske̱'nos

Book	tabernacle	Total
2 Co.	5:1, 4	2

4537. σκηνόω, ske̱no'ō

Book	dwell	Total
Jn.	1:14	1
Rev.	7:15; 12:12; 13:6; 21:3	4
Total		5

4539. σκία, ski'a

Book	shadow	Total
Mt.	4:16	1
Mk.	4:32	1
Lk.	1:79	1
Ac.	5:15	1
Col.	2:17	1
Heb.	8:5; 10:1	2
Total		7

4540. σκιρτάω, skirta'ō

Book	Oc.	leap	Oc.	leap for joy	Total
Lk.	2	1:41, 44	1	6:23	3

4538. σκήνωμα, ske̱'nōma

Book	tabernacle	Total
Ac.	7:46	1
2 Pt.	1:13, 14	2
Total		3

4541. σκληροκαρδία sklērokardi'a

Book	hardness of heart	Total
Mt.	19:8	1
Mk.	10:5; 16:14	2
Total		3

4542. σκληρός, sklẹros'

Book	Oc.	hard	Oc.	fierce	Total
Mt.	1	25:24			1
Jn.	1	6:60			1
Ac.	2	9:5; 26:14			2
Jas.			1	3:4	1
Jd.	1	1:15			1
Total	5		1		6

4543. σκληρότης, sklẹrot'ẹs

Book	hardness	Total
Ro.	2:5	1

4544. σκληροτράχηλος sklẹrotrach'ẹlos

Book	stiffnecked	Total
Ac.	7:51	1

4545. σκληρύνω, sklẹru'nō

Book	harden	Total
Ac.	19:9	1
Ro.	9:18	1
Heb.	3:8, 13, 15; 4:7	4
Total		6

4546. σκολιός, skolios'

Book	Oc.	crooked	Oc.	untoward	Oc.	froward	Total
Lk.	1	3:5					1
Ac.			1	2:40			1
Phl.	1	2:15					1
1 Pt.					1	2:18	1
Total	2		1		1		4

4547. σκόλοψ, skol'ops

Book	thorn	Total
2 Co.	12:7	1

4548. σκοπέω, skope'ō

Book	Oc.	mark	Oc.	take heed	Oc.	look on	Oc.	look at	Oc.	consider	Total
Lk.			1	11:35							1
Ro.	1	16:17									1
2 Co.							1	4:18			1
Gal.									1	6:1	1
Phl.	1	3:17			1	2:4					2
Total	2		1		1		1		1		6

4549. σκοπός, skopos'

Book	mark	Total
Phl.	3:14	1

4551. σκορπίος, skorpi'os

Book	scorpion	Total
Lk.	10:19; 11:12	2
Rev.	9:3, 5, 10	3
Total		5

4550. σκορπίζω, skorpid'zō

Book	Oc.	scatter	Oc.	scatter abroad	Oc.	disperse abroad	Total
Mt.			1	12:30			1
Lk.	1	11:23					1
Jn.	2	10:12; 16:32					2
2 Co.					1	9:9	1
Total	3		1		1		5

4552. σκοτεινός, skoteinos'

Book	Oc.	full of darkness	Oc.	dark	Total
Mt.	1	6:23			1
Lk.	1	11:34	1	11:36	2
Total	2		1		3

4553. σκοτία, skoti'a

Book	Oc.	darkness	Oc.	dark	Total
Mt.	1	10:27			1
Lk.	1	12:3			1
Jn.	6	1:5, 5; 8:12; 12:35, 35, 46	2	6:17; 20:1	8
1 Jn.	6	1:5; 2:8, 9, 11, 11, 11			6
Total	14		2		16

4554. σκοτίζω, skotid'zō

Book	darken	Total
Mt.	24:29	1
Mk.	13:24	1
Lk.	23:45	1
Ro.	1:21; 11:10	2
Eph.	4:18	1
Rev.	8:12; 9:2	2
Total		8

4555. σκότος, skot'os

Book	darkness	Total
Mt.	4:16; 6:23, 23; 8:12; 22:13; 25:30; 27:45	7
Mk.	15:33	1
Lk.	1:79; 11:35; 22:53; 23:44	4
Jn.	3:19	1
Ac.	2:20; 13:11; 26:18	3
Ro.	2:19; 13:12	2
1 Co.	4:5	1
2 Co.	4:6; 6:14	2
Eph.	5:8, 11; 6:12	3
Col.	1:13	1
1 Th.	5:4, 5	2
Heb.	12:18	1
1 Pt.	2:9	1
2 Pt.	2:17	1
1 Jn.	1:6	1
Jd.	1:13	1
Total		32

4558. Σκύθης, Sku'thẹs

Book	Scythian	Total
Col.	3:11	1

4556. σκοτόω, skoto'ō

Book	full of darkness	Total
Rev.	16:10	1

4557. σκύβαλον, sku'balon

Book	dung	Total
Phl.	3:8	1

4561. σκῦλον, sku'lon

Book	spoils	Total
Lk.	11:22	1

4559. σκυθρωπός, skuthrōpos'

Book	Oc.	of a sad countenance	Oc.	sad	Total
Mt.	1	6:16			1
Lk.			1	24:17	1
Total	1		1		2

4560. σκύλλω, skul'lō

Book	Oc.	trouble	Oc.	trouble (one's) self	Total
Mk.	1	5:35			1
Lk.	1	8:49	1	7:6	2
Total	2		1		3

4562. σκωληκόβρωτος skōlẹkob'rōtos

Book	eaten of worms	Total
Ac.	12:23	1

4563. σκώληξ, skō'lẹx

Book	worm	Total
Mk.	9:44, 46, 48	3

4564. σμαράγδινος smarag'dinos

Book	emerald	Total
Rev.	4:3	1

4565. σμάραγδος, smar'agdos

Book	emerald	Total
Rev.	21:19	1

4566. σμύρνα, smur'na

Book	myrrh	Total
Mt.	2:11	1
Jn.	19:39	1
Total		2

4567. Σμύρνα, Smur'na

Book	Smyrna	Total
Rev.	1:11	1

4570. Σόδομα, Sod'oma

Book	Oc.	Sodom	Oc.	Sodoma	Total
Mt.	3	10:15; 11:23, 24			3
Mk.	1	6:11			1
Lk.	2	10:12; 17:29			2
Ro.			1	9:29	1
2 Pt.	1	2:6			1
Jd.	1	1:7			1
Rev.	1	11:8			1
Total	9		1		10

4568. Σμυρναῖος, Smurnai'os

Book	Smyrna	Total
Rev.	2:8	1

4569. σμυρνίζω, smurnid'zō

Book	mingle with myrrh	Total
Mk.	15:23	1

4571. σοί, soi

Book	Oc.	thee	Oc.	thou	Oc.	thy	Oc.	thine own	Oc.	Not Tr.	Total
Mt.	45	2:13; 4:9; 5:26, 29, 30, 40; 6:4, 6, 18, 23; 8:13, 19, 29; 9:2, 5; 11:21, 21, 23, 24, 25; 12:47; 14:4; 15:28; 16:17, 18, 19, 22, 22; 17:4; 18:8, 9, 17, 22, 26, 29, 32; 19:27; 20:14; 21:5, 23; 25:44: 26:17. 33, 34, 35	4	17:25; 22:16, 17; 27:19							49
Mk.	21	1:24; 2:5, 9, 11; 5:7, 19, 41; 6:18, 22, 23; 9:5, 25, 43, 45, 47; 10:28, 51; 11:28; 14:30, 31, 36	2	4:38; 10:21	1	5:9			1	12:14	25
Lk.	41	1:3, 13, 19, 35; 3:22; 4:6, 34; 5:20, 23, 24; 7:14, 40, 47; 8:28, 39; 9: 33, 57, 61; 10:13, 13, 21, 35; 11:7, 35; 12:59; 14:9, 10a, 10c, 12, 14a; 15:29; 18:11, 28, 41; 19:43, 44, 44; 20:2; 22:11, 34; 23:43	6	1:14; 10:36, 40; 14:10b, 14b; 18: 22	1	8:30					48
Jn.	27	1:50; 2:4; 3:3, 5, 7, 11; 4:10, 10, 26; 5:10, 12, 14; 6:30; 9:26; 11: 22, 40, 41; 13:37, 38; 17:5, 21; 18:30, 34; 19:11, 11; 21:3, 18									27
Ac.	21	3:6; 7:3; 8:20, 22; 9:5, 6, 17; 10:6, 32, 33; 16:18; 18:10; 21:23; 22:10, 10; 23:18; 24:14; 26:14, 16, 16; 27:24	2	8:21; 26:1			1	5:4			24
Ro.	3	9:17; 13:4; 15:9			1	9:7					4
1 Co.									1	7:21	1
2 Co.	2	6:2; 12:9									2
Gal.	1	3:8									1
Eph.	2	5:14; 6:3									2
1 Ti.	5	1:18; 3:14; 4:14, 14; 6:13									5
2 Ti.	4	1:5, 5, 6; 2:7									4
Tit.	1	1:5									1
Phe.	6	1:8, 11, 11, 16, 19, 21									6
Heb.	1	8:5			1	11:18					2
Jas.	1	2:18									1
2 Jn.	1	1:5									1
3 Jn.	2	1:13, 14									2
Jd.	1	1:9									1
Rev.	15	2:5, 10, 16; 3:18; 4:1; 11:17; 14:15; 17:1, 7; 18:22, 22, 22, 23, 23; 21:9									15
Total	200		14		4		1		2		221

4572. Σολομών, Solomōn′

Book	Solomon	Total
Mt.	1:6, 7; 6:29; 12:42, 42	5
Lk.	11:31, 31; 12:27	3
Jn.	10:23	1
Ac.	3:11; 5:12; 7:47	3
Total		12

4573. σορός, soros′

4574. σός, sos

Book	Oc.	thy	Oc.	thine	Oc.	thine own	Oc.	thy goods	Oc.	thy friends	Total
Mt.	5	7:22, 22, 22; 13:27; 24:3	2	20:14; 25:25	1	7:3					8
Mk.	1	2:18							1	5:19	2
Lk.			3	5:33; 15:31; 22:42			1	6:30			4
Jn.	2	4:42; 17:17	4	17:6, 9, 10, 10	1	18:35					7
Ac.	2	24:2, 4			1	5:4					3
1 Co.	2	8:11; 14:16									2
Phe.	1	1:14									1
Total	13		9		3		1		1		27

4575. σοῦ, sou

Book	Oc.	thy	Oc.	thee	Oc.	thine	Oc.	thine own	Oc.	thou	Oc.	Not Tr.	Total
Mt.	77	1:20; 4:6b, 7, 10; 5:23a, 23b, 24, 24, 24, 29a, 29c, 29d, 30a, 30c, 30d, 36, 39, 40, 43a; 6:3b, 3c, 4b, 6, 6, 6, 6, 9, 10, 10, 17b, 18, 18, 22b, 23b; 7:3, 4a, 5b; 9:2, 6a, 14, 18, 22; 11:10a, 10b, 26; 12:2, 37, 37, 47, 47; 15:2, 4, 28; 17:16; 18:8a, 8b, 15a, 15d, 33; 19:19, 19; 20:21, 21; 21:5; 22: 37, 37, 37, 37, 39, 44b; 23:37; 25:21, 23, 25; 26: 42, 52, 73	19	2:6; 3:14; 4:6a; 5:23c, 29b, 30b, 42; 6:2; 11:10c; 12:38; 17:27; 18: 8c, 9b, 15b, 15c, 16; 21:19; 26:62; 27:13	14	5:25, 33, 43b; 6:4a, 13, 17a, 22a, 23a; 7: 4b; 9:6b; 12: 13; 18:9a; 20:15; 22: 44a	2	7:4c, 5a	2	6:3a; 19:21			114
Mk.	33	1:2a, 2b, 44; 2:5, 9, 11a; 3:32, 32; 5:34, 34, 35; 6:18; 7:5, 10, 10, 29; 9:18, 38, 43, 45; 10:19, 37, 37, 37, 52; 12:30, 30, 30, 30, 30, 31, 36b; 14:70	4	1:2c; 11:14; 14: 60; 15:4	4	2:11b; 3:5; 9:47; 12: 36a					1	5:19	42
Lk.	92	1:13, 13, 36, 38, 42, 44, 61; 2:29, 29, 30, 32, 35, 48; 4:8, 11, 12, 23; 5:5, 14, 20, 23, 24a; 6:10, 29, 41, 42a, 42e; 7:27a, 27b, 48, 50; 8:20, 20, 48, 49; 9:40, 41, 49; 10:17, 21, 27, 27, 27, 27, 27, 27; 11: 2, 2, 2, 34b, 34c, 36; 12:20a; 13:26, 34; 14:12, 12, 12; 15:19, 19, 21, 21, 27, 27, 29, 30, 30, 32; 16:2b, 6, 7, 25, 25; 17:3, 19; 18:20, 20, 42; 19:5, 16, 18, 20, 39, 42a, 42b, 44, 44; 20:43b; 22:32b, 32c; 23:42, 46	11	1:28, 35; 4:10; 7: 27c; 8:28; 9:38; 12:20b; 15:18; 16:2a; 22:32a, 33	10	4:7; 5:24b; 6: 42b; 7:44; 11: 34a; 12:58; 13:12; 19:42c, 43; 20:43a	4	6:42c, 42d; 8: 39; 19: 22	1	14:8			118
Jn.	30	4:16, 18, 50, 51, 53; 5:8, 11, 12; 7:3a; 8:13, 19; 11:23; 12:15, 28; 13:37, 38; 17:1, 1, 6, 6, 12, 14, 17, 26; 18:11; 19:26, 27; 20:27, 27; 21:18	4	3:26; 9:37; 17:7, 8	5	2:17; 8:10; 9: 10, 17, 26	1	17:11	1	7:3b			41
Ac.	33	2:28, 35, 35; 3:25; 4:25, 27, 28, 28, 29, 29, 30b; 5:9; 7:3, 3, 32, 33; 8:20, 21, 22a; 9:13, 14; 10: 4a, 31a; 11:14; 12:8, 8; 14:10; 16:31; 22:16, 18, 20; 23:5; 26:16	19	8:34; 10:22; 17: 32; 18:10; 21:21, 24, 39; 23:21, 30, 35a; 24:2, 19; 25: 26; 26:2, 3; 27: 24; 28:21, 21, 22	9	2:27; 4:30a; 5:3, 4; 8:22b; 10:4b, 31b; 13:35; 23: 35b			2	17:19; 24:11			63
Ro.	16	2:5, 25; 3:4; 4:18; 8:36; 10:8b, 8c, 9a; 11:3a; 13:9; 14:10, 10, 15, 15, 21; 15:9	2	10:8a; 11:21	4	10:6, 9b; 11: 3b; 12:20							22
1 Co.	2	15:55, 55	1	12:21									3
2 Co.			1	6:2									1
Gal.	2	3:16; 5:14											2
Eph.	1	6:2											1
1 Ti.	3	4:12, 15; 5:23a	2	4:16; 6:21	1	5:23b							6
2 Ti.	5	1:4, 5, 5; 4:5, 22	1	1:3									6
Tit.			1	2:15									1
Phe.	7	1:2, 5, 6, 7a, 13, 14, 21	3	1:4, 7b, 20									10
Heb.	10	1:8, 8, 9, 9, 12, 13b; 2:7, 12; 10:7, 9			2	1:10, 13a							12
Jas.	3	2:8, 18, 18											3
2 Jn.	2	1:4, 13											2
3 Jn.	2	1:2, 6	1	1:3									3
Rev.	40	2:2, 2, 2, 4b, 5, 9, 13, 19, 19, 19; 3:1, 2, 8a, 9, 11, 15, 18a; 4:11; 5:9; 10:9, 9; 11:17, 18, 18, 18; 14:15, 18; 15:3, 3, 4a, 4c; 16:7; 18:10, 14a, 23, 23; 19:10, 10; 22:9, 9	7	2:4a, 14, 20; 3:8b; 15:4b; 18:14b, 14c	1	3:18b							48
Total	358		76		50		7		6		1		498

4576. σουδάριον, soudar'ion

Book	Oc.	napkin	Oc.	handkerchief	Total
Lk.	1	19:20			1
Jn.	2	11:44; 20:7			2
Ac.			1	19:12	1
Total	3		1		4

4577. Σουσάννα, Sousan'na

Book	Susanna	Total
Lk.	8:3	1

4578. σοφία, sophi'a

Book	wisdom	Total
Mt.	11:19; 12:42; 13:54	3
Mk.	6:2	1
Lk.	2:40, 52; 7:35; 11:31, 49; 21:15	6
Ac.	6:3, 10; 7:10, 22	4
Ro.	11:33	1
1 Co.	1:17, 19, 20, 21, 21, 22, 24, 30; 2:1, 4, 5, 6, 6, 7, 13; 3:19; 12:8	17
2 Co.	1:12	1
Eph.	1:8, 17; 3:10	3
Col.	1:9, 28; 2:3, 23; 3:16; 4:5	6
Jas.	1:5; 3:13, 15, 17	4
2 Pt.	3:15	1
Rev.	5:12; 7:12; 13:18; 17:9	4
Total		51

4579. σοφίζω, sophid'zō

Book	Oc.	make wise	Oc.	cunningly devised	Total
2 Ti.	1	3:15			1
2 Pt.			1	1:16	1
Total	1		1		2

4580. σοφός, sophos'

Book	wise	Total
Mt.	11:25; 23:34	2
Lk.	10:21	1
Ro.	1:14, 22; 16:19, 27	4
1 Co.	1:19, 20, 25, 26, 27; 3:10, 18, 18, 19, 20	10
2 Co.	6:5	1
Eph.	5:15	1
1 Ti.	1:17	1
Jas.	3:13	1
Jd.	1:25	1
Total		22

4581. Σπανία, Spani'a

Book	Spain	Total
Ro.	15:24, 28	2

4582. σπαράσσω, sparas'sō

Book	Oc.	tear	Oc.	rend	Total
Mk.	2	1:26; 9:20	1	9:26	3
Lk.	1	9:39			1
Total	3		1		4

4583. σπαργανόω, spargano'ō

Book	wrap in swaddling clothes	Total
Lk.	2:7, 12	2

4584. σπαταλάω, spatala'ō

Book	Oc.	live in pleasure	Oc.	be wanton	Total
1 Ti.	1	5:6			1
Jas.			1	5:5	1
Total	1		1		2

4585. σπάω, spa'ō

Book	Oc.	draw	Oc.	draw out	Total
Mk.	1	14:47			1
Ac.			1	16:27	1
Total	1		1		2

4586. σπεῖρα, spei'ra

Book	band	Total
Mt.	27:27	1
Mk.	15:16	1
Jn.	18:3, 12	2
Ac.	10:1; 21:31; 27:1	3
Total		7

4587. σπείρω, spei'rō

Book	Oc.	sow	Oc.	sower	Oc.	receive seed	Total
Mt.	12	6:26; 13:3b, 4, 19a, 24, 25, 27, 31, 37, 39; 25:24, 26	2	13:3a, 18	4	13:19b, 20, 22, 23	18
Mk.	10	4:3b, 4, 14b, 15, 15, 16, 18, 20, 31, 32	2	4:3a, 14a			12
Lk.	5	8:5b, 5c; 12:24; 19:21, 22	1	8:5a			6
Jn.	2	4:36, 37					2
1 Co.	8	9:11; 15:36, 37, 37, 42, 43, 43, 44					8
2 Co.	2	9:6, 6	1	9:10			3
Gal.	3	6:7, 8, 8					3
Jas.	1	3:18					1
Total	43		6		4		53

4588. σπεκουλάτωρ spekoulat'ōr

Book	executioner	Total
Mk.	6:27	1

4589. σπένδω, spen'dō

Book	Oc.	be ready to be offered	Oc.	be offered	Total
Phl.			1	2:17	1
2 Ti.	1	4:6			1
Total	1		1		2

4590. σπέρμα, sper'ma

Book	Oc.	seed	Oc.	issue	Total
Mt.	6	13:24, 27, 32, 37, 38; 22:24	1	22:25	7
Mk.	5	4:31; 12:19, 20, 21, 22			5
Lk.	2	1:55; 20:28			2
Jn.	3	7:42; 8:33, 37			3
Ac.	4	3:25; 7:5, 6; 13:23			4
Ro.	9	1:3; 4:13, 16, 18; 9:7, 7, 8, 29; 11:1			9
1 Co.	1	15:38			1
2 Co.	2	9:10; 11:22			2
Gal.	5	3:16, 16, 16, 19, 29			5
2 Ti.	1	2:8			1
Heb.	3	2:16; 11:11, 18			3
1 Jn.	1	3:9			1
Rev.	1	12:17			1
Total	43		1		44

4591. σπερμολόγος spermolog'os

Book	babbler	Total
Ac.	17:18	1

4592. σπεύδω, speu'dō

Book	Oc.	make haste	Oc.	haste	Oc.	haste unto	Oc.	with haste	Total
Lk.	2	19:5, 6					1	2:16	3
Ac.	1	22:18	1	20:16					2
2 Pt.					1	3:12			1
Total	3		1		1		1		6

4593. σπήλαιον, spe̱'laion

Book	Oc.	den	Oc.	cave	Total
Mt.	1	21:13			1
Mk.	1	11:17			1
Lk.	1	19:46			1
Jn.			1	11:38	1
Heb.	1	11:38			1
Rev.	1	6:15			1
Total	5		1		6

4594. σπιλάς, spilas'

Book	spot	Total
Jd.	1:12	1

4595. σπιλόω, spilo'ō

Book	spot	Total
Eph.	5:27	1
2 Pt.	2:13	1
Total		2

4596. σπίλος, spi'los

Book	Oc.	defile	Oc.	spot	Total
Jas.	1	3:6			1
Jd.			1	1:23	1
Total	1		1		2

4597. σπλαγχνίζομαι, splangchnid'zomai

Book	Oc.	have compassion	Oc.	be moved with compassion	Total
Mt.	2	15:32; 20:34	3	9:36; 14:14; 18:27	5
Mk.	2	8:2; 9:22	2	1:41; 6:34	4
Lk.	3	7:13; 10:33; 15:20			3
Total	7		5		12

4598. σπλάγχνον, splangch'non

Book	Oc.	bowels	Oc.	inward affection	Oc.	tender mercy (with 1656)	Total
Lk.					1	1:78	1
Ac.	1	1:18					1
2 Co.	1	6:12	1	7:15			2
Phl.	2	1:8; 2:1					2
Col.	1	3:12					1
Phe.	3	1:7, 12, 20					3
1 Jn.	1	3:17					1
Total	9		1		1		11

4599. σπόγγος, spong'gos

Book	spunge	Total
Mt.	27:48	1
Mk.	15:36	1
Jn.	19:29	1
Total		3

4600. σποδός, spodos'

Book	ashes	Total
Mt.	11:21	1
Lk.	10:13	1
Heb.	9:13	1
Total		3

4601. σπορά, spora´

Book	seed	Total
1 Pt.	1:23	1

4602. σπόριμος, spor´imos

Book	Oc.	corn field	Oc.	corn	Total
Mt.			1	12:1	1
Mk.	1	2:23			1
Lk.	1	6:1			1
Total	2		1		3

4605. σπουδαῖος, spoudai´os

Book	diligent	Total
2 Co.	8:22	1

4606. σπουδαιότερον spoudaiot´eron

Book	very diligently	Total
2 Ti.	1:17	1

4603. σπόρος, spor´os

Book	Oc.	seed	Oc.	seed sown	Total
Mk.	2	4:26, 27			2
Lk.	2	8:5, 11			2
2 Co.			1	9:10	1
Total	4		1		5

4607. σπουδαιότερος, spoudaiot´eros

Book	Oc.	more forward	Oc.	more diligent	Total
2 Co.	1	8:17	1	8:22	2

4604. σπουδάζω, spoudad´zō

Book	Oc.	endeavour	Oc.	do diligence	Oc.	be diligent	Oc.	give diligence	Oc.	be forward	Oc.	labour	Oc.	study	Total
Gal.									1	2:10					1
Eph.	1	4:3													1
1 Th.	1	2:17													1
2 Ti.			2	4:9, 21									1	2:15	3
Tit.					1	3:12									1
Heb.											1	4:11			1
2 Pt.	1	1:15			1	3:14	1	1:10							3
Total	3		2		2		1		1		1		1		11

4608. σπουδαιοτέρως spoudaioter´ōs

Book	the more carefully	Total
Phl.	2:28	1

4609. σπουδαίως, spoudai´ōs

Book	Oc.	instantly	Oc.	diligently	Total
Lk.	1	7:4			1
Tit.			1	3:13	1
Total	1		1		2

4611. σπυρίς, spuris´

Book	basket	Total
Mt.	15:37; 16:10	2
Mk.	8:8, 20	2
Ac.	9:25	1
Total		5

4610. σπουδή, spoudē´

Book	Oc.	diligence	Oc.	haste	Oc.	business	Oc.	care	Oc.	forwardness	Oc.	earnest care	Oc.	carefulness	Total
Mk.			1	6:25											1
Lk.			1	1:39											1
Ro.	1	12:8			1	12:11									2
2 Co.	1	8:7					1	7:12	1	8:8	1	8:16	1	7:11	5
Heb.	1	6:11													1
2 Pt.	1	1:5													1
Jd.	1	1:3													1
Total	5		2		1		1		1		1		1		12

4612. στάδιον or στάδιος, stad´ion or stad´ios

Book	Oc.	furlong	Oc.	race	Total
Lk.	1	24:13			1
Jn.	2	6:19; 11:18			2
1 Co.			1	9:24	1
Rev.	2	14:20; 21:16			2
Total	5		1		6

4613. στάμνος, stam´nos

Book	pot	Total
Heb.	9:4	1

4615. στατήρ, statēr´

Book	piece of money	Total
Mt.	17:27	1

4616. σταυρός, stauros´

Book	cross	Total
Mt.	10:38; 16:24; 27:32, 40, 42	5
Mk.	8:34; 10:21; 15:21, 30, 32	5
Lk.	9:23; 14:27; 23:26	3
Jn.	19:17, 19, 25, 31	4
1 Co.	1:17, 18	2
Gal.	5:11; 6:12, 14	3
Eph.	2:16	1
Phl.	2:8; 3:18	2
Col.	1:20; 2:14	2
Heb.	12:2	1
Total		28

4614. στάσις, stas´is

Book	Oc.	sedition	Oc.	dissension	Oc.	insurrection	Oc.	uproar	Oc.	standing	Total
Mk.					1	15:7					1
Lk.	2	23:19, 25									2
Ac.	1	24:5	3	15:2; 23:7, 10			1	19:40			5
Heb.									1	9:8	1
Total	3		3		1		1		1		9

4617. σταυρόω, stauro´ō

Book	crucify	Total
Mt.	20:19; 23:34; 26:2; 27:22, 23, 26, 31, 35, 38; 28:5	10
Mk.	15:13, 14, 15, 20, 24, 25, 27; 16:6	8
Lk.	23:21, 21, 23, 33; 24:7, 20	6
Jn.	19:6, 6, 6, 10, 15, 15, 16, 18, 20, 23, 41	11
Ac.	2:36; 4:10	2
1 Co.	1:13, 23; 2:2, 8	4
2 Co.	13:4	1
Gal.	3:1; 5:24; 6:14	3
Rev.	11:8	1
Total		46

4618. σταφυλή, staphulē´

Book	grapes	Total
Mt.	7:16	1
Lk.	6:44	1
Rev.	14:18	1
Total		3

4619. στάχυς, stach´us

Book	Oc.	ear of corn	Oc.	ear	Total
Mt.	1	12:1			1
Mk.	1	2:23	2	4:28, 28	3
Lk.	1	6:1			1
Total	3		2		5

4622. στέγω, steg´ō

Book	Oc.	can forbear	Oc.	bear	Oc.	suffer	Total
1 Co.			1	13:7	1	9:12	2
1 Th.	2	3:1, 5					2
Total	2		1		1		4

4620. Στάχυς, Stach´us

Book	Stachys	Total
Ro.	16:9	1

4624. στέλλω, stel´lō

Book	Oc.	avoid	Oc.	withdraw (one's) self	Total
2 Co.	1	8:20			1
2 Th.			1	3:6	1
Total	1		1		2

4623. στεῖρος, stei´ros

Book	barren	Total
Lk.	1:7, 36; 23:29	3
Gal.	4:27	1
Total		4

4621. στέγη, steg´ē

Book	roof	Total
Mt.	8:8	1
Mk.	2:4	1
Lk.	7:6	1
Total		3

4625. στέμμα, stem´ma

Book	garland	Total
Ac.	14:13	1

4626. στεναγμός, stenagmos´

Book	groaning	Total
Ac.	7:34	1
Ro.	8:26	1
Total		2

4627. στενάζω, stenad′zō

Book	Oc.	groan	Oc.	sigh	Oc.	with grief	Oc.	grudge	Total
Mk.			1	7:34					1
Ro.	1	8:23							1
2 Co.	2	5:2, 4							2
Heb.					1	13:17			1
Jas.							1	5:9	1
Total	3		1		1		1		6

4628. στενός, stenos′

Book	strait	Total
Mt.	7:13, 14	2
Lk.	13:24	1
Total		3

4629. στενοχωρέω, stenochōre′ō

Book	Oc.	straiten	Oc.	distress	Total
2 Co.	2	6:12, 12	1	4:8	3

4630. στενοχωρία, stenochōri′a

Book	Oc.	distress	Oc.	anguish	Total
Ro.	1	8:35	1	2:9	2
2 Co.	2	6:4; 12:10			2
Total	3		1		4

4631. στερεός, stereos′

Book	Oc.	strong	Oc.	sure	Oc.	stedfast	Total
2 Ti.			1	2:19			1
Heb.	2	5:12, 14					2
1 Pt.					1	5:9	1
Total	2		1		1		4

4632. στερεόω, stereo′ō

Book	Oc.	receive strength	Oc.	make strong	Oc.	establish	Total
Ac.	1	3:7	1	3:16	1	16:5	3

4633. στερέωμα, stere′ōma

Book	stedfastness	Total
Col.	2:5	1

4634. Στεφανᾶς, Stephanas′

Book	Stephanas	Total
1 Co.	1:16; 16:15, 17	3

4635. στέφανος, steph′anos

Book	crown	Total
Mt.	27:29	1
Mk.	15:17	1
Jn.	19:2, 5	2
1 Co.	9:25	1
Phl.	4:1	1
1 Th.	2:19	1
2 Ti.	4:8	1
Jas.	1:12	1
1 Pt.	5:4	1
Rev.	2:10; 3:11; 4:4, 10; 6: 2; 9:7; 12:1; 14:14	8
Total		18

4636. Στέφανος, Steph′anos

Book	Stephen	Total
Ac.	6:5, 8, 9; 7:59; 8:2; 11: 19; 22:20	7

4637. στεφανόω, stephano′ō

Book	crown	Total
2 Ti.	2:5	1
Heb.	2:7, 9	2
Total		3

4638. στῆθος, stē′thos

Book	breast	Total
Lk.	18:13; 23:48	2
Jn.	13:25; 21:20	2
Rev.	15:6	1
Total		5

4639. στήκω, stē′kō

Book	Oc.	stand fast	Oc.	stand	Total
Mk.			1	11:25	1
Ro.			1	14:4	1
1 Co.	1	16:13			1
Gal.	1	5:1			1
Phl.	2	1:27; 4:1			2
1 Th.	1	3:8			1
2 Th.	1	2:15			1
Total	6		2		8

4640. στηριγμός, stērigmos′

Book	stedfastness	Total
2 Pt.	3:17	1

4641. στηρίζω, stērid′zō

Book	Oc.	stablish	Oc.	establish	Oc.	strengthen	Oc.	fix	Oc.	stedfastly set	Total
Lk.					1	22:32	1	16:26	1	9:51	3
Ro.	1	16:25	1	1:11							2
1 Th.	1	3:13	1	3:2							2
2 Th.	2	2:17; 3:3									2
Jas.	1	5:8									1
1 Pt.	1	5:10									1
2 Pt.			1	1:12							1
Rev.					1	3:2					1
Total	6		3		2		1		1		13

4642. στίγμα, stig′ma

Book	mark	Total
Gal.	6:17	1

4643. στιγμή, stigmē′

Book	moment	Total
Lk.	4:5	1

4644. στίλβω, stil′bō

Book	shining	Total
Mk.	9:3	1

4645. στοά, stoa′

Book	porch	Total
Jn.	5:2; 10:23	2
Ac.	3:11; 5:12	2
Total		4

4646. στοιβάς, stoibas′

Book	branch	Total
Mk.	11:8	1

4647. στοιχεῖον, stoichei′on

Book	Oc.	element	Oc.	rudiment	Oc.	principle	Total
Gal.	2	4:3, 9					2
Col.			2	2:8, 20			2
Heb.					1	5:12	1
2 Pt.	2	3:10, 12					2
Total	4		2		1		7

4648. στοιχέω, stoiche′ō

Book	Oc.	walk	Oc.	walk orderly	Total
Ac.			1	21:24	1
Ro.	1	4:12			1
Gal.	2	5:25; 6:16			2
Phl.	1	3:16			1
Total	4		1		5

4649. στολή, stolē′

Book	Oc.	robe	Oc.	long clothing	Oc.	long garment	Oc.	them (with 848)	Oc.	long robe	Total
Mk.			1	12:38	1	16:5					2
Lk.	1	15:22							1	20:46	2
Rev.	4	6:11; 7:9, 13, 14a					1	7:14b			5
Total	5		1		1		1		1		9

4650. στόμα, stom′a

Book	Oc.	mouth	Oc.	face	Oc.	edge	Total
Mt.	12	4:4; 5:2; 12:34; 13:35; 15:8, 11, 11, 17, 18; 17:27; 18:16; 21:16					12
Lk.	8	1:64, 70; 4:22; 6:45; 11:54; 19:22; 21:15; 22:71			1	21:24	9
Jn.	1	19:29					1
Ac.	12	1:16; 3:18, 21; 4:25; 8:32, 35; 10:34; 11:8; 15:7; 18: 14; 22:14; 23:2					12
Ro.	6	3:14, 19; 10:8, 9, 10; 15:6					6
2 Co.	2	6:11; 13:1					2
Eph.	2	4:29; 6:19					2
Col.	1	3:8					1
2 Th.	1	2:8					1
2 Ti.	1	4:17					1
Heb.	1	11:33			1	11:34	2
Jas.	2	3:3, 10					2
1 Pt.	1	2:22					1
2 Jn.			2	1:12, 12			2
3 Jn.			2	1:14, 14			2
Jd.	1	1;16					1
Rev.	21	1:16; 2:16; 3:16; 9:17, 18, 19; 10:9, 10; 11:5; 12:15,16, 16; 13:2, 5, 6; 14:5; 16:13, 13, 13; 19:15, 21					21
Total	72		4		2		78

4651. στόμαχος, stom′achos

Book	stomach	Total
1 Ti.	5:23	1

4652. στρατεία, stratei′a

Book	warfare	Total
2 Co.	10:4	1
1 Ti.	1:18	1
Total		2

4656. στρατία, strati′a

Book	host	Total
Lk.	2:13	1
Ac.	7:42	1
Total		2

4653. στράτευμα, strat′euma

Book	Oc.	army	Oc.	man of war	Oc.	soldier	Total
Mt.	1	22:7					1
Lk.			1	23:11			1
Ac.	1	23:27			1	23:10	2
Rev.	4	9:16; 19:14, 19, 19					4
Total	6		1		1		8

4654. στρατεύομαι, strateu′omai

Book	Oc.	war	Oc.	go a warfare	Oc.	soldier	Total
Lk.					1	3:14	1
1 Co.			1	9:7			1
2 Co.	1	10:3					1
1 Ti.	1	1:18					1
2 Ti.	1	2:4					1
Jas.	1	4:1					1
1 Pt.	1	2:11					1
Total	5		1		1		7

4655. στρατηγός, strate̱gos′

Book	Oc.	captain	Oc.	magistrate	Total
Lk.	2	22:4, 52			2
Ac.	3	4:1; 5:24, 26	5	16:20, 22, 35, 36, 38	8
Total	5		5		10

4657. στρατιώτης, stratiō′te̱s

Book	soldier	Total
Mt.	8:9; 27:27; 28:12	3
Mk.	15:16	1
Lk.	7:8; 23:36	2
Jn.	19:2, 23, 23, 24, 32, 34	6
Ac.	10:7; 12:4, 6, 18; 21:32, 32, 35; 23:23, 31; 27:31, 32, 42; 28:16	13
2 Ti.	2:3	1
Total		26

4658. στρατολογέω, stratologe′ō

Book	choose to be a soldier	Total
2 Ti.	2:4	1

4659. στρατοπεδάρχης stratopedar′che̱s

Book	captain of the guard	Total
Ac.	28:16	1

4660. στρατόπεδον, stratop′edon

Book	army	Total
Lk.	21:20	1

4661. στρεβλόω, streblo′ō

Book	wrest	Total
2 Pt.	3:16	1

4663. στρηνιάω, stre̱nia′ō

Book	live deliciously	Total
Rev.	18:7, 9	2

4664. στρῆνος, stre̱′nos

Book	delicacy	Total
Rev.	18:3	1

4662. στρέφω, streph′ō

Book	Oc.	turn	Oc.	turn (one's) self	Oc.	turn (one)	Oc.	turn again	Oc.	turn back again	Oc.	turn (one) about	Oc.	be converted	Total
Mt.	2	5:39; 16:23					1	7:6					1	18:3	4
Lk.	5	7:44; 9:55; 14:25; 22:61; 23:28			1	10:23					1	7:9			7
Jn.	1	1:38	2	20:14, 16											3
Ac.	2	7:42; 13:46							1	7:39					3
Rev.	1	11:6													1
Total	11		2		1		1		1		1		1		18

4665. στρουθίον, strouthi′on

Book	sparrow	Total
Mt.	10:29, 31	2
Lk.	12:6, 7	2
Total		4

4666. στρώννυμι or στρωννύω, strōn′numi or strōnnu′ō

Book	Oc.	spread	Oc.	straw	Oc.	furnish	Oc.	make (one's) bed	Total
Mt.	1	21:8a	1	21:8b					2
Mk.	1	11:8a	1	11:8b	1	14:15			3
Lk.					1	22:12			1
Ac.							1	9:34	1
Total	2		2		2		1		7

4667. στυγητός, stuge̱tos′

Book	hateful	Total
Tit.	3:3	1

4668. στυγνάζω, stugnad′zō

Book	Oc.	lower	Oc.	be sad	Total
Mt.	1	16:3			1
Mk.			1	10:22	1
Total	1		1		2

4669. στύλος, stu′los

Book	pillar	Total
Gal.	2:9	1
1 Ti.	3:15	1
Rev.	3:12; 10:1	2
Total		4

4670. Στωϊκός, Stōikos′

Book	Stoicks	Total
Ac.	17:18	1

4671. σύ, su

Book	thou	Total
Mt.	2:6; 3:14; 6:6, 17; 11:3, 23; 14:28; 16:16, 18; 26:25, 39, 63, 64, 69, 73; 27:4, 11, 11	18
Mk.	1:11; 3:11; 8:29; 14:36, 61, 67, 68; 15:2, 2	9
Lk.	1:28, 42, 76; 3:22; 4:7, 41; 7:19, 20; 9:60; 10:15, 37; 15:31; 16:7, 25, 25; 17:8; 19:19, 42; 22:32, 58, 67, 70; 23:3, 3, 37, 39, 40; 24:18	28
Jn.	1:19, 21, 21, 25, 42, 42, 49, 49; 2:10, 20; 3:2, 10, 26; 4:9, 10, 12, 19; 6:30, 69; 7:52; 8:5, 13, 25, 33, 48, 52, 53, 53; 9:17, 28, 34, 34, 35; 10:24, 33; 11:27, 42; 12:34; 13:6, 7; 14:9; 17:5, 8, 21, 21, 23, 23, 25; 18:17, 25, 33, 34, 37, 37; 19:9; 20:15; 21:12, 15, 16, 17, 17, 22	62
Ac.	1:24; 4:24; 7:28; 9:5; 10:15, 33; 11:9, 14; 13:33; 16:31; 21:38; 22:8, 27; 23:3, 21; 25:10; 26:15	17
Ro.	2:3, 17; 9:20; 11:17, 18, 20, 22, 24; 14:4, 10, 10, 32	12
1 Co.	14:17; 15:36	2
Gal.	2:14; 6:1	2
1 Ti.	6:11	1
2 Ti.	1:18; 2:1, 3; 3:10, 14; 4:5, 15	7
Tit.	2:1	1
Phe.	1:12	1
Heb.	1:5, 10, 11, 12; 5:5, 6; 7:17, 21	8
Jas.	2:3, 3, 18, 19; 4:12	5
3 Jn.	1:3	1
Rev.	2:15; 3:17; 4:11; 7:14	4
Total		178

4672. συγγένεια, sunggen′eia

Book	kindred	Total
Lk.	1:61	1
Ac.	7:3, 14	2
Total		3

4674. συγγνώμη, sunggnō′me̱

Book	permission	Total
1 Co.	7:6	1

4673. συγγενής, sunggene̱s′

Book	Oc.	kinsman	Oc.	cousin	Oc.	kinsfolk	Oc.	kin	Total
Mk.							1	6:4	1
Lk.	1	14:12	2	1:36, 58	2	2:44; 21:16			5
Jn.	1	18:26							1
Ac.	1	10:24							1
Ro.	4	9:3; 16:7, 11, 21							4
Total	7		2		2		1		12

4675. συγκάθημαι, sungkath′e̱mai

Book	Oc.	sat (with 2258)	Oc.	sit with	Total
Mk.	1	14:54			1
Ac.			1	26:30	1
Total	1		1		2

4676. συγκαθίζω, sungkathid′zō

Book	Oc.	make sit together	Oc.	be set down together	Total
Lk.			1	22:55	1
Eph.	1	2:6			1
Total	1		1		2

4677. συγκακοπαθέω sungkakopathe′ō

Book	be partaker of affliction	Total
2 Ti.	1:8	1

4678. συγκακουχέω sungkakouche′ō

Book	suffer affliction with	Total
Heb.	11:25	1

4679. συγκαλέω, sungkale'ō

Book	call together	Total
Mk.	15:16	1
Lk.	9:1; 15:6, 9; 23:13	4
Ac.	5:21; 10:24; 28:17	3
Total		8

4680. συγκαλύπτω
sungkalup'tō

Book	cover	Total
Lk.	12:2	1

4681. συγκάμπτω, sungkamp'tō

Book	bow down	Total
Ro.	11:10	1

4682. συγκαταβαίνω
sungkatabai'nō

Book	go down with	Total
Ac.	25:5	1

4683. συγκατάθεσις
sungkatath'esis

Book	agreement	Total
2 Co.	6:16	1

4684. συγκατατίθεμαι
sungkatatith'emai

Book	consented (with 2258)	Total
Lk.	23:51	1

4685. συγκαταψηφίζω
sungkatapse̱phid'zō

Book	number	Total
Ac.	1:26	1

4686. συγκεράννυμι, sungkeran'numi

Book	Oc.	temper together	Oc.	mix with	Total
1 Co.	1	12:24			1
Heb.			1	4:2	1
Total	1		1		2

4688. συγκλείω, sungklei'ō

Book	Oc.	conclude	Oc.	inclose	Oc.	shut up	Total
Lk.			1	5:6			1
Ro.	1	11:32					1
Gal.	1	3:22			1	3:23	2
Total	2		1		1		4

4687. συγκινέω, sungkine'ō

Book	stir up	Total
Ac.	6:12	1

4689. συγκληρονόμος, sungkle̱ronom'os

Book	Oc.	fellow heir	Oc.	joint heir	Oc.	heir together	Oc.	heir with	Total
Ro.			1	8:17					1
Eph.	1	3:6							1
Heb.							1	11:9	1
1 Pt.					1	3:7			1
Total	1		1		1		1		4

4692. συγκομίζω, sungkomid'zō

Book	carry	Total
Ac.	8:2	1

4690. συγκοινωνέω, sungkoinōne'ō

Book	Oc.	have fellowship with	Oc.	communi-cate with	Oc.	be par-taker of	Total
Eph.	1	5:11					1
Phl.			1	4:14			1
Rev.					1	18:4	1
Total	1		1		1		3

4691. συγκοιωνός, sungkoinōnos'

Book	Oc.	partake with (with 1096)	Oc.	partaker with	Oc.	par-taker	Oc.	com-panion	Total
Ro.	1	11:17							1
1 Co.			1	9:23					1
Phl.					1	1:7			1
Rev.							1	1:9	1
Total	1		1		1		1		4

4693. συγκρίνω, sungkri'nō

Book	Oc.	compare with	Oc.	compare among	Total
1 Co.	1	2:13			1
2 Co.	1	10:12a	1	10:12b	2
Total	2		1		3

4694. συγκύπτω, sungkup'tō

Book	bow together	Total
Lk.	13:11	1

4695. συγκυρία, sungkuri'a

Book	chance	Total
Lk.	10:31	1

4696. συγχαίρω, sungchai'rō

Book	Oc.	rejoice with	Oc.	rejoice in	Total
Lk.	3	1:58; 15:6, 9			3
1 Co.	1	12:26	1	13:6	2
Phl.	2	2:17, 18			2
Total	6		1		7

4698. συγχράομαι
sungchra'omai

Book	have dealings with	Total
Jn.	4:9	1

4699. σύγχυσις, sung'chusis

Book	confusion	Total
Ac.	19:29	1

4697a. συγχέω, sungche'ō

Book	stir up	Total
Ac.	21:27	1

4697b. συγχύνω, sungchu'nō

Book	Oc.	confound	Oc.	confuse	Oc.	be in an uproar	Total
Ac.	2	2:6; 9:22	1	19:32	1	21:31	4

Word 4697 has 5 occurrences.

4700. συζάω, sudza'ō

Book	live with	Total
Ro.	6:8	1
2 Co.	7:3	1
2 Ti.	2:11	1
Total		3

4701. συζεύγνυμι, sudzeug'numi

Book	join together	Total
Mt.	19:6	1
Mk.	10:9	1
Total		2

4703. συζήτησις, sudze̱'te̱sis

Book	Oc.	disputation	Oc.	disputing	Oc.	reasoning	Total
Ac.	1	15:2	1	15:7	1	28:29	3

4704. συζητητής, sudze̱te̱te̱s'

Book	disputer	Total
1 Co.	1:20	1

4702. συζητέω, sudze̱te'ō

Book	Oc.	question with	Oc.	question	Oc.	question one with another	Oc.	enquire	Oc.	dispute with	Oc.	dispute	Oc.	reason together	Oc.	reason	Total
Mk.	2	8:11; 11:14	2	1:27; 9: 16	1	9:10							1	12:28			6
Lk.							1	22:23							1	24:15	2
Ac.									1	6:9	1	9:29					2
Total	2		2		1		1		1		1		1		1		10

4705. σύζυγος, sud'zugos

Book	yokefellow	Total
Phl.	4:3	1

4706. συζωοποιέω, sudzōopoie'ō

Book	Oc.	quicken together with	Oc.	quicken together	Total
Eph.	1	2:5			1
Col.			1	2:13	1
Total	1		1		2

4710. σύκον, su'kon

Book	fig	Total
Mt.	7:16	1
Mk.	11:13	1
Lk.	6:44	1
Jas.	3:12	1
Total		4

4708. συκή, suke̱'

Book	fig tree	Total
Mt.	21:19, 19, 20, 21; 24:32	5
Mk.	11:13, 20, 21; 13:28	4
Lk.	13:6, 7; 21:29	3
Jn.	1:48, 50	2
Jas.	3:12	1
Rev.	6:13	1
Total		16

4707. συκάμινος, sukam'inos

Book	sycamine tree	Total
Lk.	17:6	1

4709. συκομωραία, sukomōrai'a

Book	sycomore tree	Total
Lk.	19:4	1

4711. συκοφαντέω, sukophante'ō

Book	Oc.	accuse falsely	Oc.	take by false accusation	Total
Lk.	1	3:14	1	19:8	2

4712. συλαγωγέω, sulagōge'ō

Book	spoil	Total
Col.	2:8	1

4713. συλάω, sula'ō

Book	rob	Total
2 Co.	11:8	1

4714. συλλαλέω, sullale'ō

Book	Oc.	talk with	Oc.	talk	Oc.	speak	Oc.	commune with	Oc.	confer	Total
Mt.			1	17:3							1
Mk.	1	9:4									1
Lk.	1	9:30			1	4:36	1	22:4			3
Ac.									1	25:12	1
Total	2		1		1		1		1		6

4715. συλλαμβάνω, sullamban'ō

Book	Oc.	take	Oc.	conceive	Oc.	help	Oc.	catch	Total
Mt.	1	26:55							1
Mk.	1	14:48							1
Lk.	2	5:9; 22:54	4	1:24, 31, 36; 2:21	1	5:7			7
Jn.	1	18:12							1
Ac.	3	1:16; 12:3; 23:27					1	26:21	4
Phl.					1	4:3			1
Jas.			1	1:15					1
Total	8		5		2		1		16

4716. συλλέγω, sulleg'ō

Book	Oc.	gather	Oc.	gather up	Oc.	gather together	Total
Mt.	4	7:16; 13:40, 41, 48	2	13:28, 29	1	13:30	7
Lk.	1	6:44					1
Total	5		2		1		8

4717. συλλογίζομαι sullogid'zomai

Book	reason	Total
Lk.	20:5	1

4718. συλλυπέω, sullupe'ō

Book	be grieved	Total
Mk.	3:5	1

4719. συμβαίνω, sumbai'nō

Book	Oc.	happen unto	Oc.	happen	Oc.	befall	Oc.	so it be	Total
Mk.	1	10:32							1
Lk.			1	24:14					1
Ac.	1	3:10			1	20:19	1	21:35	3
1 Co.	1	10:11							1
1 Pt.	1	4:12							1
2 Pt.			1	2:22					1
Total	4		2		1		1		8

4720. συμβάλλω, sumbal'lō

Book	Oc.	ponder	Oc.	make	Oc.	confer	Oc.	encounter	Oc.	help	Oc.	meet with	Total
Lk.	1	2:19	1	14:31									2
Ac.					1	4:15	1	17:18	1	18:27	1	20:14	4
Total	1		1		1		1		1		1		6

4721. συμβασιλεύω sumbasileu'ō

Book	reign with	Total
1 Co.	4:8	1
2 Ti.	2:12	1
Total		2

4722. συμβιβάζω, sumbibad'zō

Book	Oc.	knit together	Oc.	prove	Oc.	assuredly gather	Oc.	instruct	Oc.	compact	Total
Ac.			1	9:22	1	16:10					2
1 Co.							1	2:16			1
Eph.									1	4:16	1
Col.	2	2:2, 19									2
Total	2		1		1		1		1		6

4723. συμβουλεύω, sumbouleu'ō

Book	Oc.	consult	Oc.	counsel	Oc.	take counsel	Oc.	give counsel	Oc.	take counsel together	Total
Mt.	1	26:4									1
Jn.							1	18:14	1	11:53	2
Ac.					1	9:23					1
Rev.			1	3:18							1
Total	1		1		1		1		1		5

4724. συμβούλιον, sumbou'lion

Book	Oc.	counsel	Oc.	council	Oc.	consultation	Total
Mt.	4	22:15; 27:1, 7; 28:12	1	12:14			5
Mk.	1	3:6			1	15:1	2
Ac.			1	25:12			1
Total	5		2		1		8

4725. σύμβουλος, sum'boulos

Book	counsellor	Total
Ro.	11:34	1

4726. Συμεών, Sumeōn'

Book	Oc.	Simeon	Oc.	Simon Peter	Total
Lk.	3	2:25, 34; 3:30			3
Ac.	2	13:1; 15:14			2
2 Pt.			1	1:1	1
Rev.	1	7:7			1
Total	6		1		7

4727. συμμαθητής summathetes'

Book	fellowdisciple	Total
Jn.	11:16	1

4728. συμμαρτυρέω, summarture'ō

Book	Oc.	also bear witness	Oc.	testify unto	Oc.	bear witness with	Total
Ro.	2	2:15; 9:1			1	8:16	3
Rev.			1	22:18			1
Total	2		1		1		4

4729. συμμερίζομαι summerid'zomai

Book	be partaker with	Total
1 Co.	9:13	1

4730. συμμέτοχος summet'ochos

Book	partaker	Total
Eph.	3:6; 5:7	2

4731. συμμιμητής, summimetes'

Book	follower together	Total
Phl.	3:17	1

4732. συμμορφός, summorphos'

Book	Oc.	conformed to	Oc.	fashioned like unto	Total
Ro.	1	8:29			1
Phl.			1	3:21	1
Total	1		1		2

4733. συμμορφόω, summorpho'ō

Book	make conformable unto	Total
Phl.	3:10	1

4734. συμπαθέω, sumpathe'ō

Book	Oc.	have compassion	Oc.	be touched with a feeling of	Total
Heb.	1	10:34	1	4:15	2

4735. συμπαθής, sumpathes'

Book	having compassion one of another	Total
1 Pt.	3:8	1

4736. συμπαραγίνομαι, sumparagin'omai

Book	Oc.	come together	Oc.	stand with	Total
Lk.	1	23:48			1
2 Ti.			1	4:16	1
Total	1		1		2

4737. συμπαρακαλέω, sumparakale'ō

Book	comfort together	Total
Ro.	1:12	1

4738. συμπαραλαμβάνω, sumparalamban'ō

Book	take with	Total
Ac.	12:25; 15:37, 38	3
Gal.	2:1	1
Total		4

4739. συμπαραμένω, sumparamen'ō

Book	continue with	Total
Phl.	1:25	1

4740. συμπάρειμι, sumpar'eimi

Book	be here present with	Total
Ac.	25:24	1

4741. συμπάσχω, sumpas'chō

Book	suffer with	Total
Ro.	8:17	1
1 Co.	12:26	1
Total		2

4742. συμπέμπω, sumpem'pō

Book	Oc.	send	Oc.	send with	Total
2 Co.	1	8:18	1	8:22	2

4743. συμπεριλαμβάνω, sumperilamban'ō

Book	embrace	Total
Ac.	20:10	1

4744. συμπίνω, sumpi'nō

Book	drink with	Total
Ac.	10:41	1

4745. συμπληρόω, sumplero'ō

Book	Oc.	fill	Oc.	be come	Oc.	be fully come	Total
Lk.	1	8:23	1	9:51			2
Ac.					1	2:1	1
Total	1		1		1		3

4746. συμπνίγω, sumpni'gō

Book	Oc.	choke	Oc.	throng	Total
Mt.	1	13:22			1
Mk.	2	4:7, 19			2
Lk.	1	8:14	1	8:42	2
Total	4		1		5

4747. συμπολίτης, sumpoli'tes

Book	fellowcitizen	Total
Eph.	2:19	1

4748. συμπορεύομαι, symporeu'omai

Book	Oc.	go with	Oc.	resort	Total
Mk.			1	10:1	1
Lk.	3	7:11; 14:25; 24:15			3
Total	3		1		4

4749. συμπόσιον, sumpos'ion

Book	company	Total
Mk.	6:39	1

4750. συμπρεσβύτερος, sumpresbu'teros

Book	also an elder	Total
1 Pt.	5:1	1

4752. σύμφημι, sum'phemi

Book	consent unto	Total
Ro.	7:16	1

4753. συμφυλέτης, sumphulet'es

Book	countryman	Total
1 Th.	2:14	1

4754. σύμφυτος, sum'phutos

Book	planted together	Total
Ro.	6:5	1

4751. συμφέρω, sumpher'ō

Book	Oc.	be expedient	Oc.	profit	Oc.	be profitable	Oc.	bring together	Oc.	be better	Oc.	be good	Total
Mt.					2	5:29, 30			1	18:6	1	19:10	4
Jn.	3	11:50; 16:7; 18:14											3
Ac.					1	20:20	1	19:19					2
1 Co.	2	6:12; 10:23	3	7:35; 10:33; 12:7									5
2 Co.	2	8:10; 12:1											2
Heb.			1	12:10									1
Total	7		4		3		1		1		1		17

4755. συμφύω, sumphu'ō

Book	spring up with	Total
Lk.	8:7	1

4756. συμφωνέω, symphōne'ō

Book	Oc.	agree	Oc.	agree with	Oc.	agree together	Total
Mt.	2	18:19; 20:2	1	20:13			3
Lk.			1	5:36			1
Ac.	1	15:15			1	5:9	2
Total	3		2		1		6

4757. συμφώνησις, sumphō'nesis

Book	concord	Total
2 Co.	6:15	1

4758. συμφωνία, sumphōni'a

Book	musick	Total
Lk.	15:25	1

4759. σύμφωνος, sum'phōnos

Book	consent	Total
1 Co.	7:5	1

4760. συμψηφίζω, sumpsephid'zō

Book	count	Total
Ac.	19:19	1

4761. σύμψυχος, sum'psuchos

Book	of one accord	Total
Phl.	2:2	1

4762. σύν, sun

Book	Oc.	with	Oc.	beside	Oc.	accompany (with 2064)	Total
Mt.	3	25:27; 26:35; 27:38					3
Mk.	5	2:26; 4:10; 8:34; 9:4; 15:27					5
Lk.	23	1:56; 2:5, 13; 5:9, 19; 7:6, 12; 8:1, 38; 9:32; 19:23; 20:1; 22:14, 56; 23:11, 32, 35; 24:1, 10, 24, 29, 33, 44	1	24:21			24
Jn.	2	18:1; 21:3					2
Ac.	50	1:14, 14, 17, 22; 2:14; 3:4, 8; 4:13, 14, 27; 5:1, 17, 21, 26; 8:20, 31; 10:2, 20, 23; 13:7; 14:4, 4, 5, 13, 20, 28; 15:22, 22, 25; 16:3; 17:34; 18:8, 18; 19:38; 20:36; 21:5, 16, 18, 24, 26, 29; 22:9; 23:15, 27, 32; 24:24; 25:23; 26:13; 27:2; 28:16			1	11:12	51
Ro.	4	6:8; 8:32; 16:14, 15					4
1 Co.	7	1:2; 5:4; 10:13; 11:32; 15:10; 16:4, 19					7
2 Co.	6	1:1, 21; 4:14; 8:19; 9:4; 13:4					6
Gal.	4	1:2; 2:3; 3:9; 5:24					4
Eph.	2	3:18; 4:31					2
Phl.	4	1:1, 23; 2:22; 4:21					4
Col.	7	2:5, 13, 20; 3:3, 4, 9; 4:9					7
1 Th.	4	4:14, 17, 17; 5:10					4
Jas.	1	1:11					1
2 Pt.	1	1:18					1
Total	123		1		1		125

4763. συνάγω, sunag'ō

Book	Oc.	gather	Oc.	be gathered together	Oc.	gather together	Oc.	come together	Oc.	be gathered	Oc.	be assembled	Oc.	take in	Oc.	Misc.	Total
Mt.	8	3:12; 6:26; 12:30; 13:30, 47; 25:24, 26; 27:27	5	13:2; 18:20; 22:41; 24:28; 27:17	2	2:4; 22:10	1	27:62	2	22:34; 25:32	2	26:57; 28:12	3	25:35, 38, 43	1	26:3	24
Mk.	1	5:21	1	2:2			1	7:1	1	4:1					1	6:30	5
Lk.	2	3:17; 11:23	1	17:37	1	15:13	1	22:66							2	12:17, 18	7
Jn.	3	4:36; 11:47; 15:6			2	6:13; 11:52					1	20:19			2	6:12; 18:2	8
Ac.			3	4:6, 27; 20:8	2	14:27; 15:30	3	13:44; 15:6; 20:7	1	4:26					2	4:31; 11:26	11
1 Co.			1	5:4													1
Rev.	1	16:14	1	19:19	2	16:16; 20:8									2	13:10; 19:17	6
Total	15		12		9		6		4		3		3		10		62

Miscellaneous: Mt. 26:3, assemble together; Mk. 6:30, gather . . . selves together; Lk. 12:17, 18, bestow; Jn. 6:12, gather up; Jn. 18:2, resort; Ac. 4:31, be assembled together; Ac. 11:26, assemble themselves; Rev. 13:10, lead into; Rev. 19:17, gather . . . selves together.

4764. συναγωγή, sunagōgē'

Book	Oc.	synagogue	Oc.	congregation	Oc.	assembly	Total
Mt.	9	4:23; 6:2, 5; 9:35; 10:17; 12:9; 13:54; 23:6, 34					9
Mk.	8	1:21, 23, 29, 39; 3:1; 6:2; 12:39; 13:9					8
Lk.	15	4:15, 16, 20, 28, 33, 38, 44; 6:6; 7:5; 8:41; 11:43; 12:11; 13:10; 20:46; 21:12					15
Jn.	2	6:59; 18:20					2
Ac.	19	6:9; 9:2, 20; 13:5, 14, 42; 14:1; 15:21; 17:1, 10, 17; 18:4, 7, 19, 26; 19:8; 22:19; 24:12; 26:11	1	13:43			20
Jas.					1	2:2	1
Rev.	2	2:9; 3:9					2
Total	55		1		1		57

4765. συναγωνίζομαι
sunagōnid'zomai

Book	strive together with	Total
Ro.	15:30	1

4766. συναθλέω, sunathle'ō

Book	Oc.	strive together for	Oc.	labour with	Total
Phl.	1	1:27	1	4:3	2

4767. συναθροίζω, sunathroid'zō

Book	Oc.	gather together	Oc.	call together	Total
Lk.	1	24:33			1
Ac.	1	12:12	1	19:25	2
Total	2		1		3

4768. συναίρω, sunai'rō

Book	Oc.	take	Oc.	reckon	Oc.	reckon (with 3056)	Total
Mt.	1	18:23	1	18:24	1	25:19	3

4769. συναιχμάλωτος
sunaichmal'ōtos

Book	fellowprisoner	Total
Ro.	16:7	1
Col.	4:10	1
Phe.	1:23	1
Total		3

4770. συνακολουθέω
sunakolouthe'ō

Book	follow	Total
Mk.	5:37	1
Lk.	23:49	1
Total		2

4771. συναλίζω, sunalid'zō

Book	assemble together	Total
Ac.	1:4	1

4772. συναναβαίνω
sunanabai'nō

Book	come up with	Total
Mk.	15:41	1
Ac.	13:31	1
Total		2

4773. συνανάκειμαι, sunanak'eimai

Book	Oc.	sit at meat with	Oc.	sit with	Oc.	sit together with	Oc.	sit down with	Oc.	sit at the table with	Total
Mt.	1	14:9					1	9:10			2
Mk.			2	6:22, 26	1	2:15					3
Lk.	3	7:49; 14:10, 15									3
Jn.									1	12:2	1
Total	4		2		1		1		1		9

4774. συναναμίγνυμι, sunanamig'numi

Book	Oc.	company with	Oc.	keep company	Oc.	have company with	Total
1 Co.	1	5:9	1	5:11			2
2 Th.					1	3:14	1
Total	1		1		1		3

4775. συναναπαύομαι
sunanapau'omai

Book	be refreshed with	Total
Ro.	15:32	1

4776. συναντάω, sunanta'ō

Book	Oc.	meet	Oc.	befall	Total
Lk.	2	9:37; 22:10			2
Ac.	1	10:25	1	20:22	2
Heb.	2	7:1, 10			2
Total	5		1		6

4777. συνάντησις, sunan'tēsis

Book	to meet (with 1519)	Total
Mt.	8:34	1

4778. συναντιλαμβάνομαι
sunantilamban'omai

Book	help	Total
Lk.	10:40	1
Ro.	8:26	1
Total		2

4779. συναπάγω, sunapag'ō

Book	Oc.	condescend	Oc.	carry away with	Oc.	lead away with	Total
Ro.	1	12:16					1
Gal.			1	2:13			1
2 Pt.					1	3:17	1
Total	1		1		1		3

4780. συναποθνήσκω, sunapothnēs'kō

Book	Oc.	die with	Oc.	be dead with	Total
Mk.	1	14:31			1
2 Co.	1	7:3			1
2 Ti.			1	2:11	1
Total	2		1		3

4781. συναπόλλυμι
sunapol'lumi

Book	perish with	Total
Heb.	11:31	1

4782. συναποστέλλω
sunapostel'lō

Book	send with	Total
2 Co.	12:18	1

4783. συναρμολογέω, sunarmologe'ō

Book	Oc.	be fitly framed together	Oc.	be fitly joined together	Total
Eph.	1	2:21	1	4:16	2

4784. συναρπάζω, sunarpad'zō

Book	catch	Total
Lk.	8:29	1
Ac.	6:12; 19:29; 27:15	3
Total		4

4785. συναυξάνω, sunauxan'ō

Book	grow together	Total
Mt.	13:30	1

4786. σύνδεσμος, sun'desmos

Book	Oc.	bond	Oc.	band	Total
Ac.	1	8:23			1
Eph.	1	4:3			1
Col.	1	3:14	1	2:19	2
Total	3		1		4

4787. συνδέω, sunde'ō

Book	bound with	Total
Heb.	13:3	1

4788. συνδοξάζω, sundoxad'zō

Book	glorify together	Total
Ro.	8:17	1

4789. σύνδουλος, sun'doulos

Book	fellowservant	Total
Mt.	18:28, 29, 31, 33; 24:49	5
Col.	1:7; 4:7	2
Rev.	6:11; 19:10; 22:9	3
Total		10

4790. συνδρομή, sundromē'

Book	run together (with 1096)	Total
Ac.	21:30	1

4791. συνεγείρω, sunegei'rō

Book	Oc.	rise with	Oc.	raise up together	Total
Eph.			1	2:6	1
Col.	2	2:12; 3:1			2
Total	2		1		3

4792. συνέδριον, suned'rion

Book	council	Total
Mt.	5:22; 10:17; 26:59	3
Mk.	13:9; 14:55; 15:1	3
Lk.	22:66	1
Jn.	11:47	1
Ac.	4:15; 5:21, 27, 34, 41; 6:12, 15; 22:30; 23:1, 6, 15, 20, 28; 24:20	14
Total		22

4793. συνείδησις, sunei'dēsis

Book	conscience	Total
Jn.	8:9	1
Ac.	23:1; 24:16	2
Ro.	2:15; 9:1; 13:5	3
1 Co.	8:7, 7, 10, 12; 10:25, 27, 28, 29, 29	9
2 Co.	1:12; 4:2; 5:11	3
1 Ti.	1:5, 19; 3:9; 4:2	4
2 Ti.	1:3	1
Tit.	1:15	1
Heb.	9:9, 14; 10:2, 22; 13:18	5
1 Pt.	2:19; 3:16, 21	3
Total		32

4794. συνείδω, sunei'dō

Book	Oc.	be privy	Oc.	consider	Oc.	be ware of	Oc.	know	Total
Ac.	1	5:2	1	12:12	1	14:6			3
1 Co.							1	4:4	1
Total	1		1		1		1		4

4795. σύνειμι, sun'eimi

Book	be with	Total
Lk.	9:18	1
Ac.	22:11	1
Total		2

4796. σύνειμι, sun'eimi

Book	gather together	Total
Lk.	8:4	1

4797. συνεισέρχομαι, suneiser'chomai

Book	Oc.	go with into	Oc.	go in with	Total
Jn.	1	6:22	1	18:15	2

4798. συνέκδημος, sunek'dēmos

Book	Oc.	companion in travel	Oc.	travel with	Total
Ac.	1	19:29			1
2 Co.			1	8:19	1
Total	1		1		2

4799. συνεκλεκτός, suneklektos'

Book	elected together with	Total
1 Pt.	5:13	1

4800. συνελαύνω, sunelau'nō

Book	set at one again (with 1515 and 1519)	Total
Ac.	7:26	1

4801. συνεπιμαρτυρέω, sunepimarture'ō

Book	also bear witness	Total
Heb.	2:4	1

4802. συνέπομαι, sunep'omai

Book	accompany	Total
Ac.	20:4	1

4803. συνεργέω, sunerge'ō

Book	Oc.	work with	Oc.	help with	Oc.	workers together	Oc.	work together	Total
Mk.	1	16:20							1
Ro.							1	8:28	1
1 Co.			1	16:16					1
2 Co.					1	6:1			1
Jas.	1	2:22							1
Total	2		1		1		1		5

4804. συνεργός, sunergos'

Book	Oc.	fellowlabourer	Oc.	helper	Oc.	fellowhelper	Oc.	fellow-worker	Oc.	work-fellow	Oc.	labourer together with	Oc.	companion in labour	Total
Ro.			2	16:3, 9					1	16:21					3
1 Co.											1	3:9			1
2 Co.			1	1:24	1	8:23									2
Phl.	1	4:3											1	2:25	2
Col.							1	4:11							1
1 Th.	1	3:2													1
Phe.	2	1:1, 24													2
3 Jn.					1	1:8									1
Total	4		3		2		1		1		1		1		13

4805. συνέρχομαι, suner'chomai

Book	Oc.	come together	Oc.	go with	Oc.	come with	Oc.	resort	Oc.	come	Oc.	come with (with 2258)	Oc.	company with	Oc.	ac-company	Oc.	assemble with	Total
Mt.	1	1:18																	1
Mk.	2	3:20; 6:33															1	14:53	3
Lk.	1	5:15									1	23:55							2
Jn.					1	11:33	1	18:20											2
Ac.	6	1:6; 2:6; 10:27; 19:32; 21:22; 28:17	4	9:39; 11:12; 15:38; 21:16	1	10:45	1	16:13	2	5:16; 25:17			1	1:21	1	10:23			16
1 Co.	8	7:5; 11:17, 18, 20, 33, 34; 14:23, 26																	8
Total	18		4		2		2		2		1		1		1		1		32

4806. συνεσθίω, sunesthi'ō

Book	eat with	Total
Lk.	15:2	1
Ac.	10:41; 11:3	2
1 Co.	5:11	1
Gal.	2:12	1
Total		5

4807. σύνεσις, sun'esis

Book	Oc.	understanding	Oc.	knowledge	Total
Mk.	1	12:33			1
Lk.	1	2:47			1
1 Co.	1	1:19			1
Eph.			1	3:4	1
Col.	2	1:9; 2:2			2
2 Ti.	1	2:7			1
Total	6		1		7

4808. συνετός, sunetos'

Book	prudent	Total
Mt.	11:25	1
Lk.	10:21	1
Ac.	13:7	1
1 Co.	1:19	1
Total		4

4809. συνευδοκέω, suneudoke'ō

Book	Oc.	consent unto	Oc.	be pleased	Oc.	allow	Oc.	have pleasure in	Total
Lk.					1	11:48			1
Ac.	2	8:1; 22:20							2
Ro.							1	1:32	1
1 Co.			2	7:12, 13					2
Total	2		2		1		1		6

4810. συνευωχέω, suneuōche'ō

Book	feast with	Total
2 Pt.	2:13	1
Jd.	1:12	1
Total		2

4811. συνεφίστημι sunephis'tēmi

Book	rise up together	Total
Ac.	16:22	1

4812. συνέχω, sunech'ō

Book	Oc.	be taken with	Oc.	throng	Oc.	straiten	Oc.	keep in	Oc.	hold	Oc.	stop	Oc.	press	Oc.	lie sick of	Oc.	con-strain	Oc.	be in a strait	Total
Mt.	1	4:24																			1
Lk.	2	4:38; 8:37	1	8:45	1	12:50	1	19:43	1	22:63											6
Ac.											1	7:57	1	18:5	1	28:8					3
2 Co.																	1	5:14			1
Phl.																			1	1:23	1
Total	3		1		1		1		1		1		1		1		1		1		12

4813. συνήδομαι, sunē'domai

Book	delight	Total
Ro.	7:22	1

4814. συνήθεια, sunē'theia

Book	custom	Total
Jn.	18:39	1
1 Co.	11:16	1
Total		2

4815. συνηλικιώτης sunēlikiō'tēs

Book	equal	Total
Gal.	1:14	1

4816. συνθάπτω, sunthap'tō

Book	bury with	Total
Ro.	6:4	1
Col.	2:12	1
Total		2

4817. συνθλάω, sunthla'ō

Book	break	Total
Mt.	21:44	1
Lk.	20:18	1
Total		2

4818. συνθλίβω, sunthli'bō

Book	throng	Total
Mk.	5:24, 31	2

4819. συνθρύπτω, sunthrup'tō

Book	break	Total
Ac.	21:13	1

4820. συνίημι, suni'ēmi

Book	Oc.	understand	Oc.	consider	Oc.	be wise	Total
Mt.	9	13:13, 14, 15, 19, 23, 51; 15:10; 16:12; 17:13					9
Mk.	4	4:12; 7:14; 8:17, 21	1	6:52			5
Lk.	4	2:50; 8:10; 18:34; 24:45					4
Ac.	4	7:25, 25; 28:26, 27					4
Ro.	2	3:11; 15:21					2
2 Co.					1	10:12	1
Eph.	1	5:17					1
Total	24		1		1		26

4821a. συνιστάω, sunista'ō

Book	Oc.	commend	Oc.	approve	Total
2 Co.	2	4:2; 10:18a	1	6:4	3

4821b. συνιστάνω, sunistan'ō

Book	commend	Total
2 Co.	3:1; 5:12; 10:12	3

4821c. συνίστημι, sunis'tēmi

Book	Oc.	commend	Oc.	approve	Oc.	consist	Oc.	make	Oc.	stand	Oc.	stand with	Total
Lk.											1	9:32	1
Ro.	3	3:5; 5:8; 16:1											3
2 Co.	2	12:11; 10:18b	1	7:11									3
Gal.							1	2:18					1
Col.					1	1:17							1
2 Pt.									1	3:5			1
Total	5		1		1		1		1		1		10

Word 4821 has 16 occurrences.

4822. συνοδεύω, sunodeu'ō

Book	journey with	Total
Ac.	9:7	1

4823. συνοδία, sunodi'a

Book	company	Total
Lk.	2:44	1

4824. συνοικέω, sunoike'ō

Book	dwell with	Total
1 Pt.	3:7	1

4825. συνοικοδομέω sunoikodome'ō

Book	build together	Total
Eph.	2:22	1

4826. συνομιλέω, sunomile'ō

Book	talk with	Total
Ac.	10:27	1

4827. συνομορέω, sunomore'ō

Book	join hard (with 2258)	Total
Ac.	18:7	1

4828. συνόχη, sunochē'

Book	Oc.	distress	Oc.	anguish	Total
Lk.	1	21:25			1
2 Co.			1	2:4	1
Total	1		1		2

4829. συντάσσω, suntas'sō

Book	appoint	Total
Mt.	26:19; 27:10	2

4830. συντέλεια, suntel'eia

Book	end	Total
Mt.	13:39, 40, 49; 24:3; 28:20	5
Heb.	9:26	1
Total		6

4831. συντελέω, suntele'ō

Book	Oc.	end	Oc.	fulfil	Oc.	finish	Oc.	make	Total
Mt.	1	7:28							1
Mk.			1	13:4					1
Lk.	2	4:2, 13							2
Ac.	1	21:27							1
Ro.					1	9:28			1
Heb.							1	8:8	1
Total	4		1		1		1		7

4832. συντέμνω, suntem'nō

Book	Oc.	cut short	Oc.	short	Total
Ro.	1	9:28a	1	9:28b	2

4833. συντηρέω, suntēre'ō

Book	Oc.	preserve	Oc.	observe	Oc.	keep	Total
Mt.	1	9:17					1
Mk.			1	6:20			1
Lk.	1	5:38			1	2:19	2
Total	2		1		1		4

4834. συντίθημι, suntith'ēmi

Book	Oc.	agree	Oc.	covenant	Oc.	assent	Total
Lk.			1	22:5			1
Jn.	1	9:22					1
Ac.	1	23:20			1	24:9	2
Total	2		1		1		4

4835. συντόμως, suntom'ōs

Book	a few words	Total
Ac.	24:4	1

4836. συντρέχω, suntrech'ō

Book	Oc.	run	Oc.	run together	Oc.	run with	Total
Mk.	1	6:33					1
Ac.			1	3:11			1
1 Pt.					1	4:4	1
Total	1		1		1		3

4838. σύντριμμα, sun'trimma

Book	destruction	Total
Ro.	3:16	1

4837. συντρίβω, suntri'bō

Book	Oc.	bruise	Oc.	break	Oc.	broken to shivers	Oc.	brokenhearted (with 2588)	Oc.	break in pieces	Total
Mt.	1	12:20									1
Mk.			1	14:3					1	5:4	2
Lk.	1	9:39					1	4:18			2
Jn.			1	19:36							1
Ro.	1	16:20									1
Rev.					1	2:27					1
Total	3		2		1		1		1		8

4839. σύντροφος, sun'trophos

Book	brought up with	Total
Ac.	13:1	1

4840. συντυγχάνω
suntungchan'ō

Book	come at	Total
Lk.	8:19	1

4841. Συντύχη, Suntu'chē

Book	Syntyche	Total
Phl.	4:2	1

4842. συνυποκρίνομαι
sunupokrin'omai

Book	dissemble with	Total
Gal.	2:13	1

4843. συνυπουργέω
sunupourge'ō

Book	help together	Total
2 Co.	1:11	1

4844. συνωδίνω, sunōdi'nō

Book	travail in pain together	Total
Ro.	8:22	1

4845. συνωμοσία, sunōmosi'a

Book	conspiracy	Total
Ac.	23:13	1

4846. Συράκουσαι, Surak'ousai

Book	Syracuse	Total
Ac.	28:12	1

4847. Συρία, Suri'a

Book	Syria	Total
Mt.	4:24	1
Lk.	2:2	1
Ac.	15:23, 41; 18:18; 20:3; 21:3	5
Gal.	1:21	1
Total		8

4848. Σύρος, Su'ros

Book	Syrian	Total
Lk.	4:27	1

4849. Συροφοίνισσα
Surophoi'nissa

Book	Syrophenician	Total
Mk.	7:26	1

4850. σύρτις, sur'tis

Book	quicksands	Total
Ac.	27:17	1

4852. συσπαράσσω, susparas'sō

Book	tear	Total
Lk.	9:42	1

4851. σύρω, su'rō

Book	Oc.	draw	Oc.	drag	Oc.	hale	Total
Jn.			1	21:8			1
Ac.	2	14:19; 17:6			1	8:3	3
Rev.	1	12:4					1
Total	3		1		1		5

4853. σύσσημον, sus'sēmon

Book	token	Total
Mk.	14:44	1

4854. σύσσωμος, sus'sōmos

Book	of the same body	Total
Eph.	3:6	1

4855. συστασιαστής
sustasiastēs'

Book	make insurrection with	Total
Mk.	15:7	1

4856. συστατικός, sustatikos'

Book	of commendation	Total
2 Co.	3:1, 1	2

4857. συσταυρόω, sustauro'ō

Book	crucify with	Total
Mt.	27:44	1
Mk.	15:32	1
Jn.	19:32	1
Ro.	6:6	1
Gal.	2:20	1
Total		5

4858. συστέλλω, sustel'lō

Book	Oc.	wind up	Oc.	short	Total
Ac.	1	5:6			1
1 Co.			1	7:29	1
Total	1		1		2

4861. συστρατιώτης
sustratiō'tēs

Book	fellowsoldier	Total
Phl.	2:25	1
Phe.	1:2	1
Total		2

4862. συστρέφω, sustreph'ō

Book	gather	Total
Ac.	28:3	1

4859. συστενάζω, sustenad'zō

Book	groan together	Total
Ro.	8:22	1

4860. συστοιχέω, sustoiche'ō

Book	answer to	Total
Gal.	4:25	1

4864. συσχηματίζω, suschēmatid'zō

Book	Oc.	conform to	Oc.	fashion (one's) self according to	Total
Ro.	1	12:2			1
1 Pt.			1	1:14	1
Total	1		1		2

4863. συστροφή, sustrophē'

Book	Oc.	concourse	Oc.	band together	Total
Ac.	1	19:40	1	23:12	2

4865. Συχάρ, Suchar'

Book	Sychar	Total
Jn.	4:5	1

4866. Συχέμ, Suchem'

Book	Oc.	Sychem (city of Ephraim)	Oc.	Sychem (son of Emmor)	Total
Ac.	1	7:16a	1	7:16b	2

4867. σφαγή, sphagē'

Book	slaughter	Total
Ac.	8:32	1
Ro.	8:36	1
Jas.	5:5	1
Total		3

4868. σφάγιον, sphag'ion

Book	slain beast	Total
Ac.	7:42	1

4869. σφάζω, sphad'zō

Book	Oc.	slay	Oc.	kill	Oc.	wound	Total
1 Jn.	2	3:12, 12					2
Rev.	6	5:6, 9, 12; 6:9; 13:8; 18:24	1	6:4	1	13:3	8
Total	8		1		1		10

4871. σφοδρῶς, sphodrōs'

Book	exceedingly	Total
Ac.	27:18	1

4870. σφόδρα, sphod'ra

Book	Oc.	exceeding	Oc.	very	Oc.	greatly	Oc.	exceedingly	Oc.	sore	Total
Mt.	3	2:10; 17:23; 26:22	1	18:31	1	27:54	1	19:25	1	17:6	7
Mk.			1	16:4							1
Lk.			1	18:23							1
Ac.					1	6:7					1
Rev.	1	16:21									1
Total	4		3		2		1		1		11

4872. σφραγίζω, sphragid'zō

Book	Oc.	seal	Oc.	set to (one's) seal	Oc.	stop	Oc.	seal up	Oc.	set a seal	Total
Mt.	1	27:66									1
Jn.	1	6:27	1	3:33							2
Ro.	1	15:28									1
2 Co.	1	1:22			1	11:10					2
Eph.	2	1:13; 4:30									2
Rev.	16	7:3, 4, 4, 5, 5, 5, 6, 6, 6, 7, 7, 7, 8, 8, 8; 22:10					1	10:4	1	20:3	18
Total	22		1		1		1		1		26

4873. σφραγίς, sphragis'

Book	seal	Total
Ro.	4:11	1
1 Co.	9:2	1
2 Ti.	2:19	1
Rev.	5:1, 2, 5, 9; 6:1, 3, 5, 7, 9, 12; 7:2; 8:1; 9:4	13
Total		16

4874. σφυρόν, sphuron'

Book	ancle bone	Total
Ac.	3:7	1

4875. σχεδόν, schedon'

Book	almost	Total
Ac.	13:44; 19:26	2
Heb.	9:22	1
Total		3

4876. σχῆμα, schē'ma

Book	fashion	Total
1 Co.	7:31	1
Phl.	2:8	1
Total		2

4877. σχίζω, schid'zō

Book	Oc.	rend	Oc.	divide	Oc.	open	Oc.	break	Oc.	make a rent	Total
Mt.	2	27:51, 51									2
Mk.	1	15:38			1	1:10					2
Lk.	1	23:45							1	5:36	2
Jn.	1	19:24					1	21:11			2
Ac.			2	14:4; 23:7							2
Total	5		2		1		1		1		10

4878. σχίσμα, schis'ma

Book	Oc.	division	Oc.	rent	Oc.	schism	Total
Mt.			1	9:16			1
Mk.			1	2:21			1
Jn.	3	7:43; 9:16; 10:19					3
1 Co.	2	1:10; 11:18			1	12:25	3
Total	5		2		1		8

4881. σχολή, scholē'

Book	school	Total
Ac.	19:9	1

4879. σχοινίον, schoini'on

Book	Oc.	small cord	Oc.	rope	Total
Jn.	1	2:15			1
Ac.			1	27:32	1
Total	1		1		2

4880. σχολάζω, scholad'zō

Book	Oc.	empty	Oc.	give (one's) self to	Total
Mt.	1	12:44			1
1 Co.			1	7:5	1
Total	1		1		2

4882. σώζω, sōd'zō

Book	Oc.	save	Oc.	make whole	Oc.	heal	Oc.	be whole	Oc.	Misc.	Total
Mt.	13	1:21; 8:25; 10:22; 14:30; 16:25; 18:11; 19:25; 24:13, 22; 27:40, 42, 42, 49	2	9:22, 22			1	9:21			16
Mk.	10	3:4; 8:35, 35; 10:26; 13:13, 20; 15:30, 31, 31; 16:16	3	5:34; 6:56; 10:52	1	5:23	1	5:28			15
Lk.	15	6:9; 7:50; 8:12; 9:24, 24, 56; 13:23; 17:33; 18:26, 42; 19:10; 23:35, 35, 37, 39	3	8:48, 50; 17:19	1	8:36					19
Jn.	5	3:17; 5:34; 10:9; 12:27, 47							1	11:12	6
Ac.	11	2:21, 47; 4:12; 11:14; 14:9; 15:1, 11; 16:30, 31; 27:20, 31	1	4:9	1	14:9			1	2:40	14
Ro.	8	5:9, 10; 8:24; 9:27; 10:9, 13; 11:14, 26									8
1 Co.	9	1:18, 21; 3:15; 5:5; 7:16, 16; 9:22; 10:33; 15:2									9
2 Co.	1	2:15									1
Eph.	2	2:5, 8									2
1 Th.	1	2:16									1
2 Th.	1	2:10									1
1 Ti.	4	1:15; 2:4, 15; 4:16									4
2 Ti.	1	1:9							1	4:18	2
Tit.	1	3:5									1
Heb.	2	5:7; 7:25									2
Jas.	5	1:21; 2:14; 4:12; 5:15, 20									5
1 Pt.	2	3:21; 4:18									2
Jd.	2	1:5, 23									2
Rev.	1	21:24									1
Total	94		9		3		2		3		111

Miscellaneous: Jn. 11:12, do well; Ac. 2:40, save (one's) self; 2 Ti. 4:18, preserve.

4883. σῶμα, sō'ma

Book	Oc.	body	Oc.	bodily	Oc.	slave	Total
Mt.	16	5:29, 30; 6:22, 22, 23, 25, 25; 10:28, 28; 14;12; 26:12, 26; 27:52, 58, 58, 59					16
Mk.	5	5:29; 14:8, 22; 15:43, 45					5
Lk.	13	11:34, 34, 34, 36; 12:4, 22, 23; 17:37; 22:19; 23:52, 55; 24:3, 23					13
Jn.	6	2:21; 19:31, 38, 38, 40; 20:12					6
Ac.	1	9:40					1
Ro.	13	1:24; 4:19; 6:6, 12; 7:4, 24; 8:10, 11, 13, 23; 12:1, 4, 5					13
1 Co.	47	5:3; 6:13, 13, 15, 16, 18, 18, 19, 20; 7:4, 4, 34; 9:27; 10:16, 17; 11:24, 27, 29; 12:12, 12, 12, 13, 14, 15, 15, 16, 16, 17, 18, 19, 20, 22, 23, 24, 25, 27; 13:3; 15:35, 37, 38, 38, 40, 40, 44, 44, 44, 44					47
2 Co.	9	4:10, 10; 5:6, 8, 10; 12:2, 2, 3, 3	1	10:10			10
Gal.	1	6:17					1
Eph.	9	1:23; 2:16; 4:4, 12, 16, 16; 5:23, 28, 30					9
Phl.	3	1:20; 3:21, 21					3
Col.	8	1:18, 22, 24; 2:11, 17, 19, 23; 3:15					8
1 Th.	1	5:23					1
Heb.	5	10:5, 10, 22; 13:3, 11					5
Jas.	5	2:16, 26; 3:2, 3, 6					5
1 Pt.	1	2:24					1
Jd.	1	1:9					1
Rev.					1	18:13	1
Total	144		1		1		146

4884. σωματικός, sōmatikos'

Book	bodily	Total
Lk.	3:22	1
1 Ti.	4:8	1
Total		2

4885. σωματικῶς, sōmatikōs'

Book	bodily	Total
Col.	2:9	1

4886. Σώπατρος, Sō'patros

Book	Sopater	Total
Ac.	20:4	1

4890. σωτήρ, sōtēr'

Book	Saviour	Total
Lk.	1:47; 2:11	2
Jn.	4:42	1
Ac.	5:31; 13:23	2
Eph.	5:23	1
Phl.	3:20	1
1 Ti.	1:1; 2:3; 4:10	3
2 Ti.	1:10	1
Tit.	1:3, 4; 2:10, 13; 3:4, 6	6
2 Pt.	1:1, 11; 2:20; 3:2, 18	5
1 Jn.	4:14	1
Jd.	1:25	1
Total		24

4887. σωρεύω, sōreu'ō

Book	Oc.	heap	Oc.	lade	Total
Ro.	1	12:20			1
2 Ti.			1	3:6	1
Total	1		1		2

4888. Σωσθένης, Sōsthen'ēs

Book	Sosthenes	Total
Ac.	18:17	1
1 Co.	1:1	1
Total		2

4889. Σωσίπατρος, Sōsip'atros

Book	Sosipater	Total
Ro.	16:21	1

4892a. σωτήριον, sōtē'rion

Book	salvation	Total
Lk.	2:30; 3:6	2
Ac.	28:28	1
Eph.	6:17	1
Total		4

4892b. σωτήριος, sōtē'rios

Book	that brings salvation	Total
Tit.	2:11	1

Word 4892 has 5 occurrences.

4894. σωφρονίζω, sōphronid'zō

Book	teach to be sober	Total
Tit.	2:4	1

4891. σωτηρία, sōtēri'a

Book	Oc.	salvation	Oc.	that (one) be saved	Oc.	deliver (with 1325)	Oc.	health	Oc.	saving	Oc.	that (one) be saved (with 1519)	Total
Lk.	3	1:69, 77; 19:9	1	1:71									4
Jn.	1	4:22											1
Ac.	4	4:12; 13:26, 47; 16:17			1	7:25	1	27:34					6
Ro.	4	1:16; 10:10; 11:11; 13:11									1	10:1	5
2 Co.	5	1:6, 6; 6:2, 2; 7:10											5
Eph.	1	1:13											1
Phl.	3	1:19, 28; 2:12											3
1 Th.	2	5:8, 9											2
2 Th.	1	2:13											1
2 Ti.	2	2:10; 3:15											2
Heb.	6	1:14; 2:3, 10; 5:9; 6:9; 9:28							1	11:7			7
1 Pt.	3	1:5, 9, 10											3
2 Pt.	1	3:15											1
Jd.	1	1:3											1
Rev.	3	7:10; 12:10; 19:1											3
Total	40		1		1		1		1		1		45

4893. σωφρονέω, sōphrone'ō

Book	Oc.	be in right mind	Oc.	be sober	Oc.	be sober minded	Oc.	soberly	Total
Mk.	1	5:15							1
Lk.	1	8:35							1
Ro.							1	12:3	1
2 Co.			1	5:13					1
Tit.					1	2:6			1
1 Pt.			1	4:7					1
Total	2		2		1		1		6

4895. σωφρονισμός, sōphronismos'

Book	sound mind	Total
2 Ti.	1:7	1

4896. σωφρόνως, sōphron'ōs

Book	soberly	Total
Tit.	2:12	1

4897. σωφροσύνη, sōphrosu'nē

Book	Oc.	sobriety	Oc.	soberness	Total
Ac.			1	26:25	1
1 Ti.	2	2:9, 15			2
Total	2		1		3

4898. σώφρων, sō'phrōn

Book	Oc.	sober	Oc.	temperate	Oc.	discreet	Total
1 Ti.	1	3:2					1
Tit.	1	1:8	1	2:2	1	2:5	3
Total	2		1		1		4

4899. Ταβέρναι, Taber'nai

Book	taverns	Total
Ac.	28:15	1

4900. Ταβιθά, Tabitha'

Book	Tabitha	Total
Ac.	9:36, 40	2

4901. τάγμα, tag'ma

Book	order	Total
1 Co.	15:23	1

4902. τακτός, taktos'

Book	set	Total
Ac.	12:21	1

4903. ταλαιπωρέω, talaipōre'ō

Book	be afflicted	Total
Jas.	4:9	1

4904. ταλαιπωρία, talaipōri'a

Book	misery	Total
Ro.	3:16	1
Jas.	5:1	1
Total		2

4905. ταλαίπωρος, talai'pōros

Book	wretched	Total
Ro.	7:24	1
Rev.	3:17	1
Total		2

4906. ταλαντιαῖος, talantiai'os

Book	weight of a talent	Total
Rev.	16:21	1

4907. τάλαντον, tal'anton

Book	talent	Total
Mt.	18:24; 25:15, 16, 16, 20, 20, 20, 20, 22, 22, 22, 24, 25, 28, 28	15

4908. ταλιθά, talitha'

Book	Talitha	Total
Mk.	5:41	1

4910. τάξις, tax'is

Book	order	Total
Lk.	1:8	1
1 Co.	14:40	1
Col.	2:5	1
Heb.	5:6, 10; 6:20; 7:11, 11, 17, 21	7
Total		10

4909. ταμεῖον, tamei'on

Book	Oc.	closet	Oc.	secret chamber	Oc.	storehouse	Total
Mt.	1	6:6	1	24:26			2
Lk.	1	12:3			1	12:24	2
Total	2		1		1		4

4911. ταπεινός, tapeinos'

Book	Oc.	of low degree	Oc.	humble	Oc.	base	Oc.	cast down	Oc.	of low estate	Oc.	lowly	Total
Mt.											1	11:29	1
Lk.	1	1:52											1
Ro.									1	12:16			1
2 Co.					1	10:1	1	7:6					2
Jas.	1	1:9	1	4:6									2
1 Pt.			1	5:5									1
Total	2		2		1		1		1		1		8

4912. ταπεινοφροσύνη, tapeinophrosu'nē

Book	Oc.	humility	Oc.	humbleness of mind	Oc.	humility of mind	Oc.	lowliness	Oc.	lowliness of mind	Total
Ac.					1	20:19					1
Eph.							1	4:2			1
Phl.									1	2:3	1
Col.	2	2:18, 23	1	3:12							3
1 Pt.	1	5:5									1
Total	3		1		1		1		1		7

4913. ταπεινόω, tapeino'ō

Book	Oc.	humble	Oc.	abase	Oc.	humble (one's) self	Oc.	bring low	Total
Mt.	2	18:4; 23:12b	1	23:12a					3
Lk.	2	14:11b; 18:14b	2	14:11a; 18:14a			1	3:5	5
2 Co.	1	12:21	1	11:7					2
Phl.	1	2:8	1	4:12					2
Jas.					1	4:10			1
1 Pt.					1	5:6			1
Total	6		5		2		1		14

4914. ταπείνωσις, tapei'nōsis

Book	Oc.	low estate	Oc.	humiliation	Oc.	vile	Oc.	be made low	Total
Lk.	1	1:48							1
Ac.			1	8:33					1
Phl.					1	3:21			1
Jas.							1	1:10	1
Total	1		1		1		1		4

4915. ταράσσω, taras'sō

Book	trouble	Total
Mt.	2:3; 14:26	2
Mk.	6:50	1
Lk.	1:12; 24:38	2
Jn.	5:4, 7; 11:33; 12:27; 13:21; 14:1, 27	7
Ac.	15:24; 17:8	2
Gal.	1:7; 5:10	2
1 Pt.	3:14	1
Total		17

4916. ταραχή, tarachē'

Book	Oc.	trouble	Oc.	troubling	Total
Mk.	1	13:8			1
Jn.			1	5:4	1
Total	1		1		2

4917. τάραχος, tar'achos

Book	stir	Total
Ac.	12:18; 19:23	2

4918. Ταρσεύς, Tarseus'

Book	Tarsus	Total
Ac.	9:11; 21:39	2

4919. Ταρσός, Tarsos'

Book	Tarsus	Total
Ac.	9:30; 11:25; 22:3	3

4920. ταρταρόω, tartaro'ō

Book	cast down to hell	Total
2 Pt.	2:4	1

4921. τάσσω, tas'sō

Book	Oc.	appoint	Oc.	ordain	Oc.	set	Oc.	determine	Oc.	addict	Total
Mt.	1	28:16									1
Lk.					1	7:8					1
Ac.	2	22:10; 28:23	1	13:48			1	15:2			4
Ro.			1	13:1							1
1 Co.									1	16:15	1
Total	3		2		1		1		1		8

4922. ταῦρος, taur'os

Book	Oc.	ox	Oc.	bull	Total
Mt.	1	22:4			1
Ac.	1	14:13			1
Heb.			2	9:13; 10:4	2
Total	2		2		4

See page 338 for Word 4923.

4924. ταὐτά, tauta'

(Nominative or Accusative Neuter Plural of Words 3488 and 846 as Adverb)

Book	Oc.	like	Oc.	like manner	Oc.	so	Oc.	even thus	Total
Lk.			1	6:23	1	6:26	1	17:30	3
1 Th.	1	2:14							1
Total	1		1		1		1		4

4925a. ταύταις, tau'tais

(Dative Feminine Plural of Word 3678)

Book	Oc.	these	Oc.	those	Oc.	them	Oc.	that	Total
Mt.	1	22:40							1
Lk.	1	24:18	2	1:39; 6:12	1	13:14	1	23:7	5
Jn.	1	5:3							1
Ac.	1	11:27	2	1:15; 6:1					3
1 Th.	1	3:3							1
Rev.	1	9:20							1
Total	6		4		1		1		12

4925b. ταύτας, tau'tas

(Accusative Feminine Plural of Word 3678)

Book	Oc.	these	Oc.	those	Oc.	hence	Total
Mt.	1	13:53					1
Mk.	1	13:2					1
Lk.			1	1:24			1
Ac.	1	3:24	1	21:15	1	1:5	3
2 Co.	1	7:1					1
Heb.	1	9:23					1
Rev.	1	16:9					1
Total	6		2		1		9

Word 4925 has 21 occurrences.

4926a. ταύτῃ, tau'tē

(Dative Feminine Singular of Word 3678)

Book	Oc.	this	Oc.	that	Oc.	the same	Oc.	this same	Oc.	it	Total
Mt.	5	10:23; 12:45; 16:18; 26:31, 34									5
Mk.	4	8:12, 38; 14:27, 30									4
Lk.	6	11:30; 12:20; 13:7; 16:24; 17:6; 19:42	2	13:32; 17:34							8
Ac.	3	18:10; 22:3; 27:23	1	16:12							4
1 Co.	2	9:12; 15:19			1	7:20					3
2 Co.	5	1:15; 8:7, 19, 20; 11:17					1	9:4			6
Heb.									1	11:2	1
Total	25		3		1		1		1		31

4926b. ταύτην, tau′tēn

(Accusative Feminine Singular of Word 3678)

Book	Oc.	this	Oc.	the same	Oc.	that	Oc.	it	Oc.	by reason hereof (with 1223)	Oc.	her	Oc.	the	Total
Mt.	4	11:16; 15:15; 21:23; 23:36													4
Mk.	4	4:13; 10:5; 11:28; 12:10													4
Lk.	12	4:6, 23; 7:44; 12:41; 13:6, 16; 15:3; 18:5, 9; 20:2, 9, 19			1	23:48							1	24:21	14
Jn.	6	2:11; 7:8, 8; 10:6, 18; 12:27													6
Ac.	11	1:16; 3:16; 7:4, 60; 8:19; 22:4, 28; 23:13; 27:21; 28:20, 20	1	13:33											12
Ro.	1	5:2													1
1 Co.							1	6:13							1
2 Co.	2	4:1; 12:13	2	8:6; 9:5											4
1 Ti.	1	1:18													1
2 Ti.	1	2:19													1
Heb.									1	5:3					1
1 Pt.	1	5:12													1
2 Pt.	2	1:18; 3:1													2
1 Jn.	2	3:3; 4:21													2
2 Jn.	1	1:10													1
Rev.	1	2:24									1	12:15			2
Total	49		3		1		1		1		1		1		57

4926c. ταύτης, tau′tēs

(Genitive Feminine Singular of Word 3678)

Book	Oc.	this	Oc.	thereby (with 1223)	Oc.	same	Total
Mt.	2	12:41, 42					2
Lk.	6	7:31; 11:31, 32, 50, 51; 17:25					6
Jn.	3	10:16; 12:27; 15:13					3
Ac.	16	1:17, 25; 2:6, 29, 40; 5:20; 6:3; 8:22; 10:30; 13:26; 19:25, 40; 23:1; 24:21; 26:22; 28:22			1	8:35	17
2 Co.	2	9:12, 13					2
Heb.	1	9:11	2	12:15; 13:2			3
Rev.	1	22:19					1
Total	31		2		1		34

Word 4926 has 122 occurrences.

4923. ταῦτα, tau′ta

(Nominative or Accusative Neuter Plural of Word 3678)

Book	Oc.	these things	Oc.	these	Oc.	thus	Oc.	that	Oc.	these words	Oc.	this	Oc.	afterward (with 3226)	Oc.	Misc.	Total
Mt.	18	1:20; 4:9; 6:32, 33; 9:18; 11:25; 13:34, 51, 56; 19:20; 21:23, 24, 27; 23:36; 24:2, 3, 33, 34	4	10:2; 15:20; 23:23; 24:8													22
Mk.	11	2:8; 6:2; 7:23; 11:28, 28, 29, 33; 13:4, 4, 29, 30	3	10:20; 13:8; 16:17			1	16:12									15
Lk.	33	1:20; 4:28; 5:27; 7:9; 8:8; 10:1, 21; 11:27, 53; 12:30, 31; 13:17; 14:6, 15, 21; 15:26; 16:14; 18:22; 19:11; 20:2, 8; 21:6, 7, 7, 9, 31, 36; 23:31, 49; 24:9, 10, 21, 26	6	1:19, 65; 2:19, 51; 11:42; 18:21	6	9:34; 11:45; 18:11; 19:28; 23:46; 24:36	1	12:4			1	18:23	2	17:8; 18:4			49
Jn.	37	1:28; 2:16, 18; 3:9, 10, 22; 5:16, 34; 6:1, 59; 7:1, 4; 8:28; 11:11; 12:16, 16, 16, 36, 41; 13:17; 14:25; 15:11, 17, 21; 16:1, 3. 4, 4, 6, 25, 33; 17:13; 19:24, 36; 20:18; 21:1, 24	5	3:2; 5:19; 8:20; 10:21; 20:31	5	9:6; 11:43; 13:21; 18:22; 20:14			6	7:9; 8:30; 9:22, 40; 17:1; 18:1	2	5:1; 19:38	1	5:14	6	6:9; 7:32; 8:26; 10:25; 11:28; 13:7	62
Ac.	18	1:9; 5:5, 11; 7:1, 50, 54; 11:18; 12:17; 14:15; 15:17; 17:8, 20; 18:1; 19:21; 21:12; 23:22; 24:9, 22	4	10:44; 13:42; 14:18; 16:38	5	19:41; 20:36; 26:24, 30; 27:35	2	7:7; 13:20	1	28:29	1	15:16			1	17:11	32
Ro.	1	8:31	1	9:8													2
1 Co.	6	4:6, 14; 9:8a, 15; 10:6, 11	2	12:11; 13:13			1	6:8							3	6:11, 13; 9:8b	12
2 Co.	2	2:16; 13:10															2
Gal.			1	5:17a											2	2:18; 5:17b	3
Eph.	1	5:6															1
Phl.	1	4:8													2	3:7; 4:9	3
2 Th.	1	2:5															1
1 Ti.	8	3:14; 4:6, 11, 15; 5:7, 21, 6:2, 11															8
2 Ti.	2	1:12; 2:14													1	2:2	3
Tit.	2	2:15; 3:8															2
Heb.	1	7:13											1	4:8	1	11:12	3
Jas.	1	3:10															1
1 Pt.															1	1:11	1
2 Pt.	3	1:8, 9, 10													1	3:14	4
1 Jn.	4	1:4; 2:1, 26; 5:13															4
Rev.	8	7:1; 18:1; 19:1; 22:8, 8, 16, 18, 20			1	16:5	2	15:5; 20:3			2	4:1a; 7:9			4	1:19; 4:1b; 9:12; 10:4	17
Total	158		26		17		7		7		6		4		22		247

Miscellaneous: Jn. 6:9, they; Jn. 7:32, such things; Jn. 8:26, those things; Jn. 10:25, they; Jn. 11:28, so; Jn. 13:7 (with 3226), hereafter; Ac. 17:11, those things; 1 Co. 6:11, such; 1 Co. 6:13, them; 1 Co. 9:8b, the same; Gal. 2:18; 5:17b, the things; Phl. 3:7, those; Phl. 4:9, those things; 2 Ti. 2:2, the same; Heb. 11:12, him; 1 Pt. 1:11 (with 3226), that should follow; 2 Pt. 3:14, such things; Rev. 1:19; 4:1b; 9:12 (with 3226), hereafter; Rev. 10:4, them.

4927. ταφή, taphe̜′

Book	to bury (with 1519)	Total
Mt.	27:7	1

4931. ταχινός, tachinos′

Book	Oc.	shortly	Oc.	swift	Total
2 Pt.	1	1:14	1	2:1	2

4933. τάχιστα, tach′ista

Book	with all speed (with 5513)	Total
Ac.	17:15	1

4928. τάφος, taph′os

Book	Oc.	sepulchre	Oc.	tomb	Total
Mt.	5	23:27; 27:61, 64, 66; 28:1	1	23:29	6
Ro.	1	3:13			1
Total	6		1		7

4929. τάχα, tach′a

Book	Oc.	peradventure	Oc.	perhaps	Total
Ro.	1	5:7			1
Phe.			1	1:15	1
Total	1		1		2

4930. ταχέως, tache′ōs

Book	Oc.	shortly	Oc.	quickly	Oc.	soon	Oc.	hastily	Oc.	suddenly	Total
Lk.			2	14:21; 16:6							2
Jn.							1	11:31			1
1 Co.	1	4:19									1
Gal.					1	1:6					1
Phl.	2	2:19, 24									2
2 Th.					1	2:2					1
1 Ti.									1	5:22	1
2 Ti.	1	4:9									1
Total	4		2		2		1		1		10

4932. τάχιον, tach′ion

Book	Oc.	shortly	Oc.	quickly	Oc.	outrun (with 4290)	Oc.	the sooner	Total
Jn.			1	13:27	1	20:4			2
1 Ti.	1	3:14							1
Heb.	1	13:23					1	13:19	2
Total	2		1		1		1		5

4936. ταχύς, tachus′

Book	swift	Total
Jas.	1:19	1

4934. τάχος, tach′os

Book	Oc.	shortly (with 1722)	Oc.	quickly (with 1722)	Oc.	speedily (with 1722)	Total
Lk.					1	18:8	1
Ac.	1	25:4	2	12:7; 22:18			3
Ro.	1	16:20					1
Rev.	2	1:1; 22:6					2
Total	4		2		1		7

4935. ταχύ, tachu′

Book	Oc.	quickly	Oc.	lightly	Total
Mt.	3	5:25; 28:7, 8			3
Mk.	1	16:8	1	9:39	2
Jn.	1	11:29			1
Rev.	7	2:5, 16; 3:11; 11:14; 22:7, 12, 20			7
Total	12		1		13

4937. τε, te

Book	Oc.	and	Oc.	both	Oc.	then	Oc.	whether	Oc.	even	Oc.	also	Oc.	Not Tr.	Total
Mt.	3	23:6; 27:48; 28:12	1	22:10											4
Mk.	1	15:36													1
Lk.	6	2:16; 12:45; 21:11, 11; 22: 66; 24:20											1	23:12	7
Jn.	3	2:15; 4:42; 6:18													3
Ac.	97	2:3, 9, 33, 37, 40, 43, 46, 46; 3:10; 4:13, 33; 5:19, 35, 42; 6:7, 12, 13; 7:26; 8:1, 3, 6, 13, 25, 31; 9:6, 15, 18, 24a; 10:22, 28, 33, 48; 11:13, 21, 26; 12:6, 8, 12; 13:1b, 4; 14: 12, 21; 15:4, 5, 39; 16:11, 12, 13, 23, 26, 34; 17:4, 4, 5, 19, 26; 18:4, 11, 26; 19:3, 6, 11, 12, 18, 29; 20:3, 7, 11, 35; 21:11, 18, 20, 28, 30, 37; 22: 7, 8, 28; 23:10, 24, 35; 24:5, 23, 23, 27; 26:10, 11, 16b, 20, 30; 27:3, 5, 8, 17, 20, 21, 43	19	1:1, 8, 13; 4:27; 5: 14; 8:12, 38; 10: 39; 14:1, 5; 19:10; 20:21; 21:12; 22: 4; 24:15; 25:24; 26:16a, 22a; 28: 23b	2	23:5; 27:29	1	9:2					22	1:15; 2:10, 10; 5:24; 8:28; 9:24b, 29; 10: 2; 13:1a, 2; 15:9; 17:10, 14; 18:5; 19: 17; 21:25; 24:3; 25:23; 26:3, 22b; 27:1; 28:23a	141
Ro.	4	1:27; 2:19; 14:8b; 16:26	4	1:12, 14, 14; 3:9					1	1:26			9	1:16, 20; 2:9, 10; 7: 7; 10:12; 14:8a, 8c, 8d	18
1 Co.	2	1:30; 4:21	2	1:2, 24											4
2 Co.													1	10:8	1
Eph.	1	3:19	1	1:10											2
Phl.			1	1:7											1
Heb.	9	1:3; 4:12b; 6:2, 2, 4, 5; 9:1; 11:32a; 12:2	8	2:4, 11; 5:1, 14; 6: 19; 9:9, 19; 10:33							1	11:32b	4	4:12a; 5:7; 8:3; 9:2	22
Jas.	1	3:7b											1	3:7a	2
Jd.	1	1:6													1
Rev.	2	1:2; 21:12													2
Total	130		36		2		1		1		1		38		209

4941. τεκνογονέω, teknogone′ō

Book	bear children	Total
1 Ti.	5:14	1

4938. τεῖχος, tei′chos

Book	wall	Total
Ac.	9:25	1
2 Co.	11:33	1
Heb.	11:30	1
Rev.	21:12, 14, 15, 17, 18, 19	6
Total		9

4940. τεκνίον, tekni′on

Book	little children	Total
Jn.	13:33	1
Gal.	4:19	1
1 Jn.	2:1, 12, 28; 3:7, 18; 4: 4; 5:21	7
Total		9

4939. τεκμήριον, tekme̜′rion

Book	infallible proof	Total
Ac.	1:3	1

4942. τεκνογονία, teknogoni′a

Book	childbearing	Total
1 Ti.	2:15	1

4943. τέκνον, tek′non

Book	Oc.	child	Oc.	son	Oc.	daughter	Total
Mt.	12	2:18; 3:9; 7:11; 10:21, 21; 11:19; 15:26; 18: 25; 19:29; 22:24; 23: 37; 27:25	3	9:2; 21:28, 28			15
Mk.	7	7:27, 27; 10:24, 29, 30; 12:19; 13:12b	2	2:5; 13: 12a			9
Lk.	11	1:7, 17; 3:8; 7:35; 11: 13; 13:34; 14:26; 18: 29; 19:44; 20:31; 23: 28	3	2:48; 15: 31; 16:25			14
Jn.	2	8:39; 11:52	1	1:12			3
Ac.	5	2:39; 7:5; 13:33; 21: 5, 21					5
Ro.	7	8:16, 17, 21; 9:7, 8, 8, 8					7
1 Co.	1	7:14	2	4:14, 17			3
2 Co.	3	6:13; 12:14, 14					3
Gal.	4	4:25, 27, 28, 31					4
Eph.	5	2:3; 5:1, 8; 6:1, 4					5
Phl.			2	2:15, 22			2
Col.	2	3:20, 21					2
1 Th.	2	2:7, 11					2
1 Ti.	3	3:4, 12; 5:4	2	1:2, 18			5
2 Ti.			2	1:2; 2:1			2
Tit.	1	1:6	1	1:4			2
Phe.			1	1:10			1
1 Pt.	1	1:14			1	3:6	2
2 Pt.	1	2:14					1
1 Jn.	3	3:10, 10; 5:2	2	3:1, 2			5
2 Jn.	3	1:1, 4, 13					3
3 Jn.	1	1:4					1
Rev.	3	2:23; 12:4, 5					3
Total	77		21		1		99

4944. τεκνοτροφέω teknotrophe′ō

Book	bring up children	Total
1 Ti.	5:10	1

4945. τέκτων, tek′tōn

Book	carpenter	Total
Mt.	13:55	1
Mk.	6:3	1
Total		2

4946. τέλειος, tel′eios

Book	Oc.	perfect	Oc.	man	Oc.	of full age	Total
Mt.	3	5:48, 48; 19:21					3
Ro.	1	12:2					1
1 Co.	2	2:6; 13:10	1	14:20			3
Eph.	1	4:13					1
Phl.	1	3:15					1
Col.	2	1:28; 4:12					2
Heb.	1	9:11			1	5:14	2
Jas.	5	1:4, 4, 17, 25; 3:2					5
1 Jn.	1	4:18					1
Total	17		1		1		19

4947. τελειότης, teleiot′ẹs

Book	Oc.	perfectness	Oc.	perfection	Total
Col.	1	3:14			1
Heb.			1	6:1	1
Total	1		1		2

4948. τελειόω, teleio′ō

Book	Oc.	make perfect	Oc.	perfect	Oc.	finish	Oc.	fulfil	Oc.	be perfect	Oc.	consecrate	Total
Lk.			1	13:32			1	2:43					2
Jn.	1	17:23			3	4:34; 5:36; 17:4	1	19:28					5
Ac.					1	20:24							1
2 Co.	1	12:9											1
Phl.									1	3:12			1
Heb.	7	2:10; 5:9; 7:19; 9:9; 10:1; 11:40; 12:23	1	10:14							1	7:28	9
Jas.	1	2:22											1
1 Jn.	2	2:17, 18	2	2:5; 4:12									4
Total	12		4		4		2		1		1		24

4949. τελείως, telei′ōs

Book	to the end	Total
1 Pt.	1:13	1

4951. τελειωτής, teleiōtẹs′

Book	finisher	Total
Heb.	12:2	1

4952. τελεσφορέω, telesphore′ō

Book	bring fruit to perfection	Total
Lk.	8:14	1

4954. τελευτή, teleutẹ′

Book	death	Total
Mt.	2:15	1

4950. τελείωσις, telei′ōsis

Book	Oc.	performance	Oc.	perfection	Total
Lk.	1	1:45			1
Heb.			1	7:11	1
Total	1		1		2

4953. τελευτάω, teleuta′ō

Book	Oc.	die	Oc.	be dead	Oc.	decease	Total
Mt.	1	15:4	2	2:19; 9:18	1	22:25	4
Mk.	4	7:10; 9:44, 46, 48					4
Lk.	1	7:2					1
Ac.	1	7:15	1	2:29			2
Heb.	1	11:22					1
Total	8		3		1		12

4955. τελέω, tele′ō

Book	Oc.	finish	Oc.	fulfil	Oc.	accomplish	Oc.	pay	Oc.	perform	Oc.	expire	Oc.	Misc.	Total
Mt.	3	13:53; 19:1; 26:1					1	17:24					2	10:23; 11:1	6
Lk.					3	12:50; 18:31; 22: 37			1	2:39					4
Jn.	1	19:30			1	19:28									2
Ac.			1	13:29											1
Ro.			1	2:27			1	13:6							2
Gal.			1	5:16											1
2 Ti.	1	4:7													1
Jas.			1	2:8											1
Rev.	3	10:7; 11:7; 20:5	3	15:8; 17:17; 20:3							1	20:7	1	15:1	8
Total	8		7		4		2		1		1		3		26

Miscellaneous: Mt. 10:23, go over; Mt. 11:1, make an end; Rev. 15:1, fill up.

4956. τέλος, tel'os

Book	Oc.	end	Oc.	custom	Oc.	uttermost	Oc.	finally	Oc.	ending	Oc.	by (one's) continual (with 1519)	Total
Mt.	5	10:22; 24:6, 13, 14; 26:58	1	17:25									6
Mk.	3	3:26; 13:7, 13											3
Lk.	3	1:33; 21:9; 22:37									1	18:5	4
Jn.	1	13:1											1
Ro.	3	6:21, 22; 10:4	2	13:7, 7									5
1 Co.	3	1:8; 10:11; 15:24											3
2 Co.	3	1:13; 3:13; 11:15											3
Phl.	1	3:19											1
1 Th.					1	2:16							1
1 Ti.	1	1:5											1
Heb.	5	3:6, 14; 6:8, 11; 7:3											5
Jas.	1	5:11											1
1 Pt.	3	1:9; 4:7, 17					1	3:8					4
Rev.	3	2:26; 21:6; 22:13							1	1:8			4
Total	35		3		1		1		1		1		42

4957. τελώνης, telō'nēs

Book	publican	Total
Mt.	5:46, 47; 9:10, 11; 10: 3; 11:19; 18:17; 21:31, 32	9
Mk.	2:15, 16, 16	3
Lk.	3:12; 5:27, 29, 30; 7:29, 34; 15:1; 18:10, 11, 13	10
Total		22

4958. τελώνιον, telō'nion

Book	receipt of custom	Total
Mt.	9:9	1
Mk.	2:14	1
Lk.	5:27	1
Total		3

4959. τέρας, ter'as

Book	wonder	Total
Mt.	24:24	1
Mk.	13:22	1
Jn.	4:48	1
Ac.	2:19, 22, 43; 4:30; 5:12; 6:8; 7:36; 14:3; 15:12	9
Ro.	15:19	1
2 Co.	12:12	1
2 Th.	2:9	1
Heb.	2:4	1
Total		16

4960. Τέρτιος, Ter'tios

Book	Tertius	Total
Ro.	16:22	1

4961. Τέρτυλλος, Ter'tullos

Book	Tertullus	Total
Ac.	24:1, 2	2

4962. τεσσαράκοντα tessarak'onta

Book	forty	Total
Mt.	4:2, 2	2
Mk.	1:13	1
Lk.	4:2	1
Jn.	2:20	1
Ac.	1:3; 4:22; 7:30, 36, 42; 13:21; 23:13, 21	8
2 Co.	11:24	1
Heb.	3:9, 17	2
Rev.	7:4; 11:2; 13:5; 14:1, 3; 21:17	6
Total		22

4963. τεσσαρακονταετής, tessarakontaetēs'

Book	Oc.	forty years old	Oc.	of forty years	Total
Ac.	1	7:23	1	13:18	2

4964. τέσσαρες, τέσσαρα tes'sares, tes'sara

Book	four	Total
Mt.	24:31	1
Mk.	2:3; 13:27	2
Lk.	2:37	1
Jn.	11:17; 19:23	2
Ac.	10:11; 11:5; 12:4; 21:9, 23; 27:29	6
Rev.	4:4, 4, 6, 8, 10; 5:6, 8, 8, 14, 14; 6:1, 6; 7:1, 1, 1, 2, 4, 11; 9:13, 14, 15; 11:16; 14:1, 3, 3; 15:7; 19:4, 4; 20:8; 21:17	30
Total		42

4965. τασσαρεσκαιδέκατος tessareskaidek'atos

Book	fourteenth	Total
Ac.	27:27, 33	2

4966. τεταρταῖος, tetartai'os

Book	four days	Total
Jn.	11:39	1

4967. τέταρτος, tet'artos

Book	Oc.	fourth	Oc.	four	Total
Mt.	1	14:25			1
Mk.	1	6:48			1
Ac.			1	10:30	1
Rev.	7	4:7; 6:7, 7, 8; 8:12; 16:8; 21:19			7
Total	9		1		10

4968. τετράγωνος, tetrag'ōnos

Book	foursquare	Total
Rev.	21:16	1

4969. τετράδιον, tetrad'ion

Book	quaternion	Total
Ac.	12:4	1

4970. τετρακισχίλιοι tetrakischil'ioi

Book	four thousand	Total
Mt.	15:38; 16:10	2
Mk.	8:9, 20	2
Ac.	21:38	1
Total		5

4971. τετρακόσιοι, tetrakos'ioi

Book	four hundred	Total
Ac.	5:36; 7:6; 13:20	3
Gal.	3:17	1
Total		4

4972. τετράμηνον, tetram'ēnon

Book	four months	Total
Jn.	4:35	1

4973. τετραπλόος, tetraplo'os

Book	fourfold	Total
Lk.	19:8	1

4974. τετράπους, tetrap'ous

Book	fourfooted beast	Total
Ac.	10:12; 11:6	2
Ro.	1:23	1
Total		3

4975. τετραρχέω, tetrarche'ō

Book	Oc.	tetrarch	Oc.	be tetrarch	Total
Lk.	2	3:1b, 1c	1	3:1a	3

4976. τετράρχης, tetrar'chēs

Book	tetrarch	Total
Mt.	14:1	1
Lk.	3:19; 9:7	2
Ac.	13:1	1
Total		4

4977. τεφρόω, tephro'ō

Book	turn into ashes	Total
2 Pt.	2:6	1

4978. τέχνη, tech'nē

Book	Oc.	art	Oc.	occupation	Oc.	craft	Total
Ac.	1	17:29	1	18:3			2
Rev.					1	18:22	1
Total	1		1		1		3

4979. τεχνίτης, techni'tēs

Book	Oc.	craftsman	Oc.	builder	Total
Ac.	2	19:24, 38			2
Heb.			1	11:10	1
Rev.	1	18:22			1
Total	3		1		4

4980. τήκω, tē'kō

Book	melt	Total
2 Pt.	3:12	1

4981. τηλαυγῶς, tēlaugōs'

Book	clearly	Total
Mk.	8:25	1

4982. τηλικοῦτος, tēlikou'tos

Book	Oc.	so great	Oc.	so mighty	Total
2 Co.	1	1:10			1
Heb.	1	2:3			1
Jas.	1	3:4			1
Rev.			1	16:18	1
Total	3		1		4

4983. τηρέω, te̱re′ō

Book	Oc.	keep	Oc.	reserve	Oc.	observe	Oc.	watch	Oc.	preserve	Oc.	keeper	Oc.	hold fast	Total
Mt.	1	19:17			3	23:3, 3; 28: 20	2	27:36, 54			1	28:4			7
Mk.	1	7:9													1
Jn.	18	2:10; 8:51, 52, 55; 9:16; 12:7; 14:15, 21, 23, 24; 15:10, 10, 20, 20; 17:6, 11, 12, 15													18
Ac.	8	12:5, 6; 15:5, 24; 16:23; 24: 23; 25:4, 21b	1	25:21a	1	21:25									10
1 Co.	1	7:37													1
2 Co.	2	11:9, 9													2
Eph.	1	4:3													1
1 Th.									1	5:23					1
1 Ti.	2	5:22; 6:14													2
2 Ti.	1	4:7													1
Jas.	2	1:27; 2:10													2
1 Pt.			1	1:4											1
2 Pt.			4	2:4, 9, 17; 3:7											4
1 Jn.	8	2:3, 4, 5; 3:22, 24; 5:2, 3, 18													8
Jd.	2	1:6a, 21	2	1:6b, 13					1	1:1					5
Rev.	10	1:3; 2:26; 3:8, 10, 10; 12:17; 14:12; 16:15; 22:7, 9											1	3:3	11
Total	57		8		4		2		2		1		1		75

4984. τήρησις, te̱′re̱sis

Book	Oc.	hold	Oc.	prison	Oc.	keeping	Total
Ac.	1	4:3	1	5:18			2
1 Co.					1	7:19	1
Total	1		1		1		3

4985. Τιβεριάς, Tiberias′

Book	Tiberias	Total
Jn.	6:1, 23; 21:1	3

4986. Τιβέριος, Tiber′ios

Book	Tiberius	Total
Lk.	3:1	1

4987. τίθημι, tith′e̱mi

Book	Oc.	lay	Oc.	put	Oc.	lay down	Oc.	make	Oc.	appoint	Oc.	kneel down (with 1119 and 3488)	Oc.	Misc.	Total
Mt.	1	27:60	3	5:15; 12:18; 14:3			1	22:44	1	24:51					6
Mk.	4	6:29, 56; 15:47; 16:6	2	4:21; 10:16			1	12:36					1	15:19	8
Lk.	5	5:18; 6:48; 14:29; 23: 53, 55	2	8:16; 11:33	2	19:21, 22	1	20:43	1	12:46	1	22:41	3	1:66; 9:44; 21:14	15
Jn.	6	11:34; 19:41, 42; 20:2, 13, 15	1	19:19	7	10:15, 17, 18, 18; 13:37, 38; 15:13							4	2:10; 10:11; 13:4; 15:16	18
Ac.	7	3:2; 4:37; 5:2, 15; 7:16; 9:37; 13:29	5	1:7; 4:3; 5: 18, 25; 12:4	1	4:35	2	2:35; 20:28			4	7:60; 9:40; 20:36; 21:5	4	5:4; 13:47; 19:21; 27:12	23
Ro.	1	9:33	1	14:13			1	4:17							3
1 Co.	3	3:10, 11; 16:2	1	15:25			1	9:18					2	12:18, 28	7
2 Co.			1	3:13									1	5:19	2
1 Th.									1	5:9					1
1 Ti.			1	1:12									1	2:7	2
2 Ti.									1	1:11					1
Heb.							2	1:13; 10:13	1	1:2					3
1 Pt.	1	2:6							1	2:8					2
2 Pt.							1	2:6							1
1 Jn.					2	3:16, 16									2
Rev.			1	11:9									1	10:2	2
Total	28		18		12		10		6		5		17		96

Miscellaneous: Mk. 15:19, bow; Lk. 1:66, lay up; Lk. 9:44, let sink down; Lk. 21:14, settle; Jn. 2:10, set forth; Jn. 10:11, give; Jn. 13:4, lay aside; Jn. 15:16, ordain; Ac. 5:4, conceive; Ac. 13:47, set; Ac. 19:21, purpose; Ac. 27:12 (with 1012), advise; 1 Co. 12:18, 28, set; 2 Co. 5:19, commit; 1 Ti. 2:7, ordain; Rev. 10:2, set.

4988. τίκτω, tik′tō

Book	Oc.	bring forth	Oc.	be delivered	Oc.	be born	Oc.	be in travail	Oc.	bear	Total
Mt.	3	1:21, 23, 25			1	2:2					4
Lk.	2	1:31; 2:7	2	1:57; 2:6	1	2:11					5
Jn.							1	16:21			1
Gal.									1	4:27	1
Heb.	1	6:7	1	11:11							2
Jas.	1	1:15									1
Rev.	2	12:5, 13	2	12:2, 4a	1	12:4b					5
Total	9		5		3		1		1		19

4989. τίλλω, til′lō

Book	pluck	Total
Mt.	12:1	1
Mk.	2:23	1
Lk.	6:1	1
Total		3

4990. Τίμαιος, Tim′aios

Book	Timaeus	Total
Mk.	10:46	1

4991. τιμάω, tima′ō

Book	Oc.	honour	Oc.	value	Total
Mt.	4	15:4, 6, 8; 19:19	2	27:9, 9	6
Mk.	3	7:6, 10; 10:19			3
Lk.	1	18:20			1
Jn.	6	5:23, 23, 23, 23; 8:49; 12:26			6
Ac.	1	28:10			1
Eph.	1	6:2			1
1 Ti.	1	5:3			1
1 Pt.	2	2:17, 17			2
Total	19		2		21

4992. τιμή, timē′

Book	Oc.	honour	Oc.	price	Oc.	sum	Oc.	precious	Total
Mt.			2	27:6, 9					2
Jn.	1	4:44							1
Ac.	1	28:10	4	4:34; 5: 2, 3; 19: 19	1	7:16			6
Ro.	6	2:7, 10; 9: 21; 12:10; 13:7, 7							6
1 Co.	2	12:23, 24	2	6:20; 7: 23					4
Col.	1	2:23							1
1 Th.	1	4:4							1
1 Ti.	4	1:17; 5:17; 6:1, 16							4
2 Ti.	2	2:20, 21							2
Heb.	4	2:7, 9; 3:3; 5:4							4
1 Pt.	2	1:7; 3:7					1	2:7	3
2 Pt.	1	1:17							1
Rev.	8	4:9, 11; 5: 12, 13; 7: 12; 19:1; 21:24, 26							8
Total	33		8		1		1		43

4994. τιμιότης, timio′tēs

Book	costliness	Total
Rev.	18:19	1

4995. Τιμόθεος, Timoth′eos

Book	Oc.	Timotheus	Oc.	Timothy	Total
Ac.	6	16:1; 17:14, 15; 18:5; 19:22; 20:4			6
Ro.	1	16:21			1
1 Co.	2	4:17; 16:10			2
2 Co.	1	1:19	1	1:1	2
Phl.	2	1:1; 2:19			2
Col.	1	1:1			1
1 Th.	3	1:1; 3:2, 6			3
2 Th.	1	1:1			1
1 Ti.			3	1:2, 18; 6:20	3
2 Ti.			1	1:2	1
Phe.			1	1:1	1
Heb.			1	13:23	1
Total	17		7		24

4993. τίμιος, tim′ios

Book	Oc.	precious	Oc.	most precious	Oc.	more precious	Oc.	dear	Oc.	honourable	Oc.	had in reputation	Total
Ac.							1	20:24			1	5:34	2
1 Co.	1	3:12											1
Heb.									1	13:4			1
Jas.	1	5:7											1
1 Pt.	1	1:19			1	1:7							2
2 Pt.	1	1:4											1
Rev.	4	17:4; 18:12a, 16; 21:19	2	18:12b; 21:11									6
Total	8		2		1		1		1		1		14

4996. Τίμων, Ti′mōn

Book	Timon	Total
Ac.	6:5	1

4997. τιμωρέω, timōre′ō

Book	punish	Total
Ac.	22:5; 26:11	2

4998. τιμωρία, timōri′a

Book	punishment	Total
Heb.	10:29	1

4999. τίνω or τίω, ti′nō or ti′ō

Book	be punished (with 1349)	Total
2 Th.	1:9	1

5000 τις, tis (indefinite pronoun)

Book	Oc.	certain	Oc.	some	Oc.	any man	Oc.	any	Total
Mt.	3	9:3; 12:38; 21:33	3	16:28; 27:47; 28:11	5	11:27; 12:19; 21:3a; 22:46; 24:23			11
Mk.	7	2:6; 5:25; 7:1; 11:5; 12:13; 14:51, 57	5	7:2; 9:1; 14:4, 65; 15:35	5	9:30; 11:3, 16; 13:5, 21	3	8:26; 11:25b; 16:18	20
Lk.	35	1:5; 6:2; 7:2, 41; 8:2, 27; 10:25, 31, 33, 38, 38; 11:1a, 27, 37; 12:16; 13:31; 14:2, 16; 15:11; 16:1, 19, 20; 17: 12; 18:9, 18, 35; 19:12; 20:9, 27, 39; 21:2; 22:56; 23: 19; 24:22, 24	8	9:7, 8, 27; 11:15; 13:1; 19:39; 21:5; 23:8	4	14:8; 19:8b, 31; 20: 28	1	24:41	48
Jn.	3	4:46; 5:5; 12:20	7	6:64; 7:25, 44; 9:16; 11:37, 46; 13:29a	16	4:33; 6:46, 51; 7:17, 37; 9:22, 31, 32; 10: 9, 28; 11:9, 57; 12: 26, 26, 47; 16:30	3	1:46; 2:25; 7:48	29
Ac.	51	3:2; 5:1, 2; 6:9; 8:9a, 36; 9:10, 19, 33, 36; 10:1, 11, 23, 48; 11:5; 12:1; 13:1, 6; 14:8; 15:2, 5, 24; 16:1, 1, 12, 14, 16; 17:5, 6, 18a, 20, 28, 34; 18:2, 24; 19:1, 13, 31; 20:9; 21:10; 23:12; 24:1, 18, 24; 25:13, 14, 19a; 27:1, 16, 26, 39	10	5:15; 8:9b, 34; 11:20; 15:36; 17:4, 18b, 21; 18:23; 27:27	3	10:47; 19:38; 24:12	6	4:34; 9:2; 25:16; 27: 42; 28:21, 21	70
Ro.	1	15:26	6	1:11, 13; 3:3, 8; 5:7b; 11:14			3	8:39; 9:11; 15:18	10
1 Co.			12	4:18; 6:11; 8:7; 9:22; 10:7, 8, 9, 10; 15:6, 12, 34, 37	6	5:11; 7:18a; 8:10; 9:15; 10:28; 14:27	4	1:15; 6:1, 12; 7:18b	22
2 Co.			3	3:1; 10:2, 12	1	12:6a	2	11:21; 12:17	6
Gal.	1	2:12	1	1:7					2
Eph.					1	2:9	1	5:27	2
Phl.			2	1:15, 15					2
Col.					3	2:4, 8; 3:13a	2	2:23; 3:13b	5
1 Th.					1	5:15b	1	2:9	2
2 Th.			1	3:11	1	3:8a	1	3:8b	3
1 Ti.			9	1:3, 6, 19; 4:1; 5:15, 24, 24; 6:10, 21					9
2 Ti.			1	2:18					1
Heb.	2	4:7; 10:27	5	3:16; 4:6; 10:25; 11:40; 13:2	2	4:11; 12:15a	5	3:12, 13; 4:1; 12:15b, 16	14
Jas.							5	5:12, 13, 13, 14, 19a	5
2 Pt.							1	3:9b	1
1 Jn.					4	2:1, 15, 27; 5:16			4
Jd.	1	1:4							1
Rev.					3	3:20; 22:18, 19			3
Total	104		73		55		38		270

5000 τις, tis (indefinite pronoun) (continued)

Book	Oc.	one	Oc.	man	Oc.	anything	Oc.	a	Oc.	certain man	Oc.	some-thing	Oc.	some-what	Oc.	ought	Oc.	some man	Total
Mt.	2	12:29, 47	3	8:28; 22:24, 24:4	1	24:17	1	18:12							2	5:23; 21:3b			9
Mk.	2	9:38; 15:21	2	8:4; 12:19	2	11:13; 13: 15													6
Lk.	13	7:36; 8:49; 9: 19, 49; 11:1b, 45; 12:13; 13: 23; 14:1, 15; 16:30, 31; 23: 26	1	12:15	3	19:8b; 22: 35; 24:19	2	18:2, 2	3	9:57; 10: 30; 13:6	1	11:54	1	7:40					24
Jn.			9	3:3, 5; 6:50; 8:51, 52; 11: 10; 14:23; 15: 6, 13	2	7:4; 14:14	2	6:7, 9	1	11:1	1	13:29b							15
Ac.	9	5:25, 34a; 7: 24; 9:43; 10: 6; 19:9b; 21: 16; 22:12; 25:19b	1	13:41	3	17:25; 19: 39; 25:11	1	5:34b	3	15:1; 18: 7; 19:24	2	3:5; 23:18	2	23:20; 25:26b	2	4:32; 28:19	1	8:31	24
Ro.	1	5:7a	1	8:24	1	14:14													3
1 Co.	3	3:4; 5:1; 14: 24	2	4:2; 16:11	6	2:2; 3:7; 8: 2b; 10:19, 19; 14:35	1	16:7									1	15:35	13
2 Co.			3	8:12, 20; 11: 16a	2	2:10a; 3:5	1	11:16b					1	10:8					7
Gal.					2	5:6; 6:15					1	6:3b	1	2:6					4
Col.			1	2:16															1
1 Th.					1	1:8													1
2 Th.			1	2:3															1
1 Ti.			1	1:8															1
2 Ti.			2	2:5, 21															2
Tit.	1	1:12																	1
Phe.															1	1:18			1
Heb.	1	2:6	1	5:4			2	2:7, 9					1	8:3			1	3:4	6
Jas.	2	2:16; 5:19b	2	2:14, 18	1	1:7													5
1 Pt.			1	2:19															1
2 Pt.			1	2:19							1	3:16					1	3:9a	3
1 Jn.			1	4:20	1	5:14													2
Rev.			1	13:17															1
Total	34		34		25		10		7		6		6		5		4		131

5000 τις, tis (indefinite pronoun) (continued)

Book	Oc.	certain thing	Oc.	nothing (with 3656)	Oc.	divers	Oc.	he	Oc.	thing	Oc.	another	Oc.	Not Tr.	Oc.	Misc.	Total
Mt.	1	20:20															1
Mk.			1	4:22	1	8:3							1	14:47			3
Lk.													5	7:19; 11:36; 12:4; 22:50, 59	2	8:46; 24:1	7
Jn.									1	5:14			1	11:49	5	5:19; 6:12; 13:20; 20:23, 23	7
Ac.	1	23:17			1	19:9a	1	4:35	1	25:26a	2	19:32; 21:34	5	16:9; 19:14; 21: 37; 23:23; 27:8	7	2:45; 5:36; 11: 29; 18:14; 25: 8; 26:26; 27: 44	18
1 Co.													1	7:5	4	4:5; 9:12; 10: 31; 11:18	5
2 Co.			1	13:8									2	12:6b; 13:5			3
Gal.													1	6:1			1
Eph.													1	6:8			1
1 Th.															1	5:15a	1
1 Ti.															1	6:7	1
Heb.							1	10:28									1
Jas.															1	1:18	1
1 Pt.															1	4:15	1
Total	2		2		2		2		2		2		17		22		51

Miscellaneous: Lk. 8:46, somebody; Lk. 24:1, certain others; Jn. 5:19, what; Jn. 6:12 (with 3263), that nothing; Jn. 13:20 (with 1437), whomsoever; Jn. 20:23, 23 (with 302), whose soever; Ac. 2:45, every man; Ac. 5:36, somebody; Ac. 11:29 (with 2141), his ability; Ac. 18:14, a matter of; Ac. 25:8, anything at all; Ac. 26:26 (with 3656 and 3662), none; Ac. 27:44 (with 3488), broken pieces; 1 Co. 4:5 (with 3261), nothing; 1 Co. 9:12 (with 3263), lest; 1 Co. 10:31, whatsoever; 1 Co. 11:18 (with 3213), partly; 1 Th. 5:15a (with 3261), none; 1 Ti. 6:7 (with 3661), nothing; Jas. 1:18, a kind of; 1 Pt. 4:15 (with 3261), none.

Word 5000 has 452 occurrences.

See page 346 for word 5001.

5002. τίτλος, tit'los

Book	title	Total
Jn.	19:19, 20	2

5003. Τίτος, Tit'os

Book	Titus	Total
2 Co.	2:13; 7:6, 13, 14; 8:6, 16, 23; 12:18, 18	9
Gal.	2:1, 3	2
2 Ti.	4:10	1
Tit.	1:4	1
Total		13

5004. τοί, toi

Book	nevertheless (with 3203)	Total
2 Ti.	2:19	1

5005. τοιγαροῦν, toigaroun′

Book	Oc.	therefore	Oc.	wherefore	Total
1 Th.	1	4:8			1
Heb.			1	12:1	1
Total	1		1		2

5006. τοίνυν, toi′nun

Book	Oc.	therefore	Oc.	then	Total
Lk.	1	20:25			1
1 Co.	1	9:26			1
Heb.	1	13:13			1
Jas.			1	2:24	1
Total	3		1		4

5007. τοιόσδε, toios′de

Book	such	Total
2 Pt.	1:17	1

5009. τοῖχος, toi′chos

Book	wall	Total
Ac.	23:3	1

5010. τόκος, tok′os

Book	usury	Total
Mt.	25:27	1
Lk.	19:23	1
Total		2

5012. τολμηρότερον tolmerot′eron

Book	the more boldly	Total
Ro.	15:15	1

5008. τοιοῦτος, toiou′tos

Book	Oc.	such	Oc.	such thing	Oc.	such an one	Oc.	like	Oc.	such a man	Oc.	such a fellow	Total
Mt.	3	9:8; 18:5; 19:14											3
Mk.	5	4:33; 6:2; 9:37; 10:14; 13:19	2	7:8, 13									7
Lk.	1	18:16	2	9:9; 13:2									3
Jn.	3	4:23; 8:5; 9:16											3
Ac.	2	16:24; 26:29	1	21:25			1	19:25			1	22:22	5
Ro.	1	16:18	3	1:32; 2:2, 3									4
1 Co.	8	5:1; 7:15, 28; 11:16; 15:48, 48; 16:16, 18			2	5:5, 11							10
2 Co.	5	3:4, 12; 10:11b; 11:13; 12:3			4	2:7; 10:11a; 12:2, 5			1	2:6			10
Gal.	1	5:23	1	5:21	1	6:1							3
Eph.			1	5:27									1
Phl.	1	2:29											1
2 Th.	1	3:12											1
1 Ti.	1	6:5											1
Tit.	1	3:11											1
Phe.					1	1:9							1
Heb.	4	7:26; 8:1; 12:3; 13:16	1	11:14									5
Jas.	1	4:16											1
3 Jn.	1	1:8											1
Total	39		11		8		1		1		1		61

5011. τολμάω. tolma′ō

Book	Oc.	durst	Oc.	dare	Oc.	be bold	Oc.	boldly	Total
Mt.	1	22:46							1
Mk.	1	12:34					1	15:43	2
Lk.	1	20:40							1
Jn.	1	21:12							1
Ac.	2	5:13; 7:32							2
Ro.			2	5:7; 15:18					2
1 Co.			1	6:1					1
2 Co.			1	10:12	3	10:2; 11:21, 21			4
Phl.					1	1:14			1
Jd.	1	1:9							1
Total	7		4		4		1		16

5013. τολμητής, tolmetes′

Book	presumptuous	Total
2 Pt.	2:10	1

5015. τόξον, tox′on

Book	bow	Total
Rev.	6:2	1

5014. τομώτερος, tomō′teros

Book	sharper	Total
Heb.	4:12	1

5016. τοπάζιον, topad′zion

Book	topaz	Total
Rev.	21:20	1

5017. τόπος, top′os

Book	Oc.	place	Oc.	room	Oc.	quarter	Oc.	licence	Oc.	coast	Oc.	where	Oc.	plain (with 3877)	Oc.	rock (with 5038)	Total
Mt.	10	12:43; 14:13, 15, 35; 24:7, 15; 26:52; 27:33, 33; 28:6															10
Mk.	9	1:35, 45; 6:31, 32, 35; 13:8; 15:22, 22; 16:6															9
Lk.	15	4:17, 37, 42; 9:10, 12; 10:1, 32; 11:1, 24; 14:9a; 16:28; 19:5; 21:11; 22:40; 23:33	4	2:7; 14:9b, 10, 22									1	6:17			20
Jn.	16	4:20; 5:13; 6:10, 23; 10:40; 11:6, 30, 48; 14:2, 3; 18:2; 19:13, 17, 20, 41; 20:7															16
Ac.	12	1:25; 4:31; 6:13, 14; 7:7, 33, 49; 12:17; 21:28, 28; 27:8, 41			2	16:3; 28:7	1	25:16	1	27:2					1	27:29	17
Ro.	3	9:26; 12:19; 15:23															3
1 Co.	1	1:2	1	14:16													2
2 Co.	1	2:14															1
Eph.	1	4:27															1
1 Th.	1	1:8															1
1 Ti.											1	2:8					1
Heb.	3	8:7; 11:8; 12:17															3
2 Pt.	1	1:19															1
Rev.	7	2:5; 6:14; 12:6, 8, 14; 16:16; 20:11															7
Total	80		5		2		1		1		1		1		1		92

5018. τοσοῦτος, tosou'tos

Book	Oc.	so much	Oc.	so great	Oc.	so many	Oc.	so long	Oc.	as large	Oc.	these many	Oc.	so many things	Total
Mt.	1	15:33a	2	8:10; 15:33b											3
Lk.			1	7:9							1	15:29			2
Jn.					3	6:9; 12:37; 21:11	1	14:9							4
Ac.	2	5:8, 8													2
1 Co.					1	14:10									1
Gal.													1	3:4	1
Heb.	3	1:4; 7:22; 10:25	1	12:1			1	4:7							5
Rev.	1	18:7	1	18:17					1	21:16					3
Total	7		5		4		2		1		1		1		21

5001. τίς, tis (definite pronoun, interrogative)

Book	Oc.	what	Oc.	who	Oc.	why	Oc.	whom	Oc.	which	Oc.	whose	Oc.	whether
Mt.	42	5:46, 47; 6:3, 25, 25, 25, 31a, 31b; 7:9; 8:29; 9:13; 10:19, 19; 11:7, 8, 9; 12:3, 7, 11; 16:26, 26; 17:25a; 19:16, 20, 27; 20:21, 22, 32; 21:16, 28, 40; 22:17, 42a; 24:3; 26:8, 15, 65, 66, 70; 27:4, 22, 23	10	3:7; 10:11; 12:48, 48; 18:1; 19:25; 21:10, 23; 24:45; 26:68	10	6:28; 7:3; 8:26; 16:8; 17:10; 19:7, 17; 20:6; 22:18; 26:10	5	12:27; 16:13, 15; 17:25b; 27:17	1	6:27	3	22:20, 28, 42b	5	9:5; 21:31; 23:17, 19; 27:21
Mk.	34	1:24a, 27b; 2:25; 4:24, 41; 5:7, 9, 14; 6:2, 24; 8:36, 37; 9:6, 10, 16, 33; 10:3, 17, 36, 38, 51; 11:5; 12:9; 13:4, 11; 14:36, 36, 40, 63, 64, 68; 15:12, 14, 24a	9	1:24b; 2:7b; 3:33; 5:30, 31; 9:34; 10:26; 11:28; 16:3	12	2:7a, 8, 24; 4:40; 5:35, 39; 8:12, 17; 10:18; 11:3; 12:15; 14:6	2	8:27, 29			2	12:16, 23	1	2:9
Lk.	46	1:66; 3:10, 12, 14; 4:34a, 36; 5:22; 6:11; 7:24, 25, 26, 31b; 8:9, 25, 28, 30; 9:25; 10:25, 26; 12:11b, 17, 22, 22, 29, 29, 49; 13:18a; 14:31; 15:4, 8, 26; 16:3, 4; 18:6, 18, 36, 41; 19:48; 20:13, 15, 17; 21:7; 22:71; 23:22, 31, 34	20	3:7; 4:34b; 5:21, 21; 7:39, 49; 8:45, 45; 9:9; 10:22, 22, 29; 12:14, 42; 16:11, 12; 18:26; 19:3; 20:2; 22:64	12	2:48; 6:2, 41, 46; 12:26, 57; 18:19; 19:33; 20:23; 22:46; 24:5, 38	5	6:47; 9:18, 20; 11:19; 12:5	10	7:42; 9:46; 10:36; 11:5; 12:25; 14:5, 28; 17:7; 22:23, 24	3	12:20; 20:24, 33	2	5:23; 22:27
Jn.	33	1:21, 22b, 38; 2:4, 18, 25; 4:27a; 5:12; 6:6, 9, 28, 30, 30; 7:51; 8:5; 9:17, 26; 11:47, 56; 12:27, 49, 49; 13:12, 28; 15:15; 16:17, 18, 18; 18:21b, 29, 35, 38; 21:21	17	1:19, 22a; 4:10; 5:13; 6:60, 64, 64; 7:20; 8:25; 9:2, 21, 36; 12:34, 38a; 13:24, 25; 21:12	8	1:25; 4:27b; 7:19; 10:20; 18:21a, 23; 20:13, 15a	7	6:68; 8:53; 12:38b; 13:22; 18:4, 7; 20:15b	2	8:46; 21:20	1	19:24		
Ac.	29	2:12, 37; 4:9, 16; 5:35; 7:40, 49; 8:36; 9:6, 6; 10:4, 6, 17, 21, 29; 11:17; 12:18; 16:30; 17:18, 19, 20.; 19:3, 35; 21:13, 22, 33b; 22:10, 26; 23:19	8	7:27, 35; 8:33; 9:5; 19:15; 21:33a; 22:8; 26:15	11	1:11; 3:12, 12; 5:4; 9:4; 14:15; 15:10; 22:7, 16; 26:8, 14	2	8:34; 13:25	1	7:52				
Ro.	22	3:1, 1, 3, 5, 9; 4:1, 3; 6:1, 15, 21; 7:7; 8:26, 27, 31a; 9:14, 30; 10:8; 11:2, 4, 7, 15; 12:2	14	7:24; 8:31b, 33, 34, 35; 9:19b, 20a; 10:6, 7, 16; 11:34, 34, 35; 14:4	6	3:7; 8:24; 9:19a, 20b; 14:10, 10								
1 Co.	14	2:11; 4:7b, 21; 5:12; 7:16a; 9:18; 10:19; 11:22; 14:6, 15, 16; 15:2, 29a, 32	8	2:16; 3:5, 5; 4:7a; 9:7, 7, 7; 14:8	5	4:7c; 10:29, 30; 15:29b, 30								
2 Co.	6	6:14, 14, 15, 15, 16; 12:13	4	2:2, 16; 11:29, 29										
Gal.	1	4:30	2	3:1; 5:7	2	2:14; 5:11								
Eph.	8	1:18, 18, 19; 3:9, 18; 4:9; 5:10, 17												
Phl.	2	1:18, 22												
Col.	1	1:27			1	2:20								
1 Th.	3	2:19; 3:9; 4:2												
1 Ti.														
2 Ti.							1	3:14						
Heb.	5	2:6; 7:11; 11:32; 12:7; 13:6					2	3:17, 18	3	1:5, 13; 5:12				
Jas.	2	2:14, 16	2	3:13; 4:12										
1 Pt.	2	1:11; 4:17	1	3:13			1	5:8						
1 Jn.	1	3:2	2	2:22; 5:5										
Rev.	9	2:7, 11, 17, 29; 3:6, 13, 22; 7:13; 18:18	5	5:2; 6:17; 13:4, 4; 15:4										
Total	260		102		67		25		17		9		8	

5019. τότε, tot΄e

Book	Oc.	then	Oc.	that time	Oc.	when	Oc.	Not Tr.	Total
Mt.	87	2:7, 16, 17; 3:5, 13, 15; 4:1, 5, 10, 11; 5:24; 7:5, 23; 8:26; 9:6, 14, 15, 29, 37; 11:20; 12: 13, 22, 29, 38, 44, 45; 13:26, 36, 43; 15:1, 12, 28; 16:12, 20, 24, 27; 17:13, 19; 18:21, 32; 19:13, 27; 20:20; 21:1; 22:8, 13, 15, 21; 23:1; 24:9, 10, 14, 16, 21, 23, 30, 30, 40; 25:1, 7, 31, 34, 37, 41, 44, 45; 26:3, 14, 31, 36, 38, 45, 50, 52, 56, 65, 67, 74; 27:3, 9, 13, 16, 26, 27, 38, 58; 28:10	3	4:17; 16:21; 26: 16					90
Mk.	6	2:20; 3:27; 13:14, 21, 26, 27							6
Lk.	12	5:35; 6:42; 11:26; 13:26; 14:10, 21; 21:10, 20, 21, 27; 23:30; 24:45	1	16:16			1	14:9	14
Jn.	8	2:10; 7:10; 8:28; 11:14; 12:16; 19:1, 16; 20:8					2	11:6; 13: 27	10
Ac.	18	1:12; 4:8; 5:26; 6:11; 7:4; 8:17; 10:46, 48; 13:12; 15:22; 17:14; 21:26, 33; 23:3; 25: 12; 26:1; 27:32; 28:1			1	13:3	1	27:21	20
Ro.	1	6:21							1
1 Co.	6	4:5; 13:10, 12, 12; 15:28, 54					1	16:2	7
2 Co.	1	12:10							1
Gal.	3	4:8, 29; 6:4							3
Col.	1	3:4							1
1 Th.	1	5:3							1
2 Th.	1	2:8							1
Heb.	3	10:7, 9; 12:26							3
2 Pt.	1	3:6							1
Total	149		4		1		5		159

5001. τίς, tis (definite pronoun, interrogative) (continued)

Book	Oc.	whereunto	Oc.	how	Oc.	how is it	Oc.	what thing	Oc.	wherefore	Oc.	wherewith (with 1722)	Oc.	Not Tr.	Oc.	Misc.	Total
Mt.	1	11:16	1	18:12							1	5:13			4	6:31c; 14:31; 15:32; 26:62	83
Mk.	1	4:30			1	2:16	1	1:27a			1	9:50			7	6:36; 8:1, 2; 14:4, 60; 15: 24b, 34	71
Lk.	3	7:31a; 13: 18b, 20	1	1:62	2	2:49; 16:2	1	12:11a			1	14:34	1	6:9	6	1:18; 11:11; 17:8; 19:15a, 15b; 24:17	113
Jn.			1	14:22			1	10:6	1	9:27					3	7:36; 21:22, 23	74
Ac.	1	5:24			1	5:9			1	22:30					1	19:32	55
Ro.																	42
1 Co.			1	7:16b	1	14:26											29
2 Co.																	10
Gal.									1	3:19					1	4:15	7
Eph.			1	6:21													9
Phl.																	2
Col.																	2
1 Th.																	3
1 Ti.															1	1:7	1
2 Ti.																	1
Heb.																	10
Jas.																	4
1 Pt.																	4
1 Jn.															1	3:12	4
Rev.																	14
Total	6		5		5		3		3		3		1		24		538

Miscellaneous: Mt. 6:31c, wherewithal; Mt. 14:31 (with 1519), wherefore; Mt. 15:32 (with 3656), nothing; Mt. 26:62, what is it which; Mk. 6:36 (with 3656), nothing; Mk. 8:1 (with 3261), nothing; Mk. 8:2 (with 3656), nothing; Mk. 14:4 (with 1519), why; Mk. 14:60, what is it which; Mk. 15:24b, every man; Mk. 15: 34 (with 1519), why; Lk. 1:18 (with 2596), whereby; Lk. 11:11, any; Lk. 17:8, wherewith; Lk. 19:15a, how much; Lk. 19:15b, every man; Lk. 24:17, what manner of; Jn. 7:36, what manner of; Jn. 21:22, 23, what is that; Ac. 19:32 (with 1752), wherefore; Gal. 4:15, where; 1 Ti. 1:7, whereof; 1 Jn. 3:12 (with 5384), wherefore.

5020. τοῦ, tou

Book	his	Total
Ac.	17:28	1

5021. τοὐναντίον, tounanti′on

Book	contrariwise	Total
2 Co.	2:7	1
Gal.	2:7	1
1 Pt.	3:9	1
Total		3

5022. τοὔνομα, tou′noma

Book	name	Total
Mt.	27:57	1

5023. τουτέστι, toutes′ti

Book	Oc.	that is	Oc.	that is to say	Total
Mt.			1	27:46	1
Mk.			1	7:2	1
Ac.	1	19:4	1	1:19	2
Ro.	5	7:18; 9:8; 10:6, 7, 8			5
Phe.	1	1:12			1
Heb.	4	2:14; 7:5; 11:16; 13:15	2	9:11; 10:20	6
1 Pt.	1	3:20			1
Total	12		5		17

5024. τοῦτο, tou′to

(Neuter Singular Nominative or Accusative of Word 3678)

Book	Oc.	this	Oc.	therefore (with 1223)	Oc.	that	Oc.	for this cause (with 1223)	Oc.	wherefore (with 1223)	Oc.	it	Oc.	Not Tr.	Oc.	Misc.	Total
Mt.	20	1:22; 8:9; 9:28; 13:28; 15:11; 16:22; 17:21; 18:4; 19:26; 21:4; 24:14; 26:9, 12, 13, 26 28, 39, 42, 56; 28:14	9	6:25; 12:27; 13:13, 52; 14:2; 18:23; 21:43; 23:14; 24:44					2	12:31; 23:34	1	12:11					32
Mk.	9	1:27; 5:32; 9:21, 29; 11:3; 14:9, 22, 24, 36	3	6:14; 11:24; 12:24	1	13:11					2	5:43; 14:5			1	1:38	16
Lk.	29	1:18, 34, 43, 66; 2:12, 15; 3:20; 5:6; 6:3; 7:4, 8; 9:45, 48; 10:11, 28; 12:18, 39; 13:8; 16:2; 18:34; 20:17; 22:15, 17, 19, 19, 20, 23, 37, 42	4	11:19, 49; 12:22; 14:20	1	9:21					1	18:36			2	4:43; 24:40	37
Jn.	31	2:12, 22; 4:15, 54; 5:28; 6:6, 29, 39, 40, 61; 7:39; 8:6, 40; 11:26, 51; 12:5, 6, 18b, 33; 13:28; 16:17, 18; 18:34, 37, 37, 38; 19:28; 20:22; 21:14, 19, 19	13	1:31; 5:16, 18; 6:65; 7:22; 8:47; 9:23; 10:17; 12:39; 13:11; 15:19; 16:15; 19:11	5	3:32; 4:18; 11:7, 11; 14:13	2	12:18a, 27							1	20:20	52
Ac.	24	2:12, 14, 16, 33; 4:7, 22; 5:4, 24, 38; 7:60; 8:34; 9:21a; 10:16; 11:10; 16:18; 19:10, 17, 27; 20:29; 21:23; 24:14; 26:16, 26; 27:34	1	2:26	1	9:21b							1	3:6	2	19:14; 23:7	29
Ro.	8	2:3; 6:6; 9:17; 11:25; 13:6b; 14:9, 13; 15:28	1	4:16	10	1:12; 7:15, 15, 16, 19, 20; 10:6, 7, 8; 13:11	3	1:26; 13:6a; 15:9	1	5:12					1	12:20	24
1 Co.	21	1:12; 5:2, 3; 7:6, 26, 29, 35; 9:17, 23; 10:28; 11:17, 24, 24, 25, 25, 26; 15:50, 53, 53, 54, 54			1	6:6	3	4:17; 11:10, 30							3	7:37; 12:15, 16	28
2 Co.	11	2:1, 3, 9; 7:11; 8:10, 20; 9:6; 10:7, 11; 13:1, 9	3	4:1; 7:13; 13:10											3	1:17; 5:5, 14	17
Gal.	2	3:2, 17			1	6:7									1	2:10	4
Eph.	4	4:17; 5:5, 32; 6:1			1	2:8			3	1:15; 5:17; 6:13					3	6:8, 18, 22	11
Phl.	8	1:6, 7, 9, 19, 22, 25; 2:5; 3:15b			1	1:28									1	3:15a	10
Col.	2	2:4; 3:20					1	1:9							1	4:8	4
1 Th.	3	4:3, 15; 5:18	1	3:7			2	2:13; 3:5							1	3:3	7
2 Th.	1	3:10					1	2:11									2
1 Ti.	3	1:9; 2:3; 4:16			1	5:4	1	1:16							1	4:10	6
2 Ti.	2	1:15; 3:1	1	2:10													3
Phe.			1	1:15	1	1:18											2
Heb.	6	6:3; 7:27; 9:8, 20, 27; 13:19	2	1:9; 2:1	1	13:17b	1	9:15			1	13:17a			2	10:33, 33	13
Jas.	1	4:15															1
1 Pt.	4	1:25; 2:19, 20; 4:6													2	2:21; 3:9	6
2 Pt.	5	1:5, 20; 3:3, 5, 8															5
1 Jn.	2	3:8; 4:3	2	3:1; 4:5													4
3 Jn.									1	1:10							1
Jd.	2	1:4, 5															2
Rev.	1	2:6	3	7:15; 12:12; 18:8													4
Total	199		44		25		14		7		5		1		25		320

Miscellaneous: Mk. 1:38 (with 1519), therefore; Lk. 4:43 (with 1519), therefore; Lk. 24:40, thus; Jn. 20:20, so; Ac. 19:14, so; Ac. 23:7, so; Ro. 12:20, so; 1 Co. 7:37, so; 1 Co. 12:15, 16 (with 1519), therefore; 2 Co. 1:17, thus; 2 Co. 5:5, the; 2 Co. 5:14, thus; Gal. 2:10, the; Eph. 6:8, the same; Eph. 6:18 (with 1519 and 846), thereunto; Eph. 6:22, the; Phl. 3:15a, thus; Col. 4:8, the; 1 Th. 3:3 (with 1519), thereunto; 1 Ti. 4:10 (with 1519), therefore; Heb. 10:33, 33, partly; 1 Pt. 2:21 (with 1519), hereunto; 1 Pt. 3:9 (with 1519), thereunto.

5025. τούτοις, tou'tois
(Dative Plural Masculine or Neuter of Word 3678)

Book	Oc.	these	Oc.	these things	Oc.	this	Oc.	such	Oc.	them	Oc.	therein	Oc.	there-with	Oc.	those	Oc.	therewith (with 1909)	Oc.	Not Tr.	Total
Lk.					2	16:26; 24:21															2
Ac.	2	4:16; 5:35																			2
Ro.	1	15:23	2	8:37; 14:18																	3
1 Co.	1	12:23																			1
Gal.							1	5:21													1
Col.			1	3:14																	1
1 Th.	1	4:18																			1
1 Ti.									1	4:15			1	6:8							2
Heb.	1	9:23																			1
2 Pt.											1	2:20									1
3 Jn.																	1	1:10			1
Jd.	1	1:14													1	1:10			1	1:7	3
Total	7		3		2		1		1		1		1		1		1		1		19

5026. τοῦτον, tou'ton
(Accusative Singular Masculine of Word 3678)

Book	Oc.	this	Oc.	him	Oc.	that	Oc.	this fellow	Oc.	the same	Total
Mt.	2	19:11; 21:44	1	27:32							3
Mk.	3	7:29; 14:58, 71									3
Lk.	6	9:13; 12:56; 16:28; 19:14; 23:14, 18	4	9:26; 12:5; 20:12, 13			1	23:2			11
Jn.	8	2:19; 6:34, 58; 7:27; 9:39; 18:40; 19:12, 20	3	5:6; 6:27; 21:21	2	19:8, 13	1	9:29			14
Ac.	13	2:32; 3:16; 5:37; 6:14; 7:35a; 21:28; 23:17, 18, 25, 27; 24:5; 25:24; 28:26	7	2:23; 5:31; 10:40; 13:27; 15:38; 16:3; 17:23	1	2:36			1	7:35b	22
Ro.	2	9:9; 15:28									2
1 Co.	3	3:12; 11:26, 27	2	2:2; 3:17							5
2 Co.	1	4:7									1
Phl.			1	2:23							1
2 Th.					1	3:14					1
Heb.	1	8:3									1
Total	39		18		4		2		1		64

5027. τούτου, tou'tou
(Genitive Singular Masculine or Neuter of Word 3678)

Book	Oc.	this	Oc.	that	Oc.	him	Oc.	thus	Oc.	thereabout (with 3912)	Oc.	it	Oc.	thenceforth	Oc.	Misc.	Total
Mt.	6	13:15, 22, 40; 19:5; 26:29; 27:24															6
Mk.	2	4:19; 10:7															2
Lk.	4	2:17; 13:16; 16:8; 20:34	1	9:45			1	22:51	1	24:4							7
Jn.	15	4:13; 6:51; 8:23, 23; 10:41; 11:9; 12:31, 31; 13:1; 14:30; 16:11; 18:17, 29, 36, 36	2	6:66; 16:19	1	9:31					1	6:61	1	19:12			20
Ac.	13	5:28; 6:13; 9:13; 13:17, 23, 38; 15:2, 6; 17:32; 21:28; 22:22; 28:9, 27													2	25:20, 25	15
Ro.	1	7:24	1	11:7													2
1 Co.	8	1:20, 20; 2:6, 6, 8; 3:19; 5:10; 7:31															8
2 Co.	2	4:4; 12:8															2
Eph.	5	2:2; 3:1, 14; 5:31; 6:12															5
Col.	1	1:27															1
Tit.	1	1:5															1
Jas.	2	1:26; 2:5															2
1 Jn.															1	4:6	1
Rev.	4	22:7, 9, 10, 18			1	19:20											5
Total	64		4		2		1		1		1		1		3		77

Miscellaneous: Ac. 25:20 (with 3912), such manner of; Ac. 25:25, he; 1 Jn. 4:6 (with 1537), hereby.

5028. τούτους, tou'tous
(Accusative Plural Masculine of Word 3678)

Book	Oc.	these	Oc.	them	Oc.	these men	Oc.	this	Oc.	such	Total
Mt.	6	7:24, 26, 28; 10:5; 19:1; 26:1									6
Mk.					1	8:4					1
Lk.	4	9:28, 44; 19:15; 20:16									4
Jn.	2	10:19; 18:8									2
Ac.	5	2:22; 5:5, 24; 10:47; 19:37	1	21:24			1	16:36			7
Ro.			3	8:30, 30, 30							3
1 Co.			2	6:4; 16:3							2
2 Ti.									1	3:5	1
Heb.			1	2:15							1
Total	17		7		1		1		1		27

5029. τούτῳ, tou'tō
(Dative Singular Masculine or Neuter of Word 3678)

Book	Oc.	this	Oc.	him	Oc.	hereby (with 1722)	Oc.	herein (with 1722)	Oc.	Misc.	Total
Mt.	7	8:9; 12:32; 13:54, 56; 17:20; 20:14; 21:21									7
Mk.	3	6:2; 10:30; 11:23									3
Lk.	10	1:61; 4:3; 10:5, 20; 14:9; 18:30; 19:9; 21:23; 23:4, 14	1	19:19					1	7:8	12
Jn.	7	4:20, 21, 27; 12:25; 13:35; 16:30; 20:30	3	5:38; 10:3; 13:24			3	4:37; 9:30; 15:8			13
Ac.	12	1:6; 3:12; 4:17; 5:28; 7:7, 29; 8:21, 29; 15:15; 23:9; 24:2, 10	4	4:10; 10:43; 13:39; 25:5			1	24:16	1	21:9	18
Ro.	2	12:2; 13:9									2
1 Co.	4	3:18; 7:31; 11:22; 14:21			1	4:4			1	7:24	6
2 Co.	3	3:10; 5:2; 9:3					1	8:10			4
Gal.	1	6:16									1
Eph.	1	1:21									1
Phl.									1	1:18	1
Heb.	1	4:5									1
1 Pt.	1	4:16									1
2 Pt.	1	1:13							1	2:19	2
1 Jn.	4	3:10; 4:9, 17b; 5:2	2	2:4, 5a	7	2:3, 5b; 3:16, 19, 24; 4:2, 13	2	4:10, 17a			15
Rev.	2	22:18, 19									2
Total	59		10		8		7		5		89

Miscellaneous: Lk. 7:8, one; Ac. 21:9, the same; 1 Co. 7:24 (with 1722), therein; Phl. 1:18 (with 1722), therein; 2 Pt. 2:19, the same.

5030. τούτων, tou'tōn
(Genitive Plural Masculine or Neuter of Word 3678)

Book	Oc.	these	Oc.	these things	Oc.	such	Oc.	these matters	Oc.	such matters	Oc.	those	Oc.	Not Tr.	Oc.	Misc.	Total
Mt.	10	3:9; 5:19, 37; 6:29; 10:42; 18:6, 10, 14; 25:40, 45	1	6:32											1	11:7	12
Mk.	1	12:31															1
Lk.	5	3:8; 10:36; 12:27; 17:2; 21:12	6	7:18; 12:30; 18:34; 21:28; 24:14, 48													11
Jn.	6	1:50; 5:20; 7:31; 14:12; 17:20; 21:15	1	21:24													7
Ac.	10	1:21, 24; 5:32, 36, 38; 14:15; 15:28; 21:38; 26:21, 29	5	19:36; 24:8; 25:9; 26:26, 26			1	25:20	1	18:15					1	18:17	18
Ro.															1	11:30	1
1 Co.	1	13:13	1	9:15													2
1 Th.					1	4:6											1
2 Ti.	1	2:21													1	3:6	2
Tit.			1	3:8													1
Heb.	2	1:2; 10:18	1	9:6							1	13:11					4
2 Pt.	1	1:4	4	1:12, 15; 3:11, 16													5
3 Jn.													1	1:4			1
Rev.	1	9:18	1	18:15	1	20:6											3
Total	38		21		2		1		1		1		1		4		69

Miscellaneous: Mt. 11:7, they; Ac. 18:17, those things; Ro. 11:30, their; 2 Ti. 3:6, this sort.

5031. τράγος, trag'os

Book	goat	Total
Heb.	9:12, 13, 19; 10:4	4

5033. τραπεζίτης, trapedzi'tēs

Book	exchanger	Total
Mt.	25:27	1

5034. τραῦμα, trau'ma

Book	wound	Total
Lk.	10:34	1

5035. τραυματίζω, traumatid'zō

Book	wound	Total
Lk.	20:12	1
Ac.	19:16	1
Total		2

5032. τράπεζα, trap'edza

Book	Oc.	table	Oc.	bank	Oc.	meat	Total
Mt.	2	15:27; 21:12					2
Mk.	2	7:28; 11:15					2
Lk.	3	16:21; 22:21, 30	1	19:23			4
Jn.	1	2:15					1
Ac.	1	6:2			1	16:34	2
Ro.	1	11:9					1
1 Co.	2	10:21, 21					2
Heb.	1	9:2					1
Total	13		1		1		15

5036. τραχηλίζω, trachēlid'zō

Book	open	Total
Heb.	4:13	1

5037. τράχηλος, trach'ēlos

Book	neck	Total
Mt.	18:6	1
Mk.	9:42	1
Lk.	15:20; 17:2	2
Ac.	15:10; 20:37	2
Ro.	16:4	1
Total		7

5039. τραχωνῖτις, trachōni'tis

Book	Trachonitis	Total
Lk.	3:1	1

5038. τραχύς, trachus'

Book	Oc.	rough	Oc.	rock (with 5017)	Total
Lk.	1	3:5			1
Ac.			1	27:29	1
Total	1		1		2

5041. τρέμω, trem'ō

Book	Oc.	tremble	Oc.	be afraid	Total
Mk.	1	5:33			1
Lk.	1	8:47			1
Ac.	1	9:6			1
2 Pt.			1	2:10	1
Total	3		1		4

5042. τρέφω, treph'ō

Book	Oc.	feed	Oc.	nourish	Oc.	bring up	Total
Mt.	2	6:26; 25:37					2
Lk.	1	12:24			1	4:16	2
Ac.			1	12:20			1
Jas.			1	5:5			1
Rev.	1	12:6	1	12:14			2
Total	4		3		1		8

5040. τρεῖς, τρία, treis, tri'a

Book	three	Total
Mt.	12:40, 40, 40, 40; 13:33; 15:32; 17:4; 18:16, 20; 26:61; 27:40, 63	12
Mk.	8:2, 31; 9:5; 14:58; 15:29	5
Lk.	1:56; 2:46; 4:25; 9:33; 10:36; 11:5; 12:52, 52; 13:7, 21	10
Jn.	2:6, 19, 20; 21:11	4
Ac.	5:7; 7:20; 9:9; 10:19; 11:11; 17:2; 19:8; 20:3; 25:1; 28:7, 11, 12, 17	13
1 Co.	10:8; 13:13; 14:27, 29	4
2 Co.	13:1	1
Gal.	1:18	1
1 Ti.	5:19	1
Heb.	10:28	1
Jas.	5:17	1
1 Jn.	5:7, 7, 8, 8	4
Rev.	6:6; 8:13; 9:18; 11:9, 11; 16:13, 19; 21:13, 13, 13, 13	11
Total		68

5043. τρέχω, trech'ō

Book	Oc.	run	Oc.	have course	Total
Mt.	2	27:48; 28:8			2
Mk.	2	5:6; 15:36			2
Lk.	2	15:20; 24:12			2
Jn.	2	20:2, 4			2
Ro.	1	9:16			1
1 Co.	4	9:24, 24, 24, 26			4
Gal.	3	2:2, 2; 5:7			3
Phl.	1	2:16			1
2 Th.			1	3:1	1
Heb.	1	12:1			1
Rev.	1	9:9			1
Total	19		1		20

5044. τριάκοντα, triak'onta

Book	Oc.	thirty	Oc.	thirtyfold	Total
Mt.	4	13:23; 26:15; 27:3, 9	1	13:8	5
Mk.	1	4:8	1	4:20	2
Lk.	1	3:23			1
Jn.	2	5:5; 6:19			2
Gal.	1	3:17			1
Total	9		2		11

5045. τριακόσιοι, triakos'ioi

Book	three hundred	Total
Mk.	14:5	1
Jn.	12:5	1
Total		2

5046. τρίβολος, trib'olos

Book	Oc.	thistle	Oc.	brier	Total
Mt.	1	7:16			1
Heb.			1	6:8	1
Total	1		1		2

5047. τρίβος, tri'bos

Book	path	Total
Mt.	3:3	1
Mk.	1:3	1
Lk.	3:4	1
Total		3

5048. τριετία, trieti'a

Book	space of three years	Total
Ac.	20:31	1

5049. τρίζω, trid'zō

Book	gnash	Total
Mk.	9:18	1

5050. τρίμηνον, trim'e̱non

Book	three months	Total
Heb.	11:23	1

5051. τρίς, tris

Book	Oc.	thrice	Oc.	three times	Total
Mt.	2	26:34, 75			2
Mk.	2	14:30, 72			2
Lk.	2	22:34, 61			2
Jn.	1	13:38			1
Ac.	1	10:16	1	11:10	2
2 Co.	3	11:25, 25; 12:8			3
Total	11		1		12

5052. τρίστεγον, tris'tegon

Book	third loft	Total
Ac.	20:9	1

5053. τρισχίλιοι, trischil'ioi

Book	three thousand	Total
Ac.	2:41	1

5055. τρίχινος, trich'inos

Book	of hair	Total
Rev.	6:12	1

5054. τρίτος, tri'tos

Book	Oc.	third	Oc.	thirdly	Total
Mt.	7	16:21; 17:23; 20:3, 19; 22:26; 26:44; 27:64			7
Mk.	5	9:31; 10:34; 12:21; 14:41; 15:25			5
Lk.	10	9:22; 12:38; 13:32; 18:33; 20:12, 31; 23:22; 24:7, 21, 46			10
Jn.	4	2:1; 21:14, 17, 17			4
Ac.	4	2:15; 10:40; 23:23; 27:19			4
1 Co.	1	15:4	1	12:28	2
2 Co.	3	12:2, 14; 13:1			3
Rev.	22	4:7; 6:5, 5; 8:7, 8, 9, 9, 10, 10, 11, 12, 12, 12, 12, 12; 9:15, 18; 11:14; 12:4; 14:9; 16:4; 21:19			22
Total	56		1		57

5056. τρόμος, trom'os

Book	Oc.	trembling	Oc.	tremble (with 2192)	Total
Mk.			1	16:8	1
1 Co.	1	2:3			1
2 Co.	1	7:15			1
Eph.	1	6:5			1
Phl.	1	2:12			1
Total	4		1		5

5057. τροπή, trope̱'

Book	turning	Total
Jas.	1:17	1

5059. τροποφορέω, tropophore'ō

Book	suffer (one's) manners	Total
Ac.	13:18	1

5058. τρόπος, trop'os

Book	Oc.	as (with 3639)	Oc.	even as (with 2596 and 3639)	Oc.	way	Oc.	means	Oc.	even as (with 3639)	Oc.	in like manner as (with 3639)	Oc.	manner	Oc.	conver-sation	Total
Mt.									1	23:37							1
Lk.	1	13:34															1
Ac.	1	7:28	2	15:11; 27:25							1	1:11					4
Ro.					1	3:2											1
Phl.					1	1:18											1
2 Th.							2	2:3; 3:16									2
2 Ti.	1	3:8															1
Heb.															1	13:5	1
Jd.													1	1:7			1
Total	3		2		2		2		1		1		1		1		13

5060. τροφή, trophe̱'

Book	Oc.	meat	Oc.	food	Oc.	some meat	Oc.	Not Tr.	Total
Mt.	4	3:4; 6:25; 10:10; 24:45							4
Lk.	1	12:23							1
Jn.	1	4:8							1
Ac.	3	2:46; 9:19; 27:33	1	14:17	2	27:34, 36	1	27:38	7
Heb.	2	5:12, 14							2
Jas.			1	2:15					1
Total	11		2		2		1		16

5061. Τρόφιμος, Troph'imos

Book	Trophimus	Total
Ac.	20:4; 21:29	2
2 Ti.	4:20	1
Total		3

5062. τροφός, trophos'

Book	nurse	Total
1 Th.	2:7	1

5063. τροχιά, trochia'

Book	path	Total
Heb.	12:13	1

5064. τροχός, trochos'

Book	course	Total
Jas.	3:6	1

5067. τρυγών, trugōn'

Book	turtledove	Total
Lk.	2:24	1

5068. τρυμαλιά, trumalia'

Book	eye	Total
Mk.	10:25	1
Lk.	18:25	1
Total		2

5065. τρύβλιον, trub'lion

Book	dish	Total
Mt.	26:23	1
Mk.	14:20	1
Total		2

5066. τρυγάω, truga'ō

Book	gather	Total
Lk.	6:44	1
Rev.	14:18, 19	2
Total		3

5069. τρύπημα, tru'pe̱ma

Book	eye	Total
Mt.	19:24	1

5070. Τρύφαινα, Tru'phaina

Book	Tryphena	Total
Ro.	16:12	1

5071. τρυφάω, trupha'ō

Book	live in pleasure	Total
Jas.	5:5	1

5072. τρυφή, truphē'

Book	Oc.	delicately	Oc.	to riot	Total
Lk.	1	7:25			1
2 Pt.			1	2:13	1
Total	1		1		2

5073. Τρυφῶσα, Truphō'sa

Book	Tryphosa	Total
Ro.	16:12	1

5074. Τρωάς, Trōas'

Book	Troas	Total
Ac.	16:8, 11; 20:5, 5	4
2 Co.	2:12	1
2 Ti.	4:13	1
Total		6

5075. Τρωγύλλιον, Trōgul'lion

Book	Trogyllium	Total
Ac.	20:15	1

5076. τρώγω, trō'gō

Book	eat	Total
Mt.	24:38	1
Jn.	6:54, 56, 57, 58; 13:18	5
Total		6

5078. τυμπανίζω, tumpanid'zō

Book	torture	Total
Heb.	11:35	1

5077. τυγχάνω, tungchan'ō

Book	Oc.	obtain	Oc.	be	Oc.	chance	Oc.	little	Oc.	enjoy	Oc.	may be	Oc.	Not Tr.	Oc.	Misc.	Total
Lk.	1	20:35											1	10:30			2
Ac.	1	26:22					1	28:2	1	24:2					2	19:11; 27:3	5
1 Co.			1	14:10	1	15:37					1	16:6					3
2 Ti.	1	2:10															1
Heb.	2	8:6; 11:35															2
Total	5		1		1		1		1		1		1		2		13

Miscellaneous: Ac. 19:11 (with 3656), special; Ac. 27:3 (with 1958), refresh (one's) self.

5079. τύπος, tu'pos

Book	Oc.	ensample	Oc.	print	Oc.	figure	Oc.	example	Oc.	pattern	Oc.	fashion	Oc.	manner	Oc.	form	Total
Jn.			2	20:25, 25													2
Ac.					1	7:43					1	7:44	1	23:25			3
Ro.					1	5:14									1	6:17	2
1 Co.	1	10:11					1	10:6									2
Phl.	1	3:17															1
1 Th.	1	1:7															1
2 Th.	1	3:9															1
1 Ti.							1	4:12									1
Tit.									1	2:7							1
Heb.									1	8:5							1
1 Pt.	1	5:3															1
Total	5		2		2		2		2		1		1		1		16

5080. τύπτω, tup'tō

Book	Oc.	smite	Oc.	beat	Oc.	strike	Oc.	wound	Total
Mt.	2	24:49; 27:30							2
Mk.	1	15:19							1
Lk.	3	6:29; 18:13; 23:48	1	12:45	1	22:64			5
Ac.	3	23:2, 3, 3	2	18:17; 21:32					5
1 Co.							1	8:12	1
Total	9		3		1		1		14

5081. Τύραννος, Tu'rannos

Book	Tyrannus	Total
Ac.	19:9	1

5082. τυρβάζω, turbad'zō

Book	trouble	Total
Lk.	10:41	1

5083. Τύριος, Tu'rios

Book	of Tyre	Total
Ac.	12:20	1

5084. Τύρος, Tu'ros

Book	Tyre	Total
Mt.	11:21, 22; 15:21	3
Mk.	3:8; 7:24, 31	3
Lk.	6:17; 10:13, 14	3
Ac.	21:3, 7	2
Total		11

5085. τυφλός, tuphlos'

Book	Oc.	blind	Oc	blind man	Total
Mt.	15	11:5; 12:22, 22; 15:14, 14, 14, 14, 30, 31; 21:14; 23:16, 17, 19, 24, 26	3	9:27, 28; 20:30	18
Mk.	1	10:46	4	8:22, 23; 10:49, 51	5
Lk.	7	4:18; 6:39, 39; 7:21, 22; 14:13, 21	1	18:35	8
Jn.	17	5:3; 9:1, 2, 8, 13, 17, 18, 19, 20, 24, 25, 32, 39, 40, 41; 10:21; 11:37	1	9:6	18
Ac.	1	13:11			1
Ro.	1	2:19			1
2 Pt.	1	1:9			1
Rev.	1	3:17			1
Total	44		9		53

5086. τυφλόω, tuphlo'ō

Book	blind	Total
Jn.	12:40	1
2 Co.	4:4	1
1 Jn.	2:11	1
Total		3

5088. τύφω, tu'phō

Book	smoke	Total
Mt.	12:20	1

5087. τυφόω, tupho'ō

Book	Oc.	be proud	Oc.	be lifted up with pride	Oc.	highminded	Total
1 Ti.	1	6:4	1	3:6			2
2 Ti.					1	3:4	1
Total	1		1		1		3

5089. τυφωνικός, tuphōnikos'

Book	tempestuous	Total
Ac.	27:14	1

5090. Τυχικός, Tuchikos'

Book	Tychicus	Total
Ac.	20:4	1
Eph.	6:21	1
Col.	4:7	1
2 Ti.	4:12	1
Tit.	3:12	1
Total		5

5091. ὑακίνθινος, huakin'thinos

Book	jacinth	Total
Rev.	9:17	1

5092. ὑάκινθος, huak'inthos

Book	jacinth	Total
Rev.	21:20	1

5093. ὑάλινος, hual'inos

Book	of glass	Total
Rev.	4:6; 15:2, 2	3

5094. ὕαλος, hu'alos

Book	glass	Total
Rev.	21:18, 21	2

5095. ὑβρίζω, hubrid'zō

Book	Oc.	entreat spitefully	Oc.	reproach	Oc.	use despitefully	Oc.	shamefully entreat	Total
Mt.	1	22:6							1
Lk.	1	18:32	1	11:45					2
Ac.					1	14:5			1
1 Th.							1	2:2	1
Total	2		1		1		1		5

5096. ὕβρις, hu′bris

Book	Oc.	hurt	Oc.	harm	Oc.	reproach	Total
Ac.	1	27:10	1	27:21			2
2 Co.					1	12:10	1
Total	1		1		1		3

5097. ὑβριστής, hubristes

Book	Oc.	despiteful	Oc.	injurious	Total
Ro.	1	1:30			1
1 Ti.			1	1:13	1
Total	1		1		2

5098. ὑγιαίνω, hugiai′nō

Book	Oc.	sound	Oc.	be sound	Oc.	be whole	Oc.	whole	Oc.	wholesome	Oc.	be in health	Oc.	safe and sound	Total
Lk.					1	5:31	1	7:10					1	15:27	3
1 Ti.	1	1:10							1	6:3					2
2 Ti.	2	1:13; 4:3													2
Tit.	3	1:9; 2:1, 2	1	1:13											4
3 Jn.											1	1:2			1
Total	6		1		1		1		1		1		1		12

5099. ὑγιής, hugies′

Book	Oc.	whole	Oc.	sound	Total
Mt.	2	12:13; 15:31			2
Mk.	2	3:5; 5:34			2
Lk.	1	6:10			1
Jn.	7	5:4, 6, 9, 11, 14, 15; 7:23			7
Ac.	1	4:10			1
Tit.			1	2:8	1
Total	13		1		14

5100. ὑγρός, hugros′

Book	green	Total
Lk.	23:31	1

5101. ὑδριά, hudria′

Book	waterpot	Total
Jn.	2:6, 7; 4:28	3

5102. ὑδροποτέω, hudropote′ō

Book	drink water	Total
1 Ti.	5:23	1

5103. ὑδρωπικός, hudrōpikos′

Book	have the dropsy	Total
Lk.	14:2	1

5104. ὕδωρ, hu′dōr

Book	water	Total
Mt.	3:11, 16; 8:32; 14:28, 29; 17:15; 27:24	7
Mk.	1:8, 10; 9:22, 41; 14:13	5
Lk.	3:16; 7:44; 8:24, 25; 16:24; 22:10	6
Jn.	1:26, 31, 33; 2:7, 9, 9; 3:5, 23; 4:7, 10, 11, 13, 14, 14, 14, 15, 46; 5:3, 4, 4, 7; 7:38; 13:5; 19:34	24
Ac.	1:5; 8:36, 36, 38, 39; 10:47; 11:16	7
Eph.	5:26	1
Heb.	9:19; 10:22	2
Jas.	3:12	1
1 Pt.	3:20	1
2 Pt.	3:5, 5, 6	3
1 Jn.	5:6, 6, 6, 8	4
Rev.	1:15; 7:17; 8:10, 11, 11; 11:6; 12:15; 14:2, 7; 16:4, 5, 12; 17:1, 15; 19:6; 21:6; 22:1, 17	18
Total		79

5105. ὑετός, huetos′

Book	rain	Total
Ac.	14:17; 28:2	2
Heb.	6:7	1
Jas.	5:7, 18	2
Rev.	11:6	1
Total		6

5106. υἱοθεσία, huiothesi′a

Book	Oc.	adoption	Oc.	adoption of children	Oc.	adoption of sons	Total
Ro.	3	8:15, 23; 9:4					3
Gal.					1	4:5	1
Eph.			1	1:5			1
Total	3		1		1		5

5107a. υἱός, huios′

Filial Titles of Jesus Pertaining to His Deity

Book	Oc.	Son of God (with 2316)	Oc.	Son	Oc.	his Son (with 848)	Oc.	my beloved Son (with 27 and 3350)	Oc.	thy Son (with 4575)	Oc.	only begotten Son (with 3339)	Oc.	Misc.	Total
Mt.	9	4:3, 6; 8:29; 14:33; 16:16; 26:63; 27:40, 43, 54	4	11:27, 27, 27; 28:19			2	3:17; 17:5					1	2:15	16
Mk.	4	1:1; 3:11; 5:7; 15:39	1	13:32			2	1:11; 9:7					1	14:61	8
Lk.	6	1:35; 4:3, 9, 41; 8:28; 22:70	3	10:22, 22, 22			2	3:22; 9:35					1	1:32	12
Jn.	11	1:34, 49; 3:18; 5:25; 6:69; 9:35; 10:36; 11:4, 27; 19:7; 20:31	15	3:35, 36, 36; 5:19, 19, 20, 21, 22, 23, 23, 26; 6:40; 8:35, 36; 14:13	1	3:17			2	17:1, 1	2	1:18; 3:16			31
Ac.	2	8:37; 9:20							1	13:33					3
Ro.	1	1:4			6	1:3, 9; 5:10; 8:3, 29, 32									7
1 Co.			1	15:28	1	1:9									2
2 Co.	1	1:19													1
Gal.	1	2:20			3	1:16; 4:4, 6b									4
Eph.	1	4:13													1
Col.					1	1:13									1
1 Th.					1	1:10									1
Heb.	4	4:14; 6:6; 7:3; 10:29	6	1:2, 5b, 8; 3:6; 5:8; 7:28					2	1:5a; 5:5					12
2 Pt.							1	1:17							1
1 Jn.	8	3:8; 4:15; 5:5, 10a, 12b, 13, 13, 20a	5	2:22, 23, 24; 4:14; 5:12a	8	1:3, 7; 3:23; 4:10; 5:9, 10b, 11, 20b					1	4:9			22
2 Jn.			1	1:9									1	1:3	2
Rev.	1	2:18													1
Total	49		36		21		7		5		3		4		125

Miscellaneous: Mt. 2:15 (with 3350), my Son; Mk. 14:61 (with 3488 and 2128), Son of the Blessed; Lk. 1:32 (with 5210), Son of the Highest; 2 Jn. 1:3 (with 3488 and 3862), Son of the Father.

5107b. υἱός, huios′

Filial Titles of Jesus Pertaining to His Humanity

Book	Oc.	Son of Man (with 444)	Oc.	Son of David (with 1138)	Oc.	son	Oc.	his (David's) son (with 846)	Oc.	firstborn son (with 4316)	Oc.	Misc.	Total
Mt.	32	8:20; 9:6; 10:23; 11:19; 12:8, 32, 40; 13:37, 41; 16:13, 27, 28; 17:9, 12, 22; 18:11; 19:28; 20:18, 28; 24:27, 30, 30, 37, 39, 44; 25:13, 31; 26:2, 24, 24, 45, 64	9	1:1a, 20; 9:27; 12:23; 15:22; 20:30, 31; 21:9, 15	3	1:21, 23; 22:42	1	22:45	1	1:25	2	1:1b; 13:55	48
Mk.	14	2:10, 28; 8:31, 38; 9:9, 12, 31; 10:33, 45; 13:26; 14:21, 21, 41, 62	3	10:47, 48; 12:35			1	12:37			1	6:3	19
Lk.	26	5:24; 6:5, 22; 7:34; 9:22, 26, 44, 56, 58; 11:30; 12:8, 10, 40; 17:22, 24, 26, 30; 18:8, 31; 19:10; 21:27, 36; 22:22, 48, 69; 24:7	3	18:38, 39; 20:41	1	1:31	1	20:44	1	2:7	2	3:23; 4:22	34
Jn.	12	1:51; 3:13, 14; 5:27; 6:27, 53, 62; 8:28; 12:23, 34, 34; 13:31									3	1:45; 6:42; 19:26	15
Ac.	1	7:56											1
Rev.	2	1:13; 14:14									1	12:5	3
Total	87		15		4		3		2		9		120

Miscellaneous: Mt. 1:1b (with 11), son of Abraham; Mt. 13:55 (with 4945), carpenter's son; Mk. 6:3 (with 3137), son of Mary; Lk. 3:23 (with 2501), son of Joseph; Lk. 4:22 (with 2501), Joseph's son; Jn. 1:45 (with 2501), son of Joseph; Jn. 6:42 (with 2501), son of Joseph; Jn. 19:26 (with 4575), thy Son; Rev. 12:5 (with 730), man child.

5107c. υἱός, huios′

Expressing Filial Relationship of Mankind

	Spiritual Relationship of Believers				Human Relationship of Mankind Generally				Evil or Sinful Relationship								
Book	Oc.	child(ren)	Oc.	son(s)	Oc.	child(ren)	Oc.	son(s)	Oc.	child(ren)	Oc.	son(s)	Oc.	children (of Israel)	Oc.	Misc.	Total
Mt.	6	5:9, 45; 8:12; 9:15; 13:38a; 17:26			4	12:27; 17:25; 20:20a; 27:56	11	7:9; 10:37; 17:15; 20:20b, 21; 21:37, 37, 38; 22:2; 23:35; 26:37	3	13:38b; 23:15, 31			1	27:9	1	21:5	26
Mk.	1	2:19					6	3:28; 9:17; 10:35, 46; 12:6, 6							1	3:17	8
Lk.	5	5:34; 6:35; 16:8b; 20:36, 36	2	10:6; 19:9			21	1:13, 36, 57; 3:2; 5:10; 7:12; 9:38, 41; 11:11, 19; 12:53, 53; 15:11, 13, 19, 21, 21, 24, 25, 30; 20:13	2	16:8a; 20:34			1	1:16			31
Jn.	1	12:36			1	4:12	8	1:42; 4:5, 46, 47, 50, 53; 9:19, 20			1	17:12					11
Ac.	1	3:25	1	4:36	1	13:26	9	2:17; 7:16, 21, 29; 13:21; 16:1; 19:14; 23:6, 16	1	13:10			5	5:21; 7:23, 37; 9:15; 10:36			18
Ro.	1	9:26	2	8:14, 19			1	9:9					1	9:27			5
2 Co.			1	6:18									2	3:7, 13			3
Gal.	2	3:7, 26	3	4:6a, 7, 7			4	4:22, 30, 30, 30									9
Eph.							1	3:5	2	2:2; 5:6							3
Col.									1	3:6							1
1 Th.	2	5:5, 5															2
2 Th.											1	2:3					1
Heb.	1	12:5a	4	2:10; 12:5b, 6, 7a			6	2:6; 7:5; 11:21, 24; 12:7b, 8					1	11:22			12
Jas.							1	2:21									1
1 Pt.			1	5:13													1
Rev.			1	21:7									3	2:14; 7:4; 21:12			4
Total	20		15		6		68		9		2		14		2		136

Miscellaneous: Mt. 21:5, foal; Mk. 3:17 (with 1027), sons of thunder.

Word 5107 has 381 occurrences.

5108. ὕλη, hu′lē

Book	matter	Total
Jas.	3:5	1

5109. ὑμᾶς, humas′

Book	Oc.	you	Oc.	ye	Oc.	for your sakes (with 1223)	Oc.	Not Tr.	Oc.	Misc.	Total
Mt.	37	3:11, 11; 4:19; 5:11, 44, 44, 44, 44, 46; 6:30; 7:6, 15, 23; 10:13, 14, 16, 17, 17, 19, 23, 40; 11:28, 29; 12:28; 21:24, 31, 32; 23:34, 35; 24:4, 9, 9; 25:12; 26:32, 55; 28:7, 14	1	6:8							38
Mk.	14	1:8, 8, 17; 6:11; 9:19, 41; 11:29; 13:5, 9, 11, 36; 14:28, 49; 16:7									14
Lk.	39	3:16, 16; 6:9, 22, 22, 26, 27, 28, 32, 33; 9:5, 41; 10:3, 6, 8, 9, 10, 11, 16, 19; 11:20; 12:11, 12, 14, 28; 13:25, 27, 28; 16:9, 26; 19:31; 20:3; 21:12, 34; 22:31, 35; 23:15; 24:44, 49									39
Jn.	32	4:38; 5:42; 6:61, 70; 7:7; 8:32, 36; 12:35; 13:34; 14:3, 18, 18, 26a, 28; 15:9, 12, 15, 15, 16, 16, 18, 19, 19, 20; 16:2, 2, 7, 7, 13, 22, 27; 20:21	1	3:7	2	11:15; 12:30			1	14:26b	36
Ac.	21	1:8; 2:22, 29; 3:22, 26; 7:43; 13:32, 40; 15:24, 25; 18:21; 19:13; 20:20, 28, 29, 32; 22:1; 23:15; 27:22, 34; 28:20	3	14:15; 17:22; 19:36					3	17:28; 18:15; 24:22	27
Ro.	26	1:10, 11a, 13, 13; 2:24; 10:19, 19; 12:1, 14; 15:13a, 15, 22, 23, 24, 24, 29, 30, 32; 16:16, 17, 19, 21, 22, 23, 23, 25	5	1:11b; 7:4; 11:25; 12:2; 15:13b	1	11:28					32
1 Co.	35	1:8, 10; 2:1, 3; 3:2; 4:14, 15, 16, 17, 18, 19, 21; 7:5, 32; 10:13a, 13b, 27; 11:2, 3, 14, 22; 12:1; 14:6, 6, 36; 16:5, 6, 7, 7, 10, 12, 15, 19, 19, 20	5	1:7; 10:1, 13c, 20; 14:5	1	4:6					41
2 Co.	50	1:8, 15, 16, 18; 2:1, 2, 3, 4, 5, 8; 3:1; 6:11, 17; 7:4, 8, 8, 12, 15; 8:6, 17, 22, 23; 9:4, 5, 8, 14; 10:1, 1, 9, 14; 11:2, 2, 6, 9, 11, 20, 20; 12:14, 14, 15, 16, 16, 17, 17, 18, 20, 21; 13:1, 4, 13	4	2:7; 6:1; 7:11; 13:7	3	2:10; 4:15; 8:9			2	1:12; 13:3	59
Gal.	19	1:6, 7, 9; 2:5; 3:1; 4:11, 11, 17, 17, 18, 20; 5:2, 7, 8, 10, 10, 12; 6:12, 13									19
Eph.	4	2:1; 4:1; 5:6; 6:22	4	1:18; 4:17, 22; 6:11					2	1:15; 3:2	10
Phl.	9	1:7a, 8, 24, 26, 27; 2:25, 26; 4:21, 22	3	1:7b, 10, 12							12
Col.	14	1:6, 21, 22, 25; 2:4, 8, 13, 16, 18; 4:8, 10, 10, 12, 14	3	1:10; 2:1; 4:6							17
1 Th.	27	1:5a, 9; 2:1, 2, 9, 11, 12b, 18; 3:2, 2, 4, 5, 6, 11, 12, 12; 4:1a, 10, 13; 5:4, 12, 12, 14, 18, 23, 24, 27	4	1:7; 2:12a; 4:1b, 3	2	1:5b; 3:9					33
2 Th.	13	1:6, 10, 11; 2:1, 3, 5, 13, 14, 17; 3:1, 3, 4, 10	3	1:5; 2:2; 3:6							16
Heb.	6	5:12; 9:20; 13:21, 22, 23, 24									6
Jas.	2	2:6; 4:10	3	2:7; 4:2, 15							5
1 Pt.	13	1:4, 10, 12, 15, 20, 25; 2:9; 3:13, 15; 4:14a; 5:6, 10, 13							1	4:14b	14
2 Pt.	3	1:12, 13; 2:3	2	1:15; 3:11			1	3:8			6
1 Jn.	6	2:26, 27, 27, 27; 3:7, 13									6
2 Jn.	2	1:10, 12									2
Jd.	2	1:5a, 24	1	1:5b							3
Rev.	2	2:24; 12:12									2
Total	376		42		9		1		9		437

Miscellaneous: Jn. 14:26b, your; Ac. 17:28 (with 2596), your own; Ac. 18:15 (with 2596), your; Ac. 24:22, your matter; 2 Co. 1:12 (with 4214), to you-ward; 2 Co. 13:3 (with 1519), to you-ward; Eph. 1:15 (with 2596), your; Eph. 3:2 (with 1519), to you-ward; 1 Pt. 4:14b (with 2596), your.

5110. ὑμεῖς, humeis′

Book	Oc.	ye	Oc.	ye yourselves	Oc.	you	Oc.	Not Tr.	Total
Mt.	32	5:13, 14, 48; 6:9, 26; 7:11, 12; 9:4; 10:20, 31; 13:18; 14:16; 15:3, 5, 16; 16:15; 19:28, 28; 20:4, 7; 21:13, 32; 23:8, 8, 13, 28, 32; 24:33, 44; 26:31; 27:24; 28:5							32
Mk.	11	6:31, 37; 7:11, 18; 8:29; 11:17, 26; 12:27; 13:11, 23, 29					1	13:9	12
Lk.	21	6:31; 9:13, 20, 55; 10:23, 24; 11:13, 39, 48; 12:24, 29, 40; 16:15; 17:10; 19:46; 21:31; 22:26, 28, 70; 24:48, 49	1	12:36			1	9:44	23
Jn.	68	1:26; 3:28; 4:20, 22, 32, 35, 38, 38; 5:20, 33, 34, 35, 38, 39, 44, 45; 6:67; 7:8, 28, 34, 36, 47; 8:14, 15, 21, 22, 23, 23, 31, 38, 41, 44, 46, 47, 49, 54; 9:19, 27, 30; 10:26, 36; 11:49; 13:10, 13, 14, 15, 33, 34; 14:3, 17, 19, 19, 20, 20; 15:3, 4, 5, 14, 16, 16, 27; 16:20, 20, 22, 27; 18:31; 19:6, 35							68
Ac.	26	1:5; 2:15, 33, 36; 3:13, 14, 25; 4:7, 10; 5:30; 7:4, 26, 51, 51, 52; 8:24; 10:28, 37; 11:16; 15:7; 19:15; 20:18, 25; 22:3; 23:15; 27:31							26
Ro.	7	1:6; 6:11; 7:4; 8:9; 9:26; 11:30; 16:17							7
1 Co.	18	1:30; 3:17, 23; 4:10, 10, 10; 5:2, 12; 6:8; 9:1, 2; 10:15; 12:27; 14:9, 12; 16:1, 6, 16							18
2 Co.	11	1:14; 3:2; 6:13, 16; 6:18; 8:9; 9:4; 11:7; 12:11; 13:7, 9							11
Gal.	5	3:28, 29; 4:12; 5:13; 6:1							5
Eph.	6	1:13; 2:11, 13, 22; 4:20; 6:21			1	5:33			7
Phl.	3	2:18; 4:15, 15							3
Col.	6	3:4, 7, 8, 13; 4:1, 16							6
1 Th.	10	1:6; 2:10, 14, 14, 19, 20; 3:8; 4:9; 5:4, 5							10
2 Th.	2	1:12; 3:13							2
Jas.	2	2:6; 5:8							2
1 Pt.	1	2:9					1	4:1	2
2 Pt.	1	3:17							1
1 Jn.	4	1:3; 2:20, 24b; 4:4					2	2:24a, 27	6
Jd.	2	1:17, 20							2
Total	236		1		1		5		243

5111. Ὑμέναιος, Humen′aios

Book	Hymenaeus	Total
1 Ti.	1:20	1
2 Ti.	2:17	1
Total		2

5112. ὑμέτερος, humet′eros

Book	Oc.	your	Oc.	yours	Oc.	your own	Total
Lk.			1	6:20	1	16:12	2
Jn.	2	7:6; 8:17	1	15:20			3
Ac.	1	27:34					1
Ro.	1	11:31					1
1 Co.	1	15:31					1
2 Co.	1	8:8					1
Gal.	1	6:13					1
Total	7		2		1		10

5113. ὑμῖν, humin′

Book	Oc.	you	Oc.	ye	Oc.	your	Oc.	Not Tr.	Oc.	Misc.	Total
Mt.	103	3:7, 9; 5:18, 20, 22, 28, 32, 34, 39, 44; 6:2, 5, 14, 16, 25, 29, 33; 7:2, 7, 7, 12; 8:10, 11; 9:29; 10:15, 19, 20, 23, 27, 42; 11:9, 11, 17, 17, 21, 22, 22, 24; 12:6, 31, 36; 13:11, 17; 16:11, 28; 17:12, 20, 20; 18:3, 10, 13, 18, 19, 35; 19:8, 9, 23, 24, 28; 20:4, 26, 26, 27, 32; 21:3, 21, 24, 27, 31, 43; 22:31; 23:3, 13, 14, 15, 16, 23, 25, 27, 29, 36, 38, 39; 24:2, 23, 25, 26, 34, 47; 25:9, 12, 34, 40, 45; 26:13, 15, 21, 29, 64; 27:17, 21; 28:7, 20	4	18:12; 21:28; 22:42; 26:66					2	6:19, 20	109
Mk.	35	3:28; 4:11, 24, 24; 6:11; 8:12; 9:1, 13, 41; 10:3, 5, 15, 29, 36, 43, 43; 11:3, 23, 24a, 25, 29, 33; 12:43; 13:11, 21, 23, 30, 37; 14:9, 13, 15, 18, 25; 15:9; 16:7	2	11:24b; 14:64							37
Lk.	95	2:10, 11, 12; 3:7, 8, 13; 4:24, 25; 6:24, 25, 25, 26, 27, 28, 31, 38, 38, 47; 7:9, 26, 28, 32, 32; 8:10; 9:27, 48; 10:8, 11, 12, 13, 14, 19, 20, 24; 11:8, 9, 9, 9, 41, 42, 43, 44, 46, 47, 51, 52; 12:4, 5, 5, 8, 22, 27, 31, 32, 37, 44, 51; 13:3, 5, 24, 25, 27, 35, 35; 14:24; 15:7, 10; 16:9, 12; 17:6, 10, 23, 34; 18:8, 14, 17, 29; 19:26, 40; 20:8; 21:3, 13, 15a, 32; 22:10, 12, 16, 18, 26, 29, 37, 67; 24:6, 36, 44	3	6:32, 33, 34	2	16:11; 21: 15b					100
Jn.	101	1:51; 2:5; 3:12, 12; 4:35; 5:19, 24, 25, 38; 6:26, 27, 32, 32, 32, 36, 47, 53, 63, 65; 7:19, 22; 8:24, 25, 34, 37, 40, 51, 58; 9:27; 10:1, 7, 25, 26, 32; 12:24; 13:12, 15, 15, 16, 19, 20, 21, 33, 34; 14:2, 2, 3, 10, 12, 16, 17, 17, 20, 25, 25, 26, 27, 27, 27, 28, 29; 15:3, 4, 7, 7, 11, 11, 14, 15, 16, 17, 20, 21, 26; 16:1, 3, 4, 4, 4, 6, 7, 7, 12, 13, 14, 15, 20, 23, 23, 25, 25, 25, 26, 33; 18:8, 39b, 39c; 19:4; 20:19, 21, 26	2	11:56; 18:39a							103
Ac.	30	2:14, 39; 3:14, 20, 22, 26; 4:10; 5:28, 38; 7:37; 13:26, 26, 34, 38, 38, 41, 46; 14:15; 15:28; 17:3, 23; 20:20, 26, 27, 32, 35; 22:25; 25:5; 26:8; 28:28	2	5:9; 13:15							32
Ro.	15	1:7, 11, 12, 13, 15; 8:9, 10, 11, 11; 11:13; 12:3; 15:5, 15, 32; 16:1			1	16:19					16
1 Co.	43	1:3, 4, 6, 10, 11; 2:1, 2; 3:1, 3, 16, 18; 4:8, 17; 5:1, 9, 11; 6:2, 5b, 7, 19; 7:35; 9:2, 11; 10:27, 28; 11:2, 18, 19, 19, 22, 23, 30; 12:3, 31; 14:6, 25, 37; 15:1, 1, 2, 3, 12, 51			2	6:5a; 15:34			1	11:13	46
2 Co.	29	1:2, 13, 19, 21; 2:3, 4; 4:12, 14; 5:12, 12; 6:18; 7:7, 11, 12, 14, 16; 8:1, 10; 9:1, 14; 10:1, 15; 11:7, 9; 12:12, 19, 20; 13:3, 5	1	8:13	1	5:13					31
Gal.	16	1:3, 8, 8, 11, 20; 3:1, 5, 5; 4:13, 15, 16, 19, 20; 5:2, 21; 6:11									16
Eph.	8	1:2, 17; 2:17; 3:16; 4:6, 32; 5:3; 6:21									8
Phl.	13	1:2, 6, 25, 28, 29; 2:5, 13, 17, 19; 3:1, 1, 15, 18									13
Col.	11	1:2, 5, 6, 27; 2:5, 13; 3:13, 16; 4:7, 9, 16									11
1 Th.	14	1:1, 5; 2:8, 10, 13; 3:4, 7; 4:2, 6, 9, 11, 15; 5:1, 12									14
2 Th.	12	1:2, 4, 7, 12; 2:5; 3:4, 6, 7, 9, 10, 11, 16									12
Phe.	3	1:3, 6, 22									3
Heb.	7	12:5, 7; 13:7, 17, 19, 21, 22									7
Jas.	9	1:26; 3:13; 4:1, 8; 5:3, 6, 13, 14, 19									9
1 Pt.	11	1:2, 12, 13; 2:7; 3:15; 4:12b, 12c; 5:1, 2, 12, 14					1	4:12a			12
2 Pt.	8	1:2, 8, 11, 16; 2:1, 13; 3:1, 15									8
1 Jn.	23	1:2, 3, 4, 5; 2:1, 7, 8, 8, 12, 12, 13, 13, 13, 14, 14, 14, 21, 24, 24, 26, 27; 4:4; 5:13									23
2 Jn.	1	1:12									1
Jd.	4	1:2, 3, 3, 18									4
Rev.	6	1:4; 2:13, 23, 24; 18:6; 22:16									6
Total	597		14		6		1		3		621

Miscellaneous: Mt. 6:19, 20, yourselves; 1 Co. 11:13 (with 846), yourselves.

5114. ὑμνέω, humne′ō

Book	Oc.	sing an hymn	Oc.	sing praise	Total
Mt.	1	26:30			1
Mk.	1	14:26			1
Ac.			1	16:25	1
Heb.			1	2:12	1
Total	2		2		4

5115. ὕμνος, hum′nos

Book	hymn	Total
Eph.	5:19	1
Col.	3:16	1
Total		2

See Page 357 for Word 5116.

5117. ὑπάγω, hupag′ō

Book	Oc.	go	Oc.	go (one's) way	Oc.	go away	Oc.	get thee	Oc.	depart	Oc.	get thee hence	Total
Mt.	12	5:41; 8:32; 9:6; 13:44; 18: 15; 19:21; 20:4, 7; 21:28; 26:18, 24; 28:10	5	5:24; 8:4, 13; 20:14; 27:65			1	16:23			1	4:10	19
Mk.	6	5:19, 34; 6:31, 38; 14:13, 21	7	1:44; 2:11; 7:29; 10: 21, 52; 11:2; 16:7			1	8:33	1	6:33			15
Lk.	4	8:42; 12:58; 17:14; 19:30	1	10:3			1	4:8					6
Jn.	27	3:8; 4:16; 6:21; 7:3, 33; 8: 14, 14, 21b, 22; 9:7, 11; 11: 8, 31, 44; 12:35; 13:3, 33, 36, 36; 14:4, 5; 15:16; 16:5b, 10, 16, 17; 21:3	3	8:21a; 16:5a; 18:8	3	6:67; 12:11; 14:28							33
Jas.									1	2:16			1
1 Jn.	1	2:11											1
Rev.	5	10:8; 13:10; 14:4; 17:8, 11	1	16:1									6
Total	55		17		3		3		2		1		81

5118. ὑπακοή, hupakoe̱′

Book	Oc.	obedience	Oc.	obedient	Oc.	to make obedient (with 1519)	Oc.	to obey (with 1519)	Oc.	obeying	Total
Ro.	5	1:5; 5:19; 6:16b; 16:19, 26			1	15:18	1	6:16a			7
2 Co.	3	7:15; 10:5, 6									3
Phe.	1	1:21									1
Heb.	1	5:8									1
1 Pt.	1	1:2	1	1:14					1	1:22	3
Total	11		1		1		1		1		15

5119. ὑπακούω, hupakou'ō

Book	Oc.	obey	Oc.	be obedient to	Oc.	hearken	Total
Mt.	1	8:27					1
Mk.	2	1:27; 4:41					2
Lk.	2	8:25; 17:6					2
Ac.			1	6:7	1	12:13	2
Ro.	4	6:12, 16, 17; 10:16					4
Eph.	1	6:1	1	6:5			2
Phl.	1	2:12					1
Col.	2	3:20, 22					2
2 Th.	2	1:8; 3:14					2
Heb.	2	5:9; 11:8					2
1 Pt.	1	3:6					1
Total	18		2		1		21

5120. ὕπανδρος, hup'andros

Book	which hath an husband	Total
Ro.	7:2	1

5122. ὑπάντησις, hupan'tēsis

Book	to meet (with 1519)	Total
Jn.	12:13	1

5121. ὑπαντάω, hupanta'ō

Book	Oc.	meet	Oc.	go and meet	Total
Mt.	1	8:28			1
Lk.	1	8:27			1
Jn.	2	11:30; 12:18	1	11:20	3
Total	4		1		5

5124. ὑπάρχοντα, hupar'chonta

Book	Oc.	goods	Oc.	that (one) has	Oc.	things which (one) possesses	Oc.	sub-stance	Total
Mt.	2	24:47; 25:14	1	19:21					3
Lk.	3	11:21; 16:1; 19:8	3	12:33, 44; 14:33	1	12:15	1	8:3	8
Ac.					1	4:32			1
1 Co.	1	13:3							1
Heb.	1	10:34							1
Total	7		4		2		1		14

5123. ὕπαρξις, hup'arxis

Book	Oc.	goods	Oc.	substance	Total
Ac.	1	2:45			1
Heb.			1	10:34	1
Total	1		1		2

5116. ὑμῶν, humōn'

Book	Oc.	your	Oc.	you	Oc.	ye	Oc.	yours	Oc.	Not Tr.	Oc.	Misc.	Total
Mt.	62	5:12a, 16, 16, 16, 20, 37, 44, 45, 47, 48; 6:1, 1, 8, 14, 15, 15, 21, 21, 25, 25, 26, 32; 7:6, 11, 11; 9:4, 11, 29; 10:9, 13, 13, 14, 14, 20, 29, 30; 11: 29; 12:27, 27; 13:16, 16; 15:3, 6; 17: 20, 24; 18:14, 35; 19:8, 8; 20:26, 27; 23:8, 9, 9, 10, 11b, 32, 34, 38; 24:20, 42; 25:8	15	5:11, 12b; 6:27; 7:9; 12:11; 15: 7; 17:17, 17; 18:19; 21:2, 43; 23:11a; 26:21, 29; 28:20							1	23:15	78
Mk.	11	2:8; 6:11b; 7:13; 8:17; 10:5, 43; 11: 25, 25, 26, 26; 13:18	6	6:11a; 7:6; 9:19; 10:44; 11: 2; 14:18							1	7:9	18
Lk.	44	3:14; 4:21; 5:4, 22; 6:22, 23, 24, 27, 35, 35, 36, 38; 8:25; 9:5, 44; 10:6, 11, 20; 11:13, 19, 19, 39, 46, 47, 48; 12: 7, 22, 30, 32, 34, 34, 35; 13:35; 16:15; 21:14, 18, 19, 19, 28, 28, 34; 22:53b; 23:28; 24:38	20	9:41; 10:16; 11:5, 11; 12:25; 13:15; 14:5, 28, 33; 15:4; 16: 26; 17:7, 21; 21:16; 22:15, 19, 20, 27, 53a; 23:14	2	12:33; 22:10							66
Jn.	30	4:35; 6:49, 58; 8:21, 24, 24, 38, 41, 42, 44, 54, 56; 9:19, 41; 10:34; 13: 14; 14:1, 27; 15:11, 16; 16:6, 20, 22a, 22b, 24; 18:31; 19:14, 15; 20:17, 17	23	1:26; 5:45, 45; 6;64, 70; 7:19, 33; 8:7, 26, 46, 55; 12:35; 13: 18, 21, 33; 14:9, 16, 30; 15: 18; 16:4, 5, 22c, 26									53
Ac.	20	2:17, 17, 17, 17, 39; 3:17, 19, 22, 22; 5:28; 7:37, 37, 43, 51, 52; 13:41; 15: 24; 17:23; 18:6a; 19:37	15	1:7, 11; 2:22, 38; 3:16; 4:10, 11, 19; 6:3; 18:14; 20:18; 24: 21; 25:26; 27:22, 34							3	3:26; 18:6b; 20:30	38
Ro.	16	1:8a; 6:12, 13, 13, 19, 19, 19, 22; 8: 11; 12:1, 1, 2; 14:16; 15:24b; 16:19, 20a	12	1:8b, 9, 12; 6:14; 12:18; 15: 14, 24a, 28, 33; 16:2, 20b, 24									28
1 Co.	17	1:4, 26; 2:5; 5:6; 6:15, 19, 20, 20; 7: 5, 14; 9:11; 14:34; 15:14, 17, 17, 58; 16:3	16	1:11, 12, 13, 14; 4:3; 5:2; 6: 1; 7:28; 9:12; 11:24; 12:21; 14:26, 36; 16:2, 23, 24	4	5:4; 11: 18, 20; 14:18	4	3:21, 22; 8:9; 16:18			4	5:13; 7: 35; 16: 14, 17	45
2 Co.	27	1:6, 6, 14, 24, 24; 4:5; 5:11; 7:7, 7, 7, 13a; 8:14, 14, 19, 24, 24; 9:2a, 5, 10, 10, 13; 10:6, 8, 15; 11:3; 12:19; 13:9	26	1:7, 16, 16, 23; 2:3, 9; 3:1; 7: 4, 12, 13b, 14, 15; 8:16; 9:2b, 3, 14; 10:13, 14, 16; 11:8; 12: 11, 13, 14a, 15; 13:11, 14	1	1:11	1	12:14b			3	6:12; 8:7; 9: 2c	58
Gal.	4	4:6, 15a, 16; 6:18	2	3:2; 4:12	1	4:15a							7
Eph.	15	1:13, 18; 3:13b, 17; 4:4, 23, 26, 29; 5: 19; 6:1, 4, 5, 9, 14, 22	5	1:16, 16; 3:1, 13a; 4:31							1	2:8	21
Phl.	13	1:5, 9, 19, 25, 26; 2:17, 25, 30; 4:5, 6, 7a, 17, 19	6	1:3, 4, 7; 4:9, 18, 23					1	4:7b	3	1:27; 2: 19, 20	23
Col.	13	1:4, 8; 2:5, 5, 13; 3:3, 5, 8, 15, 16, 21; 4:6, 8b	10	1:3, 7, 9, 24; 2:1; 4:9, 12, 12, 13, 18							1	4:8a	24
1 Th.	13	1:3, 4, 8b; 2:17b; 3:2, 5, 6b, 7, 10, 10, 13; 4:3, 11	15	1:2, 2, 8a; 2:6, 7, 8, 9, 11, 17a; 3:6a, 9; 4:4; 5:12, 23, 28									28
2 Th.	5	1:3b, 4, 4; 2:17; 3:5	7	1:3a, 3c, 11; 2:13; 3:8, 16, 18									12
2 Ti.			1	4:22									1
Tit.			2	2:8; 3:15									2
Phe.	2	1:22, 25											2
Heb.	11	3:8, 9, 15; 4:7; 6:10; 9:14; 10:34, 35; 12:3, 13; 13:17b	9	3:12, 13; 4:1; 6:9, 11; 13:7, 17a, 24, 25									20
Jas.	19	1:3, 21; 2:2; 3:14; 4:1, 1, 3, 9, 14, 16; 5:1, 2, 2, 3, 3, 4a, 5, 8, 12	5	1:5; 2:6, 16; 4:7; 5:4b									24
1 Pt.	17	1:7, 9, 13, 14, 17, 18, 21, 22; 2:12a, 25; 3:2, 7, 15, 16b; 5:7a, 8, 9	4	2:12b; 3:16a; 4:15; 5:7b	1	4:4							22
2 Pt.	4	1:5, 10, 19; 3:1											4
1 Jn.	1	1:4											1
2 Jn.			1	1:3									1
Jd.	2	1:12, 20											2
Rev.	2	1:9; 2:23	3	2:10; 18:20; 22:21									5
Total	348		203		9		5		1		17		583

Miscellaneous: Mt. 23:15, yourselves; Mk. 7:9, your own; Ac. 3:26, his; Ac. 18:6b, your own; Ac. 20:30, your own; 1 Co. 5:13 (with 846), yourselves; 1 Co. 7:35, your own; 1 Co. 16:14, your things; 1 Co. 16:17, on your part; 2 Co. 6:12, your own; 2 Co. 8:7, your: 2 Co. 9:2c (with 1537), your; Eph. 2:8, yourselves; Phl. 1:27 (with 3912 and 3488), your affairs; Phl. 2:19, 20 (with 3912 and 3488), your state; Col. 4:8a (with 3912 and 3488), your estate.

5125. ὑπάρχω, hupar'chō

Book	Oc.	be	Oc.	have	Oc.	live	Oc.	after	Oc.	Not Tr.	Total
Lk.	5	8:41; 9:48; 11:13; 16:14, 23			1	7:25			1	23:50	7
Ac.	22	2:30; 4:34, 34; 5:4; 7:55; 8:16; 10:12; 14:8; 16:3, 20, 37; 17:24, 27, 29; 19:36, 40; 21:20; 22:3; 27:12, 34; 28:7, 18	2	3:6; 4:37			1	27:21	1	3:2	26
Ro.	1	4:19									1
1 Co.	4	7:26; 11:7, 18; 12:22									4
2 Co.	2	8:17; 12:16									2
Gal.	2	1:14; 2:14									2
Phl.	2	2:6; 3:20									2
Jas.	1	2:15									1
2 Pt.	3	1:8; 2:19; 3:11									3
Total	42		2		1		1		2		48

5126. ὑπείκω, hupei'kō

Book	submit (one's) self	Total
Heb.	13:17	1

5127. ὑπεναντίος, hupenanti'os

Book	Oc.	contrary	Oc.	adversary	Total
Col.	1	2:14			1
Heb.			1	10:27	1
Total	1		1		2

5128a. ὑπέρ, huper' (with genitive)

Book	Oc.	for	Oc.	of	Oc.	for (one's) sake	Oc.	on (one's) behalf	Oc.	in (one's) stead	Oc.	Misc.	Total
Mt.	1	5:44											1
Mk.											1	9:40	1
Lk.	4	6:28; 9:50; 22:19, 20											4
Jn.	9	6:51; 10:11, 15; 11:4, 50, 51, 52; 15:13; 18:14			3	13:37, 38; 17:19							12
Ac.	7	5:41; 8:24; 12:5; 15:26; 21:13, 26; 26:1			1	9:16							8
Ro.	18	1:5, 8; 5:6, 7, 7, 8; 8:26, 27, 31, 32, 34; 9:3; 10:1; 14:15; 15:8, 9, 30; 16:4									1	9:27	19
1 Co.	9	1:13; 4:6b; 5:7; 10:30; 11:24; 12:25; 15:3, 29, 29											9
2 Co.	15	1:6, 6, 11a; 5:14, 15, 15, 20a, 21; 7:12; 8:16; 9:14; 12:8, 15, 19; 13:8	9	1:7, 8a; 7:4, 14; 8:23; 9:2, 3; 12:5, 5	1	12:10	3	1:11b; 5:12; 8:24	1	5:20b	1	7:7	30
Gal.	3	1:4; 2:20; 3:13											3
Eph.	8	1:16; 3:1, 13; 5:2, 20, 25; 6:19, 20											8
Phl.	1	1:4	3	1:7; 2:13; 4:10	1	1:29b					1	1:29a	6
Col.	5	1:7, 9, 24a; 4:12, 13			1	1:24b							6
1 Th.	1	5:10											1
2 Th.	2	1:4, 5									1	2:1	3
1 Ti.	3	2:1, 2, 6											3
Tit.	1	2:14											1
Phe.									1	1:13			1
Heb.	11	2:9; 5:1, 1, 3; 6:20; 7:25, 27; 9:7, 24; 10:12; 13:17											11
Jas.	1	5:16											1
1 Pt.	3	2:21; 3:18; 4:1											3
1 Jn.	2	3:16, 16											2
3 Jn.					1	1:7							1
Total	104		12		8		3		2		5		134

Miscellaneous: Mk. 9:40, on one's part; Ro. 9:27, concerning; 2 Co. 7:7, toward; Phl. 1:29a, in the behalf of; 2 Th. 2:1, by.

5128b. ὑπέρ, huper' (with accusative)

Book	Oc.	above	Oc.	more than	Oc.	than	Oc.	beyond	Oc.	to	Oc.	over	Total
Mt.	2	10:24, 24	2	10:37, 37									4
Lk.	1	6:40			1	16:8							2
Ac.	1	26:13											1
1 Co.	2	4:6a; 10:13											2
2 Co.	2	1:8b; 12:6					1	8:3	1	12:13			4
Gal.	1	1:14											1
Eph.	1	3:20a									1	1:22	2
Phl.	1	2:9											1
Phe.	1	1:16	1	1:21									2
Heb.					1	4:12							1
Total	12		3		2		1		1		1		20

5128c. ὑπέρ, huper' (as an adverb)

Book	Oc.	very chiefest (with 3029)	Oc.	more	Oc.	exceeding abundantly (with 1537 and 3953)	Oc.	exceedingly (with 1537 and 3953)	Oc.	very highly (with 1537 and 3953)	Total
2 Co.	2	11:5; 12:11	1	11:23							3
Eph.					1	3:20b					1
1 Th.							1	3:10	1	5:13	2
Total	2		1		1		1		1		6

Word 5128 has 160 occurrences.

5129. ὑπεραίρομαι, huperai'romai

Book	Oc.	be exalted above measure	Oc.	exalt (one's) self	Total
2 Co.	2	12:7, 7			2
2 Th.			1	2:4	1
Total	2		1		3

5130. ὑπέρακμος, huper'akmos

Book	pass the flower of (one's) age (with 5500)	Total
1 Co.	7:36	1

5131. ὑπεράνω, huperan′ō

Book	Oc.	far above	Oc.	over	Total
Eph.	2	1:21; 4:10			2
Heb.			1	9:5	1
Total	2		1		3

5132. ὑπεραυξάνω, huperauxan′ō

Book	grow exceedingly	Total
2 Th.	1:3	1

5133. ὑπερβαίνω, huperbai′nō

Book	go beyond	Total
1 Th.	4:6	1

5134. ὑπερβαλλόντως, huperballon′tōs

Book	above measure	Total
2 Co.	11:23	1

5135. ὑπερβάλλω, huperbal′lō

Book	Oc.	exceed	Oc.	excel	Oc.	pass	Total
2 Co.	1	9:14	1	3:10			2
Eph.	2	1:19; 2:7			1	3:19	3
Total	3		1		1		5

5137. ὑπερείδω, huperei′dō

Book	wink at	Total
Ac.	17:30	1

5136. ὑπερβολή, huperbolē′

Book	Oc.	far more (with 2596)	Oc.	exceeding (with 2596)	Oc.	more excellent (with 2596)	Oc.	out of measure (with 2596)	Oc.	beyond measure (with 2596)	Oc.	excel-lency	Oc.	abun-dance	Oc.	exceeding (with 1519)	Total
Ro.			1	7:13													1
1 Co.					1	12:31											1
2 Co.	1	4:17a					1	1:8			1	4:7	1	12:7	1	4:17b	5
Gal.									1	1:13							1
Total	1		1		1		1		1		1		1		1		8

5138. ὑπερέκεινα, huperek′eina

Book	beyond	Total
2 Co.	10:16	1

5139. ὑπερεκτείνω, huperektei′nō

Book	stretch beyond	Total
2 Co.	10:14	1

5140. ὑπερεκχύνω, huperekchu′nō

Book	run over	Total
Lk.	6:38	1

5141. ὑπερεντυγχάνω, huperentungchan′ō

Book	make intercession for	Total
Ro.	8:26	1

5142. ὑπερέχω, huperech′ō

Book	Oc.	higher	Oc.	better	Oc.	excellency	Oc.	pass	Oc.	supreme	Total
Ro.	1	13:1									1
Phl.			1	2:3	1	3:8	1	4:7			3
1 Pt.									1	2:13	1
Total	1		1		1		1		1	.	5

5143. ὑπερηφανία, huperēphani′a

Book	pride	Total
Mk.	7:22	1

5144. ὑπερήφανος, huperē′phanos

Book	proud	Total
Lk.	1:51	1
Ro.	1:30	1
2 Ti.	3:2	1
Jas.	4:6	1
1 Pt.	5:5	1
Total		5

5145. ὑπερνικάω, hupernika′ō

Book	be more than conqueror	Total
Ro.	8:37	1

5146. ὑπέρογκος, huper′ongkos

Book	great swelling	Total
2 Pt.	2:18	1
Jd.	1:16	1
Total		2

5149. ὑπερπερισσῶς, huperperissōs′

Book	beyond measure	Total
Mk.	7:37	1

5147. ὑπεροχή, huperochē′

Book	Oc.	excellency	Oc.	authority	Total
1 Co.	1	2:1			1
1 Ti.			1	2:2	1
Total	1		1		2

5148. ὑπερπερισσεύω, huperperisseu′ō

Book	Oc.	much more abound	Oc.	exceeding	Total
Ro.	1	5:20			1
2 Co.			1	7:4	1
Total	1		1		2

5150. ὑπερπλεονάζω, huperpleonad′zō

Book	be exceeding abundant	Total
1 Ti.	1:14	1

5152. ὑπερφρονέω, huperphrone′ō

Book	think more highly	Total
Ro.	12:3	1

5153. ὑπερῷον, huperō′on

Book	Oc.	upper chamber	Oc.	upper room	Total
Ac.	3	9:37, 39; 20:8	1	1:13	4

5151. ὑπερυψόω, huperupso′ō

Book	highly exalt	Total
Phl.	2:9	1

5154. ὑπέχω, hupech′ō

Book	suffer	Total
Jd.	1:7	1

5155. ὑπήκοος, hupē′koos

Book	Oc.	obedient	Oc.	obey (with 1096)	Total
Ac.			1	7:39	1
2 Co.	1	2:9			1
Phl.	1	2:8			1
Total	2		1		3

5156. ὑπηρετέω, hupērete′ō

Book	Oc.	serve	Oc.	minister unto	Oc.	minister	Total
Ac.	1	13:36	1	20:34	1	24:23	3

5157. ὑπηρέτης, hupēret′ēs

Book	Oc.	officer	Oc.	minister	Oc.	servant	Total
Mt.	1	5:25			1	26:58	2
Mk.					2	14:54, 65	2
Lk.			2	1:2; 4:20			2
Jn.	8	7:32, 45, 46; 18:3, 12, 18, 22; 19:6			1	18:36	9
Ac.	2	5:22, 26	2	13:5; 26:16			4
1 Co.			1	4:1			1
Total	11		5		4		20

5158. ὕπνος, hup′nos

Book	sleep	Total
Mt.	1:24	1
Lk.	9:32	1
Jn.	11:13	1
Ac.	20:9, 9	2
Ro.	13:11	1
Total		6

5159. ὑπό, hupo′

	With the Genitive										With the Accusative				
Book	Oc.	of	Oc.	by	Oc.	with	Oc.	Not Tr.	Oc.	Misc.	Oc.	under	Oc.	in	Total
Mt.	19	1:22; 2:15, 16; 3:6, 13, 14; 4:1, 1; 5:13; 6:2; 10:22; 11:27; 14:8; 17:12; 19:12; 20:23; 23:7; 24:9; 27:12	4	2:17; 3:3; 22:31; 27:35	3	8:24; 11:7; 14:24					5	5:15; 8:8, 9, 9; 23:37			31
Mk.	7	1:5, 9, 13; 2:3; 5:26; 13:13; 16:11	2	5:4; 13:14							3	4:21, 21, 32			12
Lk.	15	2:21; 3:7; 4:2, 15; 7:30; 8:29, 43; 9:7a, 8; 10:22; 14:8, 8; 17:20; 21:17, 24	9	2:18, 26; 3:19; 5:15; 9:7b; 13:17; 16:22; 21:16; 23:8	4	6:18; 7:24; 8:14; 21:20			1	1:26	7	7:6, 8, 8; 11:33; 13:34; 17:24, 24			36
Jn.	2	10:14; 14:21	1	8:9							1	1:48			4
Ac.	22	2:24; 4:11; 10:33, 38, 41, 42; 12:5; 15:4; 16:4, 6, 14; 17:13; 21:35; 22:11, 12; 23:10, 27, 27; 24:26; 26:2, 6, 7	10	4:36; 10:22b; 13:4, 45; 15:3, 40; 16:2; 24:21; 25:14; 27:11	3	5:16; 17:25; 27:41	4	8:6; 17:19; 20:3; 23:30	1	10:22a	2	2:5; 4:12	1	5:21	43
Ro.	3	12:21; 13:1; 15:15	2	3:21; 15:24							8	3:9, 13; 6:14, 14, 15, 15; 7:14; 16:20			13
1 Co.	13	2:12, 15; 4:3, 3; 6:12; 7:25; 8:3; 10:9, 10, 29; 11:32; 14:24, 24	1	1:11							6	9:20, 20, 20; 10:1; 15:25, 27			20
2 Co.	8	1:4, 16; 2:6; 3:2; 5:4; 8:19a; 11:24; 12:11	3	3:3; 8:19b, 20			1	2:11							12
Gal.	4	1:11; 3:17; 4:9; 5:15									10	3:10, 22, 23, 25; 4:2, 3, 4, 5, 21; 5:18			14
Eph.	1	5:12	2	2:11; 5:13							1	1:22			4
Phl.	1	3:12	1	1:28											2
Col.			1	2:18							1	1:23			2
1 Th.	4	1:4; 2:4, 14, 14													4
2 Th.	1	2:13													1
1 Ti.											1	6:1			1
2 Ti.			1	2:26											1
Heb.	6	5:4, 10; 7:7; 11:23; 12:3, 5	2	2:3; 3:4			1	9:19							9
Jas.	4	1:14; 2:9; 3:4a, 6			1	3:4b					1	2:3			6
1 Pt.	1	2:4									1	5:6			2
2 Pt.			2	1:21; 3:2	2	2:7, 17			1	1:17					5
3 Jn.	2	1:12, 12													2
Jd.	2	1:12, 17									1	1:6			3
Rev.	1	6:13	1	9:18	1	6:8									3
Total	116		42		14		6		3		48		1		230

Miscellaneous: Genitive: Lk. 1:26, from; Ac. 10:22a, among; 2 Pt. 1:17, from.

5160. ὑποβάλλω, hupobal′lō

Book	suborn	Total
Ac.	6:11	1

5161. ὑπογραμμός hupogrammos′

Book	example	Total
1 Pt.	2:21	1

5162. ὑπόδειγμα, hupod′eigma

Book	Oc.	example	Oc.	pattern	Oc.	ensample	Total
Jn.	1	13:15					1
Heb.	2	4:11; 8:5	1	9:23			3
Jas.	1	5:10					1
2 Pt.					1	2:6	1
Total	4		1		1		6

5163. ὑποδείκνυμι, hupodeik′numi

Book	Oc.	shew	Oc.	warn	Oc.	forewarn	Total
Mt.			1	3:7			1
Lk.	1	6:47	1	3:7	1	12:5	3
Ac.	2	9:16; 20:35					2
Total	3		2		1		6

5164. ὑποδέχομαι hupodech′omai

Book	receive	Total
Lk.	10:38; 19:6	2
Ac.	17:7	1
Jas.	2:25	1
Total		4

5165. ὑποδέω, hupode′ō

Book	Oc.	bind on	Oc.	shod	Oc.	be shod with	Total
Mk.					1	6:9	1
Ac.	1	12:8					1
Eph.			1	6:15			1
Total	1		1		1		3

5166. ὑπόδημα, hupod′ēma

Book	shoe	Total
Mt.	3:11; 10:10	2
Mk.	1:7	1
Lk.	3:16; 10:4; 15:22; 22:35	4
Jn.	1:27	1
Ac.	7:33; 13:25	2
Total		10

5167. ὑπόδικος, hupod′ikos

Book	guilty	Total
Ro.	3:19	1

5168. ὑποζύγιον, hupodzug′ion

Book	ass	Total
Mt.	21:5	1
2 Pt.	2:16	1
Total		2

5169. ὑποζώννυμι hupodzōn′numi

Book	undergird	Total
Ac.	27:17	1

5170. ὑποκάτω, hupokat′ō

Book	under	Total
Mk.	6:11; 7:28	2
Lk.	8:16	1
Jn.	1:50	1
Heb.	2:8	1
Rev.	5:3, 13; 6:9; 12:1	4
Total		9

5171. ὑποκρίνομαι hupokrin′omai

Book	feign	Total
Lk.	20:20	1

5172. ὑπόκρισις, hupok′risis

Book	Oc.	hypocrisy	Oc.	dissimulation	Oc.	condemnation	Total
Mt.	1	23:28					1
Mk.	1	12:15					1
Lk.	1	12:1					1
Gal.			1	2:13			1
1 Ti.	1	4:2					1
Jas.					1	5:12	1
1 Pt.	1	2:1					1
Total	5		1		1		7

5173. ὑποκριτής, hupokritēs′

Book	hypocrite	Total
Mt.	6:2, 5, 16; 7:5; 15:7; 16:3; 22:18; 23:13, 14, 15, 23, 25, 27, 29; 24:51	15
Mk.	7:6	1
Lk.	6:42; 11:44; 12:56; 13:15	4
Total		20

5174. ὑπολαμβάνω, hupolamban′ō

Book	Oc.	suppose	Oc.	answer	Oc.	receive	Total
Lk.	1	7:43	1	10:30			2
Ac.	1	2:15			1	1:9	2
Total	2		1		1		4

5175. ὑπολείπω, hupolei′pō

Book	leave	Total
Ro.	11:3	1

5176. ὑπολήνιον, hupolē′nion

Book	winefat	Total
Mk.	12:1	1

5177. ὑπολιμπάνω hupolimpan′ō

Book	leave	Total
1 Pt.	2:21	1

5180. ὑπόμνησις, hupom′nēsis

Book	Oc.	remembrance	Oc.	put in remembrance	Total
2 Ti.	1	1:5			1
2 Pt.	1	3:1	1	1:13	2
Total	2		1		3

5178. ὑπομένω, hupomen′ō

Book	Oc.	endure	Oc.	take patiently	Oc.	tarry behind	Oc.	abide	Oc.	patient	Oc.	suffer	Total
Mt.	2	10:22; 24:13											2
Mk.	1	13:13											1
Lk.					1	2:43							1
Ac.							1	17:14					1
Ro.									1	12:12			1
1 Co.	1	13:7											1
2 Ti.	1	2:10									1	2:12	2
Heb.	4	10:32; 12:2, 3, 7											4
Jas.	2	1:12; 5:11											2
1 Pt.			2	2:20, 20									2
Total	11		2		1		1		1		1		17

5179. ὑπομιμνήσκω, hupomimnēs′kō

Book	Oc.	put in remembrance	Oc.	remember	Oc.	bring to remembrance	Oc.	put in mind	Total
Lk.			1	22:61					1
Jn.					1	14:26			1
2 Ti.	1	2:14							1
Tit.							1	3:1	1
2 Pt.	1	1:12							1
3 Jn.			1	1:10					1
Jd.	1	1:5							1
Total	3		2		1		1		7

5181. ὑπομονή, hupomonē′

Book	Oc.	patience	Oc.	enduring	Oc.	patient continuance	Oc.	patient waiting	Total
Lk.	2	8:15; 21:19							2
Ro.	5	5:3, 4; 8:25; 15:4, 5			1	2:7			6
2 Co.	2	6:4; 12:12	1	1:6					3
Col.	1	1:11							1
1 Th.	1	1:3							1
2 Th.	1	1:4					1	3:5	2
1 Ti.	1	6:11							1
2 Ti.	1	3:10							1
Tit.	1	2:2							1
Heb.	2	10:36; 12:1							2
Jas.	3	1:3, 4; 5:11							3
2 Pt.	2	1:6, 6							2
Rev.	7	1:9; 2:2, 3, 19; 3:10; 13:10; 14:12							7
Total	29		1		1		1		32

5183. ὑπόνοια, hupon′oia

Book	surmising	Total
1 Ti.	6:4	1

5184. ὑποπλέω, hupople′ō

Book	sail under	Total
Ac.	27:4, 7	2

5185. ὑποπνέω, hupopne′ō

Book	blow softly	Total
Ac.	27:13	1

5182. ὑπονοέω, huponoe′ō

Book	Oc.	think	Oc.	suppose	Oc.	deem	Total
Ac.	1	13:25	1	25:18	1	27:27	3

5186. ὑποπόδιον, hupopod′ion

Book	Oc.	footstool (with 4128)	Oc.	footstool	Total
Mt.	2	5:35; 22:44			2
Mk.	1	12:36			1
Lk.	1	20:43			1
Ac.	2	2:35; 7:49			2
Heb.	2	1:13; 10:13			2
Jas.			1	2:3	1
Total	8		1		9

5187. ὑπόστασις, hupos′tasis

Book	Oc.	confidence	Oc.	confident	Oc.	person	Oc.	substance	Total
2 Co.	1	11:17	1	9:4					2
Heb.	1	3:14			1	1:3	1	11:1	3
Total	2		1		1		1		5

5188. ὑποστέλλω, hupostel′lō

Book	Oc.	keep back	Oc.	shun	Oc.	withdraw	Oc.	draw back	Total
Ac.	1	20:20	1	20:27					2
Gal.					1	2:12			1
Heb.							1	10:38	1
Total	1		1		1		1		4

5189. ὑποστολή, hupostolē′

Book	of them who draw back	Total
Heb.	10:39	1

5190. ὑποστρέφω, hupostreph′ō

Book	Oc.	return	Oc.	return again	Oc.	turn back	Oc.	turn back again	Oc.	return back again	Oc.	come again	Total
Mk.	1	14:40											1
Lk.	17	1:56; 2:39, 43; 4:1, 14; 7:10; 8:39, 40; 9:10; 11:24; 17:18; 19:12; 23:48, 56; 24:9, 33, 52	1	10:17	1	17:15	1	2:45	1	8:37			21
Ac.	8	1:12; 8:25, 28; 12:25; 13:13, 34; 20:3; 23:32	2	14:21; 21:6							1	22:17	11
Gal.	1	1:17											1
Heb.	1	7:1											1
Total	28		3		1		1		1		1		35

5191. ὑποστρώννυμι hupostrōn′numi

Book	spread	Total
Lk.	19:36	1

5192. ὑποταγή, hupotagẹ′

Book	subjection	Total
2 Co.	9:13	1
Gal.	2:5	1
1 Ti.	2:11: 3:4	2
Total		4

5194. ὑποτίθημι, hupotith′ẹmi

Book	Oc.	lay down	Oc.	put in remembrance	Total
Ro.	1	16:4			1
1 Ti.			1	4:6	1
Total	1		1		2

5195. ὑποτρέχω, hupotrech′ō

Book	run under	Total
Ac.	27:16	1

5193. ὑποτάσσω, hupotas′sō

Book	Oc.	put under	Oc.	be subject unto	Oc.	be subject to	Oc.	submit (one's) self unto	Oc.	submit (one's) self to	Oc.	be in subjection unto	Oc.	put in subjection under	Oc.	Misc.	Total
Lk.			3	2:51; 10: 17, 20													3
Ro.			1	13:1	1	8:7	1	10:3							3	8:20a, 20b; 13:5	6
1 Co.	4	15:27, 27, 27, 28c	1	15:28b	1	14:32	1	16:16							2	14:34; 15: 28a	9
Eph.	1	1:22	1	5:24			1	5:22	1	5:21							4
Phl.															1	3:21	1
Col.							1	3:18									1
Tit.					1	3:1									2	2:5, 9	3
Heb.	1	2:8c									1	12:9	1	2:8b	2	2:5, 8a	5
Jas.									1	4:7							1
1 Pt.					2	2:18; 5:5b	1	5:5a	1	2:13	1	3:5			2	3:1, 22	7
Total	6		6		5		5		3		2		1		12		40

Miscellaneous: Ro. 8:20a, be made subject to; Ro. 8:20b, subject; Ro. 13:5, be subject; 1 Co. 14:34, be under obedience; 1 Co. 15:28a, subdue unto; Phl. 3:21, subdue unto; Tit. 2:5, obedient to; Tit. 2:9, be obedient unto; Heb. 2:5, 8a, put in subjection; 1 Pt. 3:1, be in subjection to; 1 Pt. 3:22, be made subject unto.

5196. ὑποτύπωσις, hupotup′ōsis

Book	Oc.	pattern	Oc.	form	Total
1 Ti.	1	1:16			1
2 Ti.			1	1:13	1
Total	1		1		2

5197. ὑποφέρω, hupopher′ō

Book	Oc.	endure	Oc.	bear	Total
1 Co.			1	10:13	1
2 Ti.	1	3:11			1
1 Pt.	1	2:19			1
Total	2		1		3

5198. ὑποχωρέω, hupochōre′ō

Book	Oc.	withdrew (with 2258)	Oc.	go aside	Total
Lk.	1	5:16	1	9:10	2

5199. ὑπωπιάζω, hupōpiad′zō

Book	Oc.	weary	Oc.	keep under	Total
Lk.	1	18:5			1
1 Co.			1	9:27	1
Total	1		1		2

5200. ὗς, hus

Book	sow	Total
2 Pt.	2:22	1

5201. ὕσσωπος, hus′sōpos

Book	hyssop	Total
Jn.	19:29	1
Heb.	9:19	1
Total		2

5203. ὑστέρημα, huster′ẹma

Book	Oc.	which is lacking	Oc.	want	Oc.	which is behind	Oc.	lack	Oc.	penury	Total
Lk.									1	21:4	1
1 Co.	1	16:17									1
2 Co.	1	11:9	3	8:14, 14; 9:12							4
Phl.							1	2:30			1
Col.					1	1:24					1
1 Th.	1	3:10									1
Total	3		3		1		1		1		9

5202. ὑστερέω, hustere′ō

Book	Oc.	lack	Oc.	be behind	Oc.	want	Oc.	come short	Oc.	be in want	Oc.	fail	Oc.	come behind	Oc.	be destitute	Oc.	Misc.	Total
Mt.	1	19:20																	1
Mk.	1	10:21																	1
Lk.	1	22:35							1	15:14									2
Jn.					1	2:3													1
Ro.							1	3:23											1
1 Co.													1	1:7			2	8:8; 12:24	3
2 Co.			2	11:5; 12:11	1	11:9													3
Phl.																	1	4:12	1
Heb.											1	12:15			1	11:37	1	4:1	3
Total	3		2		2		1		1		1		1		1		4		16

Miscellaneous: 1 Co. 8:8, be the worse; 1 Co. 12:24, part which lacked; Phl. 4:12, suffer need; Heb. 4:1, come short of.

5204. ὑστέρησις, huster′ẹsis

Book	want	Total
Mk.	12:44	1
Phl.	4:11	1
Total		2

5205. ὕστερον, hus′teron

Book	Oc.	afterward	Oc.	last	Oc.	at the last	Oc.	last of all	Total
Mt.	4	4:2; 21:29, 32; 25:11	1	22:27	1	26:60	1	21:37	7
Mk.	1	16:14							1
Lk.	1	4:2	1	20:32					2
Jn.	1	13:36							1
Heb.	1	12:11							1
Total	8		2		1		1		12

5206. ὕστερος, hus′teros

Book	latter	Total
1 Ti.	4:1	1

5207. ὑφαντός, huphantos′

Book	woven	Total
Jn.	19:23	1

5208. ὑψηλός, hupse̱los′

Book	Oc.	high	Oc.	higher	Oc.	highly esteemed	Oc.	high things	Total
Mt.	2	4:8; 17:1							2
Mk.	1	9:2							1
Lk.	1	4:5			1	16:15			2
Ac.	1	13:17							1
Ro.							1	12:16	1
Heb.	1	1:3	1	7:26					2
Rev.	2	21:10, 12							2
Total	8		1		1		1		11

5209. ὑψηλοφρονέω hupse̱lophrone′ō

Book	be highminded	Total
Ro.	11:20	1
1 Ti.	6:17	1
Total		2

5210. ὕψιστος, hup′sistos

Book	Oc.	highest	Oc.	most high	Total
Mt.	1	21:9			1
Mk.	1	11:10	1	5:7	2
Lk.	6	1:32, 35, 76; 2:14; 6:35; 19:38	1	8:28	7
Ac.			2	7:48; 16:17	2
Heb.			1	7:1	1
Total	8		5		13

5211. ὕψος, hup′sos

Book	Oc.	on high	Oc.	height	Oc.	high	Oc.	be exalted	Total
Lk.	2	1:78; 24:49							2
Eph.			1	3:18	1	4:8			2
Jas.							1	1:9	1
Rev.			1	21:16					1
Total	2		2		1		1		6

5212. ὑψόω, hupso′ō

Book	Oc.	exalt	Oc.	lift up	Total
Mt.	3	11:23; 23:12, 12			3
Lk.	6	1:52; 10:15; 14:11, 11; 18:14, 14			6
Jn.			5	3:14, 14; 8:28; 12:32, 34	5
Ac.	3	2:33; 5:31; 13:17			3
2 Co.	1	11:7			1
Jas.			1	4:10	1
1 Pt.	1	5:6			1
Total	14		6		20

5213. ὕψωμα, hup′sōma

Book	Oc.	height	Oc.	high thing	Total
Ro.	1	8:39			1
2 Co.			1	10:5	1
Total	1		1		2

5214. φάγος, phag′os

Book	gluttonous	Total
Mt.	11:19	1
Lk.	7:34	1
Total		2

5217. Φάλεκ, Phal′ek

Book	Phalec	Total
Lk.	3:35	1

5215. φάγω, phag′ō

Book	Oc.	eat	Oc.	meat	Total
Mt.	11	6:25, 31; 12:4, 4; 14:16, 20; 15:20, 32, 37; 26:17, 26	2	25:35, 42	13
Mk.	18	2:26, 26; 3:20; 5:43; 6:31, 36, 37, 37, 42, 44; 8:1, 2, 8, 9; 11:14; 14:12, 14, 22			18
Lk.	20	4:2; 6:4, 4; 7:36; 9:13, 17; 12:19, 22, 29; 13:26; 14:1, 15; 15:23; 17:8, 8; 22:8, 11, 15, 16; 24:43	1	8:55	21
Jn.	15	4:31, 32, 33; 6:5, 23, 26, 31, 31, 49, 50, 51, 52, 53, 58; 18:28			15
Ac.	6	9:9; 10:13, 14; 11:7; 23:12, 21			6
Ro.	3	14:2, 21, 23			3
1 Co.	11	8:8, 8, 13; 9:4; 10:3, 7; 11:20, 21, 24, 33; 15:32			11
2 Th.	1	3:8			1
Heb.	1	13:10			1
Jas.	1	5:3			1
Rev.	7	2:7, 14, 17, 20; 10:10; 17:16; 19:18			7
Total	94		3		97

5216. φαίνω, phai′nō

Book	Oc.	appear	Oc.	shine	Oc.	be seen	Oc.	seem	Oc.	think	Total
Mt.	10	1:20; 2:7, 13, 19; 6:16, 18; 13:26; 23:27, 28; 24:30	1	24:27	2	6:5; 9:33					13
Mk.	1	16:9							1	14:64	2
Lk.	1	9:8					1	24:11			2
Jn.			2	1:5; 5:35							2
Ro.	1	7:13									1
2 Co.	1	13:7									1
Phl.			1	2:15							1
Heb.	1	11:3									1
Jas.	1	4:14									1
1 Pt.	1	4:18									1
2 Pt.			1	1:19							1
1 Jn.			1	2:8							1
Rev.			4	1:16; 8:12; 18:23; 21:23							4
Total	17		10		2		1		1		31

5218. φανερός, phaneros′

Book	Oc.	manifest	Oc.	openly (with 1722 and 3488)	Oc.	known	Oc.	abroad (with 1519)	Oc.	spread abroad	Oc.	outwardly (with 1722 and 3488)	Oc.	outward	Oc.	appear	Total
Mt.			3	6:4, 6, 18	1	12:16											4
Mk.					1	3:12	1	4:22	1	6:14							3
Lk.	1	8:17a					1	8:17b									2
Ac.	1	4:16			1	7:13											2
Ro.	1	1:19									1	2:28a	1	2:28b			3
1 Co.	3	3:13; 11:19; 14:25															3
Gal.	1	5:19															1
Phl.	1	1:13															1
1 Ti.															1	4:15	1
1 Jn.	1	3:10															1
Total	9		3		3		2		1		1		1		1		21

5219. φανερόω, phanero'ō

Book	Oc.	make manifest	Oc.	appear	Oc.	manifest	Oc.	shew	Oc.	be manifest	Oc.	shew (one's) self	Oc.	manifestly declare	Oc.	manifest forth	Total
Mk.			2	16:12, 14	1	4:22											3
Jn.	3	1:31; 3:21; 9:3			1	17:6	2	7:4; 21:1a			2	21:1b, 14			1	2:11	9
Ro.	1	16:26			1	3:21	1	1:19									3
1 Co.	1	4:5															1
2 Co.	6	2:14; 4:10, 11; 5:11, 11; 11:6	2	5:10; 7: 12									1	3:3			9
Eph.	2	5:13, 13															2
Col.	2	1:26; 4:4	2	3:4, 4													4
1 Ti.									1	3:16							1
2 Ti.	1	1:10															1
Tit.					1	1:3											1
Heb.	1	9:8	1	9:26													2
1 Pt.			1	5:4					1	1:20							2
1 Jn.	1	2:19	3	2:28; 3: 2, 2	5	1:2, 2; 3: 5, 8; 4:9											9
Rev.	1	15:4	1	3:18													2
Total	19		12		9		3		2		2		1		1		49

5220. φανερῶς, phanerōs'

Book	Oc.	openly	Oc.	evidently	Total
Mk.	1	1:45			1
Jn.	1	7:10			1
Ac.			1	10:3	1
Total	2		1		3

5221. φανέρωσις, phaner'ōsis

Book	manifestation	Total
1 Co.	12:7	1
2 Co.	4:2	1
Total		2

5222. φανός, phanos'

Book	lantern	Total
Jn.	18:3	1

5223. Φανουήλ, Phanouel'

Book	Phanuel	Total
Lk.	2:36	1

5224. φαντάζω, phantad'zō

Book	sight	Total
Heb.	12:21	1

5225. φαντασία, phantasi'a

Book	pomp	Total
Ac.	25:23	1

5226. φάντασμα, phan'tasma

Book	spirit	Total
Mt.	14:26	1
Mk.	6:49	1
Total		2

5227. φάραγξ, phar'angx

Book	valley	Total
Lk.	3:5	1

5228. Φαραώ, Pharaō'

Book	Pharaoh	Total
Ac.	7:10, 13, 21	3
Ro.	9:17	1
Heb.	11:24	1
Total		5

5229. Φαρές, Phares'

Book	Phares	Total
Mt.	1:3, 3	2
Lk.	3:33	1
Total		3

5232. φαρμακεύς, pharmakeus'

Book	sorcerer	Total
Rev.	21:8	1

5230. Φαρισαῖος, Pharisai'os

Book	Pharisee	Total
Mt.	3:7; 5:20; 9:11, 14, 34; 12:2, 14, 24, 38; 15:1, 12; 16:1, 6, 11, 12; 19:3; 21:45; 22:15, 34, 41; 23:2, 13, 14, 15, 23, 25, 26, 27, 29; 27: 62	30
Mk.	2:16, 18, 18, 24; 3:6; 7:1, 3, 5; 8:11, 15; 10:2; 12:13	12
Lk.	5:17, 21, 30, 33; 6:2, 7; 7:30, 36, 36, 37, 39; 11:37, 38, 39, 42, 43, 44, 53; 12:1; 13:31; 14:1, 3; 15:2; 16:14; 17:20; 18:10, 11; 19:39	28
Jn.	1:24; 3:1; 4:1; 7:32, 32, 45, 47, 48; 8:3, 13; 9:13, 15, 16, 40; 11: 46, 47, 57; 12:19, 42; 18:3	20
Ac.	5:34; 15:5; 23:6, 6, 6, 7, 8, 9; 26:5	9
Phl.	3:5	1
Total		100

5231. φαρμακεία, pharmakei'a

Book	Oc.	sorcery	Oc.	witchcraft	Total
Gal.			1	5:20	1
Rev.	2	9:21; 18:23			2
Total	2		1		3

5233. φαρμακός, pharmakos'

Book	sorcerer	Total
Rev.	22:15	1

5234. φάσις, phas'is

Book	tidings	Total
Ac.	21:31	1

5235. φάσκω, phas'kō

Book	Oc.	say	Oc.	affirm	Oc.	profess	Total
Ac.	1	24:9	1	25:19			2
Ro.					1	1:22	1
Rev.	1	2:2					1
Total	2		1		1		4

5236. φάτνη, phat'ne

Book	Oc.	manger	Oc.	stall	Total
Lk.	3	2:7, 12, 16	1	13:15	4

5237. φαῦλος, phau'los

Book	evil	Total
Jn.	3:20; 5:29	2
Tit.	2:8	1
Jas.	3:16	1
Total		4

5238. φέγγος, pheng'gos

Book	light	Total
Mt.	24:29	1
Mk.	13:24	1
Lk.	11:33	1
Total		3

5239. φείδομαι, phei'domai

Book	Oc.	spare	Oc.	forbear	Total
Ac.	1	20:29			1
Ro.	3	8:32; 11:21, 21			3
1 Co.	1	7:28			1
2 Co.	2	1:23; 13:2	1	12:6	3
2 Pt.	2	2:4, 5			2
Total	9		1		10

5240. φειδομένως pheidomen'ōs

Book	sparingly	Total
2 Co.	9:6, 6	2

5241. φελόνης, phelo'nes

Book	cloke	Total
2 Ti.	4:13	1

5242. φέρω, pher'ō

Book	Oc.	bring	Oc.	bear	Oc.	bring forth	Oc.	come	Oc.	reach	Oc.	endure	Oc.	carry	Oc.	Misc.	Total
Mt.	4	14:11, 11, 18; 17:17															4
Mk.	12	1:32; 2:3; 6:27, 28; 7:32; 8:22; 9:17, 19, 20; 12:15, 16; 15:22			1	4:8											13
Lk.	3	5:18; 15:23; 24:1	1	23:26													4
Jn.	4	4:33; 18:29; 19:39; 21:10	6	2:8, 8; 15:2a, 2b, 4, 8	4	12:24; 15:2c, 5, 16			2	20:27, 27			1	21:18			17
Ac.	5	4:34, 37; 5:2, 16; 14:13													5	2:2; 12:10; 25:7; 27:15, 17	10
Ro.											1	9:22					1
2 Ti.	1	4:13															1
Heb.			1	13:13							1	12:20			3	1:3; 6:1; 9:16	5
1 Pt.	1	1:13															1
2 Pt.	1	2:11					3	1:17, 18, 21a							1	1:21b	5
2 Jn.	1	1:10															1
Rev.	2	21:24, 26															2
Total	34		8		5		3		2		2		1		9		64

Miscellaneous: Ac. 2:2, rushing; Ac. 12:10, lead; Ac. 25:7, lay; Ac. 27:15, let drive; Ac. 27:17, be driven; Heb. 1:3, uphold; Heb. 6:1, go on; Heb. 9:16, be; 2 Pt. 1:21b, move.

5243. φεύγω, pheu'gō

Book	Oc.	flee	Oc.	escape	Oc.	flee away	Total
Mt.	6	2:13; 3:7; 8:33; 10:23; 24:16; 26:56	1	23:33			7
Mk.	5	5:14; 13:14; 14:50, 52; 16:8					5
Lk.	3	3:7; 8:34; 21:21					3
Jn.	3	10:5, 12, 13					3
Ac.	2	7:29; 27:30					2
1 Co.	2	6:18; 10:14					2
1 Ti.	1	6:11					1
2 Ti.	1	2:22					1
Heb.			2	11:34; 12:25			2
Jas.	1	4:7					1
Rev.	2	9:6; 12:6			2	16:20; 20:11	4
Total	26		3		2		31

5244. Φῆλιξ, Phe̱'lix

Book	Felix	Total
Ac.	23:24, 26; 24:3, 22, 24, 25, 27, 27; 25:14	9

5245. φήμη, phe̱'me̱

Book	fame	Total
Mt.	9:26	1
Lk.	4:14	1
Total		2

5246. φημί, phe̱mi'

Book	Oc.	say	Oc.	affirm	Total
Mt.	15	4:7; 8:8; 13:28, 29; 14:8; 17:26; 19:21; 21:27; 25:21, 23; 26:34, 61; 27:11, 23, 65			15
Mk.	1	14:29			1
Lk.	5	7:40, 44; 22:58, 70; 23:3			5
Jn.	2	1:23; 9:38			2
Ac.	27	2:38; 7:2; 8:36; 10:28, 30, 31; 16:30, 37; 17:22; 19:35; 21:37; 22:2, 27, 28; 23:5, 17, 18, 35; 25:5, 22, 22, 24; 26:1, 24, 25, 28, 32			27
Ro.			1	3:8	1
1 Co.	5	6:16; 7:29; 10:15, 19; 15:50			5
2 Co.	1	10:10			1
Heb.	1	8:5			1
Total	57		1		58

5247. Φῆστος, Phe̱s'tos

Book	Festus	Total
Ac.	24:27; 25:1, 4, 9, 12, 13, 14, 22, 23, 24; 26:24, 25, 32	13

5249. φθαρτός, phthartos'

Book	corruptible	Total
Ro.	1:23	1
1 Co.	9:25; 15:53, 54	3
1 Pt.	1:18, 23	2
Total		6

5248. φθάνω, phthan'ō

Book	Oc.	come	Oc.	already attain	Oc.	attain	Oc.	prevent	Total
Mt.	1	12:28							1
Lk.	1	11:20							1
Ro.					1	9:31			1
2 Co.	1	10:14							1
Phl.			1	3:16					1
1 Th.	1	2:16					1	4:15	2
Total	4		1		1		1		7

5250. φθέγγομαι phtheng'gomai

Book	speak	Total
Ac.	4:18	1
2 Pt.	2:16, 18	2
Total		3

5253. φθόγγος, phthong'gos

Book	sound	Total
Ro.	10:18	1
1 Co.	14.7	1
Total		2

5252. φθινοπωρινός phthinopōrinos'

Book	whose fruit withereth	Total
Jd.	1:12	1

5254. φθονέω, phthone'ō

Book	envy	Total
Gal.	5:26	1

5251. φθείρω, phthei'rō

Book	Oc.	corrupt	Oc.	corrupt (one's) self	Oc.	be corrupt	Oc.	defile	Oc.	destroy	Total
1 Co.	1	15:33					1	3:17a	1	3:17b	3
2 Co.	2	7:2; 11:3									2
Eph.					1	4:22					1
Jd.			1	1:10							1
Rev.	1	19:2									1
Total	4		1		1		1		1		8

5257. φιάλη, phial'e̱

Book	vial	Total
Rev.	5:8; 15:7; 16:1, 2, 3, 4, 8, 10, 12, 17; 17:1; 21:9	12

5256. φθορά, phthora'

Book	Oc.	corruption	Oc.	to perish (with 1519)	Oc.	destroy	Total
Ro.	1	8:21					1
1 Co.	2	15:42, 50					2
Gal.	1	6:8					1
Col.			1	2:22			1
2 Pt.	3	1:4; 2:12b, 19			1	2:12a	4
Total	7		1		1		9

5255. φθόνος, phthon'os

Book	Oc.	envy	Oc.	envying	Total
Mt.	1	27:18			1
Mk.	1	15:10			1
Ro.	1	1:29			1
Gal.			1	5:21	1
Phl.	1	1:15			1
1 Ti.	1	6:4			1
Tit.	1	3:3			1
Jas.	1	4:5			1
1 Pt.	1	2:1			1
Total	8		1		9

5258. φιλάγαθος, philag'athos

Book	lover of good men	Total
Tit.	1:8	1

5259. Φιλαδέλφεια Philadel'pheia

Book	Philadelphia	Total
Rev.	1:11; 3:7	2

5260. φιλαδελφία, philadelphi'a

Book	Oc.	brotherly love	Oc.	brotherly kindness	Oc.	love of the brethren	Total
Ro.	1	12:10					1
1 Th.	1	4:9					1
Heb.	1	13:1					1
1 Pt.					1	1:22	1
2 Pt.			2	1:7, 7			2
Total	3		2		1		6

5261. φιλάδελφος, philad'elphos

Book	love as brethren	Total
1 Pt.	3:8	1

5262. φίλανδρος, phil'andros

Book	love their husbands	Total
Tit.	2:4	1

5263. φιλανθρωπία, philanthrōpi'a

Book	Oc.	kindness	Oc.	love toward man	Total
Ac.	1	28:2			1
Tit.			1	3:4	1
Total	1		1		2

5264. φιλανθρώπως philanthrō'pōs

Book	courteously	Total
Ac.	27:3	1

5265. φιλαργυρία, philarguri'a

Book	love of money	Total
1 Ti.	6:10	1

5266. φιλάργυρος, philar'guros

Book	covetous	Total
Lk.	16:14	1
2 Ti.	3:2	1
Total		2

5267. φίλαυτος, phil'autos

Book	lover of (one's) own self	Total
2 Ti.	3:2	1

5268. φιλέω, phile'ō

Book	Oc.	love	Oc.	kiss	Total
Mt.	4	6:5; 10:37, 37; 23:6	1	26:48	5
Mk.			1	14:44	1
Lk.	1	20:46	1	22:47	2
Jn.	13	5:20; 11:3, 36; 12:25; 15:19; 16:27, 27; 20:2; 21:15, 16, 17, 17, 17			13
1 Co.	1	16:22			1
Tit.	1	3:15			1
Rev.	2	3:19; 22:15			2
Total	22		3		25

5269. φιλήδονος, philē'donos

Book	lover of pleasure	Total
2 Ti.	3:4	1

5270. φίλημα, phil'ēma

Book	kiss	Total
Lk.	7:45; 22:48	2
Ro.	16:16	1
1 Co.	16:20	1
2 Co.	13:12	1
1 Th.	5:26	1
1 Pt.	5:14	1
Total		7

5271. Φιλήμων, Philē'mōn

Book	Philemon	Total
Phe.	1:1	1

5272. Φιλητός, Philētos'

Book	Philetus	Total
2 Ti.	2:17	1

5273. φιλία, phili'a

Book	friendship	Total
Jas.	4:4	1

5274. Φιλιππήσιος, Philippē'sios

Book	Philippian	Total
Phl.	4:15	1

5275. Φίλιπποι, Phil'ippoi

Book	Philippi	Total
Ac.	16:12; 20:6	2
Phl.	1:1	1
1 Th.	2:2	1
Total		4

5277. φιλόθεος, philoth'eos

Book	lover of God	Total
2 Ti.	3:4	1

5278. Φιλόλογος, Philol'ogos

Book	Philologus	Total
Ro.	16:15	1

5276. Φίλιππος, Phil'ippos

Book	Oc.	Philip (the apostle)	Oc.	Philip (the evangelist)	Oc.	Philip (Herod)	Oc.	Philippi (an adjunct of Caesarea)	Oc.	Philip (the tetrarch)	Total
Mt.	1	10:3			1	14:3	1	16:13			3
Mk.	1	3:18			1	6:17	1	8:27			3
Lk.	1	6:14			1	3:19			1	3:1	3
Jn.	12	1:43, 44, 45, 46, 48; 6:5, 7; 12:21, 22, 22; 14:8, 9									12
Ac.	1	1:13	16	6:5; 8:5, 6, 12, 13, 26, 29, 30, 31, 34, 35, 37, 38, 39, 40; 21:8							17
Total	16		16		3		2		1		38

5279. φιλονεικία, philoneiki'a

Book	strife	Total
Lk.	22:24	1

5280. φιλόνεικος, philon'eikos

Book	contentious	Total
1 Co.	11:16	1

5281. φιλονεξία, philonexi'a

Book	Oc.	hospitality	Oc.	entertain strangers	Total
Ro.	1	12:13			1
Heb.			1	13:2	1
Total	1		1		2

5282. φιλόξενος, philox'enos

Book	Oc.	given to hospitality	Oc.	lover of hospitality	Oc.	use hospitaltiy	Total
1 Ti.	1	3:2					1
Tit.			1	1:8			1
1 Pt.					1	4:9	1
Total	1		1		1		3

5283. φιλοπρωτεύω philoprōteu'ō

Book	love to have the preeminence	Total
3 Jn.	1:9	1

5284. φίλος, phi'los

Book	friend	Total
Mt.	11:19	1
Lk.	7:6, 34; 11:5, 5, 6, 8; 12:4; 14:10, 12; 15:6, 9, 29; 16:9; 21:16; 23:12	15
Jn.	3:29; 11:11; 15:13, 14, 15; 19:12	6
Ac.	10:24; 19:31; 27:3	3
Jas.	2:23; 4:4	2
3 Jn.	1:14, 14	2
Total		29

5285. φιλοσοφία, philosophi'a

Book	philosophy	Total
Col.	2:8	1

5286. φιλόσοφος, philos'ophos

Book	philosopher	Total
Ac.	17:18	1

5287. φιλόστοργος philos'torgos

Book	kindly affectioned	Total
Ro.	12:10	1

5288. φιλότεκνος, philot'eknos

Book	love (one's) children	Total
Tit.	2:4	1

5289. φιλοτιμέομαι, philotime'omai

Book	Oc.	strive	Oc.	labour	Oc.	study	Total
Ro.	1	15:20					1
2 Co.			1	5:9			1
1 Th.					1	4:11	1
Total	1		1		1		3

5290. φιλοφρόνως philophron'ōs

Book	courteously	Total
Ac.	28:7	1

5291. φιλόφρων, philoph'rōn

Book	courteous	Total
1 Pt.	3:8	1

5292. φιμόω, phimo'ō

Book	Oc.	put to silence	Oc.	hold (one's) peace	Oc.	muzzle	Oc.	be speechless	Oc.	be still	Total
Mt.	1	22:34					1	22:12			2
Mk.			1	1:25					1	4:39	2
Lk.			1	4:35							1
1 Co.					1	9:9					1
1 Ti.					1	5:18					1
1 Pt.	1	2:15									1
Total	2		2		2		1		1		8

5293. Φλέγων, Phleg'ōn

Book	Phlegon	Total
Ro.	16:14	1

5294. φλογίζω, phlogid'zō

Book	set on fire	Total
Jas.	3:6, 6	2

5295. φλόξ, phlox

Book	Oc.	flame	Oc.	flaming	Total
Lk.	1	16:24			1
Ac.	1	7:30			1
2 Th.			1	1:8	1
Heb.	1	1:7			1
Rev.	3	1:14; 2:18; 19:12			3
Total	6		1		7

5296. φλυαρέω, phluare'ō

Book	prate against	Total
3 Jn.	1:10	1

5297. φλύαρος, phlu'aros

Book	tattler	Total
1 Ti.	5:13	1

5298. φοβερός, phoberos'

Book	Oc.	fearful	Oc.	terrible	Total
Heb.	2	10:27, 31	1	12:21	3

5299. φοβέω, phobe'ō

Book	Oc.	fear	Oc.	be afraid	Oc.	be afraid of	Oc.	reverence	Oc.	Misc.	Total
Mt.	10	1:20; 10:26, 28, 28, 31; 14:5; 21:26, 46; 27:54; 28:5	7	2:22; 14:27, 30; 17:6, 7; 25:25; 28:10							17
Mk.	5	5:33; 6:20; 11:18, 32; 12:12	6	5:15, 36; 6:50; 9:32; 10:32; 16:8					1	4:41	12
Lk.	19	1:13, 30, 50; 2:10; 5:10; 8:50; 9:34, 45; 12:5, 5, 5, 7, 32; 18:2, 4; 19:21; 20:19; 22:2; 23:40	3	8:25, 35; 12:4					1	2:9	23
Jn.	2	9:22; 12:15	3	6:19, 20; 19:8							5
Ac.	10	5:26; 10:2, 22, 35; 13:16, 26; 16:38; 27:17, 24, 29	2	18:9; 22:29	1	9:26					13
Ro.	1	11:20	1	13:4	1	13:3					3
2 Co.	2	11:3; 12:20									2
Gal.	1	2:12			1	4:11					2
Eph.							1	5:33			1
Col.	1	3:22									1
Heb.	3	4:1; 11:27; 13:6			1	11:23					4
1 Pt.	1	2:17	1	3:6	1	3:14					3
1 Jn.	1	4:18									1
Rev.	6	1:17; 2:10; 11:18; 14:7; 15:4; 19:5									6
Total	62		23		5		1		2		93

Miscellaneous: Mk. 4:41 (with 5301 and 3173), fear exceedingly; Lk. 2:9 (with 5301 and 3173), be sore afraid.

5300. φόβητρον, phob'ẹtron

Book	fearful sight	Total
Lk.	21:11	1

5302. Φοίβη, Phoi'bẹ

Book	Phebe	Total
Ro.	16:1	1

5301. φόβος, phob'os

Book	Oc.	fear	Oc.	terror	Oc.	Misc.	Total
Mt.	3	14:26; 28:4, 8					3
Mk.					1	4:41	1
Lk.	6	1:12, 65; 5:26; 7:16; 8:37; 21:26			1	2:9	7
Jn.	3	7:13; 19:38; 20:19					3
Ac.	5	2:43; 5:5, 11; 9:31; 19:17					5
Ro.	4	3:18; 8:15; 13:7, 7	1	13:3			5
1 Co.	1	2:3					1
2 Co.	4	7:1, 5, 11, 15	1	5:11			5
Eph.	2	5:21; 6:5					2
Phl.	1	2:12					1
1 Ti.					1	5:20	1
Heb.	1	2:15					1
1 Pt.	4	1:17; 2:18; 3:2, 15	1	3:14			5
1 Jn.	3	4:18, 18, 18					3
Jd.	1	1:23					1
Rev.	3	11:11; 18:10, 15					3
Total	41		3		3		47

Miscellaneous: Mk. 4:41 (with 5299 and 3173), fear exceedingly; Lk. 2:9 (with 5299 and 3173), be sore afraid; 1 Ti. 5:20 (with 2192), may fear.

5303. Φοινίκη, Phoini'kẹ

Book	Oc.	Phenice	Oc.	Phenicia	Total
Ac.	2	11:19; 15:3	1	21:2	3

5304. φοῖνιξ, phoi'nix

Book	Oc.	palm tree	Oc.	palm	Total
Jn.	1	12:13			1
Rev.			1	7:9	1
Total	1		1		2

5305. Φοῖνιξ, Phoi'nix

Book	Phenice	Total
Ac.	27:12	1

5306. φονεύς, phoneus'

Book	murderer	Total
Mt.	22:7	1
Ac.	3:14; 7:52; 28:4	3
1 Pt.	4:15	1
Rev.	21:8; 22:15	2
Total		7

5307. φονεύω, phoneu'ō

Book	Oc.	kill	Oc.	do murder	Oc.	slay	Total
Mt.	3	5:21, 21; 23:31	1	19:18	1	23:35	5
Mk.	1	10:19					1
Lk.	1	18:20					1
Ro.	1	13:9					1
Jas.	4	2:11, 11; 4:2; 5:6					4
Total	10		1		1		12

5308. φόνος, phon'os

Book	Oc.	murder	Oc.	slaughter	Oc.	be slain (with 599)	Total
Mt.	1	15:19					1
Mk.	2	7:21; 15:7					2
Lk.	2	23:19, 25					2
Ac.			1	9:1			1
Ro.	1	1:29					1
Gal.	1	5:21					1
Heb.					1	11:37	1
Rev.	1	9:21					1
Total	8		1		1		10

5309. φορέω, phore'ō

Book	Oc.	bear	Oc.	wear	Total
Mt.			1	11:8	1
Jn.			1	19:5	1
Ro.	1	13:4			1
1 Co.	2	15:49, 49			2
Jas.			1	2:3	1
Total	3		3		6

5310. Φόρον, Phor'on

Book	Forum	Total
Ac.	28:15	1

5311. φόρος, phor'os

Book	tribute	Total
Lk.	20:22; 23:2	2
Ro.	13:6, 7, 7	3
Total		5

5312. φορτίζω, phortid'zō

Book	Oc.	be heavy laden	Oc.	lade	Total
Mt.	1	11:28			1
Lk.			1	11:46	1
Total	1		1		2

5313. φορτίον, phorti'on

Book	burden	Total
Mt.	11:30; 23:4	2
Lk.	11:46, 46	2
Gal.	6:5	1
Total		5

5314. φόρτος, phor'tos

Book	lading	Total
Ac.	27:10	1

5315. Φορτουνάτος Phortounat'os

Book	Fortunatus	Total
1 Co.	16:17	1

5316. φραγέλλιον, phragel'lion

Book	scourge	Total
Jn.	2:15	1

5317. φραγελλόω, phragello'ō

Book	scourge	Total
Mt.	27:26	1
Mk.	15:15	1
Total		2

5318. φραγμός, phragmos'

Book	Oc.	hedge	Oc.	hedge round about (with 3960)	Oc.	partition	Total
Mt.			1	21:33			1
Mk.	1	12:1					1
Lk.	1	14:23					1
Eph.					1	2:14	1
Total	2		1		1		4

5319. φράζω, phrad'zō

Book	declare	Total
Mt.	13:36; 15:15	2

5320. φράσσω, phras'sō

Book	stop	Total
Ro.	3:19	1
Heb.	11:33	1
Total		2

5321. φρέαρ, phre'ar

Book	Oc.	pit	Oc.	well	Total
Lk.	1	14:5			1
Jn.			2	4:11, 12	2
Rev.	4	9:1, 2, 2, 2			4
Total	5		2		7

5322. φρεναπατάω phrenapata'ō

Book	deceive	Total
Gal.	6:3	1

5323. φρεναπάτης, phrenapat'es

Book	deceiver	Total
Tit.	1:10	1

5324. φρήν, phren

Book	understanding	Total
1 Co.	14:20, 20	2

5325. φρίσσω, phris'sō

Book	tremble	Total
Jas.	2:19	1

5326. φρονέω, phrone'ō

Book	Oc.	think	Oc.	regard	Oc.	mind	Oc.	be minded	Oc.	savour	Oc.	be of the same mind (with 846q)	Oc.	be like minded (with 846q)	Oc.	Misc.	Total
Mt.									1	16:23							1
Mk.									1	8:33							1
Ac.	1	28:22															1
Ro.	2	12:3, 3	4	14:6, 6, 6, 6	2	8:5; 12:16b					1	12:16a	1	15:5			10
1 Co.	1	4:6													1	13:11	2
2 Co.															1	13:11	1
Gal.							1	5:10									1
Phl.	1	1:7			1	3:19	2	3:15, 15			1	4:2	1	2:2a	5	2:2b, 5; 3:16; 4: 10a, 10b	11
Col.															1	3:2	1
Total	5		4		3		3		2		2		2		8		29

Miscellaneous: 1 Co. 13:11, understand; 2 Co. 13:11 (with 846q), be of one mind; Phl. 2:2b (with 3488 and 1520), of one mind; Phl. 2:5 (with 3678), let this mind be; Phl. 3:16 (with 846q), mind the same thing; Phl. 4:10a, care; Phl. 4:10b, be careful; Col. 3:2, set (one's) affection on.

5327. φρόνημα, phron'ema

Book	Oc.	mind	Oc.	carnally minded (with 4461)	Oc.	spiritually minded (with 4051)	Total
Ro.	2	8:7, 27	1	8:6a	1	8:6b	4

5328. φρόνησις, phron'esis

Book	Oc.	wisdom	Oc.	prudence	Total
Lk.	1	1:17			1
Eph.			1	1:8	1
Total	1		1		2

5329. φρόνιμος, phron'imos

Book	wise	Total
Mt.	7:24; 10:16; 24:45; 25:2, 4, 8, 9	7
Lk.	12:42; 16:8	2
Ro.	11:25; 12:16	2
1 Co.	4:10; 10:15	2
2 Co.	11:19	1
Total		14

5330. φρονίμως, phronim'ōs

Book	wisely	Total
Lk.	16:8	1

5331. φροντίζω, phrontid'zō

Book	be careful	Total
Tit.	3:8	1

5332. φρουρέω, phroure'ō

Book	Oc.	keep	Oc.	keep with a garrison	Total
2 Co.			1	11:32	1
Gal.	1	3:23			1
Phl.	1	4:7			1
1 Pt.	1	1:5			1
Total	3		1		4

5333. φρυάσσω, phruas'sō

Book	rage	Total
Ac.	4:25	1

5334. φρύγανον, phru'ganon

Book	stick	Total
Ac.	28:3	1

5335. Φρυγία, Phrugi'a

Book	Phrygia	Total
Ac.	2:10; 16:6; 18:23	3

5336. Φύγελλος, Phug'ellos

Book	Phygellus	Total
2 Ti.	1:15	1

5337. φυγή, phuge'

Book	flight	Total
Mt.	24:20	1
Mk.	13:18	1
Total		2

5339. φυλακίζω, phulakid'zō

Book	imprison	Total
Ac.	22:19	1

5340. φυλακτήριον phulakte'rion

Book	phylactery	Total
Mt.	23:5	1

5341. φύλαξ, phu'lax

Book	keeper	Total
Ac.	5:23; 12:6, 19	3

5338. φυλακή, phulake'

Book	Oc.	prison	Oc.	watch	Oc.	imprisonment	Oc.	hold	Oc.	cage	Oc.	ward	Total
Mt.	8	5:25; 14:3, 10; 18:30; 25:36, 39, 43, 44	2	14:25; 24:43									10
Mk.	2	6:17, 27	1	6:48									3
Lk.	6	3:20; 12:58; 21:12; 22:33; 23:19, 25	3	2:8; 12:38, 38									9
Jn.	1	3:24											1
Ac.	15	5:19, 22, 25; 8:3; 12:4, 5, 6, 17; 16:23, 24, 27, 37, 40; 22:4; 26:10									1	12:10	16
2 Co.	1	11:23			1	6:5							2
Heb.					1	11:36							1
1 Pt.	1	3:19											1
Rev.	2	2:10; 20:7					1	18:2a	1	18:2b			4
Total	36		6		2		1		1		1		47

5342. φυλάσσω, phulas'sō

Book	Oc.	keep	Oc.	observe	Oc.	beware	Oc.	keep (one's) self	Oc.	save	Oc.	be . . . ware	Total
Mt.	1	19:20											1
Mk.			1	10:20									1
Lk.	5	2:8; 8:29; 11:21, 28; 18:21			1	12:15							6
Jn.	2	12:25; 17:12											2
Ac.	7	7:53; 12:4; 16:4; 21:24; 22:20; 23:35; 28:16					1	21:25					8
Ro.	1	2:26											1
Gal.	1	6:13											1
2 Th.	1	3:3											1
1 Ti.	1	6:20	1	5:21									2
2 Ti.	2	1:12, 14									1	4:15	3
2 Pt.					1	3:17			1	2:5			2
1 Jn.	1	5:21											1
Jd.	1	1:24											1
Total	23		2		2		1		1		1		30

5343. φυλή, phulē'

Book	Oc.	tribe	Oc.	kindred	Total
Mt.	2	19:28; 24:30			2
Lk.	2	2:36; 22:30			2
Ac.	1	13:21			1
Ro.	1	11:1			1
Phl.	1	3:5			1
Heb.	2	7:13, 14			2
Jas.	1	1:1			1
Rev.	15	5:5; 7:4, 5, 5, 5, 6, 6, 6, 7, 7, 7, 8, 8, 8; 21:12	6	1:7; 5:9; 7:9; 11:9; 13:7; 14:6	21
Total	25		6		31

5344. φύλλον, phul'lon

Book	leaf	Total
Mt.	21:19; 24:32	2
Mk.	11:13, 13; 13:28	3
Rev.	22:2	1
Total		6

5345. φύραμα, phu'rama

Book	lump	Total
Ro.	9:21; 11:16	2
1 Co.	5:6, 7	2
Gal.	5:9	1
Total		5

5346. φυσικός, phusikos'

Book	natural	Total
Ro.	1:26, 27	2
2 Pt.	2:12	1
Total		3

5347. φυσικῶς, phusikōs'

Book	naturally	Total
Jd.	1:10	1

5348. φυσιόω, phusio'ō

Book	puff up	Total
1 Co.	4:6, 18, 19; 5:2; 8:1; 13:4	6
Col.	2:18	1
Total		7

5349. φύσις, phu'sis

Book	Oc.	nature	Oc.	natural (with 2596)	Oc.	kind	Oc.	mankind (with 442)	Total
Ro.	5	1:26; 2:14, 27; 11:24a, 24b	2	11:21, 24c					7
1 Co.	1	11:14							1
Gal.	2	2:15; 4:8							2
Eph.	1	2:3							1
Jas.					1	3:7a	1	3:7b	2
2 Pt.	1	1:4							1
Total	10		2		1		1		14

5350. φυσίωσις, phusi'ōsis

Book	swelling	Total
2 Co.	12:20	1

5351. φυτεία, phutei'a

Book	plant	Total
Mt.	15:13	1

5352. φυτεύω, phuteu'ō

Book	plant	Total
Mt.	15:13; 21:33	2
Mk.	12:1	1
Lk.	13:6; 17:6, 28; 20:9	4
1 Co.	3:6, 7, 8; 9:7	4
Total		11

5353. φύω, phu'ō

Book	Oc.	spring up	Oc.	spring	Oc.	as soon as it be sprung up	Total
Lk.	1	8:8			1	8:6	2
Heb.			1	12:15			1
Total	1		1		1		3

5354. φωλεός, phōleos'

Book	hole	Total
Mt.	8:20	1
Lk.	9:58	1
Total		2

5355. φωνέω, phōne'ō

Book	Oc.	call	Oc.	crow	Oc.	cry	Oc.	call for	Total
Mt.	1	20:32	3	26:34, 74, 75			1	27:47	5
Mk.	6	3:31; 9:35; 10:49, 49, 49; 15:35	4	14:30, 68, 72, 72					10
Lk.	4	8:54; 14:12; 16:2; 19:15	3	22:34, 60, 61	3	8:8; 16:24; 23:46			10
Jn.	9	1:48; 2:9; 4:16; 9:18, 24; 11:28a; 12:17; 13:13; 18:33	2	13:38; 18:27			1	11:28b	12
Ac.	3	9:41; 10:7, 18			1	16:28			4
Rev.					1	14:18			1
Total	23		12		5		2		42

5356. φωνή, phōnē'

Book	Oc.	voice	Oc.	sound	Oc.	be noised abroad (with 1096)	Oc.	noise	Total
Mt.	7	2:18; 3:3, 17; 12:19; 17:5; 27:46, 50	1	24:31					8
Mk.	7	1:3, 11, 26; 5:7; 9:7; 15:34, 37							7
Lk.	15	1:42, 44; 3:4, 22; 4:33; 8:28; 9:35, 36; 11:27; 17:13, 15; 19:37; 23:23, 23, 46							15
Jn.	14	1:23; 3:29; 5:25, 28, 37; 10:3, 4, 5, 16, 27; 11:43; 12:28, 30; 18:37	1	3:8					15
Ac.	26	2:14; 4:24; 7:31, 57, 60; 8:7; 9:4, 7; 10:13, 15; 11:7, 9; 12:14, 22; 13:27; 14:10, 11; 16:28; 19:34; 22:7, 9, 14, 22; 24:21; 26:14, 24			1	2:6			27
1 Co.	2	14:10, 11	2	14:7, 8					4
Gal.	1	4:20							1
1 Th.	1	4:16							1
Heb.	5	3:7, 15; 4:7; 12:19, 26							5
2 Pt.	3	1:17, 18; 2:16							3
Rev.	50	1:10, 12, 15a; 3:20; 4:1, 5; 5:2, 11, 12; 6:6, 7, 10; 7:2, 10; 8:5, 13, 13; 9:13; 10:3, 3, 4, 4, 7, 8; 11:12, 15, 19; 12:10; 14:2, 2, 2, 2, 7, 9, 13, 15; 16:1, 17, 18; 18:2, 4, 22a, 23; 19:1, 5, 6, 6, 6, 17; 21:3	4	1:15b; 9:9, 9; 18:22b			1	6:1	55
Total	131		8		1		1		141

5357. φῶς, phōs

Book	Oc.	light	Oc.	fire	Total
Mt.	7	4:16, 16; 5:14, 16; 6:23; 10:27; 17:2			7
Mk.			1	14:54	1
Lk.	5	2:32; 8:16; 11:35; 12:3; 16:8	1	22:56	6
Jn.	23	1:4, 5, 7, 8, 8, 9; 3:19, 19, 20, 20, 21; 5:35; 8:12, 12; 9:5; 11:9, 10; 12:35, 35, 36, 36, 36, 46			23
Ac.	10	9:3; 12:7; 13:47; 16:29; 22:6, 9, 11; 26:13, 18, 23			10
Ro.	2	2:19; 13:12			2
2 Co.	3	4:6; 6:14; 11:14			3
Eph.	4	5:8, 8, 13, 13			4
Col.	1	1:12			1
1 Th.	1	5:5			1
1 Ti.	1	6:16			1
Jas.	1	1:17			1
1 Pt.	1	2:9			1
1 Jn.	6	1:5, 7, 7; 2:8, 9, 10			6
Rev.	3	18:23; 21:24; 22:5			3
Total	68		2		70

5358. φωστήρ, phōstēr'

Book	light	Total
Phl.	2:15	1
Rev.	21:11	1
Total		2

5359. φωσφόρος, phōsphor'os

Book	day star	Total
2 Pt.	1:19	1

5360. φωτεινός, phōteinos'

Book	Oc.	full of light	Oc.	bright	Total
Mt.	1	6:22	1	17:5	2
Lk.	3	11:34, 36, 36			3
Total	4		1		5

5362. φωτισμός, phōtismos'

Book	light	Total
2 Co.	4:4, 6	2

5361. φωτίζω, phōtid'zō

Book	Oc.	give light	Oc.	bring to light	Oc.	lighten	Oc.	enlighten	Oc.	light	Oc.	illuminate	Oc.	make to see	Total
Lk.	1	11:36													1
Jn.									1	1:9					1
1 Co.			1	4:5											1
Eph.							1	1:18					1	3:9	2
2 Ti.			1	1:10											1
Heb.							1	6:4			1	10:32			2
Rev.	1	22:5			2	18:1; 21:23									3
Total	2		2		2		2		1		1		1		11

5363. χαίρω, chai'rō

Book	Oc.	rejoice	Oc.	be glad	Oc.	joy	Oc.	hail	Oc.	greeting	Oc.	God speed	Oc.	all hail	Oc.	joyfully	Oc.	farewell	Total
Mt.	3	2:10; 5:12; 18:13					2	26:49; 27:29					1	28:9					6
Mk.			1	14:11			1	15:18											2
Lk.	7	1:14; 6:23; 10:20, 20; 13:17; 15:5; 19:37	3	15:32; 22:5; 23:8			1	1:28							1	19:6			12
Jn.	5	3:29; 4:36; 14:28; 16:20, 22	3	8:56; 11:15; 20:20			1	19:3											9
Ac.	3	5:41; 8:39; 15:31	2	11:23; 13:48					2	15:23; 23:26									7
Ro.	3	12:12, 15, 15	1	16:19															4
1 Co.	3	7:30, 30; 13:6	1	16:17															4
2 Co.	5	2:3; 6:10; 7:7, 9, 16	1	13:9	1	7:13											1	13:11	8
Phl.	7	1:18, 18; 2:28; 3:1; 4:4, 4, 10			2	2:17, 18													9
Col.	1	1:24			1	2:5													2
1 Th.	1	5:16			1	3:9													2
Jas.									1	1:1									1
1 Pt.	1	4:13a	1	4:13b															2
2 Jn.	1	1:4									2	1:10, 11							3
3 Jn.	1	1:3																	1
Rev.	1	11:10	1	19:7															2
Total	42		14		5		5		3		2		1		1		1		74

5364. χάλαζα, chal'adza

Book	hail	Total
Rev.	8:7; 11:19; 16:21, 21	4

5366. Χαλδαῖος, Chaldai'os

Book	Chaldaean	Total
Ac.	7:4	1

5365. χαλάω, chala'ō

Book	Oc.	let down	Oc.	strike	Total
Mk.	1	2:4			1
Lk.	2	5:4, 5			2
Ac.	2	9:25; 27:30	1	27:17	3
2 Co.	1	11:33			1
Total	6		1		7

5367. χαλεπός, chalepos'

Book	Oc.	fierce	Oc.	perilous	Total
Mt.	1	8:28			1
2 Ti.			1	3:1	1
Total	1		1		2

5368. χαλιναγωγέω chalinagōge'ō

Book	bridle	Total
Jas.	1:26; 3:2	2

5369. χαλινός, chalinos'

Book	Oc.	bit	Oc.	bridle	Total
Jas.	1	3:3			1
Rev.			1	14:20	1
Total	1		1		2

5370. χάλκεος, chal'keos

Book	brass	Total
Rev.	9:20	1

5371. χαλκεύς, chalkeus'

Book	coppersmith	Total
2 Ti.	4:14	1

5372. χαλκηδών, chalkēdōn'

Book	chalcedony	Total
Rev.	21:19	1

5373. χαλκίον, chalki'on

Book	brasen vessel	Total
Mk.	7:4	1

5374. χαλκολίβανον chalkolib'anon

Book	fine brass	Total
Rev.	1:15; 2:18	2

5375. χαλκός, chalkos'

Book	Oc.	brass	Oc.	money	Total
Mt.	1	10:9			1
Mk.			2	6:8; 12:41	2
1 Co.	1	13:1			1
Rev.	1	18:12			1
Total	3		2		5

5376. χαμαί, chamai'

Book	Oc.	on the ground	Oc.	to the ground	Total
Jn.	1	9:6	1	18:6	2

5377. Χαναάν, Chanaan'

Book	Chanaan	Total
Ac.	7:11; 13:19	2

5378. Χαναναῖος, Chanaanai'os

Book	of Canaan	Total
Mt.	15:22	1

5379. χαρά, chara'

Book	Oc.	joy	Oc.	gladness	Oc.	joyful	Oc.	joyous	Oc.	joyfulness	Oc.	joyfully (with 3226)	Oc.	greatly	Total
Mt.	6	2:10; 13:20, 44; 25:21, 23; 28:8													6
Mk.			1	4:16											1
Lk.	8	1:14; 2:10; 8:13; 10:17; 15:7, 10; 24:41, 52													8
Jn.	8	3:29b; 15:11, 11; 16:20, 21, 22, 24; 17:13											1	3:29a	9
Ac.	4	8:8; 13:52; 15:3; 20:24	1	12:14											5
Ro.	3	14:17; 15:13, 32													3
2 Co.	4	1:24; 2:3; 7:13; 8:2			1	7:4									5
Gal.	1	5:22													1
Phl.	4	1:4, 25; 2:2; 4:1	1	2:29											5
Col.									1	1:11					1
1 Th.	4	1:6; 2:19, 20; 3:9													4
2 Ti.	1	1:4													1
Heb.	2	12:2; 13:17					1	12:11			1	10:34			4
Jas.	2	1:2; 4:9													2
1 Pt.	1	1:8													1
1 Jn.	1	1:4													1
2 Jn.	1	1:12													1
3 Jn.	1	1:4													1
Total	51		3		1		1		1		1		1		59

5380. χάραγμα, char'agma

Book	Oc.	mark	Oc.	graven	Total
Ac.			1	17:29	1
Rev.	8	13:16, 17; 14:9, 11; 15:2; 16:2; 19:20; 20:4			8
Total	8		1		9

5381. χαρακτήρ, charaktēr'

Book	express image	Total
Heb.	1:3	1

5382. χάραξ, char'ax

Book	trench	Total
Lk.	19:43	1

5383. χαρίζομαι, charid'zomai

Book	Oc.	forgive	Oc.	give	Oc.	freely give	Oc.	deliver	Oc.	grant	Oc.	frankly forgive	Total
Lk.	1	7:43	1	7:21							1	7:42	3
Ac.			1	27:24			2	25:11, 16	1	3:14			4
Ro.					1	8:32							1
1 Co.					1	2:12							1
2 Co.	5	2:7, 10, 10, 10; 12:13											5
Gal.			1	3:18									1
Eph.	2	4:32, 32											2
Phl.			2	1:29; 2:9									2
Col.	3	2:13; 3:13, 13											3
Phe.			1	1:22									1
Total	11		6		2		2		1		1		23

5384. χάριν, char'in

Book	Oc.	for this cause (with 5027)	Oc.	because of	Oc.	wherefore (with 3639)	Oc.	wherefore (with 5001)	Oc.	forsake	Oc.	to speak reproachfully (with 3059)	Total
Lk.					1	7:47							1
Gal.			1	3:19									1
Eph.	2	3:1, 14											2
1 Ti.											1	5:14	1
Tit.	1	1:5							1	1:11			2
1 Jn.							1	3:12					1
Jd.			1	1:16									1
Total	3		2		1		1		1		1		9

5385. χάρις, char′is

Book	Oc.	grace	Oc.	favour	Oc.	thanks	Oc.	thank	Oc.	thank (with 2192)	Oc.	pleasure	Oc.	Misc.	Total
Lk.	1	2:40	2	1:30; 2:52			3	6:32, 33, 34	1	17:9			1	4:22	8
Jn.	4	1:14, 16, 16, 17													4
Ac.	10	4:33; 11:23; 13:43; 14:3, 26; 15: 11, 40; 18:27; 20:24, 32	4	2:47; 7:10, 46; 25:3							2	24:27; 25:9			16
Ro.	24	1:5, 7; 3:24; 4:4, 16; 5:2, 15, 15, 17, 20, 21; 6:1, 14, 15; 11:5, 6, 6, 6, 6; 12:3, 6; 15:15; 16:20, 24					1	6:17							25
1 Co.	8	1:3, 4; 3:10; 10:30; 15:10, 10, 10; 16:23			1	15:57							1	16:3	10
2 Co.	13	1:2, 12; 4:15; 6:1; 8:1, 6, 7, 9, 19; 9:8, 14; 12:9; 13:14			3	2:14; 8: 16; 9:15							2	1:15; 8:4	18
Gal.	7	1:3, 6, 15; 2:9, 21; 5:4; 6:18													7
Eph.	12	1:2, 6, 7; 2:5, 7, 8; 3:2, 7, 8; 4:7, 29; 6:24													12
Phl.	3	1:2, 7; 4:23													3
Col.	5	1:2, 6; 3:16; 4:6, 18													5
1 Th.	2	1:1; 5:28													2
2 Th.	4	1:2, 12; 2:16; 3:18													4
1 Ti.	3	1:2, 14; 6:21							1	1:12					4
2 Ti.	4	1:2, 9; 2:1; 4:22							1	1:3					5
Tit.	4	1:4; 2:11; 3:7, 15													4
Phe.	2	1:3, 25											1	1:7	3
Heb.	8	2:9; 4:16, 16; 10:29; 12:15, 28; 13:9, 25													8
Jas.	2	4:6, 6													2
1 Pt.	8	1:2, 10, 13; 3:7; 4:10; 5:5, 10, 12											2	2:19, 20	10
2 Pt.	2	1:2; 3:18													2
2 Jn.	1	1:3													1
Jd.	1	1:4													1
Rev.	2	1:4; 22:21													2
Total	130		6		4		4		3		2		7		156

Miscellaneous: Lk. 4:22, gracious; 1 Co. 16:3, liberality; 2 Co. 1:15, benefit; 2 Co. 8:4, gift; Phe. 1:7, joy; 1 Pt. 2:19, thankworthy; 1 Pt. 2:20, acceptable.

5386. χάρισμα, char′isma

Book	Oc.	gift	Oc.	free gift	Total
Ro.	4	1:11; 6:23; 11:29; 12:6	2	5:15, 16	6
1 Co.	7	1:7; 7:7; 12:4, 9, 28, 30, 31			7
2 Co.	1	1:11			1
1 Ti.	1	4:14			1
2 Ti.	1	1:6			1
1 Pt.	1	4:10			1
Total	15		2		17

5387. χαριτόω, charito′ō

Book	Oc.	be highly favoured	Oc.	make accepted	Total
Lk.	1	1:28			1
Eph.			1	1:6	1
Total	1		1		2

5388. Χαῤῥάν, Charhran′

Book	Charran	Total
Ac.	7:2, 4	2

5389. χάρτης, char′tes

Book	paper	Total
2 Jn.	1:12	1

5390. χάσμα, chas′ma

Book	gulf	Total
Lk.	16:26	1

5391. χεῖλος, chei′los

Book	Oc.	lip	Oc.	shore	Total
Mt.	1	15:8			1
Mk.	1	7:6			1
Ro.	1	3:13			1
1 Co.	1	14:21			1
Heb.	1	13:15	1	11:12	2
1 Pt.	1	3:10			1
Total	6		1		7

5392. χειμάζω, cheimad′zō

Book	be tossed with tempest	Total
Ac.	27:18	1

5393. χείμαῤῥος, chei′marhros

Book	brook	Total
Jn.	18:1	1

5394. χειμών, cheimōn′

Book	Oc.	winter	Oc.	tempest	Oc.	foul weather	Total
Mt.	1	24:20			1	16:3	2
Mk.	1	13:18					1
Jn.	1	10:22					1
Ac.			1	27:20			1
2 Ti.	1	4:21					1
Total	4		1		1		6

5396. χειραγωγέω, cheiragōge′ō

Book	lead by the hand	Total
Ac.	9:8; 22:11	2

5395. χείρ, cheir

Book	Oc.	hand	Oc.	Not Tr.	Total
Mt.	24	3:12; 4:6; 5:30; 8:3, 15; 9:18, 25; 12:10, 13, 49; 14:31; 15:2, 20; 17:22; 18:8, 8; 19:13, 15; 22:13; 26:23, 45, 50, 51; 27:24			24
Mk.	25	1:31, 41; 3:1, 3, 5, 5; 5:23, 41; 6:2, 5; 7:2, 3, 5, 32; 8:23, 23, 25; 9:27, 31, 43, 43; 10:16; 14:41, 46; 16:18			25
Lk.	26	1:66, 71, 74; 3:17; 4:11, 40; 5:13; 6:1, 6, 8, 10, 10; 8:54; 9:44, 62; 13:13; 15:22; 20:19; 21:12; 22:21, 53; 23:46; 24:7, 39, 40, 50			26
Jn.	15	3:35; 7:30, 44; 10:28, 29, 39; 11:44; 13:3, 9; 20:20, 25, 25, 27, 27; 21:18			15
Ac.	45	2:23; 3:7; 4:3, 28, 30; 5:12, 18; 6:6; 7:25, 35, 41, 50; 8:17, 18, 19; 9:12, 17, 41; 11:21, 30; 12:1, 7, 11, 17; 13:3, 11, 16; 14:3; 17: 25; 19:6, 11, 26, 33; 20:34; 21:11, 11, 27, 40; 23:19; 24:7; 26:1; 28:3, 4, 8, 17	1	15:23	46
Ro.	1	10:21			1
1 Co.	4	4:12; 12:15, 21; 16:21			4
2 Co.	1	11:33			1
Gal.	2	3:19; 6:11			2
Eph.	1	4:28			1
Col.	1	4:18			1
1 Th.	1	4:11			1
2 Th.	1	3:17			1
1 Ti.	3	2:8; 4:14; 5:22			3
2 Ti.	1	1:6			1
Phe.	1	1:19			1
Heb.	6	1:10; 2:7; 6:2; 8:9; 10:31; 12:12			6
Jas.	1	4:8			1
1 Pt.	1	5:6			1
1 Jn.	1	1:1			1
Rev.	17	1:16, 17; 6:5; 7:9; 8:4; 9:20; 10:2, 5, 8, 10; 13:16; 14:9, 14; 17:4; 19:2; 20:1, 4			17
Total	178		1		179

5397. χειραγωγός, cheiragōgos′

Book	some to lead by the hand	Total
Ac.	13:11	1

5398. χειρόγραφον cheirog′raphon

Book	handwriting	Total
Col.	2:14	1

5399. χειροποίητος, cheiropoi′ētos

Book	Oc.	made with hands	Oc.	made by hands	Total
Mk.	1	14:58			1
Ac.	2	7:48; 17:24			2
Eph.			1	2:11	1
Heb.	2	9:11, 24			2
Total	5		1		6

5400. χειροτονέω, cheirotone′ō

Book	Oc.	ordain	Oc.	choose	Total
Ac.	1	14:23			1
2 Co.			1	8:19	1
Total	1		1		2

5401a. χείρων, chei′rōn

Book	worse	Total
Mt.	27:64	1
1 Ti.	5:8	1
Total		2

5401b. χεῖρον, chei′ron

Book	Oc.	worse	Oc.	sorer	Oc.	worse (with 1519 and 3488)	Oc.	worse and worse (with 1909 and 3488)	Oc.	a worse thing (with 5000)	Total
Mt.	2	9:16; 12:45									2
Mk.	1	2:21			1	5:26					2
Lk.	1	11:26									1
Jn.									1	5:14	1
2 Ti.							1	3:13			1
Heb.			1	10:29							1
2 Pt.	1	2:20									1
Total	5		1		1		1		1		9

Word 5401 has 11 occurrences.

5402. χερουβίμ, cheroubim′

Book	cherubim	Total
Heb.	9:5	1

5403. χήρα, chē′ra

Book	widow	Total
Mt.	23:14	1
Mk.	12:40, 42, 43	3
Lk.	2:37; 4:25, 26; 7:12; 18:3, 5; 20:47; 21:2, 3	9
Ac.	6:1; 9:39, 41	3
1 Co.	7:8	1
1 Ti.	5:3, 4, 5, 9, 11, 16, 16	7
Jas.	1:27	1
Rev.	18:7	1
Total		26

5404. χθές, chthes

Book	yesterday	Total
Jn.	4:52	1
Ac.	7:28	1
Heb.	13:8	1
Total		3

5405. χιλιάς, chilias′

Book	thousand	Total
Lk.	14:31, 31	2
Ac.	4:4	1
1 Co.	10:8	1
Rev.	5:11, 11; 7:4, 5, 5, 5, 6, 6, 6, 7, 7, 7, 8, 8, 8; 11:13; 14:1, 3; 21:16	19
Total		23

5406. χιλίαρχος, chili′archos

Book	Oc.	chief captain	Oc.	captain	Oc.	high captain	Total
Mk.					1	6:21	1
Jn.			1	18:12			1
Ac.	18	21:31, 32, 33, 37; 22:24, 26, 27, 28, 29; 23:10, 15, 17, 18, 19, 22; 24:7, 22; 25:23					18
Rev.	1	6:15	1	19:18			2
Total	19		2		1		22

5407. χίλιοι, chil′ioi

Book	thousand	Total
2 Pt.	3:8, 8	2
Rev.	11:3; 12:6; 14:20; 20:2, 3, 4, 5, 6, 7	9
Total		11

5408. Χίος, Chi′os

Book	Chios	Total
Ac.	20:15	1

5409. χιτών, chitōn′

Book	Oc.	coat	Oc.	garment	Oc.	clothes	Total
Mt.	2	5:40; 10:10					2
Mk.	1	6:9			1	14:63	2
Lk.	3	3:11; 6:29; 9:3					3
Jn.	2	19:23, 23					2
Ac.	1	9:39					1
Jd.			1	1:23			1
Total	9		1		1		11

5410. χιών, chiōn′

Book	snow	Total
Mt.	28:3	1
Mk.	9:3	1
Rev.	1:14	1
Total		3

5411. χλαμύς, chlamus′

Book	robe	Total
Mt.	27:28, 31	2

5412. χλευάζω, chleuad′zō

Book	mock	Total
Ac.	2:13; 17:32	2

5413. χλιαρός, chliaros′

Book	lukewarm	Total
Rev.	3:16	1

5414. Χλόη, Chlo′ē

Book	Chloe	Total
1 Co.	1:11	1

5415. χλωρός, chlōros′

Book	Oc.	green	Oc.	pale	Total
Mk.	1	6:39			1
Rev.	2	8:7; 9:4	1	6:8	3
Total	3		1		4

5416. χξς (ἑξακόσιοι ἑξήκοντα ἕξ) chi xi sigma (hexakos′ioi hexē′konta hex)

Book	six hundred threescore and six	Total
Rev.	13:18	1

5417. χοϊκός, choikos′

Book	earthy	Total
1 Co.	15:47, 48, 48, 49	4

5418. χοῖνιξ, choi′nix

Book	measure	Total
Rev.	6:6, 6	2

5419. χοῖρος, choi′ros

Book	swine	Total
Mt.	7:6; 8:30, 31, 32, 32	5
Mk.	5:11, 12, 13, 14, 16	5
Lk.	8:32, 33; 15:15, 16	4
Total		14

5420. χολάω, chola′ō

Book	be angry	Total
Jn.	7:23	1

5421. χολή, cholē′

Book	gall	Total
Mt.	27:34	1
Ac.	8:23	1
Total		2

5422. χόος, cho′os

Book	dust	Total
Mk.	6:11	1
Rev.	18:19	1
Total		2

5423. Χοραζίν, Choradzin′

Book	Chorazin	Total
Mt.	11:21	1
Lk.	10:13	1
Total		2

5424. χορηγέω, chorēge′ō

Book	Oc.	minister	Oc.	give	Total
2 Co.	1	9:10			1
1 Pt.			1	4:11	1
Total	1		1		2

5425. χορός, choros′

Book	dancing	Total
Lk.	15:25	1

5426. χορτάζω, chortad′zō

Book	Oc.	fill	Oc.	be full	Oc.	satisfy	Oc.	feed	Total
Mt.	4	5:6; 14:20; 15:33, 37							4
Mk.	3	6:42; 7:27; 8:8			1	8:4			4
Lk.	2	6:21; 9:17					1	16:21	3
Jn.	1	6:26							1
Phl.			1	4:12					1
Jas.	1	2:16							1
Rev.	1	19:21							1
Total	12		1		1		1		15

5427. χόρτασμα, chor′tasma

Book	sustenance	Total
Ac.	7:11	1

5428. χόρτος, chor'tos

Book	Oc.	grass	Oc.	blade	Oc.	hay	Total
Mt.	2	6:30; 14:19	1	13:26			3
Mk.	1	6:39	1	4:28			2
Lk.	1	12:28					1
Jn.	1	6:10					1
1 Co.					1	3:12	1
Jas.	2	1:10, 11					2
1 Pt.	3	1:24, 24, 24					3
Rev.	2	8:7; 9:4					2
Total	12		2		1		15

5429. Χουζᾶς, Choudzas'

Book	Chuza	Total
Lk.	8:3	1

5431. χράω, chra'ō

Book	lend	Total
Lk.	11:5	1

5430. χράομαι, chra'omai

Book	Oc.	use	Oc.	entreat	Total
Ac.	1	27:17	1	27:3	2
1 Co.	4	7:21, 31; 9:12, 15			4
2 Co.	3	1:17; 3:12; 13:10			3
1 Ti.	2	1:8; 5:23			2
Total	10		1		11

5432. χρεία, chrei'a

Book	Oc.	need	Oc.	need (with 2192)	Oc.	necessity	Oc.	use	Oc.	needful	Oc.	necessary	Oc.	business	Oc.	lack	Oc.	wants	Total
Mt.	4	3:14; 6:8; 21:3; 26:65	2	9:12; 14:16															6
Mk.	3	2:17, 25; 11:3	1	14:63															4
Lk.	3	9:11; 19:31, 34	3	5:31; 15:7; 22:71					1	10:42									7
Jn.	1	13:29	3	2:25; 13:10; 16:30															4
Ac.	2	2:45; 4:35			1	20:34					1	28:10	1	6:3					5
Ro.					1	12:13													1
1 Co.	3	12:21, 21, 24																	3
Eph.			1	4:28			1	4:29											2
Phl.	1	4:19			1	4:16											1	2:25	3
1 Th.	1	5:1	2	1:8; 4:9											1	4:12			4
Tit.							1	3:14											1
Heb.	4	5:12, 12; 7:11; 10:36																	4
1 Jn.	1	3:17	1	2:27															2
Rev.	2	3:17; 21:23	1	22:5															3
Total	25		14		3		2		1		1		1		1		1		49

5433. χρεωφειλέτης chreōpheile'tẹs

Book	debtor	Total
Lk.	7:41; 16:5	2

5434. χρή, chrẹ

Book	ought	Total
Jas.	3:10	1

5435. χρηζω, chrẹd'zō

Book	Oc.	have need	Oc.	need	Total
Mt.	1	6:32			1
Lk.	1	12:30	1	11:8	2
Ro.	1	16:2			1
2 Co.			1	3:1	1
Total	3		2		5

5436. χρῆμα, chrẹ'ma

Book	Oc.	money	Oc.	riches	Total
Mk.			2	10:23, 24	2
Lk.			1	18:24	1
Ac.	4	4:37; 8:18, 20; 24:26			4
Total	4		3		7

5437. χρηματίζω, chrẹmatid'zō

Book	Oc.	be warned of God	Oc.	call	Oc.	be admonished of God	Oc.	reveal	Oc.	speak	Oc.	be warned from God	Total
Mt.	2	2:12, 22											2
Lk.							1	2:26					1
Ac.			1	11:26							1	10:22	2
Ro.			1	7:3									1
Heb.	1	11:7			1	8:5			1	12:25			3
Total	3		2		1		1		1		1		9

5438. χρηματισμός, chrẹmatismos'

Book	answer of God	Total
Ro.	11:4	1

5439. χρήσιμος, chrẹ'simos

Book	profit	Total
2 Ti.	2:14	1

5440. χρῆσις, chrẹ'sis

Book	use	Total
Ro.	1:26, 27	2

5441. χρηστεύομαι, chrẹsteu'omai

Book	be kind	Total
1 Co.	13:4	1

5442. χρηστολογία, chrẹstologi'a

Book	good words	Total
Ro.	16:18	1

5443. χρηστός, chrẹstos'

Book	Oc.	kind	Oc.	easy	Oc.	better	Oc.	goodness	Oc.	good	Oc.	gracious	Total
Mt.			1	11:30									1
Lk.	1	6:35			1	5:39							2
Ro.							1	2:4					1
1 Co.									1	15:33			1
Eph.	1	4:32											1
1 Pt.											1	2:3	1
Total	2		1		1		1		1		1		7

5444. χρηστότης, chrestot'es

Book	Oc.	goodness	Oc.	kindness	Oc.	good	Oc.	gentle-ness	Total
Ro.	4	2:4; 11:22, 22, 22			1	3:12			5
2 Co.			1	6:6					1
Gal.							1	5:22	1
Eph.			1	2:7					1
Col.			1	3:12					1
Tit.			1	3:4					1
Total	4		4		1		1		10

5445. χρίσμα, chris'ma

Book	Oc.	anointing	Oc.	unction	Total
1 Jn.	2	2:27, 27	1	2:20	3

5446. Χριστιανός, Christianos'

Book	Christian	Total
Ac.	11:26; 26:28	2
1 Pt.	4:16	1
Total		3

5447. Χριστός, Christos'

Book	Christ	Total
Mt.	1:1, 16, 17, 18; 2:4; 11:2; 16:16, 20; 22:42; 23:8, 10; 24:5, 23; 26:63, 68; 27:17, 22	17
Mk.	1:1; 8:29; 9:41; 12:35; 13:21; 14:61; 15:32	7
Lk.	2:11, 26; 3:15; 4:41, 41; 9:20; 20:41; 22:67; 23:2, 35, 39; 24:26, 46	13
Jn.	1:17, 20, 25, 41; 3:28; 4:25, 29, 42; 6:69; 7:26, 27, 31, 41, 41, 42; 9:22; 10:24; 11:27; 12:34; 17:3; 20:31	21
Ac.	2:30, 31, 36, 38; 3:6, 18, 20; 4:10, 26; 5:42; 8:5, 12, 37; 9:20, 22, 34; 10:36; 11:17; 15:11, 26; 16:18, 31; 17:3, 3; 18:5, 28; 19:4; 20:21; 24:24; 26: 23; 28:31	31
Ro.	1:1, 3, 6, 7, 8, 16; 2:16; 3:22, 24; 5:1, 6, 8, 11, 15, 17, 21; 6:3, 4, 8, 9, 11, 23; 7:4, 25; 8:1, 2, 9, 10, 11, 17, 34, 35, 39; 9:1, 3, 5; 10:4, 6, 7; 12:5; 13:14; 14:9, 10, 15, 18; 15:3, 5, 6, 7, 8, 16, 17, 18, 19, 20, 29, 30; 16:3, 5, 7, 9, 10, 16, 18, 20, 24, 25, 27	68
1 Co.	1:1, 2, 2, 3, 4, 6, 7, 8, 9, 10, 12, 13, 17, 17, 23, 24, 30; 2:2, 16; 3:1, 11, 23, 23; 4:1, 10, 10, 15, 15, 17; 5:4, 4, 7; 6:15, 15; 7:22; 8:6, 11, 12; 9:1, 12, 18, 21; 10:4, 9, 16, 16; 11:1, 3, 3; 12:12, 27; 15:3, 12, 13, 14, 15, 16, 17, 18, 19, 20, 22, 23, 23, 31, 57; 16:22, 23, 24	69
2 Co.	1:1, 2, 3, 5, 5, 19, 21; 2:10, 12, 14, 15, 17; 3:3, 4, 14; 4:4, 5, 6; 5:10, 14, 16, 17, 18, 19, 20, 20; 6:15; 8:9, 23; 9:13; 10:1, 5, 7, 7, 7, 14; 11:2, 3, 10, 13, 23, 31; 12:2, 9, 10, 19; 13:3, 5, 14	49
Gal.	1:1, 3, 6, 7, 10, 12, 22; 2:4, 16, 16, 16, 17, 17, 20, 20, 21; 3:1, 13, 14, 16, 17, 22, 24, 26, 27, 27, 28, 29; 4:7, 14, 19; 5:1, 2, 4, 6, 24; 6:2, 12, 14, 15, 18	41
Eph.	1:1, 1, 2, 3, 3, 5, 10, 12, 17, 20; 2:5, 6, 7, 10, 12, 13, 13, 20; 3:1, 4, 6, 8, 9, 11, 14, 17, 19, 21; 4:7, 12, 13, 15, 20, 32; 5:2, 5, 14, 20, 23, 24, 25, 32; 6:5, 6, 23, 24	46
Phl.	1:1, 1, 2, 6, 8, 10, 11, 13, 15, 16, 18, 19, 20, 21, 23, 26, 27, 29; 2:1, 5, 11, 16, 21, 30; 3:3, 7, 8, 8, 9, 12, 14, 18, 20; 4:7, 13, 19, 21, 23	38
Col.	1:1, 2, 2, 3, 4, 7, 24, 27, 28; 2:2, 5, 6, 8, 11, 17, 20; 3:1, 1, 3, 4, 11, 13, 16, 24; 4:3, 12	26
1 Th.	1:1, 1, 3; 2:6, 14, 19; 3:2, 11, 13; 4:16; 5:9, 18, 23, 28	14
2 Th.	1:1, 2, 8, 12, 12; 2:1, 2, 14, 16; 3:5, 6, 12, 18	13
1 Ti.	1:1, 1, 2, 12, 14, 15, 16; 2:5, 7; 3:13; 4:6; 5:11, 21; 6:3, 13, 14	16
2 Ti.	1:1, 1, 2, 9, 10, 13; 2:1, 3, 8, 10, 19; 3:12, 15; 4:1, 22	15
Tit.	1:1, 4; 2:13; 3:6	4
Phe.	1:1, 3, 6, 8, 9, 23, 25	7
Heb.	3:1, 6, 14; 5:5; 6:1; 9:11, 14, 24, 28; 10:10; 11:26; 13:8, 21	13
Jas.	1:1; 2:1	2
1 Pt.	1:1, 2, 3, 3, 7, 11, 11, 13, 19; 2:5, 21; 3:16, 18, 21; 4:1, 11, 13, 14; 5:1, 10, 14	21
2 Pt.	1:1, 1, 8, 11, 14, 16; 2:20; 3:18	8
1 Jn.	1:3, 7; 2:1, 22; 3:23; 4:2, 3; 5:1, 6, 20	10
2 Jn.	1:3, 7, 9, 9	4
Jd.	1:1, 1, 4, 17, 21	5
Rev.	1:1, 2, 5, 9, 9; 11:15; 12:10, 17; 20:4, 6; 22:21	11
Total		569

5448. χρίω, chri'ō

Book	anoint	Total
Lk.	4:18	1
Ac.	4:27; 10:38	2
2 Co.	1:21	1
Heb.	1:9	1
Total		5

5449. χρονίζω, chronid'zō

Book	Oc.	delay	Oc.	tarry	Oc.	tarry so long	Total
Mt.	1	24:48	1	25:5			2
Lk.	1	12:45			1	1:21	2
Heb.			1	10:37			1
Total	2		2		1		5

5450. χρόνος, chron'os

Book	Oc.	time	Oc.	season	Oc.	while	Oc.	a while	Oc.	space	Oc.	oftentimes (with 4083)	Oc.	Not Tr.	Oc.	Misc.	Total
Mt.	3	2:7, 16; 25:19															3
Mk.													2	2:19; 9:21			2
Lk.	4	1:57; 4:5; 8:27; 20: 9					1	18:4			1	8:29					6
Jn.	2	5:6; 14:9			2	7:33; 12:35											4
Ac.	13	1:6, 7, 21; 3:21; 7: 17; 8:11; 13:18; 14: 3, 28; 17:30; 18:20, 23; 27:9	2	19:22; 20:18					1	15:33					1	7:23	17
Ro.													1	7:1	1	16:25	2
1 Co.							1	16:7					1	7:39			2
Gal.	1	4:4											1	4:1			2
1 Th.	1	5:1															1
2 Ti.															1	1:9	1
Tit.															1	1:2	1
Heb.	3	4:7; 5:12; 11:32															3
1 Pt.	4	1:17, 20; 4:2, 3															4
Jd.	1	1:18															1
Rev.	1	10:6	2	6:11; 20: 3					1	2:21							4
Total	33		4		2		2		2		1		5		4		53

Miscellaneous: Ac. 7:23, old; Ro. 16:25 (with 166), since the world began; 2 Ti. 1:9 (with 166), the world began; Tit. 1:2, the world began.

5451. χρονοτριβέω chronotribe'ō

Book	spend time	Total
Ac.	20:16	1

5452. χρύσεος, chru'seos

Book	Oc.	golden	Oc.	of gold	Total
2 Ti.			1	2:20	1
Heb.	2	9:4, 4			2
Rev.	13	1:12, 13, 20; 2:1; 5:8; 8:3, 3; 9:13; 14: 14; 15:6, 7; 17:4; 21:15	2	4:4; 9:20	15
Total	15		3		18

5453. χρυσίον, chrusi'on

Book	gold	Total
Ac.	3:6; 20:33	2
Heb.	9:4	1
1 Pt.	1:7, 18; 3:3	3
Rev.	3:18; 21:18, 21	3
Total		9

5454. χρυσοδακτύλιος chrusodaktu'lios

Book	with a gold ring	Total
Jas.	2:2	1

5455. χρυσόλιθος, chrusol'ithos

Book	chrysolite	Total
Rev.	21:20	1

5456. χρυσόπρασος chrusop'rasos

Book	chrysoprasus	Total
Rev.	21:20	1

5457. χρυσός, chrusos'

Book	gold	Total
Mt.	2:11; 10:9; 23:16, 17, 17	5
Ac.	17:29	1
1 Co.	3:12	1
1 Ti.	2:9	1
Jas.	5:3	1
Rev.	9:7; 17:4; 18:12, 16	4
Total		13

5458. χρυσόω, chruso'ō

Book	deck	Total
Rev.	17:4; 18:16	2

5459. χρώς, chrōs

Book	body	Total
Ac.	19:12	1

5460. χωλός, chōlos'

Book	Oc.	lame	Oc.	halt	Oc.	cripple	Total
Mt.	4	11:5; 15:30, 31; 21:14	1	18:8			5
Mk.			1	9:45			1
Lk.	2	7:22; 14:13	1	14:21			3
Jn.			1	5:3			1
Ac.	3	3:2, 11; 8:7			1	14:8	4
Heb.	1	12:13					1
Total	10		4		1		15

5461. χώρα, chō'ra

Book	Oc.	country	Oc.	region	Oc.	land	Oc.	field	Oc.	ground	Oc.	coast	Total
Mt.	2	2:12; 8:28	1	4:16									3
Mk.	2	5:1, 10			1	1:5							3
Lk.	6	2:8; 8:26; 15:13, 15; 19:12; 21:21	1	3:1	1	15:14			1	12:16			9
Jn.	2	11:54, 55					1	4:35					3
Ac.	3	12:20; 18:23; 27:27	3	8:1; 13:49; 16:6	1	10:39					1	26:20	8
Jas.							1	5:4					1
Total	15		5		3		2		1		1		27

5462. χωρέω, chōre'ō

Book	Oc.	receive	Oc.	contain	Oc.	come	Oc.	go	Oc.	have place	Oc.	cannot receive (with 3656)	Oc.	be room to receive	Total
Mt.	2	19:12, 12					1	15:17			1	19:11			4
Mk.													1	2:2	1
Jn.			2	2:6; 21:25					1	8:37					3
2 Co.	1	7:2													1
2 Pt.					1	3:9									1
Total	3		2		1		1		1		1		1		10

5463. χωρίζω, chōrid'zō

Book	Oc.	depart	Oc.	separate	Oc.	put asunder	Total
Mt.					1	19:6	1
Mk.					1	10:9	1
Ac.	3	1:4; 18:1, 2					3
Ro.			2	8:35, 39			2
1 Co.	4	7:10, 11, 15, 15					4
Phe.	1	1:15					1
Heb.			1	7:26			1
Total	8		3		2		13

5464. χωρίον, chōri'on

Book	Oc.	field	Oc.	land	Oc.	place	Oc.	parcel of ground	Oc.	possession	Total
Mt.					1	26:36					1
Mk.					1	14:32					1
Jn.							1	4:5			1
Ac.	3	1:18, 19, 19	3	4:34; 5:3, 8					1	28:7	7
Total	3		3		2		1		1		10

5465. χωρίς, chōris'

Book	Oc.	without	Oc.	beside	Oc.	by itself	Total
Mt.	1	13:34	2	14:21; 15:38			3
Mk.	1	4:34					1
Lk.	1	6:49					1
Jn.	2	1:3; 15:5			1	20:7	3
Ro.	6	3:21, 28; 4:6; 7:8, 9; 10: 14					6
1 Co.	3	4:8; 11;11, 11					3
2 Co.			1	11:28			1
Eph.	1	2:12					1
Phl.	1	2:14					1
1 Ti.	2	2:8; 5:21					2
Phe.	1	1:14					1
Heb.	13	4:15; 7:7, 20, 21; 9:7, 18, 22, 28; 10:28; 11:6, 40; 12:8, 14					13
Jas.	3	2:20, 26, 26					3
Total	35		3		1		39

5466. χῶρος, chō'ros

Book	north west	Total
Ac.	27:12	1

5467. ψάλλω, psal'lō

Book	Oc.	sing	Oc.	sing psalms	Oc.	make melody	Total
Ro.	1	15:9					1
1 Co.	2	14:15, 15					2
Eph.					1	5:19	1
Jas.			1	5:13			1
Total	3		1		1		5

5468. ψαλμός, psalmos'

Book	Oc.	psalm	Oc.	Psalm	Total
Lk.	1	24:44	1	20:42	2
Ac.	1	13:33	1	1:20	2
1 Co.	1	14:26			1
Eph.	1	5:19			1
Col.	1	3:16			1
Total	5		2		7

5469. ψευδάδελφος pseudad'elphos

Book	false brother	Total
2 Co.	11:26	1
Gal.	2:4	1
Total		2

5470. ψευδαπόστολος pseudapos'tolos

Book	false apostle	Total
2 Co.	11:13	1

5471. ψευδής, pseudes'

Book	Oc.	liar	Oc.	false	Total
Ac.			1	6:13	1
Rev.	2	2:2; 21:8			2
Total	2		1		3

5472. ψευδοδιδάσκαλος pseudodidas'kalos

Book	false teacher	Total
2 Pt.	2:1	1

5473. ψευδολόγος, pseudolog'os

Book	speaking lies	Total
1 Ti.	4:2	1

5474. ψεύδομαι, pseu'domai

Book	Oc.	lie	Oc.	falsely	Total
Mt.			1	5:11	1
Ac.	2	5:3, 4			2
Ro.	1	9:1			1
2 Co.	1	11:31			1
Gal.	1	1:20			1
Col.	1	3:9			1
1 Ti.	1	2:7			1
Heb.	1	6:18			1
Jas.	1	3:14			1
1 Jn.	1	1:6			1
Rev.	1	3:9			1
Total	11		1		12

5475. ψευδομάρτυρ
pseudomar'tur

Book	false witness	Total
Mt.	26:60, 60	2
1 Co.	15:15	1
Total		3

5476. ψευδομαρτυρέω
pseudomarture'ō

Book	bear false witness	Total
Mt.	19:18	1
Mk.	10:19; 14:56, 57	3
Lk.	18:20	1
Ro.	13:9	1
Total		6

5477. ψευδομαρτυρία
pseudomarturi'a

Book	false witness	Total
Mt.	15:19; 26:59	2

5478. ψευδοπροφήτης
pseudoprophe̱'te̱s

Book	false prophet	Total
Mt.	7:15; 24:11, 24	3
Mk.	13:22	1
Lk.	6:26	1
Ac.	13:6	1
2 Pt.	2:1	1
1 Jn.	4:1	1
Rev.	16:13; 19:20; 20:10	3
Total		11

5479. ψεῦδος, pseu'dos

Book	Oc.	lie	Oc.	lying	Total
Jn.	1	8:44			1
Ro.	1	1:25			1
Eph.			1	4:25	1
2 Th.	1	2:11	1	2:9	2
1 Jn.	2	2:21, 27			2
Rev.	2	21:27; 22:15			2
Total	7		2		9

5480. ψευδόχριστος
pseudoch'rıstos

Book	false Christ	Total
Mt.	24:24	1
Mk.	13:22	1
Total		2

5481. ψευδώνυμος
pseudō'numos

Book	falsely so called	Total
1 Ti.	6:20	1

5482. ψεῦσμα, pseus'ma

Book	lie	Total
Ro.	3:7	1

5483. ψεύστης, pseus'te̱s

Book	liar	Total
Jn.	8:44, 55	2
Ro.	3:4	1
1 Ti.	1:10	1
Tit.	1:12	1
1 Jn.	1:10; 2:4, 22; 4:20; 5:10	5
Total		10

5484. ψηλαφάω, pse̱lapha'ō

Book	Oc.	handle	Oc.	feel after	Oc.	touch	Total
Lk.	1	24:39					1
Ac.			1	17:27			1
Heb.					1	12:18	1
1 Jn.	1	1:1					1
Total	2		1		1		4

5485. ψηφίζω, pse̱phid'zō

Book	count	Total
Lk.	14:28	1
Rev.	13:18	1
Total		2

5486. ψῆφος, pse̱'phos

Book	Oc.	stone	Oc.	voice	Total
Ac.			1	26:10	1
Rev.	2	2:17, 17			2
Total	2		1		3

5487. ψιθυρισμός, psithurismos'

Book	whispering	Total
2 Co.	12:20	1

5488. ψιθυριστής, psithuriste̱s'

Book	whisperer	Total
Ro.	1:29	1

5489. ψιχίον, psichi'on

Book	crumb	Total
Mt.	15:27	1
Mk.	7:28	1
Lk.	16:21	1
Total		3

5490. ψυχή, psuche̱'

Book	Oc.	soul	Oc.	life	Oc.	mind	Oc.	heart	Oc.	heartily (with 1537)	Oc.	Not Tr.	Total
Mt.	8	10:28, 28; 11:29; 12:18; 16:26, 26; 22:37; 26:38	8	2:20; 6:25, 25; 10:39, 39; 16:25, 25; 20:28									16
Mk.	5	8:36, 37; 12:30, 33; 14:34	4	3:4; 8:35, 35; 10:45									9
Lk.	7	1:46; 2:35; 10:27; 12:19, 19, 20; 21:19	8	6:9; 9:24, 24, 56; 12:22, 23; 14:26; 17:33									15
Jn.	1	12:27	8	10:11, 15, 17; 12:25, 25; 13:37, 38; 15:13							1	10:24	10
Ac.	10	2:27, 31, 41, 43; 3:23; 4:32; 7:14; 14:22; 15:24; 27:37	5	15:26; 20:10, 24; 27:10, 22	1	14:2							16
Ro.	2	2:9; 13:1	2	11:3; 16:4									4
1 Co.	1	15:45											1
2 Co.	1	1:23									1	12:15	2
Eph.							1	6:6					1
Phl.			1	2:30	1	1:27							2
Col.									1	3:23			1
1 Th.	2	2:8; 5:23											2
Heb.	5	4:12; 6:19; 10:38, 39; 13:17			1	12:3							6
Jas.	2	1:21; 5:20											2
1 Pt.	6	1:9, 22; 2:11, 25; 3:20; 4:19											6
2 Pt.	2	2:8, 14											2
1 Jn.			2	3:16, 16									2
3 Jn.	1	1:2											1
Rev.	5	6:9; 16:3; 18:13, 14; 20:4	2	8:9; 12:11									7
Total	58		40		3		1		1		2		105

5491. ψυχικός, psuchikos'

Book	Oc.	natural	Oc.	sensual	Total
1 Co.	4	2:14; 15:44, 44, 46			4
Jas.			1	3:15	1
Jd.			1	1:19	1
Total	4		2		6

5492. ψύχος, psu'chos

Book	cold	Total
Jn.	18:18	1
Ac.	28:2	1
2 Co.	11:27	1
Total		3

5493. ψυχρός, psuchros'

Book	cold	Total
Mt.	10:42	1
Rev.	3:15, 15, 16	3
Total		4

5494. ψύχω, psu'chō

Book	wax cold	Total
Mt.	24:12	1

5495. ψωμίζω, psōmid'zō

Book	Oc.	bestow to feed	Oc.	feed	Total
Ro.			1	12:20	1
1 Co.	1	13:3			1
Total	1		1		2

5496. ψωμίον, psōmi'on

Book	sop	Total
Jn.	13:26, 26, 27, 30	4

5497. ψώχω, psō'chō

Book	rub	Total
Lk.	6:1	1

5498. Ω, O'mega

Book	Omega	Total
Rev.	1:8, 11; 21:6; 22:13	4

5499. ὦ, ō

Book	Oc.	O	Oc.	Not Tr.	Total
Mt.	2	15:28; 17:17			2
Mk.	1	9:19			1
Lk.	2	9:41; 24:25			2
Ac.	3	1:1; 13:10; 18:14	1	27:21	4
Ro.	4	2:1, 3; 9:20; 11:33			4
Gal.	1	3:1			1
1 Ti.	1	6:20			1
Jas.	1	2:20			1
Total	15		1		16

5500. ὦ, ō

Book	Oc.	be	Oc.	may be	Oc.	should be	Oc.	is	Oc.	might be	Oc.	were	Oc.	Not Tr.	Oc.	Misc.	Total
Mt.	4	6:22, 23; 10: 13, 13	1	6:4			3	20:4, 7; 24:28									8
Mk.					1	3:14			1	5:18							2
Lk.	2	10:6; 14:8					2	11:34, 34									4
Jn.	4	3:2, 27; 9:31; 17:24	8	14:3; 16:24; 17:11, 21, 21, 22, 23, 26					1	17:19	1	6:65			1	9:5	15
Ac.	1	5:38															1
Ro.	2	2:25; 9:27			1	11:25											3
1 Co.	5	1:10, 10; 7: 29; 14:28; 16:4	3	5:7; 7:34; 15:28	1	12:25									2	2:5; 7: 36	11
2 Co.	1	13:7	2	4:7; 9:3	1	1:17							1	1:9	1	13:9	6
Gal.	1	5:10															1
Eph.	1	4:14			1	5:27											2
Phl.			2	1:10; 2:28													2
1 Ti.			1	5:7									1	4:15			2
2 Ti.			1	3:17													1
Tit.	1	3:14	1	1:9													2
Phe.					1	1:14											1
Jas.			1	1:4									2	2:15; 5:15			3
1 Jn.			1	1:4													1
2 Jn.			1	1:12													1
Total	22		22		6		5		2		1		4		4		66

Miscellaneous: Jn. 9:5, am; 1 Co. 2:5, should stand; 1 Co. 7:36 (with 5130), pass the flower of (one's) age; 2 Co. 13:9, are.

5502. ὧδε, hō'de

Book	Oc.	here	Oc.	hither	Oc.	in this place	Oc.	this place	Oc.	there	Total
Mt.	12	12:41, 42; 14:8, 17; 16:28; 17:4, 4; 20:6; 24:2, 23a; 26:38; 28:6	4	8:29; 14:18; 17:17; 22:12	1	12:6			1	24:23b	18
Mk.	8	6:3; 8:4; 9:1, 5; 13:21; 14:32, 34; 16:6	1	11:3							9
Lk.	10	4:23; 9:12, 27, 33; 11:31, 32; 17:21, 23; 22:38; 24:6	3	9:41; 14:21; 19:27			1	23:5			14
Jn.	3	6:9; 11:21, 32	2	6:25; 20:27							5
Ac.	1	9:14	1	9:21							2
Col.	1	4:9									1
Heb.	2	7:8; 13:14									2
Jas.	2	2:3, 3									2
Rev.	5	13:10, 18; 14:12, 12; 17:9	2	4:1; 11:12							7
Total	44		13		1		1		1		60

5501. Ὠβήδ, Obed'

Book	Obed	Total
Mt.	1:5, 5	2
Lk.	3:32	1
Total		3

5503. ᾠδή, ōde'

Book	song	Total
Eph.	5:19	1
Col.	3:16	1
Rev.	5:9; 14:3, 3; 15:3, 3	5
Total		7

5504. ὠδίν, ōdin'

Book	Oc.	sorrow	Oc.	pain	Oc.	travail	Total
Mt.	1	24:8					1
Mk.	1	13:8					1
Ac.			1	2:24			1
1 Th.					1	5:3	1
Total	2		1		1		4

5505. ὠδίνω, ōdi'nō

Book	Oc.	travail in birth	Oc.	travail	Total
Gal.	1	4:19	1	4:27	2
Rev.	1	12:2			1
Total	2		1		3

5506. ὦμος, ō'mos

Book	shoulder	Total
Mt.	23:4	1
Lk.	15:5	1
Total		2

5507a. ὤν, οὖσα, ὄν, ōn, ou'sa, on

Book	Oc.	being	Oc.	when . . . was	Oc.	when . . . were	Oc.	which is	Oc.	when . . . is	Oc.	who was	Oc.	Not Tr.	Oc.	Misc.	Total
Mt.	3	1:19; 7:11; 12:34					1	6:30									4
Mk.	2	8:1; 14:3											1	14:43	3	5:25; 11:11; 14:66	6
Lk.	5	2:5; 3:23; 13:16; 20:36; 22:3	2	22:53; 24:6			1	12:28			1	23:7	1	23:12	3	8:43; 14:32; 24:44	13
Jn.	9	4:9a; 5:13; 6:71; 7:50; 10:33; 11:49, 51; 18:26; 19:38	2	1:48; 20:1					1	3:4			1	10:12	4	4:9b; 9:25; 20:19; 21:11	17
Ac.	3	15:32; 16:21; 27:2	2	7:2; 27:9									5	9:2; 17:16; 18:24; 25:23; 28:17	11	7:5, 12; 8:23; 9:38, 39; 19:35, 36; 24:10, 24; 26:3; 28:25	21
Ro.	1	11:17	1	4:10	2	5:6, 10	1	16:1	1	5:13					3	4:17a, 17b; 5:8	9
1 Co.	3	8:7; 9:21; 12:12					1	8:10							1	9:19	5
2 Co.													1	8:22	2	8:9; 11:19	3
Gal.	1	2:3							1	6:3					1	4:1	3
Eph.	2	2:20; 4:18a			1	2:5									2	2:1, 4	5
Phl.															1	1:7	1
Col.	1	2:13													1	1:21	2
1 Th.															1	5:8	1
2 Th.			1	2:5													1
1 Ti.	1	3:10									1	1:13					2
Tit.	2	1:16; 3:11															2
Phe.	1	1:9															1
Heb.	2	1:3; 13:3									1	3:2			2	5:8; 8:4	5
Jas.															1	3:4	1
2 Pt.					1	1:18									1	2:11	2
Rev.													1	5:5			1
Total	36		8		4		4		3		3		10		37		105

Miscellaneous: Mk. 5:25 (with 1722), which had; Mk. 11:11, and . . . was come; Mk. 14:66, as . . . was; Lk. 8:43 (with 1722), having; Lk. 14:32, while . . . is; Lk. 24:44, while . . . was; Jn. 4:9b, which am; Jn. 9:25, whereas . . . was; Jn. 20:19, at; Jn. 21:11, for . . . were; Ac. 7:5, when . . . had; Ac. 7:12, that . . . was; Ac. 8:23, that . . . art; Ac. 9:38, forasmuch as . . . was; Ac. 9:39, while . . . was; Ac. 19:35, that . . . is; Ac. 19:36 (with 368), cannot be spoken against; Ac. 24:10, that . . . hast been; Ac. 24:24, which was; Ac. 26:3, to be; Ac. 28:25 (with 800), agreed not; Ro. 4:17a, which be; Ro. 4:17b, though . . . were; Ro. 5:8, while . . . were; 1 Co. 9:19, though . . . be; 2 Co. 8:9, though . . . was; 2 Co. 11:19, seeing . . . are; Gal. 4:1, though . . . be; Eph. 2:1, who were; Eph. 2:4, who is; Phl. 1:7, inasmuch as . . . are; Col. 1:21, that were; 1 Th. 5:8, who are; Heb. 5:8, though . . . were; Heb. 8:4, seeing that there are; Jas. 3:4, though . . . be; 2 Pt. 2:11, which are.

5507b. ὤν, οὖσα, ὄν, ōn, ou'sa, on (with 3488)

Book	Oc.	which is	Oc.	that is	Oc.	which are	Oc.	which were	Oc.	that are	Oc.	that were	Oc.	that be	Oc.	Misc.	Total
Mt.			1	12:30													1
Mk.			1	13:16			1	2:26									2
Lk.			1	11:23			1	6:3									2
Jn.	3	1:18; 3:13; 6:46	3	3:31; 8:47; 18:37			2	9:40; 11:31							1	12:17	9
Ac.	1	5:17					3	16:3; 19:31; 22:5			3	11:1; 20:34; 22:9			3	13:1; 14:13; 21:8	10
Ro.	1	7:23	1	12:3	1	16:11			2	8:5, 8			2	1:7; 13:1	2	8:28; 9:5	9
1 Co.	1	1:2			1	1:28a			1	1:28b							3
2 Co.	2	1:1a; 11:31			1	1:1b			1	5:4							4
Gal.					1	4:8											1
Eph.			1	4:18b	1	1:1									1	2:13	3
Phl.					1	1:1											1
Col.															1	4:11	1
1 Th.					1	2:14											1
1 Ti.									1	2:2							1
2 Ti.									1	2:19							1
Total	8		8		7		7		6		3		2		8		49

Miscellaneous: Jn. 12:17, that was; Ac. 13:1, that was; Ac. 14:13, which was; Ac. 21:8, which was; Ro. 8:28, who are; Ro. 9:5, who is; Eph. 2:13, who were; Col. 4:11, who are.

Word 5507 has 154 occurrences.

5508. ὠνέομαι, ōne'omai

Book	buy	Total
Ac.	7:16	1

5509. ὠόν, ōon'

Book	egg	Total
Lk.	11:12	1

5510. ὥρα, hō'ra

Book	Oc.	hour	Oc.	time	Oc.	season	Oc.	Misc.	Total
Mt.	21	8:13; 9:22; 10:19; 15:28; 17:18; 20:3, 5, 6, 9, 12; 24:36, 42, 44, 50; 25:13; 26:40, 45, 55; 27:45, 45, 46	2	14:15; 18:1					23
Mk.	9	13:11, 32; 14:35, 37, 41; 15:25, 33, 33, 34	1	6:35b			2	6:35a; 11:11	12
Lk.	13	7:21; 10:21; 12:12, 39, 40, 46; 20:19; 22:14, 53, 59; 23:44, 44; 24:33	2	1:10; 14:17			1	2:38	16
Jn.	22	1:39; 2:4; 4:6, 21, 23, 52, 52, 53; 5:25, 28; 7:30; 8:20; 11:9; 12:23, 27, 27; 13:1; 16:21, 32; 17:1; 19:14, 27	3	16:2, 4, 25	1	5:35			26
Ac.	12	2:15; 3:1; 5:7; 10:3, 9, 30, 30; 16:18, 33; 19:34; 22:13; 23:23							12
Ro.							1	13:11	1
1 Co.	2	4:11; 15:30							2
2 Co.					1	7:8			1
Gal.	1	2:5							1
1 Th.							1	2:17	1
Phe.					1	1:15			1
1 Jn.			2	2:18, 18					2
Rev.	9	3:3, 10; 9:15; 11:13; 14:7; 17:12; 18:10, 17, 19	1	14:15					10
Total	89		11		3		5		108

Miscellaneous: Mk. 6:35a, day; Mk. 11:11 (with 3698), eventide; Lk. 2:38, instant; Ro. 13:11, high time; 1 Th. 2:17, short.

5511. ὡραῖος, hōrai'os

Book	beautiful	Total
Mt.	23:27	1
Ac.	3:2, 10	2
Ro.	10:15	1
Total		4

5512. ὠρύομαι, ōru'omai

Book	roaring	Total
1 Pt.	5:8	1

5513. ὡς, hōs

Book	Oc.	as	Oc.	when	Oc.	how	Oc.	as it were	Oc.	about	Oc.	as soon as
Mt.	31	1:24; 6:10, 12; 7:29, 29; 8:13; 10:16, 16, 16, 25, 25; 13:43; 14:5; 17:2, 2, 20; 18:3, 4, 33; 19:19; 20:14; 21:26; 22:30, 39; 26:19, 39, 39, 55; 27:65; 28:9, 15										
Mk.	17	1:2, 22, 22; 3:5; 4:26; 6:15, 34; 7:6; 8:24; 9:3; 10:1, 15; 12:25, 31, 33; 13:34; 14:48			2	4:27; 12:26			2	5:13; 8:9		
Lk.	28	2:15; 3:4, 23; 6:10, 22, 40; 9:54; 10: 3, 18, 27; 11:2, 36, 44; 14:22; 15:19, 25; 17:6, 28; 18:11, 17; 21:35; 22: 26, 26, 27, 31, 52; 23:14, 26	11	1:41; 2:39; 4:25; 5:4; 7: 12; 11:1; 12:58; 19:5, 29, 41; 20:37	6	6:4; 8:47; 22: 61; 23:55; 24: 6, 35			2	2:37; 8: 42	3	1:23, 44; 22: 66
Jn.	3	1:14; 15:6; 20:11	12	2:9, 23; 4:1, 40; 6:12, 16; 7:10a; 8:7; 11:6, 32, 33; 19:33			2	7:10b; 21:8	3	1:39; 6: 19; 11: 18	4	11:20, 29; 18:6; 21:9
Ac.	18	2:15; 3:12; 7:51; 8:32a, 36; 10:25; 11:17; 13:25, 33; 16:4; 17:28; 22:5, 25; 23:11, 15, 20; 25:10; 27:30	18	5:24; 7:23; 10:7; 13:29; 14:5; 16:15; 17:13; 18:5; 19:9; 20:14, 18; 21:12, 27; 22:11; 25:14; 27:1, 27; 28:4	4	10:28, 38; 11: 16; 20:20	1	17:14	5	1:15; 5: 7; 13:18, 20; 19: 34		
Ro.	13	1:21; 3:7; 4:17; 5:15, 16, 18; 6:13; 8: 36; 9:27, 29a; 13:9, 13; 15:15			3	10:15; 11:2, 33	1	9:32				
1 Co.	36	3:1, 1, 1, 10, 15; 4:1, 7; 4:13, 14, 18; 5:3, 3; 7:7, 8, 17, 17, 25, 29, 30, 30, 30, 31; 8:7; 9:20, 20, 21, 22, 26, 26; 10:7, 15; 13:11, 11, 11; 14:33; 16:10	1	11:34			1	4:9				
2 Co.	26	2:17, 17, 17; 3:1, 5; 5:20; 6:4, 8, 9, 9, 9, 10, 10, 10, 13; 7:14; 9:5; 10:2, 9, 14; 11:3, 15, 16, 21; 13:2, 7			1	7:15	1	11:17				
Gal.	9	1:9; 3:16, 16; 4:12, 12, 14, 14; 5:14; 6:10										
Eph.	13	2:3; 3:5; 5:1, 8, 15, 15, 22, 23, 28; 6: 5, 6, 6, 20										
Phl.	5	1:20; 2:8, 12, 15, 22									1	2:23
Col.	7	2:6, 20; 3:12, 18, 22, 23; 4:4										
1 Th.	7	2:4, 6, 7, 11b; 5:2, 4, 6			2	2:10, 11a						
2 Th.	5	2:2, 2, 4; 3:15, 15										
1 Ti.	4	5:1, 1, 2, 2										
2 Ti.	4	2:3, 9, 17; 3:9										
Tit.	2	1:5, 7										
Phe.	3	1:9, 16, 17					1	1:14				
Heb.	19	1:11; 3:2, 5, 6, 8, 15; 4:3; 6:19; 7: 9; 11:9, 27, 29; 12:5, 7, 16, 27; 13: 3, 3, 17										
Jas.	5	1:10; 2:8, 9, 12; 5:5					1	5:3				
1 Pt.	27	1:14, 19, 24, 24; 2:2, 5, 11, 12, 13, 14, 16a, 16c, 25; 3:7, 7, 16; 4:10, 11, 11, 12, 15, 15, 16, 19; 5:3, 8, 12										
2 Pt.	9	1:19; 2:1, 12; 3:8, 8, 9, 10, 16, 16										
1 Jn.	2	1:7; 2:27										
2 Jn.	1	1:5										
Jd.	1	1:10										
Rev.	47	1:10, 14, 14, 15, 15, 16, 17; 2:24, 27, 27; 3:3, 21; 4:7; 5:6; 6:11, 12, 12, 13, 14; 9:2, 3, 5, 7b, 8, 8, 9b, 17; 10: 1b, 7, 9, 10; 12:15; 13:2, 2, 11; 14:2, 2; 16:3, 15; 17:12; 18:6; 19:6b, 6c, 12; 20:8; 21:2; 22:1					12	4:1; 6:1; 8: 8, 10; 9:7a, 9a; 10:1a; 13:3; 14:3; 15:2; 19: 6a; 21:21	2	8:1; 16:21		
Total	342		42		18		20		14		8	

5514. Ὡσαννά, Hōsanna'

Book	Hosanna	Total
Mt.	21:9, 9, 15	3
Mk.	11:9, 10	2
Jn.	12:13	1
Total		6

5517. Ὡσηέ, Osee'

Book	Osee	Total
Ro.	9:25	1

5515. ὡσαύτως, hōsau'tōs

Book	Oc.	likewise	Oc.	in like manner	Oc.	even so	Oc.	after the same manner	Total
Mt.	4	20:5; 21:30, 36; 25:17							4
Mk.	2	12:21; 14:31							2
Lk.	2	13:3; 22:20	1	20:31					3
Ro.	1	8:26							1
1 Co.							1	11:25	1
1 Ti.	2	3:8; 5:25	1	2:9	1	3:11			4
Tit.	2	2:3, 6							2
Total	13		2		1		1		17

5516. ὡσεί, hōsei'

Book	Oc.	about	Oc.	as	Oc.	like	Oc.	as it had been	Oc.	as it were	Oc.	like as	Total
Mt.	1	14:21	3	9:36; 28:3, 4	1	3:16							5
Mk.	1	6:44	1	9:26	1	1:10							3
Lk.	7	1:56; 3:23; 9:14, 28: 22:41, 59; 23: 44	1	24:11	1	3:22			1	22:24			10
Jn.	4	4:6; 6:10; 19:14, 39			1	1:32							5
Ac.	5	2:41; 4:4; 5:36; 10:3; 19:7					2	6:15; 9:18			1	2:3	8
Heb.			2	1:12; 11:12									2
Rev.					1	1:14							1
Total	18		7		5		2		1		1		34

5513. ὡς, hōs (continued)

Book	Oc.	like	Oc.	even as	Oc.	that	Oc.	while	Oc.	like unto	Oc.	according as	Oc.	after	Oc.	Misc.	Total
Mt.	2	6:29; 28:3	1	15:28											2	12:13; 21:46	36
Mk.	1	4:31	1	4:36											1	9:21	24
Lk.	1	12:27			1	16:1	2	24:32, 32									54
Jn.	1	7:46															25
Ac.	1	8:32b			2	17:22; 28:19	2	1:10; 10: 17	2	3:22; 7:37			3	16:10; 19:21; 21:1	5	9:23; 10:11; 11:5; 17:15; 20:24	61
Ro.					1	1:9					1	12:3			2	9:29b; 15: 24	21
1 Co.			2	3:5; 12:2											1	9:5	41
2 Co.															1	5:19	29
Gal.																	9
Eph.			1	5:33													14
Phl.															1	1:8	7
Col.																	7
1 Th.																	9
2 Th.																	5
1 Ti.																	4
2 Ti.					1	1:3											5
Tit.																	2
Phe.																	4
Heb.															1	3:11	20
Jas.																	6
1 Pt.			1	3:6											1	2:16b	29
2 Pt.											1	1:3					10
1 Jn.																	2
2 Jn.																	1
Jd.			1	1:7													2
Rev.	1	18:21							1	2:18	1	22:12			1	21:11	65
Total	7		7		5		4		3		3		3		16		492

Miscellaneous: Mt. 12:13, like as; Mt. 21:46, for; Mk. 9:21, since; Ac. 9:23, after that; Ac. 10:11, as it had been; Ac. 11:5, as it had been; Ac. 17:15, with; Ac. 20:24, so that; Ro. 9:29b, unto; Ro. 15:24 (with 1437), whensoever; 1 Co. 9:5, as well as; 2 Co. 5:19, to wit; Phl. 1:8, how greatly; Heb. 3:11, so; 1 Pt. 2:16b, for; Rev. 21:11, even like.

5518. ὥσπερ, hōs′per

Book	Oc.	as	Oc.	even as	Oc.	like as	Total
Mt.	12	6:2, 5, 7, 16; 12:40; 13:40; 18:17; 24:27, 37, 38; 25:14, 32	2	5:48; 20:28			14
Lk.	2	17:24; 18:11					2
Jn.	2	5:21, 26					2
Ac.	3	2:2; 3:17; 11:15					3
Ro.	5	5:12, 19, 21; 6:19; 11:30			1	6:4	6
1 Co.	4	8:5; 11:12; 15:22; 16:1					4
2 Co.	3	1:7; 8:7; 9:5					3
Gal.	1	4:29					1
Eph.	1	5:24					1
1 Th.	1	5:3					1
Heb.	3	4:10; 7:27; 9:25					3
Jas.	1	2:26					1
Rev.	1	10:3					1
Total	39		2		1		42

5519. ὡσπερεί, hōsperei′

Book	as	Total
1 Co.	15:8	1

5521. ὠτίον, ōti′on

Book	ear	Total
Mt.	26:51	1
Mk.	14:47	1
Lk.	22:51	1
Jn.	18:10, 26	2
Total		5

5522. ὠφέλεια, ōphel′eia

Book	Oc.	profit	Oc.	advantage	Total
Ro.	1	3:1			1
Jd.			1	1:16	1
Total	1		1		2

5520. ὥστε, hōs′te

Book	Oc.	so that	Oc.	wherefore	Oc.	insomuch that	Oc.	therefore	Oc.	that	Oc.	so then	Oc.	to	Oc.	as	Oc.	insomuch as	Total
Mt.	3	8:28; 13:2, 32	3	12:12; 19:6; 23:31	6	8:24; 12:22; 13:54; 15:31; 24:24; 27:14							2	10:1; 27:1	1	15:33			15
Mk.	5	3:20; 4:1, 32, 37; 15:5			6	1:27, 45; 2:2, 12; 3:10; 9:26	1	2:28			1	10:8							13
Lk.	1	5:7			1	12:1							1	9:52					3
Jn.									1	3:16									1
Ac.	4	16:26; 19:10, 12, 16			1	5:15			2	14:1; 15:39							1	1:19	8
Ro.	1	15:19	2	7:4, 12			1	13:2	1	7:6									5
1 Co.	2	1:7; 13:2	5	10:12; 11:27, 33; 14:22, 39			4	3:21; 4:5; 5:8; 15:58	1	5:1	2	3:7; 7:38							14
2 Co.	3	2:7; 3:7; 7:7	1	5:16	1	1:8	1	5:17			1	4:12							7
Gal.			2	3:24; 4:7	1	2:13	1	4:16			1	3:9							5
Phl.	1	1:13	1	2:12			1	4:1											3
1 Th.	2	1:7, 8	1	4:18															3
2 Th.	2	1:4; 2:4																	2
Heb.	1	13:6																	1
Jas.			1	1:19															1
1 Pt.			1	4:19					1	1:21									2
Total	25		17		16		9		6		5		3		1		1		83

5523. ὠφελέω, ōphele′ō

Book	Oc.	profit	Oc.	prevail	Oc.	better	Oc.	advantage	Total
Mt.	2	15:5; 16:26	1	27:24					3
Mk.	2	7:11; 8:36			1	5:26			3
Lk.							1	9:25	1
Jn.	1	6:63	1	12:19					2
Ro.	1	2:25							1
1 Co.	2	13:3; 14:6							2
Gal.	1	5:2							1
Heb.	2	4:2; 13:9							2
Total	11		2		1		1		15

5524. ὠφέλιμος, ōphel′imos

Book	Oc.	profitable	Oc.	profit (with 2076)	Total
1 Ti.	1	4:8b	1	4:8a	2
2 Ti.	1	3:16			1
Tit.	1	3:8			1
Total	3		1		4

THE INDEX

An Index to the English words of the King James Version of the New Testament as found in the column headings of the tabulations of this Concordance. For an explanation of the use of the Index, see the Preface to the Concordance.

THE INDEX

A

a, 1520 heis, 9
a, 3291 mia, 3
5000 tis, 10
Aaron, 2 Aarōn, 5
Abaddon, 3 Abaddōn, 1
abase, 41
abase, 4913 tapeinoō, 5
Abba, 5 Abba, 3
Abel, 6 Abel, 4
abhor, 655 apostugeō, 1
948 bdelussō, 1
Abia, 7 Abia, 3
Abiathar, 8 Abiathar, 1
abide, 390 anastrephō, 1
835 aulidzomai, 1
1304 diatribō, 5
1961 epimenō, 2
2476 histēmi, 1
3206 menō, 61
3787 paramenō, 1
4060 poieō, 1
5178 hupomenō, 1
abide in, 1961 epimenō, 1
abide in the field, 63 agrauleō, 1
abide still, 1961 epimenō, 1
4257 prosmenō, 1
Abilene, 9 Abilēnē, 1
ability, 1411 dunamis, 1
2479 ischus, 1
ability, his, 2141 euporeō with 5000
tis, 1
Abioud, 10 Abioud, 2
able, 1410 dunamai, 3
1415 dunatos, 10
2425 hikanos, 1
able, be, 1410 dunamai, 37
1840 exischuō, 1
2192 echō, 1
2480 ischuō, 6
able, make, 2427 hikanoō, 1
able to do, be, 1410 dunamai, 1
aboard, go, 1910 epibainō, 1
abode, 2650 katamenō with 2258 ēn, 1
3338 monē, 1
abolish, 2673 katargeō, 3
abominable, 111 athemitos, 1
947 bdeluktos, 1
948 bdelussō, 1
abomination, 946 bdelugma, 6
abound, 3952 perisseuō, 17
4021 pleonadzō, 6
4029 plēthunō, 1
abound, make, 3952 perisseuō, 1
abound, more, 3952 perisseuō, 1
abound, much more, 5148 huper-
perisseuō, 1
about, 1722 en, 1
1909a epi, 2 (gen.)
1909b epi, 1 (dat.)
1909c epi, 1 (acc.)
2596a kata, 3 (acc.)
2943 kuklothen, 1
3195 mellō, 1
3912a peri, 6 (gen.)
3912b peri, 25 (acc.)
4125 pou, 1
4214 pros, 2 (1 dat., 1 acc.)
5513 hōs, 14
5516 hōsei, 18
about, be, 2212 dzēteō, 1
3195 mellō, 4
about the time, 1909a epi, 1 (gen.)
above, 507 anō, 5
511 anōteros, 1
1883 epanō, 3
1909a epi, 1 (gen.)
1909b epi, 3 (dat.)
1909c epi, 1 (acc.)
3744c para, 4 (acc.)
3912a peri, 1 (gen.)
4019 pleiōn, 1
4153 pro, 3
5128b huper, 12 (acc.)
above, exceeding abundantly, 3953
perissos with 5128c huper and
1537 ek, 1
above, far, 5131 huperanō, 2
above, from, 509 anōthen, 5
above, remain over and, 3952
perisseuō, 1
above measure, 5134 huperballontōs, 1
above measure, be exalted, 5129 huper-
airomai, 2
Abraham, 11 Abraam, 73
Abraham, son of, 5107b huios with 11
Abraam, 1
abroad, 5218 phaneros with 1519 eis, 2
abroad, be noised, 5356 phōnē with
1096 ginomai, 1
abroad, blaze, 1310 diaphēmidzō, 1
abroad, come, 864 aphikneomai, 1
abroad, disperse, 4550 skorpidzō, 1
abroad, go, 1330 dierchomai, 1
1831 exerchomai, 2
abroad, make known, 1232
diagnōridzō, 1
abroad, noise, 1255 dialaleō, 1
abroad, scatter, 1287 diaskorpidzō, 2
1289 diaspeirō, 3
4396 hriptō, 1
4550 skorpidzō, 1
abroad, scattered, 1290 diaspora, 1
abroad, shed, 1632b ekchunō, 1
abroad, spread, 1831 exerchomai, 2
5218 phaneros, 1
abroad (one's) fame, spread, 1310
diaphēmidzō, 1
absence, 666 apousia, 1
absence of, in the, 817 ater, 1
absent, 548 apeimi, 1
absent, be, 548 apeimi, 6
1553 ekdēmeō, 3
abstain, 567 apechomai, 6
abstinence, 776 asitia, 1
abundance, 100 hadrotēs, 1
1411 dunamis, 1
3950 perisseia, 2
3951 perisseuma, 4
3952 perisseuō, 3
5136 huperbolē, 1
abundance, have, 3952 perisseuō, 1
abundance, have more, 3952
perisseuō, 1
abundant, 3952 perisseuō, 1
4021 pleonadzō, 1
4083 polus, 1
abundant, be exceeding, 5150 huper-
pleonadzō, 1
abundant, be more, 3952 perisseuō, 1
abundant, more, 3955 perissoteros, 3
3956 perissoterōs, 2
abundantly, 3950 perisseia with 1519
eis, 1
4046 plousiōs, 2
abundantly, more, 3953 perissos, 1
3954 perissoteron, 2
3956 perissoterōs, 4
abundantly above, exceeding, 3953
perissos with 5128c huper and
1537 ek, 1
abuse, 2711 katachraomai, 2
abuser of (one's) self with mankind,
733 arsenokoitēs, 1
accept, 588 apodechomai, 1
1209 dechomai, 2
2983 lambanō, 2
4227 prosdechomai, 1
acceptable, 587 apodektos, 2
1184 dektos, 2
2101 euarestos, 4
2144 euprosdektos, 2
5385 charis, 1
acceptably, 2102 euarestōs, 1
acceptation, 594 apodochē, 2
accepted, 1184 dektos, 3
2101 euarestos, 1
2144 euprosdektos, 3
accepted, make, 5387 charitoō, 1
access, 4218 prosagōgē, 3
accompany, 2064 erchomai with 4762
sun, 1
2192 echō, 1
4211 propempō, 1
4802 sunepomai, 1
4805 sunerchomai, 1
accomplish, 1822 exartidzō with 1096
ginomai, 1
2005 epiteleō, 2
4030 plēthō, 4
4037 plēroō, 1
4955 teleō, 4
accomplishment, 1604 ekplērōsis, 1
accord, of one, 4761 sumpsuchos, 1
accord, of (one's) own,
830 authairetos, 1
844 automatos, 1
accord, with one, 3561 homothumadon,
11
according as, 2530 kathoti, 1
2531 kathōs, 4
2596a kata, 1 (acc.)
5513 hōs, 3
according to, 2526 katho, 2
2531 kathōs, 1
2596a kata, 107 (acc.)
3488 ho, 1
4214 pros, 3
according to, fashion (one's) self,
4864 suschēmatidzō, 1
account, 2233 hēgeomai, 1
3049 logidzomai, 4
3056 logos, 8
account, put on (one's), 1677 ellogeō, 1
account worthy, 2661 kataxioō, 2
accounted, be, 1380 dokeō, 2
accursed, 331 anathema, 4
accusation, 156 aitia, 3
2724 katēgoria, 3
2920 krisis, 2
accusation, take by false, 4711
sukophanteō, 1
accuse, 1225 diaballō, 1
1458 engkaleō, 4
2723 katēgoreō, 21
accuse, falsely, 1908 epēreadzō, 1
accuse falsely, 4711 sukophanteō, 1
accused, 2724 katēgoria, 1
accuser, 2725 katēgoros, 7
accuser, false, 1228 diabolos, 2
Aceldama, 184 Akeldama, 1
Achaia, 882 Achaia, 11
Achaicus, 883 Achaikos, 1
Achaz, 881 Achadz, 2
Achim, 885 Acheim, 1
acknowledge, 1921 epiginōskō, 5
acknowledging, 1922 epignōsis, 3
acknowledgment, 1922 epignōsis, 1
acquaintance, 1110 gnōstos, 2
acquaintance, his, 2398 idios, 1
act, in the very, 1888 epautophōrō, 1
Adam, 76 Adam, 9
add, 2007 epitithēmi, 2
2018 epipherō, 1
2023 epichorēgeō, 1
4269 prostithēmi, 11
add in conference, 4223
prosanatithēmi, 1
add thereto, 1928 epidiatassomai, 1
Addi, 78 Addi, 1
addict, 4921 tassō, 1
adjure, 1844 exorkidzō, 1
3626 horkidzō, 2
administer, 1247 diakoneō, 2
administration, 1248 diakonia, 2
admiration, 2295 thauma, 1
admiration, have in, 2296 thaumadzō, 1
admire, 2296 thaumadzō, 1
admonish, 3460 noutheteō, 4
3767 paraineō, 1
admonished of God, be, 5437
chrēmatidzō, 1
admonition, 3459 nouthesia, 3
ado, make, 2350 thorubeō, 1
adoption, 5106 huiothesia, 3
adoption of children, 5106 huiothesia, 1
adoption of sons, 5106 huiothesia, 1
adorn, 2885 kosmeō, 5
adorning, 2889 kosmos, 1
Adramyttium, 98 Adramuttēnos, 1
Adria, 99 Adrias, 1
adulterer, 3332 moichos, 4
adulteress, 3328 moichalis, 3
adulterous, 3328 moichalis, 3
adultery, 3328 moichalis, 1
3330 moicheia, 4
adultery, commit, 3329 moichaō, 6
3331 moicheuō, 13
adultery, in, 3331 moicheuō, 1
advantage, 3953 perissos, 1
5522 ōpheleia, 1
5523 ōpheleō, 1
advantage, get an, 4022 pleonekteō, 1
advantageth, it, 3686 ophelos, 1
adventure, 1325 didōmi, 1
adversary, 476 antidikos, 5
480 antikeimai, 5
5127 hupenantios, 1
adversity, suffer, 2558 kakoucheō, 1
advice, 1106 gnōmē, 1
advise, 1012 boulē with 4987 tithēmi, 1
advocate, 3775 paraklētos, 1
Aeneas, 132 Aineas, 2
Aenon, 137 Ainōn, 1
afar off, 1519 eis with 3112 makran, 1
3112 makran, 2
3113 makrothen, 13
4107 porhrōthen, 2
afar off, cannot see, 3367
muōpadzō, 1
affair, 4130 pragmateia, 1
affairs, your, 5116 humōn, 1
affairs (one's), 3912a peri with 3488,
2 (gen.)
affect, 2206 dzeloō, 1
affect, zealously, 2206 dzēloō, 2
affected, make evil, 2559 kakoō, 1
affection, 3704 pathēma, 1
3706 pathos, 1
affection, inordinate, 3706 pathos, 1
affection, inward, 4598 splangchna, 1
affection, without natural, 794
astorgos, 2
affection on, set (one's), 5326
phroneō, 1
affectionately desirous, be, 2442
himeiromai, 1
affectioned, kindly, 5287 philostorgos, 1
affirm, 1226 diabebaioomai, 1
5235 phaskō, 1
5246 phēmi, 1
affirm, confidently, 1340
diischuridzomai, 1
affirm, constantly, 1340
diischuridzomai, 1
affirm constantly, 1226 diabebaioomai, 1
afflict, 2346 thlibō, 3
afflicted, be, 2553 kakopatheō, 1
4903 talaipōreō, 1
afflicted, to be, 2347 thlipsis with 1519
eis, 1
affliction, 2347 thlipsis, 17
2561 kakōsis, 1
3704 pathēma, 3
affliction, be partaker of, 4677
sungkakopatheō, 1
affliction, endure, 2553 kakopatheō, 1
affliction, suffering, 2552
kakopatheia, 1
affliction with, suffer, 4678
sungkakoucheō, 1
affrighted, 1719 emphobos, 2
affrighted, be, 1568 ekthambeō, 2
afoot, 3879 pedzē, 1
afoot, go, 3878 pedzeuō, 1
afore, prepare, 4182 proetoimadzō, 1
afore, promise, 4179
proepanggellomai, 1
afore, write, 4170 prographō, 1
aforehand, come, 4201 prolambanō, 1
aforetime, 4118 pote, 1
aforetime, write, 4170 prographō, 1
afraid, 1719 emphobos, 3
afraid, be, 1168 deiliaō, 1
5041 tremō, 1
5299 phobeō, 23
afraid, be sore, 5301 phobos with
5299 phobeō and 3173 megas, 1
afraid, sore, 1630 ekphobos, 1
afraid of, be, 5299 phobeō, 5
afresh, crucify, 388 anastauroō, 1
after, 1223a dia, 3 (gen.)
1230 diaginomai, 1
1722 en, 1
1909b epi, 3 (dat.)
1909c epi, 1 (acc.)
2517 kathexēs, 1
2596a kata, 61 (acc.)
3226b meta, 88 (acc.)
3593 opisthen, 2
3594 opisō, 22
3653 hote, 1

B

C

course, come with a straight, 2113 euthudromeō, 2
course, have, 5043 trechō, 1
court, 833 aule̱, 1
court, king's, 933 basileion with 3488, 1
courteous, 5291 philophrōn, 1
courteously, 5264 philanthrōpōs, 1
5290 philophronōs, 1
cousin, 4673 sunggene̱s, 2
covenant, 1242 diathe̱ke̱, 20
2476 histe̱mi, 1
4834 suntithe̱mi, 1
covenant breaker, 802 asunthetos, 1
cover, 1943 epikaluptō, 1
2572 kaluptō, 5
2619 katakaluptō, 3
3928 perikaluptō, 1
4680 sungkaluptō, 1
covered, 2596b kata, 1 (gen.)
covering, 3918 peribolaion, 1
covet, 1937 epithumeō, 3
2206 dze̱loō, 1
covet after, 3613 oregomai, 1
covet earnestly, 2206 dze̱loō, 1
covetous, 4023 pleonekte̱s, 4
5266 philarguros, 2
covetous, not, 866 aphilarguros, 1
covetous practice, 4024 pleonexia, 1
covetousness, 4024 pleonexia, 8
covetousness, without, 866 aphilarguros, 1
craft, 1388 dolos, 1
2039 ergasia, 1
3213 meros, 1
4978 techne̱, 1
craft, of the same, 3573 homotechnos, 1
craftiness, 3734 panourgia, 3
craftiness, cunning, 3734 panourgia, 1
craftsman, 4979 technite̱s, 3
crafty, 3735 panourgos, 1
crave, 154 aiteō, 1
create, 2936 ktidzō, 12
creation, 2937 ktisis, 6
Creator, 2936 ktidzō, 1
2939 ktiste̱s, 1
creature, 2937 ktisis, 11
2938 ktisma, 4
creditor, 1157 daneiste̱s, 1
creek, 2859 kolpos, 1
creep, 1744 endunō, 1
creep in unawares, 3821 pareisdunō, 1
creeping thing, 2062 herpeton, 3
Crescens, 2913 Kreske̱s, 1
Crete, 2914 Kre̱te̱, 5
Cretes, 2912 Kre̱s, 1
Cretians, 2912 Kre̱s, 1
crime, 156 aitia, 1
crime laid against (one), 1462 engkle̱ma, 1
cripple, 5460 chōlos, 1
Crispus, 2912 Krispos, 2
crooked, 4546 skolios, 2
cross, 4616 stauros, 28
crow, 5355 phōneō, 12
crown, 1238 diade̱ma, 3
4635 stephanos, 18
4637 stephanoō, 3
crucify, 4262 prospe̱gnumi, 1
4617 stauroō, 46
crucify afresh, 388 anastauroō, 1
crucify with, 4857 sustauroō, 5
crumb, 5489 psichion, 3
cry, 310 anaboaō, 1
863 aphie̱mi, 1
994 boaō, 11
995 boe̱, 1
1916 epiboaō, 1
2019 epiphōneō, 1
2896 kradzō, 40
2905 kraugadzō, 4
2906 krauge̱, 3
5355 phōneō, 5
cry against, 2019 epiphōneō, 1
cry aloud, 310 anaboaō, 1
cry out, 310 anaboaō, 1
349 anakradzō, 5
2896 kradzō, 19
2905 kraugadzō, 3
crying, 2906 krauge̱, 2
crystal, 2930 krustallos, 2
crystal, clear as, 2929 krustallidzō, 1
cubit, 3983 pe̱chus, 4
cumber, 2673 katargeō, 1
3949 perispaō, 1
cumi, 2891 koumi, 1
cummin, 2951 kuminon, 1
cunning craftiness, 3734 panourgia, 1
cunningly devised, 4579 sophidzō, 1
cup, 4121 pote̱rion, 33
cure, 2323 therapeuō, 5
2392 iasis, 1
curious arts, 3921 periergos, 1
curse, 332 anathematidzō, 1
2551 kakologeō, 2
2652 katanathema, 1
2653 katanathematidzō, 1
2671 katara, 3
2672 kataraomai, 6
curse, bind under a, 332 anathematidzō, 1
curse, bind under a great, 331 anathema with 332 anathematidzō, 1
cursed, 1944 epikataratos, 3
2671 katara, 1
cursing, 685 ara, 1
2671 katara, 2
custom, 1480 ethidzō, 1
1485 ethos, 7
4814 sune̱theia, 2
4956 telos, 3
custom, receipt of, 4958 telōnion, 3
custom was, as his, 1486 ethō with 2596a kata and 3488, 1 (acc.)
cut, 2629 katakoptō, 1
cut, be, 1282 diapriō, 1
cut asunder, 1371 dichotomeō, 1
cut down, 1581 ekkoptō, 2
2875 koptō, 2
cut in sunder, 1371 dichotomeō, 1
cut off, 609 apokoptō, 6
851 aphaireō, 2
1581 ekkoptō, 4
cut out, 1581 ekkoptō, 1
cut short, 4832 suntemnō, 1
cut to the heart, be, 1282 diapriō, 1
cymbal, 2950 kumbalon, 1
Cyprus, 2953 Kuprios, 3
2954 Kupros, 5
Cyrene, 2956 Kure̱naios, 3
2957 Kure̱ne̱, 1
Cyrenian, 2956 Kure̱naios, 3
Cyrenius, 2958 Kure̱nios, 1

D

daily, 1967 epiousios, 2
2184 ephe̱meros, 1
2250 he̱mera with 2596a kata, 15 (acc.)
2250 he̱mera with 2596a kata and 3856 pas, 1 (acc.)
2250 he̱mera with 2596a kata and 1538 hekastos, 1 (acc.)
2250 he̱mera with 3856 pas, 1
2522 kathe̱merinos, 1
dainty, 3045 liparos, 1
Dalmanutha, 1148 Dalmanoutha, 1
Dalmatia, 1149 Dalmatia, 1
damage, 2209 dze̱mia, 1
damage, receive, 2210 dze̱mioō, 1
Damaris, 1152 Damaris, 1
Damascenes, 1153 Damaske̱nos, 1
Damascus, 1154 Damaskos, 15
damn, 2632 katakrinō, 2
2919 krinō, 1
damnable, 684 apōleia, 1
damnation, 684 apōleia, 1
2917 krima, 7
2920 krisis, 3
damsel, 2877 korasion, 6
3713 paidion, 4
3714 paidiske̱, 4
dance, 3638 orcheomai, 4
dancing, 5425 choros, 1
danger, be in, 2793 kinduneuō, 2
danger of, in, 1777 enochos, 5
dangerous, 2000 episphale̱s, 1
Daniel, 1158 Danie̱l, 2
dare, 5011 tolmaō, 4
dark, 850 auchme̱ros, 1
4552 skoteinos, 1
4553 skotia, 2
darken, 4554 skotidzō, 8
darkly, 135 ainigma with 1722 en, 1
darkness, 2217 dzophos, 2
4553 skotia, 14
4555 skotos, 32
darkness, full of, 4552 skoteinos, 2
4556 skotoō, 1
dart, 956 belos, 1
1002 bolis, 1
dash, 4250 proskoptō, 2
daughter, 2364 thugate̱r, 29
4943 teknon, 1
daughter, little, 2365 thugatrion, 1
daughter, young, 2365 thugatrion, 1
daughter in law, 3465 numphe̱, 3
David, 1138 Dabid, 59
David, kingdom of our father, 932 Basileia, 1
dawn, 1306 diaugadzō, 1
dawn, begin to, 2020 epiphōskō, 1
day, 2250 he̱mera, 355
5510 hōra, 1
day, a great while before, 1773 ennuchon with 3029 lian, 1
day, a night and a, 3474 nuchthe̱meron,1
day, break of, 827 auge̱, 1
day, first, 4313 prōtos, 2
day, holy, 1859 heorte̱, 1
day, next, 839 aurion, 1
1206 deuteraios, 1
1836 hexe̱s, 1
1887 epaurion, 6
1966 epiousa, 2
2087 heteros, 2
day, sabbath, 4421 sabbaton, 37
day, the eighth, 3537 oktae̱meros, 1
day, this, 737 arti, 1
4494 se̱meron, 22
day, to, 4494 se̱meron, 18
day after, 1836 hexes, 1
day after, next, 1887 epaurion, 1
day before the sabbath, 4215 prosabbaton, 1
day by day, 2250 he̱mera with 2596a kata, 1
day following, 1836 hexes, 1
1887 epaurion, 2
day in which, until the, 891 achris with 2250 he̱mera and 3639e hos, 1
day star, 5359 phōsphoros, 1
day that, until the, 891 achris with 2250 he̱mera and 3639e hos, 3
day time, 2250 he̱mera, 1
day when, in the, 3639a hos with 2250 he̱mera, 1
days, four, 4966 tetartaios, 1
days of, in the, 1909a epi, 2 (gen.)
dayspring, 395 anatole̱, 1
deacon, 1249 diakonos, 3
deacon, use the office of a, 1247 diakoneō, 2
dead, 2348 thne̱skō, 1
3398 nekros, 132
dead, be, 599 apothne̱skō, 29
2348 thne̱skō, 10
2837 koimaō, 1
3399 nekroō, 2
4953 teleutaō, 3
dead, become, 2298 thanatoō, 1
dead, being, 581 apogenomenos, 1
dead, half, 2253 he̱mithane̱s, 1
dead body, 4330 ptōma, 3
dead man, 2348 thne̱skō, 1
dead with, be, 4780 sunapothne̱skō, 1
deadly, 2286 thanasimos, 1
2287 thanate̱phoros, 1
2288 thanatos, 2
deadness, 3400 nekrōsis, 1
deaf, 2974 kōphos, 5
deal, 1793 entungchanō, 1
3207 meridzō, 1
4060 poieō, 2
deal, a great, 3954 perissoteron, 1
4083 polus, 1
deal subtilly with, 2686 katasophidzomai, 1
deal with, 4274 prospherō, 1
dealings with, have, 4698 sungchraomai, 1
dear, 26 agape̱, 1
27 agape̱tos, 3
1784 entimos, 1
4993 timios, 1
dear Son, the kingdom of His, 932 basileia, 1
dearly beloved, 27 agape̱tos, 9
dearth, 3042 limos, 2
death, 336 anairesis, 2
2288 thanatos, 117
4954 teleute̱, 1
death, appoint to, 1935 epithanatios, 1
death, be at the point of, 599 apothne̱skō with 3195 mellō, 1
death, cause to be put to, 2289 thanatoō, 3
death, lie at the point of, 2079 eschatōs with 2192 echō, 1
death, put to, 337 anaireō, 2
520 apagō, 1
615 apokteinō, 6
2289 thanatoō, 4
debate, 2054 eris, 2
debt, 1156 daneion, 1
3682 opheile̱, 1
3683 opheile̱ma, 2
3684 opheilō, 1
debtor, 3681 opheilete̱s, 5
5433 chreōpheilete̱s, 2
debtor, be a, 3684 opheilō, 1
Decapolis, 1179 Dekapolis, 3
decay, 3722 palaioō, 1
decease, 1841 exodos, 2
4953 teleutaō, 1
deceit, 539 apate̱, 1
1388 dolos, 2
4006 plane̱, 1
deceit, use, 1387 dolioō, 1
deceitful, 539 apate̱, 1
1386 dolios, 1
deceitfully, handle, 1389 doloō, 1
deceitfulness, 539 apate̱, 3
deceivableness, 539 apate̱, 1
deceive, 538 apataō, 4
1818 exapataō, 4
3784 paralogidzomai, 1
4005 planaō, 24
5322 phrenapataō, 1
deceive, to, 4006 plane̱, 1
deceiver, 4008 planos, 4
5323 phrenapate̱s, 1
deceivings, 539 apate̱, 1
decently, 2156 eusche̱monōs, 1
deck, 5458 chrusoō, 2
declaration, 1335 die̱ge̱sis, 1
declare, 312 ananggellō, 3
394 anatithe̱mai, 1
518 apanggellō, 3
1107 gnōrdizō, 4
1213 de̱loō, 3
1229 dianggellō, 1
1334 die̱geomai, 3
1555 ekdie̱geomai, 2
1834 exe̱geomai, 5
2097 euanggelidzō, 1
2605 katanggellō, 2
3624 horidzō, 1
3753 paranggellō, 1
5319 phradzō, 2
declare, manifestly, 5219 phaneroō, 1
declare, to, 1732 endeixis with 1519 eis, 1
1732 endeixis with 4214 pros, 1
declare glad tidings, 2097 euanggelidzō, 1
declare plainly, 1718 emphanidzō, 1
decrease, 1642 elattoō, 1
decree, 1378 dogma, 3
2919 krinō, 1
dedicate, 1457 engkainidzō, 1
dedication, feast of, 1456 engkainia, 1
deed, 2041 ergon, 22
4062 poie̱sis, 1
4134 praxis, 4
4138 prassō, 1
deed, do, 2717 katergadzomai, 1
deed, mighty, 1411 dunamis, 1
deed, very worthy, 2735 katorthōma, 1
deed done, good, 2108 euergesia, 1
deem, 5182 huponoeō, 1
deep, 12 abussos, 2
899 bathos, 1
899 bathos with 2596a kata, 1 (acc.)
901 bathus, 2
1037 buthos, 1
deep, dig, 4526 skaptō with 900 bathunō, 1
deep thing, 899 bathos, 1
deeply, sigh, 389 anastenadzō, 1
deepness, 899 bathos, 1
defame, 987 blasphe̱meō, 1
defence, 627 apologia, 3

E

H

I

Lord (Christ), 4362 hrabboni, 1
Lord, kingdom of our, 932 basileia, 1
Lord of, be, 2961 kurieuō, 1
lord over, be, 2634 katakurieuō, 1
Lord's, 2960 kuriakos, 2
Lord's doing, the, 2962 kurios with
3744a para, 2 (gen.)
lords, 2961 kurieuō, 1
3175 megistanes, 1
lordship over, exercise,
2634 katakurieuō, 1
2961 kurieuō, 1
lose, 622 apollumi, 22
2210 dzemioō, 2
lose . . . saltness, 358 analos with
1096 ginomai, 1
lose savour, 3371 mōrainō, 2
loss, 580 apobole, 1
2209 dzemia, 3
loss, suffer, 2210 dzemioō, 2
lost, 622 apollumi, 4
lost, be, 622 apollumi, 5
lot, 2819 kleros, 8
lot, be (one's), 2975 langchanō, 1
lot, divide by, 2624 kataklerodoteō, 1
Lot, 3091 Lōt, 4
lots, cast, 2975 langchanō, 1
loud, 3173 megas, 33
love, 25 agapaō, 135
26 agape, 86
2309 thelō, 1
5268 phileō, 22
love, brotherly, 5260 philadelphia, 3
love as brethren, 5261 philadelphos, 1
love of money, 5265 philarguria, 1
love of the brethren, 5260
philadelphia, 1
love (one's) children, 5288
philoteknos, 1
love their husbands, 5262 philandros, 1
love to have the preeminence, 5283
philoprōteuō, 1
love toward man, 5263 philanthrōpia, 1
lovely, 4275 prosphiles, 1
lover of God, 5277 philotheos, 1
lover of good men, 5258 philagathos, 1
lover of hospitality, 5282 philoxenos, 1
lover of (one's) own self, 5267
philautos, 1
lover of pleasure, 5269 philedonos, 1
low, be made, 4914 tapeinōsis, 1
low, bring, 4913 tapeinoō, 1
low degree, of, 4911 tapeinos, 2
low estate, 4914 tapeinōsis, 1
low estate, of, 4911 tapeinos, 1
lower, 2737 katōteros, 1
4668 stugnadzō, 1
lower, make, 1642 elattoō, 2
lowest, 2078 eschatos, 2
lowliness, 4912 tapeinophrosune, 1
lowliness of mind, 4912
tapeinophrosune, 1
lowly, 4911 tapeinos, 1
Lucas, 3065 Loukas, 1
Lucius, 3066 Loukios, 2
lucre, 2771 kerdos, 1
lucre, for filthy, 147 aischrokerdōs, 1
lucre, given to filthy, 146
aischrokerdes, 1
lucre, greedy of filthy, 146
aischrokerdes, 2
Luke, 3065 Loukas, 2
lukewarm, 5413 chliaros, 1
lump, 5345 phurama, 5
lunatic, be, 4483 seleniadzomai, 2
lust, 1937 epithumeō, 3
1939 epithumia, 31
1971 epipotheō, 1
2237 hedone, 2
3615 orexis, 1
3706 pathos, 1
lust after, 1937 epithumeō, 1
1938 epithumetes with 1510
eimi, 1
1939 epithumia, 1
Lycaonia, 3071 Lukaonia, 1
Lycaonia, speech of, 3072 Lukaonisti, 1
Lycia, 3073 Lukia, 1
Lydda, 3069 Ludda, 3
Lydia, 3070 Ludia, 2
lying, 5479 pseudos, 2
lying in wait, 1749 enedron, 1
1917 epiboule, 1
Lysanias, 3078 Lusanias, 1
Lysias, 3079 Lusias, 3
Lystra, 3082 Lustra, 6

M

Maath, 3092 Maath, 1
Macedonia, 3109 Makedonia, 22
Macedonia, of, 3110 Makedōn, 4
Macedonian, 3110 Makedōn, 1
mad, 3130 mania, 1
mad, be, 3105 mainomai, 4
mad, make, 3130 mania with 3962
peritrepō and 1519 eis, 1
mad against, 1693 emmainomai, 1
made, be, 1080 gennaō, 1
1096 ginomai, 69
1096 ginomai with 1526
eisi, 1
1511 einai, 1
2749 keimai, 1
made, confession is, 3570 homologeō, 1
made, payment to be, 591 apodidōmi, 1
made, shall be, 2071 esomai, 1
made, thing that is, 4061 poiema, 1
made by hands, 5399 cheiropoetos, 1
made drunk, be, 3184 methuō, 1
made known, be, 319 anagnōridzomai, 1
made like, 871 aphomoioō, 1
made like to, 3567 homoiōma, 1
made low, be, 4914 tapeinōsis, 1
made ready to (one's) hand, 2092
hetoimos, 1
made rich, be, 4047 plouteō, 2
made strong, be, 1743 endunamoō, 1
made subject to, be, 5193 hupotassō, 1
made subject unto, be, 5193
hupotassō, 1
made weak, be, 770 astheneō, 1
made with hands, 5399 cheiropoetos, 5
made with hands, not, 886
acheiropoietos, 1
made without hands, 886
acheiropoietos, 2
Madian, 3099 Madian, 1
madness, 454 anoia, 1
3813 paraphronia, 1
Magdala, 3093 Magdala, 1
Magdalene, 3094 Magdalene, 12
magistrate, 746 arche, 1
758 archōn, 1
4655 strategos, 5
magistrate, obey a, 3880 peitharcheō, 1
magnificence, 3168 megaleiotes, 1
magnify, 1392 doxadzō, 1
3170 megalunō, 5
Magog, 3098 Magōg, 1
maid, 2877 korasion, 2
3714 paidiske, 3
3716 pais, 1
maiden, 3714 paidiske, 1
3716 pais, 1
maimed, 376 anaperos, 2
2948 kullos, 4
mainsail, 736 artemōn, 1
maintain, 4191 proistemi, 2
majesty, 3168 megaleiotes, 1
3172 megalōsune, 1
Majesty (said of God), 3172
megalōsune, 2
make, 1303 diatithemai, 3
1325 didōmi, 2
2005 epiteleō, 1
2076 esti, 1
2525 kathistemi, 8
2680 kataskeuadzō, 1
2722 katechō, 1
2936 ktidzō, 1
4060 poieō, 114
4300 procheiridzomai, 1
4383 hreō, 1
4720 sumballō, 1
4821c sunistemi, 1
4831 sunteleō, 1
4987 tithemi, 10
make, which, 3503 ho esti, 1
make alive, 2227 dzōopoieō, 1
make an uproar, 387 anastatoō, 1
make as though, 4264 prospoieomai, 1
make choice, 1586 eklegomai, 1
make for, the things which, 3488 ho, 1
make full proof of, 4035 plerophoreō, 1
make glorious, 1392 doxadzō, 1
make light of, 272 ameleō, 1
make like, 871 aphomoioō, 1
3566 homoioō, 2
make (one) to doubt, 142 airō with
5490 psuche, 1
make peace, 1517 eirenopoieō, 1
make rise, 393 anatellō, 1
make sit down, 347 anaklinō, 2
2625 kataklinō, 1
make sit down to meat, 347 anaklinō, 1
maker, 1217 demiourgos, 1
Malchus, 3124 Malchos, 1
male, 730b arsen, 4
malefactor, 2555 kakopoios, 1
2557 kakourgos, 3
Maleleel, 3121 Maleleel, 1
malice, 2549 kakia, 6
malicious, 4090 poneros, 1
maliciousness, 2549 kakia, 2
malignity, 2550 kakoetheia, 1
mammon, 3126 Mammōnas, 4
man, 435 aner, 156
444 anthrōpos, 552
730a arhren, 1
730b arsen, 2
1520 heis, 2
3662b oudeis with another
negative, 2
4946 teleios, 1
5000 tis, 34
man, after the manner of, 442
anthrōpinos, 1
man, aged, 4146 presbutes, 1
man, any, 1538 hekastos, 1
3267 medeis, 1
3287 metis, 1
3662a oudeis, 1
3662b oudeis with another
negative, 3
5000 tis, 55
man, blind, 5085 tuphlos, 9
man, certain, 5000 tis, 7
man, common to, 442 anthrōpinos, 1
man, dead, 2348 thneskō, 1
man, every, 303a ana, 2
1520 heis with 2596a
kata, 1 (acc.)
1538 hekastos, 39
3856 pas, 11
5000 tis, 1
5001 tis, 2
man, heathen, 1482 ethnikos, 1
man, if a, 1536 ei tis, 8
man, if any, 1536 ei tis, 35
man, impotent, 770 astheneō, 1
man, inward, 2081 esōthen, 1
man, love toward, 5263
philanthrōpia, 1
man, manner of, 686 ara, 2
man, mighty, 1415 dunatos, 1
man, neither any, 3662a oudeis, 2
man, new, 3401a neos, 1
man, no, 3261 me with 5000 tis, 6
3267 medeis, 32
3656 ou, 1
3662a oudeis, 84
3662b oudeis with another
negative, 10
man, not any, 3267 medeis, 1
man, of, 442 anthrōpinos, 1
man, old, 4145a presbuteros, 1
4146 presbutes, 1
man, poor, 4334 ptōchos, 1
man, some, 5000 tis, 4
man, strong, 2478 ischuros, 5
man, such a, 1170 deina, 1
5008 toioutos, 1
man, that no, 3261 me, 2
man, this, 846k auton, 1
846ℓ autos, 1
846m autou, 1
3678a houtos, 25
man, what manner of, 3534 hoios, 1
3597 hopoios, 1
4117 potapos, 1
man, wise, 3097 magos, 4
man, young, 3394 neanias, 5
3395 neaniskos, 10
3401b neōteros, 2
3716 pais, 1
man, younger, 3401b neōteros, 1
man can approach unto, which no,
676 aprositos, 1
man child, 730a arhren, 1
730a arhren with 5107
huios, 1
man forbidding him, no, 209 akōlutōs, 1
man of war, 4653 strateuma, 1
Manaen, 3127 Manaen, 1
Manasses (king of Judah), 3128
Manasses, 2
Manasses (son of Joseph), 3128
Manasses, 1
manger, 5236 phatne, 3
manifest, 1212 delos, 1
1552 ekdelos, 1
1717 emphanes, 1
5218 phaneros, 9
5219 phaneroō, 9
manifest, be, 1718 emphanidzō, 2
5219 phaneroō, 2
manifest, make, 5219 phaneroō, 19
manifest, that is not, 852 aphanes, 1
manifest beforehand, 4171 prodelos, 1
manifest forth, 5219 phaneroō, 1
manifest token, 1730 endeigma, 1
manifestation, 602 apokalupsis, 1
5221 phanerōsis, 2
manifestly declare, 5219 phaneroō, 1
manifold, 4064 poikilos, 2
4082 polupoikilos, 1
manifold more, 4079 pollaplasiōn, 1
mankind, 442 anthrōpinos with 5349
phusis, 1
mankind, abuser of (one's) self with,
733 arsenokoites, 1
mankind, defile (one's) self with,
733 arsenokoites, 1
manna, 3131 manna, 5
manner, 1485 ethos, 4
5058 tropos, 1
5079 tupos, 1
manner, after a godly, 2316 Theos
with 2596a kata, 1
manner, after the same, 5515
hōsautōs, 1
manner, after this, 3492 hode, 1
3679 houtō, 3
3923 periechō with
5026 touton and 5079 tupos, 1
manner, after what, 4359 pōs, 1
manner, all, 3856 pas, 2
manner, in like,
2532 kai, 1
3679 houtō, 1
5058 tropos with 3564 homoios, 1
5515 hōsautōs, 2
manner, in this, 3679 houtō, 1
manner, like, 4924 tauta, 1
manner, perfect, 195 akribeia, 1
manner, so in like, 3679 houtōs, 1
manner, what, 3534 hoios, 1
manner as, in like, 5058 tropos with
3639a hos, 1
manner of, 686 ara, 1
manner of, after the, 2596a kata,
3 (acc.)
manner of, all, 3856 pas, 11
manner of, such, 5027 toutou with
3912a peri, 1 (gen.)
manner of, what, 3597 hopoios, 1
4069 poios, 1
4117 potapos, 4
5001 tis, 2
manner of Gentiles, after the, 1483
ethnikōs, 1
manner of life, 72 agōge, 1
981 biōsis, 1
manner of man, 686 ara, 2
manner of man, after the, 442
anthrōpinos, 1
manner of man, what, 3534 hoios, 1
3597 hopoios, 1
4117 potapos, 1
manner of person, what, 4117
potapos, 1
manner was, as his, 1486 ethō with
2596a kata and 3488, 1 (acc.)
manners, 2239 ethos, 1
manners, in divers, 4087 polutropōs, 1
manners, suffer (one's), 5059
tropophoreō, 1
man's, 442 anthrōpinos, 3
846m autou, 1
man's, another, 245 allotrios, 4
manservant, 3716 pais, 1
mansion, 3338 mone, 1
manslayer, 409 androphonos, 1
manstealer, 405 andrapodistes, 1
many, 2425 hikanos, 11
4019 pleiōn, 12
4083 polus, 210
many, how, 4114 posos, 9

N

O

Q

R

ranks, in, 4137 prasia, 1
ransom, 487 antilutron, 1
 3083 lutron, 2
rashly, 4212 propetēs, 1
rather, 2228 ē, 1
 3123 mallon, 33
rather, and, 235 alla, 1
rather, but, 4033 plēn, 2
rather, have, 2309 thelō, 1
rather, the, 3123 mallon, 1
 3956 perissoterōs, 1
rather, yea, 3204 menounge, 1
rather than, 2228 ē, 2
raven, 2876 korax, 1
ravening, 724 harpagē, 1
 727 harpax, 1
reach, 190 akoloutheō, 1
 2185 ephikneomai, 2
 5242 pherō, 2
reach forth unto, 1901 epekteinomai, 1
read, 314 anaginōskō, 33
readiness, 2092 hetoimos, 1
 4188 prothumia, 1
readiness of mind, 4188 prothumia, 1
reading, 320 anagnōsis, 3
ready, 1451 enggus, 1
 2092 hetoimos, 14
 2093 hetoimōs, 3
 3195 mellō, 1
 3803 paraskeuadzō, 1
 4189 prothumos, 2
ready, be, 3195 mellō, 2
 3803 paraskeuadzō, 1
ready, make, 2090 hetoimadzō, 10
 3803 paraskeuadzō, 1
ready mind, 4188 prothumia, 1
ready mind, of a, 4190 prothumōs, 1
ready to be offered, be, 4589 spendō, 1
ready to distribute, 2130 eumetadotos, 1
ready to (one's) hand, made, 2092 hetoimos, 1
reap, 2325 theridzō, 21
reap down, 270 amaō, 1
reaper, 2327 theristēs, 2
rear up, 1453 egeirō, 1
reason, 701 arestos, 1
 1256 dialegomai, 2
 1260 dialogidzomai, 11
 3049 logidzomai, 1
 3056 logos, 1
 4702 sudzēteō, 1
 4717 sullogidzomai, 1
reason hereof, by, 1223b dia with 4926b tautēn, 1 (acc.)
reason of, by, 1223b dia, 4 (acc.)
 1223b dia with infinitive, 1 (acc.)
 1537 ek, 3
 1752 heneka, 1
reason together, 4702 sudzēteō, 1
reason with, 1256 dialegomai, 2
reason would, 3056 logos with 2596a kata, 1 (acc.)
reasonable, 3050 logikos, 1
reasoning, 1261 dialogismos, 1
 4703 sudzētēsis, 1
Rebecca, 4379 Hrebekka, 1
rebuke, 1649 elengxis with 2192 echō, 1
 1651 elengchō, 5
 1969 epiplessō, 1
 2008 epitimaō, 24
rebuke, without, 298 amōmētos, 1
receipt of custom, 4958 telōnion, 3
receive, 324 anadechomai, 2
 568 apechō, 2
 588 apodechomai, 3
 618 apolambanō, 10
 1209 dechomai, 52
 1325 didōmi, 1
 1523 eisdechomai, 1
 1926 epidechomai, 2
 2865 komidzō, 10
 2983 lambanō, 133
 3235 metalambanō, 1
 3758 paradechomai, 5
 3780 paralambanō, 15
 4227 prosdechomai, 3
 4255 proslambanō, 7
 5164 hupodechomai, 4
 5174 hupolambanō, 1
 5462 chōreō, 3
receive, be room to, 5462 chōreō, 1
receive, cannot, 5462 chōreō with 3656 ou, 1
receive . . . again, 618 apolambanō, 1
receive damage, 2210 dzēmioō, 1
receive gladly, 588 apodechomai, 2
receive mercy, 1653 eleeō, 1
receive seed, 4587 speirō, 4
receive sight, 308 anablepō, 15
receive strength, 4632 stereoō, 1
receive the law, 3449 nomotheteō, 1
receive tithes, 1183 dekatoō, 1
receive up, 353 analambanō, 3
 354 analēpsis, 1
received, he . . . , 3488 ho, 1
received, to be, 3236 metalēpsis with 1519 eis, 1
received by tradition from (one's) fathers, 3870 patroparadotos, 1
receiving, 3028 lēpsis, 1
 4256 proslēpsis, 1
reckon, 3049 logidzomai, 6
 4768 sunairō, 1
 4768 sunairō with 3056 logos, 1
recommend, 3760 paradidōmi, 2
recompence, 468 antapodoma, 2
 489 antimisthia, 2
recompence of reward, 3305 misthapodosia, 3
recompense, 467 antapodidōmi, 4
 591 apodidōmi, 1
recompense again, 467 antapodidōmi, 1
reconcile, 604 apokatallassō, 3
 1259 diallassō, 1
 2644 katallassō, 6
reconciliation, 2643 katallagē, 2
reconciliation for, make, 2433 hilaskomai, 1
reconciling, 2643 katallagē, 1
record, 3141 marturia, 7
 3144 martus, 2
record, bear, 3141 martureō, 13
record, take to, 3143 marturomai, 1
recover, 2573 kalōs with 2192 echō, 1
recover (one's) self, 366 ananēphō, 1
recovering of sight, 309 anablepsis, 1
red, 4350 purhros, 2
red, be, 4349 purhradzō, 2
Red, 2063 eruthros, 2
redeem, 59 agoradzō, 3
 1805 exagoradzō, 4
 3084 lutroō, 3
 3085 lutrōsis with 4060 poieō, 1
redemption, 629 apolutrōsis, 9
 3085 lutrōsis, 2
redound, 3952 perisseuō, 1
reed, 2563 kalamos, 11
reformation, 1357 diorthōsis, 1
refrain, 868 aphistēmi, 1
 3873 pauō, 1
refresh, 373 anapauō, 4
 404 anapsuchō, 1
refresh (one's) self, 1958 epimeleia with 5077 tungchanō, 1
refreshed with, be, 4775 sunanapauomai, 1
refreshing, 403 anapsuxis, 1
refuse, 720 arneomai, 2
 3768 paraiteomai, 5
refused, be, 579 apoblētos, 1
regard, 991 blepō with 1519 eis, 2
 1788 entrepō, 2
 1914 epiblepō, 1
 5326 phroneō, 4
regard not, 272 ameleō, 1
 3751 parabouleuomai, 1
regard to, have, 4237 prosechō, 1
regeneration, 3724 palinggenesia, 2
region, 2824 klima, 2
 5461 chōra, 5
region round about, 3966 perichōros, 5
region that lieth round about, 3966 perichōros, 1
rehearse, 312 ananggellō, 1
rehearse from the beginning, 756 archomai, 1
reign, 932 basileia with 2192 echō, 1
 936 basileuō, 20
 2231 hēgemonia, 1
reign over, 757 archō, 1
reign with, 4721 sumbasileuō, 2
reins, 3410 nephros, 1
reject, 114 atheteō, 4
 593 apodokimadzō, 7
 1609 ekptuō, 1
 3768 paraiteomai, 1
rejected, 96 adokimos, 1
rejoice, 21 agalliaō, 7
 2165 euphrainō, 6
 2744 kauchaomai, 4
 2745 kauchēma, 1
 5363 chairō, 42
rejoice, greatly, 21 agalliaō, 1
rejoice, that . . . , 1519 eis with 2745 kauchēma, 1
rejoice against, 2620 katakauchaomai, 1
rejoice in, 4696 sungchairō, 1
rejoice with, 4696 sungchairō, 6
rejoicing, 2745 kauchēma, 4
 2746 kauchēsis, 4
release, 630 apoluō, 17
relief, 1248 diakonia, 1
relieve, 1884 eparkeō, 3
religion, 2356 thrēskeia, 3
religion, Jews', 2454 Ioudaismos, 2
religious, 2357 thrēskos, 1
 4476 sebomai, 1
remain, 620 apoleipō, 3
 1265 diamenō, 2
 3206 menō, 16
 3935 perileipō, 2
 3952 perisseuō, 3
remain, which, 3062 loipoi, 1
remain, whiles . . . , 3206 menō, 1
remain over and above, 3952 perisseuō, 1
remains, it, 3063 loipon with 2076 esti, 1
remember, 363 anamimnēskō, 1
 3303 mimnēskō, 1
 3315 mnaomai, 16
 3321 mnēmoneuō, 19
 5179 hupomimnēskō, 2
remembrance, 364 anamnēsis, 3
 3317 mneia, 3
 3320 mnēmē, 1
 5180 hupomnēsis, 2
remembrance, be had in, 3315 mnaomai, 1
remembrance, bring into, 363 anamimnēskō, 1
remembrance, bring to, 5179 hupomimnēskō, 1
remembrance, call to, 363 anamimnēskō, 2
remembrance, come in, 3315 mnaomai, 1
remembrance, in, 3315 mnaomai, 1
remembrance, put in,
 363 anamimnesko, 1
 5179 hupomimneskō, 3
 5180 hupomnēsis, 1
 5194 hupotithēmi, 1
remembrance again, 364 anamnēsis, 1
remission, 859 aphesis, 9
 3829 paresis, 1
remit, 863 aphiēmi, 1
remnant, 2640 kataleimma, 1
 3005 leimma, 1
 3062 loipos, 4
remove, 142 airō, 2
 2795 kineō, 1
 3179 methistēmi, 2
 3227 metabainō, 2
 3246 metatithēmi, 1
 3811 parapherō, 1
remove into, 3251 metoikidzō, 1
removing, 3231 metathesis, 1
Remphan, 4381 Hremphan, 1
rend, 1284a diarhrēgnumi, 3
 4386a hrēgnumi, 1
 4582 sparassō, 1
 4877 schidzō, 5
rend off, 3948 perirhrēgnumi, 1
render, 467 antapodidōmi, 1
 591 apodidōmi, 9
renew, 340 anakainidzō, 1
 341 anakainoō, 2
 365 ananeoō, 1
renewing, 342 anakainōsis, 2
renounce, 550 apeipon, 1
rent, 4878 schisma, 2
rent, make a, 4877 schidzō, 1
repay, 467 antapodidōmi, 1
 591 apodidōmi, 1
 661 apotinō, 1
repent, 3238 metamellomai, 5
 3240 metanoeō, 34
repent (one's) self, 3238 metamellomai, 1
repentance, 3241 metanoia, 24
repentance, without, 278 ametamelētos, 1
repented of, not to be, 278 ametamelētos, 1
repetitions, use vain, 945 battologeō, 1
reply against, 470 antapokrinomai, 1
report, 189 akoē, 2
 312 ananggellō, 1
 518 apanggellō, 2
 3141 marturia, 1
report, evil, 1426 dusphēmia, 1
report, good, 2162 euphēmia, 1
report, have good, 3140 martureō, 2
report, obtain good, 3140 martureō, 2
report, of good, 2163 euphēmos, 1
 3140 martureō, 1
report, of honest, 3140 martureō, 1
reported, be, 191 akouō, 1
reported, be commonly, 1310 diaphēmidzō, 1
reported, be slanderously, 987 blasphēmeō, 1
reported of, be well, 3140 martureō, 2
reproach, 819 atimia, 1
 3579 oneididzō, 3
 3580 oneidismos, 5
 3581 oneidos, 1
 5095 hubridzō, 1
 5096 hubris, 1
reproach, suffer, 3579 oneididzō, 1
reproachfully, to speak, 3059 loidoria with 5384 charin, 1
reprobate, 96 adokimos, 6
reproof, 1650 elengchos, 1
reprove, 1651 elengchō, 6
reputation, be of, 1380 dokeō, 1
reputation, had in, 4993 timios, 1
reputation, in, 1784 entimos, 1
reputation, make of no, 2758 kenoō, 1
request, 155 aitēma, 1
 1162 deēsis, 1
request, make, 1189 deomai, 1
require, 154 aiteō, 2
 155 aitēma, 1
 523 apaiteō, 1
 1096 ginomai, 1
 1567 ekdzēteō, 2
 2212 dzēteō, 2
 4138 prassō, 1
requite, 287 amoibē with 591 apodidōmi, 1
rescue, 1807 exaireō, 1
resemble, 3566 homoioō, 1
reserve, 2641 kataleipō, 1
 4983 tēreō, 8
residue, 2645 kataloipos, 1
 3062 loipoi, 1
resist, 436 anthistēmi, 9
 478 antikathistēmi, 1
 496 antipiptō, 1
 498 antitassomai, 4
resolved, be, 1097 ginōskō, 1
resort, 2064 erchomai, 2
 4748 sumporeuomai, 1
 4763 sunagō, 1
 4805 sunerchomai, 2
respect, 3213 meros, 2
respect, have, 578 apoblepō, 1
respect of, in, 2596a kata, 1 (acc.)
respect of persons, 4282 prosōpolēpsia, 4
respect of persons, without, 678 aprosōpolēptōs, 1
respect to, have, 1914 epiblepō, 1
respect to persons, have, 4280 prosōpolēpteō, 1
respecter of persons, 4281 prosōpolēptēs, 1
rest, 372 anapausis, 4
 372 anapausis with 2192 echō, 1
 373 anapauō, 4
 425 anesis, 3
 1515 eirēnē, 1
 1879 epanapauomai, 1
 1954 epiloipos, 1
 1981 episkēnoō, 1
 2270 hēsuchadzo, 1
 2663 katapausis, 9
 2664 katapauō, 1
 2681 kataskēnoō, 1
 3062 loipoi, 12
 4420 sabbatismos, 1
rest, give, 373 anapauō, 1
 2664 katapauō, 1
rest, take, 373 anapauō, 2

T

U

V

west, north, 5466 chōros, 1
west, south, 3047 lips, 1
whale, 2785 kętos, 1
what, 1063 gar, 1
2228 ę, 3
3534 hoios, 1
3639a hos, 42
3639c hos with 1437 ean, 1
3645 hosos, 4
3679 houtō, 1
4069 poios, 27
4114 posos, 1
4117 potapos, 1
5000 tis, 1
5001 tis, 260
what great, 2245 hęlikos, 1
what great things, 3645 hosos, 1
what intent, for, 4214 pros with 5001 tis, 1
what is it which, 5001 tis, 2
what is that, 5001 tis, 2
what manner, 3534 hoios, 1
what manner, after, 4359 pōs, 1
what manner of, 3597 hopoios, 1
4069 poios, 1
4117 potapos, 4
5001 tis, 2
what manner of man, 3534 hoios, 1
3597 hopoios, 1
4117 potapos, 1
what manner of person, 4117 potapos, 1
what means, by,
1722 en with 5001 tis, 1
4359 pōs, 2
what on, 3488 ho, 1
what place soever, in, 3599 hopou with 1437 ean, 1
what purpose, to, 5001 tis with 1519 eis, 1
what sort of, 3597 hopoios, 1
what thing, 5001 tis, 3
what things, 3639a hos, 3
3648 hostis, 1
4069 poios, 1
what things should, 3195 mellō with 3488, 1
what things soever,
3639 hos with 302a an, 1
3645 hosos with 302b an, 1
what way, 4069 poios, 1
what would follow, 2071 esomai, 1
whatsoever,
1437 ean with 3648 hostis, 1
3597 hopoios with 4118 pote, 1
3639a hos, 2
3639a hos with 1221 dępote, 1
3639a hos with 3856 pas, 1
3639b hos with 302a an, 7
3639c hos with 1437 ean, 16
3645 hosos, 9
3645 hosos with 302b an, 7
3645 hosos with 1437 ean, 2
3648 hostis with 302d an, 4
3648 hostis with 3856 pas and 302d an, 2
3856 pas, 6
5000 tis, 1
whatsoever state, 3639a hos, 1
whatsoever thing, 3856 pas, 1
whatsoever things, 3645 hosos, 8
wheat, 4521 sitos, 12
when, 1437 ean, 2
1722 en, 3
1722 en with 3488 and infinitive, 13
1875 epan, 3
1893 epei, 1
2259 hęnika, 2
2531 kathōs, 1
3226b meta, 2 (acc.)
3598 hopote, 1
3604 hopōs, 1
3639a hos, 6
3639e hos with 1722 en, 2
3652 hotan, 115
3653 hote, 97
3657 hou, 1
4118 pote, 1
4119 pote, 12
5019 tote, 1
5513 hōs, 42
when, in the day, 3639a hos with 2250 hęmera, 1
when . . . alone, 2398 idios with 2596a kata, 1 (acc.)
when once, 3639b hos with 575 apo and 302f an, 1
whence, 3506 hothen, 1
3639a hos, 2
4059 pothen, 28
whence, from, 3506 hothen, 3
whensoever, 3652 hotan, 1
5513 hōs with 1437 ean, 1
where, 3506 hothen, 2
3599 hopou, 58
3639e hos with 1722 en, 5
3657 hou, 22
4126 pou, 37
5001 tis, 1
5017 topos, 1
where he was, 846k auton with 2596a kata, 1 (acc.)
whereas, 3599 hopou, 2
3639e hos with 1722 en, 2
whereas ye, 3648 hostis, 1
whereas . . . was, 5507a ōn, 1
whereby, 3506 hothen, 1
3639e hos with 1223a dia, 3 (gen.)
3639e hos with 1722 en, 6
3639e hos with 3912a peri, 1 (gen.)
3639e hos with 4214 pros, 1
5001 tis with 2596a kata, 1 (acc.)
whereby (one) lies in wait, 4214 pros with 3180 methodeia, 1
wherefore, 1302 diati, 4
1352 dio, 41
1355 dioper, 3
2444 hinati, 1
3506 hothen, 4
3639e hos with 1223b dia, 2 (acc.)
3639e hos with 1223b dia and 156 aitia, 3 (acc.)
3639e hos with 1519 eis, 1
3639e hos with 1909b epi, 1 (dat.)
3639e hos with 5384 charin, 1
3667 oun, 8
5001 tis, 3
5001 tis with 1519 eis, 1
5001 tis with 1752 heneken, 1
5001 tis with 5384 charin, 1
5005 toigaroun, 1
5024 touto with 1223b dia, 7 (acc.)
5520 hōste, 17
wherein, 3639a hos, 4
3639e hos with 1223b dia, 1 (acc.)
3639e hos with 1519 eis, 3
3639e hos with 1722 en, 24
3639e hos with 1909b epi, 3 (dat.)
3639e hos with 3912a peri, 1 (gen.)
3657 hou, 1
whereinsoever, 3639b hos with 1722 en and 302a an, 1
whereinto, 3639e hos with 1519 eis, 1
whereof, 3639a hos, 13
3639e hos with 1537 ek, 2
3639e hos with 1909b epi, 1 (dat.)
3639e hos with 3912a peri, 3 (gen.)
5001 tis with 3912a peri, 1 (gen.)
whereof I may glory, 2746 kauchęsis, 1
whereof (one) might trust, have, 3882 peithō, 1
whereon, 3639e hos with 1909a epi, 1 (gen.)
3639e hos with 1909b epi, 1 (dat.)
3639e hos with 1909c epi, 2 (acc.)
whereon, that, 3639a hos, 1
wheresoever, 3599 hopou, 1
3599 hopou with 302c an, 3
3599 hopou with 1437 ean, 2
whereto, 3639e hos with 1519 eis, 1
whereunto, 3639a hos, 6
3639e hos with 1519 eis, 6
5001 tis, 6
whereunto, like figure, 499 antitupon, 1
whereunto, take heed, 4237 prosechō with 3639a hos, 1
whereupon, 3506 hothen, 3
3639e hos with 1722 en, 2
wherewith, 3639a hos, 9
3639e hos with 1722 en, 2
5001 tis, 1
5001 tis with 1722 en, 3
wherewith soever, 3645 hosos with 302b an, 1
wherewithal, 5001 tis, 1
whether, 1437 ean, 3
1487 ei, 20
1535 eite, 28
2273 ętoi, 1
3639a hos with 1520 heis, 1
4120 poteron, 1
4937 te, 1
5001 tis, 8
whether, or, 1535 eite, 3
whether any, 1536 ei tis, 1
whether or not, 3279 mępote, 1
which, 846l autos, 1
846p autōn, 1
3488 ho, 413
3534 hoios, 2
3639a hos, 395
3639a hos with 302f an, 1
3639c hos with 1437 ean, 1
3645 hosos, 2
3648 hostis, 81
3648 hostis with 302d an, 1
3678c hautę, 1
4069 poios, 4
5001 tis, 17
which, by, 3639a hos, 1
which, from, 3639a hos, 2
which, in, 3639a hos, 1
which, that, 3639a hos, 20
which, that for, 3639a hos, 1
which, that thing, 3639a hos, 1
which, the things, 3639a hos, 10
which, them, 3639a hos, 1
which, things, 3639a hos, 2
which, those things, 3639a hos, 5
which concern, 3912a peri, 1 (gen.)
which thing, 3639a hos, 1
3639e hos, 1
which things, 3639a hos, 2
while, 891 achri with 3639e hos, 2
1722 en with 3488 and infinitive, 7
2193 heōs, 5
2250 hęmera, 2
2540 kairos, 1
3639e hos with 891 achri, 2
3639e hos with 1722 en, 3
3639e hos with 2193 heōs, 2
3645 hosos, 1
3652 hotan, 1
3653 hote, 2
5450 chronos, 2
5513 hōs, 4
while, a, 3297 mikron, 1
3541 oligos, 2
5450 chronos, 2
while, a great, 4083 polus, 1
while, a little, 1024 brachus, 1
3297 mikron, 9
while, any, 3719 palai, 1
while, for a, 4240 proskairos, 1
while, long, 2425 hikanos, 1
while ago, a good, 744 archaios with 575 apo and 2250 hęmera, 1
while ago, a great, 3719 palai, 1
while before day, a great, 1773 ennuchon with 3029 lian, 1
while . . . is, 5507a ōn, 1
while stands, 1519 eis, 1
while . . . was, 5507a ōn, 2
while . . . were, 5507a ōn, 1
whiles, 2193 heōs with 3655 hotou, 1
whiles . . . remain, 3206 menō, 1
whisperer, 5488 psithuristęs, 1
whispering, 5487 psithurismos, 1
whit, every, 3550 holos, 2
whit, not a, 3267 mędeis, 1
white, 2986 lampros, 2
3021 leukainō, 1
3022 leukos, 25
white, make, 3021 leukainō, 1
whited, 2867 koniaō, 2
whither, 3599 hopou, 9
3639e hos with 1519 eis, 1
3657 hou, 2
4126 pou, 10
whithersoever,
3599 hopou with 302c an, 4
3599 hopou with 1437 ean, 1
3657 hou with 1437 ean, 1
who, 846n autous, 2
3488 ho, 79
3639a hos, 84
3645 hosos, 1
3648 hostis, 30
3678a houtos, 1
5001 tis, 102
whole, 537 hapas, 3
3548 holoklęros, 1
3550 holos, 43
3856 pas, 12
5098 hugiainō, 1
5099 hugięs, 13
whole, be, 2480 ischuō, 2
4882 sōdzō, 2
5098 hugiainō, 1
whole, make, 2390 iaomai, 2
4882 sōdzō, 9
whole, make perfectly, 1295 diasōdzō, 1
whole armour, 3733 panoplia, 2
wholesome, 5098 hugiainō, 1
wholly, 3551 holotelęs, 1
wholly given to idolatry, 2713 kateidōlos, 1
wholly to, give thyself, 2468 isthi with 1722 en, 1
whom, 846m autou, 1
846o autō, 1
3639a hos, 262
3639b hos with 302f an, 3
3639c hos with 1437 ean, 3
5001 tis, 25
whom, he, 3639a hos, 2
whom, he of, 3639a hos, 1
whom, him, 3639a hos, 1
whom, to, 3488 ho, 4
3639a hos, 1
whomsoever, 3639a hos with 3856 pas, 1
3639a hos with 3907 per, 1
3639b hos with 302a an, 5
3639c hos with 1437 ean, 3
3646 hosper, 1
5000 tis with 1437 ean, 1
whore, 4104 pornę, 4
whoremonger, 4105 pornos, 5
whose, 846m autou, 2
846o autō, 2
3639a hos, 53
5001 tis, 9
whose fruit withereth, 5252 phthinopōrinos, 1
whose soever, 5000 tis with 302e an, 2
whoso, 3639b hos with 302f an, 3
3639c hos with 1437 ean, 1
whosoever,
1437 ean with 3639c hos and 3261 mę, 5
1536 ei tis, 2
3639a hos with 3856 pas, 1
3639b hos with 302a an, 35
3639b hos with 3856 pas and 302a an, 3
3639c hos with 1437 ean, 19
3645 hosos with 302b an, 2
3648 hostis, 12
3648 hostis with 302d an, 3
3856 pas, 31
whosoever not, 3262 ean mę with 3639e hos, 5
why, 1063 gar, 4
1302 diati, 23
2444 hinati, 5
3654a hoti, 2
5001 tis, 67
5001 tis with 1519 eis, 2
wicked, 113 athesmos, 2
459 anomos, 2
2556 kakos, 1
4090 ponęros, 10
wicked, more, 4091 ponęroteros, 2
wicked one, 4090 ponęros, 6
wicked person, 4090 ponęros, 1
wickedness, 2549 kakia, 1
4089 ponęria, 6
4090 ponęros, 1
wickedness, if any, 1536 ei tis, 1
wide, 4016 platus, 1
widow, 5403 chęra, 26

Y

Z

Morris
changing schools
politics